# AVIATION
## YEAR BY YEAR

# Notes on principal consultants and contributors

These notes describe the positions occupied by the consultants during the period when they were preparing this book for its first publication, which took place in 1992.

•

## Air Chief Marshal Sir Michael Armitage
*was a former Chief of Defence Intelligence and Commandant of the Royal College of Defence Studies in Britain;*

## Ian Goold
*was the air transport editor of Flight International;*

## Philip Jarrett
*was a writer and consultant on aviation and held various posts on Aerospace, Aeroplane Monthly, and Flight International Magazine;*

## Walter N. Lang
*was deputy chief of Current News Analysis and Research Service at the US Department of Defense and the author of several books, including Almanac of American Military History and Anthology of Aviation;*

## William M. Leary
*was professor of history at the University of Georgia, the author of several books about aviation, and a world authority on the history of aviation in Asia and the Pacific;*

## Michael Taylor
*was one of Britain's leading authorities on aviation. His publications included Milestones of Flight and a five-volume encyclopedia of aviation;*

## John Terino
*was for 20 years a public affairs officer in the US Air Force, serving in Vietnam and also as editor-in-chief of Defense magazine. He wrote widely on aviation and defence topics in the United States.*

•

We would like to express our sincere thanks to the museums, associations, aircraft manufacturers, and other companies around the world, too numerous to mention, that provided invaluable help with this project.

# Contents

## *Chronicle*

# Introduction

This book is possible because our planet has an atmosphere. Proportionately only about as thick as the skin on an apple, it was once toxic to life as we know it. Over millions of years its composition changed, and the presence of about 21 per cent of oxygen enabled life forms to develop. Eventually these came to include mammals that walked upright on two legs. This new species had inquiring minds. I do not know if cows ever look at birds and think "I wish I could fly like that", but certainly our ancestors did.

## First experiments

The story of human flight is replete with strange ironies. The obvious thing to do was to make wings, jump off a high place, and flap furiously. We know that quite a lot of humans tried this, and the lucky ones did nothing worse than break a limb. Even today, for all our cleverness, we have never managed to make a successful ornithopter (*see Definitions*, right). The first thing that enabled humans to fly was something that does not really exist in nature at all.

This new idea was the aerostat, in the form we call a balloon. In 1670 an Italian Jesuit priest drew a picture of a ship intended to voyage through the sky supported by spheres from which the air had been extracted. He had realised that air has a significant density, and that an evacuated sphere could be buoyant. Unfortunately, at sea level the atmospheric pressure is around 14.7 lb/sq in (1 kg/cm²), so any evacuated volume strong enough to resist being crushed would be far too heavy. Even today, such a permanently buoyant balloon is beyond our capability. Like the ornithopter, that's another thing readers can work on!

It was left to a later priest, this time in Portugal, to build the first successful aircraft.

He made a very light toy balloon, open at the bottom. Under it he put a flame, possibly a candle. Released in the royal palace in Lisbon in 1709, it amused King Jaime V until it brushed up against the royal curtains and set them on fire. Rather astonishingly, Father Laurenço never went on to make a hot-air balloon able to carry the first aeronaut into the sky. Maybe the King had said "Enough"!

## Balloon flight

Some of the ironies of flight are concerned with the unexpected people who became pioneers. Who would have thought that the brothers Joseph and Etienne Montgolfier, who made paper in the French village of Annonay, would become famous for ever? Legend has it that, in about 1780, they were intrigued by the way charred bits of paper over a bonfire always rose up towards the sky. They looked at the bonfire's smoke and wondered what magical substance it contained that held the secret of flight. Could they capture some of it in a balloon made of paper?

Joseph carried out prolonged experiments and came to the conclusion that the best materials to burn to generate the magical substance were wet straw, old shoes, cow dung, and rotting meat! He did not realize that all he needed was to heat the air to reduce its density to less than that of the surrounding colder air. I am still bemused by the fact that the brothers considered their bizarre mixture better than a roaring fire of dry wood.

Be that as it may, they went on to build huge balloons, which conveyed first animals and then people – not including themselves – into the sky. The *Montgolfière* was all the rage. Then came another irony. Within a year

***Joseph Montgolfier***
*Born in 1740, Joseph Montgolfier first created a makeshift hot-air balloon in November 1782, using a silk bag.*

## Definitions

| | |
|---|---|
| **Aerodyne** | A heavier-than-air aircraft, supported by airflow over the wings. |
| **Aeronaut** | One who flies, or flies in, an aerostat. |
| **Aeronautics** | The science of flight. |
| **Aeroplane** | UK term for an aerodyne with fixed wings and a propulsion system. |
| **Aerostat** | A lighter-than-air aircraft, buoyant in the atmosphere. |
| **Airplane** | US term for an aerodyne with fixed wings and a propulsion system. |
| **Airship** | An aerostat with a propulsion system. |
| **Autogyro** | An aerodyne with a propulsion system and free-wheeling rotor. |
| **Aviator** | One who flies an aerodyne. |
| **Balloon** | An aerostat with no propulsion system. |
| **Glider** | An aerodyne with a fixed wing and no propulsion. |
| **Helicopter** | An aerodyne lifted and propelled by a power-driven rotor system. |
| **Ornithopter** | An aerodyne with power-driven flapping wings. |
| **Sailplane** | An alternative term for a high-performance glider. |

Leonardo da Vinci sketches plans for several flying machines

First Zeppelin airship flies over Lake Constance

First flight across the English Channel

First scheduled airline flights by airplane and seaplane

| c.1500 | 1783 | 1900 | 1901 | 1902 | 1903 | 1904 | 1905 | 1906 | 1907 | 1908 | 1909 | 1910 | 1911 | 1912 | 1913 | 1914 |
|---|---|---|---|---|---|---|---|---|---|---|---|---|---|---|---|---|

The first manned balloon flight takes place over Paris

The Wright brothers make the first controlled powered flights

Airships make the first airline flights

LONDON, NEW YORK, DELHI, PARIS,
MUNICH and JOHANNESBURG

This edition first published in Great Britain in 2001
by Dorling Kindersley Limited,
80 Strand, London WC2R 0RL

First published in 1992 as *Chronicle of Aviation*
by Chronicle Communications Ltd

2 4 6 8 10 9 7 5 3 1

ISBN (UK) 0-7513-3367-0

ISBN (US) 0-7894-7986-9

A Cataloging in Publication record is available from the Library of Congress.

---

*Editorial and design updated in 2001 by*
**AMBER BOOKS LIMITED**
Bradleys Close, 74–77 White Lion Street
London N1 9PF, UK

---

**Senior Editor** • *Nicki Lampon*

**Senior Art Editor** • *Anna Benjamin*

**Managing Editor** • *Sharon Lucas*

**Senior Managing Art Editor** • *Derek Coombes*

**DTP Designer** • *Sonia Charbonnier*

**Production Controller** • *Melissa Allsopp*

**Picture Research** • *Georgina Lowin*

**Additional material for this edition** • *Hugh W. Cowin, Robert Jackson*

Colour reproduction by Colourscan, Singapore
Printed and bound by Brepols, Belgium

See our complete catalogue at

**www.dk.com**

# AVIATION
## YEAR BY YEAR

A Dorling Kindersley Book

***Early glider***
*Preparing for a flight in Lichterfelde, Berlin, in 1891, Otto Lilienthal was one of the first to fly simple gliders.*

a rival began making balloons filled with hydrogen. These worked even better than the *Montgolfière*, and the *Charlière* took over as the flavour of the month. Indeed, the hydrogen balloon was dominant for the next 175 years, during which time it played a significant role in several wars.

Then, irony yet again: someone realized that one can have a lot of fun more cheaply with a hot-air balloon. From around 1960 the gas balloon was almost completely replaced by hot-air balloons, and today many thousands of hot-air balloons – no longer called *Montgolfières* – carry people aloft in every part of the world.

Of course, the main drawback to the balloon is that it is at the mercy of the wind. Early aeronauts tried rowing with oars, but as air at sea level has a density only about one-800th that of water, the procedure was not very effective. It was better when they started cranking round propellers, and eventually, just a century ago, Zeppelin began testing rigid airships. By 1910 Zeppelins were going aloft conveying lavishly appointed restaurants patronized by the first airline travellers.

## The flying machine

By this time flying machines – the contemporary term for airplanes – were feebly spluttering aloft, but irony was to strike again. If at that time one had asked the opinion of a head of state, or an admiral or general, they would have said something like "the flying machine is fragile and useless... but the airship is going to be really important". What actually happened was that, after almost all the giant airships had crashed, in 1937 the biggest of all would be destroyed in the most public and shocking manner possible.

It was the end of a dream. Today some of my friends campaign tirelessly for giant airships. Filled with non-inflammable helium, they would be driven by highly efficient turboprops at 100 knots, whilst carrying 1,000 tons of freight containers. These they would deliver to an exact spot by a factory, or to an equally exact spot in the white hell of Antarctica, or anywhere else. I don't think they will figure in future editions of this book.

On the other hand, the feeble flying machines have made startling progress. Two

Charles Lindberg completes the first solo, non-stop Transatlantic flight

First Transatlantic flights take place

| 1915 | 1916 | 1917 | 1918 | 1919 | 1920 | 1921 | 1922 | 1923 | 1924 | 1925 | 1926 | 1927 | 1928 | 1929 | 1930 | 1931 |

Aircraft support the Allies in the Battle of the Somme

First circumnavigation of the world by air takes place

Amy Johnson is the first woman to fly from Britain to Australia, solo

*The Wright biplane*
*Wright biplanes were soon being manufactured around the world after their historic flight in 1903.*

centuries ago a Yorkshireman, Sir George Cayley, showed precisely how an airplane should be designed, with a fixed wing with an arched cross-section, and a controllable tail at the back. Much later he built a full-size glider, which he urged his coachman to fly. The coachman obeyed, and even made a controlled landing. Unaware of his importance as the world's first test pilot, he promptly resigned, saying, "Sir George, I was hired to drive".

## Flight at last

All that was missing was propulsion, and the obvious answer was to use a series of cordite-filled rockets, which had been mass-produced since the start of the century. Instead, aviators toiled to create flying machines burdened by ponderous engines, even including steam engines, with stokers shovelling coal. Not one paid attention to the vital problem of control. The French edition of this book has a headline *"Ader invente l'avion et décolle"* (Ader invents the airplane and takes off). In 1890 Clément Ader did get his bat-like machine to rise, but had he "flown" he would probably have been killed because he would have been unable to prevent it crashing.

Ader was one of a species called "chauffeurs" who believed that, having created their airplane, all they had to do was get aboard and drive it into the sky. One of the first people to realise that it might not be a bad thing to be the first to learn to fly was a German, Otto Lilienthal. Gradually he learned how to fly simple gliders, and his disciple, Englishman Percy Pilcher, not only learned to fly but, having experimented with a succession of gliders, was about to fly a powered airplane when he was killed.

It was thus left to a most unlikely pair of brothers to succeed where all before had failed. Wilbur and Orville Wright sold bicycles in Dayton, Ohio. They succeeded by the obvious process – ignored by all but Pilcher – of reading all the available literature (which they found useless), spending years learning how to build and fly controllable gliders, and then simply adding a propulsion system. By the early 20th century the spark-ignition piston engine and efficiently shaped screw propeller were known technology, and the upshot was that, having braved many hardships, including billions of stinging mosquitoes, the Wrights at last opened the age of the airplane on 17th December 1903.

Even then irony was at work. First, the secretive brothers refrained from telling and showing the world. At last, after their Paris-based rivals had got into the act, the Wrights began to reap a reward selling airplanes, but their tail-first layout was a dead end. By the

*Sir Frank Whittle*
*Now recognized as the inventor of the jet engine, Whittle spent years trying to raise interest in his invention.*

time thousands of flying machines were made, in World War I, it had been recognized that back in 1804 Cayley had been right. Airplanes settled down with the propeller(s) at the front and the tail at the back.

## Rapid development

From then on it was simply a process of development. Engines became more powerful and much more reliable. Wire-braced biplanes gradually gave way to monoplanes, and from 1930 these were increasingly made of aluminium alloys, with a so-called stressed skin that (unlike the previous fabric) carried a large part of the structural loads. This enabled airplanes to be streamlined, which in turn made it worth introducing further improvements, such as retractable landing gear, flaps, and variable-pitch propellers.

By 1935 the combination of streamlined airframes fitted with engines of 1,000 horsepower had enabled the speed of fighter aircraft suddenly to jump from 200 mph to 350 mph, and of airliners (transports) to jump from 100 mph to 200 mph. However,

Amelia Earhart flies solo, non-stop across the Atlantic

First flight by jet aircraft

The Japanese bomb Pearl Harbor

Jet fighters and bombers fly their first combat missions

Charles "Chuck" Yeager flies faster than the speed of sound

| 1932 | 1933 | 1934 | 1935 | 1936 | 1937 | 1938 | 1939 | 1940 | 1941 | 1942 | 1943 | 1944 | 1945 | 1946 | 1947 | 1948 |

The *Hindenburg* disaster ends the era of great airships

The Battle of Britain takes place in British skies

The US wins the Battle of Midway against the Japanese

B-29 bombers drop atomic bombs on Hiroshima and Nagasaki

aerodynamic drag increases as the square of the speed, so it became more and more difficult to sustain this rate of progress. Designers said they had reached "a plateau".

They did not know that in 1929 an Englishman called Frank Whittle had invented a new engine that suffered from none of the limitations of the piston engine and propeller. Like the Wrights, he was not the right sort of person to invent anything, being a physically small junior officer in the Royal Air Force. With neither money nor influence, he spent six years trying to get someone to show interest. At last, in 1936, he and some partners formed a company and, with great difficulty, built an engine. This, the world's first turbojet, ran in April 1937. British experts were astonished, disdainful, and even resentful.

## The transformation of aviation

By this time a young German, P. B. von Ohain, had had the same idea. He got instant support, and in July 1939 one of his crude engines powered the world's first jet aircraft. To say that jet propulsion transformed aviation is an understatement. Not only did it sweep away the previous limitation on speed,

but it also enabled engines to be made far more powerful, thus removing previous limitations on weight and capability as well.

To show where technology had reached at that time, half a century ago Howard Hughes was determined to build a seaplane so huge that it could serve as an unsinkable Liberty Ship to carry troops and supplies for World War II. It missed the war but flew in 1947. The span of its wing was 320 feet (almost 100 metres), the greatest of any airplane in history. Along the wing were no fewer than eight engines. Each engine was the most powerful available, an incredibly complicated mass of parts made like a watch yet weighing over two tons and putting out over 3,000 horsepower. Made of wood, this gigantic airplane could carry a load of 65 tons almost 3,500 miles at 175 mph. Today the latest 777 can carry almost twice as much payload twice as far at more than three times the speed, and do it on one-quarter as many engines!

### The airplane in WWII
*Airplanes had developed rapidly by the time of World War II and were an essential component of warfare.*

## Modern-day irony

In Europe the Airbus team are busy working on the A380, which will be as big an advance on the 747 as that famed airplane was over 30 years ago. Irony again creeps in, because the A380 is the spitting image of the projects studied by Boeing back in the 1960s before deciding on the 747. Like them, the A380 has two full-length decks. What happened in the 1960s was that Boeing were also building a huge SST (supersonic transport). It looked as if that would take all the long-haul passenger traffic, so Boeing redesigned the 747 as a freighter to carry standard 8-feet-square containers in pairs side-by-side, on one deck.

The SST was then cancelled, but Boeing were by that time about to fly the 747. No problem, the airlines were buying 747s, and for 30 years Boeing have had a monopoly at the top end of the commercial transport market. The fact that the 747 was designed to carry cargo has been forgotten, and today almost half a million passengers are airborne in 747s as I write. But recently Boeing have wished they had built the original double-deck Jumbo. Airbus would have found doing the next generation somewhat harder.

---

| The first scheduled passenger flight by a jet airliner takes place | | Pan Am's Transatlantic Boeing 707 service commences | Yuri Gagarin is the first man in space |

| 1949 | 1950 | 1951 | 1952 | 1953 | 1954 | 1955 | 1956 | 1957 | 1958 | 1959 | 1960 | 1961 | 1962 | 1963 | 1964 | 1965 |

| Airlines introduce a tourist class | First scheduled flights by turboprop airliner | | The first airliners with turbofan engines are produced | The first man-powered aircraft takes to the air |

## World War II

Irony has played a big role in military airplanes as well. World War II saw the biggest armadas of airplanes ever to fill the skies of our planet. It is inconceivable that we will ever see their like again. More than 99.99 per cent were traditional in design, though they did bring in such new things as pressurized cabins, power-driven gun turrets, and various kinds of radar and other new electronics. The other 0.01 per cent were jets.

By 1944 the Germans were facing defeat, yet they introduced two amazing new weapons that made quite an impact. The Fi 103, more commonly called the V-1 or Doodlebug, was a jet-propelled cruise missile. Extremely hard to shoot down, more than 2,400 exploded on London, and another 2,400 on the Belgian city of Antwerp, causing

enormous damage. Later in 1944 the A4, commonly called the V-2, arrived. This was a huge rocket, which climbed above the atmosphere and then arched over onto its target at a maximum speed of some 3,500 mph. Any survivors at the receiving end heard the bang, followed by the gradually diminishing thunder of its shockwaves.

## New types of fighter craft

These two weapons did not stave off Germany's defeat, but they changed the face of warfare. After World War II had been abruptly ended by two so-called "atom

bombs", defence staffs spent the 1950s trying to fit nuclear warheads into the noses of enormous intercontinental missiles. It was obvious that any fixed military installation, such as an airfield, could in any future war just be wiped off the map. Accordingly, Britain invented a new kind of warplane, the Harrier. Fitted with a clever jet engine, able to give lift as well as propulsion, the Harrier demonstrated that it could rise vertically out of a backyard, or a small clearing in a forest, or a tiny pad on a harmless-looking ship, and then fly a fighter, attack, or reconnaissance mission.

Instead of being the first of a new species of warplane, able to disperse anywhere, the Harrier was regarded as quaint. Apparently, the idea that airfields might be wiped off the map by missiles is no longer fashionable. If so, this is surely the first time in mankind's history when a capability in warfare has been demonstrated and then shelved. Today Lockheed Martin is still selling F-16s dozens at a time, and going into production with the F-22 at a price (including research and development expenditure) of some $200 million per airplane. I hope the F-22 airfields have notices saying "missiles keep out".

## The winds of change

In contrast, the technology of lightplanes has not changed dramatically in 50 years. To some degree, as a result, nations in 50 countries are today making their own, while Britain, which used to export lightplanes all over the world, is the only country to have given up. All the famous British lightplane firms, whose aircraft pioneered air travel throughout the globe, are now part of history. Even in the

***F-16 Fighting Falcon***
*A multi-role fighter, the F-16 first went into service in 1979 and has flown in air-to-air combat around the world.*

Delta-wing
Vulcans fly the
longest bombing
missions

Helicopters
play a major
part in the
Vietnam War

Neil Armstrong
and Edwin "Buzz"
Aldrin land on
the moon

First commercial
Concorde flight

The first
flight of a US
space shuttle
takes place

### Mil Mi-6
*First flown in 1957, the Mil Mi-6 was
the largest and fastest helicopter of
its time and is still in use today.*

United States the market leaders Piper, Beech, and Cessna have found life hard, particularly in the late 1980s when lunatic product-liability laws brought them to their knees.

These famous names still survive today, but in new companies. Beech vanished into mighty Raytheon, though the airplanes still retain the famous brand name. Piper went broke repeatedly, but in 2001 New Piper is prospering. Finally, hit by the product-liability threat more severely than any other company, Cessna was taken over by the giant Textron. However, its plant at Wichita is once again busy and is looking forward to delivering its 200,000th airplane.

## British planemakers

The disappearance of Britain as a planemaker, except as a partner making pieces of aircraft in multinational programmes, stems largely from the active hostility of its own home customers. For almost 50 years British Airways and its predecessor BOAC relied almost totally upon the airplanes made in Seattle. When it inherited ten small Airbuses – from an operator it took over – its chairman told the author, "We'll get rid of them, of course, they just don't fit in with the 737 fleet". In the same way, in the 1960s the RAF and Royal Navy cancelled their British airplanes and bought in US types.

### Mil Mi-6
*First flown in 1957, the Mil Mi-6 was the largest and fastest helicopter of its time and is still in use today.*

This was bad news for the once world-leading British planemakers. After these businesses had all been forced to merge into each other, the one company that was left decided to change its name to BAE Systems because "British Aerospace" might give the impression that it just made airplanes. In fact, BAE Systems is a diverse world-class company, but it would be nice to design airplanes and not just the components.

## European dominance

It is not only Britain that looks back ruefully to a time when it was great. Today the threat of the Soviet Union has vanished, and Russian and Ukrainian design teams are trying to survive in an environment of particularly harsh capitalism. Western Europe has for decades learned that, though trans-border arguments make everything take longer and cost more, there are advantages in co-operating in big multinational programmes. However, sometimes these appear to be determined to reinvent the wheel.

Having for 30 years studied how to replace the C-130 and Transall as standard airlifters, the European nations formed a succession of companies such as FIMA and Euroflag to design a new airplane. Meanwhile, by themselves, the Ukraine created the Antonov An-70. Spurning this, because it was NIH (Not Invented Here), the West Europeans now intend to spend ten years creating a rival airplane with less power and less capability.

Another area where NIH rules is helicopters. In 1957 Russian Mil designers tested the Mi-6, a helicopter able to carry ten tons at high speed. They sold 874, but none to "the West". Biggest of the current crop is the Mi-26, able to carry 24 tons, but again NIH restricts exports to places like India and Peru. Strange.

## Unidentifiable flying objects

One area where the United States has apparently made all the running is popularly known as "stealth". In 1936 Robert (later Sir Robert) Watson Watt pointed out that aircraft could be designed in clever ways to reduce their radar signature. In other words, they could be made very difficult to detect by radar. After World War II this vital fact was forgotten. Not until more than 30 years had passed did the US Air Force pick up the idea again. Lockheed became leaders in LO (low observables) technology, leading to the first flight of the F-117A in June 1981. Covered in flat reflective surfaces, this aircraft looks like something from another planet. Gradually even stranger technologies were perfected, leading to the Northrop B-2 in 1989.

Today the new buzzword is "electrogravitics". Though the subject is highly classified, an open symposium on it is in progress as I write, at the University of Sussex. Electrogravitics can make solid bodies, such as large warplanes, not only disappear but also levitate independently of the atmosphere and travel at high speed essentially without drag. We've come some way since the Wright brothers.

**Bill Gunston OBE, FRAeS**
**Editor-in-Chief**

### B-2 Stealth Bomber
*Difficult to detect and engage, the B-2 combines low-observable technology with aerodynamic efficiency.*

| 1983 | 1984 | 1985 | 1986 | 1987 | 1988 | 1989 | 1990 | 1991 | 1992 | 1993 | 1994 | 1995 | 1996 | 1997 | 1998 | 1999 |
|---|---|---|---|---|---|---|---|---|---|---|---|---|---|---|---|---|

Hundreds are killed during the worst month ever for aviation disasters

A new 'stealth' aircraft is unveiled in the US

Air attacks take place over the Gulf

First circumnavigation of the world by balloon

# Dreams of flight are inspired by myths and birds

*Since the dawn of civilization, man has been fascinated by the secret, the magic and the mystery of flight. If only he could fly, he could escape the troubles and cares of the world and be "as free as a bird". If only he could fly, he could be closer to the gods he worshipped: the Sun, the Moon, Zeus*

*and Thor all roamed the skies, where the kingdom of Heaven, with its winged angels, is still said to be. Nearly 4,000 years spent impatiently waiting for the right technology may separate Daedalus from the Wright brothers, but they have in common the same ancient yearning to conquer the air.*

## Young Icarus abandons all caution and plunges to his death

*Icarus fell because he flew too high: an engraving from a mural in Pompeii.*

*Crete, c.1700BC*

One of the best-loved and most familiar Greek myths reflects on both the desire to fly and the dangers attached to it. Daedalus, so the tale goes, was an Athenian engineer who worked for King Minos of Crete, building the labyrinth in which the monstrous Minotaur – half man, half bull – was imprisoned. When Daedalus slipped from favor, the king jailed him, with his son Icarus, in the labyrinth. The captives made themselves wings out of wax and feathers, and escaped by flying off over the sea.

But their flight to freedom ended in tragedy when Icarus ignored his father's warnings not to fly too high: the wax in his wings melted in the heat of the Sun, sending him plummeting to his death in the sea below. Daedalus completed his escape alone, landing in Naples, but swore never to fly again.

The myth is above all a cautionary tale: the sky, like the sea, is the abode of the gods and a dangerous place for mortals.

## Why imitating the birds will not work

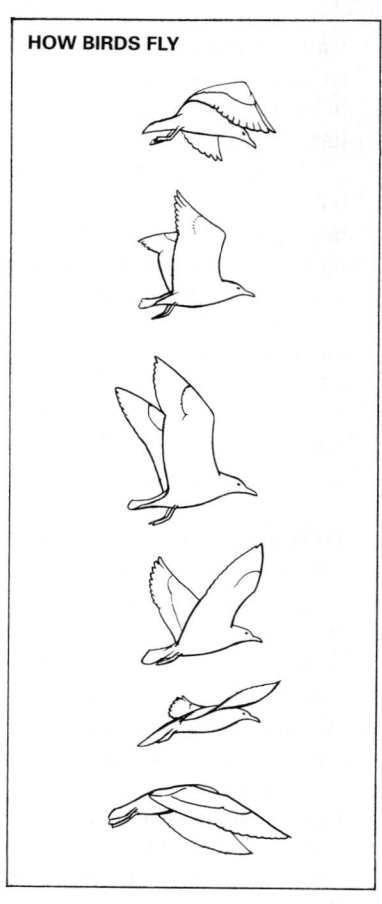

HOW BIRDS FLY

One of humanity's most ancient dreams is to be able to soar aloft like the birds. Because birds make it look so easy (apparently a simple upward and downward flapping of wings), the earliest aerial experimenters tended to attach wings to their arms and wave them violently in the hope of success. But in fact birds do much more than merely move their wings up and down. They thrust their wings forward on the downstroke, at the same time twisting the outer feathers in order to grip the air and propel the rest of the wing, and the bird's body, forward. It is impossible to observe this movement with the naked eye: birds fly too fast and too far away from the ground.

## Kings are brought low by failed attempts to conquer the air

*Britain, c.850BC*

The legendary figure of King Bladud (the father of Shakespeare's King Lear) is said to have been another victim of an early attempt to fly when his experiment went tragically wrong. A great crowd of citizens had gathered at New Troy [London] to see their ruler's brave attempt to fly over the city, but they could only watch in horror as the king lost his balance in mid-flight and tumbled to his death.

Bladud had attached wings to his arms and managed to take off when he was lifted up by a gust of wind. But as he tried to move through the air by flapping his arms, he lost his balance and crashed into the temple of Apollo, suffering horrible injuries from which he died. Known as a wizard, Bladud spread his love of

magic throughout the kingdom during his reign, says the story. But pride got the better of him when he made this attempt to fly.

A similar story of a king humiliated by failure in the air comes from Persia [Iran]. King Kai Kawus, who was the ruler of Persia in 1500BC, is said to have tied pieces of meat on to long poles attached to his throne. He then yoked four starving eagles to the throne. As they flapped in vain to reach the food, they took him up in the air and flew him all the way to China, where exhaustion overtook them. The journey ended ignominiously in a forest, and Kai Kawus renounced flying forever. These legendary failures by great and powerful men bear the same message: man was never meant to fly.

*Bladud, the legendary flying king.*

# Monk is crippled in brave gliding bid

*Eilmer of Malmesbury, with wings.*

*Wiltshire, England, c.1010*
The monk Eilmer, also known as Oliver of Malmesbury, has broken his legs in a flying accident and is now crippled. In spite of his extensive injuries, he remains resolute in his belief that people can fly, and blames his misfortune on not having added a tail to his apparatus.

The flying monk's wings were attached to his hands and feet to keep them rigid and his body horizontal during the descent. He chose to jump from the tall tower of Malmesbury Abbey, which would have sufficient up-currents to support him – or so he thought.

While he is reported to have managed an uncontroled glide of about 200 yards, he was unable to prevent himself from coming to earth with a most terrific bump.

# Marco Polo tells of man-carrying kites

*China, 1300*
Famous Venetian merchant Marco Polo, now returned from his business travels through China, has brought back a strange tale. If it is true, humans can float above the surface of the earth.

According to Polo's reports, Chinese businessmen are reluctant to board merchant ships until it has been ascertained whether or not the journey will be prosperous. To do this, a drunkard or fool is seized by the ship's crew and tied to a huge kite made of cloth and wood, attached by eight ropes to the main tethering rope, held by the crew.

When set opposite the wind, the kite rises into the sky, often with the frightened passenger screaming for pity. If the kite leans, the men on the ground pull the rope. This sets it upright once more, and by letting out more rope it rises higher. Once it is seen to fly well, the businessmen rush to the ship to sign aboard. If the kite does not fly well the merchants believe they must look for another ship, and the vessel remains in port that year.

# Bacon says people could learn to fly

*England, 1260*
Roger Bacon, 37, Franciscan monk and scientist, puts forward two methods of human flight in his book *De Mirabili Potestate Artis et Naturae* [*On the Wonderful Power of Art and Nature*].

One suggestion is "an engine for flying" with "a man sitting in the midst thereof". This would fly "by turning only about an instrument, which moves artificial wings made to beat the air, much after the fashion of a bird's flight". Alternatively, Bacon proposes that "a large hollow globe ... filled with ethereal air ... would float on the atmosphere as a ship on water".

Bacon has shown by his experiments that the atmosphere is an invisible fluid in which less dense objects could well float (→ 1680).

*Writer and inventor Roger Bacon.*

# Italian artist Leonardo da Vinci designs ingenious experimental flying machines

*Leonardo's plan for wings with flapping tips, carried on the pilot's back.*

*Florence, Italy, 1500*
Leonardo da Vinci, greatest scientist and artist of the age, has devoted a large part of his time to the problem of how people might invent a way of flying. He is reputed to have produced 500 sketches and 35,000 words on the subject of aeronautical devices.

Leonardo has considered hundreds of ideas for human flight and has sketched many of them, but he appears to have made and tested only one: this is a simple toy helicopter, with a wing of spiral shape. If a light source of power existed to propel it, this arrangement might well be made to work.

From the outset he has grasped that, unlike birds, human beings are simply not built to fly. They are too heavy and not strong enough and will never be able to fly using arms or legs alone. Accordingly, Leonardo has proposed an "ornithopter", in which two rocking beams with large flaps or paddles are driven by the wearer's arms and legs working in unison. He has also realized that a flying machine must be controled. He has added to this particular device a cruciform tail, which wires connect to the aviator's head. Movements of the head to the left or right swing the tail, as if it were a rudder, while an up or down

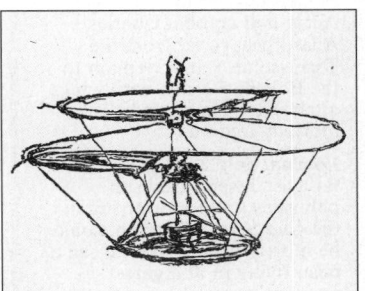
*One of the helicopter designs.*

motion controls the horizontal tail or elevator.

Leonardo has also sketched a more advanced flying machine in which the aviator lies down on a light wooden plank and works two large wings by means of hand levers and foot pedals, the latter driving the wings via cords and pulleys. In this machine Leonardo hopes to reproduce his observations on the birds' ability to camber or curve the cross-section of their wings.

Another invention from the great Florentine is a parachute, which would enable humans to descend safely from heights. But sadly, while many of his ideas appear to be basically practical, the skills and materials which would enable them to be carried out do not exist. His legacy is likely to be merely a vast gallery of sketches, products of a brilliant, fertile mind.

**Stirling, Scotland, 1507:** Italian-born John Damian launches himself from the walls of Stirling Castle, but falls to the ground, breaking several bones; he blames his failure on the fact that he used feathers from the chicken, a bird which does not fly, when he made his wings.

**London, 1638:** John Wilkins, Bishop of Chester, publishes *The Discovery of a World in the Moone*, in which he reviews ideas about flight and makes a number of suggestions for future trials.

**Lisbon, August 8, 1709:** A model hot-air balloon, designed by Father Laurenço de Gusmao, is demonstrated at the royal court in the presence of King John V (→ Nov 1782).

**St-Germain, France, c.1712:** Actor and acrobat Charles Allard tries to fly from the Terrasse de Saint-Germain to the Bois de Vésinet with wings attached to his arms; he is mortally injured.

**London, July 20, 1713:** Essayist Joseph Addison publishes a satire on flying in the *Guardian*: "Nothing would be more frequent than to see a beau flying in at a garret window, or a gallant giving chase to his mistress, like a hawk after a lark."

**Scotland, 1749:** Scientist Alexander Wilson launches a series of paper kites carrying thermometers in order to measure air temperatures at various altitudes (→ 1752).

**Württemburg, Germany, 1750:** A miller called Schweikart tries to fly from a mountain with a pair of large taffeta wings; before a large crowd he falls to the ground, smashing his wings.

**London, October 5, 1751:** Italian Andrea Grimaldi, self-styled priest of dubious reputation, exhibits a flying carriage; the machine, which remains untested, has a complex structure and a wingspan of 22 feet.

**Etampes, France, c.1770:** Canon Pierre Desforges builds a pair of feathered wings for a flying experiment; the experiment fails because the peasant to whom the wings are fixed refuses to go through with the attempt.

# Geese haul fictional flyer up to the Moon

*Hereford, England, 1638*

Bishop Francis Godwin's fictional book *Man in the Moone* has been published. It describes a fantastic journey to the Moon by Spaniard Domingo Gonsales. But the work has little, if any, basis in scientific deduction about flight.

Godwin's hero tamed a flock of wild swans which he called *gansas*, which he trained to carry burdens. By connecting each bird to a single large carrying structure, Gonsales could be raised up. To prevent this gondola from being unsteadied by birds taking off at differing times, each was tethered by string and pulley, which let out extra string to the lead birds until all were airborne.

To Gonsales's surprise, the *gansas* flew to the Moon for winter. On a 12-day flight, he had observed the daily rotation of the Earth and the Moon's mighty seas and mountains. The return journey took nine days, quicker than the outward flight because of the Earth's gravity.

*A scene from Bishop Godwin's book.*

# Would-be pilot leaps from cottage garret

*Sablé, France, 1678*

Local locksmith Monsieur Besnier has startled his neighbors by performing a successful flying experiment with a pair of wood-and-taffeta wings strapped to his back. He leapt from a cottage garret and soared over an adjoining building before coming to rest.

Besnier's "wings" consist of two wooden shafts which the pilot wears down each side of his body, attached to his arms and legs. In flight, he moves his limbs as if he were walking on the ground – swinging his right arm when he moves his left leg, and vice versa – so that when he pulls down with his right hand on the right wing, he pulls with his left leg on the left wing. The poles are fitted with hinged shutters at their ends, and these open flat on the down stroke and fold up edge-to-edge on the up stroke, to avoid drag. Besnier has sold a pair of these wings to a passing entertainer and is working on a second set.

*Besnier's design consists of two taffeta wings operated by the arms and legs.*

# Italian monk plans a flying gondola

*Brescia, Italy, 1670*

Already suspicious, the Jesuit order is now positively embarrassed by the proposal by Father Francesco de Lana that a boat could sail through the sky supported by four large copper spheres from which the air has been extracted.

De Lana has carried out experiments based on knowledge gained by Blaise Pascal and von Guericke. His idea appears sound. It seems that evacuated containers could indeed float in the atmosphere, if only they could be made light, yet strong enough not to collapse.

DE LANA'S FLYING BOAT

# Borelli argues man is too weak to fly

*Rome, 1680*

A treatise *De Motu Animalium* [*On the Movement of Living Things*], by the late Giovanni Alfonso Borelli, has been published this year. In this work Borelli uses scientific evidence to back his claims that the human being does not have the muscles needed to achieve lifting flight with wings without mechanical help.

Borelli has used the laws of dynamics and statics to assess muscular capabilities and has applied mechanical principles to the movement of various animal bodies. People are made to walk, not to fly, concludes this professor of mathematics, physics and physiology.

# French nobleman tries to fly river Seine

*"Bird-man" Bacqueville's attempted flight keeps a large crowd enthralled. He failed, by unlike so many others, he survived with only very minor injuries.*

*Paris, 1742*
The Marquis de Bacqueville is nursing his pride – as well as a broken leg – as he recovers from a gallant attempt to fly across the river Seine which went badly wrong. He came down with a great thump on a washerwoman's barge after flying less than half the distance he had intended to cover.

A large crowd watched expectantly as the marquis, with wings tied to his hands and feet, launched himself from a terrace on the side of his house in the Rue des Saints Pères, alongside the river. His plan was to swoop across the Seine and land in the Tuileries gardens about 500 feet away.

For a little while he seemed to be keeping himself aloft with vigorous strokes, but then he faltered, and plunged down toward the river where he landed on the passing barge. He has vowed never to attempt to fly again.

# British scientist finds 'inflammable air'

*England, 1766*
By mixing iron, tin and zinc shavings with oil of vitriol (sulfuric acid) in his laboratory at Clapham, south of London, British scientist Henry Cavendish has discovered a gas which burns very readily. He calls it phlogiston [inflammable air] or hydrogen [water producer] because when combined with oxygen, it makes water.

Scientists have long believed that fire is a special manifestation, or fluid, flowing out of an as yet undiscovered material. They have long sought out phlogiston, which they know must be lighter than air, because of the fact that fire and smoke rise up from a burning solid. The principal element behind them must, therefore, be lighter too. Cavendish has weighed his newly discovered gas and found it to be one-tenth the weight of air.

Moreover, it has been observed that many substances are heavier after combustion than they were before; the conclusion is that they have released their phlogiston, with its "negative weight". This negative weight could be harnessed to pull heavier objects up into the air.

# Benjamin Franklin flies a kite in test

*Philadelphia, 1752*
American scientist, politician and philosopher Benjamin Franklin has made one of the first practical experiments using flight as a tool for scientific investigation. In order to demonstrate his theory relating to the electrical element of lightning, he has flown a kite with a moist cord in a thundercloud during a storm.

The kite held a wire spike to attract the electricity, while the wet tethering string went through a metal key just above Franklin's hand, which held the string with an insulator. Friend and colleague Joseph Priestley noted the moist cord conducted electricity and the key "collected electric fire very copiously" when a spark was drawn off.

*Franklin: drawing off electricity.*

# Angelic transport dismissed as madness

*Thuringia, Germany, 1764*
Gardener's son Melchior Bauer has failed in his third attempt to obtain funds for his extraordinary "cherub wagon" flying machine. Last year he was rudely rebuffed by King George III of England and King Frederick II of Prussia. Now he has been rejected by his own ruler, Heinrich XI of Reuss.

Basing his design on the description of the angels' chariot in Ezekiel's prophecies, Bauer proposes to use a single fixed monoplane wing with dihedral and a separate means of propulsion (a system of flappers worked by the pilot). He suggests take-off from the side of a hill.

An ardent Protestant, Bauer had written to the Prussian monarch in an exalted tone, like that of the book of Ezekiel itself. A court official retorted: "The fiery fever has turned your head. If you could do that, the king would have you driven around all the days of your life in a golden coach ... Are you not fearful for your sanity ? But I pity you from the heart for having fixed such a mad scheme into your head, for to all appearances you are a sensible fellow."

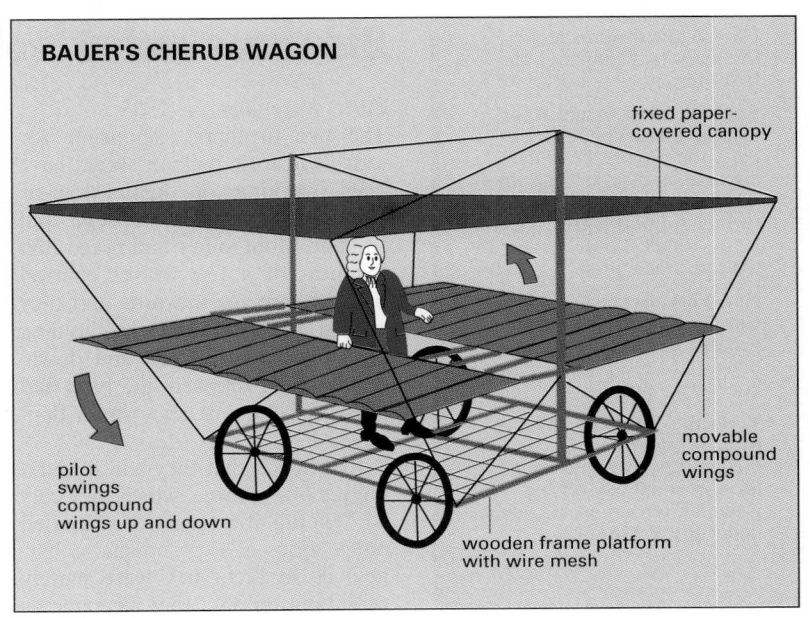

BAUER'S CHERUB WAGON

fixed paper-covered canopy

movable compound wings

pilot swings compound wings up and down

wooden frame platform with wire mesh

**Italy, 1782**: Scientist Tiberius Cavallo fills soap bubbles with hydrogen to demonstrate the lifting powers of the gas, but an attempt to fly hydrogen-filled bladders fails.→

**Avignon, France, Nov 1782**: Joseph Montgolfier carries out a first experiment with a makeshift balloon: a silk bag filled with hot air which rises to the ceiling of a townhouse.→

**Lyon, France, June 4, 1784**: Madame Elisabeth Thible is the first woman to make an untethered balloon flight; she is so thrilled by the experience that she bursts into song.

**Baltimore, Md, June 24, 1784**: Edward Warren, a boy of 13, makes the first, tethered, balloon ascent in the US; he volunteers when the craft proves too weak to lift its builder, Peter Carnes.

**London, September 15, 1784**: Italian diplomat Vincenzo Lunardi makes the first ascent in a hydrogen balloon in Britain (→ Oct 4).

**Oxford, England, Oct 4, 1784**: James Sadler becomes the first British aeronaut when he makes a flight in a Montgolfier-type balloon of 170-foot circumference.

**Kent, England, Jan 7, 1785**: Frenchman Jean-Pierre Blanchard and American Dr John Jeffries make the first crossing of the English Channel by balloon.

**Paris, April 2, 1794**: France's ruling Committee of Public Safety establishes the Compagnie d'Aérostiers [Balloonists' Company], the first military air service.→

**England, 1810**: Scientist Sir George Cayley publishes a paper on the theory of the airplane, and says: "The whole problem is ... to make a surface support a given weight by the application of power to the resistance of air" (→1849).

**New York, September 9**: Charles Ferson Durant, first professional US balloonist, makes a balloon flight of two hours over the city.

**Yorkshire, England, 1849**: A triplane glider built by Sir George Cayley succeeds in lifting a small boy off the ground after a downhill run, under tow (→ 1853).

# Montgolfier balloon makes history

## First free flight by humans is hailed

*Paris, November 21, 1783*
Adventurer Pilâtre de Rozier and the Marquis d'Arlandes, an aristo-crat, made the first manned balloon ascent today from the French capi-tal. Despite a strong wind early on, the balloon, created by the Mont-golfier brothers [*see story below*] took off from its launch site in the grounds of the royal Château La Muette in the Bois de Boulogne just before 2pm, in front of a large ex-pectant crowd.

With the aeronauts stationed on either side of the gallery to main-tain the craft's balance, the giant blue-and-gold sphere, as tall as a seven-storey building, climbed to a height estimated at 3,000 feet be-fore descending to a lower altitude and drifting gently across the Seine. But then the aeronauts realized that the fire in the wire mesh basket was burning holes in the balloon fabric and threatening the ropes connect-ing the balloon to the gallery. The two men used wet sponges to extin-guish the flames. Descending un-comfortably close to the Parisian rooftops, de Rozier and d'Arlandes threw more straw onto the brazier and rose again. Twenty-five min-utes later they landed between two millhouses, some five miles from their take-off point (→ Jun 4, 1784).

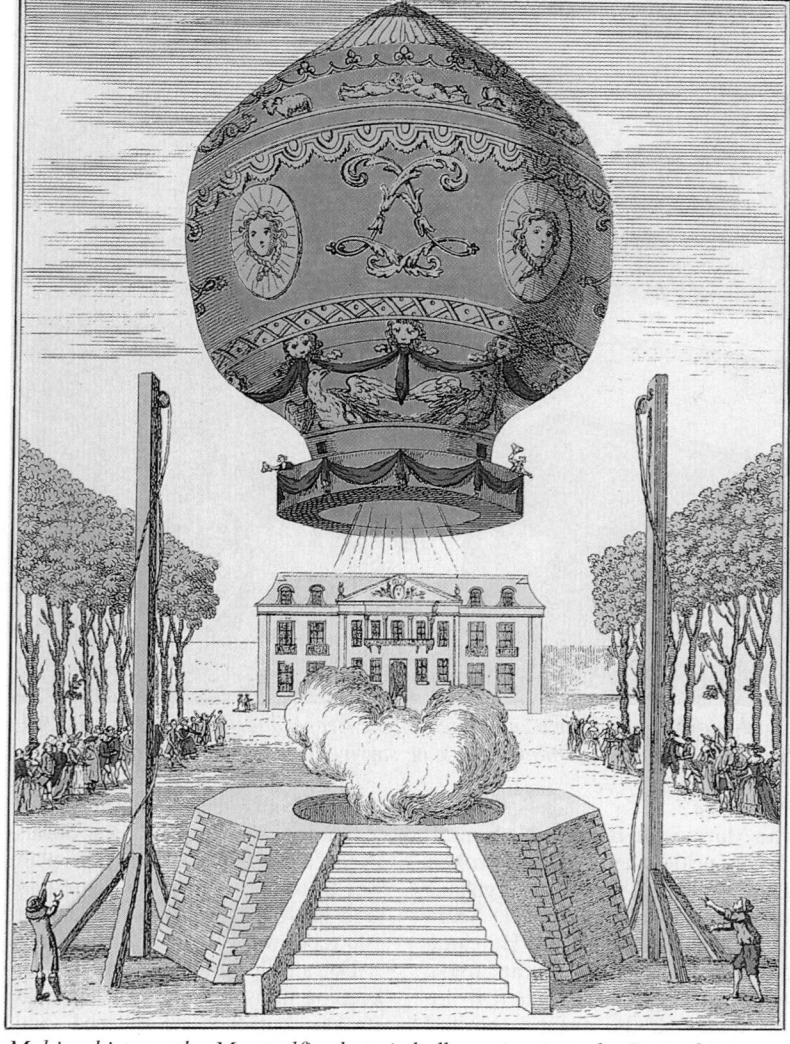
*Making history, the Montgolfier hot-air balloon rises into the Paris skies.*

## Old shoes fueled brothers' first attempt

*Paris, November 21, 1783*
The two brothers responsible for today's historic balloon ascent have been working on lighter-than-air flight for some years. Joseph and Etienne Montgolfier had noted that the heat of a fire whisks charred paper fragments upwards and they started to experiment by holding bags over a fire, open end down-ward. When released, the bags had filled with hot air and would float upward.

Convinced that they had found a unique lifting force, which they call-ed "Montgolfier gas", they carried out a series of experiments to har-ness it. In fact, they were merely exploiting the fact that air expands when heated, becoming rarefied and, therefore, lighter than the sur-rounding cold air.

On April 25, at Annonay, 40 mi-les south of Lyons, the Montgol-fiers launched their first balloon: a 35-foot-wide, paper-lined linen structure with a brazier burning straw, old shoes and rotten meat. It flew up to 1,000 feet and landed three-quarters of a mile away.

Etienne said it would have flown further if smoke had not escaped through the buttonholes which held the balloon together. The brothers then sent animals up, and on Oc-tober 15 Pilâtre de Rozier became the first man to leave the ground in a (tethered) balloon.

*An earlier trial ascent with animals.*

# Charles is first to fly in hydrogen balloon

*Paris, December 1, 1783*
Young physicist Professor Jacques Charles has made the first flight in a hydrogen-filled balloon, accompanied by Noel Roberts, one of the brothers who had built the craft. Charles overcame the problems involved in filling the balloon with sufficient gas for a flight. He and his companion flew 27 miles.

The two men jettisoned sand to maintain or increase altitude, and took with them blankets, furs and champagne to combat the cold.

Charles said after the flight: "Nothing will ever equal that moment of joyous excitement which filled my whole being when I felt myself flying away from the Earth." He took off again and became the first person to ascend solo in a balloon, reaching an estimated 10,000 feet.

Charles had launched an unmanned balloon from the Champ de Mars on August 27. It flew for 45 minutes, rose to 3,000 feet and landed 15 miles away; terrified villagers ripped it up (→ Sep 15, 1784).

*Charles and Robert are greeted by the Duke of Chartres after their triumph.*

# French army uses balloon for observation

*Fleurus, France, June 26, 1794*
Two months after the formation of the world's first airborne military service, French forces have outwitted their Austrian adversaries by observing them from a balloon. Written questions on enemy troop movements were hauled aloft and the responses sent back in a bag lowered from the balloon by cable.

The balloon *L'Entreprenant*, in the charge of scientist Captain Charles Coutelle and with General Morlot acting as observer, remained tethered aloft throughout the engagement, which lasted ten hours. French tactics were directed from the air and the Austrians, who considered the balloon evidence that the French were in league with the devil, were totally routed.

Pilots of the Compagnie d'Aérostiers [Balloonists' Company] have become the heroes of the hour. The 30-man company had been established on April 2 with the approval of France's ruling Committee of

*Getting a perspective on the action.*

Public Safety. It met with initial skepticism from the generals, who regarded chief balloonist Captain Coutelle as a charlatan. The proven success of the balloon as a weapon of war should win over the remaining doubters.

# Frenchman makes first flight in America

*An earlier triumph: Blanchard and Jeffries flying the English Channel.*

*Philadelphia, January 9, 1793*
Flamboyant French aeronaut Jean-Pierre Blanchard today took off from the town's Walnut Street prison yard in the first piloted hydrogen balloon ascent in America. Blanchard flew balloons in six European countries before fleeing here from Austria, where he had been accused of distributing seditious propaganda.

Blanchard, who speaks no English, was presented with a "passport" for today's flight by President George Washington, so that he could identify himself on landing. Charging $5 a head to witness the historic event, Blanchard ascended from the prison yard in his blue-trimmed gondola shortly after 10am. The only passenger in the balloon was a small black dog.

After a 46-minute flight, Blanchard landed 15 miles away and presented his "passport" to an illiterate farmer. The farmer did understand, however, when Blanchard offered a bottle of wine.

# Balloonists fly from London to Germany

*Germany, November 8, 1836*
Balloonist Charles Green has today successfully completed the world's longest flight when he landed near Weilburg, in the duchy of Nassau. He also became the first man to fly with a 1,000-foot trail rope, slung beneath the basket, to help control the balloon's altitude.

Green, with two passengers, British member of parliament Robert Hollond and theater producer Thomas Monck Mason, ascended from London yesterday and during the 18 hours in the air covered an estimated 480 miles. The trio flew over Kent to Canterbury – where they dropped by parachute a letter to the mayor – and Dover, crossed the English Channel and then flew over Calais and Liège before landing at 7.30am.

# Designer patents a 'steam airplane'

*England, 1843*
All England is talking about the proposed "Aerial Steam Carriage" patented this year by William Samuel Henson. It seems more like a practical flying machine than anything hitherto suggested.

Lacemaking industry engineer Henson, based in Somerset, has had a number of bright aviation ideas. This remarkable flying machine would be a monoplane, with two pusher propellers to be driven by a light steam engine of 25 to 30 horsepower. Henson actually ordered this engine from colleague John Stringfellow last year.

Even if the Aerial Steam Carriage never flies, its impact has already been tremendous. Pictures of it appear in magazines and newspapers, and it is much talked about.

# 1851

## (1851 - 1869)

**London, 1852**: James Nye publishes *Thoughts on Aerial Travelling*, which includes a design for a 337-foot balloon powered by rockets.

**Brittany, France, 1856**: Jean-Marie Le Bris pilots his winged boat *Albatros* on a short flight while it is towed by a horse on a beach near Douarnenez (→ Mar 1857).

**Brittany, France, March 1857**: Jean-Marie Le Bris crashes while attempting to fly a glider of his own design; the machine is destroyed and Le Bris is injured.

**France, 1857-8**: French naval officer Félix du Temple de la Croix experiments with a model airplane powered in one version by clockwork, and in a second by steam (→ 1874).

**Australia, February 1, 1858**: Englishman William Dean makes the first balloon ascent in Australia, flying the *Australasian* for about seven miles over Melbourne.

**USA, October 1, 1861**: The US Army Balloon Corps, consisting of five balloons and 50 men, is set up.

**Virginia, May 31, 1862**: Balloonist Thaddeus Lowe makes an aerial reconnaissance of Confederate positions which saves the Union Army from a heavy defeat at Fair Oaks.

**Essex, England, Sept 1862**: George Faux, 62, resident of Chigwell, fails in an attempt to fly from the roof of the village public house.

**Paris, October 4, 1863**: *Le Géant*, a 196-foot-high hydrogen balloon built by French photographer Nadar (Félix Tournachon), makes its first flight; it carries 12 passengers 15 miles before dropping violently to earth.→

**England, January 12, 1866**: The Aeronautical Society of Great Britain is established.→

**London, 1868**: English inventor John Stringfellow's steam-powered *Triplane*, fitted with "superposed" wings, is put on display at the Aeronautical Society's exhibition.

**Paris, 1868**: Nadar takes the world's first aerial photograph – a view of the Etoile as seen from 1,700 feet up in a tethered balloon.

# Man flies in heavier-than-air craft

*An early Cayley aircraft design, drawn on a silver disk, dated 1799.*

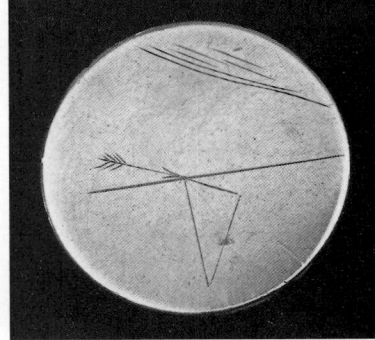

*Aerodynamics: the designer's view of the forces of lift, thrust and drag.*

*Gentleman-scientist: Sir George.*

**Yorkshire, England, 1853**

A human has flown in a heavier-than-air machine. This summer, a coachman of Sir George Cayley flew across a valley at Sir George's home at Brompton Hall, near Scarborough, in a glider built to his master's design. When he got out, he gave in his notice. "I was hired to drive, not to fly," he shouted.

What distinguishes Cayley from a host of eccentric aerial experi-menters is his grasp of aerodynamics, shown in a silver disk he engraved in 1799; on one side he sketched a diagram of the physical forces acting on a wing and on the other an airplane – complete with fuselage, elevator, tailplane and rudder – powered by flapping paddles. In 1804 he built a model glider with fixed wings and movable tail control surfaces, and also tested aerofoils on a whirling-arm device, and in 1809 he built and flew the first ever successful full-size glider.

His interest in flying rekindled by the recent strides of Henson and others, he set to work building a triplane with a tail worked by the occupant. He has also developed a tubular beam system of construction for aircraft (→ Aug 18, 1871).

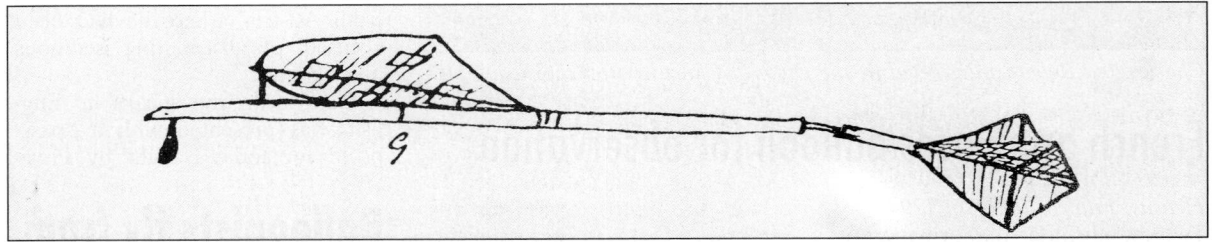

*Cayley's design for a model glider of 1804, 49 years before his man-carrying glider flew briefly near Scarborough.*

# Giffard covers 17 miles in first semi-controlled powered flight

**Paris, September 24, 1852**

In an extraordinary and successful demonstration today, Frenchman Henri Giffard made the first piloted powered flight, also involving some ability to steer. Rising from the Paris Hippodrome, he flew 17 miles to Trappes.

His cigar-shaped airship is about 144 feet in length and 39 feet in diameter at the center, with a gas volume of 88,300 cubic feet. The open car is suspended below a keel, itself attached to the envelope by ropes. The car carries both the pilot and the 3-hp steam engine, which powers the aircraft. A cloth rudder is attached above the keel, offering some control. The average speed today was 5mph (→ Aug 9, 1884).

*Henri Giffard's airship, more than 140 feet long and driven by a 3-hp engine.*

# Four Americans fly a record 800 miles

*Henderson, NY, July 2, 1859*
Four Americans, balloonist John Wise, balloon builder John La-Mountain, Vermont businessman O A Gager and St Louis journalist William Hyde, have set a new world distance record for a flight by a gas-filled balloon. They landed here today 20 hours and 40 minutes after taking off from St Louis, Missouri, having covered an estimated 809 miles.

The 120-foot-high and 60-foot-diameter balloon *Atlantic* carried a wooden lifeboat slung beneath its basket, 1,000 lb of sand ballast, a sack of express mail and copious supplies of food and drink. Wise was the only man to ride in the wicker car, while the others crammed into the lifeboat. A violent storm over the Great Lakes threatened to bring the balloon down as it crossed Lake Ontario. The passengers climbed hurriedly into the wicker car, and Wise jettisoned the lifeboat, the sack of mail, all his ballast and anything else he could find. They finally made it to land, coming down in a tree.

# Britain's aeronauts debate wing design

*London, June 27, 1866*
The first meeting of the Aeronautical Society of Great Britain, founded on January 12 this year, took place today before an earnest and dignified audience. The creation of the society reflects the growing respectability of the whole subject of aeronautics, especially the proven science of ballooning.

However, the society is clearly interested in the development of heavier-than-air flying machines, which was the principal topic of the first paper read before the society. The paper, entitled "Aerial Locomotion", was delivered by marine engineer and scientist Francis Herbert Wenham, who is especially interested in microscopy and flying. Wenham has already carried out much research into wings and, for example, reports that curved wings lift more strongly than flat ones. He also finds that long, narrow wings are better than short, broad ones.

# Confederates arrest balloonist as spy

*Thaddeus Lowe at work in the sky.*

*Unionville, SC, April 20, 1861*
A New England balloonist who has been jailed several times on suspicion of being a Yankee spy was arrested again today by Confederate troops. His arrest came just seven days after Unionist and Confederate troops clashed at Fort Sumter.

Thaddeus Lowe was released after interrogation, when an innkeeper identified him as a genuine balloonist. Lowe told his captors that he had taken off from Cincinnati nine hours earlier. His aim was to test the west-to-east wind currents on a flight from the Midwest to the Atlantic coast, prior to making an attempt to become the first man to cross the Atlantic by balloon.

# Ride of 'the Giant' comes to bumpy ending

*Paris, October 19, 1863*
There was a narrow escape today for French photographer Félix Tournachon (otherwise known as Nadar) and the eight other passengers and crew of the 196-foot-high balloon *Le Géant* [The Giant]. After a faultless flight of some 400 miles, they plummeted down to the ground, narrowly avoiding an oncoming railroad engine.

Several on board suffered broken bones, but all survived the experience. Nadar reported that the balloon hit the ground, ripped through trees and bounced across fields "like an India-rubber ball". *Le Géant* ascended yesterday in front of a crowd estimated at 500,000.

Below the balloon hung the passenger basket in its full glory. This two-story wicker "house" contained two cabins, a photography room, printing room, storeroom and a closet. Above, on the roof, was a balcony from where the passengers could enjoy the views.

Cruising at 4,000 feet, it floated over Belgium, the Netherlands and Germany. But as the Sun rose, Nadar became worried that the gas would expand and burst the envelope. Too much gas was vented; then the balloon hit a storm and could not be made to rise. Descending far too quickly, it struck the ground hard and began its alarming roll along the ground (→ 1868).

*Nadar's "Le Géant" balloon on display in London, at the Crystal Palace.*

# Englishmen soar to dizzy new heights

*England, September 5, 1862*
Two intrepid British aeronauts today ascended higher above the earth than anyone before them: Henry Coxwell, son of a naval officer, and distinguished meteorologist James Glaisher.

Today they lifted off from Wolverhampton at 1.03pm in a balloon carrying many scientific instruments. Passing through a layer of cloud, they emerged into bright sunshine and by 1.22pm had reached 10,560 feet. By 21,000 feet the air was becoming thin and cold, but still they rose. At 26,000 feet the valve line became tangled in the

*Glaisher tugs; Coxwell has fainted.*

ropes; the pair knew they would have to free it, or they would not be able to control their rapid ascent by releasing gas. Coxwell climbed high into the rigging to free the valve line. Soon they were apparently at 29,000 feet, where the air is very thin and the temperature below freezing. Glaisher found that he could no longer see to read his instruments, and then he lost the use of his arms. Finally he blacked out completely.

Meanwhile Coxwell managed to free the valve line, only to find his hands too frozen to hold it. In the end he tugged it with his teeth and began releasing gas. From a reported 30,000 feet, the unconscious men descended at last to warm oxygen-rich air below. They have now recovered (→ Apr 15, 1875).

**Paris, September 23, 1870**: Parisian aeronaut Jules Durouf pilots the balloon *Le Neptune* from the French capital, which is besieged by German forces, and carries 200 lb of mail and government papers to friendly territory.→

**Paris, August 18, 1871**: French pioneer Alphonse Penaud achieves a 13-second glide with his model glider; the horizontal stabilizer on his machine is copied from Sir George Cayley's designs.

**France, 1873**: French engineer Clément Ader begins tests of a tethered glider covered in goose feathers.→

**London, July 9, 1874**: Belgian aeronaut Vincent de Groof, known in England as "The Flying Man", is killed when his ornithopter is released from a balloon at low altitude and crashes in Chelsea.

**London, 1875**: English engineer Thomas Moy's steam-powered flying machine, the *Aerial Steamer*, makes a short hop.

**Tennessee, June 18, 1877**: Samuel Archer King makes a two-hour airmail flight of 26 miles between Nashville and Gallatin in the balloon *Buffalo*.

**Egypt, June 29, 1877**: Italian Professor Enrico Forlanini's steam-powered helicopter is tested at Alexandria.

**Montreal, July 31, 1879**: Richard Cowen and Charles Page fly the *Canadian*, first balloon to be built in Canada.

**Kent, England, 1883**: The British Army's Balloon School and Balloon Equipment Store, consisting of a small factory and a school of instruction, is set up at Chatham; the first balloon made is the *Sapper*, of 56,000 cubic feet (→ Nov 1899).

**Russia, 1884**: Tests are carried out with a steam-powered monoplane, designed by Alexander Fedorovich Mozhaiski, at Krasnoye Selo, near St Petersburg. It takes off down a short ramp and flies briefly.

**Germany, 1889**: Scientist Otto Lilienthal, who believes ornithopters – flapping-wing machines – are the key to powered flight, publishes his book *Bird Flight as the Basis of the Flying Art* (→ 1891).

## French politican is flown out to safety

*Clermont, France, October 7, 1870*
France's interior minister Léon Gambetta arrived unexpectedly today in this town northeast of Paris after escaping from the Prussian siege of the capital in a balloon, the *Armand-Barbès*. He had meant to fly to Tours, about 120 miles southwest of Paris, to organize an army and bolster the government. However, a change in wind direction forced the change in plan. He will now have to reach Tours by road.

Gambetta was cheered by thousands of Parisians as his balloon took off from the Place Saint-Pierre. The flight almost ended in disaster when the balloon lost height over a Prussian stronghold and troops opened fire. The pilot jettisoned enough ballast to gain height, although Gambetta was slightly wounded when a bullet grazed his hand. Another disaster was averted when the pilot landed near here and the basket hit a large oak tree.

Balloons are also being used by the Paris authorities to send dispatches around the country.

*Prussians fire on French aeronaut.*

# Two die on record flight

*After catastrophe at high altitude, the balloon landed near the village of Ciron.*

*Paris, April 15, 1875*
Eminent French scientists Joseph Crocé-Spinelli and Théodore Sivel died tragically today after ascending to 28,000 feet in a hydrogen-filled balloon. The only survivor was pilot Albert Tissandier.

Tissandier, a veteran flyer of the siege of Paris, had taken off with his two passengers in warm spring sunshine and under cloudless skies. At 14,000 feet, the oxygen equipment was working perfectly, but as the craft passed 23,000 feet, Tissandier noticed that both scientists were closing their eyes and panting. At 25,000 feet, the pilot tried to gulp more oxygen, but passed out. He recovered to find the balloon descending rapidly. He fainted again, but was revived by Crocé-Spinelli, who made the fatal error of jettisoning more ballast. The balloon shot up to 28,000 feet and the pilot and scientist blacked out once more.

Tissandier came to an hour later to discover both his companions dead. The balloon was now falling swiftly, but he managed to touch down safely (→ Jan 1894).

## British Army discovers balloon power

*London, August 23, 1878*
The British Army has its own balloon, which flew for the first time today at Woolwich, south-east London. It cost £71 to build, out of the £150 allocated by the War Office – the first British government military aviation budget.

Aptly named *Pioneer*, the balloon consists of a cambric envelope coated with varnish, of 10,000 cubic feet gas capacity. In charge of the balloon development, and first British air commander, is Captain James Lethbridge Brooke Templer of the 2nd Middlesex Militia, an experienced aeronaut. He owns the balloon *Crusader*, which he will lend to the War Office to begin the training program. He is paid ten shillings [50 pence] a day when employed on balloon work (→ 1883).

## French pioneer's steam-powered aircraft makes a short hop

*Brest, France, 1874*
French naval officer Félix du Temple de la Croix, 52, has built the first man-carrying powered aircraft to leave the ground. It was piloted by a young sailor whose name is not known.

Du Temple has studied winged flight for 25 years and patented his first monoplane in 1857. He spent the next two years building a succession of bird-like models, many with multi-bladed tractor (pulling) propellers powered by clockwork. After a gap of 16 years he has now built today's machine, with a wingspan of nearly 56 feet. The propeller, with a diameter of just over 13 feet, is driven by a hot-air piston engine. Du Temple put the machine at the top of a steep ramp and told the sailor how to work the rudder and hinged elevator. At the foot of the ramp the machine was airborne for a short "hop" but did not fly. Now du Temple intends to make a larger machine.

# French 'bat-plane' hops

*France, October 9, 1890*

Electrical engineer and inventor Clément Ader today managed to coax his bat-like airplane clear of the ground for a very brief hop. If it had actually flown it would surely have crashed, for Ader had provided no means for controling it in the air. He is one of the growing band of would-be aviators who concern themselves only with lift and thrust, imagining that all they have to do is to mount powerful and light enough engines aboard their machines in order to be transported into the skies.

Today's hop took place in the grounds of the Château d'Armainvilliers, near Paris. Ader started to roll along the prepared 650-foot runway at 4.04pm, and two minutes later he boosted the propeller's speed and felt himself take off with a jolt. The only witnesses, Ader's foremen Eloi Vallier and Espinosa, said that the machine was about 8 inches clear of the ground for a distance of about 165 feet.

Named *Eole* after the Greek god of the winds, Ader's aircraft has a monoplane wing of 46-foot span and a primitive tractor propeller made of bamboo and driven by a steam engine of approximately 20hp. This engine is the most impressive feature of Ader's creation: complete with high-pressure boiler and high-mounted condenser, it weighs just 145 lb. This has helped Ader keep the total weight of the Eole down to 653 lb.

Nevertheless, it is very far from being a practical flying machine. Its propeller, designed to look like four birds' feathers joined in the middle, is ineffective. It has wings like a bat's, with deeply arched camber. There is no separate tail. The pilot has to sit immediately behind the steam boiler and cannot see where he is going.

The one significant factor regarding today's hop is that the machine, which Ader calls an "avion", ran across level ground, and so it did indeed rise under its own power, albeit briefly. Previous such hops have been assisted by chutes or sloping ground. This is, therefore, an important first. But Ader himself, who now hopes to gain research funding from the French War Ministry, admits that his interesting creation has "insufficient stability" and that there exists "the necessity for further study" (→ Oct 14, 1897).

*A somewhat fanciful contemporary engraving shows the "Eole" in flight.*

# French captains maneuver their airship

*France, August 9, 1884*

This afternoon two French army captains made the first-ever fully controlled circular flight. Charles Renard, director of the French military balloon establishment at Chalais-Meudon, and Arthur Krebs ascended in their airship *La France* at 4.15pm today, and started their 9-hp Gramme electric motor when the ship had risen to 165 feet. The aeronauts first steered the airship in an easterly direction; then, over Villacoublay, they executed a neat turn and headed back to Chalais-Meudon. After 25 minutes, flying at a speed of 12/14mph, *La France* was floating 825 feet above its point of departure.

Renard and Krebs have proved that airships can be steered like sea vessels and be made to take off and land where desired. But their engine, with heavy batteries weighing 704 lb, is not really practical for aircraft.

# Eccentricity and fantasy mingle in early unsuccessful attempts to conquer skies

*Ayres' machine of 1885 depends on pedal power and compressed air.*

*New York, 1890*

Patent offices around the world are being deluged with ideas by inventors who believe they have discovered the secret of powered flight. Many of their creations will not get beyond the drawing board; certainly most of them are based on the premise that if you can create a light enough engine and aircraft, you will take off. Few address the problem of how to control the aircraft once it is airborne. However each has his own way of approaching the problem, and the sheer variety of solutions is testimony to human ingenuity.

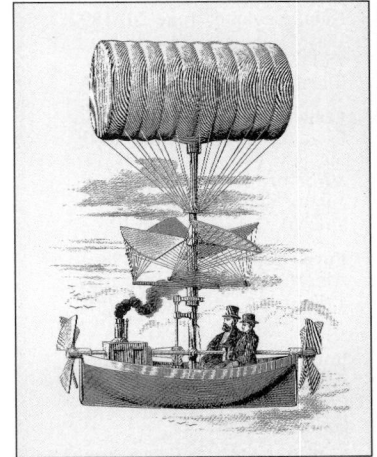

*Badgley's 1879 airship design.*

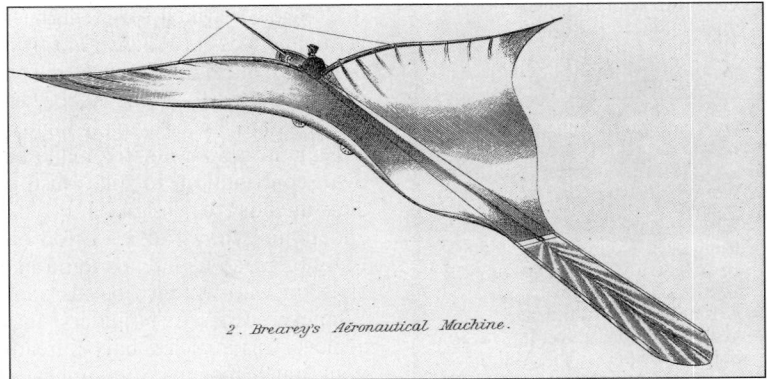

*Brearey's design of 1879 at least acknowledges the usefulness of wings.*

# Glider smash kills German 'bird man'

*Berlin, August 10, 1896*

The death today of Otto Lilienthal in a Berlin hospital robs the world of the man who can truly claim to have been the first heavier-than-air pilot. He believed, but failed to prove, that ornithopters (flapping-wing machines) rather than propellers would lift humans off the ground; it is for research on gliders that he will be most remembered.

In sharp contrast to many of the would-be aviators in this century, concerned only with building flying machines and not with the fact they had to learn to fly them, the great German knew from the start that he had to learn how to fly. Accordingly, he built a series of monoplane and biplane gliders of peeled willow wands and waxed cloth. Taking off from hills, Lilienthal made over 2,000 glides of up to 820 feet, learning to control the glider by shifting his body weight. His approach was scientific; he recorded his flights

*Otto Lilienthal: the first man to have been photographed while in flight.*

meticulously and strove constantly to improve his gliders.

Yesterday in the Rhinower hills, near Stöllen, he was caught in a gust of wind. The glider stalled, and he crashed to the ground from about 50 feet, suffering injuries of which he died at the Bergmann clinic today. "Sacrifices must be made" was a slogan of his. He has made the supreme sacrifice for the sake of his science.

## Frenchman writes history of flying

*Chicago, 1894*

Railroad engineer Octave Chanute has published a book which sets forth the entire history of human attempts to fly in heavier-than-air machines. No one could be better placed to write it; French-born Chanute has devoted his life to the study of flight and has many would-be aviators among his friends.

After building a formidable collection of literature on the subject, he began in October 1891 to contribute a series of articles to *The Railroad and Engineering Journal*. It is these articles which form the basis for the new book, *Progress in Flying Machines*, a comprehensive chronicle of the history and theory of attempts at heavier-than-air flight.

Chanute now wants to make his own contribution to that history and intends to design and build gliders himself. At 62 he is too old to fly them, so he intends to hire an assistant who will also be his pilot. Whatever Chanute's gliders may achieve, his articles have already done much to make a complicated subject accessible to a much wider audience (→ Jun 1896).

# Maxim's huge biplane hurtles briefly aloft

*Sir Hiram Maxim's giant biplane, with over 4,000 sq ft of wing area.*

*Kent, England, July 31, 1894*

Sir Hiram Maxim's giant biplane made a truly awesome sight as it took to the air today. The machine, with a wingspan of 104 feet and weighing a massive 8,000 lb, thundered down its broad-gauge launching track at 42mph. With its two 180-hp steam engines supplying great power to vast propellers, and using just 600 feet of the 1,800 feet of rail available, it lunged up-

ward. Maxim and his three-man crew held on tight. But then things went wrong.

There were wooden guard rails 2 feet above the track to restrict the flight. But the powerful machine suddenly broke through them and floated free like a giant kite. Then, just as suddenly, a length of rail fouled a propeller. To avert disaster, Maxim shut down the engines and the machine descended.

# American scientist tests model airplane

*Washington, DC, May 6, 1896*
A self-taught astronomer has today catapulted a model aircraft about 3,300 feet along the Potomac river at Quantico, and proved once and for all the possibility of powered heavier-than-air flight.

Samuel Pierpont Langley, Secretary of the Smithsonian Institution, has been building and testing his "aerodromes" for five years; only now, with *Aerodrome Nº 5*, has he met with any success. The steel model, which has a 14-foot wing-span and weighs 26 lb, was catapulted from the roof of Langley's houseboat at a height of 16 feet at 3.05pm today.

A 1-hp steam engine drove two propellers. Inventor of the telephone Alexander Graham Bell was watching as the machine flew for 90 seconds at a height of 100 feet before it ran out of steam and landed on the water. The *Aerodrome* later made another flight. It looks good; but it is only a model and has no means of control (→ Nov 28, 1896).

*"Aerodrome Nº 5", seconds after launch above the Potomac in Washington.*

# Pioneer Pilcher dies after crash of glider

*Pilcher: his tests ended tragically.*

*Leicestershire, England, Oct 2, 1899*
Britain's premier glider designer and adventurous pilot, Percy Pilcher, 32, died today. He never regained consciousness after a flying accident on September 30.

Pilcher, partner in the firm of Wilson and Pilcher Ltd, was demonstrating his glider the *Hawk* to a crowd in the grounds of Stanford Hall, Market Harborough. A bamboo spreader in the *Hawk's* tail broke; then the wing-spar failed, and the glider fell from between 30 and 60 feet. The *Hawk*, with its cambered wings and wheeled landing gear, was Pilcher's fourth and most successful glider. Pilcher had begun gliding in 1895 after building the *Bat* (→ May 17, 1900).

# Swedish balloonists disappear over Arctic

*Andrée and Fraenkel examine their balloon, forced down by a coating of ice.*

*Spitzbergen, July 11, 1897*
Three aeronauts have vanished after taking off from Spitzbergen on an attempt to make the first flight over the North Pole. Nothing has been heard of expedition leader Salomon August Andrée or his two companions Nils Strindberg and Knut Fraenkel since they lifted off from the north shore of Danes Island shortly after 1.30pm.

Observers at the launch site say three trail ropes, designed to provide ballast and keep the balloon at low altitude, fell off, allowing the balloon to fly much higher than planned. Andrée was a meticulous organizer, and he had gone to great lengths to build safety measures into his 170,000-cubic-foot-capacity balloon, the *Ornen*.

The upper hemisphere of the balloon was made of three layers of double Chinese silk and the lower of a single Chinese silk skin. Special safety features were incorporated to stop the blocking of the valves by snow and the icing up of the balloon. It is now feared that Andrée and his fellow explorers will not be able to survive in the bitter conditions of the Arctic.

**Australian Lawrence Hargrave (l) manhandles one of his box kites near Sydney in 1894; he was lifted by four of these kites towed behind a train.**

# 1900

**Paris, April 14**
The spectacular Paris International Exhibition opens. Clément Ader's *Avion III* is one of the exhibits.

**South Africa, April 25**
Observers of the British Army Third Balloon Section direct artillery fire against Boer positions near the river Vaal (→ May 7).

**Chicago, May 17**
French-born gliding pioneer Octave Chanute replies to a letter from Wilbur Wright, a bicycle manufacturer from Dayton, Ohio, and – with his brother and business partner Orville – a keen experimenter with kites. He recommends that the brothers study gliding tests carried out by a number of innovators, including Louis-Pierre Mouillard and Percy Pilcher (→ Aug 10).

**Dayton, Ohio, August 10**
Wilbur Wright informs Octave Chanute: "It is my intention to begin shortly the construction of a full-size glider" (→ Sep 6).

**Dayton, Ohio, September 6**
Wilbur Wright leaves Dayton, Ohio, for the sand dunes of Kitty Hawk, North Carolina, where he and Orville plan to test their full-size glider. Staff at the US Weather Bureau recommended the site for its strong, steady winds (→ Dec 1).

**Paris, September 19**
French oil magnate Henri Deutsch de la Meurthe, at a reception for the International Congress of Aeronautics, says: "Let us hope ... automobiles of the air will one day exceed the speeds of all automobiles on land" (→ Mar 23, 1901).

**Paris, September 22**
Brazilian-born aeronaut Alberto Santos-Dumont flies his dirigible airship *N° 4* over the Tuileries palace during a dinner for the mayors of France (→ Jul 12, 1901).

**Russia, September 30**
French aeronaut Count Henri de La Vaulx lands in his balloon at Brest Konyaski after a solo flight from France (→ Oct 9).

**Nice, France, November**
Army captain Ferdinand Ferber is appointed commander of the 17th batterie alpine. He sets to work building a platform 16 feet high on which to test his gliders (→ Dec 16).

*Octave Chanute: gliding pioneer.* ▶

*An observation balloon rises above the battlefield of Paardeberg during one of the British army's clashes with the Boer rebels in South Africa.* ▶

## Huge prize offered for flight over Paris

*Paris, March 23*

It was announced at the Aéro-Club de France today that oil magnate and financier Henri Deutsch de la Meurthe has established a generous cash prize of FF100,000 in order to encourage the further practical development of the science of aeronautics.

The prize, which is designed to mark the beginning of the new century, will go to the first pilot to fly the 11 kilometers [7 miles] from the club's headquarters at Saint-Cloud to the Eiffel Tower in under half an hour. It comes at a time when there are many in aeronautical circles who believe that the conquest of the air may well be at hand.

This belief is based on the power that is now available from internal combustion engines, a development in which de la Meurthe has also played a significant part. Among the likely favourites to win the prize are German experimenter Count Ferdinand von Zeppelin and Brazilian aviator Alberto Santos-Dumont, who is based in Paris.

By establishing the prize in Paris, the Aéro-Club is seeking to keep France, where manned flight began, in the forefront of the latest advances in aviation (→ Nov 4, 1901).

**Gas balloons muster at a French air meet. Ballooning has become a popular hobby for the rich – especially the young rich.**

# Zeppelin flies over Lake Constance

*The enormous dirigible LZ 1 floats above Lake Constance as a tug hauls it out of its special hangar.*

*Germany, July 2*

Fishermen on Lake Constance witnessed an extraordinary sight today when a great cigar-shaped object sailed above them for about 20 minutes. What the astonished locals were seeing was the first flight of the LZ 1, a powered dirigible (steerable) airship which is the brainchild of former army general Count Ferdinand von Zeppelin.

Zeppelin, 62, has been interested in airships for nearly 30 years, having seen them used in the American Civil War. It was 1893, however, before he submitted a design to the War Ministry. A government commission refused to sponsor the project, but the count went on to join up with top German engineers to found his own airship company two years ago – and the *Luftschiff Zeppelin 1* [Airship Zeppelin] is the result. Designed as a cylinder tapering to a point at each end, it is 420 feet long and 38 feet wide. Two gondolas, which today carried five men, including the count and his chief engineer, Ludwig Dürr, hang underneath the craft, with a 15-hp Daimler engine attached to each. Within the aluminum-framed enveloppe, 17 hydrogen-filled cells of rubberized cotton provide buoyancy. Despite problems with height control and steering, the airship flew for nearly 9.3 miles at 1,000 feet before returning safely to its wooden landing-stage near Friedrichshafen (→ Nov 30, 1905).

*The airship's aristocratic creator.*

## Siege of Mafeking proves value of aerial observation techniques

*In the distance: an army balloon.*

*Kimberley, South Africa, May 7*

Aerial direction of artillery from balloons manned by British soldiers has defeated Boer attempts to contain the advance of a relief column on beleaguered Mafeking.

The Boers had hoped to stop the 10th Division at Fourteen Streams, just north of the river Vaal, with artillery using smokeless powder to aid concealment. On April 25, after a six-week march from Cape Town, the 3rd Balloon Section under Lieutenant R B D Blakeney sent up observers near the river to direct fire from 5-inch howitzers of 37th Battery, Royal Field Artillery.

The spotters' corrections were shouted through a megaphone, and the results were encouraging. Five days ago the British brought up a 6-inch gun, mounted on a railway wagon. In two days its counter-battery fire, directed from the air, silenced enemy artillery.

While the attention of the Boers was concentrated on this, the main part of the British division was outflanking its enemy with a river crossing to the west. Not surprisingly, the Boers detest balloonists. Even some British soldiers believe their use to be "unfair ... against a chivalrous opponent" (→ Nov 20).

# Methodical bicycle-makers try out glider designs in windy dunes of North Carolina

*North Carolina, December 1*
A remarkable series of experiments has just been concluded on the desolate sand dunes of the North Carolina coast. For the last two months Wilbur Wright, 33, and his 29-year-old brother Orville, bicycle manufacturers from Dayton, Ohio, have been testing a biplane glider with flexible wings and forward "horizontal rudder" which enables them to maintain control in moving currents of air.

Their choice of remote Kitty Hawk was dictated by the need for a constant wind – and soft ground, in case of accidents! Advice from the US Weather Bureau indicated that such conditions, with steady 20-25-mph winds blowing on shore, were most likely to be found on the Atlantic seaboard. Most of the experiments have been conducted from the ground, with ropes attached to the wings and the glider flying much like a kite, although some involve one of the brothers lying on the lower wing.

The striking thing about the work of the pair is the quiet precision with which they approach each element of the mystery of flight. Drawing on old documents and the records of the latest experimenters, they examine and test everything in a detailed process of discovery. Most valuable to date have proved the dynamic calculations of German pioneer Otto Lilienthal, killed

*The Wrights' tethered glider flies.*

in 1896, and the work of Octave Chanute, whose rigging system the glider has used. The brothers have also introduced their own ideas, particularly the so-called "wing-warping" system for lateral control – an idea prompted by the flexing wingtips of buzzards in flight – which involves changing the profile of the wing by a system of wires.

Although the glider is a large machine with a wingspan of 17 feet, it did not generate the amount of lift predicted by Wilbur's calculations. It is understood that the brothers intend building a larger version next summer to continue their research (→ Sep 18, 1901).

## Paris hosts airmen

*Paris, September 19*
The establishment of a permanent international aeronautical commission came one step closer today as distinguished delegates gathered in the French capital for the opening of the International Congress of Aeronautics. The creation of the commission is top of the agenda for the congress, which is sponsored by the Aéro-Club de France.

There will also be debate on all aspects of aeronautics, including the possibility of heavier-than-air flight. One of the highlights is sure to be the flight planned by Brazilian Alberto Santos-Dumont in *Nº 4*, his new improved powered dirigible airship (→ Feb 15, 1901).

# Aviators experiment with lighter engines

*Paris, December 31*
With the dawn of a new century, it is suggested that the "steam" has been taken out of airplane experimentation. While only steam airplanes have so far managed to raise their pilots in brief hops, the view is now widely held that gasoline internal combustion engines may bring the day closer when airplanes will demonstrate sustained flying.

The power-to-weight ratio of gasoline engines makes them ideal for airships, where weight affects the performance. Their efficiency comes from harnessing heat inside the cylinders from the internal combustion of fuel mixture.

There have been a number of recent breakthroughs. For example, the single-cylinder De Dion-Bouton of 1889 has formed the basis of Alberto Santos-Dumont's 3.5-hp twin-cylinder engine flown

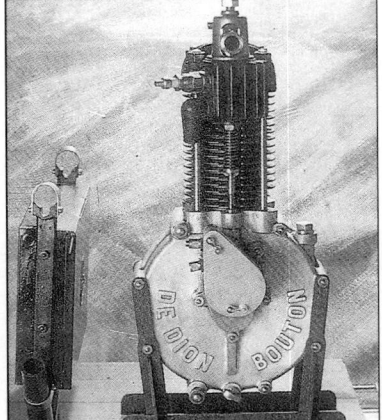
*The De Dion-Bouton 1.5hp engine.*

recently in his two airships. This weighs just 66lb, or 19lb/hp. Still greater weight savings would be made if it were somehow possible to use air, rather than water, to cool the engine.

# Frenchman sets a balloon distance record

*Russia, October 9*
French aeronaut Count Henri de La Vaulx has set a new world record for non-stop long-distance balloon flight. Today, 35 hrs and 45 mins after taking off from Paris accompanied by two other balloons flown by Count Georges de Castillon de Saint-Victor and Jacques Faure, de La Vaulx's balloon *Centaur* landed at Korostichev, near Kiev in the Ukraine – a distance of 1,200 miles. It is the second

year running that the count has won the long-distance ballooning competition organized by the Aéro-Club de France. Last month *Centaur* sailed 769 miles, a record unbroken until today. For this week's flight, which took place as part of the current Paris Exposition, the count took oxygen-breathing apparatus: the gas-filled balloon reached a maximum altitude of 2,078 feet. *Centaur's* maximum speed was 35mph.

**Alberto Santos-Dumont, born in Brazil but flying in France, puts his latest dirigible airship, "Nº 4", through its paces in the skies over Paris. A simple 7-horsepower engine is supported by the long pole below the airship, where the rather exposed inventor-pilot squats on a bicycle seat. Since his arrival in France in 1891, the famous "Santos" has been delighting and thrilling Parisians with his many remarkable aerial appearances over their city.**

# 1901

**Brussels, February 15**
The Aéro-Club de Belgique [Aero Club of Belgium] is founded.

**Widewater, Va, June 19**
American experimenter Samuel P Langley tests a quarter-scale model of his *Aerodrome*, a gasoline-driven flying machine. It makes four disappointingly short flights.

**Paris, July 12**
Alberto Santos-Dumont, making an attempt on the Deutsch prize, lands his dirigible *No 5* in the Trocadéro gardens after one of the cords controlling the rudder snaps. He uses a ladder to repair the machine where it lies before taking off again (→ Aug 8).

**Chicago, September 18**
In a talk to the Western Society of Engineers, Wilbur Wright examines the possibility of powered flight and shows photographic slides taken during his and Orville's trip to Kitty Hawk this summer (→ Oct).

**Dayton, Ohio, October**
The Wrights test a number of wing profiles with a bicycle adapted as a test platform. They also develop a wind tunnel in which they use delicate balances to measure the aerodynamic forces on a wide range of wing sections (→ Oct 28, 1902).

**London, November 15**
Frank and Vera Hedges Butler and Charles Rolls make the inaugural balloon flight of the Aero Club in the *City of York* with aeronaut Stanley Spencer (→ Feb 15, 1910).

**London, December 3**
British experimenter Sir Hiram Maxim addresses a meeting of the Aeronautical Society on the subject of "aerial navigation by bodies heavier than air". He argues that a practical airplane will be developed and will be used for "military purposes".

**France, December 16**
Artillery captain Ferdinand Ferber argues in an article on heavier-than-air engines in the magazine *Auto Vélo* for the importance of the gasoline motor (→ May 1902).

**Leeds, England, December**
Major F C Trollope inspects American ex-cowboy Samuel F Cody's man-carrying kite on behalf of the War Office (→ Dec 1902).

*Alberto Santos-Dumont.* ▶

*Santos-Dumont's trip round the Eiffel Tower on October 19 won him the Deutsch prize and ensured his place in aviation history.* ▶

SANTOS-DUMONT doublant la Tour Eiffel 1901

# German balloonists reach record height

*Germany, June 30*

At enormous personal risk, Herr Berson and Professor Süring of the *Berliner Verein für Luftschiffahrt* today established the first ratified altitude record for balloons. Their 8,510-cu ft balloon *Preussen* [Prussia] ascended to 35,435 feet above the Earth, possibly the greatest altitude at which man can survive. Although oxygen cylinders with mouthpieces were used, both men suffered loss of consciousness for short periods.

The ratification of this flight has sparked fierce controversy among those who still claim that British astronomer James Glaisher attained 36,993 feet on September 5, 1862. The dispute centres on the accuracy of Glaisher's instruments, which were damaged on landing.

Berson and Süring, with a Professor Assmann, developed very accurate instruments for balloon flight, manufactured by Bosch. These included both a specialized type of barometer and an aspirator-psychrometer that can measure air temperature without the influence of solar radiation. It was the competence of these instruments that allowed the official ratification of their flight as the highest to be upheld.

# American claims to fly

*Whitehead and his daughter pose next to his flying machine "N° 21".*

*Connecticut, August 14*

"I could fly like a bird," was the boast made by Gustave Whitehead this morning when he described a series of flights he claims to have made before dawn from a field at Fairfield, near Bridgeport.

"I was soaring above my fellow beings in a thing my own brain had evolved," he went on, describing one flight of some 1.5 miles. He also claimed to have reached a height of 200 feet.

Whitehead came to the United States from Germany in 1895. He used to live near Berlin, where he says he witnessed Otto Lilienthal's gliding experiments at first hand. He soon developed a passion to fly himself and began experimenting, at first near his home in Pittsburgh. When the local police chief found out, he banned the trials, considering them too dangerous for a populated area.

The construction of the wings on Whitehead's flying machine bears a close resemblance to that in a design by Count D'Esterno, first described in 1864. The 12-hp engine weighs 54lb, and it drives two propellers in opposite directions.

Eye-witnesses have testified that he did fly, but since it was dark at the time, and no photograph of the machine in flight exists, profound scepticism continues about the validity of his claims (→ Jan 17, 1902).

# Kite patent sought by Wild West hero

*London, November 20*

Samuel F Cody, the ex-cowboy from America who is famous for his wild west shows, has applied for a patent for a system of "war kites". The idea of using kites for military observation came to him when he heard about the British Army's problems when they used balloons in South Africa during the sieges of Mafeking and Ladysmith. Plagued by high winds and lack of hydrogen, the balloons were often unavailable when most needed.

Cody's ingenious system uses a large kite to hold the observer, while the cable is supported by several smaller kites. There is believed to be some official interest (→ Dec).

*Samuel Cody, borne by his kite.*

# Lucky Brazilian escapes death when airship crash-lands on hotel

*Santos-Dumont's first flight in the "N° 6" ended with a forced landing in the Rothschilds' Boulogne estate.*

*Paris, August 8*

Skill, tenacity and a lot of luck today saved the life of Alberto Santos-Dumont, the famous and colorful flyer, when he failed spectacularly in a second bid to win the 100,000-franc Deutsch prize [*see report on p27*].

Santos-Dumont's first attempt, on July 13, ended up in a chestnut tree. Today, as he rounded the Eiffel Tower, his airship, *N° 5*, began to lose gas. To stop the propellers severing the suspension ropes, Santos-Dumont cut the motor. Before thousands of onlookers the drooping, sinking ship fell between the two roofs of the Trocadéro hotel, and the pilot was left dangling upside down 35 feet above the street. To great cheers he skilfully clambered up to a ledge, from where he was rescued (→ Nov 4).

*A French magazine makes Santos-Dumont's dramatic accident and lucky escape its cover story.*

# Britons found club for air enthusiasts

*London, October 20*

Motoring enthusiasts led by wealthy wine merchant Frank Hedges Butler have united to form the Aero Club of the United Kingdom. Although these aeronauts are probably less scientific than learned members of the Aeronautical Society of Great Britain (founded in 1866), they make good any theoretical deficiencies with practical enthusiasm and big bank balances.

A group of enthusiasts, including Butler and Charles Rolls, discovered the joys of flight in perfect weather at Crystal Palace last month. After a two-hour, 5,000-foot ascent in a balloon named *City of York*, one said it was like climbing an invisible mountain above the Thames valley (→ Nov 15).

# Improved Wright glider still not perfect

*Wilbur soars into the air in the new glider, but he still cannot steer it.*

*North Carolina, September 1*
Returning again to Kitty Hawk, the scene of their successful experiments of last year, the Wright brothers have brought with them an improved design of glider, having a greater wingspan at 22 feet and proper arrangements for the aerial pilot to adjust the flying control surfaces as he lies on the lower wing.

But, launched repeatedly from a prime location on Big Kill Devil Hill, these improvements seem only to have introduced new problems.

Initially, lateral control proved almost impossible. Although it was mastered later, with glides of some 300 feet, attempts to turn, using the wing-warping system, sent the machine spinning to the ground.

In response, Orville and Wilbur have cut short their flying season and returned to Ohio. They fear that, despite their extensive wind-tunnel tests, their heavy reliance on the calculations of the late Otto Lilienthal may have been a great mistake (→ Sep 18).

# Santos-Dumont, flamboyant Eiffel flyer, gives away all his hard-won prize money

*The Deutsch prize judges, who had to be persuaded to award the prize.*

*Paris, November 4*
After a two-week dispute, Alberto Santos-Dumont has been awarded the Deutsch prize of 100,000 gold francs by the French Scientific Committee and the Aéro-Club de France. On October 19 he flew his airship *N° 6* from Saint-Cloud around the Eiffel Tower and back in under 30 minutes, only to be told he had failed because the airship's guide rope was not secured until past the time-limit.

The aeronaut was incensed, and the public and most of the press agreed with him; in the end the committee gave way. In an extraordinary act of generosity typical of him, Santos-Dumont is giving FF75,000 of the money to the poor of Paris and the rest to the men who built the airship (→ Jan 1903).

# Frenchman makes brief flight off scaffold

*Nice, France, December 7*
Today, France's top glider experimenter, Captain Ferdinand Ferber of the artillery corps, demonstrated a 2-second flight using his new glider, *N° 4*. Having made a brief run forward from planking on top of a specially constructed 16-foot-high wooden scaffolding tower, he dangled beneath the billowing wing as it carried him a distance of 50 feet.

Glider *N° 4* is based on the configuration of an earlier glider built by the German Otto Lilienthal, but is not so well designed or built. It has a wing surface area of 160 sq ft and weighs 66 pounds. Captain Ferber intends to use gliders as a stepping-stone to the development of a powered machine (→ 16).

*The French aviator's glider waits to be launched from its special tower.*

# Benz seaplane engine was far too heavy

*Wilhelm Kress's flying machine, complete with floats for landing on water.*

*Austria, October 15*
A piano-maker of 65 has failed in a courageous attempt to become the first person to fly a powered heavier-than-air aircraft. Vasili V Kress was 57 when he decided to study engineering at Vienna university to acquire the skills to fulfill his ambition to build an aircraft.

Construction of his craft began in 1898. It was a remarkable machine, made of carefully selected steel tubing and supported by aluminum floats. Its three pairs of wings were designed to avoid each other's airstream for maximum lift, and three rudders – for turning and lift in the air and steering on water – were controlled by just one lever.

Unfortunately, Kress's engine let him down in today's attempt to fly on Tullnerbach reservoir. He had been promised a 40-hp, 475-lb Benz motor, but got a 30-hp one of almost double the weight. The aircraft failed to lift out of the water before Kress, at the controls, saw a stone groyne looming ahead and swerved to avoid it. The wind caught the craft and capsized it. With a lighter, faster engine Kress might have made history; instead, a disappointed pioneer has seen his hopes dashed, literally, to pieces.

# 1902

**Antarctica, February**
British explorer Captain Robert Scott makes a flight in the Antarctic in a tethered balloon. He is not an experienced aeronaut and casts out too much ballast too quickly, causing the balloon to ascend rapidly to about 800 feet.

**France, May**
Captain Ferber commissions the Buchet works at Levallois-Perret to build an engine capable of delivering 5 to 6hp and weighing no more than 88 pounds (→ Nov).

**Paris, August 28**
Engineer Léon Levavasseur takes out patent number 339068 for a "motor with eight paired cylinders set in two rows at right angles". Two weeks ago, on August 15, he entered an agreement with industrialist Jules Gastambide to make an airplane fitted with a light engine (→ Dec 1903).

**Paris, October 13**
Ottokar de Bradsky and his mechanic, Morin, are killed in an accident during the first flight of de Bradsky's airship when the basket breaks away in mid-air and crashes to the ground.

**Washington, DC, October 17**
Samuel P Langley writes to Octave Chanute, asking for details of the experiments which have been carried out at Kitty Hawk by the Wright brothers (→ Aug 8, 1903).

**Nice, France, November**
Ferdinand Ferber is given permission to build an *aérodrome* in the area beyond the Promenade des Anglais. This is the new term for a place where an aircraft can take off and land (→ Dec 15).

**Moisson, France, November 12**
The *Lebaudy* semi-rigid airship, commissioned by brothers Paul and Pierre Lebaudy, reaches a speed of about 27mph on its first flight. The 190-foot ship is powered by a 35-hp Daimler engine which drives two propellers (→ May 8, 1903).

**Southern England, November 15**
Frank Hedges Butler, his daughter Vera and Charles Rolls fly the balloon *Graphic* from the Crystal Palace in London to Herriard in Hampshire in a balloon-versus-cars race organized by the Aero Club. None of the 14 participating cars is able to catch up with the balloon (→ Jul 7, 1906).

*Ferber at the controls.* ▶

Elisabeth Chemel

*December 1902: during trials at the La Californie aerodrome in Nice, the "Ferber Nᵒ 6" is suspended from its launch mast at a height of 59 feet.*

# Paris airship explodes

*The remains of the wrecked "Pax" lie scattered on the avenue du Maine.*

**Paris, May 12**
Spectators thronging Parc de Vaugirard in the French capital watched in horror as the new airship they had come to view exploded and plummeted to the ground. The crew of two, including the airship's 38-year-old Brazilian inventor Augusto Severo, were killed.

Severo's dirigible, the *Pax*, had an innovatory frame within the gas-bag. A propeller was attached to each end of the car of the two-engined airship. The tragedy was due to pilot error. As the craft climbed, Severo and his assistant, taken by surprise, threw out ballast rather than letting out gas. The ship simply climbed higher, causing the hydrogen to expand and to split the gas-bag. The explosion was then inevitable.

# Samuel Cody's 'war kites' set new record

**Suffolk, England, December**
Samuel F Cody, the wild west cowboy, has come close to death in a daring demonstration of his famous "war kites". He was testing a new system in front of a crowd of 500 people at Bury St Edmunds.

The first part of the operation went according to plan, with several tiers of "lifter kites" helping to support the heavy cable that in turn supports the main kite. But, shortly after Cody left the ground, the wind changed. The lifter kites swooped sideways and down, to treetop height. Cody could do nothing as they pulled him down in a great arc toward the ground. Then, just as it seemed that he must crash, he was blown into the branches of an oak tree. Scratched and bruised, but safely back on the ground, Cody told the anxious crowd: "Well, that's enough for today." Cody's kites are a familiar sight wherever

*Cody (r) with one of his kites.*

he takes his popular wild west show, *The Klondyke Nugget*. In August this year one of his unmanned kites reached a record height of 14,000 feet to conduct meteorological experiments, earning him a fellowship of the Royal Meteorological Society (→ Apr 16, 1903).

# First flight of an airship over London

**London, September 22**
This afternoon countless Londoners were thrilled to see a navigable balloon in the sky. The strange device was piloted by well-known aeronaut Stanley Spencer, who has spent the past three months making trial flights from the Crystal Palace.

In this, the first flight by a powered aircraft in Britain, Spencer took off from the palace grounds in south-east London at 4.15pm, passing over Tulse Hill and then setting course north-west to Clapham and Chelsea. He finally came to earth at Eastcote, west of Harrow, having covered 30 miles in three hours. Spencer's airship is 75 feet long and is driven by a 30-hp Simms gasoline engine, turning a propeller made of pinewood (→ Jun 21, 1908).

*Spencer shakes hands from the basket just before his airship takes off.*

# Riviera trials under way for new glider

**Nice, France, December 15**
French ambitions to lead Europe in the development of heavier-than-air flying have taken a step forward through the continuing efforts of Captain Ferdinand Ferber. The captain is soon to begin tethered powered airplane trials using his glider *Nº 6* with an engine.

Work on *Nº 6* began after flying with glider *Nº 5* came to an abrupt end in September, due to a bad landing through poor control. Both gliders have benefited from Captain Ferber's correspondence with engineer Octave Chanute, who brought the work of the Wright brothers to his attention.

*Nº 5* has been an important stepping-stone in Ferber's research program. Its design was influenced by the Wright gliders of 1900/01, details of which were passed on by Chanute. But it lacked the sophistication of the Wright craft in design, construction and control. The airframe was built of bamboo, and the fabric was attached in separate pieces, forming a non-rigid covering. Wing-warping as a means of lateral control, as used by the Wrights, was absent. Triangular fabric rudders were added later.

Testing of *Nº 5* began in June this year in the Alpes Maritimes area of Beuil before moving to the beaches of La Californie, near Nice. The distances flown can only be described as disappointing, the longest being just 150 feet.

*Nº 6*, as it currently appears, has a basically similar layout but lacks an elevator. Trials at La Californie continue (→ Jun 6, 1903).

# Wrights near success at Kitty Hawk

*Dayton, Ohio, October 31*

The Wright brothers have arrived home in Dayton after their third successive fall spent among the sand dunes at Kitty Hawk, North Carolina. They have returned elated, sure that they are close to a breakthrough in their pursuit of manned flight. Success comes after nearly a year of intensive scientific research in Dayton, where they used a bicycle and a wind tunnel to test their aerodynamic theories.

The season began badly in early September, when the brothers suffered an alarming series of crashes. The fault lay in the wing-warping system, by which the pilot pulls wires attached to the wings to bank the glider and right it again when the wind upsets its equilibrium. Unfortunately this increased the drag on the lower wing, slowing it down and making it drop still further, putting the glider into a spin. The problem was aggravated by the

*A breakthrough in controlled flight as the glider makes a turn to starboard.*

fixed fins which the brothers had added to their previous designs. These acted as a lever, moving the wings around the vertical axis. The breakthrough finally came when the brothers converted the fins into a moveable rudder linked to the warping cradle.

They made nearly a thousand flights, and the last few hundred were the climax of their experiments so far. The longest flight, on October 23, was 622.5 feet and lasted 26 seconds (→Dec).

## Engineer urges the brothers to try to fit engine to glider

*North Carolina, October 28*

As Orville and Wilbur Wright come to the end of another season of flying experiments and prepare to leave for home, they are considering the next logical step of adding an engine to their flying machine. Their friend, engineer Octave Chanute, urged the brothers to fit an engine when he visited their camp near Kitty Hawk earlier this month.

But adding a motor is not so easy as it sounds. The main problem is to find one that is powerful enough to drive the machine while remaining light enough to be carried by it. The Wrights need around 9hp from an engine weighing no more than

*Chanute: suggests powered flight.*

180lb. They intend to approach car manufacturers, but if that fails to produce a light enough engine Wilbur says that they may build their own.

The Wrights' first contact with French-born Chanute was in 1900. Currently based in Chicago, he has written a book, *Progress in Flying Machines*. Wilbur wrote to him, expressing the dearly held belief that "flight is possible to man" and asking for technical information. Since then they have kept enthusiastically in touch. Chanute and his associates have visited the camp several times both this year and last to watch the brothers' flights and to discuss their progress (→Oct 31).

## Steady winds help in search for perfection

*The Wright brothers make their usual careful tests on the glider "Nº 3".*

*North Carolina, October 31*

Wilbur and Orville Wright have learned to ride the wind. They have mastered the art of piloting their wood, wire and fabric gliders over considerable distances in winds of up to 30mph.

To produce lift, the wings of their gliders must have a strong, consistent airflow over them, and the Atlantic gales that blow steadily

onto the North Carolina coast have been one of the keys to their success. The wind is especially helpful when they are launching themselves off the dunes.

Despite their recent success, the brothers remain quiet, austere men. They are devoted to their preacher father; they never fly on Sundays and always wear stiff collars and ties – even when flying (→Dec).

## Dream-chasers who live only for flying

*Dayton, Ohio, December*

What makes two young men quit their prosperous business and a comfortable home each fall to spend months living in a wooden shed on a desolate beach? The answer is the pursuit of one of mankind's most ancient dreams – to fly like the birds.

Orville Wright, 35, and his brother Wilbur, 31, have pursued endeavors together since childhood. Their first joint enterprise was a family newspaper, printed on a press made by Orville. Later they built a larger press and published a local weekly and then a daily newspaper for their area of Dayton. Their business ventures culminated in 1892 when they started building bicycles. They became expert light engineers, and the Wright Cycle Company prospered. This skill came in useful when they moved on to building their first experimental gliders.

Both are single; they live with their father, Bishop Milton Wright of the United Brethren Church, and sister Katharine in Hawthorn Street, Dayton (→Sep 25, 1903).

# 1903

**Paris, January**
Alberto Santos-Dumont announces that all passengers in the dirigible airship *Nº 10* that he is currently constructing will in future be charged on a strict price-to-weight ratio: one franc per kilogram (→ Jan 2, 1906).

**Portsmouth, England, April 16**
Samuel F Cody barely escapes with his life during the naval trials of his man-carrying kite when the captain of HMS *Seahorse*, forgetting that the ship must tow the kite into the wind, turns, and both Cody and his kite are flung into the water (→ Nov 6).

**Nice, France, June 6**
After several stationary stability trials, Ferdinand Ferber makes the first full trial of his glider *Nº 6*. It fails to take off (→ Jan 10, 1904).

**Washington, DC, August 8**
Samuel Langley launches a quarter-scale model of his powered flying machine *Aerodrome* from a rail on the roof of a houseboat on the Potomac river, on a flight of 985 feet (→ Oct 7).

**Hanover, Germany, August 18**
Civil servant Karl Jatho makes an uncontrolled powered hop of 60 feet in his triplane kite. The machine, driven by a 9-hp engine, has no tail unit.

**North Carolina, September 25**
The brothers Orville and Wilbur Wright arrive at Kitty Hawk from Dayton to begin tests of their first powered aircraft (→ Dec 14).

**Perth, Western Australia, October**
It is reported that a Mr A Barr of Doodlekine, Western Australia, has patented a flying machine that will be used for military purposes.

**Paris, November 30**
Gustave Eiffel proposes that the Aéro-Club de France should set up a flying field on the Champ-de-Mars at the foot of the Eiffel Tower, with a cable for aviators to hoist themselves up to the first stage of the tower for take-off.

**Kitty Hawk, NC, December 14**
The first test of the Wright brothers' *Flyer* ends in disappointment: the machine sinks to the ground when Wilbur, at the controls, pulls too sharply on the elevator (→ 17).

*Orville (left) and Wilbur Wright.* ▶

*Wilbur Wright takes off for the first time, and the story of powered flight begins. The Wrights' achievement was to control their machine.* ▶

# Yellow airship makes historic round trip

*The "Lebaudy" on display after its flight at the Gallery of Machines in Paris.*

**Moisson, France, May 8**
Huge crowds turned out today to witness the *Lebaudy* airship make the first fully controlled aerial journey in history. Nicknamed *Le Jaune* [The Yellow One], the *Lebaudy*, crewed by Georges Juchmès and a colleague, left Moisson and flew toward Mantes, some 23 miles.

The 40-hp Benz engine worked perfectly, allowing good progress against strong winds and a fairly easy journey to Château de Rosny, where maneuvering tests were held. The elevator and rudder gave excellent control, and the separation of gas into compartments prevented gas surging. The *Lebaudy* then returned to Moisson. Its sponsors are industrialists Paul and Pierre Lebaudy, and the designer is Henri Julliot. The first fully practical airship, it is unique in being semi-rigid.

# Wright secrets are revealed to French

**Paris, April 2**
A lecture to the Aéro-Club de France by scientist and engineer Octave Chanute, born in Paris but now living in Chicago, has alarmed his former compatriots, who are anxious that the secret of heavier-than-air flight is about to be discovered in the USA.

Chanute described the American Wright brothers' successful glider trials last year, focussing on their simultaneous use of the rudder and the complex wing-twisting mechanism for flight control. This was largely dismissed, but their generally advanced work has aroused much concern (→ Nov 24, 1910).

# Kite-powered boat crosses the Channel

**Dover, Kent, November 6**
Samuel F Cody landed here at 8.30am, 13 hours after leaving Calais in a tiny boat towed by one of his large kites, which acted as a kind of sail to catch the wind. He went to France yesterday by the Channel packet, with his boat and two kites (one a spare), all made in his Alexandra Palace, London, workshops. He also had a hurricane lamp and a set of oars. He left Calais around 7.30pm yesterday in good weather, but the wind dropped and he had to haul down the kite and drift for a while. The wind freshened after sun-up and brought him safely to Dover (→ Feb 1, 1905).

# Light, high-power engine attracts praise

**Le Havre, France, December**
Great excitement in aviation circles has greeted the recent development of the Antoinette engine, designed by Léon Levavasseur. Named after the daughter of industrialist Jules Gastambide, who sponsored its development, its very light weight and high power may be the breakthrough needed to produce a practical powered airplane.

Also at Gastambide's expense, Levavasseur has built an airplane to use the engine, but it failed to fly during trials at Villorran near Chantilly. This has not dampened enthusiasm for the engine. Levavasseur received patents for his engine on August 28. Two models have been perfected so far, producing 24hp and 50hp. The larger weighs only 344 pounds.

The water-cooled Antoinette has machined-steel cylinders with brass water jackets, arranged as an eight-cylinder "V". The big-ends are placed side by side on four crankpins. Instead of a carburetor, a manifold pipe leads to each cylinder, through which gasoline drips into a tiny funnel on each cylinder. After turning the valve on, gasoline vapour and air are sucked in at the induction stroke (→ Feb 8, 1908).

# Langley's flight ends in damp disaster

*The "Aerodrome" plummets after being launched from a houseboat.*

**Widewater, Va, October 7**
Astronomer Samuel Langley, considered by many to be the United States' best hope to gain the honor of staging the first powered flight, lost his machine and very nearly his pilot this morning in the swirling waters of the Potomac river.

Langley's *Aerodrome*, a tandem-winged monoplane powered by a 52-hp gasoline engine and made of wood with steel tubing, was launched from a catapult runway placed on top of a houseboat, but it did not fly at all before plunging into the water.

Reports say that the catapult fouled the *Aerodrome* on take-off, but some observers think that this was perhaps a fortunate accident, as the inevitable break-up of the machine at least took place close to the houseboat, improving the chances of rescuing pilot Charles Manly safely. Despite this disappointment Langley hopes to try again after rebuilding the wrecked machine on shore.

*Léon Levavasseur, and his Antoinette-powered aircraft undergoing tests.*

# Dream comes true as Wright 'Flyer' leaves ground

*The dream of powered flight becomes a reality: Orville Wright coaxes his craft off the end of its wooden launch-rail, while his brother Wilbur looks on.*

*Kitty Hawk, NC, December 17*
A dream as old as history has been fulfilled: man has conquered the air. At 10.35 this morning in North Carolina the Wright brothers realized their ambition to make the world's first powered flight.

The Wrights' machine, now called the *Flyer*, took off for the first time from a 40-foot wooden rail laid out on level ground near their camp at Kill Devil Hill. With Orville at the controls, it rose into the strong, buffeting winds for a flight of 120 feet that lasted 12 seconds. The five witnesses, all local men, were not particularly impressed, as they had seen the brothers make much longer flights in their gliders over the last three years. But the Wrights were delighted; they believe they have found the key to

building a practical flying machine.

They made four flights in all, the last by Wilbur at noon. He flew for 59 seconds and covered 852 feet. The *Flyer* was then damaged when a gust of wind flipped it over before

succeed where others have failed. In their four years of gliding among the storm-battered dunes near Kitty Hawk, they have never taken unnecessary risks, always seeking to understand what they were do-

workshops in Dayton developing a suitable engine and propellers to power the *Flyer*. But on arriving at Kitty Hawk three months ago to start powered experiments, they suffered a series of delays which made them fear that they would be beaten into the air by Samuel Langley. When his *Aerodrome* crashed into the Potomac on December 8, they knew they still had a chance.

Winter was closing in. They had promised to be home for Christmas but were also determined to fly. Their first try was on December 14. The *Flyer* left the track but fell back to the ground: Wilbur was unused to the controls. Repairs were completed yesterday, but the wind was too light. Today conditions were almost ideal – and the brothers made history (→ Feb 5, 1904).

> ## 'Success four flights Thursday morning started from level with engine power alone ... inform press home Christmas'

a fifth flight could be made. The brothers decided to call it a day and hurried to telegraph the news to their father in Dayton [*see box*].

The brothers' scientific approach to their work has enabled them to

ing before attempting it and backing up their efforts with a firm grasp of aerodynamic theory.

Tests carried out last fall were very successful, and the brothers spent the winter at their bicycle

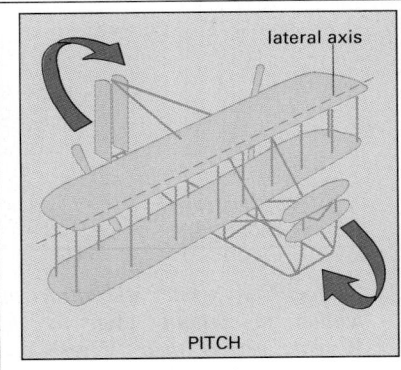

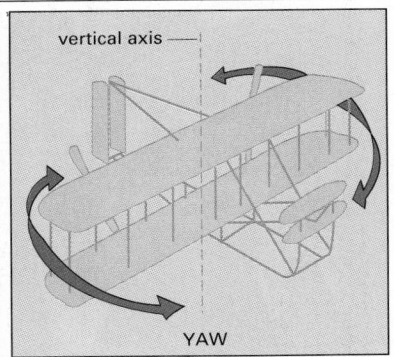

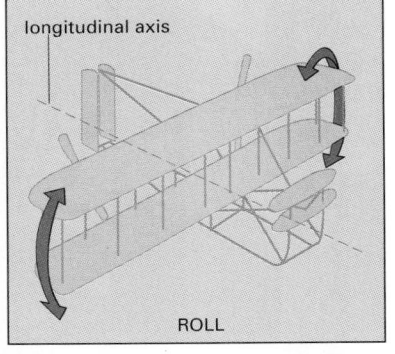

The controls of the "Flyer" enable the pilot to move it around three axes while in flight: the elevator controls pitch, the rudder controls yaw, and the ingenious system for warping the tips of the wings enables him to control roll, too. This breakthrough, being able to control movement in three dimensions at once rather than just two, marks Orville and Wilbur Wright out as the true pioneers of powered flight.

# 1904

**London, January 4**
The committee on military ballooning, established last year to consider improvements to military aviation in the light of the Boer War, publishes its report, recommending the development of dirigible (steerable) airships for the British Army.

**France, January 10**
Using Octave Chanute as an intermediary, Ferdinand Ferber writes to ask the Wright brothers if he can buy one of their machines. He has just received a letter from Orville Wright describing the brothers' success with the *Flyer*.

**Missouri, February 17**
The Wright brothers inspect the grounds where the St Louis aeronautical exposition will be held in April (→ Mar 24).

**Paris, February 22**
A glider designed by Ernest Archdeacon is examined by the technical commission at the Aéro-Club. A poor imitation of the Wright-type glider, it was constructed by Dargent at the Chalais-Meudon military works; trials are set for April.

**Dayton, Ohio, March 24**
The Wrights apply for a German patent for their airplane. Two days ago they applied for a French one (→ May 27).

**London, March**
Flying enthusiast Patrick Alexander reports to the Aeronautical Society on visits he has made to the Wright brothers in the USA, but his comments on their gliding experiments are greeted with considerable scepticism.

**Missouri, April 30**
The St Louis exposition opens. Octave Chanute exhibits a replica of his biplane glider of 1896, which he launches by using an electric winch.

**Manchester, England, May 4**
The Hon Charles Rolls, a keen motorist and flyer, enters a business agreement with Henry Royce to combine for the manufacture of motor-cars (→ Mar 15, 1906).

**France, May 9**
Ferdinand Ferber arrives at the military airfield of Chalais-Meudon, to which he has been transferred from Nice (→ Oct).

**Dayton, May 27**
Journalists invited to witness the Wright brothers' tests at their new airfield at Huffman Prairie, near Dayton, are sceptical after five days of bad weather, despite the fact that yesterday they saw Orville make the first flight of the brothers' new machine, *Flyer II*, covering some 30 feet (→ Sep 15).

**St Louis, Mo, June**
Colonel J E Capper, the officer commanding the British Army Balloon Section, visits the exposition here to ascertain American progress in aeronautics.

**Aldershot, England, June**
Official British military tests are carried out on Samuel F Cody's man-carrying kites (→ Feb 1, 1905).

**Oakland, Calif, August 3**
Thomas Scott Baldwin makes a circular flight in his dirigible airship, *California Arrow*, which is powered by an air-cooled Curtiss motor-cycle engine.

**Huffman Prairie, Ohio, Sep 15**
Wilbur Wright in *Flyer II* makes his first controlled half-circle turn in flight. For the last eight days the brothers have been using a new catapult launching device at their flying base here, also known as Simms Station. With this new device, they can take off regardless of the strength of the wind (→ 20).

**Paris, September 24**
The Aéro-Club launches a competition for manned airplanes, with a prize of FF1,500 for the first flying machine, powered or unpowered, to achieve a flight of 100 meters [328 feet] into the wind. The rules state that the difference in height between the points of take-off and landing must not be more than 17 centimeters [seven inches].

**France, October**
Ferdinand Ferber begins trials with his glider *Nº 5* at Chalais-Meudon. Trying to achieve longitudinal stability, he makes an important innovation in adding a forward stabilizer to the Chanute/Wright-type machine (→ May 25, 1905).

**Paris, November 19**
Ernest Archdeacon adds a bronze-gilt cup worth FF2,500 to the prize offered by the Aéro-Club on September 24.

*A Chanute glider at St Louis.* ▶

*Samuel Cody's kites still attract attention in Britain, even as the Wrights perfect their "Flyer" and the French test gliders.* ▶

S. F. CODY. F.R.M.S.
OF TEXAS. U.S.A.
INVENTOR OF THE FAMOUS WAR KITE.

# French not willing to believe Wrights

*Paris, 5 February*
There is barely concealed disbelief in France that the Wright brothers have achieved powered flight, as they claim. This feeling came to a head last night at a dinner at the Aéro-club, when a highly respected member, Victor Tatin, openly expressed his doubts, describing the reports as "incomplete and often contradictory".

This follows a statement by the Wright brothers on January 5 describing their four flights in detail. When the statement was reproduced in *L'Aérophile* magazine, it caused a furore. The Wrights claimed to have flown "using entirely new systems of control". Tatin is outraged at the thought that history may one day show that "aviation, born in France, only became successful thanks to the Americans" (→ 17).

# Double prize money spurs on the French

*Paris, March 25*
European aviation has received a major financial stimulus: wealthy Irish lawyer Ernest Archdeacon, president of the Aéro-Club de France, has today announced that he is going to put up FF25,000 toward a new aviation prize. This money will now be added to the FF25,000 already committed by industrialist and aviation enthusiast Henri Deutsch de la Meurthe to create the Grand Prix d'Aviation Deutsch-Archdeacon.

The new prize, which has to be won in five years from October 1, is intended to boost European aircraft developments in the wake of the Wrights' pioneering powered flight last year. It will be awarded to the first pilot who can fly an airplane around a 1-km (0.6-mile) course and land with machine intact.

# Glider lets Ferber down at Berck-sur-Mer

*Excited onlookers watch the persistent artillery captain's brief flight.*

*Berck-sur-Mer, France, April 1*
Bulky artillery captain Ferdinand Ferber, 42, continues doggedly to try to emulate the Wright brothers. Using a glider imperfectly modelled by Ernest Archdeacon on an outdated Wright design, Ferber collected bruises but no laurels as he launched himself into a short hop from a massive dune here in Normandy. In six years' experimentation, Ferber has flown no more than 16 feet. As he puts it: "To conceive a flying machine is nothing; to build it is something; to test it is everything" (→ 3).

# Voisin has better luck on Berck dunes

*At Berck-sur-Mer, Gabriel Voisin swoops down on his Archdeacon glider.*

*Berck-sur-Mer, France, April 3*
Novice aviator Gabriel Voisin from Lyon made a dramatic public début today. Flying Archdeacon's biplane glider, he was launched from the summit of Berck dune. He said afterwards: "The moment I left the ground an up-gust swept me upward irresistibly ... All the same I brought my aircraft down at the foot of the hill without incident." The demonstration has assured Voisin immediate prestige.

Voisin wanted more stability in the air, and within one hour he had modified his glider with more forward loading in a form called the *canard*, as it resembles a duck in flight. His own body-weight, as he crouched in a new position on the port side, trimmed the aircraft better. Later in the day, in a less steep area, he made several more flights lasting up to 25 seconds.

Young Voisin has scorned the efforts of Ferdinand Ferber [*see story above right*], saying he "bent" things badly and his weight was a handicap. Ferber, meanwhile, is claiming that it was after earlier tests in which Voisin was "pitched out and bruised" that the glider's designer, Ernest Archdeacon, summoned him to Normandy from Nice by telegraph to show "the new aviators" how to fly his machine.

# British colonel visits the Wrights at Dayton

*Dayton, Ohio, October 23*
Lieutenant-Colonel J E Capper, a senior officer from the British Army's Balloon Factory at Farnborough, today paid a surprise visit to the Wright brothers at their home. It was an unofficial approach, made on Capper's own initiative after travelling to the International Aeronautics Congress which was held in conjunction with the St Louis exposition.

Capper is known to have been interested in visiting the Wrights ever since the first reports of the powered flight in December last year. He is an advocate of the use of flying machines for military scouting. The Wright family courteously received their guest at their Hawthorn Street home.

Orville and Wilbur showed him photographs of some of their machines in flight, and they revealed their engine to him, but they were careful not to show him their full machine for fear that he would glean too much about their methods of flying, especially the wing-warping system.

Capper's report to the War Office will probably state that Britain is lagging far behind the US in aeronautical development (→ May 1906).

**Yet another birdman at Berck-sur-Mer: Italian designer and experimenter Lavezzari launches himself into the wind from the top of a French dune.**

# Wilbur Wright flies aircraft in a circle

*Simms Station, Ohio, Sep 20*

Wilbur Wright, by now a seasoned operator of the flying machines made by him and his brother Orville, today managed to fly in a complete circle. He was flying the second Wright *Flyer*, an improved version of the machine that made the first controlled powered flight last December. The brothers have moved from the dunes where that flight was made to a large field, owned by a dairy farmer, eight miles east of Dayton.

They have so far been content to make short straight hops. But they realize that a useful aircraft must be able to turn and have been steadily gaining experience in maneuvering their machine in the air. At first they could not turn fast enough to go round in a complete circle within the confines of the field – which has tall trees on two sides – and they have had to land in order to avoid flying over neighboring property.

Now, with increasing confidence, they are able to judge their turns. The fact that they can go round and round means they will be able to make much longer flights. The brothers shun publicity, however, and have no plans to fly any nearer Dayton itself (→ Jan 1, 1905).

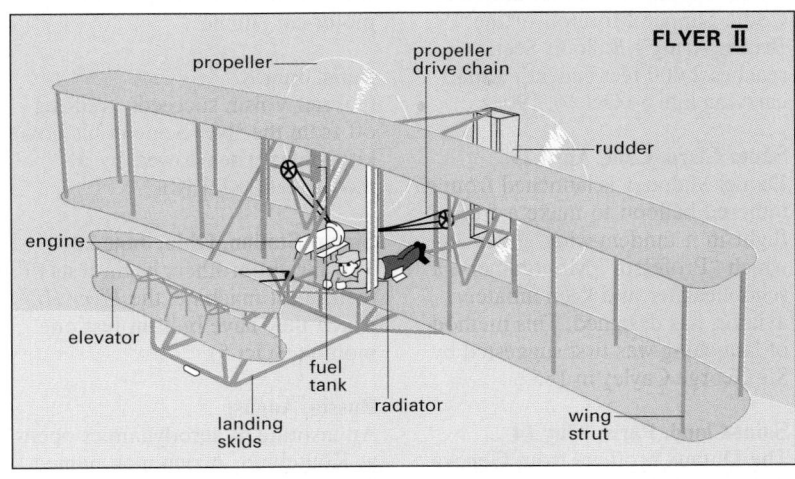

*Wilbur Wright takes the more maneuverable "Flyer II" up in the air.*

## French flyer experiments with a new control system in his glider

*Esnault-Pelterie lands his Wright-type glider, with added control surfaces.*

*France, October*

In a surprising statement, Robert Esnault-Pelterie claims that using wing-warping to maintain transverse equilibrium on gliders is too dangerous. He says: "It was possible, in our opinion, to cause magnified tension on the wires." Instead, he has invented a new device comprising two separate horizontal surfaces which are mounted forward of the wings. The pilot has a hand-operated wheel to control them. Used symmetrically, they provide longitudinal stability. Used differentially, they control lateral stability.

This is just the latest modification made to his unsophisticated copy of a 1902 Wright-type glider, which he found to be poor in its original form during maiden tests in May.

Earlier this month the glider reappeared in modified form for a second series of trials. These too were not successful. The wings had been given less curvature in section, the span reduced to 31ft 6in and the elevator removed. Wing-warping had been added, but with downward movement only. Pilot weight-shift provided pitch control.

The "new surfaces" were installed for the present third series of trials. The glider is being towed behind a car on a trolley but has so far not achieved much (→ Jan 5, 1905).

## Gasoline-engined airship goes adrift

*Missouri, October 1*

A 56-foot-long airship has thrilled spectators, but narrowly avoided disaster, at the St Louis exposition. The lumbering dirigible, named *California Arrow*, was piloted by Roy Knabenshue, who described the trip as "harrowing". He added: "We narrowly missed the fence and then we headed straight for the Brazilian building and missed it by inches, then headed straight for the Ferris wheel and I had visions of sliding down one of its spokes. By experimenting with the tiller rope I found it possible to steer."

By now, powered by Glenn Curtiss's lightweight gasoline engine, the *Arrow* was speeding along at 20mph. Knabenshue continued: "I described a wide circle and headed back. A thousand feet from the landing place, the engine died and we became a free balloon and drifted across the city and landed in Illinois."

The airship's designer, Thomas S Baldwin (a parachute jumper and showman) reckons that a lightweight power unit is a solution to many problems of powered flight. Curtiss, who built his 10-hp engine for his motorcycle racers, might have the answer. Whatever the outcome, the eventful journey of the *California Arrow* is thought to be the first circular course flown by a dirigible in the USA.

**The Parisians' favourite: a cartoon postcard of wealthy flyer Alberto Santos-Dumont.**

# 1905

**Paris, January 5**
At a conference of the Aéro-Club de France, pilot and designer Robert Esnault-Pelterie argues against the system of wing-warping. He says that it destroys the aerodynamics of the airplane. In its place he presents a design he tested last year: a pattern of independent surfaces on the wing which can be maneuvered by the pilot (→ Jan 22, 1907).

**Washington, DC, January 26**
The US Army Board of Ordnance and Fortification turns down the Wright brothers' offer to sell one of their machines to the army. In a letter to Congress, the brothers argue that airplanes can carry out reconnaissance flights and transport messages. However, they offer no proof that their machines work (→ Nov 28).

**Farnborough, England, February 1**
Samuel F Cody begins a three-month contract as a kiting instructor at the British Army's Balloon Factory, a week after the government bought two sets of kites from him on January 25: one for observation and the other for transmitting signals (→ Apr 27).

**Aldershot, England, April 27**
Under the supervision of Samuel F Cody, Sapper Moreton of the British Army's Balloon Section reaches 2,600 feet beneath a man-carrying kite (→ Oct 16, 1908).

**Santa Clara, Calif, April 29**
Daniel Maloney is launched from a tethered balloon to make a free flight in a tandem-wing glider which "Professor" Montgomery, a schoolteacher and keen amateur aviator, has designed. This method of launching was first suggested by Sir George Cayley in 1852.

**Saint-Cloud, Paris, May 14**
The Dufaux brothers from Geneva demonstrate a model helicopter. Powered by a 3-hp engine, the 37-lb machine succeeds in lifting a load of 13-lb.

**Chalais-Meudon, France, May 25**
Ferdinand Ferber makes his first aerial tests with his *N° 6 bis* glider fitted with a 12-hp Peugeot motor (→ 27).

**France, June 6**
Louis Seguin founds the Gnome engine company. His aim is to expand the workshops of the existing Gennevilliers company, which makes the German Gnom motor-car engine.

**Paris, June 8**
Gabriel Voisin succeeds in lifting off from the river Seine in his box-kite glider when towed by a motorboat (→ Jul 18).

**Simms Station, Ohio, June 23**
The Wright brothers begin tests of their latest machine, the *Flyer III*, which they have built in just one month (→ Oct 5).

**Russia, August**
An institute of aerodynamics opens at Koutchino. A rich man named Riabouchinsky has spent 100,000 roubles in building it on one of his properties.

**Dayton, November 17**
The Wrights write to Georges Besançon, the secretary-general of the Aéro-Club de France, giving a full account of their experiments with *Flyer III* (→ 28).

**Dayton, November 28**
Wilbur and Orville Wright write to the French ambassador in Washington, offering their airplane for sale to the French government as "a secret practical invention" and recommending that France send an attaché to Dayton to investigate (→ 30).

**France, November 30**
The Wrights' letter to Georges Besançon is published (→ Dec 24).

**Germany, November 30**
The Zeppelin airship LZ 2 is damaged during an abortive take-off attempt at Lake Constance. Further launch efforts are postponed (→ Jan 18, 1906).

**USA, December 5**
Colonel H J Foster, the British military attaché in Washington, breaks off negotiations with the Wright brothers for the purchase of one of their machines. The War Office has asked for an advance demonstration, but the Wrights are unwilling to show the aircraft without a guaranteed deal.

**Canada, December 28**
Dr Alexander Graham Bell's box-kite, the *Siamese Twins*, lifts off carrying pilot Neil MacDermid. It is made of 1,829 cells, each 10 inches wide.

*Ernest Archdeacon.* ▶

*Archdeacon's glider takes off at the new French airfield at Issy-les-Moulineaux. Towed by an auto, it rises 33 feet into the air.* ▶

Elisabeth Chemel

# Eye-witness account of Wright flight

*The cover of the current issue.*

**USA, January 1**

When the Wright brothers made the first powered circular flight on September 20 last year, they had a witness: Amos Root, the editor of the journal *Gleanings in Bee Culture*. In today's edition Root vividly describes what he saw in what is the first eye-witness account of a powered flight: "Imagine a locomotive that has left its track, and is climbing up in the air towards you – a locomotive ... with white wings," he gushes. He declares that the invention may one day "outrank ... all other methods of travel" (→26).

# Ferber seeks more powerful engine for his flying machine

*Chalais-Meudon, France, May 27*

Captain Ferdinand Ferber made a significant new move in his experiments today by fitting a 6-hp Peugeot engine to his *Nº 6* flying machine. It drives a single propeller just in front of the pilot's seat.

The aircraft was launched by Ferber's ingenious system of cables to give it the impetus for take-off, but the flight itself was unremarkable. The angle of the glide was shallower than his unpowered flights, around 1 in 8, suggesting that the engine had some effect, although it was clearly not powerful enough to sustain *Nº 6* in horizontal flight.

Ferber also found that the effect of the turning of the propeller made the aircraft turn towards the direction of its rotation (an effect caused by torque), making it difficult to control in the air. His airplane has no rear rudder or lateral control other than steering air brakes at the

*Ferber's persevering trial-and-error method fails to keep him airborne.*

wing tips. He has now approached engineer Léon Levavasseur to build a 24-hp engine that will turn two propellers in opposite directions to neutralize the torque. The question is whether the famous engine designer could make an engine light enough to be carried by the aircraft.

Ferber's flight is significant because it represents the first time in Europe that a powered aircraft has been in free flight, although it might be more accurately described as a "powered glide" (→Aug 1906).

# French flyers begin search for a more permanent airfield

*Paris, March 26*

Today saw the first flight at a new base for French aviators at Issy-les-Moulineaux, a suburb on the left bank of the Seine to the southwest of Paris. Finding an alternative to locations nearer the centre has become a priority in the face of a growing concern at the dangers of flights over the city.

Ernest Archdeacon, president of the Aéro-club de France, and aviation enthusiast Henry Farman have been at the forefront of the search, which bore fruit on March 20 when Farman was given permission to use the army's parade ground at Issy. It is an ideal spot: away from the city but easily accessible by *métro* and near part of Paris's old fortifications, which provide an excellent grandstand for spectators. The army has allotted the airmen special times for using the ground.

Unfortunately today's inaugural flight, by Archdeacon's second Wright-type glider, was not a success. The pilotless craft was towed aloft by a motor car but crashed after part of the tail broke away.

# Voisin forced to take a dip in the Seine

*Gabriel Voisin sits aboard his hydroglider, waiting to be towed aloft.*

*Paris, July 18*

The French aeronaut Gabriel Voisin has conducted two more flying tests with floating gliders. Two "hydrogliders" were made available to him, one by experimenter Louis Blériot, the other by Ernest Archdeacon of the Syndicat d'Aviation. Both were towed by the racing motorboat *L'Antoinette* along

an open part of the Seine between the Billancourt and Sèvres bridges.

Voisin made a brisk flight with the first glider, quickly rising 16.5 feet before suddenly coming down when the boat stopped. The second, much lighter glider became airborne as soon as the boat took the strain but crashed almost at once. Voisin was unhurt (→Nov 1906).

# Wilbur flies for a record 38 minutes

*Simms Station, Ohio, October 5*
Orville and Wilbur Wright are making amazing progress in turning their flying machines into a practical means of transport. In the past month they have made five flights, each longer than the last, and today Wilbur flew the brothers' latest machine, *Flyer III*, for 38mins 3secs, covering over 24 miles. It is the brothers' first flight of more than half-an-hour.

The *Flyer III* has the same general arrangement as the earlier designs. The Wrights have retained the superb 15/16-hp engine used in their machine last year but added new propellers. As in the previous designs, the pilot flies the machine from a prone position on the wing.

Until these recent flights, the brothers had linked their wing-warping system with the cables to the rudders at the rear, but they found that this caused the wings to

*Adjusted and tuned to perfection: the third version of the* Flyer.

slow up and lose lift on the inside of a turn. Now they have disconnected the two sets of controls, and they can put down the nose to increase speed while turning. The prolonged flights they are now able to make enable them to make dozens of turns at both ends of their test site at Simms Station, near Dayton. They now consider themselves complete masters of the new machine.

Throughout the year the Wrights have been trying to interest the military authorities in the United States and England in their flying machine for use as a scouting aircraft. So far they have not had much luck, but the success of the 37-mph *Flyer III* will encourage them to try again (→ Nov 17).

## Cagey Wrights still doubted in France

*Paris, December 24*
There were explosive scenes at a meeting of the aviation committee of the Aéro-Club yesterday when the truth about the claims of the Wright brothers to have mastered powered flight were challenged again. This follows the publication on November 30 of a letter from the Wrights to Georges Besançon, secretary-general of the Aéro-Club, describing flights of up to 38mins near Dayton this fall.

The reports of several witnesses have been verified by French journalists, yet one group within the Aéro-Club, foremost among them Ernest Archdeacon, firmly refuses to believe them. The controversy is likely to continue for as long as the Wrights refuse to fly their machine in public, for fear that their methods of construction would be revealed to competitors (→ Jan 5, 1906).

## American crashes

*Maloney, in glider, and the balloon.*

*California, July 18*
A perilous flying experiment ended in disaster today when Daniel Maloney plummeted nearly 2,000 feet to his death before thousands of spectators at San José. The experiment – launching a piloted glider from a balloon – was Maloney's third such flight this year for amateur inventor and self-publicist "Professor" John Montgomery. All went well until one of the ropes holding the balloon broke part of the glider's tail. Tragically, Maloney did not realize this and released the glider, only to plunge out of control to the ground.

## International body for flyers set up

*Paris, October 14*
Delegates attending the current aeronautical conference in the French capital have given the go-ahead for a new international body to monitor and regulate developments in aviation. The organization is to be known as the Fédération Aéronautique Internationale [International Aeronautical Federation], or FAI.

Pioneer aeronaut Count Henri de La Vaulx can claim most of the credit for bringing the FAI into existence. Along with others involved in aviation he has seen the need for some time for a universally recognized body to impose uniform standards and regulations on the proliferating number of aviators and flying clubs throughout Europe and the USA. The aims of the FAI were outlined during the Olympic Congress in Brussels in June, which called for the establishment of "a universal aeronautical federation to regulate the various aviation meetings, and advance the science and sport of aeronautics". The founding nations are Belgium, Britain, France, Germany, Italy, Spain, Switzerland and the USA.

## Aero Club founded in the United States

*New York, November 30*
A new American association reflecting the current renewed interest in the science of aeronautics has been established in New York City.

Named the Aero Club of America, it will promote the enjoyment of ballooning as a recreation, much favoured by Europeans for some years already. An exhibition of the sport is to be staged in January next year with "aerostats" (lighter-than-air craft) imported from Paris. It is hoped that this will fire the imagination of potential club pilots. The club aims to buy two balloons for hire by members.

As New York has proved a poor center for active ballooning, being close to the sea and densely built up, ascents are to be made from a field in Pittsfield, Massachusetts, where a good supply of coal gas is also available.

**The "Siamese Twins", a kite designed by Scottish inventor Dr Alexander Graham Bell, who is experimenting in Nova Scotia, Canada.**

# 1906

| | 37.85mph<br>USA<br>Wilbur Wright<br>*Flyer III*<br>Oct 5, 1905 | | 24.2 miles<br>USA<br>Wilbur Wright<br>*Flyer III*<br>Oct 5, 1905 | | 50ft<br>USA<br>Orville Wright<br>*Flyer III*<br>Sep 28, 1905 | | 855lb<br>USA<br>Wright Brothers<br>*Flyer III* | | 50hp<br>France<br>Léon Levavasseur<br>Antoinette |
|---|---|---|---|---|---|---|---|---|---|

**Paris, January 2**
Alberto Santos-Dumont enters for the Deutsch-Archdeacon prize. He has built a helicopter with an Antoinette motor for his attempt (→ Jul 23).

**New York, January 13**
The first exhibition of the Aero Club of America opens in connection with the motor show.

**Germany, January 18**
The Zeppelin LZ 2 is destroyed in a gale. It was tethered outdoors after a test flight yesterday over Lake Constance ended in a forced landing when its two engines failed (→ May 1906).

**London, January 21**
Alliott Verdon Roe writes to *The Times*, backing the Wrights' claims to have flown. The paper's engineering editor maintains that aviation is dangerous and "doomed to failure" (→ Feb 8).

**South Carolina, February 27**
Samuel Pierpont Langley, who has been overwhelmed by vigorous attacks in the press and in Congress following the failure of his experiments with the *Aerodrome*, dies after a long illness.

**London, March 15**
Rolls-Royce Ltd is registered as a public company to produce motorcars and engines.

**France, March 18**
Romanian experimenter Trajan Vuia makes a flight of 42 feet in his monoplane powered by a 25-hp carbonic acid engine – the first full-sized tractor monoplane. The uncontrolled flight, from a road near Montesson, reaches a height of 18 inches (→ Aug 19).

**London, April 7**
Charles Rolls, in his new balloon, races Frank Hedges Butler and friends aboard the *Aero Club III*. Rolls outdistances his opponents, who come down at Wimbledon, while he lands at Beaconsfield, Buckinghamshire.

**Dayton, Ohio, April 14**
The Wrights send letters to the German, Italian, Japanese and Russian ministers of war, offering to sell their airplane (→ May 22).

**London, April**
Alliott Verdon Roe leaves for the USA with British engineer G L O Davidson to work as a draughtsman on Davidson's helicopter project. He is released from his position as secretary of the Aero Club, which he took up only days ago (→ Sep 30, 1907).

**Farnborough, England, May**
Colonel J E Capper becomes superintendent of the Balloon Factory, replacing Colonel J L Templer. The army's Balloon Companies, absorbed into the Balloon School last month, are also under him (→ Dec 14).

**Germany, May**
Count Zeppelin begins building his third airship, funded by a gift of 100,000 marks from the Kaiser and a nationwide lottery raising 250,000 marks (→ Oct 9).

**Washington, DC, May 22**
The Wright brothers are granted US patent N° 821,393 for their airplane control system (→ Nov 22).

**Farnborough, England, June**
Lieutenant J W Dunne is appointed to work at the Balloon Factory. He brings designs for a tailless monoplane with swept-back wings.

**England, July 7**
Frank Hedges Butler in the balloon *Dolce far Niente*, with Col and Mrs Capper as passengers, lands just under 10 miles from the winning mark to take a 50-guinea [£52.50p] prize given by the *Daily Mail* and the *Evening News* in Britain's first official balloon race.

**Paris, July 23**
Having abandoned his helicopter project, Alberto Santos-Dumont unveils a new aircraft, the *N° 14 bis*, at Bagatelle. The odd-looking machine is dubbed *canard* [duck]

by onlookers. Santos-Dumont cannot make a test flight because *N° 14 bis* was damaged on the way to the field (→ Sep 13).

**Pennsylvania, August 11**
Mrs C J S Miller becomes the first woman passenger in an airship; the 40-hp craft is owned by her husband, Major Miller.

**Paris, August 19**
At Issy-les-Moulineaux, Trajan Vuia flies almost 79 feet at a height of just over 8 feet before his tractor monoplane, which has no means of control, crashes (→ Mar 27, 1907).

**Paris, August**
Ferdinand Ferber, who has just begun a three-year sabbatical from the army, is taken on at the Antoinette company to work with Levavasseur (→ Nov 19).

**Denmark, September 12**
Danish inventor Jakob Ellehammer makes a tethered hop-flight of 138 feet in his semi-biplane based on the designs of Otto Lilienthal. His machine, equipped with a 20-hp engine, flies around a circular track while tethered to a mast in the center.

**Paris, September 13**
Alberto Santos-Dumont takes off in his *N° 14 bis* airplane. It runs along the ground for more than 489 feet before lifting off for a flight of almost 24 feet at a height of 2 feet, ending in a crash (→ Oct 23).

**France, September 18**
Ernest Archdeacon experiments with a flying motor bicycle. In tests designed to highlight the importance of the output of the rotors, he shows that rotors driven by a 6-hp engine can lift a weight of 330 pounds at a speed of 50mph.

**Germany, October 9**
The Zeppelin LZ 3 takes off for the first time. It reaches a speed of 32mph on a flight which lasts for 2 hours and 17 minutes, carrying 11 people and 660 gallons of water as ballast (→ Oct 1, 1907).

**Paris, October 23**
Santos-Dumont flies 197 feet at a height of 6.5 feet in his *N° 14 bis* to win a 3,000-franc prize offered by Archdeacon (→ Nov 16, 1907).

**France, October 30**
French engineer Paul Cornu orders a 24-hp Antoinette engine. After tests earlier this month with a model helicopter, some 125 of his friends and acquaintances offered to put up FF100 each so that he can build a machine capable of winning the Deutsch-Archdeacon prize.

**Paris, November 10**
A banquet is held in Santos-Dumont's honor at the Aéro-Club de France (→ Nov 12).

**London, November 17**
The *Daily Mail* offers a £10,000 prize for the first flight from London to Manchester.→

**France, November 19**
Ferdinand Ferber's *N° 8* monoplane is destroyed by a violent storm at Chalais-Meudon (→ Sep 22, 1909).

**Ohio, November 22**
The Wright brothers announce that they will not display their airplane in public because of the risk of harming sales (→ May 3, 1907).

**England, December 14**
Colonel Capper reports completion of a 56-foot wind tunnel for testing air resistances of aircraft and propellers at the Balloon School, Farnborough. It is made of canvas over a wooden frame, covered in wallpaper to help make it airtight (→ May 1908).

**France, December 31**
This year has seen the perfection of the 24- and 50-hp Antoinette engines by Léon Levavasseur. Designed for motor boats in 1905, they are ideal for aviation.

*Alberto Santos-Dumont makes the first powered flight in Europe. His aircraft, the "N° 14 bis", rises high above the Parisian spectators.* ▶

# Row over American claims disrupts fine Aéro-Club dinner

*Paris, January 5*

The controversy over the Wright brothers' claim to have flown 24 miles reached a climax last night at the monthly dinner of the Aéro-Club de France. *L'Affaire Wright*, as it is known, continues to split the membership between those who believe them, led by the expatriate American Frank Lahm, and those who refuse to, led by club president Ernest Archdeacon.

The row erupted at the "moment of the cigar" and lasted until midnight. Archdeacon again pointed to the Deutsch-Archdeacon prize of FF50,000 which the Wrights could collect by flying 1 kilometer [0.62 miles]. But although skepticism persists, the view is hardening in the aeronautical press that the Wrights' claims are genuine. All that remains is for them to prove it in public (→ 21).

# Paper offers a prize for inter-city flight

*London, November 17*

The *Daily Mail* newspaper has today set aviators an extraordinary challenge, offering £10,000 to the first flyer to make "with success a journey by aeroplane from London to Manchester". Many see this as an impossible task. Five days ago Santos-Dumont was acclaimed for his flight of 722 feet [*see report opposite*], the longest distance covered in Europe. But the *Daily Mail* prize is for a flight of 200 miles.

Under the direction of its owner, Lord Northcliffe, the *Daily Mail* is proving a strong supporter of aviation. He believes that aircraft might be a priceless weapon in any future war. Today an editorial tells readers that research into flight is "vital for national reasons as well as in the cause of human progess". Last week Northcliffe blasted his editors for underplaying Santos-Dumont's flight. He warns that "there will be no more sleeping safely behind the wooden walls of old England ... if war comes the aerial chariots of the enemy will descend on British soil" (→ Apr 28, 1910).

# Powered airship flies over Montreal

*Canada, July 12*

An unusual spectacle graced the skies above Montreal today, when the American Beachey airship rose from Dominion Park on a well-publicized exhibition flight. The crowds watched with amazement as Lincoln Beachey moved fore and aft along the wooden framework gondola to alter the craft's center of gravity for ascent and descent.

Built by Beachey and Charles Earl Hess in Toledo, Ohio, and first launched this year, the craft is based on the Knabenshue airship. Its envelope is 47 feet long and power is supplied by a 5-hp Indian motorcycle engine.

# New award goes to ballooning soldier

*England, October 1*

A US Army amateur has beaten more famous rivals to win the first Gordon Bennett international balloon race. Lieutenant Frank Lahm was one of 17 contestants who ascended from Paris yesterday, including the Brazilian Alberto Santos-Dumont and Britons Frank Hedges Butler and Charles Rolls.

Lahm flew his balloon *United States* some 402 miles, including a night crossing of the English Channel, landing near York in England after 22 hours and 15 minutes, 30 miles ahead of the Italian runners-up. Santos-Dumont retired early after injuring his arm.

*Frank Hedges Butler, airborne.*

# Voisin brothers establish aircraft factory

*The Voisin-Blériot biplane, fitted with floats, is tested on Enghien Lake.*

*Paris, November*

Gabriel and Charles Voisin have founded the world's first company to build airplanes commercially. It occupies a hangar at Rue de la Ferme in the Paris suburb of Billancourt. The firm will make aircraft of their own and others' design. The new venture follows the ending of the Voisin-Blériot partnership, which last year produced a box-kite type of floatplane glider and a powered machine which would not fly. Gabriel bought out Blériot and was joined by Charles. They employ just two workers: a boat-builder and a cabinet-maker (→ Feb 28, 1907).

*Setting up on their own: Gabriel (l) and Charles Voisin.*

# British military rejects Wrights' machine

*London, February 8*

Negotiations between the Wright brothers and the British government over the sale of one of their *Flyer III* flying machines finally broke down today when C F Hadden, the director of artillery at the British War Office, wrote rejecting their terms. The final "no" from London ends months of stop-start talks during which the Wrights refused to demonstrate the machine to this or any other government in advance of a firm sale agreement, conditional on successful demonstrations. It seems that their reluctance to reveal anything about their airplane has cost them the chance of a sale.

The brothers first made contact with the British through Colonel Capper, assistant superintendent of the Balloon School at Farnborough in England. Capper visited Dayton in October 1904, when officially in the USA to attend the St Louis World Fair, and made a provisional agreement that the Wrights would supply a machine for £20,000. But the War Office rejected this deal out of hand, unconvinced of the machine's usefulness. The Wrights themselves believe that the first use of their machine will be for military reconnaissance.

Meanwhile French interest in the Wrights continues. Following their letter to the leading French aviator Captain Ferber last November, the brothers closed an agreement with a Paris syndicate – formed because the French government has been slow to act – to provide a machine for FF1,000,000 (→ Apr 14).

# Brazilian achieves first powered flight in Europe

## Donkey helps Santos-Dumont in trials

*The "Nº 14 bis" is slowly pulled along a cable by Kuigno the donkey.*

## Flight of 722 feet wins Aéro-Club prize

*An assistant crankstarts Santos-Dumont's engine before he makes his flight.*

*Paris, October 23*
A huge crowd of spectators at the Bagatelle, on the outskirts of Paris, watched in delight today as the celebrated aviator Alberto Santos-Dumont made the first sustained airplane flight in Europe. The dapper Brazilian flew his machine, the *Nº 14 bis*, for 197 feet in a straight line at a height of about 10 feet to win the Archdeacon prize of FF3,000 for the first airplane to achieve a sustained flight of over 25 meters [82 feet].

The *Nº 14 bis*, a biplane built on a fabric-covered pine frame with a 24-hp Antoinette motor at the rear and a box-like combined rudder-elevator at the front; the pilot stands upright in a wicker basket forward of the wing. Preliminary tests on July 29, in which the *Nº 14 bis* was suspended from a cable and pulled by a donkey, caused much amusement among the onlookers. But on September 13 "Santos", as he is known, lifted his machine just over two feet off the ground to make a "hop" of just under 20 feet – Europe's first powered flight. Today's more sustained effort by the Brazilian should silence those few who remain skeptical about aviation (→ Nov 12).

*Paris, November 12*
Santos-Dumont has followed up his achievements of October 23 with an even more spectacular display today at Bagatelle. At the controls of his *Nº 14 bis* – modified since its first flight by the addition of hexagonal flaps to the wings – the Brazilian made five flights of between 131 and 325 feet. But this was only a preliminary; Santos-Dumont had his eyes firmly set on the 1,500-franc prize, offered by the Aéro-Club de France in 1904 and still unclaimed, for the first airplane to fly 100 meters [328 feet]. A thousand spectators witnessed the attempt, including Ernest Archdeacon, the president of the Aéro-Club, and members of the club's committee.

Santos-Dumont sportingly invited the French aviator Louis Blériot to try for the prize first, but his machine had been damaged and "Santos" had the field to himself. *Nº 14 bis* rolled for nearly 1,000 feet before taking off and reaching 20 feet off the ground. After 21 seconds the aircraft landed, having flown just under 722 feet. Santos-Dumont was carried shoulder-high from his airplane, having surpassed all expectations.

## Brazilian-born dandy is toast of Paris

*The raffish aviator (r) makes his mark on Parisian high society.*

*Paris, November 12*
Once again the aerial feats of Alberto Santos-Dumont, or *le petit Santos* as he is affectionately called in France, have made him the toast of Paris. The five-foot-tall, 33-year-old Brazilian flyer has been one of the most popular characters on the French aviation scene for several years, not just for his impressive feats in the air as balloonist and airplane pilot but also for his sportsmanship, sense of humor and elegance of dress. Often to be seen cutting a dandified dash in modish Paris salons, the mustachioed aviator has started a fashion with his trademark of soft Panama hat and high stiff collars.

**August 19. Romanian-born inventor Trajan Vuia takes his aircraft, pictured here, for a flight of about 80 feet. The first successful monoplane with the engine in front, the bat-like "Vuia" also boasts pneumatic tyres.**

# 1907

|  | 37.85mph<br>USA<br>Wilbur Wright<br>*Flyer III*<br>Oct 5, 1905 |  | 24.2 miles<br>USA<br>Wilbur Wright<br>*Flyer III*<br>Oct 5, 1905 |  | 82ft<br>France<br>Louis Blériot<br>Blériot VI<br>Sep 17, 1907 |  | 1,151 lb<br>France<br>Voisin Brothers<br>*Voisin-Farman N°1* |  | 54hp<br>France<br>Renault<br>VB Renault |

**Nebraska, January 13**
Tests begin on the balloon which the US Army Signal Corps has purchased from France.

**Paris, January 22**
Robert Esnault-Pelterie files for a third patent for his innovative airplane controls: one lever for both ascent and descent (→ Oct 10).

**Florida, January 24**
Glenn Curtiss becomes the world's fastest man as the motorcycle he designed reaches a speed of 136.29 mph at Ormond Beach. The record is, however, not ratified. Curtiss-designed engines can be fitted on aircraft.

**Vincennes, France, February 28**
Cabinet-maker Charles Voisin begins tests of the airplane made by his company for Léon Delagrange. He takes off for a hop of several feet, but the fuselage breaks up (→ Mar 30).

**Saint-Cyr, France, March 27**
Santos-Dumont taxis his new airplane, the *N° 15*, on which the rudder is behind the engine over the pilot's head. Before he can take off, one of the wings bumps the ground and breaks (→ Apr 4).

**Paris, March 27**
Trajan Vuia begins tests of his airplane, newly fitted with steering surfaces. He makes a short flight of 33 feet (→ Jun 21).

**Saint-Cyr, France, April 4**
Santos-Dumont, disappointed by his failure on March 27 and shocked by Charles Voisin's flight of 197 feet shortly afterwards, tries again with his *N° 14 bis*. He makes a short flight of 164 feet.

**Paris, April 19**
Louis Blériot flies and crashes his powered monoplane *N° V* at Bagatelle (→ Jul 25).

**Austria, May 3**
The Wright brothers are elected honorary members of the Vienna Aviation Club (→ Feb 10, 1908).

**New York, May 18**
Wilbur Wright sails for Europe to discuss the sale of his *Flyer III* in London, Paris, Moscow and Berlin (→ May 14, 1908).

**Paris, June 21**
Romanian Trajan Vuia makes a flight of almost 66 feet, at a height of 16 feet, in his second machine which has a 24-hp Antoinette engine running on carbonic acid and has its wheels fitted with shock absorbers.

**London, June**
Englishman Horatio Phillips makes an uncontrolled flight of 492 feet in his self-built aircraft, *Multiplane II*, at Streatham. The machine has some 200 tiny aerofoils in four tandem frames.

**Paris, July 25**
At Issy-les-Moulineaux, Blériot flies 492 feet in his monoplane *N° VI*, the *Libellule* [dragonfly]. Built by Louis Peyret, the foreman at his works, it has two sets of wings in tandem. To control vertical movement, the pilot slides to and fro on a wheeled seat (→ Sep 17).

**Washington, DC, August 1**
The Aeronautical Division of the US Army Signal Corps is created. It consists of two men under Captain Charles Chandler, briefed "to study the flying machine and the possibility of adapting it to military purposes".

**England, 25 August**
Griffith Brewer tests his new balloon, *Lotus II*. It is the balloon flown by Santos-Dumont in the Gordon Bennett Cup last year, rebuilt for Brewer by Eustace and Oswald Short at their Battersea, London, works. The Short brothers are passengers on today's flight, as is Claude Moore-Brabazon.

**Canada, August**
Gliding experimenter Larry Lesh tests his second glider, based on a Chanute biplane design. He is towed by a motorboat for 7 miles on the St Lawrence river but crashes when his signal to cast off is misunderstood and the boat turns too sharply.

**Canada, September 15**
The wife of kite designer Alexander Graham Bell suggests to him and their friends, Canadian engineers John McCurdy and "Casey" Baldwin, that they form an association to carry out flying experiments (→ Oct 1).

**Paris, September 21**
Louis Breguet and Charles Richet show their gyroplane to members of the French Academy of Science.

**Paris, September 30**
After 225 failed attempts, Henry Farman takes off in his *Voisin-Farman I* biplane at Issy-les-Moulineaux; he makes a flight of some 262 feet (→ Nov 10).

**Surrey, England, September 30**
Alliott Verdon Roe tests his full-scale biplane, equipped with a 6-hp English JAP engine, at Brooklands race-track, but does not take off (→ Jun 8, 1908).

**Montreal, September**
Lincoln Beachey's flights in his airship are the main attraction at an exhibition at Sherbrooke.

**Nova Scotia, October 1**
The Aerial Experiment Association is founded at Beinn Breagh, near Baddeck, the summer home of Dr Graham Bell. Its original members are Dr Bell, F W "Casey" Baldwin, John A D McCurdy, Glenn F Curtiss and Lt Thomas E Selfridge (→ Jun 21, 1908).

**Paris, October 5**
Louis Blériot begins tests of his *N° VII* monoplane at Issy-les-Moulineaux. It is fitted with a 50-hp Antoinette engine.

**London, October 10**
Following its flight over London on October 5, the *Nulli Secundus* airship is split open at its mooring at the Crystal Palace to prevent it from tearing in the wind.

**Paris, November 5**
Léon Delagrange makes a flight of 984 feet in a semicircle at Issy-les-Moulineaux before making a crash-landing in his *Voisin-Delagrange I* biplane. He has been flying this aircraft for just five days (→ Apr 11, 1908).

**Paris, November 10**
Henry Farman makes a flight of 3,379 feet in one minute 14 seconds in his *Voisin-Farman I* – the first flight in Europe of over one minute (→ Jan 14, 1908).

**France, November 16**
Robert Esnault-Pelterie flies 1,969 feet in 55 seconds in his *REP I* monoplane (→ Jun 18, 1908).

**London, November 26**
Lord Northcliffe announces a new *Daily Mail* prize of £100 for a round flight of a quarter of a mile and back.

**USA, November 30**
Glenn Curtiss founds the Curtiss Aeroplane Company. It is the first US airplane manufacturing company (→ Aug 18, 1909).

**France, November 30**
The French army airship *Patrie* breaks free from its mooring near Verdun in a strong wind and disappears out over the Atlantic Ocean (→ Aug 25, 1908).

**USA, December 23**
Brigadier-General James Allen, the US Army's chief signal officer, produces a specification for a military airplane and requests tenders (→ Mar 2, 1909).

**Farnborough, England, December**
Samuel Cody begins constructing a biplane with a British Army grant of £50. He uses the 50-hp Antoinette engine which powered the airship *Nulli Secundus*.

*Despite the rapid progress of powered and heavier-than-air flight, ballooning remains by far the most common way to get airborne.* ▶

Official Program
of the
Second Competition
for the

GORDON BENNETT
AERONAUTIC CUP

Forest Park, St. Louis, U.S.A.
October, 1907

# Voisin biplane takes off

*The Voisins' biplane design for Léon Delagrange takes off at Bagatelle.*

*Paris, March 30*
Charles Voisin, one of the Voisin brothers whose flying machines have made them almost household names in France, today made six short flights over a large open space at Bagatelle, on the outskirts of Paris. He was flying a new biplane ordered by the French sculptor Léon Delagrange.

The *Voisin-Delagrange N° 1* made a very stable flight, covering about 197 feet. The craft was modified after an incident during a test flight two weeks ago, when it was found that the left wing had a tendency to drag. A 4.4-lb weight was placed on the right wing to counter this. Another problem they faced was the high cost of the air-craft: up to FF15,000, half of that being spent on the engine.

The Voisins design their machines with a biplane elevator at the front, biplane wings, the tail at the back and the propeller behind the wings. Delagrange's machine is powered by one of the 50-hp 8-cylinder type known as the Antoinette, designed by Levavasseur and originally installed in speedboats. The Voisins are experienced aircraft designers, having already made several gliders and flying machines. In 1905 one of their gliders was flown down the Seine towed by a speedboat. This sparked Delagrange's interest, and he asked the Voisins to make him a flying machine (→ Oct 26).

# English airplane proves to be model flyer

*London, April 6*
In the well attended and much pub-licized model airplane competition held at Alexandra Park in north London today, and sponsored by the *Daily Mail*, 29-year-old Alliott Verdon Roe swept the honors but was denied full rewards. Matched against some 200 entrants with models thought to be capable of mechanical flight, three of Roe's very large rubber-powered air-planes outflew all comers. Only half a dozen others flew well.

Unfortunately, the organizers deemed that none had flown suffi-ciently far to merit the top £150 prize, and Roe received the £75 second prize, out of £250 total award money available. He was obviously taken aback. To qualify for the main prize a minimum flight of 100 feet had been required, and his rear-tailed biplane flew the length of London's Agricultural Hall during inside trials. The hall is 100 feet long, and the model had to be restrained by a net from hitting the end wall.

Outside, on the slopes of Alexan-dra Park, it flew further. Only one of his two forward-elevator models was tested inside before lunch, but the larger 8-foot span model won the outside trials and was overall winner. The second forward-elevator model flew well outside, but the crowd made measurement impossible. Roe received the £75 magnanimously (→ Sep 30).

*Alliott Verdon Roe shows off the model airplane which won the competition.*

# French prototype helicopter lifts off for a tentative short hop

*The Breguet gyroplane has four rotors but fails to get far off the ground.*

*France, September 19*
The brothers Louis and Jacques Breguet, of a famous clock-making family, today saw their strange "gy-roplane" *N° 1* lift itself about two feet off the ground at Douai in France. This was the first piloted "flight" of a type of flying machine known as a helicopter which, unlike other aircraft, can rise vertically.

The pilot sits in the center, next to the 50-hp Antoinette engine, from which extend four long gird-ers, made of steel tubes, in the form of a horizontal cross. Each girder has a rotor on the end with four biplane blades. Four men held on to the unsteady machine (→ Sep 21).

# Bad weather stops airship polar flight

*Spitzbergen, Norway, September 2*
Bad weather has foiled an attempt by US millionaire Walter Wellman to fly his airship *America* to the North Pole. Fog, coupled with strong headwinds, forced the air-ship down onto a glacier just north of its departure point on Danes Island after only three hours in the air. The project has already been delayed for over a year owing to technical difficulties. The *America* is hydrogen-filled, 230 feet long and powered by two 90-hp engines. Although it is undamaged, no one knows if Wellman will try again.

# Blériot succeeds despite a new crash

*Paris, September 17*
Only a spectacular stunt saved the life of French aviator Louis Blériot at Issy-les-Moulineaux today, when his latest airplane, the modified tandem-wing Blériot *Nº VI* or *Libellule*, crumpled on impact with the ground and was wrecked. Blériot took off very quickly, but when he reached a height of about 80 feet, the engine suddenly cut out and the aircraft began to plummet.

A sliding seat, by which the pilot's weight could be shifted forward or backward, was intended to control the altitude of the nose of the aircraft, but it was not sufficient to right the machine. Thinking fast, Blériot left his seat to throw himself toward the tail. Just in time, the machine levelled out enough to prevent a tragic accident. Miraculously, Blériot walked away unhurt and he intends to continue flying.

The loss of the *Libellule* is unfortunate, as it seemed to hold considerable promise. In July and August it managed 11 flights, the longest, 492 feet, lasting 10 seconds. Both Blériot and his friend, Louis Peyret, shared the flying. Peyret undertook the early tests, as he had been mainly responsible for its conception.

For the latest series of trials, the *Libellule* was fitted with a 50-hp Antoinette in place of the original 24-hp engine. The 50-hp *Libellule* had made five earlier flights, the longest lasting 17 seconds and covering 603 feet (→ Dec 18).

*One of a number of botched landings of the Blériot "Nº V" aircraft.*

*The Blériot "Nº VI" or "Libellule" was a considerable improvement.*

## Robert Esnault-Pelterie is first pilot to fly with a control stick

*Robert Esnault-Pelterie waves from the cockpit of his machine, the REP.*

*France, October 10*
A remarkable new monoplane made its first tentative hop – just under 20 feet – at Buc today with 25-year-old designer Robert Esnault-Pelterie at the controls. Or rather control, because the rudderless aircraft, called the *REP* for its pilot's initials, is the first to be piloted by the use of a single, broomhandle-like lever which leaves the pilot a hand free for the engine.

The control lever is designed so that it is moved from side to side to control the warping of the wings for steering – an idea first thought of by the Wrights – and forward and backward to control climb and descent. Among the other innovations of the *REP* are its completely enclosed fuselage, made of welded steel covered in red muslin, which cuts wind drag. The airraft's nose-mounted motor, also designed by Esnault-Pelterie, is pioneering, too: it has an odd number of cylinders (seven) delivering 35hp, which makes it powerful for its small (110-lb) weight.

## 'Nulli Secundus', army airship, flies skies over London

*London, October 5*
A spectacular feat of airmanship, as unexpected as it was enterprising, brought London to a standstill this morning. The first British Army dirigible airship, boastfully named *Nulli Secundus* [second to none], flew directly over the British capital, causing thousands of people to rush into the streets. The airship left its base at Farnborough, in Hampshire, at 10.30am and concluded an epic flight three and a half hours later 50 miles away at the Crystal Palace in south London.

The craft, which first flew at Farnborough on September 10, is braced to a light framework of wooden spars and remained under

*"Nulli Secundus" above St Paul's.*

perfect control throughout, rising and dipping and circling to order. In command was Colonel J E Capper, the superintendent of the military Balloon Factory at Farnborough, assisted, as engineer, by the US-born kite-flying entrepreneur Samuel Cody, who designed the propellers and aerial controls.

As they flew toward London, Cody continually sounded a loud klaxon from the control car hung below the long, sausage-shaped gas envelope. Over the city, Capper flew low over Buckingham Palace in salute to King Edward VII and circumnavigated the dome of St Paul's Cathedral (→ Oct 10).

# Henry Farman flies Voisin biplane to set official distance record of 2,530 feet

*The "Voisin-Farman Nº 1" in full flight at Issy-les-Moulineaux, France.*

**Paris, October 26**
In tests today at Issy-les-Moulineaux, Henry Farman flew his *Voisin-Farman I* flying machine to a new, officially observed distance record of just under 2,530 feet. The son of Thomas Farman, the Paris correspondent of the London *Standard* newspaper, Henry grew up in Paris and attended the Ecole des Beaux Arts [School of Fine Arts], but turned to racing bicycles and then motorcycles and cars.

Deciding that flying would be safer, Farman visited the Voisin brothers at their Paris factory and ordered a standard example of their biplane. The Voisins have painted "HENRI FARMAN Nº 1" on the tail, but in fact Farman just as often spells his first name the English way. Small of stature, this Anglo-Frenchman has already attracted attention for his amazing energy and unflappable manner. The Voisins colorfully describe him as "manipulative skill personified".

Farman's manipulative skills are amply demonstrated by the speed with which he has learned to master the tricky flying machine. So far he has got away without a single crash. Most of the other would-be winners of the Archdeacon cup (on offer for the first officially observed flight longer than 150 meters [492 feet]) have repeatedly had to patch up their machines after crashes.

The Voisins appreciate the fact that, unlike several of their other customers, Farman has not insisted on – to their mind – ridiculous changes to the design of the machine. On the other hand, with experience, Farman could soon find that there are ways in which his machine can be improved.

Another way in which he has shown his initiative is in obtaining permission to fly on the huge military parade ground at Issy-les-Moulineaux. Large and level, it even has factory chimneys at one edge whose smoke conveniently tells the aviator the strength and direction of the wind (→ Nov 10).

*Henry Farman strikes a proud pose.*

# Cornu helicopter lifts off

*Normandy, France, November 13*
Paul Cornu, a bicycle maker at Lisieux, made a brief but triumphant vertical take-off this morning in his full-size helicopter. His short hop forward of about a foot, lasting just 20 seconds, was a cause for celebration because no manned helicopter has made a free and unassisted flight before. A piloted machine designed by Louis Breguet and Professor Richet lifted off under its own power on September 19 and 29, but it was stabilized by four helpers on the ground.

The idea behind the helicopter is to mount a propeller on top of the machine to lift it off the ground rather than one in front to pull it through the air, as is the case with an airplane. Cornu's helicopter, developed from a working model that he built last year, consists of two rotors – measuring just under 20 feet in diameter – mounted one behind the other. Each has two blades connected to a 66-foot driving belt powered by a 24-hp water-cooled Antoinette engine. The body of the machine is made of steel tubing which supports the pilot's seat and engine. Two wind vanes mounted beneath the rotors can be tilted to provide forward motion.

Cornu first tried to take off four days ago, but the driving belt broke down. This afternoon he reached a height of about five feet while his brother was standing on the frame of the helicopter.

*Paul Cornu takes the pilot's seat in his extraordinary new aircraft.*

**Inspiration for advertisers: a romantic view of life in the skies (left) and a compelling reason to purchase Abel Morrall's new hatpins (right).**

# Blériot 'Nº VII' crashes

*Blériot's new monoplane is capable of flying at a speed of 50mph.*

*Paris, December 18*
Louis Blériot, as well known for his spectacular accidents as his brief flights, crashed again at Issy-les-Moulineaux today in his *Nº VII* monoplane. It was his sixth flight in this aircraft since November 10; he had previously flown it twice for 45 seconds and covered a distance of 1,640 feet. After today's mishaps it is now likely to be abandoned.

The *Nº VII* is the third powered airplane built by Blériot. In design it is very different from the *Nº V*, which was abandoned in April after crashing at Bagatelle Meadows, and the tandem-wing *Nº VI* or *Libellule* which fell from the sky only three months ago. *Nº VII* is a monoplane with its wings low-mounted at the forward end of the fuselage, unlike the *Nº V*. It has proved inherently unstable, with only a tiny rudder and huge elevators at the tail for control. A 50-hp Antoinette engine is at the nose, driving a four-blade propeller. An unusual feature of the machine is that the entire airframe is covered with a strong paper parchment (→ Jan 23, 1909).

# Alfred de Pischoff opts for Anzani engine

*Paris, December 5*
Alfred de Pischoff, a Hungarian by birth, today made brief hops at the military parade ground of Issy-les-Moulineaux to join the short but growing list of aviators who have actually flown heavier-than-air machines.

His machine shows several novel features. A biplane, it has the engine and propeller at the front. Underneath are three wheels, two in front and one at the rear. At the back is the cruciform tail. There are no elevators or rudders in front. De Pischoff's engine is one never before used in a flying machine. Designed by a Milanese engineer, Alessandro Anzani, its three air-cooled cylinders give 25hp. This neat engine drives a beautiful propeller of carved wood – much more efficient than the bent metal sheet propellers usually seen.

The propeller was made by Frenchman Lucien Chauvière, in whose workshops the de Pischoff machine was built. The aircraft was finished last month, but then suffered various breakages which prevented it from flying. De Pischoff hopes to make more flights.

*A smiling de Pischoff shows off his airplane, with its improved engine.*

# Soldier pilots Alexander Bell's man-carrying kite on lake flight

*Nova Scotia, Canada, December 6*
Lieutenant Thomas E Selfridge, secretary of the Aerial Experiment Association, today flew in a man-carrying kite, *Cygnet 1*, across Bras d'Or Lake at Baddeck in the first experiment of its kind. The machine is also the first built by 60-year-old Dr Alexander Graham Bell, the famous Scottish-born inventor of the telephone and aviation enthusiast, who is the association's chairman and chief designer.

The design, which is made up of tetrahedral-shaped fabric panels, lacked controls, according to the pilot. The test was a limited success: the kite lifted Lieutenant Selfridge speedily from a flat barge when the steam tug took the strain, and deposited him gently back onto the lake seven minutes later after attaining a measured height of 168 feet. Unfortunately an attempt to tow the kite back ashore resulted in its destruction.

Lieutenant Selfridge's comments suggest that the thrust of experimental work will now be toward developing a glider which has full aerial control, like that of models developed in France and in the USA, with a view to adding an engine once the required skills have been acquired. Dr Bell, though, is understood to favour modifications to his tetrahedral designs.

*Members of the association, with Alexander Graham Bell seated on the left.*

# Santos flies new, lighter monoplane

*Paris, November 16*
Brazilian Alberto Santos-Dumont, the darling of Paris society, today flew his tiny monoplane, the *Demoiselle Nº 19*, at Bagatelle for 656 feet at a height of 20 feet. The airplane could hardly be more different from his biplane, which made barely a hop just a year ago.

The new machine is reputedly the smallest and lightest machine ever to navigate the air. Made mainly of bamboo and silk, it weighs a mere 243 pounds with the pilot. The 20-hp Dutheil-Chalmers engine is at the front of the wings, but the aviator sits underneath, between the wheels. He controls the machine by pivoting the tail surfaces and rocking his body from side to side to warp the wings.

# 1908

40.26mph
France
Henry Farman
Voisin biplane
Oct 30, 1908

77.48 miles
USA
Wilbur Wright
Wright A
Dec 31, 1908

361ft
USA
Wilbur Wright
Wright A
Dec 18, 1908

1,200 lb
USA
Wright Brothers
Wright A

79hp
France
Gobron-Brille
Gobron

**Paris, January 3**
The Aéro-Club de France offers a prize of FF500 to the inventor of a device to indicate horizontal level in flight.

**Paris, February 8**
Flight tests begin at Issy-les-Moulineaux for the Gastambide-Mengin monoplane, built by Léon Levavasseur and fitted with a 50-hp Antoinette engine.

**France, March 6**
Tire-makers André and Edouard Michelin offer a 20,000-franc cup, to be awarded annually for six years to the first pilot to double the flight-distance record, and FF100,000 for a flight from Paris to Puy-de-Dôme (250 miles).

**Paris, March 14**
The Renault brothers' airplane engine is tested on the Voisin-Farman *N° 1 bis* biplane at Issy-les-Moulineaux (→ Mar 21).

**Paris, March 14**
Léon Delagrange receives a new biplane, the Voisin-Delagrange *N° 2*, at Issy-les-Moulineaux and flies it just over 883 feet to win an Aéro-Club prize for a flight of 200 meters [656 feet].

**Paris, March 21**
Henry Farman covers 6,275 feet in three minutes 47 seconds in his Voisin-Farman *N° 1 bis* at Issy-les-Moulineaux (→ Oct 30).

**Paris, March 23**
French industrialist Lazare Weiller signs a contract with the Wrights establishing a Wright airplane company in France, on condition that the brothers make two demonstration flights covering 50km [31.1 miles] within an hour's flying time. They will receive FF500,000 and half the founders' shares (→ May 6).

**Paris, March 28**
Delagrange makes the first passenger flight, taking Farman aboard his *Voisin* biplane at Issy-les-Moulineaux (→ Apr 11).

**USA, April 7**
The members of the Aerial Experiment Association enter a competition sponsored by the *Scientific American*, which has offered $25,000 for a flight of over 0.62 miles. The Wrights refuse to enter because the rules state the airplane must take off without help.

**Paris, April 11**
Delagrange flies 12,878 feet in six minutes 39 seconds in his Voisin-Delagrange *N° 2* (→ May 23).

**North Carolina, May 6**
The Wright brothers fly for the first time since 1905, at Kitty Hawk. Wilbur pilots the 1905 *Flyer III*, modified so that the pilot and a passenger can sit erect, on a flight of just over 1,000 feet (→ May 14).

**North Carolina, May 14**
At Kitty Hawk, Wilbur Wright takes up Charles W Furnas of Dayton, Ohio, on a flight of 1,967 feet. Later Orville, with Furnas, covers 13,518 feet and makes a circle in just over four minutes (→ May 29).

**New York State, May 19**
Lt Thomas Selfridge makes the first solo flight by a US Army officer in the new *White Wing*, the Aerial Experiment Association's second airplane. First flown by "Casey" Baldwin yesterday, it is fitted with wing flaps, allowing the pilot to maintain lateral control in flight. Selfridge flies 237 feet.

**Rome, May 23**
French aviator Léon Delagrange makes the first airplane flight in Italy (→ Sep 6).

**Le Havre, France, May 29**
Wilbur Wright arrives from New York in order to demonstrate the Wright *Flyer* airplane in Europe (→ Jul 20).

**Farnborough, England, May**
Colonel J E Capper and Lt-Col C J Aston send a wireless signal from the balloon *Pegasus* to a point on the ground 25 miles away.

**Philadelphia, Pa, June 7**
The *Inquirer* launches the USA's first newspaper aviation column, by managing editor John T Custis.

**New York, June 10**
The Aeronautical Society of the United States is established.

**France, June 18**
On his third outing with his REP *N° 2* monoplane, Robert Esnault-Pelterie makes a forced landing after a flight of 3,937 feet at Toussus-le-Noble. The impact is softened by the pneumatic shock-absorber he has designed and fitted to the wheel axles, but he is still badly injured.

**New York State, June 21.**
The first flight of the Aerial Experiment Association's (AEA's) promising *June Bug* biplane, their third machine, takes place. It has a 40-hp air-cooled Curtiss engine.

**Turin, Italy, July 8**
Thérèse Peltier becomes the first woman to ascend in an airplane when Delagrange, whose pupil she is, takes her up. She flies about 656 feet at a height of about 13 feet.

**Florida, July 17**
The USA's first aviation legislation is passed: a municipal ordinance regulating aircraft within city limits at Kissimmee.

**USA, July 20**
Orville Wright warns Glenn Curtiss that the wing flaps used in the AEA's *June Bug* are an infringement of the Wrights' patents (→ Aug 8).

**London, July**
Capt R H S Bacon, the Royal Navy's director of ordnance, proposes the establishment of a naval air service.

**France, August 25**
The Lebaudy airship *République* bursts in mid-air and crashes in flames after a piece of the wooden propeller tears a hole through the gas-filled envelope (→ Jun 28, 1909).

**Virginia, August 28**
The US Army accepts its first dirigible; 96 feet long, with a 20-hp Curtiss engine, it has been tested by Lts Frank Lahm, Benjamin Foulois and Thomas Selfridge.

**Paris, October 9**
The Antoinette N° 4 monoplane, built in the Levavasseur factory at Puteaux, makes a successful test flight at Issy-les-Moulineaux.

**Berlin, October 11**
Colonel Shaek of the Swiss Aero Club wins the third annual Gordon Bennett international balloon race with a flight of 745 miles.

**France, October 30**
Blériot makes the first town-to-town return flight, going from Toury to Artenay, seven miles away, before returning to Toury.

**Magdeburg, Germany, November 2**
Hans Grade makes a short flight in the triplane which he built.

**Paris, November 5**
Wilbur Wright receives the Grand Gold Medal of the Aéro-Club (→ Nov 9).

**London, November 9**
The Wright brothers become honorary members of the Aeronautical Society of Great Britain (→ Dec 31).

**Paris, November**
The Seguin brothers exhibit their Gnome rotary engine at the Paris auto show.

**France, December 19**
Port-Aviation, the world's first aerodrome, built 12 miles from Paris, is finished.

---

*An unaccustomed sight in the countryside: flying over the hayricks, Henry Farman surprises a French shepherd and his flock.* ▶

# Farman wins prize for Europe's first circular flight

*Henry Farman's Voisin-Farman "Nº 1" biplane is ready for touchdown as it approaches the finishing line for the Deutsch-Archdeacon prize competition.*

**Paris, January 13**
Henry Farman made aviation history today when he flew the first circular flight in Europe at Issy-les-Moulineaux, watched by a handful of people. The feat, which he carried out in a Voisin biplane, the Voisin-Farman *Nº 1*, brings him the coveted Deutsch-Archdeacon prize of FF50,000 for Europe's first officially monitored one-kilometer [0.62-mile] circuit.

Farman ordered his *Nº 1* from the Voisin brothers in June last year, but had little success in trials in August at Issy. In September, though, after 200 attempts and some modifications to the tail construction, Farman got the aircraft to fly just over 262 feet; this was followed on October 26 by a flight of almost 2,530 feet, breaking European records. Having cracked the secret of getting his airplane aloft, Farman poured his energies into mastering the one maneuver without which powered flight would have a limited future: steering.

Farman's friendly competitor in this race, sculptor-turned-airman Léon Delagrange, managed a 984-foot semi-circular turn on November 5 in his own Voisin; Farman's first turn followed three days later. Further modifications to the Voisin-Farman were made when Farman made a crucial discovery. Working by trial and error, he found that drag is reduced and lift greatly increased when the wing's angle of attack is reduced or even eliminated. Until Farman's discovery, aircraft designers the world over had mistakenly believed that a considerable angle of attack was an absolute necessity for flight. It was in this modified craft that Farman took off for his epoch-making circuit in the dawn light. Members of the committee of the Aéro-Club de France marked the start point and, 500 meters [1,640 feet] away, the point around which Farman had to turn for his return flight. Using his rudder alone to steer – his aircraft had no wing-warping system for lateral control – Farman took off after a 164-foot run and rose to a height of approximately 40 feet before crabbing around the circuit and landing smoothly to a hero's welcome. The flight lasted one minute 28 seconds.

**London, January 14**
Farman's achievement in Paris yesterday has been greeted with excitement bordering on hysteria.

Today's edition of *The Times* of London thunders: "The Conquest of the Air – Success of an Englishman" (Farman is a British citizen, son of the Paris correspondent of the London *Standard*). January 13, declared *The Times* in a special report from Issy-les-Moulineaux, was "an epoch-making date, that of the victory before official witnesses of human intelligence in its efforts to solve the problem which brought Icarus to grief [and] which tormented the brain of Leonardo da Vinci ... Nothing of the kind has ever before been accomplished" (→ Mar 21).

**Danish inventor Jakob Ellehammer, dressed all in white, takes the controls of his "Nº IV" biplane. On January 14, this skilful and original designer flew for 578 feet in this machine. It is powered by the same 30-hp engine (of his own design) which he fitted to a previous successful triplane design last year. Ellehammer's method of controlling his aircraft is unusual: he moves the pilot's seat, which is mounted on a type of pendulum.**

## American army contracts to buy aircraft

**Washington, DC, February 10**
The US government has gone a long way to accepting the Wright *Flyer* for the Army Signal Corps. The army is inviting bids for a biplane which must be able to fly for an hour, carry two men, reach 40 mph and take fuel to cover 125 miles. Since the army invited tenders last December, 41 have arrived, most of them from cranks. The Wrights are bidding $25,000; they believe they have the only practical airplane. But they must now brush up on flying skills; they have not flown since 1905. The deal will be closed after stringent flight trials (→ May 6).

*US troops inspect an army balloon.*

# American association makes impressive progress

## 'Red Wing' crash-lands after lake flight

*The association's "Red Wing" airplane, piloted by F W "Casey" Baldwin.*

*New York State, March 12*
The *Red Wing*, the first powered aircraft developed by the Aerial Experiment Association (AEA) at its new location in Hammondsport, New York State, flew for the first time today with Canadian "Casey" Baldwin as pilot. The aircraft is largely the brainchild of one of the AEA's leading members, Lieutenant Thomas Selfridge.

Thin ice was the surprise prob-lem this morning when much of the surface of Lake Keuka, venue for the trial, was found to have thawed. A firm area was at last found and the *Red Wing*, named for its brightly colored wing fabric, was able to get airborne. It flew along steadily for some 260-295 feet at a height of 20 feet before dropping suddenly onto the ice and breaking up. Baldwin was unhurt, and another trial is planned soon (→ Jun 21).

## Crowds see 'June Bug' win distance prize

*Glenn Curtiss takes off on his way to a trophy in the "June Bug".*

*New York State, July 4*
Glenn Hammond Curtiss, motor-cycle daredevil and rising star of the Aerial Experiment Association (AEA), today succeeded in capping all his previous records – this time not on two wheels but in the new AEA flyer, the *June Bug*. Curtiss is claiming the $2,500 silver trophy offered by the journal *Scientific American* for an official flight of over a kilometer [0.62 miles]. The *June Bug* flew nearly twice the required distance, achieving 1.1 miles and alighting gently. Curtiss was delighted, seeing it as a victory for the "scientific method" of research adopted by the AEA and also by the more private Wright brothers.

The flight was watched by a large and highly excited holiday crowd at the Stony Brook Farm race-track, Hammondsport, base for the AEA experiments (→ Dec 6).

## Association's pilots show their mettle

*New York State, June 21*
The rapidly progressing group of flying experts known as the Aerial Experiment Association (AEA), brought together in the USA last year by the scientific enthusiasm of Mabel Bell, wife of telephone inventor Dr Alexander Graham Bell, is making advances by leaps and bounds. Yesterday the AEA flew its third machine, the *June Bug*, for the first time, which reflects as much on the peculiar chemistry between the members as on the simple advance of science.

Chairman of the AEA is the authoritative Dr Bell himself, aided as secretary by thoughtful soldier Lt Thomas Selfridge, and there are two energetic Canadians, pilots F W "Casey" Baldwin and J A D Mc-Curdy. And finally, adding glamor and much engineering skill, is speed motor cyclist Glenn Curtiss as director of experiments (→ Jul 4).

## Canadian John McCurdy takes up the 'Silver Dart' in the US

*New York State, December 6*
A new design from the Aerial Experimental Association is reported to have flown at their Hammondsport base. Following their resounding success this summer with the airplane *June Bug*, the new machine, to be called *Silver Dart*, is the result of a collaboration between Canadian pilot-turned-designer John McCurdy and the engine manufacturer Glenn Curtiss, both of whom are founder members of the association.

The *Silver Dart* is a conventional biplane except for its unusual wheeled undercarriage, instead of skids, which is capable of repeated field landings – an indicator of the AEA's growing confidence. It is powered by a water-cooled 50-hp Curtiss engine, a great advance on previous air-cooled motors. This drives a single twin-bladed propeller behind the pilot. Wing-tip control surfaces, now thought essential by pilots for lateral control, are larger than those on the *June Bug*. Another marked improvement is the facility to carry two people aloft, the second to sit immediately behind the pilot, who is provided with an adjustable seat to maintain the craft's centre of gravity.

If the machine is successful, McCurdy hopes to transport the *Silver Dart* back to Canada and become the first to fly a heavier-than-air machine there (→ Feb 23, 1909).

*AEA pilot John McCurdy at the controls of the "Silver Dart" which is the fourth aircraft to come from the Aerial Experiment Association stable.*

# Militant woman drops political leaflets from dirigible onto Houses of Parliament

*Air power? Suffragettes take to the air to demand a better deal for women.*

*London, June 21*
British Members of Parliament received advice from an unexpected source today when Muriel Matters, suffragette and ballooning enthusiast, flew over the Houses of Parliament dropping hundreds of "Votes For Women" leaflets. She hired Captain Spencer and his dirigible for the "bombing" raid. The idea of spreading propaganda from the air is not new. In May 1854 a Russian exile named Vladimir Engelson wrote to the French Ministry of War, suggesting that balloons be used to bombard the Russian people with messages condemning their government's campaign in the Crimea. His idea was completely ignored.

## French pilots have their wings clipped

*Paris, July 25*
French aviators were struck a blow today when the military authorities announced that all flights from the suburban army base at Issy-les-Moulineaux are to be banned. The army has become increasingly worried about the risks to local residents of an airplane accident, its fears fueled by crashes such as that of Louis Blériot's *Nº VIII* monoplane two days ago.

The ban, effective tomorrow, deprives airmen of their main experimental base. However, after pleading with the police chief, Blériot and fellow-aviator Henry Farman have won permission for flights to continue, with a police presence, between 4am and 6am.

## Farman coins a new aviation term

*New York State, September 15*
Anglo-French aviator Henry Farman, currently touring the US, has invented the term *aileron* to describe a wing's movable horizontal surfaces used for lateral control instead of wing-warping. *Ailerons* are slowly gaining acceptance.

Farman used the term when describing the Aerial Experiment Association's airplanes *White Wing* and *June Bug*, which both flew this summer. These American biplanes have a triangular *aileron* built into each wing tip, operated on the *White Wing* by a yoke attached to the pilot's shoulders. The first *ailerons* were fitted by the French aviator Robert Esnault-Pelterie to his 1904 glider.

# Briton 'hops' in test flight at race-track

*Surrey, England, June 8*
Alliott Verdon Roe, first railway apprentice and then ship's engineer, has become one of the few Britons to interest himself in flying machines. Today at the motor-race track at Brooklands in Surrey, near London, his *Roe I* biplane successfully achieved several hops.

Roe's machine originally had a six-hp JAP engine, but this proved to be too weak. Only when fitted with an Antoinette of 24hp was it able to take off. His efforts have, however, been severely hampered by the Brooklands management. They consider that the sight of so vulgar an object as a flying machine would bring the track into disrepute. Despite this, Roe has succeeded in starting a new career.

# Germans raise cash for a new airship

*Germany, August 5*
In a dramatic example of public response to aeronautical disaster, the German people have taken just one day to raise enough money to replace the LZ 4 airship, accidentally destroyed yesterday in woods near Echterdingen. The LZ 4 was the fourth craft made by airship developer Count Ferdinand von Zeppelin. It was also, clearly, a source of intense national pride.

So fast has been the public's reaction that officials at the Zeppelin works at Friedrichshafen are already calling it not "the disaster" but "the miracle" of Echterdingen. Even the German government and Kaiser Wilhelm are reported to be taking a fresh interest in the Zeppelins (→ Jul 23, 1909).

# Léon Delagrange is airborne for 30 minutes

*Léon Delagrange at the controls of his Voisin-built biplane "Nº 2".*

*Paris, September 6*
A sculptor turned aviator today became the first European to remain airborne for half an hour, when Léon Delagrange flew 15.2 miles – itself a record – in 29 minutes and 53 seconds. Delagrange, who took off from Issy-les-Moulineaux, accomplished his flight in an adapted Voisin biplane, the Voisin-Delagrange *Nº 2*.

Delagrange, who studied art and sculpture before taking up airplanes, and Henry Farman have been engaged in a friendly competition this year to get the best out of their almost identical aircraft, both built by the Voisin brothers. Delagrange has been striving to silence his critics, who accuse him of being a mere dilettante. He confidently believes that cellular biplanes can easily compete on an equal footing with monoplanes, reputed to be faster. In the end it was Delagrange who had the edge. Powered by a new 40-hp Vivinus engine, his Voisin-Delagrange *Nº 2*, now renamed *Nº 3* after the addition of side-curtains for greater lateral stability, made a number of notable flights, including an 8.7-mile circle in June, before today's outstanding effort (→ Jan 4, 1910).

# Wilbur Wright silences French doubts at Le Mans

*Wilbur Wright, at the controls of his biplane, astonishes the French with his skilled handling of an aircraft that is far superior to any French machine.*

*Wilbur Wright prepares for another take-off: minutes before the flight, the airplane is placed at one end of the wooden rail on which it will run.*

*Wilbur and a passenger, Mrs Berg.*

**Le Mans, France, August 9**
Wilbur Wright yesterday silenced those French critics who still doubted that he and his brother Orville had really achieved the flights they claimed to have made in America. Before an illustrious gathering of French air pioneers at the Hunaudières race-track near Le Mans, he made a controled circular flight of one minute 45 seconds before landing to explosive applause.

It was late afternoon when Wilbur took off from the Wrights' derrick launching-system to sweep across the late summer sky. As the crowd watched in astonishment, he turned an easy circle over the nearby trees and returned to land after a flight of nearly 2,500 feet.

This demonstration is a revelation to all aviators here, who have been able to see for the first time the Wrights' "wing-warping" method which has made it possible to make controled turns in the air. Wright's smooth curve made Henry Farman's turn in January – the first circle flown in Europe – seem clumsy and primitive.

One observer said yesterday that French aviators were "as children compared with the Wrights", while Louis Blériot declared: "For us in France, a new era of mechanical flight has commenced." Even Ernest Archdeacon, who has been among the most vocal in his doubts of the Wrights' achievements, was awed. In today's *L'Auto* magazine he writes: "For too long a time the Wright brothers have been accused in Europe of bluff ... they are today hallowed in France."

Wilbur was piloting a Wright Flyer which the brothers sent over to Le Havre in July last year. After a French syndicate arranged a deal to make Wright machines under license, Wilbur came over from the USA in June, but found that the machine had been inadvertently badly damaged by some clumsy customs officials. It has taken two months to patch up the aircraft at the local factory of a friend, Léon Bollée.

This morning, a Sunday, hundreds of people have turned up in the hope of a repeat of yesterday's performance. They will be disappointed: Wilbur is a devout Christian and never flies on the Sabbath. But he is planning a number of flights in the next few days to satisfy the crowds (→ Sep 9).

*A close-up of the Wright Flyer, showing the complex arrangement of wires, pulleys and levers used to achieve control over the airplane in flight.*

*The launching mechanism: behind the airplane is a 1,543-lb weight, which will give it a mighty pull when it drops from the height of the derrick.*

# Orville's flights delight American army

*Fort Myer, Va, September 9*
Orville Wright, America's aviation pioneer, drew gasps of admiration from the watching crowd as he flew for over an hour today through the open Virginian skies. He also took up Lt Frank Lahm, a prominent officer of the US Army Signals Corps for a short flight, making him the first military air passenger.

The aircraft, a Wright Flyer Type A, performed perfectly throughout climbing, swooping and turning with ease and grace. Most impressive was its ability to turn smoothly by tipping or "banking" its wings in a turn, rather than skidding, wings level, round the curve, as other machines do (→ Sep 17).

*Orville pilots the "Flyer" at Arlington National Cemetery, Fort Myer.*

# Soldier is first victim of powered flight

*Fort Myer, Va, September 17*
The US Army Flyer flown by Orville Wright crashed during a test flight today, fatally injuring the passenger, Lt Thomas Selfridge. The tragedy happened at 5pm after brilliantly successful trials that began two weeks ago.

Orville flew three laps at 150 feet. His passenger sat impassive, arms folded. Suddenly the machine shook and dived. The engine cut. Many of the 2,000 spectators scattered as the dust flew. W S Cline, a photographer, said later: "There was a crack like a pistol shot. I saw a piece of propeller blade twirling off." The airplane careered round the sky; then, it seemed, Wright had it under control again just before it plunged into the earth. When rescuers reached him, blood was trickling from his chin and he was limp, but conscious, just able to murmur: "Help me." Cline said that Selfridge – a member of the adjudication board – lay amid the wreckage, having hit the ground with the back of his head and base of his spine. He never recovered consciousness and died at 8.10pm; Wright is too injured to walk.

This first death through powered flight means that the trials are suspended, although it is seen as the price of progress in the dangerous business of ballooning, steam locomotion and motor cars (→ Nov 5).

# Farman links two towns

*Farman on his historic flight from Bouy, near Châlons, to Reims.*

*Bystanders try to help Wright and Selfridge out of the wrecked aircraft.*

*Champagne, France, October 30*
Anglo-French air pioneer Henry Farman has pulled off the first cross-country flight in Europe and the first flight linking two towns anywhere. Taking off from Bouy, near his base at Châlons, in a modified Voisin biplane at 3.45 this afternoon, Farman steered a course for the historic city of Reims, almost 17 miles to the north-west.

The flight went remarkably smoothly, apart from some minor problem with the aircraft's engine, which misfired from time to time. There was some anxiety as Farman approached a long avenue of tall poplars directly in his path, but he heaved his machine into a climb and cleared them easily, to the vociferous alarm of resident crows.

Flying at a height of perhaps 150 feet, Farman also successfully managed to negotiate a windmill at Mourmelon and, as he approached the outskirts of Reims, the steeple of a church at Sillery. It was a jubilant Farman who landed safely at the cavalry training ground which was his destination, his airplane dropping majestically against the magnificent backdrop of Reims Cathedral. The journey had taken 20 minutes (→ Apr 6, 1909).

**Charles Rolls poses for the photographer in the basket of his midget balloon, the "Imp", which he uses for racing.**

# English Channel is next big challenge

*London, October 5*
Flying in the face of much public ridicule, Lord Northcliffe's *Daily Mail* has offered £500 to the first aviator to fly across the English Channel in either direction in one day, before January 1. Wilbur Wright, flying daily in France, would be a favourite to win the prize, but the Wrights show no interest in flying for prize money and concentrate on selling their machine to the military or arranging European manufacturing contacts.

Two years ago the *Mail* assigned music-hall reporter Harry Harper as the first air correspondent with a fourfold pay rise to £33.12 shillings a month.

# First powered flight in Britain's skies

*Cody: showman turned engineer.*

*The British Army Aeroplane Nº 1 makes a short hop before its main flight.*

*Farnborough, England, October 16*
Samuel Cody became the first man to fly in Britain today, in a huge biplane at Farnborough in Hampshire. The flight ended in a crash. American-born Cody, not to be confused with his namesake, William F "Buffalo Bill" Cody who is now 62 years old, emerged from the wreck and apologized for the accident, but said he had "accomplished what I set out to do, constructed a machine which flies".

Cody started flying in man-carrying kites. He then worked on the airship *Nulli Secundus* and now

he has built the British Army Aeroplane Nº 1 for the British War Office, using a 50-hp Antoinette engine similar to the one which powered the airship. Cody had to await the arrival of a newly-ordered second Antoinette engine, purchased in August, before he could begin trials of his airplane.

Cody is a cautious experimenter, despite his background. Initially, he flew short hops. This morning

was different. Taxiing along Laffan's Plain at Farnborough, he noted that the machine, with its 52-foot wingspan, was already airborne. He turned, took off again downwind, leaping instantly to 30 feet. He crashed as a result of too sharp a turn 1,391 feet from take-off. The engine was still running. Cody, head bleeding, reached an arm through the wreckage to switch off (→ Dec 31, 1910).

## Canadian bows to defeat in lake tests

*New York State, November 29*
John McCurdy failed to get the Aerial Experiment Association's latest machine to fly in tests on Lake Keuka today, the first attempt at take-off from water in the US. The machine, named *The Loon*, is

powered by an eight-cylinder Curtiss engine and with two 20-foot floats of California redwood covered in oilcloth, reached 72mph. Other lakes, calmer and unobstructed for miles, may be the ideal runways of the future (→ Feb 23, 1909).

*"The Loon" afloat at the AEA's test centre at Hammondsport, NY.*

## Aircraft on display at Paris auto show

*Paris, December 24*
Crowds flocking to Paris auto show, which President Fallières opened today at the Grand Palais, came not just to see the latest motor-cars. The show's organisers, the Automobile Club de France, have devoted much of the exhibition to an important display of airplanes and other aircraft representing the very latest aviation developments.

Among the exhibits are four dirigibles and several aircraft engines, but the main focus of interest lies in the airplanes. Among these are a Wright, a Farman and a Delagrange, an Esnault-Pelterie REP, a Blériot biplane and monoplane, Levavasseur's *Antoinette* and Santos-Dumont's tiny *Demoiselle*. Also on display at the Grand-Palais are Clément Ader's *Avion* and a Breguet gyroplane.

# Wilbur Wright wins the Michelin cup

*Le Mans, December 31*
Wilbur Wright spectacularly won the Michelin trophy with its 20,000-franc prize this afternoon at Auvours barracks, near Le Mans. The cup, awarded for the longest observed circuit flight of the year, had effectively been won on December 18, when he stayed airborne for one hour, 54 minutes and 53 seconds. Nobody could match this, Wright's fourth official attempt.

Foregoing a long flight this morning owing to a fuel leak, Wilbur took off again at 2pm. He flew for 2 hours 20mins 23secs, all but 1 min 50 secs of the time round the triangular 2.2-km [1.4-mile] course. His distance was recorded as 76.5 miles (→ Mar 4, 1909).

# Novelist predicts horrors of air war

*H G Wells: a prophet of doom?*

*Britain, December 31*
"There is no place where a woman and her daughter can hide and be at peace. The war comes through the air, bombs drop in the night. Quiet people go out in the morning and see airfleets passing overhead – dripping death – dripping death." This nightmare was conjured up this year by British writer H G Wells. In his book *War in the Air*, regarded as science fantasy, he predicts that aircraft will have a profound effect on warfare, bringing death and destruction to civilians in cities far from front lines.

# 1909

47.82mph
France
Louis Blériot
Blériot XII
Aug 28, 1909

145.53 miles
France
Henry Farman
HF.1 N° III
Nov 3, 1909

1,486ft
France
Hubert Latham
Antoinette VII
Dec 1, 1909

1,367lb
France
Blériot
Model XII

89hp
France
De Dion Bouton

**Paris, January 7**
The Aéro-Club de France grants its first 15 pilots' licenses: number 1 is Louis Blériot and number 15 is Wilbur Wright (→ Jul 2).

**Paris, January 23**
Louis Blériot flies 656 feet at a speed of 47mph in his new Blériot XI monoplane, fitted with a 30-hp REP engine, at Issy-les-Moulineaux (→ May 27).

**London, January 28**
The British military publishes a report rejecting the usefulness of airplanes in war.

**Paris, February 16**
British pilot Claude Moore-Brabazon tests his Voisin-Brabazon *N° 3* biplane, fitted with a 70-hp British ENV engine. The wealthy aviator already has two other airplanes built by the Voisin brothers (→ Oct 30).

**Nova Scotia, Canada, February 23**
John McCurdy flies the Aerial Experiment Association's *Silver Dart* biplane 40 feet over the frozen Bras d'Or lake at Baddeck Bay – the first flight of a heavier-than-air machine in Canada (→ Mar 10).

**England, February**
The Aero Club of the United Kingdom and Short Brothers Ltd establish the first aerodrome in Britain – Shellbeach, at Leysdown on the Isle of Sheppey, in Kent.

**New York State, March 2**
At Hammondsport, Glenn Curtiss receives an order from the Aeronautical Society of New York for one Curtiss N° 1 Gold Bug airplane (→ Mar 20).

**Washington, DC, March 4**
President Taft approves Congressional Gold Medals for the Wright brothers (→ Mar 24).

**Canada, March 10**
John McCurdy flies the Aerial Experiment Association's *Silver Dart* for 19.9 miles in a closed circuit (→ Aug 2).

**London, March 19**
The International Aero and Motor-Boat Exhibition opens. Among the exhibits is a Wright airplane for sale at $7,000.

**USA, March 20**
Glenn Curtiss goes into partnership with the pioneer Augustus Herring to form the Herring-Curtiss Company, with an initial capital of $360,000.

**USA, March 27**
The Aero Club of America becomes the aviation section of the Automobile Club of America.

**Rome, April 15**
A crowd at the Centocelle Field sees Wilbur Wright make a 10-minute flight in which he reaches an altitude of 98 feet (→ May 4).

**Sydney, April 28**
The Aerial League of Australia holds its first meeting.

**Paris, May 27**
Louis Blériot tests a new 25-hp three-cylinder Anzani motor on his Blériot XII monoplane at Issy-les-Moulineaux. Over the last week he also tested an REP engine, but this overheated (→ Jun 12).

**Alabama, June 5**
John Berry and Paul McCullough win the US's first National Balloon Race, covering 377.9 miles – from Indianapolis to Fort Payne – in 25 hours 35 minutes.

**Paris, June 12**
Louis Blériot flies his Blériot XII monoplane at Issy-les-Moulineaux with two passengers, Santos-Dumont and André Fournier. This is the first time a pilot has flown with two passengers (→ Jul 13).

**Dayton, Ohio, June 16-17**
A two-day celebration marks the homecoming of the Wrights.

**London, June 17**
Frederick Handley Page, a designer of motor-bus engines, forms Handley Page Ltd at Woolwich,

London, with an initial capital of £10,000, in order to manufacture airplanes (→ May 26, 1910).

**Germany, June 20**
The German army receives the Zeppelin LZ 3 (→ Jul 21).

**New York, June 22**
Wykoff, Church and Partridge, a car sales firm, becomes the USA's first airplane sales agency.

**New York, June 27**
Three New York papers (the *Sun*, *Times* and *Herald*) carry the world's first advertisements of a practical airplane for sale to the general public.

**France, June**
The Lebaudy airship *Russie*, commissioned by Russia, passes its acceptance trials (→ Oct 26, 1910).

**Paris, July 2**
The Aéro-Club commission proposes a system of air routes derived from the notion of shipping lanes.

**France, July 13**
Flying 25.6 miles in his Blériot XI, Louis Blériot wins the Aéro-Club's Prix du Voyage of FF4,500. Of this, FF1,000 goes to Chauvière, the maker of the propeller, and FF1,500 to Anzani, who made the engine (→ Jul 25).

**Japan, July 30**
The *Rinji Gunyo Kikyu Kenkyu Kai* [Provisional Committee for Military Balloon Research] is formed.

**Canada, August 2**
John McCurdy demonstrates the *Silver Dart* to members of the government at Petawawa, Ontario, and takes "Casey" Baldwin up as a passenger.

**Rome, August 6**
Alessandro Anzani is awarded the Italian Order of the Crown for having built the engine used by Louis Blériot in his cross-Channel triumph.

**Saint-Cyr, France, September 16**
Santos-Dumont takes off in his *Demoiselle* in 300 feet and in 6 seconds, beating by 32 feet the record distance for a take-off set by Glenn Curtiss (→ Apr 30, 1910).

**Boulogne, France, September 22**
Captain Ferdinand Ferber is killed when he crashes his Voisin biplane during an airshow.

**Sydney, September**
George A Taylor opens an airplane factory at Surry Hills.

**USA, October 7**
Glenn Curtiss becomes the first American to hold an FAI airplane certificate (→ May 29, 1910).

**Maryland, October 27**
Mrs Ralph H van Deman flies for four minutes with Wilbur Wright at College Park, becoming the US's first woman passenger.

**Kent, England, October 30**
Claude Moore-Brabazon wins a £1,000 prize offered by the *Daily Mail* for a circular flight of 1 mile. He makes a flight of 2 mins 36.2 secs, travelling over a mile in his Short biplane *N° 2* fitted with a Green engine (→ Nov 4).

**Châlons, France, November 3**
Henry Farman wins the Michelin cup with a flight of 145.5 miles in 4 hours 17 mins (→ Mar 1, 1910).

**New York, November 6**
Orville and Wilbur Wright receive the Cross of the Legion of Honor from the French consul (→ May 25, 1910).

**France, December**
The photographer Meurisse, while a passenger in Hubert Latham's Antoinette, takes still photographs of the area of Mourmelon and Châlons.

*Louis Blériot arrives at Dover after successfully crossing the English Channel. It is the first time that two countries have been linked by air.* ▶

# The Wright brothers found a flying school

*Alabama, March 24*
The Wright brothers have founded a school in the USA to train pilots for exhibition flights. The idea will enable the brothers to win competition prize money while leaving them free for more productive work. The first pupil is a childhood friend, Walter Brookins, 21, from Dayton. Because Dayton's weather is not good enough, Orville Wright today set up the school at Montgomery, Alabama, where winds are generally light.

The Wrights set up the world's first flying school at Pau, France, in January, with Charles, Comte de Lambert, as first pupil (→ Apr 15).

*Now the Wright brothers are teaching others how to fly their airplanes.*

# De Havilland builds and test-flies biplane

*A new departure for a couple of bus engineers: the de Havilland "Nº 1".*

*Fulham, London, May 1*
A new flying machine has been created in the attic of a builder's workshop here by Geoffrey de Havilland, who has given up his steady job designing London omnibuses to do the work. Helped by his brother-in-law, motor engineer Frank Hearle, and backed by his wealthy grandfather, de Havilland, 27, has designed both the machine and its four-cylinder 45-hp engine.

It is a single-seater biplane with two pusher propellers, made of whitewood, covered in cotton stitched by de Havilland's wife. The machine is to be test-flown on the Hampshire Downs (→ Sep 10, 1910).

# Dr Bell breaks up his pioneering team

*Baddeck, Nova Scotia, March 31*
Aircraft developers and designers in both America and Europe today expressed surprise and regret at the sudden announcement, by distinguished scientist Dr Alexander Graham Bell, of the disbandment of his highly successful Aerial Experiment Association (AEA).

The association had just seemed to be "getting its wings" following the well-publicized flights of four impressive new machines over the past two years of its existence, and many suspect that the death of founder member Lt Thomas Selfridge, who died after a Wright biplane crash last September, has influenced the decision.

However, Dr Bell and AEA colleagues John McCurdy, "Casey" Baldwin and Glenn Curtiss are claiming that the original purposes of the AEA have been amply fulfilled and that any further work is best done independently.

# Henry Farman goes into aircraft design

*The tail markings make it clear that this is one of Farman's own machines.*

*France, April 6*
The first machine wholly designed by Anglo-French air pioneer Henry Farman took to the air at Bouy today. Called either the *Henry Farman III*, or, because it represents a new departure, the *HF1*, the biplane is the first aircraft to incorporate practical ailerons attached to the trailing edges of the wings. Farman decided to design his own machine after a row at the end of January with the Voisin brothers, who built his previous machines. Largely inspired by Voisin designs, the *HF1* is powered by a 50-hp Vivinus motor, but Farman plans that production models will have Gnome engines of half the weight (→ Nov 3).

# Gnome rotary engine spins with propeller

*France, June 1*
A casual observer might think that the Voisin biplane just completed at Bar-sur-Aube, near Troyes, for Louis Paulhan is normal enough. Its engine, however, is unique. Paulhan's is the first airplane to be fitted with the amazing new "Gnome", developed by brothers Louis and Laurent Seguin. The Gnome has its seven cylinders arranged radially like the spokes of a wheel. The remarkable thing is that the crankshaft is fixed to the machine while the cylinders spin around it with the propeller.

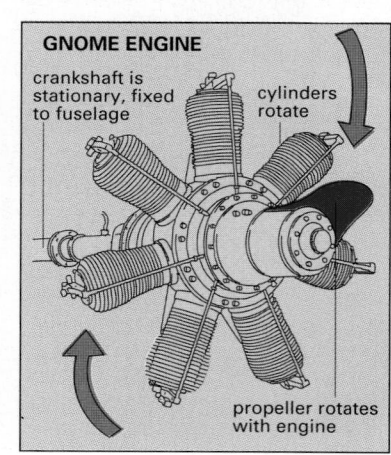

GNOME ENGINE
crankshaft is stationary, fixed to fuselage
cylinders rotate
propeller rotates with engine

# Wrights visit the Shorts

*Orville and Wilbur Wright (front, center) visit Shellbeach. The Short brothers, Oswald, Horace and Eustace, stand second, third and fourth from the left.*

**Kent, England, May 4**
Today the famed Wright brothers paid a visit to the new Short Brothers factory at Leysdown on the Isle of Sheppey, Kent. Yesterday they inspected the Shorts' works at Battersea, London. For the Wrights the main point of visiting Short is to see how work is progressing on the construction of six replica Wright Type A biplanes for members of Britain's Aero Club. This new Short factory, in which the world's first airplane production line has been established, was built between February and March on the grounds of the Aero Club's flying ground, known as Shellbeach.

Short Brothers was begun by Oswald and Eustace Short to make balloons in workshops under two railway arches at Battersea. It now includes a third brother, Horace, in the airplane business (→ Aug 2).

# Buying aircraft is preserve of wealthy

**Europe, December**
It may take bravery and not a little skill to be a pilot, but there is one thing you need above all others: money. Hand-made airframes and lightweight engines do not come cheap. And even when determined aviators have succeeded in getting off the ground, there is always the risk that they will write off their expensive machines with a single rough landing.

This year five British pilots – Charles Rolls, Alec Ogilvie, Frank McClean, Cecil Grace and Maurice Egerton – have ordered Wright Flyers (Rolls bought two). The Wrights are contracting-out the airframes to Shorts in England, who receive £200 per aircraft, and are providing French engines, costing £400 each, free to Shorts. For each complete machine they are charging a cool £1,000.

Last year, Geoffrey de Havilland had to borrow money from his grandfather to raise £250 to pay the Iris motor company for a prototype engine. He fitted it to his *No 1* biplane. Army kite-instructor Samuel Cody, who made the first flight in Britain, had to wait for the new Antoinette engine ordered by the British War Office before he could fly his airplane. This engine cost £450, and that for the *Nulli Secundus* military airship £500. In France, a 25-hp Renault engine costs FF6,000 and the 45-hp model FF14,000. The fuselage of a Blériot XI costs FF8,000.

# More than 20,000 turn out for opening of new Port-Aviation airfield near Paris

*Pilots can land into the wind, wherever it blows, at the circular field.*

**France, May 23**
Port-Aviation, the world's first purpose-built aerodrome, formally opened for business today. Over 20,000 spectators turned up to watch what promised to be a splendid flying display by leading airmen at the aerodrome, which is near Juvisy, 12 miles from Paris.

Unfortunately the huge crowd, most of which had come a long way on foot from the nearest railway station, was disappointed. Apart from the fact that only two aviators – Delagrange and Rougier – showed up out of the nine invited, stiff gusting winds meant that for most of the day only kites could fly. By the time the first airplane got off the ground, at 7pm, most of the spectators had had enough and gone home. The few who stayed were able to see Delagrange fly five circuits of the course at a singularly unspectacular height of around 15 feet. But the failure of the show should not detract from the importance of the occasion, the inauguration of the first venue built exclusively for air meetings. Blessed by the archbishop of Paris on April 1, Port-Aviation is the brainchild of France's Society for the Encouragement of Aviation. It has an elliptical 4-kilometer [2.5-mile] circuit and contains stands for 7,000 spectators.

*People on the way to the aerodrome.*

*Covered grandstands give spectators a good view at air meetings.*

# Germany's patriotic passion for airships bears fruit in international trade show

*Marvel of the skies: crowds press close to inspect a Zeppelin airship.*

*Count Ferdinand von Zeppelin.*

*The program at Frankfurt.*

*Frankfurt, July 21*
Overseas aviators are descending on the first international Zeppelin [airship] show, aware that the passenger-carrying airship is a symbol of German mastery of the air. The leading designer, Count Ferdinand von Zeppelin, made his first balloon trip while fighting in the American Civil War more than 40 years ago. His first airship flew in 1901. Since then there have been spectacular flights and disasters in Germany.

When the airship LZ 4 broke up in flames near Stuttgart last August, British politician David Lloyd George, an eye-witness, wrote: "An agony of grief swept over the massed Germans who witnessed the catastrophe. The crowd swung into the chant *Deutschland über alles* with fanatic patriotism." On May 29, the crew of LZ 5, exhausted by a 37-hour flight from Friedrichshafen on Lake Constance, failed to reach Berlin; making a forced landing after 600 miles, they hit a tree. Patched up, the ship flew on and is at Frankfurt today.

If Germany foresees a military potential for airships, the French smell profit. In the first deal of its kind, the Lebaudy brothers have built the airship *Russie* for export to Russia.

# US Army ready to put aircraft into service

*The military Flyer has all the familiar characteristics of a Wright machine.*

*Washington, DC, August 2*
The US Army has finally placed a firm order for a Wright biplane. It has exceeded the specified speed of 40mph and now commands an enhanced price of $30,000 ($25,000 plus $5,000 for exceeding speed requirement). On the evening of July 27, with Lt Frank Lahm, head of the Army Signal Corps, as passenger, Orville Wright flew 70 circuits of Fort Myer drill ground, Virginia, staying up for one hour 12 minutes and 40 seconds to cheers from spectators, among them President Taft. On July 30, with a 32-hp engine, he flew 10 miles cross-country in 14 minutes (→ Nov 6).

# First all-British machine in trial flight

*The "Avroplane" takes off during trials at Lea marshes, near London.*

*Essex, England, July 23*
Alliott Verdon Roe today took his triplane out from its hangar under an arch of a railroad bridge over the river Lea at Walthamstow, near London, took off and made a straight flight covering 899 feet. His triplane makes history: it is the first airworthy machine designed and piloted by a Briton. Shorter flights, largely ignored by the public, have been made since June 5. The triplane, named the *Avroplane* after its inventor, has only a 9-hp JAP engine. This is, however, all Roe needs, since the aircraft is extraordinarily light, weighing just 399 pounds with himself on board.

Wrapping-paper with fabric backing has been used to cover the surfaces, which saves cost as well as weight. Longitudinal control is by varying the wing angle and lateral control by warping, both achieved using a single lever in the cockpit. Roe has patented this system.

# Fearless Blériot flies 37 minutes into history

## Channel flight wins big 'Daily Mail' prize

*Blériot, in flying gear, poses next to his successful, if damaged, monoplane.*

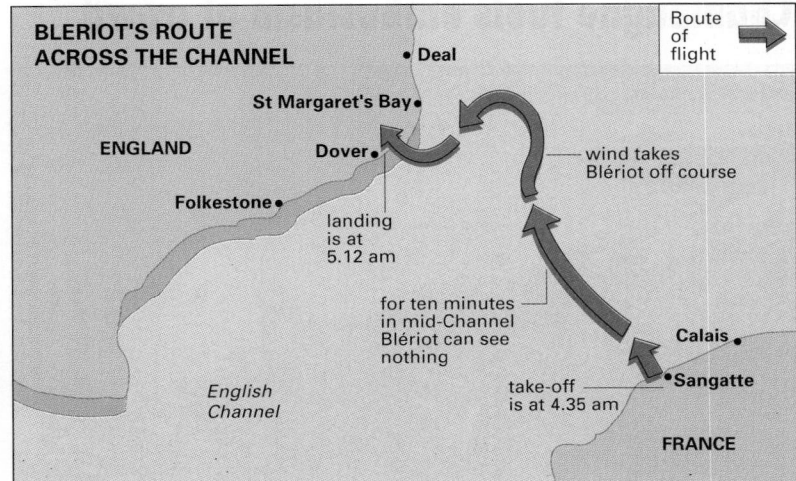

**BLÉRIOT'S ROUTE ACROSS THE CHANNEL**

Route of flight

Deal

St Margaret's Bay

ENGLAND

Dover

wind takes Blériot off course

Folkestone

landing is at 5.12 am

for ten minutes in mid-Channel Blériot can see nothing

*English Channel*

take-off is at 4.35 am

Calais

Sangatte

FRANCE

## Latham's dream comes to a watery end

*Dover, England, July 25*

Louis Blériot today became the first person to fly across the English Channel in an airplane. The flight, in his Type XI monoplane, took him under 37 minutes. This has dashed hopes of Anglo-French pilot Hubert Latham [*see story alongside*] and of Charles, Comte de Lambert; both of them were on the point of making their own attempts. Apart from his place in history, Blériot has won the £1,000 *Daily Mail* prize for the first Channel crossing by airplane in daylight.

The weather made flights look unlikely all weekend. All yesterday (Saturday) and through last night the wind stayed high and the seas rough. At Les Barraques, Blériot, who was suffering from a burn on his foot, got up at 2.30am. Everyone in Latham's camp at nearby Sangatte, meanwhile, snored on.

Blériot decided to go for a drive. Then came an amazing stroke of fortune: the weather suddenly calmed. Blériot raced back to the barn hangar at Les Barraques and ordered a test flight. His naval escort, the French destroyer *Escopette*, was notified of his imminent departure. Blériot took off at 4.35am. He had no compass or watch and flew between 150 feet and 300 feet at a speed of about 45 mph. By mid-Channel he had outpaced the escort ship with Madame Blériot on board.

Blériot tried to keep straight un-til the English shore was in sight, but, to his horror, he found that the wind had carried him north toward St Margaret's Bay. Then he spotted three ships and guessed that they were heading for Dover. He follow-ed them southward, and at an open-ing in the cliff he saw a journalist called Fontaine, from the French paper *Le Matin*, waving a French tricolor flag. This was the signal he had expected; he cut his engine and the machine dropped. The actual landing, on Northfall Meadow near Dover, was witnessed only by a police constable. "That's it," was the first thing that Blériot said to Fontaine (→ Dec 15).

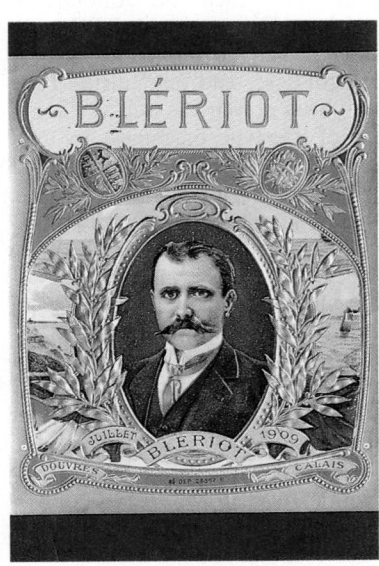

**BLÉRIOT**

*The pioneering airman is glorified.*

*Wet ending: Hubert Latham's Antoinette "Nº VII" airplane is salvaged.*

*Dover, England, July 27*

Things have not been going well for Hubert Latham. Two days after Blé-riot's exploit, this 26-year-old pilot launched his final attempt at a cross-Channel flight. Piloting his Antoinette VII, he took off from Sangatte at 5.45pm. The crossing was uneventful until he was a mere 500 yards from his goal. Then disas-ter struck: engine failure forced him to ditch in full view of his many supporters at Dover.

Latham's run of bad luck began on July 19, when a crowd assembled at Sangatte in the hope that the wea-ther would allow him to take off on his cross-Channel attempt. Léon Levavasseur, designer of Latham's Antoinette VII monoplane and 50-hp engine, had already boarded the French escort destroyer *Harpon*, which was steaming offshore. At 6.20am Levavasseur decided the weather was suitable, and the ship signalled with a gun salvo. At 6.48am Latham began his run down the slope at Cap Blanc Nez.

Just over 7 miles from France Latham's engine stopped. He was about 1,000 feet up. Fortunately the aircraft's large wing area al-lowed a gliding descent, and the machine struck the water almost horizontally at between 40 and 47mph. The machine floated. La-tham sat clear of the water, lit a cigarette and waited for the *Harpon*. The Antoinette has now been recovered by a tug (→ Jan 7, 1910).

# Reims plays host to a huge aviation meeting

## Champagne fuels enthusiasm of crowd

## Records tumble as pilots give their best

*Spectators eat, drink and make merry as aviators show off their skills.*

*Eugène Lefebvre, in a Wright Flyer, swoops low over the Reims airfield.*

**Reims, France, August 22**
Around half a million people braved wind, rain and mud today for the opening of the world's first international aviation meeting, at the plain of Bétheny, just north of the historic city of Reims in the Champagne region. The public can look forward to a week of excitement from the world's greatest aviators, brought together for the first time with money put up by the local champagne producers.

The wife of former US President Teddy Roosevelt has come to Reims, as have the British Liberal politician David Lloyd George and Lord Northcliffe, owner of *The Times* and the *Daily Mail*. Virtually every famous name in aviation is here: Blériot, Delagrange, Farman,

Ferber, Lambert, Latham and Levavasseur are among the pantheon of flyers. George Cockburn is the only pilot representing Britain; more remarkable, and disappointing to the 2,000 American visitors, is the absence of the Wright brothers: Wilbur is busy in the US, while Orville is demonstrating in Germany. America's honor rests on the shoulders of Glenn Curtiss.

Prizes worth FF200,000 are on offer at this show, and expatriate American newspaper tycoon and sports sponsor James Gordon Bennett has put up one of the biggest: FF25,000 to the fastest aviator and an "International Aviation Cup" to his country. The Gordon Bennett race is planned as the week's spectacular ending.→

**Reims, France, August 28**
Excitement is mounting for the Gordon Bennett trophy race, tomorrow's grand finale to the great "champagne" air show and the climax of a thrilling week of aerial displays which has seen many records broken and thousands of francs in prize-money won.

The airplanes which the airmen have put through their paces represent a good cross-section of the best machines available; most, not surprisingly, are French (nine Voisins plus four each of Antoinettes, Blériots, Farmans and REPs), although half a dozen Wright or Wright-types and one Curtiss have also been present, as well as a handful of one-type machines. In total over 20 machines have succeeded in getting airborne, and nearly 120 flights have been made, two-thirds of them for over 3 miles. The most spectacular flight, in terms of endurance, took place two days ago when Henry Farman landed in near-darkness after flying an astonishing 112 miles in just under 3 hours and 5 minutes. Farman won the 50,000-franc Grand Prix for this feat, which he added to the 10,000-franc prize for carrying a record two passengers.

Hubert Latham, who came second to Farman in the distance con-

test with a 96-mile flight (winning FF25,000), had the crowd gasping today when he soared to 512 feet in his monoplane to set a new altitude record and carry off a 10,000-franc prize. Apart from Farman, Latham, Blériot and Curtiss, several relative newcomers made names for themselves, including Eugène Lefebvre, Elise Deroche and, most notably, Louis Paulhan, who came third in the distance contest with an 81-mile flight in a Voisin biplane.→

*Hubert Latham's Antoinette "Nº IV" monoplane is led to the starting post.*

*Elise Deroche prepares for flight.*

# American Glenn Curtiss beats Blériot by 5.8 seconds to snatch Gordon Bennett cup

*The American airman's special machine flies to a well-deserved victory.*

*Reims, France, August 29*
Everyone expected that the Gordon Bennett trophy race would provide a thrilling conclusion to the Reims week, and they were not disappointed. In glorious sunshine 150,000 spectators turned out to watch Glenn Curtiss win a gripping contest, in which pilots representing Britain, France and the US had to complete two 10-kilometer [6.2-mile] circuits in the fastest time.

Curtiss, in his own *Reims Racer*, a pusher biplane, was the only American hope. He was first out and crossed the start line at 500 feet, so that a gradual descent would give him extra speed. With sharp turns and full throttle he did his two laps in 15 minutes 50.4 seconds, an average speed of 46.6mph.

Britain's one entrant, George Cockburn, followed Curtiss, but his slow Farman failed to manage even one lap and hit a haystack on landing. The field was thus clear for the three-man French team of Latham, Lefebvre and Blériot. Latham's Antoinette monoplane finished in 17 minutes 32 seconds, over 5mph slower than Curtiss; Lefebvre, in a Wright biplane, could coax only 34.8mph out of his machine and took nearly 21 minutes.

The cross-Channel hero took off at around four o'clock. His sleek and powerful Blériot XII monoplane knocked 10 seconds off Curtiss on the first lap. As he cruised to a perfect landing the crowd roared, and even Curtiss was sure the Frenchman had won. But then the winner's flag was raised: the Stars and Stripes. Blériot had taken 15 minutes 56.2 seconds, 5.8 seconds longer than Curtiss (→ Oct 29, 1910).

*One of the competitors in the speed trials: Louis Paulhan in a Voisin biplane.*

# A brave stunt pilot dies at the controls

*Paris, France, September 7*
Eugène Lefebvre, one of the darlings of the recent international aviation meeting here, died in an air crash at nearby Port-Aviation aerodrome this morning. He was testing a new Type A Wright Flyer.

Lefebvre, 27, was noted for daring rather than for technical innovation. He was the chief pilot for the Ariel-Wright company in France (where the American machine is built under license). His "exuberant evolutions" last week earned him repeated applause and an unofficial title as the world's first "aerial clown", or stunt pilot.

Since he was in the same program as Sommer, Latham and other adventurers (Latham broke the 100-mph barrier), this was an

*Lefebvre: killed in biplane crash.*

impressive achievement. Rather than being known for breaking records, however, the fact that Lefebvre was the first pilot to die at the controls of an airplane will assure him a place in history. He was also, as it happens, the first man to fly in the Netherlands when he took the Wright biplane there for some demonstrations on July 18.

He was not stunting on this last, fatal flight. Eye-witnesses agree that he had been airborne only a few minutes and was relatively low when the machine – the first to be fitted with wheels on the skid undercarriage – dived sharply into the ground. For some reason, so far unexplained, the controls seem to have jammed.

# Wrights file suit to defend their patent

*New York City, August 18*
The Wright brothers have today filed a suit against fellow-aviator Glenn Curtiss and the Aeronautical Society of New York. They allege that Curtiss's *Golden Flier* biplane, delivered to the society on May 29 this year, infringes patents held by the brothers on their "wing-warping" system.

The Wrights argue that aircraft with movable flaps or ailerons are derived from their own Flyer designs, and they have become increasingly embroiled in litigation to prove it. In July last year Orville told Curtiss that his *June Bug* infringed the brothers' 1906 patent and suggested Curtiss apply for a license from them. But with so many people now flying, Curtiss disputes that his machine derives from the Wrights' work (→ Oct 4).

# Hat spells disaster for Australian flyer

*Sydney, December 18*
About 50 people gathered at Victoria Park racecourse today to watch Colin Defries make another attempt to fly one of two machines recently imported by L A Adamson, headmaster of Wesley College, Melbourne. The machines are a Wright biplane and Blériot monoplane, and all attempts so far have been on the Wright. Going up in the Blériot, Defries covered about 130 feet, at heights of up to 16 feet.

All was going well until the wind started to blow Defries's hat off. He tried to keep hold of his headgear but lost control of his machine. Spectators looked on in horror as he crashed at full speed into a ditch. Although the Blériot was wrecked, Defries was rescued alive.

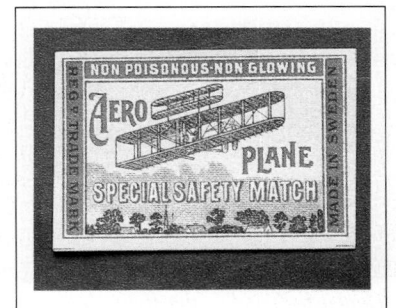

▷

# Paris air exhibition draws the crowds

*Various airplanes and balloons on display in the main exhibition hall.*

*Paris, October 1*
When the great Aero Exhibition opened at the Grand Palais in Paris on September 25, it was clear from the long wait at the turnstiles that it was going to be a huge success. And so it has turned out; within two days over 100,000 people have attended, and the exhibition looks set to remain open well into October.

This is chiefly an airplane and engine exhibition, although a Zodiac dirigible and three modern balloons are on view. Blériot's cross-Channel Type XI has pride of place, with stands of honor for two Antoinettes, an REP and a Farman. Ader's *Avion* of 1897 is another star attraction among some 30 airplanes on display.

## America celebrates its flying brothers

*Dayton celebrates its famous sons.*

*New York City, October 4*
More than a million New Yorkers had their very first glimpse of a Wright aircraft today. Wilbur Wright flew along the Hudson river from Governor's Island to Grant's Tomb and back, completing the 20-mile round trip in just over 30 minutes. The enthusiastic response of Europeans to Wilbur's successful flights at Le Mans, France, last fall has forced Americans to take notice of the Wrights' achievements, and the brothers have been widely honored since they returned to New York on May 11 this year. In their home town of Dayton, Ohio, a special two days of festivities for them were celebrated on June 16 and 17.

# All over Europe public flock to see airmen show off their skills

*Europe, November*
Flying displays have been all the rage this year. Seeing is believing, and the spectacle of watching people fly aircraft has captured the popular imagination. Ever since the success of the air show at Reims in August, crowds have flocked to air meets, and violence broke out in Paris last month when there were not enough trains to carry spectators to and from the Aero Show at Port-Aviation near Paris.

The idea of using shows to promote aircraft started in France, and French events are conspicuously better than those in other countries. Not only have they provided popular support, but the prize-money has also helped the French industry by injecting badly needed capital. Other European countries have swiftly followed suit. In September the Italian town of Brescia staged a show with prize-money totalling 100,000 lire. Massive crowds turned out, but after three days only three short flights had been made and troops had to be called out to control the angry crowd. Last month Germany offered 150,000 marks in prizes, but the meet, at Johannisthal near Berlin, was bedevilled by controversy: arguments between the promoters and pilots led to the impounding of three aircraft, and Hubert Latham hit a lamp-post while landing in the dark and was threatened with arrest for damaging public property. The meeting was saved from farce only when he managed a 6-mile cross-country flight that enthralled spectators.

There was also controversy in Britain when promoters in two towns, Doncaster and Blackpool, staged air shows over the same dates in late October. The Blackpool meet was "official", having been sanctioned by Britain's Aero Club, while the Doncaster meet was unofficial. At Blackpool, Latham made a spectacular two-lap flight around the golf course in very high winds, thrilling the crowd and winning £2,400.

But for sheer theater the prize has to go to the indefatigable Samuel Cody. In order to be eligible to compete in the *Daily Mail* competition for the first British pilot to complete a circular one-mile flight in a British aircraft, the US-born airman signed naturalization papers in public – then failed to win the £1,000 after damaging his aircraft by taxiing into a pot-hole.

*Doncaster catches the flying bug.*

*Blackpool, too, loves airplanes.*

**Aircraft racing at Belmont Park, New York, in October 1909.**

# German airline founded

*Frankfurt, October 16*

Commercial passenger airlines came a step closer today with the founding at Frankfurt-am-Main of the Deutsche Luftschiffahrts-Aktiengesellschaft [German Airship Transportation Company], or DELAG. It intends to operate giant Zeppelin airships between German cities, and it was suggested last October that London and Cologne could also be connected.

DELAG's director is Alfred Colsman, of a wealthy aluminum family, who raised three million marks capital. A major backer is Albert Ballin of the Hamburg-Amerika Line steamship company. He has promised 100,000 marks a year for advertising in exchange for becoming the sole ticket agent.

Further offers of financial backing and help in constructing airship hangars came from cities vying to become destinations, such as Frankfurt-am-Main, Düsseldorf and Baden-Baden. Services should start next year and will not be scheduled, due to the unpredictability of the weather (→ Nov 1, 1910).

# Private planes fly on army exercises

*Wiltshire, England, September 30*

Three junior British Army officers flying their own French airplanes on Salisbury Plain have persuaded commanders to accept aerial reconnaissance in fall maneuvers. Lancelot Gibbs and Bertram Dickson fly Farman biplanes and John Fulton a Blériot monoplane. The British Army has shown little interest in airplanes. The cavalry says that they frighten horses, and in February an army report saw "no trustworthy evidence" that airplanes had a future. But, as author H G Wells puts it, "the world cannot wait for the English" (→ Dec 1910).

# Austrians design a birdlike monoplane

*Austria, November 1*

There was great excitement at Wiener-Neustadt, near Vienna, today as Igo Etrich recorded the first flight of a powered airplane designed and built in Austria. The *Taube* [Dove] is a graceful, birdlike monoplane, with distinctive up-turned wingtips that look like the outstretched wings of a soaring bird. A 60-hp Austro-Daimler engine easily lifted the machine skyward. The *Taube* is the culmination of years of experimentation by Etrich and engineer Wels. Their previous aircraft, a tailless glider, flew in 1907.

# Pigs might fly – Englishman proves it!

*The aristocratic aviator pictured with his flight companion before take-off.*

*Kent, England, November 4*

The familiar British retort that "pigs might fly" to any suggestion that seems ridiculous has been well and truly turned on its head by Claude Moore-Brabazon. The aristocratic British aviator today made porcine aviation a reality by fixing a wicker cage to his Voisin biplane and carefully strapping a pig into it. He then took the bemused creature for a flight of about 3.7 miles from Shellbeach, the Short Brothers aerodrome at Leysdown on the Isle of Sheppey.

Moore-Brabazon is a sportsman of remarkable accomplishments, a scion of the British nobility whose family wealth enables him to spend his time flying airplanes. He has been interested in aviation since he was a boy and has already had a balloon and a glider made for him by the Short brothers. He is also a prominent member of Britain's Aero Club.

He learnt to fly at the flying ground at Issy-les-Moulineaux, on the outskirts of Paris. One of his early flights was pictured on the front cover of the first issue of *Flight* magazine, dated January 2 this year. Returning to England, he made flights of up to 1,476 yards at Leysdown in April and May, and then on October 30 he won the £1,000 prize offered by the *Daily Mail* for the first closed circuit of a mile in a British airplane. To do so he purchased a Short Brothers *Nº 2* aircraft. This was the only machine at the Olympia, London, air show in March which had actually been flown (→ Mar 8, 1910).

# Blériot in hospital after crash in Turkey

*Turkey, December 15*

With all the fame brought by his historic English Channel crossing in July and the commercial success this gave his airplane building business – he had taken orders for 101 monoplanes by mid-September – it seemed Louis Blériot was on the verge of giving up event flying for some time to come. But tonight he lies in a French hospital in Constantinople [Istanbul], capital of the Ottoman Empire. He has bruised ribs and possible injury to his spleen and liver following a lucky escape from death.

In August Blériot took part in the Reims aviation week, which many thought would be his last event for some time. In October, however, he flew to Budapest in Hungary and Vienna in Austria before traveling to Romania (where he was unable to fly). His ill-fated flight today, in the heart of the Ottoman Empire, was seen by a large crowd. The flying ground here is small and the winds strong. By 4pm the onlookers had become impatient, and this prompted Blériot to attempt a flight. After he had reached almost 66 feet, the wind carried him towards Tataola Hill, 2 miles from the airfield, where he was forced down. He tried to regain control but lost balance and struck the wall of a house. The airplane fell 26 feet with Blériot trapped in the cockpit. Rescuers soon arrived to drag him free.

*Blériot takes off from Taksim Square, in the centre of Istanbul.*

*The Phillips "Multiplane" featured 200 slat-like narrow-chord wings.*

*The Wright "Flyer III" flying over Huffman Prairie, Dayton, in 1905.*

*The French REP Type N used an REP engine.*

*The Bell "Cygnet 2" had a wing of some 5,500 cells. It failed to fly.*

*The 1909 Goupy is regarded as the first modern tractor biplane.*

*The world's first military airplane was a 1909 Wright of the US Army.*

*Wilbur Wright flying a standard Wright Type A at Les Hunaudières, France, in August 1908. "Canard" [duck] elevators were fitted to all early Wrights.*

*A modern replica of the diminutive Santos-Dumont "Demoiselle", one of the most famous early aircraft, sold in large numbers at a very keen price.*

*The Blériot XI monoplane was the type in which Louis Blériot crossed the Channel on July 25, 1909. It had a 25-hp Anzani engine, which overheated.*

*The Roe IV had rigid wings with elevators and ailerons for control.*

*Cody flying British Army Aeroplane Nº 1 at Farnborough, October 1908.*

*The Piggott Brothers' biplane had a pair of contrarotating propellers.*

*The Roe II triplane. A V Roe made various refinements to the aircraft.*

*Farman modified the Voisin design to produce an even better biplane.*

*The Wright Type A could carry a passenger seated beside the pilot.*

Paul Cornu's helicopter featured twin lifting rotors in tandem. On November 13, 1907, it lifted him for an untethered flight which lasted 20 seconds.

Samuel P Langley's "Aerodrome" of 1903 failed on both its take-offs.

The graceful Levavasseur-designed Antoinette VII used wing-warping.

After much trial and error, the Blériot "Nº VIII bis" of 1908 established the format which led to the 1909 Type XI and thence to today's monoplanes.

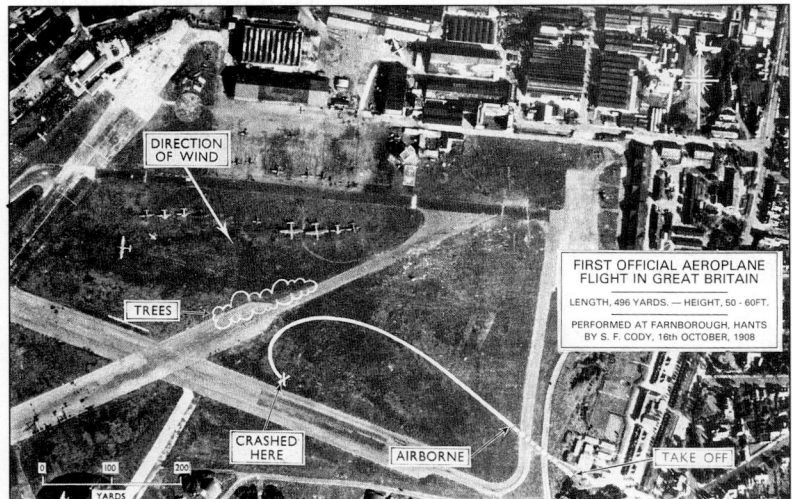

The path flown by Samuel Franklin Cody when he made the first aeroplane flight in Britain on October 16, 1908, superimposed on today's Farnborough.

Henry Farman, an Englishman living in Paris, gained fame at Reims in 1909 and was thereby able to establish a famous aircraft company.

The Blériot "Nº VII", of late 1907, was a low-winged monoplane with large tail surfaces and a covered fuselage to reduce drag. It was not a success.

Alfred de Pischoff's biplane made a flight of well over 2 miles in 1907.

Canadian J A D McCurdy's "White Wing" made five take-offs in 1908.

Santos-Dumont's "Nº 14 bis Canard": first European flight, 1906.

The Breguet-Richet "Nº 1" gyroplane needed helpers to steady it.

A V Roe's first aircraft was a biplane, which achieved its first hop on June 8, 1908. The design was abandoned, but Roe became a successful constructor.

# 1910

68.2mph
France
Alfred Leblanc
Blériot XI
Oct 29, 1910

363.34 miles
France
Maurice Tabuteau
Maurice Farman
Dec 30, 1910

10,170ft
France
Georges Legagneux
Blériot
Dec 8, 1910

2,950lb
Great Britain
Samuel Cody
Cody Michelin Cup

177hp
France
Clerget
Double Clerget 4W

**Châlons, France, January 7**
Hubert Latham flies his Antoinette
N° 7 to an altitude of 3,280 feet
(→Jun 7, 1912).

**Kiev, Ukraine, January**
Russian engineer Igor Sikorsky, 20,
begins work on a second helicopter
and an airplane. He bought two
Anzani engines in Paris recently
(→Aug 2, 1913).

**London, February 15**
King Edward VII grants the title
"Royal" to the Aero Club of the
United Kingdom.

**Germany, February**
Hugo Junkers patents an airplane
with a cantilevered wing.

**London, March 8**
Claude Moore-Brabazon receives
the Royal Aero Club's first
aviator's certificate. Charles Rolls
receives the second.

**Canada, March 10**
William W Gibson, of British
Columbia, finishes work on the
engine for the Gibson Twin-plane.

**Kent, England, March 11**
Lieutenant J W Dunne's D5 tailless
biplane is tested at Eastchurch. It
has a 60-hp Green engine and was
built by Short Brothers.

**Paris, March 20**
Photographer and balloonist
Gaspard-Félix Tournachon, alias
Nadar, dies. He took the first aerial
(ballon) photographs in 1863.

**Paris, March 26**
Plans for Aeropolis, an aerodrome
at Le Bourget, are announced.

**England, March**
To encourage military aviation in
Britain, Charles Rolls gives the
army his Wright biplane, which he
has replaced with a Short-Wright
N° 6 (→Jun 2).

**Paris, April 30**
Alberto Santos-Dumont, suffering
from multiple sclerosis, gives up
flying.

**Japan, April**
Two army officers, Captains
Tokugawa and Humazo Hino, are
sent to France and Germany
respectively to learn to fly.

**Châlons, France, May 7**
The Antoinette Company builds a
simulator at Mourmelon air school
for pilots to practice the controls on
an Antoinette monoplane.

**Paris, May 18**
International talks open to draw up
a legal basis for flight between
countries.

**Dover, England, May 21**
Frenchman Jacques de Lesseps
lands his Blériot after a 37-minute
flight from Calais to win FF12,500
and a £100 Daily Mail cup for the
second English Channel flight.

**Dayton, Ohio, May 25**
The Wright brothers fly
together for the first
time (→May 30, 1912).

**Essex, England, May 26**
Frederick Handley Page makes
several hops in his Bluebird
monoplane at Barking, but an
attempt to turn ends in a
crash.

**Milan, Italy, May 27**
Aviator Ugo Tabachi makes the
first trial flight of the Ca 1
monoplane, built by Gianni
Caproni.

**Dover, England, June 2**
Charles Rolls makes a
non-stop double crossing of
the Channel in one hour 35 mins
(→Jul 12).

**France, June 6**
Robert Martinet wins the first
cross-country air race, between
Angers and Saumur (27 miles), in a
Farman; he takes 31 minutes and
35 seconds.

**Brussels, July 7**
The War Ministry authorizes
the establishment of a flying
corps.

**New Jersey, July 9**
Walter Brookins attains an altitude
of 6,175 feet in a Wright biplane,
becoming the first to fly a mile high
and winning a prize of $5,000.

**USA, August 8**
The first aircraft tricycle
landing-gear is installed, on the US
Army's Wright airplane.

**New York State, August 20**
Lt Jacob E Fickel fires the first
shots from an airplane, at
Sheepshead Bay, scoring two hits
with a Springfield rifle in four
passes over a 3 x 3-foot target, in a
Curtiss biplane.

**Switzerland, August 28**
In his own biplane, Armand
Dufaux flies the length of Lake
Geneva (41 miles) in 56 minutes
to win a 5,000-Swiss franc prize.

**New York State, September 2**
Blanche Scott, the first woman
pilot in the US, solos at Lake
Keuka, Hammondsport.

**London, September 6**
Moisant wins the £50 prize offered
by the Daily Mail for a flight from
Paris to London (→Dec 31).

**France, September 14**
Nine airplanes take part in
French Army maneuvers; Henry
Farman has set up an army
flying school.

**Milan, October 2**
British aviator Captain Bertram
Dickson collides in mid-air with
French pilot René Thomas in his
Antoinette monoplane. Dickson is
badly injured.

**Missouri, October 11**
Ex-President Teddy Roosevelt
becomes the first US president to
fly when he is taken up at St Louis.

**Aldershot, England, October 26**
A Lebaudy airship purchased by
the British government arrives
from Moisson in France, having
made the 230-mile flight in five
hours and 30 minutes.

**New York, October 29**
Claude Grahame-White wins the
Gordon Bennett International Air
Race at Belmont Park.

**Paris, October**
Romanian Henri Coanda exhibits
a propellerless biplane,
powered by a 50-hp Clerget
piston engine, driving a
"blower"; it fails.

**Douai, France, November 5**
The Willows airship N° 3 City
of Cardiff arrives after
the first dirigible flight across
the English Channel, flying from
London in 10 hours and 30
minutes.

**Virginia, November 14**
Eugene B Ely makes the first
take-off from a ship, using a ramp
mounted on the bows of the cruiser
USS Birmingham.

**Chicago, November 24**
American aviation pioneer Octave
Chanute, 78, dies.

**Australia, December 3**
Gaston Cugnet crashes his Blériot
monoplane while demonstrating it
at Melbourne Cricket Ground.

**England, December 31**
Samuel Cody tries to win the
British Empire Michelin cup for the
longest closed-circuit flight before
January 1. He flies for four hours
47 minutes.

**New Orleans, December 31**
John Moisant is killed when his
aircraft crashes.

**India, December**
The British Army is impressed
by demonstrations by three
biplanes of the British and
Colonial Aeroplane Company,
founded at Bristol, England,
on February 19.

*Aviation meetings, such as this one
in California, give thousands the
chance to see flyers in action and
share the excitement of the air.* ▶

78

# Air show in Los Angeles

*Los Angeles, January 20*
America's first big air meeting ended today and has been declared a success, although the ten-day event, held at Dominguez Fields south of Los Angeles, was a fairly small-scale affair compared with the great Reims show last year. As well as several US aviators, including Glenn Curtiss, eminent foreign airmen were promised as the big attraction for more than 175,000 spectators. In the end Louis Paulhan was the biggest overseas name who showed up, bringing two Blériot monoplanes, two Farman biplanes, his wife and a poodle.

Paulhan, who is on a seven-month US tour, gave press tycoon William Randolph Hearst his first taste of flying. Also, to the crowd's delight, two American flyers, Eugene Ely and Philip Parmalee, made bombing demonstrations, using oranges as ordnance. Curtiss and Paulhan did not disappoint the crowds. The lanky American set a new air speed record of 54.7mph in

*After triumph: Paulhan's aircraft.*

his own biplane; in all the Curtiss team carried off $10,250 in prizes. Paulhan chalked up $10,000 with his aerial feats, including a new altitude record of 4,164 feet (in a Farman), plus a record flight with a passenger of 111.5 miles.

# Fabre hydroplane takes off in sea tests

*Henri Fabre's seaplane, equipped with three floats, at the start of trials.*

*Martigues, France, March 28*
For the first time, today, an airplane took off from water. At the controls of his *Canard* [Duck] aircraft, at Lake Berre near Martigues on the Mediterranean, was Henri Fabre, a 28-year-old engineer from Marseilles who had never flown before.

The *Canard* is a tail-first machine with a rear-mounted 50-hp Gnome engine powering one pro-

peller; it has three floats, one under the tail and one under each wing. In earlier experiments Fabre rejected a hydrofoil undercarriage because it picked up weeds and other flotsam; he has thus come up with his own design of a flat-bottomed float with a curved upper surface. On the first of four flights today the machine flew for 1,640 feet at about 13 feet. Fabre later extended this distance to 2,625 feet.

# Henry Farman makes safe night landing

*Electric lighting on the ground makes nocturnal landings less hazardous.*

*Châlons, France, March 1*
Until today no aviator had been daring or foolhardy enough to attempt to fly on moonless nights. Now Henry Farman, one of the brothers who rival Louis Blériot as the world's most successful maker of airplanes, has not only flown at night but has done so aboard a flying machine garlanded with Chinese paper lanterns.

Farman's exploit was the first officially ratified night flight. In order to help him get his bearings, he attatched the paper lanterns to the tips of his biplane's wings. These ser-

ved both as landing aids and navigation lights. Until now, airmen who wished to risk night flights had had no option but to rely on moonlight.

Farman's breakthrough has not gone unnoticed. The president of France's Aerial League, René Quinton, has suggested that towns and cities be signposted for flyers by strategically placing luminous numbers on the ground. Made of small silvery spheres, these signs would reflect ambient and artificial light, thus providing pilots with vital information about their position and altitude (→ Sep 14).

# France's Delagrange meets a tragic end

*The twisted remains of Delagrange's machine after the fatal accident.*

*Bordeaux, France, January 4*
France's much loved sculptor-turned-aviator, Léon Delagrange, died today in an accident at the official opening of the Croix d'Hins aerodrome, near Bordeaux. His accident occurred in a Blériot XI monoplane, in which he had re-

placed the 18-hp Anzani engine with a 40-hp Gnome, regardless of the greater stresses on the aircraft. The port wing collapsed while the airplane was turning at speed, and the machine fell from 59 feet onto a hangar. Delagrange was thrown out and died instantly.

## Curtiss follows the river to New York

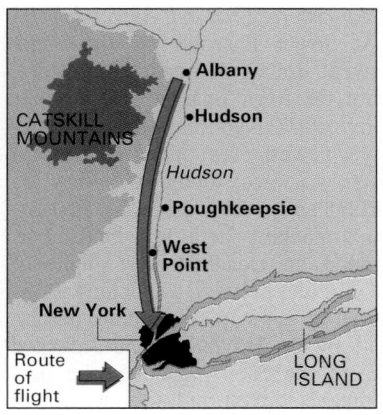

*New York State, May 29*
Today Glenn Curtiss confounded impatient doubters by flying 152 miles along the Hudson river to win the *New York World* $10,000 Hudson-Fulton Centenary prize for the first flight between Albany and New York. His flight also won him the *Scientific American* trophy for the longest flight in America; it is the third time he has won the trophy, which he now gets to keep.

Curtiss, mounting the new *Hudson Flyer* biplane and accompanied by a special train on the ground, left Van Rensselaer Island at 8am. He stopped at Poughkeepsie and Inwood before finally circling the Statue of Liberty and landing on Governor's Island. His flying time was two hours 51 minutes. Only at Catskill cliffs did he experience dangerous winds (→ Jun 30).

## Versatile 'baroness' wins pilot's license

*Paris, March 8*
Elise Deroche, the colorful self-styled Baroness Raymonde de Laroche, today became the first woman in the world to receive a pilot's license. When the Aéro-Club de France's license no 36 arrived she declared: "Flying is the best possible thing for women!" "The Baroness" is well known in Paris society for her skills as portraitist, sculptress, actress and car driver. Her test flight drew great, though in some cases grudging, admiration from male pilots, who have today publicly recognized that women can enter "their" sport.

# Tenacious Paulhan wins epic air race

*Manchester, England, April 28*
At 5.25 this morning, in the half light of a blustery dawn, crowds cheered as tenacious French aviator Louis Paulhan landed his Farman biplane to win the coveted *Daily Mail* £10,000 prize for the first flight between London and Manchester. A rival and heroic English bid, by Claude Grahame-White, had ended 40 miles away. Chilled and aching from battling against strong winds, Paulhan said he would never do it again – "not for ten times £10,000".

The 185-mile challenge, announced on November 17, 1906, was to start and end within 5 miles of the newspaper's London or Manchester offices, taking only 24 hours and with just two stops. Grahame-White's first try began last Saturday (April 23). He left Wormwood Scrubs, London, at 5.15am, but faults with the Gnome engine's inlet-valve springs and poor weather forced him to land near Lichfield, Staffordshire. He wanted to begin again from Manchester, but on Sunday a gust blew the airplane over. Repairs in London were completed yesterday. Paulhan officially began his attempt at 5.31pm yesterday

*Claude Grahame-White, ever the sportsman, leads the cheering for Paulhan.*

from Hendon, just north of London. A special train guided him along his route. Grahame-White raced to take off at 6.20pm and was closing the gap, but the two men landed for the night nearly 60 miles apart, with Grahame-White at Roade, Northamptonshire, and Paulhan at Lichfield.

Grahame-White was the first to take off this morning, having de-

cided to attempt a risky night flight. He left at 2.50am, with lamps illuminating the hedgerow. But high wind and engine trouble again robbed him of victory, and he had to land at Polesworth, Warwickshire, at 4.13am. Paulhan took off at 4am and soared to above 1,000 feet in the vain hope of escaping the wind. He landed at Didsbury, 2 miles from Manchester.

## Charles Rolls breaks neck in air show crash

*A crowd surrounds the wreckage of the airplane in which Rolls was killed.*

*Dorset, England, July 12*
The Honorable Charles Rolls, a founder of Britain's Royal Aero Club, today became the first Briton to die in an air crash, at the controls of a French-built Wright *Flyer*, on the second day of the Aviation

Week meet at Bournemouth. Rolls tried to land in a spot hemmed in by the grandstand; he approached at 70 feet in a crosswind but was too high. He put the nose down sharply, but the elevator broke off. Rolls crashed and broke his neck.

## Pilot sends radio message to ground

*New York State, August 27*
A wireless message was sent today from an airplane to a ground station 656 feet below, promising great potential for military reconnaissance. Two of Glenn Curtiss's disciples – Frederick "Casey" Baldwin and J A D McCurdy – took turns to fly and signal during a rally at Sheepshead Bay racecourse in upstate New York.

With a light transmitter in a Curtiss biplane trailing a 49-foot aerial, McCurdy used a telegraph key on the steering wheel to send a Morse message drafted by the taciturn Curtiss. It said flatly that this was "another chapter in aerial achievement". Similar tests are being run in other countries as the war potential of the mobile aerial scout is recognized. By contrast balloons are static, depending on unwieldy gas envelopes to stay up. ▷

# US Navy is shocked by aerial 'bombing'

*New York State, June 30*
Glenn Curtiss, the lean, monosyllabic speed addict who regularly upsets experts, including the Wrights, made waves in US naval circles today by dropping "bombs" on a warship-shaped target. The target, marked by buoys on Lake Keuka, was hit with 18 out of 20 dummy bombs (8-inch lengths of lead pipe) dropped by Curtiss from one of his own airplanes. Officers, including Admiral Kimball, looked on grimly as the tiny, apparently fragile flyer made pass after pass and scored a hit 15 in 17 times. Suddenly the dreadnought battleship, which so occupies the great powers of Europe, looks vulnerable to aerial attack.

Marksmanship is a new line for Curtiss. He left a village school in New York State at 14, opened a bicycle repair shop, took up motor cycles and set an unofficial land speed record of 135mph. He said that this hair-raising ride, on Ormond Beach, Florida, "satisfied my craving for speed". Another Curtiss quotation – "I hate to be beaten" – could explain his new interest in bombing the navy. He is also a shrewd businessman. His adaptation of Wright patents, and experiments with wireless and engines, all identify a man with an eye to future markets (→ Feb 1, 1911).

# Aircraft used in British Army maneuvers

*Old meets new: Robert Loraine over the ancient monument of Stonehenge.*

*Wiltshire, England, September 23*
In the teeth of opposition from many regular officers, both sides in the annual maneuvers on Salisbury Plain have accepted that they need aerial reconnaissance if they are not to be out-maneuvered. First, the defending "Red" army employed Captain Bertram Dickson (a former gunner now employed by the British and Colonial Aeroplane Company) as its scout in a Bristol biplane. Skeptics ignored him when adverse weather kept him grounded, but two days ago he took off through dawn mist and caught the "Blue" army advance between Salisbury and Amesbury.

He returned half frozen to relate the news to "Red" officers as they took a leisurely breakfast. The *Daily Mail* reported that their indifference "turned to enthusiasm as Dickson painted a far more detailed picture" than the cavalry had submitted. Later, Dickson landed on "enemy" soil to telephone his report, only to be captured by a mounted corporal named Arthur Edwards. The home secretary, Winston Churchill, soon arrived to ply Dickson with questions.

When actor-aviator Robert Loraine read the *Mail* article, he offered his services to the "Blues". After a show he drove from London to Salisbury overnight and flew Dickson's captured machine, having fitted it with a wireless Morse transmitter.

# De Havilland 'Nº 2' takes to the air

*Hampshire, England, September 10*
At Seven Barrows on the wind-swept downs of north Hampshire, not far from Beacon Hill with its important Neolithic sites, humanity's newest great invention took a step forward today. Geoffrey de Havilland, who crashed his first flying machine here last December, made an excellent first flight of 1,312 feet in his *Nº 2* machine. Powered by a 45-hp Iris engine, designed by de Havilland and salvaged from the *Nº 1* machine, the new biplane looked and sounded much better than its predecessor. Instead of four wheels it has just two, with a skid at the tail. The engine is connected to a single pusher propeller, and the framework is stronger than before (→ Jan 14, 1911).

# English flyer's effort comes to soggy end

*An actor who performs in the air.*

*Dublin, September 11*
A valiant attempt to make the first air crossing of the Irish Sea ended in a soaking today for British actor and pilot Robert Loraine. Loraine took off in his Farman biplane near Holyhead in Wales and headed for Dublin, 60 miles away. Unfortunately his machine had not been properly rigged, and its wires snapped with alarming regularity; and the Gnome engine cut out six times. Somehow Loraine made it to Dublin Bay, before the motor cut out for the last time and ditched him – 66 feet from dry land (→ 23).

# Chavez dies after making historic first flight over Swiss Alps

*Chavez makes a few final, hurried consultations before take-off at Brig.*

*Italy, September 27*
Triumph turned to tragedy today when Georges Chavez died in hospital from injuries suffered when, four days ago, he crashed at the end of a historic first flight over the Alps. The French prime minister will attend his funeral out of respect for the 23-year-old Peruvian, who was born and lived in Paris.

A 70,000-lira ($14,000) prize was on offer for the first to fly from Brig in Switzerland to Domodossola near Milan via the Simplon pass. Chavez took off at 1.29pm on September 23 in a Blériot monoplane, flew over Simplon at 6,600 feet and at about 1.50pm began his approach. Suddenly, 30 feet off the ground, something snapped, and the machine plummeted to earth.

## Airship triumphs over Channel, but Atlantic flight fails

*London, October 18*
The contrasting fortunes of two recent airship flights highlight the growing worldwide interest in lighter-than-air craft which can carry a number of people and be properly navigated.

The first flight was an attempt to cross the Atlantic by millionaire Walter Wellman in his airship *America*, which had several 330-foot steel cables secured to sea floats which were attached to the ship to assist in maintaining height during the crossing. Wellman left Atlantic City, New Jersey, on October 15 with a crew of six, but only a matter of hours after departure the *America* ran into bad weather

*Success: the "Clément-Bayard II".*

and began to pitch up and down badly as the sea floats transmitted the motion of the waves. For 86 hours the airship drifted out of control. Then a British ship, RMS *Trent*, was sighted. The crew decided to abandon the airship and were rescued by the *Trent* today, but the *America* drifted off, a total loss.

By contrast, the first airship crossing of the English Channel two days ago by the French-built dirigible *Clément-Bayard II* and its crew of seven was straightforward. The 244-mile route, from Compiègne in France to Wormwood Scrubs, London, took six hours to accomplish.

# Grahame-White, pilot and showman

*Grahame-White drops in on the President – then takes off from the street.*

## Sopwith wins his first flying prize

**Eastchurch, December 18**
Thomas Sopwith, who flew for the first time on October 22, has not wasted any time. He has just won the £4,000 Baron de Forest prize offered for the longest flight from England to the Continent by a British-built aircraft flown by a Briton. With his Howard T Wright biplane, Sopwith flew from Eastchurch to Beaumont in Belgium, a distance of 177 miles.

**DELAG's timetable for 1911.**

*New York, October 29*
Aristocratic Englishman Claude Grahame-White today won the second Gordon Bennett trophy race at Belmont Park race-track, Long Island. It was the climax of a week-long international aviation meeting, and Grahame-White was one of ten competitors. He covered the 100-kilometer [62-mile] course in his Blériot in 1 hour and 5 seconds to win $5,000 and the trophy.

Grahame-White apprenticed himself as an engineer at 16 and went into bicycles, cars and then ballooning until he saw Wilbur Wright in France and became addicted to airplanes. He learned to fly just last year but already has a name as a showman; on October 14 he surprised Washington, DC, citizens by landing in the street.

# Australians dispute who was first to fly

*Houdini, better known for his escapes, at the controls of his Voisin biplane.*

*Sydney, December 24*
The Air Carnival, Australia's first air show, opened today in Sydney. It runs until New Year's Eve, ending a momentous year which on March 18 saw Australia's first recognized powered heavier-than-air flight, by an American – none other than Eric Weiss, alias the escapologist Harry Houdini.

Houdini's 2-mile flight, which was declared an Australian first, took place in a Voisin biplane at Digger's Rest near Melbourne be-

fore nine observers. However, on the day before this flight, F C Custance claims he flew three miles at Bolivar, near Adelaide, in a Blériot XI, while George A Taylor claims he covered 292 feet at Narrabeen, NSW, on December 5 last year in his own monoplane, *Building-Australia*. His wife Florence also flew during the 29 flights made on that day, becoming, apparently, Australia's first woman aviator. These flights had no neutral observers and are unrecognized.

*Now owned by the Aviodome (the Dutch National Aerospace Museum), the Fokker "Spinne [Spider]" of 1912 was Anthony H G Fokker's first aircraft.*

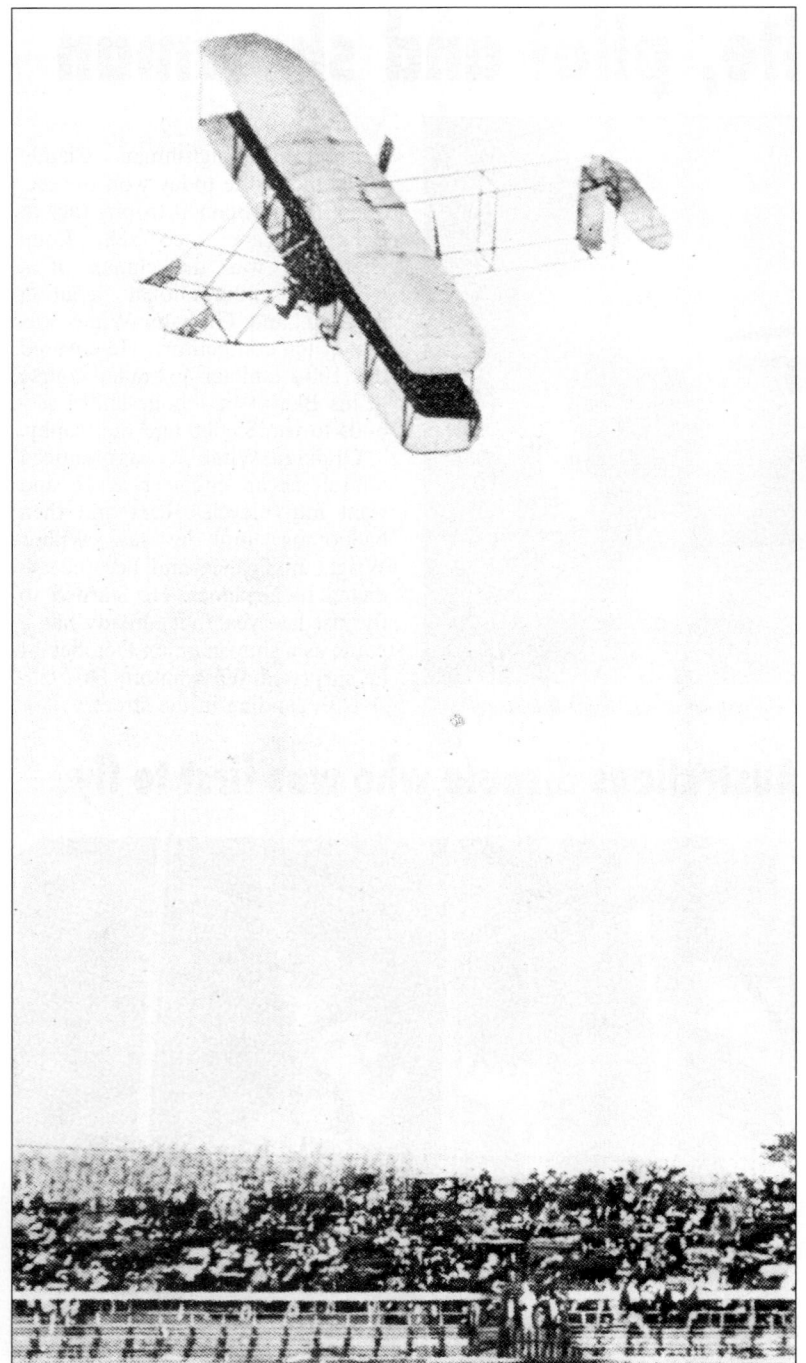

*The Boxkite was the first product of the British and Colonial Aeroplane Company. Eight shipped to Russia formed Britain's first aircraft export.*

*The "Baby Wright" of 1910 in flight at the end of an epic 92-mile flight from Springfield, Illinois, to St Louis, Missouri, piloted by Archie Hoxsey.*

*Claude Grahame-White's "Baby" was a license-built version of the American Burgess Baby. In 1913 Grahame-White became an agent for Morane.*

*The Breguet Type III (shown here), with a Renault 60-hp engine, was not as successful as his successor, the Breguet IV nicknamed "coffee-pot".*

This Paulhan biplane had a lattice girder structure for its spars and booms and could be dismantled. He did not repeat this structural exercise.

Jacob Hakkel flew his G-III biplane for the first time in 1910. It was powered by a 35-hp Anzani engine, and its top wing was smaller than its lower.

Wilbur (prominent, with bowler) and Orville Wright (right, with reversed cap) with their Model B. By this time the brothers were using rear elevators.

Englishman Geoffrey de Havilland's first successful aircraft was his "N° 2" biplane, based on a Farman design, which flew on September 10, 1910.

Ufimtsev's unusual Spheroplane featured a distinctive disc-shaped wing. Perhaps surprisingly, this aircraft flew, doing so for the first time in 1910.

The basic Blériot XI monoplane was constantly being improved. This example is an improved version of the one in which its designer crossed the Channel.

The Fabre "hydroplane", the "Canard [Duck]" was the first successful seaplane, flying on March 28, 1910. Its tail-first design was not unusual.

# 1911

 82.73mph
France
Edouard Nieuport
Nieuport Nie-2 N
Jun 21, 1911

 460 miles
France
Armand Gobé
Nieuport
Dec 24, 1911

 12,828ft
France
Roland Garros
Blériot XI
Sep 4, 1911

 2,976lb
France
Léon Levavasseur
Antoinette Monobloc

 177hp
France
Clerget
Double Clerget 4W

**Australia, January 9**
J J Hammond gives a flying demonstration in the presence of the Governor of Western Australia, reaching speeds estimated at 44-47 mph and an altitude of 2,500ft.

**Farnborough, England, January 14**
The British War Office buys the de Havilland Nº 2 biplane for £400. It is renamed the F.E.1, standing for the Farman Experimental 1, because it resembles a Farman biplane (→ Apr 1).

**San Francisco, January 15**
Lt Myron Sidney Crissy and Philip O Parmalee drop the first live bomb from an airplane in a test; it shows a 36-pound bomb dropped from 1,500 feet can impact within 20 feet of a target.

**Michigan, January 21**
Lt Paul W Beck makes the first wireless-telephonic transmission from an airplane; he sends a message from a Wright flying 100 feet over Selfridge Field.

**Massachusetts, February 1**
Burgess and Curtiss become the US's first licensed aircraft manufacturer.

**India, February 18**
Under the auspices of the British Army, French pilot Henry Pecquet makes the first official airmail flight from Allahabad to Naini Junction (→ Jul 4).

**Bristol, England, March 14**
The British and Colonial Aeroplane Company announces that Britain's War Office has purchased four of its Bristol Boxkites for the Army Air Battalion (→ Apr 1).

**Douai, France, March 23**
Louis Breguet takes up 11 passengers on a 3-mile flight in his Breguet biplane (→ Sep 1).

**Farnborough, England, April 1**
The Air Battalion of the Royal Engineers is created, amalgamating Nos 1 and 2 Airship Company.

**Maryland, April 11**
The US Army sets up its first permanent flying school at College Park (→ Mar 5, 1913).

**USA, April 12**
Lt T Gordon Ellyson becomes the Navy's first pilot (→ Nov 12, 1912).

**Paris, April 12**
Pierre Prier makes the first non-stop passenger flight, travelling from London to Paris.

**England, April 24**
Lts M Longmore and C R Samson are the first Royal Navy officers to qualify as pilots, after just two months' training (→ Dec 1).

**Essex, England, April 26**
Henry Petre makes the first tests of the Handley Page Type E two-seat monoplane at Fairlop.

**Germany, May 5**
Anthony Fokker flies his second *Spinne* [Spider] monoplane with a 50-hp Argus engine.

**Japan, May 5**
Baron Sandji Narahara makes a flight of 196.9 feet in a biplane of his own design fitted with a 50-hp Gnome engine.

**Mourmelon, France, May 11**
Edouard Niéport, a racing cyclist before he went into aircraft construction, sets a new speed record of 74.4mph flying his "Nieuport" monoplane powered by a 28-hp engine (→ Jun 21).

**Germany, May 16**
DELAG's Zeppelin LZ 8 *Ersatz Deutschland* is destroyed in an accident while docking; no one is hurt (→ Oct 17).

**Paris, May 21**
A Train monoplane crashes at the start of the Paris/Madrid air race sponsored by the newspaper *Le Petit Parisien*, killing French minister of war Maurice Berteaux and injuring aviation patron Henri Deutsch de la Meurthe.

**Florence, Italy, May**
Belgian aviatrix Hélène Dutrieu wins the Coppa del Re [King's cup], beating 14 male pilots.

**Châlons, France, June 21**
Edouard Niéport flies his Nie-2N monoplane at 87.2mph (→ Sep 15).

**France, July 6**
The Aerotechnical Institute of Saint-Cyr opens in a building rented to the University of Paris by Henri Deutsch de la Meurthe.

**Châlons, France, July 21**
Denise Moore crashes and dies on a solo flight in a Farman, the first woman killed in an airplane.

**Farnborough, England, August 18**
Geoffrey de Havilland begins test flights of the Royal Aircraft Factory F.E.2 biplane (→ Dec 4).

**Surrey, England, August 29**
Mrs Hewlett is the first British woman to win a pilot's license, at Brooklands race-track (→ Dec 22).

**Etampes, France, September 8**
Emmanuel Helen, a pilot attached to the Nieuport company, wins a Michelin cup, covering 777.5 miles in 14 hours, 4 minutes and 40 seconds, with three stops.

**Ardennes, France, September 15**
During army maneuvers, Edouard Niéport is fatally injured making an emergency landing in his own monoplane.

**New York State, September 17**
Calbraith P Rodgers leaves on a transcontinental airmail flight to California (→ Nov 5).

**Kent, England, September 18**
Francis McClean tests the Short Brothers S.39 *Triple Twin* at Eastchurch. It has two 50-hp Gnome engines, one a pusher driving one propeller, the other a tractor driving two.

**New York State, September 23**
Earle Ovington makes the first official airplane airmail flight in the US, from Nassau Air Park to Mineola, Long Island, in his Blériot monoplane; it is also the first airmail flight on a set route (→ Oct 15, 1913).

**Poland, September 25**
The Cywinski and Zbieranski biplane is piloted by a Polish aviator, Michal Scipio del Campo, on a flight of about 12 and a half miles.

**Georgia, USA, October 9**
Curtiss pilot Eugene Ely is killed in an air show at Macon.

**France, October 10**
Léon Morane and Louis Saulnier found the Morane-Saulnier aircraft manufacturers.

**Maryland, October 10**
Lt T D Milling, in a Wright, tests a new bombsight and dropping device designed by Riley E Scott, at College Park (→ Jul 5, 1912).

**London, October 17**
Flying a Bristol Boxkite, Zee Yee Lee is awarded Royal Aero Club certificate 148: he is the first Chinese pilot to qualify under the auspices of the club.

**Japan, October 25**
Captain Tokugawa makes the first flight of the Japanese Kai-1 army biplane, which has a 50-hp Gnome engine.

**Reims, France, November 26**
The Nieuport monoplane, piloted by Charles Weymann, wins the military aviation trials.

**Hampshire, England, December 27**
Geoffrey de Havilland pilots the Royal Aircraft Factory B.E.1 on its first flight, at Farnborough.

*An eagle inspects Jules Védrines on his way from Paris to Milan. He was the only one of eight competing pilots to complete the course.* ▶

# Test pilot lands his plane on deck of a US cruiser

*History made in San Francisco Bay: Eugene Ely heads for the flight deck of the USS "Pennsylvania" in his specially-adapted Curtiss aircraft.*

**San Francisco, January 18**
Eugene Ely, professional test pilot of the Curtiss company, has today notched up another success at sea. Following his daring accomplishment last November, when he flew his Curtiss Model D biplane from the light cruiser USS *Birmingham*, he has landed a similar machine on a warship at sea, widely regarded as far more difficult. The cruiser USS *Pennsylvania*, chosen for this highly dangerous experiment, was anchored in the harbor. She was modified by having a large 119-foot-long wooden platform fitted over her stern. The Curtiss lacks landing brakes, and various methods of stopping it were considered. The solution chosen – 22 ropes stretched across the platform and secured to sand bags – had previously been tested on shore. Rails had also been positioned around the whole deck area of the ship.

Ely's *Albany Flyer* took off from Tanforan Field at 10.45am and located the ship by first flying along the shoreline. Although the *Pennsylvania* was aligned to the tide, forcing a downwind landing, he chose to continue his descent directly onto the platform. Despite being buoyed up by air currents just above the deck, he was safely arrested by the ropes, which caught on hooks attached to the the Curtiss. Once aboard, Ely was cheered by hundreds of sailors clinging to vantage points on the ship (→ Oct 9).

## Moisant's flying showmen become Mexico's spies in the sky

*A Wright aircraft becomes the centre of great attention at an army base.*

**Texas, February 1**
Airplanes were today involved in warfare for probably the first time, when a group of American daredevil airmen embarked on an aerial spying mission for the Mexican government. The Mexicans hired the "Moisant International Aviators" flying troupe, who have recently been thrilling crowds on a tour of the south-western US, to fly from El Paso across the Rio Grande to spy upon rebels on the Mexican side of the river near Juarez.

René Simon, leader of the aerial circus (founder John Moisant died in a crash in New Orleans a month ago), made the first spy flight today, becoming the world's first air mercenary as well as the first airman to fly on a war mission. Known as "Fool Flyer", Simon is anything but that when he is over the rebels in his fragile Blériot. He and fellow Frenchman Roland Garros have not yet come under fire, partly because the rebels are fascinated by the flying display, but perhaps more because the airmen drop cigarettes and oranges.

The flights have aroused the interest of the US Army at Fort Sam Houston, near San Antonio. Officers, led by Lt Benjamin D Foulois, are to work with the Moisant flyers on air reconnaissance, bombardment, and evading fire. It is feared that it is only a matter of time before they face rebel bullets.

## First Irish plane is one woman's work

**Belfast, Ireland, February 1**
The first powered flying machine to be built in Ireland completed a full season of flying today. Although flying is an activity dominated by men, the machine in question has been designed, built and flown by a woman, Lilian Bland.

Bland, who has a reputation as a bit of a tomboy, has always been fascinated by the ability of gulls to soar effortlessly aloft, and after Blériot crossed the Channel she was determined to learn to fly. Last October she attended an aviation meeting at Blackpool in England to study the machines on display there. Originally she built a glider, very much in the style of the Wrights. She then bought a 20-hp engine and a propeller from A V Roe in Manchester for a powered machine, which, with a touch of wry humor, she calls the *Mayfly*. A *Mayfly II* is now planned.

# British Army forms first battalion for conducting air war

*Aldershot, England, April 1*
A new unit of the British Army came into being today: the Air Battalion of the Royal Engineers. Its formation represents a landmark in the long-running debate over the value of aircraft in waging war, which has been conducted between senior officers in the British military. It appears that the more progressive, pro-aviation officers have made a significant breakthrough.

The battalion is Britain's first fighting unit to be organized specifically to conduct war from the air. But the change in thinking has not been matched by a generous provision of resources, which suggests that the skeptics, such as Gen Douglas Haig, are still in a strong position. The new battalion has 14 officers under the command of a major, 23 non-commissioned officers, 153 other ranks (enlisted men) and two buglers; it also has four riding horses, 32 draught horses and five airplanes, which are currently out of action or obsolete. The government's Army Estimate for this year has allocated a mere £85,000 for new airplanes and airships, although it has laid out £28,000 for a new shed at the army's old Balloon Factory.

# French are victorious in Paris/Rome race

*The winners: Roland Garros (l) comes in second after André Beaumont (r).*

*Rome, June 1*
With the arrival of the celebrated airman Roland Garros here today, the Paris/Rome air race has ended in a victory for French pilots flying Blériots. Pope Pius X watched the winner, André Beaumont, reach Rome yesterday. Beaumont (whose real name is Lt de Vaisseau Jean Conneau) won the 109,000-franc main prize offered by the French newspaper *Le Petit Journal*, with a time of 82 hours and 5 minutes; Garros took 106 hours, 16 minutes.

The race began at Buc in Paris on June 28 in a highly charged atmosphere. At 6am a smoke bomb signalled the start: Garros was first to leave. Only 41 seconds later Beaumont was away, followed by 10 of the original 21 entrants. The race became a battle between Beaumont and Garros, with the former arriving ahead at Avignon on the first day and leaving early the next. Day two ended at Nice, with Garros only 38 minutes behind, despite smashing his aircraft and having to get a replacement. On the third day Beaumont's engine faltered; he could not start for Rome until the next morning. Garros reached Pisa on day three, but crashed the next day and had to find a third machine. The delay gave Beaumont the contest (→Jul 7).

# Britain acts to curb airplane casualties

*London, June 1*
The recent rapid growth in the number of flying machines, aviators and flights has prompted the British government to bring in a law to reduce what it sees as the danger to the public. The Air Navigation Bill, which was passed by Parliament today, aims to curb the worrying growth in air accidents. Last year there were 397 flights in Britain lasting over one hour, and 29 lives lost in accidents, compared with 667 flights and 35 deaths in the first five months of this year alone.

The worst aspect of the problem appears to be the reckless and irresponsible attitude of some pilots. At two traditional events on the river Thames, the Henley regatta in Oxfordshire and the boat race between Oxford and Cambridge universities in London, airplanes deliberately dived low over the river. One of the pilots, Graham Gilmour, flew to both events. During the boat race he repeatedly dived on the Oxford and Cambridge boats, stopping only when his Bristol biplane ran out of fuel and he had to make a forced landing on a nearby cricket ground. Gilmour ended up by having his pilot's license suspended by the Royal Aero Club because of his similar behavior at Henley.

# Premier impressed by flour 'bombs'

*Hendon, England, May 1*
Prime minister Herbert Asquith was today among a distinguished audience of British politicians which assembled at Hendon aerodrome, north of London, to see centuries of strategic doctrine destroyed by a sandbag. The 100-pound bag, simulating a bomb, was slung by ropes beneath the wing of a Farman biplane before being dropped on a warship-shaped target by Claude Grahame-White, daredevil founder of Hendon aerodrome. Flour "bombs", message delivery and aerial reconnaissance were demonstrated too. The visitors, including former premier Arthur Balfour and home secretary Winston Churchill, were suitably impressed.

# Freight goes by air for first time in UK

*Sussex, England, July 4*
Horatio Barber today became the first person to carry freight by air in Britain when he delivered a large box of Osram electric lamps from Shoreham aerodrome to Hove on the south coast of England. He flew in a Valkyrie monoplane of his own design and has received £100 for the flight, which was made at the invitation of the General Electric Company. Barber intends to make the £100 available to further the cause of aviation. The world's first freight flight was made in the US last November 7, when Philip Parmalee carried a consignment of silk for the Home Dry Goods Store in a Wright Model B biplane from Dayton to Columbus (→Sep 9).

**June 27. American stunt pilot Lincoln Beachey flies his Curtiss biplane over Niagara Falls and beneath the International Bridge separating the United States and Canada. A crowd of 150,000 watches spellbound as he skims along the lake before landing safely on the Canadian side of the border. Beachey's spectacular feat is made all the more remarkable by the fact that he was taught to fly – by Glenn Curtiss – only this year.**

# Frenchman wins European Circuit race

*Paris, July 7*
André Beaumont and Roland Garros have come first and second in a European Circuit race sponsored by several newspapers. Beaumont wins FF200,000. An estimated 700,000 people saw the start on June 18; Jules Védrines was first back this morning, but his flying time of 86 hours, 34 minutes and 32 seconds gives him fourth place. Beaumont's winning time is 58 hours and 38 minutes. The 994-mile circuit, from Paris to Liège (Belgium), Utrecht (Netherlands), Brussels (Belgium), Roubaix and Calais (France), London and Dover (England), then back to Paris, drew 52 entrants (→ Jul 26).

*Beaumont and Garros, friendly rivals, wait for the starting signal.*

## ... and gains another victory in a tough round-Britain contest

*Surrey, England, July 26*
French aviator André Beaumont was first out of Brooklands race-track four days ago at the start of the 1,010-mile *Daily Mail* Circuit of Britain race, and today he was the first back in. The £10,000 prize comes on top of his victories in the Paris/Rome race in June and the Circuit of Europe just over two weeks ago. The final stage from Brighton was flown in 40 minutes, and his unofficial time over all the stages is 22 hours, 29 minutes and 6 seconds.

Jules Védrines came second in his 70-hp Morane-Borel monoplane, which was faster than the winning Blériot, but he lost almost two hours finding the control stops at Glasgow and Bristol, and it cost him the race. His unofficial time is 23 hours, 38 minutes and 5 seconds. Lord Northcliffe, proprietor of the *Daily Mail*, has given him a £200 consolation prize.

Many say that this race has been tougher than the European Circuit [*see article above*]. The 21 starters have not been allowed to replace airplane or engine. Instead, five parts of the airframe and five of the engine were officially sealed at the start, two of each having to remain sealed at the end. The route from and to Brooklands took in control stops at Hendon, Harrogate, Newcastle, Edinburgh, Stirling, Glasgow, Carlisle, Manchester, Bristol, Exeter, Salisbury and Brighton.

*Edmond Audemars' team holds his airplane as it prepares for the start.*

*Collins Pizey was one of the competitors hoping to win the "Daily Mail" prize.*

# US Navy takes to the air as Curtiss delivers seaplane

*New York State, July 1*
The United States Navy took to the sky at 6.50pm today from Lake Keuka, Hammondsport. Its first airplane, the amphibious Curtiss A-1 Triad, was flown by the man who built it, Glenn Curtiss, for five minutes at a height of 25 feet.

Three other flights followed. The second flight had aboard Lieutenant Theodore G Ellyson, who made the last two flights alone. The navy's purchase of the A-1 is the culmination of Curtiss's efforts to convince it of the need for aircraft. The most crucial demonstration took place on February 17 this year in San Diego Bay, when he used another aircraft to show that an airplane could land on the water, be hoisted onto the USS *Pennsylvania*, be lowered back into the water, and take off. This led the navy to order two biplanes; one, the A-1, had to reach 45mph and touch down on land or water. Influenced by Fabre's floatplane of last year, it is the first practical seaplane (→ Jan 6, 1913).

# Airship popularity is on the increase

*Germany, October 17*
Following the lead given by the redoubtable Count von Zeppelin, the pace of developing airships to carry passengers is increasing by the day. The count's year-old company, Deutsche Luftschiffahrts Aktien Gesellschaft or DELAG, has just introduced a new airship, the *Schwaben*, despite the recent loss of the two *Deutschland* craft. DELAG has, however, learnt a lot from those accidents, according to their young operations director, former journalist Hugo Eckener.

Schütte-Lanz, another company (founded 1909), is building new, beautifully streamlined ships with plywood laminate frames in contrast to Zeppelin's aluminium. France and Italy, with its Forlanini P and M types, prefer the "soft" or "pressure" type of airship, with no frames at all. One such, Italy's P2, recently flew 153 miles from Venice to Montferrato non-stop.

# Women match men as pilots conquer the skies

*In England, members of the Women's Aerial League learn about propellers.*

*In Germany, Melli Beese gained her pilot's license despite male sabotage.*

*American flyer Harriet Quimby.*

*Belgian flyer Hélène Dutrieu.*

**Paris, December 22**
The sport of flying has attracted more than a few unusual people since its practical beginnings almost a decade ago. Cranks, wild inventors, visionaries and daredevils can be all numbered along with the more sober experimenters and brave aviators who now regularly take to the air. Perhaps surprising, in an activity dominated by men, is the extent to which women have joined them. In Europe and the Americas women from all classes of society have been rushing into the air to gain their pilot's certificates and show off their ability to manage a flying machine.

Eighteen months ago the first woman ever to gain a flying license officially, Elise Deroche (the self-styled Baroness Raymonde de Laroche) of France, proclaimed after landing her Voisin at the end of her test: "Flying does not rely so much on strength, as on physical and mental coordination." This was a comment she had some cause to regret when she crashed four months later at Reims when her machine went out of control during a competition. Undaunted, the French airwomen have this month notched up another first: a women's flying school to be run by qualified pilot Jane Herveux. Russian Lidia Zvereva, who herself first flew earlier this year, also intends teaching women to fly.

Other women stress the feeling of complete personal freedom they experience while in flight, in contrast to enforced social restrictions on the ground. Hélène Dutrieu of Belgium, a magnificent pilot sometimes known as the "Girl Hawk" of aviation, who, last May, beat all male opposition to win the Italian Coppa del Re [King's cup] in Florence, has aroused comment because she is known to prefer flying without the support of her corsets, which she says are too confining.

Blanche Stuart Scott was the first woman pilot in the US. She was taught by the great pioneer Glenn Curtiss, who, ironically, believes that a woman's proper place is on the ground. She first flew on September 2 last year, and now, despite her employer's views, is billed as the "Tomboy of the Air" and flies regularly for the Curtiss Company Exhibition team. She learned to fly before US licenses were issued. The first woman to receive one was the glamorous and mysterious Harriet Quimby, closely followed by her friend Mathilde Moisant, who has since claimed an altitude record. The first British woman to fly was Mrs Hilda B Hewlett.

Opposition to female pilots has not been confined to the US. Two months ago, in Germany, aspirant Melli Beese gained her license despite sabotage by her male colleagues, who drained her fuel and tampered with her steering prior to the test. This year also saw the tragedy of Denise Moore, who crashed her Farman at Châlons in France, becoming the first woman killed in an airplane.

*Dressed for the air: Madge Temple.*

*Hilda B Hewlett: British pioneer.*

# French aviator makes first Morocco flight

*Fez, Morocco, September 1*
Despite international tension over the French occupation of Fez and the sending of a German gunboat to Agadir, the aviator Henri Brégi today successfully carried out the first significant flight in Morocco. With the journalist René Lebaut, a reporter employed by the *Petit Journal* as passenger aboard his Breguet 11 biplane, Brégi took off from Casablanca, reaching Fez via Rabat and Meknes.

In the end it was not the threat of war which posed the biggest problem for the two men, but the absence of suitable places to land, the inability to refuel and, perhaps most of all, the stifling desert heat. Still, they made it, putting another feather in the caps of both the pilot, who last year made the first flight in South America at Buenos Aires with a Voisin biplane, and of Louis Breguet, whose airplanes have recently been piling up accolades and

*Henri Brégi stops over at Meknes.*

records. For his Casablanca to Fez flight, Henri Brégi's Breguet aircraft was powered by an 80-hp Canton Unné engine. As well as his successes in airplane design, Breguet has also advanced the development of helicopters.

# Royal Navy founds its own flying school

*In a special machine, a student learns the basics of aerial control.*

*Kent, England, December 1*
Britain's Royal Navy today set up its own permanent naval flying school, at Eastchurch on the Isle of Sheppey. It covers 10 acres, leased from the Royal Aero Club, and forms part of the naval base at Sheerness.

The establishment of this station follows the successful training of naval lieutenants Samson, Gregory and Longmore, plus Lt Gerrard of the Royal Marines, earlier this year, helped by members of the

Royal Aero Club. The Admiralty agreed to establish the school in October, after Longmore and Samson had lobbied for it, and has purchased Short S.34 and S.38 biplanes from test pilot Francis McClean as its first two machines. McClean has offered the free loan of other aircraft. Hundreds of men have applied for selection to the school, out of whom four officers have been chosen for pilot training and 12 ratings for maintenance training (→ Jun 19, 1912).

# King gives royal start to British airmail

*Hendon, England, September 9*
The first mail carried by air in the United Kingdom was successfully delivered today. The service has been commemorated by specially printed envelopes and postcards reading "1st UK Aerial Post", made available in London shops and at Hendon aerodrome, north of London, from where the first mail airplane took off. Public demand for these souvenirs has been great, and a special mail box was set up at Hendon for those wishing to have their correspondence among the first delivered.

Gustav Hamel of the Grahame-White flying school left in a Blériot at 4.58pm to make the initial flight. He took just 10 minutes to fly the 19 miles to a meadow on the royal farm at Windsor in Berkshire, as strong tail winds allowed an average speed of 105mph. His bag contained messages for King George V and other members of the British royal family. Deliveries will begin shortly. The service was conceived by Captain W G Windham, who pioneered airmail in India earlier this year, with the assistance of Britain's postmaster-general (→ Sep 23).

*Royal celebration in Britain.*

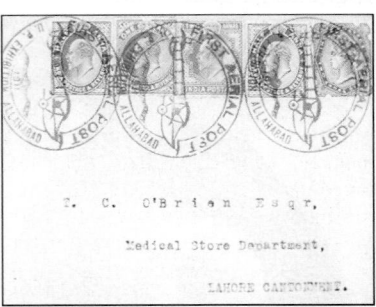
*One of the Indian Aerial Post letters.*

# Airship is broken by wind during tests

*Barrow, England, September 24*
British Admiralty officials and staff at the Vickers shipbuilding company looked on proudly today as the *Mayfly* airship, built by Vickers, was brought out of its shed at Barrow-in-Furness in north-west England for tests. However, their smiles froze in horror as the huge craft, officially His Majesty's Airship Nº1, was caught by the wind and broken. Vickers, which works closely with the Royal Navy

in supplying warships, was selected by the Admiralty in 1909 to build a rigid airship of the Zeppelin type. Nobody at the company, or anywhere in Britain, had any experience of building rigid airships, yet Vickers was asked to fulfill a demanding specification for a ship 512 feet long and capable of ascending to 1,500 feet. After many design changes, the *Mayfly* was first tested in May this year but was too heavy to take off (→ Nov 12, 1912).

*Broken dreams: the "Mayfly", pictured shortly after meeting a sorry end.*

# Rodgers makes trans-American flight

*Pasadena, Calif, November 5*
Twenty thousand people were here today to greet Calbraith P Rodgers when he became the first person to cross the US by airplane. Rodgers, draped by the crowd in an American flag, started his journey on September 17 at Sheepshead Bay, Brooklyn, New York.

Rodgers took 49 days to complete the trip, and so failed to win the $50,000 prize offered by publisher William Randolph Hearst for the first coast-to-coast trip in 30 days or less. But he will not be out of pocket. The Armour Meat Packing Company, which sponsored the flight to promote "Vin Fiz", a grape-flavoured soft drink whose name adorns his aircraft, will pay him $5 for each of the 4,321 miles that he flew: a total of $21,605.

Rodgers navigated by following railroad tracks, and his 69 stops included 16 crash-landings. He was tailed by Armour representatives, mechanics, $4,000-worth of spare parts and his wife and mother, all in a special three-car train. It is estimated that four other aircraft could have been built with the spare parts used to repair Rodgers's Wright EX airplane; only the original rudder and two wing struts are still part of the aircraft. Rodgers was airborne for 82 hours and 4 minutes, at an average speed of just under 52mph (→ Apr 3, 1912).

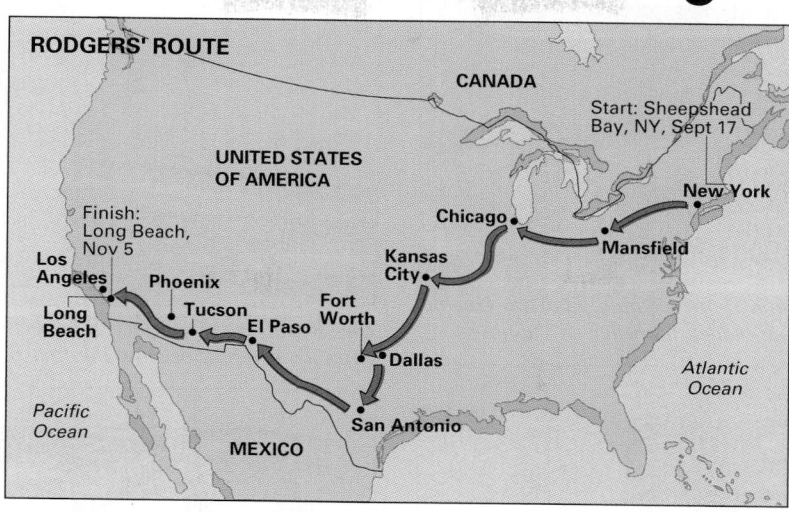

RODGERS' ROUTE

*Rodgers enjoys a pause in the long journey across the United States.*

## Libya sees world's first ever air raid

*Libya, November 1*
The airplane was used as a bomber in warfare for the first time today when Italian flyers dropped bombs on the Turks in the war to control Libya. Lt Giulio Gavotti dropped four 4.4-lb Swedish grenades from his Blériot on Turkish positions.

Italy is the first to use airplanes in a combat role, however, and has nine machines in Libya. Italians are using the most up to date models, including the Blériot XI, 300 of which have been sold this year. Six pilots arrived on October 19, and have mainly made scouting flights. The 1899 Hague Convention forbids aerial bombing from balloons, but Italy argues that this ban cannot be extended to airplanes.

## Planes go on show

*Paris, December 16*
The third Paris aviation exhibition was opened today by President Armand Fallières, and, for the first time at the show, monoplanes outnumber biplanes 29-14. All but four of the biplanes have engines in front, and nine feature enclosed fuselages. All-metal airframes are another new trend; eight machines on show have them. The Ponche and Primard monoplane is built almost entirely of metal.

# New aircraft design is put through tests

*Farnborough, England, Dec 27*
A new British airplane, the B.E.1, made its first flight here today, piloted by its designer, Geoffrey de Havilland. B.E.1 stands for "Blériot Experimental" and means that the two-seater biplane, on the Blériot model, has the engine driving a tractor propeller at the front. The machine incorporates a 60-hp Wolseley engine taken from a crashed Voisin and presented to the British War Office by the Duke of Westminster. Although it still retains the wing-warping form of lateral control, as used by the Wrights, the B.E.1 is in other respects a very modern machine. It is expected that many more will be built.

# 'Flying Dutchman' moves to Berlin

*Berlin, December 1*
Anthony Fokker has left his job as chief test pilot for Dutch airplane maker Goedecker and set up shop in a rented hangar at Johannisthal, the center of German aircraft manufacturing, near Berlin. Fokker – nicknamed "the Flying Dutchman" by the Germans – brings with him the remarkable *Haarlem Spinne* [Spider], the stable monoplane which Goedecker will continue to build for him. The *Haarlem*, so called from its showing at the Dutch city of that name in the autumn, is the third of its type, and is so stable that it has no need of lateral control and has been built without ailerons (→ May 24, 1912).

**Air test: Parisians gather at the foot of the Eiffel Tower to watch as the Hervieu parachute is tested with a dummy launched from the first story of their city's most famous monument. The voluminous cotton parachute – which weighs 40 pounds – passed its test with flying colors.**

*This strange biplane, designed by Romanian Henri Coanda, had two Gnome rotary engines coupled to drive a single four-bladed propeller on the nose.*

*The Royal Navy's Short S.38 being loaded aboard the battleship HMS "Africa", where it became the first British aircraft to fly from a ship.*

*The Short S.39 "Triple Twin", which had a typical Boxkite pusher configuration but proved surprisingly good. Its two engines drove three propellers.*

*The Grahame-White "New Baby", a development of the original Grahame-White-built Burgess Baby. Grahame-White soon developed a large business.*

*The Curtiss hydroplane (seaplane) was a pusher biplane which combined a single long main float with twin stabilizing floats under the lower wings.*

*The Breguet G.3 was a three-seater but frequently struggled aloft with more on board. Forty-one were built and exported to Britain, Sweden and Italy.*

*Gabriel Borel was at first associated with the Morane brothers but in 1911 became established as a manufacturer in his own right. His first monoplanes were similar to Morane designs, though their twin tailskids were distinctive.*

*Paul Kaufmann's 1911 monoplane – surely inspired by Santos-Dumont's "Demoiselle" – featured folding wings for easier storage. This advanced feature was to become, and remains, common for many military aircraft.*

*The Lioré monoplane had twin propellers driven by a single engine.*

*This Hanriot monoplane, built for training, handled very well indeed.*

*The streamlined Tatin-Paulhan Torpille had a propeller behind the tail.*

*Short Brothers, at that time building balloons at Battersea and aeroplanes at Eastchurch, was the first aircraft company in the world. This is the S.36, as originally completed in late 1911 with an openwork rear fuselage.*

*The Fokker "Spinne [Spider] III" allowed Anthony Fokker to gain experience in building monoplanes, which was to lead to the 1915 E.1 Eindecker fighter.*

*The Albatros M.22 was of similar appearance to the various British and French pusher Boxkite designs. Albatros soon discarded this configuration.*

*The Blackburn Mercury was a two-seater mid-wing monoplane, powered by the buyer's choice of an Isaacson, Gnome or Anzani rotary engine. This version, fitted with the 50-hp Isaacson, is shown flying at Filey, N Yorks.*

*The Avro Type D two-seater biplane, which later flew as a seaplane. With a wing-warping system for lateral control and a Green engine, it remained in service for training until 1914. By that time the Avro 504 was flying.*

# 1912

108.18mph
France
Jules Védrines
Monocoque Déperdussin
Sep 9, 1912

628.14 miles
France
Géo Fourny
Maurice Farman
Sep 11, 1912

18,405
France
Roland Garros
Morane-Saulnier
Dec 11, 1912

2,976lb
France
Léon Levavasseur
Antoinette Monobloc

197hp
France
Clerget
Clerget

**Kent, England, January 10**
Lieutenant C R Samson succeeds in taking off from a wooden runway built out over the fore gun-turret of HMS *Africa*, anchored in the river Medway, and flies his Short S.38 biplane to Eastchurch (→ May 10).

**New York, February 16**
Frank Coffyn takes aerial views of the city with a cinema camera while controling his airplane with his feet and knees.

**Surrey, England, February 17**
Graham Gilmour is killed when his Martin-Handasyde Dragonfly monoplane breaks up in mid-air at Richmond, near London, fueling concern about the doubtful safety record of the aircraft.

**St Louis, Mo, March 1**
Captain Albert Berry makes a successful trial parachute jump over Jefferson Barracks from a Benoist biplane flying at 1,509 feet. The parachute opens at 500 feet.

**Florida, March 5**
Bob Fowler flies from Los Angeles to Jacksonville. The west to east coast to coast journey has taken four months to complete.

**France, March**
French engineers Fernand Lioré and Henri Olivier found the Lioré & Olivier aircraft company.

**California, April 3**
Calbraith P Rodgers, the first man to fly coast-to-coast across the USA, dies when he crashes into the Pacific during an air show at Long Beach.

**Philadelphia, April 6**
Belgian M V de Jonckheere flies his monoplane in experiments at League Island naval base to show that airplanes can follow and attack ships at night.

**Calais, France, April 16**
Harriet Quimby, the first American woman pilot, lands after a solo flight across the English Channel from Dover (→ Jul 1).

**British Isles, April 22**
Englishman Denys Corbett Wilson flies across St George's Channel between England and Ireland.

**Sydney, May 9**
William Hart is fined £20 for "propelling for a long time an aeroplane over, upon and against the plaintiff's land" and causing a cattle herd to stampede (→ Jun 29).

**Berlin, Germany, May 24**
Anthony Fokker crashes his Goedecker-built B-1912 monoplane, killing his passenger, Lt von Schlichting. Just 10 days ago he demonstrated the machine to an army delegation (→ Dec 7).

**Maryland, June 7**
Captain Charles Chandler of the US Army Signal Corps test fires a Lewis gun fitted to a Wright Model B biplane flown by Lieutenant Thomas Milling. It is the first time a machine gun has been fired from an airplane in the US (→ Nov 27).

**Central Africa, June 7**
Pioneer Anglo-French flyer Hubert Latham is trampled to death by a buffalo while on safari. He abandoned aviation in December 1911 after the failure of the Antoinette company.

**Wiltshire, England, June 19**
The Central Flying School opens at Upavon under Captain G Paine, Royal Navy. Its costs are to be shared by the War Office and the Admiralty.

**Los Angeles, June 21**
Tiny Broadwick, 18, is the first woman to make a parachute jump from an airplane, from 1,000 feet. The pilot is Glenn Martin.

**Japan, June 26**
The Naval Committee for Aeronautical Research is formed by the Japanese government.

**Germany, June 28**
DELAG loses the Zeppelin LZ 10 *Schwaben* when a fire breaks out in its shed (→ Dec 31).

**Maryland, July 5**
Capt Charles Chandler and Lts Thomas Milling and Henry Arnold are presented with certificates qualifying them as the US's first "Military Aviators".

**Annapolis, Md, July 27**
Lt John Rodgers and Ensign Charles Maddox, in a Wright B1 *Flyer*, send the first wireless message from an airplane to a ship, the torpedo boat USS *Stringham*.

**Washington, DC, August 5**
Congress passes the Hardwick Bill, giving double pay to army officers who volunteer to train as pilots.

**Wiltshire, England, August 13**
Boer War veteran Major Hugh Trenchard wins his aviation certificate at Larkhill training ground and is posted to the Central Flying School at Upavon as an instructor.

**Châlons, France, August 15**
Frenchmen Gaubert and Scott win a 50,000-franc prize offered by the Michelin brothers to encourage the development of fighter aircraft. Flying an Astra-Wright Type E, they succeed in dropping 12 projectiles out of 15 on a dummy target 66 feet across.

**Chicago, September 9**
Jules Védrines wins the Gordon Bennett cup flying his Deperdussin monoplane at 108.16mph (→ Dec 29, 1913).

**Oxford, England, September 10**
A Bristol Coanda military monoplane crashes at Wolvercote, killing both RFC crew members.

**London, September 12**
Following a spate of crashes, the War Office bans RFC pilots from flying monoplanes (→ Feb 1913).

**Hamburg, Germany, September 19**
DELAG's Zeppelin LZ 13 *Hansa* inaugurates the company's international passenger service to Copenhagen in Denmark and Malmö in Sweden (→ Dec 13).

**Germany, October 1**
The Military Aviation Service is founded.

**England, October 12**
Samuel Cody wins the Michelin Cup offered for a flight round a 186-mile course in an all-British aircraft. To qualify, he put a 100-hp Green engine in one of his biplanes. He flew it from Farnborough via Larkhill and Newhaven and back to Farnborough. As he got lost, he flew about 220 miles to average 45-mph (→ Aug 7, 1913).

**England, October 24**
Harry Hawker wins the British Empire Michelin Cup for endurance. He achieved this with a flight of 8 hours and 23 minutes in a Burgess-Wright biplane rebuilt by Sopwith and fitted with a 40-hp A.B.C. engine.

**Washington, DC, November 12**
Lt T Gordon Ellyson pilots the Curtiss A-1 hydroplane on a successful launch from an anchored barge in the Anacostia river, using a compressed-air catapult designed by Capt W I Chambers. The first attempt at using the catapult, on July 31, was a failure.

**London, England, November 19**
The Admiralty asks Vickers to produce a biplane armed with a machine gun (→ Feb 14, 1913).

**Italy, November 28**
Italy forms an autonomous air force, the Flotta Aerea d'Italia [Air Fleet of Italy]. A colonial aviation service was formed November 19.

**Paris, December 12**
An ejector seat developed by Baron d'Odkolek is tested at Issy-les-Moulineaux: a dummy wearing a parachute is ejected by a small cannon from an airplane in flight.

*The allure of powered flight, whether in an airship or an airplane, has sparked many books on the subject, such as this by Charles Turner.* ▶

THE ROMANCE
OF
AERONAUTICS

By
CHARLES C.
TURNER

# French launch fund for military planes

*Paris, February 23*
The French newspaper *Le Matin* today launched a nationwide subscription for funds toward the development of military aircraft in France. The paper is starting the fund with a donation of FF50,000; the firm of Michelin has pledged another FF10,000. The appeal follows a meeting on army aviation at the Sorbonne on February 11, attended by 6,000 people. Soldiers and politicians spoke of the urgency of building a military air force, especially since the Germans created their own Military Aviation Service nearly six months ago.

# King approves new air force for Britain

*London, May 18*
The names of those who will run the Royal Flying Corps, the new air arm of the British forces, were made public today, a month and five days since King George V signed the royal warrant which brought the corps into being. The creation of the force follows a report by senior British commanders several months ago, which recommended setting up a single organization to co-ordinate military aviation.

Parliament has voted over £300,000 for setting up the corps, which has a naval wing and a military wing under Commander Charles Samson and Major Frederick Sykes respectively. The core of the military wing will be seven airplane squadrons with 12 machines each; at present there are three small army squadrons. The RFC took over from the former Air Battalion of the Royal Engineers five days ago. Aircraft for the naval wing are on order.

Captain George Paine heads the corps's Central Flying School at Upavon, Wiltshire, which will provide pilots for both wings and also for the RFC Reserve. The Royal Aircraft Factory at Farnborough, Hampshire, formerly the Army Aircraft Factory, also now comes under the RFC and will train mechanics as well as reconstruct aircraft and test airplanes and engines (→ Jun 19).

# Italy uses airships in the Libyan war

*Libya, March 10*
The Italian-Turkish war in Libya continues amid reports that Italian flyers are using two non-rigid airships as well as nine airplanes to drop bombs on the Turks. The airships are dropping 4.4-pound Swedish grenades; leaflets are also used. There is even some night flying. The Hague Convention of 1899 forbids bombing from balloons, but Italy argues that airplanes are exempt. Meanwhile, in the Balkans, Bulgarian pilots are also bombing the Turks; the bombs are tied to the wing and released by a rope looped round the pilot's boot.

# French army grounds Blériot monoplanes after wings collapse

*Paris, March 30*
Today the French Army took the unprecedented step of banning all its Blériot monoplanes from flying. This is the first time all flying machines of a particular make or class have been grounded and follows a recent series of fatal accidents caused by the failure of the wings of these monoplanes in flight. Indeed, Louis Blériot himself has drawn attention to the problem.

Blériot has pointed out that while the wings of his and other monoplanes are well braced by wires beneath them to take the stresses imposed by normal flight maneuvers, the wires above the wings do not offer much support to resist a download; this can be caused by turbulence or even just by taxiing over bumpy ground.

Blériot's frank publicity of the wing problem is being applauded

# Fans run amok after airman loses vote

*Védrines: cockpit campaigner.*

*South-west France, March 23*
A celebrated aviator's attempt to put aviation firmly on the political agenda ended ignominiously today, when a regiment of dragoons had to be called out to halt a riot in the streets of Limoux, near Carcassonne. Jules Védrines had lost an election to the French parliament to a local industrialist by just a few hundred votes, and his outraged supporters decided to take it out on the town, sacking the café of his opponents and generally running wild. Védrines came close to winning on account of his novel campaign, which included dropping leaflets from his airplane and landing in fields to speak to voters.

*Mechanics struggle to hold back a Blériot XI as it gathers power for take-off.*

and is considered to have enhanced his great reputation for honesty. But the fundamental nature of the issue seems likely to result in both the constructors and the customers tending to avoid monoplanes in future. This could be short-sighted, because recent monoplanes such as the Morane and Deperdussin are the fastest airplanes in the world. It remains to be seen how long the ban will remain in force.

# Wilbur Wright, aviation pioneer, dies from typhoid at 45

*Dayton, Ohio, May 30*
Wilbur Wright died at 3.15 this morning of typhoid fever at the early age of 45. The Wright home has been busy all day with callers, and there have so far been over a thousand telegrams of condolence.

Wilbur's death marks the end of an extraordinary partnership with his brother Orville, which culminated in 1903 with the first true powered flight in history. Wilbur was the practical one, Orville the ideas man; but Wilbur saw them through. His greatest personal triumph was in 1908 in France, when he showed skeptics that he and Orville really had mastered the air.

When once asked to speak at a dinner in his honor, Wilbur, a quiet man, replied that the bird who did the most talking, the parrot, could not fly very high. He had high religious and moral principles, and this led to legal battles with fellow aviators over their use of the brothers' patented system of wing-warping. These often bitter struggles cost him some friends, but he never wavered, becoming a polished courtroom performer. Yet few would disagree with what his father, Bishop Wright, wrote of Wilbur in his diary today: "A short life, full of consequences. An unfailing intellect, imperturbable temper, great self-reliance and as great modesty, seeing the right clearly, pursuing it steadfastly, he lived and died."

# Monaco hosts first seaplane contest

*Monaco, March 31*
The world's first hydroplane competition, held in Monaco over the past week, has been a runaway success for Farman biplanes. Belgian Jules Fischer is the overall winner with 112.1 points. He was one of only two non-French pilots of the eight starters and flew a Henry Farman machine. Frenchman Eugène Renaux nearly caught up and ended with 100.8 points on his Maurice Farman. Third and fourth were another Frenchman, Louis Paulhan, and American Hugh Robinson, both in Curtiss aircraft.

The competition, organized by the International Sporting Club of Monaco, has been very demanding. Farman has replaced his landing gear with floats, adding a third float at the rear of his biplane, powered by a 50-hp Gnome engine. The difficulties of taking off and landing on water are being solved. Entrants had to take off from calm water in the port of Monaco and circle buoys; land on calm water; take

*Henry Farman's hydroplane waits for the off in Monaco harbour.*

off from choppy water; and land on choppy water. On the first day only Fischer, Paulhan and Robinson managed all four tasks. There were extra points for taking passengers; yesterday Renaux took up six.

From the second day two tests were added, requiring flying from Monaco and landing between there and Mentone with a passenger, with neither pilot nor passenger getting wet feet (→ Apr 16, 1913).

# Enclosed cockpit is a success for new streamlined plane

*Surrey, England, May 1*
The first airplane to enclose the aviator inside a cabin had its first outing today in front of a large crowd at the Brooklands motor racing track south of London. Designed by A V Roe, the new machine, the Type F monoplane, is built with the principal aim of cutting down aerodynamic drag, and the fuselage is almost perfectly streamlined.

The Type F's wings pass through the aircraft at mid-fuselage, with its spars in front of and behind the pilot. The cockpit is entered through an aluminum roof hatch, and the aviator sees through celluloid windows, or, in bad weather, a circular porthole on either side. At the controls of the Type F today was a naval lieutenant, Wilfred Parke. To everyone's relief he found the cabin a success; many had predicted the windows would soon be covered with oil.

# Aircraft takes off from moving warship

*Samson's biplane takes off from the foredeck of the moving "Hibernia".*

*Dorset, England, May 10*
Commander Charles Samson of the Royal Navy is dining with King George V tonight aboard the royal yacht *Victoria and Albert* at the end of the naval review off Portland on the south coast of England. He is being hailed as the first airman to take off from a ship under way, after his flight on May 2 from the battleship HMS *Hibernia* while she steamed at 10.5 knots in Weymouth Bay.

Samson took off from the *Hiber-

nia*, which has been converted for aircraft use by the construction of a platform on her foredeck, in a Short hydroplane fitted with floats for landing on water. The display aimed to show off the capabilities of the naval arm of the new Royal Flying Corps, and follows Samson's earlier flights from stationary vessels. He made the first-ever flight from a Royal Navy ship (HMS *Africa*) on January 10, from a wooden launching-ramp on her bows.

# Pedallers try to cycle into the Paris sky

*Paris, June 2*
The French capital was the location of a bizarre aviation show today when 30 would-be flyers met at the Parc des Princes to compete for FF11,000 offered by the Peugeot brothers. But this was no ordinary air competition: the participants had to leave the ground under their own steam by sheer pedal-power.

On February 1 the Peugeots announced that FF10,000 would go to the first person to fly 10 meters (33 feet) by their own exertions, while a 1,000-franc prize was on offer for the first self-powered flight of one meter (3.3 feet). Aviators such as Gabriel Voisin, Emile Ladougne and Gabriel Poulain signed up to have a go in the contest, which drew thousands of spectators.

All sorts of ingenious machines were put through their paces: "aviettes", "cycloplanes" and converted bicycles with wings and pedal-driven propellers. Unfortunately, however, and despite a huge output of effort by the contestants, not one single machine could be coaxed off the ground.

*The Peugeot tricycle-biplane design offers an unusual approach to flying.*

# Novice wins Australia's first air race

*New South Wales, June 29*
Australia's first air race took place today, when two rival pilots vied to fly the 15.5 miles in the fastest time from the football ground at Botany, near Sydney, to Parramatta, New South Wales. The race began at 3.30pm, when William Hart took off in a Bristol Boxkite, bought, in its crate, from Bristol during the British maker's Australian mission last year.

It took him 23 minutes and 53 seconds to complete the course. Meanwhile American "Wizard" Stone, in a Metz Blériot, got lost in a raincloud and landed at Lakemba. Hart wins the £250 which each man had staked on the race, and will make up for damages he faces for landing on a market garden and stampeding a herd of cows.

The race was one of three proposed by Stone on April 14 – the other two were to be Sydney to Newcastle and back, and Sydney to

*William Hart, Australia's most successful airman, prepares for take-off.*

Melbourne – and was originally intended to be a return flight. Hart accepted the challenge on April 22, but the race, scheduled for June 16, was postponed because of bad weather. Stone is a showman, giving daredevil flying and motorcycling exhibitions. He crashed his aircraft three weeks ago while racing a motor car. Hart, holder of Australia's first aviator's certificate, learnt to fly just last year.

# Pioneer US woman aviator falls to her death at air show

*Massachusetts, July 1*
Several thousand spectators watched in horror today as Harriet Quimby, America's first woman aviator, fell around 1,500 feet to her death. Her passenger, William Willard, the father of pilot Charles Willard, also perished in a disaster that is bound to fuel new demands for improved safety for aviators. A simple belt or a parachute could have saved both victims.

The tragedy occurred at the end of the Harvard-Boston air meeting at Squantum. As a finale to the day's events, Quimby was to take up Willard senior, who organized the show, for a circuit of Boston harbor in her white Blériot XI. The machine was approaching the landing ground when, without warning, it nose-dived and passenger and pilot were hurled out.

# Parachutist dies in Eiffel Tower jump

*Paris, February 6*
Parisian cinemagoers have the chance to see a real drama tonight, when, just hours after the event, Pathé film theaters show Franz Reichelt's dramatic – and fatal – attempt to parachute from the Eiffel Tower. The cameras were on hand as Reichelt, an Austrian tailor, jumped from the first stage of the tower in a "parachute suit" of his own invention. It didn't open.

*Reichelt drops to his death.*

# Berlin cheers first flight from Paris

*Berlin, August 19*
German pilots turned out in force today to greet the first aviator to fly an airplane from Paris to the German capital. Edmond Audemars, a Swiss from Geneva, landed his Blériot at Berlin's Johannisthal airfield after a journey of 590 miles over two days. He did the trip in two roughly equal stages, stopping overnight at Bochum in the Ruhr, although mechanical worries caused him to make unscheduled landings elsewhere en route.

Audemars is a colorful character with a hallmark toothbrush moustache and bow tie. He was one of the airmen who made up the traveling show team of "Moisant's International Aviators" in the US last year, where he was nicknamed "Tiny" because of his small stature, and billed as the pilot of "the smallest and most dangerous airplane in the world". He was in the company of Frenchmen Roland Garros ("Fool Flyer") and René Simon ("Cloud Kisser"), as well as an assortment of other aerial extroverts who thrilled the American crowds with their airborne bravado.

# Pilot makes first controlled spin recovery

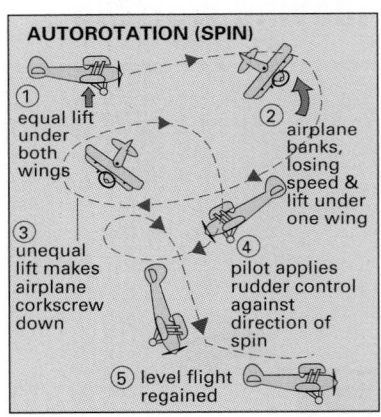

AUTOROTATION (SPIN)
① equal lift under both wings
② airplane banks, losing speed & lift under one wing
③ unequal lift makes airplane corkscrew down
④ pilot applies rudder control against direction of spin
⑤ level flight regained

*Wiltshire, England, August 25*
Today brilliant British naval pilot Lt Wilfred Parke survived one of the dreaded "spins", or spiral dives, that have claimed the lives of many aviators. Parke, who had a fellow-officer as passenger, found that he could recover from the spin by applying full opposite rudder and pushing the joystick forward, which has always seemed the wrong thing to do. He was flying the new Avro Type G biplane, which has a 60-hp Green engine and a streamlined fuselage.

**Illuminated aircraft at a night display at Hendon aerodrome, England.**

# Nations look into military role for aircraft

*A Blériot XI carries out reconnaissance during a French military exercise.*

*British soldiers restrain an airplane after the propeller has been started.*

## French flyers make an impressive sight

*Villacoublay, France, September 27*
The French Army held a review at Villacoublay today of the military airplanes which took part in the important recent maneuvers. It was an awe-inspiring sight: 72 machines, mostly flown direct from their bases, arranged in squadrons for inspection by war minister Alexandre Millerand. Every squadron was lined up, with pilots in front and motor workshops behind. Most were monoplanes of Blériot, Borel, Deperdussin, Hanriot, Morane, Nieuport, REP and Sommer types but also included Breguet, Caudron and Farman biplanes. The review took 70 minutes.

## German pilots take part in big exercise

*Germany, October 7*
Germany's air forces are developing rapidly, and today the navy's first Zeppelin rigid airship took to the air. It will be based at Johannisthal near Berlin for crew training and will carry a machine gun and wireless telegraph. The 518-foot craft could carry out long-range reconnaissance of shipping as well as bombardment. Meanwhile, on recent army maneuvers, the "Red" force used two squadrons of six airplanes each plus Army Zeppelin III, while the "Blue" force also had 12 airplanes plus a Parseval and a Gross airship. Of the 24 pilots, nine were decorated by Kaiser Wilhelm.

## British Army tests various airplanes

*Wiltshire, England, September 12*
Sixteen airplanes of the new Royal Flying Corps (RFC) are taking part in the British Army's current fall maneuvers on Salisbury Plain, 12 from the RFC's military wing and four from the naval wing. There has been one setback: the War Office grounded all monoplanes today in response to a string of fatal crashes. Military airplane trials were conducted on Salisbury Plain last month. Thirty-one aircraft were entered, and although many good French types did well, the £5,000 main prize went to Samuel Cody's *Cathedral*, a primitive biplane of huge power (→ Feb 1913).

## US Army acquires first 'flying boat'

*USA, November 27*
The aeronautical division of the US Army Signal Corps today received its first "flying boat", a Curtiss Model F, which brings the total number of aircraft accepted by the division since 1909 to just 15. Until March 1911, the only aircraft used was the army's original Wright Model A, and the recent small expansion of the division follows congressional approval for additional expenditure on air power this year. The first army maneuvers using airplanes started on August 10. The US Navy has had a tiny air strength since mid-1911, mostly for experimental uses (→ Jul 18, 1914).

# Bright future for airship line that lets passengers travel in style

*Germany, December 31*
Count von Zeppelin's passenger airship line, DELAG, is celebrating two years of constant, accident-free flying. With the introduction of three new airships the line, based at Friedrichshafen on Lake Constance, is confident of the future. More than 8,000 passengers have flown on its luxury flights between Germany's main cities. Today, at the Kaiser's urging, Admiral von Tirpitz ordered the German navy's first Zeppelin. Airships, it seems, will also have a part to play in war.

*DELAG's LZ 10 dirigible, the "Schwaben" was destroyed by fire on June 28.*

*What's the fare?*

Only a single Avro Type G biplane was ever built, but the type is historically significant: it was the first aircraft in the world to have an enclosed cabin.

The young Igor Sikorsky gained the attention of his fellow designers when his R-6A biplane won the top award at the Moscow Aeronautical Exhibition.

Luft Verkehrs Gesellschaft (LVG) produced the robust Mercedes-engined B.1, which became the primary unarmed scout for the German air service.

Short's S.45 biplane was a large training aircraft which served with the Royal Navy and at the Central Flying School until well after the outbreak of war.

The Handley Page Military Trials Aircraft, designed by founder of the Royal Australian Flying Corps Henry Petre, had a fully-cowled rotary engine.

Designed by Geoffrey de Havilland, the Royal Aircraft Factory B.E.2 was the first aircraft to reach France with the RFC at the outbreak of war in 1914.

The Maurice Farman MF 7, nicknamed "Longhorn" because of its long skids (elevator struts) projecting forward of the wings. It was a standard trainer.

This Farman seaplane crossed the English Channel for an early demonstration to the Royal Navy, which remained unconvinced of its potential.

With its Gnome rotary engine, the single-seater Short Tractor monoplane was one of the company's few early designs for a non-seafaring aircraft.

*The Blériot Type XXXIII was a strange canard, with pusher propeller behind the conventional landing gear.*

*The Curtiss A-1 Triad was another in Glenn Curtiss's series of exceedingly successful seaplanes with a large central float and wing-tip stabilizing floats.*

*Before incorporating the Cessna Aircraft Company, as we know it today, Clyde Cessna built several Blériot-derived craft including this Silver Wings.*

*At the end of 1912, Blériot produced this Type XXXVI. It had a tractor 70-hp Gnome, and a streamlined monocoque fuselage.*

*The advanced Avro Type E, depicted here, was first flown in March. It led to the Type 500, which was developed to become the legendary Avro 504.*

*The Handley Page Type E "Yellow Peril" took part in the 1912 British Military Trials Competition. It was far better than Cody's winning type.*

*The Curtiss Type F was a two-seater training flying-boat, which was also used in an observation role, powered by a pusher 100-hp Curtiss OX engine.*

*The aircraft which won the British Military Trials of this year was this outmoded Cody biplane. It won because of its 120-hp Austro-Daimler engine.*

# 1913

126.66mph
France
Maurice Prévost
Monocoque Déperdussin
Sep 29, 1913

634.54 miles
France
A Seguin
Henry Farman
Oct 13, 1913

20,079ft
France
Georges Legagneux
Nieuport II N
Dec 28, 1913

8,995lb
Russia
Igor Sikorsky
Russian Knight

217hp
France
Salmson Canton-Unné
(CU) 2M7

**Paris, January 1**
The International Federation of Aeronautics states that, by the end of 1912, 2,490 pilots had been awarded FAI licenses: 966 in France, 382 in Britain, 345 in Germany, 193 in the USA, 58 in Belgium, 27 in Switzerland and one in Egypt.

**Cuba, January 6**
The US Navy uses aircraft on maneuvers for the first time; an air camp is set up on Fisherman's Point, Guantanamo Bay, where the entire naval air fleet will be based for the exercise (→ Oct 7).

**New York, January 13**
Harry M Jones inaugurates the first regular airplane cargo service in the US, flying from Boston to New York in a Wright B. His cargo: baked beans.

**New York, January 20**
Attempting to establish a new women's altitude record, Bernetta Miller is covered with oil and temporarily blinded when her oil flow indicator smashes. She makes a safe emergency landing.

**Spain, January 24**
Swiss pilot Oscar Bider flies across the Pyrenees from Pau in southern France, reaching 11,483 feet in his Blériot monoplane; he lands at Madrid's Cuatro Vientos airfield.

**Etampes, France, January 24**
The pilot and airplane designer Charles Niéport and his mechanic Guyot are killed when their wing-warping device goes wrong.

**Gotha, Germany, February 3**
German engineers Bothmann and Glück, who founded the Gothaer Waggonfabrik [Gotha railroad wagon factory] in 1898, open an airplane division.

**London, February 14**
The Aero show opens; the Vickers shipbuilding company is exhibiting its Experimental Fighting Biplane N°1, an armed combat aircraft ordered by the British Admiralty.

**Italy, February 27**
The Caproni company's chief pilot, Slavorosov, flies from Milan to Rome on a tour organised by the paper *La Gazzetta dello Sport*. He flies over the principal towns en route to advertise the firm.

**London, February**
The War Office lifts its ban on the use of monoplanes by the RFC, imposed in September (→ Jun 1914).

**London, April 1**
The *Daily Mail* offers £10,000 for a transatlantic flight and £5,000 for a round-Britain flight in a British-designed and built airplane. Both have to be completed within 72 consecutive hours.

**Belgium, April 16**
An independent Belgian air force, the Compagnie des aviateurs [Aviators' Company] is formed.

**Cologne, Germany, April 17**
Briton Gustav Hamel lands after a non-stop flight of 4 hours and 18 minutes from Dover, England, in a Blériot XI (→ May 22, 1914).

**Panama, April 27**
In a floatplane, Bob Fowler makes the first flight with a passenger in Central America (and the first flight in Panama) when he flies with film cameraman Raymond Duhem from the Atlantic to the Pacific, flying 40 miles across the Panama isthmus in 57 minutes. En route, Duhem makes the first aerial film of Central America.

**Warsaw, June 10**
Marcel Brindejonc des Moulinais wins the Pommeroy cup for the longest flight between sunrise and sunset, flying 900 miles from Paris.

**Southampton, England, July 8**
Harry Hawker, in the Sopwith Bat Boat N° 1, completes required flight tests to win the Mortimer Singer £500 prize for an all-British amphibious aircraft, after the Bat Boat's 90-hp Austro-Daimler engine has been replaced with a British 100-hp Green (→ Aug).

**Hull, England, July 13**
Handley Page test pilot Ronald Whitehouse, who has been forbidden to fly within the city boundary on Sunday by the mayor of Hull, mocks the ban by flying just outside the boundary, to the cheers of an estimated 7,000 spectators.

**Kent, England, July 17**
The Short brothers' Folder seaplane, with a 160-hp Gnome engine, is accepted by the Royal Navy and assigned to HMS *Hermes* at Sheerness (→ Jul 18, 1914).

**Victoria, Canada, August 6**
Johnny Bryant becomes the first pilot killed in Canada when his floatplane disintegrates in flight.

**USA, August 10**
Lawrence Sperry and Lt Berringer demonstrate an automatic stabilizer in a Curtiss F flying boat. It is based on the ship's gyroscope invented by Sperry's father, Elmer Sperry (→ Jun 18, 1914).

**England, August**
Harry Hawker, the only competitor in the *Daily Mail* round-Britain hydroplane competition, attempts to fly 1,540 miles round the British and Irish coastline; he crashes near Dublin, but is awarded a special prize of £10,000 by the newspaper for showing determination and fine airmanship (→ Jan 27, 1914).

**Yorkshire, England, September 17**
Harold Blackburn, demonstrating his new Type 1 monoplane at Ripon, takes up a local woman, Mrs Leigh, who is over 70.

**England, September 18**
The prototype of the Avro 504 two-seat biplane begins flight tests, with an 80-hp Gnome engine.

**Reims, France, September 29**
Maurice Prévost flies his Deperdussin monoplane at 126.67mph to win the Gordon Bennett cup (→ Dec 31).

**Washington, DC, October**
The US Navy secretary's new Aeronautic Board recommends setting up an aeronautics center, assigning a ship for sea aviation training and testing and assigning one airplane to every major combat ship (→ Jan 10, 1914).

**France, October 15**
Lieutenant Ronin makes the first official airmail flight in France: flying a Morane-Saulnier, he carries a 22-pound sack of letters from Villacoublay to Pauillac (→ Jul 18, 1914).

**Paris, October 27**
Eugène Gilbert wins the second of three money prizes set up under the auspices of the Deutsch de la Meurthe cup, flying a closed-circuit course at St-Germain-en-Laye, on the outskirts of Paris, at a speed of 95.9mph in a Deperdussin monoplane fitted with a 160-hp Le Rhône engine.

**Paris, November 4**
The engineer Constantin patents his vented wing. A blade placed before the leading edge improves airflow over the wing.

**Los Angeles, November**
Before eager crowds, Lincoln Beachey demonstrates loops and upside-down flying in a Curtiss biplane.

**Mexico, November**
Two American mercenary pilots, Dean Ivan Lamb, flying for the revolutionary leader Pancho Villa, and Philip Rader, flying for President Huerta, exchange a dozen or so pistol shots in mid-air; neither is hit.

**England, November 30**
Captain Lushington gives Winston Churchill a flying lesson aboard his Short airplane.

*A major Belgian transport exhibition celebrates the joy of travel on two or four wheels, but even more so by airplane, airship and balloon.* ▶

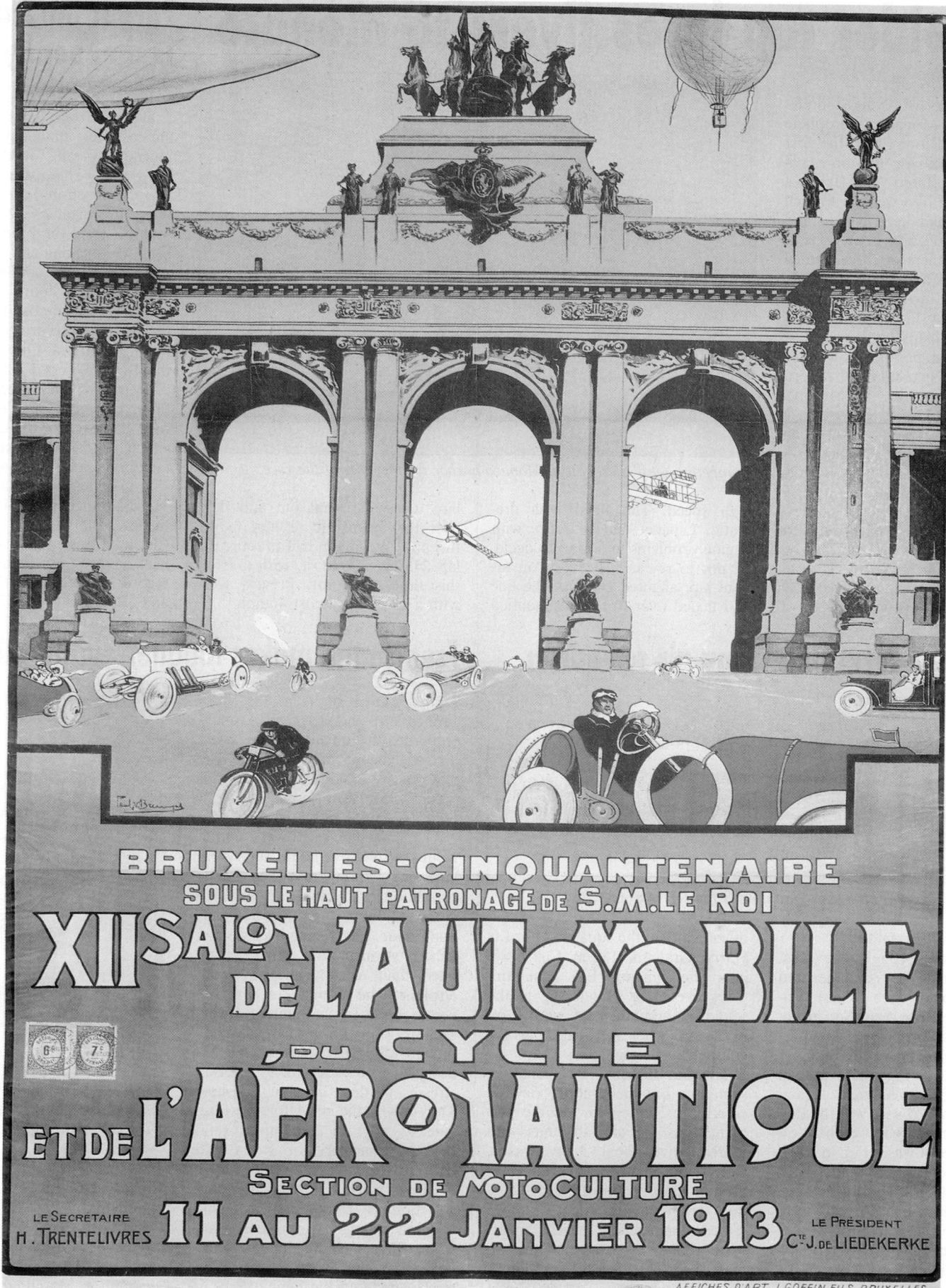

# Schneider cup lures flyers to Monaco

*Monaco, April 16*
The two weeks of flying competitions at the Monaco hydroplane meeting ended today with the first contest for the new maritime aviation cup offered by Jacques Schneider, son of a wealthy French arms maker and keen patron and organizer of aviation events. He is giving the winners of three annual events trophies and FF25,000 each.

Contestants must taxi for half of lap one and fly the remaining 173 miles over 28 laps at their fastest speeds. Taking part were Frenchmen Gabriel Espanet in a Nieuport, Roland Garros in a Morane-Saulnier and Maurice Prévost in a Deperdussin, plus American Charles Weymann in a Nieuport. A course was marked out in Roquebrune Bay.

First off was Prévost; he flew confidently. Garros taxied out next but so much water was disturbed by his airplane that his engine cut out and he had to be towed back. By now the Nieuports were flying at

*Competing seaplanes wait in Monaco harbor for the start of the race.*

high speed. The finish was dramatic. Espanet had to retire with engine problems and Garros decided not to re-enter. Prévost, on his final lap, alighted short of the line and taxied over it; this disqualified

him unless he went out and flew over the finish. He refused to do this until Weymann had to retire on lap 24. Then Prévost, with Garros this time, took off; Prévost won with a speed of almost 46mph.

# Forget the train: it is cheaper by plane

*Lyon, France, March 28*
Travelling from Paris to Lyon by air costs less than doing the same journey by rail – even if you go third class. This extraordinary fact was demonstrated in grand style today by Eugène Gilbert, when he took off from the French capital in his Morane-Saulnier monoplane and flew to the south-eastern city of Lyon in 3 hours and 10 minutes, covering almost 255 miles and setting a new record for a non-stop flight. On arrival Gilbert calculated that the five liters of oil and 60 liters of petrol he had used during the flight cost less than a third class railroad ticket for the same journey, which of course would also have taken several hours longer by train.

Gilbert has been making a name as a distance flyer. Last year he made a city-to-city flight, from Clermont-Ferrand to Brioude and back, as well as setting new speed records for distances between 217 and 373 miles (→ Oct 27).

# Americans form first army air squadron

*Two of the pioneering First Aero Squadron's first Wright aircraft.*

*Texas City, March 5*
The US Army brought the most modern part of its equipment to Texas City today when its first aviation unit, the First Aero Squadron, began operations. The squadron has nine biplanes and six pilots in addition to its commander, Captain Charles deForest Chandler.

Capt Chandler, who was the first head of the army's Aeronautical Division when it was set up in 1907, is a pioneer of army flying, as is Lt Thomas Milling, who is also here. They and Lt Henry Arnold were the first three men in the army to qualify for the title of Military Aviator, and Milling piloted one of the aircraft in army maneuvers. The

other pilots in the squadron are Lts Harry Graham, Loren Call, William Sherman and Eric Ellington. Capt Frederick Hennessey is the squadron adjutant and supply officer, and First Aero also has 51 enlisted men assigned to it.

The unit carries a provisional designation, but the aviators view its creation as a step toward the permanent use of aircraft units with more conventional army forces. The squadron will train with army ground units in the area and conduct map-making flights. Given the current rebellion in neighboring Mexico, it is expected that the aircraft will also be used for border patrol missions.

# Frenchman makes tougher, lighter planes

*France, March 3*
French airplane designer Armand Deperdussin unveiled his latest high-speed machine today. The new racer should be capable of speeds close to 125mph, giving it record-breaking potential.

The machine's power comes from its 160-hp Gnome rotary engine, but what makes it special is its revolutionary *monocoque* fuselage construction. A monocoque aircraft is ideal for racing because it is lighter, stronger and more streamlined than a conventionally built airplane. The strength of a monocoque fuselage is inherent in its shell or "skin" (in this case a "tube" of thin tulip-wood strips), which is designed to be resistant to external stresses, rather like an eggshell. This offsets the need for the fuselage to rely on a complex (and heavy) framework of struts and bars for strength.

The pioneer of monocoque construction is Deperdussin's highly talented engineer, Louis Becherau, whose first such machine was unveiled last year. Jules Védrines won the coveted Gordon Bennett race in

*The monocoque on display in Paris.*

a Deperdussin monocoque in September, setting a new world record of 108mph as well. In Britain, Geoffrey de Havilland has used a monocoque design for his latest aircraft, the B.S.1, which clocked up 90.7mph in March (→ Aug 5).

# Air mercenaries attack Mexican gunships

*Moreno, Mexico, May 30*
Dodging gunfire from the Mexican gunship *Guerrero*, which with two other government boats was guarding the city of Guaymas on the Gulf of California, Didier Masson, a French-born American mercenary in the pay of anti-government Mexican rebels, and rebel Captain Joaquin Alcalde today dropped bombs from an airplane in an attempt to sink the vessel.

On landing at Moreno, Masson reported that the bombs failed to score a hit. The airmen's inaccuracy was equalled by the ship's crew, which failed to hit the aircraft. Masson, a former instructor at the Glenn L Martin flying school in Balboa, California, flew his Martin pusher aircraft at 2,500 feet during the attack. The 30-pound bombs were made from metal piping, dynamite and steel rivets, with a detonator rod at one end and fins at the other. Masson is sure that the experience will make future raids more successful (→ May 6, 1914).

*Didier Masson, who made the perilous flight over Mexico, with a companion.*

# Russian faces jail for first ever loop

*Kiev, August 27*
A Russian aviator today became the first pilot to loop the loop when Lt Pyotr Nikolaevich Nesterov of the Imperial Russian Air Service performed this here. Nesterov's machine, a French Nieuport Type IV, completed the vertical circle at about 1,800 feet. When he landed the intrepid airman may have expected a rousing welcome for his feat, but if so he was disappointed: he was promptly arrested for endangering government property – his airplane.

The maneuver is being slammed by Nesterov's superiors as an act of "useless audacity" and he now faces up to 30 days' detention. His previous good record means he could be released sooner (→ Sep 8, 1914).

# Leading designer is arrested for fraud

*Paris, August 5*
The aviation world received a shock today when police arrested Armand Deperdussin, the noted aircraft builder and owner of Reims aerodrome, on charges of fraud and breach of trust. According to the police, Deperdussin has been responsible for embezzling the sum of FF32,000,000 from his business, which now stands on the verge of bankruptcy.

Deperdussin claims that a large part of the diverted funds went to finance further research into improving his engines. As justification he could point to the fact that for the past three years his airplanes have been at the forefront of French aviation developments, setting several records (→ Aug 1, 1914).

# Garros crosses the Med

*Roland Garros arrived with a gallon of fuel to spare and a damaged motor.*

*Bizerta, Tunisia, September 23*
Another great aviation challenge was conquered today when the French pilot Roland Garros became the first person to fly across the Mediterranean, a distance of nearly 470 miles – 20 times further than Blériot's historic cross-Channel epic. The non-stop flight was a close-run thing: Garros's Morane-Saulnier monoplane had enough fuel for an 8-hour flight and reached Tunisia 7 hours and 53 minutes after take-off.

A flight this long over water has never been made before, although the somewhat reckless Edouard Bague had two stabs at the Mediterranean crossing in 1911, on the second of which he disappeared without trace. Aware of Bague's fate, Garros left nothing to chance; he was aware of the risk of running out of fuel but confident of his ability to navigate without wasting it. With a tire inner tube as a lifesaver, he took off this morning at 5.30 from the beach near the resorts of Fréjus and St-Raphaël, southwest of Cannes, and headed out over the sea toward Corsica.

The journey was not without its troubles: less than two hours into the flight a cylinder head broke and Garros considered putting down on Sardinia, but the island was covered in cloud and he decided to press on. At 1.15pm, with a gallon of fuel left in his tank, Garros surprised the French naval garrison at Bizerta by landing triumphantly on their parade ground.

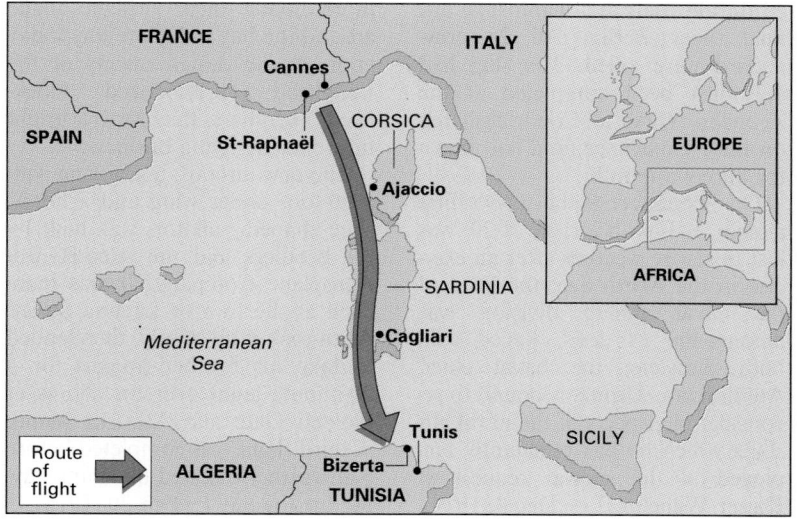

# Sam Cody dies in crash

*The debris of Samuel Cody's seaplane after the crash that killed him.*

*Farnborough, England, August 7*
Samuel Cody, Britain's Texan-born air pioneer, was hurled to his death today as his latest machine – a seaplane with a 60-foot wingspan – broke up around him at 300 feet during a routine landing at Farnborough, Hampshire. His sons Leon and Frank watched horrified as the great wings crumpled vertically and Cody and his passenger were dashed to the ground. The

aviator had hoped that his 70-mph seaplane, which he found "a lovely, easy flier, steady as a rock", would evolve into a machine to cross the Atlantic. When it crashed it was fitted with a land undercarriage.

A naturalized Briton, Cody was a pioneer in building and flying airplanes in Britain. He has died as he wished. He said recently: "I hope my death is swift ... from one of my own aeroplanes."

## Airship policy faces review after crash

*Berlin, October 17*
The future of German military airships could be in doubt following another Zeppelin tragedy today, when the Imperial navy's second airship, the L 2, blew up and crashed during trials at Johannisthal airfield, near Berlin. All 28 crew aboard were killed. The ship had only just been completed at the Zeppelin works at Friedrichshafen on Lake Constance, and had flown for barely a month.

On September 9 the navy's first airship, L 1, with a crew of 20, was lost in severe weather after an exercise in the North Sea; the head of the naval airship division was among the 14 dead. Faced with both disasters, the naval chief, Admiral von Tirpitz, is bound to reconsider all aspects of the naval airships which he has reluctantly employed at the special request of Kaiser Wilhelm II (→ Dec 4, 1914).

## Brothers show off their first airplane

*San Francisco, June 15*
After Allan Lougheed survived two crashes in Curtiss pusher-type aircraft, he and his brother Malcolm decided to design their own aircraft with the engine in the front. If the three flights their airplane made around the bay today are any indication of the design talents of the Lougheed (pronounced "lockheed") brothers, they have a bright future in the flying business.

The new aircraft, a seaplane with a 50-foot upper wing and a horseshoe shaped radiator, was built by the brothers and the Alco-Hydro-Aeroplane Company. It was launched at the foot of Laguna Street; Allan took it up briefly, then landed to take his brother aboard for a 20-minute jaunt over the shores of Golden Gate and Alcatraz island. A third flight was completed before bad weather dictated the end of flying for the day (→ Feb 20, 1915).

# Tiny biplane makes a big impression

*England, November 29*
A diminutive new biplane which takes its nickname from a compact first aid-kit delighted onlookers today at the Royal Aircraft Factory at Farnborough, Hampshire. The Tabloid, created by British designer Tommy Sopwith, with help from Fred Sigrist, is powered by an 80-hp Gnome rotary engine, and its small cockpit seats the pilot and passenger side by side, the pilot on the left. Today the Tabloid climbed to 1,200 feet in the first minute, before leveling out and reaching 92mph. This was achieved with a passenger aboard and fuel sufficient for two and a half hours' flying.

*A damaged machine is examined.*

# Sister follows the 'flying schoolgirl'

*Katherine (l) and Marjorie Stinson smile for the camera after a flight.*

*Montana, September 27*
Katherine Stinson has become the first woman in the US to make an official airmail flight. Over the past four days, she has carried 1,333 letters and postcards at the Montana State Fair in a publicity stunt to promote a Montana airmail service. Known as "The Flying Schoolgirl", she came to aviation by a strange route. Her first love was music, and she took up flying to pay for piano lessons. But she was so struck by life in the air that she abandoned all to win her pilot's license. Her younger sister Marjorie has been bitten by the bug and is following in her footsteps (→ Jul 18, 1915).

**How to beat the cold and lack of oxygen at an altitude of 33,000 feet.**

# Russia's Sikorsky defies the critics

*St Petersburg, Russia, August 2*
The world's biggest airplane today made a flight of 1 hour and 54 minutes carrying eight passengers. The machine, called *Bolshoi Baltiskii* [Great Baltic] or *Grand*, weighs over four tons and has a 92-foot wingspan. It was piloted today by its designer, Igor Sikorsky, foreman of the Russo-Baltic Wagon Works' air division. When first completed it had two 100-hp engines, biplane wings and a twin-finned tail, and it flew on March 2. Sikorsky saw that for its size more power was needed and had the machine rebuilt with four engines, two tractors and two pushers. It then made what was the world's first four-engined flight on May 10.

Sikorsky recognized that for maximum efficiency the four engines should all be tractors, arranged in a line. He has now had the giant rebuilt in this form, with a tail redesigned with four rudders so that control can be maintained if an outer engine fails.

In this third form the giant will be known as the *Russkii Vityaz* [Russian Knight]. It has confounded those who proclaimed that so large and heavy a machine could not fly. It flew to army maneuvers last month and was inspected by Czar Nicholas II (→ Feb 12, 1914).

*The "Bolshoi Baltiskii", the new giant of the air, has four engines and 16 wheels and takes eight passengers.*

## Loopy Frenchman in unrivalled aerobatics

*Buc, France, September 21*
Young French pilot Adolphe Pégoud pulled off a remarkable maneuver today when he flew in a loop during a superb display of aerobatics in his Blériot. This is not strictly the first time that a pilot has flown a loop, but Pégoud took his training seriously, spending up to 20 minutes hanging upside down inside an inverted practice cockpit. After completing his feat, he delighted the crowd by performing various daring maneuvers such as rolls and spins.

Pégoud, who has been flying for only seven months, is gaining quite a name for himself as a display pilot. On August 19, he bravely abandoned his previous Blériot at 820 feet to make the first parachute jump by a pilot to test a parachute made by Bonnet. When he reached a good height, he released the sail-like contraption and was pulled

*Pégoud is cheered after his stunt.*

from his cockpit. As he watched the Blériot spiralling to earth, he decided to try to reproduce similar aerobatics while in control of an airplane.

## French planes form a Chinese air fleet

*Peking, July 4*
The arrival of China's first fleet of aircraft has been marked with a series of demonstration flights at Peking and Tsientin by René Caudron, the French maker who has supplied the republican government with 12 new airplanes. Caudron came to Peking to oversee the delivery of his machines, and last week flew several times over the city, passing over the president's residence on one flight and dropping a letter to him.

Yesterday, with a passenger, Caudron left Peking at 5.30am and flew to Tientsin, 70 miles away, in 1 hour and 12 minutes. He returned today after some demonstration flights. The Caudrons will be based at the flying school in Peking. The first Chinese pilots to qualify will probably fight Mongolian incursions (→ Jan 1, 1914).

## French flyers are world beaters for third year running

*France, December 31*
As 1913 draws to a close, French aviators can look back on another brilliant year of achievement, with every important world record in their hands for the third year in a row. In the last four months, especially, new records have fallen thick and fast.

On September 29 Maurice Prévost carried off the 1913 Gordon Bennett trophy with a new speed record of 126.6 mph in his sleek Deperdussin monoplane. This was followed two weeks later by a new world non-stop distance record of 634.4 miles, when, on October 13, A Seguin flew his Henry Farman from Paris to Bordeaux and back. This beat Géo Fourny's 13-month-old record of just over 628 miles, although Fourny's flight, in a Maurice Farman, lasted 13 hours 22 minutes, still a record for duration.

France's latest world record was won just three days ago, on December 28, when Georges Legagneux climbed to an altitude of 20,014 feet in a Nieuport at St-Raphaël. On his ascent he became the first pilot to use oxygen in flight.

## Cairo hails aviator for 3,300-mile trip

*Cairo, December 29*
A triumphant welcome awaited Jules Védrines today when the French aviator landed in Egypt at the end of a 3,356-mile flight across Europe, Asia Minor and the Levant. It is another success for the celebrated Parisian, whose background – working-class and socialist – is untypical of most of the modern heroes of the air.

Védrines took off from Nancy in eastern France on November 20, and headed his Blériot XI for central Europe, where his main stops were Prague, Vienna and the Serbian capital Belgrade. His last stop in Europe was the Ottoman Empire capital, Constantinople [Istanbul], after which he flew over Ottoman territory around eastern Mediterranean, finally reaching Egypt via Beirut and Jaffa.

The first prototype Avro 504, an aircraft whose development potential was such that it served until well into the 1930s, almost 10,000 being built.

Sopwith's Bat Boat was an unexciting biplane flying boat, albeit the first to be built in the UK. It had a plywood "Consuta" hull sewn with copper wire.

The Grahame-White Charabanc or Aerobus, with its extended fuselage nacelle, was one of the first attempts at a passenger-carrying aircraft.

The Royal Aircraft Factory HRE2, here with a set of floats for testing.

Pilot de Waal prepares to take a passenger aloft in a Fokker M.1.

A prototype Sopwith Tabloid, later to be a successful military aircraft.

Sikorsky's impressive "Grand" first flew on March 2 this year.

Another of Blériot's strange canards was the Type XLII (42). It had an 80-hp Gnome driving a pusher propeller behind the nacelle.

The Avro Type 500 was the predecessor of the Avro 504, and was regarded by A V Roe himself as his first real success. It entered service in May 1912.

The "Ilya Muromets" had a modern fuselage, and its four engines were mounted tractor-style along the leading edge and not in push/pull pairs as on the "Grand". The RBVZ works built 80, with six different makes of engine.

The Farman F.20 was the last aircraft credited to Henry Farman alone, and it proved to be an extremely successful trainer. The usual engine was a 70- or 80-hp Gnome.

The Fokker M 2 was a neat-looking low-wing monoplane, with an unusual amount of dihedral. Soon it was to lead to the deadly E.1 Eindecker.

Geoffrey de Havilland in the cockpit of the Royal Aircraft Factory B.S.2.

The Caudron amphibian about to take to the water at Deauville. Like most flying boats and amphibians of the day, it had high-drag square-section floats.

The Sopwith Three-seater had two passengers forward and the pilot aft. It made quite a stir at the 1913 Olympia Aero Show at Earl's Court, London.

The Morane L was the first of a series of successful monoplanes.

The prototype of the R.E.1 still used wing-warping for lateral control.

The Burgess-Dunne seaplane was a US floatplane derivative of a tailless British design with pronounced wing sweepback. Three were produced.

Although famous for large land-based bombers, Friedrichshafen produced excellent seaplanes, including the 160-hp Maybach-engined FF31 of 1913.

The Royal Aircraft Factory A.E.1 was the prototype of the F.E.3, a remarkable pusher-engined fighter armed with a one-pounder cannon in the nose. It was strongly inspired by the designs of French aviators.

A rare air-to-air view of the Curtiss Model F flying boat, of which 150 were eventually built for the US Navy and about 20 were exported to Russia. It was a valuable maritime reconnaissance and training machine.

# 1914

 134.54mph
Great Britain
Norman Spratt
RAF SE.4
Jun 1914

 1,180.61 miles
Germany
Werner Landmann
Albatros
Jun 28, 1914

 26,739ft
Germany
Heinrich Oelerich
DFW
Jul 14, 1914

 10,582lb
Russia
Igor Sikorsky
Ilya Muromets A

 225hp
Great Britain
Sunbeam

**Peking, January 1**
The Chinese Army Air Arm is formed.

**Washington, DC, January 10**
The US Navy secretary says "aircraft must form a large part of our naval force" (→ Jan 20).

**Florida, January 20**
The first permanent US Navy "aeronautic station" is set up at Pensacola; the unit, transferred from Maryland, has 9 officers, 23 men and 7 aircraft (→ Jul 1).

**Australia, January 27**
Harry Hawker, the pilot who became famous abroad and returned to Australia two weeks ago, flies over Melbourne.

**France, February 12**
At Port-Aviation near Paris, Jean Ors leaps from a Deperdussin monoplane at 1,640 feet to test a parachute of his own design. Using a cord, he opens it at 1,000 feet and lands safely 39 seconds later.

**Russia, February 12**
Igor Sikorsky's giant, four-engined biplane, the *Ilya Muromets* flies. It is an improved version of last year's *Bolshoi Baltiskii* (→ Jul 11).

**Wiltshire, England, February 23**
Harry Busteed makes a first test flight of the Bristol Scout biplane at Larkhill training centre.

**Farnborough, England, March 10**
In squally weather, E T Busk flies the R.E.1 biplane without pilot control and with elevators locked, to test its stability: although unbalanced by gusts, it returns each time to stable flight.

**Florida, April**
The St Petersburg/Tampa Airboat Line goes out of business.

**Sydney, May 2**
Before a crowd of 60,000, Maurice Guillaux loops the loop ten times in succession. He has been making exhibition flights with his Blériot since April 20.

**France, May 22**
British aviator Gustav Hamel leaves Villacoublay for England in a new Morane monoplane; after flying off over the English Channel he is never seen again.

**New York, May 28**
Glenn Curtiss makes a successful flight in Samuel Langley's *Aerodrome*, which he has rebuilt and substantially altered for Mr Walcott, the secretary of the Smithsonian Institution. Curtiss and Walcott are determined to prove that a machine could have flown before the Wrights' first flight, thereby invalidating the brothers' commercially valuable patents (→ Jun 29).

**Calgary, Canada, June 25**
Tom Blakely flies the *West Wind*, a Curtiss-type biplane designed with Frank Ellis.

**England, June 27**
The Pemberton-Billing aircraft company is officially registered, using the telegraphic name *Supermarine* (→ Sep 20, 1916).

**New York, June 29**
Glenn Curtiss takes up nine passengers in his seaplane *America*, built for Rodman Wanamaker, to make an attempt on the £10,000 prize offered by the *Daily Mail* for the first transatlantic crossing in a heavier-than-air machine.

**Wiltshire, England, June**
All six squadrons of the Royal Flying Corps (RFC) are concentrated at Netheravon for a month's training (→ Aug 3).

**Washington, DC, July 1**
The Office of Naval Aeronautics is formed to oversee the air operations of the US Navy.

**Sydney, July 4**
A J Roberts pilots an Australian-built airship on a short flight, but is forced to make an emergency landing in Rushcutter's Bay.

**Washington, DC, July 14**
Dr Robert H Goddard is granted a patent for his liquid fuel rocket engine.

**Washington, DC, July 18**
The Aviation Section of the US Army Signal Corps is formed, with 60 officers, 260 men and 6 airplanes.

**England, July 28**
Royal Navy pilot Arthur Longmore launches a 14-inch torpedo from a Short seaplane.

**London, July**
Lieutenant-General Sir Douglas Haig dismisses air reconnaissance, saying: "There is only one way for a commander to get information by reconnaissance and that is by use of cavalry."

**France, August 1**
Industrialists including Louis Blériot buy out the bankrupt Deperdussin airplane company.

**Lunéville, France, August 3**
On the day that Germany declares war on France, a German airplane flies over and drops six bombs, causing slight damage.

**London, August 3**
Major Hugh Trenchard is appointed commandant of the RFC Military Wing (→ Aug 13).

**France, August 13**
Nos 1 and 2 Squadrons of the RFC arrive in France; Nos 3 and 4 are to join them shortly (→ Aug 25).

**San Diego, Calif, August 17**
Flying a Martin T, Captain Lewis Goodier begins offical tests of the Scott bomb-dropping device.

**England, September 3**
The Royal Naval Air Service (RNAS) is made responsible for British air defense (→ Oct 26).

**Germany, September 28**
The German Air Service adopts an "Iron Cross" insignia for its aircraft.

**Europe, October 26**
RNAS aircraft are ordered to display insignia based on Great Britain's Union flag (→ Dec 11).

**Australia, October 28**
Aviators in Melbourne form an Australian Aero Club.

**France, October 31**
Lt Humphreys of Nº 4 Squadron RFC finds a new method of attack when he fires 250 rounds at a German convoy when on patrol (→ Nov 20).

**France, November 20**
Field Marshal Sir John French praises the RFC's performance in the war: "Almost every day new methods for employing aircraft both strategically and tactically are discovered and put into practice" (→ Mar 12, 1915).

**Germany, December 4**
The Imperial German Navy forms its first seaplane unit.

**Russia, December 10**
The Russian Army forms its Flotilla of Flying Ships (EVK) which is equipped with *Ilya Muromets* four-engined long-range reconnaissance bombers.

**Europe, 11 December**
Royal Naval Air Service (RNAS) aircraft drop the Union flag insignia in favour of a roundel (blue and white rings with a red center) as used by the French.

**France, December 25**
In a Christmas Day prank, Captain L A Strange of Nº 5 Squadron RFC flies to the German airfield at Lille, in north-eastern France, and "bombs" it with footballs.

*The first aerial victory: on October 5, near Reims, Sergeant Frantz and Corporal Quénault, aboard a Voisin, shoot down an Aviatik.* ▶

# Passenger service opens

*Fansler (l) and Jannus flank their backer and first passenger, A C Pheil.*

**St Petersburg, Florida, January 1**
The St Petersburg/Tampa Airboat Line commenced the world's first regularly-scheduled airplane passenger flights at just after 10am today, when Tony Jannus took a Benoist flying boat into the air with passenger A C Pheil, former mayor of St Petersburg. They flew the 19 miles to Tampa in 20 minutes.

Pheil, one of the strongest backers of the airline – the idea of Percival E Fansler – bid $400 at an auction to be the first passenger. The normal fare is $5 one-way for a gross weight, including baggage, of 200 pounds. Extra weight or packages will cost six cents per pound. Four round trips a day are planned. Thomas Benoist, whose company operates the airline, hopes to add another aircraft and expand the service to Bradenton, Sarasota and Tarpon Springs (→Apr).

# Another Russian giant takes to the air

**St Petersburg, Russia, July 11**
A true giant of an airplane has just completed a 1,590-mile flight from St Petersburg to Kiev and back, carrying up to a dozen passengers on some stages. This rival for the flourishing airship trade, the *Ilya Muromets II*, is an improved version of the first *Ilya Muromets*, itself a development of the *Bolshoi Baltiskii* (or *Grand*) machine designed last year by Igor Sikorsky of the Russo-Baltic Wagon Works (air division). The colossal four-engined biplane has a wingspan of almost 100 feet and a cockpit fully enclosed by glass for the two pilots, complete with instruments to show speed and altitude. Passengers have a heated lounge and (for the brave) an outdoor promenade deck.

The *Ilya Muromets* first flew on February 12 and two days later took up a world record of 16 passengers. On June 18 its successor, *Ilya Muromets II*, set a record flight duration for pilot and six passengers of 6 hours and 33 minutes.

*Two passengers on the fuselage promenade of the "Ilya Muromets" in flight.*

# Mexicans open fire on US flying boat

**Vera Cruz, Mexico, May 6**
Mexican gunners today hit a US Navy Curtiss AH-3 flying boat on a reconnaissance mission. Neither Lt P N L Bellinger, the pilot, nor Lt R C Saufley, the observer, were injured. Bellinger, who made the first flight of the current US-Mexican hostilities on April 25 – the first time US air forces went into combat – has made regular reconnaissance flights in the area.

The US Navy brought a number of aircraft to Vera Cruz aboard the USS *Mississippi* to support US forces landed here last month in response to the arrest of American sailors in Tampico earlier this year. That incident brought to a new head the growing tension in US-Mexican relations since General Vitoriano Huerta seized power in February last year.

# Seaplanes and gunbuses are stars of the fifth British aero show

*The PB1's unusual and graceful lines attract much praise at Olympia.*

**London, March 16**
King George V today opened the Fifth Aero Show at Olympia in west London, and saw the latest models proudly displayed by British aircraft manufacturers. Various trends were in evidence, among them an increase in the number of marine aircraft on show. Avro caused a stir by installing safety belts in all its aircraft in the show. Many pilots, fearing that they would be thought less brave if they used them, took issue with this.

One of the unexpected stars has been the PB1, a new single-seat flying boat. This aircraft is the first product of a company formed by Noel Pemberton-Billing, hence the aircraft's initials. The company, based at Southampton, has the charming telegraphic address of "Supermarine". The PB1 looks an excellent start, with a shapely hull and neatly cowled Gnome 50-hp engine, but it has not yet flown.

Another British seaplane on display is a second, much improved version of the Sopwith Bat Boat, which has already proved a versatile and popular aircraft for the naval wing of the RFC. This airplane has a more powerful engine, plus room in the cockpit to house wireless equipment. The designers hope it will sell as a reconnaissance plane. The military theme is carried through by the "gunbuses" of both Sopwith and Vickers. These are "pusher" aircraft built to carry machine guns.

# Gyroscope wins big prize for American

*Sperry's stabilizing gear exposed.*

*Buc, France, June 18*
To the surprise, not to say chagrin, of many, a 21-year-old American has walked off with the first prize of FF50,000 at the French airplane safety competition. The winner, Lawrence B Sperry, is the son of Dr Elmer Sperry, founder of the Sperry Gyroscope Company. He qualified only last year as a pilot of seaplanes, and brought to the contest a Curtiss flying boat equipped with a specially designed gyroscopic stabilizer. The stabilizer is designed to keep the machine steady automatically, despite any natural disturbances which might upset it.

# North Sea crossed by air for first time

*Stavanger, Norway, July 30*
Norwegian aviator Tryggve Gran today left Scotland in an attempt to fly 300 miles across the North Sea to his homeland. His airplane, called appropriately *Nordsjöen* [North Sea], was a Blériot monoplane similar to that used for the first English Channel crossing in 1909. Gran took off but was forced back by low cloud. He then received a telegram indicating good weather at his destination, so he took off again and was able to climb above the cloud and sight the mountains of Norway to guide him in. His flight took 4 hours and 10 minutes.

# Briton carries off second Schneider trophy

*Monaco, April 20*
Howard Pixton today flew a Sopwith Tabloid biplane to victory in the second Schneider cup competition. All four entrants from last year's contest entered again this year, joined by Pierre Levasseur of France, Pixton and Lord Carbery of Britain, Ernst Burri of Switzerland, Ernst Stoeffler of Germany and William Thaw of the US.

The first shock came in the eliminating trials when last year's winner, Maurice Prévost, failed to qualify. Pixton was fourth away today and was unstoppable, reaching 86.8 mph in his flight of 2 hours and 13 seconds. Second was Burri in his FBA flying boat, taking 3 hours, 24 minutes and 12 seconds after refueling on lap 23. Espanet and Levasseur retired early, Garros broke a propeller and did not start, Stoeffler withdrew yesterday, and Thaw and Weymann did not take off. Carbery and Levasseur tried to continue on borrowed aircraft but failed to catch Pixton.

*Howard Pixton's winning Sopwith Tabloid is towed across Monaco bay.*

# Britain's first passenger service launched

*Leeds, England, July 22*
The lady mayoress of the industrial city of Leeds in Yorkshire today paid her respects to the adjacent city of Bradford in a most unfamiliar manner: she traveled from one city to the other by airplane.

The machine in which she made her flight, an 80-hp Gnome rotary-engined Blackburn Christie Type 1, was flown by Harold Blackburn, a local aero engineer and well-known designer in his own right. It was the first flight of a series, flown at half-hourly intervals, from Leeds to Bradford and back, the first scheduled airplane service anywhere in the British Isles.

# Garros triumphant

*Monaco, April 15*
Roland Garros has emerged victorious at a great air rally here, which brought together 18 French and seven German machines. It involved speed trials between Monaco and Paris, London, Brussels, Vienna, Madrid, Turin and the German town of Gotha. Seaplane-only trials were held between Genoa-Monaco and Marseilles-Monaco. Garros, in a Morane-Saulnier seaplane, was declared the winner after victory on three of the routes.

# Australia hails its first airmail flight

*Sydney, July 18*
Large crowds greeted French pilot Maurice Guillaux when he landed here this afternoon after making the first official airmail flight in Australia. Guillaux left Melbourne, Victoria, two days ago with his Blériot monoplane loaded with a cargo of 1,785 letters, some Lipton's Tea and OT Lemon Squash. He was in the air for just 9 hours and 15 minutes, but his flight was held up by bad weather. The Frenchman arrived in Australia on April 8 aboard the RMS *Orontes*, and since then has made a number of display flights. On May 2 in Sydney he performed before 60,000 spectators.

*Guillaux (l): delivering the letters.*

**February. Two of America's motorized daredevils, well-known show aviator and stuntman Lincoln Beachey and racing driver Barney Oldfield, pit their different skills against each other at a Los Angeles show.**

# How ready is Europe for warfare in the air?

## France: versatile, flexible and well-trained

*A Farman MF.11 with bomb tube.*

*France, July*
France's Aviation Militaire is well-trained and equipped but smaller than Germany's equivalent, although it has benefitted from wide-scale military maneuvers involving aircraft and is probably the more competent at reconnaissance.

There are 156 military airplanes and 15 airships; major types include slow Voisin pusher biplanes capable of bombing, and Blériot and Morane-Saulnier monoplanes. An armoured Farman has just appeared at Buc for testing. The French could produce large numbers of extra machines and engines, having been a major exporter. A French naval flying service is being established. The main naval air station will be at Fréjus, in the south, where the airplane-carrying ship *Foudre* is based.

## Germany: the largest air force in Europe

*Germany, July*
The Imperial German Military Aviation Service has the largest number of airplanes of any air arm, thought to total 246. Virtually all are two-seaters, produced by more than 20 firms. Half the total are Taube aircraft, based on the Austrian design, which have been built by 11 companies. Another standard machine is the Arrow tractor biplane. There is a major airship force, including seven Zeppelins.

Unlike the Royal Flying Corps in Great Britain, the German aircraft are under strict army control, divided between HQ and corps. The airplanes are deployed in more than 40 squadrons and flights, with four to six aircraft each. The Imperial Naval Air Service adds about 36 seaplanes to the total, as well as the Zeppelin L 3.

*Searchlights pick up a Zeppelin, star of the impressive German airpower.*

## Austria-Hungary: not well prepared

*Austria-Hungary, July*
The Austro-Hungarian empire is closely allied to Germany but is probably the least prepared European nation to fight an air war, despite being the birthplace of the Etrich Taube and Löhner Arrow. Pilots on active service have sometimes been German. Estimates of its air strength vary widely, and sources suggest it could field 110 Taube, Albatros and Löhner airplanes. Serviceability should be high due to the small number of different types, but other estimates put the strength at nearer 36 operational aircraft and one airship. The loss of the Körting M3 airship in a collision here on June 20 was a severe blow.

The empire's insistence on taking aircraft mainly from its own factories has left the air services short, not through lack of good engines but through insufficient airframe capacity. In July 1913 it was proposed to buy six Zeppelins, but this plan was abandoned. In February this year the aviation corps, under the army, was reorganized into a battalion of four companies.

## Britain: laggards in military aviation

*London, July*
Britain lags behind the other major powers in military aviation. The Royal Flying Corps is not only smaller than the air services of Germany, France and Russia; many of its aircraft are unairworthy or obsolete. The RFC was conceived as a single organization for military and naval aviation, but there has been constant bickering between the army and the navy ever since. The Admiralty is now firmly in control of naval aircraft. The RFC has a variety of aircraft, many of them French Blériots but including a growing number of British B.E.2s specially designed for reconnaissance. But of its nominal 113 airplanes, only around 70 are ready for war.

The Royal Naval Air Service has 71 aircraft and seven airships with which to carry out a range of tasks from scouting for the fleet, to protecting Britain's coastline from air attack. In addition to that, the navy has some 100-lb bombs. If aircraft are to be used for offensive bombing, the navy will do the job.

## Russia: readier on paper than in air

*Russia, July*
Russia's preparedness for an air war is hidden behind the large "paper" strength of the Imperial Russian Air Service. Nearly 250 machines are listed plus several non-rigid airships. However, this total has barely altered since last year and all but about 50 are outdated or worn out. A problem unique to Russia is the vast distances over which its forces operate.

The number of military pilots at the beginning of this year was 72, bolstered by a volunteer corps of 36 private pilots. However, three new flying schools established in 1913 may have since raised the numbers of qualified airmen. The majority of the machines are of French origin built in Russia, plus other foreign types such as Albatros, Aviatiks, Bristols and Rumplers. Both the air service and the navy have tested giant indigenous Sikorsky four-engined machines. Naval aviation is better placed. The navy's effective strength has been raised – from 20 seaplanes a month or two back to 50 now, mainly American Curtiss Fs.

## Balkan clash pushes Europe closer to war

*Europe, July*
Tension is mounting across Europe following the assassination of Archduke Franz Ferdinand, heir to the Austrian throne, at Sarajevo in Serbia on June 28.

Relations between Serbia and Austria worsened following Serbia's refusal of Austria's demands to be allowed to investigate the killing itself. Diplomatic links were broken, and Austria has now declared war on Serbia. The major powers lined up behind the protagonists – Germany with Austria, and France, Britain and Russia with Serbia.

Britain's offer to mediate has been refused. Germany's Kaiser Wilhelm II has warned Russia to stop mobilizing or Germany will do so too. Europe seems set on war, and the world is waiting to see what will happen next.

# How air power will be used in the war

*Europe, August 2*
The months of uncertainty are over. Hundreds of thousands of men across Europe are preparing to fight a major war with an array of new weapons, but few of the new technologies which have been harnessed for war have aroused as much debate as have airplanes. The pilots who fly them are eager to prove their value by flying behind the enemy lines to observe enemy troop movements. However, many senior officers, among them Generals Foch and French, have little faith in such flights. Aircraft could be used to bomb military targets and towns. This is outlawed under the 1899 Hague Convention, but that was drawn up before airplanes or dirigibles existed and (as Italy argued in its 1912 war in Libya) refers to balloons.

Most armies have experimented with bombing, but many experts agree with Brigadier-General Sir David Henderson, Britain's director of military aeronautics, that "no enemy would risk the odium such action would involve".

# French pilots bomb Zeppelin hangars

*Metz, Germany, August 14*
Two French airmen braved a ferocious bombardment today as they flew across the German border in a raid on German Zeppelin sheds near Metz. Lieutenant Cesari and Corporal Prudhommeau took off from Verdun at 5.30pm in Voisins and, as they approached Metz, ran the gauntlet of virtually every German battery in the city. Undaunt-

*Bombers at work over a town.*

ed, the pilots pressed on until they were over their target at about 7,500 feet.

Rather than dropping bombs in the usual way – by hand – they used a recent device invented by Captain Mauger-Devarennes to release 155mm shells on the airship hangars, scoring direct hits. The extent of the damage was obscured by smoke from the explosions.

# Airships easy meat for ground attack

*Zeppelins set out on a mission.*

*Liège, Belgium, August 8*
The menace of aerial bombardment from airships was countered today by prompt action from Belgian ground forces around forts at Liège. The German army Zeppelin Z 6 succeeded in its first wartime mission by dropping, by hand, some 440 pounds of artillery shells on the forts, but was driven off by sustained fire, from both Belgian light-mounted guns and infantry rifle fire, to which it seemed highly vulnerable. Having leaked a large quantity of hydrogen lifting-gas, the Z 6 was grounded, a total wreck, in a forest near Bonn.

While it now seems that the dirigible – large, slow and flying at low altitude – is a ready target for high-angle guns, the German Etrich Taube monoplane – small, capable of 62mph and an altitude of many thousands of feet – presents far more of a problem, as it can probably stay outside the range of ground defense weapons.

# Royal Flying Corps goes into action over Belgium, but missions are mixed success

*Uniforms and aircraft of the British Army's important new branch.*

*Maubeuge, France, August 19*
The Royal Flying Corps saw its first wartime action today when two aircraft were dispatched from the aerodrome at Maubeuge on reconnaissance flights into Belgium. Captain Joubert de la Ferté of Nº 3 Squadron, in a Blériot XI-2, was under instructions to reconnoiter the Nivelles and Genappe area, 16 miles south of Brussels, for friendly Belgian troop movements; his colleague, Lt Mapplebeck of Nº 4 Squadron, in a B.E.2b, had to report on a possible big German cavalry presence near Gembloux, 19 miles south-east of Brussels. They returned safely but were hampered by poor visibility. The airmen took off at 9.30am; in case of mishap they were to fly together to Nivelles, but they soon lost each other. Mapplebeck, in the faster plane, overshot as far as Brussels; he turned for Gembloux (spotting a small enemy force) and ran into thick cloud, emerging over Namur and following the river Sambre down to Maubeuge, in France.

He missed by nearly 30 miles, landing at Le Cateau, whence he returned to base at noon. Joubert de la Ferté was even less fortunate. His flight took him to Tournai and Courtrai as well as Nivelles, and he returned to Maubeuge at 5.30pm with little to report (→ 25).

*RFC cadets inspect the frame of a Royal Aircraft Factory airplane.*

# Air reconnaissance proves vital as war goes on

## Observers save British in battle at Mons

*An aerial observer keeps look-out.*

*Mons, Belgium, August 22*
The British Expeditionary Force (BEF) here has been warned by air reconnaissance of a gigantic pincer movement by two German armies. Since Brussels fell to the Germans two days ago, the French Fifth Army on the British right has retreated to avoid von Bülow in the east, leaving that flank exposed. Today the RFC flew 12 scout missions, revealing another enemy corps moving west from Brussels, probably von Kluck's First Army.

Brig-Gen Sir David Henderson, in charge of Britain's air effort, took this report to his chief, Field Marshal Sir John French, at headquarters. French promptly cancelled an offensive that could have led to his army's annihilation.

## Pilots play part in crushing German win

*Major battlefield role for airplanes: a Caudron G3 on reconnaissance.*

*Germany, August 31*
East Prussia, invaded by the Imperial Russian Army from east and south, is safely in German hands after a stunning victory at Tannenberg. A significant role in the victory was played by air observation.

Only ten days ago the German commander was planning a retreat west, across the Vistula. Kaiser Wilhelm promptly replaced him with a retired officer, Paul von Hindenburg. Hindenburg concentrated most of his 166,000-strong force for a counter-attack south, against 201,000 Russians. The problem was how to pin down the equally strong Russian army in the east. With the help of air reconnaissance, including one mission that penetrated 300 miles into Russia a week ago, the Germans held the east with a screening force, while the main force took 92,000 Russian prisoners in an epic four-day battle. Hindenberg is said to have told correspondents that his success is "totally due to air power." In fact, artillery won the battle, but airmen certainly played a crucial part.

## Flyer reports change in German tactics

*France, September 6*
As the French government flees to sanctuary in Bordeaux, and German airplanes fly over Paris every teatime, only a near-miracle can offer last minute salvation from enemy conquest. "The German army is at the gates," say leaflets dropped by Taube airplanes, "there is nothing for you to do but surrender."

This evening, as French generals berated their fliers for failing to provide useful information, a French pilot arrived with a report, soon confirmed by British airmen, that the Germans had changed their plan to cut off Paris from the south. They were seen moving, enigmatic-ally, from west to east on the river Marne, to the east of the city, exposing their flank. "Gentlemen," General Joffre pronounced, "we fight on the Marne." Aerial reconnaissance has proved its worth. In one eventful month, air observation has prevented two Allied disasters.

The Royal Flying Corps, which has four squadrons, has a mix of B.E.2 biplanes, Avros and slower Farmans. Crews fly as individuals, often landing to check positions. Intensive rifle and machine-gun fire has claimed its first casualties: one crew missing and Sergeant-Major D S Jillings, of Nº 2 Squadron, wounded in the leg.

### PILOTS SPOT TROOP MOVEMENTS

Royal
Noyon
Montdidier
FRANCE
Compiègne
*Aisne*
Soissons
•Villers-Cotterêts
Senlis
*Oise*
Château-Thierry
Rheims
*Seine*
*Marne* Epérnay
Meaux
Montmirail
*Petit Morin*
*Marne*
*Grand Morin*
Paris

Expected German advance
Actual advance
Allied reconnaissance flights

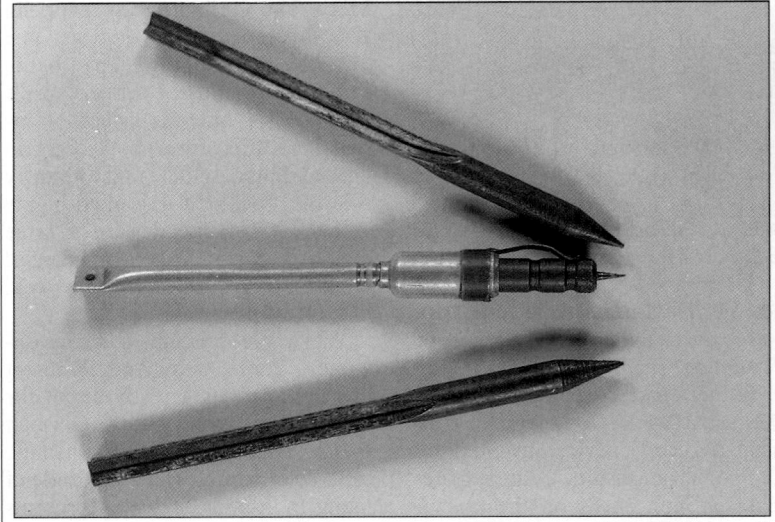

**Weapons of war: French pilots swear by steel darts called "fléchettes" which, it is hoped, will cause havoc among enemy cavalry and infantry.**

# Briton forces down first German of war

*France, August 25*
British pilots, led by the intrepid Lieutenant H D Harvey-Kelly of Nº 2 Squadron RFC, have caused the first German aircraft loss of the war. Harvey-Kelly was leading three RFC B.E.2a machines on an observation mission near the front line when they spotted a German reconnaissance airplane and gave chase, firing at it with pistols.

The chase went on for a while before the German pilot and his observer apparently decided to abandon the airplane and attempt to escape on foot. They put down in a field and were already making a dash for nearby woods as the British pilots landed and began to tear after them, brandishing their pistols in the air. The Germans' head start was too great, however, and they disappeared into the trees without being caught. Their pursuers contented themselves with burning the German airplane before heading back to base (→ Sep 24).

*The battered wreckage of a German airplane after a spectacular crash.*

# Churchill outlines four-point defense plan

*Pilot and politician: Winston Churchill in flying helmet and goggles.*

*London, September 5*
Britain's combative First Lord of the Admiralty, or navy minister, Winston Churchill, today tabled a four-point plan for his country's defense against attack by enemy airplanes or Zeppelins, as the Royal Navy is now guardian of Britain's skies as well as its coast. Churchill proposes the interception of enemy aircraft near their home bases; pre-emptive attacks on the bases by a dedicated airplane squadron in Belgium; an East Coast interception air force; anti-aircraft guns at key points; and no street lights after dark in London and other towns (a "black-out").

# Two injured as German pilot bombs Paris

*Paris, August 30*
The peace of a Parisian Sunday was shattered today when a German pilot buzzed the city center and dropped three bombs near the Gare de l'Est railroad terminal, injuring two people and causing minor damage. As stunned citizens watched the Rumpler Taube airplane disappear into the distance, leaflets and a banner, weighted with a sandbag, fell to earth with the message: "The German Army is at the gates of Paris. There is nothing for you to do but surrender. Leutnant von Hiddesen." Lt Ferdinand Von Hiddesen, the pilot, has bestowed on Paris the dubious honor of being the first capital bombed from the air. It may prove a grim precedent.

# British planes use radio to guide artillery

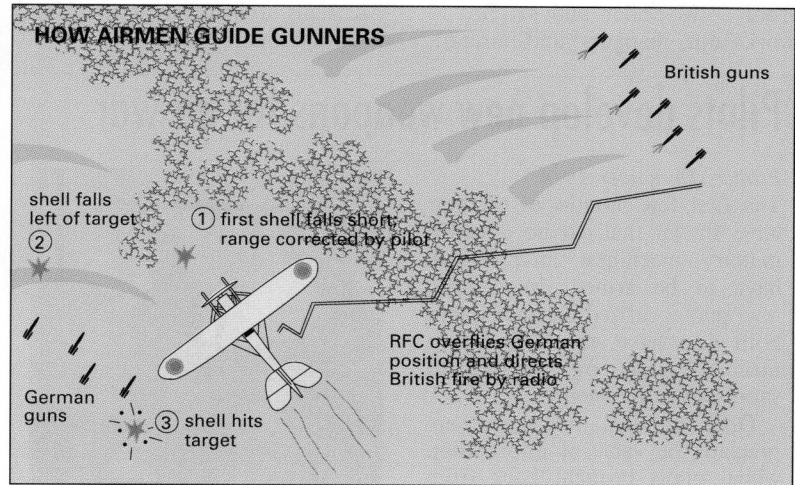

HOW AIRMEN GUIDE GUNNERS

British guns

shell falls left of target ②

① first shell falls short; range corrected by pilot

German guns

RFC overflies German position and directs British fire by radio

③ shell hits target

*Western Front, September 24*
Airplanes of the Royal Flying Corps are now being used to observe the fall of shells from Allied artillery and to send back correcting messages by wireless. In a battle at the Aisne today two lieutenants from Nº 4 Squadron, Donald Lewis and Baron James, spent the afternoon spotting for the big howitzers of the British Third Division. Their messages began:
4.02pm "A very little short. Fire!"
4.15pm "Short; over and a little left."
4.20pm "You were between two batteries. Search 200 yards each side, range OK."
4.22pm "You have them."
4.26pm "Hit! Hit! Hit!"

Different methods have been tried for air-to-ground signalling. Morse code is most usual, and this is sometimes sent by Aldis lamp. Voice telephone is thought to be a long way off (→ Oct 31).

# Japanese sink German warship from air

*Tokyo, September 17*
According to a despatch received by the Japanese government today, seaplanes which are attached to the Second Japanese Naval Squadron yesterday bombed the Austro-German fleet in the harbor at Kiaochow, China. The aircraft that were involved were two of the four Maurice Farmans from the seaplane carrier *Wakamiya Maru*.

Bombs, improvised from naval shells, were also released over wireless transmitters and electric power stations. It appears the main target was the cruiser *Kaiserin Elisabeth*, but only a smaller German warship was hit. Details are sketchy, but this vessel, the first warship to be sunk from the air by any nation, was either a minelayer or a torpedo boat. On September 5, Japanese seaplanes bombed the Austro-German barracks and the railway at Tsingtoa. One seaplane was hit but returned safely. The only opposing aircraft was a German Rumpler Taube.

# Russian rams Austrian

*Sholkiv, Russia, September 8*

A Russian squadron commander, enraged by an Austrian bombing raid on his airfield today, dramatically ended the attack by killing an enemy pilot, and himself, in an aerial collision. Staff Capt Pyotr Nesterov, 27, was in trouble with his chiefs last year for inducing a Nieuport to loop the loop. He is now a posthumous hero.

When the Austrian pilot, Baron von Rosenthal, hit the Sholkiv base from a two-seater and set fire to workshops, hangars and aircraft,

Nestorov went into a blind rage. He took off in an unarmed Morane monoplane and drove straight at his opponent. Rosenthal was leading his flight, with one aircraft on each side of him in a V-formation. All three seemed hypnotized, or unbelieving, as the Morane closed on them so that they could see their adversary's angry, unblinking stare. By the time Rosenthal had realized that he faced a suicide attack it was too late. The surviving Austrians broke off their attack and fled, horrified.

## Pilots develop new weapons for air war

*France, December 1914*

The first few months of the war have shown that, to be effective military machines, aircraft will have to be armed. In August, few pilots carried weapons, but both sides have started to mount machine guns on aircraft to shoot down the enemy.

Once soldiers began to appreciate the value of information which pilots brought back from their flights over enemy territory, they became equally keen to deny the enemy access to the skies above their own forces. In the early stages of the war, a German aircraft flying over Allied lines would be met by rifle fire – but observers could do their job well out of range.

The most effective way to counter hostile observers is to shoot them down from another armed machine. Various options have been tested. Some pilots carried pistols, rifles or shotguns to fire at their adversaries. Others dropped grenades on

*Lewis gun on Belgian airplane.*

them from above, or trailed a weighted line, trying to ensnare their opponent's propeller.

The most effective weapon has proved to be the machine gun. Many types are unsuitable for use in the air, being too heavy or too cumbersome to reload. But the Hotchkiss, which was used in the first victory in aerial combat on October 5, seems destined to be in great demand by the air services.

*An armoured German Albatros, captured by the French in August.*

# Canada creates own air service, but its one airplane is slow getting into the air

*The only Canadian Aviation Corps aircraft is a Burgess-Dunne seaplane.*

*Wiltshire, England, October*

On paper, Canada has had its own aviation corps since last month, but observers wonder if it will ever really exist. The Canadian Air Corps formally came into being when Colonel Sam Hughes, the Canadian minister of militia and defense, arranged an overseas air contingent of two officers. Capt Ernest Lloyd Janney was duly appointed provisional commander on September 16 and Lt W F Sharpe his subordinate. A budget of

C$5,000 was allocated for the purchase of one airplane and spares. This was spent on an American Burgess-Dunne tailless seaplane.

The seaplane left Champlain on September 21 to fly to Quebec City for shipment to England aboard SS *Athenia*. It was piloted by Clifford Webster, with Janney as passenger. It embarked on September 30 and in England was taken to Salisbury Plain for crew training. But it has stood there ever since without being flown, and may now be scrapped.

## Civilians killed in British raid on Cologne

*Antwerp, Belgium, October 8*

In the last aerial sorties from Antwerp before it was overrun by the German advance, flyers of the Royal Naval Air Service (RNAS) have attacked targets in Germany. Flight Lt Marix and Squadron Commander Spenser Grey, flying Sopwith Tabloids, hit Cologne railroad station and an airship base at Düsseldorf. As artillery fire came closer to Antwerp and an evacuation was prepared, the airmen waited impatiently for mist to clear. It did not, but at 1.30pm they flew anyway. Marix scored a hit from 600 feet and a hangar and an airship exploded. He crash-landed on the way back and returned by bicycle. Grey, unable to find airships in the mist, bombed Cologne, killing three civilians (→ Dec 21).

*A contemporary view shows an immaculate RNAS pilot and his craft.*

# Britain commissions first aircraft carrier

*Sunderland, England, December 9*
The Royal Navy is making a determined effort to rule the air as well as the sea, by commissioning a special warship whose sole purpose is to carry aircraft. HMS *Ark Royal* is to be the first newly built ship designed to launch, recover and house naval seaplanes. They will take off using jettisonable trolleys, land back on the sea on their own floats and be hoisted aboard into the ship's hold by crane, a technique pioneered by HMS *Hermes*, a converted light cruiser.

The hull of the *Ark Royal* is that of a merchant ship, in fact a collier, which, although too slow to keep up with the fleet, allows good deck space and a large hold area to include workshops and up to ten aircraft. These are likely to be the new Short 184 seaplane now under development, to be used primarily for gunnery spotting and maritime reconnaisance (→ Feb 17, 1915).

*"Ark Royal": slow, but can carry up to ten aircraft like this Sopwith 807.*

# Air forces take to flying in darkness

*Ostend, Belgium, December 21*
The day that saw the first German air raid on Britain – two bombs fell into the sea at Dover – has also witnessed the first night flight of the war, by Commander C R Samson of the Royal Naval Air Service. He was at the controls of a Maurice Farman biplane with a rear-mounted 130-hp Canton Unné engine for the raid on the German-held port of Ostend in Belgium.

Commander Samson intended to bomb German U-boats, but was unable to locate them in the dark. After flying around for some time Samson gave up his hunt for the submarines, but succeeded in spotting German batteries near the port. He unloaded his 18, 16-pound bombs on these before heading back into Allied territory. With only a Very flare pistol and a torch, he brought his machine safely down onto the beach at Dunkirk.

# Germans drop first bomb on England

*Dover, England, December 24*
At 10.45am today the first German bomb to fall on British soil landed perilously close to Dover Castle, an important barracks, and exploded in the back garden of Thomas Terson. This second air raid on Britain of the war [*see story alongside*] caused £40 worth of damage and left a crater 10 feet wide and 5 feet deep.

The German aircraft has been identified as a Friedrichshafen FF29 seaplane, probably from the German naval base at Zeebrugge in Belgium. It flew in alone at an altitude of about 5,000 feet, using low cloud for cover. Observers in Dover glimpsed the aircraft on its run in at about 10.30am. A Royal Navy Wight pusher seaplane was sent up from the East Promenade, but it was too slow in climbing – despite its 200-hp engine – to prevent the attack or catch the raider.

# French score victory in first air 'dogfight'

*Frantz and Quénault, winners of the first aerial combat, with their Voisin.*

*Brimont, France, October 5*
A German Aviatik two-seater became the first aircraft to be shot down in a dogfight today when it strayed into the path of Sergeant Joseph Frantz and his observer, Corporal Louis Quénault. The Frenchmen were on patrol over Reims in a rear-engined Voisin, newly fitted with a Hotchkiss machine gun at the front, when they spotted the German airplane ahead.

Part of the Voisin's mission was to test the Hotchkiss, so the chance to try it out on a real target was too good to lose.

As the Frenchmen closed in, the German pilot, Lieutenant Fritz von Zagen, opened fire. Frantz returned fire, but had loosed off two loads of ammunition when the German gun stopped. The Aviatik had been hit; it slowed down and then plummeted to earth in a ball of flame.

# British make first strategic airplane raid

*One of the aircraft is returned to its hangar after the successful bombing.*

*Germany, November 21*
The German Zeppelin sheds at Friedrichshafen on Lake Constance today became the target of the world's first strategic bombing raid by a formation of aircraft. Led by Squadron Commander E Featherstone Briggs of the RNAS, three Avro 504s took off from Belfort in France at 9.50am in sub-zero temperatures at the start of a 125-mile flight up the Rhine valley.

At 11.55am the Avros dived from 4,000 feet to drop their loads – four 20-pound bombs apiece. Several airships were damaged and a hydrogen plant blew up. The pilots all returned safely except Featherstone Briggs, who was shot down and captured (→ Dec 21).

The prototype Avro 510 two-seater seaplane built for the Circuit of Britain race. Six production aircraft were built for the RNAS and served in the war.

The Fokker M.5L was an unarmed single-seater scouting monoplane and was designated A-II in service. From it was developed a series of fighters.

The Albatros B.II was broadly equivalent to the British B.E.2c but was rather slower. It was widely used for reconnaissance duties and as a trainer.

The Short S.81 seaplane was of similar configuration to aircraft such as the Vickers Gunbus, its pusher engine allowing a forward-firing gun.

The Martinsyde S.I Scout was a small but fairly fast fighter which served with some success until 1915, when faster German types rendered it obsolete.

The Bristol Scout, probably the fastest single-seater in service at the outbreak of the war, was light and agile. It had a top speed of no less than 97mph.

The Royal Aircraft Factory B.E.2c was powered by a 90-hp engine and was used for reconnaissance, light bomber and artillery observation duties.

The Royal Aircraft Factory's streamlined little S.E.4 never progressed beyond the experimental stage, but it was the fastest aircraft of its day.

The two-seater Vickers F.B.5 (Fighting Biplane № 5) was better known as the Gunbus and had a drum-fed Lewis gun mounted on the nose of its nacelle.

The Caproni Ca 3, like the Ca 1 and Ca 2, was powered by three engines – two tractors on the wings, with a pusher at the back of the crew nacelle.

Caproni's Ca 1, 2 and 3 series of trimotor bombers proved extremely successful in wartime service and versions were reinstated in production during the 1920s.

Because it lacked forward elevator outriggers, the Maurice Farman MF 11 was dubbed "Shorthorn" by British service pilots and pupils".

The Voisin Type V was one of the most impressive aircraft built by the brothers Gabriel and Charles Voisin. The design was very characteristic of the company.

The three-engined Curtiss "America" seaplane was designed by a Royal Naval officer for an Atlantic flight attempt which was prevented by the war.

The Allgemeine Elektrizitäts Gesellschaft (AEG) B.I: an unarmed reconnaissance biplane which preceded a series of reconnaissance and bomber types.

The Short 166 was better known as the Short Folder, because it had folding wings. About 26 were built for use by Britain's Royal Naval Air Service.

The Austrian Etrich Eindecker of 1914 was a considerably updated and upgraded version of the original Taube of 1909. The type was widely used.

The Morane-Saulnier Type N was better known as the Morane Bullet and was exported to Britain and Russia in substantial numbers as a fast scout.

# 1915

| | 134.54mph<br>Great Britain<br>Norman Spratt<br>RAF SE.4<br>Jun 1914 | | 1,180.61 miles<br>Germany<br>Werner Landmann<br>Albatros<br>Jun 28, 1914 | | 26,739ft<br>Germany<br>Heinrich Oelerich<br>DFW<br>Jul 14, 1914 | | 14,000lb<br>Great Britain<br>Handley Page Ltd<br>Handley Page 0/100 | | 227hp<br>France<br>Louis Renault<br>Renault 12A |

**North Sea, January 6**
The German Navy successfully launches a Friedrichshafen FF29a seaplane from the deck of a submarine during trials to extend the aircraft's reconnaissance range (→ Feb 1, 1917).

**Poland, February 15**
Russian *Ilya Muromets* reconnaissance bombers attack along the river Vistula.

**Dardanelles, February 17**
HMS *Ark Royal*, a merchant ship converted to a carrier last year, launches Royal Naval Air Service seaplanes to reconnoiter Turkish forces (→ Aug 17).

**San Francisco, February 20**
During the Panama-Pacific Exhibition, Allan Loughead was allowed to launch an air service and flew 600 passengers across the bay in 50 days. The 10-minute flight cost $10 per passenger.

**Washington, DC, March 3**
The National Advisory Committee for Aeronautics (NACA) is set up in order to study problems of flight (→ Jul 17, 1917).

**Washington, DC, March 4**
Congress passes funding of $300,000 for army aviation in 1916 (→ Apr 2, 1917).

**San Francisco, March 14**
Renowned stunt pilot Lincoln Beachey, attempting a power dive from 3,500 feet before 50,000 people at the Panama-Pacific Exhibition, dies when the wings break off his monoplane and he falls 2,500 feet into the sea.

**England, March 27**
The kite balloon ship *Mancia* sails for the Dardanelles, equipped with a kite balloon to be used as an observation platform (→ Dec).

**Australia, April 9**
The inaugural meeting of the Australian Aero Club is held at the Café Français in Melbourne (→ Mar 16, 1916).

**Germany, April 11**
The prototype Zeppelin-Staaken VGO1 heavy bomber, fitted with one tractor and two pusher engines, flies for the first time (→ Jun 1917).

**Ypres, Belgium, April 22**
RFC aircraft save infantry from a gas attack; they spot a yellow-green cloud moving toward French troops and warn commanders, who order a retreat (→ Nov 8).

**France, May 10**
Captain L A Strange of N° 6 Squadron, RFC, falls out of his Martinsyde S.I Scout trying to free a jammed ammunition drum; he hangs on through an upside-down spiral of several thousand feet before pulling himself back into the cockpit to regain control.

**Washington, DC, May 14**
The US Navy contracts with the Connecticut Aircraft Company for its first airship.

**France, May 21**
The Spad A2 biplane fighter makes its first flight tests (→ May 10, 1916).

**Italy, May 27**
Four days after Italy declares war on Austria-Hungary, an Austrian Löhner L.I flying boat is captured off Italy and taken to Varese to be inspected by Macchi technicians.

**London, May 31**
A Zeppelin, LZ 38, makes the first air raid on London; it drops 3,000 pounds of bombs, killing seven and injuring 14 (→ Sep 8).

**Long Branch, Canada, May**
The Curtiss Aviation School, Canada's first flying school, opens for business (→ Nov 16).

**Germany, spring**
The C-type reconnaissance biplane is introduced; it is powerful (150-160hp), with a flexibly-mounted Parabellum machine gun in the rear cockpit, which is occupied by the observer. C-types are made by various firms, including Albatros, Aviatik, DFW, LVG and Rumpler.

**England, June 1**
The prototype Airco (de Havilland) D.H.2 single-seat fighter is tested. This pusher biplane has a forward-firing Lewis gun (→ Oct 1917).

**Paris, June 17**
Royal Naval Air Service hero Flight Sub-Lt R A Warneford, who was awarded the Victoria Cross after downing Zeppelin LZ 37 ten days ago, falls to his death with his passenger, American journalist H A Needham, when their aircraft rolls over during a steep turn.

**Eastern Europe, July 1**
The German Fokker E.I fighter, fitted with a machine gun synchronized to fire through the propeller without hitting the revolving blades, goes into service on the eastern front (→ Aug 31).

**Kent, England, July 13**
The Armstrong Whitworth SS (Submarine Scout) airship, which is fitted with an extra fuel tank in order to improve its range, is tested successfully at Kingsnorth (→ Jan 29, 1917).

**Chicago, July 18**
Katherine Stinson, the fearless stunt pilot, thrills onlookers by looping the loop; she is the first woman ever to perform this feat (→ Dec 17).

**Farnborough, England, August 6**
After non-stop day and night production for 12 months to meet war demands, the Royal Aircraft Factory closes for three days' rest.

**France, August 19**
Colonel Hugh Trenchard takes over command of the Royal Flying Corps from Lt-Gen Sir David Henderson (→ Dec).

**London, August 24**
Major Lanoe Hawker is awarded the Victoria Cross for his bravery on July 25, when he shot down three German Albatros biplanes (→ Nov 23, 1916).

**Germany, August 25**
Some 62 French bombers stationed at Malzéville, France, raid blast-furnaces in the Dillingen area.

**Belfort, Germany, September 14**
German pilot Ernst Udet returns safely from a bombing mission, despite losing part of the upper wing of his Aviatik B.

**USA, October 13**
The Wright airplane company is bought by a syndicate of Harry Payne Whitney, T Frank Manville and William B Thompson; Orville Wright stays on as consulting engineer (→ Aug 17, 1916).

**Harwich, England, November 3**
Flight Lieutenant H F Towler proves that a landplane can operate from an aircraft carrier when he takes off from HMS *Vindex* in a Bristol Scout.

**Pensacola, Fla, December 1**
The first US Navy flying school opens, with a commanding officer, three instructors and 12 mechanics. (→ Aug 29, 1916)

**Dessau, Germany, December 12**
The Junkers J 1, an all-metal cantilever-wing monoplane powered by a 120-hp Mercedes D.II engine, nicknamed the "Tin Donkey", makes its first flight (→ Mar 10, 1918).

**London, December 17**
Lieutenant-Commanders Stedman and Babington pilot the prototype Handley Page O/100 bomber on its first flight (→ Aug 8, 1918).

**Germany, December 21**
Claudius Dornier tests his giant Zeppelin-Lindau Rs I hydroplane on Lake Constance; it reaches a speed of 37mph, too slow to take off, before bad weather brings the trials to a halt (→ Jun 13, 1916).

---

*British defensive searchlights sweep the skies, catching the threatening presence of a German Zeppelin bound inland on a bombing raid.* ▶

124

## Civilians killed in Zeppelin air raid

*Bomb damage in Great Yarmouth.*

**Suffolk, England, January 19**
The bombardment of English towns from the air has begun. Count von Zeppelin's vision has at last been fulfilled; his airships have become lethal weapons of war.

Last night three German naval airships set out from their North Sea bases; one turned back with engine trouble, but the others dropped explosives on the undefended, fully illuminated east coast fishing port of Great Yarmouth, killing four. They flew on to bomb King's Lynn, Norfolk, and six other small towns in the area, with 20 reported killed and 40 injured. The airships also flew over the king's country home at Sandringham (→ Apr 11).

# British pilots back army in key battle

## Photos guide army

*France, March 12*
An important British push at the village of Neuve Chapelle began two days ago and has had, literally, a flying start, with Royal Flying Corps (RFC) pilots taking photos of enemy trenches. Lt-Col Sykes of the RFC, impressed by French success in this area, formed specialist sections in Nos 2 and 3 Squadrons RFC. An observer grips the plate camera by straps as he leans over the side; one exposure needs ten separate operations (→ Apr 22).

*Brave flyers: a British Avro comes to rest after a reconnaissance flight.*

## Planes go on patrol

*France, March 12*
"A solid line of cotton wool" was how the British bombardment looked to army flyers when the attack on the key village of Neuve Chapelle began two days ago. Major Blacker saw the infantry advance like "ants across a billiard table". Since then, artillery commanders report their fire on enemy guns have enjoyed "utmost assistance from the section of wireless aeroplanes ... these aeroplanes were invaluable in sending information as to positions of batteries". Air reconnaissance reported little effort, at first, by the Germans to reinforce their line, though they have 47 battalions standing by (→ Apr 22).

## Communications hit

*France, March 12*
Royal Flying Corps pilots have bombed important targets on the German supply lines during the attack on Neuve Chapelle. Captain E L Conran and Major J M Salmond of N° 3 Squadron dived to 100 feet above a command post at Fournes to drop bombs by hand. Captain G I Carmichael of N° 5 Squadron blew up a railroad junction, and Captain L A Strange of N° 6 Squadron dropped three bombs on a stationary train at Courtrai, Belgium. "As he turned to watch the result of his bombing," said one account, "he almost collided with telegraph poles." He had killed 75 troops in two coaches.

## Advances watched

*France, March 13*
As the Germans mount stiff counter-attacks on the third day of the battle for a vital salient at Neuve Chapelle, taken by the British, Captain G F Pretyman of N° 3 Squadron, Royal Flying Corps, has made two dangerous low reconnaissance flights. He saw the Germans doggedly defending a position between the village and Biez Wood, and the British defying attempts to dislodge them from the eastern edge of the village. Two crews from N° 1 Squadron, newly arrived from England with B.E.8s and Avros, bombed railroads near Douai. One pilot, Lt O M Moullin, crashed and is thought to be a prisoner (→ Apr 22).

*An RFC padre uses an F.E.2b nose cockpit for a service.*

# 'Flaming onions' protect the 'sausages'

*Western front, January*
The strain of life at the front takes a heavy toll on pilots' nerves. But it also makes for a sense of camaraderie and combative humor, and British airmen have developed a fresh and colorful vocabulary.

The strangest of the new nicknames derives from the eccentric method used by one pilot to bolster his courage when anti-aircraft shells burst around his airplane: he would sing a London music-hall song in which a woman pestered by an insistent young man cries "Archibald, certainly not!". Now everyone calls anti-aircraft fire "Archie". The long gasbags used as observation balloons were inevitably dubbed "sausages"; now the shells sent up by ground batteries to protect the balloons and attack aircraft are known as "flaming onions". The noise made by tapping the taut canvas of a barrage balloon, on the other hand, has inspired the onomatopoeic nickname "blimp".

"Dogfights" describes the tense air battles in which pilots often fight to the death. The control levers with which they fling their flimsy airplanes around have been dubbed "joysticks".

# French bombers pound German factories

*Germany, May 27*

"The finest aerial feat of arms yet accomplished": this is how the official communiqué describes the successful bombing mission which French aircraft carried out today against important German chemical factories. Led by battalion commander Louis de Goys de Mezeyrac and his pilot Etienne Bunau-Varilla, 18 Voisin biplanes of Bombardment Group N° 1 took off at three o'clock this morning from Malzéville, in eastern France, at the start of a perilous 200-mile round trip, most of it over Germany.

The bombers' targets were the two factories of the chemical manufacturers Badische Anilin und Soda Fabrik (BASF) near Mannheim in Baden. The works, at Ludwigshafen and Oppau, produce both explosives and poison gas. Despite heavy bombardment from the ground, the Voisins reached their objectives at 6.15am, and dropped 49 bombs on Ludwigshafen and 38 on Oppau, two miles away.

Three thick plumes of smoke from the two factories indicated a successful strike, and at 6.30am the airmen headed home. De Mezeyrac's Voisin was hit and had to make a forced landing; he and the pilot set fire to the aircraft before being taken prisoner (→ Aug 25).

*The pilots and observers who took part in the mission against Ludwigshafen.*

# British pilot shoots Zeppelin out of skies

*Warneford's hit: an artist's view.*

*Bruges, Belgium, June 9*

Flight Sub-Lieutenant Reginald Warneford, a Canadian in N° 1 Squadron, Royal Naval Air Service, was on a mission to bomb Zeppelin sheds near Bruges two nights ago when he spotted airship LZ 37 returning to base. In his Morane-Saulnier L monoplane he stalked LZ 37 for 40 minutes but his attacks were forced off by its gunners.

He tried again, gliding above the Zeppelin and releasing six bombs. Five missed; the sixth caused a blast so great it flipped Warneford over. LZ 37 crumpled to earth in flames: the first Zeppelin shot down. (It hit a convent near Ghent, killing four on the ground.) Warneford's motor would not restart and he landed behind enemy lines to fix it before taking off for base at Dunkirk. News of his feat soon spread: he learned today that he has won the Victoria Cross (→ Jun 17).

# Allies lose gun secret

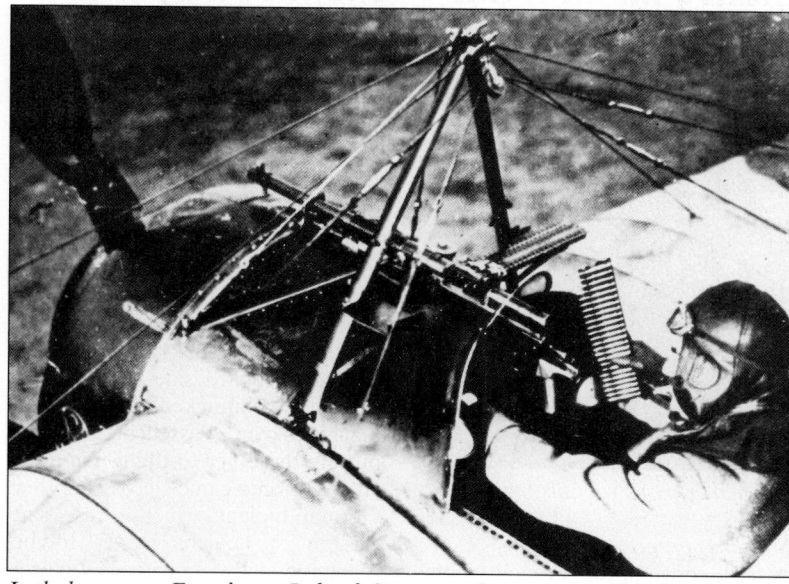

*Lethal weapon: French ace Roland Garros at the controls of his fighter.*

*Belgium, April 20*

A single bullet fired by a reservist called Schlenstedt pierced the fuel pipe of a Morane-Saulnier Type N monoplane yesterday as it flew over Courtrai in occupied Belgium, forcing the aircraft to land. The pilot failed to destroy it before he was captured, and now the Allies have lost not only one of their best airmen – Roland Garros – but also one of their top secrets: how to fire a machine gun through the disc of an airplane's propeller.

The Germans are delighted. Garros had shot down four German machines in recent weeks, and other French pilots had also boosted their success rate, apparently due to some ingenious way of firing straight past the propellor without shattering it. Now the cat is out of the bag: Garros's two propeller blades had been fitted with special steel castings to deflect bullets from the Hotchkiss gun, which would otherwise have hit it.

Garros's rather crude device, patented April 5, is the result of research with the engineer Raymond Saulnier. In the past three years or so there have been various attempts in Germany, France, Britain and Russia to invent a more efficient forward-firing system by synchronizing the gun with the propeller; so far there have been no results from these attempts (→ Oct 5, 1918).

# Fokker perfects captured firing system

*Germany, April 22*

The Germans have worked fast to improve the French forward-firing system captured three days ago. Anthony Fokker was asked to solve the problem, and at his Schwerin factory the Dutchman and his colleague Heinrich Luebbe hit on an approach first developed by Franz Schneider in 1912-13: synchronizing the gun and the airscrew so that the gun fires only when the blades are not in front of it. Fokker and Luebbe have already installed a prototype of their system, using a new Parabellum gun, on a Fokker M5K monoplane (→ Jul 1).

*A German pilot on board a Fokker.*

## Brilliant newcomer makes his first kill

*Guynemer poses with his mechanic.*

*Soissons, France, July 19*
A frail, consumptive French youth, apparently impervious to fear, stalked and killed his first enemy pilot today. A few months ago Georges Guynemer was loafing on the beach at Biarritz watching airplanes landing. When war began the army rejected him as unfit. He joined the air service as a student mechanic and started flying at Pau early this year.

On one of his first missions, an hour's reconnaissance under heavy fire, he dived at enemy guns to provoke shellbursts as background to a personal photograph being taken by the senior officer acting as his observer. Today he met a German Aviatik. "I kept about 15 meters [50 feet] from my *Boche*. In spite of all his twists I stayed with him," he said. Guynemer's gunner fired 115 shots. The pilot continued: "I had a very sweet feeling at seeing the pilot slump to the floor while his observer raised his arms to heaven in a gesture of despair and the Aviatik plunged into the abyss in flames" (→Apr 30, 1916).

## German planes are shot down by rifle

*Western front, July 25*
Major Lanoe Hawker of N° 6 Squadron, Royal Flying Corps, pulled off a spectacular hat-trick today when he saw off three German aircraft – armed only with a cavalry carbine. Hawker was on patrol at 6pm when he spotted two two-seater biplanes, both armed with machine guns. Although his Bristol Scout C was fitted with only a single-shot carbine rifle, mounted on the starboard side to avoid the propeller, he attacked, downing one machine over Passchendaele and putting the other to flight. An hour later Hawker came across another German biplane, which he also sent crashing to earth. He is to be recommended for the Victoria Cross (→Aug 19).

## Aircraft act as eyes in cruiser sinking

*East Africa, July 11*
The German light cruiser *Königsberg* has been destroyed by the Royal Navy's gun monitors *Severn* and *Mersey* in German East Africa with the aid of naval aircraft. Both land and seaplanes of the Royal Naval Air Service, including Sopwiths, Shorts, Henry Farmans and Caudrons were used to find the *Königsberg*, which was hidden up the fully defended Rufiji estuary.

The aircraft then switched to spotting for the guns of the monitors, which were unable to sight the German vessel at all throughout the action. The spotter airplanes operated in relays from a nearby captured island, sending out gunnery signals by wireless telegraphy. One machine was shot down.

## Allies fire torpedoes at Turkish ships

*The Short Type 184 – a winner in the campaign against Turkish shipping.*

*Dardanelles, August 17*
British naval aircraft taking part in attacks on Turkish shipping today sank an enemy tug and burned out an ammunition ship. It is the first time that aircraft have used torpedoes to such devastating effect.

These successes follow the sinking of a 5,080-ton Turkish supply ship five days ago in the Sea of Marmara, off Gallipoli, in which Short Type 184s, from the seaplane carrier HMS *Ben-My-Chree*, also used torpedoes. Flt-Cmdr C H Edmonds made the attack at just 15ft altitude and 900ft range. However, the ship may already have been immobilized by Royal Navy submarine E14, and another submarine claims to have struck the fatal blow at the same time.

Today's historic attacks were also made by Edmonds and Flight Lieutenant G B Dacre. It started when Edmonds spotted three Turkish steamers heading for Ak Bashi Liman. He struck at one, which caught fire and was towed away towards Constantinople [Istanbul]. Dacre's aircraft had engine problems and he was forced to land on the sea. Nevertheless, he was able to taxi to the tug, release his weapon and take off again through heavy enemy fire. The tug blew up before sinking (→Apr 1916).

## Aerobatic ace Pégoud is killed over Alsace

*Pégoud (r) being congratulated on another success by colleagues.*

*France, August 31*
France's hero Adolphe Pégoud today set his Morane Bullet down in a perfect landing before dying in the cockpit from loss of blood. He had been on a reconnaissance flight over Belfort in Alsace, Germany, and was shot in the neck and chest as he pursued a German Taube. He might have lived had he landed immediately and been taken prisoner. Pégoud was a showman, almost as popular with German pilots as with his countrymen. In February he flew against two enemy airplanes over the trenches, close enough for his observer to shoot down both with six rifle shots. His next victory was on April 1, when Allied aircraft outnumbered Germans by over two to one. In June, after his fourth victory, he was the first war pilot to be described in print as an "ace", one who had downed five enemies or more. He downed his record sixth, and last, victim, on July 11, but engaged many more.

The Germans are closing the gap on Allied airmen, owing to the Fokker synchronized forward-firing mechanism, more efficient than the Allies' deflector-plate system, which can cause bullets to ricochet in all directions (→Oct).

## Italian bombers attack Austria-Hungary

*Italy, August 20*
Heavy bombers of Italy's Corpo Aeronautico Militare today began a strategic bombing offensive against Austria-Hungary. The first attack has been against the Asiovizza airfields. It is expected to become a sustained effort to strike at major industrial and military targets, the first such campaign of the war.

Italy has been able to mount the campaign only since the arrival, earlier this month, of Caproni Ca32 triple-engined bombers. From airfields in Pordenone, Capronis can reach such targets as the German submarine base at Cattaro, the naval shipyards at Trieste, and the principal Austrian naval base at Pola on the Adriatic.

# Allies are powerless to beat 'Fokker scourge'

## New aircraft claims many Allied lives

*Western front, October*

"Fokker fodder" is the ominous term used to describe the novice Allied pilots who are sent into battle to face Germany's lethal new Fokker E.IIIs. Experienced pilots speak of the menace they represent as "the Fokker Scourge", which is now a serious enough threat to forces' morale to merit discussion in the British Parliament.

The Fokkers are armed with machine guns which fire through the propeller. To avoid hitting the revolving blades, Fokker has fitted an interrupter gear to the rotary engine which stops the gun firing when the propeller is directly in

*Victim of unequal odds: a British pilot, killed on impact, lies spreadeagled beside the wreckage of his airplane.*

*Oswald Boelcke: ruthless opponent.*

front of it. The deadly mechanism was developed in record time after the capture of French ace Roland Garros, together with his much cruder forward-firing system, on April 19 [*see report on page 127*].

German pilots quickly saw the advantage: they no longer had to fly in one direction while firing the gun to the side, but could aim the whole aircraft at their quarry, improving their aiming accuracy. On July 15, Lieutenant Kurt Wintgens first used the new gear to destroy a French Morane. Oswald Boelcke, Max Immelmann and others followed. With this development, the airplane has come into its own as a fighting machine (→ Apr 24, 1916).

## German ace Immelmann strikes at Allied airmen over the front

*Douai, France, October 17*

All the talk among the German airmen at the front is about Leutnant Max "the Eagle" Immelmann, who since August 1 has notched up four victories over Allied fliers, winning himself the Iron Cross First Class and a mention in despatches. A pilot for less than a year, he is already renowned for the brilliance with which he outwits his opponents, especially the "Immelmann turn" [*see diagram right*].

His latest victory, in his Fokker monoplane, occurred on October 12. Immelmann recorded today what happened when, after seeing off six British biplanes over Loos, he spotted another at 13,000 feet over Lille: "I fired and pursued him, firing continuous series of 20-30 rounds. When I had loosed about 300 rounds the enemy observer ceased firing. After about 400 rounds the machine fell, turning over the left wing several times as it plunged. I pursued it at once in a nose-dive, so that I was always close on its tail ... it hit a row of trees as it landed. The pilot died soon after; he had six bullets in him, while the observer had a slight leg wound. The machine was destroyed. I put its machine gun out of action at the very start by a lucky shot" (→ Feb 6, 1916).

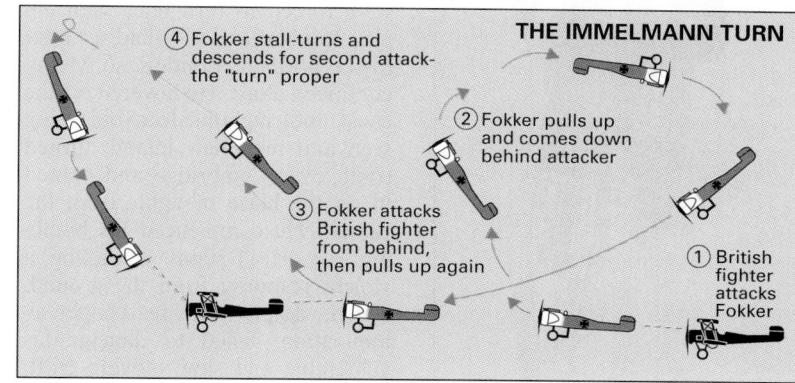

THE IMMELMANN TURN

④ Fokker stall-turns and descends for second attack- the "turn" proper

② Fokker pulls up and comes down behind attacker

③ Fokker attacks British fighter from behind, then pulls up again

① British fighter attacks Fokker

*The German "Eagle": Max Immelmann stands beside his Fokker fighter.*

# Zeppelin bombs London

*A policeman raises the alarm.*

**London, September 8**

Striking at the very heart of the British capital, the Germans tonight singled out central London as the target for the latest Zeppelin bombardment. Thirty-two civilians died in the raid, with many more injured, and material damage is put at over £500,000, all caused in less than an hour by a single airship. Targets sought by the bomber included railroad stations, the Admiralty and the Bank of England. Only one was seriously damaged: Liverpool Street station, where tracks and a bus were hit.

The German naval Zeppelin L 13, under the command of Lieutenant-Commander Heinrich Mathy, left its base at Hage in north Germany at 2.00pm loaded with almost 4,400 pounds of bombs and incendiaries, including one giant of 660 pounds. After making an aerial rendezvous with ships L 9, L 11 and L 14 over the North Sea it proceeded westward to England. L 11 and L 14 were forced to turn back with engine trouble, and L 9 had a target to the north of London, so Mathy continued alone. He hovered off the coast until nightfall to avoid being seen and then flew inland, turned south over Cambridge and homed in on the blaze of lights from the capital. He commenced his bombing run at 11.30pm, attracting a violent response from the ground, which, despite full searchlight illumination, failed to damage his vulnerable and slow moving craft. He then returned safely to base in Germany (→ May 1, 1916).

# Britain orders big boost for flying corps

**London, December**

Radical changes are sweeping the Royal Flying Corps (RFC) as the expanded needs of the "New British Army" have forced a rethink in the deployment of air power. In recent months a huge increase in the number of RFC squadrons to 100, ordered by secretary for war Field Marshal Lord Kitchener, has meant reorganization of manufacturing, purchase of more French aircraft, greater crew-training programs and a new RFC command structure. Each corps and division of the British Army now has RFC squadrons based nearby for faster reaction and direct communication. RFC "wings", which currently consist of two to four squadrons, are being doubled up into brigades, with a kite balloon wing added.

Each brigade, commanded by a brigadier-general, is self-sufficient. Wings for long-range reconnaissance and armed offensive missions are under army headquarters command. Artillery spotting and reconnaissance wings supporting the corps come under the command of corps headquarters (→ May 7, 1916).

# Catapult launches airplane from warship

**Pensacola, Fla, November 6**

United States naval aviation took a big step forward today when Lt-Cmdr Henry C Mustin piloted a Curtiss AB-2 flying boat in the first catapulted launch of an aircraft from a moving ship. The launch, announced by assistant navy secretary Franklin D Roosevelt, was from the stern of the USS *North Carolina* in Pensacola Bay. Its success opens up the prospect of warships firing at an unseen enemy, using airplanes to direct gunfire.

The catapult was built at the Washington Navy Yard. It was tested on a barge here in April and then fitted to the *North Carolina*. Yesterday a successful launch was made while the ship was anchored.

*An earlier take-off from a coalbarge tethered to the USS "North Carolina".*

# Observers see battle from balloon basket

**Western front, December**

The use of observation balloons by both sides has now made the old tactic of "gaining the high ground" for reconnaissance irrelevant. These tethered kite balloons, so called because of their aerodynamic stability, are a familiar sight along the front and are a frequent target for air and ground fire. Reeled out to as high as 6,000 feet, their observers, borne in underslung baskets, use maps, binoculars, telephone and considerable courage to assess and report the movement of troops or the impact of artillery shells. Upon attack, which happens often, they jump to the ground by parachute while the balloon explodes in flames.

*A French observation kite balloon is maneuvered by its ground crew.*

# War demand boosts airplane output

## Curtiss pilot makes flight from Toronto to New York City

*New York, November 16*

Swedish-born Victor Carlstrom, a naturalized American, today completed what must be the most significant flight so far made between Canada and the US. He covered the 485 miles that separate Toronto and New York in a flying time of 6 hours 40 minutes – a cross-country record.

Carlstrom made the journey in a Curtiss R-2 biplane. He took off from Toronto yesterday and flew around Lake Ontario before heading south-west toward New York via Hamilton. Once across the US-Canada frontier, he made stopovers in Bath, Elmira, Binghamton, Port Jervis and Cornwall before ending the day at Ridgefield Park, New Jersey. Unfortunately, the field in which he landed was too small to allow him to take off again, and the Curtiss had to be dismantled and taken to a larger area where it was reassembled before Carlstrom could complete the final few miles of his flight.

Carlstrom is an instructor with the Curtiss Aviation School in Toronto and is a very well-known aviator in Canada. He received his pilot's license in 1912 at the Curtiss school in San Diego, California, before moving north. Flying a Rex biplane, he took part in privately-run air shows in 1913 and later exhibited a Blériot (→ Nov 3, 1916).

*Constructing wooden fuselage components at the French Nieuport factory.*

*Production line: British women doping a consignment of airplane wings.*

*Europe, December*

The realization that aircraft can play a highly important role in combat has naturally led to a great increase in demand for both machines and the pilots to fly them. The experience of France, the leading country in European aviation before the war, is a good example: the number of French military squadrons leapt from 21 in November 1914 to 51 by the end of last March, and in the summer the aircraft per squadron rose from six to ten.

Head of French military aviation, Commandant Edouard Barés envisages a force twice as large: 119 squadrons with 1,190 machines and 1,400 airmen. There are problems in meeting this demand. Airplane construction has remained essentially a craft rather than a mass-production industry, each machine combining the skills of engineer, carpenter and textile worker. Output, although increasing, is thus still slow: fewer than 200 Nieuports have left the factory so far, although this is faster than in some other places: Germany has produced only 86 Fokkers, for instance. The average time between an aircraft leaving the drawing board and arriving at the airfield is nine months, so that some machines are outdated even when new.

There is a difficulty with certain parts: the French (and the British) have had to find replacements for magnetos, which came from Germany before the war (→ Dec 1916).

## British flyers in hide-and-seek drama

*St Eloi, France, November 8*

Two British airmen of the Royal Flying Corps have outwitted German artillery after being forced to hide their Vickers Gunbus biplane close to the front line overnight. Yesterday, with air mechanic G H Donald as gunner, Lieutenant Gilbert Insall set upon a German airplane and pursued it over its own lines, ignoring intensive fire and compelling it to land. The two men then shot at the crew, forcing them to flee, and bombed the aircraft.

As they flew home they dived low over German trenches, with Donald firing at them. Shots from the ground damaged the fuel tank,

so that Insall landed in a clearing in a wood just 1,600 feet inside Allied lines. The Germans proceeded to hurl 150 shells in their direction.

Undaunted, the airmen worked with concealed lanterns to camouflage and patch up the Vickers and waited for dawn. As day broke, they pushed the machine out of its camouflaged hide and, with the help of nearby soldiers, got it started. At Insall's signal the makeshift ground crew let go of the machine as he increased the power and roared out of the clearing. The frustrated Germans heard their quarry but caught no sight of it as it escaped to safety (→ Jan 14, 1916).

## Stinson loops loop

*Los Angeles, December 17*

Los Angeles residents were treated to a brilliant show tonight when Katherine Stinson looped the loop and, with magnesium flares attached to her aircraft, etched the letters "CAL" in the darkness. Always out to show that women flyers are as just as good as men, Stinson has thrilled crowds since she became the world's fourth licensed woman pilot in 1912. Tonight's flight was more spectacular than Art Smith's recent night-time loop, and makes her the first woman to loop the loop at night. She was also the first woman to do it at all, on July 18 in Chicago (→ Dec 11, 1917).

**Glenn Martin and his airplane star in "The Girl of Yesterday".**

*Macchi's L.1 two-seater flying boat had an Isotta-Fraschini engine.*

*The Halberstadt D.I fighter was armed with a single Spandau gun.*

*The Short 184 changed the face of naval warfare when it became the first aircraft to sink a warship with a torpedo. The type was widely used by the RNAS.*

*The unconventional Caudron G.IV two-seater reconnaissance biplane saw service with French, British and Italian forces during the war.*

*The elegant Nieuport 11 Bébé was the first of the Nieuport fighter line.*

*The Handley Page O/100 heavy bomber – first of a famous line.*

*The Martinsyde Elephant: a reconnaissance bomber for the RFC.*

*A total of seven massive Siemens-Schuckert R.1 bombers was built.*

*The Royal Aircraft Factory F.E.2a: a two-seater for reconnaissance.*

*The Friedrichshafen G.II proved unsuccessful as a heavy bomber.*

*The two-seater Albatros C.1 served with the German imperial air force on all fronts as scout, bomber, trainer and artillery observation platform.*

*The unusually configured Curtiss Canada had its engines suspended between the mainplanes and could accommodate three crew members in its fuselage.*

*Designed by Geoffrey de Havilland and built by the Aircraft Manufacturing Company, the Airco D.H.1 fighter featured a nose-mounted gun.*

*The Farman F.30, jointly designed by brothers Maurice and Henry.*

*The Farman F.40 bomber was used by France, Russia and Britain.*

*The peculiar Gotha G.1 had its twin engines mounted on the lower wing.*

*The AEG C.I was the first in a whole series of reconnaissance biplanes.*

*The LVG Roland C.II was a remarkably streamlined two-seater.*

*Claude Dornier designed the giant Zeppelin-Lindau Rs1 flying boat.*

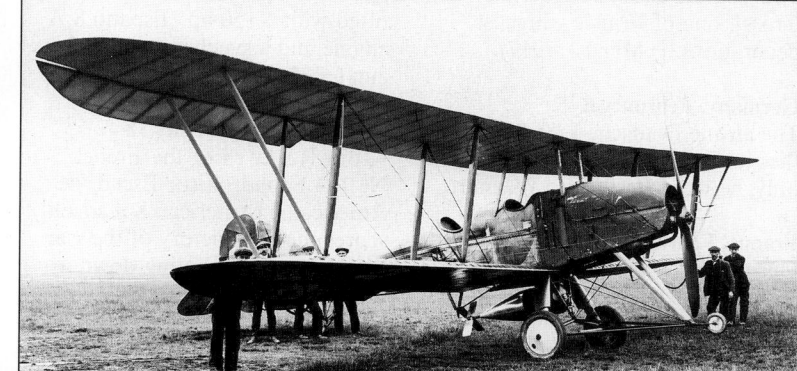

*The cumbersome Royal Aircraft Factory R.E.7 was a two to three-seater light biplane bomber, powered by an RAF 4a engine. Only about 250 were built.*

*The Armstrong Whitworth F.K.3 reconnaissance biplane, designed by Frederick Koolhoven, was essentially an improved version of the BE2c.*

*The Albatros D.I and D.II marked a major improvement over previous scouts, with their streamlined wooden monocoque fuselages and heavy punch.*

*The Paul Schmitt 7 was a two-seater biplane bomber produced in France.*

*The Rumpler C.1 reconnaissance-bomber served on all fronts.*

*The Fokker E.1 Eindecker fighter had interrupter gear fitted, allowing a gun to be fired through the propeller – with deadly results for the enemy.*

*The Sopwith 1 ½-Strutter was the first British fighter to feature interrupter gear. It was soon relegated to observation and light bombing duties.*

# 1916

134.54mph
Great Britain
Norman Spratt
RAF SE.4
Jun 1914

1,180.61 miles
Germany
Werner Landmann
Albatros
Jun 28, 1914

26,739ft
Germany
Heinrich Oelerich
DFW
Jul 14, 1914

26,265lb
Germany
Staaken
R. VI

296hp
France
Louis Renault
Renault 12F

**France, January 21**
British pilot James McCudden is awarded the Croix de Guerre [War Cross], one of France's highest decorations (→ Mar 12, 1917).

**Germany, February 6**
The airline Deutsche Luft Reederei flies its first service, which is freight only, between Berlin and Weimar.

**France, February 6**
German pilot Max Immelmann tests the Fokker E.IV fighter in battle; it has been fitted with three synchronized machine guns (→ Jun).

**Germany, February 19**
The Austrian physicist Ernst Mach, 77, dies at Haar, Munich; he did important research into the connection between aerodynamics and the speed of sound.

**Verdun, France, March 19**
The French ace Jean Navarre scores his seventh victory.

**Essex, England, April 6**
During experiments at Harwich to extend the range of fighters, Commander Porte takes off in a Porte Baby flying boat with a Bristol Scout mounted on the wing. Flight Sub-Lieutenant Day, in the "parasite" Scout, lifts off from the flying boat at 1,000 feet.

**France, April**
The Sopwith 1½-Strutter general-purpose two-seater goes into service with Nº 5 Wing, Royal Naval Air Service (→ Aug 2).

**London, May 7**
Following complaints about the record of the Royal Flying Corps, the British government announces an inquiry headed by Mr Justice Bailhache into the running of the corps (→ Aug 3).

**Kent, England, May 9**
During trials for the Short 184 seaplane at Kingsnorth, a 500-pound bomb is dropped on an armored roof target from 4,000ft, using a bombsight developed by Bourdillon and Tizard (→ May 31).

**France, May 10**
The French Air Force orders 268 Spad VII fighters. The biplane is fitted with a 150-hp Hispano 8 A engine and a synchronized Vickers gun (→ May 1, 1917).

**Alsace, Germany, May 18**
Kiffin Rockwell of the French Nº 124 Squadron (or Escadrille Américaine [American Squadron]), scores the first victory of the war by a US pilot, shooting down a German LVG (→ Jun 23).

**Germany, June 13**
The Zeppelin-Lindau Dornier Rs II hydroplane, piloted by Schröter and Schulte, succeeds in taking off from Lake Constance and makes a four-minute flight (→ Nov 4, 1919).

**Verdun, France, June 23**
Victor Emmanuel Chapman, flying with France's Nº 124 Squadron of American volunteers, becomes the first American pilot to die in the war when he is shot down and killed; H Clyde Balsley was the first American to be shot down, following a dogfight over Verdun, on June 18 (→ Dec 6).

**England, July 7**
British pilot Albert Ball is awarded the Military Cross, one of the highest British decorations for bravery (→ Aug 31).

**Belgium, August 2**
British aircraft of Nos 4 and 5 Wings, Royal Naval Air Service, try new bombing tactics during a raid near Ghent: 11 bombers attack in a line astern directed by Very signals from a Sopwith 1½-Strutter (→ Jul 1917).

**London, August 3**
The Bailhache inquiry into the administration of the air war presents its report. It concludes that a single government department should equip both the Royal Flying Corps and the Royal Naval Air Service (→ Nov 14).

**USA, August 17**
The Wright and Glenn Martin companies merge to form the Wright Martin Aircraft Corporation (→ Dec 19).

**Washington, DC, August 29**
Legislation is passed establishing a US Naval Flying Corps, with 150 officers and 350 men, and a Naval Reserve Flying Corps.

**San Diego, Calif, September 2**
During wireless tests between two aircraft in flight, messages are sent and received over two miles (→ Oct 10, 1917).

**Cuffley, England, September 2**
Schütte-Lanz airship SL 11, one of 16 raiders, is shot down just north of London by Lieutenant W Leefe-Robinson of the Royal Flying Corps in a B.E.2c; he is put forward for the Victoria Cross.

**USA, September 12**
The Hewitt-Sperry wireless-controlled flying bomb, designed by Lawrence Sperry and built by Curtiss, is tested; powered by a 10-hp engine, it has a range of up to 50 miles and can carry 300lb of bombs (→ Nov 21, 1917).

**France, September 15**
At Flers-Courcelette, Royal Flying Corps aircraft give air cover during the first assault by the new British armoured vehicle codenamed "the tank" (→ Mar 21, 1917).

**Western front, September 17**
The newly-arrived Albatros D.I fighter goes into service.

**England, September 20**
The Supermarine Aviation Works Ltd is formed; Noel Pemberton-Billing, who originally founded the flying boat company in 1914, sold his interest after being elected to Parliament on March 10.

**Hertfordshire, England, October 2**
Germany loses its most successful airship captain, Heinrich Mathy, killed when Zeppelin LZ 72 is shot down over Potter's Bar.

**London, October 5**
Although civil air operations are banned because of the war, George Holt Thomas registers the first British airline, Aircraft Transport and Travel Ltd (→ May 30, 1918).

**New York, November 3**
Victor Carlstrom completes a trial airmail flight, and the first flight from Chicago to New York, in a Curtiss R biplane; he covers the 967 miles in 8 hours 28 minutes flying time, setting new US non-stop distance (452 miles) and speed (134mph) records en route.

**France, November 16**
British Commander-in-chief in France Sir Douglas Haig asks London for 20 more air squadrons by the spring (→ Feb 2, 1917).

**France, November 21**
The prototype Breguet 14 two-seat bomber and reconnaissance biplane begins flight trials; it is fitted with a powerful 300-hp Renault engine and its innovative features include automatic full-span flaps.

**Washington, DC, December 4**
The National Advisory Committee for Aeronautics recommends authorizing the Post Office to set up airmail routes (→ Jul 17, 1917).

**France, December 6**
The name "Escadrille Lafayette" [Lafayette squadron] is adopted by the American volunteers of French air squadron Nº 124 (→ Jan 1, 1918).

**USA, December 19**
Small aircraft companies appeal to the Aero Club to control the Curtiss and Wright firms' demands for licenses and patent royalties.

**Fort Omaha, Nebr, December 20**
The US Army Balloon School is established.

*Contesting the skies: an artist's impression of air combat over the western front. Here an Albatros pilot is sent blazing away to his death.* ▶

## Popularity of air heroes: a danger to troop morale?

*Berlin, January 12*
The German authorities announced today that two of their best fighter pilots, Max Immelmann and Oswald Boelcke, have been awarded Germany's highest military honor, the order Pour le Mérite [For Merit]. Immelmann and Boelcke have won their medals for shooting down a total of eight Allied opponents each in aerial combat. They both reached this figure in the skies near the French fortress at Verdun where the German air service is playing its part in the build-up for what appears to be a new offensive.

The coveted blue-and-gold medal, and its – given the war, ironic – French title, were created in 1740 by military genius and francophile, King Frederick the Great of Prussia. The award of so great an honor to two quite junior officers represents a new step in a tendency which has been apparent for some time: to mark the exploits of individual pilots, especially fighter pilots, for special attention. This arises from a need for heroes in a war which has reached a muddy stalemate on the ground; from the trenches, the airmen's battles seem heroic, with echoes of the chivalry of medieval knights. The reality is somewhat different; the technique of the fighter pilot is to creep up on his prey unawares, pounce when the time is right and shoot him in the back before he can escape.

France instigated the title *as* [ace] for Eugène Gilbert, who had shot down five German aircraft before he was killed last summer. The British Army is not keen to follow this practice. While bravery in battle will, naturally, be rewarded, British commanders fear that it could be harmful to single out pilots as heroes: as "aces" develop auras of invincibility, so morale, when they are killed, could suffer. This dilemma could tempt senior commanders to withdraw "aces" from combat (→ Feb 6).

# Verdun push takes Allies by surprise

*France, February 21*
A huge German attack, predicted by French air scouts over a week ago, was launched today in the upper Meuse valley, centered on the French fortress of Verdun, near the German border. The offensive has caught the Allies by surprise and must be a considerable embarrassment to the French general staff, which did not believe recent aerial reconnaissance reports by its own air forces which, as late as yesterday evening, reported a huge German build-up in the region. The French commander, General Joffre, insisted that a German attack would come in the Champagne region. The defenses of Verdun, further east, have been neglected.

The French air force chief, Commandant Jean du Peuty, faces an acute shortage of aircraft and guns to meet the German onslaught. He can rely on help from his British counterpart, Major-General Hugh Trenchard, the commander of the

*A three-seater on a reconnaissance mission over the Champagne region.*

Royal Flying Corps in France, whom he met a week ago.

Trenchard thinks the best form of air defense is attack and is ready to send his own scarce guns, bullets and bombsights to aid Peuty's hard-pressed force, but he has not yet persuaded Peuty to detach his fighters from army control. Meanwhile the German commander, General von Falkenhayn, is master of the skies over Verdun (→ Mar).

## Stork is harbinger of death to Germans

*A hand of aces: the leading pilots of the French "Cigogne" [Stork] squadron.*

*France, April 30*
Among the élite squadrons created to combat the German mastery of the skies, one has already begun to achieve legendary status: N° 3 Nieuport Squadron, which has adopted the stork, traditionally a bringer of good luck, as its emblem. Stork Squadron is commanded by Captain Félix Brocard and includes several highly talented young pilots, such as Lieutenant Georges Guynemer. Their function is to "seek the enemy, engage and destroy him", harrying the Fokker squadrons which have hampered Allied observation flights over Verdun (→ Jul 5, 1917).

## French counter the German superiority

*Verdun, March*
The German army's great spring offensive at Verdun is becoming a bloody battle of attrition to "bleed France white" and the French are taking heavy casualties. The fight for control of the air above the battlefield is no less fierce.

In the early stages, German airmen had considerable success. In an attempt to deny access to the skies to Allied reconnaissance and artillery spotters, the Germans flew "barrage" patrols along the German lines to create an airborne barrier to their own airspace. But this saturation policy required virtually all the German aircraft, and French pilots, now equipped with the Nieuport II, have begun to outfight their opponents.

The key to French success lies in the aggressive tactics of French air force chief Commandant Jean du Peuty. His philosophy, which is shared by his British ally, Major-General Hugh Trenchard of the Royal Flying Corps, is simple and effective: seek out the enemy, push him back and always attack.

# Generals rely more and more on photo reconnaissance to guide battle planning

*An RFC instructor demonstrates a camera adapted for aerial photography.*

*St Omer, France, March*
After the carnage of Verdun, Allied commanders are more ready to accept the validity of photographic reconnaissance from aircraft as the basis of their front-line intelligence. British and French pre-war experiments, applied to military map making at the battle of Neuve Chapelle in 1915, led to the development of cameras fitted to aircraft, which were initially flown by Nos 2 and 3 squadrons, Royal Flying Corps (RFC). A "clock code" was also developed to guide artillery on the maps produced by air observation.

The new Vickers F.B.9 "gunbus" two-seater, now being tested at the front, is specially suited to photographic reconnaissance, carrying a plate camera instead of a machine gun in its observation position at the nose. "Photo-recce" is a risky job, requiring slow, careful flights at 5,000 feet over enemy trenches, repeated many times to build up a complete image of the lines. Since January, in response to the Fokker menace, each intelligence flight must be escorted by three fighters. For the British, this requirement has become easier to meet since the arrival of dedicated fighter aircraft such as N° 24 Squadron's D.H.2s, led by the much-decorated Major Lanoe Hawker (→ Jul 18).

*A mobile darkroom and motor-cycle messenger are essential for the task.*

# Australian flyers to join Allies in Egypt

*Australia, March 16*
Today the first complete unit of the Australian Flying Corps, N° 1 Squadron, embarked from Melbourne for service in Egypt. Its main task will be to defend the Suez Canal, and when it arrives in Egypt it will take over B.E.2 airplanes and other equipment supplied by its British counterpart, the Royal Flying Corps, at Heliopolis. The squadron has 12 airplanes which are divided into three flights of four machines each. The unit is self-sufficient and numbers 28 officers and 195 other ranks under the command of Lieutenant-Colonel E H Reynolds. The three flight commanders are Captains W Sheldon and R Williams and Lieutenant D T W Manwell (→ Aug 1, 1917).

# Air unit to avenge Mexican rebel raids

*Mexico, March 16*
US military aircraft flew their first reconnaissance mission over foreign territory today when two officers of the First Aero Squadron flew 30 miles into Mexico from Columbus, New Mexico. The squadron's commander, Capt Benjamin D Foulois, acted as observer, with Capt Townsend F Dodd at the controls. The squadron of eight Curtiss JN-3 airplanes arrived at Columbus yesterday from Fort Sam Houston, Texas, to join other US Army units under the command of Brig-Gen John Pershing, whose mission is to punish the Mexican rebel general, Francisco "Pancho" Villa, for a raid on Columbus on March 9 in which 19 Americans died (→ Sep 3, 1917).

# American volunteers join up in France

*Air heroes: a group of American volunteers for the European war.*

*France, April 18*
The first all-American air squadron in Europe was formed at the French spa town of Luxeuil-les-Bains today. Nieuport Squadron N° 124, unofficially known as the Escadrille Américaine [American Squadron], is composed of volunteers who will be under the command of a French captain, Georges Thénault.

Most of the pilots of the new squadron have spent the last two weeks undergoing intensive instruction in preparation for taking to the air in the latest Nieuport 17 pursuit aircraft. Gunnery and tactics, as well as operational procedures, have been emphasized during the training.

The formation of the Escadrille Américaine comes after a year of lobbying by Americans, both in France and the US, for the creation of their own volunteer air unit. The strength of the German attack at Verdun, which showed the need for more air squadrons, was the factor which led to the formation of the squadron (→ May 18).

# Allies move against Fokker menace

## New British fighter is big breakthrough

*Somme, France, April 24*
It looks as if Germany's Fokker monoplanes, dreaded by the Allies, have finally met their match. Today about a dozen of them were decisively beaten by the new British D.H.2 scouts of Nº 24 Squadron, Royal Flying Corps, under Major Lanoe Hawker. Since last September his 12 pilots have been in intensive training on the machines, which each have a "pusher" engine and forward-firing Lewis gun.

Today, four D.H.2s were escorting five BEs of Nº 15 Squadron when a group of Fokkers attacked. The Germans, to their surprise, encountered in the D.H.2 an opponent of great aggression, agility and firepower. The Fokker was soundly beaten in combat: the D.H.2, with the new French Nieuport Bébé, could finally end the "Fokker scourge" (→Aug 17, 1918).

## Allies plan against German air success

*Western front, March*
Major developments in the conduct of aerial fighting have been taking place over the last few months in direct response to the toll taken by the German Fokkers last year. In January, Britain's Royal Flying Corps issued an order which laid down that every machine "proceeding on reconnaissance must be escorted by at least three other fighting machines".

Until this year most pilots flew their missions alone, and combat between more than two or three aircraft was rare. Now, with six or more flying in tight formation for protection, the trend is for air battles to be much larger engagements involving whole units rather than individuals.

New, more advanced airplanes to counter the Fokkers are reaching the front, but as they do so these latest developments mean that they will be needed in much greater numbers, with ever more pilots, with ever greater skills, to fly them.

*Allied commanders hope that the Airco D.H.2 fighter will redress the balance.*

*No longer invincible: this Fokker fighter was captured by French troops.*

**HOW FORMATION FLYING PROTECTS FIGHTERS**

B flight - slightly astern A flight provides cover at 15,500 feet

C flight provides top cover at 18,000 feet

3 miles

A flight - spearhead 15,000 feet

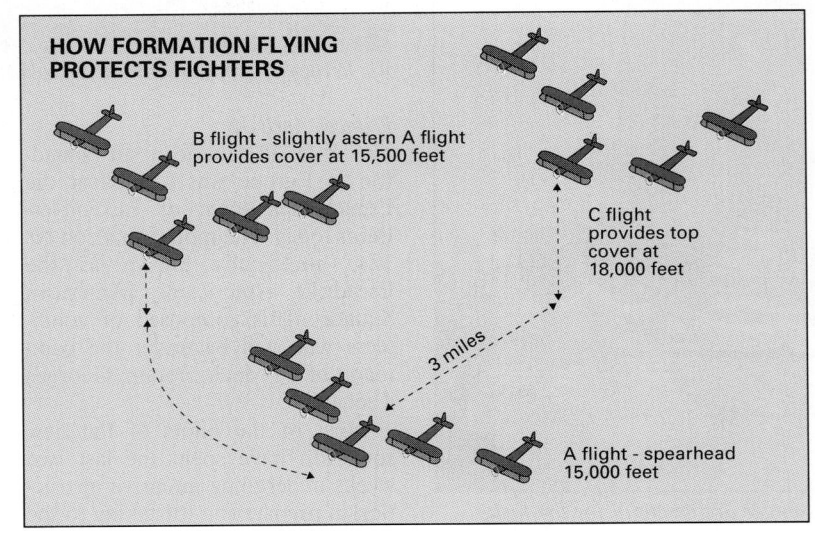

## British aircraft aid troops under siege in the Middle East

*Mesopotamia [Iraq], April*
Britain's Royal Flying Corps (RFC) and Royal Naval Air Service (RNAS) have come to the aid of a British garrison under siege from Turkish forces at Kut al Amara, providing the first ever airborne supply "bridge". Kut al Amara was captured by General Barrett after a spectacular 100-mile advance which itself would have been impossible without RFC and RNAS aircraft providing information on Turkish positions.

The Turks surrounded the city and, on April 15, RFC B.E.2cs, plus three Maurice Farman "Shorthorns" and RNAS aircraft, began flying over Turkish lines to carry in supplies. The airplanes carry food in 50-pound bags on the outside of the fuselage and 25-pound bags on the undercarriage. Other supplies have included medicine, mail, wireless parts and £10,000 of currency, including gold and silver.

## Germany prepares a 'super-Zeppelin'

*Nordholz, Germany, May 1*
Captain Strasser, dynamic head of the German Naval Airship Division, took delivery today of the magnificent L 31, the third of the new "super-Zeppelins" to emerge from the factory at Friedrichshafen on Lake Constance. The new six-engined airship is nearly 660 feet long and is capable of reaching 60mph; it has ten machine guns and, fully loaded, can carry five tons of bombs to 13,000 feet.

L 31, with two new sister airships assigned to the army, is a prototype. The Zeppelin works face at least three months more work before the super airships can be built at a wartime pace. Nevertheless Strasser sees in these aircraft the weapon which, he believes, will finally bomb Britain into submission. Others have sounded a note of caution. British naval defense fighters have been issued with new incendiary ammunition and are increasingly ready to meet the nocturnal invaders (→Sep 24).

# Airplane plays role in Jutland naval clash

*An artist's impression of the action.*

*North Sea, May 31*
An airplane played a role in a big sea battle for the first time today, when a Short 184 seaplane, launched by British seaplane carrier HMS *Engadine*, sighted German cruisers and reported their positions to the British fleet just before the battle, the largest fleet action of the war so far, began off Jutland.

The machine, piloted by Flight-Lieutenant F Rutland, with Assistant Paymaster G Trewin acting as observer, was lowered onto the water at the stern of the *Engadine* and took off toward the German fleet. It approached the ships at low level due to cloud, and although fired on by four cruisers and later forced down by a fractured fuel line, the crew transmitted three accurate reconnaissance reports.

# Mystery surrounds the death of 'Blue Max'

*Immelmann: victim of his own gun?*

*Verdun front, France, June 18*
German fighter ace Max Immelmann was downed and killed today, although the exact circumstances are unclear. Immelmann, star pupil of veteran Oswald Boelcke, and with 15 confirmed "kills" his only rival, was flying a Fokker monoplane with a forward-firing Spandau machine gun.

An examination of the wreckage of his machine has revealed that one propeller blade was shot off in line with the Spandau, raising speculation that the gun/propeller synchronizing mechanism was faulty. But the British claim that an F.E.2b of Nº 25 Squadron, RFC, piloted by Second Lieutenant McCubbin, shot Immelmann down.

In January Immelmann, known as "the Eagle of Lille", and Boelcke were the first pilots to win Germany's prestigious Pour le Mérite [For Merit] decoration. Its blue enamel earned Immelmann a new nickname: "The Blue Max".

# French pilot 'bombs' Berlin with leaflets

*Germany, June 21*
A new world record for non-stop flying of 876 miles was set today by Lieutenant Anselme Marchal on a mission to Berlin. He set out from near Nancy, in eastern France, last night and headed for the German capital, which he "bombed" with propaganda leaflets before steering a course for Russian territory. Marchal was over Poland, just 60 miles from Allied lines, when his fuel ran out and he was forced to land; he was captured shortly after.

# Ace launches solo battle

*The seemingly fearless Albert Ball.*

*France, August 31*
Nineteen-year-old British lieutenant Albert Ball, a shy loner on the ground, set new standards of aggressive airmanship this evening when he flew solo to a German air base near Cambrai determined to attack anything that dared to fly against him. From 11,000 feet he saw 12 Roland two-seaters flying in formation below and dived on them like a bird of prey, wreaking havoc.

Ball, a technician from Nottingham, was an expert shot before he learned to fly. In his Nieuport, which has special gun-mounts, he swoops below his quarry and guts him from below with a complete drum of ammunition. With his own engine shot out and no ammunition in his machine gun, he might draw his pistol, as he did today, emptying that at the enemy before gliding down to an unofficial landing field to sleep beside his machine.

Since May 16 Ball has been in combat 25 times, choosing to be outnumbered 13 times. On August 22 he took on first seven, then five German aircraft; on August 28 the sequence was four and ten. He has forced 20 opponents down and destroyed eight (→ Jun 3, 1917).

# William Boeing takes to building aircraft

*Seattle, July 15*
A new aircraft company formally came into being today when the Pacific Aero Products Company was started by timber merchant William E Boeing. Boeing, pleased with the success of his new *B&W* floatplane, believes that he can fulfill the US Navy's need for a two-seater seaplane training aircraft. The *B&W* first flew on June 29 and takes its initials from Boeing and his colleague on the project, Commander George Conrad Westervelt of the US Navy, then at Seattle naval shipyard. Westervelt went east before the *B&W* flew and is no longer involved with Boeing. The firm has three trustees. Bill Boeing is president, his cousin E N Gott is vice-president and the secretary is J C Foley (→ Apr 18, 1917).

*William E Boeing's floatplane "B&W" is made ready for its first take-off.*

# Allies win control of air as battle rages on Somme

## Pilots support major push on the ground

*Mired on the ground: troops negotiate a treacherous, muddy swamp.*

**Somme front, France, July 18**
Since the launch of a big Allied offensive on July 1, a battle has raged for about 6 miles of farmland – at a cost of about three lives per foot – on the river Somme in northern France. Despite the carnage on the ground it has been a triumph for Britain's Royal Flying Corps, which has denied the Germans air superiority while providing the British "Tommies" with direct support on the battlefield. Airmen have photographed the front line, reported the condition of wire and trenches, flown low enough to check the color of uniforms, made bomb and machine-gun attacks, and caused panic among German infantry. A big advance on the right flank is being credited to artillery aided by air observation (→ Sep 15).

## Days of Zeppelin supremacy are over

**London, September 24**
Three German naval airships bombed London last night – but only one escaped to tell the tale. The fate of the three aircraft, L 31, L 32 and L 33, seems to confirm the supremacy of Britain's air defenses over the formidable, but vulnerable, bombers.

L 31 was the lucky one. It was first over London and blasted residential areas in the south before fleeing over ground mist after blinding anti-aircraft batteries with parachute flares. L 33 struck London's industrial East End, setting off fires in a timber yard and oil storage depots near the docks, before getting caught in artillery searchlights and being pounded with shells. Sinking fast, L 33 steered for home but came down in rural Essex, where the crew was arrested by a village policeman. L 32 was set upon by a British fighter, whose pilot, Second Lt F Sowrey, poured incendiaries into the airship. It crashed, killing all 21 crew. Sowrey has been recommended for the Victoria Cross (→ May 25, 1917).

*No longer a threat: the wreckage of a Zeppelin grounded in England.*

## German air ace killed in mid-air collision

**Somme front, October 28**
Nearly five months after the death of the air ace Max Immelmann, Germany today lost his mentor, the legendary Oswald Boelcke, perhaps the greatest fighter pilot of them all. Ironically, the veteran flyer was not shot down by an Allied fighter but died in a tragic accident at the hands of one of his own comrades.

Boelcke, whose tally of 35 "kills" is more than any other airman's on either side, was engaged over the Somme battlefield with two aircraft of N° 24 Squadron of Britain's Royal Flying Corps. In a sudden moment of confusion, Boelcke and his comrade Erwin Böhme found their Albatros fighter scouts heading straight at each other, with a British airplane barring the escape route out of a collision. Before either man could prevent it, Böhme's undercarriage hit the end of Boelcke's left wing; Boelcke struggled to keep control, but the wing disintegrated and he plummeted to earth, dying instantly on impact.

After many months of Allied air successes, no unit has done more to claw back Germany's former command of the air than Boelcke's Jagdstaffel or Jasta [fighter squadron] 2, which, re-equipped with the new Albatros fighter scout, snarled into action on September 17. So far it has scored 76 "kills" for the loss of seven of its pilots – including Boelcke himself. Jasta 2 is now to be renamed Jasta Boelcke.

## German ace's rules for success in the air

**Western front, October 28**
German ace Oswald Boelcke, who died today after a mid-air collision [*see story, left*], may go down in history as "the father of aerial combat". He was the first to draw up rules for this type of warfare, laying down eight guidelines for victory in the sky which the Germans call the *Dikta Boelcke* [Boelcke Dicta]:
*Try to secure advantages before attacking. Always attack from a greater height than your opponent, if possible with the Sun behind you.
*Always carry through an attack once you have started it.
*Fire only at close range, and only when your opponent is properly in your sights.
*Always keep your eyes on your opponent, and never let yourself be deceived by ruses.
*In any form of attack it is always essential to assail your opponent from behind.
*If your opponent dives on you, do not try to evade his onslaught but turn to meet it.
*When you are over the enemy's lines never forget your own line of retreat.
*Attack in principle in groups of four or six. When the fight breaks up into a series of single combats, take care that several do not go for one opponent.

# Expanded air service and better aircraft breathe new life into German war effort

*A German LFG Roland takes off from a temporary aerodrome at the front.*

*Somme front, October*

The tide is beginning to turn against the Allies, who, after the introduction of the French Nieuport 17 and the British Airco D.H.2, enjoyed air superiority during the summer. A fundamental reorganization of the Idflieg, the German army air service, has given it greater autonomy, while new units have been established to operate greatly improved aircraft.

On October 8 General Ernst von Höppner was appointed to command a vastly expanded Idflieg on the western front, recognizing the vital importance of fighters in gaining control of the air. The German *Jagdstaffeln* or *Jastas* [fighter squadrons] are building up toward an initial target of 30 units of 14 aircraft each. Their newly-supplied Albatros D.I and D.II fighter scouts, with 160-hp engines, can climb more steeply, more rapidly and to a greater height than Allied machines, and are also faster on the level, reaching 109mph. The tiny Roland C.II two-seat fighter, is also out-performing Allied fighters although few are as yet in service.

Thirty *Schutzstaffeln* [escort squadrons] are flying C-type two-seaters, now armed with a fixed forward-firing 08/15 machine gun for the pilot as well as the flexibly-mounted Parabellum for the observer. Their main duty is protecting reconnaissance and artillery observation machines, but they also fly ground-attack, bombing or patrol missions (→ Mar 6, 1917).

# President Wilson receives aerial salute

*New York, December 17*

One of America's leading woman flyers, Ruth Law, tonight flew an illuminated aerial salute to President Woodrow Wilson aboard his yacht *Mayflower* in New York harbor. Moments before, when the president had switched on new, permanent, lighting for the Statue of Liberty, Law, with magnesium flares and an electric sign spelling "Liberty" on her airplane's lower wing, delighted the crowd by circling the famous monument. Law holds the American record for cross-country non-stop flying for her 590-mile flight from Chicago to Hornell, NY.

# Flying German baron picks off British ace

*Grandcourt, France, November 23*

An aerial duel over the western front this morning deprived Britain of its top combat pilot, Major Lanoe Hawker. Hawker, the first flyer to win the Victoria Cross, Britain's highest valor award, was killed by a young German aristocrat, Baron Manfred von Richthofen.

On patrol over the Bapaume sector, Hawker met an Albatros scout which, unusually, did not turn and run. The two fought for over half an hour, the maneuverability of Hawker's D.H.2 matched by the power and speed of the Albatros. Low on fuel, Hawker was dashing for Allied lines when a bullet from Richthofen's last drum hit him in the head (→Jan 16, 1917).

*Von Richthofen: a brilliant fighter.*

# Two years of air war realize grim vision

*France, December 31*

As the second full year of the war draws to a close, armies and navies have had to come to terms with a new dimension to warfare. In effect, much of the stark vision of air warfare predicted by British author H G Wells in his book *War in the Air* several years ago has become a reality. This has happened in two different ways.

Aircraft have become indispensable to waging war on land and at sea, mainly for reconnaissance, but also for spotting for artillery and naval gunfire and, crucially, by fighting for control of the sky over the battlefield. But, in a more sinister development, aircraft have extended hostilities beyond the battlefield, to the enemy's heartland.

The raids on French and British towns by German airships (and later by airplanes) started out as attacks on targets of military significance. But bombing is not an exact science and civilian casualties were inevitable. The damage done to the war effort by such raids has been negligible so far, but their effect on civilian attitudes and morale has been considerable, with growing calls in France and Britain for revenge raids on Germany.

*The weapons of the air war: a British crew is fitted out in an armory.*

*History in the making: Boeing's first aeroplane, the B & W floatplane.*

*The Dorand AR.1 reconnaissance bomber, with back-staggered wings.*

*The Breguet-Michelin 5 bomber did not prove a success in service.*

*Armstrong Whitworth's F.K.8 was used for reconnaissance operations.*

*The monocoque-fuselaged Albatros D.III, from a classic line of fighters.*

*The LFG Roland D.1 fighter, armed with a Spandau gun and well stream-lined, was powered by a 100-hp Mercedes engine. It saw limited production.*

*The Spad XI's poor performance made it unpopular with pilots.*

*Only one example was built of the Porte-Felixstowe Baby flying boat.*

*De Havilland's D.H.6 trainer saw regular use, but it was far from ideal.*

*Macchi's Lohner-based L.2 flying boat went into production as the L.3.*

*The Letord Type 1: a French bomber with back-staggered wings.*

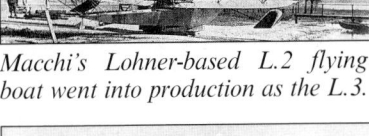

*After the Zeppelins came bombers such as this Friedrichshafen G.III.*

*A famous fighter from France: the rotary-engined Nieuport 17 was an agile and elegant mount which was flown by aces such as Charles Nungesser.*

*The prototype of the Spad VII, famous French single-seater fighter.*

*The odd Swiss Häfeli DH.1 was based on German Ago designs.*

*Another member of the Friedrichshafen family, the big G.II bomber.*

*The Breguet 4 bomber was not the cleanest of designs and proved slow.*

*The French-designed Spad XIII was one of the greatest fighter aircraft of the First World War and was flown by many French and American aces.*

*Only a few Armstrong Whitworth F.K.10 quadruplanes were made.*

*The Friedrichshafen D.I fighter carried a 160-hp Mercedes engine.*

*A prototype which led to greater things: the Bristol F.2A fighter.*

*The Gotha G.II was another German raider of the English mainland.*

*The Curtiss R-4 was a large un-gainly reconnaissance aircraft.*

*The first of a famous line of biplane fighters: the Fokker D.I.*

*Britain's Royal Aircraft Factory produced the S.E.5 scout, which proved to be an outstanding combat aeroplane. It was developed into the S.E.5a.*

*Germany's Siemens-Schuckert D.1 shows marked Nieuport influence.*

*Voisin built the wings for the Tellier flying boats, used for sea operations.*

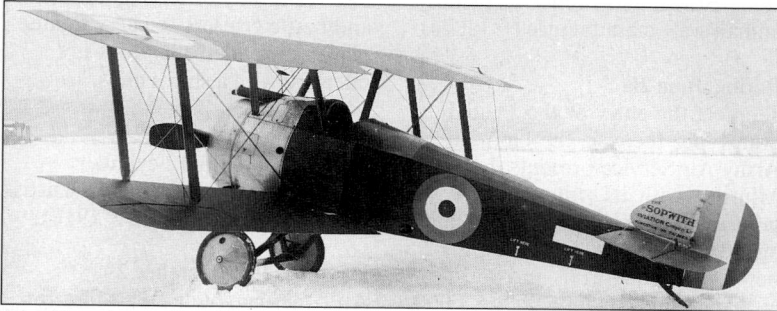

*Matchless in combat but extremely tricky to handle, the Sopwith Camel was named from the hump which covered the butts of the Vickers guns on the nose.*

*A development of the B.E.2 series: the Royal Aircraft Factory's B.E.12.*

*France's Spad VII fighter was also built under license in Britain.*

*Another German Nieuport copy was the Euler D.I; it was not ordered.*

*The ungainly AD Navyplane was designed by the British Admiralty.*

*The Hansa Brandenburg D.I featur-ed a remarkable bracing system.*

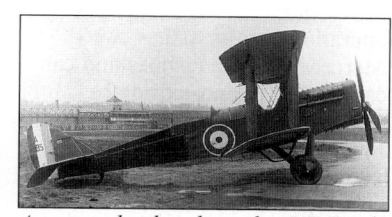

*A great day-bomber: the RFC's de Havilland-designed Airco D.H.4.*

*One of Dornier's first large craft: the Zeppelin-Lindau Rs.II flying boat.*

*Reconnaissance was the allotted task of Germany's successful DFW C.5.*

*Prototype of the famous Felixstowe boats: the Porte-Felixstowe F.1.*

*A smooth semi-monocoque fuselage distinguished the Albatros D.I.*

*A backstaggered fighter – the Airco D.H.5 from Geoffrey de Havilland.*

*An extraordinary experiment: the AD.1000 twin-fuselaged floatplane.*

*Belgium's best fighter, the Hanriot HD.1, as flown by Willy Coppens.*

*The Curtiss H-16 inspired Britain's Felixstowe long-range flying boats.*

*The French-built Breguet 14 recon-naissance and bomber aircraft.*

*Despite its good qualities, the Bristol M.1 monoplane did not find favour.*

*A great single-seater scout, much loved by its pilots: the Sopwith Pup.*

*Avro's first twin was the Pike bomber; the type was not ordered.*

# 1917

 134.54mph
Great Britain
Norman Spratt
RAF SE.4
Jun 1914

 1,180.61 miles
Germany
Werner Landmann
Albatros
Jun 28, 1914

 26,739ft
Germany
Heinrich Oelerich
DFW
Jul 14, 1914

 28,561lb
Germany
Staaken
R.VII

 400hp
USA
Packard & Hall Scott
Liberty

**Washington, DC, January 6**
A report recommends the design and construction of Zeppelin-type airships, to be funded jointly by the US Army and Navy (→ May 30).

**Berlin, January 16**
With 16 air victories to his credit, Baron Manfred von Richthofen is awarded the high German decoration Pour le Mérite [For Merit] (→ Apr 21).

**England, January 24**
N° 35 Squadron, Royal Flying Corps, the first equipped with the Armstrong Whitworth F.K.8 ("Big Ack") two-seat reconnaissance bomber, is posted to France.

**France, February 1**
The German Friedrichshafen G.III heavy bomber arrives at operational units; it has two Mercedes 260-hp engines and can carry 3,300 pounds of bombs.

**London, February 2**
The British cabinet approves a War Office plan to increase the number of RFC service squadrons from 108 to 200 (→ Sep).

**Germany, March 8**
Count von Zeppelin dies.

**London, March 12**
British pilot James McCudden wins the Military Cross (→ May).

**France, March 21**
N° 100 Squadron, Royal Flying Corps, the first British squadron formed specifically for night bombing operations, arrives in the front line, equipped with F.E.2b bombers (→ Apr 6).

**Paris, March 30**
The French aircraft maker Armand Deperdussin is jailed for five years and fined FF1,000 for embezzling FF32,000,000 from his company.

**Washington, DC, April 2**
Congress votes to declare war on Germany. The US Army Signal Corps has 250 aircraft and the US Marine Corps 54 (→ May 24).

**Kent, England, April 6**
Horace Short, 44, eldest of the three brothers who founded the Short aircraft company, dies.

**Western front, April 7**
The Royal Aircraft Factory S.E.5 single-seat fighter enters service with N° 56 Squadron of Britain's Royal Flying Corps.

**Seattle, April 18**
William E Boeing's Pacific Aero Products Company is renamed the Boeing Airplane Company.

**France, April 24**
Lt-Col William "Billy" Mitchell becomes the first US Army officer to fly over German lines (→ Sep 15, 1918).

**France, May 1**
French squadrons receive the first Spad-XIII fighters, a fast aircraft armed with two Vickers machine guns.

**North Sea, May 20**
A Royal Naval Air Service flying boat, commanded by Flight Sub-Lt C R Morrish, sinks the German *U36*, the first submarine sunk by an airplane (→ May 31).

**Paris, May 24**
French premier Alexandre Ribot asks the United States for a total of 5,000 pilots, 4,500 airplanes and 50,000 mechanics (→ Jun 16).

**Akron, Ohio, May 30**
The US Navy's B-1 dirigible arrives after an overnight flight from Chicago.

**France, May 31**
Official figures reveal that Britain's Royal Flying Corps lost 1,270 airplanes between March and May this year.

**London, June 3**
The award is announced of a posthumous Victoria Cross, Britain's highest bravery decoration, to Albert Ball.

**France, June 6**
The French fighter ace Georges Guynemer is admitted to France's prestigious Légion d'Honneur [Legion of Honour].

**USA, June 16**
The first contingent of American aviation personnel (93 civilian mechanics) sails for England to study British and French airplanes and aircraft manufacture (→ Jul 24).

**Berlin, June 26**
To meet the entry of the United States into the war, the German Army Air Service presents the War Ministry with its *Amerika-programm* [America Program], an agenda which includes creating 40 new fighter squadrons and boosting airplane output from 1,000 to 2,000 a month by March 1 next year.

**Germany, June**
The German Zeppelin-Staaken R.VI four-engined bomber enters squadron service.

**Washington, DC, July 24**
Congress approves expenditure of $640 million on military aviation. It is the largest single appropriation approved by Congress (→ Sep 3).

**Washington, DC, July 27**
The navy secretary approves a naval aircraft factory at Philadelphia.

**France, July**
Royal Flying Corps squadrons receive the Sopwith Camel single-seater (→ Jul 19, 1918).

**Australia, August 1**
A naval air fleet is set up.

**France, August 7**
The Morane-Saulnier A.I Parasol fighter airplane makes its first flight.

**France, August 11**
Canadian pilot William Bishop is awarded the Victoria Cross for bravery during a raid on a German aerodrome on June 2.

**England, September**
Special flying schools are set up to teach aerial fighting (→ Oct 17).

**France, October 11**
N° 41 Wing, Royal Flying Corps, is formed under Lt-Colonel C Newall to bomb German industrial targets.

**London, October 17**
The Admiralty orders light cruisers and battle cruisers to carry fighter planes, provided this does not interfere with a ship's guns.

**USA, October 21**
The new 400-hp 12-cylinder Liberty engine is tested on a Curtiss HS-1 seaplane (→ Aug 19, 1918).

**Dayton, Ohio, October 29**
An American-built DH-4 flies for the first time (→ Aug 2, 1918).

**Russia, November 10**
The Bolshevik regime creates the Bureau of Commissars of Aviation and Aeronautics (BKAV).

**New York, November 21**
The US Navy's N-9 flying bomb, built by Curtiss, is tested.

**England, November 30**
The prototype Vickers Vimy bomber makes its first flight.

**Cambrai, France, November**
German *Schlachtstaffeln* [battle squadrons], reorganized from the old *Schutzstaffeln* [escort squadrons], attack Allied trenches for the first time.

**California, December 11**
Katherine Stinson flies 606 miles from San Diego to San Francisco, setting a new American non-stop distance record.

**France, December 23**
British pilot James McCudden makes four "kills" in a day.

*American eagle versus German eagle: youngsters are invited to join the US Army Air Service and fight the enemy in the skies over Europe.* ▶

## French army recalls airships from front

*France, February 24*
The French army today officially stopped using airships on active service. The move follows a decision made last December in the light of much improved German defences and the low operating height of the non-rigids. The only two surviving airships, the *Champagne* and the *D'Arlandes*, are being handed over to the navy for vital anti-submarine work in the Mediterranean theater.

French army airship operations since the start of war have been dogged by losses, punctuated by a few remarkably successful missions. At the outbreak of war only five of 15 airships were operational. The *Fleurus* made the first Allied airship raid on the enemy, on August 9, 1914, and survives as a training ship. Less success attended the *Conté*, *Dupuy-de-Lôme* and *Mont-golfier*, which were hit by French "friendly fire" that month, two of them surviving with major damage.

Others were lost last year, and only yesterday the *Pilâtre de Rozier* was lost when it exploded on a reconnaissance mission. Captain Prêcheur and the rest of the crew all lost their lives in the resulting fireball.

## British night raiders hit Richthofen base

*France, April 6*
Britain's Royal Flying Corps (RFC) carried out two audacious bombing raids last night on the German airfield at Douai, home base of Baron von Richthofen's "Flying Circus" [*see story opposite*]. Four hangars were severely damaged.

The raid was carried out by the RFC's newly-formed bomber squadron, N° 100, which arrived in France from Norfolk, England, in March. It is equipped with 12 F.E.2bs and four B.E.2es. This is the first time the squadron has been on active service, and, although the raid was a success, two of its number did not return.

The raid is part of the process of "softening up" German forces ahead of a spring offensive, but it also marks a new development in RFC doctrine: hit enemy aircraft on the ground, where they are concentrated, rather than fight them piecemeal in the air (→ Apr 30).

*Bombs are checked by Australian airmen in preparation for a night raid.*

## Goering's bravado leads to a lucky escape in cemetery

*The air ace and his Albatros DV.*

*France, February*
Among the German pilots who have made a name for themselves one, Leutnant Hermann Goering, is particularly renowned for his almost reckless single-mindedness. He recently spent several months recovering from wounds following a typical action in which he chased and shot down a British bomber – and only then noticed 20 Sopwiths on his tail. Pilot and machine were soon bullet-riddled and forced into a dive; he landed in a cemetery, saved only because his pursuers had got in each other's way as they moved in for the kill (→ Jun 2, 1918).

## Germans inflict huge losses on Allied air forces in 'Bloody April'

*German onlookers surround a British airman who has been shot down.*

*France, April 30*
German air ace Baron Manfred von Richthofen went on furlough today to celebrate 52 air victories, many of them achieved this month, which British pilots are already calling "Bloody April". For their renewed offensive on the Somme, the British Royal Flying Corps (RFC) had 754 airplanes against the Germans' 264. But this roughly three-to-one superiority has been matched by a similar loss rate: since April 9 the RFC has lost 316 aircrew and the Germans 119. RFC pilots with ten hours' flying experience survive on average for just 17 hours in the air when they go into action.

The new German Albatros and Halberstadt machines outfly less powerful Allied airplanes like the Nieuport. On April 16, for example, six Nieuports met four Albatroses over the front; only two Nieuports survived (→ May 20).

**Beyond the call of duty: an artist's view of Royal Flying Corps pilot Thomas Mottershead landing his F.E.2d after being attacked; his observer survived, but he himself burned to death.**

# 'Red Baron' lets loose lethal 'circus'

*Douai, France, April*

German air ace Manfred von Richthofen has created a formidable weapon to pitch against the Allies fighting on the Somme. He has gathered an élite group of fighter pilots in single-seater Albatros machines better armed than any other force. They fly in formations of 30 or more. The core of this group, which has been dubbed "the Flying Circus", is the baron's own 11-strong Jagdstaffel or Jasta [fighter squadron] 11.

Richthofen, defying modern military convention, encourages his men to paint their machines in bright colors, almost like the shields of medieval knights. His is bright red, hence his nickname: "the Red Baron". Both the British and the French have tried for a year to combat German air superiority, with generally unsuccessful results. Richthofen's men fly as hunters and attack less capable aircraft, but dogfights can still last an hour and involve a hundred airplanes.

*Richthofen, in the cockpit, with other pilots of his famous squadron.*

## British bomber set to become fastest aircraft in the sky

*Valenciennes, France, March 6*

The first examples of a powerful new bomber were delivered here today to N° 55 Squadron of the Royal Flying Corps. The Airco (de Havilland) D.H.4 has a combination of qualities that makes it unique.

The D.H.4 is, in appearance, a conventional tractor biplane, with the pilot in front and observer (with Lewis gun) behind the main fuel tank. What makes it so exceptional

*A machine-gun post in a D.H.4.*

# German ace develops new tactics for massed flights of fighters

*Douai, France, April 30*

To ensure a "kill" French and British aces prefer to fire at near point-blank range, because their ammunition drums are limited to only 47 or 97 rounds. German airmen have more freedom owing to synchronized belt-fed twin machine guns, capable of letting off 1,000 rounds before being reloaded.

This freedom is leading pilots like von Richthofen to evolve new combat rules: shoot without being shot at; use superior speed and agility to present the smallest target; hit from above and behind without warning. Von Richthofen's motto: "Go for the kill: keep shooting."

*Deadly tactic: a German fighter swoops on a British airplane out of the Sun.*

are its very powerful engine (a 230-hp BHP, 250-hp Rolls-Royce or other types) and its superb handling. Even when laden with two 230-pound and four 110-pound bombs it can outdistance enemy fighters. In the future it is hoped that the Rolls-Royce engine will produce over 350-hp, enabling the D.H.4 to reach speeds as high as 134mph. This will make the fastest aircraft in any air force.

Already the D.H.4 is in large-scale production for Britain's Royal Flying Corps and Royal Naval Air Service. It will be used for daylight bombing, reconnaissance and submarine hunting (→ Oct 29).

# Daylight raid hits English coast towns

*Kent, England, May 25*

German Gotha heavy bombers under Captain Brandenburg today made mass-formation attacks on targets in England. Folkestone, on the coast near Dover, bore the brunt of the bombing, with Lympne airfield and the Shorncliffe army camp also taking hits. Ninety-five died and 195 were injured, and damage is put at £19,000.

The 21 aircraft were reportedly heading for London, but poor weather obscured the city. The raiders were spotted by the Tongue lightship at 4.45pm. British aircraft flew 77 defense sorties, but without success (→ Jun 13).

# Air spotters guide guns in key ridge battle

*Ypres, Belgium, June 14*

Messines Ridge, the natural fortress from which German commanders watched every Allied move on the Flanders plain, is in British hands today as a result of two lines of attack. One was a series of 20 tunnels started five months ago to put 400 tons of high explosive under enemy lines, 18 of which blew up to devastating effect.

The other was intensive air-directed artillery bombardment. In order to gain the air superiority necessary for this, formations of Royal Flying Corps Sopwith triplanes took on Albatros fighters before the battle (→ Jun 17).

# British air ace assumed dead after mystery crash

## Hero goes missing over German lines

*Vert Galand, France, May 7*
Six S.E.5 single-seater fighters of N° 56 Squadron of Britain's Royal Flying Corps (RFC) are missing tonight from a force of 11 which left on attack patrols round Arras. The top RFC ace, the much-decorated Captain Albert Ball, is among those who have failed to return.

As midnight approaches, his men are reassuring one another he has been forced to land and is a prisoner. He was last seen at dusk by Captain C M Crowe, as Ball and a red Albatros from Richthofen's "Flying Circus" disappeared into a cloud, still dogfighting.

Today the Germans outflew the S.E.5s, whose problems were compounded by engine trouble and jammed guns. Ball's Vickers gun, firing through the propeller, stopped during his first attack on a pair of Germans and he had to fire the wing-mounted Lewis gun instead. He broke off a second attack for the same reason. At dusk, near Loos, he pounced on his red opponent, but then vanished (→ May 8).

*Ball leaves London for what was to be his last tour of duty in France.*

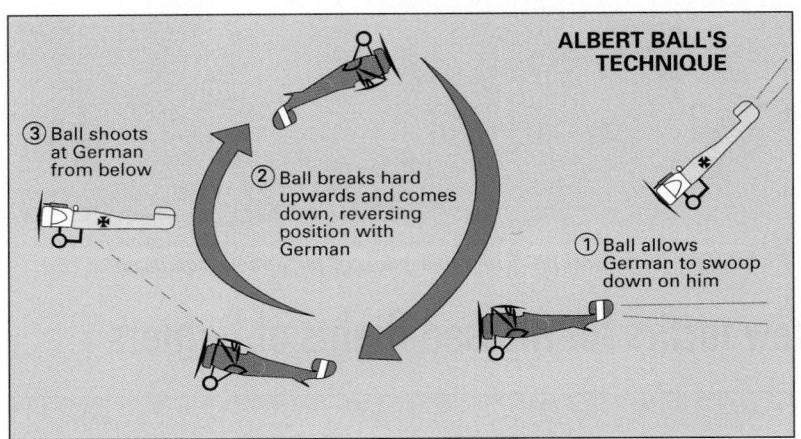

**ALBERT BALL'S TECHNIQUE**

③ Ball shoots at German from below

② Ball breaks hard upwards and comes down, reversing position with German

① Ball allows German to swoop down on him

## Ball 'plummeted to earth after a fight'

*Arras, France, May 8*
The death of Albert Ball, whom the Germans called "the English [Manfred von] Richthofen", has been unofficially confirmed by French eye-witnesses. After winning a duel with Lothar von Richthofen, Manfred's brother, Ball's S.E.5 apparently emerged from low cloud, upside-down, and dived into the ground. No more is known.

Ball inspired a generation of Royal Flying Corps pilots, including McCudden and Mannock. His airmanship was breathtaking. One technique was to expose his back to the enemy, relying on a mirror and judgement to dive at the moment the attacker was about to fire. This put him in his favorite position, below his opponent, to shoot upward. He liked flying at an opponent head on, confident that the other flyer would swerve to give way, exposing his underside to lethal burst of fire. Ball was renowned for diving alone into enemy flights, scattering them like startled pigeons, oblivious of his own safety (→ Jun 3).

# Fighter pilots working under terrible strain on the front line

*France, May*
After almost three years of warfare, the stress of unremitting combat is affecting even the most resilient pilots on both sides. Baron Manfred von Richthofen himself is not immune. Germans now captive have heard him say: "I am in wretched spirits after every battle. When I set foot on the ground I go to my quarters. I do not want to see anyone."

The horrors of warfare are taking their toll. A rising star of Britain's Royal Flying Corps (RFC), Major James McCudden, after watching an opponent burned alive, says in disgust: "We are nothing but hired assassins." His friend, Edward "Mick" Mannock, who thinks that the only good Germans are dead Germans, weeps for killed comrades in his quarters, crying their names, and carries a pistol to shoot himself with rather than perish in the flames of a burning aircraft.

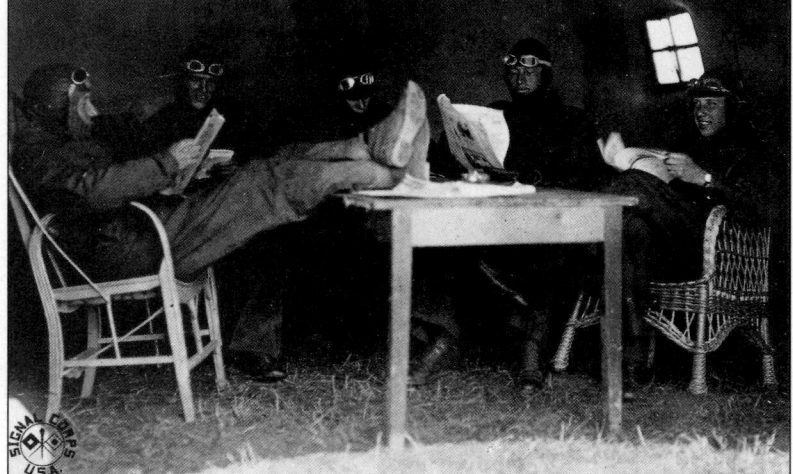

*American airmen relax in full flying gear, ready and waiting for the call.*

The RFC does not issue parachutes, nor does it plan to. Most RFC fighter pilots, young men of 19 and 20, dispel the fear when on the ground with mess "rags", indoor games of rugby, drink and noise. Others sleep when not flying and have nightmares about fire. Daily life in the cockpit starts at 4.30am (→ Sep 30).

## Ground broken for air research center

*Hampton, Va, July 17*
Ground was broken here today for the first building of the National Advisory Committee for Aeronautics (NACA) Langley Field laboratory. This is a big day for NACA, which was created by the US Congress two years ago "for the supervision and direction of scientific study of the problems of flight, with a view to their practical solution" and to "conduct research and experiment in aeronautics".

It is significant that work on the facility, which was going to be a joint project with the US Army Air Service, is continuing. The army, now fully occupied with the war, has abandoned plans – also authorized by Congress – to house at Langley Field its own specialized experimental installation, test-beds and airfield.

# Canadian air ace makes valiant attack

*France, June 2*
At 3am today Canadian William "Billy" Bishop, who has been flying Nieuport scouts with N° 60 Squadron, Royal Flying Corps, since March, got out of bed and prepared for an escapade he has planned for weeks. Taking off before dawn, he flew very low to a German aerodrome near Cambrai. His objective: to attack enemy aircraft as they took off to engage him.

Attacking alone, he weathered a storm of fire from every machine gun and rifle on the base. Soon, single-seat German scouts were being readied, and as the first one took off, Bishop shot it down. He did the same with the second, though this time he was forced to open fire from long range. Then two Germans, realizing his game, took off together, on diverging courses. He shot one down, but was attacked by the other. Bishop had no bullets left, but the second German did not press home his advantage and he escaped (→ Aug 11).

*Bishop's Nieuport 17 in action: giving chase to a German ace in an Albatros.*

# Old airplane packs punch and more power

*The F.E.2b pusher biplane: a versatile, hard-working and effective machine.*

*Suffolk, England, June 17*
In the small hours of this morning an F.E.2b of Britain's Royal Flying Corps shot down the German Zeppelin LZ 28. The "kill" underscores the value of the 1,939 machines of this type in service.

The F.E.2b is an improved version of the F.E.2a of August 1913, a 250-hp Rolls-Royce engine turning an indifferent machine into a useful night fighter/bomber, able to carry three 112-pound bombs. The squadrons of F.E aircraft have tried many ways of arming the machines, in one case having two Lewis guns aligned with a searchlight for night attacks (→ Oct 11).

# Allies to train and equip American flyers

*Le Havre, France, September 3*
The US Army's First Aero Squadron arrived here today – without airplanes. Ironically, the nation which invented the airplane will rely on its British, French and Italian allies for combat training and modern aircraft. Initial training for the newly-arrived squadron will take place at Avord.

The squadron comes from Columbus, New Mexico, where it served in action against Pancho Villa [*see page 137*]. It sailed from New York on the SS *Lapland* on August 13 (→ Feb 5, 1918).

# War clips wings of stuntman Cessna

*Kansas State, September 5*
Record-breaking stunt flyer Clyde Cessna has had his wings clipped by wartime prohibitions on flying. The 37-year-old airman is leaving the Jones motor company in Wichita for his farm in Rago.

Cessna started building and flying stunt planes because the money – up to $1,500 or more per performance – was more than he earned from farming. Not flying will make quite a dent in his pocket-book. He expected to do very well this year, especially after setting a new American speed record on July 5 in the Comet, an airplane he designed and built. Cessna flew the 76 miles from Blackwell to Wichita in 36 minutes and 35 seconds, at a speed of 124.5mph. He expected to put on 60 exhibitions this year.

# Deadly raid by German airplanes catches London unawares

*Huge German Gotha bombers, armed with several Parabellum machine guns each, line up ready for take-off.*

*London, June 13*
Last year's successes against German airships sent to bomb London [*see page 140*] lulled the city's defenses into a false sense of security. Today 162 civilians, including 18 children in a school, paid for this complacency with their lives and a further 432 were injured in a daylight raid by heavy airplanes.

Fourteen Gotha G.IV bombers, from the new *England Geschwader* [England Squadron], flying from Belgium, reached London unopposed. They bombed the area around Liverpool Street railroad station and public buildings, including the Royal Mint. The raid has sparked urgent calls for squadrons to be released from France to defend the capital (→ Sep 17).

# Triumph and tragedy as airmen show off skills

## Slow starter wins prestigious valor award

*Mannock: dressed warmly to kill.*

*Western front, July 20*
Edward "Mick" Mannock received one of Britain's top bravery decorations today, after shooting down two more Germans. Mannock, who has been awarded the Military Cross, started as a fighter pilot in April, but failed to "score". His furious commanding officer even thought he might have "cold feet".

Mannock is not typical of a Royal Flying Corps officer. A socialist, he was working as a telegraph repair man in Turkey when war broke out. He was interned there until April 1915. His first "kill" came last month. Gunnery practice and study of German tactics have now paid off (→ Jul 26).

## French ace is lost on frontier patrol

*Belgium, September 11*
French ace Georges Guynemer, with 54 victories to his credit, has disappeared on a sortie over Poelcapelle in Belgium. Guynemer's success had become an obsession in recent months; he pushed himself almost to physical breaking point and was prone to fits of anger, depression – and carelessness.

This morning he attacked a German two-seater but missed on the first pass. He flew into cloud and has not been seen since. His colleagues fear the worst.

*Guynemer in his Spad XIII fighter.*

## German hero killed in dramatic air clash

*Ypres, Belgium, September 23*
Germany is mourning the loss of one of its bravest and most gallant "knights of the air". Leutnant Werner Voss, credited with 48 victories, decorated by Kaiser Wilhelm and fêted by the people, was killed this morning after taking on, single-handedly, eight S.E.5a fighter bombers of the Royal Flying Corps (RFC). These were protected by fighters of N° 56 Squadron, RFC, making the ace's solo onslaught all the more perilous.

Voss was alone, flying a Fokker Dr.I triplane, decorated in his personal colors of black and white, when he came upon the British formation over the lines. He attacked at once, and used every trick of his legendary aerobatic skill to keep at bay such opponents as McCudden, Bowman, Rhys-Davis and Maxwell. He fought for eight desperate minutes, twisting and turning, scoring hits on most of the British formation. Then, seeing some compatriots looking for him, he broke off to lead them into the fray. But they turned tail at the sight of a massed enemy and he fought on alone. In the end numbers told. McCudden or Rhys-Davis fired a final fatal burst and Voss's machine crashed into no-man's-land.

## Navy pilot dies during deck-landing trials

*Crewmen rush to stop Dunning's Sopwith Pup toppling over the side.*

*Scotland, August 7*
Flight experiments on board HMS *Furious*, the Royal Navy cruiser which has been converted to carry aircraft by the addition of two flight decks, resulted in tragedy today. The ship's senior flying officer, Squadron Commander E H Dunning, was killed while trying to land his Sopwith Pup on the forward flight deck.

Although taking off from a ship has been achieved with some success, landing on one is more difficult, involving approaching the moving ship from behind to exploit the headwinds and then slipping in front of the bridge. Five days ago Dunning landed with the help of other pilots on deck, who grabbed rope toggles on the wings and pulled him down as he cut the engine.

Today he carried out one unassisted landing, but during an attempt to repeat the experiment the Pup had engine problems, stalling and cartwheeling overboard after a tire blew. Dunning drowned before the *Furious* could launch a rescue boat (→ Oct 17).

## British airmen match for Richthofen men

*Belgium, September 30*
Pilots of N° 56 Squadron of Britain's Royal Flying Corps have scored their 200th kill since arriving in France on April 22. Unlike the Germans, who handpick their élite squadrons, the British mix aces and novices and spread the expertise. It was by chance that B Flight of N° 56 Squadron was commanded by the legendary Albert Ball and acquired six airmen who shot down 170 Germans in four months, during which time they were opposed by Richthofen's "Circus".

The team's morale was undaunted by the disasters of "Bloody April". It scored 11 kills on August 22 and began to draw the best pilots. Major James McCudden, Ball's successor, decided to get into the squadron "under any pretense". The men of N° 56 Squadron feel much for their warrior adversaries. When German ace Werner Voss went down after taking on N° 56 Squadron alone [*see story alongside*], Lieutenant Rhys-Davis said afterwards: "If I could only have brought him down alive!" That night the British pilots drank a toast to "Von Richthofen!".

The flight has since received Britain's highest award for bravery, the Victoria Cross (VC), posthumously awarded to Albert Ball, killed on May 7. Rhys-Davis has been awarded the Distinguished Service Order, second only to the VC, while Lt G H Bowman has received the next highest award, the Military Cross, for a second time (→ Dec 23).

# Germans introduce gigantic bombers against London

*London, September 17*

Raids on London by Germany's *England Geschwader* [England Squadron] tonight included a massive new aircraft, known as the *Riesen* [giant]. This airplane, the Zeppelin Staaken R.VI, is the largest heavier-than-air machine in the world.

A 75-foot long biplane with a 141-foot wingspan, it is powered by four 260-hp Mercedes or Maybach engines in two nacelles between the wings. These permit an engineer to stay with, and even repair, the engines in flight. The crew includes front and rear gunners, wireless operator, two pilots, two engineers and commander. The pilots have night flying instruments, including an "artificial horizon", and the machine can carry 18 661-pound bombs and nearly 800 gallons of fuel (→Apr 12, 1918).

# Seaplanes help to battle submarines

*The giant Zeppelin-Lindau Dornier Rs III, a seaplane with a single, central float and four engines.*

*Seemoos, Germany, November 4*

One of the largest airplanes in the world made its maiden flight today: the Zeppelin-Lindau Rs III. The third of a series of giant flying boats masterminded by 33-year-old designer Claude Dornier, it is yet another example of the rapid progress which war has brought to aircraft construction – in this case the move from materials such as wood, wire and fabric to metal. Wherever possible, steel and aluminum have been used according to the stresses which each part will have to take.

The Rs III will need to be tough. It will serve with the German navy in the Baltic and North Seas on long-range reconnaissance and anti-submarine patrols which could last for up to 12 hours in severe weather and rough seas. Its four 250-hp Maybach MbIVa engines are arranged in push/pull pairs on struts and can be serviced during flight. There is a gunner's position in the nose, another on top of the fuselage and room to carry bombs, mines and depth charges.

# RFC bombers lead the attack at Cambrai

*This biplane is one of many aircraft that fell victim to the Allied onslaught.*

*France, November 23*

British aircraft startled German troops today when they flew just a few feet above the Cambrai battlefield to clear the way for an Allied advance by tanks and infantry. One pilot who cut through the dense mist and smoke recalled "ludicrous expressions of amazement on the upturned faces of German troops as we passed a few feet above their trenches". With German airmen grounded by fog and totally outnumbered, D.H.5s of N° 64 Squadron of Britain's Royal Flying Corps (RFC), whose members have practiced low flying in England, provoked panic with their concerted attack on the German lines. By 10.30am only two outposts were holding out, bombed and raked with gunfire by D.H.5s as Camels of N° 3 Squadron, RFC, hit German airfields. A forward airfield for the air force has been created at Bapaume (→Apr 19, 1918).

# Air-to-air radio is tested by US Army

*Langley Field, Va, October 16*

Excellent results have been achieved during the final testing of the US Army's new standard design of airborne wireless set. In experiments between two airplanes in flight, good reception was achieved over a distance of 25 miles. In air-to-ground transmissions, wireless signals were heard over as much as 45 miles.

The US Army began testing aerial wireless equipment as early as January 1912, though the first such experiments were made in 1908 by Captain Lefroy of the British Royal Engineers, with a balloon. By 1912 many tests had been made with airplanes and airships with increasing success.

The most common use of wireless in aircraft is to communicate with friendly artillery, on land or sea, and to report on the enemy's activities. Now secret experiments are in hand in which wireless signals are used to steer "flying bombs", pilotless aircraft carrying explosives. Such signals could also be used to guide pilotless aircraft for target practise.

# Autonomous British air force proposed

*London, October 17*

A secret report which could have far-reaching consequences was presented to the British war cabinet today by General Jan Smuts, military chief of the British Union of South Africa. The report recommends that an autonomous air force, quite separate from the army and the navy, should be created.

Smuts was given the task of preparing a response to the recent raids on civilian targets by German bombers which have caused outrage and demands for revenge. The German objective is to divert British fighters from France to defend London, but Smuts argues that Britain should take the offensive.

He recommends attacking German cities and says that strategic bombing will be an essential part of warfare: "The day may not be far off when aerial operations, with their destruction of industrial and population centres ... may become the principal operations of war, to which the older forms of military and naval operations may become subordinate" (→Jan 2, 1918).

Fokker's Dr.I triplane fighter was directly inspired by Sopwith's similar, but less compact, design. It proved to be one of the best fighters of the war.

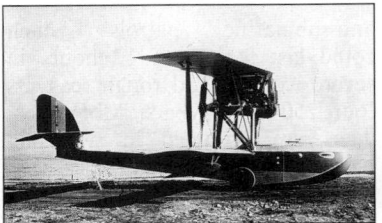

Macchi's M.7ter fighter flying boat.

The Siemens-Schuckert Dr.I triplane.

The Pfalz D.III was one of Germany's best fighters and featured a monocoque fuselage. A 160-hp Mercedes provided the power. Some 600 were built.

The Spad XIII displays its classic lines: the single-bay bracing with intermediate struts which was a unique characteristic of this widely-used fighter.

The last Nieuport fighter to see combat was the Nieuport 28, which was rejected by the French but supplied to United States Army Air Service units.

DFW's D.1 remained an experimental machine and did not see service.

There were no orders for the Labourdette-Halbronn flying boat.

The Italian SIA.7B two-seater fighter was fast and maneuverable.

The Gotha G.IV bomber cast its threatening shadow over England.

Italy's fast Ansaldo SVA.5 single-seater fighter had elegant lines.

The Ansaldo A.1 Balilla was found to be unsuitable for front-line work.

Fairey's N.10 floatplane presaged the celebrated Fairey III series.

Too late into service to take part in the war, the Vickers Vimy bomber left its mark in history when it was used for the first non-stop transatlantic flight.

From the Royal Aircraft Factory's S.E.5 was developed the S.E.5a, the mount of famous British fighter aces such as Mannock and McCudden.

Parnall's Panther fighter had a folding rear fuselage for carrier stowage.

Fairey's first own design was the F.2 twin-engined fighter; one was built.

The heavily armored Junkers J I was designed to fly contact patrols.

Fairey's Campania floatplane made reconnaissance flights from carriers.

Another backstaggered biplane – the beefy Sopwith Dolphin fighter.

The French Georges Lévy HB.2 flying boat was used for coastal patrol.

LVG C.V: a classic, widely-used two-seater reconnaissance aircraft.

The Salmson 2A2, used by France and the USA for reconnaissance.

Italy's SIA.9b served in the reconnaissance role on the Austrian front.

The French Morane-Saulnier A.I was a parasol-winged fighting scout.

Dornier's gigantic Rs.III hydroplane had four engines in tandem pairs.

The Curtiss HS-2 was a development of the H-16. It was powered by a single pusher engine in mid-span.

The Donnet-Denhaut DD.8 anti-sub flying boat: over 500 were built.

The prototype Felixstowe F.3 flying boat led to a successful series.

The Pfalz D.XII single-seal fighter reached the Front in autumn 1918.

Inelegant and ungainly: the Sopwith Rhino triplane was not ordered.

Fokker's V.VIII quintuplane made two short hops, then was scrapped.

Sopwith's Snipe fighter became a postwar stalwart of the Royal Air Force in the 1920s. It was powered by the 230-hp Bentley B.R.2 rotary engine.

De Havilland's Airco D.H.9 two-seater day-bomber was built in quantity despite its troublesome 230-hp BHP engine. It could carry two 230-lb bombs.

# 1918

163.06mph
USA
Roland Rohlfs
Curtiss Wasp
Aug 19, 1918

1,180.61 miles
Germany
Werner Landmann
Albatros
Jun 28, 1914

28,897ft
USA
Rudolph Schroeder
Bristol F.2B
Nov 18, 1918

35,053lb
Germany
Staaken
R.XIVa

700hp
Italy
Fiat
A.14

**London, January 2**
The government establishes an air ministry. Lord Rothermere is secretary of state for air; Major-General Sir Hugh Trenchard is Chief of the Air Staff (→ Apr 1).

**France, January 10**
The French "Escadrille Lafayette" [Lafayette Squadron] for American volunteers is dissolved; members join the US Army Air Service.

**France, February 2**
The first operational squadrons of the American Expeditionary Force are formed (→ May 29).

**Germany, February 5**
Stephen W Thompson, of the US Army First Aero Squadron, becomes the first US Army flyer to record a victory over a German airplane when he downs an Albatros (→ Apr 12).

**Germany, March 10**
The German Junkers J9 all-metal prototype cantilever monoplane makes its first flight.

**France, March 15**
US Army pilots fly their first patrol of the war, in Nieuport 28s; their mission is to keep German photographic aircraft away from the river Marne.

**North Sea, March 19**
Ensign Stephen Potter becomes the first US Navy airman to shoot down a German aircraft, while on patrol near Heligoland.

**London, April 2**
Major James McCudden of the Royal Flying Corps is awarded the Victoria Cross, Britain's highest decoration for valor (→ Jul 9).

**France, April 12**
The US Army First Aero Squadron is moved forward to be stationed at the front (→ May 18).

**California, April 12**
The Loughead brothers fly their seaplane, the F-1, from Santa Barbara to San Diego.

**London, April 13**
Trenchard's resignation as Britain's Chief of the Air Staff is accepted; he is going because of a personality clash with air secretary Lord Rothermere (→ Apr 25).

**London, April 25**
In the wake of Trenchard's departure, air secretary Lord Rothermere resigns.

**USA, May 15**
The US Army Signal Corps' inaugural airmail flight from Washington, DC, to New York fails; the pilot ends up in a Maryland field with a broken propeller. →

**France, May 18**
The American 96th Aero Bomber Squadron is formed at Amanty (→ May 31, 1918).

**Russia, May 24**
The Chief Directorate of the Workers' and Peasants' Military Air Fleet is established, replacing the all-Russian Air Board (→ Dec 1).

**France, May 29**
Brigadier-General Mason Patrick is appointed Chief of Air Service, American Expeditionary Force.

**London, May 30**
Passenger aviation pioneer George Holt Thomas claims a passenger service between London and Paris could be run for fares as low as £5 one way, given 40 passengers a day.

**France, May 31**
First-Lt Douglas Campbell shoots down his fifth German airplane to become the US Army's first ace (→ Jun 12).

**Germany, June 2**
Hermann Goering is awarded the decoration Pour le Mérite [For Merit] (→ Jul 7).

**France, June 12**
Eight Breguet 14s of 96th Aero Squadron bomb railyards at Dommary-Baroncourt in a day attack, the first raid of the war by US Army bombers (→ Sep 25).

**Paris, June 24**
Aircraft designer Igor Sikorsky, in flight from the Russian Revolution, offers his services to the French government (→ Mar 24, 1919).

**France, July 9**
On the day that he is appointed commander of Nº 60 Squadron, Royal Air Force, Major James McCudden dies when his S.E.5a crashes on take-off at Auxi-le-Château, near Amiens.

**France, August 2**
The first American-built Airco (de Havilland) D.H.4s go into operational service, flying an observation patrol from Ourches with the US 135th Corps Observation Squadron.

**Western front, August 7**
The Fokker E.V parasol-winged fighter goes into service with the top Jagdgeschwader [Fighter Squadron] 1.

**Cairo, August 8**
Major A S MacLaren and Brigadier-General A E Borton land their Handley Page O/400 bomber after a 12-day flight from England (→ Oct 22).

**Europe, August 10**
German fighter pilot Erich Löwenhardt, with 53 victories, is killed in a mid-air crash with another German pilot.

**North Sea, August 11**
US-born Royal Navy pilot Stuart Culley shoots down Zeppelin L 53 after taking off from a towed barge in his Sopwith Camel (→ Oct 19).

**USA, August 12**
The Post Office takes over airmail services from the army; military pilots have flown 270 flights and carried 40,500 pounds of mail.

**Los Angeles, August 17**
The Martin MB-1 bomber, designed by Donald Douglas and built by Glenn Martin, makes its first flight.

**Long Island, NY, August 19**
The first US-designed and -built fighter, the Curtiss 18-T or Kirkham triplane, is tested at Garden City; it reaches 162mph (→ Nov 27).

**Western front, September 24**
US Navy pilot David S Ingalls shoots down his fifth victim, thus becoming the US Navy's first ace.

**Ardennes, France, October 5**
French aviator Roland Garros, who escaped and returned to his unit, is killed when his Spad XIII breaks up during aerial combat.

**England, October 19**
Sopwith Cuckoo torpedo-carrying airplanes are embarked on HMS *Argus*, which has been converted from the Italian liner *Conte Rosso* into an aircraft carrier; she is fitted with a single flight deck 567 feet long (→ Nov 6).

**France, October 26**
The inter-Allied Independent Air Force is created. Marshal Foch of France is supreme commander; Britain's Major-General Sir Hugh Trenchard is commander-in-chief.

**England, November 6**
Lieutenant R E Keys pilots a Sopwith Camel in an experiment in which it is released from beneath the R23 airship at 3,000 feet.

**Compiègne, France, November 11**
The Armistice is signed at 11am.

**New York, December 17**
The Aero Club of America lifts its ban on flying over cities, and, from now on, pilots certificated as "expert" aviators will be permitted to fly over populated areas; Post Office pilots have been doing this since August.

*An illustration from the "Sphere" shows British flyers bombing and strafing German trenches, with the resulting effect on enemy morale.* ▶

# Royal Air Force is created in Britain

## Bombing force is formed to attack enemy industry

*London, April 1*

Britain took an historic step in the organization of its armed services today, becoming the first country in the world to formally acknowledge not only that a new dimension – the air – has been added to warfare but also that to fight in it a completely new armed force is needed. The Royal Air Force, which was born today, will be formed out of the army's Royal Flying Corps and the Royal Naval Air Service, but the RAF should quickly become independent of its parent services. It will ultimately have its own ministry, its own distinctive uniform and rank structure.

But the most significant thing about the RAF will be its new strategic role. While most of its 86 squadrons will continue to provide air support for the army and navy, ten have been designated "long-range". Their role will be a new one: to carry the war into the German homeland by bombing its industry and its cities.

An autonomous air force, given that specific task, was recommended by South African military chief General Smuts last year. It has political as well as military objectives, being partly a response to the public outcry for retaliation for German bombing raids on British cities, especially London.

The choice of All Fools' Day for the inauguration of the new service is seen as a wry joke in Whitehall. It reflects the widely felt hostility among the generals and admirals about the formation of the RAF. They want aircraft supporting their operations to be under their direct control (→ Apr 13).

*Members of № 1 Squadron, Royal Air Force, pose with their S.E.5a aircraft.*

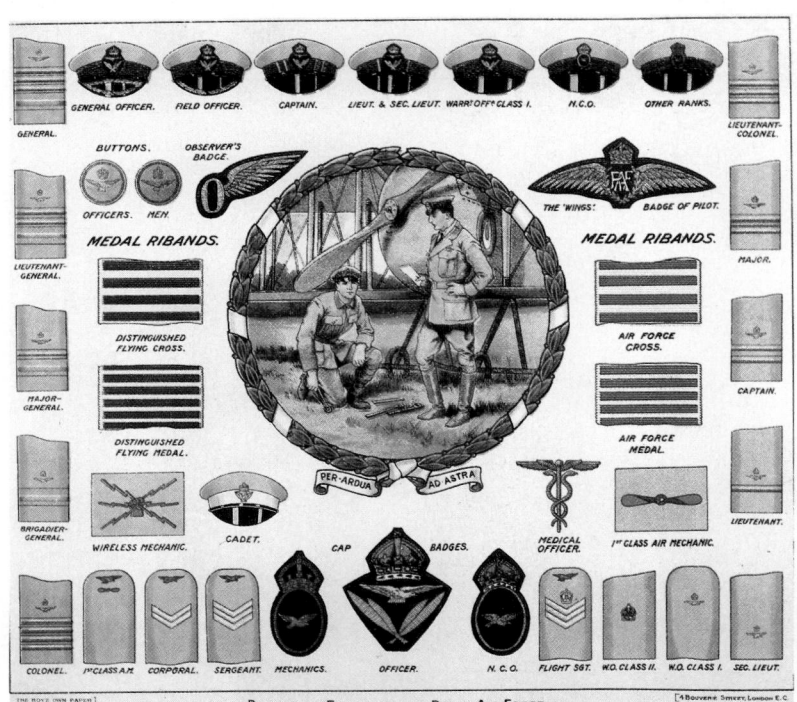

*Britain's "Boy's Own Paper" shows all the insignia of the new organization.*

*France, June 5*

There was another move in the debate over the proper use of air power today when the Independent Air Force was formed to carry the war to German cities. The IAF, under the command of Britain's former Chief of Air Staff Major-General Sir Hugh Trenchard, will operate from France, which is closer to its targets. This use of scarce bombers irks many generals, who want aircraft used only in direct support of operations on the front. But the air power theorists appear to have the upper hand, and the IAF will soon get longer-range aircraft, including the Handley Page O/400, which can carry a 1,650-pound bomb (→ Oct 26).

*Trenchard in ceremonial uniform.*

## Argentinian pilot flies over the Andes

*Argentina, April 13*

Teniente Luis C Candelaria of the Argentinian army today successfully undertook the first flight by airplane over the Andes. This spectacular feat opens up the possibility of an aerial link between on the Atlantic and Pacific coasts of the continent, hitherto separated by an impenetrable mountain range.

Flying east to west, Candelaria took off from Zapala in Argentina and landed at Cunçco in Chile, a journey of about 120 miles. He had to reach a height of 13,000 feet to clear the greatest peaks. His airplane for the flight was a Morane-Saulnier Parasol monoplane with an 80-hp Gnôme engine. The Morane is the standard advanced trainer of the Argentinian army, built by local craftsmen with only the engine imported.

Candelaria learned to fly in 1916 at Argentina's Escuola Militar de Aviacion at El Palomar.

## RFC bombers fly in to hit rebel tribesmen

*Kahan, April 19*

British airmen have played a key role in pacifying a two-month uprising in Baluchistan, India, by Marri and Khetran tribesmen. Kahan, the Baluchistani capital, is today occupied by British forces and the rebel leaders have surrendered unconditionally.

Trouble began on February 19 and 20, when Marri warriors attacked Gumbay fort. The Khetran people joined the uprising, and on March 7 colonial government buildings at Barkhan were burned and the treasury looted. A British punitive expedition was mustered, involving seven B.E.2cs of the Royal Flying Corps (RFC), but sorties were initially postponed due to severe dust storms. From March 24, Kahan was bombed daily. The first raid killed 14 armed tribesmen, and a week later the Khetran had had enough, leaving the Marri to fight on alone.

# 'Red Baron' is shot dead

*An artist's impression of the Red Baron's last pursuit by Captain Brown.*

**Le Hamel, France, April 21**

Airmen on both sides are stunned tonight at the loss of Baron Manfred von Richthofen, the greatest air ace of them all. A lively debate has already begun over who fired the bullet which killed the German aviator as he harried what would have been his 81st victim.

The end of the nobleman known from the color of his Fokker triplane as the "Red Baron" came over the Somme when 25 German Fokker and Albatros fighters met 15 Sopwith Camels of 209 Squadron, Royal Air Force (RAF). One flight leader, Canadian Captain Roy Brown, told Lieutenant Wilfred May, a schoolfriend and novice flyer, just to watch. As the fight heated up, however, May dived on a Fokker. Then his guns jammed.

As bullets struck his machine May fled, but to no avail, for he had picked a fight with Richthofen himself. May tried hedgehopping at ground level, but the red triplane stayed with him, its fire damaging

*Allies bury him with due ceremony.*

his machine and wounding him in the right arm. Brown dived, guns blazing, to aid his friend at the same time as Australian troops on the ground began shooting at the baron's airplane. Richthofen stood to check his tail, but seconds later his machine crashed into the ground. One bullet – Australian or Canadian? – had hit him in the heart.

# Canadian climbs on wing to save plane

**France, March 27**

For six days the Allies have reeled under a huge German offensive in Picardy which has already seen the fall of Arras, St Quentin and Laon and has driven a wedge between the British and French armies. The gap is being plugged by Allied fighters and bombers in one of the most crucial roles yet assigned to military aircraft.

One pilot, 2nd Lieutenant Alan McLeod, a Canadian with Nº 2 Squadron, Royal Flying Corps, was on a ground attack mission flying an Armstrong Whitworth today when eight German triplanes dived at him from 5,000 feet. By skillful maneuvering he enabled his observer to down three planes, by which time both men were wounded and the aircraft was on fire. McLeod climbed onto the lower port wing and managed to control the machine so that the flames kept on one side, allowing the observer to keep shooting while he brought the aircraft down in no-man's-land. McLeod was again hurt by a bomb while dragging his comrade to safety under fire; he is to be recommended for the Victoria Cross, Britain's highest decoration.

# German squadron is routed at sea

**England, June 4**

A unique naval battle between British flying boats and German seaplanes took place today in the North Sea, not far from the scene of the Battle of Jutland in 1916. One of five Royal Naval Air Service Felixstowe F.2.As, patrolling under the command of Captain Robert Leckie, suffered fuel failure and was forced to land on the water. Fifteen German seaplanes, looking for easy pickings, pounced on the lame duck but were surprised by the British, who turned and charged their formation head on.

In the ensuing mêlée the ponderous 5.5-ton Felixstowes were "handled like single-seat scouts", according to one witness. The British squadron sank two Germans and disabled four more, with no loss to itself.

# Paris feels force of Gotha bombing

*Young man sounds air raid siren.*

**Paris, April 12**

Parisians are living in fear following a day and night of bombing by Gotha biplanes, the twin-engined heavy German machines which are proving to be the most formidable bombers of the war. Five bombs were dropped yesterday, one of which hit a hospital and killed a mother, baby and nurse, while two people were killed by another five bombs dropped today on the city and northern suburbs.

At around ten o'clock tonight, however, a heavier attack left 26 dead and 72 injured in the heart of the city in the rue de Rivoli, which was hit by a 660-pound bomb, and the St-Paul quarter, where six bombs fell. The Gothas are clearly reserving their worst raids for darkness, when they meet less opposition from fighters (→ May 19).

*Bomb site on the rue Geoffroy.*

# US airmail service starts

*George L Boyle had a map stitched to his breeches, but still got lost.*

**Washington, DC, May 15**

The US Post Office and US Army today launched the US's first regularly-scheduled airmail service, between Washington and New York and vice versa, via Philadelphia. The army supplies the pilots and aircraft, while the Post Office takes care of the mail. By summer, the Post Office expects to provide its own pilots and airplanes and operate the service alone. Lieutenant George L Boyle made the first flight, taking off from Washington. Unfortunately, the inexperienced Boyle lost his way. Following the wrong railroad tracks and ignoring the sun, he flew south, not north, and landed in a field at Waldorf, Maryland. The other half of the flight, from Philadelphia to New York, left without the Washington mail. The New York/Philadelphia/Washington service, however, went well, with the mail arriving at 2.50pm (→ Aug 12).

# German bombers make Londoners suffer

*London, May 19*

The largest mass bombing raid on London and neighboring counties to date, by 41 German Gotha and Staaken aircraft, has provoked a loud outcry and immediate instant demands for the British Prime Minister, David Lloyd George, to recall more fighter defense squadrons from France. For over a year, monthly raids have caused death and demoralization in south-east England.

Last night 49 civilians died and 172 were injured during the raid, some victims being crushed in a mass panic as bombs fell in residential parts of London just before midnight. Regional fighter squadrons were alerted and located five Gothas and one Riesen, shooting three down (→ Aug 5).

*British air defenses brought down one of the raiding Gothas with its bombs.*

# Goering steps into Red Baron's shoes

*Ypres, Belgium, July 7*

A new commander has today been appointed to head *Jagdgeschwader* [Fighter Group] 1, the crack German band of airmen headed until his death in April by Manfred von Richthofen, the legendary "Red Baron". His mantle is being handed on to Leutnant Hermann Goering, who has become one of Germany's most celebrated air aces. In charge of *Jagdstaffeln* [Fighter Squadron] 27 since last year, Goering has over 20 victories to his name and in May was awarded his country's highest military honor, the coveted blue cross of the order Pour le Mérite, by Kaiser Wilhelm.

Goering's prestigious appointment to the air group nicknamed "Circus Richthofen" was unexpected. Richthofen's post was filled initially by Captain Reinhard. But Reinhard was killed on July 3 when the Fokker he was test-flying – Goering had flown it minutes earlier – disintegrated.

# Ship-borne aircraft destroy two Zeppelins

*The Camels sit on the deck of HMS* Furious, *waiting to fly to Tondern.*

*Tondern, Germany, July 19*

A successful air attack took place on this German coastal navy base early today. It was mounted by a special unit of Sopwith 2F.1 Camels of Britain's Royal Naval Air Service (RNAS). The seven aircraft took off from HMS *Furious* soon after 3am, each carrying two 50-pound bombs. Six reached their objective and completely destroyed the two airship hangars and Zeppelins L 54 and L 60, which were in one of them. The RNAS did not come out unscathed. One pilot was drowned, three became lost and landed in Denmark, and the others ditched near the carrier (→ Oct 19).

# British airplanes back Arab rebellion

*Palestine, September 21*

The Royal Air Force has provided great assistance to General Allenby at the start of his advance towards Damascus. On day one, September 19, RAF S.E.5 fighters and D.H.9 bombers caught the Turkish Eighth Army retreating along the Tulkeram/Nablus road and strafed it with great effect. Inflicting heavy casualties, they struck a devastating blow to the morale of Turkish soldiers who have not experienced air attack before.

The attacks continued today with raids on the Turks' main telephone exchange south of Nazareth and the headquarters of their Seventh Army at Wadi el Far'a, followed by more strafing of Turkish soldiers trapped on the heights above.

Major T E Lawrence, the British officer working with Arab irregulars, believes that aircraft "converted the Turkish retreat into a rout", and he has signalled Allenby for more air support for his forces.

## Britain loses great tactician as ace Mannock is killed

*France, July 26*

Three weeks after taking command of 85 Squadron, Royal Air Force (RAF), when he clearly needed a long rest from warfare, Major Edward "Mick" Mannock, an Irish Catholic from Belfast, threw his life away today. He scored his 73rd victory to become the top United Kingdom ace, but he broke his own rule, "never follow the Hun too low", and his aircraft was set ablaze by ground fire. His body has not been found so it is not known whether he shot himself with his own pistol to avoid being burned to death, a course he considered.

Mannock, 31, was idolized by the young pilots whom he guided, at considerable risk to himself, through their first combat. His own nerves were shot to pieces. He told a friend recently: "I don't think I will last much longer."

# American ace downs German aircraft

*Toul, France, September 25*

Captain Eddie Rickenbacker, 29, was very busy today, his first day as commander of America's 94th Aero Squadron. The famous racing-car driver turned air ace met with his unit and then took to the air to put into practise what he preaches to his pilots. The result: two more "kills" for Rickenbacker as he approaches the status of double ace with ten victories.

His prey did not come easily. Alone, patrolling over enemy lines, he spotted two Halberstadt reconnaissance planes escorted by five Fokkers. Despite the odds he did not hesitate to confront the German aircraft, and on his initial diving attack one of the Fokkers fell to his guns. In the dogfight that followed he destroyed a Halberstadt.

Rickenbacker, who has returned to duty after four months' convalescence from a severe ear infection, wants to make the 94th the very best of the US pursuit units. It will

*American air hero Eddie Rickenbacker in the cockpit of his Spad XIII.*

be a difficult task. Only three pilots, including himself, remain in the unit from the time before his illness. But he is used to challenges. He was denied enlistment as an aviator on the grounds of age, so he became a chauffeur for American Expeditionary Force air chief Brig-Gen Billy Mitchell, whom he persuaded to send him to flight school.

## German airship is shot down in North Sea

*The tangled wreckage of the L 70 is salvaged off Cromer, where it came down.*

*Norwich, England, August 5*

A last desperate attempt to bomb English towns and cities with Zeppelin airships has been foiled with the loss of the lead ship, the brand-new L 70, and its crew. This included Peter Strasser, commander of the German naval airship division. Aboard the L 70, capable of 80mph and an operational ceiling of 20,000 feet, Captain Strasser made the fatal and uncharacteristic mistake of approaching the English coast before nightfall and at a low altitude. Defending aircraft from Great Yarmouth rose to the attack and promptly sealed the L 70's fate with incendiary ammunition.

## Germans are outnumbered in air battle

*Western front, August 8*

Air activity in support of the allied offensive on the Hindenburg Line is reaching a crescendo. British and French front-line strength is 1,800 airplanes, giving them numerical superiority over the Germans with only 350. But German pilots have an outstanding fighter in the Fokker D.VII, and they are offering stiff resistance.

Even though Allied losses were 83 today, it was also one of the blackest days for the German air service – 49 machines lost. One Allied tactic is to raid German airfields, destroying machines on the ground. German pilots have found it impossible to penetrate Allied airspace in retaliation. Allied losses in the air are expected to remain high, if only because their greater numbers present more targets, but this air battle is one of attrition, and in the long term it seems inevitable that it will go the Allies' way.

*Ready for the fray, Nieuport fighters line up at a French military aerodrome.*

# US chief directs massive air assault

*Saint-Mihiel, France, September 15*
Under the direction of American Expeditionary Force (AEF) air chief Brigadier-General Billy Mitchell, a massive Allied air armada of almost 1,500 aircraft has joined with the ground forces in launching a major assault on German targets in the Saint-Mihiel salient. American, French, British and Italian air units were under the colonel's command for the carefully planned operation, which started four days ago.

Mitchell, who made daily observation flights to assess the efficacy of the operation, had 701 pursuit, 336 observation, 323 day bomber and 91 night bomber aircraft in his force. They were joined by approximately 700 French and 600 American crews and planes of various types, as well as about 100 British bombers from Major-General Sir Hugh Trenchard's units. Italian aircraft composed the remainder of the force. It is difficult to com-

*Billy Mitchell (left), architect of the air attack, poses in front of a D.H.4.*

prehend the destructive power of 1,500 aircraft. American units, 40 per cent of the force, claim 3,300 sorties in the last four days, during which over 150,000 pounds of high explosive were dropped and more than 30,000 rounds fired by machine guns. AEF commander-in-chief General John J Pershing has praised the air armada for its key role in the effectiveness of the Saint-Mihiel offensive.

## Wounded officer shows his courage

*France, October 27*
A Canadian pilot with the Royal Air Force (RAF), detached for retraining on the Sopwith Snipe, has survived a dogfight over Valenciennes against huge odds. Major William Barker had shot down three Fokkers and forced down two when, wounded, he fainted twice through loss of blood.

Barker fell 12,000 feet before he regained consciousness – to find himself in a swarm of 15 Fokkers. With bullets through both thighs and an elbow, he tried to ram the nearest Fokker, firing as he did so. The Fokker exploded in flames before he could hit it. He continued shooting as he dived, engine on fire, to crash-land just in Allied territory. Barker holds two high British decorations, the Distinguished Service Order and the Military Cross. Like the late "Mick" Mannock, he is to be recommended for the highest of all, the Victoria Cross.

# French flyer claims six victories in a day

*Leading French air ace Captain René Fonck shows off his decorations.*

*Champagne, France, September 26*
Another extraordinary feat of aerial skill has been pulled off by French ace Captain René Fonck, who today shot down six German aircraft over eastern France. It is the second time Fonck has downed six Germans in a day since joining the élite "Stork" Squadron in April 1917, and his third hat-trick. His first set

of six occurred on May 9; three of those came in 45 seconds. Fonck has a reputation for being vain and moody off-duty but razor-sharp and cool in the air. He achieved his 55th kill before the end of July, passing Guynemer's record. On August 14 he scored another hat-trick, downing three planes in one ten-second burst of fire.

# Heavy bombers hit German industrial city

*Germany, October 22*
The industrial town of Kaiserslautern in western Germany came in for a pounding by the Allies last night when it was attacked by four Handley Page O/400 bombers. The British raiders dropped 1,650lb bombs on the town, causing substantial damage in the latest in a series of heavy raids on German targets.

Apart from the physical damage caused, the raid will further depress the morale of a nation on the brink of defeat. It has proved once again

the effectiveness of the Allied air forces in general and of the Handley Page bombers, which were created to repay German attacks on England, in particular.

Developed by Frederick Handley Page and his designer George Volkert, the O/400 entered service this August with the job of hitting German industrial targets in the Ruhr valley and the Saarland. Equipped with two powerful 350-hp Rolls-Royce engines, this impressive aircraft can carry over a ton of bombs.

*The O/400 has more power and a better fuel system than its predecessors.*

# Debate begins over peacetime air roles

*Europe, December*

The Great War saw such a huge explosion in aircraft production that what began as a chronic shortage of both crew and machines has become, now the guns are silent, a chronic surplus. The question of what to do with so much equipment and expertise in peacetime is uppermost in many aviators' minds.

Inevitably there will be some wastage of surplus aircraft stock, but aviation itself probably has a bright future. Britain and France, for instance, will be interested in developing their air forces to cover their colonial empires, and the potential for civil aviation is considerable, given the distances that can now be covered easily.

As if to highlight this important point, A S MacLaren and A E Borton made the first flight from Britain to Egypt between July 28 and August 8, and on November 15 Clifford Prodger took 40 passengers up to 5,400 feet in a Handley Page V/1500. This aircraft, which was designed to bomb Berlin, entered service only after the Armistice.

*Government surplus: the Bristol Braemar arrived too late for the war.*

# Bomber flies across the British Empire

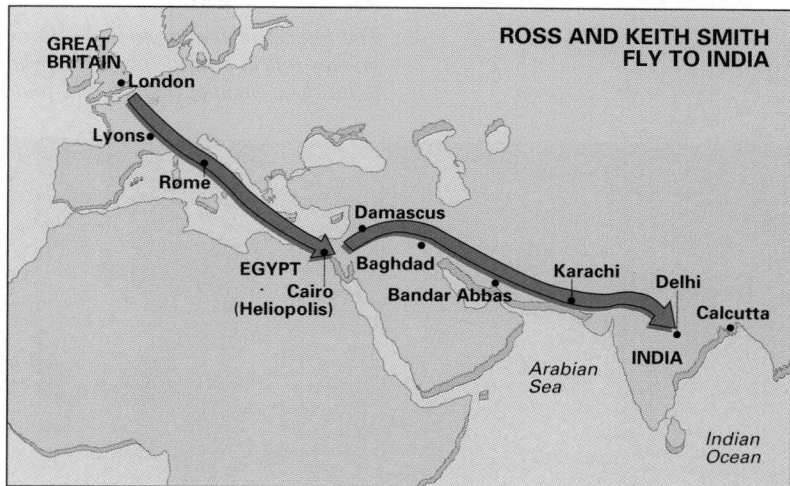

*Delhi, December 12*

The first airplane to fly from Egypt to India landed here today to a tumultuous welcome and perhaps not a little relief – the giant Handley Page O/400 bomber was carrying an important passenger in the shape of Major-General W Salmond, head of Britain's Royal Air Force (RAF) in the Middle East.

The flight from Egypt completes the RAF bomber's long trek from England, which has been carried out to survey an important new air-mail route that will link Britain with key parts of the British Empire. The first leg of the journey, from England to Egypt, took place between July 28 and August 8.

The four-man crew for the Egypt to India leg included Brigadier-General A E Borton (pilot), who was also pilot on the first leg, and Captain Ross Smith (co-pilot). The only serious problem on the flight, which began at Heliopolis on November 29, was a bad landing at Bandar Abbas, which caused some undercarriage damage.

# Curtiss flying boat carries heavy load

*New York, November 27*

The new Navy-Curtiss patrol flying boat, the NC-1, today lifted a world record 51 people (including one stowaway) into the air at Rockaway Beach.

The new machine's enormous lifting capacity bodes well for the future deployment of the flying boat – an aviation concept which has developed to meet British requirements for a machine capable of seeking out and destroying German submarines operating in the Atlantic Ocean. Such was the menace of U-boats during the war that NCs were forced to fly the Atlantic during delivery. This was partly to speed their arrival but also to prevent losses en route if transporting merchant ships were sunk.

First flown on October 4, the trimotor NC-1 has a very short hull to reduce airframe weight.

# Dutchman Fokker leaves Germany

*Schwerin, Germany, November 30*

As revolutionary unrest grips Germany, Anthony Fokker has left for his native Holland, taking with him as many of his assets as he can. Apart from sums already transferred abroad, these include 30 million marks and as many airplanes as he could organize transport for to his new base at Schiphol, near Amsterdam. His business manager will run the Fokker works in Schwerin on his behalf.

Among other equipment, Fokker got out 60 observation biplanes, 20 of the latest D.VII fighters and 400 engines. He himself left Germany in disguise, afraid, he claims, that the workers' council newly set up in his factory wanted his money and his life. However, the wily Dutchman also happens to owe the German government 14 million marks in tax (→ Jul 21, 1919).

**Surveying the skies: a French army dirigible floats serenely above the bustle of cavalry on the move through a country town. Right to the end of the war, observation balloons and airships performed the valuable task of helping not only to protect but also direct the troops on the ground.**

# Startling images reflect reality of war in the air

*The impact of the airplane on the conduct of war has been profound. These images reflect how air power has changed the face of battle, enabling nations to hit their enemies' homelands, and making a new breed of hero.*

*War as spectacle: Fokkers close up on a group of British D.H.4 bombers.*

*Excited American schoolchildren surround an airplane at Sheepshead Bay.*

*The spectacular sight of a swarm of Bristol F.2b fighters crossing the Alps.*

*F.2b pilots and observers hand over any papers which might help the enemy.*

*A balloon apron in England, designed to keep enemy aircraft away.*

*Bringing the war home: a British D.H.4 flies over enemy territory.*

*Aerial photography has revealed the true horror of wrecked cityscapes.*

*A US Army cinematographer tries to film a Nieuport 28 in flight.*

# Reconnaissance

The principal task of aircraft at the outbreak of war was military observation. It took several forms: spotting for artillery from aircraft and balloons [1] and directing the guns; low-flying contact patrols [2] to check on the progress of ground operations, and taking photographs of the front [3] to analyse changes in the disposition of the enemy. Reconnaissance aircraft were highly vulnerable to fighter attack [5], and so had to be protected by friendly fighters [4].

# Naval aviation

The task of searching for enemy ships "over the horizon" was an early role of naval aircraft. To do this, they had to fly from ships; thus the aircraft carrier [6] was born. Sea- and land-based aircraft [7] were used to attack enemy ships with torpedoes or bombs. Long-range maritime reconnaissance was carried out by aircraft and airships [12]. Aircraft [7] and smaller airships [8] were used in coastal areas to protect convoys by searching for and attacking submarines.

# Air superiority

In order to observe and attack the enemy, the opposing air forces had to fight each other for command of the skies above the battlefield. This was the task of fighters on both sides [9] and [10]. Most of the epic aerial battles of the Great War were fought to establish local air superiority. This was the job of the legendary fighter pilots and "aces" who were skilled in aerial combat. In the last two years of the war, their "dogfights" were almost daily occurrences.

# Strategic air power

The use of long-range aircraft [11] and airships [12] to attack urban and industrial centers away from the battlefield in the enemy's home country evolved steadily from 1914. To counter this development, defensive fighters had to be stationed near potential targets to intercept the bombers and shoot them down. In 1918, an Allied "Independent Air Force", dedicated to the strategic bombing of Germany, was set up to operate completely separately from land or sea forces.

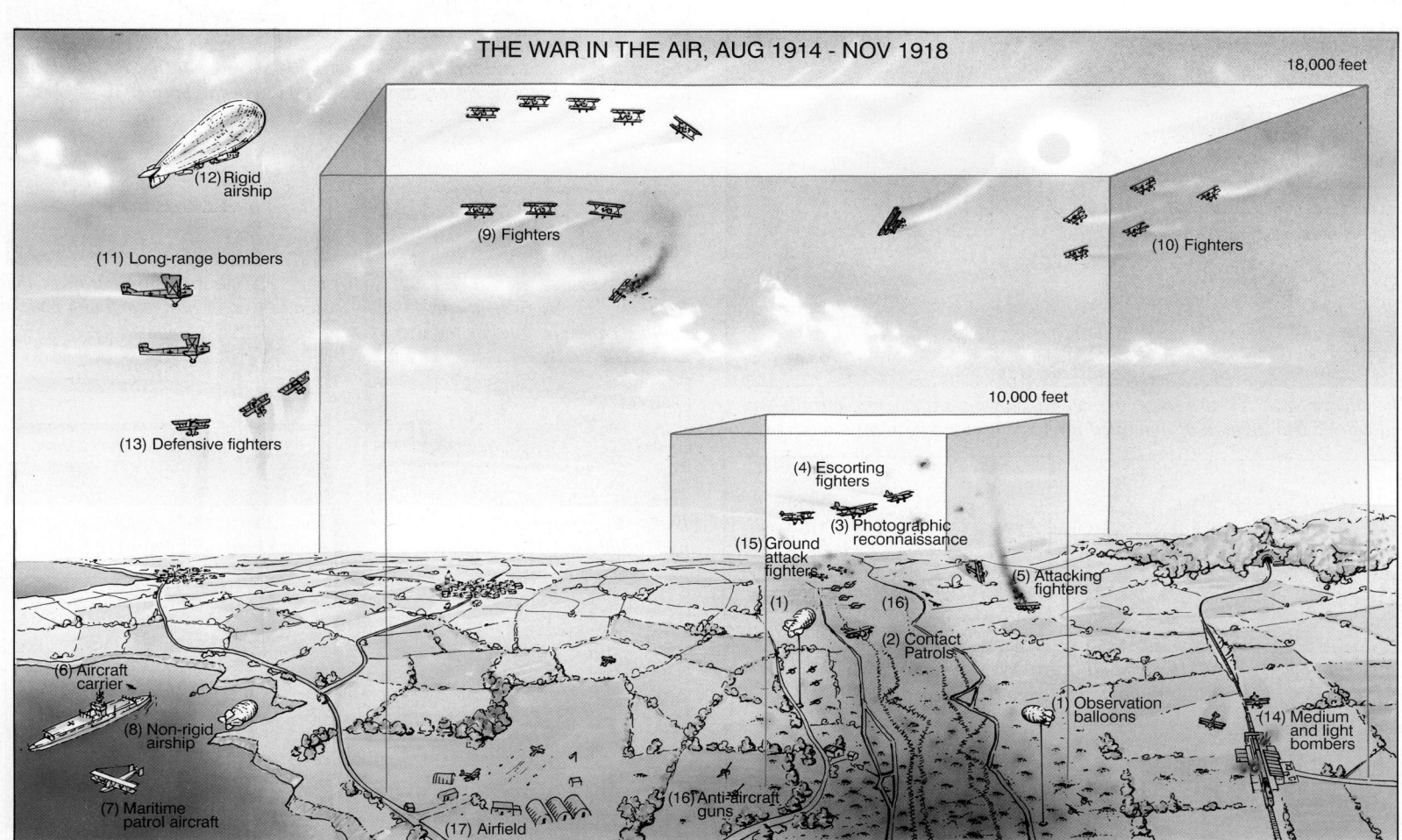

THE WAR IN THE AIR, AUG 1914 - NOV 1918

18,000 feet

(12) Rigid airship

(11) Long-range bombers

(9) Fighters

(10) Fighters

(13) Defensive fighters

10,000 feet

(4) Escorting fighters

(3) Photographic reconnaissance

(15) Ground attack fighters

(5) Attacking fighters

(1)

(16)

(2) Contact Patrols

(1) Observation balloons

(6) Aircraft carrier

(8) Non-rigid airship

(7) Maritime patrol aircraft

(16) Anti-aircraft guns

(17) Airfield

(14) Medium and light bombers

# Interdiction

Throughout the war, aircraft were used to attack the military infrastructure behind enemy lines. Light and medium bombers [14] were used against targets such as supply dumps, railroad junctions and stations, headquarters, and airfields [17]. Bomb-loads were light, and such raids had only a marginal effect on military operations.

# Ground attack

From 1917, both sides used low-flying aircraft [15] to attack enemy positions with machine guns and bombs in support of ground assaults, particularly during the opening phase. The same tactics were used to counter-attack an enemy breakthrough on the ground. Losses in this type of operation were very high.

# Performance

Aircraft speed rose during the war. In 1914/15, observation aircraft typically reached between 70 and 80mph, and fighters between 80 and 95mph. By 1918, most fighters were capable of between 120 and 135mph. In 1914, most combat took place between 6,000 and 9,000 feet; by 1918, this had increased to between 15,000 and 16,000 feet.

# Size of air forces

In 1914, Britain had 113 military aircraft, France had 156 and Germany had 246. By 1918, the comparable figures were Britain: 22,171; France: about 20,000; and Germany: 15,342. The five combatant nations, including the United States and Italy, produced 205,000 aircraft of all types during the Great War.

Germany's best First World War fighter was the Fokker D.VII, which was powered by either the 160-/180-hp Mercedes or the 185-hp BMW engine.

The Blériot-Spad XX two-seater fighter was an instant success, but the war's end caused cancellation of unlimited production; in all 95 went into service.

Large numbers of the Halberstadt multirole C.V two-seater were built.

In 1918, a number of R-4s were re-engined to become R-4Ls.

The Martin MB-1 was the first bomber built for the US Army Air Service.

The BAT Bantam fighter had a wooden monocoque fuselage.

Only one Hansa-Brandenburg W.25 single-seater seaplane was built.

Sire of a famous family: the Fairey III was to enjoy a long service life.

A flying boat on the grand scale; the massive Felixstowe Fury triplane.

One example of Sopwith's Snail fighter had a monocoque fuselage.

One of the greatest trainers ever, the Avro 504 served with the RAF well into the post-war era. Its successor, the 504N, saw use in the Second World War.

Bristol's large Braemar triplane bomber came too late for the war.

The Felixstowe F.5 became the standard RAF post-war flying boat.

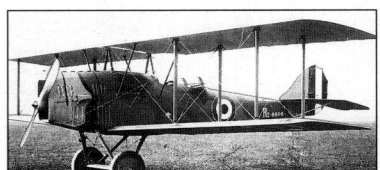

Fiat's R.2 reconnaissance biplane had a 300-hp A.12bis engine.

The Curtiss 18-T triplane set many records, but only two were built.

The LFG Roland D.XVI single-seater fighter failed to win a production order. This variant has the 200-hp Goebel rotary engine, which was not a success.

LFG's Roland D.VII single-seater fighter did not go into production.

Two Phoenix P.5 Cork flying boats were completed before the war's end.

*The Airco D.H.9A day-bomber, with a Liberty engine: a vast improvement on the D.H.9. It became one of the RAF's longest-serving inter-war aircraft.*

*The tiny Wright-Martin K-3 Scout was an unsuccessful conception.*

*De Havilland's D.H.10 Amiens day-bomber just missed action in the war.*

*The ungainly Naglo quadruplane did not find favour. The four-winged structure inhibited the pilot's view and caused a great deal of drag.*

*Fokker's promising E.V prototype was developed into the D.VIII monoplane fighter, which saw combat in small numbers alongside the famous D.VII.*

*A bold all-metal biplane with no interplane struts: Dornier's D.1.*

*The nimble Nieuport-Delage 29 saw wide service in the inter-war years.*

*Handley Page's V/1500 long-range bomber, with four engines in tandem pairs, designed to bomb Berlin: the war ended before it became operational.*

*Dornier's Cs I two-seater seaplane-fighter saw only limited production.*

*The Blackburn Kangaroo served as an anti-submarine patrol aeroplane.*

*The curious Thomas-Morse MB-1 had faired aerofoil-section bracing.*

*An experimental coastal flying boat, the Royal Aircraft Factory's C.E.1.*

*Caproni's Ca 47 – a three-engined torpedo-carrying seaplane for Italy.*

*The French Caudron C.23 saw limited production for post-war service.*

*Halberstadt's C.VIII, which appeared late in the war, was a C.V high-altitude reconnaissance airplane with a 245-hp Maybach engine. Only one was built.*

# 1919

191.1mph
France
Joseph Sadi-Lecointe
Nieuport-Delage 29v
Dec 16, 1919

1,884 miles
Great Britain
Alcock and Brown
Vickers Vimy
Jun 15, 1919

34,610ft
USA
Roland Rohlfs
Curtiss Wasp
Sep 18, 1919

44,672lb
Great Britain
WG Tarrant Ltd
Tarrant Tabor

700hp
Italy
Fiat
A.14

**Berlin, January 8**
The German air ministry approves civil flying after wartime restrictions.

**London, January 11**
Sir Hugh Trenchard is re-appointed Chief of the Air Staff, and Major-General Sir Frederick Sykes is made controller general of civil aviation (→ Jan 12).

**India, January 16**
Major A S C MacLaren and crew arrive in Delhi from England aboard a Handley Page V/1500 bomber; they left on December 13 and flew via Rome and Baghdad.

**London, February 17**
Oswald Short is told that Shorts' airship factory at Cardington is to be nationalized; it will be known as the Royal Airship Works.

**USA, February 21**
The prototype of the first US-designed fighter to enter large scale production, the Thomas-Morse MB-3 (to be made by Boeing), makes its maiden flight.

**England, March 6**
The British R.33 airship, built by Armstrong Whitworth, is launched at the company's works near Selby in Yorkshire (→ Sep 13).

**Melbourne, March 10**
The Australian government announces a prize of £10,000 for the first flight from Great Britain to Australia by Australians, which must be completed within 720 consecutive hours by the end of the year.

**France, March 24**
Airplane designer Igor Sikorsky, who fled to France after the Russian Revolution, sails for the US; the French did not take up his services (→ May 3, 1923).

**Rome, April 13**
Lieutenant Roget arrives in the city after flying his Breguet 14 the 690 miles from Paris in nine hours 40 minutes.

**Kent, England, April 13**
The Vickers Vimy Commercial, a civil version of the bomber with an enclosed fuselage capable of holding a maximum of ten passengers, makes its maiden flight (→ Dec 10).

**France, April 21**
Veteran French pilot Jules Védrines and his mechanic Guillain are both killed when their airplane suffers engine failure and crashes in the Drôme area on a flight from Paris to Rome.

**London, April 30**
The *Air Navigation Directions*, laying down rules for aircraft registration and pilot licensing, are published.

**Atlantic Ocean, May 8**
Three US Navy flying boats, under the command of Commander John Towers, launch an attempt to make the first crossing of the Atlantic, in stages (→ 27).

**Washington, DC, May 17**
The War Department orders the use of the national star insignia on all US military aircraft.

**New York, May 22**
Rich French-born hotelier Raymond Orteig offers a prize of $25,000 for the first non-stop flight in either direction between Paris and New York.

**California, June 1**
A permanent forest-fire patrol equipped with Curtiss Jenny aircraft is established at Rockwell Field, near San Diego.

**Germany, June 23**
German navy crews scuttle seven Zeppelins to stop them falling into Allied hands.

**France June 12**
France's Baroness Raymonde de Laroche breaks the women's altitude record by flying to a height of 16,896 feet (→ Jul 18).

**France, June 28**
The peace treaty is signed at Versailles; it forbids Germany to have an air force or produce military aircraft.

**London, July 18**
Britain's most successful Great War ace Major Edward "Mick" Mannock, who made 73 accredited "kills", is posthumously awarded the Victoria Cross, Britain's highest award for valor.

**Le Crotoy, France, July 18**
Self-styled Baroness Raymonde de Laroche, the first Frenchwoman to get her flying license, is killed in a flying accident in northern France.

**Holland, July 21**
Anthony Fokker founds the Dutch Aircraft Company at Schiphol, near Amsterdam (→ Nov 30, 1921).

**Canada, August 7**
Captain Ernest Hoy makes the first flight over the Canadian Rockies, in a Curtiss JN-4 fitted with an extra fuel tank; he flies from Vancouver to Calgary in 12 hours and 34 minutes' flying time.

**Germany, August 24**
DELAG inaugurates a passenger service between Friedrichshafen and Berlin.

**The Netherlands, August 28**
The International Air Traffic Association (IATA) is established at the Hague.

**England, September 13**
British airship R.33 returns from a 20-hour trip over Belgium and the Netherlands intended to demonstrate its extremely luxurious facilities to businessmen. During the flight, a splendid five-course lunch was served and a ship's newspaper was published - (→ Oct 15, 1925).

**Sydney, October 1**
The Australian Aircraft and Engineering Company is established to manufacture and sell Avro aircraft under license.

**Paris, October 13**
The International Convention of Air Navigation is signed at a conference held under the auspices of the League of Nations; a system of aircraft registration based on a five-letter call sign is established.

**London, October 24**
Frederick Handley Page is granted a patent for a controllable slot on the leading edge of an aircraft's wing; this delays the loss of lift at high angles of incidence, thereby lowering the stalling speed of the aircraft, giving greater control during landing.

**USA, October 31**
The Transcontinental Reliability and Endurance Test, conducted by the US Army Air Service since October 8, ends; seven airmen died during what amounted to an air race from New York to San Francisco and back, won on October 18 by Lieutenant Belvin W Maynard

**France, November 24**
Henri Deutsch de la Meurthe, 73, the great French promoter and sponsor of early aviation efforts, dies at Ecquevilly.

**Australia, December 12**
Captain H N Wrigley and Lieutenant A W Murphy complete the first flight across Australia. Commissioned by the Australian Defense Department to survey a route from Melbourne to Darwin, they covered the 2,500 miles between the two cities in 46 hours' flying time in an RAF B.E.2e.

**Rouen, France, December 18**
Sir John Alcock, who was knighted after his successful transatlantic flight with Arthur Brown, is killed when the Vickers Viking flying boat which he is ferrying to the Paris air show crashes.

*Honoring the Atlantic heroes: the menu for a celebration lunch thrown by the "Daily Mail" for John Alcock and Arthur Whitten Brown.* ▶

The
# TRANS-ATLANTIC
## AIR RACE
### 1919

Capt. J. ALCOCK, D.S.C.

ST. JOHN'S

Lt. A. WHITTEN BROWN

CLIFDEN

# LUNCHEON
## TO THE
# WINNER
## OF THE
# DAILY MAIL
# £10,000 PRIZE

*Savoy Hotel, June 20, 19*

# Military air service opens way to Paris

*London, January 10*
The first air service between London and Paris now separates the two capitals by little more than two hours. The Royal Air Force (RAF) N° 86 (Communications) Wing, with a fleet of eight Handley Page O/400 heavy bombers, 18 D.H.4s and three Martinsydes, is carrying mail three times a day between Hendon and Buc, most of it diplomatic post for the Versailles peace conference. The wartime destruction of the rail and road systems in northern France left no alternative but to use air transport. Other RAF teams are carrying post to Cologne for the British forces of occupation in Germany.

Two of the O/400s have been fitted out as airliners for diplomats and renamed *Great Britain* and *Silver Star*. The comfort of wicker chairs and cushions for passengers is not shared by the pilots, who are protected only by a small, semicircular windscreen during flights at a top speed of 97mph (→ Feb 8).

*An RAF D.H.4 bomber modified with an enclosed cabin for the passengers.*

# Germans lead take-off of civil airlines

*Minister Albertz boards a DLR airliner used on the Berlin/Weimar service.*

*Berlin, February 5*
The first regular, daily passenger service in the world was launched at Berlin's city airfield this cold winter's morning in an atmosphere of great excitement and activity. Aircraft and crew were feverishly prepared, engines roared to life and ground staff shouted instructions as harnesses were secured.

Germany, with its airships, first tapped the potential of commercial passenger air travel, and it is paying even more attention to it now the Allies have banned all German military aviation. A German airline, Deutsche Luft Reederei, will operate the new service. Its route is from Berlin to Weimar via Leipzig. The airline's fleet of aircraft include AEG J II biplanes with enclosed cabin for the passengers, which can carry five people at a squeeze, fewer if mail is to be taken. Two-seat DFW aircraft are also available. In good weather the flight, some 120 miles, should take around two hours and 20 minutes (→ Nov 11).

# Churchill is to head British air ministry

*London, January 12*
Winston Churchill, a staunch advocate of air power, has been appointed Britain's air minister. His interests are mainly strategic; he believes that "the first duty of the RAF is to garrison the British Empire". Some businessmen, such as George Holt Thomas and Frederick Handley Page, believe however that the empire can best be strengthened by the development of commercial flights linking Britain with India and Africa. They will try to persuade Churchill to give them government support.

He may have more pressing business. There are now 337 aerodromes in Britain, of which five are suitable for international flights, but civil flying is still prohibited by wartime regulations.

# Hardy veteran lands on roof of Paris store in dramatic stunt

*High jinks in the city: spectators look on tensely as Védrines comes in to land on the roof of the department store.*

*Paris, January 19*
Veteran French air hero Jules Védrines risked life and limb today when he won a 25,000-franc prize offered by the Galeries Lafayette, a famous Paris store. The prize, unclaimed since 1914, was for the first pilot to land on the roof of its city center building.

Védrines practiced on an airfield in a slow, highly maneuverable Caudron G-3 biplane, the only type of machine which could feasibly land on a 92-foot by 40-foot roof surrounded by a three-foot balustrade. This morning he skimmed the balustrade and braked hard on special sandbags, but no one could stop the Caudron from crashing into elevator housings and being wrecked. Védrines was unhurt (→ Apr 21).

# Commercial link for Paris and London

*London, February 8*
The capital cities of England and France have been linked today for the first time by civil air transport, thanks to the continuing vision and enterprise of Anglo-French aviation pioneer Henry Farman. A civil version of his cavernous Farman F.60 Goliath bomber made the first flight, from Toussus-le-Noble to Kenley, carrying 11 passengers, who were all military personnel – in line with current regulations.

Famous for his pioneering flying machines, Farman is now developing air routes as well as aircraft. The French are set to take a leading role in the development of airlines and services (→ Mar 29, 1920).

*Farman advertises for passengers.*

# Americans make postal flight to Canada

*Post pilots: Hubbard and Boeing, pioneers of international airmail.*

*Seattle, March 3*
Airplane builder William E Boeing and Eddie Hubbard of Hubbard Air Service have made the first international airmail flight from the US in a flight regarded as a trailblazer for a possible regular service to Canada.

Hubbard, with Boeing as passenger and carrying a sack of US mail, left Seattle, Washington State, yesterday in a Model C-700 floatplane. Flying into bad weather, they landed at Anacortes, Washington, to spend the night, and continued their trip today. They reached the Royal Vancouver Yacht Club safely with their mailsack, and collected a pouch of Canadian mail which they brought back with them to Seattle (→ May 15).

# US pilot leaps between airplanes in flight

*Atlantic City, NJ, May 24*
Visitors to the Second Annual Pan American Aeronautic Congress were amazed today when Ormer L Locklear leaped from the wing of one JN-4 to the wing of another flying alongside. The mid-air jump was a repeat of a stunt performed by the former US Army Air Service officer at Uniontown, Pennsylvania, before 10,000 people. The aircraft were flown by two of Locklear's former air service comrades.

Today's performance was another triumph for Locklear's sponsor William Hickman Pickens who has brought to the public the exploits of daredevil pilot Lincoln Beachey and motor-racing king, Barney Oldfield (→ Dec 14, 1921).

*Locklear prepares to launch himself.*

# Long-range air mail service links east to west across America

*Cleveland, Ohio, May 15*
After its accident-plagued failure last December to launch a transcontinental airmail service by flying letters from New York to Chicago, the US Post Office succeeded today with a shorter, less ambitious route from Chicago, Illinois, to Cleveland, Ohio. The flight was successful – although the load of mail carried, seven pounds, was not exactly huge – and the postal authorities are optimistic about the service's future.

By flying the mail from Chicago to meet the mail train in Cleveland, it is possible for correspondence to New York and New England states to reach its destination 16 hours faster than if it went by train alone. On return flights from Cleveland, letters taken from the mail train in the morning and flown to Cleveland can be delivered that afternoon, another 16-hour saving.

The service uses modified British D.H.4 airplanes with strengthened undercarriages, larger wheels and Liberty engines. The cockpit is set further to the rear to give the pilots a greater margin of safety. The Post Office hopes to use the same aircraft for planned services from New York to Chicago, New York to Cleveland and San Francisco to Sacramento (→ Sep 11, 1920).

**Charles Godefroy swoops under the Arc de Triomphe in Paris, in protest at the lack of an airborne tribute at the July 14 parade.**

# Flyers missing at sea for a week are safe

*London, May 25*
Joy has greeted the news that Harry Hawker and Lieutenant Commander K Mackenzie-Grieve are safe after a failed Atlantic crossing. Hawker, piloting the single-engined Sopwith *Atlantic*, took off, with Mackenzie-Grieve as navigator, at 3.48pm seven days ago from St John's, Newfoundland. About 1,400 miles out the engine cooling system failed; they ditched near a Danish steamer, the *Mary*. She had no wireless, so news of the rescue was not made known until today.

*Hawker: he was blown off course.*

# British service born

*Manchester, England, May 10*
Today the recently formed Avro Transport Company opened Britain's first scheduled air service. A fare of four guineas [£4.20] is being charged for the journey of 50 miles from Alexandra Park in north London via Southport, Lancashire, to Blackpool beach on the northwestern coast. Alliot Verdon Roe's new firm is using four of his Avro 504K aircraft, modified to carry two passengers. He hopes to replace these with the new Avro 536, with a wider four-seat cockpit.

# Determined flyers meet the Atlantic challenge

## US seaplane crosses Atlantic, in stages

*Lisbon, May 27*

A US Navy Curtiss flying boat, the *NC-4*, flown by Lieutenant-Commander Albert Read, became the first airplane to cross the Atlantic Ocean when it landed at Lisbon in Portugal today. The aircraft was the only one of three (designated *NC-1, NC-3* and *NC-4*) to complete the 3,925-mile flight. It was flown in stages, starting from Rockaway Naval Air Station in New York City, stopping at Chatham, Massachusetts, Halifax, Nova Scotia, and Trepassey Bay, Newfoundland, before setting out over the ocean for Horta in the Azores.

Everything went smoothly after the evening departure, but as dawn approached heavy rain and fog forced two aircraft down.

The *NC-1* sank, its crew plucked from the sea by a Greek ship. The *NC-3's* crew rode out the storm for 62 hours, then taxied their craft the 200 miles to the Azores. The *NC-4* managed to stay airborne through the storm and landed at Horta, staying in the Azores for ten days.

At 8.01 this evening Read landed in Lisbon, ending an historic flight with a radio message to base: "We are safely on the other side of the pond. The job is finished."

*The crew of the US Navy/Curtiss "NC-1" preparing for the flight.*

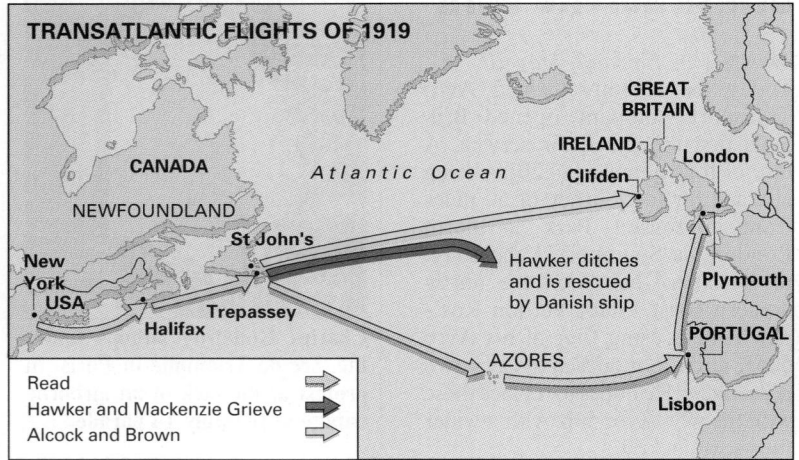

## Two Britons make first non-stop crossing

*Alcock and Brown relax over breakfast after their historic non-stop flight.*

*Ireland, June 15*

Less than three weeks after a US Navy flying boat became the first airplane to cross the Atlantic, two Britons today accomplished an even bigger challenge when they became the first to fly the Atlantic without stopping. The heroes of the flight, and winners of a £10,000 prize on offer from Britain's *Daily Mail* newspaper since 1913, are Captain John Alcock (pilot) and Lieutenant Arthur Whitten Brown (navigator).

Their ordeal, through thick cloud, pitch darkness, snow, hail and sleet, began at 4.13pm (GMT) yesterday at St John's, Newfoundland, and ended at 8.40am today when their Vickers Vimy bomber landed on Derrygimla bog at Clifden, Co Galway. It promptly sank into the ground and ended up with its nose in the bog.

The Vimy carried sufficient fuel for a 2,440-mile range; St John's to Ireland is about 1,890 miles. Start point for the heavily loaded bomber was Lester's Field, where it had been taken after assembly at Quidi Vidi. After take-off it flew over the coast at a height of 1,200 feet. The weather was poor almost from the outset, and there were several tricky moments. The most alarming came early this morning, when the Vimy went into a dangerous spiral dive; the crew pulled out just in time when they emerged from the cloud. At 8.25am they finally crossed the Irish coast and landed soon after (→Dec 18).

*The transatlantic triumph ended in an undignified landing in an Irish bog.*

## German company Junkers unveils an all-metal airliner

*Germany, June 25*

The world's most modern airliner, the Junkers F 13, made its first flight today at Dessau. The new aircraft has a semi-enclosed two-seat cockpit, while the heated cabin can seat up to four passengers. Each seat is fitted with its own restraining safety belt.

It is the structure, however, which makes this aircraft stand out, because the F 13 is made entirely of metal, with a strong, corrugated outer skin and cantilever wing structure, without struts or bracing wires. It has a 170-hp Mercedes engine, and the manufacturers intend to build the F 13 with more powerful engines. The Junkers is designed to be a versatile, durable airplane which will be sold all over the world. It can be fitted with wheels, skis or floats.

*Tough but light: the new airframe.*

# Atlantic is crossed twice

*Coming in to land: the R.34 airship arrives at Mineola, New York State.*

*England, July 13*

A British military airship operated by the Royal Air Force (RAF), the R.34, today accomplished the first two-way transatlantic air crossing. The outward journey was also the first air crossing of the Atlantic from east to west.

The airship was designed using many techniques pioneered in the German Zeppelin airships. Indeed, it was the capture of the German naval airship L 33 in 1916 which prompted the work. A sister airship, R.33 has also been built.

The R.34 took off in calm skies at dawn on July 2 at East Fortune in Scotland and, following standard ocean liner routes, flew to New York in four and a half days, fighting headwinds all the way (a fast Atlantic steamer will do it in five). It berthed at Roosevelt Field, Long Island, the ground crew being directed by an RAF officer who descended from the airship by parachute to take charge. An unexpected record – the first transatlantic air stowaway – was discovered when the airship was moored.

The R.34 left the US on July 10 to fly back. It arrived at Pulham, eastern England, three days and three hours later (→ Jan 1921).

## World's first daily air service to link London and Paris

*London and Paris, August 25*

The world's first regular daily international commercial air service was inaugurated this morning between London and Paris by the British firm of Aircraft Transport and Travel Ltd. A D.H.4a piloted by Lieutenant Bill Lawford left Hounslow, west of London, at 9.10am carrying one passenger, newspapers, leather, grouse and some Devon cream, and landed two and a half hours later at Le Bourget, Paris. The single fare is £21.

Later today a D.H.16 carried four passengers across in two and a quarter hours, while a Handley Page O/400 made a proving flight to Paris with seven journalists as passengers (→ Mar 29, 1920).

*Preparing for the historic take-off.*

## Anything to declare? Airlines get accustomed to London airport

*Middlesex, England, July 1*

London's first airport is now ready for operation on Hounslow Heath to the west of the British capital. Because it is a port of entry, with customs facilities, Hounslow will handle international flights; its customs hall has CUSTOMS over one door and its French equivalent, DOUANE, over the other.

No scheduled services have yet begun, though Aircraft Transport and Travel and others are soon to start. Handley Page Air Transport will fly from Cricklewood, which is not a port; their international flights must land at Hounslow first to clear customs (→ Aug 25).

*Welcome to London: the airfield at Hounslow with the customs sheds, left.*

## British carrier joins force fighting Reds

*Russia, July*

Britain's air services are playing a key part in the international "White" forces ranged against the Red Army in Russia's civil war. As well as the Royal Air Force, the British have sent Royal Navy ships to the White Sea and the Baltic Sea, including, most recently, a former cruiser converted into an aircraft carrier. Once HMS *Cavendish*, now HMS *Vindictive*, the vessel has been sent to join the blockade of the Russian port of Kronstadt in the Baltic. Her aircraft will fly reconnaissance missions (→ Apr 1920).

# Nomads rescue stranded French pilot

*The end of the road: Bossoutrot's Farman Goliath, breaking up in the surf.*

*Mauritania, August 21*
An attempt to link France and Dakar in French West Africa by air has ended in failure, but not, as was feared, in tragedy. A crew of six which disappeared six days ago has been found, exhausted but alive, by desert nomads near Koufra on the coast of Mauritania.

The Farman F-60 Goliath, piloted by Lucien Bossoutrot, left Paris on August 11 and reached Mogador via Casablanca on August 14. At 4pm the next day the Goliath set out for Dakar, expecting to land

around 15 hours later, but at about 6.45am the starboard propeller flew off and Bossoutrot had to land on a beach, where the crippled aircraft was wrecked by waves.

The crew managed to salvage some supplies from the aircraft and built a shelter. That night they headed south, but the next day, exhausted after they had walked 13 miles in the desert heat, they decided to turn back and wait by the wreck. Thankfully the stranded crew has not had to wait too long (→ Aug 19, 1922).

# French firm opens mail service to Morocco

*Rabat, Morocco, September 1*
The first regular airmail service between France and Morocco was inaugurated today by the Société des lignes aériennes Latécoère (Latécoère air lines company), founded by French airplane manufacturer Pierre-Georges Latécoère. Didier Daurat made the first flight of the new service; taking off from Toulouse in the south of France yesterday evening, he landed his Breguet 14 with its cargo of mail-

bags at Rabat airfield late this afternoon after an uneventful journey via Spain.

The Latécoère fleet is made up of 15 Breguets, which, like their pilots, were supplied by the French army as surplus to requirements. On today's showing the service will probably be a success, although Latécoère is hoping to renegotiate some of the terms of his contract with the French government, signed in July (→ Oct 5, 1920).

*Incoming service: Daurat's Breguet 14 shortly after its arrival at Rabat.*

# Training seen as the key to Britain's RAF

*London, December 11*
Plans for a small but specialized Royal Air Force (RAF) were endorsed today by Britain's air secretary, Winston Churchill. They were drawn up by far-sighted chief of air staff Sir Hugh Trenchard.

Central to the new regime is the opening, next year, of the RAF's own officer cadet college at Cranwell, Lincolnshire. Students there will spend two years learning how to fly and all aspects of aviation theory. A short course in air pilotage and cross-country flying will follow, and the new officers will then be posted to a service squadron. Later, pilots will be able to specialize in subjects such as navigation, engines or wireless; technical knowledge will be one qualification for high command.

The lower echelons of the force have been depleted since demobilization, and Trenchard proposes a new three-year training course for young men who will eventually join the ranks.

The report marks a change from the wartime rush to throw half-trained pilots into the sky. Some 80 per cent of air losses during the war were among pilots who had flown fewer than 20 missions, and 70 per cent of losses among pilots in their first year were from bad flying, not enemy action (→ Feb 5, 1920).

*The American "Orientator" is used to help pilots learn to fly.*

# Bad weather hits Schneider contest

*Britain, September 24*
A row over the first post-war Schneider cup race at Bournemouth, England, has ended with a compromise decision by the International Aeronautical Federation (FAI). The trophy will stay with Britain's Royal Aero Club, organizers of this year's competition, while the Royal Aero Club of Italy will organize the next contest.

The seaplane race was a farce. Mist delayed the start. Britain's Vincent Nicholl took off early in his Fairey III but beached his aircraft. Basil Hobbs's Supermarine Sea Lion tipped over when a float filled with water. France withdrew. Guido Janello, in an Italian Air Force Savoia S.13, was the only finisher, but the judges made him do an extra lap and he ran out of fuel. They refused him the trophy but relented after a storm of protest – only to have the FAI overturn their decision today (→ Aug 12, 1922).

# Passengers tuck in to in-flight hamper

*London, October 11*
British aviation entrepreneur Frederick Handley Page, famous for his development of large multi-engined aircraft, has taken a leaf out of Count Zeppelin's book in an attempt to advertise the pleasures of flying. He has begun serving luncheon hampers to his passengers en route to Brussels.

The German count did the same in his pre-war airships as they flew across Germany. While it must be admitted that the Handley Page hamper, a small basket of cold meat and salad, does not quite match the champagne and pâté de fois gras available on the Zeppelins, it is certainly, at the modest cost of three shillings [15p], more attractively priced. The only drawback seems to be that the motion of the Handley Page O/400 aircraft, coupled with noise and fumes from the engines, seems to take away the appetite of many passengers.

## Bankers join with businesses to found first Dutch airline

*The Hague, October 7*
A new Dutch airline was formally registered here today. Its name is Koninklijke Luchtvaart Maatschappij voor Nederland en Kolonien [Royal Air Travel Company for the Netherlands and Colonies], or KLM for short. Backed by powerful business and banking interests, KLM has a sound financial basis although it does not yet have any aircraft. It will be based at Amsterdam's Schiphol airport.

KLM's able managing director, Albert Plesman, began planning for the airline a few months ago. It was originally to be known as Nederlandsche en Koloniale Luchtverkeer Maatschappij [Dutch and Colonial Airline Company], but on September 12, Queen Wilhelmina authorized the use of the word royal (→ May 17, 1920).

# Brothers link England and Australia

*Australia, December 10*
Two brothers have completed the first flight from Britain to Australia, covering a distance of 11,294 miles in 27 days and 20 hours and winning a £10,000 prize from the Australian government. The prize was offered to whoever could link England and Australia by air in 30 days or less before the end of 1919.

Ross and Keith Smith, both officers in the Australian air force, persuaded the Vickers airplane company to let them use a twin-engined Vimy bomber for the attempt. Fitted with extra fuel tanks but otherwise little altered, the Vimy, carrying the Smiths and two engineers, set off in snow from Hounslow airport, west of London, on November 12. Their route took them via Italy, Crete, Egypt, Syria, the Persian Gulf, India, Burma, Siam [Thailand], Singapore, Java and Timor before the triumphant – though boring – last 500 miles

*The triumphant crew: (l to r) W H Shiers, Ross Smith, Kevin Smith, J M Bennett.*

across the Timor Sea to Darwin. The crew had some hair-raising moments, such as when the plane met a flock of kite hawks at Calcutta; one bird hit the port propeller, which, incredibly, was undamaged. The most terrifying stretch was from Rangoon and Bangkok, when Ross Smith had to fly in thick cloud (→ Apr 13, 1922).

## Germany takes the lead in civil aviation

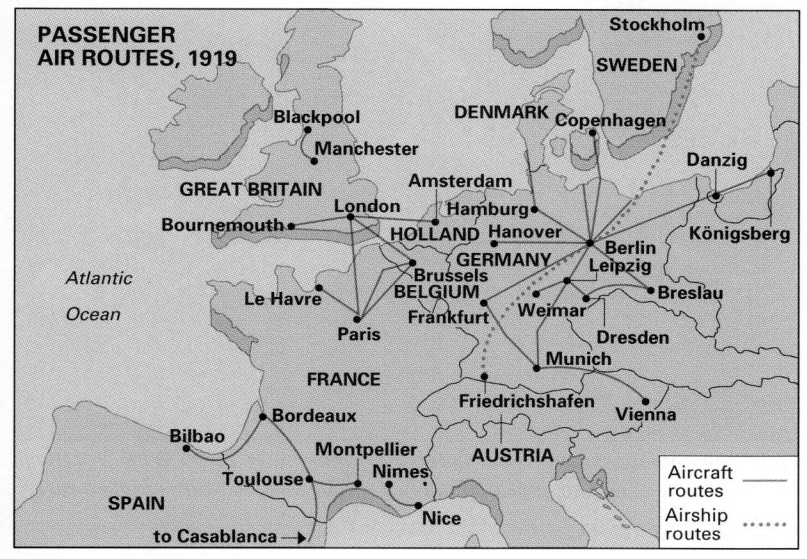

PASSENGER AIR ROUTES, 1919

Stockholm
SWEDEN
Blackpool
Manchester
DENMARK  Copenhagen
Danzig
GREAT BRITAIN   Amsterdam
London  Hamburg  Hanover  Königsberg
Bournemouth  HOLLAND  Berlin
GERMANY  Leipzig
Brussels  Breslau
Le Havre  BELGIUM
Frankfurt  Weimar
Paris  Dresden
Munich
FRANCE
Friedrichshafen  Vienna
Bordeaux
Bilbao  Montpellier  AUSTRIA
Toulouse  Nîmes
SPAIN  Nice
to Casablanca →

Atlantic Ocean

| Aircraft routes | ——— |
| Airship routes | ······ |

*Berlin, November 11*
Prevented by the new Versailles treaty from using military aircraft, the German Republic is now leading the field in civil air transport. Deutsche Luft Reederei, a joint venture of Hamburg-Amerika shipping, AEG and the Zeppelin works, was the first to start a daily passenger service. It flew initially from Berlin to Weimar and Leipzig, and has now expanded to Frankfurt and Hanover. Sächsische Luft Reederei of Saxony followed soon after, flying from Dresden to Berlin, Breslau and Leipzig, with Bayrischer Luft Lloyd of Bavaria linking Berlin with Munich, Frankfurt and the Austrian capital, Vienna.

Today sees the opening of another airline: Albatros, which will operate to Königsberg via the free city state of Danzig, again from Berlin.

## Smiths hail Vimy airplane for their success

*Darwin, Australia, December 10*
On their arrival here today from England after the first-ever flight between Britain and Australia, brothers Ross and Keith Smith said they owed their success to the Vickers Vimy aircraft which they piloted. Originally designed as a bomber for Britain's Royal Air Force, the Vimy was used by Alcock and Brown earlier this year on the first non-stop Atlantic flight. The most important factor in this success is the reliability of the two Rolls-Royce Eagle engines. Another is that the aircraft is a proven design, rather than a machine built especially for the flight.

*Victorious Vimy: the bomber boasts reliable engines for long-range flight.*

## Florida airline opens service to Havana

*Key West, Florida, November 1*
Aeromarine Airways today became America's first international airline with its inaugural flight from here to Havana. It flies from Key West at 10.30am and Havana at 3.30pm. The time saving is immense. Passengers who used to be decanted from the train only to wait eight hours for the steamer to leave on its overnight voyage can now step straight onto the flying boat and get to Havana in about 90 minutes (→ Nov 1, 1920).

*The first all-metal aircraft to enter commercial service, the Junkers F 13 was a cantilever monoplane developed from the company's military aircraft.*

*An unreliable ABC Dragonfly motor powered Sopwith's Snark triplane.*

*Nieuport's Nighthawk was ill-equipped with its Dragonfly motor.*

*Supermarine's Sea Lion I, 145-mph flying boat, was developed from a First World War design to compete in the 1919 Schneider Trophy contest.*

*The Blériot-Spad 27 commercial biplane was developed from the Spad XVIII. Although the pilot was exposed, the two passengers were housed in a cabin.*

*Anthony Fokker's wartime experience bore fruit in the immediate post-war period with the F.II monoplane, which plied the European routes.*

*The Sopwith Schneider was built for the abandoned 1919 trophy contest.*

*The Westland Weasel reconnaissance two-seater won no orders.*

*Only one Thomas-Morse S-4E aerobatic trainer was built. With a 110-hp Le Rhône rotary engine, it proved tail-heavy and was later turned into a racer.*

*Geoffrey de Havilland's Airco D.H.16 utilized standard D.H.9A components, combined with a wider fuselage to accommodate four passengers.*

The Thomas-Morse MB-3 fighter came just too late for war service.

Built in the US but designed by an Italian – the Pomilio FVL-8 fighter.

Sopwith's Dragon, with Dragonfly engine, remained a prototype only.

The Siddeley Siskin: first of a line of famous Royal Air Force fighters.

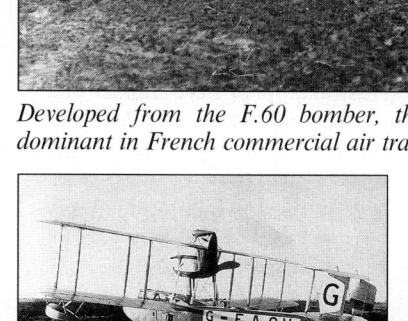

Developed from the F.60 bomber, the Farman Goliath airliner was predominant in French commercial air transport throughout the 1920s.

A successful commercial amphibian – the Vickers Viking I four-seater.

The locally-designed Häfeli DH-5 served with the Swiss air force.

The Model 6/B-1 flying boat was Boeing's first commercial design, but it failed to find buyers with so many war-surplus machines flooding the market.

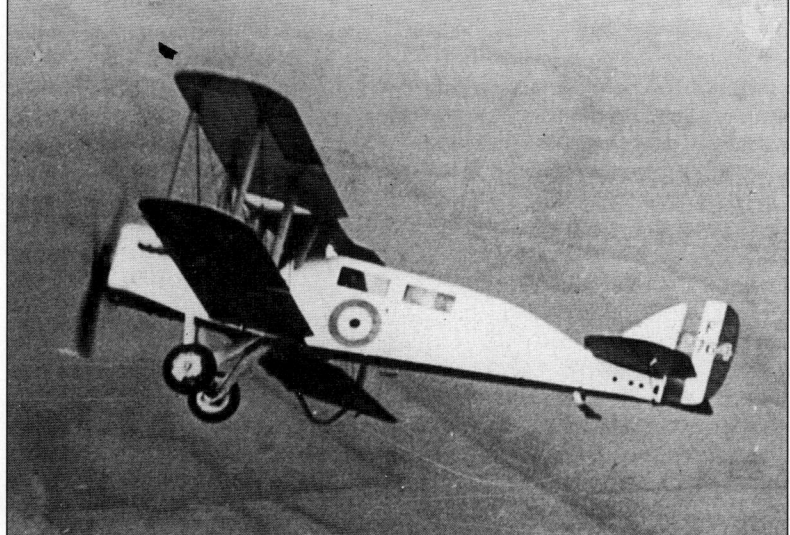

Post-war communications flights in the RAF were made by the de Havilland D.H.4A, which had a two-passenger cabin behind the pilot's cockpit.

Sopwith converted its Pup fighter to produce the aptly-named Dove civil two-seater, but there were few takers. The engine was an 80-hp Le Rhône.

Sopwith's Atlantic – built for a trans-Atlantic attempt. It was ditched.

Comfort for civil passengers: Westland's four-seater Limousine.

In Italy, Savoia produced the S.16 five-seater flying boat, a number of which were used in commercial service. S.16s were exported to many countries.

# 1920

194.49mph
France
Joseph Sadi-Lecointe
Nieuport-Delage 29v
Dec 12, 1920

1,884 miles
Great Britain
Alcock and Brown
Vickers Vimy
Jun 15, 1919

34,610ft
USA
Roland Rohlfs
Curtiss Wasp
Sep 18, 1919

44,672lb
Great Britain
WG Tarrant Ltd
Tarrant Tabor

700hp
Italy
Fiat
A.14

**India, January 24**
The British Air Ministry begins an experimental airmail service between Karachi and Bombay.

**Washington, DC, January 29**
President Woodrow Wilson appoints Orville Wright to the National Advisory Committee for Aeronautics (NACA).

**South Africa, February 1**
The South African Air Force is established.

**London, March 29**
Although it has not yet been officially opened, Croydon airport, south of London, begins operations as London's main airport, taking over from Hounslow (→ Dec 31).

**France, March 29**
The French airline CGEA introduces the splendid new Farman F.60 Goliath airliner on its service between Le Bourget (Paris) and Croydon (→ Jan 1, 1923).

**France, April 23**
The Compagnie Franco-Roumaine de Navigation Aérienne [Franco-Romanian Aerial Navigation Company] (CFRNA) is formed.

**Poland, April 25**
The Kosciuszcko Squadron of American volunteers begins operations with the Polish Air Force against the invading Red Army; the Poles have just received a consignment of Italian Ansaldo Balilla fighters (→ May 11, 1921).

**France, May 7**
The Farman brothers found the Société Générale de Transports Aériens [General Air Transport Company] (SGTA).

**England, May 15**
The Instone Air Line is formed.

**Europe, May 17**
A new service between Amsterdam and London, to be operated jointly by KLM and the British company Aircraft Transport & Travel (AT&T), opens (→ Dec 15).

**Tokyo, May 31**
An eager crowd welcomes Italian pilots Ferrarin and Masiero, after their flight of 11,250 miles from Rome in SVA.9 biplanes.

**England, May 31**
Australian pilot Bert Hinkler takes off from Croydon in an Avro Baby on the first leg of a projected flight to Australia; he lands in Turin, Italy, nine hours and 30 minutes later (→ Jun 10).

**Washington, DC, June 4**
The Army Reorganization Bill is passed, creating the US Army Air Service (→ Jul 2, 1926).

**San Antonio, Texas, June 8**
Lieutenant John Wilson makes a world record parachute jump from 19,861 feet.

**England, June 10**
Bert Hinkler arrives back in England, having given up his attempt to fly to Australia when he realized in Rome that a current war in Syria would prevent him from progressing further eastwards.

**Paris, June 12**
Jean Casale tests an oxygen-breathing device which he claims will allow pilots to make high-altitude flights (→ Jun 23, 1923).

**Japan, June 22**
Lieutenant Kuwahara takes off in his Sopwith Pup from a special ramp on the foredeck of the carrier *Wakamiya* while she is under way.

**England, July 19**
The Vickers R.80 airship, designed in an innovative streamlined shape by company designer Barnes Wallis, makes its first flight.

**Washington, July**
Boeing delivers the last of 111 converted de Havilland DH-4s ordered by the US Army Air Service.

**Madrid, August 27**
Juan de La Cierva is granted a patent for his "Autogiro".

**France, September 3**
The Deutsch de la Meurthe cup, together with the third of three cash prizes provided under the rules of a competition established August 25, 1906, is awarded to French pilot Sadi Lecointe; he flew the 118.3-mile course in 42 minutes and 53 seconds on January 3 this year (→ Oct 1, 1921).

**USA, September 11**
Edison Mouton flies into Marina Field, San Francisco, to complete the first US transcontinental airmail flight; beginning in New York on September 8, four pilots ferried mail across the US in 75 hours and 52 minutes' flying time over four days, beating the best rail-road time by 22 hours (→ Oct 15).

**Virginia, September 11**
While under radio direction, three airships succeed in flying in formation at Langley Field.

**Germany, September 30**
The prototype Zeppelin-Staaken E.4/20 monoplane, with room for 18 passengers, is completed.

**Toulouse, France, October 1**
Emile Dewoitine sets up the Société Anonyme des Avions Dewoitine [Dewoitine Airplane Company Ltd] (SAD) and begins work designing a single-seat fighter.

**USA and Canada, October 15**
Eddie Hubbard, founder of Hubbard Air Service, pilots a Boeing B-1 flying boat on the first flight of a scheduled daily international airmail service between Seattle, Washington State, and Victoria, British Columbia (→ Feb 23, 1921).

**France, October 20**
Sadi Lecointe sets a world speed record, flying his Nieuport Delage 29 at 187.99mph (→ Sep 21, 1922).

**New York, October 20**
An American-Canadian expedition to establish an air route across Alaska, which left New York on July 15, returns.

**Florida, November 1**
Aeromarine-West Indies Airways is awarded the first US foreign air mail contract.

**Tie Siding, Wyoming, November 7**
Pilot John P Woodward is killed when his DH-4 hits the side of a hill in bad weather en route from Salt Lake City, Utah, to Cheyenne, South Dakota; his death is the year's 12th fatality for the US Post Office's airmail service.

**Moscow, November 21**
Lenin allocates 35 million gold roubles to fund the establishment of a new air force.

**Germany, November 24**
The prototype Dornier Cs II Delphin flying boat, capable of carrying six passengers, makes a first test flight.

**Perth, Australia, December 2**
Pilot F S Briggs, together with his mechanic and a passenger, land their D.H.4 to complete the first east-west crossing of Australia; taking off from Melbourne on November 30, they covered the 2,169 miles in 18 hours and 12 minutes' flying time.

**Lympne, Kent, December 10**
Lympne airfield is equipped with lights for night landings.

**France, December 12**
The prototype Blériot-Spad 33 airliner makes its first flight; it can accommodate a total of five passengers.

**France, December 15**
The first of a number of flying schools to train reserve pilots for the military opens at Orly, just south of Paris.

---

*Rallying call: a colorful American poster tempts potential pilots to forget their fears and taste for themselves the thrill of the air.* ▶

# US pilot is out cold in five-mile plunge

*Dayton, Ohio, February 27*
Major Rudolph W Schroeder of the US Army Air Service set a new world altitude record today when he flew to the dizzying height of 33,143 feet – but nearly lost his life in the effort. As his Liberty-engined Packard-Le Père Lusac biplane reached its peak altitude, "Shorty" Schroeder's oxygen system failed, and a lack of oxygen combined with engine exhaust fumes caused him to black out.

The airplane plummeted five miles before Schroeder regained consciousness and was able to land. Military observers found him and the aircraft encrusted in ice; his eyes were frozen open as he sat helpless in the open cockpit.

Schroeder saved his own life. Recognizing his oxygen problem and aware he would soon black out, he switched off his engine and pushed the aircraft's nose downward to get to an altitude where he might regain consciousness. He is now recovering from his ordeal.

# Royal Air Force has school for officers

*Lincolnshire, England, February 5*
Amid modest ceremony, Britain's Royal Air Force (RAF) today opened its officer cadet training school at Cranwell on a windswept plain in eastern England. The new school, on the site of a former naval air station, reflects the determination of Sir Hugh Trenchard, chief of the air staff, to create an independent service with its own "spirit".

Trenchard has brushed off suggestions that the army and navy should train his men to be British officers and gentlemen while he just teaches them to fly. He dismisses the snobbish sarcasm of sections of the older services, who sneer that the RAF lacks "dining out power". Meanwhile he is a target for sniping from army and navy men, who accuse him of wanting enough aerodromes to create a "Royal Ground Force". But Trenchard, a distinguished career soldier before heading the air services, has the total support of air minister Winston Churchill (→ Jul 1923).

# French Sahara flight marred by tragedy

*Vuillemin and Chalus at Dakar.*

*Senegal, West Africa, March 31*
Two French airmen trying out a new route from Paris to Dakar in French West Africa, arrived today after a 21-stage flight marred by tragedy. Commandant Vuillemin and Lieutenant Chalus left Paris in a Breguet 16 on January 24, and at Tamanrasset in the Sahara they were joined by another airplane whose three crew included desert veteran General Laperrine.

The crews left for Timbuktu on February 18, but Vuillemin lost the other aircraft and landed at Menaka the next day to search for it. On March 22 it was found, crashed, with two survivors; the general had died of his injuries.

# Aircraft companies struggle in peace time

*London, 1920*
The end of the war has brought about a major slump in the global airplane industry. Many contracts for both airplanes and airships have been cancelled, with a resulting considerable loss of jobs, and world markets are clogged with surplus aircraft. Indeed, the biggest deal this year has been the purchase by the British Handley Page company of government surplus airplanes and spare parts for £1,000,000.

In Britain Vickers has slimmed down, but its Vimy is continuing to sell, and the company has won a recent air ministry design award for the next generation of amphibian airplanes. Other firms have diversified widely. Salmson in France and Armstrong in Britain are making motor cars and two other firms, including Avro, have been bought by car makers. Avro has opened an air service from London to Blackpool as well as centers giving the public joy-rides, while Handley Page runs the first scheduled air service between London and Paris.

In the US, Boeing has been greatly helped by a recent order to build military airplanes designed by other manufacturers. Anthony Fokker has fled from Germany to Holland and leading German war hero Hermann Goering is trying to sell surplus German aircraft to Scandinavia.

*War planes are lined up in Berlin, ready to be destroyed by the Allies.*

# England-Cape link dogged by mishap

*Cape Town, S Africa, March 20*
Two South African pilots have completed the first flight from Britain to South Africa. Lt-Col Pierre van Ryneveld and Squadron Leader Christopher Quintin Brand landed today at Cape Town's Wynberg aerodrome after a flying time of four days, 13 hours and 30 minutes. The two left Brooklands, near London, in a Vickers Vimy, the *Silver Queen*, on February 4. A leaking radiator caused a crash at Wadi Halfa, Sudan, and it was in a new Vimy, the *Silver Queen II*, that they reached Bulawayo in Southern Rhodesia. After crashing on take-off on March 6, they borrowed a D.H.9 for the final leg.

*Brand: one half of a winning team.*

# Britain to pull out of anti-Bolshevik war

*Russia, April*
Military sources confirm that the doomed effort by RAF "volunteers" to stem the Bolshevik advance in Russia has ended. Sopwith Camels and D.H.9s of 47 Squadron, led by Canadian war hero Major Raymond Collishaw, went disguised as a training mission to attack the Red Army.

The scheme was backed personally by air minister Winston Churchill, in spite of a failed attempt by a "relief force" in northern Russia last year. Collishaw's last raid, to attack cavalry and an armored train, was on March 28. His squadron has received nearly 30 British decorations for its efforts, and 75 from its anti-Bolshevik Russian allies.

# Colony wins air service

*King Albert flyer: a Belgian Lévy-Lepen boat seaplane moored at N'Gomé.*

**Belgian Congo, July 1**
Belgium has become the first country to launch an internal air service in a colony, with the inauguration today of regular flights between N'Gomé and Leopoldville in the Belgian Congo. Six Lévy-Lepen seaplanes will be operated by a new airline, called Lara – Ligne Aérienne Roi Albert [King Albert Air Line] – after the Belgian monarch,

who has been at the forefront of promoting the service.

The 350-mile route from Leopoldville, the capital, to N'Gomé follows the river Congo, because the aircraft cannot risk getting into difficulties over the almost impenetrable tropical forest that covers much of the colony. If the service is a success, it is hoped to extend it to Lisala and Stanleyville.

# Flying faster thanks to retractable gear

*Sadi Joseph Lecointe seated in his superbly streamlined plane.*

**Etampes, France, September 28**
Flyers today met to compete for the annual Gordon Bennett cup. The Dayton-Wright R.B. Racer, flown by American Howard Rinehart, lost but caused a sensation. It was the first time that an airplane had been fitted with retractable landing gear to improve its aerodynamics.

A simple lever system allowed the pilot to rectract the wheels after take-off. The event was won by Sadi Joseph Lecointe, who reached 167.78mph on the 300-km [186-mile] course in a Nieuport, to win the trophy a third time for France, where, under competition rules, it will now stay (→ Oct 20).

# Underwater cable becomes navigation aid

**Norfolk, Virginia, July 6**
The US Navy has just carried out an experiment which is sure to be of interest to airmen the world over. A US Navy Curtiss F-5L flying boat flew today from its base at Hampton Roads near Norfolk to the old battleship USS *Ohio* stationed 130 miles out in the Atlantic. The airplane then returned to its base.

What was special about the flight was that the pilot was able to steer straight to the battleship thanks to an electromagnetic cable lying on the sea bed. A special receiver in-

stalled aboard the Curtiss picked up the signals from the underwater cable. Using this system, the crew simply had to follow the course indicated by the signals. Whenever these were interrupted, they knew they were off course, while a constant signal meant the airplane was on the correct heading.

This simple new electromagnetic cable system could be used to keep pilots and navigators from becoming disoriented while flying at night or in thick fog, when they cannot see the ground.

*D/F equipment helps direct air traffic at London's Croydon airport.*

# Safety controls for busy Berlin traffic

**Berlin, August 10**
Berlin's Tempelhof airport has become so busy with air traffic that the safety-minded airport authorities have devised a system to announce arrivals and departures and to keep incoming and outgoing aircraft separate.

German aircraft are greeted with a prolonged wail from the control tower on arrival, while foreign or unidentified air transports get two distinct blasts on the siren. This is operated by sharp-eyed "air traffic policemen" employed solely on this duty. Others ensure that arriving airplanes stick to the "landing zone" of the airfield while departing aircraft must stay in the "take-off zone". The zones are separated by a safety area 150 feet wide.

# Two fatal crashes hit French airline

**Valencia, Spain, October 5**
Pierre Latécoère, whose company, Latécoère airlines, is hoping to open up an air route from Paris to South America via West Africa, was shocked to hear today that two of his Breguet 14 transports had crashed with loss of life. The first batch of Latécoère's 15 Breguets are ex-military machines, many still camouflaged. Their Renault engines, designed for war, have an average lifespan of only 40 hours. This is not the only problem faced by the Latécoère crews. They have to run the gauntlet of frightened or angry tribesmen in North Africa, assuming they can overcome the hostility of the authorities in Spain, which they must fly over to reach Morocco (→ May 13, 1921).

▷

# Designer Douglas sets up in Los Angeles

*Donald Douglas, in the rear cockpit, supervises work in the new factory.*

**Los Angeles, July 22**

Wealthy local sportsman and aviation enthusiast David R Davis today teamed up with airplane designer Donald W Douglas to form the Davis-Douglas Company. They aim to build the first aircraft capable of flying non-stop across the US, but before they do they will need a more suitable home than their temporary offices behind a barbershop.

Davis put up $40,000 to start the company. Douglas moved here from Cleveland, Ohio, to design transport aircraft, but has now put that work aside to collaborate with Davis. Brooklyn-born Douglas has strong aircraft design credentials. A graduate of the Massachusetts Institute of Technology, he was part of the Connecticut Aircraft Company's design team for the navy's first dirigible, the DN-1, and worked at the Glenn Martin Company in Los Angeles until it moved to the east coast in 1916.

After a short stay as chief civilian aeronautical engineer for the aviation section of the US Army Signal Corps, Douglas went back to Glenn Martin, where he was responsible for designing the army's large, twin engined MB-1 bomber and its naval and ten-passenger transport versions (→ Jun 28, 1921).

# Britain's air force pilots show off skills

*A poster advertising the RAF show.*

**London, July 3**

The British public was treated to a breathtaking display of flying today at Hendon aerodrome just north of London. The event was the Royal Air Force Pageant, held to raise money for the RAF Memorial Fund. The pageant was intended as a one-off show but, if the enthusiasm of the 40,000 spectators who jammed all roads leading to the aerodrome is anything to go by, it is unlikely to be the last.

Fighters, bombers and trainers were thrown about the sky by their pilots in daredevil smoke-trailed aerobatics. Others fought air battles, dived on mock trenches and dispatched a balloon to the ground in flames.

# Queensland airline set up by veterans

**Brisbane, Australia, November 16**

Following a marathon overland survey trip through the outback, two plucky ex-service pilots from the Australian Flying Corps have formed a new domestic air service for north-eastern Australia. The airline – Queensland and Northern Territories Aerial Services Limited or QANTAS for short – takes its place alongside some 16 other Australian airline companies, all struggling.

The pilots, Hudson Fysh and P J McGinnis, together with company chairman Fergus McMaster and mechanic W A Baird, carried out their survey across hundreds of miles of bush in a Model "T" Ford. They are determined that their fleet of two B.E.2e machines and an Avro biplane will form the basis of a continuing service to the territory, carrying mail and passengers on urgent business (→ Nov 2, 1922).

# Long Island hosts first Pulitzer race

**New York State, November 25**

A US Army Air Service lieutenant won the first Aero Club of America Pulitzer trophy air race today. Before 30,000 spectators at Mitchell Field, C C Mosley flew a Verville-Packard, designed and built in the US, over the 132-mile course in 44 minutes and 22.57 seconds at a top speed of 156.54mph. His nearest rival, Captain H E Hartney, also of the air service, followed 2.5 minutes behind him in a Thomas-Morse MB-3 fighter.

Contestants made four circuits of the course over Long Island from Mitchell Field to Lufbery Field near Wantagh, on to Henry J Damm Field near Babylon, and back to Mitchell. Sixty-three entrants vied for the trophy, which was donated by the Pulitzer brothers, publishers of the New York *World* and St Louis *Post-Dispatch* newspapers (→ Nov 5, 1921).

# Franco-Romanian airline flies to Prague

*Breaking new ground: the Potez VII which opened the Paris-Prague service.*

**Prague, October 27**

An enterprising new airline which is the brainchild of a Romanian banker is opening up even more European routes to air travel. Founded on April 23 by Aristide Blank and based in the rue de Rivoli in central Paris, the Compagnie Franco-Roumaine de Navigation Aérienne [Franco-Romanian Aerial Navigation Company] or CFRNA today opened its second service, between Paris and the Czechoslovak capital.

Blank and French colleague Pierre de Fleurieu are determined to make CFRNA the leading airline linking eastern and western Europe, and are planning services to many of the major capitals in the east. Regular daily flights to Warsaw (via Breslau in Germany) and Budapest (via Vienna) are in the pipeline, as well as an airborne version of the famous Orient Express railroad route, which will link Belgrade, Bucharest and, eventually, Istanbul in Turkey.

CFRNA, launched with the inauguration of the Paris to Strasbourg route on September 20, is the 11th airline to be created in France. It uses a fleet of SPAD and Potez aircraft which are in the charge of chief pilot and wartime air ace Albert Deullin.(→ Apr 12, 1921).

# In despair, makers turn from airships to boats and buses

*Airship frames at Short's works.*

*England, January*
British aircraft firm Short Brothers has turned its hand to building boats and motor buses. A year ago its peacetime aviation program seemed assured: it was confident of receiving a regular order for rigid airships, and the massive Short' airship shed at Cardington, Bedfordshire, made it an ideal contractor. But then things went badly wrong.

Last year the company's airship program was crippled. First the R.38 airship was cancelled and then, in April, the Cardington site was nationalized, becoming the Royal Airship Works. Consequently the R.37 has not been completed, and although the R.38 has been reinstated, the only Short' workers involved are draughtsmen.

# Capital airfields boast booming business

*London welcome: an airplane coming in to land at the new Croydon airport.*

*Britain and France, December 31*
The boom in European civil aviation means that old aerodromes need to be expanded or replaced in order to handle the growing amount of international passenger traffic. Nowhere has this need been felt more than at Europe's two largest capitals, London and Paris.

Paris has one main airport at Le Bourget, north of the city. It is perhaps the busiest in Europe, handling nearly 7,000 passengers this year. Plans are afoot to expand both passenger and aircraft facilities. Hounslow, west of London, opened for international flights in August 1919 and handled most London/Paris traffic. It proved inadequate, with wartime huts and no repair or refreshment services, so a new "London Terminal Airport" was inaugurated in March this year near Croydon, south of London. This combines two airfields, Wallington and Waddon, divided by a road; a grade crossing links the halves (→ Mar 31, 1921).

*Passenger boom: business is looking good at Le Bourget airport near Paris.*

# Cricklewood horror

*London, December 14*
A Handley Page O/400 aircraft taking off from the firm's London airport at Cricklewood crashed today, killing the pilot, engineer and two of the six passengers. Chief pilot of the airline Roger Bager was in command. He was believed to have been disoriented by the prevailing fog. The aircraft struck a tree and burst into flames on hitting the ground. Three survivors escaped through rear windows; another is reported missing. This is the first flying disaster to hit a British airline.→

# Subsidy refusal prompts British airline's collapse

*London, December 15*
Following a tragic accident here yesterday [*see report on this page*], one of Britain's leading airlines, Aircraft Transport and Travel (AT&T), has gone into liquidation.

AT&T, founded four years ago by George Holt Thomas, was competing on the London/Paris run with five other companies, including two British firms, Handley Page and the Instone Air Line. The last accounts presented by Holt Thomas's airline had shown a considerable loss, and he had been looking for financial support for some time. Knowing that the two French companies which served the same route were subsidized by the French government, he asked for help from air minister Winston Churchill, hoping that he would adopt the same approach as his counterpart in France. But Churchill refused to help, stating that the young industry should fly by its own unaided efforts.

The attitude of the British government seems extremely shortsighted in the face of evidence from the Continent of the effectiveness of subsidies in establishing the new industry.

French airlines are making remarkable progress, thanks not only to government cash to keep ticket prices down, but also to a system by which every company is allocated a specific sphere of influence, a monopoly effectively, connecting France with 12 foreign countries and French territories overseas such as Corsica, Algeria and Morocco.

Air travel is also flourishing in Germany where local communities, cities and the states, eager to be on the airline route map, contribute money in addition to central government funds.

Churchill may yet be forced to subsidize the British airlines or face the prospect of all air passengers to and from Britain being carried by foreign airlines.

*The unattractive Westland Walrus was the outcome of an attempt to turn the de Havilland D.H.9A into a naval aircraft. Only a few were built.*

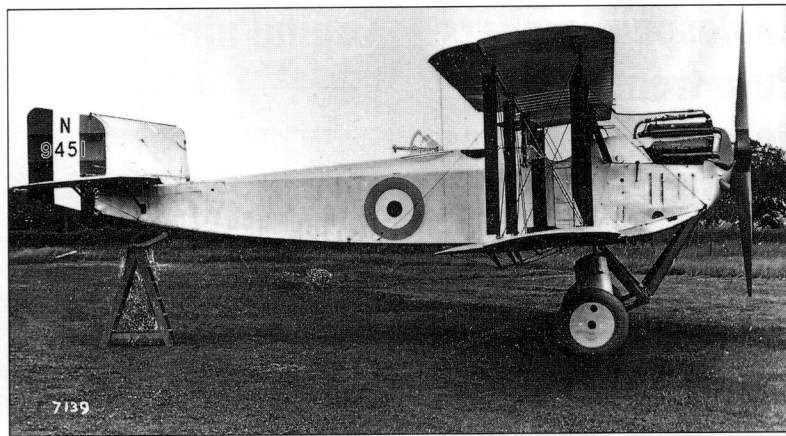

*An early member of an extremely attractive line of inter-war aircraft was the Lion-engined Fairey IIID, which was equally at home on land or water.*

*The Liberty-engined Martin NBS-1 night bomber was a development of the MB-1, the first successful twin-engined aeroplane of American design.*

*Another post-war commercial airplane that failed to find a market was the two-passenger Sopwith Antelope, with a quaint four-wheeled undercarriage.*

*Built to meet a fleet requirement, the Fairey Pintail had its fin and rudder below the tailplane to allow the gunner a clear field of fire to the rear.*

*The Saunders Kittiwake was an attempt to produce a commercial flying boat, but the prototype suffered wing structural failure on an early test flight.*

*The Blériot-Spad 34 elementary trainer was used by Argentinian, Finnish and Bolivian trainees as well as by the French pupils for whom it was built. It was powered by an 80-hp Le Rhône engine. A total of 150 were constructed.*

*Dornier's unconventional Delphin III ten-passenger flying boat had stub wings which doubled as sponsons and thus did not need wing-tip floats. The 600-hp BMW VI engine was mounted directly above the two-man cockpit.*

*A V Roe returned briefly to the triplane formula with the Type 547, but the concept was becoming outdated, and the design failed to attract orders.*

*From Bristol came the two-passenger Type 36 Seely Puma, one of many conversions of the famous Bristol two-seater fighter of the First World War.*

*The Fokker F.III, a logical development of the F.II, carried five passengers. Thirty examples were built, and it went into service with KLM in 1921.*

*The bulky Blackburn Swift carrier-borne torpedo-bomber was successful in winning orders and established its manufacturer as a builder of naval aircraft.*

*The Blériot-Spad S.33, with roomy five-seater monocoque fuselage.*

*The pilot of de Havilland's D.H.18 was located behind the passengers.*

*The Handley Page W.8b was a mainstay of the Handley Page and Imperial Airways' fleets until 1927.*

*Boulton and Paul's P.8 was built with a non-stop transatlantic crossing in mind, but it did not even get as far as making an attempt. Unlike most aircraft designed at this time, it had an enclosed cockpit. Built largely of light alloy but with a fabric covering, the P.8 was first flown on May 10, 1920. The engines were two 450-hp Napier Lions.*

# 1921

**205.22mph**
France
Joseph Sadi-Lecointe
Nieuport-Delage
Sep 26, 1921

**1,884 miles**
Great Britain
Alcock and Brown
Vickers Vimy
Jun 15, 1919

**34,610ft**
USA
Roland Rohlfs
Curtiss Wasp
Sep 18, 1919

**57,319lb**
Italy
SAI Caproni
Caproni Ca 60

**838hp**
France
Marcel Riffard
Breguet-Bugatti 32

**England, January 7**
Handley Page completes tests on the automatic stabiliser invented by Frenchman Aveline. The system helps to keep heading and altitude.

**Australia, January 16**
Citizens of Melbourne are able to read copies of the *Daily Mail* which were printed this morning in Brisbane and flown across the country in a D.H.4.

**Istres, France, January 29**
After two failures, Jean Mermoz gets his pilot's license, flying a Caudron G 3.

**London, February 6**
Vickers test pilot Stan Cockerell begins a series of tests with a Viking flying boat to investigate the possibility of flights between the river Thames in London and the river Seine in Paris.

**USA, February 23**
A team of pilots completes an experimental coast-to-coast mail flight; flying by day and night, they have linked San Francisco and Long Island in a day and a half's flying time (→ Dec 31, 1921).

**Florida, February 24**
Lieutenant William D Coney completes a solo flight from Rockwell Field, San Diego, to Jacksonville, in 22 hours and 27 minutes flying time.

**England, February 28**
Handley Page Transport and the Instone Air Line, unable to compete with French airlines backed by official subsidy, are forced to suspend their London-to-Paris services (→ Mar 21).

**Paris, March 1**
Orly aerodrome is opened, south of the city.

**England, March 21**
The Instone Air Line resumes its London/Paris service, two days after Handley Page; the airlines have each been granted a government subsidy of £25,000.

**Illinois, March 23**
Lieutenant Arthur Hamilton sets a new world record when he jumps by parachute from 24,400 feet.

**Australia, March 31**
The Air Corps is replaced by the Australian Air Force (→ Aug 13).

**Poland, April 12**
The Franco-Romanian airline CFRNA extends its Paris-Prague service to Warsaw (→ Sep 2, 1923).

**The Netherlands, April 14**
The Fokker F.III monoplane enters service with KLM.

**Washington, DC, April 14**
The Navy Department awards the Davis-Douglas Co of Los Angeles a contract worth $119,550 for three DT-1 torpedo bombers.

**Poland, May 11**
The Kosciuszko Squadron of American volunteers who fought against the Red Army is disbanded.

**Toulouse, France, May 13**
Pierre-Georges Latécoère founds the Compagnie Générale d'Entreprises Aéronautiques [General Aeronautic Enterprises Company] (→ Jan 1, 1923).

**New York State, May 15**
Laura Bromwell loops the loop 199 times in one hour and 20 minutes, setting a new womens' record for consecutive loops.

**Egypt and Iraq, June 8**
British de Havilland D.H.9As of Nos 30 and 47 Squadrons, Royal Air Force, make the first flight of a planned regular airmail service between Cairo and Baghdad; to help familiarize pilots with the new route, several land vehicles are sent ahead to make tracks in the desert sand.

**Arizona, June 12**
As part of a study of air currents, Lieutenant Alexander Pearson lands and takes off in the Grand Canyon.

**Fort Bliss, Texas, June 28**
The *Cloudster*, built by the Davis-Douglas Company, lands near El Paso after a failed attempt to fly non-stop across the US.

**Hendon, London, July 16**
Cambridge wins the first air race between Oxford and Cambridge universities, using S.E.5as.

**USA, July 21**
In an experiment to demonstrate the vulnerability of ships to air bombing, nine MB-2 bombers of the First Provisional Air Brigade, sink the unmanned ex-German navy battleship *Ostfriesland*; the cruiser *Frankfurt* was sunk on July 18 as part of the same trial, which began on June 21.

**England, August 1**
The Vickers Vernon, the first airplane designed as a troop carrier, is delivered to the RAF.

**London, August 1**
The government closes its airship program as part of expenditure cutbacks.

**Troy, Ohio, August 3**
Lieutenant John Macready finds a new use for airplanes when he sprays a patch of ground infested with caterpillars.

**USA, August 10**
The US Navy Bureau of Aeronautics is formed under the command of Rear-Admiral William Moffett.

**Australia, August 13**
The Australian Air Force is granted the prefix "Royal" by King George V.

**Germany, September 13**
Wolf Harth flies for 21 minutes in a sailplane, beating the 1911 gliding record set by Orville Wright.

**France, October 1**
The first winner of the second Deutsch de la Meurthe cup is Georges Kirsch, who achieves a speed of 172.97mph.

**Washington, DC, October 5**
Major-General Mason Patrick is appointed Chief of the Air Service.

**Seville, Spain, October 15**
The Spanish airline Compania Española de Trafico Aerea [Spanish Air Traffic Company], or CETA, flies its first service: an airmail flight to Larache in Morocco.

**Nebraska, November 5**
Bert Acosta wins the Pulitzer trophy speed race, reaching 176.7mph in a Navy Curtiss C-12 at Omaha.

**USA, November 12**
Wesley May carries out a brave in-flight refuelling experiment: with a five-gallon can of fuel strapped to his back, he climbs from the wing of a Lincoln Standard onto that of a Curtiss JN-4 and fills the tank of the second airplane.

**Berlin, November 24**
The airline Deutsch-Russische Luftverkehrs Gesellschaft [German-Russian Air Travel Company], or Deruluft, is formed by Aero Union and the Soviet government (→ May 1, 1922).

**Japan, November 30**
The Imperial Navy's aircraft carrier *Hosho* is launched; she is designed to carry 25 airplanes.

**Australia, December 5**
Western Australia Airways opens the first scheduled regular airline service in the country.

**New York State, December 29**
Edward Stinson and Lloyd Bertaud set a world endurance record of 26 hours, 18 minutes and 35 seconds flying a BMW-engined Junkers-Larsen over Roosevelt Field (→ Jul 27, 1923).

---

*Learn as you earn: a persuasive poster encouraging Americans to join up as trainee pilots and mechanics in the Army Air Service.* ▶

# Helicopter makes tentative lift-off, with the aid of a gas balloon, for brief flight

*A balloon filled with hydrogen gives the helicopter extra lifting power.*

**Valentigney, France, January 15**
A strange flying machine took to the air here today when Etienne Oehmichen, a former Peugeot engineer, flew his twin-rotor helicopter, which has a 5,000-cubic foot balloon on top. The balloon has been added just to get the machine airborne and increase its stability, and Oehmichen plans to omit it and fit a bigger engine than the current 25-hp Dutheil et Chalmers. A more powerful engine, he says, could drive four rotors. Today's flight, lasting a minute and half at a height of about 25 feet, was the first free flight of a piloted helicopter since 1907 (→ May 1, 1923).

# London's new airport is officially opened

*Now officially open: London's Croydon airport, complete with customs.*

**London, March 31**
Today, a year after the first services transferred here from Hounslow, London's new airport, south of the capital near Croydon, was officially opened. The airport is really two aerodromes: Wallington (or Beddington) on the west side of Plough Lane, Waddon and the National Aircraft Factory on the east. Most airliners have to taxi from hangars on the west field across Plough Lane to the airport buildings, the site of a future terminal, on the east side. This is in Croydon, so London's air gateway will probably be known as Croydon airport. So far, the airport buildings are like army huts, except for the control tower, which stands on tall stilts.

# Frenchwoman is first to overfly the Andes

**Santiago, April 1**
Huge crowds welcomed the first woman to fly over the Andes as she touched down at the Chilean capital today. French pilot Adrienne Bolland took off from Mendoza in neighboring Argentina early this morning in a Caudron biplane which she had had shipped to South America.

Although she had to be careful to avoid the mountain peaks which were higher than her airplane could fly, and despite the intense cold she experienced while flying at over 14,750 feet, Bolland completed the historic Andean crossing in ten hours (→ Oct 18, 1923).

*Mountain flyer: Adrienne Bolland before taking off to cross the Andes.*

# New cockpit boosts high-altitude flying

**Dayton, Ohio, June 8**
The potential of high-altitude flying could be greatly expanded if an airplane unveiled today proves successful. The aircraft, a USD-9A (US-built de Havilland D.H.9A) especially modified by the engineering division of the US Army Air Service at Dayton, has had its two open cockpits replaced by a heavy oval compartment which is designed to be pressurized by a propeller-driven supercharger attached to the lower port wing.

The army is experimenting with pressurized airplanes for use on high-altitude photographic reconnaissance missions. A pressurized cabin will be essential in the upper atmosphere where the air pressure is too low for the human body to function properly. The pilot on today's test flight, Art Smith, was unable to get the pressurizing system to work, but engineers hope to iron out the problems in due course.

**A famous passenger: film star Pearl White ready for take-off.**

# US Army chooses Boeing

*Boeing has also built two dissimilar XGA-1 armored attack triplanes.*

**Seattle, Washington, June**
A $1,448,000 contract, the largest yet awarded for military airplanes by the US government since the end of the Great War, has been won by the Boeing company. The firm has been commissioned to build 200 Thomas-Morse MB-3A pursuit aircraft for the US Army Air Service.

The contract breathes new life into a company which ended 1920 with a $300,000 deficit on its books, even though Boeing modified 111 DH-4s for the US Army last year

and more are likely to be needed in the next few years. Boeing won the contract by underbidding five competitors, including the aircraft's designers, Thomas-Morse. The contract, which will tax the capacity of the factory here, has ended the furniture-making venture that the former timberman's company started to help it survive during the post-war slump in airplane manufacturing. The firm expects to take on extra workers to fill this valuable commission (→ Jul 21, 1924).

# Color bar forces woman to go to France

*France, June 1*
Women need iron determination if they want to learn to fly, but if they are really determined, they can do so if they are prepared to take on the prejudices of a male-dominated profession. But Bessie Coleman has another obstacle in her way: she is black.

Coleman, 28, has a story to tell which is similar to that of many talented black Americans. Born in Texas, she was bright at high school but was too poor to finish college and drifted to Chicago. She opened a chili parlor, which, although successful, she found unfulfilling, and eventually she decided that what she wanted to do was train to become a pilot.

This proved easier said than done. She applied to several flying schools in the US, but found their doors shut in her face; a woman, maybe, but a *colored* woman ... Finding all paths barred she arrived this month in France, where she will begin her apprenticeship on Nieuport biplanes. The air, she says, is "the only place free from prejudices".

*Coleman, who is determined to fly.*

# Abrasive views of US air chief spark war of words with the navy

*The stricken "Ostfriesland" rolls over after being bombed by Mitchell's pilots.*

*The "Alabama", another victim.*

**Langley, Va, September 23**
US battleship *Alabama* was bombed and sunk today by the US Army Air Service. Although the ship was an agreed target for the airmen, the action has inflamed relations between the two services.

A lot of the friction is down to the outspokenness of the man in charge of the bombing trials, Brig-

adier-General Billy Mitchell. He asserts that surface ships are doomed when faced with air power, and argues that to be safe, a ship must stay beyond the reach of land-based aircraft. Because of America's remoteness, he says, the Navy should cede to the airmen its role as defender of US seaboards. The sinking of the *Alabama* will doubtless

be used to support his claims. Mitchell's leaks to the press and his ruthless bending of the trials to his favor have fueled the row.

In similar trials in July, an ex-German navy battleship, the *Ostfriesland*, was the target. Mitchell's Martin bombers sank her before a US Navy trials party could complete examination of the damage.

# Pilot conquers the summit of Europe

*Switzerland, July 30*
A Swiss pilot achieved a daring first today when he succeeded in landing his airplane on the slopes of Mont Blanc, Europe's highest mountain, in the Alps. François Durafour, from Geneva, was making a second attempt at the summit; his first, last year, ended in failure because his machine could not climb high enough.

He was luckier this time and skilfully managed to bring his Caudron G.III down on the vast snowfield of the Dôme pass on the upper slopes of the peak, nearly 16,000 feet above sea level. Just as he was about to land, a great blast of wind caught the biplane, and it seemed for one terrifying moment that Durafour would be hurled down a nearby abyss. Summoning all his skills, Durafour was able to stabilize the Caudron and came to rest safely. After a stroll to admire the view, he returned to his airplane, and took off again.

## Louis Breguet talks of visions of future

*Rouen, France, August 5*
French aircraft designer Louis Breguet astonished a scientific congress today with a visionary speech on the future of air travel. The airplane of tomorrow, Breguet said, will be "comfortable, powerful, fast and reliable". He claims airplanes will eventually carry passengers around the world at 750mph, although no aircraft has yet achieved even 250mph. Traveling long distances by sea will soon seem "as peculiar as traveling by coach and horses".

Breguet said that one key area of development needed immediate attention: safety. Despite the relative infrequency of fatal accidents, safety standards had to be improved.

*Breguet's idea of flying in the future.*

# Huge seaplane's maiden flight fails

*A magnificent failure: the huge Caproni triple triplane flying boat on Lake Maggiore shortly before the crash.*

*Lake Maggiore, Italy, March 4*
There was disappointment all round today when one of the most extraordinary aircraft ever built proved that it cannot fly. The gigantic *Capronissimo* [Great Caproni], or more properly the Caproni Ca 60, took off from the lake for a moment before nose-diving back into the water and crashing. Thankfully test pilot Semprini somehow survived.

Gianni Caproni designed the 76-foot long, 3,200-hp monster with three sets of triplane wings, hence another of its names, *Noviplano*, meaning nine wings. It is powered by eight Liberty engines, four at the front and four at the back. Capable of taking 100 passengers, it is designed as a scale model of an even bigger machine to fly the Atlantic. Undaunted, Caproni hopes to repair the wrecked machine.

## Crash at Le Bourget

*Paris, September 6*
Five people were killed this evening in the first crash at Le Bourget airport when their airplane, a Potez, hit a street near the airport during its final approach on a flight from Strasbourg. The dead included two Britons, Perkins Park and Robert Boton, and a newlywed couple, Mr and Mrs Raymond. The four died instantly and the French pilot, Jean Brosse, was fatally injured. The airline will fly as usual tomorrow.

## Over 40 die as airship crashes in trials

*Some members of the tragic crew of R.38/USN ZR-2, before disaster struck.*

*Hull, England, August 24*
The US Navy's cordial welcome of British airship R.38 to its fleet today turned to tragedy as the aircraft, newly designated USN ZR-2, broke up and crashed into the river Humber estuary with the loss of 44 lives, 16 of them American. The airship, based on the design of a wartime Zeppelin, was returning to base after final trials with a joint Royal Navy/RAF/US Navy crew. A series of violent changes of direction seem to have been too much for the huge, but delicate, lattice structure of the world's largest airship, which apparently broke its back.

According to one crewman, it "cracked in half like an eggshell and people and gear just spilled out". The front part caught fire, but the rear section sank onto a mud bar where five survivors managed to jump clear.

**At home on the ground and in the air, a "car-plane" of the future, as imagined by French engineer René Tampier. The strange vehicle is shown driving around the streets of Paris after landing from its flight.**

# Barnstorming pilots fly in search of fame and glory, but most find stardom elusive

*"Look, no hands!" A daredevil flyer hangs perilously by his teeth.*

*Omaha, Nebraska, December 14*
To the young farm lad who just saw a biplane buzz the hen house, the pilot is Sir Lancelot, Ivanhoe, and the whole of King Arthur's round table rolled into one, a knight of the air on a gasoline-powered steed: the "barnstormer".

A few, like Ormer L Locklear, who plunged to his death at night bathed in spotlights while making a movie last year, fit the romantic image. They earn up to $3,000 a day, fly daredevil feats before large crowds in new airplanes, becoming celebrities. But most of the hundreds of barnstormers who criss-cross the US are lucky if they make that much money in a year. They sleep under their airplane's wings or in a ten-cent room each night, and consider it a good day if they can attract a crowd of 50, a few of whom will pay $5 for a five-minute ride in a war-surplus Curtiss Jenny, held together by glue and wire.

*High-speed thrills, or how to transfer from airplane to car without stopping.*

# Fokker plane is seized in copyright clash

*Paris, November 30*
A row has broken out between France and the Netherlands over an aircraft on show at an aero exhibition at the Grand Palais in Paris. The aircraft has been seized by French authorities, and the stand is now guarded by six policemen. The Dutch Aircraft Company F.III is said by French designer Robert Esnault-Pelterie to use a control stick that infringes his patents. But behind the fuss may lie the fact that the F.III was designed by Dutchman Anthony Fokker, who worked for Germany during the war. He has asked the Dutch government to intervene.

# Dutch airline KLM makes name for itself

*Amsterdam, December 31*
Netherlands airline KLM has now existed, at least on paper, for more than two years. It has been operating only since May 17 last year, but already its reputation is as high as that of any airline in the world. This is chiefly due to managing director Albert Plesman. A former lieutenant in the Dutch army air service, he has shown himself to be an astute leader. Airplane manufacturer Anthony Fokker has just formed a partnership with Plesman, thus gaining an extremely useful outlet for his transport aircraft. Plesman has already ordered 13 of his aircraft (→ Nov 24, 1924).

*High-flying: KLM luxury service.*

# Travel guides issued for air passengers

*London, December 1*
"Enjoy the solitary deserts of infinite space!" So runs a line in the new booklet produced by Breguet of Paris to advertise their Croydon (London)/Paris service. More prosaic is the reassuring guide from the British firm Handley Page: "At each window there are curtains, at the end a door with the inscription "Lavatory"." All the airlines are now rushing into print, evangelists for the gospel of flight. But many say the well-publicized risks of flying ensure that their preaching reaches only the converted.

# Death toll mars record year for air mail

*Washington, DC, December 31*
Nine deaths – eight pilots and one mechanic – marred what has otherwise been another successful year of US Post Office airmail operations. The New York/Washington route was ended in May and the Minneapolis/Chicago and Chicago/St Louis routes were closed in June, leaving only the transcontinental New York/San Francisco route in operation; yet almost 45 million letters, more than double last year's volume, were carried.

Post Office pilots flew 1,713,934 miles during the year, compared with 864,128 in 1920. The ratio of miles flown to miles scheduled was 84 per cent, also an improvement on last year.

The past year has also marked the standardization of aircraft used to carry the mail. The American-built DH-4, powered by the 400-hp Liberty engine, became the sole Post Office mail plane.

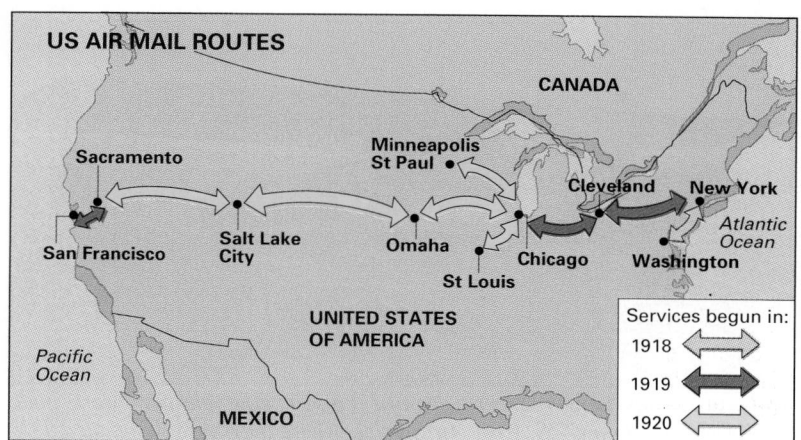

US AIR MAIL ROUTES

CANADA

Sacramento
Minneapolis St Paul
Cleveland
New York
San Francisco
Salt Lake City
Omaha
Chicago
Washington
St Louis
Atlantic Ocean

UNITED STATES OF AMERICA

Pacific Ocean

MEXICO

Services begun in:
1918
1919
1920

Only twelve Caudron C.61 airliners were built; most of them served on Romanian domestic routes. They had three 180-hp Hispano-Suiza 8A engines.

An unusual feature of the Siddeley Sinaia bomber was the accommodation of the gunners in the tails of the engine nacelles. Only one was built.

The Gloster Mars I or "Bamel", designed by H P Folland, was a single-seater racer that used many components similar to those of the Nieuport Nighthawk.

The ungainly and unsuccessful Farman BN.4 bomber had massive square wings which appeared to have been made by the mile and cut off by the yard.

Nieuport's Sesquiplan racer had a braced monoplane main wing and a smaller surface between the undercarriage legs. The engine was a 300-hp HS 8Fb.

The Breguet XIX was built for many air forces: at least 3,280 were made. It was also the first aircraft to fly non-stop from Paris to New York.

Only two ten-passenger Liberty-engined Fokker F.IV airliners were built. Both were sold to the US Army Air Service, where they were designated T-2.

The Levasseur PL-2 torpedo-bomber entered service on the French carrier "Béarn" in 1926. Its 580-hp Renault 12Ma engine was dogged by troubles.

*The Dornier Komet I was the landplane counterpart of the Delphin flying boat. It had a 185-hp BMW IIIa supercharged six-cylinder inline engine.*

*Supermarine's Seagull amphibian was designed for fleet spotting and reconnaissance. It led to the famed Walrus of the Second World War.*

*Ten examples of the Engineering Division GA-1 triplane ground-attack aircraft were built by Boeing for the US Army Air Service.*

*The Blackburn Dart torpedo-bomber featured a split-axle undercarriage which allowed for the underfuselage stowage of the 1,500-lb 18-inch torpedo.*

*After winning the Pulitzer Trophy race at 176.7mph, the Curtiss Navy Racer was developed into a successful Schneider trophy contender.*

*Designed as a "night-pursuit" fighter, the Curtiss PN-1, powered by a 6-cylinder Liberty engine, was not adopted for service use. Two were built.*

*Andrei N Tupolev's first airplane was this diminutive light monoplane, the ANT-1, powered by a radial engine. It was made mainly of light alloy.*

*The pilot of the Avro Bison fleet-spotter was positioned high up and close behind the Napier Lion engine – hence the need for the ladder on the nose.*

# 1922

|  | 224.28mph<br>USA<br>William Mitchell<br>Curtiss R-6<br>Oct 18, 1922 |  | 2,517.8 miles<br>USA<br>Kelly and Macready<br>Fokker T-2<br>Oct 6, 1922 |  | 34,610ft<br>USA<br>Roland Rohlfs<br>Curtiss Wasp<br>Sep 18, 1919 |  | 57,319lb<br>Italy<br>SAI Caproni<br>Caproni Ca 60 |  | 838hp<br>France<br>Marcel Riffard<br>Breguet-Bugatti 32A |

**Italy, January 12**
Technicians of the seaplane manufacturing concern established by German Claudius Dornier, Costruzioni Meccaniche Aeronautiche [Aeronautical Machine Constructions], set up shop in the factory premises of the Galinari Shipyard at Pisa.

**France, February 2**
The government decides to set up a network of lighthouses along commercial air routes as an aid to night flights.

**London, February 9**
The formation of the Royal Air Force Reserve is announced.

**New York, February 25**
The city is mapped in 69 minutes using a new aerial camera developed by Sherman Fairchild.

**London, March 31**
Government subsidies for British airlines are withdrawn, one year after being introduced (→ Oct 1).

**France, May**
The prototype Breguet 19 bomber/reconnaissance biplane makes a successful first flight.

**Switzerland, June 1**
The Swiss airline Ad Astra opens an international service linking Geneva and Nuremberg, Germany.

**South Africa, June 10**
The South African army uses airplanes to help crush a rebellion by the Hottentots.

**Rio de Janeiro, June 16**
Portuguese flyers Gago Coutinho and Sacadura Cabral land in their Fairey IIID *Santa Cruz* after accomplishing the first air crossing of the south Atlantic; their long and difficult journey from Lisbon, Portugal, began on March 13 in the Fairey IIIC *Lusitania*, but this airplane was destroyed en route when it crashed on the island of St Paul.

**College Park, Md, June 16**
Henry Berliner, son of the inventor, conducts helicopter flights before a US Navy delegation; the test aircraft, which has two lifting rotors in front and a tilting rotor for forward motion at the rear, ascends to seven feet off the ground three times.

**Paris, June 24**
Noted French air pioneer Léon Levavasseur, 58, who invented the Antoinette engine, dies.

**Paris, July 10**
French authorities decide that pilots going from Paris to London must fly from Le Bourget to Ecouen, then follow the Nationale 1 road to Abbeville and from there the Paris-Calais railway line (→ Dec 15, 1924).

**Paris, July 11**
An international convention for the regulation of air navigation comes into operation.

**New York City, July 21**
Police officials warn aviators that anyone breaking the law restricting flying over the city at an altitude below 2,000 feet will be arrested.

**Berlin, July 28**
Colonel Hermann Thomsen, wartime chief of staff of the German air service, admits authorship of a paper delivered anonymously in England five days ago, saying that London was defenseless against air attack.

**Washington, DC, August 9**
Captain Mustin completes tests on the gyroscopic heading repeater, an improvement on the magnetic compass.

**Italy, August 12**
British pilot Henry Biard wins the Schneider Trophy, flying his Supermarine Sea Lion to a speed of 148.19mph (→ Sep 28, 1923).

**France, August 19**
French pilot Lucien Bossoutrot, flying a Henry Farman sailplane,

makes a soaring flight in which, for the first time, he uses thermal air currents to gain and maintain height (→ Nov 17, 1925).

**Britain, September 9**
Captain F L Barnard pilots his de Havilland D.H.4A from London (Croydon) to Renfrew, Scotland, and back, averaging 123mph to win the first King's Cup air race.

**France, September 21**
French pilot Sadi Lecointe sets a new world speed record when he reaches 212mph (→ Oct 30, 1923).

**USA, September 27**
Dr Albert Hoyt Taylor and Leo C Young, scientists at the US Naval Aircraft Radio Laboratory, Anacostia, DC, make the first successful detections of objects by "radio observation".→

**San Diego, September 30**
Claude Ryan founds the Ryan Flying Company.

**London, October 1**
The three British airlines serving the London/Paris route agree that from this month Handley Page should be left to compete with the French on that route, while Daimler is given a free hand to Amsterdam and Instone to Brussels.

**London, October 1**
Government subsidies for British airlines, withdrawn in March, are restored.

**San Diego, October 6**
Lts John Macreday and O G Kelly set a new world flight endurance record, staying aloft in their Fokker T-2 monoplane for a total of 35 hours 18 minutes and 30 seconds.

**USA, October 17**
Lt V C Griffin, in a Vought VE-7SF airplane, achieves the first take-off from the USS *Langley*, America's first operational aircraft carrier.

**USA, October 26**
Lieutenant Commander Godfrey DeChevalier lands on the USS *Langley* while she is under way off Cape Henry.

**Germany, November 6**
The prototype Dornier Do J Wal flying boat makes a successful first flight (→ Dec 31, 1924).

**France, November 11**
Etienne Oehmichen makes a short flight in his helicopter N° 2 (→ May 1, 1923).

**Japan, November 12**
The first regular airmail service between Sakai (a suburb of Osaka) and Tokushima, opens; it is flown by Yokosho seaplanes of Nihon Kokuyuso Kenkyujo [Japan Air Transport Research Association].

**Spain, November 15**
Juan de La Cierva, developer of the "Autogiro", is awarded a patent for a system of rotor blades with flapping hinges (→ Jan 9, 1923).

**England, November 24**
The prototype Vickers Virginia heavy bomber makes a successful first flight.

**New York City, November 28**
Roscoe Turner uses a war-surplus fighter to write an advertisement in the sky: "Smoke Lucky Strikes".

**Ohio, December 18**
Major Thurman Bane makes a short flight at McCook Field, Dayton, in a helicopter developed by Dr George de Bothezat, a Russian working for the US Army Air Service.

**Kent, England, December 31**
A Dornier Komet lands at Lympne, the first German airplane to land in England since the end of the war.

---

*Air routes to the east: a poster advertising daily services offered by the Franco-Roumanian company from Paris to eastern Europe.* ▶ ·

# Nobleman's helicopter hovers in the air

*A complicated design: the two-rotor helicopter of Marquis Pateras Pescara.*

*Paris, January 11*
The first helicopter ever to hover above the ground for a full minute did so at the airfield at Issy-les-Moulineaux here today. The machine was the third example built by a Spaniard, Marquis Pateras de Pescara. It was flown in a hangar of France's Service Technique Aéronautique.

Powered by a 170-hp Hispano-Suiza engine, the strange-looking machine was lifted by two rotors, each with six biplane blades. The marquis has incorporated a system to alter the pitch, or angle, of the rotor blades in flight. If the engine should fail, the rotors will continue to turn due to the airflow generated by the aircraft's descent. Then, as it approaches the ground, the pilot can use a lever to suddenly increase the pitch of rotors, giving a much softer landing (→ Jan 29, 1924).

# Night service opens from London to Paris

*An airliner maneuvers before a night flight from London's Croydon airport.*

*Paris and London, June 7*
The first commercial night flight between Europe's two biggest capitals took place tonight and has been hailed as a success. A Farman Goliath of the French airline Grands Express Aériens flew from Le Bourget to Croydon and back with eight passengers on a journey which went smoothly, apart from when the airplane hit a squall on the return flight. Quite what the residents of the suburbs around Croydon airport thought of a large, noisy machine landing at 1.15am is not known.

The choice of the sturdy Goliath for the night run is not surprising; its two Salmson engines are each powerful enough to keep the aircraft flying to safety if one should break down.

# USA commissions first aircraft carrier

*Norfolk, March 20*
The USS *Langley* was commissioned today as the US Navy's first aircraft carrier. It will be a floating laboratory to study both the operation of aircraft from a ship and the design of future aircraft carriers. The *Langley*, built on the hull of a collier, is high-sided and blunt-ended with a top speed of 14 knots. To brake, incoming aircraft have hooks which catch onto cables on the deck as they come in to land. Below the flight deck is the open-sided hangar deck. A unique feature of the ship is its ability to tilt its smokestacks during flight operations (→ Dec 14, 1927).

*The USS "Langley", collier turned aircraft carrier, anchored off San Diego.*

# Six are killed in the first mid-air crash

*France, April 7*
A tragic first in civil aviation history took place today, about 60 miles north of Paris, when two airliners collided in mid-air, killing all seven people on board. Among the victims was a 16-year-old steward newly hired by the British airline Daimler Airways to serve coffee to passengers (see opposite).

The accident is being blamed on poor visibility. The pilot of the Daimler Airways D.H.18, heading for Paris from London, was flying at a few hundred feet through a valley near the town of Grand-villiers. His view was obscured by mist and the D.H.18's wide fuselage, and he failed to see a Farman Goliath of the French airline Grands Express Aériens ahead of him. The Goliath, flying from Paris to London, was following, in the opposite direction, the same route at the same altitude, and its pilot also failed to see the oncoming aircraft. The planes crashed head-on.

The disaster will intensify calls for tighter control of air traffic. At the moment pilots are left a free hand in finding routes, and many follow the same ones (→ Jul 10).

# Germans open new air route to Russia

*Moscow, May 1*
The rapid expansion of German air services is highlighted by the addition of a brand new destination to their schedules: Moscow. Deutsch-Russische Luftverkehrs Gesellschaft [German-Russian Air Travel Company], or Deruluft, a joint venture formed last year, has opened the route because of the marked increase in trade between the two countries.

The British and French supported the anti-Communists in the Russian civil war, and the Soviets are suspicious of their commercial intentions. But the Germans are welcomed, particularly if they come by air. German Fokker F.III and Junkers F 13 monoplanes have proved excellent air transports, probably a direct result of the ban on military aircraft imposed on Germany after the war: German civil airliners have been purpose-designed from scratch rather than developed from old bombers.

In any case, the young Soviet state, with vast distances and few railroads, seems determined to take advantage of German offers, whatever the political implications.

# Round-world flight ends in Indian sea

*India, August 24*
Two wet and weary British airmen, Captain Norman Macmillan and Geoffrey Malins, were rescued by ship from the Bay of Bengal today after an attempted round-the-world flight turned into a catalog of mishaps. Sponsored by the London *Daily News*, the flight started from London's Croydon airport on May 24. By the time Calcutta was reached on August 12, one crew member had left with appendicitis and Malins had taken over from another as photographer. The first D.H.9 had also been replaced.

The crew took off on the next stage, to Vancouver, in a Fairey IIIC from the Hugli river on August 19. But bad weather and engine failure forced them down near Lukhidia Char island in the Bay of Bengal, where they waited three days. As they headed for Chittagong, the engine again forced them to land. A float filled with water and the plane capsized; the men remained on the wreck for a day and a night before today's rescue.

# American dirigible flies coast to coast

*California, September 23*
History was made at 8.05 this evening when Major H A Strauss and his crew landed US Army Air Service dirigible C-2 at Ross Field, Arcadia, to complete the first crossing of the US by an airship. The C-2 departed Langley Field in Hampton, Virginia, at 12.22am on September 14 and followed railroad lines for much of the journey.

The main aim of the flight was to evaluate engine performance in varying conditions and altitudes and to test ways of mooring and maintaining airships when air service personnel and equipment are not available. The C-2's route took it over Pittsburgh, Pennsylvania; Akron, Columbus, Dayton and Cincinnati, Ohio; Belleville, Illinois; Dallas, Fort Worth, San Antonio, San Martine and El Paso, Texas; Nogales, Ajo and Yuma, Arizona, before it picked up the Southern Pacific Railroad and followed it for the final 225 miles of the journey. Total flying time during the ten-day trip was 67 hours.

# Third British airline starts Paris service

*Service with a smile from Daimler's young steward as he helps a passenger.*

*London, April 2*
The prototype of the new D.H.34 airliner, resplendent in the scarlet livery of the Daimler Hire company, opened the scheduled services of a third British airline today with a flight from London's Croydon airport to Paris. The new machine seats two pilots and nine passengers. Daimler, which will call itself The Daimler Airway, is buying four D.H.34s on hire purchase, and also has one of the earlier D.H.18s. The airline expects to begin flying soon from London to Amsterdam and Berlin, and hopes to show that subsidies can be avoided by operating intensively.

# Aéro-Club de France attracts 34 airplanes to its first rally

*France, June 18*
Thirty-four airplanes gathered at a country hotel today for the first rally organized by the Aéro-Club de France, the French state-aided aviation society. The rally, which the organizers hope will become a regular event, took place in a field next to the Bois-Joli hotel at Tillières, west of Paris.

The hotel is 104km [65 miles] from Paris, as a result of which the rally has been dubbed the "104 to 104" – 104 pilots and passengers flew 104km to the venue. Despite strong northerly winds all the aircraft had arrived by noon, and the participants made their way to the hotel for an excellent lunch at which French under-secretary of state for air Victor Laurent-Eynac presided. The meal was followed by an improvized ball on the hotel lawns and various other attractions.

The rally has been hailed as a success by Aéro-Club president André Schelcher, who believes that such events will do much to popularize aviation.

*Spectators at the rally watch a Farman Goliath as it comes in to land.*

*The Bois-Joli hotel, between Paris and Brest, where the flyers gathered.*

## Aircraft used to help troops in policing British Empire's far-flung trouble spots

*Hinaidi, Iraq, October 1*
The Royal Air Force (RAF) established a new headquarters here today to help police the British Empire. Britain holds Iraq, formerly Mesopotamia and part of the Ottoman Empire, under a mandate from the League of Nations, and has found the country is riddled with discontent as local sheikhs, such as Sheikh Mahmud in Kurdistan, seek to control their own areas.

Dealing with rebel tribes has normally been done by the British Army but the RAF won its spurs in this type of operation in a short, sharp and successful bombing campaign against tribes in Somaliland in 1920. Politicians were attracted to the idea of policing the empire from the air because it is both effective and cheaper than using the army. The procedure will be first to drop leaflets informing the dissidents that they will be bombed on a particular date if they do not cease their hostile activities.

The RAF has eight squadrons of D.H.9A bombers and Bristol Fighters. It will also have some Vickers Vernon transports which can carry up to 11 soldiers, evacuate wounded and provide a vital air link to Cairo (→ Jul 18, 1925).

## US pilots speed ahead

*Starting 'em young: Jimmy Doolittle and his son aboard the pilot's DH-4.*

## Australian pioneer dies in air tragedy

## Wireless 'can see'

*USA, September 27*
Scientists working on VHF signal technology at the Naval Aircraft Radio Laboratory at Anacostia, DC, claim to have made a breakthrough in "radio observation" today. They say that aircraft could use wireless waves to detect ships moving in conditions of poor visibility or darkness. The US Navy is interested, but cautions that further investigation is needed.

*Michigan, October 18*
The US reaffirmed its status as the fastest nation in the air today when Brigadier-General Billy Mitchell achieved a record 222.97 mph in a Curtiss R-6 at Mount Clemens. Mitchell's feat crowns six momentous weeks for US aviation, beginning on September 4 with Jimmy Doolittle's first coast-to-coast flight in under a day, in an American-built DH-4.

Doolittle completed the trip, from Pablo Beach, Florida to San Diego, California, in 21 hours and 19 minutes, stopping only once, at Kelly Field in Texas. San Diego saw another record on October 6, when Lieutenants Oakley Kelly and John MacReady set a new endurance record. They flew for 35 hours and 19 minutes in a Fokker T-2 transport, knocking six hours off the old record.

Mitchell's speed record broke one set just four days ago, when Lt Russell Maughan reached 207.7 mph in a Curtiss P-6 in Michigan to win the Pulitzer trophy. A Curtiss P-6 also came second.

*Sir Ross (l) with brother Keith.*

*England, April 13*
Australia lost one of its most famous aviators today. Sir Ross Smith was killed during a test flight of an amphibious Vickers Viking IV biplane at the new Brooklands aerodrome in Surrey. Lt Bennett, his test engineer and fellow Australian, was also killed when the airplane's engine stalled after a sharp turn.

Sir Ross and his brother, Sir Keith – both men were knighted after making the first flight from England to Australia in 1919 – were planning to attempt a round-the-world flight in the aircraft, especially ordered from Vickers. Sir Keith would have been in the same airplane, but his train from London was delayed and he arrived late. He witnessed his brother's fatal crash from the ground.

## Freight leads a boom in air traffic across the English Channel

*Wine is loaded at a Paris airport for delivery to customers in London.*

*Britain, December 1*
Figures just released show a near 50 per cent increase in the volume of passenger and freight flights across the Channel this year, with Britain increasing its market share to 58.5 per cent. Taking air traffic between Britain, Belgium, France and the Netherlands as an example, a staggering 106 per cent increase in freight carriage is recorded for the year, to 477.6 tons. Passengers carried, by comparison, went up modestly from 10,731 in 1921 to 12,359.

The increase in freight is partly due to the huge quantity of newspapers now delivered by air, amounting to nearly 78 tons for July to October alone. Mail carrying, which has been significant in helping finance new routes, is reckoned at just 9 tons across the Channel. But elsewhere mail volume is much higher. In the United States, for example, 60,487,880 letters were carried this year by Post Office aircraft over a combined flying distance of 1,756,803 miles.

The latest figures indicate a slow shift from the use of converted war-surplus aircraft that depressed the "new-build" market to modern fuel-efficient airliners carrying eight to 15 passengers or up to 2 tons of freight.

# 'Flying Dutchman' finds new success back in homeland

*The Netherlands, 1922*

Anthony Fokker, the Dutchman who built the best German fighters of the Great War, has turned his skills to commercial aviation. Fokker, nicknamed "the Flying Dutchman", was based at Schwerin in Germany during the war. In 1918 he was ordered to hand over all his aircraft to the Allies, but he hid 200 D.VII fighters and 400 engines and secretly transported them by train to Holland. He set up business at Schiphol near Amsterdam with a commercial aircraft, the five-seater F.II, built from smuggled parts. Orders from Dutch airline KLM seem likely (→Nov 7, 1923).

*A Fokker was also a showman.*

# Qantas introduces scheduled services

The Queensland and Northern Territory Aerial Services Limited.

*QANTAS's first passenger ticket cost £11 from Longreach to Cloncurry.*

*Mr Kennedy, 84, the first passenger.*

*Australia, November 2*

QANTAS, the fledgling air taxi and charter firm of Queensland and the Northern Territories, now has a real stake in the future. It has gained the airmail contract for the region, and as a result has opened its first scheduled service, flying today from its base field at Charleville to Cloncurry, 557 miles away.

After operating for two years, QANTAS won the tender for the north-east Australian region when the new Air Navigation Act of March last year regulated all British Commonwealth flying. Until then a dozen or so lone operators, mostly war veterans, had tried to offer some sort of service, generally of a fairly makeshift variety. A significant part of QANTAS's success is owing to their Armstrong Whitworth F.K.8s, which will be employed on the new two-day run, a major improvement on the elderly B.E.2es with which they started. An additional element is the connection of their north-south route with the railheads at Cloncurry, Winton, Longreach, Blackall and Charleville, which link directly to the coast (→Nov 3, 1923).

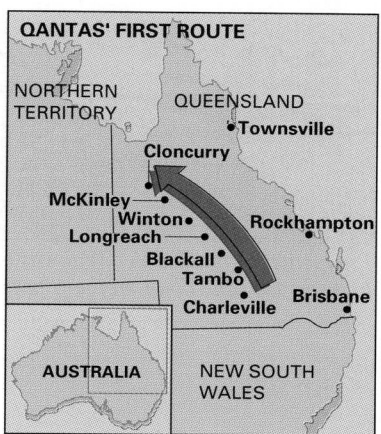

**QANTAS' FIRST ROUTE**

NORTHERN TERRITORY

QUEENSLAND

Townsville

Cloncurry

McKinley

Winton

Longreach

Rockhampton

Blackall

Tambo

Charleville

Brisbane

AUSTRALIA

NEW SOUTH WALES

# RAF aerodromes help Irish Free State to form its own air force

*Mechanics of the fledgling Irish Air Force stand to attention on parade.*

*Dublin, December*

The newly-independent Irish Free State is setting up its own air force. It already has a good start: under the Anglo-Irish treaty, Royal Air Force (RAF) aerodromes in the State have passed from British to Irish control. Even before the treaty, the Irish Republican Army (IRA) is believed to have bought a Martinsyde Type A Mk II to fly one of its leaders, Michael Collins, out of England if the truce in the Anglo-Irish conflict broke down and he faced arrest for treason. The Irish hope to obtain RAF-surplus Avro trainers, Martinsyde fighters and six D.H.9 bombers to fight IRA dissidents opposing the treaty.

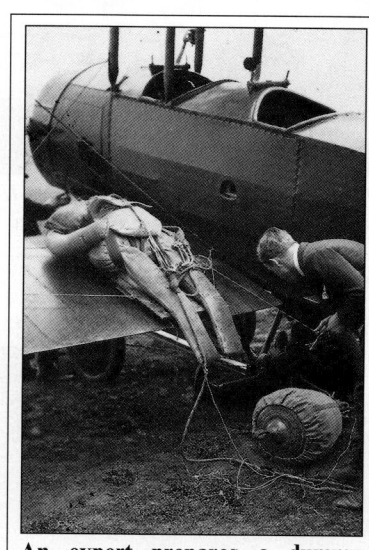

**An expert prepares a dummy for test parachute jumps.**

Powered by the three-cylinder Bristol Lucifer engine, the Junkers K 16 was a two-passenger transport which was also used for photographic survey work.

Bristol's barrel-fuselaged Type 72 racer performed disappointingly, despite its retractable undercarriage. A dangerous feature was aileron reversal.

Production of the Dornier Wal was originally undertaken in Italy by CMASA to avoid the Allied ban on the construction of this class of airplane.

The W.8, evolved from the famous Handley Page bombers of the First World War, was used first by Handley Page Transport and then by Imperial Airways.

De Havilland's D.H.34 airliner was used by Instone Air Line and Daimler Hire Ltd, and seven survived to be taken over by Imperial Airways.

The Lioré et Olivier LeO 13 was used to fly Mediterranean routes. Twenty-five were built, of which three were amphibious.

The Breguet XIX B2 No 09, powered by a Hispano-Suiza 12Ha water-cooled engine of 450hp, has been modified to fly from Villacoublay to Athens.

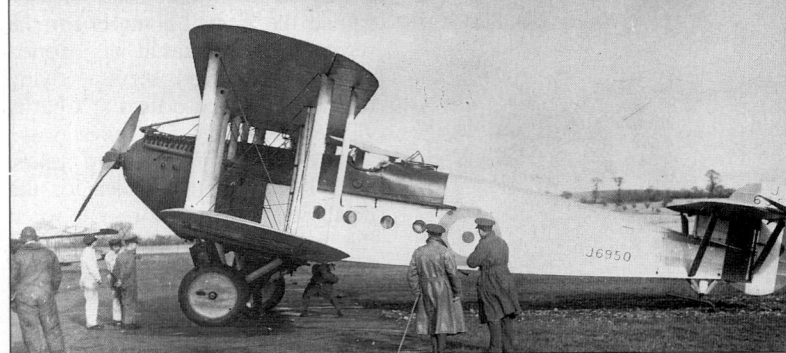

The Avro Aldershot bomber went into production in its Mark III form, but was used only by 99 Squadron of the RAF between 1924 and 1926.

One of the RAF's principal military transport aircraft of the inter-war years, the Vickers Victoria saw extensive service in the Middle East and India.

*A classic British carrier-borne or catapult-launched naval fighter of the inter-war years, the Fairey Flycatcher was equally at home on wheels or floats.*

*The Armstrong Whitworth Siskin II fighter, unlike the Mk III, was not adopted by the RAF, and only a few were built, remaining civil-registered.*

*The Supermarine Seagull III was the version which was built for the Fleet Air Arm, six being supplied. It led to the Seagull V, which became the Walrus.*

*With its all-metal fuselage and fabric-covered wing, and a speed of 158mph, the Dewoitine D.1 represented a great advance over contemporary fighters.*

*After some development from this original form, the Vickers Virginia became the mainstay of the RAF's night-bomber force from 1924 until 1937.*

*A contemporary of the Flycatcher, the Parnall Plover naval fighter did not enjoy the same success. Ten were built, for 403 and 404 Flights of the FAA.*

*The cumbersome Blackburn R.1 Blackburn carrier-borne fleet-spotter biplane entered FAA service in 1923. A Napier Lion provided the power.*

# 1923

267.16mph
USA
Alford J Williams
Curtiss R-2C-1
Nov 4, 1923

3,293 miles
USA
Smith and Richter
De Havilland DH.4B
Aug 28, 1923

36,565ft
France
Joseph Sadi-Lecointe
Nieuport-Delage
Oct 30, 1923

57,319lb
Italy
SAI Caproni
Caproni Ca 60

838hp
France
Marcel Riffard
Breguet-Bugatti 32A

**USA, February 1**
The Collier trophy, given annually for the year's greatest achievement in aviation, is awarded to the US Post Office Air Mail Service for operating the transcontinental airmail route for one year without a fatality.

**Russia, February 9**
The Soviet Council for Civil Aviation is set up (→ Mar 17).

**Le Bourget, France, February 10**
An experimental night flight arrives from Croydon, England. The pilot has given his position by radio and used the aviation light beacons to make his approach.

**Michigan, March 5**
A jettisonable extra fuel tank fitted to the bomb rack of a Boeing MB-3A fighter is shown to increase the airplane's flying range to about 400 miles (→ Jul 17, 1925).

**Washington, DC, March 17**
The US government announces that army airplanes will drop calcium arsenate to kill weevils in Louisiana cotton fields.

**Moscow, March 17**
The Council for Civil Aviation creates Dobrolet, the Volunteer Air Fleet Company (→ Jul 15).

**Italy, March 23**
The Regia Aeronautica [Board of Aeronautics] is set up.

**USA, May 16**
Amelia Earhart becomes the first woman to receive an airplane pilot's certificate from the National Aeronautic Association.

**Canada, May 26**
Lieutenant H G Crocker lands at Gordon, Ontario, to complete a non-stop transcontinental south/north flight from Houston, Texas, of 11 hours 55 minutes.

**Paris, June 6**
Three lions which were stranded on a train held up during a strike in Belgium arrive by postal airplane.

**London, June 8**
Insurance company Lloyd's of London insures American pilot and former war hero Eddie Rickenbacker for $1 million against accident or death while flying.

**New Zealand, June 14**
The New Zealand Permanent Air Force is set up.

**France, June 23**
Jean Casale, chief pilot at the Blériot company, is killed when the controls of his Blériot 115 fail during a flight and he crashes.

**San Diego, Calif, June 27**
An American-built DH-4B flown by Captain L H Smith is fully refueled in flight by pipeline from another DH-4B piloted by Lieutenant Richter (→ Aug 28).

**Santa Monica, California, July 5**
In response to a request from the US Army Air Service for proposals for an airplane capable of making a round-the-world flight, the Douglas Company presents specifications for a convertible landplane/seaplane based on its DT-2, and designated the Douglas World Cruiser (DWC) (→ Nov 23).

**Germany, July 12**
German pilot and glidermaker Ferdinand Schulz flies a glider over the 31 miles between Königsberg and Memel in East Prussia.

**Russia, July 15**
Dobrolet, the Soviet state airline, opens its first scheduled domestic service, between Moscow and Nizhniy Novgorod (→ Apr 15, 1925).

**New York, July 27**
Edward Stinson lands his Junkers at Mitchell Field after the first non-stop night flight from Chicago.

**London, July**
A British government committee under Lord Salisbury confirms the Royal Air Force's status as an independent armed service (→ Jan 22, 1926).

**Japan, July**
Kawanishi Japan Air Lines is established by airplane manufacturer Seibi Kawanashi (→ Jul 31, 1924).

**Hawaii, August 12**
US officials in Honolulu announce that airplanes have been put to use seeding forests in inaccessible areas of the islands.

**Dayton, Ohio, August 22**
The Barling XNBL-1 triplane bomber prototype, the first six-engined American airplane, makes a test flight of 28 miles, reaching a maximum 93mph.

**Moscow, August 23**
The Polikarpov Il-400 monoplane fighter makes its first flight; made entirely of wood, it is powered by a 400-hp Liberty engine recovered from a de Havilland D.H.9A.

**France, September 2**
Maurice Noguès, chief pilot of the Franco-Romanian airline CFRNA, inaugurates a night passenger service between Strasbourg and Paris (→ Oct 12).

**Lakehurst, NJ, September 3**
The US Navy's helium-filled rigid airship USS *Shenandoah* makes a successful first flight at the US Naval Air Station; its name is American Indian in origin and means "daughter of the stars" (→ Mar 30, 1925).

**USA, September 9**
The Curtiss R2C-1 racer makes a successful first flight (→ Oct 6).

**San Diego, Calif, September 10**
Scientists photograph the eclipse of the Sun from 16 US Navy airplanes; they climb to 16,000 feet.

**Middlesex, England, October 2**
A prototype of the de Havilland D.H.53 Humming Bird light airplane makes a first flight at the company's works at Edgware; it has been prepared to compete in the forthcoming *Daily Mail* Motor Glider Competitions (→ Oct 15).

**Missouri, October 6**
Curtiss R2C-1 Racers take the first two places in the Pulitzer prize contest at St Louis: Alford Williams is first at 243.63mph (a new world speed record); Harold Brow is just behind at a speed of 241.74mph.

**Yugoslavia, October 12**
People living near Belgrade's Novi Sad aerodrome complain to operators CFRNA that no rain has fallen since airplanes began using the site; scientists promise to investigate (→ Nov 14, 1924).

**Czechoslovakia, October 23**
Czechoslovak national airline Ceskoslovenske Statni Aerolinie [Czechoslovak State Airlines] makes its first experimental flight, between the cities of Prague, Bratislava, Kosice and Uzhorod; it uses small Aero A-14 biplanes, each of which is only able to carry a single passenger.

**England, October**
The Gloster Grebe fighter enters service with the RAF; it is the RAF's first new fighter since 1918 (→ Jun 3, 1925).

**Australia, November 3**
QANTAS inaugurates a new government-subsidized service linking Charleville and Cloncurry.

**Italy, December 12**
The Italian airline Aero Expresso Italiana [Italian Aero Express] is founded.

**English Channel, December 13**
American Lawrence Sperry, who demonstrated an in-flight stabilizer in 1913, is lost on a flight from London to Amsterdam (→ Apr 1924).

*Flying has really captured the public imagination. Even cartoon characters, like these from a British children's annual, are taking to the air.* ▶

# Autogyro shows off flight potential

*Madrid, January 9*
Juan de La Cierva's C.4 "autogyro" today made an officially observed circular flight of more than 2.5 miles at a height of over 80 feet. It was flown at Madrid's Cuatro Vientos military airfield by Lieutenant Alejandro Gomez Spencer.

The thinking behind Cierva's extraordinary machine is to create an aircraft with a very low stalling speed, requiring only very short runways for landing and take-off, making it ideal for short journeys. Unlike the helicopter design, the rotor on top of the autogyro is not connected to the engine. It is "self-rotating", as the name implies: the rotor turns in the airflow which is generated by the forward motion of the aircraft. This is provided in the conventional way by an engine and propeller [*see diagram*].

The autogyros are built from existing airplane components, with a rotor on top to replace the wings. The C.4 autogyro (or *Autogiro*, as Cierva has registered it) flown today has a shortened Hanriot fuselage, an 80-hp Le Rhône engine and a 33-foot rotor with four blades (→ Dec 12, 1924).

*De La Cierva's autogyro C.4, which has made a successful circular flight.*

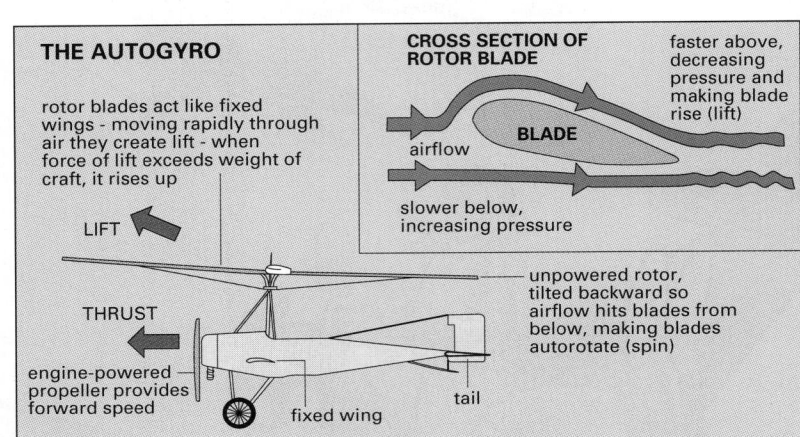

**THE AUTOGYRO**

rotor blades act like fixed wings - moving rapidly through air they create lift - when force of lift exceeds weight of craft, it rises up

LIFT

THRUST

engine-powered propeller provides forward speed

fixed wing

**CROSS SECTION OF ROTOR BLADE**

faster above, decreasing pressure and making blade rise (lift)

airflow

BLADE

slower below, increasing pressure

unpowered rotor, tilted backward so airflow hits blades from below, making blades autorotate (spin)

tail

(→ Dec 12, 1924).

## Competing airlines pool their resources

*Paris, March 16*
Today saw the merger of two leading French airlines which, until now, have been competing on some of Europe's busiest routes. With the encouragement of the French minister for aviation, Compagnie des Messageries Aériennes (CMA) and Compagnie des Grands Express Aériennes (CGEA) have fused under the name Air Union.

The joint company, which has Louis Breguet as managing director, boasts a fleet of 57 aircraft – Farman Goliaths, Breguet 14Ts and Spad 33s – flown by 17 pilots. Concentrating on the lucrative route from Paris to London, it will drop routes to the Netherlands and Belgium, leaving them to the Société Générale de Transport Aérien (SGTA), as the Farman line is now called. This fact, like the merger itself, recognizes that there are not yet enough passengers to permit several profitable carriers on a single route. French airlines, unlike their British competitors, have at least had government subsidies from the start; now they are on an even sounder footing (→ Sep 2).

# French helicopter makes stable test flight

*Helicopter builder Oehmichen.*

*Valentigney, France, May 1*
Etienne Oehmichen, the Peugeot car engineer who has become famous for his attempts to build a practical helicopter, today completed the first closed circuit to be flown by such a machine. It flew a distance of about 400 feet, making two straight runs with a 180-degree turn at each end.

Oehmichen's machine originally used a hydrogen balloon attached to the top to give it extra lift. This has now been removed, and all lift is provided by four large rotors, with other smaller rotors to provide control. A pusher propeller has been added to provide forward motion for the closed circuit flight. They are all driven by a 120-hp Le Rhône engine. Altogether the Oehmichen helicopter weighs about 1,875 pounds.

At the cost of being rather clumsy in conception, the machine has complete stability and control along every axis. Oehmichen said after the flight: "The machine is completely obedient. It flies like a boat propelled by a screw propeller and it is easy to steer." Longer flights will follow (→ May 4, 1924).

# Igor Sikorsky sets up air company in USA

*The Sikorsky S-29 under construction in the designer's open-air "factory".*

*New York, May 3*
Igor Sikorsky, the aircraft designer who fled his native Russia after the revolution, today formed the Sikorsky Aero Engineering Corporation. It will build aircraft in buildings on a chicken farm on Long Island owned by a fellow-Russian. Sikorsky, Russia's leading airplane designer before the revolution, lived in Paris for a short time before arriving in the USA in 1919. He worked on a bomber project for the US Army but lost his job due to the post-war decline in the aviation industry. He has made a living teaching mathematics and giving talks on the future of aviation.

# Boundaries pushed forward as man masters air

## Flyers cross United States – non-stop

*San Diego, California, May 3*
Another demonstration of the growing capabilities of the airplane took place today when US Army Air Service lieutenants Oakley G Kelly and John A Macready became the first to fly across the continent non-stop. Flying a single-engine Fokker T-2, they traveled 2,650 miles from Roosevelt Field on Long Island to Rockwell Field, near San Diego, in 26 hours 50 minutes. Their average speed during the long flight was 88.2mph.

The Fokker T-2, powered by a 400-hp Liberty engine, had been extensively modified in order to accomodate the 593.41 gallons of fuel needed for the non-stop flight. The fuel was stored in extra tanks built into the wings. This additional weight in turn meant that the airplane's landing gear had to be replaced. The Fokker T-2's designers were forced to borrow the considerably stronger landing gear of a Martin MB-1 bomber. Despite

this, there was some concern that the gear could collapse during the long and bumpy take-off run at Roosevelt Field.

The historic flight was followed with great interest by the American press, with one California newspaper gushing that "we have just witnessed a page of history being turned; a dream has come true". The Fokker landed at Rockwell Field shortly after midnight, but despite the late hour thousands of people turned up to cheer Kelly and Macready. In the streets of San Diego, drivers blew their horns as the Fokker landed. (→ Jul 17).

*Spanning a continent: the Fokker T-2 of army lieutenants Macready and Kelly en route from New York to San Diego.*

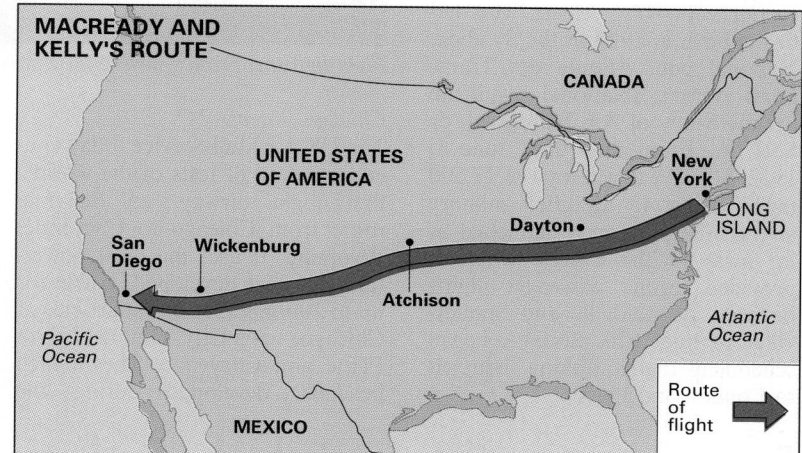

## French light plane wins Channel prize

*France, May 6*
A tiny, ultra-light airplane, the Dewoitine D.7, today won a prize offered by the French newspaper *Le Matin* for the first flight by such an airplane across the English Channel in both directions. Pilot Barbot, who started and finished near Calais, said the glider-like machine and its 16-hp Clerget engine behaved perfectly.

Emile Dewoitine is already known for his powerful fighters, but this is the first time he has gone for the potentially huge ultra-light market. The dream of owning a small, cheap airplane, especially one that can be kept in a garage with its wings folded, towed behind a car, or lifted by two or three people across a wall or hedge, is attractive to millions. It is also possible, especially in a simple machine, to grasp the basic techniques of flying after a few days' instruction.

## A ticket from Berlin to London? Just 1,300,000 marks, please!

*Berlin's Tempelhof airfield was opened for the new service to London.*

*Berlin, May 1*
The current economic crisis in Germany, and the aviation restrictions imposed by the Treaty of Versailles, has done nothing to dampen Ger-

man enthusiasm for aviation, and Germany remains in the forefront of modern aviation design. Lobbying by Berlin to have the restrictions which kept German airplanes

within German borders lifted has paid off. German air sovereignty was restored on January 1 this year, on which day a Dornier Komet of the airline Deutsche Luft Reederei (DLR) landed at Lympne in Kent, England. It was the first German airplane to land in Britain since the end of the war.

More significant is today's inauguration of a scheduled airline service between London and Berlin. For Britain's Daimler Airway it is an extension of its London/ Amsterdam route, reaching Berlin via Hamburg and Bremen. Passengers on the first flight, which lasted nine hours, have been greeted by representatives of German interests in the service, which will become reciprocal in the near future.

Pricing the service is not easy these days. A ticket from London to Berlin costs £6, while from inflation-ravaged Berlin to London the charge is an amazing 1,300,000 marks – and rising (→ Jun 30).

# Belgium launches SABENA, a national airline of its own

*Brussels, May 23*
Belgium today entered the competitive air transport world with the formation of the Société Anonyme Belge d'Exploitation de la Navigation Aérienne [Belgian Company for the Operation of Aerial Navigation] or SABENA, the country's only commercial airline network.

It was the famous Belgian pilot Georges Nélis who first discussed the plan for a Belgian national carrier with King Albert. This led to the birth in 1920 of the Syndicat National pour l'Etude des Transports Aériens [National Syndicate for the Study of Air Transport], or SNETA. From then until June 1, 1922, SNETA flew a total of 77,500 miles, using 40 modified military aircraft. Services were launched as far away as the Congo, where it provided regular passenger flights between Léopoldville and Stanleyville. In mid-1920, SNETA began scheduled flights linking Brussels to London and Paris.

# US mail proves night flying is practical

*Field lights in France, where they have been used since 1915, mark the way.*

*Chicago, August 24*
The US Air Mail Service today ended four days of tests of the world's first night airway, an 885-mile route from Chicago to Cheyenne, Wyoming. It uses the most powerful lights ever developed, visible for up to 100 miles, to mark airfields at Chicago, Iowa City, Omaha, North Platte and Cheyenne. The 36-inch beacons, developed during the Great War by the Sperry Gyroscope Company, project a 450-million candlepower beam at two degrees above the horizon. Special beacons mark 34 emergency landing fields, while 250 acetylene beacons serve as navigation markers along the way. Flights which have used the route include a coast-to-coast one of 26 hours and 14 minutes, a new record.

# Germany operates services deep into the Soviet empire

*Eastern Europe, June 30*
Building on the initial German-Soviet airline venture last year, when Deruluft introduced its service from Königsberg to Moscow, the airline Junkers Luftverkehr has extended its operations in the USSR, to Baku and beyond. This new joint venture is clearly designed to turn Moscow into the same type of domestic airline hub that Berlin has become to Germany.

Apart from the surprisingly deep Soviet involvement in a capitalist airline business, it is interesting to note the apparent lack of friction between the two competing German airline operators. Perhaps the humiliation of wartime defeat, and the subsequent ban on German military aviation, have made Germany more determined to win on the new battleground of air commerce. Few European countries have shown such flair for the design of new airliners, combined with good business sense, route planning and safe pilotage.

Junkers Luftverkehr is operating in the Caucasus with flights from Moscow to Vladikavkas and Tiflis, with mail-only flights from Rostov to Königsberg. Stimulated by these joint ventures, the new Soviet "Enterprise for Friends of the Red Air Fleet" is to fly Russian-built Ilya Muromets airplanes from Moscow next month (→ May 26, 1924).

# France spurs on pilots to win back speed records from US rivals

*France, July 17*
The French government is offering prizes of up to FF50,000 for its own aviators who can beat records held by American pilots. One reason Americans are having such success is the increasing involvement of the US government in aviation. The main French concern is the official world speed record, held until March by Frenchman Sadi Joseph Lecointe at 233mph, now taken by American Russell L Maughan at 236.5mph. The official altitude record has been in US hands for two years, set at 34,508 feet by Lieutenant John A Macready. The distance record has not been ratified by the International Aeronautics Federation since 1913, but France hopes to capture it (→ Oct 30).

The "double biplane" French Marcel Besson H.5 flying boat, which is being tested by the French navy; with its large capacity it is useful for either military operations or as a passenger or freight transport aircraft.

# Americans are tops in seaplane contest

*Cowes, England, September 28*
American pilots crushed all the opposition here today to take the Schneider seaplane trophy. First home was David Rittenhouse with a speed of 181.029mph, followed by Rutledge Irvine; both are US Navy lieutenants. Their Curtiss CR-3 racers are powered by the superb new D-12 engine. While others collided on take-off or had engine trouble, the CR-3s lapped the 186-mile course with deadly regularity and ever-increasing speed. Britain's Supermarine Sea Lion III, last year's winner, improved on its best speed by 12mph but finished third (→ Oct 6).

*Winners: Rittenhouse and the crew.*

# Proving flight by French airline paves the way for new postal service to West Africa

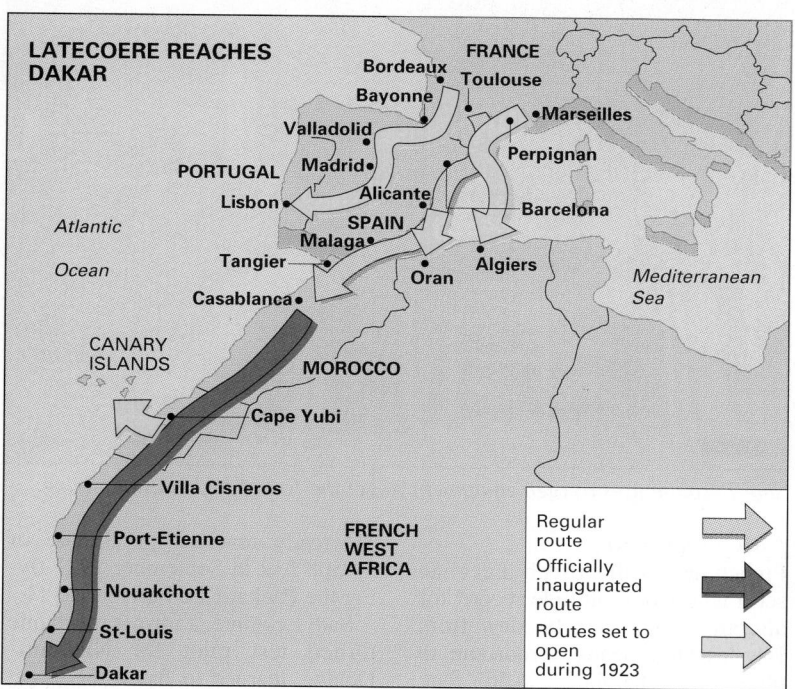

LATECOERE REACHES DAKAR

FRANCE
Bordeaux
Bayonne
Toulouse
Valladolid
Marseilles
PORTUGAL
Madrid
Perpignan
Lisbon
Alicante
Barcelona
SPAIN
Malaga
Tangier
Oran
Algiers
Casablanca
Mediterranean Sea

Atlantic Ocean

CANARY ISLANDS
MOROCCO

Cape Yubi

Villa Cisneros

Port-Etienne
FRENCH WEST AFRICA

Nouakchott

St-Louis

Dakar

Regular route
Officially inaugurated route
Routes set to open during 1923

*Dakar, May 6*
Three aircraft of the French airline Latécoère today completed the first flight down the West African coast from Casablanca in Morocco to Dakar in Senegal. The journey, under the command of Colonel Julien Roig, was intended as a preliminary flight for a new air postal route, and its success means that Latécoère is almost certain to establish a regular air mail service to Dakar.

A five-man team left Casablanca in three Breguet 14 biplanes on May 3 and headed for Dakar via Agadir, Cap-Yubi, Villa Cisneros, Port-Etienne and Saint-Louis. Colonel Roig, who traveled in the leading airplane, had carried out a reconnaissance of the route in February, setting up landing places and negotiating with local nomadic tribes. This preparation contributed much to the success of the mission. One of the mechanics had to be left at Cap-Yubi with a slight injury and Roig had to borrow some parts from the French army at Saint-Louis, but otherwise the most worrying moment came when one pilot's tropical helmet blew off and got temporarily stuck in the controls (→ May 27, 1926).

*A Breguet 14 in service to fly the mail for France's Latécoère airline.*

# Fog stops record flight

*San Diego, Calif, August 28*
A US Army Air Service airplane landed at Rockwell Field today after remaining airborne for an astonishing 37 hours 15 minutes 14.8 seconds, the longest flight ever made. The DH-4B *Liberty Plane* had been refueled in the air no fewer than 15 times, and only fog stopped the flight continuing, as it proved impossible to make contact with the tanker airplane. Crewed by Lieutenant Lowell H Smith and Lieutenant John P Richter, the airplane covered 3,293.26 miles, flying a circular route.

The tanker, another DH-4B, had a 132-US gallon fuel tank and a 50-foot hose which was fed out by a steel cable, enabling Smith and Richter to attach it to a connector in the cockpit.

*En route to a record, Smith and Richter's D.H.4B is refueled in mid-flight.*

# Mixed bunch compete for British trophy

*Alan Cobham, one of the losers, names his D.H.9 "Eileen" before the race.*

*Hendon, England, July 14*
Seventeen pilots in a spectacular array of different airplanes, from fighters to bulky airliners, lined up yesterday for the second King's Cup air race, which took place over a 794-mile course. Open to British airplanes, it has a handicap system allowing an equal chance for all types of aircraft. The race was won today by Captain Frank Courtney in a Siskin II fighter-trainer.

Air racing is drawing large crowds here and abroad, and the struggle for speed between French and US racers has caused a proliferation of new machines capable of flying at over 230mph.

# British ministry runs light airplane meet

*Kent, England, October 15*
The first British competition for light airplanes, or "motor gliders" as they are officially called, ended at the windswept airfield at Lympne today. Run by the Britain's Air Ministry, the Royal Aero Club and the *Daily Mail* newspaper, the event attracted 23 entries from Britain and four from abroad.

There were prizes for speed, altitude and landing accuracy, but the principal awards were for fuel economy: an English Electric Wren and an ANEC monoplane shared first place for flying for 73 miles on a single US gallon.

Some observers worry that the emphasis on fuel consumption is misguided. It could encourage airplanes with tiny engines, barely able to stagger into the sky which would be dangerous in high winds or bad weather. Some experts believe that a minimum engine power of 100hp is essential.

*A competitor in the Lympne competition, the English Electric Co's Wren.*

# Frenchman snatches high-flying record

*Sadi-Lecointe uses oxygen equipment to get the feel of high-altitude flying.*

*Paris, October 30*
Frenchman Sadi Joseph Lecointe set a new world altitude record for aircraft today when he flew from Issy-les-Moulineaux aerodrome to the dizzying height of 36,565 feet. Piloting a Nieuport-Delage powered by a Hispano-Suiza engine, Sadi Lecointe beat his own previous best of 35,242 feet, set on September 5, to snatch the world record from US pilot John Macready.

Macready reached an altitude of 34,508 feet in September 1921 flying the Packard-Le Père Lusac-11.

Sadi Lecointe, a former mechanic turned test pilot for Nieuport-Delage, learned to fly in the Great War. He trained for his record breaking flight in a special compression chamber, where he learned to cope with oxygen starvation and how to fly at sub-zero temperatures (→ Oct 18, 1925).

# Feisty US air chief pushes for bombers

*Hampton, Va, November 6*
America's ability to defend itself or defeat a foe on another continent rests with air power, according to Brigadier-General Billy Mitchell, director of military aviation. In an interview at Langley Field today, the controversial US Army air chief said that bigger, longer-ranged and faster bombers able to carry many bombs of 2,000 pounds and above are vital to US security.

In a statement hardly likely to please the US Navy, he said that nations can no longer rely on ships for their first line of defense because they are too vulnerable from the air. That was proved in September when bombs dropped from a Martin MB-2 bomber flying at 10,000 feet sunk the decommissioned USS *Virginia* and *New Jersey*, just as similar flights in 1921 sank the former German warships *Frankfurt* and *Ostfriesland* (→ Dec 31).

# Bolland astounds with looping stunt

*France, October 18*
Daredevil French woman pilot Adrienne Bolland has looped the loop an astonishing 98 times in just two minutes short of an hour. A former test pilot with the Caudron Company, Bolland is now a leading figure on the "barnstorming" circuit in France where, like her male counterparts, she travels from town to town to thrill the crowds with her special skills.

Bolland has acquired an enviable reputation as a pilot. She is the *enfant terrible* of the flying circus business, but her greatest achievement was two years ago when she astounded skeptics by flying over the Andes from Argentina to Santiago, the capital of Chile. During the trans-Andean flight, which took more than three hours, she reached an altitude of 14,620 feet, thought impossible in her Caudron G.III biplane (→ May 27, 1924).

# Douglas company wins US military order

*The Navy's DT-2 biplane, here pictured with floats, is a winner for Douglas.*

*Washington, DC, November 23*
The US War Department, pushing ahead with plans for a round-the-world flight next year, today awarded a $192,684 contract to the Douglas Company of California, for four aircraft and spare parts. The aircraft for the ambitious flight will be convertible landplane-seaplanes, based on the proven DT-2 design. The Liberty-engined aircraft will be delivered next March for the globe-circling flight and be called Douglas World Cruisers; a prototype has been tested at McCook Field near Dayton, Ohio, and at Hampton Roads, Virginia (→ Mar 11, 1924).

# Fifty feared dead in airship disaster

*The ill-fated French airship "Dixmude", which made the longest flight by any aircraft just three months ago.*

**Toulon, France, 21 December**
The *Dixmude*, the biggest airship in the French fleet, is assumed lost with all hands after disappearing over the Mediterranean in violent weather. The bodies of its commander, Lieutenant Jean du Plessis de Grenedan, and one unidentified crewman have been recovered, with some wreckage. The other 50 crew members are presumed dead. The *Dixmude*, a Zeppelin appropriated from Germany as part of war reparations, was returning home after a successful stay in North Africa. Its crew was in high spirits, looking forward to Christmas leave. Flying over the Sahara, the airship had increased the world endurance record to 118 hours 41 minutes.

The crew reported bad weather early this morning, but all transmissions ceased after a call at 3.30pm which said that fuel was low and de Grenedan would attempt an emergency landing in a gale, something requiring extraordinary skill without ground support. It seems likely that the airship broke up and exploded.

## Daredevil doings of flying circuses take heavy toll of flyers

*USA, December 31*
The growing popularity of show flying around the world is ensuring huge crowds for daredevil pilots and aerial stuntmen but is also exacting a heavy toll of those taking part in "flying circuses". This year alone, for instance, 85 stunt flyers have been killed and 162 injured.

The US is the home of airborne showmen. The most famous troupe is Gates' Flying Circus, run by tough Californian Ivan Gates, known to his employees as "the pope". The death-defying antics of Gates's three stuntmen and three pilots, who use Standard J-1 biplanes, include formation looping, flying upside down (a specialty of chief pilot Clyde Pangborn), climbing out and hanging from the undercarriage, walking on the top wing, or crossing from one airplane to another in flight.

# Mussolini says state and private sectors should boost air force

*All lined up: Italian air force machines laid out for inspection by leading members of the country's military hierarchy.*

**Rome, December 31**
Benito Mussolini, Italy's Fascist premier, has announced a big boost for the Italian air force. The dictator known as Il Duce [The Leader] has decreed that government funding, wedded to the engineering genius of big corporations such as the Fabbrica Italiana di Automobili Torino [Turin Italian Automobile Factory] or Fiat, will boost Italy's already impressive military air arm.

The air service was given independent status only in March, but it has a long pedigree: the Italians were the first to use airplanes for aerial bombardment, against the Turks in Libya before the Great War.

Italy has long been one of the leading aviation nations; last May the country was represented on an international airship flight over the North Pole, while Celestino Rosatelli worked on an "entirely Italian" fighter. Mussolini has been influenced by fellow Italian Major-General Giulio Douhet, author of *Command of the Air*, a seminal book published in 1921 which argues that air power will dominate future battles. His views coincide with air force chiefs', notably Brigadier-General Billy Mitchell of the US Army Air Service and Sir Hugh Trenchard of Britain's Royal Air Force (→Sep 5, 1925).

## Will air age navies invest in carriers?

*Washington, DC, December 31*
The debate over the vulnerability of battleships to air attack continues in the wake of the successful bombing demonstrations by the US Army's Brig-Gen Billy Mitchell. Admirals are divided between those who put their faith in battleships and those who see aircraft carriers as the future capital ships.

Rear-Admiral William Moffett of the US Navy has been countering Mitchell's views by arguing for more shipborne aircraft, both to protect the fleet from bombers and to attack the enemy's ships. Ironically, Moffett's arguments received a boost as a result of last year's Washington Treaty which limits the number of battleships allowed to each of the maritime powers – the US, Britain and Japan. Under the treaty, heavy cruisers (up to 33,000 tons) under construction can be converted into aircraft carriers. The admirals could hardly object, despite the $22.5m price tag, since the alternative would be to scrap them. Two are now being converted (→Jul 24, 1928).

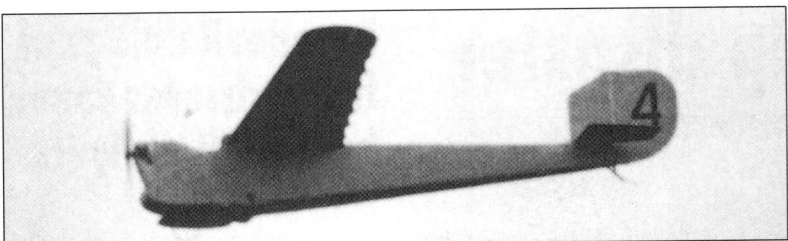

*The minimally-powered English Electric Wren light aeroplane needed still weather and short grass if it was to be flown. It did 87 miles per gallon.*

*Typical of the many sporting biplanes of the era, the Great Lakes Sports Trainer, fitted with a variety of engines, was popular with private owners.*

*The de Havilland D.H.50 became Australia's first flying-doctor aircraft.*

*A military development of the W.8 airliner, the Handley Page Hyderabad night-bomber served in four RAF home-based squadrons from 1925 to 1930.*

*Most of the 229 FBA 17 flying boats manufactured by Schreck were supplied to the French navy, but others served as civil aircraft or were exported.*

*The manufacturer built two production examples of the Blériot 115 airliner, which had four 180-hp Hispano-Suiza engines. There were many derivatives.*

*Because of the complex problems involved, helicopter development was slow. The designs of Marquis Pateras Pescara left the ground but went nowhere.*

*In Spain, La Cierva's first successful autogyro, the C.4, proved the practicability of the concept. Most of the subsequent development was in the UK.*

*Like all the light aeroplanes of the period, de Havilland's D.H.53 Humming Bird was underpowered and therefore not suitable as a club aircraft.*

*The Junkers A 20, designed to carry mail and freight, closely resembled its wartime forebears. It served with Deutsche Luft Hansa and Ad Astra Aero.*

Fairey's N.4 flying boat was impressively large, but not impressive enough to win orders; only two – the "Titania" and the "Atalanta" – were finished.

Czechoslovakia's Aero A.11 was a two-seater general-purpose biplane which was built in many variants to suit specific roles. Finland also used it.

Hawker's Woodcock fighter was not a success in its original two-bay form, but single-bay wings and other changes resulted in a production order.

A 55-hp Walter NZ radial engine powered the Avia BH.9 two-seater trainer; an example with increased tankage set a Czechoslovakian duration record.

One of the ugliest aeroplanes of 1923, the Armstrong Whitworth Wolf was designed as a two-seater reconnaissance machine but failed to win an order.

After entering RAF service, the Gloster Grebe fighter was found to suffer from flutter problems and had to be strengthened. The engine was a Jaguar.

The Boeing Model 15/PW-9 was the first of the company's fighters to be operated by the US Army Air Service. The engine was a 440-hp Curtiss D-12.

Curtiss built racers for the US Army as well as the US Navy. The clean lines of the 266-mph R-8 (originally the Navy's R2C-1) are well displayed here.

Appearing in 1923, the Curtiss PW-8 made the first dawn-to-dusk crossing of the US on June 23, 1924. Illustrated is the XPW-8 prototype 23-1201.

# 1924

278.47mph
France
Florentin Bonnet
Bernard Ferbois V2
Dec 11, 1924

3,293 miles
USA
Smith and Richter
De Havilland DH.4B
Aug 28, 1923

36,565ft
France
Joseph Sadi-Lecointe
Nieuport-Delage
Oct 30, 1923

57,319lb
Italy
SAI Caproni
Caproni Ca 60

1,000hp
Great Britain
Napier
Cub

**London, January 22**
Lord Thompson becomes secretary of state for air in Britain's first Labour government (→ Nov 7).

**Paris, January 29**
Pateras Pescara's Nº3 helicopter, fitted with a 180-hp Hispano engine, makes a flight of 10 minutes 10 seconds.

**Dakar, February 20**
Lieutenant-Colonel Tulasne, Captain Gama and Lieutenant Michel land their Breguet 14 airplanes after a round flight to Colomb-Béchar, thus completing the first trip across the Sahara desert and back.

**Nebraska, March 4**
Two Martin and two de Havilland bombers finally succeed in breaking an ice jam in the Platte river at North Bend, after six hours of bombardment.

**USA, March 7**
Lieutenant E H Barksdale and his navigator B Q Jones fly an American-built DH-4B the 575 miles from McCook Field, Dayton, Ohio, to Mitchell Field, New York, on instruments only (→ Jul).

**California, March 11**
The Douglas Company delivers the last of four Douglas World Cruisers (DWCs) ordered by the US Air Service for its planned round-the-world flight (→ Mar 19).

**Seattle, March 19**
The four DWCs set off on their travels (→ Apr 6).

**England, March 25**
Squadron Leader A S C MacLaren, Flying Officer W N Plenderleith and Sergeant R Andrews take off from the Calshot seaplane base in a Vickers Vulture II to attempt a round-the-world flight (→ Aug 2).

**London, April 2**
The day after state-owned Imperial Airways starts operation, a deputation from the newly-formed pilots' union, the Federation of Civilian Air Pilots, visits the secretary of state for air in an attempt to solve a dispute over pay and employment rights (→ Apr 28).

**Schiphol, Amsterdam, April 11**
Hermann Hess pilots the prototype Fokker F.VII monoplane on a test flight (→ Aug 21).

**London, April 28**
Imperial Airways inaugurates its London/Paris service (→ May 3).

**London, April**
The Fleet Air Arm (FAA) of the Royal Air Force (RAF), responsible for all shipborne and seaplane operations, is established; air spotting and reconnaissance duties are to be performed by Royal Navy aircrew on detachment to the RAF, which retains overall control of the FAA and supplies aircrew for other flying duties.

**Florida, May 2**
A Douglas DT-2 torpedo bomber is launched by catapult from the carrier USS *Langley* at anchor in Pensacola Bay.

**London, May 3**
Imperial Airways opens a service between London and Cologne via Brussels (→ Mar 30, 1926).

**France, May 4**
Etienne Oehmichen flies for 7 minutes 40 seconds in his helicopter Nº2, covering over a kilometer [0.6 miles] for the first time.

**New York, May 4**
In an experiment designed to prove that there are methods of defense from air attack, an airplane lays a smokescreen over Manhattan from 700 feet, cutting off a view of the city from the sea.

**Port Mollier, Alaska, May 11**
Frederick Martin and Alva Harvey, missing from the US Army Air Service round-the-world attempt after their DWC airplane crashed into a mountain, reach safety after a ten-day walk through a blizzard (→ Jul 15).

**Melbourne, May 19**
Wing-Commander S J Goble and Flying Officer I E MacIntyre land after a 8,568-mile flight around Australia in a Fairey IIID floatplane; they left Melbourne on April 6.

**Paris, May 27**
Adrienne Bolland wins the women's record for looping from Laura Bromwell, performing the feat 212 times in 1 hour 1 minutes in her Caudron 127.

**France, June 11**
Armand Deperdussin, the French aircraft designer, commits suicide; founder of what became the Spad airplane construction company, he was jailed for fraud and ended his days in extreme poverty.

**Tokyo, June 17**
French pilot Pelletier d'Oisy and his mechanic Besin land after a flight from Paris; they left on April 24 and covered the 12,677 miles in 12 legs in 120 hours' flying time, changing airplanes in Shanghai.

**Germany, June 23**
The prototype Focke-Wulf A 16 monoplane makes its first flight. Capable of carrying four passengers, it is the first product of Focke-Wulf Flugzeugbau GmbH [Focke-Wulf Airplane Construction Company] set up in January by Heinrich Focke and Georg Wulf with the backing of Bremen bankers (→ Sep 29, 1927).

**Siberia, Russia, August 2**
British aviators MacLaren, Plenderleith and Andrews abandon their round-the-world flight when their Vickers Vulture is wrecked in a forced landing at sea off the Siberian coast near Nikolski.

**Arctic, August 24**
The USS Richmond picks up Italian flyers Locatelli, Crossio, Farcinelli and Fraccini, who were forced down near Cape Farewell by bad weather during a flight across the North Atlantic in a Dornier Wal flying boat (→ Dec 31).

**Italy, August**
The prototype Savoia-Marchetti S.55 twin-hull flying boat makes its first flight.

**Canada, September 11**
Laurentide Air Services begins flying mail between Haileybury, Ontario, and Rouyn, Quebec. This is Canada's first scheduled air service.

**Lakehurst, NJ, October 15**
The Zeppelin ZR 3 airship, which has been built by the Germans for the US Navy under the Great War reparations scheme, arrives at the US Naval Air Station after making an 81-hour flight from the Zeppelin factory at Friedrichshafen on Lake Constance, on the German/Swiss border.

**Rome, November 4**
The new Fiat CR.1 fighter is demonstrated during the annual review of Italy's air forces at Centocelle airport.

**London, November 7**
Sir Samuel Hoare becomes secretary of state for air, replacing Lord Thompson (→ Mar 17, 1925).

**New York, November 7**
Dutch airplane manufacturer Anthony Fokker arrives to set up a plant in Hasbrouck, New Jersey, in order to manufacture airplanes for the US government (→ Nov 24).

**USA, December 13**
First Lieutenant Clyde Finter pilots a Sperry Messenger on an attempt to hook on to the US Army's dirigible TC-3; the attempt fails, and he makes an emergency landing.

**Bremerton, Wash, December 14**
A Martin MO-1 airplane is launched from the USS *Mississippi* by explosive catapult.

*Heroic homecoming: President Coolidge welcomes one of the pilots of the Douglas World Cruisers home after his round-the-world flight.* ▶

# THE SPHERE

AN ILLUSTRATED NEWSPAPER FOR THE HOME

With which is incorporated
BLACK & WHITE

Volume XCVIII. No. 1287.  Price One Shilling.  Postage { Inland, 1½d.; Canada and Newfoundland, 1½d.; Foreign, 3d. }  London, September 20, 1924.

## PRESIDENT COOLIDGE WELCOMES THE WORLD FLIERS ON THEIR RETURN

On March 17 the American aviators set out to fly round the world. Nearly six months later, after many adventures by sea and land, they again set foot on their native land for the comparatively easy task of making the final portion of their flight across America back to the starting-point in California. Everywhere in the United States they have been received with tremendous enthusiasm, and in Washington President Coolidge awaited their arrival for four hours in the rain. The picture reproduced here shows Mr. Coolidge shaking hands with Lieutenant Smith, while behind them is seen Secretary of War Weeks

# New British airline is grounded by strike action

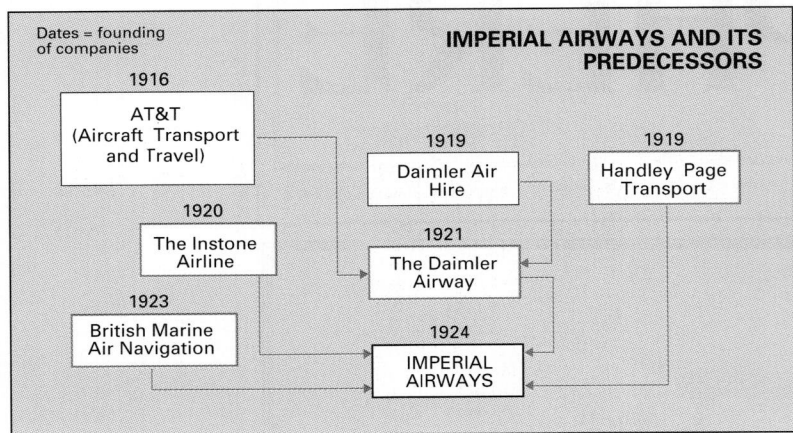

Dates = founding of companies

**IMPERIAL AIRWAYS AND ITS PREDECESSORS**

1916 — AT&T (Aircraft Transport and Travel)
1919 — Daimler Air Hire
1919 — Handley Page Transport
1920 — The Instone Airline
1921 — The Daimler Airway
1923 — British Marine Air Navigation
1924 — IMPERIAL AIRWAYS

*Imperial carrier: a Handley Page W.8 aircraft of the new national airline.*

**Croydon, England, April 28**

Britain's new national airline, Imperial Airways, started flying from London to Paris today, nearly a month after its formation. The delay has been caused by striking pilots who are demanding better pay and conditions. Imperial was formed on April 1 by the amalgamation of four pioneering British airlines: Handley Page Transport, Daimler Airway, Instone Airline and British Marine Air Navigation. The new company, capitalized at £1,000,000, will take over the aircraft, pilots, stewards and ground personnel of the old companies. State ownership now seems the only way to ensure the future of air travel in Britain.

The privately owned companies had great difficulty operating at a profit, even in the summer months when traffic is at its highest and despite the fact that, since October 1922, they have not been competing with each other. Each had its own route: Handley Page flew to Paris, Daimler to Amsterdam and Instone to Brussels.

Their main continental rivals have long enjoyed a high level of government support, including subsidies on ticket price, making the four British carriers' struggle to survive even more difficult. Amalgamation and state cash should improve the financial results: in addition to the capitalization, the government has agreed to a further £1,000,000 over the next ten years, £137,000 of it this year.

The new airline is a statement of confidence in the industry. It is hoped that, when the strike is over, it will become a flag-carrier for Britain not just in the empire but all over the world.

*Celebrations marking a new era.*

## Le Bourget boasts new control tower

**Paris, February 15**

Le Bourget aerodrome, to the north-east of the French capital, has become so busy that the need for new, stricter controls of air traffic into and out of the airport has become urgent. A big step in the right direction was taken today when the world's first "control tower" was inaugurated on the edge of the airport, with a commanding view of the landing area and its approaches. It will add to Le Bourget's growing reputation as Europe's most efficient airport.

At the top of the tower an airport official with binoculars signals the approach of airplanes and identifies the airline to which they belong. Alongside him, wireless operators maintain radio contact with pilots, establishing their positions through goniometers, special wireless direction finders (→ Jun 30).

## Canadians form their own Royal Air Force

*The crew of a Royal Canadian Air Force Vickers Viking, ready for action.*

**Ottawa, April 1**

Canada's own air force was created today. The history of Canadian military flying is one of great airmanship defeated by absent resources. In 1918 there were 13,000 Canadians in Britain's Royal Air Force, including three Victoria Cross winners; the new Royal Canadian Air Force (RCAF) has 68 officers and 307 airmen. RCAF tasks will include mapping, flying "treaty money" to native Canadians, hunting smugglers and illegal immigrants, and carrying mail and injured persons (→ Dec 24, 1927).

## Pilots leave Seattle to fly around world

**Seattle, Wash, April 6**

Today, after a year of planning, four US Army Air Service single-engined DWCs (Douglas World Cruisers), named *Seattle, Chicago, Boston* and *New Orleans*, set off in formation at the start of the longest air journey in history. Their plan is to circumnavigate the world, with the first leg to Prince Rupert, British Columbia, Canada.

This is a highly organized expedition, perhaps secretly aimed at recovering army prestige after the US Navy made the first ever transatlantic flight in 1919. Everyone speculates whether it is possible. The US Army thinks so, and huge quantities of spares – from screws to replacement undercarriages and 15 Liberty engines – have been sent ahead to keep the airplanes flying. Each DWC carries 600 US gallons of fuel (→ May 11).

# Flyers look forward to taking it easy on long-haul flights with 'automatic pilot'

*France, April*
An automatic system which allows aircrew to relax on long flights has been developed by French engineers. The idea is by no means new: five years ago inventor and aviator Max Boucher created the first "hands-off" airplane, but it was not a commercial success.

The principal problems have now been overcome, enabling the equipment to maintain a horizontal flight path and fly the aircraft to a preset destination. The objective of stable, horizontal flight is achieved by using gyroscopes to keep the craft on an even keel. Any deviation from the horizontal is detected by the gyroscopes and relayed, by a system of cables, to electric motors which make the necessary adjustments to the controls. The pilot feeds a program of the flight path into the control system, which automatically corrects it as required.

If the trials now under way prove satisfactory, it is expected that the "automatic pilot" will be fitted to commercial airplanes within the next year or so.

*The three servo-motors which are at the heart of the new control system.*

# US postal pilots are the world's best paid

*USA, 1924*
Civil aviation pilots find it hard to shake off the assumption that they fly because they love to, yet many are forced to put up with conditions and wages which vary greatly from one company to another. US Post Office airmail pilots, who fly around 60 hours a month on a dangerous job in all weathers and terrain, are undoubtedly the best paid in the world. Base pay is from $2,000 to $2,800 a year (the US average wage is $1,300), with increments for experience of up to $3,600. They are rewarded by the mile, according to the terrain which they have to cover, from 5 cents (flat terrain) to 14 cents (mountains). Four pilots have taken over $4,000 in mileage pay alone this year, and one, H T Lewis, has earned $5,582.

In England, the new national airline Imperial Airways almost crashed before it took off this spring, when the pilots of the airlines absorbed into the new operator struck over conditions. In the end they accepted a low basic retainer plus payment for each hour in the air. The French airline Latécoère pays by results. On top of a retainer, its flyers receive supplements on the basis of output, number of stages flown and tickets sold. Keeping to the timetable will be rewarded with a bonus (→ Feb 2, 1925).

# Germany is model for new Tupolev ANT-2

*A strong construction: the Tupolev ANT-2 all-metal transport airplane.*

*Moscow, May 26*
Impressed by the sheer comfort and reliability of German airplanes, which are carrying passengers in Soviet skies, the USSR has built a modern machine of its own. The ANT-2, which made its first flight today, is named after its designer, Andrei N Tupolev. Its all-metal construction is similar to that pioneered by Junkers whose aircraft Tupolev has been involved in building in the Soviet Union for some time.

The ANT-2 has the familiar Junkers-type corrugated metal fuselage, slung below a high wing, to make the enclosed two-seat passenger cabin. The pilot sits out front in the open, behind a single 100-hp Bristol Lucifer three-cylinder radial engine (→ Nov 29, 1925).

# US government keeps Boeing plant busy

*Fuselages under construction in the Boeing factory at Seattle, Washington.*

*Seattle, Wash, July*
The Boeing Airplane Company has a lot of work in hand rebuilding the American-built DH-4s for the government and filling the US Navy's 49-airplane order for two versions of its own training aircraft. They feel confident for their future.

Besides the Navy order, Boeing will provide the US Post Office with an aircraft based on the trainer design, powered by a Liberty engine. The post office intends to buy an experimental mail airplane from every company willing to build one to meet its specifications. The most important new venture for Boeing, however, is its experimental PW-9 pursuit plane. If the PW-9, now undergoing US Army Air Service trials at McCook Field near Dayton, Ohio, is successful, the company will have proved its ability to provide high performance military aircraft. The Curtiss PW-8, which has already been ordered by the Air Service, is the PW-9's major competitor (→ Jul 1).

# Speedy pilot beats Sun

*A Curtiss PW-8 pursuit airplane of the sort used by Lieutenant Maughan.*

*San Francisco, June 23*
With only one minute to spare before the Sun set, US Army Air Service (USAAS) Lieutenant Russell L Maughan touched the wheels of his airplane down in San Francisco to complete the first one-day, daylight crossing of the US. His "race against the Sun" took 21 hours 48 minutes 30 seconds.

Maughan's achievement is all the more noteworthy because low cloud at Mitchell Field, Long Island, where he started out at dawn,

delayed take-off for 36 minutes. Then a further hour was lost in Dayton, Ohio, when a fuel filler sheared off after being over-tightened by a zealous mechanic and had to be replaced.

The flight was made in order to prove the assertion of USAAS bosses that their aircraft, even PW-8 Curtiss pursuit planes powered by single 450-hp engines like the one used today, can be deployed anywhere in the country within a single day (→ Jan 1925).

# First round-Australia flight is completed

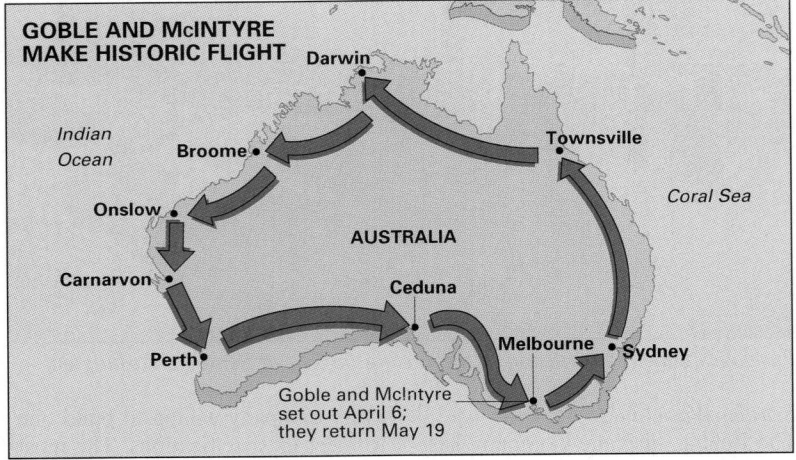

GOBLE AND McINTYRE
MAKE HISTORIC FLIGHT

Indian Ocean · Broome · Darwin · Townsville · Coral Sea · Onslow · AUSTRALIA · Carnarvon · Ceduna · Melbourne · Sydney · Perth · Goble and McIntyre set out April 6; they return May 19

*Melbourne, Victoria, May 19*
The entire coastline of Australia has been circumnavigated by air. The feat has been accomplished by two Royal Australian Air Force officers, Wing-Commander Stanley Goble and Flying Officer Ivor McIntyre, who were awarded the prestigious Britannia trophy for their flight. They set off from Point Cook on April 6 to find suitable

sites coastal defense airfields. The two men covered 8,568 miles in a total flying time of 93 hours. The airplane used was a British Fairey IIID reconnaissance and general purpose biplane. It used the same Rolls-Royce Eagle VIII engine throughout the flight and on arrival back here today, Goble cabled his superiors to say that the machine remained fit for service.

# US airmail launches coast-to-coast run

*Night light: an airfield beacon.*

*Washington, DC, July 1*
With $2.75 million authorized by Congress, the US Post Office today began a transcontinental air mail service between New York City and San Francisco. The east/west mail flight will take about 35 hours and the west/east trip, which usually benefits from favorable tail winds, about 30 hours.

Modified de Havilland DH-4s, fitted with lights for night flying, will carry the mail. Official confidence in the service is based on trials last August and the addition of extra beacons to guide the pilots along the route. The trip will be flown in relays, with fresh pilots and aircraft provided six times along the route (→ Feb 22, 1925).

# Bear flies to Berlin and a bull to Paris

*Germany, August 21*
A rather unusual passenger disembarked today at Königsberg in East Prussia from a Fokker F.VII of the Dutch airline KLM: a Russian bear. He seemed to be none the worse for his flight from Moscow and will soon be taking off for the second leg of his journey from the Soviet Union to Berlin, where he will join the German capital's famous zoo.

The wide-bodied, high-winged Fokker F.VII monoplanes are proving to be ideal for carrying such live cargo. On July 9, for instance, a large stud bull called Nico V was flown in an F.VII by KLM from Rotterdam in the Netherlands to Paris.

# Japan circled by air

*Osaka, Japan, July 31*
Two Japanese airmen, Yukichi Goto and his flight engineer Minezo Yonezawa, today returned to Osaka after completing a remarkable first: a flight around Japan. The distance covered by the two men was 2,727 miles. The flight was sponsored by Nippon Koku KK and the newspaper *Daimai Tonichi Shimbun*.

Leaving Osaka in the Kawanishi K-6 seaplane on July 23, they took in Kagoshima, Hakata, Kanazawa, Akita, Minato, Kasumigaura and Yokaichi. Flying time was 33 hours 48 minutes (→ May 1, 1925).

**Royal Air Force mechanics inflate a kite balloon which will be used to help police direct traffic going to the Derby, the classic English horse-race.**

# Globe-girdling team makes the world smaller

## Three out of four aircraft reach Paris

*Paris, July 15*

The six airmen remaining on the US Army Air Service (USAAS) round-the-world flight are pausing in France today. They made a special effort to arrive in time for the Bastille Day celebrations yesterday when they dropped flowers on the tomb of the Unknown Warrior, accompanied by French aviators.

The three Douglas World Cruisers, the *Boston*, *Chicago* and *New Orleans*, reached France after flying from the United States by way of Alaska and Japan, then across Asia to Europe. Their crews have

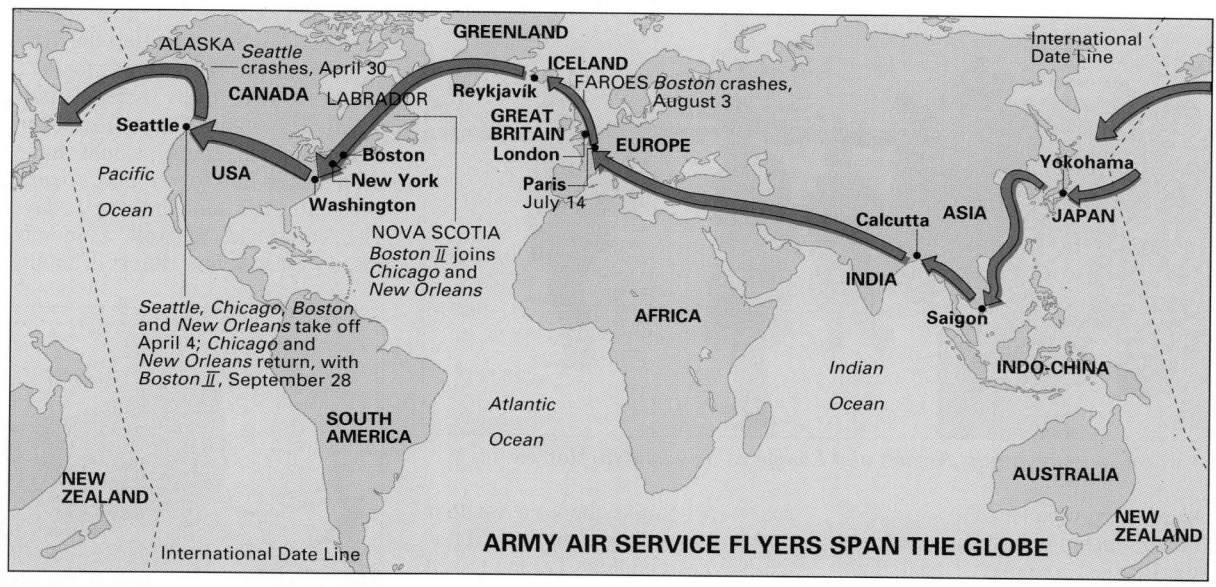

ARMY AIR SERVICE FLYERS SPAN THE GLOBE

*The pilots gather around a globe before setting out on their trip.*

had many adventures on the way. The aircraft can be fitted with either wheels or pontoons depending on whether they were flying over land or water. On the leg from Japan to Shanghai in China, they had pontoons fitted, but found they had to search the harbor for a space to land as it was teeming with junks and sampans.

The fourth DWC of the original team, the *Seattle*, was lost on April 30 when it struck a mountain in mist on the Alaskan peninsula. It had smashed its float struts at Prince Rupert, Canada, and been given a new engine in Chignik. Major Frederick L Martin, the flight commander, and Sergeant Alva L Harvey took ten days to walk to civilization. With Martin out of the flight, command passed on to Lieutenant Lowell Smith.→

## 'Boston' succumbs on the way to Iceland

*Faroe Islands, Sweden, August 3*
Following the loss of the *Seattle* on April 30 [*see story, left*], another DWC airplane was lost today on the US Army Air Service world tour. Reaching England on July 16, the remaining three were overhauled and fitted with floats instead of wheels, then flew to the Orkney Islands before the long North Atlantic leg to Iceland. They left yesterday, but fog prevented all but the *New Orleans* from reaching Reykjavik. Today the *Chicago* and the *Boston* tried again. But the *Boston* developed oil pump failure and had to make an emergency landing. A trawler came to the rescue, later handing over to the USS *Richmond*. The *Boston* was towed towards the Faroes but capsized and sank. The crew was unhurt.→

*The airmen caught during their stop at Croydon aerodrome, near London.*

## Pilots return home as national heroes

*Seattle, Wash, September 28*
Great excitement and much national pride greeted the return to Seattle of the US Army Air Service (USAAS) DWCs *Chicago* and *New Orleans* today. The historic first circumnavigation of the world by air is complete. The journey of over 26,345 miles has taken 175 days, with the loss of two machines.

The crews also recorded the first staged Pacific and east/west South Atlantic crossings. Flying time was 363 hours. Accompanying successful crewmen lieutenants Lowell Smith and Leslie Arnold (the *Chicago*) and Erik Nelson and John Harding (the *New Orleans*) were Wade and Ogden, whose DWC *Boston* was lost on August 3. They flew today in the prototype DWC, now named *Boston II*, after joining up in Nova Scotia for the final flight across the USA.

Iceland to Frederiksdal in Greenland had been the longest non-stop stage, about 875 miles. The crews touched down again in North America on Labrador, on August 31. Their first welcoming reception was at Boston on the 6th, where 20,000 well-wishers turned out and US Navy guns sounded their approval. The crews also took in New York and Washington, DC, where they met President Coolidge.

# Pilots brave freezing cold to fly to Russia

*A warm welcome awaits Noguès and Laulhé as they land at Moscow.*

**Moscow, November 14**

Two Frenchmen have braved freezing weather to make a trial flight from Paris to Moscow for the Compagnie Franco-Roumaine de Navigation Aérienne (CFRNA), which operates routes from France to eastern Europe. CFRNA halts flights from November 1 to February 15 because the cold weather makes flying dangerous; but Maurice Noguès and Jean Laulhé risked it, and left Paris in a Caudron C81 on November 7 for Moscow via Prague, Warsaw, Vilno [Vilnius], Minsk and Smolensk. Despite engine troubles from the cold they arrived safely today (→ Jan 1, 1925).

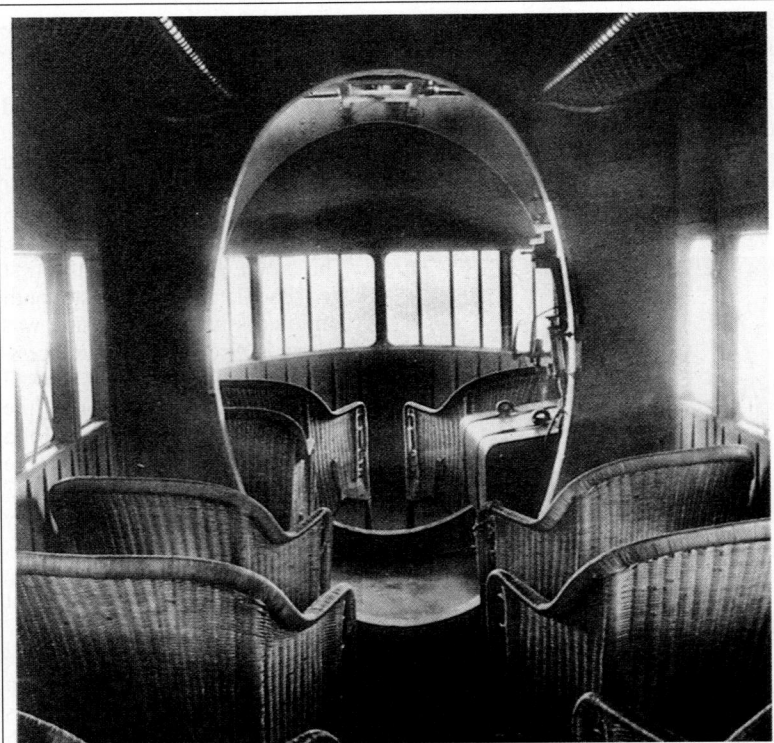

**Keeping travellers in the style to which they are increasingly becoming accustomed: the spacious interior and luxurious fittings on board the Farman F.3X Jabiru (also known as the F.121), which last year won France's prestigious 500,000-franc Grand Prix des Avions Transports. The Jabiru's comfortable wicker armchairs are arranged so that each of the nine passengers has a good view through the airplane's large windows. Four Hispano-Suiza 8Ac 180-hp engines supply the power.**

# KLM beats a path for East Indies flights

**Java, November 24**

A KLM Fokker F.VII today touched down in Batavia after the first flight from the Netherlands to Java in the Dutch East Indies [Indonesia]. The 55-day flight, a trial for a commercial route, would have been faster but for engine seizure over Bulgaria on the third day. The crew had to wait a month for a replacement. Pilots Captain A Thomassen à Thuessink van der Hoop and Lieutenant van Weerden Poelman, with P van den Broeke as engineer, began the first stage to Prague on October 1. Because of the halt in Bulgaria, Constantinople [Istanbul] was only reached on November 3 and Sumatra on November 21. Total flying time for the 9,552-mile flight was 127 hours 16 minutes (→ Sep 4, 1925).

*Eastern trailblazer: a Fokker F.VII, as used on the Netherlands to Java flight.*

# Explosives blast US Navy plane off ship

**Bremerton, Wash, December 14**

The noise of detonating explosives drowned out the roar of the engine today as the US Navy successfully hurled an aircraft into the sky from the forward turret of the battleship USS *Mississippi*. The aircraft was launched by a catapult charged with 14 pounds of smokeless gunpowder. Today's flight, by Lieutenants L C Hayden and W M Fallers in a Martin MO-1 observation plane, is the US Navy's latest attempt to perfect ways to catapult an aircraft from a ship. Past efforts have employed various means ranging from block-and-tackle to compressed air.

Until now, ships other than aircraft carriers have had to halt and lower airplanes into the water by crane before they could take off. Judging by today's demonstration, however, it should be possible for a fleet under way to launch aircraft without slackening speed and making itself vulnerable (→ Jul 1, 1926).

# London to Paris air route mapped out

**Le Bourget, December 15**

Since 1922, when a British and a French airliner collided head-on over France while flying on reciprocal courses between London and Paris, ways have been sought to reduce the danger of air collision. Now a one-way system has been set up. This requires aircraft leaving Le Bourget to go via Ecouen, Abbeville, Etaples and Oxted to Croydon (→ Sep 1, 1925).

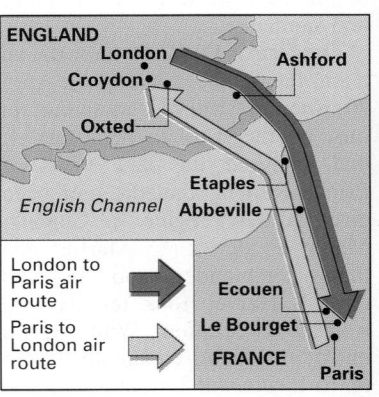

# European operators flock to buy Dornier 'Whale' flying boats

*Airlines are queueing up to buy the Dornier Do J Wal [Whale] flying boat, which is living up to its promise.*

*Italy, December 31*
Speaking at aircraft makers Costruzioni Meccaniche Aeronautiche at Marina di Pisa today, Professor Claudius Dornier declared: "The future rests with the flying boat". Since the Great War the German designer's Italian-based company has built some of the world's best flying boats.

The type that is proving to be a hit all over the world is the Type J, named the Wal [Whale]. This is by no means as big as some wartime giants, but it has the qualities airlines and air forces want. It is big enough to carry nine passengers, or 14 for shorter distances, yet is not unwieldy, with a rectangular wing spaning less than 74 feet. It is powered by two powerful and reliable engines in tandem, such as Rolls-Royce, Napier, Hispano-Suiza, Lorraine and Fiat. Not least, its structure is entirely of the light but particularly strong metal called Duralumin, making it tough and seaworthy.

The first Wal prototype flew in November 1922. Despite the restrictions imposed on aircraft production by the post-war Treaty of Versailles, the Wal is being made in Germany, as well as Switzerland, Italy, Spain, the Netherlands and Japan. With a steady stream of new customers, Dornier's order books for the Wal will be full for some time to come.

# Beech and Cessna join in new venture

*Wichita, Kansas, December 24*
Three leading names in the US airplane industry came together here today to form the Travel Air Manufacturing Company. The deal ends months of negotiations between Walter Beech, Clyde Cessna and Lloyd Stearman, which began soon after Beech and Stearman walked out on the Swallow Airplane Manufacturing Company, where Beech was sales officer and test pilot and Stearman chief mechanic.

Beech and Stearman wanted Swallow to use a steel airframe developed some years ago in Detroit, but the company rejected the idea and the two men decided to quit. They paid a call on Cessna, an airplane builder already well-known in Wichita, and convinced him to invest most of the capital for a new company. Travel Air will concentrate on building biplanes to be used for two passengers and mail.

# Weathermen offer new service for pilots

*Keeping an eye on the weather.*

*Paris, June 30*
After years of lobbying by pilots, almost the whole of the English-speaking world as well as the whole of western Europe, is now linked into an international system of weather reporting. Such a meteorological system has been made essential by the growth in commercial air services. Pilots need information that is not only accurate, but also right up to date.

There are still many difficulties. Pilots need to know the weather not only at their airport of departure, but also all the way along their route to the destination airport. Moreover, they need to have information not only at sea level but also at the height at which they will fly. Thanks to the work of ICAN, the International Commission for Air Navigation, every major airport now not only sends out weather reports but also receives them.

Thus, here at Le Bourget airport in Paris for example, a huge map shows the northern half of France as well as Belgium and southern England. Arrows dotted over it show the direction of the wind and its strength, while other symbols show cloud and fog. Other symbols indicate the height of the cloud base above ground.

The weather, being a natural phenomenon, can change after an airliner has taken off. Mist can descend without warning, and at present there is no sure way of landing an airplane in thick fog, which can often form in minutes. There is a pressing need for some kind of system which will be able to guide airplanes safely to the airfield in minimum visibility (→ Dec 15).

# Autogyro makes a flight across Madrid

*Madrid, December 12*
The Cierva C.6A autogyro, a peculiar hybrid of an Avro 504K trainer airplane and a helicopter, today flew for over 7.5 miles. The aircraft, which has been under development for over four years, was piloted by Captain Joaquin Loriga Taboada. The 8-minute 12-second journey was between Cuatro Vientos and Getafé in Madrid. Earlier this year the C.6A flew to an altitude of 655 feet and showed a speed range of 16 to 68mph (→ Jan 16, 1925).

AIR UNION — AIR UNION

FREIGHT SERVICE

THE FASTEST GOODS EXPRESS TO THIRTY EUROPEAN CITIES

TRAVEL BY AIR

PLEASURE
COMFORT
SPEED
REGULARITY
SAFETY

**An advertising pamphlet for the major French airline Air Union.**

Built for the Lympne light aeroplane competitions, the Bristol Brownie performed well on its limited power; but engine reliability was a problem.

One of the smallest all-metal twin-engined flying boats ever to appear, the single-seater Short Cockle did not go into production, only one being built.

In France, Avions Michel Wibault was also building all-metal aircraft, epitomized here by the square-fuselaged, parasol-winged Type 7C1 fighter.

Hawker's entry for the Lympne competitions was the elegant little Cygnet biplane, the work of promising young British designer Sydney Camm.

The Junkers G 23 all-metal airliner, with its trimotor layout, low wings and corrugated all-metal skinning, presaged the larger and famous Ju 52/3m.

All-metal construction was also being tried in the USSR. The inelegant Tupolev ANT-2 displays corrugated skinning reminiscent of Junkers practise.

The first successful design to come from Heinrich Foche and Georg Wulf was the three-passenger Focke-Wulf FW 16, powered by a 75-hp Siemens engine.

Trailblazer of metal commercial airplanes in the US was Bill Stout, whose 2-AT airliner received the financial backing of businessman Henry Ford.

The Fokker C.V sesquiplane was produced in Amsterdam. It was nice to fly, robust and easily maintained, and it could use a wide variety of engines.

Some 4,000 examples of the Potez 25 general-purpose and reconnaissance biplane were built, testifying to the success of this widely-exported design.

Looking ill-proportioned, but revealing the shape of things to come, the American Curtiss XO-1G Falcon was a two-seater observation aeroplane.

Fokker's D.XIII single-seater fighter clearly reveals its descent from the First World War D.VII. The company adhered to the biplane for some time.

Macchi's M.24 flying boat, evolved from First World War designs, went into production as both a bomber or torpedo-carrier and a six-passenger airliner.

The snub-nosed, radial-engined Koolhoven FK.31 was powered by a 400-hp Bristol Jupiter engine. It proved to be too slow for the Netherlands air force.

The Blériot-Spad S.51 C1 single-seater fighter featured a smooth wooden monocoque fuselage and fabric-covered metal wings. Poland bought 50.

Produced in limited numbers for the RAF, the Fairey Fawn day-bomber was one of the few new types supplied to the service in the lean post-war years.

The Aero A.24 night-bomber, Czechoslovakia's first twin-engined aircraft and its most ambitious design so far, had two 245-hp Maybach engines.

# 1925

278.47mph
France
Florentin Bonnet
Bernard Ferbois V2
Dec 11, 1924

3,293 miles
USA
Smith and Richter
De Havilland DH.4B
Aug 28, 1923

36,565ft
France
Joseph Sadi-Lecointe
Nieuport-Delage
Oct 30, 1923

57,319lb
Italy
SAI Caproni
Caproni Ca 60

1,000hp
Great Britain
Napier
Cub

**Paris, January 1**
The airline CFRNA changes its name to the Compagnie Internationale de Navigation Aérienne (CIDNA) (→ Mar 6).

**Madrid, January 16**
Captain Joaquin Loriga Taboada, demonstrating the Cierva C.6A autogyro to a delegation from the British company Vickers, suffers a complete engine failure at an altitude of 196 feet, but still lands safely (→ Mar 24, 1926).

**Washington, DC, February 2**
President Coolidge signs the Kelly Bill, which authorizes the contracting of air mail services to private companies (→ Jun 1).

**Los Angeles, California, March 1**
Ryan Airlines, founded by commercial aviation pioneer Tubal Claude Ryan, launch the first year-long scheduled passenger service in the US. Each day, there are two flights from Los Angeles to San Diego. Tickets for return flights cost $22.50.

**Europe, March 16**
Forbidden by Germany to fly in its airspace, the French airline CIDNA is forced to make a detour by way of Zurich and Vienna on the Strasbourg/Prague section of its Paris/Istanbul service (→ Jun 30).

**London, March 17**
Sir Sefton Brancker, the British government's director of civil aviation, returns from a round trip to Rangoon, Burma, to survey air routes to the East. He left London, with pilot Alan Cobham, on November 20 last year.

**New York, March 30**
Morris Titterington of the Pioneer Instrument Co demonstrates his earth inductor compass. Using a coil instead of a magnet to point the needle, it has been fitted to the airship USS *Shenandoah* (→ Sep 3).

**Ukraine, April 15**
Ukvozduchput airline starts flying from Kharkov to Kiev (→ Jul 13).

**Japan, May 1**
The Japanese army air corps is established (→ Sep 28).

**Toulouse, France, May 3**
Clément Ader, early French aircraft pioneer whose *Avion* machine gave the French their word for airplane, dies.

**Europe, May 15**
The Swedish airline AB Aerotransport introduces the new Junkers G 23 three-engined all-metal transport on its service between Malmö and Amsterdam.

**Germany, May 16**
The M-17 Ello, the first airplane constructed by the Messerschmitt company, makes its first flight. Coming in to land, the airplane hits a high tension wire and crashes, injuring both the pilot and company founder Willy Messerschmitt, who is on board.

**Norway, May 21**
Roald Amundsen and Lincoln Ellsworth and their crews take off from Kings Bay in two Dornier Wal flying boats, heading for the North Pole (→ Jul 15).

**Detroit, Mich, May 21**
Howard E Coffin announces the formation of National Air Transport; with capital of $10,000,000 it is an ambitious newcomer on the air transport scene (→ Apr 17, 1926).

**Croydon, England, May 29**
Alan Cobham lands the prototype de Havilland D.H.60 Moth after flying 1,000 miles to Zurich and back in a single day (→ Jul 21).

**San Francisco, June 1**
A car dealer covers himself in stamps worth $718 in a bid to be sent airmail to New York; the US Post Office refuses to accept him.

**New York City, July 1**
The US Air Mail Service begins overnight flights between New York and Chicago over the Allegheny mountains (→ Oct 7).

**Seattle, Wash, July 7**
The Boeing Model 40 mailplane makes its first flight at the company's works; designed primarily to carry mail, it has been adapted to take two paying passengers in order to cut operating costs (→ Feb 13, 1927).

**USA, July 15**
Dr A Hamilton Rice's expedition to the Amazon, the first exploration by airplane, returns; Lieutenant Walter Hinton piloted a Curtiss Seagull (→ Oct 26).

**Lancashire, England, July 21**
The first production de Havilland D.H.60 Moth is delivered by Alan Cobham to the Lancashire Aero Club at Woodford, one of five founded with an Air Ministry subsidy at the behest of Sir Sefton Brancker, Britain's director of civil aviation (→ Oct 15).

**USA, August 14**
Jack Rickman, 17, hitches a lift by sneaking on to the wing of a California National Guard airplane flying from Las Vegas to Los Angeles; the airplane completes its journey safely, and Rickman climbs down unhurt.

**France, September 1**
A wireless station is opened at Viry-Châtillon, near Orly; it directs the movements of airplanes on the 900-meter band, which was agreed on August 15 by Britain, France, Belgium and the Netherlands as a common waveband.

**Basle, Switzerland, September 2**
Swiss airline Basler Luftverkehr [Basle Airways] is established.

**The Netherlands, September 4**
The prototype Fokker F.VIIa-3m three-engined monoplane makes its first flight.

**Texas, September 5**
Colonel (formerly temporary Brigadier-General) Billy Mitchell, posted to San Antonio when his term as US Army Air Service chief

expired in April, publicly blames the state of military aviation on "incompetency, criminal negligence and almost treasonable administration by the War and Navy Departments" (→ Oct 28).

**Washington, DC, September 12**
President Calvin Coolidge appoints a board of inquiry under Dwight Morrow to determine federal aviation policy.

**France, October 18**
France pilot Sadi Lecointe wins the Beaumont cup with a speed of 194.165mph (→ Apr 10, 1926).

**Croydon, England, November 16**
Alan Cobham leaves in a D.H.50 fitted with two extra fuel tanks to make a survey of possible civil air routes over Africa; he is accompanied by engineer A B Elliott and photographer B W G Emmott (→ Jan 24, 1926).

**France, November 17**
French pilot Jean Boussoutrot pilots the Farman Super-Goliath F 140 BN6 to a height of 11,745 feet while it is carrying a load of almost six tons.

**Middlesex, England, November 18**
The Holt Autochute is publicly demonstrated for the first time at Stag Lane airfield, Edgware; a small "pilot" parachute pulls the main chute out of the pack.

**Russia, November 24**
The prototype Tupolev ANT-4 twin-engined monoplane bomber makes its first flight (→ Jan 1, 1926).

**Washington, DC, December 17**
Colonel Billy Mitchell is found guilty of discrediting the US Army by his public comments on the state of military aviation; he is sentenced to five years' suspension of rank, pay and command (→ Feb 1, 1926).

*A flight timetable for the German Junkers airline. Flying remains the preserve of the few but is becoming a more common mode of travel.* ▶

# War surplus Curtiss Jenny, still favorite, might yet outlive US's 'flying circuses'

*The versatile Jenny is ready to lend a hand spraying crops on the farm.*

**USA, January**
The countless teams of barnstormers swarming over the countryside to earn a precarious living, still choose the ageing, but reliable Curtiss Jenny as their favorite mount. War surplus, it is cheap, ideal for so-called "gipsy flyers", who often belong to traveling flying circuses with as few as two pilots and one airplane.

But the Jenny has a serious side. The Curtiss Exhibition Company flew 100,000 miles in 1924, partly on Jennies. It carried over 3,000 passengers, instructed pilots, and undertook film work, air photography and fast deliveries. There are so many Jennies still around that the company has even given free machines to graduates.

If their airplane still has a future, that of the aerial entertainers themselves is bleak. Accidents are common, and the public will now only pay $3 or $5 for a joyride instead of $12.50 when the circuses were more of a novelty (→ Jul 15).

# Trimotor metal Junkers airliner is a hit

**Malmö, Sweden May 15**
A new German airliner, the Junkers G 23, started its career here today with Swedish Air Lines. It follows the practice pioneered by Junkers of building all-metal monoplanes. Its debut marks another first for the company: the G 23 is the first three-engined aircraft to carry passengers anywhere in the world. Three-engined airliners are likely to proliferate: Fokker is working on a similar design which is expected to fly later this year.

**At Bolling Field, Washington, DC, aircraft designer Igor Sikorsky (5th from left) attends a performance on a piano which has been flown from Long Island on the biplane S-29 he has built with other Russian refugees.**

# French pioneer South American air routes

*Recife, Brazil, March 6*
One of the most outstanding French achievements of recent years has been the development of air services from France to West Africa and South America. The French airline CGEA has been a major pioneer.

Its first exploratory mission to South America took place last May, under the leadership of Captain Julien Roig, who had previously inaugurated a route between Casablanca, Morocco, and Dakar, Senegal. Roig conducted surveys, making ten stops between Buenos Aires, Argentina, and Natal in Brazil. He met officials in Brazil Argentina and Uruguay.

A second mission set off last December to make demonstration flights and establish bases. For the last few months, pilots have been surveying the 2,858 miles between Buenos Aires and Recife. Two of the pilots, named Hamm and Vachet, today completed the last leg in their Breguets (→ Mar 16).

*In Montevideo, Captain Roig offers flowers to the French ambassador's wife.*

# De Havilland tests new two-seater Moth

*London, February 22*
The British aircraft maker Geoffrey de Havilland flew his latest design, the D.H.60 Moth, on its maiden flight here today. The prototype performed well, and may set new standards for light aircraft.

After watching the performance of ultra-light airplanes at recent Air Ministry competitions, de Havilland came to the conclusion that a practical two-seater for air club and private use needed a powerful engine. The Moth uses a 60-hp Cirrus engine, but he intends to fit it with the 85-hp Cirrus II soon.

The Moth is a clever balance between low weight and tough wooden construction, with a ply-skinned fuselage, folding wings, reliable engine and good fuel capacity. The fully laden Cirrus/Moth prototype weighs no more than 1,240 pounds (→ May 29).

# Sky movies offered on German airlines

*Berlin, March*

Passengers on several German airlines now have something else to look at apart from the landscape: movies. Passengers unable to read or sleep, due to the motion of the machine, are apparently happy to be entertained by moving pictures, although what they can do about a feature they dislike is unclear. Single-reel "shorts" are generally shown due to weight limitations. The fact that the films are silent makes them ideal for showing in an airliner: the engine noise is so great that it is difficult for passengers to hear anything even at the best of times.

*Watching the first in-flight movie.*

# Ford Motor starts its own air service

*Dearborn, Mich, April 3*

The Ford Motor Company launched an airline today when the *Maiden Dearborn* carried cargo between Detroit and Chicago. The Stout monoplane will make a round trip between the cities every other day, and a route between Detroit and Minneapolis will start soon.

The venture represents the start of the first regular commercial flights in the USA and reflects Henry Ford's confidence in commercial aviation. The company has built a terminus with facilities for airplanes and airships at Dearborn, just outside Detroit – hence the punning name of the airplane. Ford's commitment to the airline is emphasized by reports that he is bidding for a franchise to run an air mail route (→ Aug 21, 1926).

# French airplane does without an airstrip

*River landing: Bajac's Schreck amphibian on the Thames in west London.*

*London, June 30*

Do airlines need airfields? French airline Air Union has decided to experiment with an alternative: aircraft that float. An Air Union Schreck FBA 19HMT 3, flown by company chief pilot Robert Bajac, took off from the river Seine in Paris, then landed on the river Thames in London.

The Schreck can land wherever there is a sizeable body of water and is able to deliver passengers right to the heart of any city with a river. But it is unlikely to have any effect on commercial services due to its small passenger and freight load, in this case just two paying passengers or one plus freight.

At the moment Air Union has only one FBA 19HMT 3. It has a 350-hp Hispano-Suiza engine giving the machine a maximum speed of almost 100mph, making it more suitable for fast dispatch-carrying than passengers (→ Apr 14, 1926).

# Polar explorers' airborne expedition fails

*Spitzbergen, Norway, 16 July*

Roald Amundsen, the first man to reach the South Pole, returned here today from a dramatic attempt to fly over the North Pole. With American colleague Lincoln Ellsworth and four crew, he set out on May 21 hoping to navigate two ice-adapted Dornier Wal flying boats to the Pole. They returned with just one aircraft, using their combined fuel. Fog beset them on their outward journey, and they lost their way. After eight hours flying they set down 150 miles from their goal. Unable to take off, they labored for 26 days to build an ice runway from which to take off (→ May 14, 1926).

*At rest on the ice, a Dornier flying boat of Amundsen's polar expedition.*

# RAF flyers are lent a royal hand during annual air pageant

*RAF airmen rehearsing on D.H.9As.*

*Hendon, England, June 3*

Pilots at the Royal Air Force (RAF) display today were given instructions from an unusual source: King George V. Using the latest ground-to-air wireless, the king personally directed Grebe fighters of 25 Squadron during the five-year-old annual pageant, which is inspired by Sir Hugh Trenchard. Trenchard's optimism for the service he did more than anyone to found even led him once to rewrite a bad weather forecast for the RAF show. The weather promptly improved (→ Oct 21, 1926).

# Soviet airplanes fly Moscow to Peking

*Peking, July 13*

Soviet airmen have pulled off a considerable coup by completing a formation flight from Moscow to Peking in China. Six airplanes set off on June 10 and five arrived on July 13, having covered 4,375 miles. With the crews were eight reporters.

The expedition, sponsored by the airline Dobrolet and the organization "Friends of Aviation", had two main purposes. One was to pioneer an air route across the unconquered Gobi desert to China, and the other to show the strength of Soviet aviation. However, only one aircraft, the AK 1, was of Russian design. The other machines consisted of two Junkers F.13s and copies of the de Havilland D.H.4 and D.H.9A built as R-1 and R-2s. One Junkers was wrecked at Kalgan.

## RAF gets used to role as Britain's imperial police

*Hinaidi, Iraq, July 18*
The role of Britain's Royal Air Force as an imperial sword of judgement was demonstrated literally today, when a low-flying Bristol F.2b fighter decapitated a Turkish cavalryman who was part of a unit trying to infiltrate British-controlled Iraq.

It was at Churchill's Cairo conference in March 1921 that the RAF was, in effect, appointed the British Empire's policeman. Airmen had won "the cheapest war in history" the year before by defeating the "Mad Mullah" in Somaliland [Somalia] in a mere three weeks at a cost of £77,000.

Air power was tested again in 1922, when new Turkish leader Mustapha Kemal Atatürk tore up the treaty signed by his defeated country after the Great War. His army, threatening Gallipoli and Constantinople [Istanbul] halted when faced with air attack.

Last year, after dropping the usual warning leaflets, RAF bombers attacked tribes in Waziristan, in the lawless North-West Frontier region between India and Afghanistan.

In Iraq, the Kurdish leader Sheik Mahmud, secretly backed by Turkey, is running a constant guerrilla war. Recently, to secure the major Kurdish town of Sulaymaniyah, RAF D.H.9s and other machines dropped 28 tons of bombs in 48 hours, destroying most of the houses. Given these responsibilities it is hardly surprising that one RAF officer, Squadron Leader Arthur Harris, should complain that defense cuts in Britain mean "filthy food" for his men.

These are not wars for weak stomachs. Airmen carry what they call "goolie" chits promising a reward for safe passage if they crash. But many tribesmen cannot read, and their response is often to castrate a prisoner before killing him and stuffing the amputated parts into the corpse's mouth (→ Sep 1, 1926).

## American airmen brave the Arctic wastes

*Northern Canada, August 12*
Four members of an expedition sponsored by the National Geographic Society became the first flyers to land an aircraft in the Canadian Arctic today when they touched down in two Loeing amphibians at Hayes Fjord on the east coast of Ellesmere Island.

The aircraft were under the command of Lieutenant-Commander Richard E Byrd, detailed to the expedition by the US Navy. Byrd and Floyd Bennett were in one airplane and Lieutenant-Commander E F McDonald, captain of one of the expedition's ships, and his pilot in the other (→ May 9, 1926).

*Flight leader: Lt-Cdr Richard Byrd.*

## Submarine finds missing seaplane crew

*The US Navy's Hall PN-9 seaplane shortly after leaving San Francisco.*

*Hawaii, September 10*
Five airmen who disappeared over the Pacific 11 days ago on a flight from San Francisco to Hawaii have been found safe and well. Commander John Rogers and his crew were discovered by a submarine, sitting on the floats of their seaplane, drifting 15 miles off the east coast of the island of Kauai.

They left San Francisco on a regular flight on August 31, then 300 miles into their journey radioed back to report a lack of fuel; then there was radio silence. An extensive search was mounted, then abandoned after six days when there appeared to be no hope of finding them alive. In fact Rogers had managed to land the seaplane in calm seas. The crew then ripped fabric from one of the wings to erect a makeshift sail.

The submarine came across them when the shipwrecked crew were within sight of the island, but drifting away from it. They had survived by carefully rationing the provisions they had taken with them when they set out.

## Lindbergh survives parachute drama

*Kelly Field, Texas, March 6*
There is a saying much used by airmen the world over that Charles Lindbergh is now not likely to forget: "If you ever need a parachute and you don't have one, you'll never need one again."

During a advanced training session at Kelly Field today, Lindbergh and several other Ameican pilots were simulating an aerial attack on a group of "enemy" bombers. He dived from high altitude on a de Havilland, then, just as he pulled out of the dive, his airplane was violently hit by a descending one flown by a young fellow officer. Although both aircraft were badly damaged in the mid-air collision, they continued flying sufficiently long enough for the two pilots to bail out and land safely.

In fact, this unfortunate incident was the very first time that the intrepid Charles Lindbergh, now known as "Lucky Lindy" among his friends, had ever made use of a parachute.

*A lucky Charles Lindbergh (left).*

## Five companies win air mail contracts in American competition

*Washington, DC, October 7*
The Air Mail Act, signed by President Calvin Coolidge in February, took effect today, when five contracts were granted to companies to fly the US mail. Airmail, at present transported on US Post Office aircraft by government pilots, will soon all be carried by private airlines. The five companies named today and the routes they bid for are: Colonial Air Transport (Boston/New York); Robertson Aircraft Corporation (Chicago/St Louis); National Air Transport (Chicago/Dallas); Western Air Express (Salt Lake City/Los Angeles); and Varney Speed Lines (Elko/Pasco).

While today's law, known as the Kelly Act, requires that airmail be moved by private companies, it is questionable whether they can be as effective as the US Post Office has been (→ Apr 10, 1926).

# Storm rips US Navy airship apart

*A front part of the disaster-stricken airship USS "Shenandoah" – the rear part fell in another field.*

*Ava, Ohio, September 3*
After almost four terror-filled hours in the sky, the last piece of the storm-wracked airship USS *Shenandoah* settled to earth at 6.45am today with the last seven survivors from its 43-man crew. They were among the lucky 14 who lived; the rest, including the *Shenandoah*'s captain, Lt-Cdr Zachary Lansdowne, perished when the airship was torn apart. Crew members said the flight was normal until 3am, when they flew into a storm. Gale-force winds brought the *Shenandoah* to a halt before inflicting a series of rapid, wrenching ascents and descents.

Lansdowne realized the airship was breaking up and let crewmen leave the cars suspended beneath it. Many took refuge in the forward and aft hull sections where the gas bags were. When the craft broke apart these sections floated to earth and the men in them survived. The captain and the remaining men plunged to the ground in the control and radio cars.

The use of non-flammable helium saved many lives. If hydrogen had been used, the *Shenandoah* would certainly have exploded, as the French airship *Dixmude* did with the loss of its crew of over 50 last December.

# Airship carries pilot to mid-air launch

*Pulham, England, October 15*
A Royal Air Force (RAF) pilot in a light airplane was released from under the R.33 airship today as it flew at 3,800 feet. He dived away to gain speed, flew two loops and hooked back on board.

This feat marks the start of Britain's latest trials with "parasite" airplanes. In fully-developed form, parasite warplanes have the potential to defend the craft to which it is attached and to extend greatly the scope of reconnaissance flights.

During 1918, a Sopwith Camel was launched from airship R.23, but the advent of peace brought experiments to a premature end. In the current tests, RAF de Havilland D.H.53 Humming Bird airplanes have each been given an elaborate tubular structure above the fuselage for hooking on to a trapeze attached to the R.33.

Today, for the first time, the R.33 lifted off with the Humming Bird beneath. The D.H.53 pilot, Squadron Leader de Haga Haig, used a ladder to climb from the airship into his cockpit.

# Doolittle races to Schneider Trophy win

*Chesapeake Bay, October 26*
A US Army test pilot today ensured that the Schneider trophy for seaplanes stays in the USA. The victorious airman is Lieutenant James H Doolittle, who flew a Curtiss R3C-2 biplane.

Doolittle easily won the world's premier seaplane race over the bay with an average speed of 232.56–mph. The event, said one spectator, was more a procession than a race. The British had an adventurous monoplane design with cantilever wings in the Supermarine S.4, but it was subject to wing flutter. It stalled and sideslipped into the water during trials and a Gloucester biplane was used instead. Italy also entered a monoplane, the M.33, which was withdrawn due to engine trouble.

*Doolittle poses with the seaplane in which he won the Schneider trophy.*

# American air chief speaks out of turn, faces court-martial

*Washington, DC, October 28*
The trial of Colonel William "Billy" Mitchell, who some say is the prophet of air power and others call an unrealistic fanatic, began today. The former US Army air chief faces a court-martial for making public statements contrary to military order and discipline.

The wonder is that his outspokenness has not had him in court before now. His clamoring for a larger US Army Air Service and demands for a separate air arm equal to the army and navy, like Britain's RAF, have particularly riled his superiors. His rebuke of

*Mitchell at his court martial.*

the navy secretary, who claimed that recent crashes of US Navy aircraft on long flights (including that of the USS *Shenandoah* – see report, left) proved the country could not be attacked from the air, was the immediate cause of the court-martial. Mitchell told reporters that the crashes arose from "incompetency, criminal negligence and almost treasonable" actions by the War and Navy Departments. Officers close to the Great War hero believe this astonishing outburst has sealed his downfall. But he could well use the trial as another opportunity to make the public aware of his views (→ Dec 17).

Dornier's high-winged Merckur eight-to-ten passenger airliner, with a BMW VI engine. Deutsche Luft Hansa had many, and there was a seaplane variant.

Developed for carrying the mail, the Douglas M-4 had purposeful lines.

Fokker's Universal monoplane in its original form, with an open cockpit.

Tupolev's tough ANT-4 all-metal cantilever monoplane bomber.

A revolution in light aviation was heralded by the maiden flight of Geoffrey de Havilland's D.H.60 Moth, with its 60-hp, 4-cylinder ADC Cirrus engine.

The single-engined Fokker F.VIIa was an outstandingly successful eight-passenger or cargo-carrying airliner widely used on European internal routes.

The Boeing Model 40 formed the basis of a successful family of commercial transports. Its capacious cargo compartment could hold 1,000 pounds of mail.

Fokker's Universal in its standard form, with a fully enclosed cockpit.

This Fokker T-2 achieved the first US non-stop coast-to-coast flight.

The Fokker F-10A was the final development of the F.VII series. It was very popular with US domestic airlines in the late 1920s and early 1930s.

The Westland-Hill Pterodactyl Ia was a tailless experimental airplane.

Czechoslovakia's Letov S-16 two-seater reconnaissance bomber.

The Westland Yeovil bomber did not find favour with the RAF.

Armstrong Whitworth's Atlas, conceived with British Army help.

The Armstrong Whitworth Siskin IIIA was one of the best fighters used by the RAF in the inter-war years. It had an Armstrong Siddeley Jaguar engine.

The Curtiss P-1 was the first of the company's Hawk series of single-seater fighters. It is seen here with an experimental Allison V-1410 installation.

The three-engined F.4X is one of numerous versions of the broad-winged Farman Jabiru airliners. Other variants have four engines.

Ahead of its time and ahead of the fighters: the Fairey Fox bomber.

Savoia's odd twin-hulled S.55 maritime bomber was built in quantity.

The successful Supermarine Southampton maritime patrol seaplane.

The Hawker Horsley, designed as both a day- and a torpedo-bomber.

In its original form the Fairey Firefly fighter was not a success, but the Mark II, which was considerably modified, was built under license in Belgium.

The civil-registered Tupolev ANT-3 made a tour of Europe in 1926.

The Fiat BR.2 displays its distinctive Warren girder interplane bracing.

Gloster's attractive Gamecock fighter was another of the RAF's front-line fighters of the interwar years; it was a Grebe powered by a Jupiter engine.

# 1926

278.47mph
France
Florentin Bonnet
Bernard Ferbois V2
Dec 11, 1924

3,352.92 miles
France
Costes and Rignot
Breguet 19 GR
Oct 19, 1926

36,565ft
France
Joseph Sadi-Lecointe
Nieuport-Delage
Oct 30, 1923

57,319lb
Italy
SAI Caproni
Caproni Ca 60

1,000hp
Great Britain
Napier
Cub

**Russia, January 1**
Germany and the USSR sign a top-secret agreement to open a military flight center at Lipetsk, 220 miles from Moscow, to enable the Germans to train military pilots in defiance of the terms of the Treaty of Versailles.

**Berlin, January 6**
Airlines Deutscher Aero Lloyd and Junkers Luftverkehr merge to form Deutsche Luft Hansa (DLH) (→ Apr 6).

**Southern Africa, January 24**
Alan Cobham and crew visit the Victoria Falls on their flight to the Cape; Cobham skillfully flies the D.H.50 over the falls so that his cameraman Emmott can get a good shot (→ Feb 17).

**Washington, DC, February 1**
Secretary of War Dwight Davis accepts the resignation of ex-air chief Billy Mitchell from the US Army Air Service (→ Feb 5).

**Washington, DC, February 5**
Appearing as a civilian, Billy Mitchell urges the House Committee on Military Affairs to base the nation's defense on airplanes rather than on ships.

**Buenos Aires, February 10**
Spanish commander Ramon Franco and crew land in their Dornier Wal seaplane *Plus Ultra* after crossing the South Atlantic from east to west; they left Melilla in Spain on January 22 (→ Sep 30).

**London, February 10**
The Handley Page W.10 airliner makes its first flight in the hands of test pilot Hubert Broad at Cricklewood, north-west London.

**South Africa, February 17**
Alan Cobham and crew arrive at Cape Town on their route-testing flight (→ Mar 13).

**Hampshire, England, March 24**
Juan de La Cierva sets up the Cierva Autogiro [sic] Company Ltd near Southampton (→ May 1, 1927).

**Miami, Florida, April 1**
Florida Airways, set up by Reed Chambers and Eddie Ricken-backer, opens a mail route from Atlanta, Georgia, to Miami (→ Mar 14, 1927).

**Saint Louis, Missouri, April 10**
Lindbergh becomes chief pilot for Robertson Aircraft Corp, flying a Saint Louis to Chicago mail route.

**Paris, April 14**
France and Germany sign an air treaty; since 1923, the Germans have seized 15 airplanes of the French-based airline CFRNA (now CIDNA) which were forced to land on German soil (→ May 25).

**USA, April 17**
Western Air Express starts its service between Los Angeles and Salt Lake City (→ Jun 18).

**Berlin, May 25**
French airline SGTA and German airline DLH agree to pool services between Paris and Berlin via Cologne (→ Nov 11).

**England, June 30**
Alan Cobham and mechanic Arthur B Elliott, in a de Havilland D.H.50, leave Rochester, Kent, on a route-testing flight from Britain to Australia (→ Jul 5).

**England, June**
While the de Havilland D.H.66 airliner is still under construction, its type name is decided by a competition in *Meccano Magazine*: the winner is a schoolboy, E F Hope-Jones of Eton College, who suggested giving it the name Hercules (→ Sep 30).

**Croydon, England, July 1**
Imperial Airways introduces a new airliner, the Armstrong Whitworth Argosy, into service on the London/Paris route (→ May 1, 1927).

**Washington, DC, July 2**
The Air Corps Act becomes law; it renames the US Army Air Service the US Army Air Corps.

**Iraq, July 5**
Alan Cobham's flight engineer Arthur Elliott is killed by a bullet fired at their de Havilland D.H.50 while over the desert between Baghdad and Basra en route for Australia (→ Aug 15).

**USA, July 28**
During experimental operations, the US submarine *S-1* surfaces and launches a seaplane flown by Lieutenant D C Allen, then recovers the airplane and submerges once more.

**Hampshire, England, July 29**
Avro test pilot Frank Courtney flies the Avro Type 587 (Cierva C.6D) two-seater autogyro on a short flight with Juan de La Cierva as passenger – the first passenger flight in the rotary-winged autogyro (→ Feb 7, 1927).

**Melbourne, August 15**
Large crowds greet Alan Cobham and flight engineer Sergeant Ward as they land their D.H.50 after their flight from England (→ Oct 1).

**Kent, England, August 17**
The duralumin-hulled Short Singapore flying boat, built for the air ministry, makes its first flight, from Rochester, piloted by John Lankester Parker (→ Jan 14, 1927).

**Peking, August 30**
Two Junkers G 24s with German pilots arrive from Berlin; they left Germany on July 24 crewed by Soviet-German teams, but the Soviet pilots were refused entry to China because they had incorrect visas (→ Apr 13, 1927).

**Minnesota, September 1**
Colonel Lewis H Brittin founds Northwest Airways, based in Minneapolis, Minnesota. Harold H Emmons is named as the company's president (→ Oct 1).

**London, September 30**
The de Havilland D.H.66 Hercules makes its first flight, piloted by Hubert Broad; the new airliner can carry 14 passengers (→ Jan 1, 1927).

**Germany, September 30**
The prototype Dornier Do R Super Wal flying boat begins flight tests (→ May 7, 1927).

**Sahara desert, November 11**
North African tribesmen kill two pilots and one crew member when their airplane is forced down while flying airmail for the French company CGEA (→ Jul 30, 1927).

**Minnesota, October 1**
Northwest Airways begins regular air mail flights between Chicago, Illinois, and Minneapolis, using two rented open-cockpit biplanes (→ Jul 5, 1927).

**Gloucestershire, England, Nov 11**
The Gloucestershire aircraft company changes its name to Gloster: the old name caused pronunciation problems for foreigners.

**Bombay, India, November 15**
The Arab gunman whose stray shot killed Alan Cobham's mechanic Arthur Elliott in July is convicted of manslaughter (→ Jan 8, 1927).

**Michigan, November 15**
The Ford company opens a 60,000-square foot factory to produce the Trimotor transport airplane; the Ford "progressive" system of mass production will be used for the first time to build aircraft (→ Feb 15, 1927).

**Hollywood, Calif, December**
American airplane designer Allan Loughead founds a new aircraft company, called "Lockheed" to avoid confusion over the pronunciation of his name; his previous aircraft company was dissolved in 1921 (→ Jul 4, 1927).

*Returning to a hero's welcome: Alan Cobham flies in to land on the river Thames in London at the end of his round flight to Australia.* ▶

# Briton hailed after triumphant flight to Cape and back

PLAYER'S CIGARETTES.

SIR ALAN COBHAM.

*Cobham graces a cigarette card.*

*Croydon, England, March 13*
Alan Cobham, whose name is now linked with long-distance flights to Africa and beyond, landed here today at the end of a thrilling four-month marathon to Cape Town, South Africa, and back. En route he encountered intense heat, sand storms and swamps.

As the red and silver de Havilland D.H.50J touched down, crowds smashed through police barriers to mob and carry him shoulder high. He has been commanded to appear at Buckingham Palace to deliver a letter from the Governor-General of South Africa to King George V.

Accompanied by Gaumont photographer B W G Emmott and irrepressible engineer Arthur Elliott, Cobham left on November 16. His purpose was to survey a route across Africa from Cairo to Cape Town, about 8,000 miles. Flying via Athens, along north Africa to Cairo, Khartoum and Kenya, he reached Cape Town on February 17, having checked out 27 possible landing sites. Accumulated flying time was over 94 hours. Nine days later, he set off for the faster return journey, beating the SS *Windsor Castle* back to England (→ Jun 2).

# Scientist claims rocket breakthrough

*Auburn, Mass, March 16*
Dr Robert H Goddard, who has speculated that it will one day be possible to launch a rocket to the moon, fired his latest propulsion device today in a field. Its flight lasted 2.5 seconds. It reached a speed of 70mph, traveled 184 feet and attained an altitude of 41 feet.

Despite these modest performance figures, Goddard is claiming it as a very significant accomplishment: the first successful launch of a liquid-fueled rocket, a concept he has been working on since 1921. The device flown today weighed 5.75 pounds, before being loaded with 4.5 pounds of fuel. Goddard, who used liquid oxygen and gasoline this time, has previously concentrated on solid propellant to fuel his rockets. His work on these began during the Great War, when his efforts to develop bombardment weapons were successfully demonstrated to the US Army at the Aberdeen Proving Grounds in Maryland. Funds for those experiments came from the army and the eminent Smithsonian Institution.

That work finished with the end of war, but the Smithsonian has continued to support Goddard's rocket research.

*Goddard with his liquid-fuel rocket.*

## Merged German airline is leaner and fitter

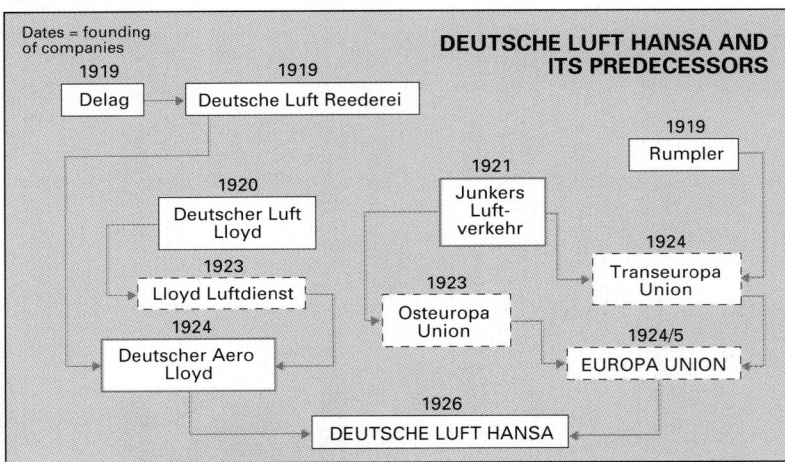

Dates = founding of companies

DEUTSCHE LUFT HANSA AND ITS PREDECESSORS

- 1919 Delag
- 1919 Deutsche Luft Reederei
- 1919 Rumpler
- 1920 Deutscher Luft Lloyd
- 1921 Junkers Luftverkehr
- 1923 Lloyd Luftdienst
- 1923 Osteuropa Union
- 1924 Transeuropa Union
- 1924 Deutscher Aero Lloyd
- 1924/5 EUROPA UNION
- 1926 DEUTSCHE LUFT HANSA

*Berlin, April 6*
Three months to the day after its creation from the merger of two competing German airline consortia, Deutscher Aero Lloyd and Junkers Luftverkehr, German national airline Deutsche Luft Hansa today made its first commercial flight. DLH, as it is to be known, is now in the very best position to take advantage of the ever-growing demand for European air travel, now that damaging competition between domestic and international German airlines has been removed and airlines have combined as a national flag carrier. Other nations will have to look to their laurels if they want to stay up with the Germans. DLH already has an air fleet of over 100 Junkers, Fokker, and Rohrbach aircraft, with Dornier flying boats for sea and lake service (→ Aug 30).

## New York/Paris air attempt is planned

*New York, June 10*
US aviators will make the first non-stop flight from New York to Paris, to claim the Orteig prize of $25,000, if naval Lieutenant-Commanders Richard E Byrd and Noel Davis have their way.

Noted Arctic flyer Byrd will use a Fokker Trimotor similar to the one he used on his flight over the North Pole in May. Department store tycoon Rodman Wanamaker has put up $10,000 to cover all expenses of the flight.

Davis, meanwhile, has $10,000 from the US ex-servicemen's organization, which sees the flight as a natural complement to its Paris convention next year. He will use a modified Keystone biplane bomber, to be named *The American Legion* after his sponsors.

The Americans face stiff competition from French war air ace Charles Nungesser, who plans to fly in the opposite direction in a biplane equipped with a single water-cooled engine (→ Sep 21).

## American army pilot sets distance record gliding to safety

*Dayton, Ohio, April 10*
Lieutenant John A Macready of the US Army Air Service (USAAS) failed today in his bid to set a new world altitude record for airplanes. Instead, having run out of fuel while still at 37,000 feet, he glided to safety and in doing so established a world distance record for gliding. Macready had previously set a world altitude record here on September 18, 1921, in a Packard-Le Père, at 34,509 feet.

Then Frenchman Sadi Joseph Lecointe beat it in a Nieuport two years later, reaching 35,242 feet on September 5, 1923. On October 30, 1923, Sadi Lecointe bettered his own record, reaching 36,564 feet. Macready tried to better this on March 13 this year, but he only reached 37,579 feet. Today was his final attempt to regain the record, as he is leaving the USAAS.

# Determined air crews blaze trail over frozen Arctic

## American pilots fly Fokker to North Pole

*The Arctic flyer "Josephine Ford" in a flight before the expedition set off.*

**Spitzbergen, Norway, May 9**
Just as Roald Amundsen was preparing for another crack at flying over the North Pole, a US Navy officer has apparently captured the honor of being first. It was a blow for the Norwegian explorer who was the first man to reach the South Pole, but he sportingly embraced the victor. Lieutenant-Commander Richard E Byrd's expedition took off just after midnight from King's Bay, Norway, with Floyd Bennett as pilot and Byrd navigating. The team claim to have circled the pole at 9.02am in their Fokker F.VII-3m *Josephine Ford*, named after the daughter of owner Edsel Ford, the attempt's co-sponsor, who is the son of industrialist Henry Ford. John D Rockefeller was the second backer.

The only scare of the 16-hour, 1,535-mile return flight came when an oil leak developed in one engine.

Byrd, a polar veteran, used all his skill to navigate, as flying close to the true pole makes a magnetic compass useless. He used the barely visible Sun and dead reckoning.→

*Byrd is well-equipped for the cold.*

## 'Norge' airship comes in a close second

*Amundsen's dirigible "Norge" coming in to moor at King's Bay, Norway.*

**Teller, Alaska, May 14**
The Norwegian explorer Roald Amundsen landed here today after an airship flight from Spitzbergen lasting 70 hours. Having been beaten by Byrd in making the first flight by any aircraft over the North Pole, it is some consolation that he has made the first flight over the pole by airship, and the first flight across the whole Arctic, some 2,485 miles. He and helmsman Oskar Wisting are the first to visit both poles.

Amundsen's airship, the N1 *Norge* [*Norway*], sustained some damage to its envelope, probably caused by lumps of ice spinning off the propellers, and on landing. It cannot fly and may be abandoned, in which case Amundsen will lose the $46,000 return price from the Italian government, who owns the airship. The *Norge*'s commander was Italian Colonel Umberto Nobile, appointed as a condition of borrowing the *Norge*, and there are other Italians in the crew. One US crewman, Lincoln Ellsworth, took part in Amundsen's first polar attempt by air a year ago.

*Amundsen, conqueror of the poles.*

# Italians seize Schneider Trophy in Virginia

**Norfolk, Va, November 13**
Earlier this year British designers said a new airplane to challenge US dominance in the Schneider Trophy race could not be built before the next competition. Italy's dictator, Benito Mussolini, thought differently, declaring that Italy must win the Schneider this year. He gave state backing to airplane builder Macchi and engine makers Fiat. Designer Mario Castoldi produced a total of five very fast M.39 monoplanes. On the start line, the Italians faced a US Navy team, with three Curtiss machines at full strength despite two deaths in training. Each lap produced ever faster times. US Navy Lieutenant George Cuddihy produced a remarkable 232.42mph lap before running out of fuel. The Italians seized their opportunity, and Major Mario di Bernardi finally risked blowing up his engine to produce an unbeatable 246.5mph.

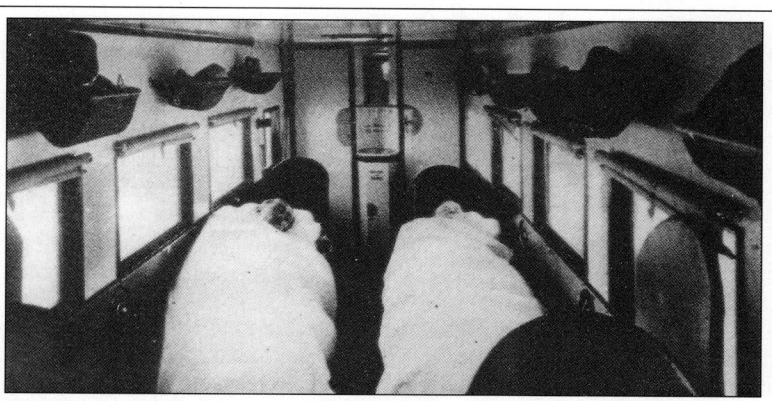

**Sleeping berths have been introduced by Deutsche Luft Hansa (DLH).**

# Airmail network grows

*One of the new airmail carriers, a Douglas M-2 of Western Air Express.*

**USA, April 10**
Airmail delivery has become big business in the United States. The last Contract Air Mail, or CAM route has just been sold. The Kelly Act allows postal authorities to sell exclusive airmail route rights to private companies. Hopeful candidates for a CAM have for some time been desperately seeking the funding necessary to purchase the aircraft they require to set up an efficient airmail service.

CAM-1, covering the lucrative New York City to Boston, Massachusetts, route, was sold to William Rockefeller, Cornelius Vanderbilt Whitney, and Juan Trippe, an ambitious young businessman. The CAM-2 route, flying from Saint

Louis, Missouri, to Chicago, Illinois, was attributed to the Robertson brothers, former fighter pilots who borrowed the funds from a Saint Louis businessman. Western Air Express purchased the CAM-4 route linking Los Angeles, California, to Salt Lake City, Utah, with money provided by Harry Chandler, publisher of the *Los Angeles Times*. The CAM-5 route was snapped up by Varney Air Lines, now flying between Elko, Nevada, and Pasco, Washington State.

Some of the CAM operators also carry passengers. However, should there be enough mail along the route to displace passengers, they must be prepared to leave the flight (→ Dec 31).

**British pilot Alan Cobham and crew with their seaplane at Port Darwin, Australia, during their round trip from London to Australia and back.**

## Moroccans demand ransom for pilot

*Morocco, May 27*
Intrepid French pilot Jean Mermoz has been released by his Moorish captors for a ransom of 1,000 pesetas. Mermoz was flying from Casablanca to Dakar, on an established mail route, when his airplane was forced down with technical problems. He crash-landed in the desert and was promptly bound hand and foot and put in a cage. It was three days before an Arab chieftain agreed to accept a ransom for him. Mermoz is no stranger to adventure – when he flew his test flight for the Latécoère mail company, he looped the loop, made a series of steep turns and slipped into a landing (→ Apr 15, 1927).

*Safe: Mermoz (r) in Casablanca.*

## Kurd rebel kidnaps two RAF crewmen

*Iraq, September 1*
Kurdish nationalist leader Sheik Mahmud has fled from British vengeance in Iraq to sanctuary in Persia [Iran]. This is not the first time: he did this before when the Royal Air Force broke the resistance of his army and civilians with low-level machine-gun attacks and bombing raids. The difference now is that he has two hostages, the crew of a D.H.9A bomber, seized when their machine landed due to engine failure on June 14.

The crew are thought to be still alive, to be used as bargaining counters in a political checker game. Money alone is unlikely to secure the release of such a valuable prize for Mahmud. The British released him from prison four years ago and settled him in the neighboring British dependency of Koweit [Kuwait] with a generous pension. He has made war against them ever since.

This summer, encouraged by his example, Arab tribes in southern Iraq also rebelled in the belief that the RAF could not handle more trouble. Squadron-Leader Arthur Harris, an advocate of air bombardment, thought otherwise. He had holes sawn in the noses of previously unarmed Vernon cargo airplanes. In just nine attacks they let fly 6.5 tons of high-explosive bombs, 4,000 incendiaries and 2,000 machine-gun rounds at the rebels, who soon gave up the unequal struggle.

# Beech airplane wins top reliability award

*Detroit, Mich, August 21*
For the second year running, the tough Ford Reliability Tour trophy, one of the most coveted in aviation, has been won by Walter H Beech. President of the Travel Air Manufacturing Co, of Wichita, Kansas, Beech could ask for no better advertizement for his three-seat biplane, powered by a 220-hp Wright Whirlwind engine. Beech's partner in this year's trial was pilot G Goldsborough. The annual tour was organized by the Ford company to help convince the public of the safety and reliability of American flying (→ Feb 15, 1927).

*Travel Air's Walt Beech, and friend.*

# Fonck's dream ends before it has begun

*New York, September 21*
A bid by French Great War ace René Fonck to fly the Atlantic and win the $25,000 Orteig prize for the first flight from New York/Paris or vice versa ended in tragedy today. Fonck was to start from Roosevelt Field, where his new Sikorsky S-35 trimotor biplane was overloaded with 28,860 pounds of fuel. As Fonck headed down the mile-long runway he realized he could not take off and tried to abort, but the S-35 cartwheeled and burst into flames. Fonck and American co-pilot Lieutenant Lawrence Curtin jumped clear, but the French wireless operator and the Russian mechanic perished (→ Apr 26, 1927).

*The blazing wreck of Fonck's dream.*

# Cobham is hero after Australia flight

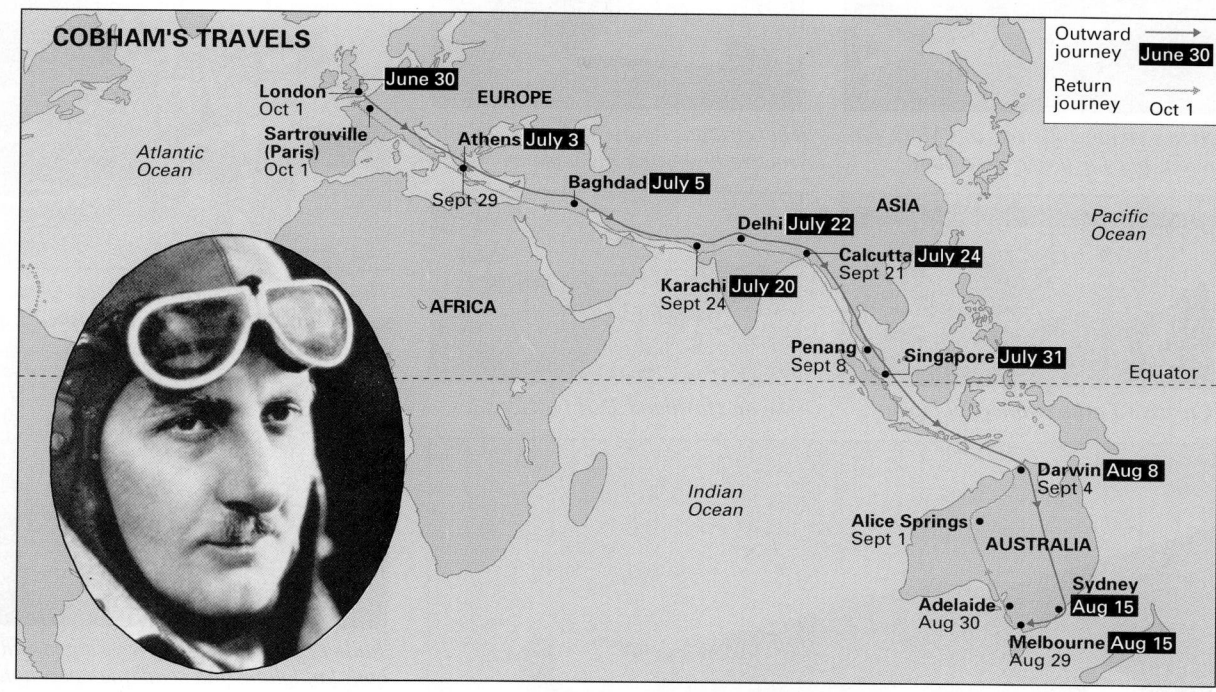

**COBHAM'S TRAVELS**

| | |
|---|---|
| Outward journey | **June 30** → |
| Return journey | **Oct 1** |

London — June 30 / Oct 1
Sartrouville (Paris) — Oct 1 / Sept 29
Athens — July 3
Baghdad — July 5
Delhi — July 22
Karachi — July 20 / Sept 24
Calcutta — July 24 / Sept 21
Penang — Sept 8
Singapore — July 31
Darwin — Aug 8 / Sept 4
Alice Springs — Sept 1
Adelaide — Aug 30
Sydney — Aug 15
Melbourne — Aug 15 / Aug 29

*London, October 1*
British members of parliament and their friends were among spectators who watched Alan Cobham make a spectacular landing alongside the Houses of Parliament on the river Thames today. It was the end of his 26,703-mile flight from England to Australia and back.

It was a triumph marred by the death on the outward leg of his engineer and friend of long standing, Arthur Elliott. Cobham and crew left from the river Medway, Kent, on June 30, in the same de Havilland D.H.50J he had used to reach Rangoon and Cape Town, modified as a seaplane. It carried a boomerang as mascot.

The extremes of weather added to Cobham's discomfort and uncharacteristic depression on the flight. The Elliott tragedy occurred over Iraq near the Persian Gulf, when he was shot by a Bedouin tribesman. A severe sandstorm had forced the aircraft to fly low, making it an easy target. After the bullet ripped through the airplane, Elliott passed a note to Cobham saying a petrol pipe had burst and he himself was "bleeding a pot of blood". Cobham landed at Basra, but Elliott died in hospital that same night.

Royal Air Force Sergeant Ward took over, and Darwin in Australia was reached on August 5. Converted back into a landplane, the D.H.50J passed through Sydney, Melbourne and Adelaide before Cobham headed home on the return leg of the flight.

# Italy enjoys boom in airline network

*Italy, December 31*
Italy is at last catching up with the rest of Europe in developing an airline network. Two new Italian companies have been formed this year: SA Navigazione Aerea, SANA, which covers the Genoa/Rome/Naples routes and Transadriatica which flies from Rome to Venice and on to Vienna. The oldest Italian airline is Società Italiana Servizi Aerei (SISA), which began operations on the Trieste/Pola/Zara/Ancona and Turin/Venice/Trieste routes, while in August Aero Expresso Italiana inaugurated a Brindisi to Constantinople service.

# Federal regulation for US operators

*Washington, DC, December 31*
US airlines are hailing 1926 as the year they got the federal regulation they had long asked for. The Air Commerce Act, signed by President Coolidge on May 20, followed a report of an inquiry set up last year under Dwight W Morrow into federal aviation policy. The act has created a new Bureau of Aeronautics, under an assistant secretary of state within the Commerce Department. The first man in the post, William P McCracken Jr, will oversee the development and safe operation of a national air transportation system.

**A hardy design: the sturdy lines of the Ford 4-AT Trimotor, which made its first flight on June 11 this year. The 4-AT is a tough transport airplane which can take plenty of knocks. Its all-metal fuselage is encased in corrugated aluminum sheeting like a Junkers transport – hence its nickname of "Tin Goose". It uses a successful high-wing monoplane design and is fitted with three powerful 300-hp Wright Whirlwind engines. It should prove to be a reliable "pack-horse" on long-distance services.**

*Avro's Avian followed the Moth formula, but far fewer were built.*

*The civilian Ryan M-1 was an attractive high-wing monoplane.*

*Curtiss's Lark commercial biplane.*

*The de Havilland D.H.66 Hercules.*

*The French-designed Lioré et Olivier LeO 213 airliner had a distinctive square-cut nose which distinguished it from the similar Farman Goliath.*

*Junkers' rugged cantilever-winged, all-metal W 33 monoplane was used for both landplane and seaplane operations, a total of 199 being built.*

*Despite a patent dispute with Junkers, the Ford 4-AT trimotor saw widespread use across the USA, and it proved to be a reliable and tough workhorse.*

*The speedy Macchi M.39 claimed the 1926 Schneider Trophy for Italy.*

*Alan Cobham used this D.H.50J to survey the aerial route to Australia.*

*The Ryan B.1 Brougham was an attractive monoplane derived from Charles Lindbergh's famous "Spirit of St Louis" in which he flew solo to Paris.*

*Production Dornier Super-Wals were normally powered by four 500-hp Bristol Jupiter VIII radials in tandem pairs, but other powerplants were also used.*

*The Parnall Peto submarine-borne scout did not prove a success.*

*Another sporting two-seater from the US: the Laird Model LC-B.*

No fewer than 320 Lioré et Olivier LeO 20 night-bombers served in the French Aéronautique Militaire. It was also supplied to Brazil and Romania.

The three-seat Levasseur PL 7 torpedo-bomber suffered from some structural problems which led to modifications. It featured a watertight keel.

Fiat's CR.20, with a 410-hp Fiat A20 engine, was one of the company's most successful inter-war fighters. Production totalled more than 670 aircraft.

The prototype Blackburn Iris first flew in September 1926. Designed as a long-range reconnaissance flying boat, the Mark III served in the RAF.

Both Czechoslovakia and Lithuania used the dumpy Letov S-20 fighter.

Dewoitine's D.27 fighter was exported to Sweden and Yugoslavia.

Fairey's IIIF, seen here in prototype form, proved to be a great success.

The Boulton and Paul Sidestrand bomber flew with only one squadron.

Boeing's XF2B-1 carrier-based fighter was used on the USS "Langley".

Some 20 Vought FU-1 single-seat fighters were built for the US Navy.

The Boeing F2B-1 featured a steel and duralumin fuselage and tail.

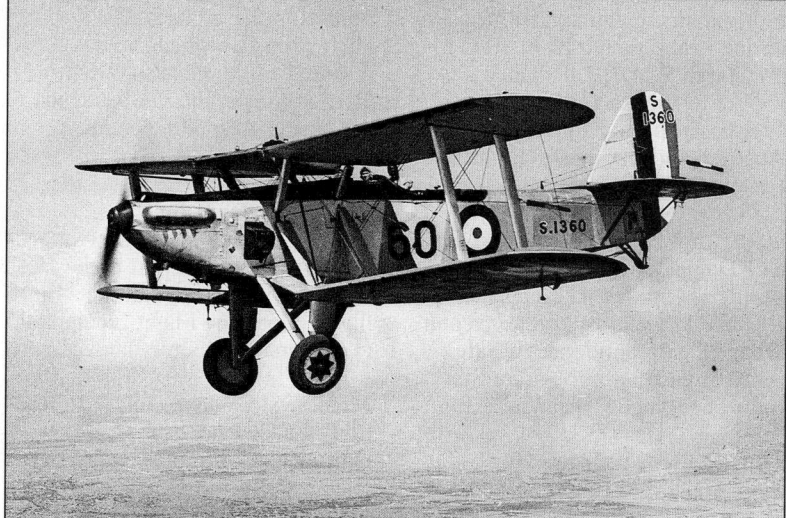

The big Short Singapore flying boat was developed for RAF service.

Unlike the W 33, the Junkers W 34 monoplane had an enclosed cockpit.

The Blackburn Ripon torpedo-bomber was adopted for Fleet Air Arm service. The Ripon II, which is shown here, was more refined than its predecessor.

# 1927

297.83mph
Italy
Mario de Bernardi
Macchi M.52
Nov 4, 1927

3,911 miles
USA
Chamberlin and Levine
Bellanca
Jun 6, 1927

38,418ft
USA
CC Champion
Wright Apache
Jul 25, 1927

57,319lb
Italy
SAI Caproni
Caproni Ca 60

1,000hp
Great Britain
Napier
Cub

**Hampshire, England, February 7**
During a test flight of the British-built Cierva C.6C (the Avro 574), a rotor blade breaks off and the machine crashes and is wrecked; afterward, injured pilot Frank Courtney ends his association with designer Juan de La Cierva.

**Washington, DC, February 7**
Georgetown University medical school offers the first aviation medicine course in the USA.

**California, February 25**
Charles Lindbergh places a down-payment of $1,000 with Ryan Airlines, who begin work on the M-2 airplane he has ordered for his attempt on the $25,000 Orteig prize for a flight between New York and Paris (→ May 11).

**Athens, March 10**
Following the first flight of the *Chelidon* [Swallow], entirely Greek designed and built at the Old Phaleron factory established by Britain's Blackburn company, company founder Robert Blackburn is invested with the Insignia of the Golden Cross of the Order of the Redeemer by the king of the Hellenes.

**Munich, Germany, April 13**
German airline Deutsche Luft Hansa (DLH) inaugurates a service to Milan in conjunction with Italian airline Avio-Linee Italiane (ALI); on March 21 DLH launched a service to Vienna via Dresden and Prague, in partnership with Austrian and Czechoslovak airlines (→ Aug 5).

**USA, April 20**
The Daniel Guggenheim Fund for the Promotion of Aeronautics, founded last year by copper tycoon Guggenheim, announces a Safe Aircraft Competition with a first prize of $100,000 (→ Jan 6, 1930).

**Langley Field, Va, April 26**
Noel Davis and co-pilot Stanton Wooster, chasing the Orteig prize, crash on take-off for Paris and are killed instantly.

**Alaska, April 28**
The first airmail service north of the Arctic Circle begins between Fairbanks and Wiseman (→ Sep 1).

**Missouri, May 11**
Charles Lindbergh lands his new Ryan airplane, the *Spirit of St Louis*, in St Louis after a record non-stop overnight flight from San Diego of 14 hrs 25 mins (→ May 21).

**New York, May 13**
Colonial Air Transport offers a sight-seeing trip from Teterboro, New Jersey, around the city for just $8, less than the price of a similar trip in a taxi (→ Sep 1).

**Croydon, England, May 29**
Charles Lindbergh, hero of the first non-stop solo Atlantic crossing, arrives from Paris in the *Spirit of St Louis*; excited crowds break through barriers and swarm over the runway (→ Jun 16).

**Germany, June 5**
Several space enthusiasts found the Verein für Raumschiffahrt [Society for Space Travel], or VfR. The society plans to experiment with liquid-fueled rockets.

**Ontario, June 6**
W R Turnbull sells the patent rights for the controllable-pitch propeller which he has invented to the Curtiss-Wright Corporation in the USA and to the Bristol Aeroplane company in Britain.

**Suffolk, England, June 7**
The Supermarine S.5 racer, constructed to take part in the 1927 Schneider cup race, makes its first flight, piloted by Flight Lieutenant O E Worsley (→ Sep 20).

**Middlesex, England, July 5**
Lady Bailey establishes a new light airplane altitude record of 17,283 feet, in a de Havilland D.H.60 Moth, at the company's airfield in Edgware, Middlesex (→ Apr 30, 1928).

**Nicaragua, July 17**
Five DH-4 bombers of the US Marine Corps go into action against the guerrilla forces of General Augusto Sandino, which have surrounded the US garrison at Ocotal; this is the first organized dive-bombing action in combat (→ Aug 24).

**Paris, July 30**
French airline Air Union opens its luxury Golden Ray service to London, flying Lioré et Olivier 213s, to compete with the Silver Wing service of Imperial Airways (→ Oct 26).

**Suffolk, England, August 12**
Four prototype flying boats leave Felixstowe on a tour of Baltic seaports to help the RAF decide which type it should put into service; they are the Supermarine Southampton, the Blackburn Iris, the Short Singapore and the Saunders-Roe Valkyrie (→ Oct 16).

**Hawaii, August 17**
Hollywood stunt man Art Goeble and US Navy pilot W V Davis land in Honolulu to win the Dole air race, flying their Travel Air Woolaroc from Oakland, California, in 26 hrs 17 mins 33 secs; two of the four competing crews, including one flying the Lockheed Vega prototype *Golden Eagle*, are missing at sea.

**Riga, August 26**
Australia's Bert Hinkler sets a non-stop distance for light air-planes by flying from Croydon, England, to Riga, Latvia (→ Feb 7, 1928).

**USA, September 1**
Following Boeing Air Transport's takeover of the Chicago/San Francisco portion of the transcontinental air mail route on July 1, National Air Transport takes over the New York/Chicago portion; this marks the end of the US Air Mail Service, whose routes have now all been placed with private operators (→ Oct 14).

**USA, September 1**
American Railway Express and major US airlines begin air express operations.

**Wichita, Kan, September 8**
The Cessna Aircraft Company is established.

**Cape Town, S Africa, September 28**
Lieutenant Dick Bentley of the South African Air Force lands his D.H.60X Moth after the first solo flight from Britain to the Cape. He left London on September 1.

**USA, October 11**
Southeastern Airlines, founded last July by Reed Chambers and Richard F Hoyt, is officially registered in Delaware under the name of Atlantic Gulf and Caribbean Airways (→ Jun 23, 1928).

**Suffolk, England, October 14**
Four Supermarine Southampton II flying boats under Group Captain Cave-Brown-Cave fly to Singapore where they will form 205 Squadron, Royal Air Force (→ Nov 17).

**Kent, England, November 17**
Sir Alan Cobham leaves Rochester in a Short Singapore flying boat; he is to make the "Sir Charles Wakefield Flight of Survey Round Africa" (→ May 5, 1928).

**USA, December 14**
The US Navy's third aircraft carrier, the USS *Lexington*, is commissioned; the second, the USS *Saratoga*, was commissioned on November 16.

**Germany, December 29**
Georg Wulf, co-founder of the Focke-Wulf aircraft construction company, is killed when the tail-first Focke-Wulf Fw 19, in which he is making a demonstration flight, crashes.

*Safely arrived in Paris, Charles Lindbergh poses proudly by his aircraft after his non-stop flight across the Atlantic from New York.* ▶

# Flying risk is 'less than from mules'

*Washington, DC, January 3*
The prospector's old faithful friend, the mule, has been dragged in to support the efforts of gold-digging US Army and airline chiefs eager to capture more supporters for their speculative ventures. Captain H Stevens of the US Army Air Corps today gave an unusual statistic to the American Society for the Promotion of Aviation: last year some 80 people in the state of Missouri were kicked to death by mules; over the same period only eight commercial pilots lost their lives. Fine, so long as one remembers that mules probably outnumber airplanes by about 100,000 to one.

# Doolittle wins orders for Curtiss

*Buffalo, NY, January 12*
The Chilean government has given the Curtiss Company its largest order since the Great War, and Lieutenant James Doolittle of the US Army Air Corps, who is confined to hospital in Washington with two broken ankles, deserves the credit for the sale of the P-1 pursuit aircraft.

Doolittle became involved in the Chilean sale when, following a request from Curtiss, the army gave him leave of absence to demonstrate the pursuit plane. Curtiss explained that no other pilot was equal to the task. With German, English and Italian firms present in Santiago, competition for the Chilean order was keen. Unfortunately, Doolittle went to a party with some Chilean army officers where he fell from a balcony and shattered his ankles. The doctor at the hospital in Santiago placed his legs in heavy casts and confined him to bed for several weeks.

Doolittle knew that without him there would be be no demonstration of the Curtiss plane. He left the hospital, was carried to the airplane, had his cast-covered feet literally fastened to the rudder pedals and took off. Despite intense pain, he put the plane through its paces, thoroughly outperforming the European competition and winning the contract for Curtiss (→ May 24).

# Imperial opens first stage of India service

*An Imperial Airways de Havilland Hercules en route to Basra, Iraq.*

*Delhi, January 8*
A de Havilland D.H.66 Hercules airliner arrived here today after a route-testing flight from Britain for Imperial Airways. For the next few months the service will terminate at Basra, Iraq, but the British government ultimately intends the route to continue all the way to Australia, linking the empire by air.

The Hercules is powered by three of the supremely reliable Bristol Jupiter engines. Carrying seven passengers and mailbags, it has been specially designed for Imperial's routes over harsh terrain often inhabited by hostile tribesmen. The fleet of five will eventually handle the sector from Cairo to Karachi. The first 1,100 miles, to Basra, are over some of the most featureless terrain in the world. The Royal Air Force had to plow a furrow across the desert to guide aviators. →

# Tiny Moth receives an Indian welcome

*India, January 8*
The first light airplanes to fly from London to India arrived at Karachi today. It was a sensational feat for two little 85-hp-engined de Havilland D.H.60 Moth biplanes, each of which carried extra fuel in the front cockpit and was flown as a single-seater. Captain T Neville Stack and B S Leete left Croydon, London, on November 16 to attempt the 5,540-mile journey.

The Moths have aroused much interest among the locals, and many joyriding flights are expected to be demanded as they tour Indian cities. Since first appearing two years ago, the Moth has taken British aviators by storm. They have found it an ideal club machine: cheap, strong and simple to maintain. Its secret lies in having been designed from the very outset in close collaboration with a particular engine-maker, ADC (→ Jul 5).

# French pilot Dagnaux clips his wings during flight across Africa

*Jean Dagnaux stops over in Northern Rhodesia to tackle a broken wing.*

*Northern Rhodesia, Jan 18*
French aviator Jean Dagnaux took off from Broken Hill in the British colony of Northern Rhodesia today on the next stage of his Paris to Madagascar flight – minus part of a wing. When attempting to take off from Broken Hill two days ago, his Breguet 19 biplane hit a large tree, badly damaging the lower right wing. He managed to bring the airplane down safely and set about patching it up. Despite a lack of tools, Dagnaux straightened out the leading edge, shortened the damaged aluminum wing and finally sealed the surface with glue. Next stop: Mozambique.

# African adventure hailed as triumph for seaplane potential

*Paris, January 14*
Adolphe Bernard returned to Paris in triumph today after completing a 14,444-mile trip through Africa. The flight has been hailed as proof, particularly by French seaplane manufacturers, that a seaplane is the only form of rapid transport for the trans-African route to the French protectorate of Madagascar in the Indian Ocean. Bernard's route took him via Morocco, the Canary Islands, Cameroon, the Congo, Nyasaland and Mozambique to Madagascar.

In the course of its flight, the seaplane also made landings on the rivers Senegal, Niger, Benoue, Chari, Ubanghi, Congo and Zambezi, as well as on Lakes Nyasa and Tanganyika. Accompanied by a mechanic, Bernard was fêted on his arrival in Madagascar by the French governor, who held a grand reception to which 80,000 people were invited.

After a week's rest and recuperation on the island, the two men began the return journey to their homeland. This time they crossed East Africa, reaching the Mediterranean via Lake Victoria and the river Nile (→ Aug 12).

# Pratt & Whitney engines power Boeing

*Hartford, Conn, February 13*
The new Pratt & Whitney 420-hp air-cooled Wasp engine won another major order today when Boeing Air Transport announced it would use the engine on its Chicago to San Francisco mail run which starts on July 1. The new company is the brainchild of F B Rentschler, who has been convinced of the merits of air-cooled radial engines for some time. This conviction stems from his successful experience with the Wright Whirlwind engine.

In fact, it was Rentschler's wife who invented the name Wasp for the new engine when she heard its characteristic rasping roar. But it was its weight which won over Bill Boeing. The Pratt & Whitney engine is all of 220 pounds lighter than the watercooled, wartime Liberty engines which powered his earlier models and which had initially been meant to power the Boeing 40A airplane.

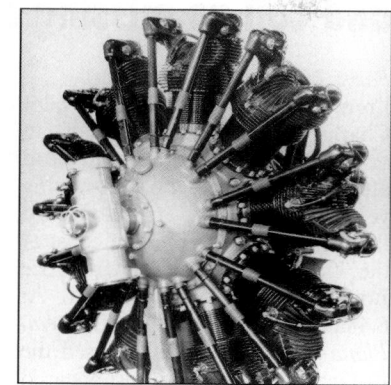
*An air-cooled, radial Wasp engine.*

Securing the engines is a coup for Bill Boeing. He can now tender for the mail contract at $1.50 for the first 1,000 miles, then 15 cents for each additional 100 miles – giving him a significant price advantage over his competitors. The Post Office will not be paying more to fly its mail halfway across the country that it now pays for a New York City to Boston flight.

# The new Aéropostale takes over CGEA

*France, April 15*
One of the pioneers of French civil aviation, Pierre Latécoère, has just sold 93 per cent of the shares of his company, CGEA, to the Franco-South American Civil Engineering Company owned by Marcel Bouilloux-Lafont. This deal, concluded four days ago, is worth 30 million gold francs. The new owner has renamed the company Aéropostale, and the sale of CGEA was today granted official government approval.

Latécoère's decision was motivated by the fact that profits had been decreasing, while he knew that large sums would have to be spent to replace the fleet of ageing Breguet airplanes. Another factor was the realisation that setting up an efficient infrastructure in South America was bound to be costly. The French government, which is seeking to set up a strong airmail operation in order to fight off foreign competitors, had been pres-

*Aéropostale, flying to Morocco.*

sing Latécoère to hand over the reins of his company, offering state grants as an inducement. As for Bouilloux-Lafont, he is already making plans to use the Aéropostale as a means to conquer the commercial aviation market.

# Cessna decides to form its own company

*Wichita, Kan, February 15*
The Travel Air Manufacturing Company partnership of Clyde Cessna, Lloyd Stearman and Walter Beech, which was formed in 1926, ended today when Cessna left to form his own company. Beech, who is currently president of Travel Air, said the parting was amicable.

Clyde Cessna said that from now on he wants to concentrate on building monoplanes, while his former partners wish to focus on biplane transports. Ironically, Travel Air has had considerable success with several high-wing, enclosed cabin aircraft. While no site for his new company has been chosen, Cessna expects no trouble with building up business because he has been flying, designing and manufacturing airplanes for more than a decade (→ Sep 8).

# Passengers fêted by luxury in the air

*Imperial Airways is piling on the luxury on its London/Paris route.*

# The tasks of Pan American Airways

*New York, March 14*
A new airline was officially born today. Its name is Pan American Airways Incorporated. The incorporation formalities for the company, begun only six days ago, have just been completed under the laws of the State of New York.

The airline was set up by a young army officer, Captain J K Montgomery, who has great ambitions. Foremost among these is to use Florida as a base for developing the United States' commercial aviation world-wide. Montgomery can already count on strong financial support, as he has won the backing of Richard Bevier, a son-in-law of the banker Lewis Pierson, and of George Grant Mason. At the request of Peter Von Bauer, president of the Colombia-based German airline SCADTA, Montgomery is seeking to clinch a contract to carry airmail to South America via the West Indies. Montgomery is not the only one to be after that lucrative deal. Juan Trippe has also shown interest in it, although Pan American Airways is well placed to win, since Cuban dictator Gerardo Machado has granted Grant Mason exclusive landing rights in Cuba (→ Oct 30).

*Croydon, England, May 1*
Imperial Airways' new "flying railroad car", the splendid Armstrong Whitworth Argosy biplane *City of Glasgow*, today added a touch of the Orient Express railroad to its London/Paris noon flight: the Silver Wing service.

A first-class buffet, silver service and courteous waiter now replace the earlier lunch baskets handed out before take-off. Hot soup is followed by a variety of cold meats and other dishes ordered from the cabin steward and served at the seat tables during the two-and-a-half hour flight of this new service. The silver and blue Argosy airliner carries up to 20 passengers plus two pilots.

*Relaxing on board the airliner, Silver Wing passengers admire the view while enjoying refreshments.*

# Dornier's flying boats attract admirers

*Germany, July*

The German aircraft industry is acquiring a name for the reliability and flexibility of its airplanes, and in the van of its progress is Dornier's Wal [whale] flying boat. In February 1925 it broke no less than 22 payload, speed, height and distance records; later that year Roald Amundsen used one on his polar expedition, and another made the first east/west crossing of the South Atlantic. Deutsche Luft Hansa used Wals in May last year for new routes from Stettin to Stockholm and Oslo. In March this year a Wal made the first flight from Lisbon to Rio, and the Japan Air Transport Company has now become Dornier's latest customer.

*German Junkers and Dornier Wal airplanes of Colombian Airlines.*

# Doolittle does it again with 'outside loop'

*Dayton, Ohio, May 24*

US Army Air Corps pilot Jimmy Doolittle has stunned the aviation world again. Holder of the Schneider Trophy and the seaplane world speed record, he today became the first flyer to perform an "outside loop" at Wright Field.

Asked why he had attempted what many believed to be a fatal maneuver, he said he did it "just on the spur of the moment". But in fact he has been been building towards the attempt since leaving hospital after breaking his ankles in Chile. Doolittle dived the 450-hp Curtiss fighter from 10,000 feet. Reaching 280mph, he bottomed out upside down, climbed and completed the loop (→ Sep 24, 1929).

# France in shock as pioneers Nungesser and Coli go missing over the Atlantic

*Paris, May 10*

French wartime fighter pilot Charles Nungesser and his navigator François Coli are believed dead after having been reported missing yesterday during an attempted flight from Paris to the east coast of the USA. They took off from Le Bourget yesterday at 5.17am. At 6.48am, their airplane *L'Oiseau Blanc* [*The White Bird*] crossed the French coastline and disappeared into cloud over the English Channel. Five hours later they were sighted off the coast of Ireland but, contrary to earlier weather forecasts, they were said to be flying into headwinds.

It has been estimated that winds of only 25mph will have reduced their speed to little more than 75mph. Such winds will cut their range by 400 miles, and they are flying with a fuel-thirsty engine. At the moment, there are no reports of the fate of the two airmen. Nungesser is a flamboyant figure, who distinguished himself during the Great War by driving an armored car he had singlehandedly captured from the Germans back to his own lines. He shot down 45 German airplanes and received 17 wounds. He was made a member of the prestigious French Légion d'Honneur [Legion of Honor] and received medals from a dozen other grateful Allied nations.

After the war things were not easy for the air hero. His marriage to American Consuelo Hatmaker failed. One ambition, however,

*The two missing French airmen.*

grew more and more: to fly the Atlantic. Nungesser managed to persuade the aircraft designer Pierre Levasseur to build him an airplane that would do the job. Levasseur tailored a PL-8, originally designed for the French navy, for the attempted crossing. The aircraft has a 12-cylinder, water-cooled, 450-hp Lorraine-Dietrich engine, capable of maintaining a 100-mph cruising speed, and carried 886 US gallons of fuel.

*The undercarriage of Nungesser and Coli's "L'Oiseau Blanc" was released shortly after take-off to reduce the heavily-laden machine's weight.*

# Lindbergh flies 'Spirit of St Louis' into history

## Pilot flies non-stop New York to Paris

*Paris, May 21*

Captain Charles A Lindbergh, a US Army reserve officer, landed at Paris today to fulfill what many thought was the impossible dream: flying the Atlantic Ocean, solo, without stopping. His flight from New York makes him the 92nd person to fly the Atlantic, but he is the very first to manage it alone and has become an instant hero. Lindbergh wins the $25,000 Orteig prize for the trip, which, at 3,614 miles, is also an unratified world record.

Lindbergh seized the opportunity of high pressure over the Atlantic and consequent fair weather. Yesterday in the early hours he was at Roosevelt Field, NY, to see his airplane, the Ryan NYP *Spirit of St Louis*, towed and pushed to the 5,000-foot runway.

With so much fuel on board the tires bulged and sank into the clay,

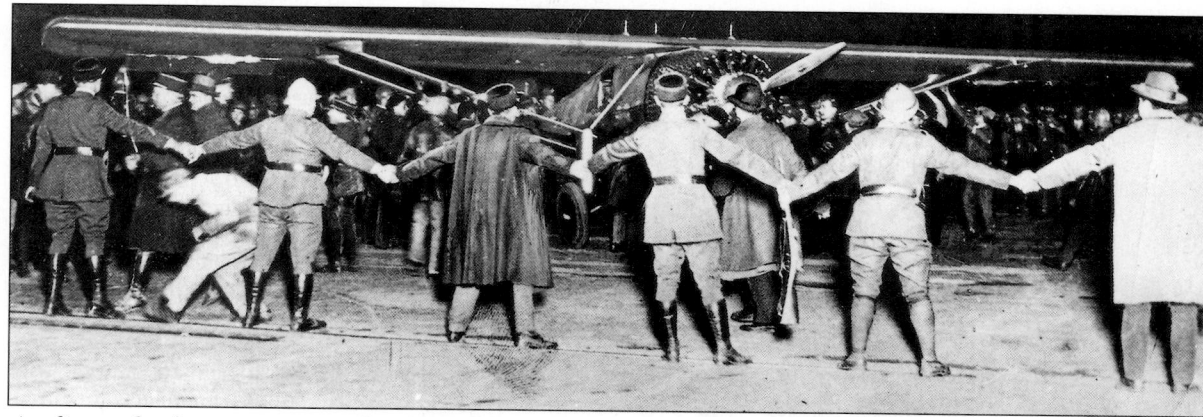

*A police cordon has to protect Lindbergh's aircraft to stop Parisian souvenir hunters stripping all its fixtures.*

but at 7.54am Lindbergh started his take-off run. The *Spirit of St Louis* strained under its load, but Lindbergh lifted it into the air with very little runway to spare. He flew over Nova Scotia, where a storm pounded the aircraft. The weather cleared and he passed St John's, Newfoundland, before heading out to sea. With over a day's flying ahead, Lindbergh's greatest battle was staying awake; he had already not slept for 36 hours before the flight. Ice was a hazard, and he even considered turning back. "There's no alternative but death and failure," he repeated. Feeling his eyes close, he would stick his face into a rush of cold air from outside.

Several times he veered off course. Once the airplane flew on its side in the darkness; another time fog forced him to fly just above the waves. After 28 hours land appeared: Valentia Island, off Ireland. He was close to his dream but still had six hours to go. The light faded, but Paris was lit like a beacon; the Seine sparkled, and the Eiffel tower shone with advertizing signs. The headlamps of hundreds of cars heading to greet him at Le Bourget led him all the way to the airport. At last, after 33 hours, 30 minutes and 29.8 seconds, he landed – in the pages of history.

## Ryan provides airplane suited to task

*Pilot and airplane are mobbed shortly after landing at Le Bourget, Paris.*

*Paris, May 21*

Lindbergh's success has catapulted the little Ryan Airlines Inc of San Diego, builder of the *Spirit of St Louis*, into world recognition. A Ryan was not his first choice, but he could not buy a Bellanca.

Ryan based the NYP on its M-1, but to fly 4,650 miles, including a safety margin, meant 2,700 pounds of fuel. This meant placing a huge tank in front of the cockpit, block-

ing all forward vision except by periscope and side windows. A 237-hp Wright J-5C Whirlwind engine was fitted. Wing span was extended, and the gross airplane weight came out at a staggering 5,250 pounds. Flight instrumentation was basic, with magnetic and earth inductor compasses, a drift sight and turn-slip indicator. It took less than two months to build, and cost just $6,000.

## The man who fought to the end of his dream

*Paris, May 21*

Charles Augustus Lindbergh, or "Lindy", is a private, self-contained man. Dick Blythe, one of two pressmen assigned to cover Lindbergh's preparations for the flight, describes their sharing a room as being like two strange wildcats, each in his own hole.

Twenty-five years old, over 6 feet tall, clean cut, good-looking, enigmatic Lindbergh shuns publicity, a peculiar characteristic for someone who has put his name in every newspaper headline. But he was a barnstorming stunt pilot at 22 years of age, has been a US Army Air Service/Corps Reserve pilot since 1925, has baled out of three crashing airplanes, and inaugurated the US Post Office's CAM-2 air mail route between St Louis and Chicago last year.

Brought up in Minnesota, as a boy, Lindy had a passion for airplanes. His early life was as unusual as his later years. At six he had an 0.22 rifle; he drove the family Ford Model "T" at 11 and ran the family farm at 16. Having been coerced

*Lindbergh: challenger of the skies.*

into taking a mechanical engineering course at the University of Wisconsin in 1920, he proved a poor student and left. In a brief interlude between leaving university and traveling to Nebraska "Lindy" learned to fly, purchasing his own warsurplus Jenny in 1922 (→ May 29).

# Transatlantic trip ends in a wheatfield

*Clarence Chamberlin did not reach Berlin, but he flew further than Lindbergh.*

*Germany, June 6*

Clarence Chamberlin has followed his friend Charles Lindbergh in crossing the Atlantic without stopping. In doing so he has beaten "Lindy's" record non-stop distance by 300 miles with a staggering total of 3,911 miles.

Flying a Wright-engined Bellanca monoplane named *Columbia* and accompanied by owner Charles Levine, he took off from Roosevelt Field, NY, on June 4. Forty-three hours later they ran out of fuel and were forced to land in a German wheatfield, 100 miles short of their objective, Berlin. Otherwise the Bellanca, widely regarded as one of the best airplanes in the world, driven by the 200-hp J-5C Whirlwind engine, performed to order. The only real threat came when Chamberlin allowed Levine to take the controls so he could snatch some sleep. Levine's inexperience became apparent, and the aircraft was soon in a spiral dive from 20,000 feet. Chamberlin woke up just in time to bring the airplane back on an even keel.

# Americans flock to see hero Lindbergh

*New York, June 16*

America's newest hero today received a ticker-tape welcome here in the city which saw the start of his epic journey. "I am genuinely glad to be back," said Charles "Lindy" Lindbergh as he arrived in Washington on June 11 to meet President Calvin Coolidge and receive the first Distinguished Flying Cross to be awarded. Lindbergh has already been rewarded with promotion from captain to colonel in the US Army Air Corps Reserve.

The President had sent the US Navy cruiser *Memphis* to bring Lindbergh back. Down the gangplank he walked, alone and in front, to a huge welcome. His mother Evangeline followed, escorted by Rear-Admiral Benjamin Hutchinson and the secretaries of war and of the navy behind. No royalty was better received (→ Mar 3, 1929).

*Broadway greets the returning hero.*

# Luft Hansa gets South America foothold

*Brazil, May 7*

Luft Hansa has finally gained a foothold in South America. The powerful German airline's subsidiary in Brazil, the Syndicato Condor, has just founded VARIG [Viaçao Aerea Rio Grandense], which holds the franchise for the route between Santa Catarina and Rio Grande State. Luft Hansa has thus stolen a march on France's Aéropostale, which is also seeking to set up air routes between Europe and South America. The German company's strategy is to create local subsidiaries. The first of these, SCADTA, has been operating in Colombia since 1919. As for the Syndicato Condor, founded in 1924 it has until now limited its operations to South America. The company now plans to use VARIG to set up a network between Europe and South America (→ Dec 12).

**Six Royal Air Force parachutists jump together in a striking demonstration during the annual RAF pageant and display at Hendon, England.**

# American pilots head west across the Pacific to link California and Hawaii

*Honolulu, Hawaii, June 29*
A beautiful Hawaiian sunrise and the Kilauea Lighthouse on Kuai greeted US Army Air Corps lieutenants Lester J Maitland and Albert F Hegenberger en route to their landing in a tropical downpour at Wheeler Field today, where they became the first aviators successfully to fly from the mainland US to Hawaii. The flight took 25 hours 50 minutes.

Their achievement ranks with Charles Lindbergh's New York to Paris crossing last month, because of the difficulty they had in finding somewhere to land at the end of the 2,407-mile flight. The army flyers' Fokker, the *Bird of Paradise*, had a new wireless designed to receive the beam from a directional transmitter that would guide them to Hawaii. The receiver failed shortly after they took off from Oakland, California, and they had to fall back on standard navigational equipment and Hegenberger's skill to complete the flight safely (→ Jul 15).

*Hawaii-bound: Maitland and Hegenberger's Fokker leaves San Francisco.*

# North Pole hero makes Atlantic flight

*"America" before the emergency, seen at Ver-sur-Mer, in northern France.*

*Normandy, France, July 1*
Commander Richard Byrd and his crew had an ignominious end to their non-stop transatlantic crossing today when they ditched in the sea off the coast of Calvados, France. Unhurt but shocked, they used a rubber raft to paddle through the surf to the beach, safeguarding the 150-pound bag of US mail that was the first to cross the Atlantic by airplane. It took an hour to raise help.

With Byrd (who was navigator) in the Fokker C-2 *America* were Bert Acosta (pilot), Bernt Balchen (co-pilot) and Lieutenant George Noville (engineer and wireless operator). They left New York on June 29 but encountered thick cloud, which stayed with them. By the time they crossed the French coast, fuel was becoming low.

Fog obscured Paris. After vainly circling in the hope of spotting a landmark, Balchen, the only one trained to fly on instruments, took over the controls from a weary Acosta and headed back to the coast for an emergency ditching. Their eventful flight had lasted 46 hours 6 minutes (→ Nov 29, 1929).

# Boeing Airplane founds in-house airline

*Chicago, July 1*
The Boeing Airplane Company's new airline, Boeing Air Transport, began operations today. It has taken over the western portion of the transcontinental airmail service from the US Post Office, carrying mail and passengers from Chicago to San Francisco. Reporter Jane Eads of the Chicago *Herald and Examiner* was the first passenger for the new airline when its inaugural flight departed at 9.30pm.

Hardly surprisingly, the company flies only Boeing aircraft, and the very latest models at that: single-engined Model 40As. The airplanes feature an enclosed passenger compartment which seats two; the pilot sits in an open cockpit above and behind the compartment (→ Jan 1, 1928).

*Good business: Boeing Air Transport is operating with Boeing airplanes.*

# Lockheed unveils its streamlined Vega

*Inglewood, Calif, July 4*
For the young Lockheed Aircraft Company today was not only US Independence Day but also the start of flight testing of the new Lockheed Vega. Perhaps the most streamlined airplane yet built, the Vega, built in a rented workshop in Hollywood, is expected to approach 200mph with its 220-hp Wright Whirlwind engine, even with four passengers aboard. Company founder Allan Loughead and chief engineer Jack Northrop hope eventually to fit a Vega with the new 425-hp Pratt & Whitney Wasp engine (→ Aug 17).

*The Vega's streamlined cowling.*

# Crash ends single-engined Hawaii flight

*Molaki, Hawaii, July 15*
They may not have reached their intended destination of Honolulu, but today, just two weeks after the first successful flight to Hawaii, two more Americans, Ernest L Smith and Emory B Bronte, duplicated that feat when they arrived at Molaki from Oakland, California. They ran out of fuel and had to land in a brush-covered area. Neither pilot was injured in the landing, but their single-engined Travel Air monoplane was destroyed.

# RAF reviews its air strength at exercises

*British air strength: a formation of Bristol Bulldog fighters of the RAF.*

*Hampshire, England, July 25*
Britain's annual air defense exercise at Andover has produced an embarrassing result for the defenders. Thanks to an American engine (a Curtiss D-12), a new Royal Air Force (RAF) bomber called the Fairey Fox flew 50mph faster than any interceptor aircraft. The Curtiss is not only more powerful but also helps Fairey to build a unique-

ly clean aerodynamic form, reducing the effects of drag.

The result will not displease RAF chief Sir Hugh Trenchard, who argues that in air war the best defense is pre-emptive attack on enemy facilities without regard to a front line. When he set up the RAF two years ago, Trenchard created three bomber squadrons for every one of fighters.

# Will Gipsy engine revolutionize the Moth?

*Middlesex, England, August 24*
De Havilland's D.H.71 Tiger Moth monoplane caused a stir today when it set a new speed record for light airplanes of 186.47mph flown by Hubert Broad. The airplane, which made its first flight at the company's airfield at Edgware this summer, is the first powered by the new engine known as the Gipsy.

Until now all the de Havilland Moth biplanes have been powered by the 60-hp Cirrus engine. This was designed by Major Frank Halford, who managed to keep the costs down by converting wartime Renault engines. But as sales of D.H.60 Moths have been brisk, and

supplies of Renault parts have started running low, so Halford has embarked on the design of a more powerful engine from scratch after long talks with de Havilland. The new engine follows the same layout as the Cirrus, with four air-cooled cylinders in line, but it develops twice the power output at 135-hp.

The new de Havilland engine will power the next generation of Moths, including the D.H.60G, but for the moment only two special racing engines have been made, one of which flew in the first D.H.71 today. The first D.H.60Gs, due next year, will inevitably be known as Gipsy Moths (→ Sep 28).

*The new engine is destined to replace the Cirrus seen on this earlier D.H.60.*

# Luft Hansa service now reaches Venice

*Berlin, August 5*
The rise of German national airline Deutsche Luft Hansa, known as DLH or, increasingly, just Luft Hansa, is underlined by the opening today of another new service to Italy, to the cultural city of Venice. Not many taking the airplane to Venice can be businessmen or diplomats. These are tourists, forsaking boat and train for speed and security in the air.

Recent events such as the scrapping of the 1921 London Agreement which forbade the manufacture of aircraft in Germany, the introduction of larger all-metal aircraft, and the rigorous new training of Luft Hansa pilots in "blind pilotage" and "radiolocation" in bad weather have helped to bring reliability to a service whose timekeeping is said to match that of Swiss railroads (→ Jan 5, 1928).

# Northwest Airways sells first ticket

*Minneapolis, Minnesota, July 5*
Byron G Webster today became the first passenger for Northwest Airways, when the mayor of nearby Saint Paul had second thoughts and refused to fly as promised. Colonel Lewis H Brittin, the founder of Northwest, selected a young businessman named Webster from a small crowd that had gathered to see the mayor off.

"Speed" Holman, the pilot, helped Webster aboard the Stinson Detroiter biplane and then hoisted his own 6 foot 6 inch frame aboard. Then they were off for Chicago. This is the first time an airline has operated a closed cockpit airplane for passenger service.

An engine failure found the duo marooned in a farmer's field. On a second attempt, after braving thunderstorms, they arrived in Chicago after a 12 hour 30 minute flight.

# Briton Webster speeds to Schneider win

*Britain's Schneider team at a celebration dinner: Webster is in the front row, second from the right.*

*Venice, Italy, September 20*
A Royal Air Force team flying the slender Supermarine S.5 has set a new world speed record for seaplanes of 281.65mph to win the Schneider Trophy competition set up in 1912. Two S.5s were the only

machines to finish the seven-lap course. The American entrant withdrew before the race, and the best of the Italians were stopped by mechanical trouble. A British Short Crusader crashed in practise.

The British victory reflects the sort of national determination seen in earlier years in Italy and the US. A special RAF High Speed Flight was set up and equipped with three S.5s, three Gloster IVs and the Mercury-engined Crusader – the largest number of machines built by a single nation for such an event. The race was won by British pilots Flight Lieutenant S N Webster and Flight Lieutenant O E Worsley, who were particularly good at making steep banks around pylons marking virtual 180-degree turns. After the very last turn Webster, in the lead, flew an unnecessary eighth lap over the 31-mile course. As it happened, he had just enough fuel to make it.

## Fight for control of Caribbean sky

*United States, September 30*

Three American airlines are fighting for a major contract. At stake is nothing less than the monopoly of air trafic in the West Indies.

The three groups are headed by Reed Chambers and Eddie Rickenbacker, co-founders of Florida Airways, J K Montgomery of the German-owned SCADTA, who organised Pan American Airways last March, and the founder of the Aviation Corporation of America (Avco) Juan Trippe. On July 16, President Machado of Cuba granted Pan Am exclusive airmail rights on the Miami/Havana route. However, Trippe has won this round, obtaining monopoly landing rights in Cuba from Machado. Montgomery and Trippe will now have to work together (→ Jun 27, 1928).

# French cross South Atlantic non-stop

*Natal, Brazil, October 15*

After a flight lasting 18 hours and 5 minutes, Captain Dieudonné Costes and his navigator Lieutenant Commander Le Brix landed here today to record the first ever non-stop air crossing of the South Atlantic. The 2,100-mile flight started at Saint-Louis in Senegal, West Africa. The two Frenchmen had made an even longer flight, including stops, in order to reach Senegal for the crossing, leaving Le Bourget in France five days ago.

The two officers plan to leave here tomorrow for Rio de Janeiro and Buenos Aires, before flying up to New York, their final destination. Their airplane is a Breguet-Hispano XIXGR, *Nungesser et Coli*, named after the two French flyers lost on an attempted transatlantic flight earlier this year.

*A hero from the skies, Costes is mobbed by a crowd of Argentinian admirers.*

## Florida Airways backed by bankers

*Miami, Fla, September*

Organised by Eddie Rickenbacker and Reed Chambers early last year, Florida Airways has enjoyed the backing of a very impressive group of American bankers.

These are all men with an strong interest in pioneering air services, and they have been looking closely at the possibility of several southern routes, towards the Caribbean and South America. Among these East Coast financiers are such names as Charles Hayden, Percy A Rockefeller, Anne Morgan, Carles Stone, George Mixter, the vice-president of Stone and Webster Bank, and Richard F Hoyt.

# Pan American Airways saves mail contract at the last minute

*Key West, Fla, October 19*

Pan American Airways Inc has just had a narrow escape. The airline came within an inch of being in breach of its contract to fly mail to Cuba.

By not doing so, it has saved its reputation and a $25,000 deposit. The problem began when no airplane was available to fly 30,000 letters from Florida to Havana. Luckily, *La Nina*, a small Fairchild FC-2 seaplane operated by West Indian Aerial, made a refueling stop at Key West. Its pilot, Cy Caldwell, agreed to fly the mail to the Cuban capital for a fee of $145.50. Caldwell's unexpected mission was accomplished within the hour (→ Jun 23, 1928).

*Cy Caldwell's Fairchild FC-2 was at the right place at the right time.*

**On December 31, American pilot Arthur C Goebel wins the Dole Race and a $25,000 first prize by flying his monoplane Woolaroc from the west coast of the United States to Honolulu.**

## Trippe, a Yale boy with high ambitions

*Key West, Fla, October 19*

He is running his fourth airline, was a US Navy pilot, played football at Yale, is the son of a New York banker, bears a distinctly Latin name but traces his descent from Englishmen who came to America in the 1600s: he is Juan Terry Trippe, president of Pan American Airways. He is aged 28.

Aviation has been his life since 1917. He then left Yale to become a Navy bomber pilot: when he returned he started a flying club. Later, he bought seven surplus US Navy seaplanes, for $3,500, to start a charter service to ferry tourists to resorts. With a group of wealthy Yale friends, young Trippe founded Eastern Air Transport and merged it into Colonial Air Transport. Not satisfied with this, he now has designs on Pan American Airways (→ Jun 27, 1928).

# Flyers are Hollywood hit

*Actress Clara Bow is given the cold shoulder in the latest hit,"Wings".*

**USA, December 31**

The Great War has started again – on the battlefields of Hollywood. American motion-picture makers are finding that military exploits, especially the aerial deeds of the great aces, make good movies with everything in them that audiences want to see: action, suspense, heroism and romance.

This year's air movies include *The Lone Eagle*, *Now We're in the Air*, *Sky-high Saunders*, *Three Miles Up* and *Wide Open*. But one film, *Wings*, has thrilled audiences above

all with its tale of the derring-do of two airmen, played by Richard Arlen and Charles "Buddy" Rogers. The film, which also stars Clara Bow and Gary Cooper, was directed by William A Wellman and produced by Paramount. It was largely shot at Camp Stanley in Texas, where the makers paid $300,000 for US Army engineers to build a reconstruction of a western front battlefield. *Wings* and other films are adding to the legend of the ace as a chivalrous, fearless, fast-living knight of the air.

 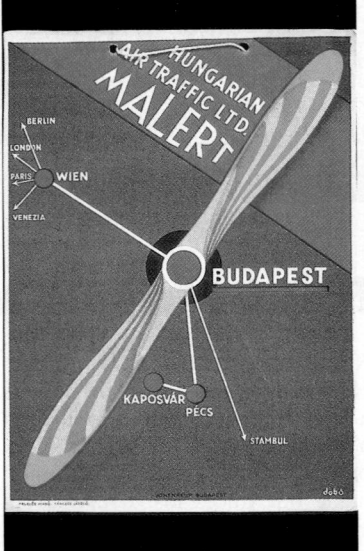

**Attracting passengers: two posters advertising airline services, (l) for French company Farman, (r) for Hungarian company Malert which represents capital city Budapest as the center of a giant propeller.**

# Price war spells good news for travelers

*Paris, October 26*

What looks like an airline price war seems to be under way following today's announcement by leading French carrier Air Union that it is cutting fares on the busy Paris/London route and creating a new, cheaper, "second-class" service on its airplanes.

Air Union's move is a response to the introduction this month by Im-

perial Airways, the leading British carrier, of a second-class economy service on its own London/Paris flights. Those who cannot afford to fly as first-class passengers, with access to a bar and service by an air steward, now have the opportunity to travel more cheaply. Whatever Imperial's next move against its competitor will be, the air traveler looks certain to benefit.

*Meanwhile, in first class, no luxury is too great for the well-heeled.*

# New Spanish airline has German connection

*A Junkers aircraft of Luft Hansa's Brazilian subsidiary Syndicato Condor.*

*Madrid, December 12*

Following its usual business methods, pioneered by its predecessor companies with the USSR earlier in the decade, the German national airline Luft Hansa has entered into a joint venture to start a Spanish airline: Compania Aerea de Transportes, which commenced operations today, flies from Madrid to Barcelona. The new airline's aircraft will be German, although

some may be built in Spain. The schedules will soon be interlinked with the Europe-wide Luft Hansa network, and the pilots will train in Luft Hansa's own flying schools.

At present joint venture operations or agreements exist with the Soviet Union, Austria, France, Austria, Italy, Norway, Poland and now Spain. Other Luft Hansa subsidiaries also exist in countries such as Brazil.

# Atlantic challenge brings out determined flyers

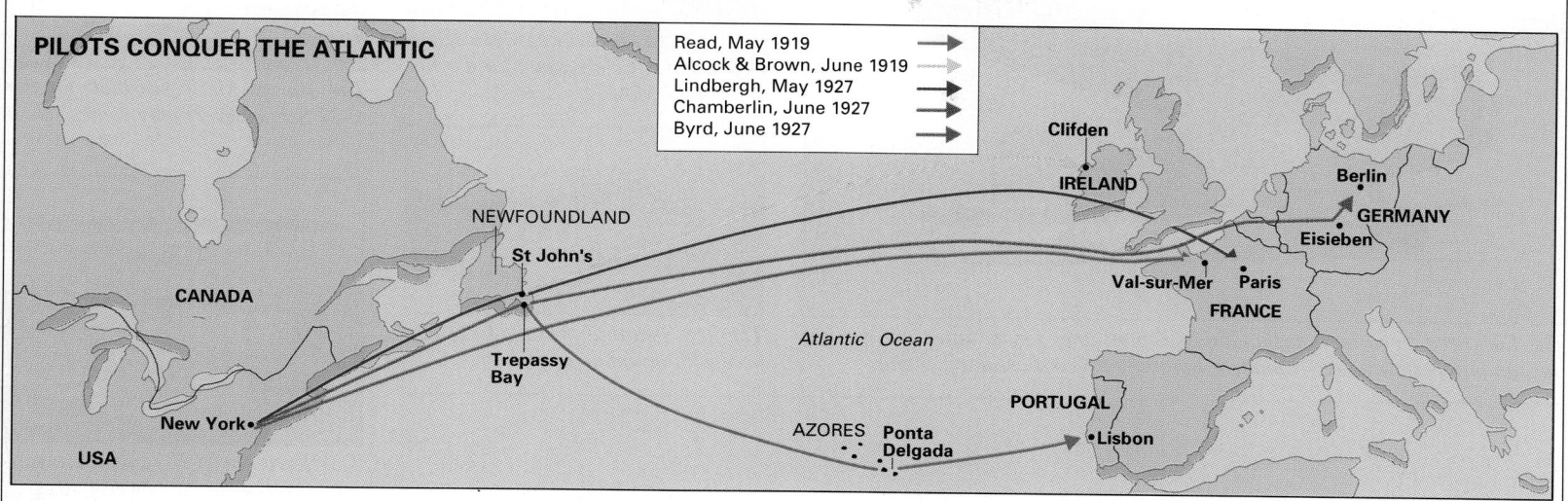

**PILOTS CONQUER THE ATLANTIC**

| | |
|---|---|
| Read, May 1919 | → |
| Alcock & Brown, June 1919 | → |
| Lindbergh, May 1927 | → |
| Chamberlin, June 1927 | → |
| Byrd, June 1927 | → |

## Atlantic bids, 1927: crews and aircraft

**April 26**: Davis and Wooster, Keystone Pathfinder.
**May 8**: Nungesser and Coli, Levasseur PL.8.
**May 20**: Lindbergh*, Ryan NYP.
**May 20**: De Pinedo*, Savoia S.55, with stops.
**June 4**: Chamberlin and Levine*, Bellanca.
**June 29**: Byrd*, Fokker C-2.
**August 1**: Chamberlin, Bellanca.
**August 14**: Loose, Köhl and

Fitzmaurice, Fokker F.VII.

von Hünefeld, Junkers W 33.
**August 14**: Ristics, Edzard and Knickerbocker, Junkers W 33.
**August 28**: Brock and Schlee*, Stinson.
**August 29**: Tully and Medcalf, Stinson.
**August 31**: Minchin, Hamilton and Löwenstein, Fokker F.VIIa.
**September 1**: Tully and Medcalf, Stinson.

**September 2**: Givion and Corbu, Farman biplane.
**September 3**: Courtney, Little, Downer, Hosmer; Dornier Wal.
**September 5**: Tully and Medcalf, Stinson.
**September 6**: Bertaud, Hill and Payne, Fokker F.VII.
**September 7**: Schiller and Wood, Stinson.
**September 16**: McIntosh and

**October 11**: Haldeman and Ruth Elder, Stinson.
**October 14**: Loose, Starke, Loewe, Fritzler and Dillens, Junkers G 24.
**October 23**: Hultz, Grayson and Goldsborough, Sikorsky.
**November 4**: Merz, Rohde and Bock, Heinkel 800.
**December 23**: Omdal, Koehler, Goldsborough and Grayson, Sikorsky.
[* = *successful flight.*]

## Disappearance of a Princess

*Atlantic, August 31*
Three more flyers, including the first woman to attempt the crossing, have perished over the Atlantic. The missing woman, Princess Löwenstein-Wertheim, 60, daughter of Count Mexborough, was part of the crew, consisting also of Lt-Col Minchin and Capt Leslie Hamilton, of the Fokker *Saint-Raphael* (G-EBTO) heading for the US from Britain. There has been no news from the plane, which has a 500hp Bristol engine, since take-off. The crew of a tanker has reported seeing the plane somewhere between Britain and Newfoundland. Since that sighting, there has been no news and the worst is feared.

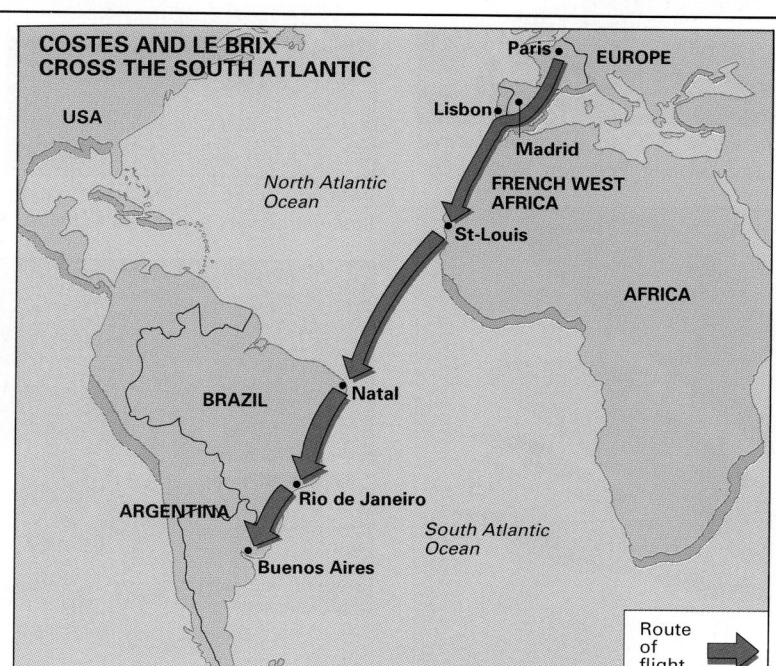

**COSTES AND LE BRIX CROSS THE SOUTH ATLANTIC**

*The Paris to Buenos Aires route flown by Costes and Le Brix. Their trip, in October, was one of the great challenges left to pilots. Previous crossings of the South Atlantic had always been flown with mid-ocean stops.*

## Model escapes from crash

*Atlantic, 12 October*
Another lady has met trouble in an attempt to be the first member of her sex to cross the Atlantic, although in her case the mishap was not fatal. Ruth Elder, a young fashion model aged 23, was next to pilot George Haldeman when he took off from New York in the *American Girl* on October 11 at 5.04pm. The aim was to reach Paris via the Azores. However, the plane's oil pressure fell to zero some 400 miles from the islands. Miss Elder sent out an SOS from the Stinson's small radio. The distress signal was picked up by the Dutch tanker *Barendrecht* which rescued the two survivors.

The Lockheed Vega had outstandingly elegant lines for its time, and was an outstanding performance. It made a number of record-breaking flights.

Deutsche Luft Hansa had ten Focke-Wulf A.17 Möwes.

The first Stearman was the C-3, seen here with an inline engine.

The Macchi M.52 was built for the 1927 Schneider Trophy contest.

The Waco Model 10 could use a variety of radial-engine powerplants.

The H-47 Metalplane, another all-metal design from the United States.

Charles Lindbergh's Ryan NYP, the "Spirit of St Louis" carried its intrepid pilot safely from New York to Paris on the first non-stop flight.

The Fokker F.VIII (two Jupiter engines) saw only limited production.

Boeing's Wasp-engined Model 40A could carry passengers and mail.

The Bach 3CT Air Yacht had three radial engines. Very few were built.

Fairchild's FC-2 multirole cabin monoplane was popular in Canada.

Supermarine's S.5 seaplane, winner of the 1927 Schneider Trophy.

Armstrong Whitworth's attempt to produce a three-engined airliner resulted in the ungainly Argosy, which served Imperial Airways for ten years.

Adolph Rohrbach's answer to a similar need appeared as the Roland all-metal monoplane, which had cleaner lines. Surprisingly, few were sold.

*The Stinson Detroiter, powered by a 300hp Wright Whirlwind radial, had an outstanding performance and set duration and endurance records.*

*The Bristol Bulldog fighter proved promising, and in its Mk II form was adopted by the RAF and other air services. The engine was a Bristol Jupiter.*

*A small number of the Swiss Comte AC-4 Gentleman were built.*

*The Junkers K 37: a military aircraft disguised as a mailplane.*

*The Avro 504N was used as a trainer in both military and civil roles.*

*The Canadian Vickers Velos survey aircraft proved rather tricky to fly.*

*Although the Westland Wapiti Mk I was built largely of wood, the Mk II had an all-metal airframe. It replaced progressively the D.H.9A in the RAF.*

*The US Navy had 74 F3B-1 fighters developed from the PW-9C.*

*Handley Page's Hinaidi night bomber, with two Jupiter engines.*

*The Douglas T2D-1 was a twin-engined Navy torpedo bomber.*

*Boeing's PW-9C was derived directly from the PW-9. The US Army Air Corps took delivery of 40 examples. It led to much better Wasp-engined versions.*

*The distinctive Nieuport-Delage NiD 52 sesquiplane fighter.*

# 1928

318.57mph
Italy
Mario de Bernadi
Macchi M.52bis
Mar 30, 1928

4,763.81 miles
Italy
Ferrarin and del Prete
SIAI-Marchetti S.64
Jul 5, 1928

38,418ft
USA
CC Champion
Wright Apache
Jul 25, 1927

57,319lb
Italy
SAI Caproni
Caproni Ca 60

1,000hp
Great Britain
Napier
Cub

**California, January 1**
Boeing Air Transport buys majority shareholding in American airline Pacific Air Transport, owned by Vern Gorst (→ Feb 1, 1929).

**Stuttgart, Germany, January 5**
German airline Deutsche Luft Hansa (DLH) opens a service to Barcelona, Spain, to link up with the service from Madrid operated by its Spanish subsidiary Iberia; passengers can now fly all the way from Berlin to Madrid on DLH services, a route of 1,305 miles (→ Mar 30).

**USSR, January 7**
The prototype Polikarpov U-2 training biplane makes its first flight.

**Quilali, Nicaragua, January 7**
US Marine Lieutenant C F Schilt uses his Vought Corsair biplane as a flying ambulance to rescue wounded colleagues; the first use of military aircraft as ambulances was in British Somaliland [Somalia] in 1919.

**Rome, February 7**
Australian pilot Squadron Leader Bert Hinkler, who left Croydon, England, this morning in his Avro Avian light plane for Australia, lands at the end of the first leg of his flight and is immediately arrested: he has mistakenly touched down at a military airfield (→ Feb 22).

**Kent, England, February 15**
The new Short flying boat, the S.8 Calcutta, makes its first flight in the hands of John Lankester Parker at Rochester.

**Argentina, March 1**
French pilot Jean Mermoz takes off from Buenos Aires for Rio de Janeiro in Brazil on the first leg of French company Aéropostale's new airmail service from South America to France. Aéropostale's agreement with Argentina stipulates that under normal circumstances delivery must be made in no more than seven-and-a-half days (→ Mar 13).

**Cameri, Italy, March 3**
The new Savoia-Marchetti S.64, built by SIAI, is demonstrated. Due to a low power-to-weight ratio, the aiplane has to use a sloping, 4,000 foot runway to take off.

**Sydney, March 12**
Squadron Leader Bert Hinkler receives news that his solo flight to Australia has earned him the Air Force Cross, which is awarded to Royal Air Force officers for bravery away from the battlefield (→ Nov 27, 1931).

**Canada, March 13**
Eileen Vollick is the first Canadian woman to be licensed as a pilot.

**France, March 13**
Aéropostale pilot Elisée Négrin lands at Montaudran with the company's first load of airmail from South America; the inaugural flight from Buenos Aires to Toulouse has taken 12 days 20 minutes, longer than agreed with Argentina.

**Zehden, Germany, March 30**
Local resident Samuel Schwartz asks German airline DLH for rent for the airspace above his house, citing the law that says his rights extend to the "space above and the ground beneath" his property (→ Nov 6, 1929).

**Australia, April 27**
Dr K St Vincent Welsh is appointed aerial medical officer for the Northern Territory.

**Cape Town, South Africa, April 30**
British pilot Lady Mary Bailey lands to complete a flight from England; she left on March 9.→

**Devon, England, May 5**
Alan Cobham and crew land after completing the Sir Charles Wakefield Africa Survey (→ Aug 31, 1931).

**Australia, May 9**
QANTAS starts the first daily service here, between Brisbane and Toowoomba (→ May 15).

**Croydon, England, May 17**
Lady Heath lands her Avro Avian to complete the first solo flight from South Africa to Britain; she left Cape Town on February 12.

**London, May 21**
Admiral Madden, Royal Navy chief of staff, circulates his refutation of Marshal of the Royal Air Force Lord Trenchard's claim that to defeat an enemy nation the Royal Air Force should attack its citizens directly.

**San Francisco, May 31**
Charles Kingsford Smith and his crew set off in their Fokker F.VIIb-3m *Southern Cross* for Honolulu, on the first leg of a flight to Australia (→ Jun 9).

**Dübendorf, Switzerland, June 3**
The Dewoitine D.27 fighter has its first flight (→ Jun 18, 1932).

**Germany, June 11**
Friedrich Stamer pilots a rocket-powered glider for a mile during experiments directed by aerodynamicist Alex Lippisch, financed by Fritz von Opel (→ Sep 30, 1929).

**Britain, June 15**
As a publicity stunt, an Imperial Airways AW Argosy piloted by Gordon Olley races the London and North Eastern Railway's *Flying Scotsman* train the 390 miles from London to Edinburgh; the Argosy takes 84 minutes to refuel twice en route and beats the train by only 15 minutes.

**Oklahoma, June 20**
Paul Braniff inaugurates a daily passenger service between Tulsa and Oklahoma City.

**Brazil, July 5**
Italian airmen Arturo Ferrarin and Carlo del Prete land their Savoia S.64 on a beach near Natal after a 4,466-mile non-stop flight from Rome, which they left on July 3.→

**Manitoba, Canada, August 28**
"Punch" Dickins and Lieutenant-Colonel MacAlpine leave on a survey flight across northern Canada; they plan to make the first flight across the Barren Lands.

**Newark, New Jersey, October 1**
Newark Municipal Airport is officially opened (→ Mar 12, 1932).

**Washington, DC, October 6**
US Navy Secretary Curtis Wilbur signs a contract with the Goodyear-Zeppelin Corporation of Akron, Ohio, for two giant dirigibles.

**Japan, October 30**
Japan Air Lines, a single national airline, is formed from the merger of Tozai Regular Air Transport Society and Kawanishi Japan Air Lines.

**Arizona, November 4**
Captain C B Collyer and Harry Tucker, who set a speed record of 24 hours 5 minutes between New York and Los Angeles on October 25, die when their Lockheed Vega crashes into Canyon Creek during an attempt to set a west/east speed record between the two cities.

**Texas, December 12**
In a demonstration of paratroop techniques at Brooks Field, a six-man machine-gun team jumps from a six-airplane formation.

**Washington, DC, December 17**
The Boeing Airplane Company merges with Pratt & Whitney Aircraft and Chance Vought to form United Aircraft and Transport Corporation.

**Afghanistan, December 23**
Royal Air Force aircraft begin the evacuation of citizens under attack in Kabul (→ Feb 25, 1929).

**Honduras, December 29**
Pan American is granted exclusive airmail rights by the Honduran government (→ Jan 25, 1929).

*The dream of flight has truly inspired this magazine artist in his commemoration of the 25th anniversary of the Wright brothers' take-off.* ▶

# New Zealand flyers missing on flight across Tasman Sea

*Richmond, Australia, January 10*
It is feared that two New Zealand airmen, Lieutenant John Moncrieff and Captain George Hood, have died while attempting to fly from Australia to Wellington, New Zealand, across the Tasman Sea. The last wireless signal from the Ryan B.1 *Aotearoa* was at 2.52pm local time, 12 hours 8 minutes after leaving Richmond, New South Wales.

Nothing more has been heard, but the captain of the steamer *Kaiwarra* reported seeing the aircraft off Porirua, on the west coast of New Zealand's North Island, over four hours later. A ground mist had developed. They are feared to have crashed in a mountainous area or into the sea.

*Crashed? Moncrieff (l) and Hood.*

# England to Australia epic sets five records

*Hinkler lifts off the engine's cowling before showing it to the spectators.*

*Darwin, Australia, February 22*
Australian Bert Hinkler landed at Fanny Bay today after an epic 11,000-mile solo flight from England, to the sort of welcome his countrymen usually reserve for their international cricketers. He is the first to make such a trip, setting four other new records: longest solo flight, longest light plane flight, first non-stop flight from London to Rome and fastest journey from Britain to India.

Squadron Leader Hinkler took off from Croydon, England, on the morning of February 7 and flew via Rome, Malta, Libya, India, Burma and Singapore. As his journey progressed, the anticipation in Australia mounted to a fever pitch, with every stage seeming to pose additional hazards to the diminutive and retiring Hinkler and his tiny Avro Avian biplane. Like American aviator Charles Lindbergh, Hinkler is a thorough man, working on his machine every day, checking to ensure it is airworthy. This, he says, is what helped him to win through in the end (→ Mar 12).

# US airship makes rendezvous with carrier

*Newport, RI, January 27*
Two of the US Navy's newest ships, one of the air and the other of the sea, met off the coast here today when the airship USS *Los Angeles* showed off its maneuverability by landing on the aircraft carrier USS *Saratoga* without the benefit of a mooring mast.

The *Los Angeles* proved that it was feasible for a lighter-than-air craft to moor to a ship when it was guided to the mast-equipped steamship *Patoka*. Today's accomplishment was probably only made possible because of the airship's five reversible engines, which have a combined 2,625-hp output. The *Los Angeles* was moored to the stern of the aircraft carrier's flight deck. It transferred passengers to the *Saratoga* and delivered fuel and supplies, demonstrating that in the future airships may be able to accompany the fleet.

*The "Los Angeles" at its mast.*

# French heroes get New York welcome

*New York, February 11*
French pilot Dieudonné Costes and his navigator Lieutenant-Commander Joseph Le Brix today received a hero's welcome on their arrival here after a 22,500-mile flight from Paris. The epic journey, in a green-painted Breguet XIX, named *Nungesser et Coli* after two famous French flyers lost last year, has taken 125 days at an average speed of 125mph.

Costes and Le Brix flew via Africa and South America. They set out on October 10 on the first leg of their flight to Senegal. Flying across the South Atlantic, they landed at Rio de Janeiro before heading south to Buenos Aires, then north-west to La Paz (where the airfield height is 13,450ft) and Panama before the final leg to New York. Costes and Le Brix now plan to cross the USA to San Francisco and thence to Japan (→ Sep 3, 1930).

# Italian smashes his own speed record

*Venice, Italy, March 30*
Major Mario de Bernardi of the Italian air force today smashed his own world air speed record. He took his Macchi M.52R seaplane to an impressive average of 318.57-mph during six runs over the 1.86-mile measured course at Venice's Lido. This is the first time an aircraft has exceeded 500km/h [310.7-mph]. The M.52R is a sleeker version of the M.52, with reduced wing and tailplane areas, but a similar Fiat 1,000-hp AS.3 engine.

As he already held the world record, de Bernardi was reluctant to take the risk of an unnecessary attempt. However, he went ahead for two reasons: firstly, because British pilots were threatening his record speed of 300.93mph, set in a Macchi M.52 here late last year; secondly, because Mussolini told him to. Only 18 days ago, Flight Lieutenant Kinkead of the Royal Air Force's High Speed Flight lost his life while attempting the record in a Supermarine S.5. He dived into the sea in misty conditions. Another attempt may be made later.

## Pilots fly across the icy Arctic wasteland

*Spitzbergen, Norway, April 21*
Australian explorer Hubert Wilkins and his American pilot Carl Ben Eielson arrived here today after making the first ever crossing of the Arctic by airplane. They left Point Barrow, Alaska, on April 15 in their Lockheed Vega. Having flown for around 20 hours, they were beset by storms and were forced down on Dead Man's Island, 5 miles from Spitzbergen. They spent five days inside the aircraft before the storm passed. Then they found that the Vega's skis had sunk into the soft snow and Wilkins had to push the airplane to get it moving. Eielson took off without him, then landed again and, at the second attempt, they got away together.

# Non-stop from Ireland to Labrador

*The Junkers "Bremen" prepares to take off on a difficult Atlantic crossing which ends on Greenly Island, Labrador.*

*New York, April 14*
Great relief has greeted today's news from Labrador that the four men are safe. The four include three Germans, pilots Carl Spinder and Hermann Köhl, and their passenger, Baron von Hunefeld, as well as an Irish navigator, Commandant James Fitzmaurice. They had failed to arrive at Mitchell Field, New York, yesterday after an attempted non-stop, east/west Atlantic crossing. Even at the best of times, the prevailing westerly headwinds make an east/west crossing a difficult challenge, and the worst was feared.

The airmen left Baldonnel, Ireland, in their Junkers W 33 *Bremen* on the 12th. But problems with their compass and bad lighting, plus headwinds reaching 100mph and patchy fog, forced them to land yesterday on Greenly Island, Labrador, some 1,200 miles from New York. They also had to contend with a snowstorm that raged for most of the night. For hours, the two pilots had to stuggle to keep the Junkers in the air. Just as the men were reaching the end of their tether, an island appeared on the horizon. They landed safely after a flight lasting 37 hours, although the propeller snapped and the landing gear collapsed.

## Earhart is first woman to fly the Atlantic

*Amelia Earhart (in flying clothes, left) is warmly congratulated after her triumphant transatlantic flight.*

*Barry, Wales, June 18*
Amelia Earhart, American former holder of the world altitude record, today became the first woman to fly across the Atlantic. She was one of three crew who took off from Trepassey, Newfoundland, bound for Ireland.

The noted pilot had to content herself with being just a passenger in the Fokker F.VIIb-3m *Friendship* flown by Wilmer Stultz and "Slim" Gordon. At 2.51pm [British time] yesterday, the airplane took off. Earhart sat between fuel tanks and kept a log, her writing shaken by the vibration as the airplane battled through fog, rain and, later, darkness, with its engine exhausts like "glowing meteors". The crossing took 24 hours and 49 minutes. With just 50 US gallons of fuel left, the airplane landed on the other side of the ocean – but in Wales, not Ireland (→ Apr 8, 1931).

## Sick Australians look to the skies for help

*An injured person, rescued from the outback, is transferred to an ambulance.*

*Cloncurry, Australia, May 15*
A new method of bringing doctor to patient is being tested in Australia's northern bushland. The "flying doctor" service is run by The Revd John Flynn's Australia Inland Mission in collaboration with QANTAS. One of their D.H.50 aircraft is to fly Dr K St Vincent Welsh to any distant bedside.

# 'Smithy' flies 'Southern Cross' to Pacific triumph

*Thousands press close to see the transpacific Fokker "Southern Cross" after its landing near Brisbane, Australia.*

*Pilots Ulm and Kingsford Smith.*

*Brisbane, Australia, June 9*
Two Australian pilots have pulled off the breathtaking feat of flying across the largest ocean in the world. Charles "Smithy" Kingsford Smith and Charles Ulm, with Americans Harry Lyon and James Warner as navigator and radio operator, landed at Brisbane's Eagle Farm airfield this morning after their 7,316-mile flight from America via Hawaii and Fiji.

The four left San Francisco on May 31 in their Fokker F.VIIb-3m *Southern Cross.* Flying westward through the night they landed at Wheeler Field, Honolulu, after 27 hours in the air. But when the *Southern Cross* had been refueled it was too heavy to take off from the short runway. It had to be moved to a beach, and took to the sky again on the morning of June 3, bound for Fiji.

En route the radio failed and one engine ran badly, but the worst threat was the weather, with storm clouds forcing detours of many miles. After 34 tough flying hours they landed in Suva. When they were airborne again their compass failed; then they ran into more severe weather, including thunderstorms, which rocked the Fokker violently. The crew fought for control of the airplane and nearly lost it, but after four desperate hours the storm subsided and, 21 hours later, they touched down triumphantly at their destination (→ Sep 11).

## Manufacturers compete to build aircraft for private flyers

*Britain, April 30*
The arrival in Cape Town yesterday of Lady Mary Bailey in her de Havilland D.H.60 Moth, after a solo flight from England, highlights the extraordinary impact this little airplane has had on private flying in Britain. For several years after the Great War, those keen on flying their own airplane could easily get one from the large stocks of war-surplus machines. But this supply eventually dried up and its designs became obsolete, so the search was on for a new, safe, easy-to-fly machine.

De Havilland stood alongside other manufacturers in the race to capture this market. Avro produced the Avian, Blackburn the pretty Bluebird and de Havilland the Moth, with its ultra-light 122-pound Cirrus engine. One unusual feature of all these airplanes is their ability to fold back their wings so that they can be trailed behind cars. In France, Caudron has produced its C-232 and, in America, where the old Curtiss Jenny still reigns supreme, a wide range of companies have also built new airplanes for private buyers.

But it seems de Havilland has stolen the honors. People fly Moths from the new private clubs subsidized by Britain's Royal Aero Club, taking them on "Grand Tours" of Europe or, as Lady Bailey has done, further afield as well. Some believe that light airplanes like the Moth, which sells for around $1,500, will replace motor cars (→ Jan 10, 1929).

*An English pilot and his airplane camped down for the night in Wiltshire.*

## Italians reach Rio on non-stop flight

*Natal, Brazil, July 5*
Two Italian air force pilots have set a new long-distance non-stop record of 4,466 miles on a flight from Montecelio, near Rome, to Port Natal, Touros Bay, on the Brazilian coast, where they landed safely today. Captain Arturo Ferrarin and Major Carlo P del Prete left Rome at eight in the evening two days ago in a Savoia Marchetti pusher monoplane.

Their final destination was Rio de Janeiro. But when they reached Port Natal after the transatlantic crossing, they chose not to risk flying on and decided to stop before nightfall. The landed here at 4pm [local time] and proceeded to make some minor repairs on their airplane before taking off again for Rio. Their record breaking flight lasted a total of 58 hours and 35 minutes.

# Trippe controls Pan American Airways

*Wilmington, Del, June 27*
Juan Trippe has finally played his trump card. Pan American now has a monopoly on all the major Latin American routes.

However, the young American pilot's task has not been an easy one. He faced an uphill struggle until, on June 23, Trippe's Aviation Corporation of America agreed to merge with Montgomery's group, Pan American Airways, and the Atlantic, Gulf and Caribbean group run by Charles Stone, Richard Hoyt and Percy Rockefeller. The three groups merged by forming the Aviation Corporation of the Americas, a subtle change of name of Trippe's company. The new holding company was then incorporated under the laws of the State of Delaware, 40 per cent of the stock being held each by Trippe's and Hoyt's groups, and 20 per cent by Pan American. It was Hoyt who broke the deadlock when he laid down two basic principles: no one party was to be in control, and everything must be paid for in cash. Today, Trippe purchased Pan American's assets for $500,000, thus taking over the airline's airmail routes.

Pan American is now set to be the dominant airline in the Caribbean and South America. Trippe intends to use the exclusive Cuban landing rights he secured when the company started the mail service from Key West to Havana as a model for future expansion (→ Dec 29).

*Pan Am's "General Machado", one of the Fokkers used on the Cuban run.*

# London's new-look Croydon airport opens

*The opening of the new terminal.*

*Croydon, England, May 2*
Lady Maud Hoare, the wife of Britain's air secretary, Sir Samuel Hoare, today declared London's revamped Croydon airport officially open. It is claimed to be the first custom-built airport in the world.

In the Great War there were two airfields here, separated by a public road, 10 miles south of central London near the growing suburb of Croydon. The two were combined as London's terminal airport in March 1921, with a few sheds on one side of the road and maintenance hangars on the other. Now the whole area has been turned into one big airfield, with splendid new terminal buildings on the east side, including a first-class hotel.

# North Pole expedition ends in tragedy

*Cold but safe, four survivors of Nobile's failed North Pole expedition.*

*Norway, July 12*
Tragedy surrounds the rescue of survivors of the airship *Italia*, which crashed on to the polar ice north of King's Bay, Spitzbergen, on May 25. Veteran airship commander Umberto Nobile and his crew of 16 had completed surveys of Nicholas II Land, Gillis Land and the North Pole, and they were returning to King's Bay in strong headwinds when ice formed on the airship's exterior, jamming the elevator in a nosedown position. When the *Italia* hit the ice, the control car broke off with ten men, then the remains of the airship floated away with six others who were never seen again. An international rescue effort was mounted and supplies were dropped on June 23. Nobile was rescued the next day and two crew were rescued by Soviet icebreaker *Krassin* today, but polar explorer Roald Amundsen and five others were lost.

# Daily Mail turns an airplane into office

*London, August 1*
Time was when the only transport a newspaper reporter had was a bicycle. Now the London *Daily Mail* has bought a transport airplane and fitted it out as a flying office, with every possible kind of equipment for sending back stories from anywhere in Europe. It is a de Havilland D.H.61, powered by a 500-hp Bristol Jupiter engine. On board are not only a desk and typewriter, but also a motorcycle for speeding to the scene of events and a photographic darkroom so that prints are ready when the aircraft lands.

**Passengers of leading German airline Deutsche Luft Hansa (DLH) are welcomed by the driver of a special bus service, on hand to cut traveling time by delivering them right to Berlin's airport. DLH now offers a wide range of services from the German capital: since March last year, the company has been flying to Prague, Czechoslovakia, and Vienna, Austria.**

# US Navy carriers receive Boeing fighters

*This Boeing F3B-1 Sqn is to be embarked aboard the "USS Langley".*

*Seattle, November 11*
The last of 74 F3B-1 fighter bombers ordered by the US Navy for its aircraft carriers were delivered today by the Boeing Airplane Company. But, as the year began, there had been serious doubt that the airplane would be produced at all.

Very similar in appearance to the company's successful F2B-1, the XF3B-1 prototype was a private venture built by Boeing in 1927 to be offered to the Navy as the successor to its earlier fighter plane. Unfortunately, when it took to the air in March 1927, it proved heavier and slower than its predecessor. Boeing was given a second chance, and the prototype was returned to the factory to be redesigned. With a greater payload, longer range, higher rate of climb, speed equal to the F2B-1 and the ability to carry two .30 caliber machine guns and five 25-pound bombs, it emerged from the factory in February.

# New US carrier has a powerful punch

*San Diego, July 24*
The US Navy's latest aircraft carrier, the USS *Saratoga*, is getting a final mechanical shakedown here while her crew undergo extra training. The *Saratoga* and her sister ship, the USS *Lexington*, were originally planned to be 43,500-ton battle cruisers, armed with eight 16-inch guns instead of aircraft. They were under construction when the Washington Treaty was signed in 1922. This limited the number of battleships which each of the major powers could have, so the navy decided to convert them into carriers.

*The US Navy's "USS Saratoga".*

# Crowds flock to see Los Angeles show

*A US Navy stunt team at the show.*

*Los Angeles, September 16*
For the past eight days, a former barley field has been the center of American Aviation as more than half a million people have flocked to the National Air Races and International Aeronautical Exposition at Mines Field, Los Angeles.

In addition to the races, in which cash prizes totalling $80,000 were at stake, flying exhibitions captivated the crowds. Thrilling viewing was provided by the US Army Air Corps's "Three Musketeers" and the Navy's "Three Sea Hawks".

# Graf Zeppelin crosses the Atlantic Ocean

*Lakehurst, NJ, October 15*
The world's biggest airship, the *Graf Zeppelin*, arrived here today after crossing the Atlantic. It had left Friedrichshafen, Germany, on October 11. Commanded by Dr

*The plush fittings of the lounge.*

Hugo Eckener, the airship had a full load of 20 passengers. Six were newspaper reporters; London socialite Lady Grace Drummond, representing Hearst newspapers, was the only woman aboard. In making the flight, she became the second woman to cross the Atlantic by air and the first to do so in an airship.

Right from the start, the 775-foot aircraft appeared jinxed. Bad weather kept it from heading west across the Atlantic. Eckener followed the Rhône valley and the east coast of Spain, passing over Gibraltar before heading for Bermuda. On the third day, a squall tore part of the fabric cover from the airship's 60-foot-long horizontal fin.

Eckener idled the engines and crew members, including his son, climbed on to the fin to make repairs. In order to prevent further damage, the airship flew at reduced speed for the rest of the trip.

# Death strikes Santos-Dumont fans off Rio

*Rio de Janeiro, December 4*
Rio de Janeiro's high society is in a state of shock. What was supposed to be a joyful occasion has been marred by tragedy.

Six members of the country's intelligentsia have been killed in an airplane crash as they flew to welcome the aviation pioneer Alberto Santos-Dumont back to his homeland. The six Brazilians had flown out over Rio de Janeiro Bay in a large seaplane to greet Santos-Dumont's liner, the *Cap Arcona*; while the aircraft was banking, one wing tip of the three-engined Junkers G 24 hit the water and the plane broke up in a huge explosion of spray. All six passengers were killed outright.

An already ailing and distressed Santos-Dumont has now asked local officials to cancel all celebrations in his honor.

**The KLM desk at Croydon airport's new terminal: passengers can book tickets for the many destinations covered by the Dutch airline.**

# ...ted seaplane speeds mail to US

*..., September 13*
...periment in speeding mail ... the Atlantic was successfully ...pleted today, when an aircraft ...apulted from ocean liner *Ile de ...ance* landed in New York har-...r, reducing the time for mail ...om Europe by a whole day.

It is a joint operation between the ...ompagnie Général Transatlan-...ique and the Société Transatlan-...ique Aérienne. A single-engined

Lioré et Oliver LeO 198 amphibian biplane, strengthened to withstand catapulting, was used in the experiment. It was launched from the stern of the *Ile de France* 466 miles from New York, and the flight took 4 hours 15 minutes. This hybrid air and sea arrangement is an ingenious way to speed the mail but, before long, aircraft may be able to span the Atlantic direct, speeding it up even more.

*The mailplane is launched from the French ocean liner "Ile-de-France".*

# Crew acclaimed for perilous sea flight

*New Zealand, September 11*
"Panic was very near – I almost lost my head," said Charles Kingsford Smith, the Australian long-distance aviator, who landed today at Christchurch after a wild, first-ever crossing of the Tasman Sea. While the flight was far shorter than his recent epic Pacific crossing, the Tasman Sea's weather is notorious and severely tested his Fokker Trimotor *Southern Cross*.

He took off on a pleasant evening yesterday with co-pilot Charles Ulm, navigator Litchfield, and a radio operator from New Zealand, T McWilliam. However, the night brought worse weather. The airspeed indicator iced up, the wireless was plagued by lightning and the aircraft was tossed around by turbulent air. A relieved crew landed at 9.20am after a flight of 14 hours 12 minutes (→ Jun 26, 1930).

# RAF punishes Arab rebel chief in Aden

*Aden [South Yemen], December*
Britain's Royal Air Force (RAF) has imposed the colonial will on another rebellious tribal leader. The latest unruly subject to be punished is the Imam of Yemen, a warrior prince from the hills extending from Yemen to the port of Aden, the vital refueling stop for British ships en route to India.

With 6,000 regular troops commanded by Turkish mercenaries and as many guerrillas, the imam could have tied up a land army for years and cost Britain millions of pounds. Since January, however, the RAF has had the job of defending Aden. Only 12 RAF bombers of Group Captain W G S Mitchell's Aden Command were needed to convince the Imam, for now, that the desert and mountains are no defense. The cost was slight: one airplane accident.

# La Cierva crosses the Channel in triumph for first international flight of autogyro

*The autogyro comes of age: could it become a familiar sight in our skies?*

*Paris, September 18*
Juan de La Cierva, inventor of the autogyro, pulled off a triumph today when he flew one of his unusual machines – the C.8L-III, powered by a 180-hp Lynx engine – across the English Channel with a passenger on board. La Cierva was accompanied on this first international flight by autogyro by Henri Bouché, editor of French magazine *L'Aéronautique*.

They crossed the English coast at a height of 4,000 feet and landed at Calais before flying on to Le Bourget airport near Paris, where La Cierva gave a flying display, in particular showing off the autogyro's ability to land easily in confined spaces (→ Oct 8, 1929).

**Deutsche Luft Hansa offers service as good as that on the railroads.**

The Soviet Polikarpov Po-2 began its long career in 1928, and when it ceased, to be built 25 years later, some 40,000 had rolled off the production lines.

There were numerous variants of the CAMS 55 military flying boat, and 29 were still serving when the Second World War broke out in September 1939.

Though it first flew in 1928, the Hawker Hart led to over 3,000 aircraft of some 56 versions.

The functional Vickers Vildebeeste torpedo-bomber first flew in April.

Gloster's Jupiter-engined Gambet fighter remained a prototype only.

There were many variants of the Lioré et Olivier LeO H-25 series of bombers, including seaplanes, and the type remained in service until as late as 1940.

Built with record breaking in mind: the Fairey long-range monoplane. It had a 570-hp Napier Lion engine.

The Gloster Gnatsnapper was an experimental deck-landing fighter.

The Bristol Bulldog II first flew in 1928 and joined up with the RAF.

An experimental metal aircraft: the underpowered Beardmore Inflexible.

The versatile Fairchild 71 proved a good "bush" aircraft in Canada.

Boeing's Model 80A grew from the Model 80. It carried 18 passengers and had P&W Hornet engines.

The Consolidated Commodore was a commercial transport development of the PY-1 patrol flying boat which won a US Navy design competition.

The epitome of the rich man's airplane: Grover Loening's Air Yacht.

Boeing Air Transport's Model 40B mail carrier: a modified Model 40.

The Bellanca CH series of cabin monoplanes was popular in the US.

High twin-tail-booms characterized Sikorsky's S-38 amphibian biplane.

Boeing's experimental XP-9 fighter relied on ample external bracing.

The Cierva C.8L-II was the first autogyro to cross the Channel.

The Kalinin K-4 six-passenger airliner saw only limited production.

The proven Ford Trimotor formula was further developed in the 5-AT, which could accommodate 14 or 15 passengers within its corrugated fuselage.

The Boeing Model 95 was designed as an express mail and cargo carrier.

Breda's neat Ba 15 monoplane tourer – light aircraft, Italian-style.

C W Holman poses proudly with his sporting Laird Speedwing LC-R.

Transcontinental travel in comfort: the Travel Air 6000 from the US.

Focke-Wulf's tail-first F 19a Ente, which made its first flight in 1928, is demonstrated at Hanworth, England, during a European tour in 1931.

Imperial Airways' first Short Calcutta flying boat floats on the Thames at Westminster, London, awaiting an inspection by Members of Parliament.

# 1929

362mph
Italy
Giuseppe Motta
Macchi M.67
Aug 22, 1929

4,989.26 miles
France
D. Costes, and P. Codos
Breguet 19
Dec 17, 1929

41,795ft
Germany
Willi Neuenhofen
Junkers W 34
May 26, 1929

123,457lb
Germany
Dornier
Do X

1,900hp
Great Britain
Rolls-Royce
R

**Warsaw, January 1**
Polish airlines are nationalized, creating one commercial operator, Polskie Linje Lotnicze [Polish Air Lines] or LOT.

**Nice, France, January 1**
George Holt Thomas, son of owner of the *Daily Graphic* and founder of Airco, dies.

**Croydon, England, January 10**
Lady Mary Bailey lands to complete an 18,000-mile round-trip to Cape Town and back.

**Sydney, January 23**
Aircraft carrier HMAS *Albatross*, the first warship built in Australia, is commissioned; she is equipped to carry six Supermarine Seagull amphibians.

**USA, January 25**
Pan American Grace Airways (PANAGRA) is incorporated; jointly owned by Pan Am and shipping and banking corporation W R Grace & Company, the airline will operate an airmail service between the Panama Canal and Argentina (→ May 19).

**New York, February 5**
Frank Hawks and Oscar Grubb land their Lockheed Air Express after a record flight from Los Angeles of 18 hours 20 minutes.

**Washington, DC, February 28**
An amendment to the Air Commerce Act, effective in June, provides for federal licensing of flying schools.

**Croydon, England, March 30**
Imperial Airways' silver-winged Armstrong Whitworth Argosy, *City of Glasgow*, leaves for Basel, Switzerland, on the first leg of the airline's service to India (→ Apr 6).

**Karachi, India, April 6**
The airmail of the first Imperial Airways service to India, which left Croydon on March 30, arrives in a Short Calcutta flying boat, the *City of Alexandria*; it was transferred between airplanes en route.→

**Paris, April 9**
French airline Air Union starts to operate a nightly service from Paris to London.

**Karachi, India, April 27**
Sqn Leader A G Jones-Williams and Flight Lieutenant N H Jenkins complete the first non-stop flight from England to India; they flew the 4,130 miles in 50 hours 37 minutes in a Fairey Long-Range Monoplane (→ Dec 16).

**Langley Field, Va, May 13**
Harold Pitcairn lands after flying from Pennsylvania in a Cierva C.8 Mk IV autogyro.

**Mollendo, Peru, May 19**
A Fairchild monoplane of new airline PANAGRA completes the first direct air connection between the USA and Peru; on May 14, a mailplane left Miami, Florida, for Cristobal, whence a Pan Am S-38 on contract to PANAGRA took the mail to Talara, where the Fairchild took over.

**Englewood, NJ, May 20**
Charles Lindbergh marries Anne, daughter of Dwight W Morrow, US ambassador to Mexico and author of an influential report on American aviation (→ Oct 27).

**Panama, May 22**
Pan American Airways inaugurates a new passenger service. The journey from Miami, Florida, takes 56 hours, with stops at Belize and Managua. The aircrafts are F.VII/3ns.

**English Channel, June 17**
Imperial Airways' Handley Page W.10 *City of Ottawa* crashes into the sea, killing four. Up to now the Handley Page fleet has flown 3.9 million miles without an injury or a fatality to any of its passengers.

**Caracas, July 3**
Venezuela's parliament approves a five-year exclusive airmail contract to French company Aéropostale (→ Mar 31, 1931).

**Spokane, Wash, July 10**
Nick Mamer and Art Walker land after a 7,200-mile non-stop return flight to New York in their airplane *Spokane Sun God*, which was refueled in flight.

**Lisbon, July 11**
Spaniard Luis Rambaud Goma lands in a Cierva C-12 autogyro, after flying 350 miles non-stop from Madrid.

**Washington, DC, September 1**
The Aeronautics Branch of the US Department of Commerce rules that all licensed US aircraft used in foreign commerce must display the international designation "N" on their wings and rudder, followed by prescribed symbols.

**Teterboro, NJ, September 11**
The Fokker F-32 four-engined luxury airliner makes its first US flight at Teterboro Airport.

**Amsterdam, September 12**
Dutch airline KLM inaugurates an experimental, long-range airmail service to Djakarta. The 9,000-mile trip, flown by a Fokker F.VII, takes 12 days (→ Dec 12).

**Hampshire, England, September 12**
Just days after the British triumph in the Schneider Trophy race, Squadron Leader Orlebar sets a new world speed record of 357.7mph in a Supermarine S.6 floatplane.

**United States, October 8**
Juan de La Cierva demonstrates the first autogyro manufactured by the Pitcairn-Cierva Autogiro Company of America (→ Nov 11, 1930).

**New York, October 21**
The Colonial Flying Service and Scully Walton Ambulance Co organize USA's first civilian air ambulance service.

**Middlesex, England, October 25**
Norman Macmillan pilots the Fairey Fox II light bomber on its first flight at Northolt.

**Mediterranean Sea, October 31**
The Italian government withdraws Imperial Airways' right to use Italian ports; the British airline refuses to share profits on its Genoa-Alexandria seaplane route with the Italians.

**New York, November 1**
The Tupolev ANT-4 *Strana Sovietov* [Land of the Soviets] heavy bomber lands here after a 12,300-mile flight from Moscow. It left on August 23.

**Cape Town, S Africa, November 11**
British staff arrive on a joint Imperial Airways/Air Ministry survey of a route between England and South Africa.

**Canada, November 30**
Western Canada Airways merges with the Aviation Corporation of Canada to form Canadian Airways Ltd.

**Netherlands, December 12**
KLM ends an experimental two-weekly mail service to the Dutch East Indies (→ Feb 16, 1931).

**Siam, December 16**
Air Asia opens its airmail service between Bangkok and Saigon; operated by Potez 32s, it takes two days (→ Jul 8, 1930).

**Tunisia, December 16**
Squadron Leader A G Jones-Williams and Flight Lieutenant N H Jenkins are killed when their Fairey Long-Range Monoplane crashes during an attempt to set a new long-distance record for a straight-line flight.

**Karachi, India, Dec 20**
The Indian State Air Service, an extension of Imperial Airways' routes, opens its inaugural service, from Karachi to Delhi.

*A Pan Am advertising poster shows an S-40 flying boat loading passengers for one of the company's many long-range routes.* ▶

# 'Question Mark' finds endurance answer

*The crew of the "Question Mark" and tankers pose with fuel for the flight.*

*Los Angeles, January 7*
Two pilots of the US Army Air Corps (USAAC), Major Carl Spaatz and Captain Ira C Eaker, today claimed a world flight endurance record by staying aloft for more than 150 hours. The two pilots and their three-man crew used a mid-air refueling technique first developed in 1923.

Their Fokker C-2A, powered by three 220-hp Wright Whirlwind engines and called *Question Mark*, took off from Los Angeles on New Year's Day. It was refueled in flight from one of a team of back-up airplanes, and Spaatz and his crew landed back at Los Angeles 150 hours 40 minutes 15 seconds after take-off. The endurance record is one of a number set in recent years by the USAAC – 18 months ago two pilots set a non-stop long-distance record of 2,418 miles.

# The Chinese get their 'Spirit of St Louis'

*China's "Chu Kiang", based on the four-seat Ryan Brougham.*

*Peking [Beijing], January 14*
China has acquired one of its first aircraft, an exact copy of the Ryan Brougham, and thus resembling to Charles Lindbergh's *Spirit of St Louis*. Piloted by Chang Wai-chung, the 250-hp *Chu Kiang* recently completed a 2,500-mile flight across China. Equipped with floats, the airplane followed a route marked out by rivers, canals and lakes. The first airplane built here was a two-seater biplane reconnaissance trainer, constructed for the Kwangtung revolutionary government in 1923.

# Air force lifts civilians out of Afghanistan

*Kabul, February 25*
The world's first major air evacuation came to an end today when Britain's Royal Air Force (RAF) flew out the last of 586 civilians from the high, windswept airfield of Kabul to the safety of India.

The airlift, which involved nationals of about 20 countries, has hit the headlines worldwide. It took place as a result of a rebellion against Afghanistan's King Amanullah by Muslim fundamentalists, who saw the westernized ruler as a puppet of the British. By December, Kabul was under siege. The airlift began on December 23 and involved an RAF fleet of seven lumbering Vickers Victorias and one Handley Page airplane, which flew a total of 28,160 miles over high mountains (→Apr 25, 1932).

*Royal Air Force transports used to airlift foreign citizens from Kabul.*

# French pilots safe after Andes flight

*Chile, March 12*
Two French pilots and a passenger have turned up safe and sound 48 hours after it was feared their airplane had crashed high up in the Andes. Jean Mermoz and his mechanic Andre Collenot, flying with Count de La Vaulx, took off from San Antonio on March 2 in their Latécoère 25 parasol-winged, single-engined monoplane, bound for Santiago.

Engine trouble forced them down on a 10,000-foot high plateau, but they finally arrived in the Chilean capital. On the return trip they decided to fly a more northerly route. Trouble began at 13,000 feet over the Andes, when gale-force winds forced their plane down on a rocky precipice; the undercarriage was bent, and then the water pipes froze up and split. Mermoz and Collenot took three days to repair the plane, using whatever they had on board, including string and strips of clothing.

When it came to take off, Mermoz knew that one false maneuver would send them all into the abyss. The take-off was successful, and Mermoz was able to glide down to a landing site at Copiapo, 200 miles north of Santiago (→May 13, 1930).

# 'Lindy' and fiancée land with a bump

*Mexico, March 3*
Pioneer aviator Colonel Charles Lindbergh and his fiancée Anne Morrow, daughter of the US ambassador to Mexico, had a narrow escape today when their light airplane crash-landed at Valbuena Field. Lindbergh dislocated his right shoulder, but Anne escaped uninjured.

The couple had flown for a private picnic and were returning home in a borrowed 110-hp Stinson Junior monoplane, when one of its landing wheels fell off. The ace pilot managed to bring the Stinson down on one wheel, but after some yards the naked axle touched ground. The wing tipped down and the airplane turned over. Lindbergh crawled out of the upside-down plane and then Anne emerged unscathed. It turned out that her fiancé, seeing he would have to crash-land, had packed cushions around her to soften the impact. Although the accident was hardly the fault of Lindbergh, the Mexican ministry of war apparently felt it should protect his reputation. Soon after the crash, the ministry sent troops to confiscate still and motion-picture film from photographers who had witnessed the incident (→May 20).

# Trains join planes for coast-to-coast

*Los Angeles, July 8*

Transcontinental Air Transport (TAT) today became the second US airline to offer an airplane-and-train service from New York to Los Angeles. Universal Aviation Corporation first offered the service on June 14. TAT has spent more than a year in preparing for the inauguration of the route, which was planned by a technical committee chaired by transatlantic hero Colonel Charles Lindbergh.

Lindbergh is very familiar with coast-to-coast flying from his work as an airmail pilot, and has chosen routes and emergency landing fields for the Robertson Aircraft Corporation. TAT will use Ford Trimotors to transport passengers during the daytime flights. For the overnight portion of the journey, passengers will transfer to trains with sleeping cars on the Pennsylvania and the Atchison, Topeka and Santa Fe Railroads. The journey will take about two days.

Prominent industrialists formed TAT specifically to provide transcontinental transportation on May 16 last year. Substantial holdings in TAT are owned by companies with interests in aviation and transportation, such as Wright, Curtiss and Pennsylvania Railroad. TAT's president, Clement M Keys, heads the Curtiss Group (→Jul 16, 1930).

*TAT's first eastbound departure is seen off by Mary Pickford (with flowers).*

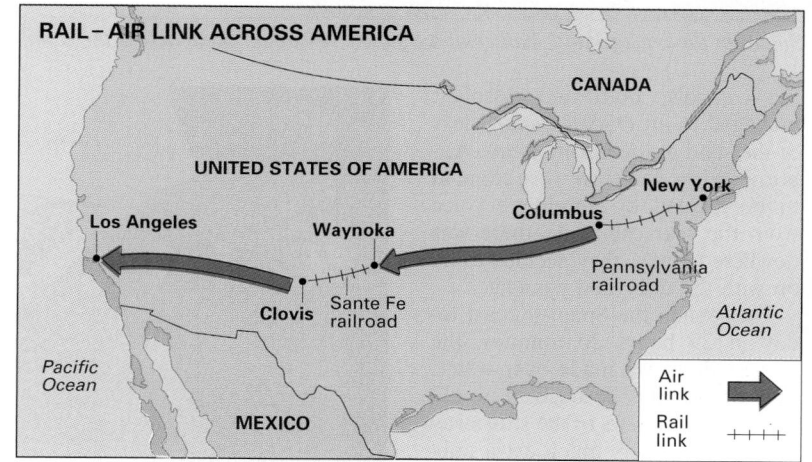

**RAIL–AIR LINK ACROSS AMERICA**

CANADA

UNITED STATES OF AMERICA

New York

Columbus

Los Angeles    Waynoka

Clovis    Sante Fe railroad    Pennsylvania railroad

Atlantic Ocean

Pacific Ocean

MEXICO

Air link
Rail link

# Ed Link invents new ground-based trainer for pilots

*Binghamton, NY, April 14*

Airline pilots can now now learn the basic skills needed to fly before they even leave the ground, thanks to a device patented today by Binghamton resident Ed Link, son of the owner of Link Piano and Organ Company, which makes player-pianos and nickelodeons.

Link, who is a pilot and aircraft owner, has been working on his flight trainer in the basement of the family factory for a year and a half. It consists of a cockpit fitted with the basic controls and instruments found in any airplane. The cockpit is mounted on a joint, which allows movement in any direction, and bellows and motors simulate the motions of flight in response to the stick and rudder controls. Link claims the trainer will reduce the time it takes to learn to fly; he also sees it as a big attraction for amusement parks.

# Bigger is better for air industry giants

*USA, August*

Merger mania is overtaking the US airline and airplane manufacturing industries as Wall Street flexes it financial muscles in the air transport business. In the process, two of the great pioneering companies in American aviation, those of Wright Brothers and Glenn Curtiss, have been brought together this month in a single $220m concern: the Curtiss-Wright Corporation. Such giant companies, headed by financiers, such as Clement M Keys of Curtiss and Richard Hoyt of Wright, and including airlines, airframe and engine manufacturing interests, will be able to finance expansion in the industry.

With passenger traffic set to increase and new, longer range aircraft planned, the airline business is becoming transcontinental, with little room for the smaller, local operators. At the beginning of last year there were 25 airlines in America's skies; now there are just 14 and the mergers seem destined to continue.

# Three aircraft (and a train) complete scheduled service to India

*One of the D.H.66 Hercules aircraft used on Imperial's latest service.*

*Karachi, India, April 6*

Britain's Imperial Airways today completed its first scheduled passenger flight from London to India. The service has been planned for many years and is seen as a major addition to the British Empire's air routes. The service began on March 30 when an Armstrong Whitworth Argosy, the *City of Glasgow*, took off from London's Croydon airport carrying three VIP passengers and about 1,200 letters. After a stop at Paris it went on to Basel, Switzerland, where passengers boarded a train for Genoa, Italy. From Genoa one of Imperial's new Short Calcutta flying boats, the *City of Alexandria*, continued the route via Ostia, Naples, Corfu, Athens, Suda Bay and Tobruk to Alexandria in Egypt.

Here one of the passengers and the mail transferred to a D.H.66 Hercules landplane, the *City of Jerusalem*, which, after more stops and a delay due to sandstorms, reached Karachi today. Tomorrow another Hercules, the *City of Baghdad*, will leave with three passengers and mail on the return flight (→Feb 28, 1931).

# Stowaway joins transatlantic jaunt

*The crew are welcomed after arriving in Spain; in the background, bulls pull a Spanish rescue airplane across the sand.*

**Comillas, Spain, June 14**
Three French airmen fought fiercely to get airborne for a non-stop Atlantic flight yesterday, unaware that the extra weight was caused by a stowaway. The trio of Assolant, Lefèvre and Lotti were destined for Spain from Old Orchard beach, Maine. The stowaway, American journalist Arthur Schreiber, slipped aboard their Bernard 191 G.R.H.2 *Oiseau Canari* while the crew were bidding their supporters farewell.

First trouble came when, with the engine roaring flat out, the fuel-heavy machine refused to leave the ground. Fortunately, the beach was long and, with a mighty heave of

the controls, Lotti and Assolant managed to lift *Oiseau Canari* clear of the sand at the last moment. Airborne at last, the crew were stunned to be greeted by Shreiber's voice from the rear cabin. As there was nowhere to land, they decided to fly on with the uninvited passenger.

They made the Spanish coast today in 29 hours 20 minutes, the longest flight yet made over water. The aircraft has been given a wild reception and news of the stowaway brought the flyers much extra publicity. Shreiber, having stolen a ride, has now stolen the show, much to the chagrin of his unwilling French hosts.

*The flyers pose with the stowaway.*

**Britain's graphic artists make the most of the glamor of the air. "The Ace" (r) is a board game.**

## Farman pilot soars to altitude record

*France, July 26*
Johnny Burtin, test pilot for French aviation company Farman, today set a new world altitude record of 26,531 feet for airplanes with a 1-ton load on board. He was flying a modified version of the Breguet 19 powered by a 12-cylinder 550-hp Farman engine, coupled to a supercharger built by Rateau-Leparmentier.

Burtin's successful flight also had a commercial purpose. At high altitudes, fuel consumption drops considerably and wind resistance is reduced, making high-altitude flying more economical and therefore more profitable.

## Fearless Doolittle makes 'blind' flight

*New York, September 24*
Fog, the greatest enemy to safe, reliable and frequent air travel, may be a problem of the past, following an important flight by Lieutenant James Doolittle today. Fog has grounded airplanes and caused many to crash-land. It has made schedules impossible to keep and lost much revenue for airlines.

Pilots encountering fog can use a gyroscopic turn-and-bank indicator and a magnetic compass to fly blind. But landing blind has usually spelt disaster; Doolittle set out to prove it can be accomplished safely. He took off from Mitchell Field today (with "sighted" safety pilot Benjamin S Kelsey), flew for 15 miles over an irregular course and landed, all without seeing anything outside the cockpit of his specially prepared Consolidated NY-2.

This was no stunt, but the culmination of nearly a year's careful research at the Full Flight Laboratory set up by Harry Guggenheim and Captain Emory Land. Crucial to the today's success was the development by Paul Kollsman of an accurate barometric altimeter capable of measuring height within a few feet, a Sperry artificial horizon and directional gyroscope, and a radio receiver and vibrating reed indicator to pick up approach signals from the long-range beacons at Mitchell Field (→Sep 3, 1932).

# Tanager supreme in safe-airplane contest

*The winner's amazing lower wings have variable incidence as seen here.*

**New York, November 22**

The Curtiss Company has just won a hotly-disputed $100,000 international competition to design and build the safest possible aircraft, beating entries from the United Kingdom, Germany and France. The British airplane vying for the prize money was the Handley Page *Gugnunc*. The American entry to the competition, sponsored by the Guggenheim Foundation, is known as the *Tanager*.

This high-winged, single-engined biplane won the low speed test by flying at only 34.8mph without stalling. This extraordinary performance is made possible by the airplane's full-span flaps and ailerons and its variable-incidence lower wings, which combine to increase lift by as much as 50 per cent. It also performed well during the compulsory high speed test, flying at 109,9mph. The *Tanager* is powered by a 185-hp Curtiss Challenger five-cylinder radial engine. This is powerful enough for it to fly over a 33-foot high obstacle placed only 500 feet from where it starts its take-off roll.

Curtiss is delighted with the result of the competition, although the company needs to find buyers for the *Tanager*, which cost more than $100,000 to develop. Unfortunately, the US is in the throes of an economic crisis.

# Wireless beacons signal the way for flyers

*A wireless receiver of c.1929.*

**Abbeville, France, October 1**

A system for guiding airplanes by wireless, developed by French engineers, was tested for the first time here today. Using a rotating wireless beacon, the system is able to plot an airplane's position accurately to within two degrees of the London/Paris route. The beacon sweeps through 360 degrees once a minute, emitting a tone for 50 seconds, followed by its identification signal. By using a stopwatch to measure the time elapsed between due north, when the tone is loudest, and the point when his equipment detects it passing his aircraft, the pilot can work out his bearing. The system is not yet able to measure the distance of the aircraft from the beacon (→ Jun 24, 1930).

# RAF wins Schneider Trophy for second time

**Southampton, England, Sep 7**

Britain retained the coveted Schneider trophy today, fighting off a strong Italian challenge and setting a world speed record of 328.629mph. The US Navy refused to let Lieutenant Al Williams compete as a private individual.

Britain won with a new streamlined seaplane, designed by R J Mitchell, with a supercharged Rolls-Royce 1,900-hp engine burning a potent mix of fuels. The aircraft, the Supermarine S.6, is a low-wing monoplane flown by Royal Air Force pilots and known to be capable of much higher speeds than those achieved today.

In perfect weather, Flying Officer H R D Waghorn started first, used full throttle to lift out of the water and lapped the course at up to 331mph. On the last lap his engine cut out and he landed short, unaware that he was in fact flying an extra, seventh, lap of honor. The Italians were hit by dangerous de-

*The program issued for the contest.*

fects. Lieutenants R Cadringher and G Monti, in Macchi M.67s, were choked and blinded by exhaust fumes, a fault thought to have caused a death in practice recently. Monti was also severely scalded by engine coolant (→ Jan 30, 1931).

*An RAF pilot who wins the Schneider Trophy should not get his feet wet.*

# 'Graf Zeppelin' tours the world in 21 days

**Lakehurst, NJ, August 29**

The first circumnavigation of the globe by airship was completed today when the German *Graf Zeppelin* arrived at Lakehurst, which it left on August 8 on its 21,150-mile journey. It has completed the flight in 21 days 5 hours 31 minutes, although actual flying time was 12 days 12 hours 40 minutes. The airship flew at an average speed of 70.23mph. W R Hearst, the American newspaper magnate, financed the trip in exchange for exclusive coverage rights for his pressmen. Among the passengers were the US Navy's dirigible expert, Commander Charles E Rosendahl, Australian Arctic explorer Sir Hubert Wilkins and scientific and Soviet and Japanese naval representatives.

# Junkers builds metal giant of the sky

*The enormous and extremely luxurious G 38 designed by Hugo Junkers.*

*Dessau, Germany, November 6*
German airplane makers have come up with a second gigantic all-metal airliner this year – the Junkers G 38.

The impressive new machine, which made its maiden flight here today, is a landplane. Though large by any standard, its metallic fuselage is dwarfed by enormous wings. Like Dornier, Junkers has pioneered the use of metal in aircraft construction, particularly the tough alloy Duralumin. The Junkers G 38 has a wingspan of 144 feet with four Junkers engines, two of 400hp and two of 750hp. Twenty-six of the 34 passengers it will carry for Deutsche Luft Hansa will be accommodated in the fuselage, with cabins for three more in each root of the wings, and two seated right in the nose. The six passengers flying in the wings enjoy excellent visibility tanks to the windows built into the leading edges.

# Dornier flying boat has twelve engines

*The massive Dornier Do X flying boat can fly at a speed of 130mph.*

*Lake Constance, October 21*
A German giant took of from the Swiss side of this lake today with its first load of passengers. The Dornier Do X flying boat, the world's largest and heaviest aircraft, took off with 150 passengers, a crew of ten and nine stowaways.

Designed by Claude Dornier, the flying boat was completed at the Altenrhein works, on the Swiss side of Lake Constance. The Do X, which flew for the first time on July 25, has a wingspan of 157 feet, and is powered by a dozen 525-hp Bristol Jupiter engines arranged in push-pull pairs above the wings. The ten-man crew is housed in the upper deck, while the lower deck has been split into seven particularly luxurious lounges. Its streamlined hull gives it good landing and take-off performance, despite the weight of the 21,099 gallons of fuel it carries on take-off, stored in its six huge tanks.

# New York crowd hails South Pole flight

*Antarctica, November 29*
In a perilous 17-hour 26-minute flight over a forbidding landscape, Commander Richard Byrd, USN, this morning led the first flight over the South Pole. Byrd, who left from New Zealand, helped to set up a base in Antarctica, practically on the same spot where Norwegian explorer Roald Amundsen had stopped 18 years ago.

Byrd took off from his base, Little America, on the Ross Ice Shelf in his Ford 4-AT Trimotor, named *Floyd Bennett* after the pilot who flew with Byrd over the North Pole in 1926. To clear the ice cliffs of the Queen Maud Range, Byrd and his crew had to throw out their survival packs to lighten the aircraft. Circling over the pole, they dropped a stone from Bennett's grave wrapped in the US flag, and then reported their success to base by wireless. The message was instantly relayed to Times Square and rebroadcast to a huge waiting crowd over loudspeakers.

*Commander Byrd's base, Little America, is a place of refuge in the Antarctic.*

# Fighter makes night landing on carriers

*Valletta, Malta, November 26*
Last night, a Royal Navy pilot from HMS *Courageous*, Owen Cathcart-Jones, carried out one of the most difficult flying maneuvers: landing on an aircraft carrier in darkness. It is the first time a fighter has made a night landing on an aircraft carrier. For this experiment, he flew one of the Royal Navy's best established fighters, a Fairey Flycatcher. He took off from Hal Far airfield and touched down uneventfully on the carrier's deck while she was at anchor in Valletta harbor. Jones's most celebrated flying exploit to date took place earlier this year when he bombed the bridge of flagship HMS *Queen Elizabeth* with lavatory paper.

# Six die at Croydon

*Surrey, England, November 6*
The death of six people in an air crash today has come as a blow to the reputation for safety held by the airline Deutsche Luft Hansa. Eyewitnesses in nearby Caterham reported hearing explosions and, according to one, a "noise like the crushing of tin cans" as the Junkers G 24, which had just taken off from Croydon for Berlin, hit the hillside at Foster Downs and blew up less than five miles from the airport. An RAF officer at the scene said the monoplane was seen "struggling to gain height" (→ Jul 1, 1931).

# New British airship

*Bedfordshire, England, October 2*
The first of Britain's two new airships was unveiled at Cardington today. The 722 foot-long, diesel-powered R.101 was built under state management, while its sister ship, the R.100, was privately constructed. The R.101 has attracted great publicity, mainly because of its size: 2 miles of girders, 6 miles of booms and 8 miles of struts were used to build a structure held together by 450,000 rivets and laced with 11 miles of cable and 27 miles of tubing. The airship's cost is expected to reach £700,000 (→ Oct 14).

## Pan Am bathes in Lindbergh's glory

*New York, October 27*

Pan American Airways chief Juan Trippe is steadily advancing the influence of his airline through Central and South America. In doing so, he has at his disposal the expertise of one of the world's greatest and best-known aviators, Colonel Charles Lindbergh, whom he hired as a consultant earlier this year both for his flying expertise and for his publicity value.

Lindbergh was heavily involved with opening up the Cuba/Panama airmail route recently. First he surveyed the route, flying over the mountains and jungles to identify sites for airfields and navigation equipment, then he made the inaugural flight. Two years after his solo transatlantic epic, he is still mobbed by cheering crowds wherever he lands. When he gets out of an airplane that carries the Pan Am logo, this popular hero generates goodwill for the company with both government officials and with the local population (→ Aug 26, 1931).

## Hawaii gets own island-hopping airline

*Betty Judd, daughter of the governor, baptizes one of the two Sikorsky S-38s.*

*Honolulu, November 11*

A new airline to link the islands of Hawaii was born this morning. With thousands of people looking on, Hawaii's governor Lawrence M Judd hailed "the march of progress" while his daughter Betty christened the new airplanes of Inter-Island Airways. Forty US Army Air Corps aircraft flew overhead as part of the festivities. The airline will use two twin-engine Sikorsky S-38 amphibians to fly up to eight passengers from John Rogers Airport here on Oahu to the islands of Maui, Hawaii and Kauai.

## Fritz von Opel invents and flies a rocket-driven craft

*Germany, September 30*

Fritz von Opel, one of Germany's leading automobile manufacturers, briefly turned his hand to aeronautical experiment today by making a spectacular flight in a rocket-powered glider: the Opel-Sander-Hatry Rak I. Trailing a billowing plume of smoke, he made a dipping and diving flight of about a mile, reaching a speed of between 95 and 100mph before gliding in to land. The aircraft is powered by sixteen Sander solid fuel rockets, each of which supplies 55lb thrust, arranged in banks of four just behind the pilot's seat. They were fired in stages. It proved an extremely difficult machine to control.

Detractors say that Opel made the flight purely for the publicity. If that is so, then he certainly succeeded, for an enormous crowd gathered to watch. It is the third Opel rocket plane; the first, the *Ente* [Duck], was a tail-first design conceived by Professor A M Lippisch and flown by Fritz Stamer over 1,400 yards in 70 seconds on June 11, 1928.

The Rak I was built with funds provided by the German Society for Space Travel. Interest in using rocket power to fly into space has been growing ever since French aviation pioneer Robert Esnault-Pelterie gave a lecture on the subject on 8 June 1927 entitled *The Exploration by Rockets of the Upper Atmosphere and the Possibility of Interplanetary Travel.*

## Private-enterprise airship floats to compete with state effort

*Humberside, England, Nov 16*

The first flight took place today of Britain's second new giant rigid airship, the R.100. Built by the privately-owned Airship Guarantee Company, it is cheaper than the state-built R.101 and has been less publicized, yet may prove the better airship. The R.100 has been built with largely semi-skilled labor in the wartime shed here at Howden, which was so cold in winter that ice formed on the airship's girders. Conversely, the R.101 was assembled by skilled workers at the government-owned works at Cardington, Bedfordshire. The company has also had to bear overrun costs on a very tight budget. One compensation has been the leadership of Commander Burney and the presence of brilliant designer Dr Barnes Wallis.

The R.100 is designed along traditional lines, except for its unique criss-cross skeleton structure, which gives it great strength. Its six engines give 4,200hp, compared with the R.101's 2,900hp, allowing twice the load (→ Jan 16, 1930).

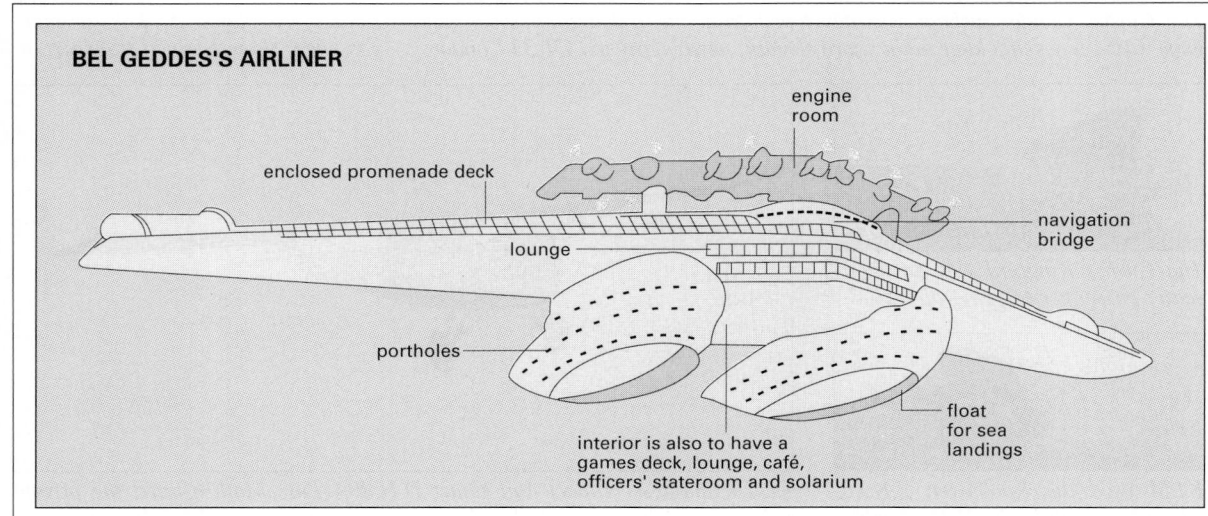

**BEL GEDDES'S AIRLINER**

enclosed promenade deck

engine room

navigation bridge

lounge

portholes

interior is also to have a games deck, lounge, café, officers' stateroom and solarium

float for sea landings

## Colossal luxury

This huge airliner has been conceived by American industrial designer Norman Bel Geddes to transport "a thousand luxury lovers from New York to Paris fast". Bel Geddes envisages a 700-ton airplane with a wingspan of 577 feet, an extra wing to carry 20 engines and two pontoons to hold crew, lifeboats and two smaller airplanes. The machine will hold 451 passengers and 155 crew. However, the machine's price-tag of $9 million may put off potential investors.

The Hall XPH-1 patrol flying boat attracted small orders from the US Navy. A couple of Wright R-1820 Cyclone radial engines provided the power.

The US Fokker F-32: the US's first four-engined commercial airliner.

Cessna's Model A was the company's first production aeroplane.

The US-designed Fokker F-14 was unusual in having a parasol wing.

Consolidated's Fleetster: a parasol wing and monocoque fuselage.

The Aeronca C single-seater in an unusual form: as a seaplane.

Only one Wasp-engined Heinkel He 57 amphibian was constructed.

Dornier's ten-passenger Do K displays its unusual low-slung engines.

Twelve engines mounted overwing in tandem pairs made the ponderously massive Dornier Do X unmistakable. It was the largest flying boat in the world.

The Boeing Model 203 was designed to serve as a single-engined trainer.

Macchi's M.67 seaplane failed to win the Schneider trophy in 1929.

The Avro Tutor was destined to have a long career as an RAF trainer.

The Curtiss Condor airliner was developed from the B-2 night-bomber but gave way a few years later to the more elegant, newly designed CT-32 Condor.

Andrei Tupolev's ANT-9: a nine-passenger three-engined transport.

Two Fokker F.IXs went to KLM, and it was also built as a bomber.

The Curtiss Kingbird was an eight-seater passenger-carrying aircraft.

The Kellett Autogyros: based on principles laid down by de La Cierva.

KLM used the Koolhoven F.K.40, which was built in the Netherlands.

De Havilland's compact and smart D.H.80A Puss Moth offered the private owner the luxury of an enclosed cabin to protect him from the elements.

The massive Junkers G 38 could accommodate six of its 34 passengers in the roots of its wings. The two built served with Deutsche Luft Hansa.

In the US, Stearman's C-3R Speedster sporting biplane fought for customers in a depressed economy and a market flooded with similar designs.

A famous Boeing product of the inter-war years was the P-12 fighter.

The Westland Wessex IV, from Yeovil, was a small feeder liner.

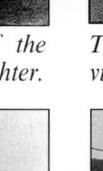

Gloster's AS.31 was designed for aerial surveying. Only two were built.

Tupolev's twin-engined ANT-7 was essentially a scaled-down version of the TB-1 bomber.

Gloster's experimental SS.18 fighter carried four machine guns.

Fritz von Opel carried out early rocket-propulsion trials using a glider.

The Levasseur P.L.10 was a carrier-borne reconnaissance aircraft.

Louis Breguet's distinctive Bre.27 was designed for observation duties.

Morane-Saulnier's MS.230 military trainer continued this French manufacturer's successful series of parasol-winged designs. Over 1,000 were built.

Thirty Levasseur P.L.14 reconnaissance seaplanes were constructed.

The Fokker D.XVI single-seater biplane fighter was based on the C.V.

Any performance advantage that Boeing's XP-15 fighter might have gained from being a monoplane was largely negated by the complex wing-struttery.

The streamlined Lockheed Sirius monoplane was ahead of its time.

Pulawski's revolutionary PZL P-1 fighter prototype had a gull wing.

The shape of the Fury to come: Hawker's Hornet prototype – winner in official trials, and one of the most beautiful biplanes ordered for the RAF.

Consolidated's XPY-1 patrol flying boat won orders from the US Navy.

Fokker's XO-27 observation monoplane was designed for the US Army.

# 1930

**Paris, January 1**
From today the International Aeronautical Federation (FAI) will recognize as world records only the best performances in the following categories: duration, distance in a closed circuit and in a straight line, altitude and speed.

**Florida, February 25**
Ralph O'Neill lands in Miami on the first mail service of American airline New York, Rio and Buenos Aires Line (NYRBA) between Buenos Aires and New York after a difficult 6-day flight from Argentina (→ Aug 19).

**New Jersey, April 18**
French pioneer aeronaut Count Henri de La Vaulx, president of the International Aeronautical Federation (FAI), dies when the airplane in which he is traveling strikes a power line and crashes at Hackensack Meadows.

**Cape Town, South Africa, April 19**
Mary, Duchess of Bedford, lands at Maitland aerodrome with co-pilot C D Barnard and T Little in a Fokker F.VIIa monoplane, *The Spider*, after a record 10-day flight from Britain to the Cape. The Duchess's Fokker is powered by a single Bristol Jupiter engine.

**USSR, April 29**
Soviet designer Nikolai N Polikarpov's VT-11 biplane fighter makes its maiden flight; the Soviet authorities had placed Polikarpov and his colleagues under house arrest while they were designing the airplane as an incentive to encourage productivity. The VT-11 is the fastest fighter so far developed in the Soviet Union, and should lead to a production version.

**Croydon, England, May 3**
British typist Amy Johnson, flying a second-hand de Havilland Gipsy Moth, the *Jason*, takes off on the first leg of a planned flight to Australia (→ May 10).

**Natal, Brazil, May 13**
Jean Mermoz, in a Latécoère 28 hydroplane, lands after flying from St Louis, Senegal, on the ocean sector of French company Aéropostale's first airmail service from Toulouse, France, to Rio de Janeiro; Mermoz's flight across the South Atlantic took 20 hours 50 minutes. →

**London, June 3**
Amy Johnson is made Commander of the Order of the British Empire (CBE) (→ Aug 4).

**Bucharest, Romania, June 19**
An international competition for fighter airplanes ends; the all-metal Polish fighter, the Panstwowe Zaklady Lotnicze (PZL) P-1, has been the star of the show, winning eight of the 15 prizes. This is a triumph for the brilliant designer Zygmund Pulawski, whose aircraft consistently out-performed those of his rivals.

**Washington, DC, June 24**
Dr Albert Taylor and Leo Young of the Aircraft Research Laboratory, near Bolling Field, succeed in tracing the position of airplanes in flight using wireless detection equipment (→ Dec 31, 1933).

**Hertfordshire, England, July 7**
The Handley Page company's new airfield at Radlett is opened; during the ceremony, Tom Harry England demonstrates the ability of the H.P. Gugnunc to make a slow take-off: he starts the airplane's engine inside the hangar, and is airborne as he passes through the doors. Radlett has actually been in use since June 12 when company chief test pilot Jim Cordes made the first flight of the H.P.38 Heyford bomber.

**USA, July 25**
Famous designer Chance Vought dies at the early age of 40. A simple extraction of a tooth led to fatal blood poisoning. Chance Vought Aircraft is part of the giant United Aircraft Corporation.

**USSR, August 2**
A 12-man detachment of military parachutists makes a successful experimental jump, leaping in two waves from a Farman F-60 Goliath airplane during summer maneuvers at Voronezh.

**Los Angeles, August 5**
Poncho Barnes sets a new women's air speed record of 196.1mph.

**USA, August 19**
Pan American Airways takes over the New York, Rio and Buenos Aires Line (NYRBA), thereby eliminating its only serious commercial rival on the eastern coast of South America (→ Oct 1).

**Chicago, Illinois, August 27**
Lockheed's chief test pilot Wiley Post arrives after flying a Lockheed Vega airplane from Los Angeles, California, in 9 hours and 9 minutes (→ Jul 1, 1931).

**Bradford, Penn, September 10**
Built by the Taylor Aircraft Company, the Taylor E-2, a single-seater light aircraft, makes its first flight. Powered by a Brownback Tiger Kitten 20-hp engine, the small airplane, designed by Charles Gilbert Taylor and William Thomas Piper, is named the Cub.

**London, October 2**
The R.101 is given a certificate of airworthiness (→ Oct 5).

**Rome, October 13**
A two-rotor helicopter designed by Corradino d'Ascanio makes a successful first flight of two-thirds of a mile, reaching an altitude of 42 feet.

**Cape Town, October 13**
Lieutenant R F Caspareuthus of the South African Air Force lands after flying from England in a record time of 8 days 10 hours 30 minutes; he left Lympne, Kent, on October 5.

**USA, October 25**
Transcontinental and Western Air (TWA) inaugurates its all-air, coast-to-coast service with simultaneous departures from Newark, New Jersey, and Los Angeles; the route includes a 12-hour stopover in Kansas City (→ Nov 18, 1932).

**Washington, DC, November 6**
In recognition of 25 aerial victories in the Great War, President Hoover presents the Congressional Medal of Honor to the USA's "Ace of Aces", former Lieutenant Edward Rickenbacker.

**Hertfordshire, England, Nov 17**
The new Handley Page H.P.42 airliner is demonstrated by pilot Tom Harry England (→ Jul 11, 1931).

**Dayton, Ohio, November 18**
The Boeing XP-9 monoplane fighter makes its first flight.

**France, November 20**
The Dewoitine D.33 single-engine long-range monoplane makes its maiden flight.

**Harmondsworth, England, Nov 25**
The Fairey Hendon monoplane bomber makes its first flight.

**Berlin, December 17**
German army officers, including Colonel Karl Becker, who proposes to use rockets as weapons, meet to launch a rocket research program.

**Europe, December 19**
French airline Société Générale des Transports Aériens (SGTA) makes the first use of an automatic pilot during a commercial flight, on its service from Le Bourget, France, to Dortmund, Germany.

**USSR, December 22**
The Tupolev ANT-6 heavy bomber makes its first flight.

---

*The pilot becomes muse: a music-sheet for a song composed to celebrate British flyer Amy Johnson's great flight to Australia.* ▶

# Swiss explorer flies to unseen summit

*Mittelholzer poses with his camera.*

*Tanganyika [Tanzania], January 8*
Suffering from severe altitude sickness and with his airplane being buffeted in freezing high winds, Swiss explorer and photographer Walter Mittelholzer today became the first person to see and film the yawning crater of Kibo, the highest peak of Mount Kilimanjaro. The extinct volcano has, he says, "sheer walls of ice and rock". Pilot Alfred Künzle approached the volcano from the South but encountered downdrafts. From the North, he met upcurrents, which enabled the Fokker F.VII-3m to reach 21,100 feet where they circled several times. The flight started from the Serengeti Plain, where Mittelholzer is on safari with Baron de Rothschild.

# Airline mergers create big new US carrier

*Wilmington, Del, January 25*
The merger here today of what were once 12 independent local airlines into one major transcontinental carrier, is part of the continuing rationalization of the airline industry. American Airways has been created by the Aviation Corporation out of regional operators Universal, Colonial, Southern, Interstate and Embry-Riddle. The new airline links over 50 large north American cities, including New York, Boston, Chicago, Los Angeles and Toronto, with mail, passenger and freight services.

The process of amalgamation is being actively encouraged by the postmaster general, Walter Folger Brown, as part of his plan to improve mail services and encourage commercial aviation.

# Quiet Kiwi shows mastery of air navigation

*Darwin, Australia, January 25*
A quietly-spoken New Zealander, Francis Chichester, proved today that he is both an outstanding navigator and an excellent long-distance flyer. Chichester has emulated the triumph of Australian Bert Hinkler, who flew from England to Australia two years ago, to become the second man to fly the route solo in a light airplane. He flew his D.H.60G Gipsy Moth tourer *Madam Elija* from London to Darwin in five weeks. He was delayed in Libya before Christmas with major repairs.

Although a redoubtable pilot, Chichester considers himself more of a pioneer of air navigation, which has so far borrowed much from maritime techniques. He feels it needs more development, and intends to fly his airplane from New Zealand to tiny Norfolk Island, 700 miles across the Tasman Sea, which will test his abilities to the full.

*Francis Chichester at the controls of his biplane, and ready for anything.*

# Air ferries start in San Francisco bay

*One of Air Ferries' "flying trams".*

*San Francisco, February 1*
San Francisco's first air ferry service came into operation today, cutting journey time across the Bay to 6 minutes. The ferry flies from San Francisco to Alameda, and from Oakland to Vallejo. Air Ferries, run by Vern Gorst, formerly of Pacific Air Transport, hopes to carry 60,000 passengers a year.

The Loening amphibians used on the route take just two minutes to turn round for the start of the return journey. Gorst hopes to make the route "the busiest air transport line in the world". It remains to be seen what impact the proposal to build a bridge from San Francisco across the Bay to Oakland will have on the service.

# Whittle seeks patent for new 'turbojet'

*London, January 16*
A patent for a new kind of airplane engine was filed today by a junior officer in Britain's Royal Air Force (RAF). Flying Officer Frank Whittle, a flying instructor and former fighter and test pilot, believes that aircraft can be powered by what he calls a "turbojet", a gas turbine engine which creates a propulsive jet of hot gas. According to Whittle the turbojet could enable airplanes to fly very much higher and faster than they can today. But he lacks the money to build his engine. Nobody appears able to disprove his calculations, but he has been unable to arouse any interest in the RAF, the Air Ministry or the aircraft industry.

# Eastern Air rises from ashes of Pitcairn

*Atlanta, Ga, January 17*
Pitcairn Airline became Eastern Air Transport Incorporated today. Company officials explained that the name change was meant to distinguish the flying operation from its previous owner, Philadelphia-based Pitcairn Aircraft Inc., which sold off its airline and contract airmail routes some time ago. Eastern will continue to fly the fleet of Pitcairn PA-5 biplanes it has inherited, but main stockholder Curtiss-Wright is expected to introduce other types of aircraft as well.

Industry observers say that the new company, which currently flies between New York, Atlanta, Miami and Tampa, is seeking to expand beyond these routes.

# New 'hostesses' tend to the air traveler's needs

*San Francisco, May 15*
United Air Lines has become the first airline to introduce female attendants on its passenger flights. The first travelers to benefit from this exclusive service are those on the San Francisco/Cheyenne route.

Ellen Church, a registered nurse, persuaded Boeing to adopt the idea. She has become the first of eight attendants to be taken on by the company. She and her seven colleagues, all nurses, will wear white uniforms during the flight, and green woollen twill suits, with capes and berets, on the ground. The scheme has been sanctioned by Boeing on a three-month trial basis. Ellen Church has not only designed the uniforms for the attendants, but has also laid down various rules – including that the attendants should be no taller than 5 feet 2 inches, no heavier than 115 pounds and no older than 25. They should also be "positive and reassuring".

The role of the new "air hostesses" is mixed: they have to check that seats are fixed firmly to the floor, make sure the passengers do not throw rubbish out of the window, and generally look after their needs. Above all, they must advise travelers not to confuse the door of the washroom with the exit.

At the end of the flight, the hostesses' work is by no means over. When they have seen the passengers off, they are expected to clean the aircraft and even help the mechanics to push it into the hangar. The pay is $125 a month, for 100 hours' work.

*Nurse Ellen Church (far left) with the world's first team of air hostesses.*

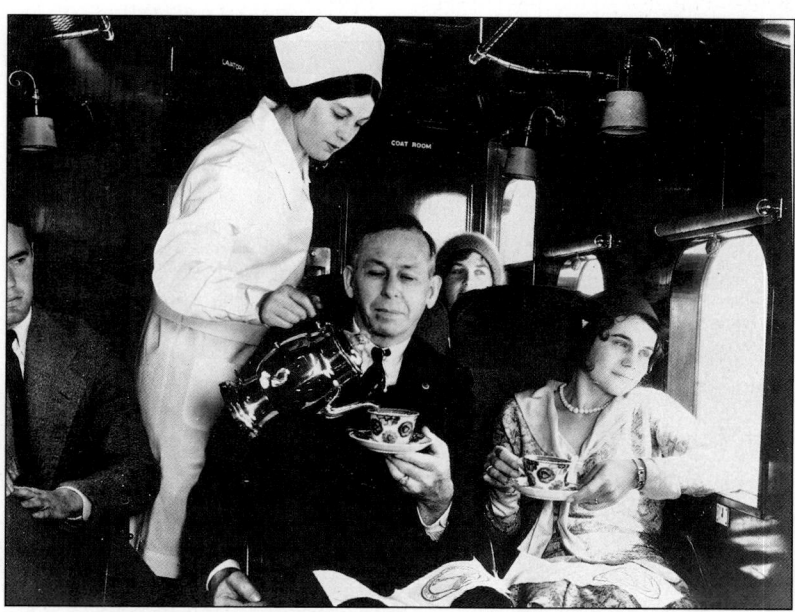
*All in white, the ministering angel of the skies serves tea to passengers.*

## Boeing shows off multi-colored mailplane

*Seattle, May 22*
Painted a garish green, grey and orange, a revolutionary, all-metal, single-engine, low-wing, monoplane mail carrier flew for the first time today: Boeing's model 200 Monomail.

The Monomail breaks with traditional airplane design and employs the most advanced streamlining possible. There are no external braces for the cantilever wing, and a drag-reducing ring surrounds the 575-hp Pratt & Whitney engine; the landing gear retracts into the wing with only half of the wheel exposed during flight; and the fuselage is nearly circular in cross-section. The Monomail is 41 feet long and has a wingspan of 58 feet. It has 220 cubic feet of space for mail and cargo, cruises at 135mph with 60 per cent power and has a range of 530 miles.

*The Monomail is able to carry passengers in the hold instead of post.*

## Pioneer Glenn Curtiss dies after operation

*America's first licensed pilot will be buried at Hammondsport, where he flew.*

*Rochester, NY, July 23*
Glenn Curtiss, holder of the Aero Club of America's pilot's license No 1, died today of a blood clot on the lung following an operation for appendicitis. He was just 52 and, although he retired in 1921, retained a seat on the board of the Curtiss-Wright company. The man who did more than anyone else to spread the gospel of aviation in the US during the first two decades of this century still loved flying. Two months ago he retraced the route of his historic Albany/New York flight of 1910 in a new Condor.

▷

# Northrop changes the shape of airplanes

*Burbank, California, May 1*
American aircraft designer J K Northrop believes that future airplanes will have no tails and no fuselages; they will be composed of just a "flying wing".

Northrop, who heads the Northrop Aircraft Corporation division of United Aircraft and Transport Corporation, has designed, built and flown an experimental plane with a 30-foot wingspan, which is a first step in turning his concept into reality. A single engine and the cockpit are completely enclosed in the wing of the airplane. But it is not a pure flying wing. Two slender booms extend from the trailing edge of the wing. At their ends are a horizontal stabilizer and twin rudders. Northrop says that these control surfaces prevent handling problems, and that as the fuselage has been eliminated, they too will disappear as the aircraft's design evolves.

*Northrop's experimental "flying wing" is powered by a 90-hp engine.*

# Air battle movie is a hit

*Actress Jean Harlow outshines the flyers in a scene from "Hell's Angels".*

*Hollywood, June*
Long lines have formed outside every movie house in the country this month to watch the most talked-about motion picture of the year. *Hell's Angels*, directed by oil magnate Howard Hughes, features sky battles so vivid they put the audience in the very cockpit of Great War fighter planes. *Hell's Angels* has been four years in the making, and it has cost $4,000,000 and the lives of three men.

The film grew from Hughes's obsession with airplanes. Not surprisingly, the aerial combat scenes are magnificent. Over 60 obsolete aircraft were rounded up, including the Sikorsky S-29A made to look like a German Gotha bomber. One of the three who died, an air mechanic, was killed when this aircraft crashed. The movie was completed last year, but the addition of sound put another $1,000,000 on the budget. *Hell's Angels* is the second outstanding air-war movie to appear in a few months; it follows the success of Howard Hawks's *Dawn Patrol*, made last year.

# Italy's Caproni puts world's biggest landplane through its paces

*Milan, Italy, February 22*
Caproni's huge Ca 90 bomber today made a flight lasting 1 hour 31 minutes, in the course of which it set new records for altitude and duration carrying a useful load. With a load of 10 tonnes [22,046 pounds] it climbed to 10,600 feet.

First flown almost a year ago from Milan's Taliedo airfield, the Ca 90 is the biggest landplane in the world, dwarfed only by the Dornier Do X flying boat. Its lower wing has a span of over 152 feet, and the machine has six 1,000-hp Isotta-Fraschini engines, arranged in tandem push/pull pairs. However, only one Ca 90 has been built. It is basically an outdated fabric-covered machine, braced by struts and wires and too slow for modern air forces.

*The Ca 90's airframe is 39 feet high, and its wheels are taller than a man.*

# Australian makes it across the Atlantic

*Newfoundland, June 26*
The *Southern Cross* has done it again. Smashed during the Wilkins 1926 Arctic survey, bought by Australian Charles Kingsford Smith for his 1928 transpacific epic, the Fokker F.VIIb-3m yesterday completed a transatlantic flight from Portmarnock Strand, Ireland, to Harbour Grace, Newfoundland. It flew on to New York today.

"Smithy" and his three crew meant to reach New York yesterday, but fuel shortage forced a diversion. Bad weather then forced them so low that at one point their dangling aerial touched the sea. Later the wireless compass faltered and another airplane guided them over the coast (→ Apr 25, 1931).

# Buy yourself an airplane at Selfridges

*London, December 15*

For the man, or woman, who has everything, the most unusual gift this Christmas must be: an airplane! With a few hundred pounds to spend, anyone can walk into Selfridges, London's biggest department store, and buy themselves the machine of their dreams. In March, the store opened a showroom at Kensington, about two miles from the huge main store in Oxford Street. London's top retailers believe that light aircraft will soon be as popular as cars. Harrods pushed the Blackburn Sidecar, displaying it while mannequins modeled flying garb. Moths, Avians and Bluebirds are reported to be among the strongest sellers.

*An enthusiast tries out a de Havilland Moth in Selfridges' London showroom.*

# Civil aircraft dominate Paris exhibition

*Paris, December 13*

Military and civil aircraft share equal billing at the 12th International Aeronautical Exposition, which opened here today. Of the 21 military craft on show, 18 are landplanes and three are seaplanes. But it is the commercial planes, particularly airliners, which are getting all the attention. There are more civil aircraft at the show than at any time since the Great War. Seventeen transport airplanes, ranging from 120hp to 2,600hp, and in weight capacity from 1,568 pounds to 10 tons, are lined up alongside a variety of light aircraft for clubs and private owners. Experts are predicting sales of between 250 and 350 a year.

*An airplane for the exposition is maneuvered into the Grand Palais in Paris.*

# Formation stunts and flying lions excite the crowds as daredevils show off skills

**A team of US Navy pilots performs the extraordinary and dangerous aerobatic feat of flying in formation when linked together by a cable.**

**A British cameraman, firmly strapped to the wing of a Vickers Virginia, braves the wind as he prepares to take footage of a parachute jump.**

**Barnstormer Roscoe Turner, pictured with fearless co-pilot Gilmore, the flying lion. The intrepid pair caused a sensation at the National Air Races this year, but now – after logging 30,000 air miles – Gilmore is growing too big for the cockpit and is bound for the zoo.**

A line of classic light aircraft originated with the first Taylor Cub in 1930. As the Piper Cub it continued in production well into the post-war years.

The speedy little Swift was designed by Nick Comper for private owners.

The engines of the Douglas Dolphin were set high, well clear of spray.

Futuristic trends in the Lockheed Orion high-speed airliner included a cantilever wing, retractable undercarriage and variable-pitch propeller.

The Wibault-Penhoët 280 series of airliners became familiar sights at European airports in the 1930s. Air Union and Air France operated the type.

Bellanca's Pacemaker had aerofoil-section bracing struts for added lift.

The parasol-winged PWS-10 single-seater fighter, designed in Poland.

Boeing's Model 200 Monomail high-performance mailplane had a semi-retractable undercarriage. The engine was a 575-hp Pratt & Whitney Hornet.

It was possible to travel to Europe and across the British Empire in comfort in the Handley Page H.P.42, provided one was not in too much of a hurry.

Bellanca's unconventional P-200 was best described as a semi-biplane.

A transport built by the American Airplane & Engine Corporation.

The neat Potez 39 observation aircraft served with the Armée de l'Air.

Fairchild's F-100 continued the company's successful line of aircraft.

Tupolev's massive ANT-6 heavy bomber underwent constant revision during its service life. Many ended up as unarmed G-2 paratroop transports.

The Douglas YO-31A was designed as an observation aircraft for the US Army but was ordered only in small numbers. Its successor was the O-46A.

The Sikorsky S-41 was a fifteen-passenger development of the S-38.

A monoplane with a fabric-covered metal airframe, the Fairey Hendon bomber served with the RAF. It had a pair of Rolls-Royce Kestrel engines.

The Fairey Seal was the Fleet Air Arm version of the RAF's Gordon.

Boeing's XP-15 performed disappointingly and failed to win orders.

Developed from the Calcutta, the Short Rangoon served with the RAF.

A distinctive design, if somewhat dated: the Handley Page Heyford bomber carried its bombs in the lower wing's specially deepened centre section.

For naval fighter-reconnaissance Hawker produced the Osprey, developed from the RAF's Hart bomber. It could be launched by a ship's catapult.

Designed specifically to break long-distance records, the Dewoitine D.33 was the heaviest aircraft that could be flown by its single 580-hp engine.

# 1931

**Wellington, NZ, January 7**
Australian Guy Menzies lands his Avro Avian after a 1,200-mile flight from Sydney of 12 hours 15 minutes to complete the first trans-Tasman solo flight in a light aircraft, beating Charles Kingsford Smith's record of 14 hours 25 minutes.

**Washington, DC, January 9**
US Army chief of staff General Douglas MacArthur and US Navy chief of operations Admiral William Pratt announce an agreement on their air forces: naval flyers are to be attached to the fleet and will move with it to provide support; army flyers will perform all other functions.

**Washington, DC, February 5**
The US Navy accepts for service a tiny airplane developed by Grover Loening for use with submarines; it can be dismantled and fitted into an 8-foot tube.

**Kent, England, February 24**
John Lankester Parker makes the first flight of the prototype Short S.17 Kent flying boat, from the river Medway.

**Poland, March 21**
Polish airplane designer Zygmunt Pulawski dies when the PZL P.12 amphibian which he is flying crashes.

**Washington, DC, April 2**
The US Navy awards a contract to Grumman for a prototype of the USA's first naval fighter with a retractable undercarriage.

**Croydon, England, April 4**
An experimental airmail service leaves for Australia; the first leg of the new service is the existing scheduled airmail flight to Karachi, India (→ Apr 19).

**Hertfordshire, England, April 8**
The Iraqi Air Force makes its inaugural flight when five military de Havilland Moths, flown by the first British-trained Iraqi pilots, leave Hatfield for Baghdad.

**Pennsylvania, April 8**
Amelia Earhart climbs to a record altitude of 18,415 feet in a Pitcairn autogyro at Willow Grove, near Philadelphia (→ Jun 8).

**Koepang, Timor, April 19**
Imperial Airways' experimental airmail service from England to Australia hits trouble when the D.H.66 Hercules *City of Cairo*, which took on mail in India on April 13, crashes (→ May 14).

**USA, May 4**
Following the tragic crash of a Transcontinental and Western Air Fokker F.10A trimotor on March 31, the aircraft is taken out of passenger service; it is a major blow to the reputation of the Fokker Aircraft Corporation.

**Kaaden, Czechoslovakia, May 5**
German pilot Günther Groenhoff lands after a 165-mile glider flight from Munich (→ Jul 23, 1932).

**Croydon, England, May 14**
The first return mail arrives on Imperial Airways' experimental service between Britain and Australia.

**Augsburg, Germany, May 27**
Swiss physicist Auguste Piccard and assistant Paul Kipfer reach a world record altitude of 51,775 feet in a balloon; it has a sealed cabin gondola fitted with an internal supply of oxygen.

**Langley Field, Va, May 27**
A full-scale wind tunnel goes into operation at the NACA Laboratory.

**Ottawa, May 31**
The Canadian government announces that airmail services will be canceled because of a $6,000,000 operating deficit.

**Canada, June 2**
American pilot Ruth Nichols crashes her Lockheed Vega *Akita* at St John, New Brunswick, on an attempted transatlantic flight to Paris; she suffers five broken vertebrae (→ Feb 14, 1932).

**New York, June 23**
Former airmail pilot Wiley Post and navigator Harold Gatty take off from Roosevelt Field, Long Island, on the first leg of a round-the-world flight (→ Jul 1).

**Berlin, July 1**
Deutsche Luft Hansa introduces 34-passenger Junkers G.38 airliners into service between Berlin, Hamburg and Cologne.

**Hungary, July 16**
Pilots Alexander Magyar and György Enders land 12 miles short of their target, Budapest, when they run out of fuel after a 3,200-mile flight from Newfoundland, Canada in their Lockheed Orion.

**Chicago, July 27**
The Air Line Pilots Association of the USA is founded; David Behncke is first president.

**Tokyo, August 6**
Amy Johnson and mechanic Jack Humphreys land their de Havilland Moth *Jason II* after a flight from England; they left Lympne, Kent, on July 28.

**London, August 7**
Jim Mollison lands after flying from Australia in 10 days, knocking two days off the existing record (→ Mar 28, 1932).

**Hampshire, England, August 31**
Alan Cobham and crew return from a 12,300-mile survey of the Nile and Africa's lakes in a Short Valetta seaplane (→ Apr 12, 1932).

**Newark, NJ, September 4**
Major James Doolittle wins the $10,000 Bendix Prize after flying across the country in 11 hours 16 minutes and ten seconds, at an average speed of 223mph.

**Hampshire, England, September 29**
At Calshot, Flight Lieutenant George Stainforth sets a new world speed record in the Supermarine S.6B seaplane; over six circuits of a set course he achieves an average speed of 407.5mph.

**Wenatchee, Wash, October 5**
Clyde Pangborn and Hugh Herndon Jr land their Bellanca Skyrocket *Miss Veedol* to complete the first non-stop flight from Japan to the USA; they left Sabishiro Beach on October 3, covering the 4,465 miles in 41 hours 13 minutes.

**Anacostia, Wash, DC, October 12**
President Hoover's wife christens *American Clipper*, a Sikorsky S-40 flying boat, using water instead of champagne due to Prohibition.

**Pennsylvania, October 13**
Canadian pilot Godfrey Dean performs the first loop in an autogyro, at Willow Field, near Philadelphia.

**France, October 21**
Official flight tests for the Latécoère 290 torpedo bomber begin at St-Raphaël, near Nice.

**Lakehurst, NJ, November 2**
The USS *Akron*, a purpose-built aircraft-carrying airship, is commissioned (→ Apr 5, 1933).

**Cape Town, S Africa, November 5**
British débutante Peggy Salaman and Gordon Store land their D.H.80A Puss Moth *Good Hope* to set a record for a flight from England of 5 days, 6 hours 38 minutes.

**Senegal, November 27**
Australian pilot Bert Hinkler lands his D.H.80A Puss Moth *Karohi* to complete the first west/east crossing of the South Atlantic; flying time from Natal, Brazil, was 25 hours 5 minutes (→ Jan 7, 1933).

**USSR, December 3**
V S Vakhmistrov's Zveno-1 is test flown; it consists of a TB-1 heavy bomber with an I-4 "parasite" fighter mounted on each wing, which can take off when the TB-1 is in flight.

*This advertisement plays on the airlines' greatest advantage over land transport: that flying gets you to your destination more quickly.* ▶

# Patriotic lady pays for trophy attempt

*Lady Houston, Britain's benefactor.*

*London, 30 January*
The wealthy widow of a shipping magnate is to finance Britain's entry in the Schneider Trophy competition this year after Britain's Labour government pulled out of a promise to support the effort to win the trophy permanently with one more victory. Lady Houston, who is putting up $453,000, believes "one Englishman" is "equal to three foreigners", and that Labour wants to reduce Britain to a third-rate power.

Her money will go towards the production of a 2,350-hp Rolls-Royce "R" engine to secure the distinctively shaped trophy, which Royal Aero Club members have dubbed "the hat rack" (→ Sep 13).

# German rocket flies

*Dessau, Germany, March 14*
Scientist Johannes Winkler, one of a band of visionaries who believe that space travel is the next step after the conquest of the air, has successfully tested a 2-foot rocket powered by methane and liquid oxygen fed by compressed nitrogen. The vehicle reached an altitude of 1,800 feet and is being hailed as the first liquid-fueled rocket to be flown in Europe.

Scientists at two research centers, one at Reinickendorf near Berlin and the other in Austria, are working to develop this new form of aviation. The Berlin team includes a brilliant young scientist called Wernher von Braun.

# Federal support is boost to US airlines

*USA, February*
Public confidence that an airmail letter posted in Miami today will be in Havana tomorrow, or that one posted in New York will be in Los Angeles in two days, owes much to the US government. The growth and efficiency of US airlines is directly attributable to support by the government in the shape of the US Post Office, which awards the airmail contracts guaranteeing airlines a certain amount of income.

Federal support enables the airlines, which have Post Office contracts, to fly more than 100,000 miles each day this year on mail routes within and outside the country. Most importantly for the expansion of civil aviation, airlines will seize the opportunity handed to them to provide a passenger and cargo service on every airmail flight. By the end of the year, the total amount of money spent by the Post Office in 14 years of airmail operations, and the amount the Department of Commerce invests per air mile, will be less than a third of the money spent per road mile. Even more remarkably, it will be only 2.94 per cent of federal investment per railroad mile.

# The Aéropostale is liquidated

*France, March 31*
Aéropostale, the French company which pioneered regular mail flights between Europe, North Africa and South America, has gone into liquidation. The company has been making a loss since 1927.

Company head Marcel Bouilloux-Lafont was banking on French government intervention to save his ailing group. However, the Wall Street crash of 1929 and the 1930 revolution in Brazil dealt a fatal blow to his hopes. The 1929 crash had serious repercussions in the whole of South America, and the Brazilian political situation forced Aéropostale to suspend operations for several months. The combination of events was too much for the company, and by mid-March Bouillox-Lafont was unable to meet his bank repayments.

# KLM is forced to do a deal with Air Orient

*A KLM poster shows the ground crew busily loading an F.VIII with cargo.*

*Amsterdam, February 16*
Dutch airline KLM has been forced to do a deal with French airline Air Orient, following the refusal of the French authorities to licence their fleet of new Fokker F.VIIs. The configuration of the airplane's engine mountings does not conform to current standards, say the French.

KLM director Albert Plesman has hired out three of his existing fleet to Air Orient, which wanted to boost its capacity and open up a new route from Marseilles to Saigon. In return, KLM will run a ten-day route from Amsterdam to the Dutch East Indies, flying via Bangkok to Medang in Sumatra and thence to its final destination of Batavia in Java.

On its homeward journey, the KLM airplane will connect with the Air Orient plane at Baghdad and transfer cargo destined for France. The two planes will return to Europe by different routes, the former to Amsterdam and the latter to Marseilles, France, arriving at the same time. The arrangement allows both airlines to fulfill their obligations.

# Imperial Airways opens new African route

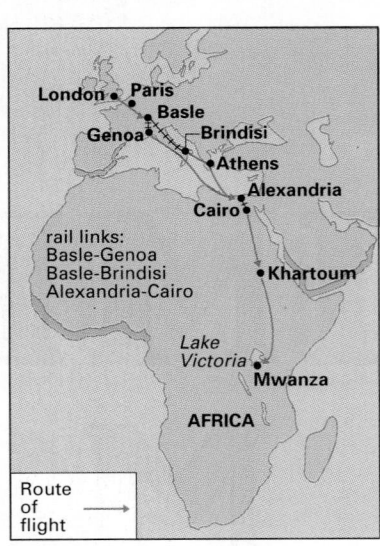

*Croydon, England, February 28*
Britain's Imperial Airways today began regular weekly services over a 5,114-mile route to Mwanza on Lake Victoria, Tanganyika. The new route was opened by an Armstrong Whitworth Argosy three-engined airliner. It was bound for Basel, Switzerland, where passengers transfer to the railroad for the journey to Genoa or Brindisi in Italy.

The Mediterranean section of the route, from Genoa to Alexandria, Egypt, is flown by Imperial's new four-engined Short Kent flying boats, named *Scipio*, *Satyrus*, and *Sylvanus*. The Argosy takes over to continue the route down the Nile as far as Khartoum in the Sudan.

For the moment this is the terminus for passengers; mail and cargo transfer to a Short Calcutta flying boat for the stages to Mwanza. Before long, however, both mail and passengers will be able to fly through to Cape Town. The last sectors, south of Mwanza, will be flown by D.H.66 Hercules landplanes (→ Apr 27, 1932).

# Light plane makes world solo flight

*Croydon, England, February 20*
An aristocratic Englishwoman arrived here today after a lengthy trip around the world in a light airplane. The Honorable Mrs Victor Bruce aroused much skepticism when, with just 40 solo flying hours under her belt, she announced that she was going to fly around the world. She was undeterred, and left Heston, near London, on September 25 in her Blackburn Bluebird IV biplane.

Mrs Bruce, who carried a transmitter to send a Morse signal every 15 minutes, made three forced landings, near Istanbul, in the Kohimborak Hills of Oman, and near Bangkok. Her intrepid flight stopped short of tackling the Pacific or the Atlantic. The aircraft was shipped from Tokyo to Seattle and from New York to Le Havre, France, via Plymouth, England, reaching France on February 16.

*Mrs Bruce during a stop in Tokyo.*

# Rockne killed in crash

*South Bend, Indiana, March 31*
Americans in general and the university of Notre Dame in particular are in mourning tonight following the tragic death of Knute Rockne, the coach of the Flying Irish football team, which brought the university to national prominence. He was one of eight who died when a TWA Fokker F.10A Trimotor crashed into a hillside in Baazar, Kansas.

Rockne was en route to Los Angeles and Hollywood. He took a train from Chicago to Kansas City, where he boarded the airplane, which left at 9.15am. Eyewitness on the ground near the crash site in Indiana said they saw the wing of the aircraft tear off before the Fokker plummeted into the ground.

Notre Dame and Rockne were synonymous. He played football while a student there and graduated *summa cum laude*. The death in an air crash of a personality like Rockne is sure to hurt passenger traffic for the troubled TWA, which has been losing $200,000 per month for some time. The tragedy is a blow to Fokker's reputation as the manufacturers of excellent, reliable airplanes (→ May 4).

## 'Smithy' saves the post – and the day

*The Mail for Australia goes aboard a Handley Page 42 at Croydon airport.*

*Koepang, Timor, April 25*
Charles Kingsford Smith, the veteran Australian aviator, today rescued the passengers, crew and mail of a stranded airliner of Britain's Imperial Airways bound for Australia. The D.H.66 Hercules *City of Cairo* was on an experimental airmail flight from England. After leaving Batavia, Java, it ran into strong headwinds, ran out of fuel, and made an emergency landing on Timor. "Smithy" was cabled from London and flew his Fokker *Southern Cross* to Timor. People and mail were recovered safely.

# Swissair is created from airline merger

*Zurich, March 26*
Two Swiss airlines, Balair and Ad Astra, have combined to form Schweizerische Luftverkehr [Swiss Airways], which will be known as Swissair. The new company is small by any standards, with nine pilots and 12 other crew to fly its fleet of six Fokker F.VIIb planes, which are the core of its fleet.

The Swiss are following the lead of other small European countries, such as Belgium and the Netherlands, by starting a national airline in the same way that the bigger nations have done. Every country wants to have a flag-carrying airline, not only for economic reasons, but also as a symbol of technological advancement. Without its own aircraft industry of its own, Swissair will look to buy the best machines. One option would be to buy American, with Lockheed and Douglas as two potential suppliers.

# Navy approves of new landing gear

*Washington, DC, March 21*
Following exhaustive tests using a Vought Corsair observation airplane, the US Navy has announced that it is pleased with the amphibious float invented by Grumman Aircraft Engineering. The float incorporates two wheels which retract into the floats in the air, but can be lowered by the pilot for landing on airfields. The testing included catapult launches from and arrested landings on the carrier USS *Lexington* and the battleship USS *Tennessee*.

Grumman is now concentrating on demonstrating how the retractable wheels can be designed into a high-speed fighter. Work is going ahead on the prototype Grumman XFF-1, called Fifi in the factory, which, although a two-seater, promises to be faster than any single-seat fighter in the US Navy. Grumman hopes to fit the retractable landing gear to single-seat fighters able to reach speeds as high as 250mph. Because of its new features, this one airplane will cost the navy $73,975. Production models will be much cheaper (→ Apr 2).

# US award for aviation achievement goes to modified autogyro

*Washington, DC, April 22*
An autogyro piloted by James Ray of the Pitcairn-Cierva Autogiro Company of America descended gently on to the south lawn of the White House today as part of the Collier trophy award ceremony. President Herbert C Hoover presented the trophy for the greatest achievement in aviation in the USA in the past year to Harold Pitcairn and the people who helped him to build the autogyro. Spanish inventor of the machine Juan de La Cierva was absent today because of political problems in his homeland.

Pitcairn and his staff were awarded the trophy for refinements to de La Cierva's basic design made at his factory at Willow Grove, Pennsylvania, this year. Pitcairn is hoping to attract the well-to-do with a new and convenient, not to mention fashionable, way of getting around. With its nose-mounted radial engine for power, and four unpowered, rotating blades on top of the fuselage as its main lifting device, the autogyro can take off and land in very short distances – which came in useful for today's landing at the White House.

Newspapers could use autogyros to speed film from the scene of an event, and they may also be used as crop-dusters, since their ability to fly as slow as 20mph allows for safer and more accurate pesticide spraying (→ Jun 8).

# Armada of planes upsets peace lobby

*US Army airplanes fly in formation over the Capitol in Washington, DC.*

*New York, May 23*
Thousands of people crowded the New Jersey Palisades and the rooftops and highways along the Hudson River today to see US Army Air Corps bomber, pursuit, attack and observation airplanes fly past en route to the dedication of Floyd Bennett Field in Brooklyn. At the same time as the fly-past, about 400 people rallied at Cooper Union Square in Lower Manhattan in protest at the largest armada of warplanes the city has ever seen.

Religious anti-war groups claim the display glorifies war, and that the expenditure it cost should have been used to help the unemployed. "The way of Jesus and Gandhi is stronger than guns", said Reverend Eliot White at Brookwood Labor College.

# Huge 'Hannibal' joins Imperial Airways

*Imperial is putting great faith in the strongly-built, reliable H.P.42s.*

*Croydon, England, July 11*
The first of a fleet of eight giant Handley Page H.P.42 transports, among the largest airliners in the world, carried fare-paying passengers for the first time today from London to Paris. The new airliner, named *Hannibal*, started proving flights on the route on June 6. The huge biplanes, powered by four 525-hp Bristol Jupiter engines, will eventually come with two different passenger layouts depending on whether they are destined for the western or eastern area of operations. The western type, for use in Europe, seats 38 passengers, while the eastern type, to be based at Cairo, seats only 18 passengers, but will carry far more luggage.

# Earhart flies coast to coast in autogyro

*Los Angeles, June 8*
Amelia Earhart, the noted airwoman who wed George Putnam last February 7, arrived here today believing she was the first to fly across the USA in an autogyro. But Johnny Miller of Poughkeepsie, New York, in a Pitcairn PCA-2, the same model as Earhart's, beat her to the honor last week.

Earhart was disappointed. Her flight was delayed several weeks while she recovered from a tonsilectomy. She plans to return to New York immediately to become the first person to make a west/east transcontinental autogyro flight. Earhart, who claimed a world altitude record for autogyros of 19,000 feet on April 8 at Pitcairn's airfield at Willow Grove, Pennsylvania, is sponsored by the makers of Beechnut chewing-gum. With Beechnut Gum boldly stenciled on its sides, the autogyro is a flying billboard. As she crossed the country, Earhart and her mechanic Eddie de Vaught distributed giant packages of gum (→ May 21, 1932).

*Amelia Earhart with her husband.*

# Severed head ends missing flyer riddle

*Dutch New Guinea, August 1*
Tribesmen cleared up the mystery of a missing airman here today – by displaying the pilot's head to the man sent to replace him. It happened at the airstrip built by mining airline Guinea Airways, which operates various Junkers aircraft to the Bulolo gold mines.

Ian Grabowsky, recently hired to replace pilot Les Trist, who had been missing for three months, was working at Lae base aerodrome when he was approached by a group of tribesmen. They carried a bag which they held out to him, making gestures suggestive of a zooming airplane. When they opened the bag the grisly truth emerged. But despite their reputation as headhunters, the tribesmen had not killed Les Trist. They had found his body in the wreckage of his airplane and cut off his head to take it "home" to his airstrip. Later today, they led a party to the crash site. It seems Trist had tried to fly blind through a rocky pass and had hit a mountain.

# Captain, remember your flags...

*The "Heracles" flying its pennants.*

*Le Bourget, France, July*
Airports are becoming busier every day and aircraft on the ground must fly two pennants from their cockpits, that of the host country and that of their airline. Some pilots, busy with their pre-take off checks, have forgotten to remove the pennants. It is then up to an airport official to point out the oversight to the crew.

# Wiley Post speeds home

*Wiley Post: taking on the world.*

*New York, July 1*

American endurance flyer Wiley Post landed in triumph here today after a record flight round the northern hemisphere of 8 days, 15 hours and 51 minutes. He and navigator Harold Gatty left Roosevelt Field, New York, on June 23 in Wiley's much loved, barrel-shaped, high-wing Lockheed Vega monoplane *Winnie Mae*.

They refueled at Harbour Grace, Newfoundland, before crossing the Atlantic and flying across Britain, Germany, the USSR, Alaska and Canada on a trip of 15,474 miles, which took 175 days when it was first flown seven years ago.

The personal pilot of Oklahoma oil tycoon F C Hall, Post, who is blind in one eye, specializes in flying the Lockheed Vega, a favorite with pilots for endurance flights. Last year, in *Winnie Mae*, he beat four other Vegas to win a non-stop race from Los Angeles to Chicago. His comment afterward, "It takes a Lockheed to beat a Lockheed", delighted the company, which ranks it with that other quip, "What's good for Ford is good for America" as a publicity slogan.

Amelia Earhart, America's most famous woman aviator, has flown her own Vega on several record-breaking flights. Ruth Nichols has roused much less attention with her transcontinental and altitude records (28,743 feet) for women in a Vega 5 Special. The airplane's reliability makes it a natural choice for commercial fleets, including Braniff. It is even finding work as an aerial ambulance. Post believes he and *Winnie Mae* have even greater successes ahead. He plans an assault on the record for a round-the-world solo flight, as well as on the altitude record.

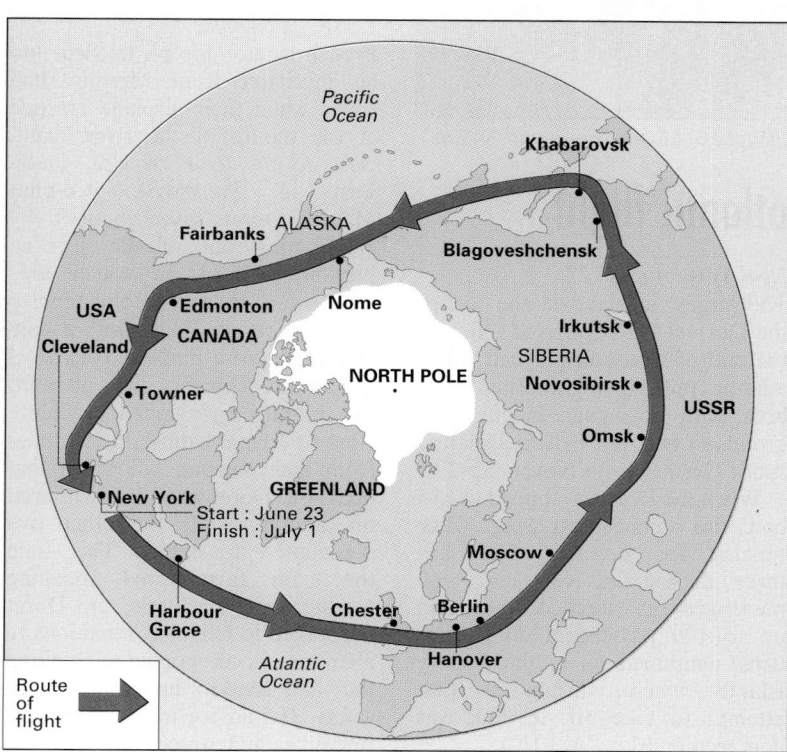

Route of flight →

# How to launch a seaplane from a sub

**The British M.2 submarine comes to the surface, its hangar closed.**

**A Parnall Peto seaplane is brought out of the hangar before launching.**

**The Peto is launched by catapult and must gain speed before climbing.**

**After landing, the seaplane taxis beneath the crane on board the M.2.**

**Hauled on board, the machine is readied to go back in the hangar.**

# Britain wins the Schneider for good

*Hampshire, England, September 13*
The streamlined Supermarine S.6B seaplane proved supreme today, winning the Schneider Trophy outright for Britain. After the failure of US, Italian and French engineers to get aircraft ready in time, the British accepted no delays and produced three machines.

Watched by tens of thousands in fine weather on the beaches of Hampshire and the Isle of Wight, Flight Lieutenant J N Boothman took off from Calshot in aircraft S1595. With the throttle fully open, he completed his first circuit at 344-mph, but noticed overheating and slowed down. He knew that at that speed, he could expect the 2,350-hp V-12 Rolls-Royce engine to melt on its mounts after 45 to 90 minutes. Boothman's average speed on this unchallenged "flyover" over the 62-mile circuit was 340.08mph, enough to retain the trophy. Flight Lieutenant G H Stainforth then flew a straight 1.8-mile course to set a world record of 379.05mph. He is confident of exceeding 400mph.

The competition has not fulfilled the dream of its founder, Jacques Schneider, who died in 1928, of promoting fast, reliable flying boats for passengers. Instead, it has led to the rapid creation of ever-faster machines, envisaged by military men as potential fighters. So far research and test flights have cost the lives of 12 pilots: three Britons, two Americans and seven Italians.

*Britain's machine for the Schneider seaplane trophy, the Supermarine S.6B.*

*From l, Stainforth and Boothman with colleagues Orlebar, Long and Snaith.*

## Dornier lands in New York after wave-top transatlantic flight

*The Statue of Liberty welcomes the Do X flying boat to New York harbor.*

*New York, August 27*
The largest airplane in the world, the Dornier Do X, arrived today at the end of a trouble-plagued transatlantic proving flight. The flying boat, with 12 engines in push/pull groups of two, left Friedrichshafen, south Germany, on November 2.

When the Dornier stopped at Lisbon, fire damaged its wing. After repairs, the aircraft, which has three decks and can carry 66 passengers on extended flights and up to 100 passengers on shorter trips, continued on to the Canary Islands, where, during its first attempt to take off, its hull was damaged (→ May 24, 1932).

# Lindberghs fly to Tokyo on 'vacation'

*Tokyo, August 26*
Colonel Charles Lindbergh has successfully linked the capitals of the USA and Japan by air by flying his single-engined Lockheed Sirius seaplane from Washington to Tokyo with his wife Anne as wireless operator. The Lindberghs left North Haven, Maine, in late July and followed the Great Circle route between the two cities.

They crossed Hudson Bay, then flew along the northern coast of Canada to Point Barrow and Nome in Alaska, then across the Bering Strait and down the Siberian coast to Petropavlovsk. Their arrival in the Kurile islands was delayed when severe weather forced them to land on the sea, 100 miles from their scheduled stopover, and spend the night on the storm-tossed sea.

Despite flying over some of the most desolate regions of the world, the Lindberghs call it a vacation. Colonel Lindbergh said it "had no start or finish, no diplomatic or commercial significance, and no records to be sought" (→ Nov 19).

## Noted French pilot killed in the USSR

*USSR, September 12*
French aviator Joseph Le Brix and his mechanic René Mesmin died today when their airplane crashed at the mouth of the river Tanit, close to the town of Ufa, southwest of Sverdlovsk. Co-pilot Marcel Doret saved himself by parachuting out of the stricken Dewoitine D.33, in which they were trying for the second time to enter the record books with a nonstop flight from Paris to Tokyo.

The Frenchmen's first attempt, two months ago, ended in failure close to Nizhni-Udinsk, 3,750 miles from their starting point. On that occasion, Doret was slightly injured on landing, while the other two parachuted to safety. This time the team encountered appalling weather over the Urals, and Doret felt forced to tell his companions to abandon the monoplane. Thinking they had done so, he parachuted to safety. His advice to his colleagues proved sadly correct.

# Airship dubbed 'Queen of the Skies'

*Akron, Ohio, September 23*
The US Navy's latest airship, the *Akron*, is a craft of awesome proportions, already dubbed by an admiring public the "Queen of the Skies". The behemoth, which flew for the first time today, is 785 feet long and powered by eight engines with propellers that can be swiveled up or down to help launch and recovery. It is borne aloft by 6.5 million cubic feet of helium and has a crew of 113 sailors and civilians.

The airship, officially the ZRS-4, is named after the city where it was built by the Goodyear-Zeppelin Company. It was christened by President Hoover's wife last month in front of 25,000 people, who learned that the *Akron* is not so much an airship, more of a flying aircraft carrier. Five F9C fighters are stored in a hangar amidships, and they can be launched and recovered in flight. The role of the *Akron* will be long-range maritime reconnaissance. Observation can be carried

*The huge airship "Akron" edges out of its specially-built hangar in Ohio.*

out by its lookouts, or its fighters can be launched to search for enemy battleships. It will work closely with the surface fleet, extending the fleet's eyes and ears over the horizon. Its ability to lift 200 tons could offer other useful possibilities to the US Navy. Following today's launch, the *Akron* will carry out coast-to-coast test flights under the command of Lieutenant-Commander C E Rosendahl (→Nov 2).

# Tiger Moth trainer put through paces

*London, October 26*
Having scored a great hit among civilian clubs and private owners with its Moth family, Britain's de Havilland company seems set to repeat its success with the D.H.82 Tiger Moth, the prototype of which made its first flight here today.

Unlike the original Moth, the D.H.82 is designed to meet a Royal Air Force (RAF) specification for a trainer, and therefore has dual pilot controls. To enable the instructor in the front cockpit to abandon the aircraft quickly, all struts and wires are ahead of his cockpit, which in turn means the upper wing is swept backwards. The new, inverted Gipsy Major engine has exhausts underneath, enabling both cockpits to be fitted with fold-down doors on both sides. Provision will also be made for a blind-flying hood to be placed over the rear (pupil) cockpit. An RAF-type instrument panel will be fitted to Tiger Moths on service models. The D.H.82 bears no relation to the D.H.71 Tiger Moth monoplane of 1927.

# Charles Lindbergh pilots giant Clipper

*One of Pan Am's latest Clippers, seen over New York during a test flight.*

*Miami, November 19*
Colonel Charles Lindbergh launched a new era in air travel today when he made the first flight by a Pan American Airways Sikorsky S-40 flying boat from Miami to the Panama Canal Zone.

Pan Am has three of the new four-engined aircraft, which will replace its Consolidated Commodores. The S-40 has a crew of six and weighs 34,000 lb – twice as much as the Commodore. It also carries twice as many passengers (40) as the older airplane. Each aircraft will include the word "Clipper" in its name, for example *Southern Clipper*. The designation has been chosen because it is hoped that the flying boat offers the speed and efficiency of its sailing ship namesake of earlier times.

# US airways given federal subsidy as routes boom

*USA, December*
The huge potential for air travel inside the United States is set to launch US airlines, and with them the US civil aircraft manufacturing industry, on a new period of expansion.

Americans were slower than Europeans to take to the air as passengers, but since Charles Lindbergh's flight in 1927 there has been extraordinary growth in passenger traffic in the US. In 1928, 38 domestic airlines carried 48,312 passengers. In 1929 the numbers flying had nearly quadrupled: 34 airlines carried 161,933 passengers. Last year saw a more than twofold increase on that, with 43 domestic airlines carrying 384,506 passengers. Today over half of all airline passengers carried anywhere in the world fly on US domestic routes.

Over the same period there has been a steady consolidation of the airline industry. This has been brought about by US postmaster-general Walter Folger Brown. He believes that the national interest is best served by larger, well-financed airlines rather than many small, badly-financed operators. He wants to develop transcontinental routes and provide an impetus to the development of new commercial aircraft.

Since the passage of the McNary-Watres Act of 1930, the US Post Office has had powers to award lucrative mail contracts, on which the airlines depend for much of their income, to those who are prepared to cooperate with its strategy. The act has also changed the way the airlines are paid for carrying mail: instead of payment by weight, the airlines will be paid $1.25 per mile for the space provided for mail.

This money, effectively an indirect subsidy to the industry, will eventually find its way through to US airplane makers as airlines look around for new, faster aircraft.

The Boeing B-9 bomber embodied many advanced technical features.

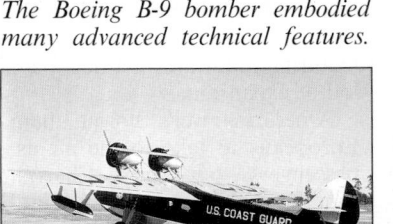

Douglas produced the RD (Dolphin) amphibian for the US Coast Guard.

Heinkel's He 46, built for reconnaissance and army cooperation.

The Berliner-Joyce OJ-2 was a catapult-launched observation aircraft.

The French Amiot 143 multi-seat combat aircraft: built in quantity.

The Heinkel He 59 torpedo-bomber, also used for air/sea rescue work.

The Focke-Wulf A.47 was a prototype for meteorological observation.

Heinkel's He 50 could be used as a dive-bomber or for reconnaissance.

The Arado Ar 65 single-seater fighter entered Luftwaffe service in 1933.

A prototype attack monoplane, the Curtiss A-8 Shrike of the USAAC.

Five Douglas YIO-35 observation aircraft were supplied to the USAAC.

The Curtiss XF9C-1 carrier-fighter was adapted to produce the F9C-2 Sparrowhawk, operated from the airships "Akron" and "Macon".

A seaplane torpedo-bomber, Latécoère's Hispano-Suiza-powered Laté 29-0 displayed a strong similarity to the Laté 28 commercial monoplane.

Breguet's 410M was typical of the boxy designs produced to meet the French Multiplace de Combat requirements, which turned out to be ill-founded.

De Havilland's Tiger Moth: a great and famous trainer makes its debut.

The Saunders-Roe Cloud amphibian served in military and civil roles.

The epitome of fighter biplanes, the Hawker Fury formed the front-line equipment of three of the RAF's premier fighter squadrons from 1931 to 1939.

The Tupolev ANT-14 had five M-22 (Bristol Jupiter) engines.

The Fokker F.XII airliner was also built under license as a bomber.

A development of the formula established by the S.55, the Savoia-Marchetti S.66 was a 14-passenger twin-hull flying boat for commercial operations.

Grumman's FF-1 two-seater was the first US Navy fighter to have a retractable undercarriage. It launched a long association of company and customer.

Poland's RWD-5 was used for a Dakar/Natal South Atlantic flight.

Sikorsky's S-40 airliner was the world's largest amphibian in its day.

The General Aircraft Monospar had a patented form of wing-structure.

A classic among transports, the corrugated Junkers Ju 52/3m was built in larger numbers than any other European transport aircraft before or since.

The Arrow Active was intended as a fighter trainer. Only two were built.

Blackburn's B-2 trainer had side-by-side seating for pilot and pupil.

An eight-passenger commercial tri-motor: the Savoia-Marchetti S.71.

Macchi's sleek MC.72 still holds the world speed record for seaplanes.

The American Pilgrim 100-A: used for internal feeder-liner services.

The Focke-Wulf Möwe series ended in the A.38, with a 510-hp Jupiter VI.

# 1932

406.94mph
Great Britain
GH Stainforth
Supermarine S.6.B
Sep 29, 1931

6,587.45 miles
France
Bossoutrot and Rossi
Blériot 110
Mar 26, 1932

43,976ft
Great Britain
Cyril F Uwins
Vickers Vespa
Sep 16, 1932

123,457lb
Germany
Dornier
Do X

3,058hp
Italy
Fiat
AS.6

**Croydon, England, January 20**
Imperial Airways' Handley Page
H.P.42 *Helena* leaves for Paris on
the first leg of the company's new
mail service to Cape Town.

**Paris, January 24**
French pilots Paul Codos and
Henri Robida land after flying from
Hanoi in French Indochina in
a record time of 3 days 4 hours.

**Dorset, England, January 26**
The British M.2 submarine, which
was converted to carry an airplane
[*see page 287*], sinks with the loss of
the entire crew. Both hangar doors
had been left open.

**China, February 5**
Two Nakajima Type 3 fighters
leave the carrier *Hosho* to take on
Chinese fighters over Shingu, in the
first air battles fought by Japanese
air forces (→ Feb 26).

**New York, February 13**
The Goodyear blimp *Columbia* is
battered and destroyed by high
winds as it attempts to moor at
Holmes airport, Queens.

**New York, February 14**
Ruth Nichols flies her Lockheed
Vega from Floyd Bennett Field to
an altitude of 19,928 feet, a new
world record for diesel-engined
airplanes.

**New York, February 28**
French aero engineer Robert
Esnault-Pelterie's attempt to
enforce his patents covering the
"stick and rudder control" of
airplanes is thrown out of a
Brooklyn court after a long
hearing.

**Washington, DC, March 1**
The US government announces an
amendment to its air-commerce
regulations: pilots of scheduled
airliners must pass tests in blind
flying and the use of radio aids in
navigation.

**South Africa, March 28**
Jim Mollison lands near Cape
Town after flying from London in

4 days 17 hours 30 minutes – a
new record; he is so tired at the end
that he has double vision and
cannot land at the airport because
the lights dazzle him, so he puts
down on a beach, where the
incoming tide damages his
D.H.80A Puss Moth (→ May 9).

**Washington, DC, March 31**
The Collier trophy for 1931 is
awarded to the Packard Motor Car
Co for developing the diesel
aircraft engine.

**Wichita, Kansas, April 1**
Walter Beech and his wife Olive
Ann found the Beech Aircraft
Corporation (→ Nov 4).

**Kent, England, April 8**
Eustace Short, one of the three
founders of Short Brothers aircraft
manufacturers, dies of a heart
attack just after landing his Short
Mussel seaplane at Rochester.

**Hanworth, London, April 12**
Sir Alan Cobham, veteran of many
flights to Africa and Australia,
opens his National Aviation Day
tour. He plans to visit British
towns, exhibiting his airplanes and
taking people up on flights.

**Iraq, April 25**
Aircraft of Britain's Royal Air
Force go into action in support of
Iraqi forces against Kurdish rebels.

**Croydon, England, April 27**
Imperial Airways inaugurates
passenger services between London
and Cape Town, with simultaneous
departures at both ends of the
route; the return fare is £234.

**Darwin, Australia, April 28**
British pilot Charles Scott lands
after a record flight of 8 days 20
hours 54 minutes from England in
a de Havilland Gipsy Moth.

**Germany, May 1**
German airline Deutsche Luft
Hansa (DLH) inaugurates a daily
express service from Berlin to
Rome, via Munich and Venice
(→ Apr 29, 1933).

**Moscow, May 1**
Nine of the latest Soviet TB-3
heavy bombers take part in the Red
Square May Day celebrations;
each has four engines and ten
machine-guns.

**Germany, May 7**
The Dornier Do 11 twin-engined
bomber makes its first flight; the
aircraft is disguised as a mail/cargo
transport because of post-Great
War restrictions.

**London, May 9**
Celebrated British aviators Amy
Johnson and Jim Mollison
announce their engagement after
lunch in London's smart Quaglino's
restaurant (→ Jul 29).

**USA, May 12**
Truck driver William Allen finds
the corpse of a 20-month-old baby
boy just 4 miles from Hopewell, the
family home of famous pilot
Charles Lindbergh. It is identified
as that of the pilot's son, Charles
Augustus, who was kidnapped on
March 1; Lindbergh had just made
a ransom payment of $75,000.

**Friedrichshafen, Germany, May 24**
The giant German Dornier Do X
flying boat lands at the end of a
19-month world tour.

**Hanworth, London, May 31**
Juan de La Cierva, inventor of the
autogyro, opens a flying school;
the first pupil to enrol is 68-year-
old James McCullen.

**Toulouse, France, June 18**
Marcel Doret pilots the Dewoitine
D.500 cantilever-wing fighter on
its first flight.

**USA, June 21**
Financier Robert E Gross takes
control of Lockheed. He wants to
build an airplane to rival Boeing's
planned 247.

**New York, July 5**
American pilots James Mattern
and Bennett Griffin leave on an
attempt to break the record for a
round-the-world flight (→ Aug 17).

**Wasserkuppe, Germany, July 23**
German glider pilot Günther
Groenhoff is killed when his Fafnir
glider crashes.

**Massachusetts, August 13**
The Granville Brothers' Gee Bee
R-1 racing airplane makes its first
flight, at Springfield (→ Sep 3).

**USSR, August 14**
Alexei Cheremukhin pilots the
TsAGI 1-EA helicopter to an
altitude of 1,985 feet.

**England, September 14**
The third version of the Fairey
Queen unmanned radio-controlled
gunnery target is successfully
launched from HMS *Valiant*.

**Bristol, England, September 16**
Cyril Uwins flies a Vickers Type
210 Vespa Mk VII to a world
record altitude of 43,976 feet.

**Croydon, England, September 26**
Imperial Airways puts the
Armstrong Whitworth Atalanta
into service on the London -
Cologne route (→ Jul 1, 1933).

**Alaska, October 15**
After buying two small airlines,
Pan American sets up Pacific
Alaska Airways Inc.

**Wichita, Kansas, November 4**
Beech Aircraft Corporation's first
airplane, the Model 17, makes its
first flight.

**USA, November 30**
Pan American Airways announces
that it has signed contracts for two
flying boats, one from Sikorsky and
one from Glenn L Martin.

**Croydon, England, December 18**
Amy Johnson lands her D.H.80A
Puss Moth *Desert Cloud*, after a
flight of 7 days 7 hours 5 minutes
from South Africa.

*First woman to fly solo across the
Atlantic, Amelia Earhart salutes the
crowd after her triumphant flight
from Newfoundland to Ireland.* ▶

# Radio airplane test makes a false start

*Portsmouth, England, January 30*
In a new twist to the debate about sea-air strategy, Britain's admirals have tried to catapult an aircraft without a pilot from the deck of a warship in the river Solent. The experiment was a failure, but an interesting one.

The aircraft, a Fairey III, was intended to be a moving target. Britain's admirals are still worried by tests in the USA a few years ago which demonstrated how vulnerable a big warship can be when it comes under air attack, and have been keen to develop the skills of naval gunners. A Fairey landplane was fitted with floats last year and rigged for control by radio.

Today, the Fairey III was controled by radio autopilot and gyroscope. Watched from the bridge, the machine sped along the movable gantry on HMS *Valiant* and was hurled skyward. It soared upward for about 12 seconds, before, as the controler struggled to bring the machine level, it pointed its nose down and dived into the sea about 6 seconds later.

The Royal Navy is not wholly disappointed, because its scientists know why they failed: the gyroscope, acting like a human sense of balance, had insufficient time to respond to sudden acceleration. More aircraft are available for further experiments.

# Japanese carrier airplanes attack China

*The Nakajima A1N carrier fighter: launched by the Japanese against China.*

*Shanghai, China, February 26*
The Asian mainland has been attacked from the air for the first time, by Japanese naval aircraft. Four days after shooting down an American pilot flying for China, airplanes from the Japanese carrier *Kaga* today bombed Chinese airfields. Over Hangchow eight Japanese Nakajima A1N fighters took on five Chinese interceptors and claim to have shot down three.

In the February 22 incident, Robert Short, flying a Boeing 218 demonstration fighter, intercepted a torpedo bomber from the *Kaga* and killed its gunner. Short died soon after when three A1Ns pounced on him. The current fighting began last year when the imperial Japanese army seized Chinese Manchuria without even consulting its own government in Tokyo. The imperial Japanese navy, smelling blood, has now also waded into the conflict. The danger signs have been evident for years in Japan's betrayal of pacts with the USA and Britain, which put a brake on its naval expansion, and in the remarkable evolution of a naval air arm. From a modest 7,500-ton carrier in 1919, Japan, aided by a British mission in 1921, has since completed two 30,000-ton carriers, *Akagi* and *Kaga*, and is now building its own light bomber, the Kawasaki 88, without Western help.

# 'Lindy's' son taken

*Hopewell, NJ, March 2*
The 20-month-old son of aviator Charles Lindbergh has been kidnapped. Last night his mother Anne and his nursemaid put him to bed in the upstairs nursery of the family's isolated Sourland Mountain home. Two hours later the nurse found his crib empty. Lindbergh said a ransom note on the window frame demanded $50,000 for the return of Charles Jr. The baby was taken while the family dined downstairs; Lindbergh heard a noise "like an orange crate smashing". Now 100,000 police and volunteers have joined the search. President Hoover said he would "move heaven and earth" to find Charles Jr.

# Future of air war is discussed at Geneva meeting

*Geneva, February 2*
The threat of air power to world security is high on the agenda of the international conference on disarmament, which opened here today under the auspices of the League of Nations. Armies and navies are reasonably contained by recent treaties. Air forces are another matter. Governments fear that their cities will be razed and torched in the first hours of hostilities, but no-one can agree on a solution.

The British, for instance, would limit the size of airplanes, but reserve the right to use bombers for "police work in outlying regions", that is, to put down rebellions in the British Empire. The Germans want equality with France, regardless of any formula, but the French fear the Germans and demand an edge to preserve their security. They therefore demand a British guarantee backed by military preparations.

France also suggests an international civil air transport system, which would prevent pilots and airplanes from falling into the hands of air force generals. Military professionals, with one eye on Japan's invasion of Manchuria and another on the rise of the militaristic Nazi Party in Germany, do not trust any disarmament scheme to be adhered to by those nations.

French and British intelligence reports reveal German evasions of the limits imposed on its construction of military aircraft, against the good intentions of the League of Nations. The Treaty of Rapallo, between Germany and the USSR ten years ago, is suspected of leading Germany to open up secret air training schools on Soviet territory. There are also "front" companies making German weapons in Sweden, Finland, Turkey and elsewhere. The Allied Control Commission, set up after the Great War to supervise the Versailles Treaty, speaks of "brazen violations".

**American pilots Halliburton and Stevens fly their humorously-named airplane "Flying Carpet" over the magnificent Taj Mahal, near Agra, India. The pair completed a flight around the world this year.**

# New Jersey airport installs landing aids

*Permission to take off or land is signaled to the pilot with an electric light.*

**Newark, NJ, March 12**
New landing aids have been installed at Newark airport, the busiest airport in the world, to supplement the night landing facilities already in existence there. Wires stretched at right angles to the runway emit signals which allow the pilot of an incoming airplane to know his or her precise position on the approach. Newark airport has had lights to mark the center of its runway for several years.

Construction work at Newark began in February 1928 on an expanse of marshland. In nine months and at a cost of $1,750,000,

Newark Municipal Airport was created with a 1,600-foot-long, northeast-to-southwest asphalt runway. The airport opened officially on October 1, 1928, although a Ryan monoplane had made the first landing there in August.

Newark was designated as the New York metropolitan airmail terminus in the same year, and four airlines began scheduled passenger services from there. By the autumn of 1930, Newark was said to be the world's busiest airport. In that year, there were some 28,000 landings and the airport handled 20,000 passengers.

# 'Code Q' is international language of air

**London, April 30**
An international code of air traffic communication was formally established today, following the decision to do so at a 1927 conference in Washington, DC. The move has become necessary because of the increase in the number of countries operating international airline services, and the widespread use of radio-telegraphy aboard aircraft.

The long delay in implementing a decision made five years ago has been caused by the detailed discussions between countries on how best to structure the code. It had to be easily recognizable and allow for the fact that pilots did not speak each other's languages. The new code is based on a series of three-

letter codes starting with the letter "Q", such as the following:
QAA: Estimated arrival time is ...
QAB: I am en route for ...
QAC: I am returning to ...
QAH: My altitude is ...
QAL: I am going to land at ...
QBA: Visibility is ...
QBF: I am in the clouds.
QBU: Your message is unclear.
QCJ: I am not receiving you.
QGH: Ground pressure is ...
QRD: I will go to ...
QRF: I am turning back.
QRK: Receiving you clearly.
QRL: I am busy.
QRQ: Transmit faster.
QRS: Transmit more slowly.
QRT: Cease transmission ...
QSY: I am changing frequency.

# Soviets launch Aeroflot

**Moscow, March 25**
Today the USSR inaugurated a major expansion of its modest airline Dobroflot into a potentially gigantic nationwide civil air arm. Strictly called the Grazhdanskii Vozdushnyi Flot [Civil Air Fleet], the airline will use the more manageable title of Aeroflot.

The USSR is the biggest country in the world and, as it industrializes rapidly, Aeroflot could easily become the world's largest airline. It

is far more than just a passenger carrier, because it has been charged with every civil task which involves airplanes, such as fighting forest fires, patroling power lines and pipelines, surveying and photoraphy, crop dusting and ambulance work.

Aeroflot is administered by 11 regional directorates. It is planned to open up the Arctic, as well as large areas of remote Siberia. It will mean a great expansion in Soviet civil aircraft production.

*The Soviets believe that each town should have its own well-equipped airport.*

# Italian air force performs for Mussolini

**Rome, May 27**
Italian air minister Italo Balbo today laid on a spectacular air show for Italy's "Duce", Benito Mussolini. Four hundred airplanes staged a daring show of aerobatics and mock combat which testified to Balbo's impressive achievements in revitalising Italian aviation. Flyers from 11 nations were invited to witness the display.

Mussolini, with a characteristic grasp of propaganda, insisted that all the planes were Italian, in order

to show off his country's flying power. German manufacturer Dornier set up an Italian plant in order to satisfy him, and Italian Dornier Wals put on a good display at today's show. Savoia-Marchetti demonstrated its S.71 trimotor commercial monoplane, which can take eight passengers. At the other end of the aviation spectrum, Macchi's Schneider trophy-winning M.39 seaplane, with its 800-hp, 12-cylinder Fiat AS2 engine, attracted great admiration.

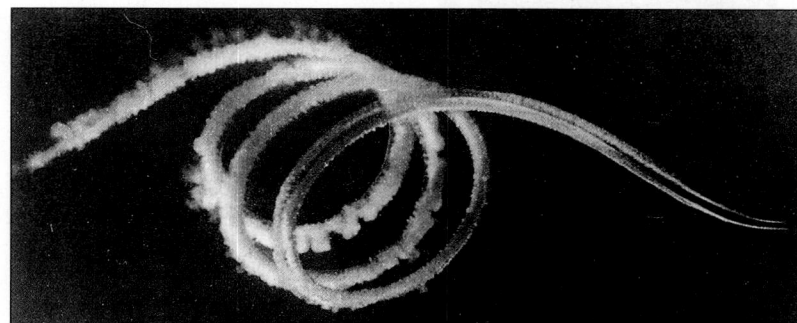

*A superb spiral pattern created by two aerobatic performers in tight formation.* ▷

## Ocean flyer saved from a watery death

*Lou Reichers: forced down at sea.*

*Atlantic Ocean, May 13*
Lou Reichers, who sped from Montreal to Havana in just 9 hours 3 minutes two weeks ago, had his hopes of halving Lindbergh's time to Paris dashed today by winds, mechanical problems and a shortage of fuel. He was saved from death by the quick action of the SS *President Roosevelt*.

The ship saw Reichers's single-engine Lockheed Altair monoplane *Liberty* plunging into the sea. Despite rough seas, a boat was lowered which took Reichers off the sinking plane 47 miles west of Fastnet Light, off Ireland. He suffered a broken nose and facial lacerations. Reichers covered the leg from Newark, New Jersey, to Harbour Grace, Newfoundland, in the record time of 6 hours 19 minutes.

# Earhart finds glory over the Atlantic

*Northern Ireland, May 21*
Danny McCallion and his cows provided the welcoming committee when Amelia Earhart landed in Gallagher's pasture at Culmore, near Londonderry, today, and became the first woman to fly solo non-stop across the Atlantic.

Earhart's trip, which began at Harbour Grace, Newfoundland, was not uneventful. Her altimeter, vital to instrument-flying at night and in bad weather, failed. She encountered a thunderstorm. Trying to climb above the clouds, her Lockheed Vega became covered with ice and went into a 3,000-foot spin. For the last two hours of the flight, she watched flames visible from a split engine manifold, hoping that the fumes from fuel dripping from a leaky gauge into the cockpit would not ignite.

The time for her Atlantic crossing, 14 hours 54 minutes, beats Alcock and Brown's record of 16 hours 12 minutes. At the same time, she has established the record for the longest non-stop flight by a woman, 2,026 miles (→ Aug 25).

*Well-wishers press close to congratulate Amelia after her arrival in Ireland.*

## The Farman 1000 has a pressurized cabin

*The Farman 1000 airplane was especially built for flights at high altitudes.*

*Villacoublay, Paris, June 25*
Farman company test pilot Lucien Coupet has just taken off in the new Farman 1000, designed to gain the high-altitude record for France. It is only the third aircraft to be fitted with a sealed pressurized cabin for the pilot, which also accommodates an observer.

Powered by a 350-hp Farman 8Vi engine, the Type 1000 has a huge wing to provide lift in the thin air at the altitude it aims for, 32,800 feet. The engine is progressively more supercharged as the aircraft climbs, and the cabin is pumped to a pressure of 2.85 pounds per square inch to maintain the interior at conditions found at 11,500 feet. The pilot has no external view except through small side windows. For take-off and landing, which are not easy operations, the pilot has to open a roof hatch.

## Army pilot makes 'blind' flight solo

*Dayton, Ohio, May 9*
US Army Air Corps Captain A F Hegenberger has become the first pilot in the world to make a "blind" landing using instruments alone, with no back-up co-pilot on board. A blind landing has been a goal of experiments funded by philanthropist Daniel Guggenheim since Jimmy Doolittle made the first ever blind flight in September 1929, with Ben Kelsey as safety pilot.

Like Doolittle, Hegenberger flew a modified 220-hp Consolidated NY-2 biplane trainer. The key to his successful landing were two Kreusi radio compass transmitters (locators), each with a VHF marker beacon, enabling him to pinpoint the runway accurately.

Blind flying with a check pilot on board is now becoming recognized as an essential element of pilot training. Britain's Royal Air Force, for example, has been using Avro 504Ns for instrument flying training since last September.

# Lost pilots saved in bush by aborigines

*Australia, June 28*

Two German aviators, missing since May 15, have been found alive in the Australian bush six miles south of Cape Bernier, after being looked after by aboriginal tribesmen. The Junkers seaplane of Captain Hans Bertram and mechanic Adolph Klauseman crashed on the last leg of a flight from Germany to Australia.

A team of police searchers found the two men today, some 12 miles from where they had abandoned their seaplane on June 24. The two men are said to be as well as can be expected, although suffering from malnourishment. They had survived on a meager diet of snails, kangaroo flesh, eucalyptus leaves, red berries and lizards, washed down with water from the airplane's cooling system.

*Bertram was saved by aborigines.*

# British flyers Johnson and Mollison wed

*Famous flyers Amy and Jim are toasted by guests at their wedding reception.*

*London, July 29*

Britain's favorite woman flyer, Amy Johnson, today married rival record-breaking aviator Jim Mollison at St George's church, off London's Hanover Square. The pair love speed in marriage as in the rest of life: Jim proposed to Amy after just a few hours in her company. Amy told her family only yesterday evening, and her parents and sisters drove overnight from Yorkshire through heavy rain. They arrived as the bride was leaving the church, but Amy, in a black coat with silver fox fur, did not see them as the couple left in a Rolls-Royce. The honeymoon was a weekend in Scotland before Jim's bid to fly the Atlantic both ways (→ Aug 20).

# Polish airman safe after ordeal at sea

*North Atlantic, June 11*

"Thanks very much, Captain": That is all that the Polish airman Stanley Haussner managed to blurt out this evening before collapsing from exhaustion and exposure onto the deck of the *Circe Shell*.

Before being rescued, he had drifted for seven days aboard a tiny life raft in the North Atlantic, some 600 miles from the coast of Europe. Flying the *Rose Marie*, a single-engine Bellanca airplane, Haussner had left New York on June 3 to fly non-stop to Warsaw. However, a leaking fuel tank forced him down a week ago. While adrift at sea, a total of 15 ships passed within sight of him, but his calls for help went unnoticed.

Towards the end of the seventh day, as the pilot was nearing the end of his tether, Haussner was spotted by the *Circe Shell's* officer of the watch. Despite the failing light and a dangerously heavy swell, the ship's crew, which had sailed from the Belgian port of Antwerp, was able to hoist the exhausted airman aboard.

# Earhart seizes three women's records in transcontinental flight

*Newark, NJ, August 25*

Amelia Earhart continues to rewrite the record books. At 11.31 this morning she landed here to establish three more records for woman flyers, including one for the first woman to fly across the USA non-stop. Flying the same Lockheed Vega which she used to cross the Atlantic in May, she set a women's distance flying record of 2,478 miles.

Her coast-to-coast time of 19 hours 5 minutes broke the record she set last month by almost ten minutes. On that flight she was forced to land at Columbus, Ohio, with a faulty fuel line. Despite her success today, she failed to better Frank Hawks' five-year-old record of 18 hours 22 minutes.

# Pioneer Santos-Dumont takes own life

*Santos-Dumont: driven to suicide.*

*Guaryja, Brazil, July 23*

Alberto Santos-Dumont, one of the world's great aviation pioneers, has been found dead at the age of 59 while suffering from depression. He committed suicide by hanging. Santos-Dumont, who had multiple sclerosis, became famous when he lived in Paris for flying all three types of machine – balloon, airship and airplane. He was known to be deeply upset by the use of flying machines for military purposes. In Brazil, he was considered the father of aviation, an engineering genius and a global ambassador for peaceful air commerce.

**Englishman Charles Scott is welcomed home after his flight to Australia.**

## Americans applaud flyers' brave effort

*A New York official greets the flyers.*

*New York, August 17*
Two Americans, James (Jimmy) Mattern and Bennett Griffin, may have failed in their bid to break the round-the-world record, but they certainly had a heroes' welcome today. Thousands of New Yorkers cheered their return on the SS *Leviathan* escorted by four Army planes.

Their bid to beat last year's record, set by Wiley Post and Harold Gatty, ended in a dramatic crash-landing at Minsk, USSR, on July 7. The pilots were hurt and their Lockheed Vega *Century of Progress* twisted and buckled. The day before they had made a sensational 18-hr 41-min run from Newfoundland to Berlin, ten hours inside the previous best (→ Jun 2, 1933).

## Mollison goes west on Canada flight

*New Brunswick, Canada, August 20*
An exhausted Jim Mollison landed his de Havilland Puss Moth *Heart's Content* in a field at Pennfield Ridge today, completing the first solo east/west transatlantic flight. The trip from the east coast of Ireland lasted 31 hours 20 minutes, making it the fastest-ever westbound crossing. Mollison kept himself going on nips of brandy during what turned out to be the longest flight ever in a light airplane. The Puss Moth is only half the size of the Ryan monoplane Charles Lindbergh used on his famous west/east crossing five years ago (→ Nov 18).

# 'Flying family' found among ice-caps

*Greenland, September 13*
All four members of the flying Hutchinson family have been found safe and well on a desolate part of the Greenland coast, 38 miles south-west of Angmagsalik. Their Sikorsky seaplane, however, is completely wrecked.

Colonel Hutchinson, his wife Blanche and their two young daughters, Kathryn and Janet Lee, took off from Baltimore on August 23, in what was described as a foolhardy attempt to fly to England. The family and five-strong crew were forced down by violent storms off the coast of Greenland, from where they sent out an SOS, which was picked up by a British trawler. They were finally found after a five-day search.

*Mrs Hutchinson and daughters stare at their wrecked airplane in Greenland.*

## Doolittle seizes record in 'touchy' Gee Bee

*Cleveland, Ohio, September 3*
Major James Doolittle set a new world speed record for landplanes today, averaging 294mph over a three-kilometer [1.86-mile] course in his Granville Gee Bee R-1 monoplane. In the Thomson Trophy speed race, Doolittle lapped all the contestants except Jimmy Wedell in his Wedell-Williams Special.

His achievement has been hailed as a rare feat of airmanship, as the Gee Bee is notoriously dangerous and suffers from directional instability. Built for outright speed, the Gee Bee has a massive engine, a stubby, barrel-shaped fuselage, short wings and a tiny, vertical fin. Doolittle has called it "the touchiest plane I have ever been in".

Practising pylon turns at 5,000 feet, instead of the racing height of less than 250 feet, Doolittle found that the airplane went into snap rolls if banked too sharply. To overcome this problem during the race, he used the plane's power to seize the lead at take-off, allowing him time to bank wide of the three pylons.

*Jimmy Doolittle's compact Gee Bee racer flashes to a new speed record.*

## Douglas wins big contract from TWA

*USA, November 18*
Transcontinental and Western Air (TWA) signed a contract today with the Douglas Aircraft Company for a new transport plane to be called the DC-1. TWA will pay $125,000 for the first aircraft with an option to purchase more in batches of between 10 and 20 for $58,000 each, excluding engines.

TWA had approached Boeing to buy a fleet of its 247 model, which is due to fly next year, but Boeing was unwilling to help TWA, since it belongs to the same group of companies as United Airlines and was under contract to sell the first 75 to United. TWA's vice-president Jack Frye therefore went to Douglas with a design specification aimed at bettering the 247.

The 247 is a development of the single-engined 200 Monomail, never taken into service. None the less it provided Boeing with the experience of building an all-metal, stressed-skin monoplane expressly designed for transport use. Douglas is now determined to build an airliner even better than the Boeing 247. The eventual beneficiaries of this competition between airplane builders will be the airlines and, ultimately, their passengers as airliners improve in speed, comfort and safety (→ Jul 1, 1933).

# Amy takes ten hours off husband's record

*Cape Town, November 18*

British airwoman Amy Mollison, née Johnson, has grabbed the world record for a flight from Britain to the Cape – from her husband Jim. Soon after they married four months ago she said: "I'm going to try to beat Jim's Cape record; just a sporting effort." The "sporting effort" demanded a 6,700-mile flight in her de Havilland Puss Moth *Desert Cloud* from Edgware, near London, down the west coast of Africa. She did it in 4 days, 6 hours and 56 minutes, ten hours faster than her husband. She hopes to break another record on the return flight.

Her worst moments, she says, came about midway, flying by night through thunderstorms. The brief course she had taken back home in "blind" flying, on instruments only, proved useless for coping with fatigue, turbulence and driving rain. Her advice to her family, though, had been that if she went missing, they need not worry since Jim would come and find her in his own Puss Moth (→ Feb 9, 1933).

*Amy's father films, and her mother watches, as her airplane comes down.*

# British statesman warns of bomber power

*London, November 10*

The prospect of civilians being bombed from the air was vividly illustrated in a speech today by Stanley Baldwin, the former premier who is leader of the Conservatives in Britain's coalition National government. He said: "The bomber will always get through."

Baldwin was speaking against the background of the deadlocked Geneva Disarmament Conference, which has so far failed to find a way to ban, or even limit, the size of the bomber fleets of the major powers. His speech reflects a growing fatalism about the threat which long-range bombers pose, and he was skeptical of the ability of international conferences to provide an answer. He said: "Will any form of prohibition of bombing by convention, treaty or agreement or anything else you like, be effective in war?" He went on to provide his own answer to the question: "The stern test of war will break down all conventions."

If international agreement will not work, and since the airplane cannot be uninvented, the only hope of finding an effective deterrent to aerial bombers must lie in human ingenuity. History shows that for every offensive weapon developed, a defense is eventually found, though usually only after much pain and suffering.

# British aim to make better parachutes as advances are made in military potential

*Dropping in for a chat: an artist's bright idea of a future use for parachutes.*

*London, November*

British entrepreneurs Raymond Quilter and James Gregory are trying to set up a company to make better parachutes. They hope to sell chutes of an improved, cheaper design, not only to Britain's Royal Air Force (RAF) but also to private flyers and airlines. They also envisage their use for air drops of troops, weapons and other cargoes.

It is only six years since Leslie Irvin opened his factory at Letchworth, Hertfordshire, to produce all parachutes for the RAF. Other air forces adopted parachutes much earlier, especially during the Great War, and it has been calculated that the lack of such equipment cost the lives of over 6,000 British flyers. British developments in the military use of parachutes do not compare with those of the USSR, where hundreds of assault troops, complete with machine guns and even light artillery, have been parachuted on to their objectives.

This year also saw a parachute altitude record of 24,000 feet, set in Germany by Frau Schroter.

# Wrights honored by granite monument

*Kitty Hawk, NC, November 19*

If the Wrights had tried to take the *Flyer* out today, their fragile craft would have been been destroyed by the strong winds and heavy rains that swirled around Kill Devil Hill. But the only mishap today was that spectators got wet during ceremonies to unveil a monument to the Wrights' achievement.

With 61-year-old Orville, the surviving brother, watching, aviatrix Ruth Nichols unveiled the 61-foot, triangular granite pylon, inscribed: "In commemoration of the conquest of the air by the brothers Wilbur and Orville Wright, conceived by genius, achieved by dauntless resolution and unconquerable faith."

**A model tries a leather flying suit, with gloves to match.**

*Civil variant of the Farman F.220, used on South Atlantic services.*

*Deutsche Luft Hansa used only four Junkers Ju 60 six-passenger liners.*

*Designed by the Günter brothers, the beautifully streamlined Heinkel He 70 set a totally new standard in European aircraft technology.*

*A distinctive and durable design: the Beech Model 17, known as the "Stagger-wing" for obvious reasons. The series remained in production until 1948.*

*The General Aviation GA-43 ten-passenger airliner had clean lines.*

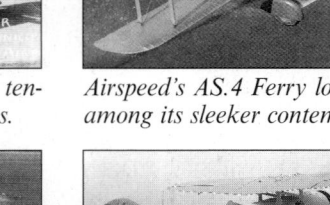

*Airspeed's AS.4 Ferry looked quaint among its sleeker contemporaries.*

*Fokker's 14-seater F.XVIII, power-ed by three Pratt & Whitney Wasps.*

*Consolidated's Type 20 Fleetster: chiefly a mail and express aircraft.*

*Armstrong Whitworth's A.W.15 Atalanta, used by Imperial Airways.*

*The de Havilland Fox Moth, domestic transport and feeder liner.*

*Edgar Percival's Gull found a niche in the private-aircraft market, and was used for a number of outstanding record-breaking long-distance flights.*

*Focke-Wulf's Fw 44 Stieglitz served as a Luftwaffe primary trainer.*

*Savoia-Marchetti's S.72: a bomber/transport trimotor monoplane.*

*The Martin 123, later the US Army B-10, revolutionized bomber design.*

*The Lioré et Olivier 206, with tandem pairs of Gnome-Rhône radials.*

*Five Junkers Ju 46 two-seater commercial seaplanes were used by DLH.*

*The Czech Letov S-328 observation and light bombing aeroplane.*

*The F11C-3 Goshawk was the last Curtiss fighter used by the US Navy.*

*Gloster's giant TC.33 troop transport was not put into production.*

*Fiat kept to Warren girder-bracing in its curvaceous C.R.30 fighter.*

The square-cut Farman F.220 series of bombers saw the Armée de l'Air right through to the Second World War, by which time they were outmoded.

Lithuania's Anbo IV, used for general purposes and reconnaissance.

Morane-Saulnier's MS.225 fighter adhered to the parasol-wing layout.

The Nimrod was the Fleet Air Arm's counterpart to the Hawker Fury.

Lioré et Olivier's LeO 203 bomber failed to win production orders.

Although Dewoitine's D.500 series of fighters had some advanced features, their fixed undercarriages and open cockpits dated them in the early 1930s.

The Berliner-Joyce Y1P-16 won a limited order from the USAAC.

Heinkel's He 45: a general-purpose two-seater for the Luftwaffe.

The Loire 43, 45 and 46 fighters had stressed skins and gull wings, but their complicated wing and undercarriage struttery inhibited performance.

Supermarine's Scapa flying boat: a greatly modernized Southampton.

The Blackburn Baffin replaced the Ripon in Britain's Fleet Air Arm.

Consolidated's P2Y-1 patrol flying boat was ordered by the US Navy, and 23 entered service. The later P2Y-3 had its engines in the wing leading edges.

The Boeing P-26 "Peashooter" was the company's first and last production monoplane fighter. A 600-hp Pratt & Whitney Wasp provided the power.

# 1933

423.82mph
Italy
Francesco Agello
Macchi-Castoldi MC-72
Apr 18, 1933

6,587.45 miles
France
Bossoutrot and Rossi
Bléroit 110
Mar 26, 1932

44,816ft
France
Gustave Lemoine
Potez 50
Sep 28, 1933

123,457lb
Germany
Dornier
Do X

3,058hp
Italy
Fiat
AS.6

**Croydon, England, January 7**
Australian airman Bert Hinkler leaves in an attempt to fly to Australia (→ Apr 28).

**Seattle, February 8**
Boeing's 247 twin-engined, all-metal airliner makes its maiden flight (→ Mar 30).

**Natal, Brazil, February 9**
Jim Mollison arrives in his de Havilland Puss Moth *Heart's Content* at the end of a flight from Kent, England.

**Middlesex, England, March 21**
Fairey's TSR.1 torpedo spotter-reconnaissance airplane makes its first flight at Harmondsworth.

**Newark, NJ, March 21**
The first cross-country test of blind flying and landing is made by James L Kinney from College Park, Maryland, to Newark.

**India, April 1**
The Indian Air Force is formed.

**Essex, England, April 14**
At Southend, Sir Alan Cobham launches his second National Aviation Day tour of British towns and cities (→ Oct 8).

**Berlin, April**
The Junkers Ju 52/3m enters service with airline Deutsche Luft Hansa (DLH).

**France, May 17**
Four carriers – Air Orient, CIDNA, Air Union and SGTA – merge to form the Société Centrale pour l'Exploitation des Lignes Aériennes (SCELA), as a preliminary to discussions with the government over the planned nationalization of France's airlines, announced April 14 (→ Oct 31).

**Los Angeles, June 1**
A United Airlines Boeing 247 flies from coast to coast in 19 hours and 45 minutes, compared to the 26 hours needed for TWA's three-engined Fords.

**New York, June 2**
US airman Jimmy Mattern leaves Brooklyn in his airplane *Century of Progress* to try to fly solo round the world in six days or less (→ Jun 15).

**Washington, DC, June 6**
The US government receives a Douglas monoplane with luxurious fittings for VIP passengers, which is to be put at the disposal of President Franklin D Roosevelt.

**Russia, June 15**
Mattern leaves Khabarovsk, Siberia, headed for Nome, Alaska, on his solo round-the-world flight attempt (→ Jul 6).

**Russia, June 22**
The Tupolev ANT-25 monoplane, designed to win the world long-distance record for the USSR, makes its first flight.

**Santa Monica, Calif, July 1**
Carl Cover pilots the prototype of the Douglas DC-1 all-metal airliner on its first flight (→ Dec).

**Croydon, England, July 1**
Imperial Airways' Armstrong Whitworth Atalanta *Arethusa* leaves with the first consignment of through mail for Calcutta, thus extending Imperial's route to Australia by one stage (→ Dec 9).

**USSR, July 3**
The giant Soviet TB-4 bomber (the ANT-16) makes its maiden flight.

**Los Angeles, July 4**
A Fokker airliner escorted by six Boeing pursuit airplanes delivers the guest of honor, actress Mary Pickford, to the National Air Races at Los Angeles; Mrs May Haizlip wins the trophy for women pilots in her Wedell-Williams racer.

**New York, July 6**
The *New York Times* receives a wireless message from pilot Jimmy Mattern, who went missing shortly after leaving Khabarovsk on June 15: "Safe at Anadyr, Chukotka, Siberia, Jimmy Mattern."

**Chicago, July 15**
A formation flight of 24 Italian seaplanes under the command of General Italo Balbo land on Lake Michigan for the World's Fair; they left Italy on July 1 and crossed the Atlantic in easy stages in 47 hours 52 minutes flying time.

**New York, July 15**
Wiley Post leaves in his Lockheed Vega *Winnie Mae* on an attempt to fly around the world (→ Jul 22).

**Germany, July 17**
Lithuanian pilots Stephen Darius and Stanley Girenas die tragically at the end of a successful flight from the USA, when they crash-land in East Prussia after losing their way in a thunderstorm and running out of fuel.

**Atlantic City, NJ, July 28**
Albert Forsythe and Clifford Anderson land at Atlantic City to complete the first return flight to the West Coast by black pilots.

**Seattle, August 5**
The Boeing Airplane Company is renamed the Boeing Aircraft Company.

**Rayak, Syria, August 7**
French pilots Maurice Rossi and Paul Codos land after flying from New York to set a world distance record of 5,657 miles.

**Kent, England, August 15**
A young woman dies when an RAF airplane mistakes her rowing boat for a target and shoots her.

**Berlin, August 21**
Nazi aviation minister Hermann Goering announces a ban on aerial photography over Germany.

**USA, August**
The first practical variable-pitch, two-position propeller, made by Hamilton Standard, is introduced on the Curtiss Condor transport.

**New York, September 2**
Italian flyer General Francesco de Pinedo is killed when he crashes on take-off from Floyd Bennett Field, Brooklyn, on a planned transatlantic fight.

**England, October 8**
Sir Alan Cobham's second National Aviation Day Tour ends with two displays west and east of London at Staines, Middlesex, and Romford, Essex.

**Western Australia, October 20**
Hot on the heels of Charles Kingsford Smith, who set a new record of 7 days 5 hours between England and Australia on October 11, his former navigator Charles Ulm lands with crew after flying from England in just 6 days 17 hours.

**Palermo, Sicily, November 6**
Fishermen say they have located the skeleton of the French dirigible *Dixmude*, which disappeared over the Mediterranean in December 1923.

**Croydon, England, November 19**
The Croydon Controlled Zone scheme, under which pilots are required to get radio clearance before entering a specified area of airspace around the airport, is introduced.

**Bridgeton, NJ, November 20**
Lieutenant-Commander Thomas Settle and Major Chester Fordney land at Bridgeton in their balloon after attaining a world record altitude of 61,237 feet.

**Singapore, December 9**
Imperial Airways' service is extended to the territory.

**USSR, December 31**
The prototype Polikarpov I-16 fighter makes its first flight; it has a cantilever monoplane wing, fully cowled M-22 radial engine and retractable landing gear.

*Flying over the "roof of the world": an Italian magazine here depicts the scene as Lord Clydesdale's Westland biplane approaches Everest.* ▶

# LA TRIBUNA ILLUSTRATA

Abbonamenti Interno · Anno L. 15 · Semestre L. 8
Estero · Anno L. 30 · Semestre L. 15
Per gli abbonamenti rivolgersi all'Amministrazione
de LA TRIBUNA, via Milano, 69 · Roma

Supplemento illustrato de "La Tribuna„
Proprietà letteraria e artistica riservata secondo le leggi

Per inserzioni rivolgersi all'Ufficio Pubblicità de
LA TRIBUNA, via Milano, 69, telef. 41-161 Roma (3).
Per l'Alta Italia Agenzia GOLFREDO BRESCHI, via
Salvini 10 telef. 20-907 Milano (113)

Anno XLI — N. 16.

16 aprile 1933 — Anno XI.

Cent. 30 il numero.

# 'Rainbow' spans the sky to South America

*The "Arc-en-Ciel": a revolutionary design by Frenchman René Couzinet.*

**Natal, Brazil, January 16**
The last link in the air route from Paris to South America was put in place today when an Aéropostale crew, headed by Jean Mermoz, made a direct crossing of the South Atlantic from St Louis, Mauritania, to Natal in Brazil. The transatlantic leg from Africa to the northern coast of Brazil coast took 14 hours 27 minutes. Crossing by ship takes five days, so the total journey time from Paris to Buenos Aires has been cut from eight days to just over three.

The airplane, named the *Arc-en-Ciel* [*Rainbow*], was a Couzinet 70 powered by three 650-hp Hispano-Suiza engines. The crew consists of pilot, engineer, navigator and wireless operator and, on this occasion, M Couzinet himself.

# Disaster hits world's largest airship

*The US Navy's ill-fated "Akron".*

**Barnegat, NJ, April 5**
The world's largest airship, the USS *Akron*, plunged into the Atlantic here shortly after midnight last night in a storm. Seventy of the 73 persons aboard perished.

The *Akron* left Lakehurst, New Jersey, last night to join the fleet off Delaware. At 00.23am the crew of a German ship saw lights heading toward the sea at a 45-degree angle. They vanished and then were sighted on the surface. The ship sailed towards the lights and its crew manned the lifeboats. They were able to pull four men from the water, one of whom died (→ Jun 23).

# Flyers go over Everest

**Purnea, India, April 3**
In a remarkable fight against the elements, two British airplanes today succeeded in flying over the world's highest mountain, Mount Everest. Having battled for every foot of altitude, they remained near the peak for 15 minutes.

The first over Everest was a Westland PV.3, sponsored by Lady Houston and piloted by the Marquis of Douglas and Clydesdale with observer Lieutenant-Colonel Steward Blacker. Britain's Air Ministry supplied the other plane, a Westland Wallace, crewed by Flight Lieutenant David McIntyre and cameraman Sidney Bonnett. Both airplanes carried mapping cameras. To combat the thin air and cold, the crews had oxygen masks and heated flying suits.

The Westlands took off at 8.25 am. They broke through thick haze at 19,000 feet, at last seeing the daunting white reaches of Makalu, Everest and Kanchenjunga. Caught in a plunging downdraft and then

*Flying over the towering Himalayas.*

an upcurrent, the PV.3 juddered as it pierced Everest's summit cloud, and flew over the peak with 500 feet to spare. McIntyre had even greater difficulty rising, repeatedly using updrafts to clear the peak.

*The Everest aircrew pose (right) by Puss and Fox Moths.*

**The Heinkel He 70** Blitz **is Europe's fastest passenger aircraft.**

# The Boeing 247, a new type of airliner

*Boeing's twin-engined model 247 made its first test flight last February 8.*

**Seattle, March 30**
United Airlines today began operating what can only be considered as the world's first truly modern airliner.

Based on the B-9 bomber and Monomail mailplane, Boeing's model 247 is a remarkable aircraft which flew for the first time on February 8. The 247 is way ahead of all contemporary designs. It is the first all-metal streamlined monoplane transport. This single-aisle, low-wing, stressed-skin airplane has fully retractable landing gear. It introduces control surface trim tabs, automatic pilot and wing and tail de-icing. Powered by Pratt & Whitney Wasp 550-hp radials, the 247 is the first twin-engine airplane able to climb on one engine with a full load of 10 passengers and three crew. It is also the first multi-engined transport to use supercharged engines of the type formerly confined to military airplanes. Its top cruising speed of 155mph and range of 485 miles make it possible to fly across the USA in less than 20 hours. The 247 introduces cabin air conditioning and a soundproofed fuselage. Its passengers have individual reading lights and a toilet is provided.

# TWA interested by the Northrop Gamma

*Lincoln Ellsworth's high-performance, long-range Northrop Gamma. Northrop and Douglas have used similar technology in the DC-1 airliner.*

**USA, September**
Any aircraft capable of carrying freight and six passengers across the United States in under 12 hours is bound to catch the eye of TWA executives.

The airline has just bought three of Northrop's new Gamma airplanes and plans to use them on airmail routes. These are low-wing monoplanes of all-metal construction, developed jointly by Northrop and Edward Heinemann from an earlier model, the Alpha, which first flew three years ago. Both models are basically mail airplanes modified to carry passengers in the front half of the fuselage, with the pilot occupying an open cockpit aft of the wing. The Gamma benefits from two important construction techniques. The first are wing fillets (fairings) fitted at the juncture of wing and fuselage to increase aerodynamic efficiency. The second is a revolutionary multicellular stressed-skin wing which dramatically increases the aircraft's strength.

The Gamma is powered either by a Wright Cyclone radial engine or by a Pratt & Whitney Wasp. It has a maximum speed of 177mph, a top cruising speed of 145mph and a fully-laden range of 1,650 miles.

# Robbery attempt could have caused Imperial Airways tragedy

**Dixmude, Belgium, March 28**
Stunned Imperial Airways officials and crash investigators are rushing to Belgium today to visit the scene of devastation surrounding the crash of the *City of Liverpool*, one of the airline's Armstrong Whitworth Argosy airliners. En route from Brussels to London, the tri-motor was seen by observers on the ground to be belching smoke from the rear section and descending rapidly. Shortly before it hit the ground, the fuselage broke in two and caught fire. All on board, 12 passengers and three crew, died in the flames.

This is the first fatality to strike what has so far proved a useful and wholly safe airliner. Imperial has said: "Our policy of using airliners of proven biplane design with three or more engines illustrates our fullest commitment to air safety." The fact that the fire seems to have started in the rear of the aircraft points perhaps towards passenger involvement in the accident. No working machinery which could cause a fire is located in that part of the cabin.

The baggage included a consignment of silver bullion, which ended up scattered all around the accident site. There is speculation that the cabin fire was part of a botched attempt at aerial robbery by forcing the airplane down to steal the cargo of silver.

*The fire-scarred remains of the "City of Liverpool" in a field near Dixmude.*

# New German plane named by Goering

**Berlin, April 29**
A band played briskly and soldiers and officials saluted today as Hermann Goering, air transport minister in the new National Socialist government, performed a naming ceremony on a giant airplane of airline Deutsche Luft Hansa (DLH). In a style every bit as grand as launching a ship, the second Junkers G 38 "flying wing" aircraft, which has been in service for over a year, was named *Generalfeldmarschall von Hindenburg* after the German president.

Since his appointment, Goering, a wartime fighter ace, has been making his presence felt. His stated intention, and that of German chancellor Adolf Hitler, is to make DLH the top airline in the world, by continually expanding its operations and influence.

# Independent French air force created

*Paris, April 1*
French air minister Pierre Cot today signed documents creating the country's independent air force, L'Armée de l'Air [Air Army]. It takes the airborne wing of the services out of the control of the army and puts all three branches of the military on an equal footing.

Supporters of this move have argued since 1918 in favor of a separate air arm like Britain's Royal Air Force. Five changes at the top of the Air Ministry have repeatedly frustrated their cause; now their appeals have been heeded.

The new air force is still woefully short of modern aircraft, despite the fact that in terms of numbers it is one of the largest air forces in the world. If the government goes ahead and nationalizes the majority of the aircraft industry, as is being planned, production of new airplanes will be stepped up dramatically. Many French politicians see this as an urgent task if France is to have an effective air force.

# Australian airman found dead in Italy

*Italy, April 28*
Australian pioneer aviator Bert Hinkler is dead. This morning Italian charcoal burners came across his decomposed body lying in a mountain stream, close to the wreckage of his silver de Havilland Puss Moth. It had crashed in the Prato Mago hills above Florence.

His widow was told the news aboard the liner *Strathaird*, berthed in Fremantle, Western Australia. She burst into tears, never having given up hope that he might be alive, but questioning why he had flown in such bad weather. Hinkler had not been seen since taking off from Feltham aerodrome, near London, on January 8, on an attempt to fly to Darwin in record time. It is likely that heavy cloud forced him to descend too soon before he had completely cleared the Dolomite mountains.

His body will lie in state in Florence before being taken to his homeland for a state funeral in Brisbane.

# American Airways needs stewardesses

*With alcoholic drinks still prohibited, a Coca-Cola is the next-best thing.*

*Chicago, May 4*
Four attractive young women will attend to passengers on the direct air service which American Airways began today between New York, Detroit and Chicago. Working in the 18-seater Curtiss Condors, they will serve a menu that includes sandwiches, green salad vinaigrette, pistachio ice-cream, coffee and cake. The one-way fare on the route, a trip of 5 hours 49 minutes to New York and about 30 minutes longer to Chicago, is $47.50. There is a 10 per cent discount on round-trip tickets.

# Propaganda aircraft flies in Soviet Union

*The crew of the ANT-14 improvises a political meeting on the landing ground.*

*Moscow, August 14*
One of the world's largest transporter aircraft, the Tupolev ANT-14, made its first flight here today. Able to carry 26 passengers, it is powered by five M-22 engines, Soviet versions of the Bristol Jupiter. Construction of the giant was speeded up by using wings from the ANT-6 heavy bomber. The ANT-14, named *Pravda*, is much bigger than Aeroflot, the Soviet civil airline, needs. In fact, no more will be built and the plane will become the flagship of the Maxim Gorkii propaganda squadron.

# Refueling problem solved by Germans over the Atlantic

*Atlantic Ocean, June 6*
The problem of operating a safe and regular air service across the Atlantic, something that would bring in millions to anyone who could achieve it, has not yet been solved. Most believe that the answer lies with airships such as the German *Graf Zeppelin*. Others believe the solution rests in bigger and better seaplanes or flying boats. Again it seems to be the Germans who have come up with at least a partial solution.

They have fitted several of their well-known Dornier Wal flying boats with long-range tanks and

*A Wal runs on to the Heine mat deployed by "Westfalen".*

then stationed a seaplane tender, the *Westfalen*, permanently in mid-Atlantic. After rendezvous, the Wal is lifted from the sea, refueled and then sent on its way. The first trials of the *Westfalen* took place successfully today when a Wal flying boat flew from Bathurst in West Africa to Brazil.

The 4,900-ton *Westfalen* is a cargo ship with a special flexible Heine mat and ramp to take the flying boat alongside before being swung aboard. After refueling, the 8-ton aircraft is shot from the deck by catapult to a speed of over 100mph. Airline Deutsche Luft Hansa hopes to introduce a regular three-and-a-half day service to Rio soon.

# USA boasts new airship

*Lakehurst, NJ, June 23*
The US Navy's $2.4 million airship USS *Macon* was commissioned today. Like its sister ship the *Akron*, which crashed at sea on April 4, the *Macon* can lower five fighter planes from a bay in the hull on a trapeze-like device, for in-flight launch and recovery.

But the *Macon*, which reached 85mph on its first flight on April 21, is lighter and more streamlined. Weight was saved by using a gelatin-latex material developed by Goodyear for the gas cells instead of rubberized fabric, and by improvements to the eight engine mounts, the electrical system and other components. Air resistance was lowered by the use of two to four smaller helium valve hoods on each gas cell, instead of the lone large ones employed on the *Akron*'s cells.

*USS "Macon" approaches its mast.*

## Mussolini's propaganda planes fly home

*Ostia, Italy, August 12*
Massive crowds lined the banks of the river Tiber today to welcome General Italo Balbo's armada of seaplanes when they landed triumphantly at the conclusion of their formation flight to the USA.

Italy's Fascist leader, Benito Mussolini, pleased at the international recognition generated by the flight, which was to mark the tenth anniversary of his regime, greeted the airmen, who saluted him with the cry "God save the Duce!" Mussolini promised them a parade under the Arch of Constantine to equal the triumphs given to victorious Roman legions

2,000 years ago. Balbo and almost 100 men left Orbetello on July 1 in 25 twin-engined Savoia S.55s. One airplane was lost and a crewman killed when they landed in Amsterdam. Their route then took them to Ireland, Iceland, Labrador, and Montreal before they dazzled the crowds when they arrived at the Chicago World's Fair on July 15. Four days later, again in perfect formation, they flew to New York for another welcome. A second airplane and pilot were lost in the Azores on the return trip. At all times during the flight the aviators held their tight formation, even in thick fog.

*Balbo's armada flies in to a tumultuous welcome at the port of Ostia.*

# New York gives Wiley Post huge welcome

*New York, NY, July 22*
A famous partnership of pilot and airplane scored again tonight when Wiley Post and the *Winnie Mae*, his Wasp-powered Lockheed Vega, landed after dark at Floyd Bennett Field, Brooklyn, to a tumultuous welcome. This was their second trip round the globe, setting a new record of 7 days 18 hours and 49 minutes.

Wiley and the *Winnie Mae* made the journey two years ago, accompanied by navigator Harold Gatty,

when it took 21 hours more. This time Wiley became the first to fly the journey alone. On the first leg he became the first to fly New York/Berlin non-stop in 25 hours 45 minutes. His route home went via Moscow and Siberia. Near the end, he was lost for seven hours in storm clouds over Alaska, damaging his propeller and undercarriage while landing to check his location. The *Winnie Mae* was patched up for a triumphant return to its home base.

*Wiley stands proudly by his round-the-world flyer, the Vega "Winnie Mae".*

## Spanish pair make non-stop Cuba trip

*Havana, June 11*
Two Spanish aviators, Captain Mariano Barberan and Lieutenant Joaquin Collar, landed at Camaguey today after making the first non-stop flight between Seville, Spain, and Cuba. It is also the first time the Atlantic has been crossed to the West Indies.

A distance of about 4,500 miles was covered in a flying time of 39 hours 55 minutes. Only 30 US gallons of fuel remained in the large tanks when the aircraft finally touched down. The airplane, a Breguet Super Bidon, named *Cuatro Vientos* [*Four Winds*], is a variant of the French Breguet XIX family, and was built under license in Spain by CASA at Getafe near Madrid. The splendid French-designed, 600-hp Hispano-Suiza water-cooled engine was also of Spanish construction. The airplane's two crew members sat in tandem beneath enclosing canopies.

## Lindbergh seaplane lands on Seine

*Paris, October 26*
This is not the first time that Charles Lindbergh has come to Paris, but the American pilot had never before landed on the the river which flows through France's capital.

A large crowd turned up at Les Mureaux, on the outskirts of the city, to welcome the famous flier. 'Lucky Lindy' had a surprise for them: he climbed out of his Lockheed Sirius accompanied by his wife, Anne Morrow-Lindbergh. Waving shyly at the crowd, she left for central Paris with her husband. During her stay here, Mrs Lindbergh avoided all public engagements except for a reception at the US Embassy, where she was mobbed by photographers.

Colonel Lindbergh's visit is not all pleasure, however. He has been hired by Pan American, and is checking North Atlantic routes with a view to setting up the first US/Europe passenger service.

# Air France, French national airline, is launched

*Air Minister Cot makes a speech at Air France's inauguration ceremony.*

*Ready for action: crews pose before one of the new company's Wibault 282s.*

*France, October 31*

France now has a single, national airline. The country's air minister, Pierre Cot, today formally inaugurated the airline, Air France.

The birth of Air France is part of the process of merging the small pioneering airline companies into bigger businesses, which is happening on both sides of the Atlantic. Cot acted following the government's refusal to continue subsidizing airlines whose status was often ambiguous. Many had close links with aircraft manufacturers who have in the past demanded that such airlines buy their planes. Cut-throat competition between the airlines also impeded their development. The first step in this process came on May 31, when four airlines, Air Orient, Air Union, CIDNA and SGTA (Farman), joined forces to create the Société Centrale pour l'Exploitation des Lignes Aériennes (SCELA), in order to negotiate with the government over its plans to nationalize French carriers, which were announced in April. On August 30, SCELA formally became Air France, a limited company with a capital of FF120,000,000. The process was completed today with the buying up of mail carrier Aéropostale's assets.

Air France's first priority will be to rationalise its fleet. It inherits 259 aircraft of 35 different types, of which no fewer than 172 are single-engined machines.

## TWA takes delivery of new Douglas DC-1

*USA, December*

Transcontinental and Western Air (TWA) has taken delivery of the new 12-seat airliner, the Douglas DC-1. It is the only airplane of its type, but TWA has already ordered 20 of its 14-seater derivative, the DC-2. The DC-1 cost $306,778 to develop and has been sold to TWA for $125,000. It is arguably the world's most modern airliner. It has been built to TWA specifications following the airline's inability to secure Boeing 247s owing to Boeing's connection with rival United Air Lines. Douglas will be keen to see how it compares with the rival Boeing machine.

*The fine lines of the Douglas DC-1 are exhibited at Glendale, California.*

One of the final scenes from the movie "King Kong", where the eponymous hero – precariously perched on the summit of New York's Empire State building – faces up to an attack by a fleet of airplanes. Here he takes a measure of revenge by reaching out to smash one of the machines. The movie, which has taken the US by storm, was produced by Merian C Cooper, a veteran aviator who won his spurs in the Great War in Europe. Perhaps it was partly his experience of aerial attacks which made these sensational scenes look so convincing. The airplane has come to the movies, and directors and audiences have both fallen under the spell of the air.

# Giant Soviet plane falls from the sky

*Ukraine, November 20*
The USSR, home of big monoplane bombers and airliners, witnessed a tragedy today of huge proportions when the Kalinin K-7 was seen to break up in the sky and plummet to the ground, where it burst into flames. The K-7 was on its ninth test flight since first taking to the air on August 11. Its immense size had created something of a legend in the Kharkov region, where it excited crowds whenever it flew over.

Designed by K Alexeievitch Kalinin and built over four years, advancing technology had already passed it by. Its 174-foot wings supported no fewer than six 750-hp M-34F engines, with a seventh placed as a pusher between the two tailbooms. It was the right boom that broke today, after the tail began oscillating wildly. Plans for an airliner variant, able to carry 120 passengers in wing cabins, may now be shelved.

# William Boeing's plane is a Douglas

*Los Angeles, December 31*
The Douglas Aircraft Company sold another of its luxury Dolphin seaplanes today to a most unlikely buyer: William Boeing, the man who heads its arch rival in the large transport aircraft market. William Boeing will take delivery of a custom-outfitted Dolphin next year.

Douglas officials explained that the purchase makes sense because Boeing does not manufacture a small seaplane. In addition, they pointed out that some very prominent people use the twin-engined Dolphin, including a French industrialist who gave Douglas a check for $57,000 and some specific ideas about the configuration of his airplane – including the installation of a bar. In fact, the combination of luxury and reliability available in the airplane led to a five-passenger version being purchased for the use of President Roosevelt. The basic design of the Dolphin has been in production for a number of years. The US Army Air Corps uses a more austere version.

# Now every nation wants military aircraft

*A Fleet Air Arm Baffin torpedo bomber on exercise with Britain's Royal Navy.*

*A fleet of Dragons built for Iraq.*

*London, December*
Military aircraft are increasingly seen as an essential part of any military or naval force, and its not only the major powers whose security requirements include having an air force these days. One example is Iraq, until recently controlled by Britain, which has begun to establish its own military air arm – equipped by Britain.

Meanwhile, Britain and America, like the other maritime powers, are steadily integrating aircraft and aircraft carriers into their navies. For historical and political reasons, the Royal Navy's aircraft carriers and their aircraft are nominally under the control of the RAF, though the navy has always been keen to see the Fleet Air Arm brought under its direct control.

# Pilots find their way with Morse code

*Le Bourget, France, December 31*
The progressive introduction of radio aids to safer flying has this year seen the Radio Range installed along several of Europe's busiest air routes, including that from here via Abbeville and Lympne (Kent) to London's Croydon airport.

First developed in the USA, the Range requires special radio stations to be built along each route. Each station has towers transmitting narrow beams directed at the next station up to 100 miles away. Flying along this beam, the pilot hears in his headphones an "A" in Morse on one side of the center line and an "N" on the other. Along the center the signals merge to give a continuous note.

In Germany, the Lorenz company is using a similar process to provide guidance beams for aircraft landing in bad weather.

# Airports boom in USA as air traffic grows and grows

*Washington, DC, December 31*
One cannot use an aircraft without an airport. Few people are aware of the important contributions made by communities and companies which have built and maintained airports, and by the US government's continued development of the Federal Airways System.

When US pilots take to the air today they can land at 558 municipal and 650 commercial airports. There are also 55 US Army, 18 US Navy and 85 other federal, state, and private airports available. California, with 211 airfields, has more of the nation's 1,366 airports than any other state. Texas, with 144, and Ohio, with 117, follow.

But America's busiest airport of all is in New Jersey. Newark airport, with 74 scheduled flights daily and an average of 15,584 passengers per month, holds that distinction, followed by Chicago with 72 and 15,534 and Cleveland with 70 and 14,716. If all kinds of flying are taken into account, nobody is sure just which airport is the most active, but Floyd Bennett Field in Brooklyn, New York, has seen more than 51,800 landings this year.

While the number of airports, flights and passengers have grown, so has the government's Federal Airways System, which now has 19,992 miles of routes with 18,635 miles equipped with 1,510 rotating and 286 flashing beacons for night flying.

Pilots receive weather data from 68 radio stations and keep on course with the aid of 94 radio range beacons. Weather information is collected at airports and weather stations and relayed to airports over 13,000 miles of teletypewriter circuits. Teletypewritten weather maps, an experiment in 1932, are now transmitted every four hours. Flying has certainly come a long way from the days of "follow the railroad and watch out for black clouds".

From Boeing came the 247 airliner, with retractable undercarriage and monocoque construction. Even so, it was quickly overshadowed by the DC-2.

A celebrated line of light aircraft was launched with the Miles M.2 Hawk.

A new monoplane from de Havilland was the D.H.85 Leopard Moth.

One step from undying fame: the Douglas DC-2, developed specially for TWA, proved an instant success and won orders from airlines world-wide.

Supermarine's Walrus amphibian began as the Seagull V for Australia.

A fast passenger-carrying version of the Northrop Gamma: the Delta.

Only one Dewoitine D.332 was produced, and it served with Air Orient.

Airspeed's AS.5 Courier five-seater boasted a retractable undercarriage.

The Breguet 393T trimotor airliner went into production for Air France.

Northrop's Gamma: a fast single-seater designed to carry freight.

A comfortable private aircraft for the family airman: the Stinson Reliant.

Tupolev's ANT-25: designed for record-breaking, it flew 6,306 miles.

Avro's two-seater Club Cadet had a limited number of buyers in the UK.

The Douglas DC-1 airliner made its first flight on July 1, 1933.

The first Vultee V-1A made test flights on American Airlines' routes.

The Northrop Alpha was a speedy six-passenger cabin monoplane.

A sporting monoplane from Germany – the popular Klemm K1.25.

The Loire 70 maritime reconnaissance flying boat: an unusual design.

The Klemm KL.32: a three-seater powered by a Siemens SH.14a.

The Belgian-designed Stampe S.V.4c had more elegant lines and was better for aerobatics than its British lookalike, de Havilland's Tiger Moth.

Flown on the last day of 1933, the Polikarpov I-16 was the world's first cantilever monoplane fighter with retractable landing gear.

Heinkel's He 60 was an armed reconnaissance and trainer biplane.

US Marines used the Great Lakes BG-1 carrier-based dive-bomber.

The Gloster Gauntlet was the last open-cockpit fighter biplane to serve with the RAF. In 1937 it equipped a total of 14 Fighter Command squadrons.

The Curtiss XSBC-1 monoplane was the prototype of the Helldiver.

The Armée de L'Air used Bloch's ungainly Type 200 night-bomber.

The Heinkel He 51 was the new Luftwaffe's first single-seater fighter.

The Fleet Air Arm adopted the Blackburn Shark torpedo-bomber.

Large numbers of Heinkel He 72 trainers were used by the Luftwaffe.

The Blackburn Perth flying boat succeeded the Iris in RAF Service.

Grumman's JF-2 amphibian had a distinctive extended central float.

Breguet's 521 Bizerte was developed from the Short Calcutta. The 30 examples built served with "Exploration" squadrons of the French Aéronavale.

The Dornier Do 23 was the first heavy bomber for the Luftwaffe.

Czechoslovakia's attractive Avia B.534 fighter was built in quantity.

Grumman's dumpy F2F carrier-based fighter won a production order from the US Navy, and 54 were built. The engine was a 700-hp Pratt & Whitney.

The US Navy found Boeing's XF7B-1 fighter too advanced for service.

The second step towards the SBC Helldiver was the Curtiss XSBC-2.

# 1934

440.68mph
Italy
Francesco Agello
Macchi-Castoldi MC-72
Oct 23, 1934

6,587.45 miles
France
Bossoutrot and Rossi
Blériot 110
Mar 26, 1932

47,352ft
Italy
Renato Donati
Caproni Ca 113 AQ
Apr 11, 1934

123,457lb
Germany
Dornier
Do X

3,058hp
Italy
Fiat
AS.6

**Berlin, January 1**
The airline Deutsche Luft Hansa changes its name to Lufthansa.

**Seattle, January 10**
The Boeing P-26 makes its first flight; the US Army Air Corps has ordered 111 of the monoplane fighters.

**Wichita, Kansas, January 10**
The directors of Cessna Aircraft Co vote to reopen the plant, which was closed on January 31, 1931, because of the Depression.

**France, January 14**
An Air France Dewoitine D.332 en route from Indochina, piloted by Maurice Noguès, crashes near Corbigny. All on board are killed, including France's director of civil aviation.

**London, January 16**
Conservative member of parliament and former navy and air minister Winston Churchill makes a radio speech in which he argues that Britain is now, as a result of the "hideous curse" of air war, less well defended than for hundreds of years; the least the country needs, he adds, is an air force equal to that of its potential enemies.

**Buenos Aires, February 9**
Arrival of a consignment of mail which left Berlin six days ago. The mail was flown to Seville, Spain, by Heinkel 70, then to the Gambia aboard a Junkers 52/3m. A Dornier seaplane then flew it across the Atlantic to Natal, Brazil, making a mid-ocean refueling by the ship *Westfalen*. A Junkers belonging to the Condor Syndikat flew the mail from Natal to Buenos Aires. The service, run by German airline Lufthansa, is 36 hours faster than that of French airline Aéropostale (→ May 28).

**Australia, February 17**
Charles Ulm makes the first airmail flight from New Zealand, crossing the Tasman Sea in 14 hours 10 minutes in his Avro Ten.

**New Jersey, February 18**
Eddie Rickenbacker and Jack Frye land in Newark from Los Angeles after flying the last load of airmail to be transported under the private contract system, abolished by President Roosevelt with effect from tomorrow; flying in the Douglas DC-1, they made the journey in a record 13 hours 4 minutes (→ Feb 19).

**USA, February 19**
China officially takes delivery of the first of the 24 Northrop Gamma bombers it ordered.

**USA, February 22**
US Army pilot Durwood Lowry is killed when his airplane crashes near Toledo on a scheduled mail run; two other Army mailmen are rescued from the ocean off Rockaway Point, NY (→ Mar 9).

**USA, March 9**
Four US Army mail pilots die in crashes (→ Mar 19).

**USA, March 19**
After being grounded for a week in the wake of the deaths of March 9, the US Army resumes its airmail service (→ May 3).

**Rome, March 24**
Benito Mussolini, Italy's air minister, rescinds a decree which made it illegal for airmen belonging to the country's armed forces to marry.

**Russia, April 13**
Seven pilots are created "Heroes of the Soviet Union" for their actions last month in rescuing 109 survivors from the icebreaker *Chelyuskin*, which sank after a collision (→ Jun 17).

**Washington, DC, May 3**
The Post Office announces the award of 15 airmail contracts to private companies (→ Jun 1).

**New York, May 27**
French airmen Paul Codos and Maurice Rossi land their Blériot 110 after a flight from Paris.

**Washington, DC, May 29**
The Collier trophy for the year's outstanding aviation achievement is awarded to Hamilton Standard Propeller Company for the development of the controllable-pitch propeller.

**Middlesex, England, August 9**
Leonard Reid and James Ayling land their D.H.84 Dragon at Heston after the first non-stop flight from Canada; their flying time was 30 hours 50 minutes.

**Toulouse, France, August 14**
Marcel Doret pilots the Dewoitine D.510 fighter on its first flight.

**Cleveland, Ohio, September 3**
The National Air Races are hit by tragedy when Douglas Davis, the winner of the Bendix trophy and the Shell speed dash earlier in the meeting, crashes and is killed while leading on the eighth lap of the Thompson Trophy race; Roscoe Turner, who was second, goes on to win the Thompson in his Wedell Williams racer (→ Sep 7, 1936).

**Hertfordshire, September 8**
The first de Havilland D.H.88 Comet, ordered by Jim and Amy Mollison for the MacRobertson air race to Australia, makes its first flight (→ Oct 24).

**Malta, September 22**
Sir Alan Cobham, attempting a non-stop flight from Portsmouth, England, to Karachi, India is forced to land after the throttle of his airplane, an Airspeed AS.5 Courier specially equipped for in-flight refueling, comes away in his hand (→ Sep 30).

**Essex, England, September 30**
Sir Alan Cobham's third National Aviation Day Tour of British towns and cities comes to an end at Romford.

**Cairo, September**
Airline Misr Air, founded by the Egyptian Misr bank, lays on flights to Jeddah for the annual Muslim religious pilgrimage to Mecca.

**USSR, October 7**
The Tupolev ANT-40, or SB-1, tactical bomber makes its first flight.

**Suffolk, England, October 20**
Twenty aircraft leave Mildenhall for Australia at the start of the MacRobertson air race (→ Oct 24).

**Guyancourt, Paris, November 30**
French airwoman Hélène Boucher, holder of the women's world speed record, is killed when her Caudron Rafale crashes in bad weather.

**Algiers, December 6**
North African Air Lines (LANA) start a regular passenger service to Oran.

**London, December 20**
The British government announces details of its new "Empire Air Mail Scheme", under which all mail sent between those parts of the British Empire which are currently being served by national carrier Imperial Airways would automatically be dispatched by air; the scheme is scheduled to come into operation in three years' time (→ Oct 1937).

**USA, December 22**
Charles and Ann Lindbergh leave for Europe in order to escape the blaze of publicity surrounding the controversial death sentence passed on German immigrant Bruno Hauptmann, who was found guilty of kidnapping and killing their baby son in 1932 (→ Apr 3, 1936).

**Istres, France, December 25**
French pilot Raymond Delmotte sets a new world speed record for landplanes of 314.33mph, flying a Caudron 460 (→ Sep 13, 1935).

*Around the world: the cover of a souvenir booklet published to mark the MacRobertson air race from England to Australia in October.* ▶

# French airline backs safety on sea route

*The "Croix du Sud" sails into Natal, Brazil, after its transatlantic flight.*

*Natal, Brazil, January 4*
Since the wreck of its Latécoère 28 flying boat, the *Comte de La Vaulx*, in July 1930, France's Aéropostale has opted for safety as well as speed in its bid for the lucrative South American run. The policy of using a multi-engined aircraft paid off today with the safe landing here from Dakar, Senegal, of a Latécoère 300 flying boat, the *Croix du Sud* [*Southern Cross*]. It was the first time that a Latécoère 300 had attempted a crossing of the South Atlantic.

The French crew, made up of Bonnot, Gautier, Emont and Duruthy brought the plane into Natal after an eventless flight of 1,726 miles in 19 hours 7 minutes. The flight's success means that the

Aéropostale company has secured the mail contract for the route, beating its chief rival, the German carrier Lufthansa, which took six days to make the crossing on its first attempt last February. The Latécoère 300 is powered by four large 640-hp Hispano-Suiza engines mounted in tandem pairs. The huge airplane is constructed out of light alloy, and its hull, which measures 137.8 inches at its widest point, is stabilized by two lateral sponsons.

A prototype of the Latécoère 300 aircraft was successfully tested in 1933. It covered the first leg of the flight which ended today, from France to Senegal, in just 23 hours, beating the world distance record (→ Feb 9).

The Curtiss Condor "sleeper": its cabin is insulated from engine noise by three layers of special material. A four-berth compartment has been installed just aft of the aircraft's flight deck.

# New airline hopes to compete with Dutch

*Brisbane, Australia, January 18*
Today, QANTAS joined forces with Britain's Imperial Airways to create QANTAS Empire Airways. The new company forms part of Imperial's plan to compete with Dutch airline KLM in the Far East and beyond.

In May last year, the Dutch provided a regular service to the British colony of Singapore, to the embarrassment of Imperial Airways, whose routes ceased at Karachi. From there, the Delhi Flying Club and Tata Airlines provided only oc-

casional links to Delhi and Bombay. It was December before Indian Transcontinental Airways, in association with Imperial, extended the British service to Singapore.

Now QANTAS Empire Airways will add the final leg to this route of over 12,500 miles by flying D.H.86s from Singapore to Brisbane. The joint venture is carefully worked out. Each company holds 49 per cent of the capital; the remaining two per cent is in the hands of a neutral "umpire". Services should start later this year (→ Apr 20, 1935).

*One of KLM's Fokker F.XXII aircraft, designed for the eastern routes.*

# US Navy planes fly to non-stop record

*Pearl Harbor, Hawaii, January 11*
Flying records fell today when Lieutenant-Commander Knefler McGinnis of the US Navy, leading a squadron of six Consolidated P2Y-1 flying boats, completed a non-stop, 2,399-mile flight from the Golden Gate in San Francisco to the base here in a record 24 hours 35 minutes.

It was the longest non-stop formation airplane flight in history, but McGinnis emphasized that it was not a stunt but a routine squadron transfer to an overseas base. The aircraft left the Golden Gate in clear weather yesterday afternoon, but they were in fog by 7pm and had to rely on radios and instruments to maintain their course and formation until early morning. They were aided by six US warships stationed along the route.

# Pilot scrapes home on wing and prayer

*Miami, Fla, January 14*
A world record and a breathtaking near accident marked the four days of the sixth annual all-American air races that ended today. Jack Wright of Utica, NY, set the world light-cabin-plane closed-course speed record of 167.48mph, but he was slow compared to pilots in other events with more powerful aircraft. Hollywood film producer Howard Hughes hit 185.707mph in the sportsman free-for-all, and Lee Miles topped 194.511mph on a 15-mile triangular course. Jimmy Wedell was even faster, reaching 253.717mph over two laps.

Local flyer W H Grevemeyer brought the gasping crowd to its feet when the wingtip of his J-4 Cessna touched the ground at 145mph during a turn. He went on to win the Curtiss trophy (→ Sep 3).

# US airmail service rocked by scandal and tragedy

## President orders military to fly the mail

*Washington, DC, February 19*
Allegations of collusion and favoritism between the US government and commercial airlines mean that from today the US Army Air Corps (USAAC) will fly the mail across the US. The army has been drafted in to cope with what amounts to a state of national emergency following President Roosevelt's order of February 9, giving the go-ahead for the US Post Office Department to cancel its airmail contracts.

The order, affecting 26 routes flown by 12 companies, directs the secretary of war to provide the postmaster-general with USAAC airplanes, airfields, and pilots to carry the mail. USAAC chief Major-General Benjamin D Foulois says his pilots and planes are capable of doing the job.

The clamp-down comes in the wake of probes by the US Post Office Department and by a Senate special committee chaired by Senator Hugo L Black, which claim that under the Hoover administration airmail contracts were awarded on a corrupt basis. The collusion took place, according to US Postmaster-General James A Farley, at meetings called "Spoils Conferences" which awarded $78 million in airmail contracts to selected carriers. In all, 18 out of 20 contracts went to consortia controlled by United Aircraft, Aviation Corporation and North American-General Motors (→ Feb 22).

*Members of Congress cast an official eye over a military airfield.*

## 'Legalized murder' ends the army role

*Washington, DC, June 1*
The US Army Air Corps (USAAC) stopped flying airmail for the US Post Office Department today, ending what US Great War ace and airline executive Eddie Rickenbacker called a period of "legalized murder". He and others point to the 11 deaths and 66 crashes which have marred the Army's record since it took over airmail flying from private carriers.

When the Army began airmail flights on February 19 it did not have enough aircraft to do the job and initially could fly only 14 of the 26 routes formerly contracted to private carriers. Its aircraft, Curtiss A-12 Shrike attack monoplanes, were not designed to carry mail and lacked the instruments needed for night- and bad-weather flying, of which USAAC pilots had little or no experience. Flights were stopped on March 10, after nine pilots and passengers had died in accidents, to give the service time to overhaul its aircraft and retrain pilots. Flights restarted on March 19.

Despite these accidents, the USAAC carried 768,215 pounds of mail, flew over 1.7 million miles and logged over 47,000 flying hours on airmail-related business.

## Roosevelt imposes a new deal for mail

*Roosevelt: cleaning up the airmail.*

*Washington, DC, June 12*
President Roosevelt today signed legislation to prevent the abuses that led to the cancellation of airmail contracts in February. This move comes after Congress approved the Black-McKellar Bill which provides for the handing over of airmail contracts to private carriers.

The new law is aimed at giving small private carriers a chance, although they will have to show that they can operate safely and efficiently. The private carriers will now be awarded one-year contracts with extensions based on performance. Airlines awarded temporary contracts from April will not have to reapply.

However, some of the major aircraft manufacturers are less than happy with the clause calling for the separation of airlines from their subsidiaries involved in building airplanes. Boeing is a case in point, as the company has made no secret of the huge profits made by its transport division under the earlier contract system.

The new contracts will cost taxpayers up to 50 per cent less than those of the Hoover administration, although, ironically, many airlines are the same ones as before. United, American, TWA and Eastern are expected to corner most of the airmail contracts. This means that the new airmail network will closely resemble the old system (→ Sep 26).

# Italian smashes airplane altitude record – but pays a price

*An Italian artist's view of Donati's record-breaking high-altitude flight.*

*Rome, April 11*
Commander Renato Donati of the Italian air force had to be lifted from his cockpit today after setting a new world altitude record for airplanes of 47,360 feet. It was more evidence that the human body cannot function properly at such heights. His Caproni Ca 113 biplane, its wingspan increased by 12 feet to 46 feet 5 inches, is powered by a supercharged Bristol Pegasus engine made under license by Alfa Romeo; it drives a four-bladed propeller. Donati beat the record in 1927, by 183 feet, too small a margin to count as a new record. To fly at such altitudes, aircraft will need pressurized cabins or pilots will need pressure suits (→ Sep 28, 1936).

# Saigon-Paris flight crashes near Lyons

*Corbigny, France, January 14*
The Air France Dewoitine D.332 *Emeraude* took off from Marseilles shortly after 3pm for Lyons, the final stop before reaching its destination, Paris. The flight had been plagued with bad luck ever since it set out from Saigon on January 5 and its passengers were anxious to get home. Among those aboard were Maurice Balazuc, chief of Air France's operations, Governor Pasquier of French Indochina, and Emmanuel Chaumié, director of France's civil aviation. First, the flight was delayed by engine problems in Calcutta. Then repairs had to be carried out on the aircraft's landing gear in Gwadar, northern India. Finally, bad weather in Marseilles delayed the departure for Lyons. After a brief stop there, the *Emeraude* took off. A few minutes later, flying at an altitude of 5,500 feet, it was caught in a snowstorm. Ice quickly formed on the wings and the aircraft crashed in the mountainous Morvan region, just north of Lyons. All seven passengers and three crew died.

# Lockheed stakes future on new Electra

*Burbank, Calif, February 23*
Hired test pilot Marshall Headle was in good spirits as he climbed out of the new Lockheed Model 10 Electra here this morning. The sleek, stressed-skin, all-metal monoplane looks like being a real winner, and is already backed by $250,000 worth of advance orders, including an order for six from new Venezuelan airline LAV.

The Electra is the resurrected Lockheed company's first twin-engined airplane, and the firm is banking on its success: it has borrowed over $140,000 to build it. Designers Hall L Hibbard and Clarence L Johnson aimed to develop a 200-mph, ten-passenger transport selling for two-thirds of the price of the 14-passenger Douglas DC-2. The DC-2 is the only other twin-engine airliner capable of 200mph.

Lockheed has targeted the Electra at smaller airlines. Despite this, however, Pan Am and Northwest have placed orders and several other big airlines are negotiating for the airplane (→ May 11).

# Sikorsky's flying boat designed on the back of a menu fits the bill for Pan Am

*Bridgeport, Connecticut, August*
At the Sikorsky aircraft factory there is considerable pride in the latest flying boat which the company has built for Pan American Airways. The magnificent S-42 is a tribute to the efforts of the workforce, many of whom, like Igor Sikorsky, are Russian emigrés.

Its aerodynamic appearance was the result of conversations between Sikorsky and Charles Lindbergh during the inaugural flight of its predecessor, the S-40, when the two men sketched out the details on the back of a menu. Its stressed-skin, monoplane design uses a minimum of external bracing, and its four 700-hp Pratt & Whitney Hornet engines are mounted in nacelles in the wing instead of on a forest of struts and wires. The S-42 has a maximum speed of just over 190mph.

The first S-42, delivered this month, is set to take over many of Pan American's South American routes, but clearly it is an aircraft with transoceanic potential. Pan Am president Juan Trippe would like to use it for a transatlantic service to Britain or France, but neither country has the aircraft to open a reciprocal service and international agreements prevent one country from opening a service until the other is able to do so. If such frustrations continue, Trippe may look to the Pacific where the S-42 can pioneer new routes to the Orient (→ Apr 17, 1935).

*Lockheed's new twin-engined Electra on a landing ground in Venezuela.*

*The Sikorsky S-42, a long-range flying boat which cruises at 140mph.*

# Batten beats Amy Johnson by four days

*Darwin, Australia, May 23*
New Zealander Jean Batten has beaten the England/Australia record set by Amy Johnson (now Mollison) in May 1930. She flew from Lympne, Kent, to Darwin in 14 days 22 hours 30 minutes, beating Johnson's time by more than four days. Batten intends to turn around straight away and head back for England in order to claim a double record.

Both women used the same type of airplane, one which has proved a favorite with flying clubs around the world, as well as with long-distance flyers: the de Havilland D.H.60 Moth. Johnson's aircraft *Jason* was the "G" version, Batten's the later "M" (→ Nov 13, 1935).

*Long-distance flyer Jean Batten.*

# TWA puts new Douglas DC-2 into service

*TWA's new DC-2, the airline's latest attempt to outpace the competition.*

**Los Angeles, May 11**
The first Douglas DC-2 bought by Transcontinental and Western Air (TWA) took to the air today. It is the first of an initial order for 20 aircraft by the airline, on the strength of which Douglas put it into production. TWA will use the new Douglas transports to make three daily round trips between Los Angeles and New York, with intermediate stops at Kansas City and either St Louis or Chicago. The DC-2 is scheduled to make the transcontinental flight in 16 hours.

TWA also plans to fly two round flights a day between Kansas City and New York via Chicago, and make one round trip between Chicago and New York.

The DC-2 is a descendant of the DC-1, with its fuselage stretched by two feet and more powerful Wright Cyclone engines. These allow for an extra row of seats, bringing the DC-2's passenger capacity up to 14 and enabling it to cruise at 170mph. It is also soundproofed, with a heated cabin and the latest Sperry autopilot (→ Sep 28).

# Air France is the fastest to South America

*The "Arc-en-Ciel" gets stuck in mud and a tractor has to haul it out.*

**South Atlantic, May 28**
Two aircraft are playing a critical role in Air France's counterattack against German airline Lufthansa in the battle for the South Atlantic business. Until recently, Dornier Wal flying boats have dominated the competition, but now the French Latécoère 300 flying boat *Croix du Sud* [*Southern Cross*] is outpacing its German rival together with the Couzinet 71 *Arc-en-Ciel* [*Rainbow*] landplane.

The prototype Latécoère 300 was designed to carry 2,205 pounds of

mail between Dakar, Senegal, and Natal, Brazil. The prototype first flew in 1931, but sank near Marseilles. It was salvaged and rebuilt as the *Croix du Sud*. The flying boat set up a record for marine aircraft by flying 2,285 miles from France to St Louis, Senegal, in just under 24 hours.

The Couzinet 71 is a development of the 10-01 monoplane designed by René Couzinet. It's plywood fuselage curves from a squat forward section to sweep up gracefully to form the fin (→ Sep 28).

# Giant Soviet propaganda plane even has its own onboard cinema

**Moscow, May 19**
Muscovites could hardly believe their eyes when the giant object, looking like some enormous hawk, floated into view. The *Maxim Gorkii* or ANT-20 by its official name, is a propaganda tool. Its fuselage contains a kitchen, photo lab, radio studio, printing unit and an aerial cinema. Tupolev built the plane at the Fili plant with money raised by the Union of writers and editors to celebrate the anniversary of Gorkii's literary debut. The propaganda machine with its crew of 20 can carry 50 passengers, who can admire the view or watch films. The ANT-20 is the largest landplane ever built (→ May 18,1935).

*The "Maxim Gorkii" has eight engines, six on the wings, two on the fuselage.*

# KLM drops Fokker and goes for DC-2

**Amsterdam, September 28**
In a shock announcement today, Dutch national airline KLM said it will go for US-built airplanes to form its fleet over the next ten years. Up to now KLM has bought Dutch-built airliners, and with good reason: the aircraft produced by Anthony Fokker's factory in Amsterdam have been in the vanguard of the expansion in European routes over the last 15 years. The current thinking is that they are good planes, but expensive to run. KLM's choice for the future is the new Douglas DC-2. Shiny, sleek, fast and quiet, it looks the part of a modern airliner.

# Swissair stewardess is first in Europe

*Swissair stewardess Nelly Diener.*

*Zurich, Switzerland, July 28*
Her name is Nelly Diener and today she became Europe's first air stewardess.

The young brunette's first flight, aboard a comfortable Swissair Curtiss Condor airplane, had a total of 15 passengers, who flew from Zurich to Berne via Basel and Geneva. The new stewardess will now be working on flights to Berlin, with stopovers in Stuttgart and Leipzig. There are no galleys on those flights and passengers will be asked to pay a small supplement to cover the cost of the refreshments and sandwiches served by the stewardess. Under the Swiss carrier's regulations, passengers will be permitted to tip the young woman.

# Kingsford Smith defies Pacific hazards

*Oakland, Cal, November 4*
Pilot Charles Kingsford Smith and navigator Patrick Gordon Taylor today became the first to fly from Australia to the USA, a total distance of 7,230 miles.

Flying a single-engined Lockheed model 8D Altair, the *Lady Southern Cross*, they took off from Brisbane on October 20. Despite the huge distances covered, the two airmen only stopped off twice before reaching their destination, once in the Fiji Islands and once at Honolulu, Hawaii. Their aircraft is in fact based on a Lockheed Vega whose wings have been modified to accomodate the retractable landing gear. This has the effect of improving speed and reducing fuel consumption. The *Lady Southern Cross* is powered by a 450-hp Pratt & Whitney engine with a variable-pitch propeller.

# William Boeing bows out from business

*Seattle, September 18*
William E Boeing, whose name has become synonymous with aviation over the past two decades, has decided to throw in the towel and retire from a business he started in 1916, operating from a wooden building near central Seattle.

Rumor has it that his decision is motivated at least in part by criticism over the US Air Mail scandal earlier this year. Newspapers accused him of having reaped vast profits at the expense of his fellow citizens. Boeing's resignation has come a few days before his group of companies is split up, in accordance with the Black-McKellar Act. This calls for the separation of carriers and aircraft manufacturers. William Boeing has made an important contribution to aviation and his name will continue to be a household word.

*William Boeing with Board members.*

# British 'Comet' wins race to Australia

*Scott and Campbell-Black's Comet is led in after landing at Melbourne.*

*Melbourne, Australia, October 24*
A British airplane has won the 11,333-mile MacRobertson handicap race from England to Australia. The de Havilland D.H.88 Comet *Grosvenor House* landed at the Melbourne racecourse yesterday, 2 days, 22 hours and 54 minutes after setting off from Mildenhall, Suffolk. The race marks the centenary of the state of Victoria and is sponsored by Sir MacPherson Robertson.

The winners, Charles Scott and Tom Campbell-Black, pushed the twin 230hp-engined Comet, one of three built for the race, to an average speed of 158.9mph. The *Black Magic*, Amy and Jim Mollison's airplane, retired in India, while the third Comet is still en route.

More astonishing than the Comet's performance was the showing of the Douglas DC-2 airliner *Uiver* of Dutch carrier KLM. Piloted by K D Parmentier and J J Moll, it flew three passengers and 420 pounds of mail over the route in 3 days 18 hours 17 minutes to finish second behind the racer.

# United Aircraft forced to split into three

*Washington, DC, September 26*
The United Aircraft and Transport Corporation, a vast conglomerate of aircraft manufacturing and airline interests, is being forcibly broken up into its component parts. It was not involved in the collusion which led to the cancellation of airmail contracts in February this year, but it must abide the Black-McKellar Act which is designed to prevent such abuses in the future. The law now stipulates that airlines must be entirely separate companies from airplane makers if they wish to be eligible for lucrative airmail contacts.

The break-up of United Aircraft has been a rapid process and the company hopes it will not suffer unduly from it. The part of the group which includes Hamilton Aero, Standard Steel Propeller, Pratt & Whitney, Chance Vought and Sikorsky Aircraft, will remain under the United Aircraft Corporation's control. This company is part of the huge Boeing empire set up in 1928 by William Boeing and his friend Frederick B Rentschler, who merged Boeing and Pratt & Whitney before going on to set up United Aircraft and Transport.

Other US companies are also being affected by the new laws. The Aviation Corporation was forced to change the name of American Airways to American Airlines Incorporated on April 11, while TWA became TWA Incorporated six days later, despite the fact that it had no links whatsoever with an aircraft manufacturer. Finally, North American Aviation, initially set up by the Curtiss Aeroplane company, changed the name of Eastern Air Transport to Eastern Air Lines (→ Jan 14, 1935).

# Mail service links London and Brisbane

*London, December 8*
Seasonal greetings from England mailed today should be in Australia in time for Christmas, if the British Post Office's new airmail service to Australia, started today, stays on schedule. Letters from the King and Queen to the Australian governor-general were included in the mail sacks loaded into Imperial Airways airliner *Hengist* this mor-

ning before it took off for Paris on the first stage of the journey. Mail flown to Australia is expected to take 12 days, a considerable saving on the six weeks taken by sea.

From London to Singapore, the mail will be carried by first Imperial Airways and then Indian Trans-Continental Airways. QANTAS picks it up for the final flight to Brisbane, Australia (→ Dec 20).

*The longest airmail route in the world is officially opened at Croydon airport.*

# Italian seaplane flashes to speed record

*Lake Garda, Italy, October 23*
After years of tribulation and fatal crashes, the Macchi MC.72 racing seaplane has twice pushed up the world speed record. On April 10 last year Warrant Officer Francesco Agello set the new mark at 423.8mph. Today the same pilot

and seaplane reached the exceptional average speed of 440.68mph. This record will be hard to beat and could stand for years.

The MC.72, designed by Mario Castoldi, is powered by two huge Fiat engines joined end-to-end to form one 3,100-hp unit (→ Dec 25).

*The Macchi seaplane in which Francesco Agello broke the world speed record.*

# Corporations cash in on aviation image

*USA and Europe, December 31*
Aviation, with its glamorous combination of speed and travel to distant lands, has become one of the biggest themes in advertising. The trend received a boost from Charles Lindbergh's transatlantic flight, which sparked the sale of everything from "Lindbergh" slippers to

light bulbs with airplanes inside. It seems that Britons will buy more cigarettes if the packets contain picture cards depicting the great airliners or airplanes in exotic settings across the British Empire. Liquor is among many other diverse products using airplanes to attract those all-important sales.

# Lufthansa has flown a million passengers

*Germany, September 28*
Lufthansa is a fast-growing airline. Today, the German national carrier celebrated a milestone in its short history: its millionth paying passenger, who was rewarded with a portrait of Hitler. The airline, which changed its name to Luft-

hansa on January 1, provides regular services to a long list of destinations abroad, as well as to every major city in Germany, often using the Junkers 52. On May 1, it added Warsaw to its existing network. At home, young pilots are flocking to its training center at Staaken.

# British enthusiast launches air guide

*London, November 1*
With scheduled air services covering more and more of the globe, it was inevitable that sooner or later a comprehensive airline timetable would be produced. Bradshaw's, British publishers of one of the world's most popular railroad timetables, has produced just such a book. After a century of producing its world-famous guide to the rail systems of Europe and Asia, it has created an *International Air Guide* which gives details of scheduled flights together with local times and currencies.

Pilots are familiar with the rail guide. "Flying by Bradshaw's" refers to the practise of following railway lines to reach a destination; so too, in bad weather, does the much-used expression "faith, hope and Bradshaw's".

# Richey is the USA's first mail airwoman

*Detroit, Mich, December 31*
The mailman turned out to be a woman today when Central Airlines' flight from Washington, DC, landed here with Helen Richey at the controls of a Ford Trimotor. Richey is the USA's first female airline pilot.

Although many of her male counterparts say women do not have the strength and stamina to pilot a heavy transport airplane, Richey has very impressive credentials. Last December, with Frances Marsalis, she established a new women's endurance record. By refueling in flight from another aircraft, the airwomen managed to remain aloft over Miami for 9 days 22 hours. Richey also won the Fairchild trophy at the first women's national air meet at Dayton, Ohio (→ Jul 11, 1935).

The elegant Lockheed L.10 Electra ten-passenger high-speed airliner entered service with Northwest Airlines in August 1934, and 149 were produced.

The Aeronca L series were low-wing monoplanes with trousered wheels.

The Savoia-Marchetti S.M.79 prototype: a typical trimotor of the 1930s.

A total of 737 de Havilland D.H.89 Dragon Rapides were built.

De Havilland's D.H.87 Hornet Moth was made for private owners.

The Savoia-Marchetti S.73 commercial transport carried 18 people.

KLM had the only Fokker F.XXXVI 32-passenger airliner to be built.

A smart cabin monoplane from Phillips & Powis, the Miles Falcon.

In a later form, the S.M.79B was a twin-engined high-speed bomber.

The Luftwaffe's last operational biplane fighter was the Arado Ar 68.

Three Martin M.130 flying boats served with Pan American Airways.

Short Brothers built only two Scyllas (derived from the Kent flying boat).

The Potez 29: the Armée de l'Air used as many as 120 as ambulances.

Savoia-Marchetti's S.62 "bis" was built in the USSR as the MBR-4.

Poland's PZL P-23 Karas reconnaissance bomber saw wide service.

Stylish travel for Pan Am passengers in ten Sikorsky S-42s.

External strut-bracing marred the lines of the Stinson A Trimotor.

The Airspeed AS.6 Envoy: a twin-engined development of the Courier.

The de Havilland D.H.86A Express Airliner served with QANTAS.

Fieseler's Fi 97 four-seater was built for the 1934 Challenge de Tourisme.

The Loire 130 military pusher flying boat could be catapult-launched.

The Italian CRDA Cant Z.501: gunner's position in the engine nacelle.

Messerschmitt's Bf 108 Taifun four-seater was to lead to a great fighter.

The Dewoitine D.37 parasol-winged fighter was sold to five customers.

Avia of Czechoslovakia produced the B122, a great aerobatic aircraft.

By the time it went into service the Lioré et Olivier H-43 was obsolete.

Japan's Mitsubishi G3M bomber remained operational throughout the Second World War. More than a thousand were built in a range of versions.

The RAF's last biplane fighter was the very agile Gloster Gladiator.

Breda's 236-mph Ba 27 fighter was supplied to China in small numbers.

A reconnaissance flying boat, the Saro London entered service in 1936.

The Levasseur P.L.14 was a seaplane version of the P.L.7.

The Henschel Hs 121 single-seater advanced trainer found no buyers.

Polikarpov's I-17 had an imported 760-hp Hispano-Suiza V12 engine.

Fairey's Swordfish torpedo-bomber, which began life as the TSR.II, outlived its supposed replacements and earned fame in the war despite a dated design.

The Hawker Hind day-bomber was an interim replacement for the Hart.

The last Westland-Hill Pterodactyl built was the Mk V turret-fighter.

L'Armée de l'Air had 283 Bloch 210 bombers, but by the time the last were delivered the design was obsolete. A 1,730-kg bomb load could be carried.

The Caudron Goëland was still made after the Second World War.

The twin-finned Junkers Ju 86: first a ten-seat transport, then a bomber.

Northrop's A-17 attack-monoplane was supplied to two USAAC groups.

A fighter which found few orders – the Armstrong Whitworth Scimitar.

"The Flying Pencil": Dornier's Do 17 served in Spain and formed part of the Luftwaffe's front-line equipment at the start of the Second World War.

Propaganda uses: Tupolev's 207-ft-span ANT-20 "Maxim Gorkii".

The Bü.131 Jungmann, a fine aerobatic trainer: Bücker's first product.

Gotha's Go.145 was a primary and advanced trainer; 10,000 were built.

Cessna C-34 production began in January 1934, about 42 being built.

# 1935

 440.68mph
Italy
Francesco Agello
Macchi-Castoldi MC-72
Oct 23, 1934

 6,587.45 miles
France
Bossoutrot and Rossi
Blériot 110
Mar 26, 1932

 47,818ft
USSR
Vladimir Kokkinaki
Polikarpov TsKB-3 (I-15)
Nov 21, 1935

 123,457lb
Germany
Dornier
Do X

 3,058hp
Italy
Fiat
AS.6

**Chicago, January 14**
United Air Lines decides to equip its fleet with a de-icing system for airplane wings, following successful tests on a Boeing 247.

**Gauting, Germany, February 3**
German engineer Dr Hugo Junkers, pioneer of the construction of all-metal airplanes, dies, aged 76.

**Kagamigahara, Japan, February 4**
Mitsubishi's A5M monoplane fighter, powered by a 580-hp Nakajima (Bristol Jupiter) engine, begins test flights.

**New York, February 11**
Lou Reichers makes a successful flight in a twin-engine Uppercu-Burnelli transport with a Ford automobile strapped between the wheels of its landing gear; the stunt is intended to demonstrate the potential of the airplane for transporting vehicles in an emergency.

**Point Sur, Calif, February 12**
The US Navy airship *Macon* crashes into the sea off the Californian coast, killing two of the crew of 83 (→ Mar 13).

**Paris, February 27**
Latécoère's giant seaplane *Santos-Dumont* lands with a cargo of mail after a record flight from Natal, Brazil, of 53 hours 4 minutes, with two stops en route.

**Lakehurst, NJ, March 13**
The US Navy's only surviving airship, the *Los Angeles*, is damaged while taking part in tests of mooring techniques.

**Kent, England, March 14**
The Percival Gull makes its maiden flight (→ Nov 13).

**Berlin, March 17**
German authorities make the color-coding of vital aircraft parts obligatory; red for fire circuit-breakers, green for temperature regulators, yellow for throttles and brown for hydraulic circuits.

**Bethpage, NY, March 22**
The Grumman XF3F-1 naval fighter makes its first flight; it is a variant of the Grumman F2F, nicknamed "Flying Barrel" because of its portly fuselage.

**Augsburg, Germany, March 28**
Hans Knoetzsch pilots the Messerschmitt Bf 109V1 prototype on its first flight (→ Sep 17).

**Zürich, Switzerland, April 1**
Swissair opens a regular passenger service to Croydon airport, England.

**Los Angeles, Calif, April 15**
The Douglas XTBD-1 naval torpedo-bomber prototype, the first with hydraulically-operated folding wings, makes its first flight.

**Honolulu, Hawaii, April 17**
Pan Am Sikorsky S-42 flying boat *Oriental Clipper* arrives after a route-proving flight from Alameda, California (→ Nov 22).

**London, April 20**
The first passengers leave for Australia on a new Imperial Airways/QANTAS service; the first Australian departures were made from Brisbane on April 17.

**Washington, DC, May 8**
The US Commerce Department announces that blind-landing radio equipment developed by a US Army Air Corps team under Captain Albert Hegenberger is to be installed at all major airports between New York and Los Angeles; this follows the serious crash of a TWA airliner at Kansas City two days ago (→ Jul 30).

**London, May 22**
The British parliament votes to treble the number of front-line military airplanes over the next two years; this amounts to an increase of 1,500 airplanes (→ Sep 10).

**Bridgeport, Connecticut, June 5**
Sikorsky's S-43 twin-engined Baby Clipper amphibian makes a first flight of 9 minutes.

**Washington, DC, June 29**
The US government awards the Consolidated Aircraft Corporation a contract worth $6 million for 60 PBY-1 flying boats; it is the largest official order for airplanes since the end of the Great War.

**Burbank, California, July 11**
Laura Ingalls arrives after a flight from Floyd Bennett Field, New York, in 18 hours 19 minutes 30 seconds, becoming the first woman to fly east/west across the USA.

**Suffolk, England, July 24**
A group of British research scientists carries out a successful experiment with "radio direction finding" equipment by which airplanes in flight can be traced on a cathode-ray tube; in today's secret test a Hawker Hart is tracked by the equipment for a distance of 34 miles, and a formation of airplanes is located and counted (→ Sep 9).

**Seattle, Washington, July 28**
The Boeing Model 299 prototype bomber makes its first flight, piloted by Leslie Tower (→ Oct 30).

**Villacoublay, France, August 8**
French pilot Michel Détroyat flies the prototype Morane-Saulnier MS.405 fighter on its first flight (→ Mar 5, 1936).

**Alaska, August 15**
American comedian Will Rogers and round-the-world flyer Wiley Post are both killed when their Orion Explorer hybrid aircraft stalls and crashes into a frozen lake (→ ).

**England, September 10**
The Vickers company is awarded a British Air Ministry contract for a total of 96 monoplane bombers with the type name Wellesley (→ Nov 6).

**Germany, September 17**
The Junkers Ju 87 prototype dive bomber makes its maiden flight.

**Baltimore, Md, October 9**
The Glenn L Martin Co hands over the Martin M-130 flying boat to Pan Am; the aircraft cost $417,000, compared with $242,000 for the Sikorsky S-42 and $78,000 for the Douglas DC-2 (→ Nov 22).

**Croydon, England, November 2**
A German-developed Lorenz blind-landing system is installed at the Croydon airport.

**Kent, England, November 11**
David Llewellyn and Jill Wyndham land at Lympne in a Parnell Heck airplane after a record flight of 6 days 12 hours 17 minutes from the Cape (→ Feb 9, 1936).

**Natal, Brazil, November 13**
Jean Batten completes a flight from Lympne, England, setting a new record for the route of 2 days 13 hours 15 minutes over the route in her Percival Gull Six *Jean*.

**Manila, November 29**
Pan American M-130 flying boat *China Clipper* completes the first transpacific airmail service after a flight of 4 days from San Francisco (→ Jan 25, 1936).

**Newark, NJ, December 1**
The first airway traffic control center opens, operated by staff of Eastern Air Lines, United Air Lines, American Airlines and TWA.

**USA, December 15**
After a poll of its customers, American Airlines announces that it will not serve alcohol on its flights; airline chief C R Smith says "public opinion is against the practise".

**Hawaii, December 27**
Five US Army Air Corps pilots bomb Mauna Loa volcano in an effort to stop its lava flow from reaching the town of Hilo.

---

*The DST "Skysleeper" has room for 14 passengers, seated or lying on berths, while the DC-3 version will accomodate 21 seated passengers.* ▶

## La Guardia plans a showcase airport

*New York, January 5*
New York's air-travel-minded mayor Fiorello La Guardia, who has long chafed at having to land at Newark Airport in New Jersey when flying to New York, today opened a new city airport on Flushing Bay in Queen's. Municipal Airport 2, only eight miles from Times Square, Manhattan, is easily accessible by the Queensboro Bridge across the East River.

However, the 105-acre airfield, which was once part of the Gala Amusement Park, is hardly a first-rate facility. It has been a private flying field since 1929, at first named Glenn H Curtiss Airport, then North Beach Airport. It has three graded runways, a few hangars, and a seaplane slipway. Sources close to the mayor say that the size of the airfield will be increased to more than 500 acres, mainly by filling in a portion of the bay and with some purchase of additional land.

La Guardia also plans to ask his fellow-Democrat President Roosevelt to help fund new facilities, which will turn the airport into an aviation showcase. He is determined that New Yorkers, who live in the greatest city in the world, will also possess the greatest airport in the world.

## American air corps gains more power

*Hampton, Va, March 1*
A General Headquarters (GHQ) Air Force was inaugurated here today at Langley Field, with Brigadier-General Frank M Andrews in command. The creation, for the first time in the US, of anything called an "air force" is being hailed as a major step toward making the US Army Air Corps (USAAC) an independent service on equal terms with the US Navy and US Army. Proponents of air power will be pleased that aviation is now starting to break free of being a mere subdivision of America's existing military services.

All tactical aircraft will be removed from the control of the US Army's nine corps area commanders and assigned to the new GHQ Air Force. The airplanes will be concentrated in three operational wings based at Langley, at Barksdale Field, Louisiana, and at March Field, California. This will unify combat air units and establish a structure for integrated training in peacetime and coordinated wartime operations. General Andrews will report to the army general staff through USAAC chief Major-General Benjamin D Foulois. In the event of war, GHQ Air Force will come under the control of the commander of army field forces.

# Boom in flying boats

*An artist's sketch of the pilot's cabin on board the giant Laté 521.*

*USA and Europe, March 28*
As the airlines face the challenge of long-distance, transoceanic flying, the flying boat is proving to have a significant advantage over the landplane for such routes. There are a number of reasons for this, the main one being that there are very few airports which can take landplanes of the size which would give them the range for such flights. Flying boats can also land and take off near seaports, which are where passengers want to go. Their greater spaciousness also makes them more attractive to passengers.

Pan American is buying giant Martin 130 flying boats for the Pacific, and Britain's flag-carrier Imperial Airways is ordering no fewer than 28 Empire-type flying boats from Short Brothers to carry passengers and mail throughout the British Empire. French carrier Aéromaritime will also use flying boats for mail flights between Dakar, Senegal, and Brazzaville, the Congo, under a contract signed today. The airline, created for this operation by the giant French shipping line Compagnie des Chargeurs Réunis, hopes to carry passengers and mail from Paris down the West African coast to Pointe Noire, the most southerly French city in Africa. Latécoère and Lioré will probably provide most of the necessary aircraft (→ Jul 7).

**The aircraft-carrying airship USS "Macon", which carried out a series of successful maneuvers for the Navy before crashing on February 12.**

*The Latécoère 521 "Lieutenant de vaisseau Paris" first flew on January 10.*

# Earhart is first woman to cross Pacific

*Earhart: bored by the Pacific fog.*

**San Francisco, January 12**
Today leading American airwoman Amelia Earhart, at the controls of a Lockheed Vega, became the first woman to fly the Pacific alone. A crowd of over 10,000 converged on Oakland to see her land after an 18-hour flight from Wheeler Field, Honolulu, Hawaii.

Throughout her flight, Earhart was able to tune her powerful transmitter into radio stations along the Pacific coast of the US and give regular broadcasts. At one point, listeners were shocked to hear her voice fading with the words: "I am feeling so tired." Many thought she had collapsed at the controls. But later she came back on to reassure her audience: "I just got tired of flying over fog."

# Speedy British monoplane makes debut

**Bristol, England, April 12**
Test pilot Cyril Uwins of the Bristol Aeroplane Co made the first flight of the Bristol 142 at Filton airfield here today. The 142's all-metal, stressed-skin construction gives it a futuristic appearance.

The airplane has been ordered by aviation-loving newspaper tycoon Lord Rothermere, owner of the *Daily Mail*, as his eight-passenger personal transport, but it has obvious potential as a bomber or even a long-range fighter. Powered by two 650-hp Bristol Mercury engines, it can exceed 300mph, 80mph faster than the RAF's quickest fighter, and has a range of 1,000 miles. The new 142 has been named *Britain First* (→ Jun 25, 1936).

*Special order for a British press baron: the Type 142 "Britain First".*

# British try out airplane detection system

**London, September 9**
British scientists are using radio signals in experiments to detect airplanes over the horizon. Exact details are scarce because the work is secret. The British hope to reflect waves off the metal fuselages of aircraft, mirrored as "blips" on a cathode-ray tube, as a way of alerting air defenses. They are also planning tall transmitter masts on military coastal sites. In 1885, German scientist Hertz succeeded in bouncing electromagnetic pulses off a metal object. In 1931, engineers in a radio-tower reported a "flutter" in reception when airplanes flew past (→ Mar 13, 1936).

# Nazis unveil air secrets

*The powerful prototype Heinkel He 111 bomber, dressed as a civil transport.*

**Berlin, March 9**
Less than five years after the last Allied troops left Germany, Nazi leader Adolf Hitler has admitted that his country has an air force: the Luftwaffe. Aviation experts have long suspected that such a force existed in secret, despite the Treaty of Versailles.

Luftwaffe commander Hermann Goering has 11,000 men and 1,800 planes, which have been forged into an instrument of war under the guise of belonging to flying clubs. Military aircraft production, including bombers able to reach the Ural Mountains, is engaging Germany's foremost designers: Heinkel, Dornier, Messerschmitt and Junkers. The 250-mph Heinkel He 111, which flew for the first time on February 24, is presented as a civil transport, but it could easily be converted to a bomber capable of carrying a heavy payload.

Goering has said that the Luftwaffe will only "defend the Fatherland", but it is difficult to see how long-range bombers can be used defensively; by their very nature they are weapons of offense, not only on the battlefield but also against an enemy nation's industry and population (→ May 22).

# Hermann Goering to run new Luftwaffe

*Luftwaffe chief Hermann Goering.*

**Berlin, March 10**
An air ace of the Great War with 20 kills to his credit has been put in charge of the new Luftwaffe. Hermann Goering, last commander of the legendary "Circus Richthofen" group of fighter aces, was a civilian flyer in Scandinavia after 1918 and joined the National Socialist German Workers' Party (Nazis) in 1922. The portly, upper-crust son of a judge, Goering has a taste for hunting, narcotics and good food, lending a touch of flamboyance to his party, in contrast to the rather shabby thugs who make up much of the Nazi membership. His dedication to the Luftwaffe is not lessened by his mercurial temperament and variable health.

Strategists are split about the role of Goering's Luftwaffe. Chief of Staff Walther Wever believes it should follow Britain and build bombers to deter attack, while Goering's deputy Erhard Milch (founder of Deutsche Luft Hansa airline) says it should back ground forces in a short "lightning war" or *blitzkrieg* (→ Jun 3, 1936).

# Research teams rely on wind tunnels

*The prototype Gauntlet fighter in the wind tunnel at Farnborough.*

*Hampshire, England, April 4*
British secretary of state for air Lord Londonderry opened the largest wind tunnel in Britain at the Royal Aircraft Establishment at Farnborough today.

The atmospheric tunnel has a working section 24 feet across and is large enough for useful testing to be carried out on full-scale aircraft, even if their wingspans are greater than 24 feet. For example, the first series of tests in the new tunnel will be to investigate the cooling of the Bristol Mercury cowled radial engine fitted to a Royal Air Force Gloster Gauntlet fighter. Other countries already

have, or are in the process of building, tunnels wider than 24 feet. At Chalais-Meudon in France, Guidonia in Italy, Langley Field in the United States and Göttingen in Germany there are wind tunnels which surpass the new one at Farnborough. The most productive is without doubt the 60-foot one at Langley Field, which was opened in 1931.

The huge fans in these tunnels are driven by powerful electric motors. Everything possible is done to straighten the flow of air and facilitate observation of any problems in order to ensure the most accurate results.

# American pays 79,500 dollars for the DST

*New York, July 8*
American Airlines president Cyrus Smith today announced an order for ten passenger transports of a new design from the Douglas Aircraft Company. The aircraft, the Douglas Sleeper Transport (DST), will cost $79,500 each. Smith chose the DST to replace his fleet of three-engined Fokker aircraft and his Curtiss Condor "sleepers".

Because its Curtiss Condor twin-engined biplanes were losing business to airlines using the faster Douglas DC-2 monoplane, American Airlines asked Douglas to build an airplane capable of carrying a greater payload than the DC-2, with more cabin volume for berths on each side, sufficient range for

non-stop New York to Chicago and four-stop only transcontinental flights, and more positive directional control.

Although Douglas was reluctant to change the DC-2 design, he agreed to the request. He began work on the DST prototype last year after American Airlines secured a loan of $4.5 million from the Reconstruction Finance Corporation. The DST has a rounded fuselage which is 26 inches wider and 30 inches longer than the DC-2's, and its 95-foot wingspan is 10 feet longer. It can take 14 overnight passengers. Without the berths, the DST will be known as the DC-3 and will be able to accomodate 21 passengers (→ Dec 17).

# World's worst airplane crash claims 48

*The "Maxim Gorkii" during a demonstration flight, with escort fighters.*

*Moscow, May 18*
The USSR's flying mammoth, the ANT-20 *Maxim Gorkii*, crashed today at the Tushino airbase near Moscow, killing all 48 people on board. Two people were also killed on the ground. The tragedy happened when an escort fighter hit the *Maxim Gorkii's* wing during filming intended to promote the airplane. Built on Stalin's orders, the airplane had a printing press, photographic laboratory and movie cinema on board, and it could blast out music and inspirational messages through loudspeakers as it flew. The little fighter was being flown

alongside for visual contrast when pilot Nikolai Blagin ignored orders to keep his distance, saying over the radio: "I'll show you how good a flyer I am."

Blagin tried to loop round the wing of the bigger machine but crashed into it instead, sliding along the fuselage into the rudder. Both aircraft hit the ground in a spectacular explosion. The fighter pilot was also killed.

What was intended as a showcase for the Soviet political system and its aviation industry was turned instead into a public relations disaster, all in a matter of seconds.

# Breguet-Dorand helicopter takes off

*Ground staff duck as the twin-rotor Breguet-Dorand prepares to take off.*

*Villacoublay, France, June 26*
More than 20 years after his first helicopter experiments, Louis Breguet appears to have succeeded at last. His *Gyroplane* made its first flight here today, and appears to be a complete success.

The *Gyroplane* is officially the Breguet-Dorand 314, and the test pilot assigned to it is Maurice

Claisse. The machine has two rotors, mounted one above the other, rotating in opposite directions. The helicopter has cyclic and collective pitch controls enabling the pilot to vary the angle of the rotor blades in flight. This is a significant advance in helicopter design, giving better control over the altitude and the direction of flight (→ Jun 26, 1936).

# Howard Hughes slashes speed record

# French airline opens services in Senegal

*Millionaire flyer Howard Hughes beside his superb homebuilt Hughes Racer.*

*Santa Ana, Calif, September 13*
Millionaire film producer and amateur air racer Howard Hughes shattered the world landplane speed record no less than six times today, reaching an average speed of 352.38mph. The previous record of 314mph was set a year ago by French pilot Raymond Delmotte.

Hughes had a narrow escape on the fifth circuit, when his engine failed at a speed of nearly 560mph and the racer crashed into a field. When spectators rushed to the site, they found he was unharmed. His

aircraft was built in secrecy at a reported cost of some $100,000. A team of engineers took 18 months to complete the task. Before construction began, he had a model of the plane tested in the wind tunnel of the California Institute of Technology.

The racer, designated the H-1, has a wingspan of 25 feet and is powered by a Pratt & Whitney Twin Wasp Junior air-cooled engine rated at 700hp at 8,500 feet but able to deliver 1,000hp for racing (→ Jan 14, 1936).

*Dakar, July 7*
The French airline Aéromaritime, which began operations in March with a regular weekly service between Dakar and the French Congo, launched a new service today into the interior of Senegal. The new route, from Cotonou to Niamey, will add another section to the internal network in francophone Africa built up by airlines Compagnie Transafricaine and Sabena.

Pierre Janet was at the controls of the Caudron *Pélican* which made today's inaugural flight along the route. His journey was not an easy one. Besides having to use make-

shift airfields, he was faced with bad weather and problems with his radio reception. After take-off, the *Pélican* flew into a hurricane and had to put down on marshy ground 30 miles from Cotonou. Taking off once more (and only narrowly avoiding the surrounding treetops as he did so), Janet reached Niamey 7 hours later.

Aéromaritime was set up by the Fabre brothers. Since early 1929, they had been seeking to add an airline service to their shipping business. After failing to buy up Aéropostale stock, they decided to found their own airline.

*Refuelling Janet's Pélican at Cotonou, on the route in West Africa.*

# British Airways is formed by merger

*London, October 29*
A new British airline called British Airways was created today from the amalgamation of three other airlines, Hillman, Spartan and United Airways.

It does not intend to be a rival to established British flag-carrier Imperial Airways. Imperial primarily serves the British Empire, while British Airways aims to achieve a foothold in Europe and, in particular, to take some trade from the Germans. The new airline also owns two domestic subsidiaries, Highland Airways and Northern and Scottish. British Airways expects to begin operations in the New Year (→Apr 5, 1937).

**The Douglas DC-2, shown here in Swissair livery, offers new levels of passenger speed and comfort.**

# Italian air power pounds Abyssinians

*Abyssinia [Ethiopia], October 3*
The invasion of Abyssinia began yesterday when 100,000 Italian and native troops crossed the border from Eritrea. International fury at Mussolini's aggression has been increased by his use of air power against near-defenseless troops: his bombers are dropping mustard gas and high explosive on tribesmen who answered Emperor Haile Selassie's call to arms.

The Italians are reported to have bombed a hospital in the border town of Adowa, the first target for Caproni 101 bombers. Abyssinia itself has a few obsolete reconnaissance biplanes and light sports aircraft manned by foreign mercenaries. Some of their machines were destroyed on the ground by Italian fighters (→ May 9, 1936).

*A gunner is ready to fire during a reconnaissance by Ca 101s over Abyssinia.*

## TWA opens a school for air hostesses

*Los Angeles, December 6*
An air academy with a difference has just opened at TWA's California headquarters. The school aims to train air hostesses in the art of mid-air passenger care.

The women, who have been taken on to fly in TWA's new prestige DC-2 and DC-3 airliners, must be qualified nurses and "possessed of a pleasant manner". Their training covers everything from dusting out an airplane to the correct loading of baggage, a prime responsibility. They also serve out boxed meals to passengers, and must provide bags in case of air sickness. The air hostesses have been generally welcomed, though some pilots' wives have apparently expressed reservations.

# Pilot error blamed for crash of Boeing B-299 Army prototype

*The doomed Boeing was designated as the XB-17. Its crash means the winner is the rival Douglas B-18.*

*Wright Field, October 30*
Tragedy struck at Wright Field today when Boeing's highly-acclaimed, four-engined Model 299, or XB-17, an entrant in the US Army Air Corps's bomber competition, crashed. The pilot, Major Pete Hill, was killed and two others were seriously injured in a disaster caused apparently by the pilot failing to unlock the tail control surfaces, thus forcing the plane into its fatally steep climb. Eye-witnesses said the plane climbed at a much steeper angle than normal, eventually losing flying speed, stalling and falling to the ground. This should have been a routine flight for Boeing was favorite over Martin's B-12 and Douglas's B-18. Then over-confidence struck, most probably the result of the flight from Seattle to Dayton last month when Boeing's chief test pilot Leslie Tower beat speed records by covering the 2,100 mile, non-stop flight at an average speed of 232 mph, faster than that of most of the pursuit planes. The doomed plane was a one-off 432,000 dollar example. Its loss means financial difficulties for Boeing. The destruction of the plane that was the favorite in the competiton means that the Martin B-12 and the Douglas B-18 are now the Army's choices. The Boeing was called the Flying Fortress because of its machine guns and Plexiglas nose (→ Mar 1, 1937).

## Navy airman lands blind on a carrier

*San Diego, July 30*
Landing an airplane on an aircraft carrier is not easy in the best of circumstances. Today, however, Lieutenant Frank Akers of the US Navy did it without seeing the sky, the water or the ship, to become the first person to make a "blind" landing at sea. The Lieutenant flew a Berliner-Joyce OJ-2 biplane with a hooded cockpit in which he could see only his controls and instruments.

Akers took off from San Diego Naval Air Station to find the USS *Langley*, knowing only that she was somewhere at sea about 150 miles away. Using his flight instruments and radio, he found the ship and landed successfully. Akers's system involved the use of a "localizer", "glide slope" and marker beacon developed by Washington Institute of Technology (→ Nov 2).

# Wiley Post is killed in flight over Alaska

*Point Barrow, Alaska, August 15*
Lockheed test pilot Wiley Post and his friend, comedian Will Rogers, were both killed today when their seaplane, the *Orion Explorer* crashed into a frozen lake near Point Barrow, on the northernmost tip of Alaska. They had been flying at low altitude to look for a whale hunter when the aircraft, thrown off balance by its large floats, stalled and crashed. The seaplane had been hastily assembled following the sale on June 15 of Post's *Winnie Mae* to the Smithsonian, which bought the airplane for $25,000.

# Buy a life insurance before boarding

*USA, December 18*
Despite the constantly improving air safety standards, there are a number of Americans who are still afraid of flying.

Some of these are simply scared of climbing aboard flying machines, while others, such as businessmen, worry about the effect on their company of the lost of a hard to replace executive. Six major insurance companies are currently drawing up contracts that will provide insurance for passengers and pay compensation to the bereaved relatives of accident victims.

# Douglas DST undertakes test flight

*Clover Field, Cal, December 17*
Today's test flight could not have been more successful.

Douglas test pilot Carl Cover, along with assistants Fred Stineman and Franck Collbohm, took off from here aboard the DST for a crucial proving flight. The test lasted 1 hour and 40 minutes and the aircraft handled beautifully.

Things went so well that American Airlines has already increased its order from ten to 20 Douglas airplanes. The airline with thus be purchasing eight Douglas Sleeper Transports (DST) and 12 DC-3s. The DST, developed thanks to a $4.5 million government loan, is capable of carrying 14 passengers in comfortable berths built into the cabin in superposed groups of two. In its DC-3 configuration, the aircraft will accomodate up to 21 seated passengers. For the uninitiated,

*The DST sleeper plane, forerunner of the DC-3, at Glendale, California.*

the easiest way of telling the two airplanes apart is to count the number of windows on the fuselage. The DC-2 has seven of these, while the DC-3 has eight. Both aircraft appear likely to be excellent profit earners for operators such as American Airlines since the DC-3's operating costs are only 10 per cent higher than those of the DC-2.

## 'Smithy' is missing over Indian ocean

*Singapore, November 9*
A massive air and sea search is under way for the Lockheed Altair piloted by veteran Australian aviator Sir Charles Kingsford Smith after he failed to arrive here this morning on a flight from India. With co-pilot Tommy Petheridge, "Smithy" was seeking to set a new Britain/Australia record in the *Lady Southern Cross*. They had made good time from Hamble, Hampshire, to Baghdad, but a sudden sandstorm on the next leg, from Baghdad to Allahabad, had put them behind schedule.

The airplane was last seen by pilot H F Broadbent who reported that the Altair had flown past him in the Bay of Bengal and that he had seen jets of flame spurting from its exhaust pipe. Hopes of finding the crew alive are now fading.

## San Francisco to Manila with Pan Am

*Manila, November 29*
Pan Am's *China Clipper* NC 14716 touched down today off Manila carrying 58 mail bags on the inaugural service between the US and the Philippines. The flying boat, which left San Francisco on November 22, covered the 8,210 miles in 59h 48m flight time with stops in Honolulu, Midway, Wake and Guam. The mail bags contained 110,865 letters, some 44,346 for Manila. In all, 200,000 commemorative stamps have been printed for the occasion and many letters are destined to be redirected to the senders as souvenirs. Captain Edwin Musick's flight followed the award in April to Pan Am of the trans-Pacific airmail contract. In October the airline was given a 25-year authorization by the Philippines to transport passengers ánd mail between the islands and the US. Passenger services are to begin next year. The *China Clipper* is the first of three new Martin M-130s purchased by Pan Am for the Pacific run. Pan Am has invested heavily at stopovers notably at Wake where coral in the lagoon was dynamited so that the Clippers can land.

## Britain catches up with monoplane trend

*London, November 6*
Hawker Aircraft Company test pilot P W S "George" Bulman today took up Britain's F.36/34 fighter on its first flight.

At present known only as the Hawker High-Speed Monoplane, but possibly to be named the Hurricane, the airplane could, if tests are satisfactory, represent the start of a new generation of British monoplanes. It brings Britain up to date with the latest designs followed by the USSR with the Polikarpov I-16, the US with the Boeing P-26 and Curtiss-Wright 75, Germany with the Messerschmitt Bf 109 and France with the Morane-Saulnier MS.405.

Powered by the new Rolls-Royce PV.12 engine, in the 1,000-hp class, the Hawker shows that even Britain is becoming convinced that the days of the biplane are coming to an end. The new monoplane has a fully retractable undercarriage, flaps and even an enclosed cockpit, with a sliding Perspex canopy. The aircraft's armament is top secret, but it is expected to be heavier than the traditional two machine guns in the fuselage.

*Trippe and Lindbergh flew the "China Clipper" during test flights.*

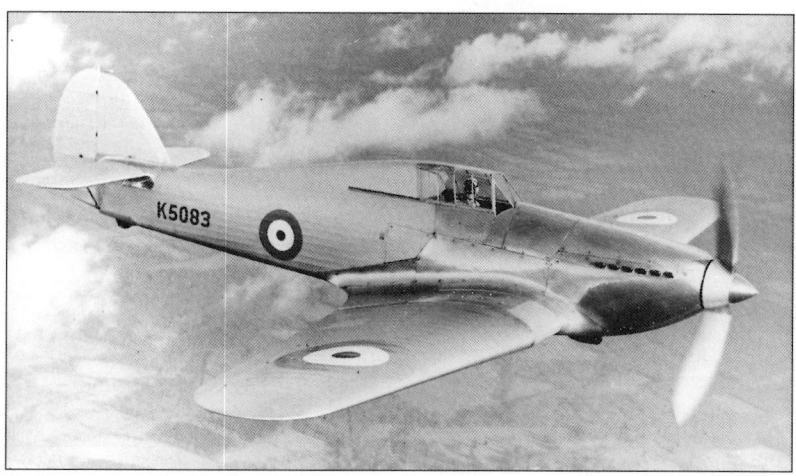
*Bulman tests the Hawker F.36/34, the RAF's first monoplane fighter.*

Armstrong Whitworth built a single A.W.23, forerunner of the Whitley.

Three Koolhoven F.K.50 eight-seat airliners served the Swiss line Alpar.

Douglas developed the DC-2 into the DC-3 for American Airlines.

The 1,500-hp Sikorsky S-43 amphibian could carry up to 18 passengers.

Macchi MC.94 12-passenger flying boats were built for Ala Littoria.

Fairchild's Canadian subsidiary constructed 11 ten-seater Model 82s.

Air France received 16 Bloch 220 high-speed 16-passenger airliners.

Caudron designed the C.641 Typhon as a high-speed mail-carrier.

Breguet's 521 Bizerte was preferred to the Laté 582 by the French navy.

Nardi F.N.305 200-hp touring aircraft, also built as fighter/trainers.

The prototype Dornier Do 18 transocean flying boat, made for DLH.

First prototype Heinkel He 112 fighter, powered by Rolls-Royce Kestrel.

Fairchild 91 and A-942 amphibians were supplied to Pan American.

A Klemm Kl 35 trainer modified as a closed-cockpit single-seater.

French government-sponsored flying clubs had 155 Potez 60s built.

Focke-Wulf's Fw 159 fighter lost the Luftwaffe contract to the Bf 109.

The last Luftwaffe operational biplane was the Henschel Hs 123B.

Forerunner of the Miles Magister was the Miles M.2X Hawk Trainer.

Savoia-Marchetti S.73 18-seat airliners saw wartime military service.

Heston Aircraft built five examples of the attractive five-seater Phoenix.

Noorduyn Aviation's Norseman was ideal for bush operations in Canada.

The Seversky SEV-X-BT was an ancestor of the prototype P-35 fighter.

Vultee's V-11 light bomber: sold to China, USSR, Turkey and Brazil.

Supermarine's Stranraer 165-mph general reconnaissance flying boat.

Vickers built 177 Wellesley light bombers for the Royal Air Force.

First customer for the Caproni Ca 135 was the Peruvian Air Force.

One Messerschmitt Bf 109 tested engine-mounted MG 17 and FF guns.

Savoia-Marchetti S.M.81 Pipistrello, used in the Abyssinian campaign.

Unsuccessful competitor with the Ju 87 Stuka: the Heinkel He 118 V4.

Breda Ba 65s were used for close-support and reconnaissance duties.

Forerunner of the BT-9 trainer: the prototype North American NA-16.

The USAAC received 240 North American O-47s for observation.

A 20mm cannon was built into the engine of the Yugoslav Ikarus IK-2.

The Focke-Wulf Fw 58 Weihe communications/crew-training aircraft.

Bristol Bombays were used as both night-bombers and troop-carriers.

By 1945, 12,731 Boeing B-17 Flying Fortress heavy bombers were built.

Six 860-hp engines were fitted to the sole 70-passenger Latécoère 521.

Morane-Saulnier built 17 MS.405s; production version was the MS.406.

Douglas TBD: first US Navy production carrier-based monoplane.

The Dutch military ordered 68 Koolhoven F.K.51 advanced trainers.

A Curtiss P-36A pursuit in 1939 USAAC "war games" camouflage.

Avro Ansons were used in coastal reconnaissance and training roles.

The Curtiss Model 76, tested by the US Army Air Corps as the XA-14.

The Hawker F.36/34 High-Speed Monoplane led to the Hurricane.

The fourth production prototype Junkers Ju 87 Stuka dive-bomber.

The Consolidated XP3Y-1 was modified into the PBY-5 Catalina.

Some Naval Aircraft Factory N3N Canary trainers were floatplanes.

The Douglas B-18A bomber, derived from the DC-2 transport.

Heinkel He 111s were built as civil transports, not originally as bombers.

Fieseler completed only a single prototype of the Fi 98a dive-bomber.

PZL P-37 Los [elk] medium bomber with later twin vertical tail surfaces.

# 1936

440.68mph
Italy
Francesco Agello
Macchi-Castoldi MC-72
Oct 23, 1934

6,587.45 miles
France
Bossoutrot and Rossi
Blériot 110
Mar 26, 1932

49,944ft
Great Britain
S.R. Swain
Bristol 138
Sep 28, 1936

123,457lb
Germany
Dormier
Do X

3,058hp
Italy
Fiat
AS.6

**USA and England, January 25**
Pan American and Imperial Airways sign an agreement to cooperate in the development of transatlantic flights (→ Oct 27).

**Africa, February 9**
Imperial Airways opens a service from Khartoum, Sudan, to Kano, Nigeria (→ Mar 14).

**Cape Town, S Africa, February 9**
Tommy Rose lands at Wingfield Aerodrome after a record flight from England of 3 days 17 hours 38 minutes (→ May 7).

**New York, February 19**
Former US Army Air Service general Billy Mitchell, a advocate of strategic air power, dies.

**London, March 2**
RAF officer Frank Whittle sets up Power Jets, with a capital of £10,000, to develop a turbojet airplane engine (→ Apr 15).

**Germany, March 4**
The German Zeppelin Company's LZ 129 *Hindenburg* makes its maiden flight; at 803.8 feet long and with a maximum diameter of 134.5 feet, it is the largest rigid airship in the world (→ May 14).

**London, March 14**
Imperial Airways opens a weekly service to Hong Kong.

**Germany, March**
Scientist Wernher von Braun's liquid-fuel rocket-motor, mounted on a Heinkel He 112, makes a test flight; the airplane explodes, but test pilot Erich Warsitz is hurled clear (→ Oct 13).

**New Jersey, April 3**
Bruno Hauptmann, who was convicted of murdering the baby son of Charles and Anne Lindbergh, is executed.

**Marienehe, Germany, April 15**
Development of a turbojet engine is begun at the Heinkel plant under engineers Hans Pabst von Ohain and Max Hahn (→ Apr 13, 1937).

**Germany, April**
The prototype Fieseler Fi 156 *Storch* [*Stork*] short take-off and landing monoplane makes its first flight.

**England and Australia, May 6**
Imperial Airways and QANTAS upgrade their London/Brisbane run into a twice-weekly service.

**Cape Town, S Africa, May 7**
Amy Mollison lands at Wingfield Aerodrome, Cape Town, to set a new record of 3 days 6 hours 26 minutes for a flight from England; she followed a new route down the west coast of Africa in a Percival Gull Six (→ May 15).

**Germany, May 12**
Rudolf Opitz pilots the first flight of the twin-engined Messerschmitt Bf 110 prototype fighter (→ Jun 3).

**Frankfurt, Germany, May 14**
The new German airship LZ 129 *Hindenburg* returns after a round-trip to New Jersey, USA; it left Friedrichshafen on May 6, flying outward in 2 days 13 hours 50 minutes and back in 2 days 1 hour 3 minutes (→ Dec 18).

**Dublin, May 27**
Aer Lingus Teoranta, registered five days ago, inaugurates a daily service to Bristol, England; the service is operated in conjunction with British-registered Blackpool and West Coast Air Service, which put up the capital for the Irish airline.

**Dresden, Germany, June 3**
Walther Wever, first Luftwaffe chief of staff, dies in an air crash.

**West Sussex, England, June 6**
A grass aerodrome beside the London/Brighton railway is officially opened as Gatwick Airport, although it has been in use for flights since 1930.

**USA, June 7**
Major Ira C Eaker flies entirely by instruments from New York to Los Angeles in a Boeing P-12.

**Surrey, England, June 15**
The Vickers B.9/32 bomber prototype, built using a very strong "basket-work" frame conceived by designer Barnes Wallis, makes its first flight, piloted by "Mutt" Summers, at Brooklands.

**Bristol, England, June 25**
The prototype of a fast bomber, the Bristol Blenheim Mark 1, makes its first flight; it is based on the Bristol 142 *Britain First*, which was offered to the Royal Air Force by owner Lord Rothermere.

**Australia, July 1**
Holyman's Airways, Airlines of Australia, Adelaide Airways and West Australia Airways merge to form Australian National Airways.

**Morocco, July 19**
Captain Cecil Bebb of British airline Olley Air Service flies a secret mission to transport Spanish rebel leader General Franco here from the Canary Islands; Bebb was hired by autogyro inventor Juan de La Cierva and Spanish newsman Luis Bolin (→ Jul 20).

**Morocco, July 20**
A major airlift of rebel Spanish Nationalist troops and equipment to Seville begins using German Ju 52/3ms; the operation is organized by General Franco (→ Jul 29).

**London, July 30**
Viscount Swinton announces the formation of a Volunteer Reserve for the Royal Air Force.

**Cadiz, Spain, August 7**
Six Heinkel He 51 fighters, despatched by the German government, arrive to support General Franco and the Nationalists (→ Aug 14).

**Paris, August 8**
Louis Blériot, the first man to fly across the English Channel and one of France's most renowned air pioneers, dies of a heart attack at the age of 64. He was almost destitute since the failure of his aircraft manufacturing company.

**Villacoublay, France, Sept 22**
Test pilot Maurice Claisse flies the Breguet-Dorand helicopter to an altitude of 518 feet.

**Cartagena, Spain, October 13**
A consignment of Soviet I-15 fighters, despatched by Stalin's government, arrives to support the Republican forces in the Spanish civil war (→ Oct 29).

**Paris, October 16**
French air minister Pierre Cot announces that all factories manufacturing airplanes and aircraft engines under contracts for the French government are to be nationalized.

**Spain, October 30**
The German Kondor [Condor] Legion of fighter, bomber and reconnaissance airplanes, led by General Hugo Sperrle, is created to support Franco's Nationalists in the civil war (→ Nov 4).

**Mediterranean, October 30**
Imperial Airways puts its first Short C-class flying boat, the *Canopus*, into service on the route between Alexandria, Egypt, and Brindisi, Italy.→

**Washington, DC, November 10**
President Franklin D Roosevelt bans exports of US military airplanes of the latest design.

**South Atlantic, December 7**
Air France pilot Jean Mermoz, known as "*L'Archange de la Ligne* [the Archangel of the Line]", disappears while piloting the Latécoère 300 *Croix du Sud* between Dakar and Brazil.

**Dessau, Germany, December 21**
The first prototype Junkers Ju 88V-1 high-speed bomber makes its maiden flight.

---

*Passenger night flights have become commonplace in Europe. Note the mandatory flag flown by each Air France Wibault aircraft.* ▶

# Hughes crosses USA in under ten hours

*Newark, NJ, January 14*
Tycoon and air enthusiast Howard Hughes left Burbank airport, California, at lunchtime yesterday, and landed here in time for a midnight snack early today. He did it by averaging 259mph, setting a new non-stop, coast-to-coast speed record of 9 hours 26 minutes 10 seconds, and a world speed record for the distance covered.

Hughes flew a Northrop Gamma monoplane powered by a 1,000-hp Wright G Cyclone radial engine. His radio was useless because the antenna snapped off during take-off, and he had to use oxygen when bad weather forced him up to 18,000 feet. But he was helped by strong tail winds which enabled him to complete the 170 miles between Indianapolis and Columbus in 35 minutes, and the 160 miles between Columbus and Pittsburgh in 32 minutes (→ Feb 19, 1937).

# France mapped by aerial photography

*A mapping camera with nine lenses.*

*France, February 1*
French army cartographers have set out to create an aerial map of France on a scale of 1/50,000, a marathon task that is likely to take more than 20 years. The estimated size of France, including Corsica, is 213,000 square miles. Relief will no longer be represented by shading, but by contour lines following the same height. An entire squadron is to be devoted to the undertaking, and several years have been spent on developing the cameras which will be used.

# New rules for travel confound passengers

*Croydon, England, March 17*
Smoking in an airliner's toilet is as serious an offense as smoking at school. An Imperial Airways passenger, caught red-handed while lighting up against airline regulations in a Handley Page HP.42 en route from Paris to London, was fined £10 in a Croydon court today. This is the first case of its kind to come before the British courts, and it seems the severity of the fine is designed to deter others.

The incident highlights some of the restrictions imposed on airplane travelers which are generally not found on trains or ships. In flight, they must remain seated almost the whole of the time and, if standing, resume their seats instantly at the command of the pilot. Hold and cabin baggage must still be separated, as aboard ship, and luggage is also restricted in size and weight, not easy for possessors of large wardrobes. Passengers themselves are weighed before being let on board, which some regard as a great indignity. Mid-air snacks are

*Happy landings for meek travelers.*

frowned upon, unless they are supplied by the airline, and vacuum flasks and other items liable to be affected by changes in atmospheric pressure are completely forbidden.

# Radio device plots high-altitude flight

*Suffolk, England, March 13*
British scientists are believed to have detected an aircraft flying at 15,000 feet at a distance of 60 miles using an array of radio aerials recently erected on the coast above the research station in a stately home at Bawdsey.

The lonely spot is home to a a combined civilian/RAF team which is ideal for secret experiments. The 250-foot-high masts transmit an invisible curtain of radio waves. When an airplane, such as the Hawker Hart used today, penetrates it, a luminous spot shows on a fluorescent cathode-ray tube. The whole system has been dubbed "radio direction finding" (RDF) by the Scotsman in charge of the project, Robert Watson Watt. He will not say if the airplane's direction is shown as well as its altitude.

The first experiment using an aircraft to cause a "blip" on such a screen was at Daventry on February 26 last year.

# Supermarine unveils its high-performance monoplane prototype

*Southampton, England, March 5*
Chief test pilot "Mutt" Summers expressed delight today at Southampton's Eastleigh aerodrome when he landed the prototype of Supermarine's latest fighter, to be known as the Spitfire. "Don't touch anything," he said after a highly successful first flight. The aircraft is not just a joy to fly but also a joy to behold: small and powerful, with superb, clean lines, it looks like a thoroughbred fighting machine.

Stressed-skin construction has been used throughout; the aircraft has beautiful elliptical wings and landing gear that is retracted by hand pump. The radiator is under the left wing, the oil cooler under the right. Its armament will consist of a battery of up to eight machine guns mounted inside the wing but well clear of the propeller arc.

The Rolls-Royce PV.12 engine with which it is fitted is at present rated at 990 hp, but has the potential to give well over 1,000 hp with further development. But it drives an obsolete two-blade fixed-pitch propeller (→ Jun 11, 1937).

*King Edward VIII is shown the cockpit of Supermarine's fighter prototype, the Model 300, to be named Spitfire.*

## Major US airlines seek 'superplane'

*Los Angeles, March 23*
Five major airlines agreed today to provide $500,000 to aircraft manufacturer Douglas to develop a super airliner. The aim is to produce an airplane that can carry double the number of passengers twice as far as existing transports.

The airlines – American, Pan American, Eastern, United and TWA – will each put up $100,000 for research and development. Initial studies indicate that they want Douglas's creation, designated the DC-4, to have four engines and a range of up to 2,000 miles. They want a pressurized, air-conditioned cabin for flight above bad weather, slotted flaps, triple fins and rudders for extra stability if two engines are shut down on one side, power-assisted controls and a nose wheel rather than a tail wheel. The airliner will have to carry at least 42 daytime passengers in two rows of double seats and sleep up to 30 at night (→ Sep 18).

# Italian air power conquers Abyssinia

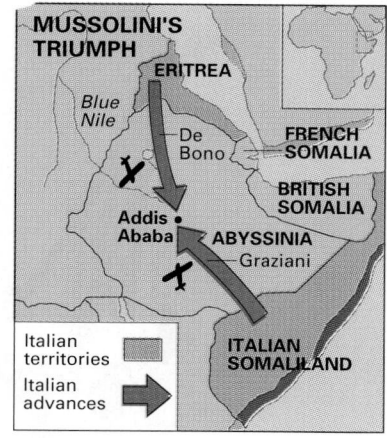

*Count Ciano (r), Italy's propaganda minister, aboard a Caproni airplane.*

*Addis Ababa, May 9*
The war in Abyssinia [Ethiopia] is over. The defending forces have put up a brave resistance for seven months, but now Emperor Haile Selassie is on his way into exile, and his country has been annexed formally by Benito Mussolini, Italy's Duce [Leader].

The war was a victory for numerically inferior forces, which owed their success to their command of the air. It is also the first fruit of the *blitzkrieg* theory of war, in which land and air operations combine in a surprise attack to overwhelm an opponent before effective defenses can be organized.

In view of Mussolini's savage bombing campaign against poorly equipped tribal armies, the surprise is not that the war is over after seven months, but that it lasted so long. As it was, the Duce sacked his first commander, General de Bono, replacing him with Marshal Pietro Badoglio. He did not, however, sack his son Vittorio for dropping 40 bombs on a hospital. It was virtually all over when Italian troops entered Addis Ababa four days ago, allowing Mussolini to declare Abyssinia part of his new empire.

## Gutsy Amy smashes South Africa record

*Cheering crowds congratulate Amy as she is driven away from Croydon.*

*Croydon, England, May 15*
Amy Mollison touched down at Croydon today to universal acclaim for her persistence in breaking the record for a flight from London to Cape Town and back. Her time of 3 days 6 hours 28 minutes slices 11 hours off Tommy Rose's record set in February this year.

She made an attempt last month, but it nearly ended in tragedy at Colomb Béchar, Algeria, when her Percival Gull, heavy with extra fuel, slewed off the runway in what she described as "a stupid accident". After five days waiting for spare parts from England, she flew back to Britain with Sabena to collect them, and then flew back to the Gull and started out all over again. It is for such determination that she is so admired (→ Oct 1).

## Taylor's popular Cub is child's play to fly

*Savannah, Ga, May 15*
"So easy, even a child could fly it" was the proud boast of Taylor Brothers Aircraft manufacturing company about its Taylor Cub monoplane. To prove it was right, it brought in 11-year-old Billy Lee, who flew solo in the Cub today and landed almost perfectly as skeptical pressmen watched and then cheered. Billy was taught to fly the Cub by his father at Augusta. The simple airplane, designed by oil-man Piper, is easy to fly, although with its original Brownbach 20-hp engine it was somewhat underpowered. But fitted with an air cooled, 32-hp four-cylinder Continental engine, the improved Cub sells well at $1,325. Piper saw his design as a popular "people's plane" before the Depression; he now hopes that the Cub can be sold by the firm Piper Aircraft (→ Dec).

*The people's plane: the Taylor E-2 Cub is cheap to buy, and very easy to fly.*

# New Guinea prospectors fly the gold trail

*Lae, New Guinea, May*
When gold was discovered in New Guinea in 1927, the opportunity for an airline entrepreneur was obvious. The overland journey to the goldfields involved a risky hike through dense jungle and a climb over a 4,000-foot-high ridge, made even more hazardous by the presence of cannibalistic tribesmen. That same year, former patrol officer C J Levien founded the airline New Guinea Gold No Liability with a D.H.37. It started regular services to Wau, using an inland airstrip which was only just suitable, situated at a height of 3,700 feet and with a 4-degree slope.

Since then companies have multiplied, and today even local Christian missionaries get around in their own private aircraft.

*An Austin Seven car is loaded on to one of Guinea Airways' Junkers G 31s.*

# Air France opts for conservative airliner

*France, June 6*
Air France has gone for a sturdy if outmoded trimotor as the latest addition to its fleet. Eight Dewoitine D.338 airliners went into service today after the company's chief pilots had proclaimed the all-metal, low-winged monoplane to be the ideal machine for all routes. An initial order for 21 has been placed.

The D.338 is descended from the tough D.332 *Emeraude*, which entered service with the airline three years ago. Its three 650-hp, nine-cylinder Hispano-Suiza radial engines provide exceptional power and a cruising speed of 144mph, slow compared with the world's most advanced airliners in service, the Boeing 247 and Douglas DC-2.

The D.338 can carry 22 passengers on European services, 15 on African routes or 12 on the Far-Eastern route, six of them having sleeper-seats. It will be used initially on domestic routes, but will later serve on the line from Toulouse to Casablanca and Dakar.

*Part of Air France's latest order, the Dewoitine D.338 "Clément Isaure".*

# German helicopter makes promising start

*The creation of Professor Focke and Herr Achgelis takes to the air.*

*Bremen, Germany, June 26*
Exactly a year after the first flight of France's Breguet *Gyroplane* helicopter [*see page 326*], the Focke-Wulf company today flew a machine which it claims to be superior. Test pilot Ewald Rohlfs predicts a great future for it.

The German machine's designation is Fa 61, the Fa standing for designers Professor Heinrich Karl Focke and Gerd Achgelis. Like the Breguet, the Fa 61 has two rotors, but they are side-by-side, mounted on long outrigger struts. The fuselage has a 160-hp Siemens radial engine at the nose, driving not only the rotors (via long shafting) but also a propeller to keep the engine cool. At the back is an airplane-type tail, and the machine has tricycle landing gear.

Today's flight lasted only 28 seconds, but Rohlfs said there is every reason to believe the Fa 61 will be able to achieve much longer flights. The immediate task is to perfect stability and control. Focke must also demonstrate safe landing after engine failure (→ Sep 22).

# Airwomen triumph in coast-to-coast race

*Los Angeles, September 4*
It was not planned that way, but it was "Ladies' Day" at the National Air Races today as Mrs Louise Thaden became the first woman to win the prestigious coast-to-coast Bendix trophy race. To the chagrin of their male colleagues, women took three of the first five places, with Laura Ingalls second across the line and Amelia Earhart fifth.

Thaden's victory is unique, not just because she is a woman but because she flew an enclosed-cabin Beech Model 17 "Staggerwing" bi-plane instead of a sleek monoplane racer like most of the other contestants. With co-pilot Blanche Noyes, Thaden flew from New York to Los Angeles in 14 hours 55 minutes. Her time was well over Roscoe Turner's 1933 east/west record of 11 hours 30 minutes, but

*Louise Thaden savors her victory.*

it did set the mark for women. At various times since 1928 she has held women's endurance, altitude and speed records.

Last year's winner Benny Howard and his wife both broke their legs when their racer – built by Benny – crashed 30 miles north of Crown Point, New Mexico, in a Navajo reservation (→ Sep 7).

# Air forces go into action as civil war splits Spain

## Nationalist troops moved to Spain by air

*Spanish Morocco, July 29*
As Spain slides towards civil war, air power has already been a decisive factor. At first the Nationalist uprising against the elected government lacked both firm leadership and an experienced army. Now the airplane has provided them.

On July 19 General Francisco Franco flew in from the Canary Islands (where he had effectively been exiled by the government) to take charge. Among his first acts was to ask Adolf Hitler for transport aircraft. Yesterday the world's first large-scale military airlift of troops began as thousands of Span-ish Moroccan soldiers and Spanish foreign legionnaires began crowding into Junkers Ju 52/3m transports in batches of between 30 and 40 to make the short journey across the Straits of Gibraltar.

The Spanish navy is loyal to the government and would have blocked the movement of Nationalist forces by sea. Much of the air force, with most of the aircraft, is with the government too, but many experienced pilots have joined Franco. What the general now needs is aircraft, and he is looking to Fascist Germany and Italy to provide him with them.→

*Ready for action: the first German squadron of Arado 68F Fighters.*

## Air back-up arrives for General Franco

*Nationalist leader General Franco.*

*Spain, August 14*
Hitler and Mussolini have responded quickly to Franco's request for aircraft. Heinkel He 51 fighters, with volunteers from the Luftwaffe to fly and service them, have been arriving in Spain since early August, and today the first Fiat CR.32 fighters arrived from Italy. Foreign pilots have been advisers to date, but without any notable success by Spanish pilots; the first combat mission by German crews took place today: a Ju 52, converted into a bomber, scored two hits on the Republican battleship *Jaime I*, putting it out of action (→ Oct 30).

## Writer establishes 'Spanish Squadron'

*Merida, Spain, August 14*
Republican morale was boosted today when a makeshift squadron of old airplanes and foreign pilots, organized by young French writer André Malraux, strafed a column of Franco's troops near here. The column failed to link up with its allies. Malraux knows little of flying, but he has thrown himself into creating his "Spanish Squadron". It is a gallant gesture, but experts do not rate its chances against Franco's highly-trained German and Italian "volunteers" (→ Oct 13).

*Malraux: backing the Republicans.*

# The Lysander can take off from even the shortest of runways

*Yeovil, England, June 10*
The tiny aircraft soars into the sky after an incredibly short take-off run. Westland's new two-seater Lysander aircraft is being taken through its paces by test pilot Harald Penrose. Powered by an 890-hp Bristol Mercury IX engine, the Lysander only needs a 490-foot take-off run to be able to fly over a 50-foot obstacle at the end of the runway. Such performance, added to the fact that its cockpit has excellent all-round visibility and that twin Browning machine-guns can be mounted on its fixed landing gear, gives the Lysander a wide range of military or civilian uses.

*The Lysander high-winged monoplane has Dowty internally-sprung wheels encased in large spats. To these can be attached machine-guns and stub-wings for bombs or supply containers.*

**Mrs. Richardson, Air France's 100,000th passenger this year, receives a rousing welcome.**

# Douglas' spacious day-or-night airliner puts American ahead of the competition

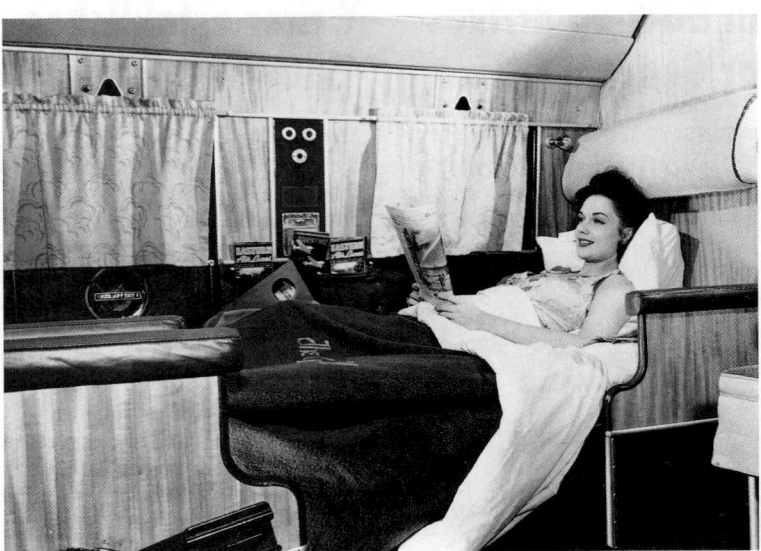

*The Douglas Sleeper Transport offers passengers a good night's rest.*

*New York, September 18*
American Airlines today put the new Douglas Sleeper Transport (DST) into service on the transcontinental route between New York and Los Angeles. The flying time between the two cities is now 16 hours. The spacious new model, both in the DST sleeper format and in its DC-3 day version, offers greater speed and comfort than other airliners, and it looks set to place American ahead of main rivals TWA, United and Eastern. American has operated DSTs since June 25 and DC-3s since August 18.

*Oakland, Calif, December 5*
United Air Lines, which has been operating some Douglas DC-2s, has ordered eight DC-3s. The airline however asked Douglas to provide a more powerful version. Douglas will replace the 900-hp engines with 1,100-hp ones. This new model, which got its certification on November 11, will go into service on the Los Angeles/San Francisco route on January 1. Today, stewardesses began using the galley built aboard United airliners to prepare hot meals for their passengers.

*United hostesses promise to continue working after they are married.*

# Beryl Markham triumphs over Atlantic

*Baleine, Nova Scotia, September 5*
Englishwoman Beryl Markham, 34, twice married and twice divorced, has added yet another chapter to her colorful life. After leaving Abingdon, England, yesterday, Mrs Markham landed in Nova Scotia today to become the first woman to fly solo east/west across the Atlantic. The little airplane, powered by a 200-hp Gipsy Six engine, flew the 2,612 miles in 21 hours 25 minutes.

As she approached Nova Scotia, unusually high winds exhausted what remained of the fuel, and she crash-landed in a swamp at Baleine Cove, Cape Breton Island, but without injury. Her airplane, a Percival Vega Gull called the *Messenger*, ended on its nose in six feet of mud.

Mrs Markham is a British expatriate who lives in Kenya, where, when still plain Beryl Clutterbuck, she set up horse-racing stables while still a teenager. Two marriages and a child have done little to quell her antics as a member of the Nairobi "high set", which include hunting elephants by air.

*A welcoming committee with Beryl Markham on her arrival back in England.*

# DLH opens luxury service to Bermuda

*Bermuda, September 10*
Lufthansa today began a series of experimental transatlantic flights with luxury Dornier Do 18 seaplanes powered by twin Diesel engines. The route is from Berlin to New York, with the flying boats heading from Lisbon to the Azores and then on to the mid-Atlantic seaplane tender *Schwabenland*. Passengers can then fly on direct to New York or via Bermuda. As ever, the Atlantic weather, and thus the ability to dock safely at the *Schwabenland*, will be the ruling factor in all DLH's transatlantic operations (→Jun 16, 1937).

# Army unimpressed by rocket research

*Roswell, N Mex, October 13*
The US Army Air Corps (USAAC) paid a visit to scientist Robert Goddard today to assess the value of the rocket pioneer's research. The Army, in the shape of junior officer Lieutenant John W Sessums, was primarily interested in the possible military applications of Goddard's work.

Sessums was not greatly impressed and he is preparing to report to his superiors that liquid-fuel rockets have little military value, but appear useful for driving turbines for shaft-power, and for the propulsion of targets (→Jul 1937).

# Frenchman grabs American speed trophy

*Bystanders admire the sleek lines of the extraordinary Caudron C.460 racer.*

**Los Angeles, September 7**
Two of the top speed trophies awarded at this year's National Air Races will be taken to France by Michel Detroyat, who stunned his American colleagues when he won the Greve and Thompson trophies.

Detroyat flew a Renault-powered Caudron C.460, a sleek aircraft with a much smaller engine than the 750-hp and 1,000-hp engines of the American planes. He took the Thompson trophy with a speed of 264.13mph and the Greve with 247.3mph. Harold Neumann was also impressive in his Folkerts Special. He came second to Detroyat and was placed in three other races.

The performance of the French aircraft should not have been a surprise for the Americans. A C.460 racer was piloted by Raymond Delmotte to the then world landplane speed record of 314mph in December 1934. Delmotte also took the 1935 Deutsch cup in the C.460, achieving the creditable speed of 275.93mph on that occasion.

# Soviet planes enter Spanish Civil War

**Madrid, November 4**
Pilots of two Italian Fiat fighters shot down over the Spanish capital today probably never knew what hit them. They were victims of the first Soviet air action of the Spanish Civil War.

Stalin's support for the Republicans arrived slowly compared with the swift help sent to Franco by Hitler and Mussolini. It finally arrived in the form of ten I-15 biplanes led by Ukrainian ace Pavel Rychagov, 25. The Soviet intervention is a state secret, though reporters at southern ports have for weeks witnessed the unloading of cargoes of I-15s, some 50 of which have now been assembled. They are fast, maneuverable fighters designed by Polikarpov. Launched for the first time today to intercept an Italian reconnaissance airplane, they succeeded in shooting down the two escorts.→

# Madrid is target of sustained bombing

**Madrid, November 9**
Madrid has earned a sad place in history: the first major city to be subjected to sustained aerial bombing. For three days waves of German bombers have bombarded the city around the clock with high-explosive and incendiary bombs, the night attacks guided by the fires started during the day.

The original purpose of the raids was to dislodge Republican defenders, opening the way for a Nationalist attack, but it turned into a test of the theory that air power could so demoralize a population that it would surrender without a land attack. In this sense the victory went to the people of Madrid: they did not succumb. The bombing has brought a greater spirit of defiance. The cry that echoed round the city last night was: "No pasaran [they shall not pass]." And, so far, they have not (→ Feb 18, 1937).

# RAF pilot soars to new altitude record

**Hampshire, England, September 28**
After being in French and Italian hands for three years, the world altitude record has returned to Britain. In a 2-hour flight from Farnborough today in the new Bristol 138A monoplane, Squadron Leader S R D Swain reached what he reckoned as 49,944 feet. His instruments indicated well over 50,000 feet.

With its 66-foot span, the Bristol took some time to reach 35,000 feet, where the second of the superchargers of the Pegasus engine came into use. Thirty-five minutes were needed to attain 40,000 feet, and twice this time passed before the record height was reached. On the way down Swain's oxygen ran out, and he had to break the glass of his pressure-suit helmet in order to breathe (→ May 7, 1937).

*Swain had to wear a pressure suit.*

# Imperial Airways acquires new seaplanes

*Imperial Airways' "C" class flying boat "Canopus" lifts off for a test flight.*

**Brindisi, Italy, October 30**
The flying boat *Canopus*, the first of a fleet of 28 being bought by Britain's Imperial Airways, today made its first scheduled flight with the airline. It arrived here from Alexandria, Egypt, after a journey of 7 hours 30 minutes.

Officially called Short S.23s, but universally known as the "C" class from their names, these flying boats set a standard for both the airline and the British aircraft industry. Powered by four 910-hp Bristol Pegasus engines, each driving a Hamilton-type, variable-pitch propeller, the flying boats are monoplanes – thus extremely clean aerodynamically – and can cruise for long distances at 164mph. They can carry 17 passengers in comfort and 2 tons of mail.

The decision to buy no fewer than 28 of these impressive planes underscores Imperial's determination to use water-based transports throughout its entire route network. The second aircraft off the production line at the Short factory in Rochester will be equipped with additional fuel tanks for flights across the Atlantic (→ Feb 8, 1937).

# Pan Am opens service to the Philippines

*Pan Am's luxurious "Hawaii Clipper" is launched in a formal ceremony.*

*Manila, October 27*
The Pan American Airways *Hawaii Clipper* NC 14714 flying boat arrived here today, marking the start of regular passenger flights between the US and the Philippines. The flight, carrying 11 passengers, left San Francisco on October 21 and stopped at Honolulu and Midway, Wake and Guam islands.

Pan Am has been preparing for the flight since last November,

when it began airmail flights to Manila. The carrier says it has invested $5 million in preparing the new transpacific passenger service. Since the airmail run started, the airline has been training crews, expanding its fleet of Martin M-130s and building facilities beyond Hawaii, including luxury hotels on the barren Midway and Wake islands. Passengers paid $799 each for the 8,200-mile flight (→ Jun 16).

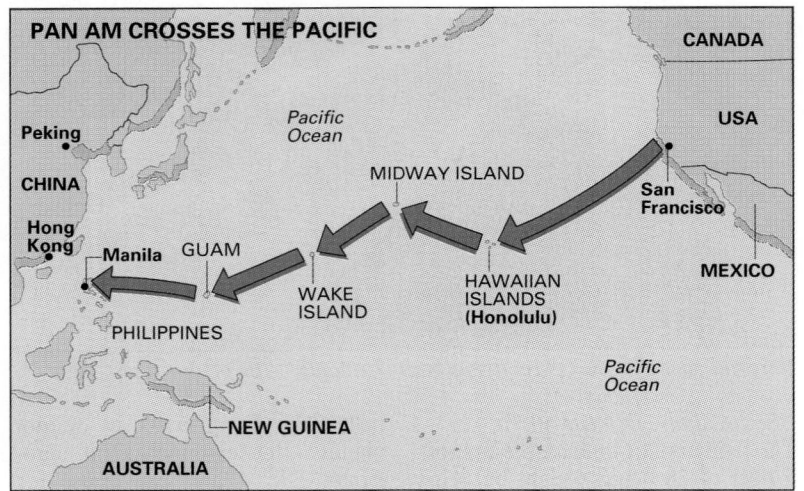

PAN AM CROSSES THE PACIFIC

# Light aircraft are in strong demand

*Lock Haven, Pa, December*
The world light airplane industry is booming. Taylor Aircraft's production line here has delivered 761 J-2 Cubs this year, and good results have been reported by builders in the US and Europe. In Europe, the leaders are Morane-Saulnier, Caudron and Potez in France; Miles,

Percival and de Havilland in Britain; and Klemm, Focke-Wulf and BFW in Germany. German output has been boosted by orders for trainers for the Luftwaffe. Most of the trainers are fabric-covered biplanes, but BFW's Bf 108 typifies the new breed of stressed-skin monoplanes.

# US Navy buys new Consolidated PBYs

*San Diego, November 2*
Consolidated Aircraft today received an order for 66 of its latest long-range seaplane, the PBY-3, from the US Navy. The purchase means that modernization of the Navy's fleet of patrol bombers is continuing at a rapid pace.

So far 176 of the twin-engined seaplanes have been ordered since the initial order for 60 PBY-1s was placed in June last year. That was followed by an order for 50 PBY-2s four months ago, and now this one for PBY-3s. All of the airplanes ordered are similar, the main difference in the PBY-3s being the engines, 1,000-hp Pratt & Whitney R-1830-66 Twin Wasps. The first

fully equipped operational squadron to fly the new PBYs will be VP-11, based in Hawaii.

The purchase means the end for the biplane flying boats which have been standard in the US Navy for years. The PBY has a parasol-mounted wing and a stressed skin which eliminates external bracing except for a pair of struts between the hull and the wing on each side. Unique stabilizing floats toward the end of each wing fold upward to form the wing tips in flight.

The PBY can carry 2,000 pounds of bombs and three machine guns. This makes the PBY-3 very effective as a patrol bomber, especially against submarines.

*The seaplane Patrol Bomber PBY from Consolidated Aircraft Corporation is costing the US Navy $95,000, $15,000 less than the Douglas version.*

# Jean Batten gets huge welcome in Auckland

*Auckland, October 16*
A traffic queue stretched from Auckland's airfield right back to the city today as people flocked to see Jean Batten landing at the end of the fastest solo flight from Britain to New Zealand.

Since leaving Lympne, Kent, Batten has pushed herself and her Percival Gull Six, aptly called *Jean*, to the limits of endurance, covering the 14,000-mile route in 11 days 1 hour 25 minutes. As she flew, records have fallen at her feet. Jean's first aim was to beat her rival H F Broadbent's time for a flight between England and Australia. She started before dawn on October 5. Five days 21 hours 3 minutes later she reached Darwin, having endured sandstorms and typhoons to slash the solo flight record by an amazing 1 day 16 minutes.

But her ultimate goal remained her native New Zealand, and even the offer of money to tour Australia would not induce her to change her mind. The last leg of her journey,

between Richmond, Victoria, and New Zealand, was another triumph. Batten flew it in a record-breaking time of 10 hours 36 minutes (→ Oct 18, 1937).

*Jean in England before the flight.*

# Mollison's plane seized after record flight

*"Miss Dorothy" taxis at Croydon, England, after last month's record flight.*

**Delaware, November 4**
In a bizarre twist to the triumph of his recent transatlantic crossing, British airman Jim Mollison has had his Flash monoplane *Miss Dorothy* repossessed by its manufacturer, Bellanca. It is said that his sponsor, the Irish Hospitals Trust, has defaulted. It is more bad news for the pilot, whose marriage to Amy Johnson is crumbling. Mollison's transatlantic attempt began in New York on October 28. The following day he took off from Harbour Grace, Newfoundland, and reached the Irish coast after just 9 hours 15 minutes. Four hours 3 minutes later he arrived at Croydon airport, achieving an average speed of 225mph (→ Mar 22, 1937).

# Ansett switches from buses to airplanes

**Melbourne, Australia, December**
A new airline, created to get round officialdom, is now an established airmail and passenger carrier here in south-eastern Australia. Determined that the railroad was going to be the only means of public transport in Victoria, the state's transport board issued a banning order to stop bus operator Reg Ansett establishing a regular service from Melbourne to Hamilton.

Undaunted, Ansett bought himself a Fokker Universal, called it *Austral Star*, and flew his first scheduled service on February 17, carrying six passengers. Having secured an airmail contract in May, he has ambitions to expand in Victoria and beyond.

**Three actors try out a mock-up of the airplane of the future, which was built by a film studio in Hollywood to take part in one of its features.**

# Spanish autogyro pioneer dies in England

**Croydon, England, December 9**
In Britain's worst-ever aircraft accident, a DC-2 of Dutch airline KLM crashed on take-off into a row of houses in thick fog today, killing the pilot and all 13 passengers on the flight. The DC-2 and one house were totally destroyed and several neighboring buildings suffered heavy damage.

Among the dead was Juan de La Cierva, Spanish pioneer of the autogyro, whose C.30 had recently reached 110mph. He succeeded in turning the early, crude designs for gyroplanes into sophisticated aircraft that could take off and land on the spot and hover in mid-air. He was also a passionate advocate of air safety.

*The wreckage of the crash at Croydon in which Juan de La Cierva died.*

# Soviet Polikarpovs pound Kondor Legion

**Spain, November**
The Spanish Civil War is presenting an unrivalled opportunity for Germany, Italy and the Soviet Union (which supports the Republicans) to test their military aircraft and tactical theories about air power in combat.

On October 29, the first Soviet Tupolev SB-2 bomber fell to the guns of an Italian Fiat CR.32 fighter flown by Spaniard Angel Salas. Despite such reverses, the recently deployed Soviet Polikarpov I-15 and I-16 fighters are beginning to inflict considerable losses on Germany's pro-Franco Kondor Legion, providing a badly needed morale boost for anti-Franco forces. These squat, powerful Soviet biplanes flying under Republican colors are proving superior to the German He 51s and Junkers Ju 52s, as well as the Italian CR.32 and Ro.37 fighters. The Polikarpovs can also provide good air cover for ground troops.

*Soviet Polikarpov I-15 fighters are providing support to the Republicans.*

The low-cost Miles' M.11 Whitney Straight two-seater monoplane.

A single Loire 102 four-engined flying boat was built for Air France.

An S-42-inspired Kawanishi Navy H6K Type 97 Flying Boat Model 22.

The Romano R.82 trainer: 110 were built for the French armed forces.

Mitsubishi Ki-21 Army Type 97 six-seater Heavy Bomber Model 1A.

Bristol's prototype Blenheim light bomber, also used as a night-fighter.

Vought's SB2U Vindicator: the first US Navy monoplane dive-bomber.

Short Brothers had an order from Imperial Airways for 28 Empire or "C" class flying boats, for passengers and mail, before the prototype had flown.

Bristol's Type 138A single-seater high-altitude research aircraft.

Handley Page's Hampden medium bomber (two Pegasus): 1,430 built.

The prototype Supermarine Spitfire was the first of 22,890 aircraft of numerous variants which were manufactured for the RAF between 1936 and 1947.

Lockheed's L-12A Electra in wartime service with 24 Squadron, RAF.

Fairey Battle light bombers replaced Hawker Hind biplanes.

Junkers' Ju 89 bomber was abandoned and became the Ju 90 airliner.

Breda's Ba 88 Lince light bomber: 105 were made but little used.

Third prototype Heinkel He 115 with an extended canopy and revised nose.

Arado produced the Ar 95L wheeled version of the Ar 95A floatplane.

Early Fiat B.R.20 Cicogna bombers took part in the Spanish Civil War.

The Luftwaffe never received Messerschmitt's Bf 162 light bomber.

Fairey Seafox reconnaissance seaplanes were catapult-launched.

Built to British bomber specification B.9/32, the Vickers Type 271 was the ancestor of the Wellington. Almost every part was later to be redesigned.

Lioré et Olivier's H-47 for Air France served as an ocean patroler.

Fiat's BGA medium bomber, whose prototype disappointed on test.

Focke-Achgelis Fa 223 Hornisse prototype, developed from the FW 61.

Henschel Hs 126A-1: useful STOL short-range reconnaissance aircraft.

Petlyakov Pe-8 (ANT-42): USSR's only Second War heavy bomber.

Fokker's D.XXI fighter: 93 were license-built in Finland by 1944.

Best and most numerous Luftwaffe bomber was the Junkers Ju 88.

The developed SB-2 "bis" version of the Tupolev ANT-40 fast bomber had more powerful M-103 engines. SB-2 production totalled 6,656 aircraft.

Fokker's G.1 fighter: 36 were supplied to the Netherlands army air service and were also used for ground-attack operations. One escaped to Britain.

Prototype Tupolev ANT-37 (DB-2) long-range record-breaking bomber.

An early production Heinkel He 111B-2 bomber (civil-registered).

This Bloch MB-175B-3 served at Oran in 1942 (last one made 1950).

Just 16 LWS.4 Zubr [bison] bombers were built for the Polish air force.

Aeroflot's Tupolev ANT-35 (PS-35) ten-passenger airliner.

Heinkel He 114 reconnaissance seaplane (Germany and Romania).

Handley Page H.P.54 Harrow bombers became wartime transports.

Fieseler's Storch could virtually hover against a 25-mph headwind.

Westland Lysanders were used for army cooperation and air/sea rescue duties. Special versions were used to transport agents and supply the Maquis.

# 1937

440.68mph
Italy
Francesco Agello
Macchi-Castoldi MC-72
Oct 23, 1934

6,587.45 miles
France
Bossoutrot and Rossi
Blériot 110
Mar 26, 1932

53,937ft
Great Britain
MJ Adam
Bristol 138
Jun 30, 1937

123,457lb
Germany
Dornier
Do X

3,058hp
Italy
Fiat
AS.6

**Rome, January 12**
Italian dictator Benito Mussolini performs standard military tests to qualify as a Service pilot; he has been a private pilot for years.

**Wichita, Kansas, January 15**
Walter Beech, having bought out his partners in the Travel Air company, witnesses the first flight of the Beechcraft Model 18 all-metal, twin-engined monoplane.

**Yorkshire, England, February 7**
The prototype Blackburn B.24 Skua two-seat fighter/dive-bomber makes its maiden flight, piloted by "Dasher" Blake at Brough; it is Britain's first dive-bomber.

**Hampshire, England, February 8**
Imperial Airways opens a regular non-stop flying boat service from Southampton to Alexandria, Egypt, using Short S.23 Empire flying boats (→ Jun 2).

**Spain, February 18**
Ben Leider, American volunteer pilot for the Republicans, is killed when he crashes into a hillside after a dogfight with three German Heinkels; he is the first American pilot to die in the Spanish Civil War.

**East Anglia, England, March 22**
Britain's "Flying Duchess", 72-year-old Mary, Duchess of Bedford, goes missing in a snowstorm after taking off from Woburn, Bedfordshire, in her de Havilland 60 Gipsy Moth to view the frozen fens.

**Trollhättan, Sweden, April 2**
Swedish airplane manufacturer Svenska Aeroplan Aktiebolaget (SAAB) is established.

**Santa Monica, Cal, April 5**
The Douglas Aircraft Company takes over Northrop.

**Croydon, England, April 5**
British Airways introduces the Lockheed Electra into service on its London/Paris route; it can carry ten passengers (→ May 7).

**Lima, April 18**
Commander Armando Revoredo Iglesias lands to complete a solo flight to Buenos Aires and back.

**Atlantic Ocean, April 30**
An attack by Republican airplanes sinks Nationalist battleship *España*.

**Croydon, England, May 2**
Imperial Airways' Handley Page H.P.42 *Heracles* makes the airline's 40,000th cross-Channel flight.

**El Ferrol, Spain, May 8**
Oberleutnant Adolf Galland arrives after a 14-day journey aboard a Panama-registered steamer. He is to take command of the Kondor Legion's 3rd Staffel, with *Mickey Mouse* mascot.

**New York, May 14**
American journalists Dick Merrill and John S Lambie land at Floyd Bennett Field after a 5-day round flight to London in their Lockheed Model 10 the *Daily Express*; they set a new record for the fastest return trip over this route, but the main purpose of their journey was to be in London for the coronation of King George VI.

**New York, May 25**
A letter posted in Manhattan on April 19 is delivered after being misdirected by way of San Francisco, Hong Kong, Penang, Amsterdam and Rio de Janeiro.

**Hampshire, England, June 2**
Imperial Airways' Short S.23 flying boat *Canopus* leaves Southampton on the company's first through service by flying boat to Durban, South Africa (→ Jul 6).

**Reykjavik, June 3**
Iceland forms an airline, Flugfelag Akureyrar; it consists of a single seaplane.

**England, June 11**
Reginald Mitchell, designer of Supermarine's much-praised new Spitfire fighter, dies of cancer, aged 42.

**Paris, June 16**
Air France and Lufthansa sign an agreement for cooperation on their transatlantic passenger services.

**Atlantic Ocean, June 16**
Imperial Airways and Pan Am open a joint service between Bermuda and New York (→ Jul 6).

**Farnborough, England, June 30**
Royal Air Force Flt Lt M J Adam flies his Bristol 138 to a world altitude record of 53,937 feet; the cockpit canopy cracks, but he is saved by his pressure suit.

**Singapore, June**
A new combined airport is opened with a grass landing area and slipways for flying boats.

**Washington, DC, July 6**
The War Department signs a $4,133,550 contract to buy 210 Curtiss P-36 fighters. On June 10, the department ordered 177 Douglas B-18 bombers at a cost of $11,651,948.

**Hawaii, July 19**
The official search for missing flyers Amelia Earhart and Fred Noonan is abandoned.

**London, July 30**
After a long fight the Royal Navy takes control of the Fleet Air Arm from the RAF.

**Germany, July**
The German Air Ministry establishes Projekt X under Dr Alexander Lippisch; its aim is to produce a rocket-powered research airplane.

**England, August 11**
The prototype Boulton Paul Defiant fighter, with a four-gun turret, makes its first flight.

**Marienehe, Germany, August 27**
A Heinkel He 112 fitted with both piston and rocket motors takes off and makes a flight on the power of the rocket motor alone; Erich Warsitz is the pilot.

**Britain, October 1**
Safety belts become compulsory for passengers aboard British civil airplanes.

**France, October 1**
Following a series of accidents in which 11 people have died over the past year, the fore and aft wings of the popular *Pou du Ciel* (Flying Flea), designed and built by Henri Mignet, are modified to avoid nose-diving at speed. The tiny aircraft costs less than 4,000FF to manufacture.

**Kent, England, October 18**
Jean Batten arrives at Lympne from Darwin, Australia, in her Percival Gull *Jean*, setting a new speed record of 5 days 18 hours 15 minutes over the route.

**Le Bourget, France, November 12**
Le Bourget airport, a small collection of hangars when Charles Lindbergh landed his *Spirit of St Louis* here in 1927, is reopened by French air minister Pierre Cot after a program of major rebuilding work.

**Moscow, November 19**
Soviet aircraft designer Andrei N Tupolev is arrested in Stalin's "terror". The reason being that he gave Germany the design of the Bf 110.

**Croydon, England, November 20**
London club-owner Betty Kirby-Green and RAF pilot Arthur Clouston land their D.H.88 Comet, *The Burberry*, after flying to South Africa and back in 5 days 17 hours 29 minutes, knocking four days off the previous record, held by Amy Johnson.

**China, December 12**
Japanese aircraft attack and sink the gunboat USS *Panay* near Nanking.

---

*Under Mussolini, Italy has built some of the fastest aircraft to date, and the Italian love of aviation is shown in this exhibition poster.→*

# Intrepid Hughes flies into another record

*Hughes in his aircraft, dubbed "Winged Bullet", after his record flight.*

*Newark, NJ, February 19*
When Howard Hughes lands here he often sets a record. Today was no exception. Despite having to circle Newark airport for 20 minutes before he could land, the 30-year-old millionaire movie-maker still managed to establish a new transcontinental speed record from Los Angeles of 7 hours, 28 minutes and 25 seconds.

The dynamic Hughes used the same aircraft in which he set the landplane speed record in October 1935, the custom-built, wind–tunnel-tested H-1, which now has larger wings, an engine supercharger and special oxygen equipment to make it better suited for longer, high-altitude flight.

Hughes' problems in landing were mostly his own fault for not having a radio. When he arrived at Newark he could not talk to the control tower and had to communicate his wish to land by flying past the tower and waggling his wings. Even with the delay, he still averaged 332mph over the 2,500-mile route (→ Jul 14, 1938).

# Saharan convoy is monitored from air

*Algiers, February 22*
France has employed air power in its latest show of strength in the Sahara. Since 1879, Paris has sent expeditions to try to link the French colonies north and south of the desert, fighting savage guerrilla wars against local tribes. There was even a scheme to build a railway from the Mediterranean to Timbuktu. Now troops have driven in convoy from French Sudan to Algeria, guarded during the 12-day trip by a Bloch aircraft from the south, and two Potez covering the northern leg of the journey. There is no clear strategic value in this exercise except to show that French North Africa could be reinforced overland from the equatorial colonies.

# Earhart's world bid ends on the runway

*Honolulu, Hawaii, March 20*
An attempted round-the-world flight by leading US woman aviator Amelia Earhart ended dramatically at dawn today when the starboard tyre of her Lockheed Electra airliner burst during take-off. The heavily loaded $80,000 airplane spun round and belly-flopped, causing so much damage that the expedition has been temporarily abandoned.

Fortunately Earhart herself, navigators Captain Harry Manning and Frederick Noonan and engineer Paul Mantz were all uninjured. The first leg from Oakland, California, to Honolulu on March 17 was made in 16 hours, an east/west record (→ Jul 2).

# Flying Fortress boosts American force

*Hampton, Virginia, March 1*
The Second Bombardment Group of the US Army Air Corps (USAAC) here at Langley Field received the first of its 13 Boeing YB-17A Flying Fortresses today. The unit expects to have all its new planes by the beginning of August.

The aircraft is the USAAC's first four-engined bomber, possibly the most advanced aircraft of its type in the world. It is also the first airplane to fulfill the concept of an effective all-weather, long-range bomber. When the prototype, the Model 299, was destroyed in a crash at Wright Field in October 1935, it could have been the aircraft's death knell. But it was recognized that the accident was due to pilot error. Re-engined by four 1,000-hp Wright Cyclones, the YB-17A can cruise at 30,000 feet at 256 mph, has a range of between 1,360 and 3,300 miles and a maximum take-off weight of 42,600 pounds.

*Three of the US Army Air Corps's sleek new YB-17A heavy bombers.*

# China welcomes the arrival of US fighters

*Nanking, China, February 18*
With Japan poised menacingly on China's doorstep, four daughters of city officials here in Nanking had good reason today to crack bottles of wine over 18 American fighter planes. This was in celebration of their arrival in the cause of national salvation. They had been paid for by Chinese living abroad.

Considerable progress has been made in China to strengthen the central (Nanking) government air force since General Chiang Kai-shek's wife became air minister in 1936. Growing national unity, last year's desertion of the rebel Kwantung air force to the government (which brought 90 airplanes and crews), and General Chiang's 50th birthday, for which he was presented with 50 modern warplanes, have helped. New aerodromes have been built, and the Italian air mission has been active in improving training facilities. However, the rebel Kwangsi air force at Liuchow still poses a threat.

*A group of Curtiss Hawks delivered to China by the US stand at the ready.*

# Nazi bomber fleets pound Guernica without mercy

*Ground crews load He 111 bombers of Germany's Kondor Legion.*

*A dazed survivor looks up at the skies from which German bombs rained down.*

## Civilians die in indiscriminate bombing

*Guernica, Spain, April 26*
This morning Guernica was a bustling country town, its streets crowded for market day. This evening the Sun has set on a smoldering skeleton of smashed streets, strewn with the broken corpses of its defenseless citizens.

Never has aerial bombing of such intensity been seen anywhere in the world. The attack was ostensibly to destroy a bridge of alleged military significance. In reality, it was scientifically calculated as a bombing experiment by Germany's Kondor Legion, allies of General Franco. Guernica's church bells rang out a warning at 4.30pm, but before anyone could dive for cover, the streets were raked by machine-gun fire from low-flying Heinkel He 51 fighters. Heavy bombing by Heinkel He 111s and Junkers Ju 52s was followed by a wave of incendiaries which set fire to what was left.

Shaken observers argue that the merciless four-hour onslaught required several squadrons. No ground or air defense was evident. The bridge is undamaged.→

## World shocked by brutality of air war

*Madrid, April 27*
The world has a new name for the horror of war: Guernica. Yesterday's unleashing of all the force of modern aerial warfare on defenseless civilians has shocked international opinion. As one reporter at the scene wrote: "The raid on Guernica is unparalleled." Protests pouring in are said to have alarmed Franco. Reports say he is angered by the carnage. German propaganda boss Joseph Goebbels claims that "no German airplane took part in this bombing". This might surprise chief of staff Wolfram von Richthofen, head of the Kondor Legion, who is said to have reported his "success" to Berlin.

Military strategists believe Hitler wanted to test the effect of saturation bombing on a civilian center. The bitter lesson of Guernica will be noted elsewhere (→ Apr 30).

## Sport club becomes Hitler's flying corps

*Berlin, April 20*
To celebrate his birthday today, Adolf Hitler has changed the name of the Air Sport Association (the amateur flyers' organization) to the Nazi Flying Corps. The German chancellor is keen to make his country more "air minded".

The amateur flying movement played an important role in the resurgence of military aviation in Germany by providing "ghost" squadrons, which later became part of the Luftwaffe before it was officially unveiled two years ago. The move is consistent with Hitler's policy of identifying technical progress of any kind with the Nazi Party.

## 'Kamikaze' marks coronation with record Japan to London flight

*The brave Japanese flyers and the "Kamikaze" are welcomed to Croydon.*

*Croydon, England, April 9*
To mark next month's coronation of King George VI, one of the latest Japanese airplanes has flown from Japan to England in a record-breaking flying time of 2 days 3 hours 17 minutes. The aviators have been warmly welcomed, with crowds almost rioting to get near the prototype Mitsubishi Type 97 *Kamikaze* [*Divine Wind*].

The flight, which began in Tachikawa on April 6, was sponsored by Tokyo newspaper *Asahi Shimbun*. The crew for this arduous journey were pilot Masaaki Iinuma and navigator-mechanic Kenji Tsukagoshi. The total elapsed time over the 9,542 miles was 3 days 23 hours 17 minutes.

▷

# 'Hindenburg' blows up

*Panic spreads on the ground as the "Hindenburg" explodes over Lakehurst.*

*Lakehurst, NJ, May 6*
The German airship *Hindenburg* arrived overhead at 7.25pm. Suddenly, the aircraft became a fireball and sank to the ground. Within a minute it was no more than a skeleton of white-hot metal: 36 people were dead, but 61 others were saved.

The airship had been delayed by headwinds and was forced to circle the airfield to wait for a thunderstorm to clear. A witness reported seeing a glow inside the tail. Then, a jet of flame shot through the fabric and the hydrogen blew up. The *Hindenburg's* tail sank to the ground. The cause of the fire is unknown, but some believe that static electricity ignited the gas.

**Old meets new: British music-hall veteran Charlie Coburn before being taken up on a flight over London in celebration of his 85th birthday.**

## Lockheed's pressurized plane flies high

*Burbank, Calif, May 7*
The specially-adapted Lockheed Electra, *The Boiler*, with its pressurized cockpit left here today for successful, high-altitude tests. There was little to indicate anything out of the ordinary, except that the aircraft's normal, rounded fuselage windows had been replaced by tiny slits. The airplane, designated XC-35, and powered by twin Pratt & Whitney 550-hp turbo-supercharged XR-1340 Wasp radial engines, has been built for the US Army Air Corps as the first American pressurized plane. Designers failed totally to pressurize the aircraft. They used a thickened fuselage skin, with neoprene tape to seal joints, to provide the same pressure at all higher altitudes as that found at 12,000 feet. The six crew members need no oxygen or special clothing.

*Lockheed's XC-35 prototype is a pressurized version of the Model 10 Electra.*

## British turbojet engine has its first trials

*Warwickshire, England, April 13*
Unknown to the outside world, junior Royal Air Force officer Frank Whittle today tested the new type of engine he invented over seven years ago. Called a turbojet, it is a gas turbine which, instead of driving a propeller shaft, creates a high-velocity jet of hot gas. The test at Rugby had some success, but at one point bystanders were seriously alarmed when the engine appeared about to explode.

*Not ready yet: Frank Whittle's test engine needs some further research.*

## London's imperial airmail scheme grows

*London, October*
The British government's Empire Mail Scheme is in full flight and expanding rapidly. Britain's flag-carrier Imperial Airways, as the world's largest carrier of airmail, is building up to the day when it can carry letters and postcards anywhere in the British Empire for just one-and-a-half pence per ounce.

The first service under the scheme set off on June 29, with the Short "C" class flying boat *Centurion* carrying 3,500 pounds of mail bound for South Africa. This month has seen the scheme extended to India, with the *Clio* carrying mail from Southampton to Alexandria, Egypt. At Alexandria the *Calypso* takes over for the leg to Karachi, India. The *Camilla* arrived at Southampton to complete the first return journey from India today.

The scheme was the brainchild of S A Dismore, then secretary of Imperial Airways, in 1933. The aircraft may be modified to carry up to two tons of mail by removing a smoking cabin (→ Feb 23, 1938).

# Amelia Earhart lost over the Pacific

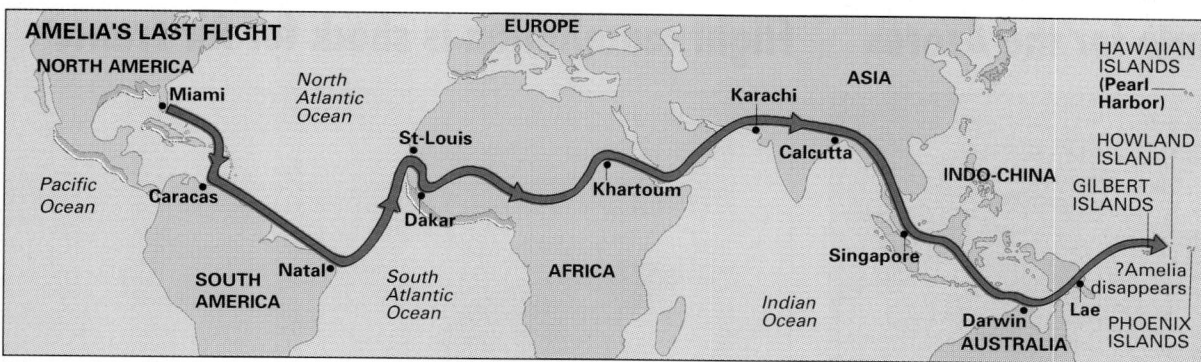

**AMELIA'S LAST FLIGHT**

*Pacific, July 2*
Amelia Earhart radioed "We are flying north-east". Nothing more has been heard from her Lockheed Electra as she headed east across the Pacific in her bid with navigator Fred Noonan, to circumnavigate the globe near the Equator. President Roosevelt has ordered a huge search around Howland Island for America's favorite airwoman. Also to be searched are the Phoenix Islands, where an emergency landing could have been made, and the Gilberts, which Earhart may have favored if she was unable to find Howland. The flier had prepared everything carefully, except perhaps her radio, for she left behind a long antenna in Miami from where she headed for the Pacific via

Puerto Rico, Venezuela, Brazil, Senegal, Sudan, India, Singapore, Darwin and Lae, New Guinea. Contact was lost yesterday. Her last message was picked up by the US Coast Guard cutter *Itasca* at 8.43am, an hour after she had reported just half an hour of fuel remaining. Her plan had been to land on Howland. Some believe the pair's best chance of survival rests on whether their Lockheed Electra has been able to float on its empty tanks after ditching her and her navigator in the Pacific. Waters in that region are shark-infested. There have been reports of faint radio distress signals, but there seems little hope of finding the fliers in the wide expanse of the ocean despite the rescue operation (→ Jul 19).

*Amelia during a pause in Africa.*

## US women's speed record is broken by Jacqueline Cochran

*USA, July 26*
Crack flyer Jacqueline Cochran set a new speed record for women today, hitting 203.89mph over a set course in a modernized Beech D-17W "Staggerwing" biplane.

In the five years since Walter H Beech and wife Olive Ann founded the Beech Aircraft Corporation at Wichita Municipal Airport, several versions of their Model 17 have gone into production. The prototype first flew on November 4, 1932, and won the Texaco Trophy at the Miami Air Races in the following year. The next version, the B-17, with back-staggered wings, went into production in 1934 and 36 aircraft were built in 1935.

In 1935, the design was improved, with wing flaps relocated and shorter undercarriage legs fitted. The tail unit of the more powerful versions was also modified to give a cleaner airflow (→ Sep 3, 1938).

*Record breaker: Jackie Cochran.*

# Russians fly further than anyone in trip over Pole to California

*The Soviet crew in Moscow before taking off on the North Pole route.*

*California, July 14*
Californians have just realised that they are a mere 6,306 miles away from Moscow if an aircraft flies over the North Pole. A single-engined Tupolev ANT-25 monoplane touched down today at San Jacinto, California, breaking the International Aeronautical Federation (FAI) world distance record. It had been airborne for an amazing 2 days 14 hours 17 minutes and had covered 6,306 miles. The crew members – M Gromov, S Danilin and A Yumashyev – left Moscow on July 12. They flew non-stop over the North Pole in a journey free from mechanical and weather problems and landed with 3,300 pounds of fuel left. This is in marked contrast to the attempt in June, when the ANT-25 limped into Vancouver, Washington state, after battling against mechanical troubles and bad weather. That was, however, the first transpolar flight.

The ANT-25 was conceived solely for the purpose of breaking distance records. A specially-sloped runway was built at Shchyelkovo to help take-off. Two attempts to gain closed-circuit distance records in 1934 failed before a 75-hour flight produced a record of 7,730 miles that September. Two over-Pole, straight-distance attempts in August 1935 and July 1936 also failed, the second after 56 hours.

## France nationalizes its aircraft industry

*France, July 15*
In a move prompted by rapid German rearmament, the French government has nationalized much of the country's arms and aircraft industry. Many famous names will disappear under new titles: Loire Nieuport, for instance, is now Société nationale de constructions aéronautiques de l'Ouest [Western Aeronautical Company] or SNCAO, and Bloch, Potez, Farman and Dewoitine face a similar fate, as have engine companies Hispano-Suiza and Gnome et Rhône.

# Airlines jostle to set up routes across the Atlantic

## Lufthansa chooses a route for the Azores

*A Lufthansa Blohm und Voss Ha 139 is catapulted over the Atlantic.*

**New York, November 18**
Lufthansa has ended a remarkable series of seven experimental return flights between the Azores and New York prior to a proposed North Atlantic route. By far the most interesting aspect has been the use of four-engined Blohm und Voss Ha 139 seaplanes, catapulted from depot ships at take-off and hoisted back on board later. The Ha 139 for the first trial, on August 15, was *Nordmeer* (North Sea). East/West times varied from under 15 hours to 19 hours. After 39 meters, the catapulted plane had sufficient speed for take-off with its four-man crew. One particular flight to New York took some 17h 24min. Earlier in June, Lufthansa had used the Focke-Wulf Fw 200 for a test run.

## Flight cancellation is shock for Air France

*The flying boat, "Lieutenant de vaisseau Paris", is readied for take-off.*

**Paris, September 24**
France's attempt to be present on the North Atlantic has been delayed by a decision by the Portuguese authorities to deny landing rights in the Azores for the giant, six-engined Latécoère 521 *Lieutenant de vaisseau Paris*. The plane had been specially repaired for the flight after being downed during a typhoon on a trial crossing last year. This was to have been the inaugural service of Air France Transatlantique to New York. The Azores stopover is essential. The planned route was via Saint-Pierre-et-Miquelon. The flight was Air France's attempt to catch up with its rivals over the North Atlantic. This last-minute cancellation, a surprise for all concerned, means that France will be absent over the North Atlantic.

## Imperial uses extended-range 'Caledonia'

**Newfoundland, January 6**
The Short Empire *Caledonia,* of Imperial Airways, with greater fuel capacity to increase its range, has flown between Foynes, Ireland and Botwood, Newfoundland, in sixteen hours nine minutes. The flying boat, with its range of 3,300 miles, was undertaking an experimental commercial North Atlantic crossing. The *Caledonia* will fly on to New York. Future regular services will be operated jointly with Pan American, whose Sikorsky S-42B *Clipper III* flew simultaneously in the opposite direction. The two companies already cooperate between New York and Bermuda. For the flight extra fuel tanks took the place on board of seats. Imperial and Pan Am now lead over the ocean.

## Pan American Airways in Atlantic talks

**Dublin, July 26**
A four-way conference was held here between Pan American Airways, Imperial Airways and the British and Irish governments to work out the infrastructure for joint commercial services across the Atlantic in the light of recent, highly successful trials. London gave Pan American the go-ahead on February 22 for a joint service to Britain with Imperial Airways. American studies have shown that the ideal is a pressurized landplane rather than a flying boat. Pan American in March ordered the Boeing 307. The wide-ranging discussions here included airmail and meteorology. Pan American's Atlantic Division, formed earlier this year, is based at Port Washington.

*The "Caledonia", off Foynes, before its departure for Newfoundland.*

*The Sikorsky S-42B lands at Foynes in Ireland after an Atlantic crossing.*

# Airplane lands with automatic controls

*Dayton, Ohio, August 23*
Wright Field saw the first totally automatic aircraft landing in aviation history today. The feat was watched by director and assistant director of the US Army Air Corps (USAAC) instrument and navigation laboratory, Captains Carl Crane and George Holloman, and project engineer Raymond Stout.

Their invention, a combination of electrical and radio instruments, brought a USAAC cargo plane safely to the ground. The automatic landing system requires a pilot only to determine the plane's altitude and to bring it within 20 miles of an airport having special radio equipment. Two gyroscopes allow the pilot to compensate for any vertical or horizontal variation in course. Even if the aircraft is flying away from its intended destination it will be guided to the runway.

# Trans-Canada line takes to the skies

*Canada, September 1*
Trans-Canada Air Lines (TCA) inaugurated its first scheduled services today. Flying by the airline actually started some months ago, on July 7, with a survey flight from Vancouver to Seattle. This is the route chosen for the service launched today, which will be for airmail only. TCA has a fleet of Lockheed Electra monoplanes.

TCA was founded on April 10 by an act of the Canadian Parliament, with stock held by Canadian National Railways (CNR). Canadian Pacific Railways (CPR) was also expected to become a major shareholder in TCA along with CNR and the federal government. But CPR refused to take part in the venture, since it holds a substantial stake in the existing Canadian Airways, which is one of the new airline's competitors.

# Japanese flyers bombard Chinese targets

*A Japanese Mitsubishi Ki-1-II bomber prepares itself to take off on a mission.*

*China, September 21*
Japan struck from the air again today when 12 bombers, escorted by 15 fighters, attacked China's Tienho and Paiyun airfields. Tokyo claims 12 victories on the ground and ten US-built Curtiss Hawks shot down. Five *Hosho* fighter escorts ditched in the sea on the way back to their carriers. Later, planes from the carrier *Ryujo* claimed five more Hawks.

Since the publication of a photograph of a baby crying alone in the wreckage of Shanghai rail terminus after an air raid on August 29, the world has been forced to recognize Japan's burgeoning air power. Its Navy air corps has 400 planes, including twin-engined Mitsubishi

G3M bombers, eight out of 18 of which were shot down by Hawks in a raid on Nanking on August 14. The Army has 500 machines and is also ready to take heavy losses.

On August 17, only one torpedo-bomber out of 12 attacking Shanghai survived. On August 22, the odds shifted. The new Mitsubishi A5M monoplane fighter joined the action from the carrier *Kaga*, driving the Chinese from the skies over Shanghai. Soon after, operating from a land base and using long-range fuel tanks, A5Ms escorted the bombers back to Nanking. Three days ago, 27 of the new machines claimed 11 out of 16 Chinese interceptors shot down over that city.

# Demand for Douglas DC-3 exceeds supply

*Santa Monica, Calif, October 31*
The Douglas Aircraft factory in the suburbs of Los Angeles today delivered the 198th DC-3. The airliner may well become one of the world's best-selling transports; Douglas is building one every three days and cannot keep up with demand.

The DC-3 opens up a new era in airliner design. It is the first airplane whose 700,000 components are manufactured separately and then delivered for final assembly. It takes some 500,000 rivets and 8,000 feet of wire to build a DC-3. The leading edges of the DC-3's wings have a rubber boot which the pilot can inflate with pressurized air to crack any ice that has accumulated. The airliner's ventilation system pumps 989 cubic feet of air per minute (→ Feb 24, 1938).

*DC-3 wings stacked up ready for delivery in Douglas's Santa Monica factory.*

# German Bf 109 sets new speed record

*Augsburg, Germany, November 11*
Smashing the record set by American Howard Hughes in September 1935, the latest fighter airplane from German manufacturer BFW today soared to a speed of just over 379mph.

The Bf 109 is a sleek monoplane with a retractable undercarriage and Daimler-Benz engine. Its success has sent shockwaves through military circles in Europe, as it is feared that it may be a tuned production aircraft and not merely a racer. At present, no air force has anything which can compare in speed to the new German fighter.

**An attentive airline official notes down a passenger's weight before she takes off on a service from Croydon airport, England.**

Lockheed's L-14 Super Electra 12-passenger 235-mph airliner.

Beech's Model 18 six-passenger light transport, produced until 1969.

The Luscombe Model 8 Silvaire 2-seater outlasted five constructors.

Fairchild Canada developed the Sekani twin-engined utility aircraft.

Phillips & Powis Kestrel private venture trainer led to the Miles Master.

Potez 62-0 Courlis 16-passenger airliners were built for Air France.

The third prototype Junkers Ju 90 four-engined 40-passenger airliner, delivered to Deutsche Lufthansa.

De Havilland built seven D.H. Albatross – two mail, five passenger.

Short's prototype S.25 Sunderland anti-submarine patrol flying boat.

North American's NA-16 prototype, forerunner of the AT-6 Texan.

Lockheed's XC-35: an experimental high-altitude pressurized Electra.

Blohm und Voss Ha 140 floatplane. Three prototypes were constructed.

Fiat G.50 Freccia fighters flew in the Spanish Civil War with little success.

Caproni's Ca 310 Libeccio colonial aircraft triggered a prolific family of twin-engined military monoplanes.

Focke-Wulf's Fw 200 Condor prototype, later an anti-shipping aircraft.

Ilyushin DB-3/Il-4 long-range bomber. Altogether 5,256 were built.

Amiot 350 series aircraft were used in reconnaissance and bomber roles.

Boulton Paul's Defiant two-seater fighter (powered four-gun turret).

Focke-Wulf's Fw 187A-0 two-seater fighter never entered service.

A captured Nakajima B5N2 Naval Type 97 Attack Bomber Model 12.

The Boeing XB-15 heavy bomber was intended to have a 5,000-mile range. Cruising speed was 152mph.

The US Navy used Grumman's G-21 Goose eight-seater amphibian.

The Romanian air force used IAR 37 three-seater light bombers.

The Curtiss-Wright CW-19R 350-hp light fighter-trainer.

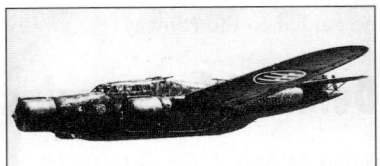

Some CRDA CANT Z.1007 "bis" Alcione bombers had twin fins.

The prototype Blackburn Skua carrier-based fighter/dive-bomber.

Breguet's 462 Vultur: a French "Multiplace de Combat" design.

The Dornier Do 24 was designed for the Royal Netherlands Naval Air Service for use in the East Indies.

Intended for carrier-based fighter/bomber duties: the Arado Ar 97.

Koolhoven's F.K.52: two-seater general-purpose biplane (Mercury).

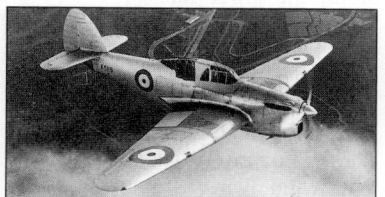

Gloster Aircraft built 200 Hawker Henley dive-bombers as target tugs.

Waco YPT-14 trainer was developed from the civil Model UPF-7.

Brewster F2A-2 Buffalo was the production version of the XF2A-1.

Grumman's F4F-4 Wildcat carrier-based US Navy fighter was to see plenty of action in the Pacific.

The Vought XOS2U-1 Kingfisher observation floatplane prototype.

Macchi MC.200 fighters used the low-powered Fiat A.74 RC.38 engine.

Consolidated's XPB2Y-1 was later developed into the Coronado.

The Erco Ercoupe was a supposedly stall-proof all-metal two-seater.

Arado's Ar 196A coastal patrol and reconnaissance floatplane.

The second prototype Blohm und Voss Bv 138 reconnaissance flying boat, nicknamed "Flying Shoe".

A total of 8,586 Airspeed AS.10 Oxford trainers were built by four firms.

Sikorsky's Model VS-44 XPBS-1 military flying boat: sole example.

Heinkel and Weser delivered 138 He 115 reconnaissance seaplanes.

Bloch's 150 was a French front-line fighter developed into the 152C-1.

The Barkley-Grow T8P-1, first flown in April 1937 with land undercarriage, was a feeder line aircraft.

The third prototype Heinkel He 119 engine testbed ended as a seaplane.

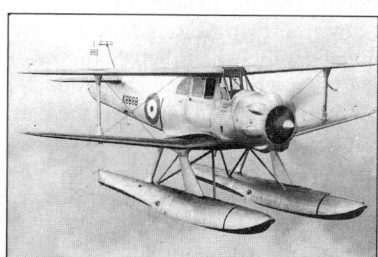

Airspeed AS.30 Queen Wasp radio-controlled pilotless target-drone.

Three test Curtiss Y1P-36s preceded 178 P-36A and 31 P-36C fighters.

The prototype CCB-26, which led to 1,528 Ilyushin DB-3 bombers.

Bell's YFM-1 Airacuda carried a crew of five as a multi-place fighter.

Prototype Gloster F.5/34 eight-gun fighter (Bristol Mercury engine).

The Lioré et Olivier LeO 451 bomber had a retractable ventral gun-turret, but its engines were not reliable.

# 1938

 440.68mph
Italy
Francesco Agello
Macchi-Castoldi MC-72
Oct 23, 1934

 7,239 miles
Japan
Takahashi and Sekine
Koken
May 16, 1938

 56,046ft
Italy
Mario Pezzi
Caproni 161bis
Oct 22, 1938

 123,457lb
Germany
Dornier
Do X

 3,058hp
Italy
Fiat
AS.6

**Pacific Ocean, January 11**
Captain Edwin Musick and six crew members die when their Sikorsky S-42 flying boat disappears in mid-ocean during a survey flight for Pan American from San Francisco to Auckland, New Zealand (→ Jul 30).

**Middlesex, England, February 10**
Squadron-Leader Gillan lands at Northolt after a flight from Edinburgh, Scotland, in the new Hawker Hurricane; his average speed of 408mph was assisted by a following wind of 50mph.

**Southampton, February 23**
An Imperial Airways flying boat leaves Hythe on a new service extending the Empire Air Mail service to India, Burma, Ceylon and Malaya (→ Oct 24).

**USA, February 24**
Mitsui & Co, US subsidiary of Japanese firm Mitsui Bussan Kaisha, pays $90,000 to build and sell Douglas DC-3s under license in Japan and Manchuria.

**Langley Field, Va, February 27**
A goodwill flight of six Boeing Y1B-17 bombers under Lieut-enant-Colonel Robert Olds lands after an 11,800-mile flight to the Panama Canal Zone and back via Miami and Lima.

**Berlin, March 1**
Field Marshal Hermann Goering is named chief of staff of the Luftwaffe today, German Air Force Day (→ Oct 18).

**Kent, England, March 26**
Arthur Clouston and Victor Ricketts land their D.H.88 Comet *Australian Anniversary* at Gravesend to complete a 26,500-mile flight from England to New Zealand and back in a record 10 days 21 hours.

**London, May 25**
British air minister Lord Swinton is sacked in response to public criticism of Britain's failure to achieve parity with German air strength (→ Jun 9).

**USA, May**
Some 220 airplanes take part in maneuvers to test whether an air force can repel an attack against the US eastern seaboard without the help of the US Navy; the results are promising (→ Dec 31).

**Seattle, June 7**
The first of six Boeing Model 314 flying boats, built under contract for Pan American, makes its first flight.

**London, June 9**
The British government announces that it is to buy 200 airplanes from US manufacturers Lockheed and North American; a commission was sent to the USA in April to study military airplanes (→ Oct 31).

**Germany, June 20**
Focke-Achgelis company test pilot Karl Bode flies the Fa 61 helicopter a record distance – for such an aircraft – of 143 miles.

**Washington, DC, June 23**
President Roosevelt signs the Civil Aeronautics Act which creates a Civil Aeronautics Authority, Administrator and Air Safety Board; it marks the start of comprehensive federal regulation of airlines (→ Jun 11, 1940).

**Sydney, July 5**
QANTAS's first Short "C" class flying boat, the *Cooee*, enters service, on the Australia/England route.

**USSR, July 11**
The Soviet air force goes into action as fighting breaks out against the Japanese over territory on the frontiers of Korea, Manchuria and Siberia (→ Aug 24).

**New York, July 21**
The Short S.20 seaplane *Mercury*, the upper component of the Short-Mayo composite airplane, lands after a transatlantic flight; the aircraft was launched from the Short S.21 flying boat *Maia* over Foynes, Ireland; total flying time was 22 hours 29 minutes (→ Oct 8).

**Bogota, July 24**
Thirty-four die when a military airplane crashes into a crowd during celebrations marking the opening of the Campo de Marte military airfield.

**New York, August 8**
Lufthansa's Blohm und Voss Ha 139 seaplane *Nordwind*, powered by four 600-hp Junkers Jumo 205C diesel engines, lands at Port Washington after a record flight from the Azores to New York of 15 hours 50 minutes.

**New York, August 11**
The prototype Focke-Wulf Fw 200 Condor, flown by Lufthansa pilot Kurt Henke, lands after a non-stop flight of 24 hours 36 minutes from Staaken airport, Berlin, demonstrating that landplanes are as capable of ocean crossings as flying boats.→

**Kehl, Germany, August 13**
A Czechoslovak airliner en route from Prague to Paris crashes into a mountain, killing 16.

**China, August 24**
Thirteen passengers and one crew member are killed when Japanese aircraft shoot down a China National Aviation Corporation DC-2 en route from Hong Kong to Chungking; this is the first civil airliner to be lost to hostile air attack (→ Aug 8, 1939).

**Cleveland, Ohio, September 3**
Jacqueline Cochran flies in from Burbank, California, to win the Bendix Trophy, having covered 2,042 miles in 8 hours 10 minutes 31 seconds.

**Cleveland, Ohio, September 5**
Roscoe Turner wins the Thompson Trophy again, with an average speed of 283.42mph (→ Sep 5, 1939).

**Burbank, Calif, September 21**
US Army Air Corps Chief Major-General Oscar Westover is killed in an airplane crash at Lockheed Airport.

**France, October 2**
The Dewoitine D.520 fighter makes its first flight.

**South Africa, October 8**
Captain D C T Bennett and Flying Officer Ian Harvey land their Short S.20 seaplane *Mercury* at Alexander Bay when they run out of fuel on their way to Cape Town; they were launched by the Short S.21 *Maia*, the lower half of the Short-Mayo composite, near Dundee, Scotland, on October 6.

**Yeovil, England, October 11**
The prototype Westland Whirlwind twin-engined, single-seat fighter flies for the first time.

**USA, October 14**
The Allison-engined Curtiss XP-40 prototype fighter makes its maiden flight.

**Berlin, October 18**
On Hitler's behalf, Luftwaffe chief Hermann Goering invests Colonel Charles Lindbergh with the Order of the German Eagle, with star, following the famous US aviator's tour of German aircraft factories and facilities (→ Sep 15, 1939).

**Croydon, England, October 24**
British national carrier Imperial Airways puts the Armstrong Whitworth A.W.27 Ensign into service on its Paris route (→ Aug 4, 1939).

**Germany, December 8**
Germany officially launches its first aircraft carrier, the 280-foot by 89-foot *Graf Zeppelin*; the world count currently stands at Britain: seven; United States: six; Japan: five; France: one; and Germany: one.

*A colorful recruiting poster tries to persuade patriotic young Americans to become "eagles" by joining up with the US Army Air Corps.→*

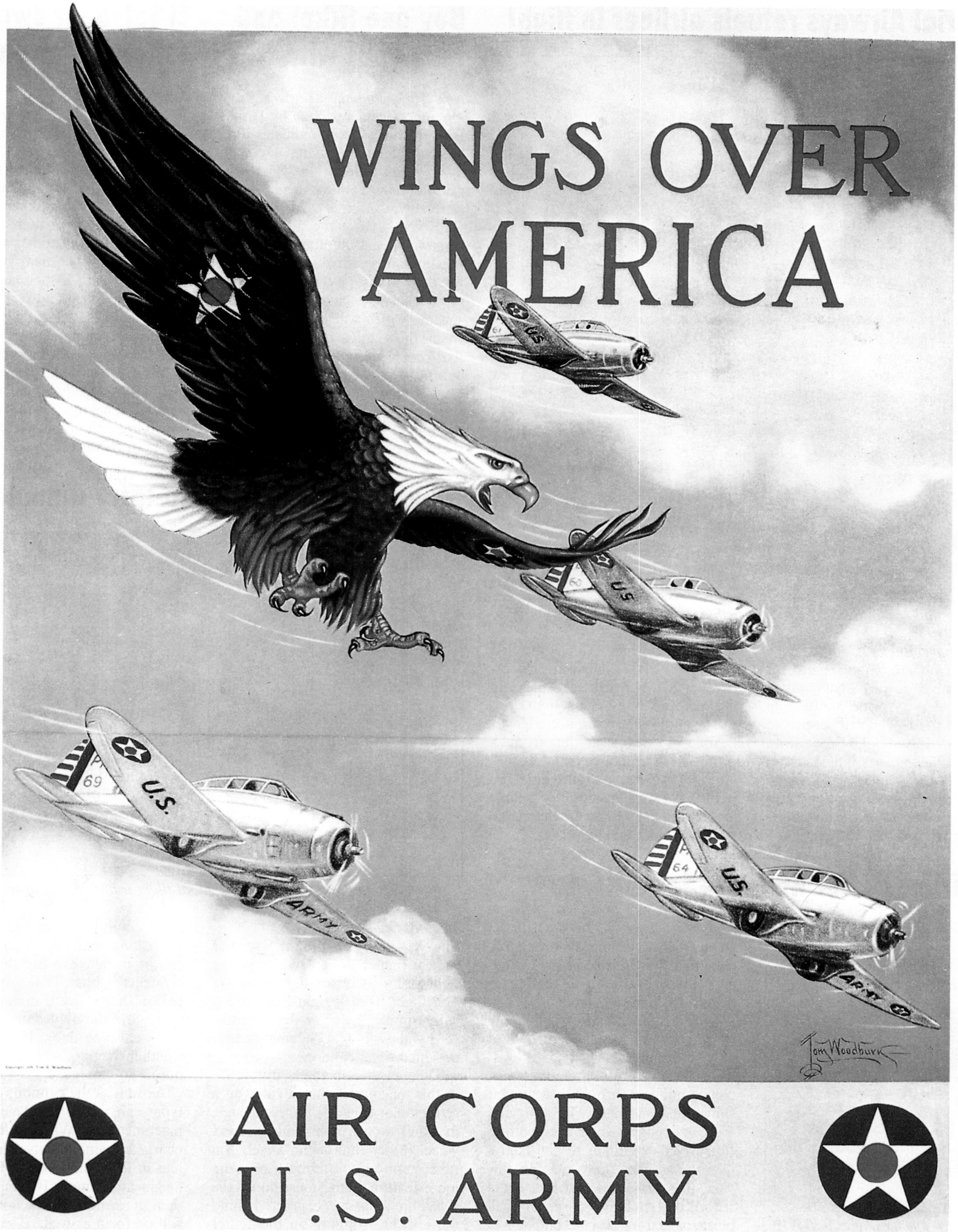
WINGS OVER
AMERICA
U.S.
U.S.
69
U.S.
ARMY
64
U.S.
ARMY
Tom Woodburn
AIR CORPS
U.S. ARMY

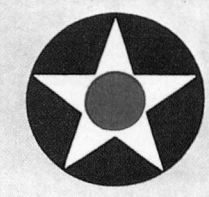

# Imperial Airways refuels airliner in flight

*A Harrow tanker pumps 920 gallons of fuel into the flying boat "Cambria".*

**Southampton, England, January 20**
Sir Alan Cobham, an evangelist for British air power, has taken Imperial Airways one more step down the road of global service to the British Empire. His new firm, Flight Refuelling, has linked up an Imperial Airways "C" class flying boat to an Armstrong Whitworth A.W.23 tanker in flight, enabling the airliner to refuel without interrupting its journey. This is the first in a series of in-flight refueling experiments which will take place in all weathers to test the system.

The aircraft are connected by a flexible hose reeled out from a drum. Sir Alan hopes that "feeder" aircraft can be stationed on Imperial Airways routes to enable long-distance, non-stop flights to become routine (→ Feb 23).

# US airlines offer half fare for children

*Checking propeller blades at TWA.*

**New York, June 26**
In an effort to generate more family passenger traffic, American, United and TWA are offering half-price tickets for children from next Friday. The reduced fares will apply to youngsters between two and 12 years of age.

The fare cut announcement comes midway through a year that shows airlines in the US carrying more passengers than ever before. If travelers continue to fly as frequently as they have so far this year, it is projected that last year's record of 1,102,707 passengers will be surpassed by 20 per cent.

# Buy one ticket and take your wife free

*New York, January 27*
An announcement today by United Airlines and TWA indicates they believe interstate flying faces its most serious threat not from the railroad but from women – more especially, the wives of businessmen who want to use the aircraft as a fast way of getting about the country, but whose anxious spouses fear for their safety.

The carriers have brought in a scheme which will give passengers' wives the chance to fly with them free over certain interstate and coast-to-coast routes. It is hoped the wives will enjoy the experience, be happier about their husbands' flying and choose the same airlines themselves (→ Jun 26).

# El Salvador swops coffee for airplanes

*Central America, March 7*
The Italian government has signed a contract with El Salvador under which Italian airplanes are to be swapped for consignments of Salvadorean coffee. The Italians' aim in making this unusual agreement is not so much to get their hands on Salvador's finest export, as to gain access to the potentially huge Central and South American market for their military and civil airplane manufacturers.

German manufacturers led the way in using the barter system to establish a foothold in South America. It is ideally suited for commercial dealings with countries which are rich in material resources but poor in cash (→ Jul 24).

# New Airacobra is first to carry cannon

*The Bell XP-39 prototype makes its initial flight trials without armaments.*

*Dayton, Ohio, April 6*
The XP-39 Airacobra, the second radical fighter design by the young Bell Aircraft Corporation, made its first flight from Wright Field today with Jimmy Taylor at the controls. It is the first US single-seater designed for a cannon.

The most obvious difference in this machine is that it rides on a retractable tricycle undercarriage, in other words, one with a nose-wheel rather than a tail-wheel. Another unusual, although not unique, feature is the location of the 1,150-hp Allison engine, behind the cockpit, roughly on the center of gravity. It drives the propeller via a long shaft. A 37-mm cannon can be installed to fire through the propeller's boss. The Airacobra's cockpit has a fixed, streamlined canopy, and the pilot enters by opening a car-type door. It is not clear whether the pilot will be able to bail out in an emergency.

As well as the cannon, the prototype can carry fuselage-mounted machine guns. With a turbo-supercharged engine, it can reach 20,000 feet in four minutes and fly at that height at 390mph. It remains to be seen if armed production models will perform as well.

# Two-in-one airplane has trial separation

*The S.20 "Mercury" lifts dramatically off in mid-air from the S.21 "Maia".*

**Kent, England, February 6**
Witnessed by only a few people on the ground near the river Medway, Britain's unique Short-Mayo composite aircraft separated in flight for the first time today. The combination consists of a heavily loaded seaplane riding on top of a much larger flying boat. The idea, by Major Robert Mayo, is that the bigger airplane will be able to lift a seaplane so heavily loaded that it

could not take off by itself. The lower, or parent, aircraft *Maia* is a four-engined Short S.21, similar to the S.23 "C" class Empire flying boats but broader, to give greater buoyancy. The upper plane *Mercury* is an S.20 floatplane powered by four 340-hp Napier engines. Cruising at 180mph, it is expected to carry sufficient fuel for 6,000 miles. Both pilots take part in the separation (→Jul 21).

# Troubled Eastern is sold to Rickenbacker

*Rickenbacker, Eastern's new owner.*

**New York, April 22**
America's wartime air hero Captain Eddie V Rickenbacker has bought Eastern Air Lines for $3.5 million. The purchase follows extensive negotiations with Eastern's former owner General Motors and its operating subsidiary, North American Aviation.

Making the airline profitable will be a challenge for Rickenbacker and his associates. Its routes from New York to Miami and Atlanta, from Chicago to Atlanta and from Atlanta to New Orleans are prone to bad weather which, without modern aircraft such as Boeing 247s or Douglas DC-2s, has made the service unreliable.

Rickenbacker managed Eastern for North American prior to the sale, and becomes president of the new company. Kuhn, Loeb and Company put up the money needed for the purchase.

# Hughes flies the world

**New York, July 14**
Flamboyant flying tycoon Howard Hughes flew into Floyd Bennett Field today at the end of a flight around the northern hemisphere. By keeping his stops to a minimum, Hughes has smashed the old record of fellow American Wiley Post by almost four days, setting a time of 3 days 19 hours 8 minutes. Hughes used all the modern technology available, and concedes that almost any pilot could now repeat the 14,791-mile journey provided he has the right airplane.

"Howard, the weather looks good all the way and should hold. Go!" These words sent him soaring away at 7.30pm on July 10. They were relayed from the New York World's Fair, where a radio relay

system had been set up to collate international weather information and transmit it to wherever the Lockheed 14-N Super Electra *New York World's Fair 1939* happened to be. The Lockheed was specially built for Hughes, with a maximum range approaching 5,000 miles. Refueling stops, which took up a total of 18 hours, were limited to Paris, Moscow, Omsk and Yakutsk in the Soviet Union, Fairbanks in Alaska and Minneapolis. Accurate navigation was aided by prearranged signals from radio stations around the world.

With Hughes was co-pilot and navigator Lieutenant Thurlow, second navigator Harry Cannon, radio operator Richard Stoddard and mechanic Edward Lund.

*Admirers congratulate Hughes and his crew on their return to New York.*

# Hughes' navigator afraid of unlucky 13

**New York, July 10**
For the superstitious, the number 13 has long had particular significance. When such a person comes across two 13s just prior to a dangerous undertaking, he may well prefer to stay in bed.

Lieutenant Thomas Thurlow, who is about to fly as navigator with Howard Hughes when they take off from here this evening to attempt a round-the-world flight, has always been superstitious. This morning, as Thurlow went to pay the hotel bill for himself and the other Hughes crew members, his blood ran cold when he was told that he owed 13

dollars and 13 cents. As his bewildered friends looked on, fearing that the navigator would refuse to take part in the flight, Thurlow rushed back up to his room.

There, he grabbed the telephone and made several local calls before returning downstairs to join his fellow airmen. On going back to the front desk, he was told that his bill now amounted to 14 dollars. As far as Thurlow was concerned, the curse of the unlucky 13 had been broken. The young officer now feels that it will be perfectly safe for him to set out aboard Hughes's specially-built Lockheed Super Electra.

# 'Wrong-Way' Corrigan lands in hot water

*Douglas "Wrong-Way" Corrigan: crossed the ocean instead of the land.*

*New York, July 18*
Federal aviation officials here, who believed that Douglas Corrigan was returning to California, were not amused with the explanation that his "compass must have been wrong" when he landed today in Dublin instead.

Already dubbed "Wrong-Way" Corrigan, the impish aviator may face disciplinary action on both sides of the Atlantic. He has violated US regulations by making an unauthorized ocean crossing and Irish ones by failing to obtain permission to land on Irish soil. Cor-

rigan has come to no harm, but US air-safety officials are saying that the questionable structural integrity of his nine-year-old Curtiss Robin aircraft means he was lucky to make it across the Atlantic.

Corrigan told workers at Floyd Bennett Field, Brooklyn, that he was headed west. He got into the plane, secured the door with a piece of wire (it had a broken latch), took off and headed east – to the astonishment of those on the ground. For his nerve, Corrigan has been made a life member of the Wisconsin Liars' Club.

# French flying boat completes ocean trial

*New York, August 31*
Five French airmen are resting in the luxury of the Waldorf Astoria Hotel tonight after a marathon 2,800-mile crossing of the Atlantic by flying boat. The giant 43-ton Latécoère 521 *Lieutenant de vaisseau Paris* had taken off from Horta eight hours earlier and touched down at Port Washington on the Hudson river opposite the Statue of Liberty.

The total flying time by the airplane from the Azores to Port Washington, around 2,400 miles, was 22 hours 48 minutes, slow compared with what US, British and German airplanes can achieve. An Atlantic gale meant a five-day wait

at Horta and a spectacular take-off over a heavy swell with 6-foot waves. The two-minute take-off run involved a high level of skill by pilots Henri Guillaumet and Henri LeClaire.

The outsize and rather outmoded 521 is powered by six 650-hp Hispano-Suiza 12Nbr engines. It can carry 76 passengers (though not very far) on its two internal decks. The *Lieutenant de vaisseau Paris* first flew on January 17, 1935, and it was rebuilt after sinking on its first attempt at an Atlantic crossing. Before today's crossing, the aircraft had set both load-over-distance and load-to-altitude records for flying boats.

*Air France's "Lieutenant de vaisseau Paris" in dock at Biscarosse.*

# Supermarine's speedy Spitfire goes into RAF squadron service

*Pilots of 19 Squadron stand proudly by the first batch of Spitfire fighters.*

*England, August 4*
The first of 310 revolutionary Supermarine Spitfire fighters, developed from 1934 by the late Reginald Mitchell from his Schneider Trophy winners, entered service with 19 Squadron of Britain's Royal Air Force (RAF) at Duxford today.

The Spitfire, with its thin, elliptical wing set low in the fuselage, is one of the fastest of the new breed of fighters, and it performs superbly in tight turns. With its 1,030-hp Rolls-Royce Merlin engine, the fighter dives at over 500mph. It has eight guns and provides the RAF with a machine almost certainly superior to its nearest rival as a fighter, the German Messerschmitt Bf 109. It is easy to fly, confirming the maxim that "good wing equals good airplane" (→ Oct 16, 1939).

# Pan Am Clipper is missing in Pacific

*Pacific, July 30*
Pan Am flying boat *Hawaii Clipper* has been reported missing over the Pacific on a scheduled flight between Guam and Manila. The airplane, with six passengers and nine crew members, failed to report yesterday, and the worst is feared.

For Pan Am, the world's biggest and arguably most experienced airline, a tragedy would be a serious blow. The giant Martin Clipper is a four-engined monoplane flying boat designed for transoceanic services. The *Hawaii Clipper* was one of three aircraft which began service in October 1936 on the route from San Francisco to the Philippines via the islands of Midway, Wake and Guam (→ May 23, 1939).

# Nazis limit flights in German airspace

*Berlin, September 10*

The Nazi authorities today imposed tight limits on foreign aircraft entering German airspace. Airlines have been forbidden to fly over German territory, except in strictly-defined corridors. Any carriers who stray from them will lose all rights to fly over the country.

It is believed here that foreign governments have been using civil airplanes to monitor German military activity. If so, they are not the only spies. Some Lufthansa aircraft, too, are thought to have been adapted to gather military intelligence (→ Jul 25, 1939).

# Franco's brother is killed in air crash

*Mediterranean Sea, October 28*

Generalissimo Franco's brother, Ramon, was killed today when his Italian-built Cant Z.506 seaplane, loaded with 550 pounds of bombs, crashed into the sea.

Lieutenant Colonel Franco, who is in command of the pro-Franco air force in the Balearic Islands, lost control of the seaplane when one of its three engines failed. He had set off from the Balearics, to which he had been posted after being recalled by his brother from a diplomatic posting in Washington, DC, on a mission to bomb the city of Valencia, eastern Spain.

# Douglas DC-4 offers last word in luxury

*The DC-4 looks set to transform services on the Los Angeles/New York route.*

*Los Angeles, September 25*

Vice-president and chief engineer of Douglas Aircraft Arthur E Raymond said today that the huge new DC-4 transport "has exceeded the predictions of its designers". The biggest commercial transport in the world, the DC-4 has flown 46 times since its maiden flight on June 7.

Essentially a bigger, four-engined version of the DC-3, the DC-4 spans 138 feet. Along the wing are mounted the four 1,450-hp Pratt & Whitney Twin Hornet engines. New features include a tricycle undercarriage and a triple-finned tail.

The DC-4 is being developed to meet the future needs of the four biggest US airlines, Eastern, United, American and Pan American. It will seat 52 day passengers or sleep 30 in bunks by night, with hot and cold running water, a fully-equipped galley and even an air-to-ground telephone (→ Jun 30, 1939).

# Airplane shuttles Prime Minister to talks

*"Peace for our time": Chamberlain makes his speech on arrival home.*

*London, September 30*

Gaunt and exhausted, the British Prime Minister today returned from Munich and said "I believe it is peace for our time." He flew both times by British Airways, first in a Lockheed Electra and today in a Lockheed 14.

The flights, Chamberlain's first, represent the start of a new era in international relations, not just because they have taken place in the looming shadow of a European war, but also because they demonstrate how quickly statesmen and diplomats from different nations can come together in a crisis. It is to be hoped that Chamberlain's airborne diplomacy has a lasting effect, as Nazi troops march into Czechoslovakia tomorrow under the Munich agreement.

While all eyes are on the politicians and hopes for peace, the Royal Air Force (RAF) is preparing for war. It has just ended a big exercise with 945 planes in which a mass-bomber attack was simulated. "Eastland", with 36 bomber squadrons, attacked "Westland", with 23 fighter squadrons. Secret radio-location methods were tested and judged "highly satisfactory" by RAF chiefs.

# Flying cures sufferers of whooping cough

*France, September*

French doctors are prescribing an unlikely new treatment for the highly infectious infant disease of whooping cough. Physicians cannot explain why, but a short flight at an altitude of about 7,000 to 9,000 feet in an unpressurized airplane has cured the illness in a number of children. Worried parents willing to try out the new miracle cure can now enrol their offspring at local flying clubs for special "whooping-cough flights".

**A Short Sarafand adds its weight to this person's birthday greetings.**

# Sturdy new bomber joins up with the RAF

*Suffolk, England, October 31*
Following the delivery today of the first twin-engined Wellington bomber to 99 Squadron of the Royal Air Force at Mildenhall, production of the aircraft is to increase dramatically. The reason: air chiefs do not trust their politicians, who have caved in to Hitler at Munich. Airmen know that they are racing the Germans to build a war-winning fighter and a strategic bomber. The air marshals think the Spitfire is the fighter and hope the Wellington will be the bomber.

Barnes Wallis, who designed the Wellington drew on his experience three years ago with the Wellesley, a single-engine bomber that flew 7,000 miles non-stop. The Wellington is even more efficient, built using the same geodetic principles of construction, or "basket-work" design as it has been popularly called, which is very strong for its relatively low weight.

The RAF's top brass are wary of the design in spite of the fact that a prototype turned in a performance twice as good as they had specified, doubling the 1,500-mile range prescribed and carrying twice the required bomb load of 1,000 pounds. Their attitude may change if the machine's structure can take more punishment than others (→ Nov 1).

*One of the tough new Wellington bombers engaged in air exercises.*

# RAF switches from bombers to fighters

*London, November 1*
Head of Royal Air Force Fighter Command Air Marshal Sir Hugh Dowding is to boost British fighter-aircraft production. Up until April this year, bombers were given priority in aircraft procurement, the idea being to deter Germany from launching an air attack. The government has now agreed to give priority to fighters, although the number of bombers on order, about 1,360, will stay the same. The ratio of bombers to fighters will rise from 2:1 to 1.7:1.

Dowding forced through the Supermarine Spitfire and backed another excellent fighter, the Hawker Hurricane (→ Sep 3, 1939).

# British pilots claim long-range record

*Darwin, Australia, November 7*
The world distance record of 6,306 miles, set last year by a Russian ANT-25, was today beaten by men of the Royal Air Force's Long-Range Flight. After a harassing 48 hours in the air, two Vickers Wellesleys landed here after flying a total of 7,157.7 miles.

Three bombers had taken off from Ismailia, Egypt, two days ago, piloted by Squadron-Leader Kellett, Flight-Lieutenant Hogan and Flight-Lieutenant Combe. Bad weather and headwinds dogged their progress over the Bay of Bengal and the South China Sea. Hogan had to land early at Kupang, Timor, to refuel.

# Caproni airplane breaks altitude barrier

*The Ca 161 "bis" has a specially designed propeller for high-altitude flying.*

*Montecelio, Italy, October 22*
In the latest episode of a long-standing rivalry with British pilots flying the much more modern-looking Bristol 138 monoplane, Lieutenant-Colonel Mario Pezzi has flown the Caproni Ca 161 *bis* biplane to a new world altitude record of 56,046 feet. This recaptures the record lost by Italy in June last year. For protection at such an altitude in the open cockpit, Pezzi wore a pressure suit.

Fundamental to the remarkable performance of the Ca 161 *bis* is its 700-hp Piaggio P.XI RC.100 radial engine, which is far more powerful than the Bristol 138 Pegasus engine. Developed from the Ca 113 trainer, the Ca 161 *bis* has twice the power and a much greater wingspan than its predecessor.

# Curtiss delivers cheap new P-36 fighters

*The XP-40's new 12-cylinder engine gives it a longer nose than the P-36.*

*USA, October 11*
In July 1937, the US War Department ordered 210 Curtiss model 75 fighters, designated P-36 by the military. This single-seat fighter is being sold, without its engine, for the low unit price of $19,500 specified in the contract.

Designer Don Berlin has already spent five years developing this modern fighter, with a stressed-skin airframe and main landing gears which retract backwards, the wheels turning 90 degrees to lie inside the wing.

Curtiss has a choice of three engines, all in the 1,000hp class. The P-36 will have an air-cooled radial, either the P&W Twin Wasp or a Wright Cyclone. But Curtiss has just flown the prototype XP-40, which has the new liquid-cooled Allison V-1710 which totally alters the fighter's appearance.

## Politician warns: 'US lagging behind'

*Washington, DC, December 31*
US assistant secretary of war Louis Johnson, citing the bombing in China and Spain, says that "the United States must be awakened" to its weakness against hostile aircraft and is "convinced" it must spend money for protection from that threat. He warned today that other nations have many more military aircraft and deplored current US construction and the existing procurement program for aircraft as falling far short of supplying the airplanes needed. The US may even have lost its lead in technology, and "research and development programs must be accelerated ... to regain our position of technical leadership" (→ Feb 26, 1940).

## RAF buys Hudsons

*Burbank, Calif, December 10*
A military version of the Lockheed 14, ordered by Britain's Royal Air Force as a long-range reconnaissance aircraft, started flight trials here today. The B14L, or Hudson, prototype has two Wright 1,100-hp engines and a glazed nose to house the navigator.

The RAF is impressed both by the excellence of the Hudson and by the Lockheed Corporation's ability to fulfill its needs quickly and more cheaply than rivals Boeing and Douglas. As a result it has placed a order for 200 Hudsons – at £17,000 each.

# The Condor is a transatlantic airliner

*One of the Focke-Wulf Fw 200's good features is that an engine can be changed in just 30 minutes during a stopover.*

*New York, August 11*
Proof of the capability of Germany's renascent airplane industry was provided at Roosevelt Field here today, when a four-engined Focke-Wulf Fw 200 Condor transport landed after flying non-stop from Berlin. The distance of 4,075 miles was flown against strong headwinds in a time of 24 hours 36 minutes.

The Fw 200 is one of two types of modern, stressed-skin, four-engined cantilever monoplane transports now flying in Germany, the other being the even bigger Junkers Ju 90. Both are to be used by state airline Lufthansa. The Fw 200 has also been ordered by Denmark's airline DDL, and other export contracts are expected to be confirmed soon.

The airplane that flew here today was, in fact, the first prototype, powered by 875-hp Pratt & Whitney Hornet engines and laden with extra fuel instead of a payload. In normal service, Condors will be powered by 850-hp BMW 132G engines, similar to the Hornet, and will seat about 26 passengers. In a typical configuration, there would be a 17-seat main cabin and a smoking cabin forward with nine seats.

The Condor was designed by Professor Kurt Tank. He is so confident of its basically sound design and good performance that he ordered a pre-production batch of nine aircraft to be laid down even before the first prototype had flown. Not many airlines are ready for such large and costly equipment, but the Fw 200 has the potential for military development.

# Boeing unveils its new pressurized, comfortable Stratoliner

*Seattle, December 31*
Boeing's New Year baby arrived a few hours early today when the most advanced passenger aircraft in the world, the model 307 Stratoliner, made its first test flight at the company's base here.

The four-engined aircraft, which brings the wings and tail surfaces of Boeing's B-17 Flying Fortress to a new, pressurized cylindrical fuselage, will carry up to 33 passengers in comfort at between 14,000 and 20,000 feet, cruising at 245mph well above the turbulence and weather encountered by current planes. So far, orders have been placed for ten of the Stratoliners, which cost $315,000 each: five for TWA, four for Pan American and one for record-breaking flying film tycoon Howard Hughes (→ Jul 8, 1940).

*A Stratoliner copes well with what was once a catastrophic event: engine failure. Here the model 307 flies with two propellers feathered on one side.*

Twelve Boeing 314 and 314A Clipper passenger flying boats were built for Pan American Airways' pioneer non-stop routes across the North Atlantic.

Armstrong Whitworth A.W.27 Ensigns were built for Imperial Airways.

Ala Littoria flew Savoia-Marchetti S.M.83 high-performance airliners.

Auster liaison aircraft were derived in Britain from Taylorcraft designs.

Martin-Baker MB.2 single-seater fighter prototype (Napier Dagger).

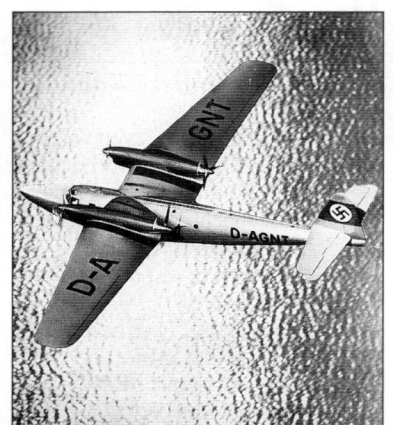
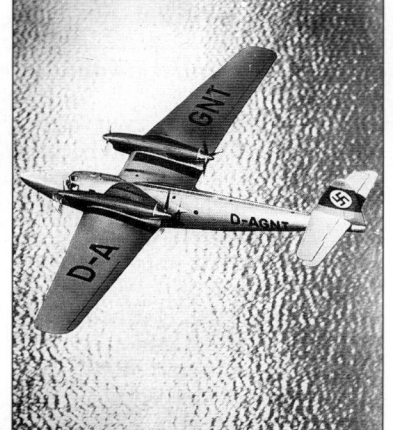

The Dornier Do 26A, for Deutsche Lufthansa's Atlantic mail services.

Dornier's Do 217E was first production version of the medium bomber.

Avia's Av-35 was developed as the Av-135, 12 of which were completed.

The prototype Blohm und Voss Ha 142 landplane version of the Ha 139.

The Potez-CAMS 141 four-engined flying boat.

The Saro Lerwick general reconnaissance flying boat (twin Hercules engines) proved totally unacceptable.

Bell's XP-39 had an Allison V-1710 engine installed behind the cockpit.

The Rogorzarski SIM XIV-H seaplane, 18 of which saw operational service before the German invasion.

The triple-finned prototype Douglas DC-4E was designed for five major US airlines, but the production DC-4 was a smaller and simplified development.

Boeing's Model 307 Stratoliner had the distinction of being the world's first pressurized airliner to enter service. The first airline to use it was TWA.

The Miles Mentor communications and radio trainer: 45 were built.

An Allison V-1710 vee-12 engine was fitted to the Curtiss XP-40.

Bristol's Beaufort torpedo-bomber prototype (two Taurus engines).

Supermarine Sea Otters were used from 1944 for air/sea rescue duties.

*Focke-Wulf's Fw 189 V2 Uhu, for short-range reconnaissance.*

*Aichi's D3A Navy Type 99 Carrier Bomber, called "Val" by the Allies.*

*The unique asymmetric configuration of the Blohm und Voss Bv 141.*

*Blackburn's Botha four-seater torpedo-bomber saw little combat.*

*The French Dewoitine D.520 fighter: 891 had been built by the time production ceased in August 1944. A few were converted post-war as two-seater trainers.*

*The prototype Messerschmitt Me 209, which set a world absolute airspeed record of 469mph, had an innovative low-drag engine-cooling system.*

*Westland Whirlwinds (two 885-hp Rolls-Royce Peregrine engines) were among the world's first single-seater twin-engined fighters to enter service.*

*Reggiane's Re 2000 Falco I single-seater fighter of Regia Aeronautica.*

*Messerschmitt's Me 210 fighter-bomber/reconnaissance aircraft.*

*The Douglas SBD Dauntless carrier-borne dive-bomber: 5,936 were built, for the US Navy, the Marine Corps and the US Army (as the A-25).*

*L'Armée de l'Air used three-seater high-performance Breguet 690s.*

*Heinkel's He 100 435mph high-speed fighter never entered service.*

*Arado Ar 196A floatplanes were based on larger German warships.*

*The Netherlands delivered 18 Koolhoven F.K.58 fighters to France.*

*The Fiat C.R.42 highly agile biplane fighter; 1,781 were manufactured.*

*Blackburn's Roc development of the Skua, with Boulton Paul gun-turret.*

# 1939

 469.22mph
Germany
Fritz Wendel
Messerschmitt Me 209 V1
Apr 26, 1939

 8,038 miles
Italy
Tondi, Degasso, Vignoli
Savoia-Marchetti S.M.75
Aug 1, 1939

 56,046ft
Italy
Mario Pezzi
Caproni 161bis
Oct 22, 1938

 123,457lb
Germany
Dornier
Do X

 1,200lb thrust
Germany
Pabst von Ohaim
Heinkel HeS 3B

**North Atlantic, January 21**
Ten of the 13 people aboard the Imperial Airways flying boat *Cavalier* are rescued by the oil tanker *Esso Baytown*. The plane was forced down at sea by iced-up engines during a flight from New York to Bermuda.

**Kent, England, February 9**
British flyer Alex Henshaw lands his Percival Mew Gull at Gravesend after a record flight to Cape Town and back in 4 days 10 hours 20 minutes.

**New York, February 11**
Lieutenant Ben Kelsey flies in from March Field, California, in the Lockheed XP-38 prototype in a record 7 hours 45 minutes; he is injured when the engines fail to respond as he approaches East Hempstead, Long Island, and he crashes on to a golf course.

**Spain, March 28**
The civil war ends as Madrid and Valencia surrender to the Nationalist forces of General Franco (→ Jun 6).

**Oranienburg, Germany, March 30**
Hans Dieterle flies the Heinkel He 100V-8 fighter at 463.82mph, a new world speed record (→ Apr 26).

**Kagamigahara, Japan, April 1**
The prototype Mitsubishi A6M1 Zero fighter makes its first flight; it is intended for service with the imperial Japanese navy.

**Augsburg, Germany, April 26**
Fritz Wendel snatches the four-week-old world speed record from compatriot Hans Dieterle, flying the Messerschmitt Me 209 V1 racer to a speed of 469.225mph.

**New Brunswick, Canada, April 29**
Soviet flyers Vladimir Kokkinaki and Mikhail Gordienko are forced by bad weather and dwindling fuel to make a landing on Miscou Island in the Bay of Chaleur; they left the Soviet Union yesterday in an attempt to fly non-stop to New York.

**USSR, May 7**
The Petlyakov VI-100 fighter makes its first flight.

**Washington, DC, May 11**
The US Navy orders the Curtiss XSB2C Helldiver carrier-based dive-bomber.

**Kent, England, May 14**
John Lankester Parker pilots the prototype Short Stirling four-engined bomber on its first flight; the promising machine is wrecked in a landing accident in which no one is hurt (→ Aug 2, 1940).

**England, May 24**
The Imperial Airways Short seaplane *Cabot* is successfully refueled in mid-air by a Handley Page bomber modified to carry 891 gallons of aviation fuel.

**Paris, June 16**
Air France inaugurates flights "every hour on the hour" to London (→ Oct 11).

**Peenemünde, Germany, June 20**
Erich Warsitz pilots the Heinkel He 176 rocket-powered airplane on its first flight; it was designed by Ernst Heinkel, with a power plant developed by the Walther firm (→ Aug 27).

**London, June 28**
The Women's Auxiliary Air Force (WAAF) is created when 48 companies of the Auxiliary Territorial Service (ATS) are transferred from the Army to the Royal Air Force (RAF).

**Los Angeles, June 30**
United Airlines returns the DC-4 prototype to Douglas, unhappy with the airliner's performance. Pan American, TWA and American Airlines have also decided not to purchase the DC-4 (→ Feb 25, 1942).

**England, July 25**
The Avro 679 Manchester heavy bomber, powered by two Rolls-Royce Vulture engines, makes a 17-minute maiden flight.

**Berlin, July 25**
German airline Lufthansa opens a fortnightly service to Bangkok. The service was opened by Ju 52/3m D-AGAK.

**London, July 31**
The Air Ministry takes delivery of a PBY-4 from the Consolidated Aircraft Corporation. The seaplane, which is to undergo a series of evaluation tests, had been flown to England from California (→ May 10, 1941)

**England, September 1**
All RAF squadrons are put at war readiness, and RAF reservists are called up; in addition, the Auxiliary Air Force is activated, and the Air Transport Auxiliary is formed to move airplanes and equipment from the factories where they are manufactured to operational units (→ Nov 11).

**Silesia, Poland, September 3**
As part of the German offensive, paratroopers drop behind Polish lines in the first reported use of parachutists in war.→

**South-east England, September 6**
A fault in the air-traffic reporting system causes British fighters to scramble in the belief that a major German air attack is imminent; in the confusion, RAF Spitfires shoot down two RAF Hurricanes, and one Spitfire is lost to anti-aircraft fire.

**France, September 9**
The last of 13 Royal Air Force squadrons which have been transferred since September 4 arrive to complete the air component of the British Expeditionary Force; 14 squadrons of an Advanced Air Striking Force are also due.

**Atlantic Ocean, September 18**
Two Short Sunderland flying boats from Plymouth rescue the 34 crew of torpedoed steamer *Kensington Court* who are clinging to a lifeboat approximately 70 miles west of the Scilly Isles.

**Sydney, September 21**
Two Imperial Airways Short "C" class flying boats, which were here when war was declared, are handed over to the Royal Australian Air Force; Imperial will take on two airplanes from the QANTAS fleet in exchange.

**British Empire, October 10**
The Empire Air Training Scheme is set up to train Australian, New Zealand and Canadian air crews.

**London and Paris, October 11**
Air France and Imperial Airways resume services between the cities, suspended when war was declared.

**South Atlantic, October**
The Farman F.223.0 stratospheric research airplane *Camille Flammarion* flies secret missions to locate German battleships *Graf Spee* and *Admiral Scheer*; officially, the F.223.0 is making reconnaissance flights for Air France.

**Lorraine, France, November 6**
Nine Curtiss H.75As of the French II/5 fighter squadron take on 27 Messerschmitt Bf 109s, claiming eight "kills" and two possibles; this is hailed as proof of the superiority of US-made French airplanes.

**Marienehe, Germany, Nov 19**
The Heinkel He 177 Greif heavy bomber makes its first flight.

**Westminster, London, Nov 24**
The BOAC Act, establishing the British Overseas Airways Corporation by the merger of Imperial Airways and British Airways, comes into force.

**San Diego, December 29**
The Consolidated XB-24 prototype four-engined heavy bomber makes its first flight, at Lindbergh Field.

---

*Last preparations: beside his Messerschmitt Bf 109E fighter, a German pilot fastens his lifejacket before taking off on his next mission.* ▶

# Lockheed launches high-speed fighter

*The XP-38 has a striking twin-tail-boom layout with a short central nacelle.*

*March Field, Calif, January 27*
Lockheed's new high-speed XP-38 fighter made its first flight today. However, the 24-minute test nearly ended badly.

As Lieutenant Benjamin Kelsey was bringing the aircraft in to land here, he pulled on a lever in the cockpit to deploy the Fowler flaps, but the cable snapped. The fighter came in much too fast and Kelsey was only able to bring the XP-38 to a halt by resorting to emergency braking. The pilot was nonetheless enthusiastic about the airplane, which is powered by two V-12, liquid-cooled, 1,000-hp Allison V-1710 engines which give it a maximum speed of 420mph. Designed by "Kelly" Johnson, the sleek new fighter's engines are mounted inside twin booms which house the cooling radiators and also support the twin-fin tail. The cockpit is in the central section. The XP-38 features tricycle landing gear. Production models will have turbo-superchargers for high-altitude performance, and will carry heavy armament (→ Feb 11).

# Japanese carriers to have a new fighter

*Japan, April 1*
A completely new Mitsubishi fighter should soon be deployed aboard Japan's aircraft carriers.

Designated the A6M1, the prototype of this airplane made a successful first flight today. The fighter, ordered by the Imperial Japanese Navy in May 1937, is powered by a 780-hp Mitsubishi Zuisei 13 engine. Mitsubishi won the contract when its rival manufacturer, Nakajima, decided to back out of the deal. The low-winged, metal-fuselaged fighter is armed with twin 20-mm cannon and twin 7.7-mm machine-guns. For increased pilot safety, its fuel and oil tanks are protected by reinforced fire walls. The enclosed cockpit has a sliding Plexiglas canopy, above which is the radio antenna. The aircraft also has fully retractable, inward-folding landing gear.

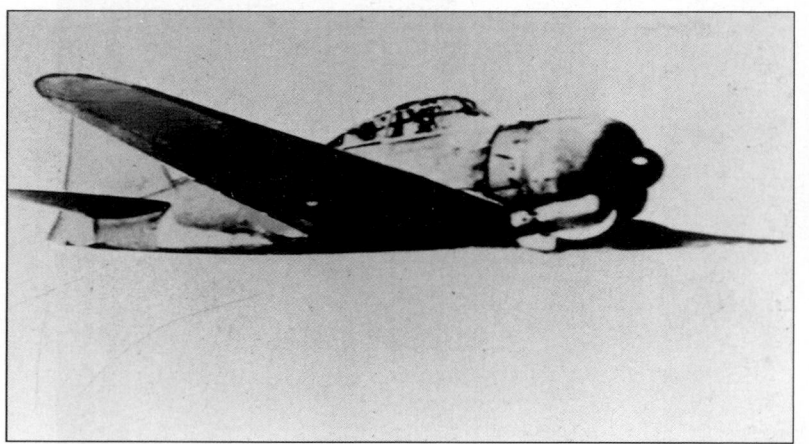

*The Mitsubishi A6M1 has been designed to have unprecedented range.*

# Mail pilots pick up letters without landing

*In a few moments, the mailbags (arrowed) will be hauled up into the airplane.*

*Coatesville, Pa, March*
Before a crowd of more than 2,500 spectators, a bright red Stinson Reliant SR-10 aircraft of All American Aviation today proved the theory of Dr. Lytle S Adams of Chicago by swooping from the sky to drop and, at the same time, pick up a sack of mail.

All American Aviation founder Richard C Dupont had first observed the system of cables, hooks and winches at the Chicago Exposition, "A Century of Progress", which opened in May 1933. Dupont is today convincing US Postal officials of its potential. He believes that this area of remote mountainous terrain can at last have its own efficient air mail service.

Although the first dropped sack landed in the middle of an automobile graveyard, the next two trials were right on target.

# Trans-Canada flies across the continent

*Montreal, April 1*
The publicly owned Trans-Canada Airlines (TCA) began transcontinental passenger services today with a flight to Vancouver. The price of a ticket is $255, four times the average monthly wage. TCA stewardesses are all trained nurses and earn a relatively high salary of $140 a month, although they have to buy their own uniforms, which cost $40. The service incorporates a full-scale overnight airmail operation.

The airline operates a fleet of Lockheed 14H ten-passenger aircraft as well as 14-seater Lockheed Lodestars (→ May 16, 1942).

*Welcoming cabin crew stand by.*

# Europe buys American

*France, May 13*
The arrival today of the first batch of Curtiss H.75A fighters, which were ordered by the French air force last year, is part of an urgent drive for rearmament by Britain and France alike. Both countries have realized that their home production of military aircraft is insufficient to meet the growing threat of a well-armed German air force.

Their solution: buy American. The RAF and Royal Navy are evaluating a number of US aircraft, including the B-17 bomber and the new Grumman G-36. Last year the RAF ordered 200 North American Harvard single-engined trainers and the same number of Lockheed Hudson reconnaissance aircraft.

In February this year, France ordered 100 Douglas DB-7 bombers, a move which was backed by President Roosevelt himself. He is said to see France as the first line of America's defense (→ Nov 4).

*American-built Hudsons are loaded in New York prior to the trip to Europe.*

# Germans test superb Focke-Wulf fighter

*Bremen, Germany, June 1*
Germany's new Focke-Wulf Fw 190 fighter made its first flight at the airport here today. Intended to supplement the Bf 109, the Fw 190 is more advanced in conception.

The airplane's engine is a BMW 139 radial of about 1,600hp, installed in a tight cowling to which cooling air is admitted via the huge hollow hub of the propeller. Another advanced feature is that almost every item on board is electric. Aircraft designer Kurt Tank in-tends the 190 to be the fastest and most formidable fighter in the world. The planned armament of four 20-millimeter cannon in the wings, and two machine guns in the fuselage, represent a tremendous firepower for so small an aircraft. Future versions are also likely to be heavily armored and to carry bombs, so they will need airfields which allow a long take-off run.

Test pilot Flugkapitän Hans Sander said today his only problem was excessive heat in the cockpit.

# Top German squadron returns from Spain

*Lt. Hans Schmoller-Haldy in the cockpit of his Messerschmitt Bf 109E-3.*

*Berlin, June 6*
Men of Germany's Kondor Legion, which helped General Franco to victory in the Spanish Civil War, have returned home to find tacticians and designers eager to apply the lessons of that campaign. Spain has been a test-bed for the Luftwaffe's best men and machines. The Messerschmitt Bf 109 fighter was very successful against Soviet Polikarpov I-15 and I-16s, and German designers are increasing its firepower. The Heinkel He 111 bomber outflew enemy interceptors. The Junkers Ju 87 dive-bomber hit its targets with pinpoint accuracy and was used as a form of aerial artillery, coordinated with the advance of ground forces.

# Fly from New York to Marseilles for $375

*New York, June 28*
The world's first scheduled transatlantic passenger flights began at twelve minutes past three this afternoon when Captain R O D Sullivan lifted Pan Am's Boeing 314A *Dixie Clipper* flying boat into the sky from Port Washington on the Hudson. His 22 passengers, bound for Marseilles, France, via the Azores and Lisbon, have paid $375 single or $675 return for the trip. Flights to England, which are due to begin on July 8, will cost the same.

Passengers should get their money's worth. With its ship-style staterooms, and an elegant dining room with well-trained, attentive stewards, the *Dixie Clipper* is the ultimate in luxury (→ Sep 13, 1940).

**The Commonwealth Wirraway, based on the North American NA-33, is the first aircraft to be mass-produced in Australia. The first of these two-seater, general-purpose trainers was delivered to the RAAF in July.**

# 'Yankee Clipper' blazes Atlantic trail

## Imperial joins Pan Am for new service

*Southampton, England, August 11*
Regular passenger and mail flights between the US and Britain are now a reality. America, in the form of Pan American, has had an aircraft capable of the flight for some time, but it was agreed that no service would start until Britain had one too. Pan American led the way on May 20 with the Boeing 314A flying boat *Yankee Clipper*, which left New York on the first scheduled transatlantic airmail flight. Britain's Imperial Airways joined the fray using the Short S.30 flying boat *Caribou* commanded by Captain Kelly Rogers, which arrived back in Southampton today after the first return transatlantic flight by a British airline. The flights will run once a week to New York via Foynes, Ireland, Botwood, Newfoundland, and Montreal.

But Pan American was first. The May 20 flight, from Port Washington, New York, to Southampton via the Azores, Lisbon and Marseilles, France, took just under three days including overnight stops. Captain Arthur LaPorte commanded the historic flight, which carried 1,804 pounds of mail.

The *Yankee Clipper*, with Harold Gray as captain, left New York next on June 24 using the northern route with 1,743 pounds of mail and 21 government and industry observers. The flight, via Shediac, New Brunswick, Botwood and Foynes, included a delay at Shediac because of fog at Botwood. The aircraft reached Southampton on June 28. On the same day, Pan Am launched the first scheduled transatlantic passenger service, from New York on the *Dixie Clipper*, which arrived in Marseilles on June 30 [*see story on page 367*].

Captain LaPorte and the *Yankee Clipper* also made the first scheduled transatlantic flight via the northern route from Port Washington to Southampton. He started on the morning of July 8 with 19 passengers and arrived 27 hours later. But even as it gets under way, the service is threatened as war clouds gather over Europe (→ Sep 21).

*Pan Am's powerful Boeing 314 flying boat roars across the water just before take-off. The Boeing's four engines can each produce 1,550-hp take-off power.*

*In the nerve center of the "Clipper" the flight engineer supervises the engine controls of the flying boat, which is capable of flying for 30hrs at 145mph.*

*Dinner is served aboard the "Yankee Clipper" at an altitude of 10,000 feet.*

## US flyers set off to 'wild blue yonder'

*Washington, DC, July 15*
General Henry "Hap" Arnold has chosen a stirring anthem for his US Army Air Corps. The words and music of *The Army Air Corps*, by airman Robert Crawford, evoke the bravado of fighting in the air:
"Off we go, into the wild blue yonder
Climbing high into the Sun;
Here they come, zooming to meet our thunder
At 'em boys, give 'er the gun!
Down we dive, spouting our flame from under,
Off with one helluva roar,
We live in fame or go down in flame, hey!
Nothing'll stop the Army Air Corps!" (→ May 19, 1941).

## BOAC is new airline for Britain's empire

*London, August 4*
Britain is to get a new flag-carrying airline following the decision to merge two existing competitors, Imperial Airways and British Airways. The new state-owned airline will be called British Overseas Airways Corporation (BOAC). Its formation follows a hard-hitting report from Lord Cadman, published last year, which highlighted "poor staff relations, inefficient operations and the use of obsolete equipment" in Imperial Airways in particular. Imperial's general manager, George Woods-Humphrey, has resigned in protest at the merger plan (→ Aug 11).

## French pilots steal top German fighter

*France, May 10*
A daring escapade ended in tragedy today when French brothers Jean and Xavier Oettil were killed in the crash of a Bf 110 fighter, which they had stolen from the Messerschmitt factory. They escaped from Germany, but lost their way and crashed in thick fog near Villers-sous-Chalamont. French officials will still welcome the chance to examine the wrecked fighter.

# Invisible 'Chain Home' offers air defense

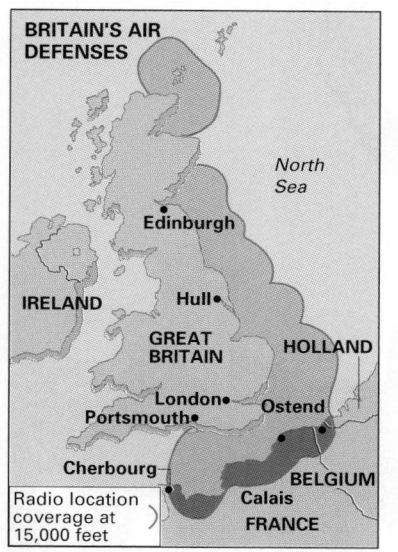

BRITAIN'S AIR DEFENSES

North Sea

Edinburgh

IRELAND   Hull

GREAT BRITAIN   HOLLAND

London   Ostend
Portsmouth

Cherbourg   BELGIUM
Calais

Radio location coverage at 15,000 feet   FRANCE

*Middlesex, England, April 4*
The French have their much-vaunted Maginot Line, said to be able to stop an invading army in its tracks. For its part, the British government is relying on radar as one of its main lines of defense against German air aggression. Britain's invisible defense against enemy air attack is the "Chain Home" Radio Direction Finding (RDF). It is made up of stations built round the coast which use radio beams to detect enemy aircraft approaching the country. The network has been constructed in stages from December 1936.

Bentley Priory, Stanmore, has been transformed into the nerve center of an air-defense system under the command of Air Chief Marshal Hugh Dowding. This system includes the Observer Corps – which is stationed throughout the British Isles to spot attacking aircraft visually – anti-aircraft guns, numerous barrage balloons and, crucially, RAF Fighter Command, which provides the Spitfires and Hurricanes to intercept the incoming enemy.

# Avro Manchester has 1,950-hp engines

*Manchester, England, July 25*
The British aircraft manufacturer A.V.Roe started flight testing its powerful new bomber today.

The Avro Manchester, known as Type 679, is a twin-engined, monoplane heavy bomber designed to be capable of striking distant targets. It can carry an effective payload of 10,300 pounds of high-explosive bombs and has a maximum range of more than 1,200 miles. This puts targets in Germany well within its range. The Avro Manchester is powered by two Rolls-Royce Vulture engines of 1,950-hp each. It has nose, dorsal and tail power-driven turrets, and an extremely large and unobstructed bomb bay.

The new warplane was designed and built following the British Air Ministry's call, made in May 1936, for a new generation of heavy, long-range penetration bombers. Avro's design seems to have fulfilled the ministry's specifications. The only worry is that the engines are complex and undeveloped.

# Germans test new jet-powered airplane

*Heinkel's jet-powered He 178 has an engine of 1,050-lb maximum thrust.*

*Marienehe, Germany, August 27*
Heinkel test pilot Captain Erich Warsitz today flew a strange and exciting new kind of airplane at the airfield here, not far from the city of Rostock.

The Heinkel He 178 has no propeller; instead it has a turbojet. This revolutionary type of engine, which was first pioneered by Frank Whittle in Britain, consists of a gas turbine burning ordinary kerosene fuel, with a turbine driving a compressor which sucks in air through a large inlet located in the airplane's nose. Thrust is generated when a jet of hot gas is expelled from a nozzle at the tail of the aircraft.

The new "jet" aircraft has been built quickly and in secret. It made a brief hop here three days ago, but today saw the first real flight. On take-off it sucked in a bird.

The engine, called the HeS 3B, is the brain-child of Hans Von Ohain, who has been developing it with Heinkel backing since 1936. His first test rig burned hydrogen gas from the laboratory. Early this year, a proper engine was tested slung under a He 118 dive bomber. An improved version of this engine is fitted in the 178. So far, Ernst Heinkel has not succeeded in firing the Berlin Air Ministry with enthusiasm, but his aircraft designers are planning a fighter with two of the revolutionary new engines.

# A British fighter that can play many roles

*Filton, England, July 17*
The biggest gap in the Royal Air Force looks like being filled at last. Today, the Bristol Aeroplane Company flew the prototype model 156, which they have named Beaufighter. A powerful twin-engined fighter, it has long range, devastating armament (4 cannons and 6 machine guns) and is big enough to carry the newly invented radar for fighting at night. The prototype has 1,650-hp Bristol Hercules engines, and can reach 330mph. With luck, Fighter Command could form a squadron in late 1940.

*The Avro 679 Manchester is the world's most powerful twin-engined bomber.*

*The RAF's multi-role combat aircraft, the Bristol Beaufighter Type 156.*

# RAF launches air war with raid on fleet

*London, September 4*
Britain's Royal Air Force (RAF) started its war last night with a raid on Germany's industrial Ruhr area by Whitley bombers. Their 13-tons loads consisted only of propaganda leaflets, in accordance with an undertaking not to bomb civilian targets, made by the belligerents at the suggestion of President Roosevelt.

However, the RAF also made its first raid on a military target last night when 29 Wellington and Blenheim bombers went to bomb the German fleet at Wilhelmshaven and elsewhere. The raid was not a great success: ten attackers did not find the target, and seven were shot down by anti-aircraft fire. London is playing down the fact that the damage to prize targets, such as the battleship *Admiral Scheer*, is minimal. The RAF's iron bombs would not penetrate her armor. A crippled Blenheim aimed at the *Emden* caused more serious damage.

*A crew member drops the leaflets.*

*The leaflet shows that Hitler and Stalin differ only in their hairstyles.*

# McDonnell sets up new Missouri firm

*St Louis, Mo, September 25*
The McDonnell Aircraft Corporation opened for business today in a rented building owned by American Airlines at Lambert Field, near St Louis.

The company, incorporated in Maryland on July 6, now intends to concentrate on designing and building aircraft for the US Army Air Corps and US Navy. Aeronautical engineer James Smith McDonnell heads the new company. Originally from Little Rock, Arkansas, McDonnell, who is just 40 years old, brings extensive experience in design and manufacture to his company. He worked for Ford, designed his first *Doodlebug* aircraft in 1929 and was chief project engineer for the Glenn L Martin Company in Baltimore, Maryland, until December last year, when he decided to form his own firm.

# Turner wins trophy and takes his leave

*Turner after breaking his own east/west speed record across the US.*

*Cleveland, Ohio, September 5*
Flamboyant US airman Roscoe Turner, who gained fame by carrying a lion cub on his flights, ended his air-racing career today with a two-lap victory in the National Air Races Thompson Trophy event. It was Turner's third Thompson win.

Turner started poorly today. He was last on the first lap of the 30-lap, 300-mile race. But by the ninth lap he had taken the lead and lapped the rest of the field.

He won his first Thompson in 1934, and was forced out of the 1935 race, barely escaping death when his engine's supercharger exploded. He could not compete in 1936 because a crash-landing destroyed his machine. He came third in 1937 in an airplane of his own design and, after modifying this aircraft, won the Thompson last year.

Turner also came first and second in the transcontinental Bendix race in 1933 and 1935 respectively, and has set several coast-to-coast records. When he landed today, Turner called for photographers and announced his retirement. He said: "Pylon racing is a young man's game. I am 43."

**Russian-born aircraft designer Igor Sikorsky makes a tethered flight of his VS-300 helicopter at Stratford, Connecticut. Two tethers attaching the machine to the ground are very faintly visible as diagonal lines.**

# German 'Blitzkrieg' shatters Poland

*Polish youths look to the sky as wave after wave of German bombers roll in.*

## Huge Luftwaffe air raid pounds Warsaw

*Poland, October 6*
Poland has been defeated, dismembered and divided up between Nazi Germany and Soviet Russia in a campaign lasting 36 days. Air power has played a key role in that victory, first by supporting the *Blitzkrieg* [see below], then by reducing the city of Warsaw. The Luftwaffe initially committed two *Luftflotten*, comprising 648 level-bombers, 219 dive-bombers, 30

ground-attack aircraft, 210 single-engined and twin-engined fighters and 474 reconnaissance aircraft, plus transports and army liaison aircraft. Against them the Poles could only muster 159 fighters, 154 bombers and 84 observation machines, some obsolete. Lessons of the campaign are clear: any country without effective air defenses, or a strategic air force to deter Hitler, is vulnerable (→ Apr 9, 1940).

*Junkers Ju 52/3ms of the Luftwaffe played a major role in defeating Poland.*

## Luftwaffe planes support army in German Blitzkrieg tactics

*Berlin, September 14*
The secret of the rapid German advance into Poland, the *Blitzkrieg* [lightning war], lies in the use of airplanes in co-operation with ground forces. Goering's Luftwaffe is working in close concert with the German army, using coordinated battle plans to keep air and ground forces

well connected and moving forward together smoothly, with air support available as close as 300 yards from the leading armored columns. One commander explained it thus: "We always have an air waveband with a Luftwaffe officer in the leading tank and make sure that everybody keeps talking to each other."

The pinpoint accuracy of Stuka dive-bomber attacks just in front of advancing troops is a matter of fierce pride with their pilots, rated in Germany even above fighter pilots for courage and dash; they always release their bombs at the very last possible moment to ensure maximum accuracy (→ Sep 27).

## Poland isolated as Soviets join attack

*Warsaw, September 27*
Poland is in its death throes today. Following a massive air raid on Warsaw two days ago, a huge pall of smoke still hangs over the city which is decked out with white flags this morning, signalling its surrender to the Luftwaffe.

Warsaw held out heroically for several days, but it was doomed once the Polish air force, which put up a spirited defense of the capital, despite a great inferiority in equipment and size, had been ground down by the Luftwaffe. Following the Soviet invasion on September 17, the remnants of Poland's combat aircraft were flown to sanctuary in Romania.

With the skies over the city open, cousin of the Great War ace and commander of the Special Purposes Air Command General Wolfram von Richthofen saw his chance to prove what air power alone could do. As former commander of the Kondor Legion during the Spanish Civil War, he was keen to use the terror tactics he had used there. At first the German high command refused to countenance the raid, but when the defenders of the city showed no signs of weakening it was authorized.

At 8am two days ago, the first of over 1,000 bombers began dropping high-explosive and incendiary bombs, setting the city alight. For two nights the glow of burning buildings could be seen for miles around. German losses were two Stukas and a single Ju 52. The Luftwaffe's commanders are ecstatic, as their tactical doctrine is apparently well-founded (→ Oct 6).

## LaGuardia airfield opens for business

*LaGuardia: ready for business.*

*Flushing, NY, October 15*
With more than 300,000 people looking on, New York mayor Fiorello La Guardia today dedicated what many call the finest airport in the world. It was also one of the costliest to build: $45 million.

The airport will be known as LaGuardia Field in honor of the mayor who – as both congressman and mayor – has been a staunch supporter of aviation. The new airport, built primarily on filled-in portions of Flushing Bay as well as what was formerly a dirt airfield and amusement park, covers 558 acres. It has four runways, water for seaplanes to land on, and it is expected that 2,000 or more passengers each day will use the airport in its first year of operations.

**John F Kennedy, seen here with his father, the US ambassador to Great Britain.**

# Spitfires draw first blood over Britain

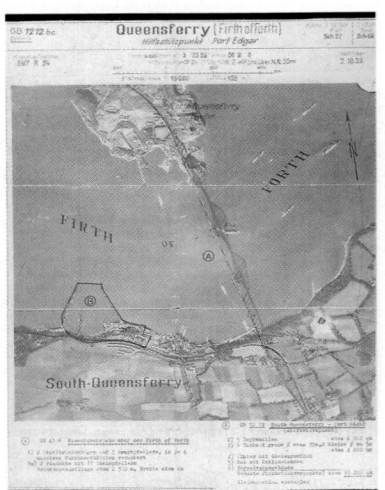

*Luftwaffe target map, Edinburgh.*

Edinburgh, October 16
The first "kills" by British pilots in battle over Britain were credited today to reserve pilots of Auxiliary Air Force Squadrons 602 and 603, based in Glasgow and Edinburgh. Flying Supermarine Spitfires, they took on a force of Junkers Ju 88 bombers flying over the Scottish capital to attack warships in the Firth of Forth. A destroyer was hit and some crewmen killed, but the Spitfires shot down two Ju 88s and harried the rest without loss to themselves (→ Oct 28).

# Chinese negotiate to set up own air force

China, December 16
With the advent of war in Europe, the Soviet Union has withdrawn its fighter and bomber squadrons, flying instructors and other personnel who had been supporting General Chiang Kai-shek's Nationalist forces in the Sino-Japanese war. The Soviet pilots had been effective, but since their departure their Chinese pupils have proved less so.

Tough former US Army Air Corps officer Claire Chennault has stepped into the breach, and he is now trying to forge an effective Chinese air force. He had been trying to convince the Chinese to set up a strong flying training program, but with the Soviet presence his advice was ignored until now.

To plug the gap his Chinese masters persuaded him to hire mercenaries, and nine men – three Americans, four Frenchmen, one Dutch and one German – were taken on to fly with Chinese pilots in 30 Vultee V-11 bombers. But before they could be made into an effective unit the Japanese discovered their base at Tsinan and sent in a force of bombers to destroy all the airplanes (→ Apr 15, 1941).

*General Claire Chennault (l), with Madame Chiang and Chiang Kai-shek.*

# Sensitive electronics discovered in downed German airplane

Scotland, October 28
The first German bomber to be brought down on British soil since 1918, a Heinkel He 111P-1, was forced down almost intact on the hills near Dalkeith today by Spitfires of 602 (City of Glasgow) and 603 (City of Edinburgh) Squadrons of the Auxiliary Air Force. It was riddled with bullet holes. Two of the crew were killed before it touched down, and the pilot was wounded; the observer was unhurt. British scientists will be eager to examine the aircraft and may be able to discover if the Luftwaffe is using radio beams to guide its bombers. They will be particularly keen to find out more about the Heinkel's sensitive Lorenz blind-landing system (→ Jun 1, 1940).

*Local people and officials gather to inspect the wreckage of the German Heinkel which came down in Scotland.*

# Allies freed to buy airplanes from USA

Washington, DC, November 4
Britain and France will receive nearly 3,000 badly-needed aircraft following President Roosevelt's signing today of a new Neutrality Act. The act repeals the embargo on the export of arms to countries at war and allows the release of weapons and aircraft which were ordered by the Allies before the European war broke out.

Nearly 400 aircraft, ranging from Harvard trainers to Hudson bombers, are awaiting delivery to Britain. In theory, Germany, too, can buy weapons and aircraft, but the Royal Navy will try to ensure that traffic will be confined to the democracies (→ Nov 6).

# Women are keen to win wings in ATA

*Women want to do their bit too.*

London, November 11
In a speech today Queen Elizabeth urged the women of Britain to keep up their war work "in every field of national service". This now includes flying every type of aircraft, from fighters and bombers to light transports, in the Air Transport Auxiliary. The ATA was set up on September 1 to ferry aircraft from the factories to RAF airfields, relieving the fighter and bomber pilots of the task. It is an ideal war job for experienced women pilots, and the first women are now preparing for the job. Among them is Pauline Gower, who has been pressing for women to join the ATA.

# Soviets bomb Helsinki

*Until the war started Luftwaffe He 111 bombers often flew over Finland.*

*Helsinki, December 9*
The Soviet air force today sent planes to attack the Finnish capital, clearly aiming at civilian targets. Stalin's propaganda insists, however, that the air force is dropping food to starving Finns, who have thus given the nickname "Molotov's breadbaskets" to the incendiary bombs which can wreak havoc on entire suburbs of their traditional wooden-built houses.

It is nine days since Stalin ordered his forces to invade Finland, after the Finns refused to hand over part of their territory. The Soviets have found it tougher going than they thought, both on the ground and in the air. The tiny Finnish air force, a motley collection of 145 airplanes, some of them British, German and Italian fighters and a few French scouts, is giving a good account of itself. The Soviets, using I-15s and I-16s recently returned

*An air-raid siren sounds in Helsinki.*

from their Manchurian campaign, have lost several aircraft. But the Finns have few defenses against the heavy bombers. Even the ancient TB-3 has been able to do its work with little opposition (→ Dec 16).

## First empire air force flies in to boost RAF

*New South Wales, December 26*
The first British Empire air force unit to be committed to the European war theater flew into Britain today. The main body of 10 Squadron of the Royal Australian Air Force (RAAF) was introduced to the Short Sunderland flying boats that it will fly with RAF Coastal Command. Australia joined the war in September.

The nine Sunderlands allotted to the Australians are armed with

front and rear machine-gun turrets and dorsal mountings for single guns on each beam. Sunderlands are primarily anti-U-boat weapons, but they have proved to have a useful rescue capacity. In September three Sunderlands based in Wales picked up an SOS from a torpedoed tramp steamer and rescued the crew of 34. Orders are about to go out forbidding such rescues because of the danger of Sunderlands breaking up in the Atlantic swell.

# 'Blimps' provide defense against attack

*London, December*
Barrage balloons filled with hydrogen, tethered to vehicles on the ground and linked by cable "curtains", have now become part of Britain's air defenses. Designed to slice the wings off intruding Luftwaffe bombers, the balloons, which are known as "blimps", appeared in 1938 around major towns, cities and airfields throughout the south of England. They are manned by RAF ground units.

The purpose of the balloons is to drive bombers to higher altitudes at which they can be more easily tackled by anti-aircraft weapons. Despite the steel cable tethers, several have broken free in high winds and been mistaken by radar for hostile bombers.

*A balloon defending British skies.*

# British lose 12 bombers in single air raid

*Germany, December 18*
Britain's Royal Air Force (RAF) has lost 12 Wellington bombers in a disastrous raid on German warships at Wilhelmshaven. Three more crash-landed on return to base. After the loss of five other bombers four days ago, it is clear that even Wellingtons, with five machine guns, are easy prey in daytime for cannon-firing Messerschmitt fighters.

Today 24 bombers, led by Wing Commander Richard Kellett of 149 Squadron, flew on the combined reconnaissance and strike mission. As they crossed the North Sea, the Luftwaffe was waiting for them, suggesting the Germans have a radio-direction finding system. Bf 109 and 110s hit from the flanks, ripping apart the Wellingtons, ten of which crashed immediately with another two ditching on the way home. Little damage was caused by the RAF raiders.

Such a costly operation will surely lead to a reappraisal of bomber invincibility on daylight raids without fighter escort (→ May 20, 1940).

**The leading players in "The Lion Has Wings", a stirring propaganda film about the RAF – the first British feature film of the war.**

*Three Short "G" class flying boats were delivered to Imperial Airways.*

*Three 26-seat Macchi MC.100 flying boats were built for Ala Littoria.*

*Curtiss built 32 CW-21s for China and 24 for the Dutch East Indies.*

*The most prolific Japanese fighter was the Mitsubishi A6M Zero-Sen.*

*Short Stirlings were Royal Air Force bombers, transports and glider-tugs.*

*Martin's Model 167 XA-22 three-seater attack-bomber (Maryland).*

*Intended to be used by Air Afrique: the Bloch 160 12-passenger airliner.*

*Just one Latécoère 611 flying boat was completed before the Armistice.*

*The prototype Fokker D.23 with a pair of push/pull Lorraine engines.*

*Vultee Model 48 Vanguards: supplied to China as Lease-Lend P-66s.*

*Fiat produced 152 R.S.14 twin-float seaplanes for the Italian air force.*

*Vultee Valiant trainer: 11,537 were built as military BT-13s and BT-15s.*

*Klemm Kl 35D trainers were built under license for Sweden's air force.*

*Henschel Hs 129B ground-attack and anti-tank aircraft: 859 built.*

*The imperial army's Mitsubishi Ki-46 reconnaissance aircraft.*

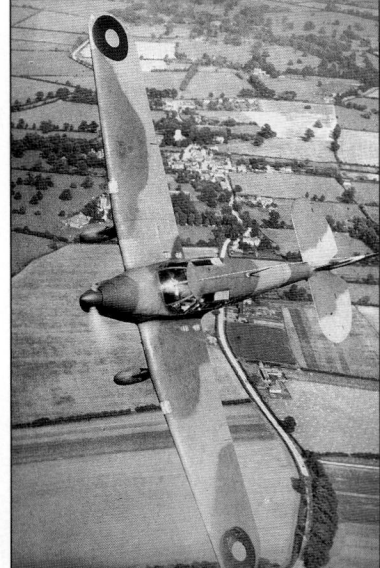

*Percival Proctor, a radio trainer and communications aircraft.*

*Kawasaki built a total of 1,977 Army Ki-48 Type 99 Light Bombers.*

*More than 18,000 Consolidated B-24 Liberator bombers were built.*

*Nakajima's Army Ki-49 Donryu, the last and best of its bombers.*

*Seversky-Republic's XP-41 experimental fighter, based on the P-35.*

*North American's private-venture NA-40, forerunner of the B-25.*

*The Luftwaffe's Bücker Bestmann training/liaison aircraft.*

*Heinkel's He 177 Greif [Gryphon] was to have been a strategic bomber.*

*The Heinkel He 178 was the first aircraft to fly purely on turbojet power.*

*The Commonwealth Wirraway, a development of the NA Harvard.*

*Nakajima's Ki-43 Hayabusa fighter. It carried just two 12.7mm guns.*

*Ilyushin's original Il-2 Shturmovik single-seat ground-attack aircraft.*

*Igor Sikorsky's VS-300 helicopter, with the designer at the controls.*

*Bristol Beaufighters quickly became successful night-fighters with radar.*

*Avro's Manchester twin-engined bomber, the Lancaster's forerunner.*

*The least successful production Douglas transport was the DC-5.*

*The Stinson Voyager, a two-seat cabin monoplane for private owners.*

*The Vickers Warwick, designed to replace smaller Wellington bombers.*

*Lockheed's P-38 Lightning was a successful long-range escort-fighter.*

*Lockheed's 14-seat L-18 Lodestar, developed from the Lockeed 14.*

*Focke-Wulf's prototype Fw 190; in all, 20,001 of them were produced.*

*Martin's XPBM-1 Mariner gull-winged flying boat patrol-bomber.*

*Lioré et Olivier's LeO 100 warplane had a cannon in the rear cockpit.*

*The Douglas B-23 Dragon bomber: 38 were constructed for the USAAF.*

*Complete failure: Curtiss's SO3C Seamew scout/observation seaplane.*

*A dorsal turret was a feature of the Savoia-Marchetti S.M.82 Canguro.*

*Piaggio's P.108B bomber: the Regia Aeronautica had 163.*

*Handley Page's four-engined Halifax heavy bomber (first prototype).*

*Kawasaki's Ki-45 Toryu two-seater twin-engined long-range fighter.*

# 1940

469.22mph
Germany
Fritz Wendel
Messerschmitt Me 209 V1
Apr 26, 1939

8,038 miles
Italy
Tondi, Degasso, Vignoli
Savoia-Marchetti S.M.75
Aug 1, 1939

56,046ft
Italy
Mario Pezzi
Caproni 161bis
Oct 22, 1938

123,457lb
Germany
Dornier
Do X

1,200lb thrust
Germany
Pabst von Ohaim
Heinkel HeS 3B

**River Dangu, Belgian Congo, Jan 6**
Imperial Airways pilot Captain Kelly Rogers finally takes off in his Short Empire flying boat *Corsair*, which crashed here on March 14 last year; nine months of hard work by local people resulted in the construction of a waterway 50 yards wide, from which he got airborne (→ Jun 19).

**France, February 3**
Flight Lieutenant Robert Jeffe becomes the first Royal Air Force (RAF) officer decorated by France when he is awarded the Croix de Guerre for downing the first Heinkel He 111 bomber over French soil on November 2.

**England, February 24**
The 2,000-hp prototype Hawker Typhoon fighter makes its first flight.

**New York, February 26**
The US Air Defense Command is formed at Mitchell Field.

**Middlesex, England, March 9**
The Operations Room of RAF Fighter Command is established in the basement of Bentley Priory, near London.

**USA, March 25**
Airplane manufacturers contracted to the US Army Air Corps (USAAC) are authorized to sell modern warplanes to countries fighting the Axis; the planned expansion in production should help the USAAC too (→ May 16).

**Russia, April 5**
The prototype Mikoyan-Gureyevich I-200 fighter flies for the first time.

**Anchorage, Alaska, April 25**
McGee Airways pioneers the transportation of fresh meat and milk to the Alaskan interior (→ May 5, 1944).

**Auckland, April 30**
Tasman Empire Airways, founded just four days ago, opens its first service, to Sydney.

**France, May 12**
RAF 264 Squadron takes delivery of the first Boulton Paul Defiant fighters; the two-seater Defiant is unusual in having its armament in a turret behind the pilot.

**Stratford, Conn, May 13**
Russian-born Igor Sikorsky's VS-300 helicopter makes its first free flight (→ May 6, 1941).

**London, May 16**
Despite protests yesterday by Sir Hugh Dowding that too many fighters needed for Britain's defense are being sent to France, the transfer of four more squadrons is authorized by new Prime Minister Winston Churchill (→ May 19).

**Washington, DC, May 16**
President Roosevelt calls for the production of 50,000 airplanes a year in the US (→ Oct 11).

**London, May 19**
Churchill rules that no more British fighter squadrons are to be sent to France (→ Jun 18).

**Stratford, Conn, May 29**
Lyman Bullard pilots the Vought XF4U-1 Corsair naval fighter-bomber on its first flight.

**Italy, June 10**
Italy joins Germany in declaring war on the Allies, closing down the Mediterranean to civil air transport and blocking flights from England to Australia (→ Aug 14).

**Washington, DC, June 11**
The Civil Aeronautics Authority becomes the Civil Aeronautics Board (→ Mar 20, 1941).

**Brittany, France, June 19**
Some 108 pupils of the Morlaix flying school respond to General de Gaulle's call for Free French pilots, leaving Douarnenez for London on board a fishing boat (→ Jul 8).

**Manchester, England, June 21**
The director of military operations opens the Central Landing School to train paratroopers.

**Fort Benning, Ga, July 5**
A test platoon is formed to begin training as an airborne combat unit; they are America's first paratroopers (→ Aug 29).

**Middle East, July 8**
Provisional head of Forces Aériennes Françaises Libres [Free French Air Force] Admiral Muselier puts the first squadrons in place: N° 1 at Aden [Yemen] and N° 2 at Haifa (→ Nov 15, 1941).

**New York, July 8**
TWA begins operating Boeing 307-B Stratoliners on the San Francisco/New York route. The flight takes 13 hours 40 minutes, two hours faster than by DC-3.

**Leeming, England, August 2**
No 7 Sqn RAF receives the first Short Stirling to be delivered.

**USA, August 19**
The prototype of the North American B-25 Mitchell bomber makes its first flight.

**Germany, August 20**
Luftwaffe chief Hermann Goering orders: "The enemy is to be forced to use his fighters by means of ceaseless attacks" (→ Sep 14).

**England, August 26**
Bomber Command airplanes return after the first RAF raid on Berlin, retaliating for the Luftwaffe bombing of London on the night of August 24-25 (→ Jul 9, 1941).

**Milan, Italy, August 28**
The Camproni-Campini N.1 experimental jet-propelled airplane makes its first flight.→

**Chungking, China, September 13**
Japan's Mitsubishi A6M1 Zero fighters make their combat début, shooting down 27 Chinese and Soviet fighters without loss.

**San Francisco, September 13**
Pan Am begins scheduled passenger flights to Auckland; an airmail service over the same route began on July 12 (→ Aug 18, 1941).

**Yorkshire, England, September 19**
US volunteer pilots form the Eagle fighter squadron, within the RAF, at Church Fenton (→ Dec 2, 1941).

**Gibraltar, September 25**
Eighty Vichy French bombers operating from Africa drop 55 tons of bombs in reprisal for the British attack yesterday on the French fleet at Dakar (→ Jul 28, 1941).

**Hampshire, England, September 26**
Supermarine's Woolston factory is wrecked in a Luftwaffe raid.

**USA, October 11**
Organized transatlantic ferry flights of US-built airplanes to Britain begin (→ Mar 27, 1941).

**USA, October 26**
The prototype North American NA-73 fighter, designed to meet a request by Britain, makes its first flight (→ Nov 30).

**England, November 11**
Italy makes its first major air attack on Britain, although some Italian planes are believed to have taken part in a smaller attack on September 7 (→ Nov 2).

**Hatfield, England, November 25**
Geoffrey de Havilland Jr pilots the D.H.98 Mosquito on its first flight (→ Sep 20, 1941).

**New York, December 8**
The city experiences its first blackout and anti-aircraft exercise, around the Brooklyn Navy Yard.

**Orkney, Scotland, December 25**
Two Grumman Martlets of 804 Squadron, Fleet Air Arm, become the first US-built airplanes to destroy a German airplane in the war, bringing down a Ju 88 over Scapa Flow.

*Together with the Hurricane (the two middle aircraft), the Spitfire lay behind Britain's success in keeping the Luftwaffe at bay in 1940.* ▶

# Airmen of several nations arrive in Britain

*RCAF ground crews arriving in England demonstrate their sky-high morale.*

*Britain, March 1*
Royal Canadian Air Force (RCAF) pilots and crew along with mechanics and support teams docked today at Liverpool. Their arrival is the first tangible evidence of a deal involving Britain, Canada, Australia, S Rhodesia and New Zealand to train pilots, navigators and gunners from all these countries. The RCAF entered the war with 4,000 men, but is now besieged by volunteers.

Meanwhile, some pilots who fled Poland when Germany invaded are now in Paris, where their government-in-exile is based, and have joined the French air force. Squadrons of Koolhoven FK.58 and Caudron 714 fighters are flown by Poles. Other Poles have chosen Britain and are being absorbed into the Auxiliary Air Force. Of these, 609 Squadron, based in Yorkshire, includes citizens of Britain, Canada, Poland, New Zealand, Australia and the United States. The question mark looming over these airmen now is how fast the volunteers and the machines can be welded into coherent fighting units (→ Mar 1, 1941).

**An RAF Coastal Command Sunderland flying boat. Most of its missions are long-range maritime reconnaissance patrols, although the Sunderland is sometimes used for rescue operations at sea.**

# 'Wrong island bombed' claim Germans

*London, March 20*
RAF Bomber Command officers are wondering how to respond to German claims that a raid on a seaplane base last night went humiliatingly wrong. Reacting to a Luftwaffe strike on a British naval base four days ago, the RAF targeted a night raid by 50 Whitleys and Hampdens on Sylt, off the German North Sea coast. The morning after the bombing, there is no obvious damage to Sylt, but the neutral Danish authorities on Bornholm island, 260 miles away in the Baltic, are furious about apparently being bombed by the RAF. After the Wilhelmshaven débâcle [*see page 373*] the RAF is learning that night bombing is no pushover either.

*RAF pilots pore over a map before taking off on their night mission.*

# American battalion makes trial airlift

*California, January 23*
The US Army today demonstrated for the first time that it can move a unit of combat troops swiftly to where it is needed by air, when the 2nd Battalion of the 65th Coast Artillery was flown from Hamilton Field, near San Francisco, to March Field, Riverside. The 500-mile movement was accomplished using 38 Douglas B-18A bombers of the 7th Bombardment Group, which is stationed at Hamilton Field. The soldiers, many of whom had never even flown before, were in full uniform complete with field packs and rifles.

Using the bombers in a transport role is not as unusual as it may seem: the twin-engined aircraft has many of the features of the Douglas DC-2 and DC-3 airplanes used by airlines throughout the world (→ Feb 26).

# Italian jet aircraft disappoints in tests

*Taliedo, Italy, August 28*
Today a strange airplane was flown for the first time from this airfield near Milan. Known as the N.1, it was built by Italian makers Caproni to test a method of jet propulsion which has been invented by Secondo Campini. In Campini's jet, an ordinary piston engine drives a ducted fan which pumps air out of a nozzle at the tail. Extra fuel can be burned in this airflow to boost the speed of the aircraft.

But test pilot Mario de Bernardi was not impressed. The N.1's maximum speed is barely 200mph and its normal cruising speed is only 130mph – slower than it would fly if the engine drove only an ordinary propeller. The N.1 is the result of years of research, yet its performance today was poorer than that of even trainers and transports. Part of its trouble is the size of the aircraft – the N.1 is large and clumsy and has a wingspan of 52 feet – but the propulsion system itself is mainly at fault.

# Nazi air power pummels Norway and Denmark

## German paratroops spearhead attacks

*Germans parachute into Norway from Junkers Ju 52/3m aircraft.*

*Denmark, April 9*
In a grim day for the freedom of Europe, Germany has invaded Denmark and Norway in a sea and air operation codenamed Operation Weserübung. Both countries are neutral. The invasions were spearheaded by paratroopers, and in Denmark their primary objectives were the airbase at Aalborg in the north and a river bridge in Copenhagen; both were needed for reinforcement by air and sea. A 30-man platoon of paratroops captured Aalborg, while two platoons were needed to secure the bridge.

The Norwegians put up a stronger defense: at Sola airfield, near Stavanger, a full company of German paratroops was dropped, but it took more troops, flown in by Junkers Ju 52/3ms, to take the base, and the Germans suffered heavy losses. It was the same at Fornebu, near Oslo: when the slow-moving transports arrived to land reinforcements, they were riddled by Norwegian groundfire (→ Apr 26).

## Luftwaffe crucial to success of invasions

*German Stuka dive-bomber pilots being briefed before a new mission.*

*Oslo, April 26*
With the capitulation of Denmark within 24 hours of being attacked, its Aalborg airbase is being used as a stepping-stone for German reinforcements on their way to Norway. German fighters and bombers are operating from Sola and Fornebu, while some 350 Ju 52/3ms maintain a shuttle service from Germany bringing in infantry and supplies. Operating from Norway, the 330 German bombers are now up to 400 miles closer to the Allied warships in the North Sea, enabling the Luftwaffe to attack Allied forces sent to help Norway.

On April 24, RAF Gloster Gladiators arrived on the frozen Lake Lesjaskog, having taken off from the aircraft carrier HMS *Glorious*. It was an heroic effort but they were virtually wiped out by the Luftwaffe (→ May 10).

## Dive-bombers surprise German cruiser

*Bergen fjord, Norway, April 10*
In an operation by men of Britain's Fleet Air Arm (FAA), Blackburn Skuas of 800 and 803 Squadrons today sank the 6,000-ton German cruiser *Königsberg* in a dive-bombing attack at dawn by Skoltegrund mole, in Bergen fjord. This is the first time in the war that a capital warship has been sunk by airplanes alone. The Skuas are normally based on the carrier HMS *Ark Royal* but are temporarily ashore at Hatston in the Orkney Islands. To mount the attack, the pilots had to fly across 300 miles in darkness. Only one failed to return. The seven Skuas of 800 Squadron were led by Captain R Partridge, and the nine of 803 by Lieutenant W Lucy.

## William Boeing buys a Douglas DC-5

*Los Angeles, Calif, April 19*
William Boeing has just purchased a Douglas DC-5 to replace the Douglas Dolphin he had bought for his own use in 1933. This is a surprising choice since the DC-5 has not yet proved itself. This twin-engined aircraft is derived from the DB-7 bomber designed by Ed Heinemann in 1938 and it cannot accomodate more passengers than the DC-3. The Douglas DC-5 is not pressurized and cannot be considered as an improvement on the DC-3. It is powered by 1,100-hp Wright engines and has tricycle landing gear. One of its assets is its capacity to use short runways. The US Navy has ordered three DC-5s, designated R3D-1.

*The Royal Navy's Skua dive-bombers often attack ships out of the Sun.*

*The twin-engined Douglas DC-5 made its first flight on February 12, 1939.*

# German 'Blitzkrieg' conquers the Low Countries

## Luftwaffe leads assault on Netherlands

*A Junkers Ju 87B Stuka in action.*

*The Netherlands, May 10*
At dawn today Germany applied its *Blitzkrieg* formula to neutral Belgium, Luxembourg and the Netherlands. The opening stages of the invasion are now chillingly familiar: aerial bombardment followed by paratroop assaults on key military targets ahead of a land invasion. With over 1,100 He 111, Do 17 and Ju 88 level bombers, 385 Stuka dive bombers, some 1,300 Bf 109 and 110 fighters and around 1,000 reconnaissance and transport aircraft, it has been a day of intense air activity for the Luftwaffe.

Dutch military airfields, such as Waalhaven, were early targets, as were bridges. At Rotterdam, shock troops landed on the Maas river in 12 He 59 seaplanes to seize three bridges. But the Germans have not had it all their own way. Dutch Fokker T.V bombers hit Ju 52 transports on the ground at Ockenburg airfield, and RAF fighters gave a good account of themselves. By the end of the day, 304 Luftwaffe aircraft had been destroyed, 51 damaged and 267 airmen killed. However, the boldness and efficiency of the German assault still give an aura of invincibility.→

## Swift glider strike takes Belgian fort

*A Junkers Ju 52/3m drops material and supplies to forward troops.*

## Allied air strikes fail to halt the Germans

*Hasselt, Belgium, May 12*
About 17 Allied aircraft have been lost in failed endeavors to dislodge German forces from bridges over the Albert canal, 35 miles from the German border. The bridges, which were seized by airborne troops two days ago and immediately protected by anti-aircraft guns, are vital to the German advance.

Today, six RAF Battle bombers escorted by Hurricanes attempted to break the principal bridge, but were torn apart by flak. Only one Battle survived. The pilots' courage surprised even the Germans. Flying Officer D E Garland and navigator Sergeant T Gray are to be recommended posthumously for the Victoria Cross, Britain's highest valor award. Belgium lost seven aircraft in the air and many more on the ground. France's air force lost five in air combat (→May 14).

*Liège, Belgium, May 10*
Glider-borne German commandos have snatched an "impregnable" fort obstructing today's Nazi invasion of Belgium. Eben Emael, built in 1935 close to Liège, on the left bank of the River Meuse, is a mass of reinforced concrete, bristling with guns and defended by 1,200 men. Eleven 68-foot wingspan DFS 230 gliders lifted off near Cologne, Germany, at dawn, towed by Junkers Ju 52s. They carried 84 men of the élite "Granit" assault group, plus 5,000 pounds of explosive and 30,000 rounds of ammunition. Two of the gliders, including one carrying operation leader Oberleutnant Witzig, fell short. The other nine achieved total surprise, thanks to their silent approach, and landed on top of the fort.

The first wave seized anti-aircraft guns and destroyed heavy cannon with special munitions. Witzig joined the fight three hours later. As the fort surrendered, its Belgian commander, Major Jottrand, shot himself. Six Germans died in the assault (→May 12).

*Hawker Hurricanes of the Belgian air force (two 0.5in and two 0.303in guns).*

*Five Belgian Fairey Battles, distinguished by their chin radiators.*

# At dawn, the Luftwaffe strikes throughout France

## France's airfields are the primary targets

*The view from the forward machine-gunner's station on a Heinkel He 111.*

**France, May 10**
About 400 bombers of the 1st, 2nd and 5th Fliegerkorps left Germany before first light on a mission to destroy Allied air forces on the ground.

Air raid sirens rang out in the Paris region at 4.45am as German aircraft flew over the Oise valley. A total of 72 airfields, 47 of them in northern France, were targeted. This first strike by the German air force does not however seem to have been entirely successful, since only about 60 French and British airplanes were destroyed on the ground and only four airfields put out of action by the Luftwaffe's bombs.

## French pilots fly 360 missions in one day

*Sub-lieutenant Plubeau's Curtiss H.75A (P-36) on the day of the attack.*

**France, May 10**
French fighters began to take off as soon as news of the German attack reached their bases.

Morane 406, Bloch 152, Dewoitine 520 and Curtiss H.75A fighters rushed to attack the Luftwaffe's bombers. They took advantage of the fact that the German raiders were not protected by escorting Bf 109 or Bf 110 fighters. German bombers were also hampered by heavy fog over many of their targets. At the end of a day of non-stop combat operations, French fighter pilots, who have flown a total of 360 sorties, are claiming the downing of 44 enemy aircraft.

## Canada becomes a center for air training

**Ottawa, April 29**
The Empire Air Training Scheme, set up to coordinate air crew training in the British Empire, has begun. Canada is building 29 pilot schools, together with ten observer, ten bombing and gunnery and two air navigation schools. They will train British, Canadian, Australian and New Zealand crews and US volunteers. Australia and New Zealand have 29 schools for their nationals, and Southern Rhodesia and South Africa are training some RAF crews. The target is to train 28,000 pilots, navigators, bomb aimers and air gunners a year. The massive air training scheme follows an agreement signed by Australia, Britain, Canada and New Zealand on December 17 1939. Article XV of the agreement calls for the formation of distinct national squadrons in the war theaters of Europe.

## A fortune in cash rains down from the sky

**Lille, France, May 26**
While British troops were beginning their retreat from Dunkirk, Fernand Carles, the prefect of the northern French city of Lille, sent a message to Paris to urgently request funds.

For security reasons it was decided to send the money by aircraft and two Martin 167 bombers were assigned to transport a fortune in notes. Unfortunately, anti-aircraft gunners in the Lille region were not familiar with that type of airplane. They opened fire as soon as the two American bombers came into range. It was only when the aircraft were directly overhead that they realized their mistake and ceased firing, but it was too late. Both airplanes were shot down, with only one crew member parachuting to safety amid a cloud of large-denomination notes.

*New pilots march past a Battle and an Oxford at Camp Borden, Canada.*

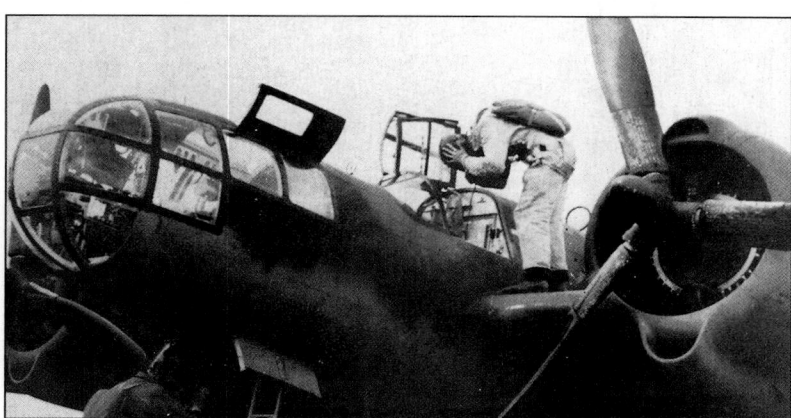

*A Martin 167-B3 bomber similar to the two mistakenly shot down near Lille.*

# RAF and Luftwaffe learn lessons at Dunkirk

## RAF provides cover for retreating troops

*British troops march through a smoking scene of devastation in Dunkirk.*

**Dunkirk, France, 1 June**
Thousands of British troops massed on the beaches here had ringside seats yesterday evening as Spitfires of 609 Squadron, RAF, engaged the Luftwaffe above their heads. At around 7.45pm German bombers came over Dunkirk at 15,000 feet, just as the RAF fighters arrived. British anti-aircraft fire was already thick as the fighter pilots quickly opened their throttles and climbed to over 20,000 feet. Flight Lieutenant F J Howell and his flight spotted a Ju 88, twisting and turning to get out of the fire. They dived toward it firing. Howell's six-second burst silenced the gunner, and his wingman set an engine alight; then they converted speed to height to join in the dogfight above. Just as they were closing in on the battle they saw a Heinkel He 111 below them trying to escape toward the Netherlands. They dived again, but anti-aircraft fire opened up once more, and they were on the receiving end of it for 30 seconds before the gunners recognized they were Spitfires. They poured the last of their ammunition into the Heinkel, setting one engine on fire, and then headed home across the Channel (→ Jun 4).

## Luftwaffe is beaten off for the first time

*Dover, England, June 4*
The evacuation of the British Army from Dunkirk, codenamed Operation Dynamo, is now complete. Winston Churchill sees "a victory inside this deliverance, gained by the air force".

This is true, but the Royal Air Force was aided in its task by both the over-confidence of Hermann Goering and the weather. For the first time the Luftwaffe's reputation for invincibility has been dented. Once the British were on the beaches, Goering saw an opportunity for his air force to destroy them by the use of air power *alone*. He persuaded Hitler to stop the advance of the tanks, but he had underestimated the effect of the weeks of intense operations on the Luftwaffe; then the weather closed in, making the task even harder. Goering had also not counted on disciplined intervention by RAF fighters, including for the first time Spitfires, which managed to beat off several raids. The result was that out of the nine days of the operation there were less than three when the Luftwaffe could intervene, enabling an armada of small boats to bring home a third of a million men from the beaches (→ Sep 26).

*An RAF Lockheed Hudson makes a reconnaissance flight near Dunkirk.*

## French bomber carries out first raid of the war on Berlin

*France, June 8*
French Lieutenant-Commander Henri Daillière has triumphantly landed his Farman NC.223-4 *Jules Verne* back on home soil this morning after making France's first bombing raid of the war against Berlin. With two other air crew he took off from Bordeaux-Mérignac, south-western France, at 3pm yesterday, planning to reach the German capital at about midnight. Under strict instructions not to hit the city center, he made several passes over Berlin, before unloading his bombs over the suburbs. Built as a long-range mailplane, this NC.223-4 is the only one actually to receive bombing equipment.

*Squadron B5 personnel make final external checks to the "Jules Verne".*

# RAF bombs Italian plants

*A Whitley returns from a gruelling ten-hour mission across the Alps.*

*Italy, August 14*
A total of 32 RAF Whitley heavy bombers last night struck at the heart of Italy's aircraft industry. The raiders crossed the Alps by moonlight and dropped explosives and incendiary bombs upon the aircraft works of the cities of Turin and Milan.

At Turin the main target was the huge Fiat facility, producer of the C.R.42 Falco and G.50 Freccia fighters. Crews are claiming many direct hits. The blaze acted as a beacon for a second wave of bombers. The Caproni works at Milan

Taliedo are also badly damaged. One raider was said to have dropped incendiaries along the ridge of a workshop roof. There were also claimed to have been direct hits on hangars adjoining the factory.

These assaults seem to have taken the Italians by surprise. Resistance was light, and flak was less than expected. One damaged bomber ditched near the English coast on the way back, but the crew was rescued. The RAF has been in action against Italian targets since June 11, a few hours after Italy joined the war (→ Nov 11).

# The fighting is over for France's air force

*France, June 25*
After having endured the Luftwaffe's *Blitzkrieg* for 47 harrowing days, French air force pilots have finally ceased fighting.

The Luftwaffe has total air superiority over France. On June 16, General Joseph Vuillemin, commander-in-chief of l'*Armée de l'Air* [the Air Army], ordered his last remaining aircraft to withdraw to North Africa to avoid further

losses. As from today, there is no longer an operational French air force in mainland France. Despite outdated fighter aircraft such as the Morane-Saulnier M.S.40b, French pilots have destroyed a total of 733 enemy airplanes. French losses are staggering. German attacks resulted in the destruction of 852 French aircraft. Of these, 504 were fighters, 211 were bombers and 137 were reconnaissance airplanes.

*Giving the Germans air superiority, the powerful Messerschmitt Bf 110.*

# US bomber makes totally blind flight

*Hampton, Va, April 6*
The ability of US Army Air Corps (USAAC) long-range heavy bombers to take off and land when visibility at an airfield is zero, and to fly to distant targets that are equally obscured, was successfully demonstrated tonight when commander of the 20th Bombardment Squadron Major Carl McDaniel landed his B-17 Flying Fortress here.

Major McDaniel, in a hooded cockpit with only instruments to guide him, took off from Mitchell Field, outside New York, and finally set the large, four-engined aircraft down at Langley Field. If he had been flying a combat mission, several tons of bombs could have been dropped "blind" onto an enemy target.

The trip was completed in 2 hours 2 minutes. In addition to the major, the B-17 had a co-pilot who was not under the hood, a navigator, and four other crewmen. One member of the squadron said the pioneering flight was accomplished "with all the smoothness of a routine flight".

# Single Junkers conquers British islands

*Relaxed soldiers watch the swastika hoisted over the Channel Islands.*

*Channel Islands, June 30*
Guernsey, second largest of the Channel Islands, the British islands in the English Channel near France, today surrendered to Germany without a shot being fired. In compliance with German orders a white cross had been painted on the small airport; a Junkers Ju 52/3m transport brought the delegation to

accept the surrender this morning.

Prime minister Winston Churchill accepted weeks ago that the islands could not be defended. All troops were withdrawn, and large numbers of the islanders also managed to escape to mainland Britain. Neighboring Jersey, the biggest of the Channel Islands, may be occupied tomorrow.

# War forces changes to routes of BOAC

*Durban, South Africa, June 19*
A Short "C" class Empire flying boat of the British Overseas Airways Corporation (BOAC) – the airline formed last year from Imperial Airways and British Airways – left Durban today to open a weekly service to Australia on the "Horseshoe Route". It will fly up the east coast of Africa and then via India and Burma. At about the same time a flying boat left Sydney to fly the route in reverse.

The route is a result of Axis control of most western European and Mediterranean airspace. This has cut off BOAC's routes from Britain to destinations south and east of Cairo (where today there are 16 BOAC flying boats), although it is hoped to open a route from England to Lisbon and Lagos, Nigeria, and thence across Africa. A few flights have already been made to Lisbon, including one by flying boat today, but tomorrow BOAC's staging post at Biscarosse, on France's Atlantic coast, will be evacuated. Future flights must be made non-stop (→ Mar 3, 1941).

# RAF defiant as Hitler orders massive invasion

The nerve center of British defenses.

**Berlin, July 16**
Hitler has ordered the invasion of England, but first the RAF has to be swept from the skies to give the Luftwaffe air superiority over the English Channel and the beaches where any landings would occur.

Hitler still appears to have some hopes for a negotiated peace with Britain, so he has ruled out strategic attacks on London. Instead the Luftwaffe will attack shipping, RAF airfields and radar stations in an attempt to neutralize Fighter Command on the ground. Luftwaffe intelligence chief Oberleutnant "Beppo" Schmidt believes that Fighter Command is down to just 400 airplanes, with only 200 a month being produced, making its destruction assured.

But for a supposedly doomed force, the RAF remains remarkably active. Photo-reconnaissance Spitfires and Lockheed Hudsons are flying hundreds of sorties over Europe from Norway to Spain. Efforts by Dornier bombers to hit a Channel convoy and to bomb mainland targets were disrupted by Hurricanes yesterday. So many British fighters were in the air – one estimate suggests 400 sorties, equating to the RAF's entire alleged fighter force – that doubt is being cast on Berlin's figures (→ Sep 16).

Luftwaffe airmen plotting victory.

## RAF Spitfires intercept German bombers

**Dover, England, July 29**
The Luftwaffe, intent on extending its current mastery of the sky to the English Channel, had quite a surprise today when a raid of 30 Ju 87 Stuka dive-bombers, escorted by 50 Bf 109 fighters, launched an attack on a British convoy in Dover harbor.

In Poland and France the Stuka gained an enviable reputation for destroying its targets, but against a modern, disciplined force such as the RAF, fighting on its home ground, it is proving considerably less effective, even vulnerable. Today's raid was detected by radio location long before it reached the port. Spitfires and Hurricanes were scrambled in plenty of time to intercept it before the German pilots could line up for an accurate bombing run, and the raid was split up in the fierce dogfight which ensued. Some of the Stukas made it to the harbor, where they made a spectacular display of waterspouts but did little damage.

At 5pm, 20 more Stukas went for Harwich, Essex; they were intercepted by 151 Squadron with similar results. The tally for the day: six Stukas shot down for the loss of three RAF machines. The Spitfires are proving more than a match for the Bf 109s, while the Hurricanes, which lack their performance, concentrate on the bombers.

## 'Eagle Day' air offensive is damp squib

Be like the eagle: German fighter pilots seem confident that they will win.

**London, August 13**
"Adler Tag [Eagle Day]", meant to be the beginning of the end of the RAF, has ended up with the Luftwaffe getting a bloody nose. Bad weather made Goering try to recall 74 Dornier Do 17s on their way to Eastchurch this morning, but only the Bf 110 fighter escorts got the message and went home, leaving the bombers to the mercy of 74 Squadron, RAF, which cut them to pieces. When radar detected a later raid, 609 Squadron Spitfires dived through the Bf 109 escorts to rip into Ju 87 Stukas. Some RAF airfields were damaged, but at the end of the day the RAF had lost 13 aircraft to the Luftwaffe's 45, and that is the figure which counts.

## First American airman with the RAF is killed

**London, August 17**
US Olympic champion William Fiske, who drove four-man bobsleds to victory in 1928 and 1932, died today of wounds received over Tangmere, Sussex, yesterday. He is the first American pilot with the RAF to be killed in action. His squadron of RAF Hurricane fighters engaged a mass formation of German bombers. The RAF said that although he was wounded, Fiske flew his damaged aircraft back to base. Fiske, educated in England, was married to the Countess of Warwick.

An RAF Spitfire climbing to attack a German Ju 88 bomber from behind.

# Luftwaffe switches its attack to London

*London, September 8*

In a dramatic change of strategy, the Luftwaffe has switched from bombing the RAF's airfields to attacking London. It is a surprising move for an air force trained and equipped to cooperate with land forces rather than to operate alone as a strategic air force.

Some 650 bombers, escorted by 1,000 fighters, hit London's docklands during the day and long into the night, dropping 650 tons of high-explosive bombs and thousands of incendiaries, killing 448 people. It was a frustrating day for Fighter Command, which had been deployed to meet attacks on its airfields rather than a stream of aircraft heading for London. British pilots shot down 41 German machines, but in the process lost 28 of their own, with 19 of the pilots missing. The loss of pilots is a blow. Aircraft can be replaced quickly; training pilots takes months.

The reason for changing policy is clear: revenge. On August 24 a German bomber accidentally dropped its load on London. The following night the RAF bombed Berlin, and other German cities have had the same treatment since. Hitler was outraged, and on September 4 he vowed to "erase" British cities. Today's raids may be the start of a concerted attack designed to bludgeon the British into submission.

*Londoners bed down for the night in Piccadilly underground station.*

# British airmen win vital breathing space

*London, September 16*

The switch from bombing the RAF to bombing London appears to have been a major blunder by Hitler and Goering. Yesterday they made their maximum effort. In response Fighter Command's entire strength was committed to the battle, and German aircrews were left in no doubt that the RAF had the upper hand, thanks mainly to the respite from attacks on its airfields.

German losses have mounted since September 7: 321 aircraft shot down to the RAF's 174. More importantly, the bombing has not disrupted Britain's war potential, and German hopes that Britain would sue for peace in the face of the *blitz* have proved wrong. In fact, British morale remains high, while the Luftwaffe has suffered a blow to its pride. The blame has been placed firmly on the shoulders of the Luftwaffe's fighter pilots for failing to protect the bombers, which have been the RAF's main target. But the fighter pilots argue that their orders to stay close to the bombers are wrong; they want to be free to maneuver as much as possible. With the RAF still intact, Hitler has ordered the postponement of the invasion plans.

# Tedium, tension and terror are all in a day's work for Britain's battling pilots

*"Scramble!": RAF Hurricane pilots race towards their waiting machines.*

*Southern England, August 20*

Prime minister Churchill today paid tribute to the RAF fighter-pilots "who, undaunted by odds, unwearied in their constant challenge and mortal danger, are turning the tide of the world war ... never in the field of human conflict was so much owed by so many to so few".

Life for the young pilots is a strange mixture of tranquility punctuated by short periods of intense activity and moments of sheer terror. In the evenings they can go to the pub for a pint; at night they sleep between clean sheets in their own beds; part of the summer's day could be spent playing cricket on the mown grass of the airfield, or lounging in chairs puffing pipes and swapping jokes. But all ears are cocked for the telephone and the order "Squadron scramble!".

Minutes later they could be diving on a German bomber, waiting to get really close before opening fire. Or they may suddenly feel the sickening impact of a German fighter's cannon shells tearing their aircraft apart. Many will survive being shot down to fight again the next day; a few will die, adding to the strain on the survivors.

*Pilots sleep whenever they can.*

*RAF crews are briefed for battle.*

# Air forces count cost of Battle of Britain

*Anti-aircraft guns blaze in London.*

**London, October 31**

The price of victory over the Luftwaffe has been high. Since July 10 the RAF has lost 915 fighters, with 415 pilots killed. But the Germans have lost nearly twice that number: 1,733 aircraft, mostly bombers with three or four crew members.

Claims on both sides are much higher than the actual figures shot down. This, coupled with the confusion of air battles, makes it difficult to be certain who the top-scoring RAF pilots are, and the RAF has always been reluctant to single out its "aces". But the top-scoring RAF pilot during the battle was most likely Czech air force pilot Josef Frantisek with 17 kills, who escaped first to Poland and then to Britain, where he served with 303 (Polish) Squadron. Next was Pilot Officer Eric Lock with 16, then with 15 Sergeant James "Ginger" Lacey, one of the non-commissioned pilots who make up 40 per cent of Fighter Command's strength. Top-scoring German pilot of the battle was Major Helmut Wick, with 56 victories.

*The wreckage of a Messerschmitt Bf 109E-4 shot down in Kent, England.*

# RAF airplane downs opponent by night

**Sussex, England, November 20**

Two German airmen are prisoners and two more are dead after their Ju 88 bomber crashed at East Wittering last night.

Their aircraft was severely damaged over Oxfordshire after a raid on Birmingham. The after-dark kill was made by a Bristol Beaufighter of 604 Squadron, RAF, specially equipped as a night-fighter with an on-board system called "Airborne Interception" (AI) which has been under development since 1936. As the Luftwaffe moves to night attacks to avoid the costly attention of Fighter Command during the day, so German losses have fallen. The action over Oxfordshire last night could spell the start of a way of redressing the balance in favor of the fighters once more by giving them badly needed "night vision". RAF pilot Flight Lieutenant John Cunningham was guided to within visual range of his quarry by Airborne Interception operator Sergeant J Phillipson, making them the first crew to achieve a kill using the system.

# The warlords who plot the air battles

*Dowding: Fighter Command chief.*

*Goering: head of the Luftwaffe.*

**London, September 14**

The Battle of Britain has been won. The instrument of victory was Fighter Command, but the architect was Air Chief Marshal Sir Hugh Dowding. Known irreverently as "Stuffy", he is a quiet, unassuming man of 58 with deep spiritual beliefs coupled with a scientific approach to warfare. He fought for the funds to make radio direction-finding a priority, giving the RAF the winning advantage.

Hermann Goering, 47, his opponent, is very different: flamboyant, with a taste for exotic uniforms and luxury trains from which to conduct operations, and a long-time member of the Nazi Party. In July he was made *Reichsmarschall* by Hitler for the Luftwaffe's performance to that date, but his lack of judgement since has contributed heavily to the British victory.

# German guided bomb could be a threat

**Germany, December 18**

A formidable new weapon, the Henschel Hs 293A guided bomb, made its first successful flight here today. If mass-produced, the bomb could have a serious effect on Allied shipping and other targets. The Hs 293A resembles a miniature airplane, with a wingspan of about 10 feet. The nose is formed by an SC 500 explosive warhead, and slung underneath is a rocket motor. Bombers such as the Do 217, He 177 and Fw 200C will carry at least two of the weapons. Seeing a target, the crew will drop a missile. The bomb-aimer will watch flares in the missile's tail and keep these aligned with the target, steering the bomb by a radio link controlling ailerons and elevators. The rocket motor enables the missile to be released from as low as 1,300 feet, though for long range (up to 11 miles) a higher altitude is needed. The bomb flies at 560-mph, so it is very difficult to shoot down (→ Oct 3, 1942).

*The Henschel Hs 293 guided bomb was tested for the first time on December 18. The weapon operates with a radio control system.*

# Italian navy is pounded

*The blistering attack on Taranto, as painted by artist Laurence Bagley.*

*Taranto, Italy, November 12*
In the early hours of this morning, 18 Fairey Swordfish of Britain's Fleet Air Arm returned to their aircraft carrier after an historic air assault. For the first time, airplanes – and slow old biplanes at that – have cripped an entire naval fleet.

Reconnaissance had shown the Italian navy ensconced at Taranto, protected by guns, submarine nets and barrage balloons. With five Swordfish from HMS *Eagle* on board to supplement her own Swordfish, the Royal Navy carrier HMS *Illustrious* sailed to within 170 miles of the port. At 8.35pm

the first 12 airplanes left the deck, followed an hour later by the first of eight more aircraft. Half of them carried torpedoes to strike at battleships in the outer harbor area; the rest had bombs to hit depots and ships in the inner harbor.

A few also carried flares, which they dropped just before 10pm to light the harbor. Then the attack began; two airplanes were lost, but the rest pressed home their surprise attack. The mission was a great success, with one battleship and two auxiliary vessels sunk and six battleships, cruisers and destroyers badly damaged (→ Nov 28, 1942).

# Radio systems lead Luftwaffe to target

*Coventry, England, November 14*
The Luftwaffe's raid on the city of Coventry tonight depended for its success on a secret weapon. This is *Knickebein* [crooked leg], a radio beam which guides the pilot to his target by tones heard in his headphones, enabling him to carry out a "blind-bombing" raid accurate to within one mile in 180.

The pilot flying a true course hears a steady sound in his headset. If he strays he is warned by Morse code. Near the target he crosses a second, intersecting beam and hears a signal to drop his bombs. Another, more elaborate system, *X-Gerät* [x-device], decides when to drop bombs and even takes over the task of releasing them.

# US Army parachute soldiers on show

*Fort Benning, Ga, August 29*
The US Army's experimental parachute unit, which started training in June, gave a demonstration today of how troops can jump from aircraft such as the B-18 bomber. Major William Lee, who was directed to form the unit, used an amusement ride from the New York World's Fair to train his men. Built by the Safe Parachute Company, the ride has a high tower with wire guides. A similar tower has been built here. The army abandoned the idea of parachute soldiers a decade ago, but with the success of German paratroops in Europe it seems the US Army has a place for them, and there are plans to form an operational unit (→ May 6, 1941).

# Coventry suffers a devastating air raid

*Coventry, England, November 14*
Coventry, a city in Warwickshire famous for its medieval buildings, but also important for its factories producing munitions, arms and engines for tanks and aircraft, has suffered a devastating air attack. It began at 7.20pm.

Led by 13 Heinkel He 111 pathfinders of KGr 100 Squadron, 449 bombers dropped incendiaries, parachute mines and high explosives to destroy or damage 60,000 of Coventry's estimated 75,000 buildings. The Gothic cathedral is a smoking shell. Of 568 dead, mainly civilians, 400 were burned beyond recognition and will be buried in a mass grave. Some died as the medieval center was annihilated by a horrific "firestorm", pulling victims into the inferno as the flames sucked in oxygen. The raid, which shows the terrible power of a concentrated aerial attack on a relatively small, densely-populated area, has spawned a new German verb, *koventrieren*, to "coventrate" a city from the air.

The city's defenses were ineffective. Forty anti-aircraft guns plus light guns and mobile batteries were backed up in 120 sorties by obsolete Gladiator biplanes and modern Beaufighters, but the Germans lost only one aircraft.

*German bombers, guided by special beams, wreaked havoc in Coventry.*

# North American builds fighter in 102 days

*Inglewood, Calif, November 30*
US airplane manufacturer North American Aviation (NAA) has just performed a remarkable feat. The Company has designed and built the NA-73X prototype fighter in just 102 days. Late delivery of the Allison V-1710 engine delayed the first flight for another 20 days. NAA had been asked by Britain to build the Curtiss P-40 or P-46 under license, but replied that it could design a better fighter. The US Army will receive two aircraft, designated XP-51, for evaluation. NAA hired Vance Breeze to make the first three test flights. Then NAA test pilot Paul Balfour took over. He selected an empty fuel tank, resulting in a forced landing.

*The damaged NA-73X prototype.*

Republic's P-43 Lancer fighter was developed for USAAF service but was also used by the Royal Australian Air Force and China; 272 were built.

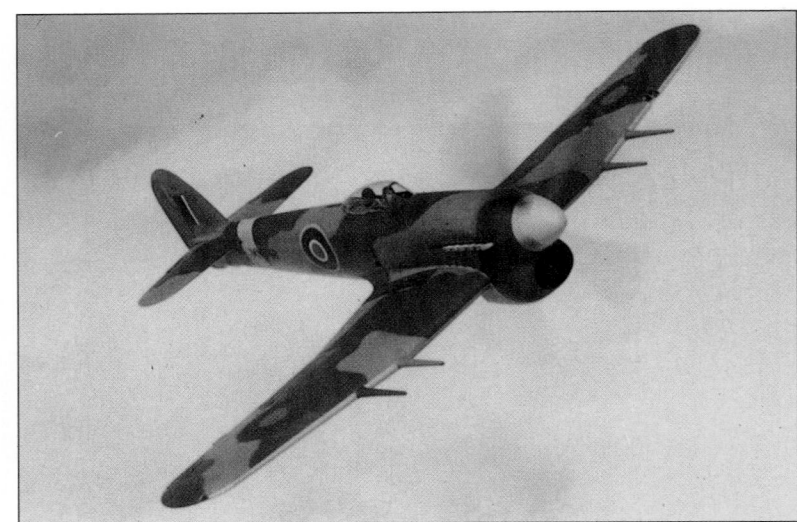

Originally designed as an interceptor, the Hawker Typhoon became a most successful fighter bomber for the Royal Air Force. Production totalled 3,330.

Arado's Ar 240, designed to use a remote-controlled gun-turret.

The Caproni-Campini N.1, said to be Italy's first jet aircraft. Its piston engine drove a fan which forced air through a jet pipe in which fuel was burned.

The Stearman (Boeing) Kaydet trainer was made in vast numbers.

The Yak-1, Yakovlev's first fighter, powered by a 1,100-hp Klimov engine, had a cannon and two guns.

Northrop's N-3PB patrol/bomber: 24 were produced for Norway.

Vought built 12,571 F4U Corsair carrier-based fighters in many variants from 1940 until 1952. The prototype, pictured, was the first 400-mph fighter.

Three Avia B-35 single-seat fighters led to the production version, B-135.

Yokosuka's D4Y Suisei Navy Type 2 carrier/reconnaissance-bomber.

Designers Mikoyan and Gurevich collaborated on the MiG-1 fighter.

Airspeed's AS.39 Fleet Shadower did not achieve production status.

A total of 9,816 North American B-25 Mitchells were built; the original design pictured here exceeded a USAAF specification for a medium bomber.

North American designed the NA-73 Mustang to meet a Royal Air Force requirement; later it was adopted by the USAAF as the P-51, 15,586 being built.

Aichi was given a requirement by the Japanese navy for a pilot-and-crew-trainer flying boat to train Kawanishi H8K1 crews. The result was the H9A.

Avio-Linee Italiane acquired three 14-passenger Fiat G.12C airliners.

This floatplane version of the Fiat C.R.42 fighter was not widely used.

Starting life as the Curtiss CW-20 36-passenger airliner, the C-46 Commando then achieved great success with the US Army Air Transport Command.

The US Navy and Marine Corps used 7,200 Curtiss SB2C Helldivers.

Of all-wood construction, the de Havilland D.H.98 Mosquito was designed as an unarmed bomber relying on its high speed to avoid interception.

Designed to a Deutsche Lufthansa transoceanic flying-boat requirement, Blohm und Voss's Bv 222 Wiking became a Luftwaffe transport aircraft.

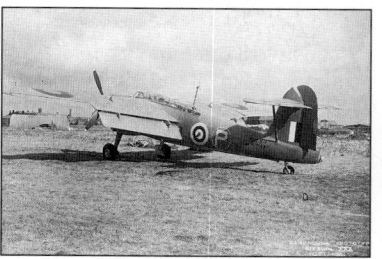

The Fairey Barracuda high-wing monoplane torpedo/dive-bomber.

Mikoyan-Gurevich I-250 fighter, virtually a piston/jet aircraft.

Macchi MC.202 Folgores were powered by the DB 601A engine.

Nakajima's Ki-44 Shoki interceptor: Japanese Army Type 2 Fighter.

The Fairey Fulmar naval fighter.

One of the least-known wartime aircraft was the highly capable North American XB-28, of which this was the second prototype.

Armstrong Whitworth Albemarles were used primarily as glider-tugs.

# 1941

623.85 mph
Germany
Heini Dittmar
Messerschmitt Me 163 A
Oct 2, 1941

8,038 miles
Italy
Tondi, Degasso, Vignoli
Savoia-Marchetti S.M.75
Aug 1, 1939

56,046ft
Italy
Mario Pezzi
Caproni 161bis
Oct 22, 1938

123,457lb
Germany
Dornier
Do X

1,650lb thrust
Germany
Walter HWK
R11

**Manchester, England, January 9**
The Avro Lancaster four-engined heavy bomber makes its first flight in the hands of test pilot 'Bill' Thorn; Avro managing director Roy H. Dobson, watching, exclaims: "Oh boy, oh boy, what an aeroplane!" (→ Mar 3, 1942).

**Berlin, February 6**
Hitler issues War Directive N° 23, which calls for the concentration of air attacks against the British arms industry, ports and shipping.

**Naples, Italy, February 8**
A fleet of Junkers Ju 52/3ms inaugurates the German Operation *Sonnenblume*, to transport General Rommel's troops to North Africa.

**Yorkshire, England, March 1**
The first Royal New Zealand Air Force fighter unit, 485 Squadron, is formed at Driffield.

**Fort Benning, Ga, March 6**
Sergeant Floyd Beard is killed when his parachute fails to open on a training jump; he is the US Army's first parachute fatality.

**Washington, DC, April 15**
Central Aircraft Manufacturing Company (CAMCO), organized by businessman William Pawley, signs a contract with the Chinese government to administer the projected American Volunteer Group (AVG) in China, to which President Roosevelt has given approval; the AVG, under Colonel Claire Chennault, will receive 100 Curtiss P-40 fighters and US service pilots (→ Dec 20).

**London, April 16**
Last night, in the city's heaviest German raid so far, 500 bombers dropped 890 tons of high explosive and 151,230 incendiaries.

**Washington, DC, April 28**
Colonel Charles Lindbergh resigns from the US Army Air Corps Reserve, claiming his isolationist views have been misinterpreted as disloyalty.

**Greece, May 2**
The evacuation of British forces after the German conquest of Greece is completed; the RAF has lost 151 airplanes in this arena since April 6 (→ Jun 1).

**Stratford, Connecticut, May 6**
Igor Sikorsky pilots the Sikorsky VS-300 helicopter on a flight of 1 hour 32 minutes 26 seconds, a world endurance record for a helicopter.

**USA, May 6**
The prototype of the Republic P-47B Thunderbolt fighter makes its first flight.

**Scotland, May 10**
Hitler's deputy, Rudolf Hess, lands by parachute near Glasgow after flying a Messerschmitt Bf 110 from the Messerschmitt works at Augsburg; in custody, he claims he has come on a peace mission.

**Iraq, May 18**
Arab troops loyal to Britain relieve RAF Habbaniyah which, defended by outdated training aircraft, has been besieged by the pro-German forces of General Rashid Ali and attacked by Bf 110s and He IIIs.→

**USA and Britain, May 29**
The US Army Air Corps (USAAC) Ferrying Command is formed to fly US airplanes to Britain; the British Ministry of Aircraft Production has set up an Atlantic Ferry Organization this month to fly war material from the US and to return USAAC ferry crews (→ Jun 20).

**Baghdad, May 30**
General Rashid Ali flees to Iran after Axis aid for his anti-British rebellion fails to materialize.

**Washington, DC, June 16**
National Airport opens.

**Washington, DC, June 20**
The US Army Air Corps is renamed the United States Army Air Forces (USAAF), under the command of Major-General Henry H "Hap" Arnold.

**London, July 9**
The air staff issues a directive to RAF Bomber Command to commit bombers to "dislocating the German transportation system and to destroying the morale of the civilian population" (→ Nov 9).

**Paris, July 28**
Secretary of state for aviation in the Vichy government General Bergeret signs an agreement for the construction in France of 2,275 airplanes for Germany.

**California, July**
The first successful rocket-assisted take-off in the USA was made this month at March Field by Lieutenant H A Boushey in an Ercoupe equipped with rockets.

**Romania, August 1**
The Soviet air force puts its "parasite" I-16SPB dive-bombers into operation for the first time during an attack on Constanza; the machines are carried under the wings of TB-3 heavy bombers and released near the target.

**Pisa, Italy, August 7**
The Duce's son, Bruno Mussolini, is killed while flying a Piaggio P.108 heavy bomber near here.

**Washington, DC, August 18**
President Roosevelt announces that Pan Am has agreed to ferry lend-lease US warplanes to British bases in the Middle East; this operation will involve devising an airway across Africa in a short time.

**Baltic Sea, September 14**
The huge Messerschmitt 321 Gigant troop-carrying glider sees service for the first time during the German attack on Saaremaa island.

**France, September 20**
The de Havilland D.H.98 Mosquito I photo-reconnaissance airplane makes its operational début with the RAF on a mission from England to Brest and Bordeaux to photograph harbor installations (→ Sep 25, 1942).

**Kronstadt, USSR, September 23**
German Junkers Ju 87 Stuka dive-bombers attack the Soviet Baltic fleet; Leutnant Hans-Ulrich Rudel sinks the battleship *Marat*.

**Britain, September 24**
BOAC takes over the North Atlantic air ferry service from the Atlantic Ferry Organization, which started in May (→ Oct 12).

**Peenemünde, Germany, October 2**
The Messerschmitt Me 163A rocket-powered fighter is launched at 13,000 feet and piloted by Heini Dittmar to a world record speed of 623.85mph (→ Jul 18, 1942).

**Southampton, England, October 12**
BOAC launches a commercial flying-boat service from England to Cairo via Lisbon, Gibraltar and Malta.

**Washington, DC, December 13**
President Roosevelt places all civil aviation under the control of the US War Department.

**Philippines, December 18**
Lieutenant "Buzz" Wagner of the US Army Air Forces becomes the first US air ace of the war when he shoots down his fifth Japanese airplane.

**Kunming, China, December 20**
US pilots of Claire Chennault's American Volunteer Group, flying Curtiss P-40s, down three Japanese Kawasaki Ki-48 bombers in their first engagement; another Ki-48 is reported shot down en route to Hanoi, while the AVG loses one aircraft when it runs out of fuel and is forced to crash-land (→ Jan 3, 1942).

**Japan, December**
The prototype Kawasaki Ki-61 Hien fighter, fitted with a liquid-cooled engine, makes its first flight.

*A recruiting poster for Britain's Women's Auxiliary Air Force (WAAF), in which women carry out essential non-combatant duties.* ▶

# Amy Johnson dies in a mysterious way

*A Portrait of Amy Johnson in 1938.*

*London, January 5*
Britain was shocked today by the loss of its great air heroine, Amy Johnson. She seems to have made an error of judgement in taking off while Britain was covered in dense cloud. Flying a twin-engined Airspeed Oxford, she ran out of fuel over the Thames estuary. She bailed out, but a frantic attempt to save her from the freezing waters failed, costing the life of a Royal Navy skipper who dived in after her.

Six months ago, Johnson joined Britain's Air Transport Auxiliary (ATA), which ferries airplanes to RAF bases throughout the country, and from the US and Canada. Her former husband Jim Mollison is also an ATA pilot.

# Millionth passenger for American Airlines

*Washington, DC, March 20*
The US Civil Aeronautics Board (CAB) said today that traveling by air is safer than ever. CAB points to American Airlines, established five years ago, which recently flew its one millionth passenger without a fatal accident. The safety of air travel is attributed to the use of better aircraft and engines, typified by the widely flown Douglas DC-3, and to the flying aids now available to pilots. These range from weather information and advanced navigation instruments to radio guidance equipment (→ Dec 13).

# Mammoth cargo glider Gigant lifts off

*Leipheim, Germany, February 25*
One of the Luftwaffe's new secret weapons was flown today for the first time. Test pilot Karl Baur took Messerschmitt's new Me 321 glider, dubbed the Gigant [Giant], up for 22 minutes. He found the controls very heavy.

The Gigant can take a staggering 22 tons of cargo. Its original specification was for a glider to carry the Wehrmacht PzKW. IV medium tank with crew, fuel and ammunition. It will also carry an 88-mm gun and tractor or up to 120 troops.

The fuselage is made of wooden hoops and welded steel tubing with fabric stretched over to form a cavernous, whale-like hull entered through front "clam-shell" doors. The wings, which span 180 feet, are also mainly of wood. The Gigant is towed by one Ju 290 transport or three Bf 110 fighters (→ Sep 14).

*The giant Messerschmitt Me 321 glider can move tanks, men, and supplies.*

# US 'Lend-Lease' will boost RAF air power

*The production line of trainers at North American's factory in Los Angeles.*

*Washington, DC, March 27*
The US Congress today promised $7 billion to help Britain buy 16,000 military aircraft from US makers. The funds have been pledged following the passage of the Lend-Lease Act, which became law on March 12, under which Britain and its allies are relieved, for the time being, of the burden of paying for US war material. This will enable Britain to pay for its orders with US firms, which include French orders which it took over when France fell.

Lend-lease will allow Britain to take full advantage of the more liberal war exports policy adopted by the US last year, which authorizes the sale to foreign states of certain modern aircraft, as soon as the US Army Air Corps takes delivery of a superior type.

# BOAC starts secret flights to Stockholm

*Flying supplies in secret: the fast Lockheed 14 Super Electra.*

*Scotland, March 2*
Using night for cover, the British Overseas Airways Corporation has restarted regular flights to Stockholm to help the war effort. Flights to the capital of neutral Sweden were halted after Germany invaded Denmark and Norway.

The service employs a single Lockheed 14, which was flown from Poland to Scotland in 1939 when the Germans invaded. Civil registered and with a civilian crew, the unarmed airliner carries not only diplomats, agents and other VIPs, but also Swedish-made ball bearings that are vital to Britain's armaments industry. The plane flies over the Skagerrak, the channel between Norway and Denmark. The last two letters of its civil registration, G-AGBG, have spawned the nickname "Bashful Gertie, the terror of the Skagerrak" (→ Sep 24).

# The Halifax has an unlucky first mission

*Bomber Command has begun operating its first Halifax heavy bombers.*

*Linton-on-Ouse, England, May 11*
The crews of RAF Bomber Command's 35 Squadron who took part in last night's operation are not pleased with themselves this morning, after their return to their Yorkshire base.

The first mission using the new four-engined Handley Page Halifax heavy bomber was far from a success. They had been ordered to bomb the harbor at Le Havre, northern France. Since it was a short flight, each airplane took off with 12,980 lb of bombs. However, one aircraft failed to find either Le Havre or its secondary target, Boulogne, so it dropped its bombs on Dieppe. A second Halifax also failed to find Le Havre and dropped its bombs in the English Channel on its way back. A third bomber's mission was successful, but it was shot down by an RAF fighter, which failed to recognize the new bomber, on the return flight. Two crewmen were, however, able to parachute to safety.

# Frank Whittle's jet engine flies at last

*Lincolnshire, England, May 15*
Today, seven years later than it might have done, Britain has finally put a jet airplane into the sky. Chief test pilot of Gloster Aircraft Gerry Sayer flew the E.28/39 at Cranwell for 17 minutes.

The observers on the airfield included RAF officer and former test pilot Frank Whittle, who invented the revolutionary turbojet engine in 1929. He could get no one interested then, and he only managed to build an engine and start testing in 1937. The E.28/39 has an improved form of the 1937 engine, which gives a thrust of about 1,000 pounds. The airplane is designed to carry, in theory, four machine guns, but is only a test-bed. Gloster is designing a larger production airplane, powered by two Whittle engines, that will be able to carry six 20mm cannon (→ Apr 21, 1942).

*The compact little Gloster E.28/39, Britain's first jet-powered airplane.*

# Flying Fortresses head for Hawaii base

*The Boeing B-17 Fortress gives the Army Air Corps a strategic capability.*

*Hamilton Field, Calif, May 13*
Twenty-one US Army Air Corps (USAAC) B-17D Flying Fortress heavy bombers left here today for Hickam Field, Hawaii. This is the third action taken this year to bolster US strength in Hawaii. In February, 31 Curtiss P-36 Hawk planes were sent there aboard the carrier USS *Enterprise*, and 55 Curtiss P-40 Warhawks followed in April. Whether or not to send the B-17s, which have to be flown 2,400 miles to Hawaii, has been hotly debated. Fear of the flight's failure – it has never been done before – was overcome as the need to provide a strong force in the Pacific appeared more urgent.

The US Navy has placed ships at 500-mile intervals along the route to aid any aircraft in trouble, while commercial radio stations in San Francisco and Honolulu are transmitting homing signals for the flight. Fifteen of the airmen will remain in Hawaii to train the crews who will fly the B-17s (→ Aug 1).

# B-24 Liberators flown across the Atlantic

*England, May 4*
Captain Donald Bennett of the RAF has just flown across the Atlantic to deliver the first B-24 Liberator long-range bomber to Britain's Coastal Command.

Captain Bennett flew the heavy machine, manufactured by Consolidated Aircraft, at an average speed of 280mph and an altitude of 33,000 feet. The Liberator, a bomber which can also be used for maritime reconnaissance patrols and anti-submarine warfare missions, is one of the 164 B-24s ordered by the British government. The RAF has, however, decided to use its Liberators, which have long range, as heavy transport aircraft rather than in a combat role. Since the airplane first flew, on December 29 1939, the US Army Air Corps (USAAC) has ordered 43 of them and the French government 120.

*Coastal Command's B-24 Liberator is a long-range, four-engined bomber.*

## Navy Swordfish seal fate of 'Bismarck'

*A Fairey Swordfish drops a torpedo.*

*North Atlantic, May 27*
Ensign Leonard B.Smith, US Navy, had no idea that his routine mission, yesterday, would lead to the sinking of the *Bismarck*.

His orders were to train pilots of Catalina seaplanes. Flying a PBY-5 of 209 Squadron, and accompanied by Dennis Briggs of the RAF, he took off before noon. As they were flying just above sea level, Smith spotted the German battleship *Bismarck* and Briggs radioed for assistance. It was one of 14 Fleet Air Arm Fairey Swordfish biplanes from the Royal Navy carrier HMS *Ark Royal* which delivered the fatal blows.

One of two torpedo hits put the rudders out of action. This left the *Bismarck* circling helplessly as British ships closed in. Today, at 10.36am, the *Bismarck* sank; she had been completely destroyed by RN warships (→ Nov 30).

# Crete falls to airborne Nazi invasion

*Crete, June 1*
Allied troops have abandoned the key strategic Mediterranean island of Crete less than two weeks after the Germans launched the first airborne invasion in military history. Although German losses are high, they have succeeded in capturing the island by air power alone.

The first stage of Germany's Operation *Merkur* was to bomb RAF bases on Crete; by May 19 the six RAF planes which survived the attacks had been withdrawn to Egypt. The next day waves of German fighters and bombers attacked Crete's defenses from bases in Greece, to be followed by 493 Junkers Ju 52 transport planes and 80 DFS gliders. They were carrying no fewer than 15,750 paratroopers and airborne troops.

Immediate targets for the Germans were Maleme and Heraklion airfields. The Allied troops, mostly Australians and New Zealanders, fought fiercely, particularly around Maleme, but German reinforce-

*German paratroops descend to Crete while their Ju 52/3m transport crashes.*

ments flown in on May 22 proved decisive. By May 29 the Allied evacuation had begun. Germany has, however, paid a heavy price for victory in this first-ever airborne invasion. An estimated 3,600 troops and 320 Luftwaffe crew have died. Half the transport aircraft have been destroyed, along with large numbers of gliders. Crack parachute division Fliegerkorps XI has been almost eliminated.

# World's first twin-engined jet airplane makes inaugural flight

*Marienehe, Germany, April 2*
The world's first twin-jet airplane has flown. Fritz Schäfer flew the Heinkel He 280V-1 fighter prototype once round the airfield at a maximum height of 900 feet, because only a little fuel was carried. Powered by two Heinkel-Hirth HeS 8A 1,320-pound thrust turbojets, the jet flew with engine cowlings removed and undercarriage down. It has a compressed-air ejection seat (→ Oct 2).

*The jet engines are slung underneath each wing of the Heinkel He 280V-1.*

# Allies exempted from US fuel export ban

*Washington, DC, August 1*
In the latest of a series of initiatives designed to back Britain's war effort, President Roosevelt today banned the export of aviation fuel from the US to all places except Britain and other unoccupied countries which are resisting the Nazis.

This decision will be a particularly harsh blow to the Japanese, whose continuing war against China is a great drain on their resources. It will do nothing to improve relations between the US and Japan at a time of rising tension

between the two countries. The ban comes in the wake of this year's Lend-Lease Act, signed into law on March 12 and backed with $7 billion funding by Congress on March 27 [*see story on page 392*]. Such moves, which place American sympathies fairly unequivocally behind the British cause, are meeting with some opposition from US isolationists. They contend that the measures compromise US neutrality and make it harder for the US to avoid being dragged into the war against its will (→ Dec 7).

**A British badge for those who have given up pots and pans for Spitfires.**

# Soviet air force reels under massive German attack

*USSR, June 23*
Luftwaffe aircraft have delivered what may be a knock-out blow to the Soviet air force after just one day of war on Germany's eastern front. Operation Barbarossa, the attack against Germany's former ally, began at 3.15am yesterday. By noon around 1,200 Soviet airplanes had been destroyed, most on the ground before they could even get into combat.

Over three million men were hurled by Hitler into an attack along an 1,800-mile front. Aircrews flying Heinkel He 111, Junkers Ju 88 and Dornier Do 17 bombers immediately attacked 66 Soviet airfields. They flew in flights of three planes to a target and used fragmentation bombs to cause maximum damage. In many cases the unsuspecting Soviets had left their planes lined up on the ground,

wide open to attack. Following up the surprise attack by the bombers came Stukas and Messerschmitts, attacking airfield targets with greater precision.

The few Soviet aircraft which got into the air were outgunned. The Polikarpov I-15 and I-16 fighters were no match for the Messerschmitt Bf 109s. Relative freedom of the air enabled the Luftwaffe to bomb and strafe targets almost at will ahead of the advancing land forces. Mines were also dropped in the Black and Baltic Seas, while five Soviet cities came under sustained bombardment: Kovno, Minsk, Rovno, Odessa and Sevastopol.

After a day's fighting the Soviet air force had lost over 1,800 planes – 80 per cent of them on the ground. German losses, by contrast, are reported to be no more than 35 aircraft (→ Jan 24, 1942).

*Soviet SB-2 bombers hit by the pre-emptive strike of Operation Barbarossa.*

## Cochran recruits women transport pilots

*Trainee women pilots are given a technical briefing on engine maintenance.*

*USA, August 31*
Famous American speed flyer Jacqueline Cochran was today hired on a special mission to recruit US women pilots to fly delivery missions for the British government. The volunteer flyers are to join the Air Transport Auxiliary (ATA) in Britain to fly airplanes and war equipment from factories to operational units.

Cochran has been trying for some months to set up a similar scheme to the ATA in the USA, in

order to take advantage of the skill and commitment of her country's 650 qualified women pilots. But her attempts to interest the US Army Air Force's (USAAF) hierarchy met with little enthusiasm. Nevertheless, she did achieve a first, limited, success at the end of last month when USAAF chief General Henry H "Hap" Arnold agreed to take on 50 of the most experienced women pilots to fly on a trial basis for USAAF Ferrying Command, which was set up in May.

## French pilots begin operations from Britain

*Britain, November 15*
Although a few French pilots fought alongside Britons in the Battle of Britain, along with Poles, Czechs, Americans and Canadians, there was no specifically French squadron – until today. The Allied and Free French conquests of the Vichy French territories of Syria and the Lebanon last summer made it possible to form a French bomber group, Lorraine, and fighter group, Alsace, in the Middle East. Today, despite the shortage of aircraft and mechanics, two new Free French

units, Paris and Versailles Squadrons, became airborne in Britain.

Together they make up the Ile de France Group under Colonel Martial Valin, a follower of General Charles de Gaulle who in September announced the formation of a London-based French government in exile. Valin is the man behind the creation of the Forces Aériennes Françaises Libres [Free French Air Forces]. His squadrons, flying Blenheims and Hurricanes, hope to build up their own ground support from the French naval air arm.

*The crew of a Bristol Blenheim bomber of the Free French Lorraine Group.*

# RAF strikes a blow against the U-boats

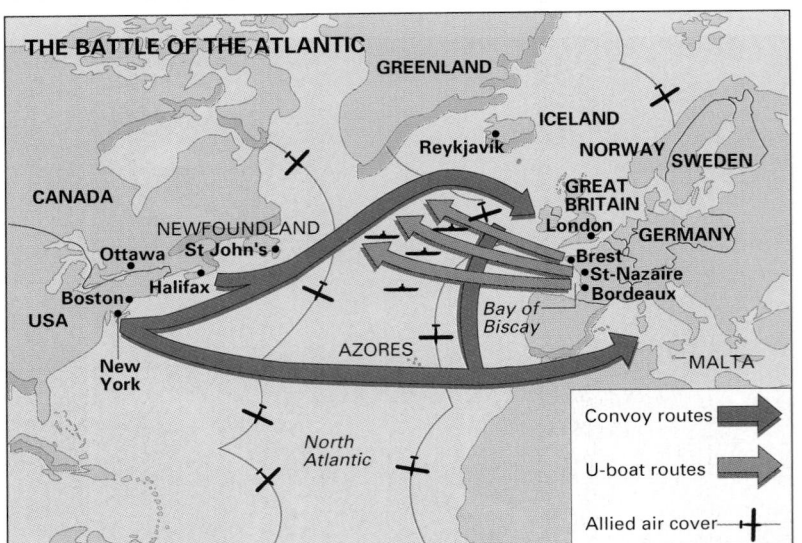

THE BATTLE OF THE ATLANTIC

GREENLAND

ICELAND

Reykjavik

NORWAY
SWEDEN

GREAT
BRITAIN

CANADA

NEWFOUNDLAND

Ottawa    St John's

London    GERMANY

Brest

Halifax    St-Nazaire

Boston    Bordeaux

USA    Bay of
Biscay

New
York    AZORES

North
Atlantic    MALTA

Convoy routes

U-boat routes

Allied air cover

**Bay of Biscay, November 30**
RAF Coastal Command has today achieved its first unaided sinking of a U-boat. The attack on *U206*, as it headed through the Bay of Biscay, owes its success to code-breakers and a new air-to-surface (ASV) radio direction-finding system. An Armstrong Whitworth Whitley bomber of 502 Squadron was sent to look for the U-boat after British code-breakers had intercepted a signal from the submarine. The aircrew located the U-boat at a distance of 5 miles and sank it with depth charges.

# Aircraft are now equipped with radar

**USA, July 18**
It is reported that some RAF airplanes can now rely on the new air-to-surface (ASV) Mark I radar system to help them find their targets. The radar operator watches a screen which shows the echo made when a very high frequency pulse bounces off a target. The system is particularly efficient at sea since there are no natural obstacles to give false echoes. The ASV, designed by British engineers and in operation since early 1940, has been adapted for use by night-fighters and coastal surveillance airplanes. It is not used when flying over Germany to avoid it falling into enemy hands. The more efficient Mark III system should be operational soon.

*A Bristol Beaufighter equipped with Mk IV radar for night combat missions.*

# US volunteers show British their worth

**Britain, December 2**
Since they first saw combat here on July 2, the pilots of 71, 121 and 133 Squadrons of the RAF – the American-manned "Eagle Squadrons" – have become a vital part of Britain's air defense. The men who are risking their lives for the British cause by joining the RAF are also risking the loss of their citizenship; this is one of the potential penalties, under US law, for fighting for another nation.

Many officers of Fighter Command at first felt that the Americans were too undisciplined to be effective warplane pilots. That opinion is seldom heard any more, and a look at their accomplishments tells why. In October and November, 71 Squadron, the first US unit to go into action, led all RAF squadrons in combat ratings and numbers of enemy planes destroyed. Pilot officers Bill Dunn and Gus Daymond became the first and second American aces of the war by downing five German planes each. Three Americans, Daymond, Pete Peterson and Red McColpin, have earned the Distinguished Flying Cross (→ Sep 29, 1942).

*American "Eagle Squadron" pilots pose with one of their Hurricane fighters.*

# RAF planes caught by German 'boxes'

**London, November 9**
Heavy losses in raids on Germany last night have prompted a review by the RAF of its current bombing strategy. A total of 380 airplanes attacked Berlin, Cologne, Mannheim and targets in the industrial area of the Ruhr. Of these, 34 were lost in the raids. Germany is using a defense system known to the British as the Kammhuber Line with great effectiveness. It involves a series of ground-controlled interception "boxes" along the flight paths used most frequently by the Allied bombers. Within each "box" a German night-fighter patrols, waiting to attack (→ Feb 14, 1942).

THERE ARE NO DISTANT LANDS
...BY FLYING CLIPPER

ALASKA

HAWAII
ORIENT

EUROPE

AUSTRALASIA    MEXICO · CENTRAL
AMERICA    WEST INDIES    SOUTH AMERICA

PAN AMERICAN AIRWAYS SYSTEM

**Shrinking the world: Pan Am claims that the Clipper flying-boat compresses long distances.**

# Surprise Japanese air attack brings US into war

*Japanese A6Ms and B5Ns on a carrier, ready for the attack on Pearl Harbor.*

*Looking on in a state of shock after the Japanese assault on Hickam Field.*

## Americans watch as fleet goes up in smoke

*Pearl Harbor, Hawaii, December 7*
Smoke from burning military installations obscures the sunset this evening after this morning's attack by Japanese aircraft on Pearl Harbor. The surprise assault has virtually destroyed all the battleships of the US Pacific Fleet and has severely hit the US Army Air Forces (USAAF) in Hawaii. The US has one compensation: the Japanese failed to hit its aircraft carriers, which were away on maneuvers.

In all, 365 fighters, bombers and torpedo aircraft from six Japanese aircraft carriers sank five battleships, severely damaged three others, and sank or damaged ten other warships or auxiliaries in Pearl Harbor. US dead are reported to stand at 2,403 sailors, soldiers and airmen killed. Japanese losses are put at 100 men, 28 aircraft and five midget submarines. Of 394 US military aircraft here, 188 were destroyed and 159 damaged.

Boeing B-17D bombers, which were sent here to thwart a naval attack, and Curtiss P-40 Warhawk pursuit planes, which were supposed to stop an air assault, were mostly caught on the ground. Four pilots got their P-40s airborne and shot down seven Zero fighters; four were downed by Lieutenant George Welch (→ Feb 21, 1942).

## US air force will be tough match for Japan

*Washington, DC, December 8*
The US declared war on Japan today, and Tokyo, supreme in yesterday's attack on Pearl Harbor, now faces the real might of vastly superior US air power. Japan's army and navy have about 2,700 aircraft and 6,000 pilots. Training programs will provide 3,000 pilots per year, while aircraft production stands at 5,000 per year. By comparison, this year the US trained 11,000 pilots and built more than 19,445 military aircraft, and it aims to increase production threefold.

The latest US airplanes are considered superior to the majority of Japanese. Japan has no long-range, four-engined heavy bombers; the US has both the B-17 and the B-24. Other Japanese airplanes, greatly influenced by the designs of Japan's German allies but of inferior quality, sacrifice crew-safety features such as self-sealing fuel tanks and armor.

Japanese aircraft are used as an adjunct to overall ground and sea operations without any thought to strategic deployment, a basic tenet of the US Army Air Forces (USAAF). In fact, the biggest challenge for the US as the war progresses will be crossing the vast expanse of the Pacific to bring its air power to bear on Japan.

## B-17s hit back at ships in the Philippines

*Philippines, December 10*
US Army Air Forces B-17 bombers and P-40 and P-35 fighters today attacked Japanese ships landing troops and supplies on the beaches at Vigan on the north-west coast of Luzon, the largest island in the Philippines. One Japanese transport was sunk; two were damaged.

A significant event of the day was the attack by a single B-17 piloted by Captain Colin Kelly, who dropped three 600-pound bombs on the flagship of the Japanese Third Fleet, the heavy cruiser *Ashigara*. The cruiser was last seen stopped in the water with black smoke pouring from her. As Kelly prepared to land at Clark Field, the B-17 was attacked by enemy fighters. With his plane in flames and his left rear-gunner dead, Kelly ordered the surviving crew to bail out while he stayed at the controls. They survived, but Kelly perished when the airplane exploded.

## US Far East air strength dealt bitter blow

*Philippines, December 13*
Less than a week after the attack on Pearl Harbor, Japanese bombers arrived over Clark, Ibu and Nicholls airfields near Manila and, just as their comrades had in Hawaii, found US warplanes parked close together in neat rows, providing a perfect target.

A year of concentrated effort to build a formidable air arm for US commander in the Philippines General Douglas MacArthur was ne-gated in minutes. The US Army Air Forces here had grown from a handful of antiquated P-26, B-10, and B-18 aircraft to an armada of 300 planes including P-35s and the latest P-40s and B-17s. The attack, which has wrecked half the US Far East Air Force, claimed more than half the 35 B-17s as well as 56 of 72 P-40s. The question remaining to be answered is: after Pearl Harbor, why was no action taken to disperse these aircraft?

The Gotha Go 242 transport glider served with six special squadrons.

Affectionately known as "the Jug", Republic's P-47 fighter first flew as the XP-47B on May 6, 1941. By the time production ended 15,683 had been built.

A captured Nakajima B6N2 torpedo-bomber is tested in the US.

A Hawker Hurricane is rocket-launched from a merchant ship to prove the system as a means of convoy defense. The pilot later had to ditch and pray.

The rocket-boosted Sukhoi Su-7 was a high-altitude interceptor.

The Brewster SB2A Buccaneer (RAF Bermuda) was a failure.

Built as a bomber, the Douglas XB-19 was relegated to transporting.

Designed for French and British requirements: Martin's Baltimore.

In its prototype form, the Avro Lancaster heavy bomber had triple fins and no dorsal or ventral turrets. The central fin was deleted on production models.

The Vultee Vengeance dive-bomber was initially ordered by the British, but the US Army also had it, though it used the type mostly for target-towing.

Consolidated's XTBU-1 Sea Wolf torpedo-bomber never saw action.

The first flight of the Heinkel He 280, the first turbojet fighter.

Junkers' Ju 288 advanced medium bomber first flew in January 1941.

Messerschmitt's enormous Me 321 Gigant glider spanned 180ft 5in.

A flying observation post: the Fane T.1/40 was not ordered in quantity.

The Kawanishi H8K was Japan's equivalent of the Short Sunderland.

Britain's first jet aircraft was the Gloster (Whittle) E.28/39, which made its maiden flight on May 15, 1941. Two subsequently did much test flying.

Begun as a private venture, the Junkers Ju 188 was distinguished by its pointed wing-tips. It served in the bomber, torpedo-bomber and reconnaissance roles.

Nakajima's J1N1 Gekko reconnaissance aircraft: the first prototype.

Kawasaki's Ki-61 Hien fighter featured a V-12 liquid-cooled engine.

One of the Second World War's greatest torpedo-bombers: the Grumman TBF Avenger became operational on June 4, 1942, in the Battle of Midway.

Messerschmitt's Me 163B rocket-propelled interceptor caused consternation among US bomber crews, but was just as dangerous to those who flew it.

Junkers' Ju 252: almost the last of the company's trimotor transports.

Airspeed's AS.45 Cambridge trainer proved to be far from ideal for the task, and the two machines built did little flying once the test program was ended.

The Curtiss XP-60 was basically an improved P-40. It was not ordered.

# 1942

623.85mph
Germany
Heini Dittmar
Messerschmitt Me 163A
Oct 2, 1941

8,038 miles
Italy
Tondi, Degasso, Vignoli
Savoia-Marchetti S.M.75
Aug 1, 1939

56,046ft
Italy
Mario Pezzi
Caproni 161bis
Oct 22, 1938

140,000lb
USA
Boeing
XB-29 Superfortress

2,006lb thrust
Germany
Junkers Motoren
Jumo 004 B

**Washington, DC, January 10**
The US Army announces the delivery of its first troop-transport gliders.

**Pacific Ocean, January 11**
In the first Japanese use of airborne troops, the airfield at Menado, Celebes islands, is seized from its Dutch defenders.

**Darwin, Australia, February 19**
Japanese bombers attack shipping in the harbor here, forcing Australians into an awareness of their country's vulnerability to long-range raids.

**Buckinghamshire, England, Feb 22**
Air Marshal Arthur Harris takes over as commander-in-chief of RAF Bomber Command at its HQ near High Wycombe (→ May 4).

**London, February 23**
Brigadier-General Ira Eaker takes charge of the US Eighth Army Air Force Bomber Command, which is to be based in Britain (→ Jun 18).

**Newfoundland, March 1**
Ensign William Tepuni, US Naval Reserve, becomes the first US pilot of the war to destroy a German submarine when he hits the *U656* in the Cape Race area.

**North Sea, March 3**
The Avro Lancaster heavy bomber makes its operational début in a mine-laying mission off Heligoland with 44 Squadron, RAF (→ Oct 17).

**Kasumigaura, Japan, March 20**
The Mitsubishi J2M1 Raiden naval fighter makes its first flight.

**France, March 20**
The prototype of the six-engined Potez-CAMS 160 seaplane flies for the first time.

**Yorkshire, England, March 27**
The General Aircraft Hamilcar glider makes its first flight; this remarkable, all-wooden transport weighs 18,000 pounds and is capable of carrying 17,500 pounds of troops and materials.

**Germany, March 29**
After having tested the Gee system over the city of Cologne during a night mission on March 13 and 14, Bomber Command sends 234 bombers over Lübeck. They are guided by 10 equipped with the Gee system. The raid is successful.

**Italy, April 19**
The Macchi C.205 fighter prototype makes its first flight; it is powered by a 1,250hp Fiat R.A. 1050 RC.58 Tifone engine, and is capable of a speed of 399mph.

**Hertfordshire, England, April 21**
The second experimental Gloster E.28/39 jet airplane is demonstrated to prime minister Winston Churchill and senior members of the air staff; Frank Whittle, inventor of the jet engine, is not invited (→ Mar 5, 1943).

**USSR, May 1**
Squadron N° 588 of the Soviet air force, an all-woman night-bombing unit equipped with Polikarpov Po-2 biplanes, is formed.

**Canada, May 16**
Ten small airlines merge to form Canadian Pacific Airlines.

**Connecticut, May 18**
The Sikorsky XR-4 experimental military helicopter, built to a US Army Air Forces specification, leaves for official tests at Wright Field, Dayton, Ohio (→ May 7, 1943).

**USA, May 26**
The Northrop XP-61 Black Widow night fighter prototype flies for the first time.

**England, June 18**
Major-General Carl Spaatz takes command of the US Eighth Army Air Force.

**USA, June 26**
The prototype of the Grumman F6F Hellcat naval fighter is flown for the first time (→ Aug 31, 1943).

**China, July 4**
The American Volunteer Group (AVG), nicknamed "the Flying Tigers", is dissolved; its commander, Colonel Claire Chennault, was recalled to active USAAF duty in April and promoted brigadier-general.

**San Francisco, Calif, July 7**
Second lieutenant Richard Bong loops the loop with his P-38 around the central arch of the Golden Gate Bridge. He then flies up Market Street a few dozen feet off the ground, sending a local woman's laundry flying. His commanding officer, General Kenney, orders the young pilot to re-wash the laundry as a punishment to fit the crime.

**Leipheim, Germany, July 18**
The prototype of the Messerschmitt Me 262 turbojet fighter makes a successful first flight in the hands of Fritz Wendel; a piston-engined version of the same airplane flew on April 18 last year.

**Louisiana, August 16**
The 82nd Airborne (All American) paratroop Division is formed.

**Oregon, September 9**
A Japanese Yokosuka E14Y1 seaplane, launched at sea by the submarine *I-25*, makes a fire-bombing raid which starts a number of forest fires; it is the first Japanese air raid on the mainland United States.→

**Seattle, September 21**
The Boeing XB-29 prototype heavy bomber, which US officials hope will win the war in the Pacific, is piloted by Eddie Allen on its first flight; the huge airplane is fitted with four Wright Duplex Cyclone engines and has three pressurized cabins.→

**Oslo, September 25**
Gestapo headquarters in the Norwegian capital is destroyed in a daylight raid by de Havilland Mosquito bombers of 105 and 139 Squadrons, RAF (→ Dec 20/21).

**England, September 29**
American volunteers serving in the RAF's "Eagle Squadrons" are transferred to the USAAF Fourth Fighter Group (→ Mar 13, 1943).

**North Africa, October 26**
An Italian convoy bringing supplies and fuel to General Rommel is struck outside Tobruk harbor by RAF Wellington bombers; such attacks on supply lines are proving crucial to the success of the Allied land campaign (→ Apr 18, 1943).

**Eastern front, November 24**
The Luftwaffe begins an airlift operation to supply German troops encircled at Stalingrad (→ Nov 26).

**Turin, Italy, November 28/29**
The city is bombed by the RAF with the first 8,000-pound bombs of the war (→ Dec 4).

**South East Asia, December 1**
The USAAF Air Transport Command assumes responsibility for the India-to-China air route over the Himalayas ("The Hump").

**Naples, Italy, December 4**
Consolidated B-24s of the US Ninth AAF carry out a successful bombing raid against the Italian fleet and docks here; it is the first attack by US bombers on Italy in the war (→ Jun 11, 1943).

**The Netherlands, December 20/21**
The British precise navigational aid "Oboe" is used for the first time on a night raid by Mosquitoes of 109 Squadron, RAF, against a power station (→ Jan 1943).

**London, December 23**
The British government establishes a committee under pioneer aviator J T C Moore-Brabazon, now Lord Brabazon of Tara, to consider Britain's needs for civil airplanes in the immediate post-war period.

---

*Avro Lancaster bombers of N° 44 Sqn, RAF. The aircraft first flew on January 9, 1941 and made its first combat mission on March 3, 1942.*

# Sikorsky launches single-rotor helicopter

*Sikorsky (l) and the Army machine.*

*Connecticut, January 14*
A major breakthrough in the development of helicopters was marked today when the Sikorsky VS-316A single-rotor helicopter made its maiden flight. Also known by its US Army designation of XR-4, this promises to be the first helicopter put into front-line service in large numbers. Based on Igor Sikorsky's pioneer VS-300A, the 316 is a production model, with more power and with two seats in an enclosed cabin. The new machine would make a good trainer, and could also be adapted to do other useful tasks, particularly in the humanitarian field (→ May 18).

# Churchill crosses Atlantic in a Boeing 314

*Boeing's 314A "Berwick" is a flying palace, both luxurious and very roomy.*

# Beaten pilot steals his opponent's fighter

*Stalingrad, January 21*
There cannot be many pilots who take off on a combat mission and return in another aircraft, but 23-year-old Lieutenant Kuznetsov managed it today. He was flying his Sturmovik attack-bomber back to base from a mission when he was set upon by a German Messerschmitt Bf 109, which shot him down.

With great skill he managed to recover for a crash-landing in an open field near a wood. He clambered out and took cover as his airplane blew up. A few moments later he was surprised to hear the snarl of a Daimler-Benz engine and, peering out of the foliage, was astounded to see his recent opponent land his fighter next to the burning plane, perhaps to grab some trophy as proof of his feat. While the German was poking inside the smoldering wreckage, Kuznetsov crept out of cover and walked up to the Messerschmitt. Vaulting into the pilot's seat, he had the propeller turning in a moment and, to the undoubted dismay of the German, took off for home in a swirl of snow with his captured prize (→ Jul 1).

*Devon, England, January 17*
British prime minister Winston Churchill landed at Plymouth today after a narrow escape.

As it approached Plymouth, a small formation of RAF Hurricanes nearly attacked his airplane, mistaking it for a German bomber. Churchill, returning from seeing President Roosevelt, chose to fly rather than undertake the long crossing by Royal Navy ship. His airplane was the BOAC Boeing 314A flying boat *Berwick*, one of the three received last year from Pan American as well-appointed transatlantic VIP transports. Leaving on January 15, he flew from Norfolk, Virginia, to Bermuda, where he stopped overnight.

*Winston Churchill (l) relaxes with the crew prior to take-off.*

# 'The Flying Tigers' take on Japanese

*Washington, DC, January 3*
Chiang Kai-shek was today appointed commander-in-chief of Allied forces in China as his country, which has been at war with Japan since 1937, formally aligned itself with the US, which entered the war last month. Some US pilots are already fighting for Chiang Kai-shek's Chinese Nationalist forces.

Around 100 volunteers, now known as "the Flying Tigers", formed the American Volunteer Group under the command of Texan Colonel Claire L Chennault, 51, last August. They were all retired officers of the US Army and Navy Air Forces, or

*Patch as worn by the "Tigers".*

serving officers granted leave without loss of seniority.

The "Tigers" saw their first combat last month when, flying their Curtiss P-40s, they shot down three Kawasaki Ki-48 bombers over the city of Kunming. A fourth Ki-48 is reported to have gone down en route to Hanoi (→ Jul 4).

*The showy sharks' teeth motif was later used by many other air forces.*

# US Army Air Force takes on Douglas DC-4s

*The USAAF has asked that some C-54s be made into flying ambulances.*

*Santa Monica, Ca, March 20*
The US Army Air Force (USAAF) received their first Douglas C-54-DO transport airplane today. Another 23 are to follow. The C-54 is the military designation for the redesigned DC-4 airliner, which Douglas had just begun building for airlines at the time of the Pearl Harbor attack. But production is now for the US War Department.

Before the C-54 first flew on February 14, the military were mainly interested in the smaller DC-3. The four-engined DC-4 is now seen as ideal for heavy transport duties over the Atlantic and Pacific. The first 24 C-54s are being finished to airline standard, except for auxiliary fuel tanks and 26 seats. Later versions will be prepared for cargo handling.

Back in 1938, Douglas designed the original DC-4 for the four largest American airlines (TWA, Eastern, United Airlines and American Airlines). The result was an aircraft with unattractive characteristics, which, redesignated DC-4E (for Experimental) was sold to Japan. The redesigned airplane is very much simpler in its structure and systems. Its cabin is fully air conditioned, but not pressurized, and it is powered by four 1,400hp Pratt & Whitney R-2000 Twin Wasp engines.

# Doolittle's 16 B-25 Mitchells hit Tokyo

*Washington, DC, April 21*
When bombs fell on Tokyo, Yokohama, Kobe, Osaka and Nagoya three days ago, they shattered their citizens' belief in Japan's invincibility. The US War Department has said little about the raid, except that it was made by 16 USAAF B-25 Mitchell bombers – never intended for carriers – led by Lieutenant-Colonel Jimmy Doolittle.

Doolittle's raiders flew from the carrier USS *Hornet*. They were supposed to take off 500 miles from Japan, but were spotted by a picket boat and launched from 650 miles. One B-25 landed in the USSR, one at sea, and the other 14 in China. Most of the captured crews, including Doolittle, are believed to be safe in Chinese hands. The raid followed months of preparation at Eglin Field, Florida. Problems included reducing aircraft weight, installing extra fuel tanks and perfecting carrier take-offs (→ May 8).

*One of Doolittle's B-25 raiders takes off for Tokyo from the USS "Hornet".*

# Five-in-one O'Hare stuns the Japanese

*South-west Pacific, February 21*
Five twin-engined Japanese bombers shot down in flames within five minutes is good shooting for a fighter squadron, let alone one man. Lieutenant Edward "Butch" O'Hare of the US Navy achieved this astonishing feat today in his Grumman F4F Wildcat.

His aircraft carrier, the *Lexington*, was on her way toward New Britain and had just destroyed nine Japanese bombers when a second flight was detected. O'Hare and a colleague took off and attacked. His partner's guns jammed and he broke away, but O'Hare picked off the last airplane on one side of the formation, got another, and then moved to the other side to empty his guns into three more (→ Apr 21).

# Wildcat or Martlet: what's in a name?

*Washington, DC, January 3*
The US Army Air Force (USAAF) decided to follow the British example today and give names to all their aircraft types rather than just numbers.

Pilot cadets in the USAAF, for example, will now get instruction on the North American Texan rather than the AT-6, which the Royal Air Force calls the Harvard. On aircraft carriers, US pilots will fly Wildcats while Royal Navy flyers have Martlets; except for their external paint, these fighters are identical Grumman F4Fs. The Douglas C-47 and Curtiss P-40 will be known as the Skytrain and the Warhawk respectively to the USAAF, but as the Dakota and Kittyhawk to the RAF.

# RAF gives new role to American Mustang

*Sussex, England, May 5*
The North American Mustang I saw action for the first time today, with the RAF's 26 Squadron based at Gatwick. The Mustang arrived in Britain last October, five months after the first production model made its maiden flight. At low altitudes the Mustang I performs better than any Allied fighter. It is faster, at 390mph, but at high altitudes it is handicapped by the lack of power of its Allison engine. The RAF has therefore decided to use it as an armed reconnaissance fighter. The Mustang will be used to take photographs and attack targets in France with its eight guns.

*The prototype Mustang, AG345, will remain at North American's facilities.*

# Aircraft fight sea battle

*An artist's view of the Japanese carrier "Shoho" sinking in the Coral Sea.*

*South-west Pacific, May 8*
A Japanese attempt to seize Port Moresby, New Guinea, was thwarted today after the first sea battle in which ships neither saw each other, nor engaged each other with gunfire; all the US combatants were carrier-borne aircraft. This battle in the Coral Sea gives the American forces their first victory in the war against the Japanese navy.

The countdown to the engagement began when US intelligence learned that a large Japanese convoy, escorted by two task forces with three aircraft carriers, had left Rabaul, New Britain, to attack Port Moresby. A US task force, with the carriers USS *Lexington* and USS *Yorktown* and other US and Australian warships, was sent to intercept the invaders. On May 7 the fighting began. Japanese carrier airplanes sank a destroyer and an oiler

separated from the main US force. Meanwhile aircraft from the *Lexington* and *Yorktown* found one of the Japanese task forces and sent the light carrier *Shoho* to the bottom. That afternoon, land-based bombers struck unsuccessfully at US and Australian cruisers southwest of the Louisiade islands.

At dawn today the battle between the task forces, which have remained 100 to 200 miles apart, resumed. Carrier aircraft from both sides attempted to sink each others' ships. When the day ended, the *Lexington* had to be abandoned, the Japanese carrier *Shokaku* had been severely damaged, and the *Zuikaku* had lost many aircraft. Each side lost about 30 aircraft, and neither can claim an absolute victory; but the invasion fleet, wary of being attacked by US carrier airplanes, has reversed its course (→ Jun 5).

*Wreckage of a Japanese A6M Zero fighter, which was shot down in the battle.*

# Spitfires fight valiantly to rebuff the Axis fighters in battle to win control of Malta

*Malta, May 9*
With German and Italian forces tightening the noose around this strategically vital, British-held island in the Mediterranean, the bomb-battered population of Malta was cheered today by the arrival of 62 Supermarine Spitfire fighters on board the aircraft carriers HMS *Eagle* and USS *Wasp*.

Last month 17 Spitfires were destroyed on the ground by German attacks soon after their arrival on Malta. But today the pilots were briefed about safe landing areas where eager ground crew were waiting to refuel them for action. Within 35 minutes of landing, some fighters were airborne.

An Italian bomber formation with a defensive fighter screen was located flying at high altitude. The superior Spitfires blasted through the fighters, sending several aircraft spiraling to earth. At low level, Luftwaffe Junkers Ju 87 Stuka dive-bombers met equally heavy punishment from other Spitfires. Seven Axis aircraft have been confirmed as destroyed and seven recorded by the RAF as "probables".

Yet Malta's position remains perilous, dependent for supplies on convoys and bombed daily by Axis aircraft from bases in Italy, Greece and North Africa. The lack of fuel and spares adds to the problems of Malta's Spitfire crews (→ Aug 15).

*An RAF Spitfire (tropical VC, four cannon) leaves the "Wasp" for Malta.*

## 'Baedeker' towns targeted by beams

*Exeter, England, May 4*
This cathedral city was bombed for the second time in two weeks last night. It was the latest in a series of reprisal raids by the Germans. The historic towns of Bath, Norwich and York have also been attacked in what are called "Baedeker" raids – after the German guide books.

RAF chiefs believe that the Luftwaffe is using a new type of electronic beam to guide its planes to their targets. However, Germany lacks sufficient bombers to turn this new technology to full advantage. RAF fighters are destroying many enemy bombers (→ May 31).

**BACK THEM UP!**

**A British poster calls for support for bombers and their crews.**

# RAF stages its first 1,000-bomber raid

*Wellington Mk IC bombers were used in force on the "1,000-bomber" raid.*

*Cologne, Germany, May 31*
The heart of this ancient city on the Rhine is a smoking ruin today after suffering the biggest air raid in the history of air warfare. The raid, Operation Millenium, was masterminded by head of RAF Bomber Command Air Marshal Arthur Harris. He sent every serviceable bomber of his five first-line groups, 1,047, including many from training units. They were told to turn for home 90 minutes after zero hour, whether they had dropped their bombs or not. In the event, some 868 aircraft did bomb Cologne, dropping 1,455 tons of explosives – two-thirds were incendiaries, and aircrew claimed that fires could be seen 150 miles away. More than 5,000 people were killed or injured and 45,000 left homeless. This was the first time that any German city had endured anything like Guernica, Warsaw, Rotterdam or London.

# A Lightning pilot invents 'fuel bomb'

*Pacific Ocean, June 1*
At the controls of his Lightning P-38, an American pilot today bombed soldiers manning positions on a Japanese-held Pacific island. His P-38 was carrying auxiliary fuel tanks. Although these still had some fuel left in them after the raid, he decided to jettison them before the return flight. When they hit the ground, he noticed that the explosion was far more devastating than his bombs.

# China orders 800 Curtiss fighters

*Peking, May 15*
Curtiss P-40 fighters are selling like hot cakes and are taking part in air combat in many theaters of war.

Britain, where it is known as the Kittyhawk, has just ordered another 1,300 of the increasingly popular aircraft, in its P-40F version. China has now decided to purchase 800 of the Curtiss fighters, opting for the P-40K version which is powered by a new 1,325-hp Allison engine.

# Captured Fw 190 yields its secrets

*South Wales, June 23*
One of the most valuable prizes of the air war inadvertently landed this evening at the RAF station at Pembrey: a Focke-Wulf Fw 190 fighter, flown by Leutnant Arnim Faber of the Luftwaffe, based at Morlaix, Brittany.

After engaging Spitfires of a Polish wing over Devon, Faber had apparently become disoriented. Mistaking the Bristol Channel for the English Channel, he headed north for Wales.

The captured Fw 190, of the A-3 sub-type, is the first of its type to fall into Allied hands. For a year the radial-engined fighter has established a worrying level of combat superiority over RAF squadrons equipped with Spitfire Vs. Except perhaps in its turning circle, the Luftwaffe fighter is better in every respect. Now this perfect specimen will be taken to test sites at Farnborough or Boscombe Down to be tested against the new Spitfire IX and analysed. It has a new 1,700-hp BMW 801D-2 engine in a fan-cooled installation, and the heavy armament of four cannon and two machine guns.

# Sikorsky seaplane flies across Atlantic

*Foynes, Ireland, June 20*
A Vought-Sikorsky VS-44A Excalibur flying boat carrying 16 passengers landed on the River Shannon, near here, today after completing its first non-stop flight across the Atlantic. The four-engined aircraft is being operated on the New York to Ireland route by American Export Air Lines (AEAL). In January, this company was authorized by the US Navy to use the North Atlantic route under contract from the Naval Air Transport Service. Anxious to break into the lucrative long-distance passenger service, the airline ordered three VS-44As in 1939. Its plans were delayed by the outbreak of war, but are now well on the way to being fulfilled.

*The Vought-Sikorsky VS-44A made its maiden flight on January 18.*

# RAAF Beaufort bombers on first mission

*Papua New Guinea, June 25*
Five Beaufort bombers of the Royal Australian Air Force (RAAF) had their first taste of war today.

They had been scrambled after a Japanese warship was reported off Lae, on the island's Japanese-occupied northern coast. Despite the loss of one bomber, which was hit by anti-aircraft fire, the RAAF raid was successful. While two of the Beauforts bombed and machine-gunned Japanese ground positions at nearby Salamaua, the other aircraft disabled the warship. One of the four remaining bombers then experienced mechanical problems and made a belly-landing at Port Moresby, but the other three returned to base safely.

*The Royal Air Force in England received 1,380 Beauforts made by Bristol.*

# American flyers grab victory in Midway sea battle

## Aircraft carriers do battle in the Coral Sea

## Dive-bombers are heroes – and victims

*Its wing torn off by a direct hit, a B6N torpedo bomber crashes at sea.*

*An SBD Dauntless about to take off for a bombing raid on Japanese targets.*

**Coral Sea, May 8**
Few if any naval battles have, like this one did, relied so entirely on carrier-borne aircraft. The battle for control over the vital Coral Sea sector is unique in the annals of modern warfare insofar as it was a duel between aircraft carriers in which other warships played no direct role.

Tactically, the victory is Japan's, but, strategically, it was the US Navy who won the day, since it succeeded in preventing Japan from achieving its goal of capturing Port Moresby, on Papua New Guinea's south-eastern coast. This would have given the Japanese the means of completely cutting off Australia from outside help. The US Navy's partial success was, however, a costly one. The aircraft carrier USS *Lexington* was sunk, with the loss of 33 airplanes. Another carrier, the USS *Yorktown* was damaged, while the destroyer USS *Sims* was sunk. Japanese losses include the light aircraft carrier *Shoho*. A second Japanese carrier suffered heavy damage.

Learning from their mistakes, US naval commanders are now planning to increase the ratio of fighters to bombers (→ Jun 6).

**Midway, Pacific Ocean, June 6**
American dive-bombers were the heroes – and the victims – of the bloody battle at Midway.

Diving from as high at 12,000 feet, the pilots plunge for half a minute or more before releasing a high-explosive bomb at between 1,500 and 2,000 feet and attempting to pull out against intense centrifugal pressure. Many of the US Navy pilots had never seen combat before – and many were to die. All 15 of the lumbering Devastator bombers in the USS *Hornet's* Torpedo Squadron 8 were shot down, and only pilot Ensign George Gay survived. He and his comrades lost their fighter escort and were easy prey for the far faster Zero fighters. None managed to release their bombs or torpedoes. Ensign Gay clambered out of his plane into a floating seat cushion, drifting helplessly while the battle raged around him until he was eventually rescued.

Despite heavy losses, Dauntless dive-bombers took only five minutes two days ago to destroy half of the Japanese carrier force. Today, the battle of Midway is won and Japan's navy has lost its superiority in the Pacific.

*During the battle, crew save a Hellcat which caught fire returning to its ship.*

*A Japanese ship off Midway streams smoke as US SBDs launch an attack.*

# Aeroflot pilots save besieged Sevastopol

*The Lisunov Li-2 is the Soviet-built version of the Douglas DC-3.*

**Sevastopol, Crimea, July 1**
The DC-3 has proved its worth again, this time in the hands of Soviet pilots. The Soviet Li-2 version has helped to stave off the German attack on Sevastopol, with Soviet airline pilots running the gauntlet of enemy fire at the controls of their aircraft. Since June 21, 218 tons of vital supplies have been flown into the besieged Crimean port, and 2, 162 people have been taken out, including 1, 542 wounded.

American lend-lease airplanes are bolstering the Allies' fight. None has done better than the DC-3, known as the Dakota to the RAF, the C-47 or R4D to the US military and the PS-84 or Li-2 to the Soviets (→Nov 26).

# RAF's new force shows bombers the way

**Wyton, England, August 19**
The new RAF bomber unit, the Pathfinder Force (PFF), is evaluating the results of its first operation, a raid on a German submarine facility at Flensburg last night. Based in East Anglia, the PFF will fly ahead of the bombers to drop parachute flares on the target. PFF commander Group Captain Don Bennett believes this will increase the accuracy of bombers. The RAF are also using the Gee, a ground-based, area-coverage, pulsed navigation system developed by Robert Dippy of the Telecommunications Research Establishment at Worth Matravers, Dorset. The Gee system has a range of about 450 miles.

*Bennett: in charge of the new force.*

# Britain's heavy bomber proves its worth

**France, October 17**
At nightfall today, 94 Avro Lancasters of the RAF flew across France to attack the Schneider gun factory at Le Creusot, 170 miles south-east of Paris. The attack was a success; even though they had no fighter cover, all but one of the bombers returned safely.

The raid is the latest success for the RAF's new heavy bomber, which undertook its first operation – laying mines in the Heligoland Bight – on March 3. In the Lancaster, the single huge weapon bay can carry any conceivable type of bomb or other store up to a weight of 22,000 lb. The Lancaster's four 1,280-hp Merlin XX or 1,650-hp Hercules engines can carry 14,000 pounds of bombs up to 1,660 miles at a cruising speed of 210mph.

# US bomber chief leads attack on Rouen

**England, September 17**
The first daylight precision bombing mission to the European continent was flown today by 12 US Army Air Forces (USAAF) B-17 Flying Fortresses. The B-17s successfully struck at the Rouen-Sotteville marshaling yard just inland from the French coast.

Head of US Eighth AAF Bomber Command Brigadier-General Ira C Eaker showed his confidence in his men's ability to bomb in daytime by flying on the strike aboard the B-17E *Yankee Doodle*. RAF Spitfires escorted the bombers on the carefully planned raid. The weather was clear in the target area, where the B-17s dropped 36,900 pounds of bombs. The Spitfires downed two German fighters, but suffered two losses; all the B-17s returned safely, although two were slightly damaged.

Commander-in-chief of RAF Bomber Command Air Marshal Arthur Harris congratulated Eaker on the success of the mission with the message: "*Yankee Doodle* certainly went to town" (→Oct 17).

*One of the first arrivals, a B-17F, back from the USAAF's first raid on Europe.*

# Hawker Tempest could be new triumph

**Langley, England, September 2**
Test pilot Philip Lucas took the Hawker Tempest fighter on its first test flight at Langley, west of London, today. Although based on the existing Hawker Typhoon, it has a much thinner wing of distinctive elliptical form. With this and other changes, the Tempest promises to be one of the world's best fighter-bombers. At low levels, the Tempest can probably beat any airplane it will meet in combat, but its main role may be to carry bombs and rockets against ground targets on the battlefield.

The fighting in North Africa has taught the RAF a great deal about tactical airpower, and the Tempest could prove to be an excellent all-rounder, with a speed of 440mph and heavy armor and armament.

*The Hawker Tempest Mk I has radiators in the leading edges of its wings.*

# Americans shocked as Japan hits USA

*Mount Emily, Oregon, September 9*
Isolated from the fighting by distance, Americans received a shock today when news broke that a Japanese airplane had bombed the mainland. Although it was suggested that a bomb-carrying balloon could be the culprit, the raid was, in fact, carried out by a Japanese navy Yokosuka E14Y seaplane launched from the submarine *I-25*. It carried out two attacks, dropping four 168-pound phosphorus bombs which started a forest fire. A crater has been found at the coastal town of Brookings.

# Luftwaffe airlifts to army in Stalingard

*Dropping supplies over Stalingrad.*

*USSR, November 26*
More than a quarter of a million German troops are now trapped inside Stalingrad, dependent upon the Luftwaffe for their fuel, food and ammunition. German air chief Hermann Goering has assured Hitler that the Luftwaffe can meet the challenge, but it faces daunting obstacles. Virtually its entire fleet of transport aircraft would be needed to airlift the 500 tons of fuel and ammunition required each day by the trapped Sixth Army under General Friedrich Paulus. Yet many are in action in the Middle East, many more unserviceable, the weather is worsening, and the only two airfields open to the Germans are under intense Soviet attack.

# Bell XP-59A takes USA into the jet age

*The first American jet airplane, the Bell XP-59A Airacomet, in flight.*

*Muroc Dry Lake, Calif, Oct 1*
Following the lead of Germany and Britain, the first jet-propelled airplane to be produced in America made a successful maiden flight at a remote US Army test field here in the Californian desert today. It is the Bell XP-59A Airacomet, and it was flown on this occasion by Bell test pilot Bob Stanley.

Bell Aircraft had previously planned a P-59 fighter with an ordinary piston engine. To preserve secrecy, the new jet was trucked here with a dummy propeller fixed on the nose; its actual engines are under the wings where they join the fuselage. Made by General Electric, they are US versions of the Whittle turbojet designed in Britain. Designated I-A, each engine has a thrust of 1,250 pounds. With these engines, the XP-59A has a top speed of about 400mph.

# FIDO relied on to clear fogbound runways

*An RAF Lancaster bomber lands safely after FIDO has cleared the way.*

*Britain, November 4*
In another winter at war, Allied bomber crews are once more having to face the added danger of fog on landing after a long and tiring mission. To a battle-damaged airplane, the risk is even worse, and many crews have been lost to the weather after surviving combat.

But British inventors working for the government have now come up with Fog Investigation Dispersal Operation (FIDO). FIDO consists of underground pipes carrying petrol to burners along the edges of a runway. When needed, the burners are lit, dissipating fog and lighting the airstrip.

Initial plans call for FIDO to be installed at runways at Carnaby in Yorkshire, Manston in Kent, and Woodbridge in Suffolk. Damaged bombers can be guided to these air bases by radio.

# SAS is formed for secret operations

*Cairo, November 1*
Cloak-and-dagger commandos specializing in raids on Luftwaffe airfields, and destroying more planes on the ground in a night than the RAF can manage in the air in a week, have come of age. From obscurity as "L" detachment of a fictitious "Special Air Service Brigade", the team of 65 daredevils recruited by gangling Scots Guards Captain David Stirling and trained at Kabrit last year is now 1 SAS Regiment. Alongside 500 Britons are 94 Frenchmen, 114 soldiers of the Greek Sacred Squadron and 55 amphibious special forces men of the Special Boat Section.

Stirling wants more than pinprick raids in the German rear. His theory is that small, élite special forces' teams, living for long periods in enemy territory, can hit important targets such as dams, air bases, supply dumps and key VIPs. His motto: "Who Dares Wins."

# Eddie Rickenbacker found in Pacific

*Pacific Ocean, November 14*
Leading US fighter ace of World War I Captain Eddie Rickenbacker is credited with saving the lives of six men who were with him on board a B-17 which crashed in the Pacific on October 23. US Navy Catalina flying boats today plucked the men from the sea where they had been adrift on rubber rafts for 22 days. An eighth man succumbed to his ordeal several days ago.

Rickenbacker had been on a US War Department mission to see how US aircraft perform around the world. He was en route to a Pacific site when, 12 hours out of Honolulu, the B-17 he was flying suffered mechanical problems and ditched. All eight persons aboard escaped the sinking aircraft. Exhibiting the same iron will he showed as an air ace over Flanders, where he scored 26 "kills", 52-year-old Rickenbacker literally threatened and taunted his companions into surviving. He took charge of the party, rationed the food they had, caught a seagull and fish, and, when it rained, collected water.

# Airplanes lead Allied offensive in North Africa

*F4Fs and SBDs at the ready on the carrier USS "Ranger" off North Africa.*

*A German Bf 109E in local colors.*

## Air power tilts the balance to Allies

*North Africa, November 12*
Rommel's retreat from El Alamein, Egypt, just four days before the Allies launched Operation Torch further west in North Africa, has highlighted a shortcoming for the Luftwaffe that might yet prove critical. Over the past months hundreds of Junkers Ju 52/3m transports have been diverted to the eastern front, badly affecting the supply line for the Afrika Korps.

Even more devastating for Rommel has been the close-support tactics in the western desert of Allied Hurricane IIDs with 40mm guns and Curtiss Kittyhawks, which are bursting open Afrika Korps armor. Air commander-in-chief in the Middle East Sir Arthur Tedder has enjoyed clear air superiority, with 1,500 aircraft against some 350 serviceable German and Italian airplanes in Africa. The Allied airplanes have also been used to attack Axis ships attempting to send supplies across the Mediterranean.

*North Africa, November 12*
Since the Allied landings in Algeria and Morocco under Operation Torch four days ago, the use of air power has been essential in offering air cover and in moving airborne forces to new objectives. The three Allied beach-landing task forces met strong resistance, with French warplanes loyal to the Vichy government strafing those troops unloading landing craft.

At 7.51am on November 10, Vichy French fighters flew into battle against US Navy Wildcats from the carrier USS *Ranger*. Airplanes flying from offshore US Navy and Royal Navy carriers have been essential to operations, while the RAF has flown from the specially extended runway on Gibraltar. However, with the taking of the Maison Blanche and Blida airfields near Algiers on the first day, RAF Hurricanes were able set up forward operating bases.

Allied airborne forces are spearheading the race against the Axis to Tunisia. Yesterday paratroopers of the 509th Parachute Battalion were dropped from Douglas C-47 transports. Their task was to bolster the forces attempting to take the La Senia and Tafaraoui airfields on the outskirts of Oran.

Today Allied paratroopers from 26 US C-47s, escorted by the RAF, took the airfield and port at Bône, Algeria, outmaneuvering the Germans, while yesterday Bougie fell. The Allies are now coming under German air attack.

## Long-range Superfortress could hit Japan

*Seattle, September 21*
In what is probably the biggest airplane manufacturing program of all time, the prototype Boeing B-29 Superfortress heavy bomber made its first flight here today. The crew was headed by Boeing company test pilot Eddie Allen.

The B-29 is not only enormous but is also packed with new technology. The 2,200-hp Wright Duplex Cyclone engines are the biggest and most powerful ever used, and each expels its exhaust through two large turbosuperchargers to maintain power at altitudes never previously approached by any bomber. At over 30,000 feet, the crew will sit in comfort in warm pressurized cabins. The gun turrets are controlled from remote sighting stations.

Not least, the B-29 is designed to have a very long range, enabling it to bomb the heartland of Japan. Boeing, Bell and Martin are each going to produce these giant bombers by the hundred, if not by the thousand (→ Feb 18, 1943).

## Heinkel night-fighter takes to the skies

*Marienehe, Germany, November 15*
This modest airfield near Rostock, which has already seen the first flights of two types of jet airplane, was today the setting for the first flight of the Heinkel He 219. Powered by piston engines of the most powerful type, the 1,850-hp DB 603A, the new Heinkel looks set to become a very formidable all-round warplane. It was originally planned in 1940 to do various tasks, but thanks to the RAF its future role is already decided. Carrying radio direction-finding equipment and heavy cannon it will be a night-fighter, perhaps among the best in the world.

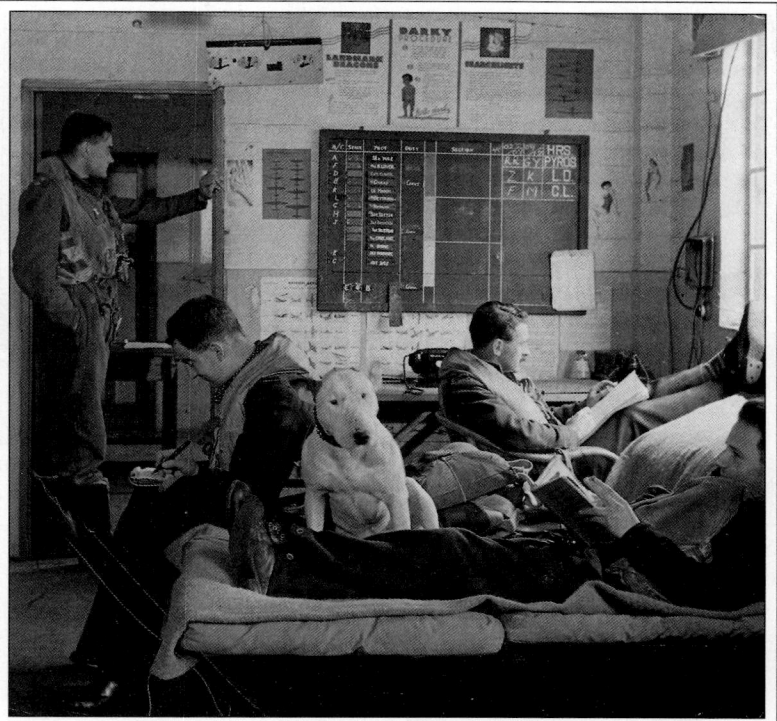

**Dressed for action, RAF pilots relax as best they can while they are waiting to be ordered up on a fighter sweep mission. The squadron mascot seems willing to lend an ear to whatever they have on their minds.**

Lockheed's XP-49, a P-38 Lightning with Continental engines.

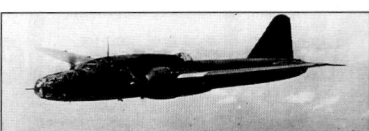

The Mitsubishi Ki-67 was the best Japanese bomber of the Pacific war.

The Grumman F6F Hellcat succeeded the Wildcat as the US Navy's premier carrier-borne fighter. It went into action over Marcus Island in August 1943.

Lavochkin's La-7 was an improved development of the mass-produced La-5. Armament comprised two (sometimes three) fuselage-mounted cannon.

The Aichi B7A Ryusei: the last Japanese carrier-borne attack-bomber.

Heinkel's He 219 Uhu interceptor became a specialized night-fighter.

An outstanding Swedish twin-engined bomber – the Saab B18A.

Stearman's Model X-91 basic trainer failed to win production orders.

Some 1,100 Messerschmitt Me 410s were produced for a variety of roles.

Nine production Latécoère 631 46-passenger flying boats were built after the war, the Germans having confiscated the prototype during the occupation.

The first all-jet flight by a Messerschmitt Me 262 was made by the V3 prototype on July 18, 1942. A pair of Junkers Jumo 109-004B turbojets provided power.

The P-63 Kingcobra followed the Airacobra on Bell's production line.

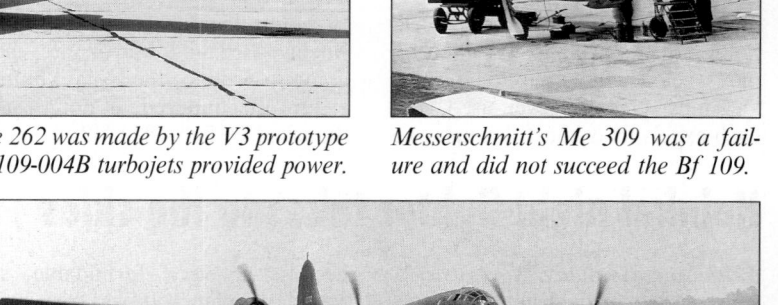

On September 21, 1942, the Boeing XB-29 took to the air for the first time, initiating a production run of 3,627 Superfortresses of all variants.

Northrop's first P-61 Black Widow night-fighter flew on May 26, 1942.

The Messerschmitt Me 264 was developed for long-range operations.

Messerschmitt's Me 309 was a failure and did not succeed the Bf 109.

The Boeing XPBB-1 was the largest twin-engined flying boat ever built.

Avro's York transport married the Lancaster's wings to a new fuselage.

The US Army's first four-engined transport: Douglas's C-54 (DC-4).

Grumman's F5F Skyrocket fighter got no further than the prototype.

Martin-Baker's MB.3 fighter had six cannon but failed to win orders.

The Martin Mars began as a bomber but became a heavy cargo transport.

Westland manufactured more than 60 Welkin high-altitude fighters.

The Australian Commonwealth Boomerang fighter: 250 were made.

The USA's first jet aircraft, the Bell XP-59A Airacomet: powered by two General Electric turbojets developed from the British Whittle gas turbine.

Fiat's G.55 Centauro: one of Italy's best Second World War fighters.

The first US helicopter to enter series production – Sikorsky's R-4.

Mitsubishi's J2M Raiden: a land-based single-seater interceptor.

Blackburn's Firebrand strike-fighter could carry a torpedo, bombs and/or rockets. The original Napier Sabre engine gave way to the Bristol Centaurus.

Macchi's MC.205V Veltro fighter, basically an MC.202 powered by a license-built Daimler-Benz DB.605, saw little action before the Italian surrender.

Douglas's XA-26 light bomber/reconnaissance aircraft was produced as the Invader for the USAAF and, as the B-26, saw service in Korea and Vietnam.

# 1943

**New Guinea, January 28**
In a vital operation, Douglas C-47 (Dakota) transports fly 57 sorties under Japanese fire to drop two Australian battalions on the besieged town of Wau.

**Berlin, January 30**
In the RAF's first daylight raid on the German capital, de Havilland Mosquito bombers of 105 and 139 Squadrons attack the radio station and succeed in holding up a broadcast by Nazi propaganda minister Josef Goebbels for more than an hour (→ Nov 27).

**Solomon Islands, February 13**
The Vought F4U Corsair naval fighter makes its operational debut, escorting PB4Y-1 Liberators (the US Navy's version of the B-24) raiding Bougainville (→ Apr 18).

**Seattle, February 18**
Boeing test pilot Eddie Allen and his crew are killed when the second prototype B-29 bomber develops an engine fire and crashes (→ Jun 1).

**Bismarck Sea, March 2**
US and Australian bombers led by Lieutenant-General George Kenney pioneer "skip-bombing"; flying low-level attacks just above the waves, they sink eight Japanese transport ships and four destroyers by skipping bombs across the water to the target (→ Apr 29).

**Gloucestershire, England, March 5**
The prototype Gloster Meteor twin-jet fighter flies for the first time (→ Jul 12,1944).

**China, March 10**
The US 14th Air Force is activated under the command of former "Flying Tigers" chief Major-General Claire L Chennault.

**USA, March 13**
Consolidated Aircraft merges with Vultee Aircraft to form the Consolidated-Vultee Aircraft Corporation (Convair). The company, which numbers 100,000 employees, plans to manufacture more than 10,400 aircraft this year.

**Cambridgeshire, England, April 1**
Nº 1409 (Meteorological) Flight RAF is formed for long-range weather reconnaissance duties for Bomber Command and the Eighth Air Force.

**Germany, April 21**
The RAF bombs Stettin, Rostock and Berlin to mark Adolf Hitler's 54th birthday.

**Kent, England, April 29**
Barnes Wallis's experimental "bouncing bomb" is successfully tested at Reculver; the normally reserved Wallis is so overjoyed he dances in the rain (→ May 17).

**Long Island Sound, NY, May 7**
The US Navy concludes tests into the feasibility of helicopter operations at sea, in which Colonel Frank Gregory has made take-offs and landings in a Sikorsky XR-4 aboard the tanker *Bunker Hill*.

**Aberdeenshire, Scotland, May 9**
A Junkers Ju 88R night fighter lands, delivering a working FuG 202 Liechtenstein radar set; the German crew appears to have come over to the Allies (→ Jul 13, 1944).

**Atlantic Ocean, May 23**
A Fairey Swordfish from the Royal Navy escort carrier HMS *Archer* sinks the German U-boat *U752* in the first successful use of a rocket launched by an aircraft against a submarine.

**English Channel, June 1**
A KLM DC-3 flying from Lisbon to England is shot down by German Ju 88s, killing all 17 on board, among them British actor Leslie Howard; the Germans believed Winston Churchill was on the aircraft.

**Marietta, Georgia, June 1**
The USAAF's 58th Very Heavy Bombardment Wing is established; it is to be equipped with Boeing B-29 Superfortresses for strategic attacks on Japan (→ Dec 15).

**The Netherlands, June 6**
German pilot Major Werner Streib shoots down five RAF bombers in a single sortie in a Heinkel He 219.

**Mediterranean, June 11**
The 11,000-strong Italian garrison on Pantelleria surrenders after a week-long Allied onslaught by aircraft alone (→ Jul 10).

**Rheine, Germany, June 15**
The prototype Ar 234 V1 jet bomber makes its first flight.

**Indian Ocean, June 29**
QANTAS flies its first service from Perth to Colombo; passengers on the 127-mph Catalina are given a certificate of membership of "The Rare and Secret Order of the Double Sunrise" for being airborne for over 24 hours (→ Jun 17, 1944).

**Florida, July 18**
The US Navy *K-74* becomes the first airship shot down in the war when it is hit by the German U-boat *U134*; the submarine is damaged in the conflict and forced back to base (→ May 31, 1944).

**Montreal, July 22**
Trans-Canada Airlines begins flights to London via Iceland using Lancaster bombers converted for passengers; they will carry mainly military personnel and VIPs.

**Hamburg, Germany, July 24/25**
The RAF uses "Window" (metal foil dropped to confuse German radar) for the first time; 700 aircraft get through to bomb the city (→ Aug 3).

**USSR, August 1**
Junior-Lieutenant Lydia Litvyak of the Soviet 73rd Guards Fighter Regiment is shot down and killed; she had 12 victories to her credit.

**Bay of Biscay, August 17/18**
The German Henschel Hs 293-A1 remote-controlled bomb sees action for the first time, during a Luftwaffe raid on Royal Navy warships (→ Oct 28).

**Germany, September 15**
RAF Lancaster bombers of 617 Squadron hit the Dortmund/Ems canal with 12,000-lb bombs.

**Hertfordshire, England, Sept 29**
The de Havilland Vampire jet fighter prototype makes its first flight at Hatfield (→ Mar 23, 1948).

**France, October 18**
Wing Commander Bob Hodges and Pilot Officer John Affleck fly a secret mission in Lockheed Hudsons, taking in four Allied agents and bringing out a record 18.

**Baltimore, Md, November 2**
The US Navy receives the first Martin Mars 70-ton, four-engined flying boat; it can carry 133 soldiers or 40 civilian passengers and has a range of 4,600 miles.

**England, November 3**
Head of RAF Bomber Command Air Marshal Arthur Harris writes to prime minister Winston Churchill that 19 German cities have been "virtually destroyed" by his bombers; he promises that they could "wreck Berlin from end to end" if the USAAF came in on the project (→ May 31, 1944).

**East Prussia, Germany, Nov 26**
Hitler inspects a Messerschmitt Me 262 jet fighter at Insterburg and orders its mass production – as a bomber (→ Jun 30, 1944).

**Hartford, Conn, November 26**
Pratt & Whitney announces it has perfected a water injection system which gives engines a surge of extra power on demand.

**France, December 24**
The US Eighth Air Force sends 670 B-17s and B-24s to hit German V-1 rocket sites in the Pas-de-Calais area (→ Jun 12/13, 1944).

---

*RAF ground crew load a Lancaster Mark 1 bomber prior to a raid. Five British factories were engaged in the production of Lancasters in 1943.* ▶

# Constellation 'a winner', say test pilots

*Burbank, Calif, January 9*
The world's heaviest, fastest and most powerful airliner made a successful maiden flight here today. Test pilots Eddie Allen and Milo Burcham are delighted with the Lockheed Constellation. Its four 2,200-hp Wright Duplex Cyclone engines power huge Hamilton propellers. It is fully pressurized, has a range of 2,400 miles and is intended to carry 65 to 90 passengers in comfort at over 300mph. Distinctive features include a graceful fuselage and triple-finned tail. The Constellation, nicknamed the "Connie", was ordered and paid for by Howard Hughes, for his airline TWA. Jack Frye assisted Hughes in getting the specification right.

However, instead of being a gleaming airliner for TWA, the first "Connie" is painted olive drab, and bears military insignia. Because of the war, the whole output of Constellations has been assigned to the US Army Air Force, where it will be known as the C-69 (→ Feb 18).

*The US Army's C-69 (to the rear) is prepared for its first flight at Burbank.*

# Renowned Lafayette Squadron is reborn

*Tunisia, January 15*
US pilots flew French army fighters in the last war in their own unit, the Lafayette Escadrille [Squadron]. Today, the famous squadron took to the air again for its first encounter with the Luftwaffe, but with a difference: the resurrected Lafayette Escadrille is made up of French pilots flying US airplanes.

They shot down two Germans for the loss of one French airman.

Because of its distinguished lineage the Lafayette Escadrille, designated GC II/5, was the first Free French unit to be equipped by the US. The famous Sioux Indian insignia which marked its predecessor's biplanes is now displayed on the squadron's P-40 Warhawks.

*Curtiss P-40 fighters of the Lafayette Escadrille line up at Algiers airport.*

# 'Oboe' is music to ears of RAF bombers

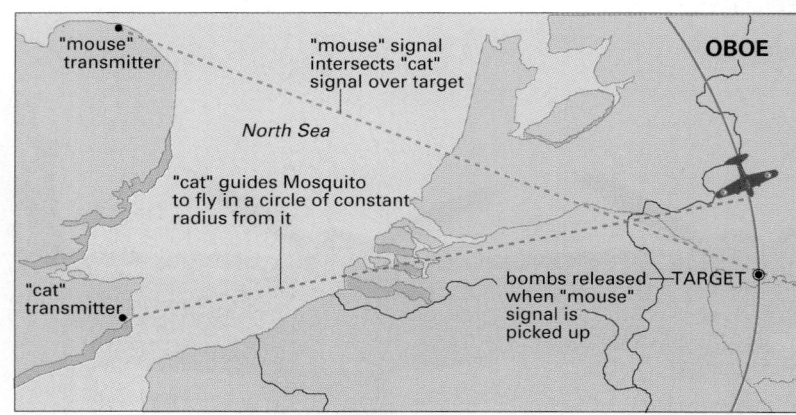

*England, January*
Since the start of the war, RAF pilots had been longing for an efficient and, above all, precise navigation aid.

This requirement appears to have at last been met, despite strong opposition from top people in London, many of whom did not believe the idea would work. Two new navigational aids have been used by the RAF over the last month to improve bomber accuracy. One of these, known as the "Oboe" system, is used by Mosquitoes of the Pathfinder Force which flies ahead of the bombers. The system involves radio pulses from two stations in England to establish the location of the target. The stations guide aircraft along the exact arc of a circle passing over the target. About one minute before bomb release, the pilot hears sequences of dots and dashes, followed by one long dash. He releases his bombs at the end of this transmission. The "Oboe" system is accurate to within the size of a factory.

The "H2S", a downward-looking rotating radar (RDF) transmitter, gives a navigator a picture of the ground he is flying over on a cathode-ray tube. Its chief drawback is that bombers must carry special equipment weighing 4,000 lb.

**Built mainly out of wood, the de Havilland Mosquito B IV went into service with the RAF in May 1942. It relies on speed for safety.**

# American bombers make first raid on targets in Germany

*Germany, January 27*
US heavy bombers attacked Germany for the first time today when 84 B-17 Flying Fortresses and seven Liberators of the US Eighth Air Force, based in England, struck the North Sea naval base of Wilhelmshaven and the submarine yards at Emden. Colonel Frank Armstrong, who in August led the first US daylight bombing raid of the war, on Rouen, was once again in the lead B-17.

To reduce their chance of detec-

*A B-24J Liberator drops its load.*

tion until as late as possible, the bombers flew a carefully planned route far over the North Sea to avoid the enemy coast. When the formation turned toward Germany and climbed to 25,000 feet, the weather began to deteriorate. The submarine yards were obscured by clouds, so only two bombers attacked Emden. Other targets in north-western Germany were hit, but Armstrong directed the bulk of his force – 55 bombers – toward Wilhelmshaven. It, too, had cloud cover and a smoke screen, but there were enough gaps to bomb these key navy docks.

No fighters met the B-17s on their way in, and the anti-aircraft fire over Wilhelmshaven was light and inaccurate, but an estimated 50 to 75 Bf 109s and Fw 190s intercepted the formation on the way back. Three of the Flying Fortresses failed to return home (→ Jun 19).

# Women only at Avenger training center

*Avenger trainees Leila Mather and Martha Thomas in a Vultee BT-15.*

*Avenger Field, Texas, May 11*
American pilot Jackie Cochran's flying school has just been transferred from Houston to Avenger Field, near Sweetwater, in the broiling Texas desert.

The new US Army Air Force (USAAF) experimental training center, under the command of General Arnold, is reserved exclusively for women pilots, who will train on modern aircraft such as North American AT-6s and Beech AT-17s. However, Avenger Field is far from an easy posting for the trainees, who are housed in uncomfortable wooden shacks and sleep six to a dormitory. The young

women – the first batch of trainees are aged from 18 to 35 – are woken at dawn by the sound of an army bugle. After a breakfast in the mess, they are herded outside for morning exercises before attending endless flying instruction classes. Their day is a long one – an average of 16 hours. In fact, the women are undergoing exactly the same regime as their male counterparts.

By the end of the course, each trainee was initially expected to have accumulated a minimum of 200 hours' flying time, but this has been reduced to 75 hours. Despite the rigors of Avenger, Cochran hopes to recruit more women.

# US fighters down Admiral Yamamoto

*Solomon Islands, April 18*
A USAAF P-38 Lightning today shot down Admiral Isoroku Yamamoto, head of the Japanese navy and commander of all Japanese air forces in the Pacific. Captain Thomas G Lanphier downed the Mitsubishi G4M1 "Betty" bomber carrying the man who planned the attack on Pearl Harbor. The mission was possible because the US Navy broke Japanese codes and knew the date, time, destination and type of Yamamoto's flight. Lanphier hit the "Betty", which crashed in the jungle (→ Nov 5).

*Admiral Yamamoto: shot down by the 339th Fighter Squadron.*

# Lysanders take the 'moonlight squadrons' to occupied Europe

*France, April 16*
Guided only by torch signals, a black-painted RAF Lysander made a perilous landing on a field near Rouen last night. It picked up downed USAAF airman Captain Ryan and British undercover agent Wing Commander Forest Yeo-Thomas, to complete yet another mission to occupied Europe for the "moonlight squadrons". Westland Lysanders have now lifted 400 escapees and agents out of France in the past two years. The pilot of one Lysander got home with 30 bullet holes in the fuselage of his airplane and one in his neck.

The Lysander is highly maneuverable. Pilots can land safely at 60mph in the dark and take off in just 36 yards. With its massive fixed

*The trusty Lysander, veteran of many top-secret night missions into France.*

undercarriage and stubby wings, this inelegant machine can turn, its pilots boast, on a postage stamp. Navigation is mainly by dead reckoning from a fixed point on the

French coast and, allowing for wind drift and distance, is often approximate. Torches or flares lit by the Resistance mark the fields that serve as runways (→ Oct 18). ▷

# US airplane factories work all-out for the Allies

*Mechanics, including women, put the finishing touches to B-24 Liberators.*

*Production workers busy on B-17 bomber fuselages in Boeing's Seattle factory.*

**USA, May 11**
In 1940, before the US was at war, President Roosevelt vowed that America would be "the great arsenal of democracy". Today, as Winston Churchill arrives in Washington for talks on Allied strategy in North Africa, that promise is being amply fulfilled. Every seven minutes an airplane rolls off a US production line, and virtually every one of America's allies is fighting the Axis with US-built aircraft. Britain's RAF uses such US planes

as P-51 Mustangs, B-24 Liberators, PB2Y Coronados, SB2C Helldivers and F4U Corsairs. In Africa the French have P-40 Warhawks, P-38 Lightnings and B-26 Marauders; in the USSR there are P-39 Airacobras and C-47 Skytrains; the Chinese fly B-25 Mitchells, and the Canadians use PT-17 Kaydets and AT-17 Bobcats.

Considering that US aircraft manufacturers told the government in 1939 that the industry's maximum output was 5,500 planes per

year, today's 5,500 aircraft per *month* is phenomenal. To get from the production levels of 1939 to that of today required more factories, more machine tools and more workers. This would have been a difficult enough task in peacetime; in war it must have seemed nearly insurmountable, especially when production had to exceed America's own needs by up to 33 per cent to supply its allies.

But it has happened. Factory floor space devoted to aviation has

grown from 9,605,936 square feet in January 1940 to over 41 million square feet now. Production techniques have improved: the number of man-hours taken to build a B-17 has dropped from 50,000 to 19,000.

The workforce has expanded from under 100,000 in 1940 to nearly 200,000 at the start of 1941 and 660,000 last January. Women have made a vital contribution to this expansion. They now account for 28 per cent – 170,000 – of aviation workers (→ Oct 20).

## 'Shuttle' raids extend range of bombing

**London, June 24**
Allied bombing strategy gained a new dimension this month with the first "shuttle" mission in which crews left England for long-range targets in southern Germany before flying to be refueled in North Africa. The bombers returned to England yesterday after hitting targets in Italy on their way home. This tactic brings some Axis targets within range of Allied bombers for the first time and augments continuing day and night raids by the USAAF and RAF on the Ruhr.

The first shuttle bombing raid also had the advantage of confusing German fighters, which often try to attack bombers on their way back to England. The target this time was the old Zeppelin works at Friedrichshafen, Lake Constance. Intelligence reports say this is now

used as a factory for radar (radio direction-finding) equipment.

Lancasters of RAF Bomber Command's No 5 Group undertook the raid on the night of June 20/21. Sixty aircraft took part in the attack, which is said to have done great damage to the factory. The bombers then flew to Blida, Algeria, from where, after a day's rest, they attacked the Italian naval base of La Spezia on the long flight back to England. A dense smoke-screen put up by the Italians meant that the port had to be bombed blind, so the damage is unknown.

Eight Lancs' stayed in Algeria for repairs. The problem of servicing Lancasters in North Africa will limit the frequency of such raids, but the tactic reflects Allied determination to press home the air war all over Axis Europe (→ May 31, 1944).

## French pilot was 'too old' to fly a Lightning

*Saint-Exupéry at the controls of a Lightning. His old leg injuries prevented him applying full pressure on the aircraft's brake pedals.*

**Tunisia, August 11**
The USAAF today grounded one of Free France's most famous pilots because he is too old to fly. Antoine de Saint-Exupéry, one of the great mail pilots of the 1920s and 1930s, but best known outside France as author of the novels *Night Flight* and *Flight to Arras*, had been flying P-38 Lightnings on missions over occupied France.

Ten days ago he had to make an emergency landing at La Marsa airfield, where pilots must use all of the short 1,600-ft runway and brake hard if they are to stop in time. Saint-Exupéry did neither and ended up in a nearby vineyard. USAAF Colonel Harold Willis, who saw the accident, was furious to learn that the Frenchman, 43, is 13 years older than the upper age limit for P-38 pilots.

# Bouncing bombs smash two dams

*Germany, May 17*

A huge wall of water last night thundered through breaches in two dams supplying electricity to many German war factories. The Möhne and Eder dams, in the Ruhr, were thought invulnerable until 19 RAF Lancasters of special "dambusting" unit 617 Squadron based at Scampton, Lincolnshire, came in low bearing the "bouncing bomb".

Each cylindrical, 5-ton bomb, designed by Barnes Wallis, was carried slung beneath the bomber. As the airplane approached the target a motor set the bomb spinning, and at 60 feet it was released. Because of its spin, it skipped along the surface until it hit the dam and sank, exploding under pressure 40 feet down, like a depth charge. The Möhne and Eder dams were hit in the first wave, causing floods which drowned nearly 1,300 people and disrupted power to factories. In a separate wave two other dams were attacked; one, the Sorpe, was breached, but only above the water.

The raid, under the leadership of Wing Commander Guy Gibson, was costly. Fifty-three out of 133 airmen were feared dead as eight Lancasters were lost: four downed by flak, two hitting power lines, one crippled by its own bomb and crashing, and one hitting a tree.

*Artist Frank Wootton's view of the RAF's remarkable "dambusting" raid.*

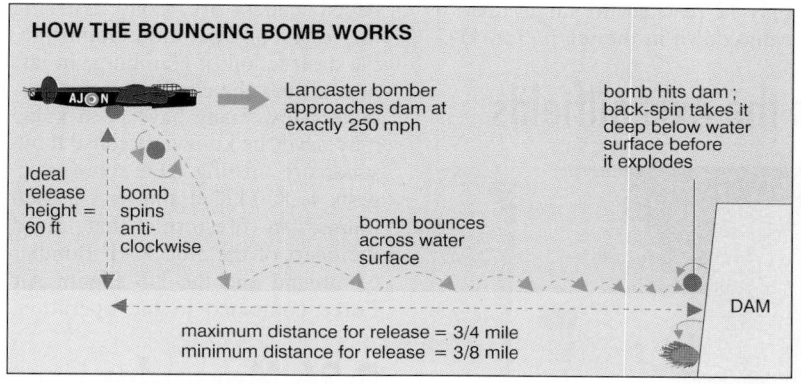

**HOW THE BOUNCING BOMB WORKS**

Lancaster bomber approaches dam at exactly 250 mph

bomb hits dam; back-spin takes it deep below water surface before it explodes

Ideal release height = 60 ft

bomb spins anti-clockwise

bomb bounces across water surface

maximum distance for release = 3/4 mile
minimum distance for release = 3/8 mile

DAM

## Germans evacuate Ruhr area after punishing British air raids

*RAF crewmen watch as their Stirling is "bombed up" ready for a raid.*

*Ruhr, Germany, June 25*

RAF Bomber Command's current intensive bombing of the industrial Ruhr valley and Rhineland in western Germany prompted the Nazi government to declare the areas war zones today. About a million non-combatants – women, children, the elderly and invalids – are to be evacuated from these urban centers, upon which the RAF has been raining around a thousand bombs on most nights since March.

It appears that what German newspapers call the "Battle of the Ruhr" is affecting the morale of troops with families in the area. British prime minister Winston Churchill has ordered the RAF to continue the bombing campaign. He has also approved daylight operations by the British-based US Eighth Air Force.

## 'Flak jacket' helps save airmen's lives

*London, July 8*

Chief surgeon of the US Eighth Air Force Colonel Malcolm Grow received the US Legion of Merit today for developing a life-saving body armor for airmen.

A study of wounds suffered by aircrew showed that 70 per cent came from low-velocity bullets and anti-aircraft shell fragments. Grow was directed to Wilkinson Sword, an old British steel firm specializing in swords and armor. Together they came up with the 20-lb "Flak Suit", formed of two-inch laminated manganese steel plate squares with a quick-release mechanism. Both US and British bomber crews are using the "flak jacket" and a helmet.

## US fighters savage German air convoy

*Tripolitania, Libya, April 18*

In what could be called an aerial massacre, USAAF 57th Fighter Group today destroyed 59 out of 90 Junkers Ju 52 transports bringing supplies from Sicily to what is left of the German Afrika Korps trapped in Tunisia. Some 47 P-40 Warhawks were patrolling the Gulf of Tunis when they encountered the formation of Ju 52s and attacked. As well as the 59 confirmed "kills", 20 more of the trimotors were probably destroyed or damaged, and 16 Messerschmitt fighter escorts were also downed. The USAAF lost six Warhawks (→Aug 1).

**My Goodness My GUINNESS**

# Air disasters mar start of Sicily invasion

*Training for the Sicily landings.*

*Syracuse, Sicily, July 10*
Allied troops have landed on Sicily today by air and by sea, but a storm caused problems for the invaders with a near disaster for the airborne attackers. Paratroops were to be the first wave of the attack, Operation Husky, but they hit problems soon after their C-47s took off from their bases in North Africa.

Pilots taking 2,781 paratroops from the US 505th Parachute Regiment fought the storm, dust, anti-aircraft fire and enemy fighters. Navigators aboard 226 Douglas C-47s were working at night from daytime photographs. As a result, the US paratroops landed over a 50-mile radius of southern Sicily.

Their British counterparts fared even worse. Of 137 Horsa gliders aiming to capture the key strategic Ponte Grande bridge near here, only 12 reached the target area; 69 came down in the sea (→ Jun 11).

# Long-range raid targets the Axis oilfields

*A B-24 Liberator flies on as the Ploesti oil refinery is engulfed in black smoke.*

*Benghazi, Libya, August 1*
American B-24 Liberator bombers flew from here today to attack the oilfields of pro-Axis Romania, which provides much of Germany's oil supplies. Their target was the Ploesti oilfield north of Bucharest, seven hours flying time away across the Mediterranean.

The plan was to attack at rooftop height to surprise the Romanians. Intelligence predicted light flak, but got it wrong. One survivor said: "It was like flying through hell." Among the first bombers hit was that of Colonel Addison Baker, leader of 93rd Group. He and co-pilot John L Jerstad refused to save themselves but flew on, leading the attack until their machine exploded around them. Of 178 bombers on the raid, 53 have been destroyed, with 310 airmen killed and over 100 taken prisoner. Some refineries were disabled by the raid; others are still working normally.

# Allied bombers raze the city of Hamburg

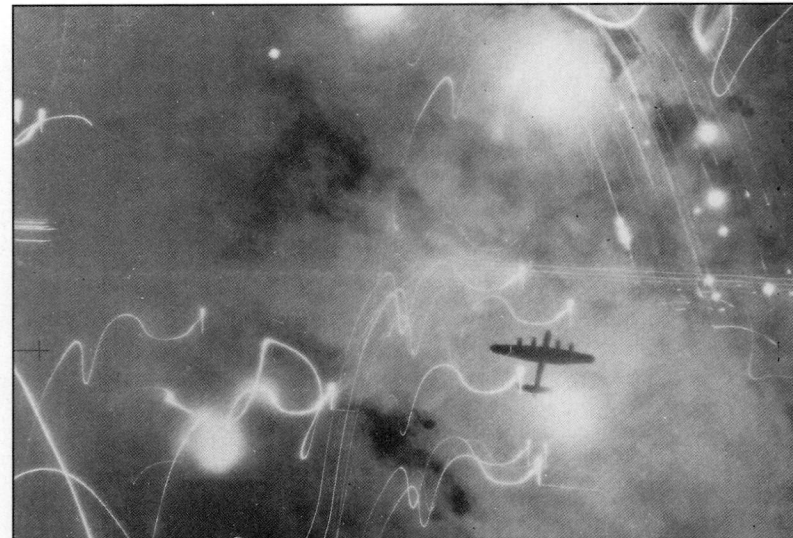

*A Lancaster outlined against a background of fire and flak over Hamburg.*

*Hamburg, August 3*
Allied leaders are today assessing the results of Operation Gomorrah, the destruction of Hamburg. In just over a week the city has been devastated. How many have been killed may never be known, because thousands are missing. One report suggests 41,800 killed and over 37,000 injured in firestorms that razed the heart of the city. RAF Bomber Command and the US Eighth Air Force combined in the operation.

Aluminium foil strips, called "Window" by the RAF and "Chaff" by the Americans, were used to confuse the German defenses. The strips are released in clouds which appear on German radar screens like formations of airplanes. The raids began on the night of July 24/25. Except for one night, when 705 bombers went to bomb Essen, the attacks were almost non-stop. The RAF made 3,095 sorties, dropping 9,656 tons of bombs.

# B-26 Marauder proves less dangerous

*England, December 20*
Among RAF and American pilots, the Martin B-26 Marauder had earned a reputation as a dangerous airplane. Some even called the bomber a "widow maker". This reputation has now improved, as the B-26 has just made its 500th sortie with only three per cent losses. It seems that the accidents that occurred after its first flight, on November 25, 1940, were due to the pilots' lack of experience rather than to design faults. Since then, the B-26 has undergone several modifications. It can operate at an altitude of up to 20,000 feet, out of reach of anti-aircraft guns, and its armor plating provides added protection.

*A formation of US B-26 Marauders. The RAF also operates similar aircraft.*

## US airline pilots help ferry planes

*Karachi, India, May 8*
The US Air Transport Command sometimes suffers from a shortage of pilots to ferry aircraft or military equipment. To remedy this, it calls on airline pilots. Four and a half days ago, 30 Curtiss C-46 Commando cargo aircraft left Miami, Florida, and headed west. At the controls were five USAAF pilots, 10 from TWA and 15 from Northwest. All 30 twin-engined C-46s landed here safely today after flying over the Himalayas.

## US pilots to have sea-survival kits

*USA, May 8*
The US Army Air Force is improving the chances of survival of pilots downed at sea. It has decided that inflatable life-rafts will be equipped with a radio transmitter that will automatically send signals as soon as the dinghy is deployed. Known as the "Gibson Girl" by pilots, it will speed up rescue efforts.

**British customs keep a close eye on goods arriving from the US. Here, an RAF pilot shows a pair of priceless nylon stockings.**

# Douglas C-54s mass-produced in Chicago

*The gigantic C-54 assembly-line at the Douglas factory in Chicago.*

*Chicago, Illinois, October 1*
The Douglas Aircraft Company today started to deliver the first of the 155 C-54 Skymaster multipurpose long-range transport aircraft to come off the busy assembly line of its new factory here.

The factory was built with government funding, as part of the national policy of increasing aircraft production. Unlike the Douglas manufacturing centers in Santa Monica, California, and Tulsa, Oklahoma, the Chicago plant is being rented to the company for the duration of the war. The C-54, which is in fact the military version of the DC-4A, is playing an ever-increasing role in the US war effort. It can be used to transport men, large quantities of cargo or as a casualty evacuation airplane. Its four powerful Pratt & Whitney R-2000 Twin Wasp engines (1,400-hp each) and huge freight door just aft of the wing make it ideal for ferrying heavy and cumbersome loads. There are already several versions of the C-54, the most recent being the C-54-DO and the C-54-DC, whose extra wing tanks give it a fuel capacity of 3,110 gallons.

Douglas has also built just one VC-54C-DO, capable of carrying 4,510 gal (3,750 Imp gal) of fuel. Called the *Sacred Cow*, it will be used by President Roosevelt. An electric elevator under the fuselage has been added to lift the commander-in-chief's wheelchair.

# Hellcats, Avengers beef up Allied strength

*Pacific Ocean, August 31*
A new high-performance fighter, the Grumman F6F Hellcat, made its operational debut today with US Navy squadron VF-5, flying from a US Navy aircraft carrier. The 2,000-hp Hellcat promises to cut a swathe through all the lightly built Japanese warplanes it meets and to outfly them, which earlier Allied fighters were unable to do.

The Hellcat is by no means the only new piece of equipment for Allied carrier-based squadrons. Thanks to decisions taken before the bombing of Pearl Harbor, several new combat aircraft are now making their mark. Perhaps an even better fighter than the Hellcat is Vought's bent-wing F4U Corsair, now in action with island-based US Marine units. This tough 400-mph fighter-bomber will soon be entering service on aircraft carriers of Britain's Royal Navy.

Another newcomer from Grumman is the massive TBF Avenger torpedo-bomber, which is already causing destruction to Japanese ships. So, too, is the Curtiss SB2C Helldiver, which after many initial problems is now being introduced into service by the hundreds. Britain is also introducing its own new naval warplanes. From the Fairey company come the Barracuda torpedo/dive-bomber and the Firefly two-seater fighter.

## 'Flying bomb' site revealed by aerial photo unit of RAF

*London, October 28*
An RAF photo-reconnaissance aircraft today returned to England with what appears to be evidence of a launch site for Hitler's latest secret weapon, a "flying bomb" or rocket. This site was at Abbeville, France, well within the presumed range for attacking London.

The British government has been aware of a German rocket program for some months. Aerial photographs identified Peenemünde on the Baltic as a possible site for development work. Pictures taken last April showed an object protruding from one of several mysterious buildings; four seconds later it had disappeared, leaving only a puff of smoke. The RAF raided Peenemünde on August 18.

Also in August, what appears to have been a smaller rocket landed in Denmark, where an Allied agent photographed it before it could be recovered. A French agent has also sent London plans of a launch site, giving renewed impetus to the hunt for actual sites. The RAF's Photographic Reconnaissance Unit, set up in April 1940, uses specially adapted Spitfires and Mosquitoes with cameras with 20-inch lenses. An interpretation unit at Wembley, London, uses stereoscopic viewing instruments to seek clues from the photographs (→ Dec 24).

**Hollywood star and USAAF captain Clark Gable has participated in raids on Germany's Ruhr area.**

## Women pilots to fly delivery missions for US air services

*Doris Marland, who is a WASP.*

San Antonio, Texas, October 20
The pilot delivering a new aircraft to Randolf Field USAAF base here is likely to be a woman, following today's announcement of the formation of the Women's Air Force Service Pilots (WASP). With airmen needed for combat overseas, the USAAF does not want to use them to ferry planes from factories to bases. The WASPs, headed by veteran pilot Jacqueline Cochran, are one of two groups of women organised along the lines of Britain's Air Transport Auxiliary (ATA) for non-combat roles; the other is the Women's Auxiliary Ferrying Squadron, under Nancy H Love.

*British ATA girl meets Barracuda.*

# Planes spearhead 'island-hopping'

*South-west Pacific, November 5*
At 11.15am over 100 US torpedo planes, dive-bombers and fighters from the carriers USS *Saratoga* and *Princeton* appeared over the island of New Britain and launched the first Allied air attack on Rabaul, the Japanese HQ in the south-west Pacific. The surprise attack caused severe damage to three cruisers and three destroyers, and all but ten raiders returned safely.

The damaged ships were preparing to assault US forces newly established on Bougainville as part of their "island-hopping" campaign in the Solomon Islands. The campaign has been a very costly war of attrition for Japanese air power in the area. Since August last year, when US Marines landed on Guadalcanal, US Army, Navy and Marine land and carrier aircraft have pummeled Japanese air bases.

Guadalcanal was a springboard for moves up the Solomons to Bougainville, the largest island in the group. Each step has followed the same pattern: incessant bombardment by New Hebrides-based US

*USAAF personnel unload steel mats to build an airfield on Guadalcanal.*

13th Air Force heavy and medium bombers and shorter-range planes from Henderson Field, Guadalcanal, has been followed by surprise amphibious landings, the quick repair of existing airfields or the con-

struction of new ones, the securing of the objective, and then on to the next island. Each island captured has cost the Japanese airfields, and the air battles have lost them 3,000 aircraft and pilots (→ Feb 17, 1944).

## Memphis belle greets the 'Memphis Belle'

*Memphis, Tennessee, June 19*
Captain Robert K Morgan and the *Memphis Belle*, the first B-17 Flying Fortress to complete 25 missions in Europe, landed here today to be greeted by Morgan's fiancée Margaret Polk, after whom the bomber was named. The story of Captain Morgan, his nine crewmen and their B-17 is one of courage, skill and, as they admit, luck. They came together in September in Bangor, Maine, flew here for Polk to christen the B-17 and crossed the Atlantic to join the US Eighth Air Force in England.

The bomber's 25 missions began with a raid on submarine pens at Brest, France, on November 7, and ended with an attack on the shipyard at Wilhelmshaven, Germany. During that time the crew survived anti-aircraft fire, fighters and bombs dropped onto the bomber formations while delivering more than 60 tons of bombs and shooting down eight confirmed and five probable German fighters. Only the tail-gunner suffered so much as a

*Captain Morgan is congratulated.*

minor wound, but the *Memphis Belle* was frequently riddled with bullets and anti-aircraft fire. Five times it limped back to England on three engines. But it was patched up and even given a new wing so that it could fly back home to the USA today (→ Aug 17).

## Berlin is pounded in Lancaster raid

*Berlin, November 27*
After a night of ceaseless bombing, Berliners climbed from their cellars this morning to find much of the German capital in ruins. RAF heavy bombers, supported by Mosquitoes, had made their fourth big raid of the week, dropping at least 5,000 tons of high explosive and incendiary weapons.

The first estimates of casualties number the dead at over 4,000, with 400,000 homeless. The administrative heart of Berlin has been severely hit, including the Air Ministry, Admiralty and Hitler's Chancellery. A house was destroyed when a bomber crashed on to it, killing 92 people in an air-raid shelter.

But the RAF is paying a high price in lost aircraft and aircrews. Of the 450 Lancasters and Halifaxes that set out, 42 failed to return. Fourteen of them limped back across the English Channel only to crash in Britain, sometimes within sight of their home airfields.

# Germans develop advanced air weapons

*Germany, December*

Allied reconnaissance aircraft are finding increasing evidence of radical new types of airplane on trial for the Luftwaffe at test establishments throughout Germany.

At Rechlin, narrow lines scorched in the grass and over tarmac show where the extraordinary Me 163B Komet, powered by the Walter 109-509A-2 rocket engine, has been tested. This tiny airplane is distinctive in having swept-back wings but no horizontal tail. It has already been assigned to combat units and will see action next year.

Broader scorch marks on the ground indicate the testing of turbojets. Two Jumo 004B engines power both the Messerschmitt Me 262A fighter and the Arado Ar 234B reconnaissance-bomber. Both are likely to cause the Allies some headaches in the coming year.

At Peenemünde, on the Baltic coast, the V-1 flying bomb and V-2 rocket [*see story on page 419*] have been developed. The rocket, in particular, might prove dangerous to the Allies, as at present no defense against it exists. At Karlshagen, near Hanover, air-launched missiles are being tested. They include the Hs 293 guided rocket-bomb, the powerful FX 1400 guided bomb and the Bv 246 glider-bomb; these have not been detected by Allied reconnaissance (→ Oct 30, 1944).

*Production of the turbojet-powered Messerschmitt Me 262 began last month.*

# Air war intensifies in battle for China

*China, December 25*

The air war is escalating in China as the Nationalist forces, bolstered by the USAAF, clash with Japan. The battle is particularly fierce in the northern Hunan province, where Chinese troops today recaptured Kung-an, a town which was lost two months ago when 100,000 Japanese soldiers invaded the area. Air power is playing a vital role in the campaign, as Japan tries to prevent Chinese troops from moving south to support the Allied forces in Burma.

American and Chinese pilots have been used to drop supplies and to airlift artillery to the battle zones. A sign of their success has been increased attention from the Japanese air force. Two weeks ago, a major night attack on Allied airfields at Changte destroyed 40 US and Chinese airplanes.

# 'Superfortresses' bound for China

*China, December 15*

China is preparing furiously for the arrival early next year of a new superbomber: the Boeing B-29, dubbed "Superfortress" after the older B-17 Flying Fortress. Laborers are working round the clock to prepare the runways of more than a mile in length needed by the new bomber, which it is hoped will bring Japan to its knees. Boeing is running behind schedule with the manufacture of the B-29 due to delays in the supply of components, but even so the first aircraft should be delivered some time in March.

It is an awesome machine. With pressurized cabins and a bomb load of nearly 5 tons, it can fly 3,250 miles at 35,000 feet, well out of reach of Japanese defense fighters. The British in India are also expecting B-29s, which will be flown by the USAAF (→ Jun 5, 1944).

# USA leads the field as combatants boost aircraft output for another year of war

*Lines of Soviet Yak fighters are turned out at a factory in the USSR.*

*Washington, DC, December*

As the world prepares for another bitter year of fighting, Allied and Axis aircraft manufacturers are achieving almost unbelievable production records. The US has nearly doubled last year's figures with a staggering total of 85,898 aircraft rolling from the assembly lines. The Soviets have built 34,900 against last year's 25,436; and, despite the Allies' constant night and daylight bombing raids, the Germans have succeeded in building 24,807 aircraft, an increase of nearly 10,000 in a year.

Japanese workers doubled their production from 8,861 to 16,693, while Britain has made the smallest increase, from 23,672 to 26,263.

In the battle of war economies, the Allies have a clear advantage with the US as their arsenal. In human terms, too, the Axis has problems. Most Japanese pilots who were serving at the time of Pearl Harbor are now dead, and many of their successors are young and inexperienced. The Germans, too, are being forced to draw upon younger and younger pilots.

*Lancasters are built in England (here by Austin Motor) and also in Canada.*

The Lockheed Constellation transport was designed for TWA, but was quickly impressed as the USAAF C-69, in which guise it could carry 94 troops.

The wooden Curtiss C-76 Caravan.

The Junkers Ju 352 trimotor was a Ju 252 redesigned in wood.

Lavochkin's La-7 was one of the most successful Soviet fighters.

Junkers's six-engined Ju 390 strategic bomber was an enlarged Ju 290.

The Hughes D-2 was developed into the XF-11 reconnaissance aircraft.

The Hawker Tempest II fighter did not reach the RAF until 1945.

Dornier's Do 335 Pfeil [Arrow] fighter featured pusher and tractor Daimler-Benz DB 603 power plants, and its pilot sat on a primitive ejector seat.

The all-wing Northrop XP-56 Black Bullet proved too tricky to handle.

The Fisher XP-75 Eagle used many components from other aircraft.

The Consolidated PB4Y-2 Privateer was a long-range maritime patrol-bomber development of the B-24 Liberator with numerous major changes.

The Nakajima Ki-84 Hayate [Hurricane], "Frank" to the Allies, was much faster and better armed than the earlier Mitsubishi A6M Zero of the navy.

Savoia-Marchetti's S.M.95 transport enjoyed a long post-war career.

Junkers Ju 388J: a night fighter with nose-mounted radar array.

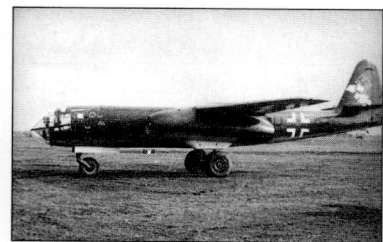

*Arado's Ar 234B-2: the first in-service jet reconnaissance-bomber.*

*Sikorsky's R-5 helicopter flew with the US Navy in 1945 as the HO2S-1.*

*The de Havilland DH.100 Vampire was originally dubbed "the Spider Crab" and did not enter service until after the war. Because de Havilland was so busy all production for many years was handled by English Electric at Preston.*

*The Supermarine Spitfire Mk XII was the first Griffon-engined version of this classic fighter. The later Mk XIV had a more powerful two-stage Griffon.*

*The Saab 21A pusher-engined fighter: 299 were later converted into jets.*

*Curtiss produced three CW-24 XP-55 Ascender prototypes.*

*The Gloster F.9/40 Meteor became the only operational Allied jet fighter of the war. This prototype flew in 1943 with Metrovick F.2 axial engines.*

*Kawanishi's N1K2 Shinden fighter, the land-based version of N1K1.*

*Focke-Wulf constructed its Ta 154A night fighter of film-bonded wood.*

*Curtiss's XP-62 high-altitude fighter prototype. It took six 20mm cannon.*

*The Junkers Ju 388K bomber had a pressurized crew compartment.*

*The Grumman F7F Tigercat was the first US twin-engined carrier fighter. Its P&W R-2800 Double Wasps gave it 4,000hp – more than enough!*

*The Miles M.39B Libellula, powered by two Gipsy engines, tested the aft-wing concept, much of the lift coming from a flapped foreplane.*

# 1944

623.85mph
Germany
Heini Dittmar
Messerschmitt Me 163A
Oct 2, 1941

8,038 miles
Italy
Tondi, Degasso, Vignoli
Savoia-Marchetti S.M.75
Aug 1, 1939

56,046ft
Italy
Mario Pezzi
Caproni 161bis
Oct 22, 1938

207,981lb
Germany
Blohm & Voss
V238 V1

4,410lb thrust
Germany
Walter HWK
109-509 C

**Europe, January 6**
Lieutenant-General Carl Spaatz takes command of the US Strategic Air Forces in Europe (USSAFE), a new grouping amalgamating the US Eighth Air Force in Britain and the US 15th Air Force in Italy; he has responsibility for all long-range bombing of Germany (→ 31).

**Frankfurt, January 7**
US movie star James Stewart leads the USAAF 445th Bomb Group in a raid on the city.

**Atlantic, January 11**
Two Grumman TBF-1C Avengers from the USS *Block Island* make the first US attack with forward-firing rockets, on a German U-boat; the rockets, slung beneath the fighter's wing, increase the chance of hitting a target because they have much greater power than guns.

**London, January 21/22**
Over 440 Luftwaffe bombers launch Operation Steinbock, a new wave of attacks (→ Apr 18/19).

**Pacific Ocean, February 17**
In the first night-bombing attack from a US aircraft carrier, 12 US Navy Grumman Avengers from the USS *Enterprise* hit several Japanese ships during the battle for the Marshall Islands (→ Jun 15).

**Berkshire, England, March 2**
Operation Sailor, a rehearsal for Neptune, the airborne operation which is to accompany the planned Allied invasion of northern France, takes place; 97 gliders land waves of British and US troops at ten-second intervals with 100 per cent success (→ May 6).

**Germany, March 23**
RAF Flight Sergeant Nicholas Alkemade jumps without a parachute from his stricken Lancaster bomber at 18,000 feet, but lands in a snow bank without breaking a single bone after his fall is broken by a fir tree.

**The Hague, April 11**
Six RAF de Havilland Mosquito bombers of 613 Squadron make a brilliant precision attack on the Kleizkamp art gallery, used by the Gestapo, destroying records of the Dutch Resistance.

**Seattle, Washington, May 2**
After many years of being known first as McGee Airways, then as Star Air Lines and Alaska Star Airlines, the name of this pioneering carrier is once again changed to Alaska Airlines.

**Japan, May 6**
Eisaku Shibayama pilots the Mitsubishi A7M1 Reppu [Hurricane] on its first flight; the fighter is designed to replace the famous Zero.

**Eastern Europe, June 2**
US bombers fly their first "shuttle" bombing raids of the war; they take off from bases in Italy to hit communications targets in Hungary before landing at three new USAAF bases in the USSR.

**Bangkok, June 5**
The Boeing B-29 Superfortress bomber makes its operational debut in a raid on the city from bases in India.

**California, June 10**
The second prototype of the Lockheed Shooting Star is flown for the first time, by test pilot Tony LeVier. Larger and heavier than its predecessor, its 3,810-lb thrust jet engine can propel it at over 580mph at an altitude of 39,300 feet (→ Dec 6).

**USA, June 12**
The Civil Aeronautics Board awards United Airlines and TWA the right to serve Boston; in May last year these airlines won the right to serve Washington, DC, on transcontinental flights. Both these routes were previously the sole preserve of American Airlines.

**Somerset, England, July 12**
Two Gloster Meteor F.1 fighters are delivered to 616 Squadron at Culmhead – the first operational jet-powered airplanes to serve with the RAF (→ Sep 20, 1945).

**Coutances, France, July 17**
USAAF P-38 Lightnings use napalm incendiary material for the first time, during a raid.

**California, August 1**
The US Army Air Force renames the Mojave Desert facility at Rogers Dry Lake, calling it the Muroc Flight Test Base, commonly known as Muroc Dry Lake; the word "Muroc" is the name Corum spelled backwards. In 1910, two brothers, Ralph and Clifford Corum, became the first humans to settle permanently in the area and founded a small community, calling it Muroc (→ Jan 27, 1950).

**Germany, August 16**
The Junkers Ju 287 V1 prototype jet bomber, which features forward-swept wings, is flown for the first time.

**London, September 10**
The Luftwaffe flies its first photo-reconnaissance mission over the city since January 10, 1941; RAF Fighter Command has kept these aircraft away for 38 months.

**Maryland, September 10**
The first aircraft of the war designed solely for cargo, the Fairchild C-82, makes its first flight, at Hagerstown.

**Germany, September 18**
The Messerschmitt Me 262 undergoes operational tests and Walter Nowotny sets up a jet fighter unit, the Erpro-bungskommando 262, based at Achmer (→ Nov 8).

**England, September**
The 12,780th – and last – Hawker Hurricane fighter built in Britain is delivered.

**Germany, November 8**
Major Nowotny dies after crashing his Me 262. His squadron, JG7, will bear his name.

**Croydon, England, November 13**
The airport is reopened for civil operations; the first service is flown by a Railway Air Services D.H.86B to Belfast via Liverpool.

**English Channel, December 5**
The UC-64 aircraft bearing US band leader Major Glenn Miller from Bedford to Paris disappears over the Channel.

**Vienna, December 6**
The Heinkel He 162 Volksjäger [People's Fighter], a wooden-winged jet designed and built in 69 days, makes its first flight.

**Chicago, December 7**
The International Civil Aviation Conference ends; delegates from 52 countries have held talks since November 1 to work out post-war standards for civil aviation.

**Utah, December 17**
The USAAF 509th Composite Group is formed under Colonel Paul Tibbets to practice dropping atomic bombs; the unit will also modify aircraft to carry the bomb.

**Liège, Belgium, December 24**
In the world's first operation by jet bombers, German Arado Ar 234B-2 Blitz [Lightning] bombers led by Captain Dieter Lukesch hit a factory and marshaling yards.

**Pacific Ocean, December 24**
The people of the Philippines receive a surprise when airplanes of 43rd Bombing Group fly over to drop a million Christmas cards; each one contains the words: "Merry Christmas and Happy New Year 1944 – General Douglas MacArthur."

*Nothing shall stop them: a stirring poster for the USAAF represents the members of the bomber force as defenders of the world's freedom.* ▶

# 'Lulu Belle' will be named Shooting Star

*"Lulu Belle" was transported from Burbank to Muroc Dry Lake for the tests.*

*Muroc Dry Lake, Calif, January 13*
This time, the prototype XP-80 flew perfectly. It climbed at such a rate during its test at the USAAF base here that the military have decided to call the jet *Shooting Star*.

Today's flight was better than the one made on January 8 by Lockheed test pilot Milo Burcham. He nearly crashed when the flaps kept retracting due to the pressure of air at high speed. The landing gear also refused to retract. Nicknamed *Lulu Belle* by the Lockheed design team

headed by Hall L Hibbard and C L "Kelly" Johnson, the XP-80 was built in 143 days. It is expected to achieve a speed of more than 500-mph in sustained level flight. The XP-80 is the country's second jet-powered aircraft, after the Bell XP-59 Airacomet, which first flew on October 2, 1942. When the *Lulu Belle* took to the air today it was equipped with six machine guns in its nose and powered by a 3,000-lb thrust de Havilland H.1B turbojet (→ Jun 10).

# Sikorsky R-4 helicopter in mercy mission

*The two-seater Sikorsky R-4 is designated HNS by the US Coast Guard.*

*Sandy Hook, NJ, January 3*
Igor Sikorsky's belief that his helicopter will play a humanitarian role in aviation was justified here today. Over 100 sailors had been injured in an explosion on a destroyer; blood plasma was desperately needed, but a snowstorm had grounded fixed-

wing aircraft. Flying a Sikorsky R-4, Commander Frank Erikson of the US Coast Guard flew the plasma from New York. The R-4 has seen service with the USAAF in Alaska and Burma. It is the first helicopter to be operated by British forces, as the Hoverfly I (→ Apr 23).

# Doolittle cuts fighter escorts for bombers

*Vapor trails reveal the position of high-flying aircraft to the enemy.*

*England, January 31*
General Jimmy Doolittle of the British-based US Eighth Air Force is making a high-stakes gamble in the air war against Germany. He has ordered that on future bombing raids some aircraft of the US bombers' fighter escort should abandon their defensive duties and instead peel off and take on attacking Luftwaffe fighters directly.

Doolittle, who led the astonishing B-25 bombing raid against Tokyo in April 1942, knows the

dangers faced by the bomber pilots and crews in their slow machines. Although a number of US bomber crews have complained bitterly that the new policy is a risky one and could backfire, Doolittle is relying on the tactical gamble that his fighters can knock out the enemy before US losses reach an unacceptable level.

He is also following a longer-term objective: to soften up the Luftwaffe before the planned Allied landings in France (→ Feb 25).

# Pilotless bomber lands in family's garden

*Cambridge, England, February 23*
The Riglesford family had a shock tonight when they found a fully-laden German Dornier bomber in their garden. They entered their shelter when they heard air-raid sirens signalling that Luftwaffe bombers were on their way to attack London, and heard nothing to indicate that the airplane had landed. Inspecting the machine with caution, they realized that it was

only by a miracle that they had escaped with their lives. The Dornier's bomb bays contained its full load of incendiary bombs, and there was plenty of petrol in the tanks, which might have turned the Riglesfords' house into an inferno.

The bomber's cabin was badly damaged but empty – the pilot and crew had bailed out, and been picked up by the police some 30 miles away.

*Almost undamaged, the Do 217M-1 was the first of its type to be captured.*

# Americans rebuild Japanese Zero fighter

*The USAAF has made a close study of Japan's remarkable Zero fighter.*

*Dayton, Ohio, February 12*
By building a Japanese Mitsubishi A6M Zero fighter from the remains of five aircraft shot down in the Pacific theater, USAAF engineers at Wright Field near here have learned the secrets of its combat success and exposed its weaknesses.

The Zero has good maneuverability (especially at low-to-medium altitude), a high rate of climb and a top speed of over 330mph. All this is achieved with a small 950-hp, 14-cylinder radial Nakajima NK1C Sakae engine, which appears to be practically identical to a mid-1930s Pratt & Whitney powerplant. The aircraft's performance is largely due to the Zero's light weight, which is a liability as well as an asset. As has been demonstrated by the US Navy, which recovered and tested an almost intact Zero in 1942, heavier US aircraft like the P-40 Warhawk and F4F Wildcat, while unable to climb and turn with the Zero, can gain an advantage by diving.

The Mitsubishi A6M is very light because it omits armor from key parts of the airframe, including the cockpit, and self-sealing fuel tanks. These omissions make the Zero vulnerable in combat and more likely to be destroyed by hits which US aircraft would survive (→ May 6).

# More than 1,800 aircraft clash over Berlin

*Boeing built 4,035 B-17Gs, Douglas manufactured 2,395 and Vega 2,250.*

*Berlin, March 6*
Berlin and nearby towns were struck today by 658 B-17s and B-24s of the US Eighth Air Force. Despite an escort of about 700 fighters, 69 US bombers were shot down by German fighters. Because it took a long time to get so many planes into the air over East Anglia, they were easily detected by German radar, allowing fighters to be sent to intercept them. The Germans saw that the escort fighters were concentrated at the ends of the 60-mile-long flight of bombers and sent small groups of fighters to tackle them. Meanwhile, a force of 400 Bf 109s and Fw 190s ravaged the bombers in the formation's unprotected center. When the raiders reached Berlin, partial cloud cover meant that most of the bombs hit the city's suburbs and nearby towns rather than the capital's center (→ Mar 31).

# Allied bombers devastate Monte Cassino

*Monte Cassino, Italy, February 15*
Allied aircraft have bombed the 700-year-old monastery of Monte Cassino, which stands in the way of the Allied advance through Italy.

The Americans were against a raid on the building, but Lieutenant-General Sir Bernard Freyberg, whose New Zealand Corps is leading the ground assault, was convinced it was being used as an observation post by German artillery.

However, Allied supreme commander in the Mediterranean General Sir Henry Maitland-Wilson gave the go-ahead for the air raid. The onslaught was carried out by 142 B-17 Flying Fortresses, B-25 Mitchells and B-26 Marauders, which dropped 400 tons of high explosive on the monastery, now a shattered ruin after a day and a night of bombardment. There were in fact no Germans in the building, only the abbot and a handful of monks; ironically, the 3rd German Paratroop Regiment is now moving into the ruins.

*P-51 and A-36 Mustangs played a major role at Monte Cassino.*

# RAF bombs Amiens jail to free prisoners

*Amiens, France, February 18*
In a breathtaking display of precision bombing, 19 RAF Mosquito fighter-bombers today brought the walls of Amiens jail down in the aptly-named Operation Jericho. The aircrews needed split-second timing to drop their 500-lb bombs onto the 3-foot-thick, 20-foot-high walls. The first three bombers missed the outer wall, but the two following were on target. The next pair bombed the guards' dining room before the main prison block was hit. Several aircrew were lost, including the raid's leader, Group Captain Charles Pickard, shot down by an Fw 190. On the ground, 56 Resistance prisoners were killed, many shot by guards. But 258 Frenchmen escaped, almost all having faced execution next day (→ Apr 11).

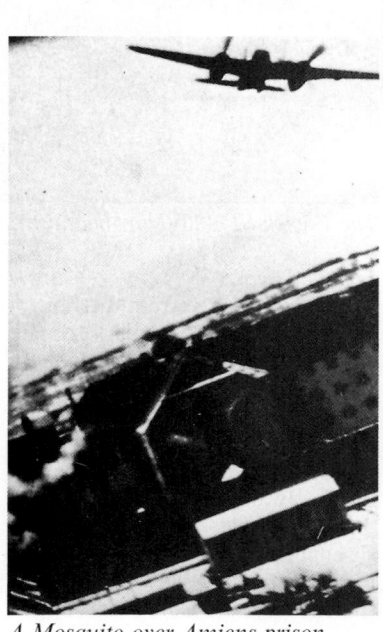

*A Mosquito over Amiens prison.*

# Howard Hughes flies a C-69 Constellation

*Constellations built for the commercial market are designated L-049.*

*Washington, DC, April 17*
Billionaire Howard Hughes landed a four-engined Lockheed C-69 Constellation at 1.54pm here today. Along with navigator Howard Bolton, TWA chief Jack Frye and two other crew, Hughes had taken off from Burbank, California, yesterday at 3.57am. The 2,299-mile non-stop flight took six hours 57 minutes 51 seconds, giving an average speed of 331.54mph. Aboard the Constellation were 12 VIPs invited by Hughes, the USAAF and Lockheed. Since Hughes became a majority shareholder in TWA six years ago, he has sought to qualify to fly all the airline's airplanes. He however had some difficulty in gaining his qualification on the Constellation, but finally succeeded after training at Palm Springs.

# Swiss get 12 fighters they can't use

*This twin-engined Bf 110G-4 night fighter is fitted with C.2 and SN.2 radars.*

*Switzerland, May 20*
The Swiss government has to a certain extent been hoist on its own petard. On April 28, a German Messerschmitt Bf 110G-4 night fighter was forced to make an emergency landing at Dübendorf, near Zurich, due to engine problems. The aircraft was fitted with top secret radar systems and sophisticated oblique-firing guns. Germany, desperate to stop the plane falling into Allied hands, offered Switzerland 12 Messerschmitt Bf 109G-6s in exchange for the destruction of the Bf 110. The Swiss agreed, but first thoroughly inspected the grounded fighter. However, when the 12 Bf 109s were delivered today, the Swiss found they needed overhaul: not one of them was operational.

# RAF destroys commandeered flying boats

*The French SE.200 flying-boat can take off with a total weight of 71 tons.*

*London, April 17*
The radio message from the French Resistance was simple enough: "Suzanne and Louise have gone on holiday." It was passed on to "Vernon" – alias Henri Ziegler, Free French chief of staff in London. He knew what it meant: the Luftwaffe had commandeered three valuable French prototype six-engined flying boats, taking them from Marseilles to Friedrichshafen, on Lake Constance. Engineers and pilots at the Marignane base had long wished they could fly the aircraft – an SE.200, a Latécoère 631 and a Potez-CAMS 631 – to freedom. They could not, so when Luftwaffe crews arrived to ferry them to Germany two Resistance fighters sent the innocuous message about "Suzanne" and "Louise". Today, as the three giants were being refueled, six RAF Mosquitoes swooped down and riddled them with cannon fire. The flying boats sank to the bottom of the lake.

# US helicopter rescues secret service men

*Burma, April 23*
A US Sikorsky YR-4 helicopter is back at its secret base behind Japanese lines in northern Burma after a daring rescue of four British special operations troops. This is the latest rescue involving US special forces airmen and Britain's "Chindit" guerillas and Special Operations Executive. Pilot Lieutenant Carter Harman had to lift four men out of a tight jungle corner in which their aircraft had crashed. Knowing his engine did not have enough lift to take them all up at once, he snatched them one at a time and used full throttle at the critical moment to get airborne.

**A patched-up Chinese DC-3, flying with the right wing of a DC-2! The DC-3's original wing was damaged on the ground in a bombing attack.**

# More than 11,000 planes fight it out over Channel

## RAF destroys all German radars but one

*The Typhoon weighs seven tons and is a valued ground-attack aircraft.*

*Cherbourg, France, June 5*

An RAF raid by 25 Typhoon 1B aircraft today destroyed the German radar station at Cap de La Hague, near here. This has left Germany with just one operational radar station between here and Boulogne, at Boulogne itself. It was spared so that it would spot the aluminum "chaff" to be ejected off Boulogne just hours before the Allied landings. Typhoons, designed by Sydney Camm of Hawker, are well-armed, heavy attack planes whose cockpits stand more than eight feet above the ground.

## Why air power holds key to Allies success

*London, England, June 7*

The importance of air power in the D-Day invasion is seen in the chain of command: the overall deputy to supreme Allied commander General Dwight Eisenhower is not a general, nor an admiral, even though this was the greatest seaborne invasion in history. Eisenhower's number two is an airman – Air Chief Marshal Sir Arthur Tedder. Now that a beach-head has been established, fighters and medium bombers, operating from England, will be crucial in providing direct fire support to the armies as they fight their way inland. As soon as airfields can be made available they will operate from France, moving with the advancing armies.

*Air support: a Republic P-47 Thunderbolt with a fire-bomb beneath its wing.*

## US warplanes get special D-Day paint job

*England, June 5*

As last-minute preparations for the Allied invasion are under way, all warplanes involved in D-Day operations are beginning to look like zebras.

As paratroops and aircrew await the 'go' order, every aircraft is getting black and white stripes painted on its wings and fuselage. Allied commanders hope that such highly-visible markings will prevent the airplanes being hit by friendly fire from the ground, as was the case a year ago during the Allied landing on Sicily, when US Navy gunners mistakenly shot down 27 Douglas C-47s.

*A-20 Havoc with new stripes.*

## RAF Spitfires over the Normandy beaches

*Normandy, France, June 6*

Almost four years after the Battle of Britain, Spitfires of the RAF have been transformed. In 1940 all were powered by Rolls Royce Merlin engines of 1,030-hp, or 1,290-hp on 100-octane fuel.

Today, thousands of far more formidable "Spits" are almost darkening the sky over the Allied invasion force landing on the beaches of Normandy. Not all have the famed Merlin engine, and not one retains the eight machine guns of 1940. Almost every RAF Spitfire is armed with two wing-mounted 20mm Hispano-Suiza long-barreled cannon, plus either four .303 or two .5 machine guns. Those Spitfires equipped with the "Universal" wing can carry two drop tanks or 500-lb bombs, although one squadron has already begun ferrying in externally-slung barrels of beer.

No fewer than 60 squadrons fly the Mk IX, with the two-stage Merlin. Others fly the Mk XVI, with the Packard Merlin, pointed rudder and teardrop canopy. Many have low-altitude fighter (LF) clipped wings. By far the most awesome are the Mk XIVs. A 2,050-hp Rolls-Royce Griffon engine drives a huge five-bladed propeller and it has an operational ceiling of 40,000 feet. Spitfire Mk XIVs have quickly become the masters of German Bf 109s or Fw 190s.

*Starting in 1941, a total of more than 6,500 Spitfire Mk Vs were built.*

# US spotter plane is armed with bazooka

*An American pilot rests against his maneuverable Piper L-4 light plane.*

**Normandy, June 10**

"Grasshoppers" – as the Piper Cub light airplanes, normally used for artillery-spotting and observation, are officially named – have found a new role in battle as "tank-busters". Fitted with bazooka anti-tank rockets, the highly maneuverable L-4B is able to fly at grasstop height and land almost in its own length. Major Charles Carpenter of the US Fourth Army Division has

fitted six of these rocket weapons under his L-4 and destroyed five German tanks.

On June 7 a squadron of Piper L-4s fitted with supplementary fuel tanks flew across the English Channel to guide naval bombardment of enemy positions. The 65-hp Cubs are now helping the Allied advance by spotting for the artillery and looking for concentrations of German armored forces.

# US bombs Japan after two-year break

*Yawata, Japan, June 15*

In the first US attack on mainland Japan since the daring Doolittle raid of April 1942, 47 B-29 Superfortresses flying from Chengtu, China, today bombed the imperial iron and steel works at Yawata. One B-29 was destroyed on the ground at Neihsiang airfield by enemy fighters when engine trouble forced it down.

Today's raid is the culmination of an effort which began late last year. At that time it was decided to exploit the Superfortress's 1,600-mile radius by basing B-29s in

India and staging them through China for attacks on Japan. It is hoped that they will eventually attack Japan from the Marianas, when this Pacific island group has been recaptured by US forces.

Creating bases in China and India to support the B-29s has been a big task. Construction and maintenance equipment and materials, munitions and fuel all had to be transported great distances before the bombers could go on the offensive. The B-29s themselves helped; they ferried in supplies as soon as runways were usable (→ Jun 18).

*The B-29, with 1,600-mile radius, has made attacks on Japan more feasible.*

# QANTAS speeds up service to Ceylon

*Colombo, June 17*

With two sunsets on the westbound flight and two sunrises on the return, the QANTAS service from Perth to Ceylon [Sri Lanka] was the world's longest scheduled flight. Flying Catalina flying boats especially adapted for the task, QANTAS formed an important link in the chain of air routes connecting Britain's colonies and dominions.

Until today the non-stop, 3,513-mile flight from Australia to Ceylon lasted on average 27 hours, and often more than 30 hours. It had few passengers and was used mainly as a mail service, with a payload restricted to 1,200 pounds. In October 1943 the service was extended to Karachi.

The introduction of Liberator landplanes today will reduce the flight time to 17 hours, including a stopover at Exmouth Gulf, 600 miles north of Perth (→ Jun 2, 1945).

# Hitler's V-1 'reprisal weapon' brings death to heart of London

*London, June 13*

Hitler's first *Vergeltungswaffe* [reprisal weapon] struck London's East End last night, killing six people in Grove Road, Bethnal Green. The V-1, more properly the Fieseler Fi 103, is a flying bomb – a miniature pilotless airplane. In the nose is a devastating warhead

loaded with 1,870 lb of high explosive. In the middle are the fuel tanks and small wings. The tail contains autopilot controls, and on top, at the rear, is the deafeningly noisy pulsejet that powers the weapon. This engine is programed to cut out after a flight time that would put it over London; the V-1 then

falls silently on its victims. The V-1s will fly at 1,000 feet at speeds of around 400mph, so they will be difficult to catch. Hitler wanted to launch the V-1 last year but was delayed by RAF raids on its launch and production sites. Now launch sites are vulnerable to any Allied advance from Normandy.

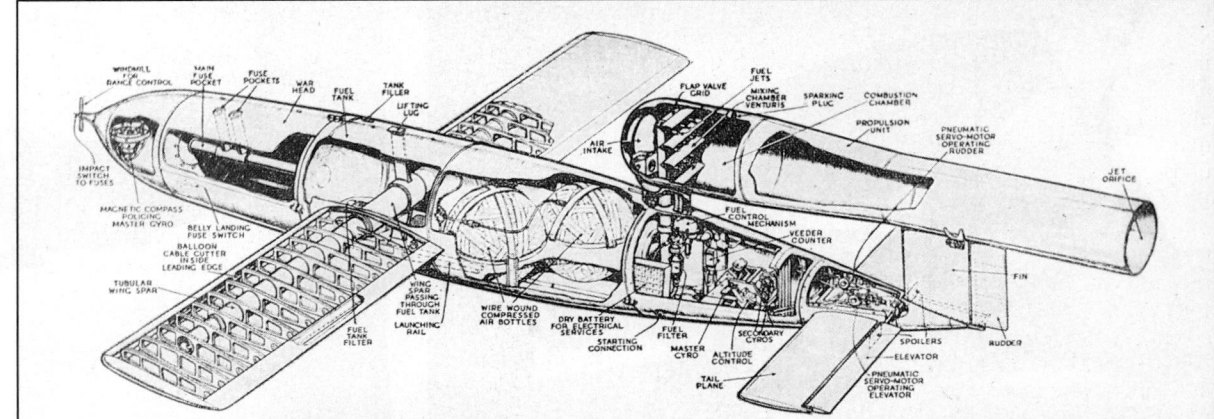

*A 1944 drawing by Max Millar of "Flight" of the V-1 flying bomb – or "doodlebug", as it was nicknamed by the British.*

# Pacific battle becomes 'turkey shoot'

*A suicide attacker just misses.*

*The Curtiss SB2C Helldiver dive-bomber, one of TF58's lethal weapons.*

*Philippine Sea, June 20*
Japanese air power in the Pacific has been dealt a savage blow in the last two days by Vice-Admiral Marc Mitscher's Task Force 58 (TF58). In what the Americans are nicknaming "the Marianas turkey shoot", warplanes from TF58's seven heavy and eight light aircraft carriers have ravaged Japanese land-based aircraft on the ground on Guam and the other Mariana Islands. They have also repulsed attacks by airplanes from nine Japanese carriers and destroyed most of Japan's remaining carrier-borne air strength in this part of the Pacific.

In two days the Japanese have lost 480 aircraft, almost as many pilots, and three aircraft carriers.

The US force has lost 129 planes and 76 pilots, while three ships have been slightly damaged. Vice-Admiral Ozawa's force never had a chance. The 500 land-based airplanes he was depending on to support his 600 carrier aircraft had been hit on the ground. With over 900 aircraft TF58 outnumbered the opposition, and shipboard radar enabled the aircraft to counter attacks. Yesterday 402 Japanese airplanes were lost, either in the air or on board two carriers which were sunk by US submarines. TF58 lost only 29 aircraft, and half of the downed US pilots were rescued.

Today 216 of TF58's planes went after the Japanese fleet, sinking the heavy carrier *Hiryo* and damaging two heavy and two light carriers, one battleship and one heavy cruiser. They destroyed 78 more Japanese planes for the loss of 20 US aircraft, although a further 80 US warplanes were either lost on the long night flight back or crash-ed landed on their carriers. Almost three-quarters of the 200 aircrew involved were rescued (→ Aug 9).

## Saipan is set to be latest air-led 'island-hopping' US victory

*Pacific Ocean, June 18*
US ground forces have seized control of Aslito on the Japanese-held island of Saipan in the Marianas, which they stormed yesterday. The invasion followed a heavy air attack a week ago in which some 200 Japanese aircraft were damaged. It is one of many similar air-led assaults upon Japanese island bases in the Pacific, by means of which the Americans hope to gain a satisfactory base for long-range bombing raids on Japan.

General MacArthur's forces won control of the Admiralty Islands off New Guinea on May 18 after a similar operation. Each new island taken serves as a base for an attack on the next in the chain (→ Jun 20).

*US Marine Corps F4U Corsairs ready for take-off from Espiritu Santo.*

## Germans form first jet unit for combat

*Lechfeld, Germany, June 30*
A special Luftwaffe unit was form-ed today to fly the jet-propelled Messerschmitt Me 262A-2a high-speed bomber. Known as Kommando Schenk, or 1/KG 51, it is the world's first jet combat unit, although 616 Squadron of Britain's Auxiliary Air Force is about to become operational with Gloster Meteors. When the new unit is combat ready, it will move to Châteaudun, France.

The Me 262 was designed as a fighter, but at Hitler's insistence it has been produced as a bomber, carrying two 551-lb bombs.

## Rocket airplane is taken on test flight

*Muroc Dry Lake, Calif, July 5*
Previously known only as secret Project 12, the Northrop MX-324 rocket-powered "flying wing" has just made its first powered flight with test pilot Harry Crosby lying inside the wing in an unconventional face-down position. The MX-324 is not a warplane but a research aircraft. Neither is it particularly fast; it has fixed landing gear and is not intended to exceed 300mph. It is powered by a Reaction Motors rocket fed with aniline and concentrated nitric acid.

## Pilot error hands vital secrets to RAF

*Suffolk, England, July 13*
Mist still hung over Woodbridge RAF base this morning when an aircraft was heard approaching from the sea. Assuming it to be a lost Mosquito, the duty officer fired a flare, giving permission to land. To his amazement – and delight – the plane was in fact a Junkers Ju 88G night-fighter with a three-man crew, which had got lost on a training mission. The Ju 88 is said to be packed with "every imaginable" kind of radio and radar, such as FuG220. This radar device is not fooled by "Window", the tinfoil strips expelled by RAF bombers to confuse conventional systems.

▷

# RAF jet fighter wins duel with V-1 bomb

*One of the second batch of Gloster Meteors, a Mk III.*

**Manston, England, August 4**
Flying Officer P J "Dixie" Dean of 616 Squadron RAF took part in the first combat between jet-powered aircraft today when his Gloster Meteor fighter destroyed a German V-1 flying bomb (or "doodlebug", as it is known to Londoners) in flight. Capable of 493mph, thanks to its Rolls-Royce 1,700lb-thrust engines, the Meteor is one of few aircraft fast enough to intercept the pilotless V-1s. In today's encounter, Dean's 20mm cannon jammed when he tried to shoot the V-1 down. He flew alongside the missile, slipped his wing-tip under its wing and banked sharply to flip the missile up, sending it crashing into woodland (→ Sep 8).

# George Bush bails out into Pacific Ocean

*A Grumman Avenger torpedo-bomber taking off from an aircraft carrier.*

**Bonin Islands, Japan, September 2**
US Navy carrier pilot Lieutenant George Bush has had a second narrow escape.

Today, as he flew his Grumman Avenger on a bombing raid against a Japanese radio station at Chi Chi Jima Island, near here, his airplane was hit by ground fire. Bush, who is the sole survivor among the torpedo-bomber's three-man crew, managed stay in the air just long enough to bail out over the ocean and he was quickly picked up by a US Navy submarine.

Last June, Bush's machine was hit by enemy fire shortly after take-off from the aircraft carrier *San Jacinto*, but the young officer was able to crash-land at sea.

# Only one pilot for Mistel's two airplanes

*The pilotless, explosive-filled Junkers Ju 88 with an Fw 190 fighter on top.*

**St Dizier, France, June 25**
A special Luftwaffe squadron flew its first combat mission last night. It is the first to be equipped with a new "piggy-back" system of two airplanes called Mistel [mistletoe]. This is made up of a Bf 109 or Fw 190 fighter mounted on top of a pilotless Junkers Ju 88 with its crew section filled with a giant 8,380-pound warhead. The composite aircraft takes off and flies toward its target controlled by the fighter pilot. Nearing the target, he aims the Ju 88 at it, then releases it from a distance which, in theory, allows it to glide to the target and strike home. However, the Junkers is uncontrolled during its descent, and the accuracy of the glider bomb is poor. The attack last night, against invasion shipping in the Seine Bay, was foiled when an RAF Mosquito night-fighter intercepted the Mistel, forcing the German pilot to jettison his Ju 88.

# New German aircraft arrive, but too late

**Germany, October 30**
Today the first regular Luftwaffe pilots to fly the Arado Ar 234B-2 jet-bomber began training. The speedy twin-engined Arado will give the Luftwaffe a capability no air force yet has. The Ar 234B-1 is already flying reconnaissance missions over Britain and Italy.

Of other advanced new German aircraft, both the Messerschmitt Me 163B Komet rocket-powered interceptor and the Me 262 twin-jet fighter and attack-bomber are entering service in increasing numbers. Dornier's factory at Oberpfaffenhofen is producing the initial version of the Do 335 push/pull fighter, and the radical Bachem Ba 349 Natter semi-expendable interceptor is well advanced. Plans are being rushed ahead to build a new *Volksjäger* [people's fighter] at the rate of 4,000 per month. (→ Dec 24).

*A rocket engine enables the Me 163 Komet to climb at 11,800 feet per minute.*

# RAF Lancaster bombers sink the 'Tirpitz'

*Famous victory: the sinking of the "Tirpitz", painted by Gerald Coulson.*

**Norway, November 12**
The German battleship *Tirpitz* has been sunk by RAF Lancasters in the northern Norwegian port of Tromsö. In icy conditions, 31 bombers of 9 and 617 Squadrons, led by Group Captain Tait, flew from Lossiemouth, Scotland, this morning. Each aircraft carried a single 12,000-lb Tallboy bomb designed to be capable of piercing the vessel's armor plate. This was the second hit on the *Tirpitz* with the same type of bomb. In September, RAF Lancasters scored one direct hit with a Tallboy. No longer seaworthy, the *Tirpitz* was moved to Tromsö to serve as a floating fort for coastal defense. The RAF finished the job today with two direct hits from 14,000 feet. Half her crew of 1,800 were killed in the attack.

**To mark the 5,000th P-38 Lightning to come out of the Burbank factory, this P-38J was given a special coat of red paint and the name** Yippee. **Its four engine-cooling radiators are placed far behind the engines.**

# Suicide bombers hit American warships

*Pacific Ocean, October 25*
The US Navy escort carrier *St Lo* was sunk today and four others were damaged when Japanese pilots flew their bomb-laden airplanes into them near the Philippines. There have been isolated instances of planes on both sides deliberately ramming enemy targets, but usually only when the pilots were mortally wounded. Today's attacks were different, with the pilots making no attempt to release bombs. The aircraft belonged to new suicide units called *kamikaze* [divine wind] after a typhoon which saved Japan from a Mongol invasion in 1281 (→Mar 10, 1945).

# 'Shooting Star' has a difficult début

*Muroc Dry Lake, December 6*
Lockheed's *Shooting Star* has once again been involved in an air crash. As test pilot Perry Claypool was flying the jet-powered fighter over this Californian test center tonight, the YP-80A crashed in mid-air into a twin-engined B-25. There were no survivors.

On October 24, Lockheed test pilot Milo Burcham, flying a prototype YP-80A on its first flight, was killed when the fuel supply to the GE I40 turbojet failed. He had no time to eject because the aircraft was flying at an altitude of only 295 feet. It seems certain that *Shooting Star* will need modifications.

# WASPS of Ferry Command head for home

*Four women pilots of the WAFS leave their B-17s at Lockbourne, Michigan.*

*USA, December 20*
The war is finally over for WASPS (Women's Air Force Service Pilots) and their unit, the women's Auxiliary Ferrying Squadron (WAFS) has been officially disbanded with little ceremony.

The US government seems somewhat reluctant to pay tribute to these womens' contribution to the war effort and it has never given them full military status. A recently-published official report states only that the WAFS' contribution during the 27 months since it was set up is difficult to evaluate. Over this time, the WAFS ferried a total of 12,650 aircraft of 77 different types, from heavy bombers such as B-17s to the most modern fighters. The WASPS covered 9,221,580 air-miles in all. They lost 38 pilots, 12 being killed during training and 26 others while on flying missions. The US Ferrying Division initially numbered 120 women pilots, then this quickly increased to 303. Last July however, 123 of the WASPS were transferred to the Air Training Command. Since September, there have only been 140 WASPS. Over the 27 months of its existence, 916 women pilots have served at one time or another in the WAFS.

The Ilyushin Il-12 served as a troop/paratroop- or freight-transport with the Soviet air force and saw commercial service with Aeroflot, CSA and LOT.

A Danish four-seater: Kramme and Zeuthen's KZ VII Lark monoplane.

The Boeing XF8B-1 carrier-based fighter/bomber failed to win orders.

The jet-powered Heinkel He 162 Salamander, popularly known as "the People's Fighter", was designed to use as few strategic materials as possible.

Grumman's agile F8F Bearcat succeeded the Hellcat as the US Navy's premier carrier-borne fighter; production was cut back because of the war's end.

The Royal Navy was supplied with 20 Miles M.33 Monitor target-tugs.

RAF Bomber Command's Avro Lincoln succeeded the great Lancaster.

The wing and tail of the Boeing B-29 were married to a new double-bubble fuselage to create the XC-97 transport, which entered service as the C-97A.

Three Northrop MX-324s were used to test flying-wing aerodynamics.

Fairchild's distinctive C-82 Packet transport first flew on September 10.

For all its good looks and impressive performance the Martin-Baker MB.5 fighter failed to win a production contract, and only one took to the air.

Production of the Nakajima G8N Renzan bomber was abandoned.

In 1944, deliveries of the Il-2m Shturmovik reached 36,163.

Only 151 Martin Mauler carrier-based attack aircraft were produced.

The odd Messerschmitt Me 328 was a pulse-jet-powered attack aircraft.

France's Morane-Saulnier MS.470 intermediate trainer: 500 were built.

Ryan's FR Fireball naval fighter had a jet as well as a piston engine.

Bell's XP-77 all-wood fighter proved underpowered and was canceled.

Blohm und Voss's Bv 155 interceptor was further developed as the Me 155.

The Lockheed P-80 Stooting Star was the first jet accepted for operational service by the USAAF. It first flew at Muroc Dry Lake on January 8, 1944.

Focke-Wulf's Ta 152H, the final development of the Fw 190, met a Luftwaffe requirement for a high-altitude interceptor based on a production airframe.

The Bristol Brigand ground-attack bomber served in the Middle and Far East, and made bomb and rocket attacks against Malayan terrorists in the 1950s.

Another rocket-propulsion experiment: the compact Junkers Ju 248.

The Blohm und Voss Bv 238 long-range flying-boat spanned 197ft.

Equally at home on floats or wheels: the Curtiss Seahawk patrol aircraft.

The unique Vultee XA-41 attack aircraft first flew on February 11, 1944.

A four-engined jet-bomber with forward-swept wings, the Junkers Ju 287 had only reached the prototype stage when the war's end halted the program.

De Havilland's D.H.103 Hornet was the RAF's fastest piston-engined fighter. It served in Fighter Command until 1951, and then the Far East Air Force.

# 1945

623.85mph
Germany
Heini Dittmar
Messerschmitt Me 163A
Oct 2, 1941

8,038 miles
Italy
Tondi, Degasso, Vignoli
Savoia-Marchetti S.M.75
Aug 1, 1939

56,046ft
Italy
Mario Pezzi
Caproni 161bis
Oct 22, 1938

207,981lb
Germany
Blohm & Voss
V238 V1

4,410lb thrust
Germany
Walter HWK
109-509 C

## Western Europe, January 1
Some 900 German aircraft attack 15 Allied air bases in Belgium and northern France as the Luftwaffe launches Operation Bodenplatte; 194 British and US aircraft are destroyed on the ground and 400 are damaged, but the Germans lose 300 machines and over 255 aircrew.

## The Philippines, January 7
Major Thomas MacGuire is killed in air combat. He was credited with 38 "kills" while flying his P-38.

## Hyakurigahara, Japan, January 8
The Mitsubishi J8M1 rocket-fighter makes its first flight.

## USA, February 25
The Bell XP-83 fighter prototype, a long-range development of the P-59 Airacomet, makes its first flight.

## The Congo, March 1
Belgian airline Sabena starts regular services from Leopoldville to Lagos, Gao and Algiers.

## Bielefeld, Germany, March 14
An RAF Lancaster bomber of 617 Squadron drops the first 22,000-lb "Grand Slam" bomb on the viaduct here; the earthquake effect of the huge bomb causes over 100 yards of viaduct to collapse.

## Berlin, March 18
The city is raided by the largest bomber strike force ever assembled – 1,251 B-24s and B-17s, escorted by 645 Mustang fighters, which drop 3,000 tons of bombs on the German capital.

## USA, March 18
The Douglas XBT2D-1 Skyraider dive-bomber, intended for the US Navy, makes its first flight.

## Pacific Ocean, April 1
The US battleship *West Virginia* and the British carrier HMS *Indefatigable* are among vessels badly damaged in the first successful missions flown by Japanese Yokosuka Ohka purpose-built suicide airplanes.→

## England, April 5
Jet engine inventor Frank Whittle receives an interim award of £10,000 from the Ministry of Aircraft Production; his case – that he should be properly rewarded for the invention – is to be examined further by the Royal Commission on Awards to Inventors.

## Havana, April 19
The International Air Transport Association (IATA), an inter-airline body to fix rates and ensure cooperation on safety procedures, is formed; it succeeds the International Air Traffic Association, set up in 1919.

## Germany, May 5
The destruction of German airports by Allied bombing and the current chaos in the country force the airline Lufthansa to suspend its operations. The final flight, from Oslo to Flensburg, Germany, landed today (→ Apr 1, 1955).

## France, June 4
French test pilot Georges Detré flies a prototype Stampe SV.4, designed by a Belgian, Jean Stampe. Powered by a 140-hp Renault engine, it is an excellent training and aerobatic aircraft.

## Surrey, England, June 22
At Wisley, test pilot Mutt Summers flies the prototype airliner Vickers-Armstrongs Viking. Derived from the Wellington bomber, it has the same wings, landing gear and engine cowlings.

## Paris, June 26
Air France is nationalized by the government of the Fourth French Republic; it has been under government control since France was liberated last year.

## USA, June 28
The Cessna 140, designed as a private plane, makes a successful first flight. It is powered by a Continental C-25 engine and has simple spring-steel landing gear.

## Paris, July 7
The Arsenal VB 10, designed by French engineers Vernisse and Badre, flies for the first time at Villacoublay, near here. It is powered by two massive 24-cylinder engines in tandem.

## New Mexico, July 16
Manhattan Project scientists at the Alamogordo desert range test the plutonium bomb known as Fat Man (→ Aug 9).

## Japan, August 7
Japan's first jet-fighter, the Nakajima Kikka, makes its first flight; its design is based on the Messerschmitt Me 262.

## South Pacific, August 15
Lieutenant-Commander Reidy of the US Navy shoots down a Nakajima C6N1 in the last confirmed air victory of the war.

## Australia, August 16
The Australian National Airlines Act is passed, providing for the establishment of a national commission to operate interstate and territorial air services.

## USA, September 2
Since August 16, the US industry has had over 42,000 aircraft cancelled.

## England, September 20
A Gloster Meteor fighter fitted with Rolls-Royce Trent turboprop engines makes a successful experimental flight; the pilot is Eric Greenwood.

## Le Bourget, France, September 22
Air France resumes regular flights between this airport and London.

## Singapore, October 4
The Qantas C-class flying boat *Coriolanus* completes the airline's first post-war service from Sydney.

## Paris, October 11
The French wartime air transport organization reopens its service between Le Bourget and London using ex-Luftwaffe Ju 52/3ms.

## USA, November 6
A Ryan Fireball fitted with both piston and jet engines makes the first jet-powered landing on an aircraft carrier when Ensign Jake West lands on the USS *Wake Island*; he has to rely on the jet when the piston engine fails.

## Seattle, November 27
Boeing factories, where 78,000 people worked last year, now only number 44,000 employees.

## Seattle, November 28
Boeing receives a contract worth $24.5 million from Pan Am for a total of 20 B-377 Stratocruiser airliners.

## England, December 2
Two British transport prototypes, the Bristol Type 170 Freighter and the Handley Page Hermes, make their first flights on the same day; the Hermes crashes, killing pilot Flight Lieutenant J R Talbot and flight observer E A Wright.

## England, December 3
A de Havilland Sea Vampire fighter becomes the first purely jet-powered airplane to operate from an aircraft carrier when Lieutenant-Commander E M "Winkle" Brown lands his aircraft on HMS *Ocean*.

## New Zealand, December 7
New Zealand National Airways Corporation is founded with the amalgamation of Union Airways, Air Travel and Cook Strait Airways.

## Wichita, Kansas, December 22
Beechcraft's prototype Beech 35 Bonanza flies for the first time. This single-engined aircraft with a butterfly tail can carry up to five people.

*The B-29 bomber has a pressurized fuselage, remote-controlled gun turrets and four enormous double turbo-supercharged engines.* ▶

# Boeing Stratofreighter sets speed record

*The Boeing XC-97 has proved itself to be the fastest transport in the world.*

**Washington, DC, January 9**
In spite of its huge, bluff-nosed fuselage, the new Boeing XC-97 is the fastest transport airplane in the world. It arrived here today after a record non-stop 3,323-mile flight from the Boeing plant at Seattle of just 6 hours 3 minutes, with a payload of 20,000 lb.

The XC-97, or 367-1-1, is a transport version of the B-29 Superfortress bomber. Its enormously enlarged fuselage is fully pressurized, enabling it to cross the US at an altitude of over 30,000 feet, where today it took advantage of favorable winds to reach 383mph. The USAAF expects to procure the

C-97 in quantity. Some may be equipped as 34-seat passenger carriers or 83-patient medical evacuation transports, but most will probably be freighters, with "clamshell" double doors under the tail through which cargo can be loaded, unloaded or dropped by parachute.

The first XC-97 is closely based on the B-29 and has the same 2,200hp Wright R-3350 engines. Later production C-97s are expected to have 3,500-hp Pratt & Whitney R-4360 Wasp Major engines, a taller tail and other improvements. Boeing is also marketing a civil airline version, the 377 Stratocruiser, which will include a bar.

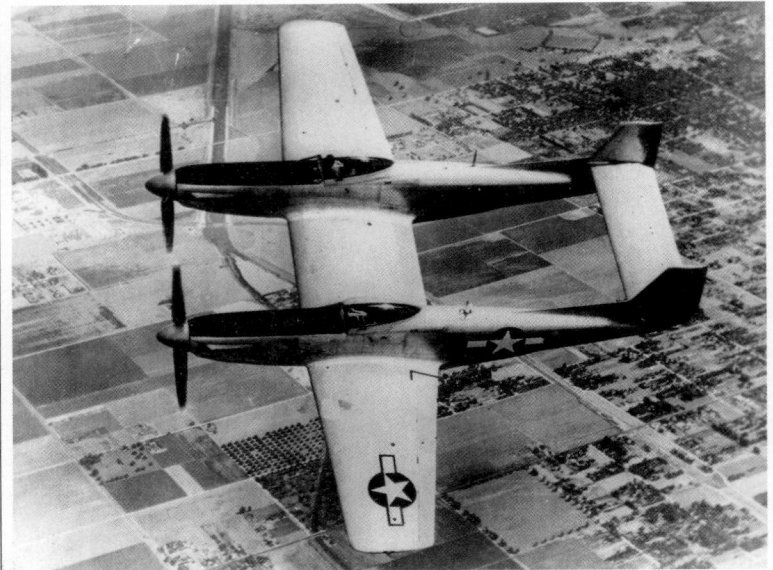

**The North American XP-82 Twin Mustang uses two enlarged P-51 fighter fuselages joined by a rectangular wing section, powered by two Packard Merlin 1,860-hp engines. It is a long-range fighter for escort missions lasting up to 12 hours, for which two pilots are needed to share the load.**

# Jet and propeller join forces in XP-81

*Muroc Dry Lake, Calif, February 7*
A huge experimental fighter, the Convair XP-81, strange-looking and strange-sounding, made its first flight today at the USAAF's desert flight test center. It has been designed to meet the USAAF's requirement for a long-range fighter to escort B-29 bombers on missions to Japan. It has also been designed to combine that range with the speed of a jet. The range and endurance of jet fighters is still short.

The solution (also being tried with the US Navy's Ryan FR-1) is to use two different types of engine: a turbojet for speed and a turboprop for fuel economy. Eventually it will have a General Electric I-40 turbojet in the tail and a General Electric T31 turboprop in the nose, which would give it a power output equivalent to the B-29s it has been designed to escort and a top speed of over 500mph. However, the turboprop is not ready yet, so for today's flight a Packard Merlin V-1650 piston engine was used in the nose instead.

The XP-81 is one of the biggest fighters ever built: its wingspan is over 50 feet, and it weighs 24,650 pounds. There are fears that this might make it not agile enough in combat, but the war may be over before it can be tested in service.

*The XP-81 has jet engines, a propeller and a pressurized cockpit for the pilot.*

# Roosevelt flies to war summit in a DC-4

*The "Sacred Cow" and its crew.*

**Yalta, Crimea, February 4**
US President Franklin D Roosevelt touched down at this Crimean resort today in his presidential airplane *Sacred Cow* for a crucial summit with British prime minister

Winston Churchill and Soviet leader Joseph Stalin. The leaders are meeting to discuss terms for Germany's surrender and the shape of post-war Europe.

The *Sacred Cow* is a Douglas VC-54C-DO, a military version of the DC-4 civil transport specially modified to serve the needs of the President and his staff of 14; it is not only a means of transport, it is also a mobile home and office. There are three conference rooms, a presidential state room with six adjoining sleeping compartments for his aides, complete with shower facilities. It has also been fitted with an electric elevator for President Roosevelt's wheelchair. Standard fuel capacity for the type is 3,580 US gallons, but for its long-range role, and for safety, the *Sacred Cow* carries 4,510 US gallons.

# Sabena reopens Brussels-Congo route

*Sabena's Lockheed Lodestar is welcomed at Brussels' Haren airport.*

**Brussels, July 10**
The arrival here this morning of a Sabena Lockheed Lodestar, piloted by Jo Van Ackere, marked the resumption of regular flights between Léopoldville and the Belgian capital. The flight, which took two days, was the first since the start of the war. The French government has granted Sabena permission to fly over the Mediterranean Sea from Algiers, while the Allies have allowed Sabena flights to land in Brussels, which is still an unauthorized sector for civil aviation. Today's flight, the first of a weekly service, also stopped in Gao and Marseilles, France.

# RAF Lancasters leave Dresden in ruins

**Dresden, Germany, February 14**
This largely unbombed city was the target of the most devastating raid of the war so far. Its population of 700,000 was swollen by around 500,000 refugees and estimates of casualties range from 50,000 to 200,000.

Starting last night at 10.15pm, a total of 773 RAF Bomber Command Lancasters and Halifaxes, followed by 450 USAAF B-17s and B-24s dropped over 3,000 tons of high explosive and incendiary bombs on the city and its suburbs. The massive raid, which lasted 14 hours and was carried out in two main waves, created deadly firestorms throughout Dresden. Today, USAAF Fortresses attacked yet again, but there was only rubble left to bomb.

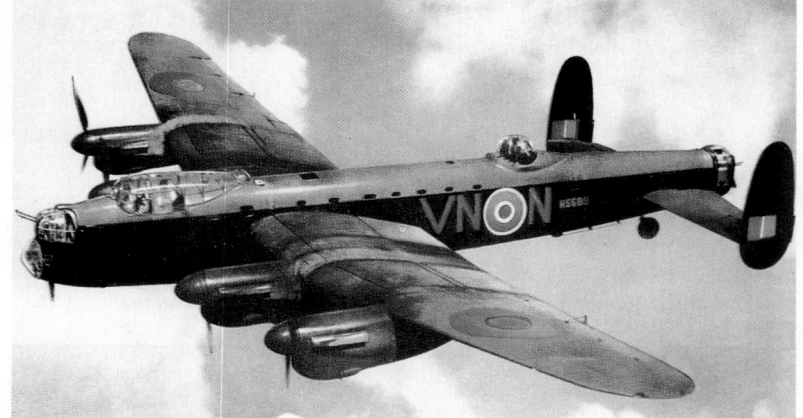

*The Lancaster can carry 6.5 tons of bombs over a distance of 1,740 miles.*

# Japanese mass-produce kamikaze planes

**Okinawa, Japan, April 12**
Japanese suicide missiles scored their first success off this island today when they sank the destroyer USS *Mannert L Abele*. On April 1 they caused some damage to the battleship USS *West Virginia* and other vessels, including the British carrier HMS *Indefatigable*.

With the designation of Yokosuka MXY-7 Model 11 or Ohka [Cherry Blossom], and known to the Allies by the Japanese name Baka [Fool], these missiles are the first designed to be flown by suicide pilots. They have had little success. The brainchild of naval pilot Ensign Mitsuo Ohta, the MXY-7 is a 2,646-lb warhead fastened to a tiny airplane propelled by three solid-fuel rockets. It must be carried to the target slung under a Mitsubishi G4M bomber. Once the missile has been released, however, it can dive on its target at up to 576mph (→ May 5).

*Several Okha flying bombs have been discovered on captured airfields.*

# Germans experiment with vertical flight

**Germany, February 28**
The difficulty of achieving precise rocket navigation and the time needed to manufacture fighters have led German scientists to look for something in between these two types of machine. Erich Bachem and his team of engineers believe they have a viable solution. The Ba 349 Natter (viper) is fired almost vertically. The pilot makes a single pass at enemy bombers, firing a battery of 55-mm rockets. Then he fires charges separating the aircraft, the motor and tail being recovered by parachute while he has his own parachute. A BA 349 was launched today, with Lothar Siebert at the controls. However, seconds after the launch, the canopy came loose and killed the pilot. Despite this setback, German military planners still hope that the Ba 349 can be deployed in Germany as a last-ditch counter to the waves of Allied bombers pounding the country.

*The Bachem Ba 349 has no ailerons, but independently-moving elevators.*

# Superior US air might smashes Tokyo

*Aircrew and armorers on a Pacific island load an RNZAF Avenger.*

*The ruins of Osaka, flattened by crushing Superfortress bombing raids.*

*Tokyo, March 10*

In the Japanese capital's most devastating raid of the war, incendiary bombs dropped last night by 279 B-29 Superfortresses of Major-General Curtis E LeMay's 21st Bomber Command have turned the largely wooden-built city into a raging inferno. Between 80,000 and 130,000 people are dead, with over a million homeless. Almost 16 square miles of Tokyo are in flames.

The attack by wave after wave of B-29s from three islands in the Marianas – Saipan, Tinian and Guam – lasted four hours. Pilots in the last waves said it was difficult to control their aircraft because of the violent updrafts from the intense fires below.

Yesterday's raid succeeded because LeMay changed tactics. He abandoned high-altitude precision bombing, in which the B-29s would drop high explosive from above 25,000 feet, partly because of frequent cloud cover and high winds. LeMay realized that Japanese industry depended on parts produced in small shops and homes around industrial plants and ordered low-altitude blanket bombing of the manufacturing areas from 5,000 to 10,000 feet. He recalled Japanese incendiary attacks on Chinese cities and reasoned similar results would be achieved. He gambled that fighters would not be a problem at night, and that, without radar, anti-aircraft fire would be ineffective. LeMay was right: last night each B-29 managed to drop 12,000 lb of incendiaries. Only 14 planes were lost; five crews were rescued from the Pacific (→ Apr 1).

## Turret gunner bags two German jets!

*Metz, France, April 20*

USAAF Lt James L Vining is resting tonight in the Army hospital here, despite having his right leg blown off by 30mm shells from an Me 262. Happier is his dorsal turret gunner, Sgt Ed S Tyszkiewicz. He is credited with two Messerschmitt Me 262 twin-jets, and has been recommended for the Silver Star.

Their Martin B-26 Marauder was one of a formation from the 9th AF's 323rd Bomb Group, which this morning attacked the marshalling yard at Memmingen. Suddenly they were set upon by about 15 of the enemy jets. Three bombers went down at once, and 12 more (almost the whole formation) were damaged. Vining's B-26 was badly damaged, and the right engine had to be feathered. Seeing this, several of the 262s closed in for the kill, but the dorsal gunner's accurate fire resulted in two confirmed claims. Against the 262, this is unprecedented. The fastest fighters of the Allies are outpaced by 100mph.

## US glide-bomb fired

*Borneo, April 23*

Missiles which home on ships automatically were used for the first time today when US Navy PB4Y-2 Privateers launched ASM-N-2 Bat unpowered glide-bombs at Japanese shipping in Balikpapan Harbor. These anti-shipping missiles carry 1,000-lb explosive charges and self-contained guidance systems made up of radar transmitters and receivers, and are reliably reported to be accurate to within 150 feet of the aiming point.

## London seems safe from threat of V-1

*London, March 29*

Allied service chiefs with access to top-secret intelligence sources are now almost certain that Britain has seen the last of the V-1 "doodle-bugs" launched by Hitler on Britain since June in a final attempt to sap British morale. The number of missiles has been dropping over the last few months, although two days ago one of them killed over 130 Londoners, many of them in an apartment block. Anti-aircraft gunners in Suffolk downed what could be the last of them today.

The deafening throb of the V-1's ramjet engine, followed by an ominous silence when it cuts out, have become familiar to Londoners. It has claimed the lives of 2,745 civilians and 2,900 servicemen during its reign of terror, but with the fuel shortages afflicting Germany, Allied armies have overrun the launch sites, and during recent weeks, England has been attacked by bombs launched from hastily converted He 111s.

## Dauntless II packs a powerful punch

*Los Angeles, March 18*

The US Navy's newest dive-bomber and torpedo-plane, the Douglas XBT2D-1 Dauntless II, which flew today for the first time, bears little resemblance to the three-man Dauntless now fighting with the fleet. For a start, it has only one crew member, which saves weight. More weight is saved and the complexity of the aircraft is reduced by having no internal weapons bay.

These weight savings give the Dauntless II greater ordnance-carrying ability. But with a large, 2,500-hp Wright R-3350 engine, a wingspan of over 50 feet and a length of 38 feet, it is not by any means a small airplane. The weight savings and the big engine will allow the new aircraft to carry a variety of weaponry totalling up to 8,000 lb, in addition to its four wing-mounted 20mm cannon. The Dauntless II has a maximum level speed of more than 300mph and a range of 900 miles.

# Bombing crews will not get any medals

*Berlin, May 7*
Germany surrendered to the Allies today. It was defeated in a ground war and not, as some people thought possible, by air power alone. In the attempt to bomb Germany into submission, the RAF flew 1.44 million bombing sorties, dropping 3.02 million tons of bombs. The USAAF/RAF campaign killed over 300,000 people. Germany's major cities have suffered badly. The RAF lost 22,000 aircraft, the USAAF 18,000 and the Luftwaffe 57,000. The USAAF lost 78,265 personnel and the RAF 78,281, of whom 47,268 (over 55,000 including British Commonwealth Air Forces) were from Bomber Command. No campaign medal will be struck for aircrews who took part in the offensive.

# American airlines to share Atlantic run

*Washington, June 1*
Pan American Airways' monopoly of the potentially lucrative transatlantic route ended today when the US Civil Aeronautics Board allowed two other major US airlines to compete on them.

The move comes despite objections from Pan Am chief Juan Trippe, who before the war had the only permanent license for the routes. American Airlines' new subsidiary, American Overseas Airlines, and TWA are Pan Am's competitors. United did not express an interest in the route.

# Allied air chief promises to end the war

*The Pacific war: USS "Missouri" is attacked by a Japanese suicide airplane.*

*Mariana Islands, Pacific, May 29*
Back in March, after hitting Tokyo with the greatest incendiary raid in air history, Major-General Curtis LeMay of 21st US Bomber Command signalled to his superiors: "Destruction of Japan's ability to wage war lies within the capability of this command."

Japan's warlords do not see it that way. They took 6,821 US lives on tiny Iwo Jima island in a month and are now prepared to fight equally hard for Okinawa, impervious to the appeals for Japan to surrender dropped from US planes. The warlords think the US will not sacrifice a million men to conquer Japan, in which case it must settle for less than unconditional surrender. LeMay's view is that air power can do

the trick, with more fire-bombings and a blockade, using anti-shipping mines to cut off Japan's oil. US air power is awesome: at Tokyo in March, LeMay's B-29 Superfortresses killed at least 83,000 people and took out a vast area of central Tokyo. Osaka, Kobe, Nagoya and Toyama have also been torched.

Japanese fighters, when not grounded by lack of fuel, fly *kamikaze* missions; women, boys and old men are ready to defend beaches with bamboo stakes. Three days ago 429 B-29s dropped 4,000 tons of incendiaries on Tokyo, burning the imperial palace. With the high cost in US lives of invading Japan, blasting it into submission instead remains attractive to the Allies (→ Jun 17).

# Last Liberator rolls off production line

*Detroit, Mich, May 31*
Today the world's greatest aircraft production line stopped abruptly with the cancelation of an order for 5,168 Consolidated B-24N Liberator bombers. With the European war ended, these bombers are simply not needed.

Although it received much less publicity than the B-17 Flying Fortress, which was designed almost five years before the Liberator appeared in 1939, the now discontinued B-24 was actually built in

*The last B-24 is rolled out in Detroit.*

greater numbers, 18,188 in all, in many versions for many purposes. This compares with just 12,731 B-17s, almost all of which were bombers. The B-24 was more complex and more demanding, but could fly a little faster and further than the B-17. Because of its range the B-24, unlike its partner, served in large numbers in the Mediterranean and Pacific war theaters. Its contribution to the impending Allied victory has been tremendous.

# Northrop Flying Ram fails to get airborne

*Muroc Dry Lake, Calif, June 30*
The Northrop company's extraordinary XP-79 Flying Ram ran into trouble at the USAAF test base today even before getting off the ground: its tires burst while it was taxiing. Powered by two of the new Westinghouse 19B turbojets, each giving 1,600 lb of thrust, the XP-79 is intended to collide with enemy bombers and slice off their wings or tails. For this purpose its wing is made of very thick magnesium, with a leading edge tough enough

to survive the collision. It is another of Jack Northrop's "flying-wing" designs. The pilot lies prone inside the leading edge, looking out through an unusual transparent "nose" between the jet inlets. The XP-79's speed is expected to be around 550mph, which should even give it an edge over enemy fighters and bombers, but its maneuverability has yet to be investigated. However, it seems that the Flying Ram has arrived too late to take part in the war.

**June 18: Chinese infantrymen of the Sixth Army march across an airfield in Burma to the airplanes that are to fly them across the Himalayas to China, the first time an entire army has been moved by air.**

# British airline resumes Australian route

*A Lancaster bomber, reborn in BOAC colors as the Lancastrian airliner.*

**Sydney, June 2**
A former Lancaster bomber, now rebuilt as a civil Lancastrian, touched down here today after a 63-hour flight from Hurn near Bournemouth, England. The route, the longest in the world, is being shared by BOAC and Qantas, with stopovers at Lydda, Palestine [Israel], Karachi, Colombo and Learmouth.

The first flight from Sydney leaves today.

The England/Australia express service has been organized to carry important mail only, but other Lancasters – some with wartime bombing experience – are being fitted out with nine passenger seats (or six bunks) along their starboard sides (→ Oct 4).

# Thirteen die when bomber hits skyscraper

**New York, July 28**
A B-25 Mitchell bomber crashed into the fog-shrouded Empire State Building here today, killing 13 people and injuring 26 others. It hit 915 feet above the street, at the level of the 78th and 79th floors of the world's tallest building.

The impact sheared off the airplane's wings while the engines and body punched an 18-foot-wide, 20-foot-high hole in the building. One engine tore across the 78th floor, through the opposite wall, and destroyed a penthouse on the roof of a neighboring 12-story building. Flaming fuel rushed into the two floors and stairwells, trapping and killing many of the young women clerical workers in its path.

*The gaping hole left by the B-25.*

# Richard Bong dies in Shooting Star crash

**Burbank, California, August 6**
Ace pilot Major Richard Bong was killed near here today while test flying a Lockheed P-80 Shooting Star. The crash happened just after take-off, when the aircraft's jet engine suddenly lost power at low altitude. Bong joined the US Army Air Force in June 1941. During combat operations he flew a Lightning P-38, like his friend Major Thomas MacGuire, and scored more "kills" than any other USAAF fighter pilot [see page 446].

# 'Fighting Lady' and 'Way to the Stars' among film hits of 1945

*USA and Britain*
The heroism of pilots at sea and on land has proved a rewarding subject for movie-makers this year. In the United States, the carrier USS *Yorktown* starred in the Academy-award-winning documentary *The Fighting Lady* by veteran German-American director William Wyler, who directed last year's documentary *Memphis Belle* about a USAAF bomber. In Britain the saga of an RAF airfield in Yorkshire, *The Way to the Stars*, was one of the most popular films of the year. Scripted by British playwright Terence Rattigan, this film examined the tensions and friendships between American and British servicemen and took a poignant look at the effects of the air war on loved ones left behind.

*Action stations: an F6F prepares to take off from the "Fighting Lady".*

*"The Way to the Stars", released in the US as "Johnny-in-the-clouds".*

# Two B-29 bombers plunge world into a new era

*Colonel Paul Tibbets, the pilot of the USAAF B-29 Superfortress "Enola Gay", only told his crew the precise details of their mission after take-off.*

*Hiroshima, Japan, August 6*
When Col Paul Tibbets, commanding the 509th Composite Group, and his crew of 11 took off at 2.45am from Tinian Island in the Marianas, all aboard the USAAF B-29 Superfortress very soon knew that this mission was like none they had ever undertaken before.

Tibbets, flying *Enola Gay*, named after his mother, knew its 9,000-lb uranium-238 bomb "Little Boy" was special, but just how special only became clear 50 seconds after they released it over the industrial city of Hiroshima from 31,000 feet, at 8.15am. Tibbets put the plane into a diving turn to get clear as a purple-black mushroom cloud rose almost level with them. The bomb exploded 1,000 feet over the city in a fireball three times hotter than the Sun and with a power greater than that of 20,000 tons of TNT. The

force of the blast was unlike anything ever seen before. Around 80,000 people were killed outright. Many who survived are now dying from intense radiation burns. Two-thirds of the city of 290,000 inhabitants was reduced to blackened wasteland by the first atomic bomb ever dropped.

*Nagasaki, Japan, August 9*
The USAAF unleashed an atomic bomb on Japan again today. This time the target was the city of Nagasaki, a major shipbuilding port of 250,000 inhabitants in western Kyushu. Again, it was a B-29 Superfortress, named *Bock's Car* and flown by Major Sweeney, that

launched the devastating attack which has killed around 50,000 people and wiped out two-thirds of the city. The 10,000-lb bomb, plutonium-charged and nicknamed "Fat Man", was dropped on Nagasaki only because the primary target, a military arsenal at Kokura, was obscured by cloud.→

## American aircrews undergo special training for A-bomb raids

*Tinian Island, Pacific, August 9*
For two months, men of the USAAF's 509th Composite Group were a mystery to other flyers here. They had come from a remote training base in the Utah desert in 15 B-29s fitted with modified bomb bays, and they refused to discuss their business.

When other B-29s went to Japan, the machines of 509th tagged along but always peeled off at the last moment to find their own targets. Now the secret is out. The special team was dropping blast bombs which were lookalike A-weapons in rehearsal for the deliveries to Hiroshima and Nagasaki. Most aircrew involved did not know exactly what this was about, either. Only their chief, Colonel Paul Tibbets, had a good idea of the real weapon, though not of its target, or when it would be delivered.

Dropping the atomic bomb was the sole purpose of 509th when it was set up a year ago. The first place targeted was Germany, but by the time the device could be test-

*The ground and flight crews of the "Enola Gay" after the mission.*

ed successfully, in New Mexico 25 days ago, Europe's war was over. The Nazis might have had the A-bomb, but Hitler derided the idea as a product of "Jewish physics". Japan had its own atomic program. But the Allies got there first, and the Mexico test crowned the three-

year-long Manhattan Project, created to split the atom and release its awesome energy. As soon as he got the test result, President Truman ordered that the "special bomb", be dropped. Winston Churchill gave British approval. War is unlikely to be the same again (→Aug 15).

*Mushroom cloud over Hiroshima.*

# Meteor first plane to use turboprops...

*The turboprop-powered Gloster Meteor also has a sideways-hinged canopy.*

**England, September 20**

A Gloster Meteor today became the first aircraft to fly powered by turboprops.

Rolls-Royce engineers studying the basics of turboprop operation and control systems have placed a reduction gearbox on a Rolls-Royce Derwent turbojet engine. This meant raising the propeller shaft above the center-line of the engine. They then found that there was not enough room to install a normal propeller, so instead used an extremely small, five-bladed one. The aerodynamics of the resulting machine were far from ideal and extra fins had to be fitted. The first flight nearly ended in disaster when the pilot shut the throttles only to find this resulted in a near-stall at low altitude.

# but can reach 600mph with jet engines

**England, November 7**

A Gloster Meteor jet fighter of the RAF's newly reformed High Speed Flight smashed through the 600-mph barrier today to set a new speed record of 606mph.

The F.4 version of the fighter, powered by two Rolls-Royce Derwent V engines, differs from its predecessors in its shorter wing-span (37 feet 2 inches) which improves its speed. The first Meteors, powered by Rolls-Royce Welland turbojets, were used against German V-1 flying bombs, but only 20 of this model were ever made. A few interim Mark 3 Meteors flew operations over Germany during the closing stages of the war, but the British plane – the only Allied jet-propelled aircraft to go into active service before Germany's surrender – never met its German counterpart, the Messerschmitt Me 262, in air-to-air combat. Dogfights between jet-propelled airplanes will have to wait for a future war.

*Group Captain H J Wilson at the controls of the record-breaking Meteor.*

# ATA girls have delivered 308,567 planes

*ATA pilots and crew checking their navigation maps before a delivery flight.*

**England, November 30**

Women pilots of the Air Transport Auxiliary (ATA) have had a busy war, delivering a total of 308,567 aircraft from the factories to front line squadrons since January 11, 1940. Initially, the Women's Section of the ATA only numbered nine pilots under the command of Pauline Gower. By 1941, this number had risen to 100, including women from New Zealand, Australia, the US, Poland and France. One world-famous air ace, Amy Johnson, was killed in January 1941 when the aircraft she was ferrying for the ATA crashed into the Thames Estuary.

# US airline restarts transatlantic flights

**Dorset, England, October 24**

A new era in air travel was ushered in today when a C-54 of American Overseas Airlines (AOA) arrived at Hurn airport, near Bournemouth, from New York via Gander, Newfoundland, and Shannon, Ireland. The crossing, which marks the start of the first scheduled transatlantic service by landplanes, took place in the record flying time of 14 hours 5 minutes. The C-54, which started as a civil transport, the DC-4, before the war, was taken over by the military and mass-produced as a long-range transport. C-54s are no strangers to the Atlantic, having been used to ferry supplies and VIP passengers, which makes them ideal to open up the route for civil traffic. On June 1 the US authorities awarded AOA – a subsidiary of American Airlines – and TWA the right to compete on North Atlantic routes, ending the monopoly held hitherto by Pan Am.

*A DC-4 flies over Brooklyn before landing at New York's LaGuardia airport.*

# Superfortress sets non-stop flight record

*The first B-29 bomber to return from Japan is welcomed in Washington, DC.*

*Washington, DC, November 20*
The B-29 bomber *Pacusan Dreamboat* landed here today after an astonishing non-stop flight which began at the island of Guam in the Pacific Ocean. The Superfortress had set a new non-stop distance record of 7,916 miles.

The *Pacusan Dreamboat* is one of many veteran Superfortresses making their way back to the US from the Pacific arena. When Japan surrendered in September, most of the bombers were kept in place to fly supplies to Allied prisoners of war. Now they are coming home – and in style. On November 1, four B-29s blazed the trail ahead of the *Pacusan Dreamboat*, completing a non-stop flight to Washington from Hokkaido, their base in Japan, in just 27 hours 30 minutes.

# Speedy jet fighter goes into service

*Riverside, Calif, December 3*
A new sound was heard at March Field here today as the first P-80 Shooting Star arrived at 412th Fighter Group. The unit is the first in the USAAF to be equipped with a jet-fighter. The P-80, which is said to be capable of over 550mph, was developed in the closing stages of the war to counter the German Messerschmitt Me 262 jet fighter. Although four service-test YP-80As were sent to Europe early this year to demonstrate their capabilities, they saw no combat. The new fighter has a pressurized cockpit and jettisonable 165-gallon wing-tip fuel tanks.

*The Shooting Star, with six guns, is the USAAF's latest front-line fighter.*

# US civil flying revives ...

*USA, December 31*
It was inevitable that the war would end with the US dominant in civil aviation. US manufacturers concentrated on developing long-range transports, suitable for conversion to civil use, while Britain built combat aircraft. The US also has a huge domestic market for civil aircraft with no competition, save between US companies, to supply it.

It was a Lockheed Constellation that opened the transatlantic route for TWA on December 4 by flying from Washington, DC, to Paris via Gander and Shannon in 12 hours 57 minutes. The transformation of this military aircraft to a civil airliner took less than three months.

In Seattle, Boeing engineers, who initiated a transport version of the B-29 Superfortress as long ago as 1942, are working on the airliner counterpart, the 337 Stratocruiser, which will carry 100 passengers over a range of 4,000 miles.

## ... as British committee plans new planes

*Brabazon: planning the future.*

*London, December 31*
British civil aviation enters the post-war world woefully short of the right aircraft. For long-haul operations BOAC will have to rely on converted wartime bombers or go on buying American until new British types are available.

In 1944 the government set up a committee under Lord Brabazon to examine Britain's post-war needs, and the new Labour government has backed the types it recommended, which range from light aircraft, to feed the major cities of the empire from its distant outposts, to a turbojet mailplane, which could become the world's first jet-airliner.

# Fighters disappear in Bermuda area

*Fort Lauderdale, Fla, December 5*
Five US Navy Avenger torpedo-bombers on a routine training flight off the east coast of Florida went missing today in unexplained circumstances. The Martin Mariner flying boat dispatched to search for the lost flight has also disappeared. It is believed all aircraft went missing in an area to the south-west of Bermuda.

The last word from the Avengers came when flight commander Lieutenant Taylor reported: "We can't see land anymore. We're lost." He then broke contact. Nothing was heard from the Mariner except routine climbing reports shortly after take off. All aircraft were equipped with tested magnetic compasses and fuel well in excess of their planned requirements.

**Trainee gunners in B-29 bomber fuselages direct their remote-controlled turrets at flying targets at an academy near Las Vegas.**

# Roll of honor: the war's top-scoring fighter pilots

*America's top-scoring fighter pilot.*

## Richard I Bong

Major Richard Ira Bong, a farm boy from Poplar, Wisconsin, shot down 40 Japanese aircraft on 146 missions to become America's top-scoring ace. Never a good shot, he simply flew his P-38 Lightning straight at his targets before opening fire at point-blank range.

He loved the P-38 for both its "fire-power wallop" and its ability to climb "like a homesick angel". Awarded the Medal of Honor, he returned to the US late in the war. He was killed testing a P-80 jet on August 6, 1945.

## Erich Hartmann

Major Erich Hartmann shot down 352 airplanes, mostly Russian, to become the greatest ace the world has ever seen or is ever likely to see. He crashed on his first operational flight and did not open his score until November 5, 1942; his second kill took him another four months, but from then until the end of the war planes fell before his aggressive flying and brilliant marksmanship.

"Bubi" Hartmann's Bf 109 was easily recognizable by its black nose, and he became known as the "Black Devil" to the Soviets, who put a price of 10,000 roubles on his head. On one occasion he crashed and was captured but escaped. It was not until the end of the war that the Russians caught him and made him serve ten years in a labor camp.

## Joseph J Foss

Major Joe Foss, another of America's farm-boy aces, was a brilliant marksman, and he shot down 26 Japanese planes in three months to become the Marines' top scorer. His success was all the more remarkable because he was flying the outclassed F4F Wildcat and suffering from severe malaria.

He was invalided to the United States and awarded the Medal of Honor but eventually returned to action in command of an F4U Corsair squadron. He later became Governor of South Dakota.

*Foss downed 26 enemy aircraft.*

## H Nishizawa

The Japanese did not accord their aces the same public praise as the other warring countries, and so it was not until after the war that it became known that Sub-officer Hiroyoshi Nishizawa was Japan's leading ace. Flying the nimble A6M Zero fighter he scored 103 victories, 90 of them over Americans.

Nishizawa was a cadaverous, aloof man afflicted with a number of tropical diseases, but when he climbed into his Zero he became an aerobatic artist, exciting admiration among the seasoned pilots who flew with him in the élite wing that operated from Lae in New Guinea.

He died at the controls of an unarmed transport, shot down by Hellcats while flying a group of pilots to pick up new Zeros.

*Pattle: deadly in an antique biplane.*

## 'Pat' Pattle

Squadron Leader Marmaduke St John "Pat" Pattle gained 23 official kills in North Africa and Greece but is believed to have shot down over 20 more. This makes him the RAF's top scorer, albeit unofficially. He was a superb marksman, but what made his success remarkable was that he flew an ancient Gladiator biplane. Re-equipped with a Hurricane, he shot down five Germans in a day. On April 22, 1941, he destroyed three German fighters, but was riddled by two Bf 110s and vanished into the Aegean.

## Marcel Albert

Captain Marcel Albert, who shot down 23 German aircraft over the Russian front and was awarded the title of Hero of the Soviet Union, was the top-scoring ace of the Free French Normandy Squadron. The French pilots, flying Soviet Yak fighters, took part in the battles to liberate White Russia and Lithuania and did so well in the battle for the Niémen river they were allowed to add the name of Niémen to their squadron's title.

Albert and his fellow pilots were in action for three years. They lost 42 killed and missing but were credited with 273 victories. On one day alone they shot down 26 Germans without loss to themselves. At the war's end the Russians allowed them to fly their Yak-3s to Paris.

## Hans-J Marseille

Captain Hans-Joachim Marseille became a Luftwaffe legend by shooting down 158 RAF aircraft. He fought in the Battle of Britain, but his skill flowered later over the desert where he ruled the skies in his yellow-nosed Bf 109. On September 1, 1942, he achieved the unique feat of shooting down 17 aircraft in one day. He received his country's highest award, the Knight's Cross with Oak leaves, Swords and Diamonds, but died later that month when he baled out and was struck by the tailplane.

*Marseille shows what happened.*

## David McCampbell

Captain David McCampbell, the US Navy's leading ace with a score of 34 Japanese aircraft shot down, was not only a superb marksman but also a great leader and tactician. These qualities were recognized by his superiors, who made him Air Group Commander on board the carrier USS *Essex*.

On October 24, 1944, with over a hundred Japanese planes coming in to attack, McCampbell abandoned his command duties and led seven Hellcats to intercept them. He shot down nine of them; none at all got through. Career officer McCampbell was awarded the Medal of Honor, the Navy Cross, the Silver Star, the Legion of Merit, the Distinguished Service Cross and the Air Medal.

# Bold men – and a woman – who flew to glory

## Ivan Kozhedub and Lydia Lityvak

*Lydia Lityvak (with map) flew with the men straight to the heart of battle.*

Major Ivan Kozhedub, three times a Hero of the Soviet Union, was the top-scoring Russian ace with 62 victories. This peasant boy, flying an La-5, opened his account with a Ju 87 Stuka dive-bomber during the Battle of Kursk in July 1943. Later, flying the more powerful La-7, he accounted for an Me 262 jet fighter. Most of his kills were Fw 190 and Bf 109 fighters. Kozhedub survived the war to become a general and command the Soviet fighter pilots fighting for the north in the Korean war.

Another Soviet ace who did not survive the war was Lydia Lityvak, who, with 12 kills, was the leading Soviet woman fighter pilot. Some 1,000 women pilots fought with distinction, most of them in all-woman units. One unit, the "Night Witches", flew Po-2 biplanes at

*Kozhedub: survived 120 dogfights.*

night over the battlefield. Other women pilots flew alongside men in fighter regiments. The blonde, blue-eyed Lityvak was one of these. Flying a Yak, she was shot down and killed on August 1, 1943.

## Adolf Galland

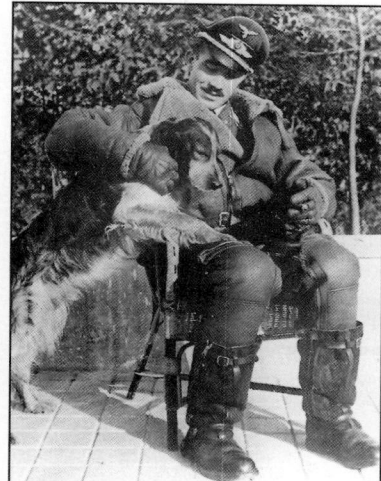

*Galland relaxes with a friend.*

Major Adolf Galland was one of the brilliant fighter pilots who "mixed it" in the skies over southern England during the Battle of Britain. Galland, one of Hermann Goering's favorites, once had the nerve to tell the Luftwaffe chief that he wanted a squadron of Spitfires. He had fought in the Spanish Civil War and was the epitome of the bemedalled Luftwaffe officer. He shot down a remarkable 104 enemy aircraft and was appointed general of fighters.

## 'Ginger' Lacey

*Lacey: Battle of Britain ace.*

Freckle-faced James Harry "Ginger" Lacey was not at first considered "officer material" by the RAF because of his grammar-school education. It was not until he had fought over France and in the Battle of Britain, winning 15 kills and a Distinguished Flying Medal with bar, that he was commissioned. Among his exploits was shooting down the He 111 that bombed Buckingham Palace. He finished the war in Burma with a final official tally of 28.

## Midway's hero: the story of George Gay

When Ensign George "Tex" Gay flew his lumbering Devastator torpedo-bomber off the USS *Hornet* on June 4, 1942, to attack the Japanese fleet he knew it was going to be dangerous. Just how dangerous he had no idea. Every plane in his unit, Torpedo 8, was hacked out of the sky by Zeros protecting the Japanese carriers. Gay's plane plummeted, on fire, into the sea; but,

although he was wounded, he escaped from the wreckage, grabbed a seat cushion and held on to it while the Battle of Midway raged all round him. He watched as another wave of American planes died and then saw the Japanese carriers *Akagi*, *Kaga* and *Soryu* all destroyed by Dauntless dive-bombers. The following day he was rescued by a Catalina flying boat.

G/C George "Screwball" Beurling (l) was a hero of the air defense of Malta, and the highest-scoring Canadian ace of the war with 31 victories. G/C Clive "Killer" Caldwell (r) won his spurs in the Western Desert in 1941 and was Australia's top ace of the war with 28 "kills".

*Most of the 45 Sud-Ouest SO.30 Bretagnes saw French military use.*

*Sikorsky's S-51 was the first in a long line of commercial helicopters.*

*The Sud-Est SE.161 Languedoc was the production version of the pre-war Bloch 160; 100 were built. It was used by Air France on several major routes.*

*The first post-war British airliner to enter service, the Vickers Viking initially used Wellington bomber parts. British European Airways was a major user.*

*De Havilland's D.H.104 Dove eight/ ten-seater local service airliner.*

*Bristol 170 Freighters had clamshell nose doors for bulky loads and cars.*

*Cessna introduced a metal fuselage on its Model 120 private two-seater.*

*The cabin of the Miles M.57 Aero-van could accommodate a vehicle.*

*Northrop designed the XP-79 Flying Ram flying-wing fighter to slice off the tails of enemy aircraft. The wing was of magnesium and steel armour plate.*

*Bell's Model 47 was awarded the first US Type Approval Certificate for a commercial helicopter. It remained in production in the USA until 1974.*

*Powered by 1,600-hp GR14 engines, the 23-seat Breguet 500 Colmar.*

*The 50-seat Handley Page Hermes 2 was produced only as a prototype.*

*The prototype of the Avro Tudor 1: the first British pressurized airliner.*

*Twenty Martin JRM-1 Mars flying boats were ordered; five were built.*

*The Nakajima Kikka single-seater twin-jet fighter with Ne-20 turbojets.*

*The Pilatus P-2 trainer – 53 were supplied to the Swiss air force.*

The twin-engined Miles M.65 Gemini was an extremely good 4-seater.

The Douglas C-74 Globemaster was succeeded by the superior C-124.

Bell XP-83 experimental jet fighter, developed from the P-59 Airacomet.

More than 320 four-seat Saab 91s were built, mainly for military use.

The FAA's last piston-engined fighter was the Hawker Sea Fury. The prototype's fixed wings were replaced by folding wings on production Sea Furies.

The Douglas XBT2D-1 was the first single-seat US Navy carrier-based dive-bomber and torpedo-carrier. As the Skyraider, it won its spurs in Korea.

Farman built the only Heinkel He 274 high-altitude bomber.

Northrop's F-15A Reporter, the reconnaissance version of the P-61.

Nord's 1201 Norécrin three-seater monoplane (Renault 4P01 engine).

Yokosuka Navy Yard, Japan, produced the MXY-7 suicide aircraft.

Fairey's Spearfish torpedo-bomber, designed to replace the Barracuda.

A vertical-launched piloted missile: the Bachem Ba 349 Natter [Adder].

The 18th production Gloster Meteor F.1 became the Trent-Meteor. With two Rolls-Royce Trent engines, it was the world's first turboprop-powered aircraft.

The first prototype Short Sunderland Mk IV was later converted into the prototype Seaford, which formed the basis of BOAC's civil Short Solent.

Yakovlev's simple Yak-15 was one of the first two Soviet jet fighters.

Lockheed's prototype P2V Neptune patrol and anti-submarine aircraft.

The Grumman XTB3F Guardian in its radar-equipped AF-2W variant.

The Convair XP-81, powered by a jet and also a TG-100 turboprop.

449

# 1946

 623.85mph
Germany
Heini Dittmar
Messerschmitt Me 163A
Oct 2, 1941

 11,235 miles
USA
Thomas D Davies
Lockheed P2V-1 Neptune
Oct 1, 1946

 56,046ft
Italy
Mario Pezzi
Caproni 161bis
Oct 22, 1938

 310,000lb
USA
Convair
XB-36

 6,000lb thrust
USA
Reaction Motors Inc
XLR 11-RM-5

**Britain, January 1**
The British Civil Aviation Act establishes state airlines British Overseas Airways Corporation (BOAC), British European Airways (BEA) and British South American Airways (BSAA). A BSAA Lancastrian makes the first commercial departure from the new London Airport at Heathrow, 20 miles west of the city centre (→ May 31).

**New York, January 26**
Colonel William H Councill lands his Lockheed P-80R Shooting Star at LaGuardia after a record flight of 4 hours 13 minutes from Long Beach, California (→ Jun 22).

**England, January 31**
A BOAC Short Sunderland reopens the airline's flying-boat service to Singapore (→ Apr 2).

**Paris, February 6**
A TWA Lockheed Constellation lands at Orly airport from LaGuardia, New York, to complete the airline's first scheduled international flight (→ Feb 15).

**Bermuda, February 11**
Representatives of the US and Britain sign a bilateral agreement to regulate air traffic between the two countries (→ Mar 27).

**USA, March 1**
United Air Lines begins a New York/San Francisco service.

**Washington, DC, March 8**
The US Civil Aeronautics Administration (CAA) awards its first civil helicopter certificate, to the Bell Model 47 (→ Oct 30).

**New York, March 27**
An air agreement is signed by France and the US giving Air France the right to serve the cities of Boston, New York, Washington, DC, and Chicago (→ May 21).

**Belgrade, April 1**
Yugoslavia's national airline Jugoslovenski Aerotransport (JAT) is established.

**Tokyo, April 2**
A BOAC Short Sunderland III Hythe flying boat, which left England on February 17, completes a 35,313-mile route-survey flight via Australia, New Zealand, Hong Kong and Shanghai (→ May 12).

**USA, April 24**
Winged Cargo Inc opens an unusual freight service in which goods are carried in a Waco CG-4A glider towed by a DC-3.

**New York, May 9**
The New York Yankees baseball club becomes the first Major League team to travel to scheduled games by air when it contracts to travel exclusively on United Airlines for the 1946 season.

**Muroc Dry Lake, Calif, May 17**
Bob Brush makes the first flight in the experimental Douglas XB-43; it is the USA's first jet bomber (→ Mar 17, 1947).

**The Netherlands, May 21**
KLM inaugurates a scheduled service to New York (→ Jul 1).

**London, June 1**
A Pan Am Constellation lands at the newly opened Heathrow Airport; it is the airline's first scheduled flight from New York to London (→ Jun 17, 1947).

**Schenectady, NY, June 22**
Two P-80 Shooting Stars take off with the first airmail carried by jet, one flying to Washington, DC, the other to Chicago (→ Jun 20, 1948).

**Australasia, June 24**
British Commonwealth Pacific Airlines is founded to operate transpacific services from Australia and New Zealand to the US.

**Muroc Dry Lake, Calif, June 25**
The Northrop XB-35 bomber lands after an 85-mile maiden flight from Hawthorne, Los Angeles; the first bomber of "flying wing" design, it can carry 28 tons of bombs and has a range of about 10,000 miles (→ Oct 21, 1947).

**Washington, DC, June 26**
The knot and the nautical mile are adopted by the US Navy and USAAF as units for aeronautical speed and distance; the nautical mile is about 1.15 land miles; the knot is one nautical mile per hour.

**Wichita, Kansas, July 5**
Al and Art Mooney, along with G C Yankey and W L McMahon, set up the Mooney Aircraft company (→ Jan 5, 1953).

**Washington, DC, July 12**
The CAA grounds all Lockheed Constellations after an in-flight fire led to the crash of a TWA aircraft at Reading, Pennsylvania, yesterday (→ Sep 20).

**Washington, DC, July 25**
US air power advocate Brigadier-General Billy Mitchell is posthumously awarded the Congressional Medal of Honor.

**India, July 29**
Tata Air Lines changes its name to Air India Ltd and is converted to a public company (→ Mar 8, 1948).

**Scandinavia, July 31**
Scandinavian Airlines System (SAS), a collaboration between the three national airlines of Sweden, Denmark and Norway, is established.

**Dayton, Ohio, August 17**
In the first manned test of an ejector seat in the United States, USAAF Sergeant Lawrence Lambert abandons a Northrop P-61 Black Widow at 302mph, landing safely (→ May 30, 1949).

**Melbourne, Australia, September 9**
Trans-Australia Airlines (TAA) inaugurates its first trial service, to Sydney (→ May 5, 1947).

**Sydney, September 15**
Australian National Airlines opens a regular fortnightly service with Douglas DC-4s from Sydney to Vancouver, Canada, via Fiji, Canton Island, Honolulu and San Francisco.

**Italy, September 16**
Aerolinee Italiane Internazionali (Alitalia) is established, with the newly formed British European Airways holding 30 per cent of the shares; Linee Aeree Italiane (LAI) is formed on the same day, with the US airline TWA holding a 40 per cent stake.

**Washington, DC, September 20**
The CAA lifts its order of July 12 grounding all Constellations; the problem has been traced to the aircraft's cabin blowers.

**Hong Kong, September 24**
Cathay Pacific Airways, formed in February by a group of US and Australian pilots, is incorporated.

**Chicago, October 1**
A joint exercise is launched by the US Post Office and the USAAF to study the feasibility of helicopter airmail deliveries (→ Oct 8, 1947).

**China, October 25**
Major-General Claire L Chennault and Whiting Willauer establish CNRAA Air Transport to fly relief supplies to China.

**Massachusetts, November 13**
Vincent J Schaefer of General Electric flies into a cloud over Greylock Mountain and "seeds" it with dry-ice pellets, causing the first artificial snowstorm.

**Sweden, November 16**
The Saab 90 Scandia, a DC-3 class transport with two 1,800-hp Pratt & Whitney Twin Wasp engines, makes its first flight.

**Shanghai, December 25**
Today is promptly nicknamed "Black Christmas" as three airliners crash trying to land in bad weather, killing 72 people. It is the worst day so far in the history of Chinese civil aviation.

*One of TWA's stewardesses offers service with a smile: meals are now becoming an element in transatlantic flight competition.* ▶

# Rivalry reborn as DC-3 lands in London

*London, January 2*
The old rivalry between British and French airlines on the London/Paris route hotted up today with the arrival of an Air France DC-3 from Le Bourget. France has run a limited Paris/London service since hostilities ended, using former Luftwaffe Ju 52/3ms, but this is the first proper Air France flight since the war began. The airline plans to replace the DC-3s with SE 161 Languedocs and 44-seat DC-4s. The UK's newly-created British European Airways (BEA) will respond soon, also with DC-3s. It too has Ju 52/3ms in an inventory which includes the de Havilland D.H.89 Rapide, a pre-war, fabric-covered, biplane light transport (→Feb 4).

*A Caudron C.449 Goëland in Air France livery; it only carries six passengers.*

# New Orleans airport named for early flyer

*New Orleans, January 13*
Recalling both its French roots and a pioneer who died at the city's first aviation meeting on December 31, 1910, New Orleans has named its new airport John B Moisant Field. Moisant was famous in Europe for carrying his cat as a passenger between Paris and London and for flying his mechanic across the English Channel, the first passenger to do so. The new airfield is actually at Kenner, between the Mississippi and Lake Pontchartrain. It covers 1,500 acres, five times the area of the old airport, meeting the city's current needs with plenty of room for expansion.

**Australian National Airways' new Skymaster goes on view to the public.**

# Sikorsky helicopter reaches new heights

*The record-breaking Sikorsky R-5 helicopter has a payload of 1,100lb.*

*Stratford, Connecticut, January 10*
A US Army Sikorsky R-5 set a new unofficial altitude record for helicopters today when it reached 21,000 feet on a test flight. The R-5 is a much improved version of the R-4, which was the first helicopter to go into full-scale production, seeing service in the war. The rotors have been improved, and it has a 450-hp engine compared with the R-4's 145-hp. The R-4's fuselage was covered in fabric while the R-5 has an all-metal fuselage and a new crew layout with two seats in tandem; a rescue version will be fitted with a powered hoist. The R-5 is a military design, but it has already been adapted as Sikorsky's first civil machine, the four-seater S-51, which goes into production this year. Under a license agreement with Westland, it will also be the first helicopter built in Britain.

# Republic launches its Thunderjet fighter

*XP-84: the first new US fighter to have its maiden flight since the war's end.*

*Muroc Dry Lake, Calif, February 28*
America's second jet fighter made its debut here today, flown by Major William Lien. The Republic XP-84 Thunderjet looks a worthy successor to the company's piston-engined P-47 Thunderbolt which made such a name for itself during the war as a fighter/bomber.

Alexander Kartveli, the designer for Republic, had originally studied the possibility of installing a General Electric TG-180 turbojet in a modified version of the P-47. However, he started afresh last year with a new, slimmer design and a 3,750-lb thrust GE J35-GE-7 engine. The USAAF has ordered 85 P-84Bs, to be powered by the 4,000-lb thrust Allison J35-A-15C turbojet and armed with four 0.50-in machine guns.

# Hughes flies the stars to New York

*Los Angeles, February 15*
Billionaire, pilot and film producer Howard Hughes brought off a sensational publicity coup for his airline today when he personally took command of a TWA Lockheed Constellation, packed with Hollywood's finest, non-stop from Los Angeles to New York.

Edward G Robinson, Linda Darnell, Paulette Goddard, William Powell and Walter Pidgeon, among others, joined journalists at nearly 30,000 feet in the pressurized cabin and reported favorably on the service and the airplane. The flight was to publicize TWA's scheduled services on the route, which begin on March 1, and to take the limelight from United Airlines, whose San Francisco/New York service, in the unpressurized DC-4, begins on the same day (→ Jul 12).

*Stairway to Heaven: stars board the TWA Constellation in party mood.*

## New British airline shows way to Paris

*Northolt, England, February 4*
British commercial aviation took a big step along the road to post-war recovery today as British European Airways (BEA) started scheduled services to Paris, Amsterdam, Brussels, Madrid, Lisbon, Stockholm and Helsinki. Next month it will add Oslo, Copenhagen, Gibraltar, Rome and Athens to its network, and its board confidently expects to take over German airline Lufthansa's pre-war position as the Continent's premier carrier.

At present BEA is the European division of BOAC, but under the Civil Aviation Act of January 1 it will become independent in the summer. BOAC will continue to fly long-haul intercontinental routes. Both airlines will remain fully owned by the state (→ Sep 1).

# Strategic force gives USAAF a longer range

*A B-29 Superfortress, part of the USA's ambitious peace-keeping scheme.*

*Andrews Field, Md, March 21*
The advent of the long-range bomber and the atomic bomb has led US defense planners to take the first steps in creating an independent air force within the USAAF.

The Strategic Air Command (SAC) came into being today with a mission "to conduct long-range offensive operations in any part of the world independently of, or in cooperation with, land or naval forces". This move comes when the USA, though it has a monopoly on the atomic bomb, is aware that it is no longer out of the range of improved bombers. General Carl Spaatz, Commanding General of the Army Air Forces, said: "Attacks can now come across the Arctic – the next Pearl Harbor might be Chicago."

Two other commands recognize other roles for military aircraft: Tactical Air Command to support land operations, and Air Defense Command to defend US skies from enemy bombers.

# New DC-6 aims to rival Constellation

*Santa Monica, Calif, February 15*
When America went to war in 1941 the USAAF was able to take full advantage of the development work initiated by the airlines to build the Douglas DC-4 airliner, turning it into a superb military transport, the C-54. Today the opposite happened when John F Martin made the first flight in what should have been the C-54's successor airplane, the XC-112A, developed at the expense of the USAAF. But with the war over and military requirements drastically cut, Douglas sees the future of the airplane not as a military transport, but as an airliner to be designated DC-6.

It will have a pressurized cabin with seating for 86 passengers, giving Douglas a competitor for the Lockheed Constellation which is already available. It will have equally powerful engines, better de-icing and upgraded radio and electronic aids. The DC-6 should fly in June. American Airlines and United Air Lines are impressed enough with it on paper to order 50 and 20 respectively (→ Apr 27, 1947).

*Douglas hopes that its DC-6 will prove a rival to the Lockheed Constellation.*

# Pan Am bids farewell to flying-boat era

*The Boeing B-314A "Dixie Clipper" flying boat began operating in 1939.*

**San Francisco, April 9**
There were tears in a few eyes here today when Pan American flying boat *American Clipper* touched down for the last time after a flight from Honolulu. The airline will no longer use the trusty and well-loved B-314s on its Pacific routes. Few in the airline industry now doubt that the new range of economical, fast landplanes, like the Lockheed Constellation and the Douglas DC-4, have dealt the flying boats a deadly blow.

As if to underline that point, a Constellation which left Honolulu at the same time as the *American Clipper* arrived here four hours sooner. The landplanes can also take more passengers, so fares have

dropped – from $278 to $195 for a single fare.

BOAC has recently retired the last of its three Boeing B-314 flying boats serving the Bermuda/Baltimore route. However, the British airline is still using converted wartime Short Sunderlands on its routes to South Africa and India and will soon introduce the new Solent flying boat, based on the military Seaford, on long-haul flights. It is also evaluating the Saunders-Roe Princess, a 100-ton flying boat powered by ten turboprops. BOAC's conversion to landplanes (outside the North Atlantic route, where it plans to fly Constellations and Avro Tudors) will perhaps be less decisive than Pan Am's.

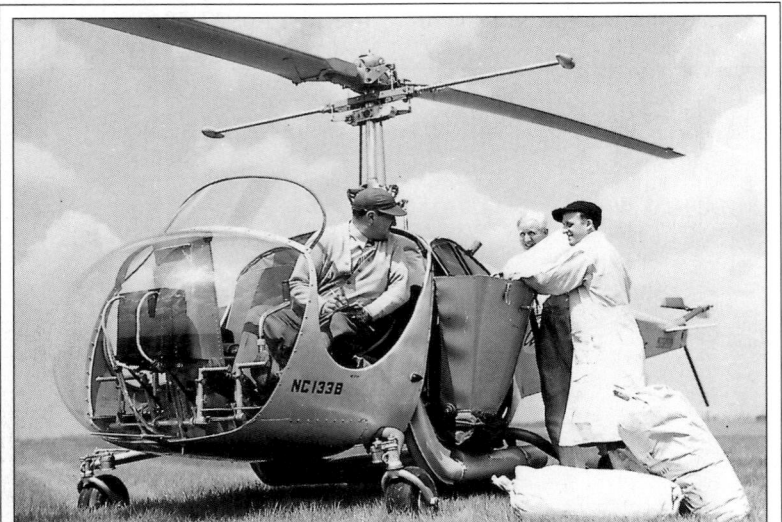

**Bell's Model 47, here shown in a crop-spraying version, has won the first commercial helicopter certificate from the CAA. It has a bright future.**

# Soviets base new jets on German designs

**Chkalovskaya, USSR, April 24**
Following months of activity, two jet fighter prototypes made their first flights at this airfield today. They have been made possible by German jet-engine technology.

The first to be ready was the Yakovlev Yak-15, but Stalin decreed that both aircraft should be flown together. In the event, the second jet, the twin-engined MiG I-300, the prototype of the MiG-9, flew first,

designer Artyom I Mikoyan having won the toss of a coin. The MiG has RD-20 engines, based on the German BMW 003A, while the Yak has a single RD-10, based on the German Jumo 004B. Both can exceed 500mph and carry heavy caliber cannon. The MiG was flown by A N Grinchik and the Yak-15 by M I Ivanov. Both jets flew well; this will please Stalin, who is eager to get them into service (→ Oct 31).

*The Soviet Yak-15 jet fighter, for which Stalin showed much enthusiasm.*

# Vampire fighters lead Victory Day fly-by

**London, June 8**
The British public had a first opportunity to view the RAF's latest fighter today when a squadron of de Havilland D.H.100 Vampire Mk I jets flew over Buckingham Palace and the City at the head of the Victory Day celebration fly-by. The little twin-tailed jets belonged to RAF Fighter Command's N° 247 Squadron, the first unit to be equipped with the aircraft.

The Vampire, the world's first fighter capable of over 500mph, is a symbol of the new post-war jet age. The prototype flew in September 1943, but it took until April last year for a production airplane to fly and it did not enter service before the war ended (→ Mar 23, 1948).

*Lancasters fly over Parliament.*

# France is reaching for the stratosphere

**Toussus-le-Noble, France, June 6**
A pure research aircraft, the NC 3021 *Belphégor*, designed to explore the problems of flying in the stratosphere at well over 40,000 feet, has made its first flight here at the former Farman works with Johnny Burtin at the controls.

Had it been designed today it might have been a jet, but no such engines were available when design started during the war. Instead the

*Belphégor's* engine is a 2,950-hp Daimler-Benz 610 driving a huge, four-bladed propeller similar to those on the Heinkel He 177 bomber. Its cabin is a pressurized drum, accommodating five crew members who monitor a wide range of instruments which show the performance of its 24-cylinder double engine at great heights, cabin pressure and variations in outside air pressure and temperature.

## Heathrow Airport opens for business

*Middlesex, England, May 31*
The first overseas passengers to arrive at Heathrow, London's new airport which opened for business today, thought they had arrived at an army camp. Business tycoons, film stars and diplomats have to queue on wooden-slatted floors to protect them from the mud in a "tent city" at the ex-RAF and Fairey Aviation airfield to house customs and immigration.

Long-haul traffic, mainly from the US, has been arriving at Hurn, near Bournemouth, since flights re-started after the war, but American airlines have complained that this means passengers still have 100 miles to travel once they reach Britain, so the government agreed to the use of Heathrow, which is 20 miles from the city center (→ Jun 6).

*Makeshift facilities at Heathrow.*

# European airlines head for New York

*Heathrow, July 1*
British flag-carrier BOAC today became the third European airline since May to begin flights to New York. The new twice-weekly service, using Lockheed Constellations, is yet another sign of the growing importance of the North Atlantic as the premier air route in the post-war world, making New York the air gateway to America.

Dutch airline KLM was first off the mark on May 21, with a 25-hour service from Amsterdam to New York using DC-4s, making stopovers at Prestwick, Scotland, and Gander, Newfoundland. A week ago Air France opened its Paris/New York route, also using DC-4s, flying via Shannon, Ireland, and Gander. Three US airlines – Pan Am, TWA and American Overseas Airlines – have all been flying the route for some time.

The International Air Transport Association (IATA) has set the round-trip fare from London to New York at £156, but despite the high price traffic is expected to grow. A new airport is under construction at Idlewild near New York City with several 10,000-foot runways, which are planned to cater for up to 360 airplanes an hour when it opens in 1948. Other European airlines are likely to join in the North Atlantic rush before long. Scandinavian Airlines System (SAS), which ordered its DC-4s in November 1943, expects to start flying between Stockholm and New York in a few weeks time. But while there is competition between US and European airlines for passengers, American manufacturers remain the only source of aircraft suitable for the job (→ Jun 4, 1947).

*KLM is the first European airline to open post-war flights to New York.*

*Air France has the reputation of offering one of the best on-board services.*

## Howard Hughes cheats death in air crash

*Los Angeles, July 7*
One of the US's greatest aviation pioneers, Howard Hughes, 41, is critically ill with burns and multiple injuries after his XF-11 twin-engined reconnaissance aircraft crashed on a test flight today. He was attempting to crash-land on a golf course when the 6,000-hp aircraft plowed into a house.

Hughes had spent much of the day on taxi trials, getting the feel of the advanced controls. His take-off on the short runway was perfect, and it was not until he was flying at 400mph over the Pacific that disaster struck. The XF-11 suddenly swung violently to the right; only later did the pilot learn that the rearmost of the starboard pair of contra-rotating propellers had gone into full reverse pitch. Nothing had registered on the instrument panel (→ Nov 2, 1947).

## British pilot tests 'ejection seat' in flight

*Chalgrove, England, July 24*
Bernard Lynch became one of the few men to have been "shot" out of an airplane today, in the first airborne test of a British "ejection seat". He did it from the rear cockpit of a modified Gloster Meteor F.3 flying at 8,000 feet and 320mph. The need for such a dramatic means of escape arose in the war as airplanes grew faster and the "G" forces made it difficult to climb out of the cockpit. Even if a pilot managed it, he was likely to be smashed against the tail, a problem even more acute with the arrival of jet aircraft. This life-saver, made by Martin-Baker, consists of a seat, with a built-in parachute, on rollers which run up a guide rail. The pilot activates it by pulling a screen over his face which fires a charge in a tube, propelling him up and away from the aircraft (→ Aug 17).

# Helicopters sell well in the United States

*The popular S-51 helicopter.*

*Bridgeport, Conn, October 30*
Commercial sales of Sikorsky helicopters are growing steadily. The four-seater S-51 model was chosen for the first experimental use of helicopters to deliver mail, which took place in the suburbs of Chicago today. Greyhound Skyways of Michigan will receive two S-51s next month, while the US Navy has just ordered for an Antarctic expedition which is planned for later on this year.

On August 19 Sikorsky delivered its first commercial helicopter to Helicopter Air Transport Inc of Camden, New Jersey, the world's first helicopter airline. Its total of three S-51s are used to carry passengers between airports and city hall in Philadelphia (→ Jun 26, 1947).

# Convair tests the world's largest bomber

*Fort Worth, Texas, August 8*
Convair test pilots Beryl Erickson and Gus Green today took the prototype of the largest bomber in the world, the B-36, on a 38-minute first flight. Originally called Model 37, the giant was designed to bomb Germany from bases in North America in the event that Hitler succeeded in invading Britain. The USAAF specification called for an aircraft which could carry a 10,000-pound bomb-load to a target 5,000 miles away and return to base without refueling. It also made exacting demands for both speed and altitude.

The result is the huge Consolidated Vultee XB-36. Everything about it is enormous: the wingspan is 230 feet, and it is powered by six 3,500-hp Wasp Major engines driving huge pusher propellers. Production models will have 17 cannon, 12 in turrets which retract into the fuselage (→ Mar 26, 1949).

*Even the B-29 Superfortress is dwarfed by the enormous size of the XB-36.*

# BOAC agrees to share routes with Qantas

*Dorset, England, May 12*
Today marks the start of a new air link between England and Australia shared between BOAC and Qantas Empire Airways. It may be new, but the concept is old; they are using converted wartime Sunderland flying boats, renamed Hythes. BOAC will fly the inaugural leg from Poole in the *Hudson*, which will go as far as Singapore where, the *Hobart* will take over for the second stage to Sydney. The one-way trip takes over five days.

Flying boats used to be the only way to fly long distances, but with the better landplanes brought about by the war they now hark back to a more leisurely age in air transport which cannot be revived.

# BEA replaces DC-3s with British Vikings

*London, September 1*
British European Airways (BEA) today put its new 21-seat Vickers Viking airliner into service between Northolt, now London's Continental services airport, and Kastrup airport, Copenhagen. Captain James was in command on this, its first commercial flight.

The Viking was conceived during the war as a means of turning swords into plowshares while revitalizing British civil aviation as quickly as possible. As such it was always considered an interim design, its original name being the Wellington Continental as it was based on the Wellington bomber, with a stressed metal fuselage and other key modifications. For example, it carries freight in holds underneath the cabin.

By replacing the DC-3, BEA has cut the journey time to Copenhagen by 35 minutes to just 3 hours 25 minutes, and the airline will introduce it on services to the Netherlands and Norway tomorrow.

# Meteor jet sets new world speed record

*Sussex, England, September 7*
Britain's jet fighter, the Gloster F.4 Meteor, set a new world speed record of 616mph along a course off the coast today. Pilot Group Captain Edward Donaldson of the RAF's High Speed Flight added 10mph to last year's record held by the same team, and beat another attempt today by a USAAF pilot in a P-84 Thunderjet, who set a new American record of 611mph in the course of his attempt.

The RAF's new F.4 version has a pressurized cockpit, new Rolls-Royce Derwent engines and, as originally designed, a 43-foot wingspan. However, the wings have now been shortened to just over 37 feet.

All but a very few F.4s have "clipped" wings. The Meteor has kept Britain in the forefront of jet airplane developments: one was used for ejection-seat trials [*see page 455*], while another made 32 trial landings on the aircraft carrier HMS *Implacable* (→ Dec 9, 1950).

**The Curtiss C-46 Commando, the rival to the DC-3: it was developed for the USAAF and US Navy in the Pacific campaign. Many of the 3,180 built have gone into commercial use after the war as the CW-20E.**

# Canadian airline puts faith in North Star

*A pressurized version of the North Star, in service with TCA over the Atlantic.*

*Montreal, July*

Canadian manufacturer Canadair is trying to make a workable marriage between a successful American airframe, the DC-4, and the famous British Rolls-Royce Merlin engine. The idea is that this will meet the needs of both the Royal Canadian Air Force (RCAF) and Trans-Canada Airlines (TCA).

The ultimate goal is to produce a pressurized version of the DC-4 using supercharged Merlins to fly at high altitudes where they are more efficient. But to get the project going, it was decided to use unpressurized DC-54 military fuselages with four liquid-cooled 1,725-hp Merlin 620s. The first of these hybrids, to be named North Star, was flown this month by Bob Brush of Douglas and Al Lily of Canadair and will be one of an order for 24 by the RCAF. TCA is expected to order up to 50 of the pressurized versions (→ Jul 13, 1949).

# France's first jet, Triton, takes to the air

*The first French jet uses a Junkers Jumo 004B engine of 1,980 lb thrust.*

*Orléans-Bricy, France, Nov 11*

Working in secrecy in what they describe as "appalling conditions" in an old hangar here, engineers have finally produced the first French jet aircraft, the Triton, which made its first flight today. Designer Lucien Servanty and his team have been working on this unusually-shaped aircraft with its bulbous fuselage and razor-like wings since 1943. Servanty was waiting by the hangar as test pilot Daniel Rastel brought the Triton out of the low cloud at 1,000 feet to make a perfect landing. The engineers had wagered that the Triton would be ready for the 17th Paris Air Show, which opens in four days. They have won their bet.

# De Havilland killed in test flight crash

*Hertfordshire, England, Sep 27*

The staff of de Havilland Aircraft at Hatfield are mourning the tragic loss of their chief test pilot today – none more so than Sir Geoffrey de Havilland himself, the company's founder, for the man who died was his eldest son, Geoffrey. The tragedy happened when Geoffrey junior was engaged in high-speed diving trials in a D.H.108 tailless swept-wing research aircraft.

This had been made to explore the possibility of supersonic flight. Fitted with a 3,300-lb thrust Goblin engine, it was thought capable of supersonic speed. De Havilland planned to dive to low level and then make a full-throttle run up the Thames estuary in preparation for an attempt on the world speed record. At first the flight seemed to go as planned; then, according to eye-witnesses, the aircraft broke up and fell into Egypt Bay, northeast of Gravesend, Kent. The catastrophe probably resulted from forces associated with the shock wave which builds up around an aircraft flying close to the speed of sound, the so-called "sound barrier" (→ Dec 31).

*The D.H.108 tailless jet involved in the fatal crash during transonic testing.*

# US bomber takes shorter polar route

*Cairo, October 6*

The Boeing B-29B *Pacusan Dreamboat* proved the feasibility of USAAF flights over the top of the world today when it landed here at the end of a 10,873-mile, non-stop, unrefueled flight across the Arctic from Honolulu.

Pilot Colonel Clarence S Irvine said the flight showed that a global air force is possible: it confirmed that the Arctic route, which he called "the shortest route to most places" from the US, is "navigable" and "communication can be maintained with ships and shore".

However, US War Department sources and military experts offered the somber observation that the flight also proved America's vulnerability to an attack via the Arctic (→ Dec 1, 1948).

# Soviets put German scientists to work

*Moscow, October*

Since the war ended, over 3,000 German scientists and engineers have so far been put to work in the USSR on the same kind of research they were doing when they worked for Hitler's Germany. Others are working in Britain, the US and France, but in the USSR conditions are different: German expertise is more desperately needed, and the Germans have no status, except as prisoners of war. It will be years before they are free men.

The three areas on which they are working are: transonic aerodynamics and swept-wing aircraft design; rockets and jet engines; and large ballistic rocket missiles. In all these fields, the Soviets feel they are running a race against their former allies (→ Aug 3, 1947). ▷

# 'Truculent Turtle' breaks distance record

*The not so truculent Lockheed Neptune, a winner despite weather difficulties.*

*Columbus, Ohio, October 1*
Describing their flight from Perth, Australia, as "just like a hard patrol", four US Navy airmen climbed out of their Lockheed P2V Neptune patrol bomber here today. Their record non-stop, un-refueled, 11,236-mile flight had taken 55 hours 15 minutes.

The P2V, which averaged about 200mph, was nicknamed "the Truculent Turtle". It carried 8,600 US gallons of fuel, giving it a gross take-off weight of 85,500 lb, way above the plane's intended gross weight of 58,000 lb. To get it airborne, four JATO (jet-assisted take-off) rocket units added 4,000 lb of thrust to the Turtle's two 2,300-hp Wright R-3350 engines.

There were headwinds throughout the flight across the Pacific. Bad weather over the Seattle area caused them to divert south toward

Red Bluff, California, about 100 miles north of San Francisco, where they crossed the coast. On this stretch, Commander Thomas C Davies almost feathered the port engine when an instrument indicated problems, only to realize that the instrument was faulty and the engine was fine. Moments later a real problem occurred when ice stopped the engine; the crew used an alternative heating system and restarted it in 30 seconds.

The crew had thought the airplane could reach Washington, DC, but landed here because it was low on fuel – there were about 25 US gallons left in the tanks. Without the headwinds and freezing weather, which at one point caused the wings to be covered with an estimated 1,000 lb of ice, Davies believes the aircraft could have reached as far as Bermuda.

**A postcard from LaGuardia airport, which serves New York City.**

# Underpowered, the Constitution takes off

*Muroc Dry Lake, Calif, Nov 9*
Personnel turned out in force here today to watch test pilot Joe Towle land the prototype of the huge Lockheed Constitution after a maiden flight of 2 hours 17 minutes.

The 189-foot wingspan giant was originally planned before the war as a large-capacity, long-range airliner for Pan American, which had already seen the advantages of landplanes over flying boats for much of its transoceanic network. During the war it was taken over by the US Navy and designated XR6O-1. The 156-foot "double-bubble" fuselage can hold up to 204 military personnel, and in its civilian configuration, it would carry 51 seated passengers and 58 in sleeping berths. But at 92 tons it is one of the heaviest aircraft in the world, too heavy possibly even for its four 3,500-hp Pratt & Whitney R-4360 double turbo-charged engines.

Its vital statistics are impressive, but it is performance which counts. It seems that its current engines simply will not have the power to make it viable for the airlines.

*The Constitution could take up to 204 passengers – given the right engines.*

# Tinseltown pays screen tribute to flyers

*USA, December 31*
Hollywood film studios this year paid tribute to a US pioneer of flight and to the problems faced by the veterans of the air war. Columbia released *Gallant Journey*, the story of John J Montgomery, the Californian glider designer who claimed to have made history's first controlled winged flight in August 1883, some 20 years before the Wright brothers.

The outstanding success of 1946, however, was *The Best Years of Our Lives*, an unflinching view of the return of three war veterans, including a bomber pilot, to civilian life in a world changed by the war. The film was sensitively directed by veteran German-American director William Wyler, who was responsible for many successful pre-war features and for two popular wartime aviation documentaries, *The*

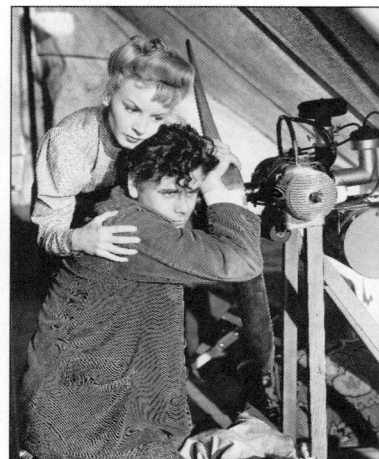

*Glenn Ford in "Gallant Journey".*

*Fighting Lady* (1945), about a US aircraft carrier, and *Memphis Belle* (1944), about a USAAF bomber and its crew stationed in Britain [see reports on page 442].

# US pulls ahead in the supersonic race

*Goodlin stands before the XS-1: he could be first to break the sound barrier.*

## Rocket-powered Bell XS-1 nears Mach 1

*Muroc Dry Lake, Calif, Dec 9*
Supersonic flight edged a little closer today when company test pilot Chalmers "Slick" Goodlin made the first powered flight in the Bell XS-1. He touched Mach 0.79 (79 per cent of the speed of sound) during the flight to 35,000 feet.

The straight-winged XS-1 is a joint venture between the National Advisory Committee for Aeronaut-ics (NACA), the USAAF and Bell. Three XS-1s have been built; un-able to take off under their own power, they have been borne aloft by B-29 and dropped while starting their engines. Today's flight was made in the second XS-1, using the wings and tail of the first, which will have a thinner tail and wings for its assault on the "sound bar-rier" (→ Oct 14, 1947).

## British research jet airplane is shelved

*England, December 31*
It has been a disappointing year for British supersonic efforts. In Sep-tember Geoffrey de Havilland Jr died in the D.H.108, and now it seems that the top-secret Miles M.52 was axed last February, end-ing British hopes of building the first supersonic aircraft.

The specification for the M.52 was drawn up in 1943, giving Miles the task of building an airplane which could take off under its own power to reach 1,000mph at 36,000 feet. Frank Whittle designed the W2/700 jet engine with an after-burner, and all seemed set for suc-cess. But the M.52 had straight wings, and captured German re-search suggested that very fast air-craft need swept-back wings.

Although the US equivalent, the Bell XS-1, has straight wings, Brit-ish officials decided to scrap the M.52 and instead play with small Vickers models. Unless de Havil-land can achieve something with the D.H.108s, the first man through the sound barrier will be American (→ May 30, 1947).

## American airlines enjoy a post-war passenger boom

*Business is good at US airports.*

*USA, December 31*
In the first full year of peace, the US has consolidated its position as the world leader in civil avia-tion. With its huge domestic market, it is now set to leap ahead in both the airline busi-ness and aircraft manufacture. Europeans will have to work hard to compete.

Most European airlines were forced to close down by the Sec-ond World War, while US do-mestic carriers continued to fly; in fact, the number of passengers carried by US domestic airlines increased from 4 million in 1944 and 6.5 million in 1945 to 12.2 million this year. This last figure represents two-thirds of all pas-sengers carried worldwide.

During the war, Europe's avi-ation industry concentrated on fighters and bombers. In the US, Boeing also made bombers, but Douglas and Lockheed devel-oped their four-engined air-liners, the DC-4 and the Con-stellation, albeit for military use.

America is building on this strong base while the European industry is still struggling to adapt to peacetime conditions. Meanwhile, the Europeans have little option but to buy Ameri-can. Once the US establishes a grip on the industry, it could be hard to loosen (→ Dec 31, 1947).

# Shock waves pose problem for researchers into the unknown

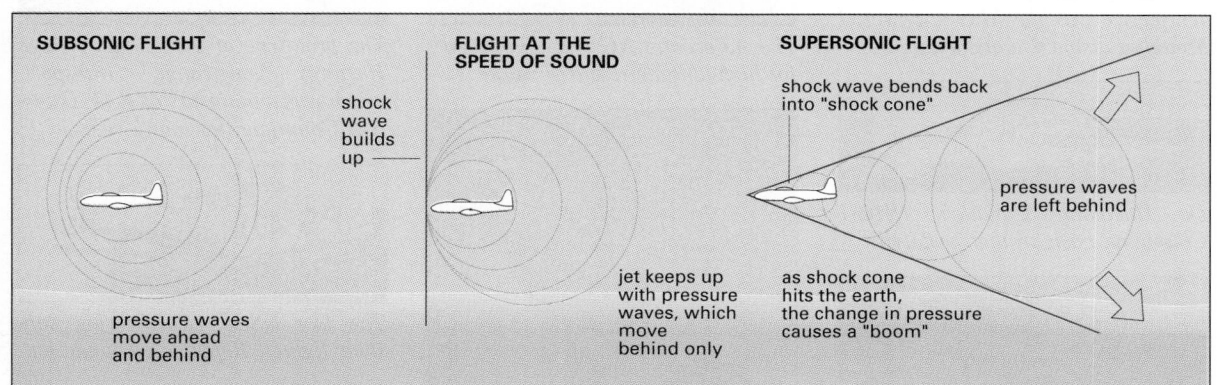

*Muroc Dry Lake, Calif, December*
Flying at speeds never before achieved, especially in the face of what is known about the possible hazards of what is called the "tran-sonic region" from about Mach 0.8 to Mach 1.2, is a dangerous busi-ness. Before men risk their lives, scientists would like to find out more by testing models in wind tun-nels, but this is impossible. Models can be tested at below Mach 0.8 and at speeds beyond Mach 1.2, but near the speed of sound itself shock waves from the model block the tunnel airflow. Many pilots died in the later part of the war flying at speeds approaching Mach 1.0 where extreme buffeting led to loss of control and structural failure.

The expression "Mach 1.0" is used to describe the "local" speed of sound, which varies with the temperature of the air. Thus Mach 1.0 equals 760mph at sea level at 59°F, while at 36,000 feet it falls to 659mph at minus 60°F.

Douglas built the XC-112A pressurized development of the C-54 Skymaster to meet USAAF needs, but it became better known as the DC-6 airliner.

The first US post-war-designed twin-engined airliner to receive type approval was the unpressurized Martin 2-0-2, 31 of which were delivered to airlines.

One of the first Soviet jet fighters to enter service was the MiG-9, powered by two RD-20 engines supplied with air through a distinctive divided intake.

The Chrislea C.H.3 Super Ace, for the private owner, had a unique system for flying controls but failed to win substantial orders.

De Havilland Canada's DHC-1 Chipmunk basic trainer prototype.

The double-decker fuselage Lockheed R6O Constitution seated 167.

Convair's prototype Model 110 30-seat airliner, parent to the CV 240.

Production of Saab's 90 Scandia totaled 17 in addition to the prototype.

Aeronca's first post-war model was the neat 7AC Champion two-seater.

SAI produced the four-seat KZ.VII with a Continental flat-four engine.

The Aérocentre NC 3021 Belphégor, for high-altitude research work.

The prototype of the Northrop XB-35 flying-wing long-range bomber.

The Sud-Ouest SO 6000 Triton was the first French jet aeroplane to fly.

Grumman's Mallard amphibian appealed to wealthy private owners.

The Percival Prentice became the standard basic trainer for the RAF.

The prototype of the Handley Page Hastings long-range transport, which was a mainstay of RAF Transport Command for many years.

The last USAF straight-wing subsonic fighter, Republic's Thunderjet.

The first Argentinian twin-engined aeroplane was the I.Ae 24 Calquin.

*Yakovlev's Yak-12: a simple four-seat general-purpose light aircraft.*

*The Royal Navy's Westland Wyvern single-seat turboprop strike-fighter.*

*The turboprop-plus-jet experimental Ryan XF2R-1 single-seat fighter.*

*The first US Air Force jet bomber, the Douglas XB-43, won no orders.*

*Yakovlev's Yak-18 aerobatic trainer was mass-produced for 20 years.*

*Supermarine's Attacker naval fighter (powered by Rolls-Royce Nene).*

*Short's Sturgeon, designed as a carrier-based reconnaissance-bomber.*

*The original straight-wing North American FJ-1 Fury naval fighter.*

*Chance-Vought's F6U-1 Pirate: 30 production models, three prototypes.*

*The de Havilland D.H.108 was built to investigate the control and stability characteristics of swept-back wings, particularly for the D.H.106 Comet.*

*Tupolev based the Tu-75 transport on Boeing's B-29 Superfortress.*

*Martin's XP4M Mercator bomber used both piston and jet engines.*

*The first prototype Convair XB-36 six-engined bomber with the original faired cockpit, replaced on the second and 382 production aircraft by a raised roof.*

*The Chance Vought XF5U-1's wing was of virtually circular plan-form.*

*The prototype of the FMA I.Ae 30 Namçu twin-engined escort-fighter.*

*The Commonwealth CA-15 was a possible successor to the Mustang.*

*Boeing's EB-17G, used as a flying testbed for Wright's XT35 turboprop.*

*The Bell X-1 was built to investigate supersonic flight characteristics, and on October 14, 1947, it became the first aircraft to exceed the speed of sound.*

# 1947

891.07mph
USA
Charles Yeager
Bell X-1
Nov 6, 1947

11,235 miles
USA
Thomas D Davies
Lockheed P2V-1 Neptune
Oct 1, 1946

56,046ft
Italy
Mario Pezzi
Caproni 161bis
Oct 22, 1938

400,000lb
USA
Hughes Aircraft Co
H-4 Hercules

6,000lb thrust
USA
Reactions Motors Inc
XLR 11-RM-5

**USA, January 30**
TWA inaugurates an innovative all-freight transatlantic service to Europe (→ May 17, 1950).

**France, February 1**
The airline Air France introduces Lockheed Constellations on its flights from Paris to New York, via Shannon, Ireland, and Gander, Newfoundland.

**Norrköping, Sweden, March 10**
The first prototype of the Saab J 21R jet fighter makes its maiden flight; it is a version of the piston-engined J 21 which has been fitted with a de Havilland Goblin turbojet (→ Sep 1, 1948).

**USA, March 17**
The USAAF's first multi-engined jet reconnaissance bomber, the North American XB-45 Tornado, is flown for the first time.

**London, April 15**
BOAC opens its first regular service to Canada; it is a weekly flight by Constellation to Montreal.

**New York, April 27**
United Airlines is the first carrier to put the new Douglas DC-6 into service, when it flies on the New York/San Francisco service.→

**St Louis, Missouri, May 5**
An experimental ramjet helicopter known as the Little Henry and built by McDonnell for the USAAF, begins tests; the ramjets are attached to the tips of the rotors, increasing the efficiency of the rotor system.

**Bangkok, May 25**
Pacific Overseas Airlines (Siam) is formed.

**Brussels, June 4**
Sabena launches a regular service to New York (→ Oct 8).

**New York, June 17**
Pan Am opens the first round-the-world air service; it flies eastbound to San Francisco with Lockheed Constellations (→ Apr 15, 1948).

**Wiltshire, England, June 17**
Mike Lithgow takes the Supermarine Attacker F.1 jet fighter on its first flight, at Boscombe Down.

**Mount Rainier, Wash, June 24**
Pilot and businessman Kenneth Arnold claims to see nine oddly shaped aircraft which resemble "saucers skipping over the water" moving at high speed near here; his report gives rise to the term "flying saucer" (→ Dec 27, 1949).

**Seattle, June 25**
The Boeing B-50A strategic bomber, an uprated version of the B-29 with 3,500-hp Wasp Major engines, makes its first flight (→ Mar 2, 1949).

**Ruislip, England, June 26**
British European Airways orders three Sikorsky S-51 and two Bell 47D helicopters in preparation for opening a Helicopter Experimental Unit at Yeovil, Somerset.

**Washington, DC, July 1**
The USAF takes delivery of a Douglas VC-118 (DC-6) airliner for use by the President; it is named *The Independence* for the Missouri home town of Harry S Truman (→ Mar 7, 1948).

**Seattle, July 8**
The prototype Boeing Model 377 Stratocruiser, a luxury civil version of the US military's C-97 Stratofreighter transport, makes its first flight (→ Jan 31, 1949).

**Minneapolis, July 15**
Northwest Airlines begins a service to the Far East on the "Great Circle" route, taking in Anchorage, Tokyo, Seoul, Shanghai and Manila (→ Oct 17, 1949).

**USSR, July 24**
The brothers V K and K K Kokinakki test-fly Ilyushin's new four-engined jet bomber, the Il-22 (→ Aug 3).

**Santa Monica, Calif, August 9**
The last DC-4 to be built by Douglas is delivered to South African Airways; the company has closed the DC-4 production line in order to concentrate on other models (→ Nov 4, 1948).

**Toronto, Canada, August 16**
The prototype of the all-metal de Havilland Canada DHC-2 Beaver, the company's first STOL bush transport, makes its first flight, at Downsview.

**Muroc Dry Lake, Calif, August 20**
US Navy Commander Turner Caldwell flies the Douglas D-558-1 Skystreak to a new world speed record of 644.663mph; he breaks the previous record made on June 19 by Colonel Albert Boyd, who reached 623.738mph in a Lockheed P-80R (→ Aug 25).

**Washington, DC, September 18**
W Stuart Symington is sworn in as the first Secretary of the US Air Force, which now officially exists as an independent service within the new unified US armed forces.→

**Oxfordshire, England, Sep 22**
A Douglas C-54 Skymaster from Wilmington, Ohio, lands manually at the RAF base at Brize Norton after making a fully-autopilot flight from Stephenville, Newfoundland.

**Washington, DC, September 25**
General Carl "Tooey" Spaatz is named as the first Chief of Staff of the USAF (→ Nov 5, 1948).

**Los Angeles, October 1**
Los Angeles Airways opens the world's first regular airmail service by helicopter, using Sikorsky S-51 machines; Russian-born designer Igor Sikorsky himself witnesses the event (→ Jun 1, 1948).

**Paris, October 8**
Air France opens its Golden Comet Deluxe Service to New York, an all-sleeper night route flown by Lockheed Constellations, carrying 11 passengers (→ Apr 28, 1948).

**Muroc Dry Lake, Calif, Oct 21**
The Northrop YB-49 prototype "flying wing" jet bomber begins flight tests (→ May 4, 1950).

**Cherry Point, NC, October 24**
The first US Marine Corps jet-fighter squadron, VMF-122, is established; it is equipped with McDonnell FH-1 Phantom aircraft.

**Croydon, England, November 1**
British European Airways (BEA) makes its last scheduled flight from the airport here.

**Muroc Dry Lake, Calif, Nov 24**
The USAF's first swept-wing jet-fighter, the North American XP-86, successfully completes its initial flight tests (→ Nov 30, 1948).

**Sydney, December 1**
Australian carrier Qantas opens its first landplane service to London, with the Lockheed L-749 Constellation *Charles Kingsford Smith*; L-749s Constellations are scheduled to take four days, as opposed to seven by flying boat.

**Hong Kong, December 2**
Hong Kong Airways, founded in March, begins its first scheduled service, to Shanghai.

**Teterboro, NJ, December 10**
Clifford Evans and George Truman land back here after a 123-day round-the-world flight in two Piper Super Cruiser light planes.

**USSR, December 30**
The prototype of the second Mikoyan Type S fighter, an early version of the MiG-15, makes its first flight; it has an imported Rolls-Royce Nene 2 jet engine.

*Air France has 160 destinations throughout the world. This fanciful depiction of some European ones should whet travelers' appetites. ▶*

## 'Ski-planes' ready for Antarctic snow

*Antarctica, January 29*
In 1929 Commander Richard Byrd of the US Navy made the first flight over the South Pole. Today, a flight of six US Navy aircraft landed at Byrd's former base, Little America on the Ross Ice Shelf, to support new US Antarctic expeditions.

They are all naval versions of the versatile Douglas DC-3 – or, as the Navy calls them, R4D-5Ls. They started their journey south on board the aircraft carrier USS *Philippine Sea*. Once they were within range, they had to use jet-assisted take-off (JATO) to launch themselves from the deck. They have been specially adapted for the job, with retractable ski undercarriages with a little wheel/ski at the tail for landing on the ice.

They are expected to stay about a month on this visit, but as the US establishes a greater presence on Antarctica, so aircraft will play an increasingly important part in opening up the icy continent. One day an airplane may even land at the South Pole (→ Oct 31, 1956).

## Convair 240: almost a 300mph airliner

*Convair's CV-240 is expected to be the first of a family of Convair-Liners.*

*San Diego, California, March 16*
Today Consolidated-Vultee Aircraft at Lindbergh Field achieved a successful first flight with the CV-240, which will be marketed as the Convair Liner. It replaces the Convair 110, which flew on July 9 last year.

The 110 was inadequate, but the Convair 240 looks likely to become a world-wide best-seller. Powered by two 2,400-hp Pratt & Whitney Double Wasps, with long exhaust pipes giving useful forward thrust from nozzles over the trailing edge, the new airliner has a tubular pressurized fuselage seating 40 passengers in 10 rows of four. With broad "paddle-blade" propellers the cruising speed is expected to be almost 300mph. First deliveries will go to American Airlines early next year. Other customers include KLM and Trans-Australia. The Pentagon expects to order transport and crew-training versions.

## Post-war boom for Australian airlines

*Sydney, May 5*
Last year all records in the numbers of passengers flown on Australian airlines were broken: 640,666 passengers were carried, representing some 280 million passenger miles.

This follows the creation of a state-owned airline last year by the Labor government to establish interstate services. Trans-Australia Airlines (TAA) began operations in September with a Sydney/Melbourne service, with Hobart, Canberra, Brisbane and Adelaide all being served by December. It started with a fleet of 11 war-surplus C-47s and DC-3s, to which four-engined DC-4s were added to establish a night service between Melbourne and Perth on December 2. This year has seen further expansion, and today TAA started a service from Adelaide to Sydney via Mildura and Canberra.

With vast distances between its major cities, often with open bush in between, Australia is an ideal country for an airline industry to expand even further (→ Jun 30).

## Last DC-3 to be built joins the Sabena fleet

*The last "workhorse of the skies" has gone into civilian service with Sabena.*

*Santa Monica, Calif, March 21*
With due ceremony – and not a few tears shed – the great hangar doors opened here today to allow the very last DC-3 to make its test flight before being handed over to a civilian airline. DC-3 OO-AWH has gone into service with Belgian airline Sabena, which already has 100 of the aircraft. Few airplanes have been built in such numbers or earned such affection as the versatile DC-3. General Eisenhower called it one of the war's great weapons for its vital supply service from India "over the Hump" – the Himalayas – to China. Since 1935 Douglas has made 10,654 DC-3s, 960 of them here, 5,409 at Oklahoma City and 4,285 at Long Beach. All but 607 were orders for the C-47 military version, although many C-47s have been converted for civil use (→ Mar 2, 1948).

## Plans drawn up for a smarter Heathrow

*London, May 31*
Hundreds of workmen are toiling hard to turn the six and a quarter square miles of what looks like a muddy wasteland at Heathrow into the very model of a modern international airport. Much of the effort is going into completing the nine runways which are arranged in three parallel sets running in different directions; they are not expected to be completed until 1950.

While work on the "airside" is progressing, the passenger accommodation still leaves much to be desired. Up to the end of last year, 63,151 passengers passed through Heathrow, far more than anticipated. Plans for the terminal building have been constantly under revision, and one year to the day after the airport was opened there are still no permanent buildings on the site. The tents which greeted the first pasengers have been replaced by temporary prefabricated huts to house the reception area, departure lounge, restaurant and bar (which has yet to get its license to sell alco-

*The prefab buffet at Heathrow.*

holic drinks!). London has three other airports: Croydon, which is surrounded by houses, has little room for expansion and must close when other capacity has been found; Gatwick, which is further from central London than most passengers like; and the small RAF station at Northolt.

# Skystreak takes off under its own power

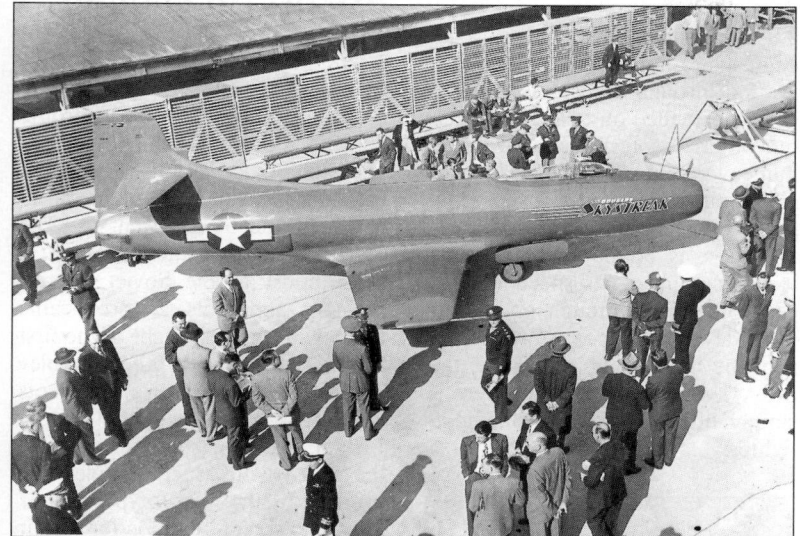

*The Douglas Skystreak: specially designed to withstand transonic buffeting.*

*Muroc Dry Lake, Calif, April 15*
Douglas test pilot Eugene F May today piloted the D-558-1 Skystreak on its first flight. It was a difficult flight: first, the Skystreak suffered a partial power loss, which meant he had to cut the test short; then the left brake disintegrated on landing. Like the Bell XS-1, it has been built to explore transonic speeds. The big difference is that the jet-powered D-558-1 can take off under its own power rather than be dropped from an airplane. It has been designed by a team under Ed Heinemann who says: "So much of

it is completely new that it was like working on our first airplane."

Aware of the tremendous forces found in the transonic region, Heinemann has designed the D-558-1 to withstand 18 Gs, and it is one of the strongest aircraft in the world. With a little more thrust than the 5,000lb delivered by its Allison J35 turbojet engine, Heinemann believes it could fly supersonically. It should reach 650mph, fast enough for an attempt on the world speed record. Heinemann is working on a Mach 2 successor, the D-558-2 (→ Jun 19).

# Comet will have to fly higher than most

*Hertfordshire, England, July*
Jet propulsion is the one area of aeronautics in which Britain has a real lead over the US, and one of the few ways open to Britain to wrest the lead in civil aviation back from America would be to build the world's first commercial jet airliner.

During the war the Brabazon Committee, set up to ponder Britain's post-war civil aircraft needs, proposed two new aircraft, one using turboprop engines, in which a gas turbine turns a propeller, and the other, the Brabazon IV, to be a pure jet airliner. With such an airplane, it was argued, Britain could leap ahead of the world. De Havilland got the job of building the jet air-

liner, and chief designer Ronald E Bishop and engine designer Frank Halford have recently settled on the general layout of what has been called the D.H.-106 Comet, which has been named for the successful de Havilland Comet Racer of 1934.

To get the range from its four Ghost engines, the Comet will have to fly higher than piston-powered airliners, well into the stratosphere, at 35,000 feet in the cold, thin air where jet engines are at their most efficient. Building a pressurized cabin to operate at that height means taking airliner technology into new realms, a pioneering step for which de Havilland should be congratulated (→ Jul 7, 1949).

# Air power hits Viet Minh

*South-east Asia, April 15*
France is using air power to help its efforts to re-establish its colonial authority in Indo-China, which has been challenged by Communist Viet Minh rebels since the Second World War. Before that the Viet Minh had led popular resistance to the Japanese occupation.

Only days after Japan's surrender in August 1945, Britain's RAF parachuted French special forces into Tay Ninh to tackle the rebels. In January this year came Operation Dedale, a night drop on Nam Dinh.

Today 500 paratroopers dropped on Hoa Binh in Operation Papillon. The French are using DC-3s and some captured Ju 52s, escorted by ex-Japanese Oscar fighters and ex-RAF Spitfires.

Last month Ju 52s and Spitfires broke an enemy force in Laos, on the Mekong river, and two days ago, in the first strikes by French carrier-borne aircraft, dive-bombers covered amphibious landings. Other countries are watching France's efforts with air power against insurgent forces with interest.

*France makes use of the air in an effort to beat guerillas in the jungle war.*

# New body set up to oversee air traffic

*Montreal, April 4*
The International Civil Aviation Organization (ICAO) was officially founded here today. It is an inter-governmental organization, established to regulate air transportation on a worldwide basis, its authority restricted only by the number of signatory nations. Already well over 50 countries have become members, and this figure is expected to rise rapidly. The ICAO stems from a convention agreed at a Chicago conference in late 1944.

The ICAO has many functions, among which is to ensure that all member states have equal opportunities in international airline operations. It has the necessary powers to regulate areas such as safety, navigation, telecommunications, meteorology and air charts. The ICAO can also licence aircraft airworthiness, operations, personnel and airport facilities.

# Britain's A1 rocket test is damp squib

*Cornwall, England, May 30*
Following the cancellation of the manned Miles M.52 [see page 459], it was decided to carry out research into aerodynamics at transonic speeds using models. This research suffered a blow today with the loss of one of these models, the A1, before it could even be tested.

The A1 was the first of 24 models ordered from Vickers-Armstrongs (Aircraft) under a £500,000 contract. These expendable rocket-powered craft carry autopilots, radar transponders and telemetering units to supply data before dropping into the sea. The models have either straight or swept wings.

Today, as part of Operation Neptune, the 11-foot-long A1 was carried under a de Havilland Mosquito to 20,000 feet. But the airplane flew into a storm cloud and went out of control. The A1 broke free and was lost (→ May 27, 1948).

# Shooting Star flies to air speed record

*Pilot Col Albert Boyd climbs aboard.*

*Muroc Dry Lake, Calif, June 19*
USAAF Colonel Albert Boyd streaked over the desert here today in a Lockheed P-80 Shooting Star to set a new world air speed record of 623.738mph. His aircraft, carrying the designation XP-80R, was a specially modified version of the versatile fighter that is now in service throughout the USAAF. It flew without external fuel tanks and had minimum fuel, no guns, and a smaller canopy.

The P-80 is now serving with American interceptor units, and a reconnaissance version is being developed. In November last year it became the first jet fighter to provide close air support for ground forces, in exercises in California. The P-80 also set the record for 1,000 kilometers [621 miles] when it covered the distance in 1 hour 20 minutes 30 seconds on June 3, last year (→ Aug 20).

# Jet flying boat debut

*Isle of Wight, England, July 16*
Following extensive ground testing, Geoffrey Tyson, test pilot for the Saunders-Roe company, this evening made the first flight of the SR.A/1 jet-fighter. What makes it unique is the fact that it is a flying boat. It was designed by a team led by Henry Knowler to meet an official specification, drawn up when it was thought that a long-range fighter seaplane would be needed in the Pacific war theater.

The A/1 is a jet, but no attempt has been made to use advanced transonic aerodynamics. Its two 3,850-lb thrust Metrovick axial engines are housed in the hull, and are fed through a nose inlet, which can be extended on take-off to keep out water. Tyson is pleased with the maneuverability of this odd machine, although its size – the wingspan is 46 feet and the length over 50 feet – is bound to tell against it in air combat. Its speed will exceed 500mph, although given current developments even this will soon be inadequate. All in all, the SR.A/1 may be a mistake. There is simply little call for a flying-boat-fighter.

*Unique, but a mistake: the Saunders-Roe jet flying boat, the SR.A/1.*

# Britain's first helicopter, Sycamore, flies

*Bristol, England, July 27*
The first British-designed and built helicopter made its maiden flight at Filton today. Alan Marsh flew the Bristol 171 Sycamore on several short flights, some with passengers. It has been designed for both military and civil markets.

Research and development have been carried out over two years by a team under Raoul Hafner, who experimented with helicopters in Austria before coming to Britain in 1933. The Sycamore is a five-seater machine, with a three-blade main rotor which has a relatively high speed of rotation. This prototype is powered by an American 450-hp Pratt & Whitney Wasp Junior as no British engine was available. Later versions will be powered by the British 545-hp Alvis Leonides.

# Row as Soviet jets use British engines

*USSR, June 27*
In a move widely regarded as at best naive and at worst catastrophic, the Labour government has supplied the Soviet Union with the latest Rolls-Royce jet engines: 25 Nene 2s and 30 Derwent 5s. The first evidence that they represent a great boost to the Soviet aircraft industry, and to its air force, came today with the first flight of the first Soviet jet bomber, the Tupolev Tu-77, powered by two Derwents which give it a speed of 487mph. Britain has no jet bomber yet, and the speed with which Tupolev has produced the prototype Tu-77 shows how keen Stalin is for his air force to go jet. It cannot be long before Nenes, or Soviet copies of them, power Soviet fighters.

Britain has been very generous with jet-engine technology: it has supplied Hispano-Suiza in France, and General Electric and Pratt & Whitney in the US, with the means to produce engines against which British engine-makers will have to compete for orders. The Soviet deal means the RAF may even have to fly against MiGs with engines derived from British designs (→ Jul 24).

# Australian government nationalizes Qantas Empire Airways

*Australia, June 30*
Today saw the beginning of a new era in Australian civil aviation when the federal government nationalized Qantas to create a state-owned flag carrier.

Moves to create a national airline for Australia began last December. The Australian end of the route to Europe is operated by Qantas Empire Airways (QEA), which was jointly owned by Qantas and Britain's BOAC. In December the Australian government passed a bill enabling Qantas to buy BOAC's 50 per cent holding in QEA. Now the government has control, and tomorrow Hudson Fysh will take over as managing director on a five-year contract with a salary of $A3,500 a year. His task will be to give Australia a world-class airline, and the first step in that direction came in October last year.

This was when QEA ordered four Lockheed Constellations to replace the converted Lancaster bombers and Hythe flying boats which presently fly the London/Sydney route, taking a week. The Constellations are expected to come into service later this year, nearly halving that time (→ Dec).

# Pride of Soviet air force displayed

*The Ilyushin Il-12 is a piston-engined airliner which can take 21 passengers.*

**Moscow, August 3**
The Soviet Aviation Day display at Tushino was expected to be a revealing occasion, but few had anticipated the appearance of so many new airplanes in a mix of technologies which reflects Stalin's crash program to match the West.

Early on, though, disaster nearly struck three Tupolev Tu-4s, copies of America's B-29 bomber. An air traffic control error meant that they buzzed the crowd at just 200 feet.

A derivative of the Tu-4, the Tu-70, a 72-seat airliner for Aeroflot, the state-owned airline, also came from Tupolev. Aeroflot has the daunting task of maintaining civilian services while the needs of the military take priority. What makes its task even more difficult is that in a vast country like the Soviet Union it plays an unusually important role in national economic plans while still backing up the military.

Also on display were Ilyushin's four-jet Il-22 and Tupolev's twin-jet Tu-77 bombers [*see opposite*]. New single-seater jet-fighters came from Lavochkin, Sukhoi and Yakovlev, mostly with Soviet RD-10 and RD-20 turbojets copied from German originals.

## A second Skystreak breaks record after only five days

*A proud wink from Major Carl.*

**Muroc Dry Lake, Calif, August 25**
The world air speed record fell for the second time in five days here when Major Marion Carl of the US Marines flew a Douglas D-558-1 Skystreak at an average speed of 650.8mph in four passes over a low-level, 3-kilometer course.

The previous record, 640.663-mph, was set by US Navy Commander Turner Caldwell on August 20 in another Skystreak. In that flight, he passed USAF Colonel Al Boyd's mark of 623.738mph, achieved on June 19 in a modified Lockheed P-80 [*see opposite*].

Unlike Boyd's airplane, which was designed as a fighter and modified for its record setting flight, the D-558-1s flown by Carl and Caldwell were designed specifically for high-speed research between Mach 0.75 and 0.85 from sea level to 40,000 feet. A US Navy/NACA requirement called for a non-military aircraft capable of the maximum speed possible with an existing powerplant, which could take off and land by itself with a pilot and up to 500 pounds of test equipment.

This produced a tubular aircraft powered by a 5,000-lb thrust J35-A-11, an Allison-built version of the General Electric TG-180 turbojet (→ Oct 14).

# Royal Navy adds piston-engined Sea Fury to carrier-borne force

**England, August 31**
At a time when other air forces are ordering jets, Britain's tradition-minded Royal Navy has brought into service a piston-engined fighter. This is the Hawker Sea Fury, a folding-wing version of the machine which first flew on February 21, 1945, but which the RAF canceled before the war ended. The navy's Fleet Air Arm believes that outside Europe its carrier-borne air fleet will not be in danger of encountering the most modern combat jets.

The first 50 of 615 machines to be ordered went into service with Britain's carrier fleet this month. The aircraft is derived from the formidable Tempest fighter/bomber; this shot down 20 Me 262 jets while serving in Europe during the war. Navy pilots recall this when asked what will happen if they tangle with a more modern opponent.

Despite giving up India, Britain still has many overseas territories

*The Hawker Sea Fury has a 2,575-hp Bristol Centaurus sleeve-valve radial.*

vital to Western interests, such as the Suez Canal Zone (occupied jointly with France), Cyprus, East and West Africa, Malaya and the Persian Gulf protectorates, including Aden and Kuwait. These are areas where a carrier-borne air force might make a vital difference as nationalist, possibly communist-inspired unrest boils over.

## US Air Force set up as separate, independent arm

*Washington, DC, September 18*
The dream of the late Brigadier-General Billy Mitchell, that the US should have an air force independent of the army and the navy, came true today as Stuart Symington was sworn in as the first Secretary of the Air Force by Chief Justice Fred Vinson of the US Supreme Court. The US Air Force is now a separate service with equal status to the other two forces as a result of the National Security Act, passed by Congress earlier this year and signed by Harry Truman on July 17 aboard the presidential DC-4. The Act was a major reform of the US defense establishment. It abolished the old US War Department and created in its place a Department of Defense (DoD) and three military departments for the army, navy and air force, each headed by a civilian Secretary appointed by the President.

The first action of the new Department of the Air Force has been to transfer all the existing US Army Air Forces, their personnel, aircraft and other equipment, to the USAF. The former USAAF commander General Carl "Tooey" Spaatz is now the head of the new service as Chief of Staff. The new service will retain the army's rank structure, but it is to receive new uniforms, which will be blue (→ Sep 25).

*Truman: sanctioned the USAF.*

# Pilot flies faster than speed of sound

*The Bell X-1 (previously XS-1) dropped from an NB-29 "mother ship".*

*Supersonic Yeager (l) tells his story.*

*Muroc Dry Lake, Calif, October 14*
American fighter ace and test pilot Captain Charles "Chuck" Yeager is today thought to have become the first man to fly faster than sound. Reliable sources indicate that he "broke the sound barrier", that invisible obstacle which has claimed the lives of some brave pilots, by reaching 670mph, Mach 1.015, at 42,000 feet in the Bell X-1.

Yeager, 24, replaced Bell test pilot "Slick" Goodlin last summer when the USAF and NACA took over the test program from the company. He christened the airplane *Glamorous Glennis* after his wife, the same name he gave his P-51 Mustang in the war. He had a number of close calls during the test program, including one virtually blind landing when the windshield froze over due to vapor trapped inside the cockpit.

Since August he had been building up speed slowly, reaching Mach 0.997 before trying the supersonic run. On today's flight the X-1 went through the usual buffeting as it approached Mach 1.0; then suddenly that stopped as he went faster than sound, into a realm of aeronautics where nobody had any experience.

The flight remains secret, as does the fact that, yesterday evening, Yeager broke two ribs in a wild party and has told nobody (May 26, 1948).

## US tests its first swept-wing fighter

*Muroc Dry Lake, Calif, October 1*
Today, America's first swept-wing fighter, the North American prototype XP-86, took to the air. It takes advantage of captured German data which suggests that swept-wings would be a great advantage at speeds approaching Mach 1.0.

The first flight of the XP-86 lasted almost an hour, longer than scheduled because test pilot George Welch had trouble getting the nosewheel down. One of the disadvantages of sweepback is that handling the aircraft at slow speed, especially when landing, becomes tricky, but North American's engineers solved the problem with slats on the wings' leading edges, which open automatically, enhancing lift and lowering the aircraft's stall speed, then retract as speed increases. The USAF hopes that it will fly beyond the speed of sound (→ Nov 24).

# Huge bomber to equip US deterrent force

*The XB-47 takes off with rockets.*

*Seattle, December 17*
Today, the 44th anniversary of the Wright brothers' first flight, the world's most advanced jet bomber flew for the first time. The USAF's sleek Boeing XB-47 Stratojet bomber will become the backbone of the new Strategic Air Command (SAC) the US's atomic deterrent bomber force, which was created in March last year.

The Stratojet employs the same German-derived, swept-wing technology as was used in the advanced North American XP-86, which first flew two months ago [*see story left*]. It has a top speed of over 550mph, making it faster than most fighters now flying. The new bomber is powered by six engines, in pods suspended from the wing. Unlike the existing B-29 and B-50 bombers, which have ten-member crews, the XB-47 has a crew of just three: the pilot, the co-pilot and the bombardier/navigator.

# Howard Hughes' gigantic 'Spruce Goose' hops into history

*The H-4 Hercules needed all of its 24,000-hp to lift its enormous bulk and weight into the air.*

**Long Beach, Calif, November 2**
Piloted by its creator, aviator-tycoon Howard Hughes, the biggest airplane in the world made a stately hop of about a mile across the harbor here today. In front of thousands of spectators and boats full of pressmen, Hughes has done what he said he would: flown the gigantic H-4 Hercules, although the huge flying boat never climbed above an altitude of about 70 feet. Hughes, who had publicly threatened to leave the US and never to return if the H-4 was prevented from flying, is delighted.

In May 1942 Hughes joined with shipping tycoon Henry J Kaiser to build "unsinkable Liberty ships" in the form of huge HK-1 flying boats, each able to carry bulky cargoes or 700 troops. Kaiser pulled out, and the US War Department lost interest, but for Hughes the project was a matter of honor. At a cost of $25 million he finished the Hercules. The project cost Hughes $7 million of his his own money, while the US Government contributed the remaining $18 million. Powered by eight 3,000-hp Pratt & Whitney R-4360 Wasp Major engines, the Hercules is made entirely of wood, hence the media's nickname of "Spruce Goose". Its wingspan of 320 feet and height of 79 feet are unlikely to be exceeded for many years to come, though in such matters as gross weight (400,000 lb) and power, the mighty flying boat will probably be beaten by future jet airplanes.

Today's short flight gave every indication of being successful. But running this mighty airplane is expensive, even to a billionaire such as

*Hughes at the controls of the H-4.*

Hughes, the owner of TWA. It remains to be seen whether he will go on to complete its civilian certification so that it can be put into commercial service.

## American airlines celebrate good year

*USA, December 31*
Americans are taking to the air like never before. This year 12,890,208 paying passengers flew on domestic airlines, an increase of more than 875,000 passengers over 1946. The battle for customers grew more intense this year with the advent of the pressurized Douglas DC-6. Now American, United and TWA all offer eastbound and westbound services.

*American Airlines' hostesses line up.*

## Mi for Mikoyan G for Gurevich

*Soviet Union, December 30*
Artyom I Mikoyan, aged 42, and 55-year-old Mikhail Gurevich have worked together for ten years at their experimental Design Bureau (OKB). Their latest airplane, the MiG-15 (Nato codename Fagot), made a successful first flight today. This all-metal, stressed-skin, mid-wing monoplane is the first operational Soviet swept-wing aircraft. The MiG-15, powered by a Rolls-Royce Nene jet engine, has a speed of 670mph. Last year the MiG-9 (Fargo), the first MiG jet fighter, entered service with the Soviet air force (→Jan 13, 1950).

# 'Flying kangaroo' Constellation logo enters Qantas service

*The new luxury Lockheed L-749 Constellation bearing the Qantas logo.*

*Sydney, December*
To promote Qantas' latest "leap" forward – a regular Australian link to Britain with the new luxury Lockheed Constellation airliner – the airline has adopted a new logo: a flying kangaroo. "Kangaroo" is also the name given to this service to Australia.

The first through service to London, flown by the Constellation *Charles Kingsford Smith*, left Sydney on December 1, and the return left on December 7. The service will be operated weekly. Passengers and pilots are delighted with the Constellation (→Apr 2, 1949).

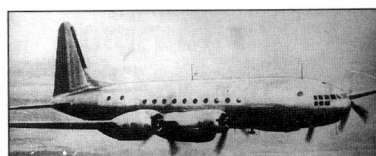

*Ilyushin's original Il-18 was a piston-engined 60-seater.*

*De Havilland of Canada built 1,657 examples of the DHC-2 Beaver 1.*

*The Percival P.48 Merganser transport preceded the P.50 Prince.*

*The wooden Hughes Hercules was the largest flying boat ever built.*

*The Convair XC-99 was a transport derivative of the B-36 bomber.*

*Eight Allison J35 jet engines powered the Northrop YB-49 flying wing.*

*The elegant Armstrong Whitworth A.W.52 tailless research aircraft.*

*The 47-seat Airspeed AS.57 Ambassador was ordered only by British European Airways, and 20 production aircraft followed three prototypes.*

*The Hawker P.1040, prototype of the Sea Hawk naval jet fighter.*

*The Fairchild C-119 Boxcar was derived from the XC-82B prototype.*

*Convair's L-13: employed for liaison and casualty-evacuation duties.*

*The Martin XB-48 was powered by six underwing Allison J35 engines.*

*Tupolev's Tu-14T land-based naval attack-bomber bore two torpedoes.*

*Convair developed the twin-engined Model 240 40-passenger airliner from the 30-seat Model 110. Nearly 1,000 CV-240 and successor types were built.*

*The rotund Sud-Ouest SO 95 Corse II was built for the French navy.*

*Boeing built the Model 377 Stratocruiser airliner, with a downstairs bar, as a derivative of the C-97 military transport, itself a version of the B-29.*

*The Vickers Valetta was the military version of the Viking civil airliner.*

*The Boeing B-47 Stratojet was the world's first swept-wing jet-bomber.*

*More Antonov An-2s were built than any other transport type in history.*

*The Scottish Aviation A.2/45, an observation and liaison aircraft.*

*The North American B-45 Tornado.*

*Rolls-Royce's Nene jet engine powered the I-310, the prototype MiG-15.*

*The Saunders-Roe SR.A/1 was the world's first jet-fighter flying boat.*

*Argentina's I.Ae 27 Pulqui 1: the first indigenous Latin American jet.*

*Avio-Linee Italiane ordered the Fiat G.212 post-war version of the G.12.*

The Dassault M.D.315 Flamant, the initial production version of the proto-type M.D.303 trainer. Flamants were subsequently built for crew training.

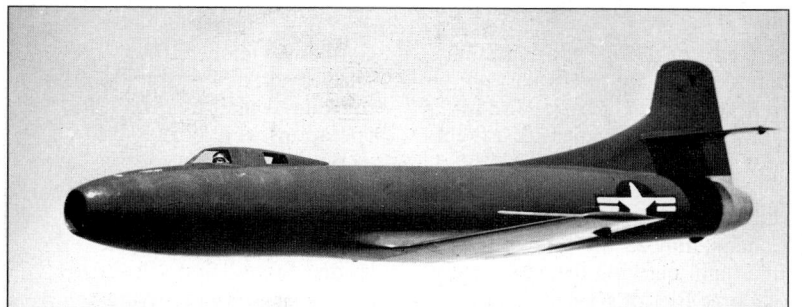

Three Douglas Skystreak high-speed research aircraft were built, and one of them set an absolute world speed record of 640.63mph on August 20, 1947.

Grumman's XJR2F-1 Albatross am-phibian, later redesignated SA-16.

Boeing's B-50 was an improved B-29 fitted with more powerful engines.

Sikorsky's S-52 was the first US heli-copter to have metal rotor blades.

The first Soviet-built jet-bomber was the straight-winged Tupolev Tu-12.

McDonnell's XF2H-1 Banshee proto-type fighter for the US Navy featured marked tailplane dihedral.

Bristol's Type 171 Mk 1 became the Sycamore 4-seat liaison helicopter.

The Soviet Bratukhin Omega G-4 was a purely experimental helicopter.

A Rolls-Royce Nene engine, later built under license as the Pratt & Whitney J42, powered Grumman's first jet fighter, the compact XF9F-2 Panther.

The McDonnell XH-80 Little Henry featured tip ramjets on the blades.

A Russian-built RR Derwent engine powered the Lavochkin La-15.

Nord's unusual 2100 Norazur twin-pusher-engined transport prototype.

Saab evolved the jet-powered 21R fighter from the piston-engined 21A.

Convair built a single prototype of the streamlined XB-46 jet bomber.

Boeing-Wichita designed the XL-15 Scout US Army liaison aeroplane.

Warsaw Pact air forces built more than 300 Yakovlev Yak-23 fighters.

The North American XP-86 Sabre was the USAF's first swept-wing fighter and was the first to exceed the speed of sound, if only in a shallow dive.

# 1948

957mph
USA
Charles Yeager
Bell X-1
Mar 26, 1948

11,235 miles
USA
Thomas D Davies
Lockheed P2V-1 Neptune
Oct 1, 1946

64,000ft
USA
Charles Yeager
Bell X-1
May 26, 1948

400,000lb
USA
Hughes Aircraft Co
H-4 Hercules

6,041lb thrust
USSR
Klimov
VK-1

**Atlantic Ocean, January 29/30**
A British South American Airways Avro Tudor 4 disappears on a flight from the Azores to Bermuda with a complement of six crew and at least 28 passengers (→ Jan 20, 1949).

**Spain, February 18**
Spanish airline Aviacion y Comercio SA (Aviaco) is established, initially to operate cargo services.

**Winston-Salem, NC, Feb 20**
Piedmont Airlines, established on January 1, begins passenger services.

**London, March 2**
Nineteen die when a DC-3 of Belgian airline Sabena – the last DC-3 built – crashes while attempting to land after a flight from Brussels (→ Apr 5).

**New Delhi, March 8**
Air India begins overseas operations and changes its name to Air India International.

**Berlin, April 5**
A Soviet Yak fighter collides with a BEA Viking which is coming in to land, killing the Russian pilot and all 14 on board the British airliner; the Soviets express deep regret and say there is no policy to obstruct flights through the agreed air corridor to Berlin (→ Apr 15).

**Hampshire, England, April 14**
A new terminal for BOAC's flying boats, which have been transferred from Poole, Dorset, opens at Hythe, Southampton (→ Dec 6, 1949).

**Ireland, April 15**
A Pan Am Lockheed Constellation crashes near Shannon airport, killing 30 (→ Jun 17).

**LaGuardia, New York, April 28**
The first non-stop Paris/New York flight is made by an Air France sleeper Constellation; the journey from Orly airport, near Paris, takes 16 hrs 1 min.

**Muroc Dry Lake, Calif, May 3**
Howard C Lilley, test pilot for the National Advisory Committee for Aeronautics (NACA), dies when his Douglas D-558-1 Skystreak crashes; he is the first NACA pilot killed on duty.

**Palestine [Israel], May 20**
The air force of the Israeli defense forces goes into action for the first time when it attacks the Egyptian army at Samakh (→ May 27).

**California, May 26**
Charles "Chuck" Yeager flies the Bell X-1 to a new altitude record of 64,000 feet (→ Jan 5, 1949).

**London, May 27**
On recommendation of the Royal Commission on Awards to Inventors, Air Commodore Frank Whittle will receive £100,000 for his invention of the jet engine (→ Jul).

**Muroc Dry Lake, Calif, June 5**
During a test flight, the prototype Northrop YB-49 disintegrates, killing all aboard, including Captain Glen Edwards (→ Jan 27, 1950).

**Maidenhead, England, June 28**
A Fairey Gyrodyne helicopter, piloted by Squadron Leader Basil Arkell, achieves a record speed for rotary-winged aircraft of 124.31mph.

**Chicago, Illinois, June 30**
Butler Aviation sets up as the first FBO (fixed base operator) at Midway Airport here to service business and private aviation.

**Middlesex, England, July 4**
An RAF Avro York collides with a Scandinavian Air Lines DC-6 in bad weather over Northolt; all 39 on board die in Britain's worst peacetime disaster (→ Aug 1).

**Labrador, July 14**
Six RAF Vampires land at the end of the first transatlantic flight by jet; they left Britain two days ago, and their staged journey was made via Iceland and Greenland.

**Surrey, England, July 16**
Vickers' Type 630 Viscount, the first transport designed from the outset with turboprops, makes its first flight piloted by "Mutt" Summers at Wisley (→ Jul 29, 1950).

**Scotland, July 20**
Sixteen Lockheed Shooting Stars complete the first west/east transatlantic flight by jet aircraft, landing at Stornoway after a flight of 9 hours 20 minutes from Selfridge Field, Michigan.

**London, July 25**
In a flight marking the anniversary of Louis Blériot's 1909 Channel crossing, Joseph "Mutt" Summers pilots the Nene Viking, a Vickers Viking airliner powered by two Rolls-Royce Nene turbojets, on a trip to Paris and back in a record flying time of 1 hour 10 minutes 30 seconds (→ Apr 16, 1950).

**London, July**
Frank Whittle is knighted.

**Atlantic Ocean, August 1**
A giant Air France Latécoère 631 flying boat disappears on a flight from Martinique to Senegal in West Africa; all 52 on board are feared lost (→ 29).

**Muroc Dry Lake, Calif, August 16**
The Northrop XF-89 Scorpion makes its first flight; it is planned as the USAF's first all-weather jet interceptor (→ Dec 8, 1949).

**Winona, Minnesota, August 29**
A Northwest Airlines Martin 2-0-2, losing its left wing, crashes in a violent storm, killing all 37 on board and raising questions about the safety of twin-engined transports (→ Oct 21).

**Cleveland, Ohio, September 5**
The US Navy's Martin JRM-2 *Caroline Mars* flying boat arrives from its Patuxent River base with a record payload of 68,282 lb.

**Germany, September 15**
The Royal Australian Air Force joins the Berlin airlift (→ Oct 15).

**Scotland, October 21**
A Lockheed Constellation operated by Dutch carrier KLM crashes a mile from Prestwick airport after hitting a power line; 34 of the 40 people on board are killed in the accident (→ Feb 5, 1949).

**Germany, October 15**
The Royal Air Force and USAF coordinate their Berlin airlift operations as a joint task force (→ Apr 16, 1949).

**New York, November 4**
Capital Airlines opens the United States' first scheduled coach-class service, flying 60-passenger DC-4s on its Chicago route and charging only 4c per mile ($33 one way) instead of the usual 6c.

**Washington, DC, November 5**
The marking "USAF" is officially approved for all US warplanes except those operated by the US Navy, Marine Corps, Army, National Guard and Military Air Transport Service (MATS) (→ Jan 25, 1949).

**Tel Aviv, Israel, Nov 15**
Israeli airline El Al is officially created.

**Miami, Florida, November 20**
National Airlines pilots end their 295-day strike.

**Muroc Dry Lake, Calif, Nov 30**
The USAF takes delivery of its first F-86 Sabre single-seat fighter (→ Mar 4, 1949).

**USSR, December 26**
I V Fedorov becomes the first Soviet pilot to break the sound barrier. He achieves the necessary speed by diving his Lavochkin La-176 jet, powered by a Rolls-Royce Nene engine, at full throttle.

---

*Flying wings: Northrop B-35s line up at Hawthorne, Calif. Nine of the all-wing bombers await conversion into eight-jet YB-49s.* ▶

# Pioneer of flight Orville Wright dies

*Dayton, Ohio, January 30*
Today the city of Dayton lost its most distinguished citizen when Orville Wright, the first man to fly a powered airplane, died peacefully at the age of 76. He suffered a heart attack three days ago. On December 17, 1903, Orville was at the controls of the *Flyer*, built by him and younger brother Wilbur (who died in 1912), when it made the first powered, controlled, heavier-than-air flight at Kill Devil Hill, on the shore of North Carolina.

Minutes beforehand he had set up a camera, which was operated seconds after the take-off by John Daniels from the nearby lifesaving station. The camera captured the dawn of the age of human flight, with Orville lying on the lower wing, fighting to control the biplane against the stiff breeze, and Wilbur running alongside.

For years Orville busied himself with his laboratory and with papers

*Pioneer: Orville Wright, 1871-1948.*

and records. Part of his work concerned dismantling his wind tunnel, and arranging the return of the *Flyer* from London's Science Museum to the Smithsonian Institution in Washington, DC (→ Dec 17).

# Airline pilots strike over air-safety fears

*Miami, Florida, February 3*
All 145 pilots and co-pilots at National Airlines went on strike at 11pm today, grounding the carrier's 22 aircraft. The dispute is mainly over air safety. The pilots' concerns arise from the walkout two weeks ago by National mechanics, who refused to cross the picket

lines of striking clerical workers. A spokesman for the pilots' union, the Air Lines Pilots' Association, said the walkout was an "inevitable climax to two years of notoriously poor pilot-management relations". The firing of a pilot involved in an accident two years ago is also an issue in the dispute (→ Nov 20).

# US services set up joint transport unit

*Washington, DC, February 4*
The airlift components of the USAF and the US Navy were combined today with the creation of MATS – the Military Air Transport Service – under the command of USAF Lt-Gen Laurence S Kuter. The new service will integrate the Air Transport Command and the smaller Navy Air Transport Service into an organization which will fulfill the air transportation needs of all US military services. MATS will be more cost-effective than the two separate commands because it will keep the best features of the USAF and US Navy structures, while eliminating duplicate areas of operation (→ Nov 5).

**S-51 is by far the quickest way to get supplies to the Wolf Rock lighthouse off the British coast.**

# First 'flying car' rolls into the skies

*San Diego, January 29*
Is it a bird? Is it a plane? Yes, it is a plane, but it is also – a car. More precisely, it is the Hall Flying Automobile, which flew here today for the first time.

Theodore P Hall, after two years of research backed by former employer Consolidated-Vultee Aircraft Corporation (Convair), where he was chief development engineer, is pressing ahead with his idea for a car which converts into an airplane. His design combines a four-passenger rear-engined sedan with a detachable wing and a boom leading to a cruciform tail. A 190-hp Lycoming engine mounted on the wing provides the power for flight. The wings are attached to the car at three points and carry jacks to support them when not in use. The curious hybrid cruises at 100mph in the air, 67mph on the road.

*The Hall Flying Automobile, a novel hybrid of the car and the airplane.*

# French firm Jodel gives birth to 'Baby'

*Beaune, France, January 21*
Braving the snow which covers the little airfield here, Edmond Joly took his new light monoplane, the D.9 Bébé [Baby] Jodel, on its first flight today. He quickly found himself airborne, and was pleasantly surprised by how well the little airplane handled during its short flight. The D.9 will be marketed either made up or in kit form. If it sells it will represent a new departure for Joly and partner Jean Délémontez, whose company has until now been concerned with aircraft repair and overhaul.

*Flying the Bébé Jodel is as easy as driving a car – and it is not much bigger.*

# Four-jet fighter could be last for Curtiss

*The Curtiss Blackhawk, the world's first four-engined jet fighter.*

*Muroc Dry Lake, Calif, March 1*
What may prove to be the last airplane built by the ailing Curtiss company made its first flight here today. It is the XP-87 Blackhawk, a giant four-jet night fighter.

The Curtiss-Wright empire has found itself without the top management and design expertise to compete in the new field of high-speed jets. The XP-87 has a wingspan of 60 feet and is 62 feet long, and not even the four 3,000-pound thrust Westinghouse J34 engines will give it adequate performance or maneuverability.

Perhaps taking this into account, the plane's four 20mm cannon will be mounted on a pivoting platform in the nose, made by Martin.

# Helicopter delivers the airmail to Britons

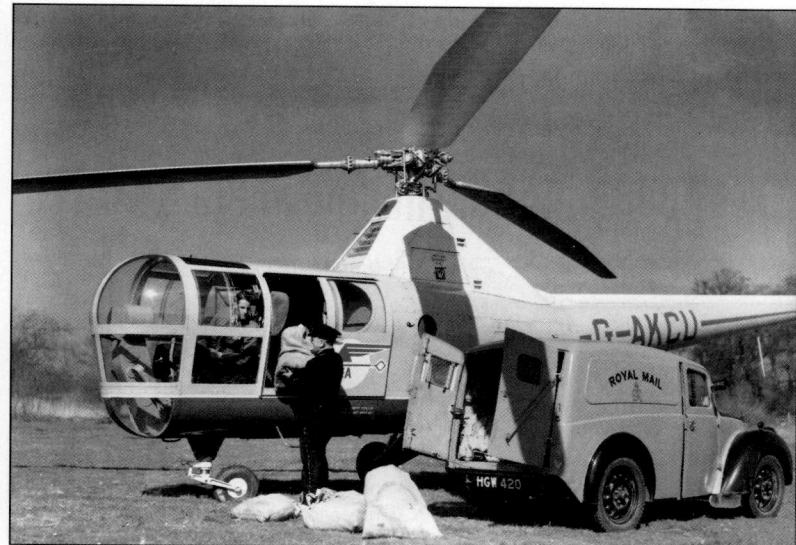

*One of the three Westland-Sikorsky helicopters delivering the Royal Mail.*

*East Anglia, England, June 1*
Today marked the inauguration of the first helicopter airmail service in Britain. Flown by British European Airways (BEA), the operation is based in Peterborough because of the city's position on the arterial railroad route which links London and the north of Britain. Among the places served by BEA's helicopters are the important Norfolk towns of Great Yarmouth, King's Lynn and Norwich. Taking its lead from US airline Los Angeles Airways, BEA ordered three Sikorsky S-51 and two Bell Model 47D helicopters in June last year.

The following month, the airline established its Helicopter Experimental Unit in Somerset, and ran a trial service earlier this year. So far BEA is only planning daytime flights, but a future night service is under consideration.

# Vampire sinks teeth into altitude record

*Hertfordshire, England, March 23*
Former night-fighter ace Group Captain John Cunningham today flew Britain's diminutive de Havilland Vampire jet fighter to a new world altitude record. Piloting the third production Vampire F Mk 1, he took off from Hatfield and reached 59,446 feet. This is the first world absolute altitude record set for over nine years, and the first to be established by a jet. But, amazingly, it beats by only 400 feet the record held by the 1938 piston-engined Caproni 161 *bis*. The Vampire flown today differs from other F Mk 1s in having 4-foot extensions to its wing-tips and a metal canopy, and it was prepared as a high-altitude test bed for the new 5,000-lb thrust de Havilland Ghost 45 2/2 engine (→ May 26).

*John Cunningham, who has set the first world altitude record in a jet.*

# Clean bill of health for grounded DC-6

*Washington, DC, March 7*
The US Civil Aeronautics Administration (CAA) today gave the go-ahead for Douglas DC-6 airliners to resume flying. They can take to the air as soon as modifications are completed to prevent a repeat of two in-flight fires last fall, which were caused by fuel leaking into the cabin heaters.

The first fire broke out on a United Airlines airplane, which crashed in Utah killing all 52 on board. The second was on an American Airlines plane, but the airliner was able to land safely. Both airlines are now expected to resume DC-6 services within two weeks. Others will follow (→ Jun 17).

# US Navy shows that jets can use ships

*Rhode Island, May 5*
US Navy Squadron VF-17A today qualified as the world's first carrier-based jet-fighter unit. In three days of operations on board the USS *Saipan* off the US coast, each of its pilots has completed at least eight take-offs and landings in McDonnell FH-1 Phantoms. The Phantom also has the distinction of being the first US-designed jet-fighter to take off from and land on an aircraft carrier.

The FH-1 has two 1,600-lb thrust Westinghouse J30-WE-20 jets. It has a maximum speed of 479mph at sea level, cruises at 248mph and is armed with four 0.50-in machine guns.

## From clandestine beginning, Israeli air force is born

*Israel, May 27*

Jerusalem is besieged, and air-war veterans from around the world are rallying to the newly born state of Israel. Nothing quite like this has happened since airmen of the 1930s signed up with the International Brigade in Spain. The new state's recruits are not all Zionists. Many are not even Jews. They are *mahals* [foreign volunteers] who want a fair deal for the race which Hitler tried to exterminate. Like other idealistic fighters, such as the Americans who joined the French army to fly with the Lafayette Squadron in the First World War, these men are not overly concerned with the political small print.

With the partition of British-controlled Palestine, the Jews – one-third of the population – got 57 per cent of the land. Hours after the state of Israel was proclaimed on May 15, Arab forces attacked it. However, the Arabs could find only 15,000 fighting men aided by 22 light tanks, ten Spitfires and a few C-47 transports.

Israel's air force, the Chel Ha'vir, which came into being today, is a joke, with about a dozen Auster air-observation machines which under British rule were easily disguised on the civil register as sports planes. But the joke may not last long: Israelis are now scouring the world for fighters, be they Spitfires, Bf 109s or Mosquitoes. If a complete machine is not available, they will cannibalize parts from a scrap heap or air crash, to be transformed into something that, with luck, will fly. Civilianized B-17s are to be restored as bombers. The Israelis are also looking for Harvard trainers. But as the world's official arms suppliers give them the cold shoulder, Israeli pioneers are learning to use arms black markets and ruses, such as forming bogus film companies ready to shoot air-war epics, to get what they need (→ Jan 7, 1949).

# Crashes raise questions of air safety

*Nineteen people died when a Sabena DC-3 crashed in fog at London airport.*

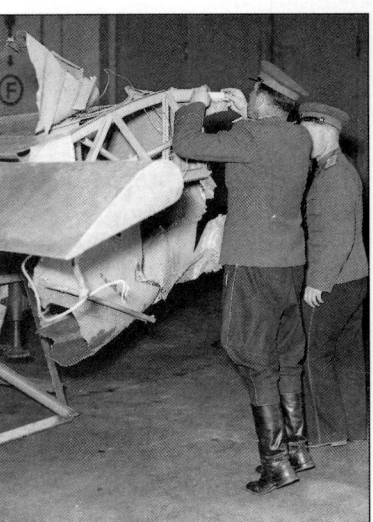

*Studying the crashed Viking's wing.*

*Mount Carmel, Penn, June 17*

The subject of air safety is again on everyone's lips after the loss today of a United Air Lines DC-6. With 39 passengers and four crew it had left San Diego, California, yesterday for New York. It did not arrive. Horrified onlookers watched as the plane came down with its port wing belching smoke. Captain George Warner battled to find a safe area to land, but the airliner struck a 60,000-volt electricity transformer and disintegrated. The wreckage burned out north of here; no one survived. The grounding of DC-6s, following two in-flight fires, was only lifted in March [*see page 475*].

The crash follows a string of tragedies in Europe in recent months On March 2 a DC-3 of Belgium's Sabena crashed at London's Heathrow airport, killing 19 of the 22 on board. The DC-3 – the last one built – had been attempting to land when ground visibility was just 600 feet, using the airport's ground-controlled approach radar (GCA) system. (To counter accusations of blame, the British Ministry of Civil Aviation issued a statement that GCA was not a blind-landing service, but only a guide to pilots on approach.) On April 5 a BEA Viking airliner collided with a Soviet Yak fighter over Berlin. All were killed. On April 15 a Pan Am Constellation crashed near Shannon airport, Eire, killing 30 (→ Jul 4).

# Massive Anglo-US airlift gives Berlin its only lifeline to the West

*Children at Gatow watch the C-54s bringing supplies to the blockaded city.*

*Berlin, June 26*

Operation Vittles – what might prove to be the world's most ambitious airlift – has begun on the orders of General Lucius Clay, military commander of the US zone of Berlin. For two days, two million people living in the Western sector of the city have been effectively under siege since the Soviet authorities severed all road, rail and canal links to West Germany.

The row started with an argument about currency reform among the occupying powers in Berlin. But the Western Allies see in the blockade an attempt to force them to abandon this pocket of democracy behind the Iron Curtain. The three Western zones need thousands of tons of food and fuel. The USAF is airlifting supplies from Frankfurt and Wiesbaden, with the RAF doing the same from Wunstorf and Bückeburg (→ Sep 15).

# Idlewild airport opens in New York

*New York, July 31*
What was still the marshy, reed-filled wetland of Jamaica Bay, 15 miles from Times Square, three years ago was dedicated today as New York International Airport, the largest airport in the US. The growth of air travel into and out of New York and the expectations for the future led to the creation of the new Idlewild airport. At 4,900 acres, it dwarfs the city's older 558-acre LaGuardia Field, which was opened in 1939.

The new airport takes its name from the former Idlewild Beach golf course, which was razed as part of the airport development. But the majority of Idlewild's land did not exist when the first dredging contract to fill in the portion of the bay bordered by the borough of Queens was awarded back in 1942. Commercial operations from the airport, which has six runways, began on July 1 with a series of test and service flights.

The first scheduled airliner to use the airport was a Peruvian International Airways DC-4 on July 9, followed by an Air France transatlantic service on July 14. Officials anticipate that in the airport's first year of full operations it will handle about 18,000 aircraft movements and 220,000 passengers.

# British plane breaks through sound barrier

*Hertfordshire, England, Sep 6*
A British jet broke the sound barrier today for the first time. But it was done inadvertently and with the airplane briefly out of control.

De Havilland test pilot John Derry took off from Hatfield this morning in the third D.H.108 to carry out a series of high-speed dives, edging closer to Mach 1.0.

He climbed to 45,000 feet and pushed the nose down into a 30-degree dive. At Mach 0.96 the nose felt very heavy, but instead of pulling out he pushed, making the dive steeper. At 38,000 feet the jet went into the vertical and out of control. But Derry managed to recover by 23,500 feet and, in the process, the Machmeter indicated Mach 1.04.

# Wrights' historic 'Flyer' returns to US

*Washington, DC, December 17*
Today, the 45th anniversary of the the Wrights' first heavier-than-air flight, the airplane which made it went on display at the Smithsonian. The return of the Wright *Flyer* marks the end of the late brothers' feud with the institution. The argument ended in 1943, when the Smithsonian at last conceded that the *Flyer*, and not S P Langley's *Aerodrome*, was the first heavier-than-air craft capable of powered flight. Until then, the Wrights had refused to let the Smithonian have the machine. War delayed its return from London's Science Museum, where it had been since 1928.

*Handing over the original Wright "Flyer" at the Science Museum, London.*

# Swedish jet fighter is European landmark

*The Saab J 29's barrel-like fuselage makes it unlikely to exceed Mach 1.*

*Linköping, Sweden, September 1*
Squadron Leader Robert Moore, British test pilot with the royal Swedish air force, today made the first flight in the Saab J 29, probably Europe's fastest and most advanced fighter. It has swept-wings and can reach more than Mach 0.9.

Saab has already tested the swept-wing at low speeds on a Safir light plane. The J 29 is thus largely a known quantity, though it is not known if it could dive faster than the speed of sound. This is unlikely, because its British-designed Ghost engine makes the fuselage portly, hence its Swedish nickname "*Tunnan* [Barrel]". The aircraft will be armed with four 20mm cannon. The Swedish air force expects to buy several hundred J 29s in fighter and reconnaissance versions.

# In-flight refueling is perfected by Boeing

*Seattle, December 1*
The ability of USAF Strategic Air Command bombers to strike an enemy anywhere in the world will be improved by a new system which will make in-flight refueling both safer and faster.

It replaces the British hose system currently used by the USAF with a telescoping boom at the tanker aircraft's tail and a special fuel socket on the receiver aircraft. The boom will be lowered and extended into the receiver aircraft's socket by a crewman on the tanker. Miniature wings on the boom, called "ruddervators", will be used to guide it into the socket. The new system will be more efficient and faster than the hose method.

# Free food is taken off Western menu

*Salt Lake City, Utah, December 12*
From New Year's Day, passengers on Western Air Lines' flights are likely to feel a bit peckish by the time they land. The airline announced today that no in-flight meals will be served after the end of this month.

Passengers will save about 5 per cent on fares, according to Western president Terrell C Drinkwater. Western, it seems, has come full circle. In 1928 it was the first airline to offer free in-flight meals. "It is perhaps appropriate that we are the first to take them off," Drinkwater observed. However, in a highly competitive industry, service becomes a discriminator.

**September 15: Jet pioneer Sir Frank Whittle addresses an International Air Transport Association meeting in Belgium.**

The 32-seat Vickers V.630 Viscount prototype was the world's first turboprop-powered transport aeroplane, being fitted with four Rolls-Royce Darts.

Britain's first post-war civilian amphibian was the Short Sealand.

Piper updated the pre-war J-3 Cub to produce the PA-18 Super Cub.

The Aero Design and Engineering Corporation was established to produce a prototype executive aircraft known as the Aero Commander L-3805.

The first production Percival P.50 Prince medium-range transport.

The four-seat Model Cessna 170 was an enlarged and improved 140.

The three-seat Model 360 was the first production Hiller helicopter.

Supermarine designed the Seagull to replace the Sea Otter and Walrus.

SNCA du Sud-Ouest designed the SO 6020 Espadon jet fighter to carry armament comprising two 30mm cannon and four 12.7mm machine guns.

The second prototype Boulton Paul Balliol used a Mamba turboprop.

McDonnell's XF-85 Goblin parasite fighter was carried inside a B-36.

North American's XAJ-1 was designed for carrier-based nuclear strike.

Supermarine's experimental 510 was effectively a swept-wing Attacker.

Ilyushin Il-28 tactical bombers, powered by a pair of Nene-derived Klimov VK-1 turbojets, were exported to several countries, including Finland.

The Saab J29 was Europe's first swept-wing jet fighter to achieve large-scale production. The Swedish and Austrian air forces took delivery of 661 of them.

*The McDonnell XF-88 Voodoo was the forerunner of the F-101 Voodoo.*

*The Convair XF-92A was later developed into the F-102 Delta Dagger.*

*Northrop's tailless X-4 Bantam, for research into subsonic stability.*

*Northrop's first prototype XF-89 Scorpion twin-jet fighter.*

*Extended nacelles carried the tail surfaces of the Aérocentre NC.1071, powered by two HS Nene turbojets.*

*The Beech 45 or T-34 was a tandem trainer development of the Bonanza.*

*From the single-seat F-80 Shooting Star fighter Lockheed derived the TF-80C two-seat lengthened-fuselage trainer, which was later redesignated T-33A.*

*The first Soviet series-production helicopter was the Mil Mi-1, which was built in quantity and later produced in Poland by WSK-PZL Swidnik as the SM-1.*

*Swept-wing research was the role of the Douglas D-558-2 Skyrocket. It had a Westinghouse J34 turbojet and a Reaction Motors XLR-8 rocket motor.*

*Vought's unconventional F7U Cutlass had combined pitch and roll controls in the form of wing elevons, and the vertical tail surfaces were wing-mounted.*

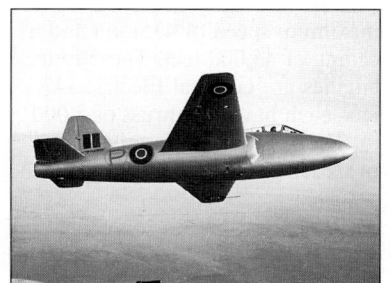

*Development of the Gloster E.1/44 was halted in favour of the Meteor.*

*The Douglas F3D Skyknight: the US Navy's two-seat jet night-fighter.*

*The Arsenal VG 70 was of mixed construction and had a wooden wing.*

*The Martin P5M Marlin was the US Navy's last operational flying boat.*

*Four Westinghouse turbojets powered the Curtiss XP-87 Black Hawk.*

# 1949

957mph
USA
Charles Yeager
Bell X-1
Mar 26, 1948

23,093 miles
USA
James Gallagher
Boeing B-50A
Mar 2, 1949

71,902ft
USA
Frank Everest
Bell X-1
Aug 8, 1949

400,000lb
USA
Hughes Aircraft Co
H-4 Hercules

6,500lb thrust
Great Britain
Rolls Royce
Avon 100

**Muroc Dry Lake, Calif, January 5**
Major Charles "Chuck" Yeager sets an unofficial climbing speed record of over 13,000 feet per minute in the Bell X-1 experimental rocket aircraft; this is also the first ground take-off of a rocket-propelled research aircraft.

**Israel, January 7**
Israeli air force C-210s, Czech-built Messerschmitt Bf 109 fighters, shoot down four RAF Spitfire Mk XVIIIs during a clash near the Egyptian border.

**Oakland, Calif, January 13**
Pilot William B Odom lands here after flying a Beechcraft Bonanza from Honolulu, Hawaii, a distance of 2,407 miles. The flight lasted 22 hours.

**London, January 20**
Following the disappearance of another Avro Tudor 4, British South American Airways' *Star Ariel*, on a flight from Bermuda to Jamaica, the aircraft is withdrawn from passenger service.

**USA, January 25**
The USAF officially adopts blue uniforms, in place of army olive buff, to enhance its identity and, therefore, it is hoped, boost morale and aid recruiting; seven leading designers submitted USAF uniforms in colors including light gray, green and blue (→ Jan 23, 1950).

**Chicago, USA, January 26**
US carrier American Airlines equips its entire fleet of aircraft with a passenger loudspeaker system which allows the pilot to provide passengers with flight or emergency information.

**Seattle, USA, January 31**
Pan Am receives the first Boeing Model 377 Stratocruiser to be delivered (→ Apr 1).

**New York, February 5**
An Eastern Air Lines Lockheed Constellation lands at LaGuardia at the end of a flight of 6 hours 18 minutes from Los Angeles, a coast-to-coast record for transport aircraft (→ Oct 27).

**Washington state, February 14**
An Aeronca reconnaissance airplane inexplicably takes off without a pilot from Gray army airfield, Fort Lewis; the wind carries it to a farmer's field near Kittikas, where it lands with only slight damage (→ Apr 26).

**USA, March 4**
The 1st Fighter Wing of the USAF begins operating F-86 fighters. A competition is organized to find a name for the single-seat jet aircraft. Sabre is chosen among the 78 names suggested. The USAF's 4th and 81st Fighter Wings also receive F-86 Sabres.

**San Diego, Calif, March 26**
The USAF's first ten-engined aircraft, the B-36D, makes its first flight; a Convair B-36 with four extra jet engines in paired pods beneath the wings, it has a maximum speed of 435mph and a ceiling of 45,000 feet. These four engines are General Electric J47 jets, each having a thrust of 5,000 lb. The six R-4360 piston engines provide 3,500-hp each.

**Australia, April 2**
Australian airline Qantas hands over all domestic services, including the Flying Doctor Service based in Charleville and Cloncurry, to Trans-Australian Airlines (→ Mar 3, 1950).

**Port Angeles, Washington, April 6**
A Sikorsky S-51 completes a record helicopter flight of 3,750 miles from Elizabeth, New Jersey.

**Berlin, April 16**
On the busiest day of the airlift so far, West Berlin receives 12,940 short tons of supplies from the West in 1,398 sorties (→ May 12).

**USA, April 18**
Colonial Airlines sets a new record for passenger safety, completing 19 years of scheduled services without a single fatality or serious injury to passengers or crew.

**China, April 21**
An RAF Sunderland lands on the Yangtse river to take a doctor and supplies to the British frigate HMS *Amethyst*, which has been attacked by Chinese Communist forces.

**Berlin, May 12**
The USSR ends its blockade; the Western airlift continues to build up supplies in the city (→ Sep 30).

**Lancashire, England, May 13**
Roland Beamont pilots Britain's first jet bomber, the English Electric A.1 Canberra, on its first flight, at Warton (→ Dec 1950).

**New York, May 18**
The city's first heliport, built on Pier 41 by the Hudson River, opens.

**San Diego, California, May 19**
US Navy flying boat *Marshall Mars* lands after flying from Alameda, near San Francisco, with a record 301 passengers.

**New York, June 29**
Eastern and Pan Am are said to be testing the feasibility of using phonographs as a means of in-flight entertainment.

**Canada, July 13**
The Canadair North Star *Empress of Sydney* inaugurates Canadian Pacific Air Lines' first international service, from Vancouver to Sydney.

**London, July 30**
BOAC absorbs British South American Airways.

**Toronto, August 10**
The Avro Canada C-102 Jetliner, the world's second jet airliner, makes its maiden flight; it is powered by four Rolls-Royce Derwent engines.

**Berkshire, England, September 19**
The Fairey Gannet carrier-based anti-submarine aircraft makes its first flight, at Aldermaston.

**Minneapolis, October 17**
Northwest Airlines announces that it will serve alcoholic drinks to passengers, the first US airline to do so on domestic flights.

**Azores, October 27**
An Air France Constellation crashes on a flight from New York, killing 48; celebrated young violinist Ginette Neveu and French boxing champion Marcel Cerdan are among the victims (→ Nov 1).

**Arlington, Va, November 1**
A USAF P-38 fighter hits an Eastern Airlines DC-4 over Washington National Airport, killing all 55 on board the airliner as well as the pilot of the P-38; it is the worst air disaster to date in the USA (→ Mar 12, 1950).

**Stratford, Conn, November 10**
The Sikorsky S-55 successfully makes its first flight; it is the first helicopter to have the engine in the nose rather than in the center of the fuselage, allowing greater cabin space.

**Washington, DC, December 5**
The USAF announces that it is to build a radar network in Alaska and elsewhere, to warn of the approach of hostile aircraft up to 300 miles away.

**USA, December 27**
US carriers American Airlines and TWA begin coast-to-coast coach-class flights with 60-passenger DC-4s, charging $110 one-way.

*The weekly magazine "Aeroplane" of June 3, 1949; its price was one shilling [5p]. The advertisement shows the Bristol Brabazon I.* ▶

# Americans fly round the world non-stop

*The B-50A "Lucky Lady II" touches down after its record-breaking flight.*

**Fort Worth, Texas, March 2**
The USA's global deterrent power was demonstrated today when a Boeing B-50A, the *Lucky Lady II*, landed at Carswell Air Force Base to complete the first non-stop round-the-world flight.

The bomber was not stripped down for the flight but carried a normal crew of 13 and defensive armament of 13 0.50-in machine guns. During the 94 hours and one

minute it was airborne, the *Lucky Lady II* was refueled in flight four times by KB-29 tankers.

The 23,453-mile flight shows that, in addition to its six-engined, 10,000-mile-range B-36, which is the only bomber capable of reaching a target on another continent and returning to base without refueling, the US B-29 and B-50 medium bombers can now deliver nuclear weapons anywhere.

# Tudor airliner goes missing off Bermuda

**Bermuda, January 17**
A British South American Airways Tudor 4B airliner, *Star Ariel*, with a crew of seven and 33 passengers on board was declared missing and presumed lost today.

The aircraft had taken off from here and was heading for Kingston, Jamaica. At 1.52pm, the aircraft sent a radio message to inform air traffic control that it was 125 miles southwest of Bermuda and flying at an altitude of 18,000 feet. The crew

made no mention of any problems aboard. Search and rescue operations were begun at 7.15pm, as the Tudor was already long overdue. So far there is nothing to explain the airplane's mysterious disappearance. This is the second time that an airliner of this type and operated by the same British company has vanished off Bermuda. Two years ago, a third airliner, a DC-3, also went missing for unknown reasons in this sector (→ 20).

*Aviation authorities are trying to piece together* Star Ariel's *last moments.*

# Leduc ramjet airplane shoots aloft

**Toulouse, France, April 21**
René Leduc's ramjet-powered O.10 research airplane flew today for the first time, with pilot Jean Gonord squeezed into the cramped cockpit in the conical nose.

The ramjet engine cannot propel an airplane from a standing start because it relies on forward motion to provide compressed air for combustion. For this reason it is necessary for the O.10 to be carried aloft on the back of a large parent aircraft – today it was a Languedoc four-engined transport flown by

Commandant Jean Perrin. At 13,100 feet the aircraft was released into a shallow dive at 267mph, and its burners were lit. Gonord, pinned to the back of his seat by the force of the engine, put the O.10 into a climb at 400mph. The fuel ran out after nine minutes.

On later flights more fuel will be carried, which should enable higher speeds to be reached. Leduc wants to design a ramjet fighter which can exceed Mach 2, although this must be some years off. The take-off problem also remains to be solved.

*The instant when the O.10 ramjet detached itself from the parent aircraft.*

# Bonanza airplane flies to new record

**Teterboro, New Jersey, March 8**
A magnificent non-stop flight of 56 hours and 2 minutes has put Captain William Odom in the record books. Leaving Honolulu, Hawaii, he covered a distance of 4,957.25 miles before landing here today to gain the world record in Class C-1-c for light aircraft.

His airplane, the *Waikiki*, was a Beechcraft Model 35 Bonanza, a diminutive four-seater machine with a distinctive "V"-shaped tail. The Bonanza has been a runaway success for its manufacturer since first flying on December 22, 1945. Before production even got under way in 1947, the company had received orders for 1,500 of the monoplanes. By the end of that year about 1,000 of them had already been delivered.

# Six weeks in the air for 'Sunkist Lady'

**USA, April 24**
Breaking records in aviation has increasingly become the province of the major aviation companies backed by multi-million-dollar defense research and development contracts from national governments. But today light plane pilots Bill Barris and Dick Reidel flew their way into the history books in their Aeronca Chief *Sunkist Lady*.

They set a new world record for flight-refueled endurance of 1,008 hours 1 minute, just a minute over six weeks. To take on fuel they had to swoop low four times a day, flying just above a Jeep racing along the ground from which they hauled up Jerry-cans. The same Jeep provided the pilots, who took it in turns to fly, with all their food and other vital supplies.

# Stratocruisers set new standards of airline luxury

*Even with engines at their loudest, normal conversation may be carried on.*

*The comfort of the forward stateroom. The seats can be made into divans.*

*San Francisco, April 1*

Pan Am took a leap ahead of its great rival TWA today when the latest addition to its fleet, the luxurious Boeing Stratocruiser, went into service. The new airliner made its debut on Pan Am's busiest route, carrying 86 passengers from San Francisco to Honolulu.

The Stratocruiser is a civil development of the USAF's C-97, which was itself based on one of the great workhorses of the last war, the B-29 Superfortress bomber. The airliner's fuselage, built to the same novel "double-bubble" design as the C-97 (it resembles a figure "8"

in cross-section), accommodates two decks which are linked by a spiral staircase. The main cabin, on the upper deck, seats up to 100 passengers and can be fitted with 28 berths as well as private compartments and two changing rooms. Downstairs is a spacious cocktail bar and lounge, where 14 people can relax in comfort.

Pan Am, which ordered 20 of these high-status airliners in November 1945, has announced that the Stratocruiser will begin transatlantic services to London on June 1 this year. This new President service will be first-class only.

*Pan Am's giant double-deck Stratocruiser "Flying Cloud" lands at London.*

*The galley can serve passengers and crew three times a day without reloading.*

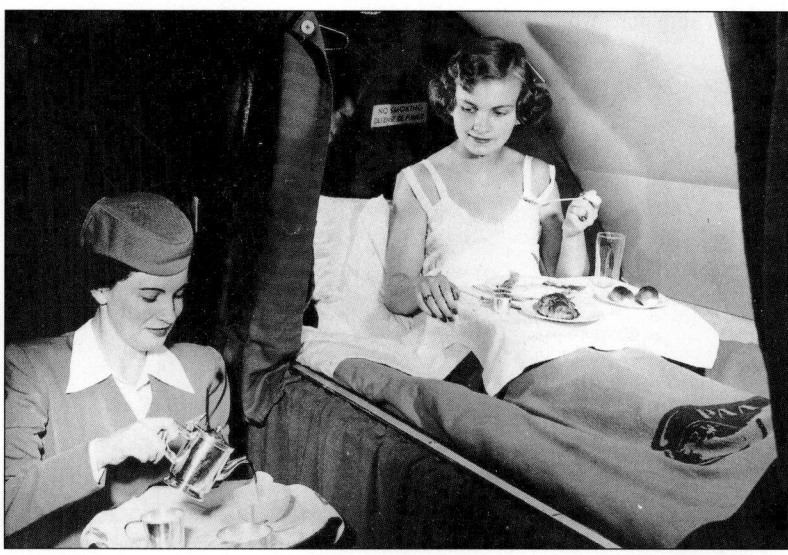

*Breakfast in bed on board the "Clipper Mayflower" on the President service.*

## Pilot ejects from airplane in flight

*Baginton, England, May 30*
The first use of a Martin-Baker ejection seat in a genuine emergency occurred today when pilot J O Lancaster abandoned an Armstrong Whitworth "flying wing" jet airplane. The seat worked perfectly well.

Armstrong Whitworth investigated flying-wing aircraft with the camouflaged wooden AW.52G glider, first flown in March 1945. This underpinned the design of two white-painted all-metal AW.52s, one powered by two Rolls-Royce Derwent turbojets and the other by two Rolls-Royce Nenes. Lancaster ejected from the Derwent aircraft, first flown on November 13, 1948. It was during a test flight today that a dangerous flutter developed in one wing-tip. After Lancaster had ejected, a so-far inexplicable thing happened. The flutter seemed to stop, and the aircraft resumed a normal flight attitude, gliding to land in an area of open countryside and sustaining little damage. Aerodynamics experts are totally baffled by this.

# Comet opens the era of jet transport

*Hertfordshire, England, July 27*
The hangar doors at Hatfield have opened to reveal the sleek lines of an aircraft that heralds the age of commercial jet travel. The veil of secrecy has been lifted from the de Havilland D.H.106 Comet – the world's first jet airliner – which flew for the first time today.

The Comet is a pressurized, four-jet, 36-seat airliner with which Britain hopes to steal the initiative from the dominant US aircraft manufacturers. If all goes as planned, airlines wishing to use gas-turbine airplanes will have to look to Britain, in the short term at least. Two Comets have already been ordered by the British Ministry of Supply. Each airliner is powered by four 4,450-lb thrust de Havilland Ghost 50 turbojet engines housed in pairs at the roots of the wings. The wings themselves are swept back at 20 degrees and carry large flaps, ensuring good handling at all speeds. The Comet's controls are hydraulically powered.

Inside the fuselage are two cabins, pressurized to the equivalent of 8,000 feet when flying at an altitude of 35,000 feet. The aircraft's cruising speed is an impressive 490mph. The pilot for today's first flight was John Cunningham, who was joined by three other crew.

*A proud day for Britain: the first Comet, G-ALVG, is unveiled at Hatfield, and a new era in aviation history begins.*

## Avro 707 points way forward as Brabazon looks backward

*Bristol, England, September 4*
The largest airplane ever built in Britain, the Bristol Brabazon, made a successful first flight from Filton today with chief test pilot Bill Pegg at the controls. Four pairs of coupled Centaurus piston engines, which drive four contra-rotating propellers, powered it, and it lumbered into the air in a stately manner which surely belongs to another age. In order to get the 140-ton monster into the air, the runway at Filton was lengthened to 8,250 feet which involved rerouting a road and demolishing the village of Charlton. Intended to carry 100 passengers across the Atlantic in luxury, the concept seems out of date.

In contrast, and 50 miles to the east, S E "Red" Esler flew the Avro 707 for the first time today at Boscombe Down.

The 707, a scale-model of the future Avro 698 bomber, built to explore the potential of delta wings, points the way forward. Avro at Manchester is building further 707s, including a two-seat trainer to teach pilots how to handle deltas.

*The Brabazon, which in fact only needed 2,500 feet of runway to take off.*

*Avro's 707 delta-wing research aircraft shows the very latest technology.*

# Berlin airlift crisis ends

*Unloading 25 tons of flour from a C-74 Globemaster at Tempelhof airport.*

*Berlin, September 30*
The USAF today made the last official flight of "Operation Vittles" – the Berlin Airlift. There have been 277,569 flights since the Soviet blockade of West Berlin began 15 months ago; the last RAF flight was on September 23 and the last civil flight on August 16.

US and British planes have poured supplies into Berlin night and day, flying so close together that one radar operator saw an endless "string of pearls" on his screen. Aircraft landed and took off with one minute's clearance, and airspeed had to be accurate within one knot. On any day an average of 380 aircraft were airborne, including Skymasters, Halifax bombers and even Sunderland flying boats, which landed on Berlin's lakes. Over 2.3 million tons of cargo were carried, and around 57,000 personnel took part. The USAF lost 27 personnel in accidents, the RAF 18 plus seven German passengers, and charter aircraft ten. In May the Soviets conceded defeat, but the airlift continued in case they tried again. Even after today, unofficial flights will continue for a short time.

# Farnborough air show thrills the crowds

*Hampshire, England, September*
Although nothing at this year's annual Farnborough show of the Society of British Aircraft Constructors could break the sound barrier, it was still a memorable occasion. Many of the aircraft on display herald the shape of things to come.

Pride of place went to the de Havilland Comet, the first jet airliner. Backing it up are the world's first four turboprop airliners, the Hermes 5, Armstrong Whitworth Apollo, Marathon 2 and, best of all, the Vickers Viscount. For sheer size nothing can surpass the majestic Bristol Brabazon; for peculiarity nothing resembles the huge Cierva Air Horse helicopter, lifted by three rotors. For excitement the star was the new Canberra bomber. Test pilot Roland Beamont gave a breathtaking demonstration in this agile twin-jet.

*On display at Farnborough air show, British aviation's showcase to the world.*

# BOAC thinks twice about flying boats

*Poole, England, December 6*
The sedate and luxurious days of BOAC's flying-boat services may be coming to an end. Faster, more economical landplanes are the new masters. Boeing Stratocruisers joined BOAC's fleet today, hot on the heels of the Argonauts introduced on August 23. With an unenviable reputation for noise, the Argonaut is now on the airline's London/ Hong Kong route – a far cry from the Sandringham service.

The Argonaut is basically a pressurized version of the Douglas DC-4, built by Canadair as the DC-4M. Its cost attracts BOAC: some dollar savings are made by using Rolls-Royce Merlin engines and much British equipment.

# Paratroopers rain nuts on Belgian town

*Joining in the "nutty" celebrations.*

*Bastogne, Belgium, December 22*
The burghers of this town in the Ardennes were taken by surprise today when it began to rain – nuts. They came with the compliments of the US 101st Airborne Division which was celebrating the fifth anniversary of the siege of Bastogne during the embattled German army's last offensive in the west.

But why nuts? They recall the reply of 101st's commander in the siege, General Anthony McAuliffe, to his German counterpart. With low cloud cover making supplies from the air impossible the 101st's situation looked hopeless, and the Germans demanded surrender. But McAuliffe's terse response, which became an instant classic among military communications, was simple: "Nuts."

# Transatlantic flight carries record 103

*Norfolk, England, November 18*
A giant USAF C-74 Globemaster transport landed at Marham today with 103 people on board. It is the first airplane to cross the North Atlantic with a complement of more than a hundred.

The 23-hour flight from Mobile, Alabama, proved that by using the C-74 aircraft the US could rapidly deploy large military forces to Europe to support its Nato allies in the event of Soviet aggression. The C-74 has a much greater capacity than the largest airliners flying in the US. Douglas, the manufacturer of the C-74, also builds the fast DC-6 transport, yet the latter can only carry about 60 people, barely half the Globemaster's capacity.

The SIPA S.901 Minicab light plane proved economical and reliable.

The Breguet 761 Deux Ponts transport featured two passenger decks.

The Sud-Est SE 2010 Armagnac proved uneconomical and was soon withdrawn from service with TAI, although seven later served with SAGETA.

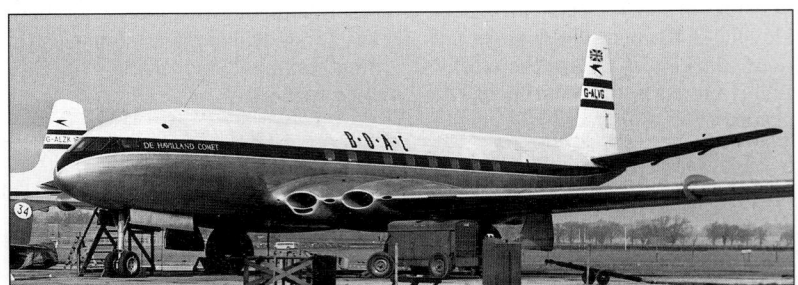

The de Havilland Comet I was the world's first successful in-service jet-airliner, although serious structural problems led to the type being grounded.

The Avro Shackleton remained in front-line RAF operation until 1991!

Beechcraft's Twin Bonanza was also made as the YL-23 for the USAF.

Saunders-Roe's Skeeter: a British Army lightweight AOP helicopter.

Moulton B. Taylor's Aerocar: an attempt to produce a roadable plane.

The Avro Canada C-102 Jetliner was conventional in appearance and had four Rolls-Royce Derwent engines paired in underwing nacelles.

The Bristol Brabazon, conceived as a transatlantic airliner but killed off by the dawning of the jet age and mismanagement by the British government.

The French Fouga C.M.8-R Sylphe was basically a jet-powered glider.

The Nord 1402 Noroit was a twin-engined reconnaissance flying boat.

Morane-Saulnier's neat MS.730 was designed as a primary trainer.

The twin-boom Sud-Ouest SO. 6020 Narval, intended as a naval fighter.

The Royal Navy used Fairey's Gannet, powered by Coupled Mambas.

The three-jet Martin XB-51 proved inferior to the B-57 (Canberra).

Fairchild's C-123 Provider was a tactical assault transport for the USAF.

The Vickers Varsity advanced RAF pilot and aircrew trainer aircraft.

English Electric's Canberra: British post-war aircraft industry's success.

The mixed-power-plant Republic XF-91: fastest US fighter of its day.

The unsuccessful Arsenal VG 90, designed as a ground-attack fighter.

De Havilland's Venom: re-winged, re-engined multirole Vampire.

Lockheed's experimental XF-90, designed as a "penetration fighter".

The Leduc O.10 was a ramjet-powered experimental aircraft, air-launched from a parent aircraft to provide sufficient speed to ignite the engine.

The Sikorsky S-55 12-seat utility helicopter was built in large numbers.

The prototype of Nord's 2501 Noratlas, a versatile military transport.

The Nord 2200 was intended as a naval jet fighter but won no orders.

The graceful Armstrong Whitworth Apollo prototype turboprop airliner.

The French Dassault Ouragan proved to be an effective ground-attack aircraft, and large numbers were built for L'armée de l'Air, Israel and India.

Douglas's YC-124 Globemaster II was developed from the C-74 and shared the same wings and tail, coupled to a new fuselage with clamshell nose-doors.

North American produced the T-28 to replace the T-6 Texan (Harvard).

The Convair T-29 navigation trainer was a version of the Convair 240.

Lockheed's XF-94 Starfire, a night-fighter version of the proven F-80/T-33 Shooting Star family. The F-94 saw active service during the Korean War.

The Northrop Pioneer: developed into the C-125 Raider for the USAF.

CASA's C 201 Alcotan: first Spanish-designed turboprop transport.

# 1950

**Sonoma, California, Jan 15**
Former commander of US Army Air Forces General Henry H "Hap" Arnold, 63, dies.

**Washington, DC, January 23**
The USAF Air Research and Development Command is established.

**Muroc Dry Lake, Calif, Jan 27**
The USAF installation here is renamed Edwards Air Force Base in honor of Captain Glen Edwards, who died in a crash two years ago.

**USA, February 1**
Eight Grumman F9F Panthers land on the USS *Valley Forge* to complete the first aircraft carrier night-landing trials by jets.

**Antarctic, February 18**
The first International Antarctic Expedition, launched on January 31, ends; the joint British, Swedish and Norwegian venture used two Auster light aircraft for exploration flights.

**Wichita, Kansas, March 1**
The first production six-engined Boeing B-47A Stratojet swept-wing bomber rolls off the line at the Boeing factory here; the prototype's six 3,750-lb-thrust General Electrics J35 engines have been replaced by J47s of 5,200 lb thrust.

**Sydney, March 3**
Qantas inaugurates a passenger service from Sydney to Tokyo.

**Dallas, Texas, March 14**
The first production example of the US Navy's new twin-jet semi-tailless fighter, the Chance Vought F7U-1 Cutlass, makes a successful first flight.

**Dallas, Texas, March 16**
The USAF orders very high frequency (VHF) radio systems worth a total of $7 million, from the Collins Radio company; these systems are deemed more reliable than low-frequency radios.

**Norfolk, England, March 22**
Four B-29 Superfortresses, known to the RAF as the Washington, are delivered to 149 Squadron, RAF, at Marham; they are the first of 70 supplied to the RAF under the US Military Aid Program.

**Baltic Sea, April 8**
A US Navy Consolidated PB4Y-2 Privateer is shot down by Soviet MiG-15 fighters; all ten crew-members are lost (→ Nov 1, 1951).

**Brussels, April 12**
Lorne Welch, who took off from Redhill, England, lands to complete the first glider crossing of the English Channel.

**London, April 16**
British European Airways (BEA) begins operations from Heathrow airport with a Vickers Viking flight to Paris (→ Oct 31).

**Washington, DC, April 18**
The USAF announces plans to acquire 1,250 new airplanes at a cost of $1,203 million.

**Birkenhead, England, May 3**
Queen Elizabeth launches the new aircraft carrier, HMS *Ark Royal*.

**USA, June 1**
Frontier Airlines is launched as a result of the merger of Arizona Airways and Challenger Airlines.

**New York, June 23**
Charles Lawrance, 67, designer of Lindbergh's Wright Whirlwind engine, dies at East Islip.

**Korea, June 27**
USAF Lieutenant William Hudson downs the first North Korean aircraft of the war; Staff-Sergeant Mickey Nyle is co-pilot of the F-82G Twin Mustang fighter.→

**Korea, June 28**
Taking off from Japan in a Lockheed RF-80A to survey North Korean troop movements, Lieutenant Bryce D Poe II completes the USAF's first combat reconnaissance mission by a jet.

**Korea, June 29**
Douglas B-26 Invaders carry out the first USAF bombing raid against North Korea, attacking the military airfield at Pyongyang.

**Korea, July 3**
Panthers, Corsairs and Skyraiders from the USS *Valley Forge* and Firefly FR.1s from HMS *Triumph* carry out the war's first strikes by naval aircraft when they raid military facilities in Pyongyang; two Yaks are downed by Panthers.

**London, August 3**
BEA orders 20 Vickers-Armstrongs Type 701 Viscounts.

**Korea, August 5**
Major Louis J Sebille deliberately crashes his airplane into a North Korean position threatening US troops near Hanchang; he is to be posthumously recommended for the Congressional Medal of Honor, the US's most distinguished award for valor.

**China, August 23**
The US Central Intelligence Agency (CIA) buys Civil Air Transport from Claire Chennault and Whiting Willauer; it is the first in a planned worldwide network of CIA-owned airlines.

**Europe, August 27**
Nato's first large-scale air exercise, codenamed Cupola, ends after three days.

**Korea, September 4**
The first helicopter rescue of a downed pilot behind enemy lines takes place when First Lieutenant Paul Van Boven and Corporal John Fuentz pick up Captain Robert E Wayne, an F-80 pilot shot down on his 95th mission (→ Dec 1).

**Alice Springs, Australia, Sept 9**
"The School of the Air" broadcasts its first lessons through the Flying Doctor Service; the "school" aims to reach children on remote cattle stations spread over the Northern Territories.

**USA, September 25**
Pan American takes over the assets of American Overseas Airlines.

**Ceylon [Sri Lanka], October 10**
The Royal Ceylon Air Force is created, with British assistance.

**Korea, October 20**
The first paratroop assault of the war is launched over Sukchon and Sunchon by the US 187th Airborne Regiment from Kimpo airfield; in one hour, 71 C-119s and 40 C-47s drop 2,860 men and over 300 tons of equipment.

**London, October 31**
A BEA Vickers Viking crashes in fog at Heathrow, killing 28.

**New York, November 1**
Continental Airlines has flown 1,204,000 passengers without a single fatality in 16 years.

**Wichita, Kansas, November 29**
Walter H Beech, founder of the Beechcraft Corporation, dies of a heart attack.

**Korea, December 1**
US Mobile Army Surgical Hospital (MASH) units, which have been in operation since July 7, receive unarmed Bell 47 helicopters equipped for carrying casualties.

**College Station, Tex, December 1**
Test pilot C W von Rosenberg completes the first test flight of the Texas A&M AG-1 agricultural monoplane, which can carry dust, seed or fertilizer in a 27-cubic-foot hopper.

**Korea, December 17**
On their first day in action, North American F-86A Sabres claim four MiG-15s 10 miles south-east of the Yalu river, in the first encounter between swept-wing aircraft.

*The fuel tanks at the tip of each wing enable the Lockheed L-1049G Super Constellation to make non-stop transcontinental flights.* ▶

# Rising world tension boosts US military spending as new aircraft take to the air

*Washington, DC, June 1*
Cold-war tension between the USA and the Soviet Union has led the USAF to start a civilian Ground Observer Corps to watch for attackers. It will supplement the $50 million worth of radar which the US is building in Alaska in response to the testing of a Soviet atomic bomb last August, and the USSR's construction of Tu-4 bombers.

Soviet backing for the unrest in Greece and Turkey, the Berlin blockade and the reported downing of a US Navy reconnaissance plane over the Baltic on April 8 have focused US attention on the Communist threat to Europe. This has triggered the accelerated purchase of B-47 jet bombers, the supply of 70 B-29s to Britain in March, and the development of the advanced F-89 and F-94 interceptors and the B-52 intercontinental jet bomber.

Another portent of increased tension, this time in the Far East, is the build-up of the US Navy's carrier force. The stalwart is the P2V-2 or P2V-3 Neptune, whose rocket-assisted take-offs thunder off the decks of carriers such as the USS *Franklin D Roosevelt*. Now more modern fighters are coming on stream, including the Douglas F3D Skyknight and the Grumman F9F Panther. The Skyknight is a radar-equipped night fighter seating pilot and radar operator side by side.

*The Neptune fires its rockets ...*

*then, with its wing flaps lowered ...*

*it reaches the end of the deck ...*

*at the right speed for take-off.*

# TWA changes its name but keeps logo

*USA, May 17*
Transcontinental & Western Air today changed its name to Trans World Airlines, a title which better reflects the international nature of the big US airline's business. TWA was a leading pre-war domestic carrier, and its crews began making military transatlantic flights to Britain in 1942 with Stratoliners which had been taken over by the USAAF. This experience, together with the its early order for Lockheed Constellations, which passed back into airline control when peace returned, gave TWA the airplanes and crews it needed to compete over the Atlantic. Regular flights to Paris began on February 6, 1946, to Cairo on April 1, and to Madrid a month later. Routes to Asia have followed since.

# Cuts mean short life for new flying wing

*The YRB-49A, built as a bomber, will end up as a reconnaissance aircraft.*

*Hawthorne, California, May 4*
The first flight today of the prototype Northrop YRB-49A "flying wing" airplane should have been an exciting day. But with the USAF's flying-wing reconnaissance bomber program canceled, enthusiasm was muted.

The YRB-49A was to have been the first of nine jet-powered conversions of YB-35 piston-engined flying-wing bombers ordered early last year. The USAF finally opted for the Convair B-36 instead. Since 1946, 200 Martin-built production B-35A bombers, the eight-jet B-49 and an order for 30 YRB-49As have been axed.

The cancelation of the flying-wing program means an end to the dream of designer Jack Northrop, who believed that such a design would be faster and more efficient than conventional aircraft. But the US Air Force will use the giant B-36 instead.

# Doolittle, Cochran are flyers of decade

*Washington, DC, July 5*
Famous US flyers Jimmy Doolittle and Jacqueline Cochran were today named aviator and aviatrix of the decade by the Harmon International Aviation Awards committee.

Doolittle, now a director of Shell Oil, began the last decade as president of America's Institute of the Aeronautical Sciences. He was probably the most famous Army pilot between the world wars, and held a world speed record. He awarded the Congressional Medal of Honor for leading the B-25 raid on Tokyo in 1942, and later in the war, as a lieutenant-general, he commanded the US Eighth AAF. He became first president of the Air Force Association. Celebrated pre-war pilot Cochran organized and headed the Women's Airforce Service Pilots, or WASPS.

# Helicopter service launched in Britain

*Liverpool, England, June 1*
British European Airways (BEA) is no stranger to innovation. Having inaugurated Britain's first helicopter mail route two years ago, it today began operating a scheduled helicopter passenger service. The first flight between Speke (Liverpool) and Cardiff, via Wrexham, took 2 hours 20 minutes. It carried dignitaries, including BEA Chairman Lord Douglas of Kirtleside, and a consignment of penicillin. British civil aviation minister Lord Pakenham opened the proceedings and flew in one of the Westland-built Sikorsky WS-51 helicopters used today.

From May 9 to May 19 a WS-51 operated the world's first scheduled helicopter passenger service between London and Birmingham during the British Industrial Fair.

# Air forces square up as conflict erupts in Korea

## Fighters shot down as battle is joined

*South Korea, June 27*
Two days after the start of the war, seven North Korean aircraft were shot down by US Fifth Air Force fighters while attempting to attack C-54 and C-47 transports. The transports were evacuating Americans from the South Korean capital of Seoul in the face of the advancing Communist North Korean army. USAF fighters flying from Japan have been covering the evacuation from Seoul and Inchon.

The first North Korean attack was at midday. Five Yak-7s attacked Seoul's Kimpo airfield and were intercepted by five F-82 Twin Mustangs, which were providing protective cover for the airfield. In less than five minutes, three of the Yaks were in flames. Lieutenant William G Hudson is credited with shooting down the first Communist aircraft of the conflict. An hour later, eight of North Korea's Ilyushin Il-10 attack aircraft tried to hit Kimpo. Four USAF F-80 Shooting Star jet fighters, which had replaced the piston-engined F-82s, shot down four Il-10s, two of which were downed by Lieutenant Robert E Wayne. They were the first jet victories of the war.

*Night maintenance for a B-29 Superfortress preparing for a dawn raid.*

*A medical evacuation HO3S helicopter hovers above marines near the front.*

## Lives saved by new use of helicopters

*South Korea, August 8*
While United Nations forces are besieged on the Pusan peninsula by North Korean troops, the North Korean air force has been practically destroyed by US air power. This has allowed B-29 and B-26 bombers, as well as USAF and US Navy fighter/bombers, to help Pusan's defenders keep the North Koreans at bay until reinforcements arrive. The USAF's 1,000 modern aircraft have easily overwhelmed the Communists' 132 Second World War combat aircraft.

Meanwhile, helicopters have found a valuable new role in moving wounded troops from the inaccessible, mountainous terrain of the front line to Mobile Army Surgical Hospital (MASH) units a few miles to the rear. Sikorsky S-51s were at first used for reconnaissance, with a pilot, a co-pilot and a bench for three passengers at the rear. By taking out a window and fixing a strap across the opposite side of the cabin, a stretcher can be secured in the helicopter and a wounded soldier flown out – with his feet sticking out of the window. Specially adapted Bell 47s, expected in the coming months, should give a more comfortable ride (→ Sep 4).

## MiG downed in first jet-to-jet dogfight ...

*Ammunition is loaded into an F-80.*

*Korea, November 8*
The first aerial combat between jet fighters was won today by the USAF when an F-80C Shooting Star from 51 Fighter Interceptor Wing (FIW), piloted by Lieutenant Russell J Brown, shot down a Chinese MiG-15.

The unit was escorting B-29s when a number of MiGs crossed the Yalu river and dove upon the formation. The F-80s turned to meet the MiGs, all but one of which used their superior climbing speed to escape. But the heavier F-80 is slightly faster than the MiG-15 in a dive, and Brown overtook the straggler. A five-second burst from his six 0.50-in machine guns sent the MiG to the ground.

## ... then Navy wins second jet combat victory

*Korea, November 9*
Flying an F9F-2 Panther, Lieutenant-Commander Tom Amen became the first US Navy jet pilot to claim another jet today when he shot down a Chinese MiG-15. Yesterday, the USAF claimed the first "kill" in a duel between jet fighters [see left].

Amen commands Fighter Squadron VF-111, based on the aircraft carrier USS *Philippine Sea*. He was attacking bridges on the Yalu river which link North Korea to Manchuria in the Sinuiju area. The aerial battle was joined when a number of MiGs took off from their Manchurian sanctuary across the Yalu at Antung in Communist China to challenge the US Navy jets.

*A Corsair sets off to fight MiGs.*

# Viscount brings turbine smoothness

*The Viscount makes its debut as the first turbine-driven passenger airplane.*

## Britain's answer to the big US airliners

*Britain, July 29*
Long-range, pressurized piston-engined airliners, developed in the US during the war, gave American civil plane makers the lead. Britain now believes it can fight back using its lead in turbojet and turboprop technology. The turboprop uses a gas turbine to drive a propeller, giving it the versatility of a piston engine but offering more power for weight, longer life, cheaper fuel, easier maintenance and almost vibration-free flight. The turbojet uses the gas turbine to generate a stream of hot gases, which propels the aircraft forward and gives almost limitless speed.

# New ground radar promises safer and quicker landings

*Washington, DC, June 8*
The US Civil Aeronautics Administration has today awarded a $1 million contract to Bendix Aviation to develop a more precise ground-controlled approach radar (GCA). GCA gives air-traffic controlers an accurate picture of approaching aircraft in plan and elevation, which allows them to watch the downward progress of an aircraft toward the runway, even if the pilot is flying blind. The pilot watches his airspeed and obeys commands from the ground to move left or right, up or down. At the last moment he can look ahead and land visually. US airports are also being linked by a nationwide network of VOR stations – VHF radio beacons, each of which gives pilots reliable and immediate data on their bearing.

# Turboprop prototype whisks lucky passengers to Paris in style

*Middlesex, England, July 29*
Sir Frank Whittle, the inventor of the jet engine, watched with pride today from the cabin of the new Vickers Viscount when the four-engined turboprop airliner took off on a scheduled flight to Le Bourget airport, Paris. This is an historic day in the annals of civil aviation. Certificated only two days ago, the

Viscount 630 prototype today carried 14 BEA paying passengers and 12 guests on its flight from Northolt. This marks the first scheduled passenger service by a gas-turbine-engined airliner. Cruising at 300mph, the airplane took 1 hour 10 minutes, 20 minutes faster than normal. Vickers still awaits orders from British European Airways

(BEA) to launch the airliner into full production. The Viscount has changed a good deal since first conceived in 1945 as the 24-seat VC-2 Viceroy. The first example has been built as the Viscount 630, with 32 seats and 1,000-hp Rolls-Royce Dart 502 turboprops. The 40-48 seat Viscount 700 should fly in about two months (→ Aug 3).

# Jet fighter achieves a transatlantic first

*Limestone, Maine, September 22*
A USAF F-84E Thunderjet landed here at 7.02pm to complete the first non-stop transatlantic flight by jet. The pilot was Second World War ace Colonel David C Schilling. Schilling was accompanied by another F-84 flown by Lieutenant-Colonel William D Ritchie. However, Ritchie failed to make a successful refueling and had to bail out over Labrador when he ran out of fuel. He was rescued by a helicopter, bruised but otherwise unhurt.

Schilling said bad weather and high winds throughout the flight from Manston, Kent, England, cut their planned speed very substantially. There were three aerial refuelings: over Prestwick, Scotland, by an RAF Lancaster; over Keflavik, Iceland, by an RAF Lincoln; and over Labrador by a US KB-29. Schilling also had problems refueling and did not get a full load at the final rendezvous. He was ordered to land here instead of at his planned destination, Mitchell Air Force Base, New York, where there was poor weather. The flight lasted 10 hours 1 minute.

# World's worst air crash kills 80 in Wales

*Llandow, Cardiff, March 12*
Seventy-five Welsh rugby football fans and five crew died today in the world's worst civil air crash. They were returning from a game in Dublin when eye-witnesses saw the plane skim over a field west of Cardiff. It climbed again, but the engines stopped and it nosedived into a field. There were three survivors.

The plane, a four-engined Avro Tudor 5, had logged 1,400 hours during the Berlin airlift. Developed from the Lancaster bomber, the Tudor has caused growing anxiety in the past two years over its safety record. The inquiry into the accident is bound to ask why the airplane's seating capacity was increased from 72 to 75, and why it was apparently three passengers over this limit (→ Oct 31).

*Eighty people died in this wreckage.*

# Gremlins mar flight of French Growler

*Toulouse, France, April 30*
France's powerful jet fighter, the Grognard [Growler], has run into trouble during tests. The SE.2410 has two Hispano-Suiza (RR) Nene engines one above the other, fed by an air-intake behind the cockpit. It began to experience serious buffeting at only Mach 0.53 when test pilot Pierre Nadot put it through its paces here today. It has been returned to the SNCASE works.

Not even his greatest fan would agree that designer Pierre Satre has produced a beautiful aircraft. With its fat belly, slim wings and odd tail – the horizontal element unusually low – the Grognard would have flown earlier but for tire problems.

# Super Constellation shows its paces

*The Lockheed Super Constellation, a stretched version of the "Connie" (in rear), can take more passengers further.*

*Burbank, California, October 13*
A test crew headed by J White today completed the maiden flight of the Lockheed Super Constellation. Known as the L-1049, it differs from the familiar C-69 Constellation or "Connie" chiefly in that extra sections have been put into the fuselage to increase the airliner's length, from 95 feet 2 inches to 114 feet 7 inches. This "stretching" process may well be applied to

many aircraft in future. In this case, it has actually enhanced the airplane's appearance and, given its 2,700-hp Wright R-3350 engines, has done nothing to harm the performance. The tourist-class passenger capacity has gone up from 69 to 92, with only very minor changes in operating costs.

This Super Constellation is actually the "old Nº 1961", the first C-69, first flown on January 9,

1943, and since used for many development tasks. Adding 18 feet 5 inches in front of and behind the wings has demanded renumbering all the fuselage frames and stations. Care was needed to avoid sudden discontinuities, because of the nose-to-tail curvature of the original fuselage. Among other changes planned, the round windows on the prototype will be replaced with square ones on production models.

## Pan Am's radio net circles the world

*Washington, DC, November 12*
The first globe-girdling air-to-ground voice radio system is complete. The US Civil Aeronautics Administration today approved voice radio communications between Pan Am aircraft and ground radio stations on the airline's Basra/Karachi/New Delhi run.

The $2 million network's 32 high-frequency ground stations span 16 continents and islands in a 19,687-mile chain. The project began in Pan Am's Latin American Division in 1945 when it was allowed to replace slower radio/telegraph systems on its routes between Miami, Havana and Nassau. By the end of that year Pan Am had extended the service to its transatlantic routes. The voice radio network has been established with the cooperation of other international airlines, as well as several governments and communications equipment manufacturers. New stations have been constructed in Los Angeles, San Francisco, Seattle, Anchorage, Honolulu, Okinawa, Tokyo, New Delhi and Karachi.

# RAF prepares to put Canberra into service

*A plug for the Canberra bomber.*

*Lincolnshire, England, December*
All is now prepared at the air base at Binbrook for the RAF's 101 Squadron to begin conversion, next month, from the Lincoln to the new twin-jet English Electric Canberra bomber. Among other things, the

aircraft will put four men from each existing crew out of a job; it needs only a pilot, a signaller and a navigator/bomb-aimer.

The Canberra was meant to have a crew of only two and to carry a complex radar bombsight. This has not yet materialized, and so navigation and bomb-aiming are done by traditional methods. But in almost every other respect the Canberra is utterly new. Perhaps rather unexciting in appearance, it is anything but in performance.

Two 6,500-lb thrust Rolls-Royce Avon engines give it a top speed of about 580mph. Even more significantly, the Canberra can climb very quickly to about 50,000 feet, a height which jet fighters such as the Meteor and the F-80 cannot reach.

Interest in the Canberra has been shown by a number of air forces, the most significant being the USAF, which has confirmed that it wants it built under license in the US, the first British aircraft in 40 years to be produced in this way.

**The smart image of efficiency: British European Airways hostess Freda Moore checks in a passenger's luggage at Northolt airport. BEA chief executive Peter Masefield has cut costs and brought in special off-peak family fares for flights within the United Kingdom, which have helped nudge the airline into profit this year, after it made a loss in 1949.**

The Vickers Viscount 700 was the first production version and, with the Series 800, it became Britain's best selling airliner, with 444 manufactured.

FMA's Ae 33 Pulqui [Arrow] II: an Argentinian jet fighter prototype.

North American's YF-93A: F-86 re-engined, with bifurcated intakes.

The MiG-17 Fresco was an improved MiG-15 - three forward-firing 23-mm cannon plus bombs and rockets made it a formidable ground-attack fighter.

The single-seat Avro 707B experimental delta was an aerodynamic test-vehicle for the Vulcan bomber. It had a single Rolls-Royce Derwent turbojet.

The twin Derwent-powered Nord 1601: a pure research jet aircraft.

Most Avro 706 Ashtons (jet-Tudors) tested high-altitude bomb systems.

Piper's last high-wing lightplane was the PA-18 Super Cub. Over 10,000 were made, and it became one of the longest-running production aircraft of all time.

De Havilland's D.H.114 Heron feeder-liner seated 14 passengers in airliner comfort. Nearly 150 were built in 1952-1964, many serving with royal Flights.

Blackburn's YB-1 (Double Mamba engine) lost out to Fairey's Gannet.

Boulton Paul's P.111 was a tailless delta-winged research-work aircraft.

Armstrong Whitworth produced the Meteor NF.11, the backbone of the RAF's first jet night-fighter force, with nose-mounted airborne interception radar.

A Goblin turbojet powered the de Havilland Vampire T.11 jet trainer.

Avro Canada's two-seat CF-100 prototype all-weather jet fighter.

Two prototypes were built of the single-seat Sud-Est Grognard strike aircraft. Two Nene turbojets were mounted one above the other in the rear fuselage.

Fairchild's XC-120 Pack-Plane had a detachable 12,500-lb cargo-pod.

The five-seat Scottish Aviation Pioneer, designed for STOL operations.

Hawker's P.1081 was a rebuild of the P.1052, its technology half-way between straight-wing Seahawk and swept-wing Hunter. It had one RR Nene engine.

The US Navy Convair XP5Y (later R3Y) Tradewind flying-boat was designed for Pacific island-hopping. After beaching, the drive-in nose visor opened.

Percival P.56 Provost T.1 trainers replaced the RAF's North American Harvards. The prototype had a Cheetah engine, production models Leonides.

Douglas's A2D-1 Skyshark carrier-based attack-bomber was built for the US Navy. The Allison XT40 coupled turboprop drove co-axial propellers.

Republic modified an existing "straightwing" F-84 to produce the first F-84F Thunderstreak. Production F-84s were more powerful.

General Aircraft's GAL.60, later the RAF's Blackburn B.101 Beverley.

The Fouga C.M.100, a powered version of a military transport glider.

# 1951

1,240.89mph
USA
William Bridgeman
Douglas D-558-2
Aug 7, 1951

23,093 miles
USA
James Gallagher
Boeing B-50A
Mar 2, 1949

79,494ft
USA
William Bridgeman
Douglas D-558-2
Aug 15, 1951

400,000lb
USA
Hughes Aircraft Co
H-4 Hercules

9,7000lb thrust
USA
Pratt & Whitney
J57-P-3

**Paris, January 20**
Air France follows British airlines BEA and BOAC in deciding to paint the upper fuselage of its airliners white; tests carried out in Britain and the USA have shown that this will reduce the cabin temperature by up to 20 degrees when aircraft are on the ground in hot countries.

**Isle of Wight, England, January 22**
East Cowes-based Saunders-Roe absorbs the Cierva autogyro company (→ Sep 2, 1952).

**Newfoundland, February 21**
An English Electric Canberra B.Mk 2 bomber lands at Gander after the first unrefueled, non-stop transatlantic crossing by jet; it took off from Aldergrove, Northern Ireland (→ Aug 26, 1952).

**Wiltshire, England, March 12**
The Fairey F.D.1 experimental delta-winged aircraft makes its first flight, at Boscombe Down, piloted by Group Captain R G Slade.

**LaGuardia, New York, March 29**
Flight Safety Inc. begins operations at the Marine Air Terminal here with just one secretary and rented late night hours on a Link trainer simulator.

**Washington, DC, March 31**
The US Navy issues a contract to Convair for the design and construction of an experimental vertical take-off and landing (VTOL) fighter, the XFY-1.

**Korea, April 12**
Forty-eight USAF B-29 bombers attacking a rail bridge on the Yalu river are engaged by 75 MiG-15 fighters, and three of the B-29s are shot down.

**Korea, April 21**
Two MiG-15s are shot down over North Korea by the gunner of a USAF B-29 based in Okinawa, Japan; this is the first time jets have been downed by bomber fire.

**Korea, May 1**
Eight US Navy Skyraiders and 12 Corsairs from the USS *Princeton* attack the Hwachon dam; the resulting flood stops Communist forces crossing the Pukhan river.

**Wisley, England, May 18**
The Vickers-Amstrongs 660 Valiant bomber prototype, capable of over 560mph, makes its maiden flight (→ Aug 30, 1952).

**Karachi, May 25**
Pakistan orders three Lockheed Super Constellations as the basis for its new airline, Pakistan International Airlines.→

**Fairbanks, Alaska, May 29**
Captain Charles Blair lands in his F-51 piston-engined Mustang after making the first solo flight across the North Pole in a single-engined aircraft, from Bardufoss, Norway, covering 3,375 miles in 10 hours 29 minutes; he earlier flew from New York to London in a record 7 hours 48 minutes.

**Long Island, NY, May 31**
Roosevelt Field, from which Lindbergh's 1927 transatlantic crossing and other pioneering flights took off, is closed down after 40 years in use; it was named for President Roosevelt's son Quentin.

**London, June 1**
BEA inaugurates a helicopter service from Heathrow to Birmingham; passenger flights will start on June 4.

**California, June 20**
The first of two Bell X-5 research jets makes its maiden flight at Edwards Air Force Base; derived from the uncompleted Messerschmitt P.1101, it has variable-sweep wings (→ Jul 27).

**Korea, July 6**
Four US RF-80As, based at Yokota, Japan, are refueled by a KB-29 tanker during a reconnaissance flight over North Korea; this is the first in-flight refueling under combat conditions.

**Tokyo, August 1**
Japan Air Lines is formed as a private company to fly internal services; because of a post-war ban on Japanese aircraft and pilots, it will make use of airplanes and crew loaned by US carrier Northwest Airlines (→ Oct 25, 1952).

**Wiltshire, England, August 5**
The first production prototype of the Supermarine Swift single-seat interceptor fighter makes its first flight at Boscombe Down.

**Sussex, England, August 22**
The first Fleet Air Arm (FAA) jet powered by the Rolls-Royce Nene engine, the Supermarine Attacker, enters service with 800 Squadron, at Ford; it is the FAA's first front-line jet fighter.

**Washington, DC, August 24**
The first Medal of Honor, America's highest valor award, to go to an airman in Korea is awarded posthumously to Major Louis J Sebille, who was killed in action last year.

**Korea, August 25**
US Navy jets escort a bombing mission for the first time when 12 F2H-2 and 12 F9F-2 fighters, from the carrier USS *Essex*, fly with 30 B-29 bombers on a raid of targets at Rashin.

**Korea, September 21**
The first mass movement of troops to the battlefront by helicopter takes place when 228 US Marines are airlifted in 12 Sikorsky S-55s to a hilltop in central Korea.→

**Key West, Florida, October 3**
The US Navy's first anti-submarine helicopter squadron, HS-1, is commissioned.

**USA, October 22**
The US Navy is studying a one-person rocket-powered helicopter, says inventor Gilbert Magill; the 100-lb machine is strapped on to the back of the user, who straddles a bicycle seat and steers with a joystick.

**Santa Monica, California, Nov 2**
The 175th and last Douglas DC-6 transport is delivered to Braniff Airways (→ Feb 11, 1954).

**Gloucestershire, England, Nov 26**
The first of three Gloster GA.5 prototypes makes its first flight at Moreton Valence; it is the world's first twin-engined, delta-winged jet fighter and Britain's first fighter designed for all-weather operation.→

**New Mexico, November 27**
A rocket intercepts an airplane for the first time during tests at White Sands; the missile is detonated about 25 feet from the 300-mph target aircraft, which is flying at 33,000 feet (→ Mar 19, 1952).

**Europe/USA, December 5**
The 11 airlines operating the North Atlantic route announce that "tourist-class" fares are to be introduced on it (→ Dec 15).

**Windsor Locks, Conn, Dec 10**
The first turbine-engined helicopter, the Kaman K-225, makes a successful first flight (→ Jul 24, 1953).

**Seattle, Wash, December 12**
Alaska Air becomes the first airline to fly over the North Pole. The flight was made in a DC-4 aircraft.

**New York, December 17**
The first Lockheed L-1049 Super Constellation enters airline service on Eastern Air Lines' New York to Miami route (→ Oct 20, 1953).

**USA, December 31**
This year, for the first time, air passenger miles flown (10.6 million) have exceeded passenger miles traveled in Pullman cars on the railroad (10.2 million).

*Ready for service: TWA likes to emphasize the important role of its cabin staff in ensuring that passengers have a pleasant flight.* ▶

# English jet finds an American market

*Baltimore, Maryland, April 18*
An agreement was signed today for the licensed production in the US of Britain's English Electric Canberra light bomber. Construction will be undertaken by the Glenn L Martin Company.

The Canberra, or B-57 as the USAF will call it, is the first British-designed airplane to be built in the US since 1918, and the first US service airplane of foreign design accepted since 1945. An early Canberra B.Mk 2 flew to the US for evaluation against four US bombers. It flew the Atlantic on February 21 in a unofficial record time of 4 hours 37 minutes, at an average speed above 450mph. This was the first non-stop, unrefueled Atlantic flight by a jet. Following trials at Andrews Air Force Base, the Canberra has been selected on March 6 (→Aug 23, 1953).

*The Canberra has RR Avon engines; the B-57 will have J65 Sapphires.*

# France tests home-grown jet transport

*The SO.30R, a piston-engined airliner revamped as an experimental jet.*

*Villacoublay, France, 15 March*
Keen to join the passenger jet race, the French have modified a Sud-Ouest SO.30P Bretagne, a piston-engined airliner of the 1940s, as a flying test bed. Called the SO.30R, the test aircraft is powered by two Rolls-Royce Nene jet engines, built under license by Hispano-Suiza, housed in nacelles beneath the wings. It made its first flight here today to become the world's fourth jet transport to fly, after the Nene-Viking, D.H. Comet and the Avro Canada Jetliner.

The SO.30R performed quite well, but the Sud-Ouest company, based in Toulouse, is reported to be working on an even more interesting jet airliner. Currently called the X-210, this aircraft's design is believed to place the jet engines at the rear of the fuselage or even in the tail.

# Designers of new Mystère swept-wing jet-fighter win admirers

*Istres, France, February 23*
After a morning of taxiing and braking tests here today, Dassault test pilot Constantine Rozanoff lined up the company's latest jet fighter for its second take-off of the day. This time he took the MD.452.01 Mystère – a plane which has aroused the interest of several governments, even at the design stage – up for 40 minutes, and expressed delight with the aircraft.

The designers of the Mystère, intended as a competitor of the Grognard [*see page 492*], hope it will eventually be capable of supersonic speeds. Its engine is a 5,070-lb thrust Rolls-Royce Nene, built under license by Hispano-Suiza. In keeping with Dassault's tradition of developing an aircraft directly from a predecessor (thus reducing technical risk), the Mystère is based on the Ouragan, with swept-back wings and other improvements. The good reputation of the Ouragan has helped to attract interest; the fighter will enter service with the French Armée de l'Air in 1955 (→Jun 27, 1954).

# New DC-6 version can carry up to 102

*Santa Monica, Calif, February 2*
Keeping a finger on the pulse of its airline customers, the Douglas Aircraft Company has responded to the need for greater passenger capacity with its new DC-6B. The aircraft, which flew for the first time today, is based on the DC-6A freighter, which has a "stretched" fuselage 5 feet longer than the original DC-6. This offers a 7 per cent increase in passenger capacity at a modest 4 per cent increase in operating cost.

The DC-6B accommodates 54 passengers and has larger galleys and other facilities than the 64-seat domestic model. But with a high-density seating arrangement, the capacity could rise dramatically to 92 or even 102. Fundamental to the enlarged airliner has been the adoption of more powerful 2,400-hp Pratt & Whitney R-2800-CB16 or 2,500-hp R-2800-CB17 Double Wasp engines. With one CB17 installed, take-off weight is raised to 106,000 lb (→Aug 24).

*France's sleek swept-wing Mystère II fighter, which is powered by a Rolls-Royce Nene built under license.*

# USAF orders new Boeing heavy bomber

*Washington, DC, March 1*
The USAF has issued a letter of intent for production of Boeing's eight-engined intercontinental jet bomber, the B-52 – even though the prototype is not yet ready to fly. The advance order is based on concerns for national security as well as positive design studies and wind-tunnel tests of the bomber.

With the Korean War well under way, harassment of US military aircraft in the Arctic and other areas adjacent to the USSR, and the continued growth of the Soviet nuclear capability, military leaders view the B-52 as vital to maintaining US military superiority. They point out that it will be several years before the medium-range B-47 force is fully operational, and the B-36 will soon be obsolete. Failure to lay the groundwork now for a new intercontinental bomber force, capable of a deterring aggression by threatening a devastating nuclear strike on the USSR, will, it is argued, leave the US vulnerable, especially if foreign bases close to the USSR are lost (→ Apr 15, 1952).

*The prototype of the B-52 jet bomber, ordered into production by the USAF.*

# Hawker pins hopes on high-speed P.1067

*Surrey, England, July 20*
Those in the know are already calling it a masterpiece from the hands of the master. Britain's latest jet fighter prototype, the new Hawker P.1067, powered by a single Rolls-Royce Avon engine, flew for the first time today at Dunsfold, showing off the clean lines and smart handling which are typical of Hawker's chief designer, Sydney Camm, who has been designing aircraft for the Hawker Company since it first came to public notice back in the early 1920s. The P.1067 is the latest in Camm's long line of excellent models, starting with the biplane Hawker Hart and Hind. Perhaps his most famous aircraft, the Hawker Hurricane, proved its worth as the RAF's chief front-line fighter during the Battle of Britain.

The RAF needs an airplane to replace the Gloster Meteor, the twin-engined machine which pioneered the development of British jet fighters in the Second World War. Hawker's reservations about depending on a single engine have been allayed by Rolls-Royce's assurances about the Avon's reliability. In any case, a proportion are to have Armstrong Siddeley Sapphire engines.

Armed with four 30mm Aden cannon and capable of 700mph, the RAF's new P.1067 should prove a match in any battle with Soviet jet-fighters. Test pilot Neville Duke is delighted with its sweet handling (→ Sep 7, 1953).

*The Hawker P.1067 on a test flight.*

# Catalina flies from Australia to Chile

*Valparaiso, Chile, March 26*
An Australian Catalina flying boat has landed here after flying 8,450 miles from Sydney, achieving the first direct link between Australia and South America. It stopped at several places on the way, including Easter Island.

The machine which made the journey was specially adapted for the journey with auxiliary rockets for take-off. But even the production model has gone through many successful reincarnations in the 18 years since Isaac Laddon designed the first Consolidated PBY for the US Navy. The RAF gave it the name Catalina, which the Americans were to adopt, in 1939. The dependable airplane now serves in many countries as a sea-rescue and fire-fighting machine.

# Thunderjet is ready for action in Korea

*Farmingdale, New York, June 15*
The latest version of the USAF's Thunderjet fighter-bomber was unveiled at Republic Aviation here today. The chief new feature of the F-84G is a receptacle in the leading edge of the left wing, which enables it to be refueled in flight using the Boeing Flying Boom method.

First flown just after the Second World War, the original F-84 was superior to Lockheed's F-80 but suffered from maintenance difficulties which kept half of them grounded at any one time. It has been through many modifications, most notably the F-84F, which has swept-back wings. In-flight refueling gives the F-84G an extended range which will make it ideal as a long-range escort for the B-29 bombers in Korea (→ Mar 18, 1952).

# Jabara becomes the first jet-fighter ace

*A Lockheed F-80C takes off from a United Nations airfield in Korea.*

*Suwon, Korea, May 20*
USAF Captain James Jabara downed two MiG-15s today, his fifth and sixth "kills" of the Korean War, to become the America's first jet ace. Jabara, who did not return to Japan with his own unit when it rotated on May 7, has been flying from Suwon with the 335th Fighter Interceptor Squadron, waiting to add to his total of victories.

He got his chance today when 50 MiGs crossed the Yalu river to engage 36 US F-86 Sabres. Jabara was in one of two flights which came to their aid. He quickly got his F-86 on the tail of one of the enemy MiGs and peppered it with his six 0.50-in machine guns, until the pilot ejected at 10,000 feet. Jabara then sent a second MiG down in flames.

Jabara was able to score his victories despite being handicapped by an airplane which retained its auxiliary fuel tank after he had hit the jettison switch. Normally, this is enough reason to avoid combat, because of the limits it puts on the performance of an aircraft.

# Bell X-5 adjusts its wings in flight

## Olive Beech named woman of the year

*Wichita, Kansas, May 30*
President of the Beech Aircraft Company Olive Ann Beech was today elected Woman of the Year by The Women's National Aeronautical Association of the US. Beech took control of the company when husband Walter H. Beech died last year, and has kept it firmly on course despite her profound grief and the pressures of being a busy mother. She and Walter founded Beech Aircraft in 1931.

Olive started in 1921 as a secretary in the Travel Air Manufacturing Company, and was rapidly promoted to assist Walter Beech. They were married in 1930 and set out to realize a dream to "make the best airplanes in the world".

## Flying doctor finds final resting place

*Flynn: linked flying and doctoring.*

*Alice Springs, Australia, May 23*
The man who established Australia's Flying Doctor Service, John Flynn, has achieved his final ambition: to be buried in the heart of the outback which he served so well. Flynn, who died on May 5, was today buried 4 miles from Alice Springs, within sight of Mount Gillen. "Flynn of the inland" worked untiringly for the people of the outback after his first visit in 1912, setting up a radio network and a church patrol, as well as the doctor service (→ Mar 1, 1952).

*The wing's angle of sweep can be changed as the Bell X-5 gathers speed.*

*California, July 27*
Today over Edwards Air Force Base, test pilot Jean "Skip" Ziegler "redesigned" his airplane in flight. For the first time, the wings of his Bell X-5 were fully swept back to 60 degrees for high-speed flight and then forward to 20 degrees again for landing. The first in-flight wing sweeping took place on July 16, when the X-5's wings were pulled back from 20 to 30 degrees.

German aerodynamicists publicly explained in 1935 how sweeping the wings back could reduce the problem of compressibility of high Mach numbers, thus improving aircraft speed. This discovery was ignored in other countries until 1945, when US troops at Oberammergau, Germany, found the Messerschmitt P.1101, which was designed to test wings at different sweep angles, adjusted on the ground prior to take-off.

Today's X-5, one of two built by Bell, is in effect a P.1101 with the wings developed to change their sweep angle in flight. It is not intended to exceed about 700mph, but it will assist the design of later aircraft. Pivoted wings can be fitted with high-lift devices to assist take-off and landing.

## Airlines stunned by crash of new DC-6B

*Los Angeles, August 24*
The civil airline industry was stunned by the crash today of a United Air Lines Douglas DC-6B, which had entered service with the airline only on August 1. The airliner, en route from Boston to San Francisco, crashed into a hill 20 miles from Oakland airport, killing 50.

Powered by 4 R-2800 2,500-hp piston engines, the DC-6B is a version of the DC-6A freighter, itself a "stretched" version of the DC-6. The DC-6B first flew in February this year [*see page 498*]. Today's tragedy will arouse fears that the DC-6B may suffer fatal problems like the DC-6, which was grounded soon after entering service in 1947. This followed two fires, the first of which led to 52 deaths. The problem, fuel spilling into heaters, was solved and the DC-6 resumed flying in March 1948 (→ Nov 2).

## Viscount orders boost Vickers' confidence

*Surrey, England, November*
BEA was the first customer for the Vickers Viscount turboprop airliner, ordering 20 in August 1950. This month two more airlines have followed suit; within weeks of each other, Air France ordered 12 and Aer Lingus ordered four. The order from the French flag-carrier is particularly pleasing for Vickers-Armstrongs because sales to big foreign airlines are just the kind of breakthrough it is looking for.

No other manufacturer has anything comparable, and once some of Europe's, and possibly America's, airlines have turboprop travel, others will have to follow suit.

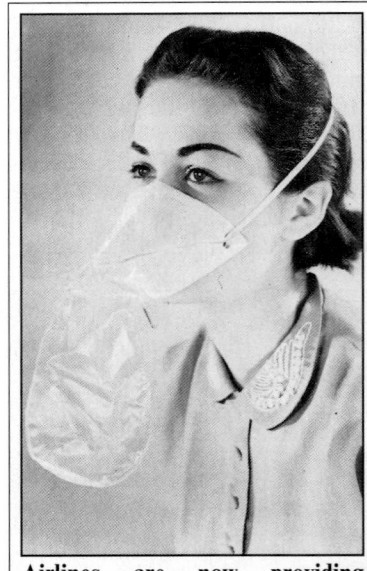

**Airlines are now providing oxygen masks for passengers, made of porous paper with a bag of polythene film. When needed, the masks can easily be made to drop down, already connected to the oxygen supply.**

# Skyrocket soars to two new records

*The all-rocket Skyrocket is released from its parent ship, a Boeing PB2B-1S.*

*Pilot William B "Bill" Bridgeman.*

*California, August 15*
Bill Bridgeman can claim to be not only just the world's fastest, but also its highest-flying pilot. Having flown the second Douglas D-558-II Skyrocket to Mach 1.88 eight days ago, today he took it from Edwards AFB up to 74,494 feet. Three Skyrockets were built to investigate supersonic flight with swept-back wings. Each was to use

both a Westinghouse J34 engine and a Reaction Motors bi-propellant rocket.

The Skyrocket was designed to be capable of airfield takeoffs, but to save fuel for maximum performance, it has to be carried aloft under an NB-52.

Last year the second Skyrocket had its turbojet removed and a 6,000-lb thrust XLR-8-RM-6 roc-

ket motor, fueled by diluted ethyl achohol and liquid oxygen, installed. The restarted program began disastrously. In December, three attempted air launches failed, then on Jan. 26 Bridgeman was released too early because of a communications failure. He saved the day by igniting the rocket, climbing to 40,000 feet, then landing back at Edwards.

## Latest figures show US airplane makers lead world market

*Washington, DC, October 9*
Figures from the US Civil Aeronautics Board (CAB) show that if you travel by air anywhere in the world you probably fly in an airplane built in the US. Eighty per cent of the world's airliners are American, with Douglas building 56 per cent of those. America's Aircraft Industries Association says that, in 1950, 759 aircraft were exported and this year the figure has risen to 894. Since 1948, aircraft worth $165 million have been exported to the rest of the world.

The percentage of Douglas transports is likely to fall. Douglas built large numbers of its popular DC-3 and DC-4 designs as the military C-47 and C-54 respectively. Many of these war-surplus airplanes became commercial airliners, but are now growing obsolete. The more modern DC-6 is very popular, but other airliners, such as the Lockheed Constellation, Convair 240 and 340, Martin 4-0-4 and Boeing Stratocruiser, are challenging the market dominance won for the Douglas Company by the DC-3 dating back to the 1930s.

## Korean airlift of US Marines proves combat value of helicopters

*Korea, September 21*
A helicopter lift of a US Marines company today to a peak northwest of Kansong, heralds a new development in airborne warfare. The operation began when six Sikorsky HRS-1 helicopters, the Marines' version of the USAF's H-19, hovered just above the 3,000-foot peak. Marines scrambled down ropes and used axes and shovels to clear a landing area for 15 more helicopters, which brought troops and 9 tons of equipment.

Four hours later the "choppers" were gone and the 228 Marines had set up defensive positions. The helicopters allowed the Marines to be landed as a group, rather than have them scattered as they would have been had they been dropped by parachute. They were also able to bypass the tough mountainous route, catching their North Korean adversaries off guard (→ Dec 16, 1952).

*In Korea even the small S-51 is fulfilling a vital role as an aerial ambulance.*

## US completes radar warning network

*Syracuse, New York, October 10*
The General Electric Company announced today that it has installed a network of the largest radar systems ever produced, in the Arctic and other areas, for the USAF. The radars will warn the US and Canada of any Soviet air attack from the polar region.

The cost, locations, and number of radar stations was not revealed. General Electric did say that about 400 men were required to keep each station in operation 24 hours a day. It also said that the radars were the most sophisticated ever built and were capable of detecting several raids simultaneously. In the Arctic regions, the radars are housed in radomes resembling colossal golf balls. Made of inflated rubberized fabric, they provide protection from the severe Arctic weather.

# British Comet jet flies impressive tests

*BOAC technicians carry out last-minute checks on the Comet's jet engines.*

**Hampshire, England, August 1**
Testing of the de Havilland Comet jet airliner continues to go well. The company is completing development flying from Hatfield, Hertfordshire, prior to the aircraft receiving its certification for use by public air carriers, which is expected early next year. At the same time, the Comet Unit of leading British airline BOAC, based at Hurn near Bournemouth, is half-way through a 500-hour program of route proving and crew training.

It has been established that there are no problems on the BOAC routes which the Comets will fly, and route proving has taken place to Johannesburg, Beirut, Karachi, New Delhi, Singapore and Jakarta. So far, the revolutionary airliner has set intercapital records between London and Rome, Copenhagen and Cairo (→ Jan 22, 1952).

# NACA finds formula for low transonic drag

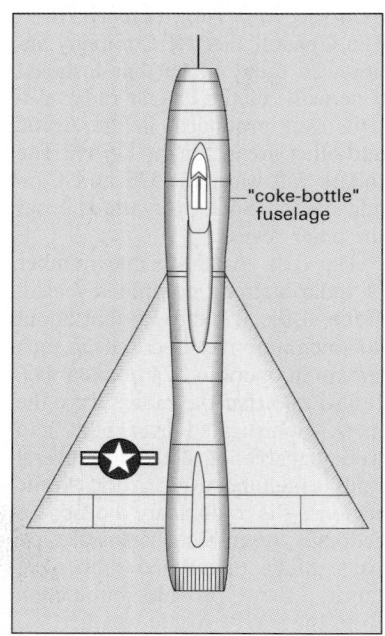

"coke-bottle" fuselage

*Langley, Virginia, December*
Experts here at the chief aerodynamic research center of America's National Advisory Committee for Aeronautics (NACA), are urgently searching for rules which can be applied to help the designers of jet aircraft. Since the middle of the Second World War, scientists have been concerned at the lack of knowledge of the transonic region, between about 0.8 and 1.2 times the speed of sound. The result is a crop of jets which are slower than expected and which experience buffeting or a tendency to dive, climb or roll.

It is known that if the fuselage is curved in at the root of the wings, giving it a so-called "Coke-bottle" shape, the airflow is improved. NACA's Richard Whitcomb is trying to draw a general rule from this discovery (→ Dec 21, 1954).

# Airlines race to update

*Los Angeles, October 30*
Lockheed's new L-1049 Super Constellation – the first production model of which flew on July 14 – has brought the company over $100 million in orders. Seven airlines have ordered 65 of the sleek transports. Eastern Air Lines, with 30 aircraft, is the biggest buyer and other orders have come from TWA (ten), KLM (nine), Air France (ten) and Trans-Canada (five). The "stretched" L-1049 is 18 feet 5 inches longer than the older Constellation, carries almost a third more passengers and is more powerful, with greater range.

The demand for these airplanes reflects a massive modernization going on in the US airline industry as carriers compete for passengers. TWA has 40 twin-engined Martin 4-0-4s on order, and Delta Air Lines is buying ten Convair 340s. Eastern is also buying 60 Martins as part of a $100 million fleet-replacement program. American Airlines, as well as the 17 DC-6Bs it will

*Variants of the "Super Connie".*

receive this year, has ordered 24 more and six DC-6As from Douglas, which has orders for almost 100 more. The L-1049 and the DC-6B may represent the peak of development of the propeller-driven airliner; the next leap forward in civil aviation is widely expected to be jet powered (→ Dec 17).

*All is serenity and comfort in the first-class cabin of the Super Constellation.*

# USAF orders an atomic-powered aircraft

*Washington, DC, September 5*
The USAF has awarded contracts today for the world's first nuclear-powered airplane. Convair, the manufacturer of the ten-engined, long-range B-36 bomber, will design the airplane while the world leader in power systems and jet engines, General Electric Company, will build the nuclear power plant. Sources said they expect the aircraft to be about the size of the B-36 with the power plant driving turboprop-type engines. Its flying time will be limited only by the endurance of its crew.

# Pakistan orders fleet for new state airline

*Karachi, May 25*
While much of the Third World's flying is based on small aircraft, mainly used for agricultural purposes and often paid for by foreign aid, there is also a growing passenger trade. Pakistan today ordered a fleet of Lockheed Super Constellations to form the basis of a new, state-owned flag carrier, Pakistan International Airways. It will supplement the activities of Orient Airways, which has been operating ser-

vices between East and West Pakistan, 1,500 miles apart.

The number of airlines in Asia has grown astonishingly since the war: in India alone, 11 companies have been licensed to fly on 51 routes. They have provided a wide variety of services, including forced mass movements of people, particularly between India and Pakistan when the two countries were partitioned after their independence from Britain.

*An aircraft used for spraying locusts is unloaded at Karachi, Pakistan.*

# Alouette helicopter passes flight trial

*Marseille, France, July 31*
The trim SNCASE SE.3120 Alouette [Lark] helicopter made its first flight today, piloted by Henri Stakenburg. There was just enough bodywork to write the registration, F-WGGD; the rest of the machine is an assembly of light tubes and a huge windcreen with a 203-hp Salmson piston engine.

Today's machine is a development of the SE.3110 test rig. The French army has already shown some interest, but chief engineer Jacques Lecarme is convinced that helicopters will soon be transformed by gas-turbine engines, which will improve their power, safety and reliability.

# Airlines introduce new tourist class

*London and Paris, December 15*
Facing competition from non-scheduled airlines which offer low fares for a no-frills service, many scheduled airlines are now taking coach or tourist class more seriously. British European Airways (BEA) and Air France announced today that they would start new tourist-class services between London and Paris next October.

The move follows the announcement on December 5, during an International Air Transport Association (IATA) conference in France, at Nice, that the 11 airlines flying the North Atlantic would introduce tourist class on transatlantic flights next May 1 (→ May 1, 1952).

# Javelin spearheads delta-wing design

*Gloucestershire, England, Nov 26*
The prototype of the world's first twin-jet, delta-winged warplane, the Gloster GA.5 Javelin, flew for the first time today at Moreton Valence. It is designed as a high-performance, long-endurance interceptor fighter capable of reaching high altitudes and high subsonic speeds. Its sophisticated electronics and radar should enable it to fly day and night in all weathers.

During today's 34-minute test flight, pilot Squadron Leader W A Waterton experienced severe buffeting of the rudder. On the ground, oil streaks revealed that the efflux from the Armstrong Siddeley Sapphire engines had interfered with the airflow at the rear of the fuselage; this could be prevented by extending the nozzle fairing.

# Catapult hurls navy planes into the air

*Portsmouth, England, December 31*
A revolutionary steam-powered catapult, which is now being tested by the Royal Navy carrier HMS *Perseus* for launching aircraft, is attracting attention from several navies. The device is based on a simple catapult, with below-deck piston rams providing the thrust. A complex system of steam valves adjusts the "throw" of the catapult to the weight of the aircraft. A towing bridle is hooked to a strong part of the machine, falling away as it clears the deck.

As warplanes have become heavier, navies have grown aware of the need for extra launch power. The US Navy favors a compressed-air and jet-fuel combustion catapult, but US sailors fear explosive consequences (→ Apr 30, 1952).

**A United Air Lines stewardess at LaGuardia airport, New York, comes to the end of an exhaustive check of her appearance before going on duty.**

De Havilland Canada constructed 465 robust DHC-3 Otter bushplanes.

Sud-Est's SE 3120 Alouette I prototype, powered by a Salmson engine.

Fouga's C.M.88-R Gemeaux I: two C.M.8-R Cyclopes, siamesed.

The Brochet M.B.80 two-seat light aeroplane had a 75-hp Minie engine.

The sleek Sud-Ouest SO 4000 jet bomber employed two Nene engines.

TWA and Eastern Air Lines were joint launch customers for the 40-passenger Martin 4-0-4. The only other customer for the 103 built was US Coast Guard.

Only 24 Lockheed L-1049 Super Constellations were built for launch customers Eastern and TWA. The first 92-seat production model flew in July.

No tail rotor: Sud-Ouest's SO 1120 Ariel III three-seat jet helicopter.

The J47-powered Chase XC-123A: first jet transport to fly in the US.

This CV-340 was used as the YC-131 Allison turboprop testbed.

The Sud-Est SE 3110 helicopter featured a pair of "butterfly" tail rotors.

The prototype of the Swift was the Avon-engined Supermarine 541.

Fiat's first jet-powered airplane was the G.80 two-seat fighter-trainer.

North American XA2J-1 experimental carrier-based turboprop bomber.

The Italian air force used Piaggio's P.148 side-by-side primary trainer.

McDonnell's F3H-1 Demon naval fighter was a failure.

The Supermarine 508 prototype naval fighter featured a butterfly tail.

Douglas's AD-4 Skyraider proved an outstandingly versatile airplane.

Fairey designed the small F.D.1 jet to research tailed delta-wing design.

*Max Holste's five-seat M.H.152 preceded the M.H.1521 Broussard.*

*The first Dassault MD.452 Mystère, an Ouragan with more sweep.*

*The Vickers-Armstrongs Valiant was the first of Britain's V-bombers; 111 were built, for bomber, photo-reconnaissance and tanker roles.*

*Douglas's XF4D-1 Skyray carrier-based jet-fighter featured a tailless delta wing based on research by Dr Alexander Lippisch; the US Navy had 420.*

*Chance Vought built 290 F7U-3 Cutlass variants for the US Navy.*

*The Sud-Ouest SO 6026 Espadon used a turbojet/rocket power plant.*

*Saab's 210 light jet was used to evaluate the double-delta-wing concept.*

*Gloster's GA.5 Javelin high-tailed delta-winged all-weather fighter.*

*The Panther with swept wings: the Grumman G-93, XF9F-6 Cougar.*

*The Handley Page H.P.88 tested the Victor bomber's crescent wing.*

*The two-seat Fokker S.14 Mach-Trainer: the first Dutch jet aircraft.*

*Short's four-engined SA.4 Sperrin: built to test jet-bomber technology.*

*The Avro 707A was the third of a family of five delta research aircraft.*

*Two Bell X-5 research aircraft were built for the USAF to investigate variable-sweep wings. The design was based on the wartime Messerschmitt P.1101.*

*India's first primary trainer was the Hindustan HT-2 tandem two-seater.*

*Commonwealth's CA-22 Winjeel: the RAAF's basic trainer prototype.*

*The Hawker P.1067, the prototype of the Hunter, nearly 2,000 of which were built before production ended in the mid-1970s. It had a single Avon turbojet.*

*De Havilland's 110, later the D.H.110 Sea Vixen naval fighter.*

*The Breguet 960 Vultur had a Mamba/Nene dual propulsion system.*

# 1952

1,240.89mph
USA
William Bridgeman
Douglas D-558-2
Aug 7, 1951

23,093 miles
USA
James Gallagher
Boeing B-50A
Mar 2, 1949

79,494ft
USA
William Bridgeman
Douglas D-558-2
Aug 15, 1951

420,000lb
USA
Boeing
B-52A Stratofortress

9,7000lb thrust
USA
Pratt & Whitney
J57-P-3

**California, January 1**
This state now has the highest number of civil aircraft registrations in the nation (9,845). Texas has 6,404 while Vermont only has 168.

**Cornwall, England, January 13**
The first of 52 Lockheed Neptune MR.1 twin-engined maritime reconnaissance aircraft, called the P2V-5 by the US Navy, arrive at St Eval for 217 Sqn.

**Sweden, January 21**
The Saab 210 experimental delta-winged research aircraft makes its first flight.

**London, January 22**
The de Havilland Comet 1 is awarded the first Certificate of Airworthiness to go to a jet airliner (→ Apr 15).

**Australia, March 1**
Trans-Australia Airlines takes over the Northern Territories' Flying Doctor Service based at Darwin and Alice Springs.

**London, March 13**
BEA introduces the Elizabethan-class Airspeed Ambassador into scheduled service, on its London/Paris route.

**Neubiberg, Germany, March 18**
Two USAF F-84 Thunderjets land after the longest sustained jet flight; they flew 2,800 miles from the USA in 4 hours 48 minutes, without refueling (→ Mar 10, 1953).

**Frankfurt, Germany, March 22**
A KLM airliner crashes while attempting to land in rain and fog, killing 44.

**Chicago, March 28**
United Air Lines becomes the first carrier to take delivery of the twin-engined Convair 340 airliner, an improved CV-240.

**Hertfordshire, England, April 8**
BOAC takes delivery at Hatfield of the first of an order of ten de Havilland Comet 1s (→ May 3).

**Seattle, Washington, April 15**
The Boeing YB-52 heavy bomber prototype flies for the first time; it is powered by eight turbojets carried in four pods under the wings (→ Apr 18).

**Washington, DC, April 30**
Following successful trials abroad Britain's HMS *Perseus*, the US Navy announces that it will install steam catapults on its own carriers starting with the USS *Hancock* (→ Jun 1, 1954).

**New York/London/Paris, May 1**
TWA, BOAC and Air France launch the world's first scheduled tourist-class flights on their transatlantic routes (→ May 2).

**North Pole, May 3**
A USAF Douglas C-47 transport equipped with a wheel/sky landing gear makes the first successful landing by an aircraft at the North pole; Lieutenant-Colonels William Benedict and Joseph Fletcher have to start the engines every fifteen minutes in order to stop them freezing while they carry out geological tests.

**Baltic Sea, June 16**
A Swedish air force PBY-5A Catalina amphibian is shot down by two Soviet fighters, wounding two of the crew, who are rescued by a German freighter; the Catalina was looking for the eight crew of a Swedish DC-3, which the Soviets shot down in the area three days ago while it was officially on a training flight (→ Mar 12, 1953).

**Washington, DC, July 2**
The USAF announces the existence of the Lockheed F-94C Starfire interceptor. This is the first USAF fighter to have no guns; the two-seater jet carries 48 Mighty Mouse rockets.

**Yokota, Japan, July 29**
A USAF North American RB-45 completes the first non-stop transpacific flight by jet; the plane refueled twice during the flight from Elmendorf, Alaska.

**Korea, August 9**
Lieutenant Peter Carmichael of the Fleet Air Arm, in a piston-engined Hawker Sea Fury FB Mk11, scores the first British "kill" of the war when he downs a MiG-15.

**London, August 11**
BOAC begins a weekly service with the Comet 1 jet-airliner between London and Colombo, Ceylon [Sri Lanka] (→ Oct 14).

**Dallas, Texas, August 16**
Braniff Airlines becomes America's sixth-biggest airline when it takes over Mid-Continent Airlines.

**North Atlantic, August 26**
An RAF Canberra bomber makes the first return crossing of the Atlantic in a single day; the eastbound flight from Gander, Newfoundland, to Aldergrove, Northern Ireland, takes a record 3 hours 25 minutes in a total time, including turnaround, of just over ten hours (→ Feb 1954).

**Woodford, England, August 30**
The prototype Avro 698, the RAF's new delta-winged long-range V-bomber, flies for the first time (→ Dec 24).

**Sydney, September 1**
Qantas introduces its Wallaby service between here and Johannesburg, via Perth, the Cocos Islands and Mauritius (→ Oct 16).

**Thule, Greenland, September 18**
The US and Denmark announce the completion of a huge Arctic airbase here.

**London, October 14**
BOAC starts flying a Comet 1 jet-airliner service from London to Singapore (→ Oct 20).

**Melun-Villaroche, France, Oct 16**
The two-seat Sud-Ouest SO.4050 Vautour [Vulture] fighter/light bomber, the first French twin-engined transonic warplane, flies for the first time.

**Australia, October 16**
Qantas inaugurates its first service to Europe, extending its route to Cairo on to Frankfurt via Beirut (→ Oct 1, 1953).

**New York, October 20**
Pan Am announces that it is to buy three Comet IIIs for delivery in 1956 (→ Oct 26).

**Korea, October 23**
In the war's biggest air battle so far, ten USAF B-29s escorted by 89 fighters are intercepted by about 150 MiGs while attacking Namsi airfield; three B-29s are shot down and three damaged beyond repair, while six MiGs are shot down.

**Tokyo, October 25**
Japan Air Lines begins operations with its own DC-4s and Japanese crews (→ Nov 23).

**Rome, October 26**
Doubts about the safety of the Comet airliner are raised for the first time when a BOAC Comet 1 is badly damaged in an accident during take-off (→ Apr 3, 1953).

**California, October 28**
The Douglas XA3D-1 Skywarrior carrier-based heavy attack-bomber flies for the first time from Edwards Air Force Base.

**Sweden, November 3**
The Saab-32 Lansen all-weather fighter makes its first flight.

**North Korea, November 3**
The US Navy Douglas F3D Skyknight flown by Commander Stratton downs a North Korean Yak-15; it is the first night "kill" in combat between jet fighters.

**USA, December 16**
The first US helicopter squadron begins operations as part of USAF Tactical Air Command.

*Lockheed's F-80 Shooting Star, the USAF's first operational jet-powered aircraft in 1945, is being used to test Marquardt ramjets.* ▶

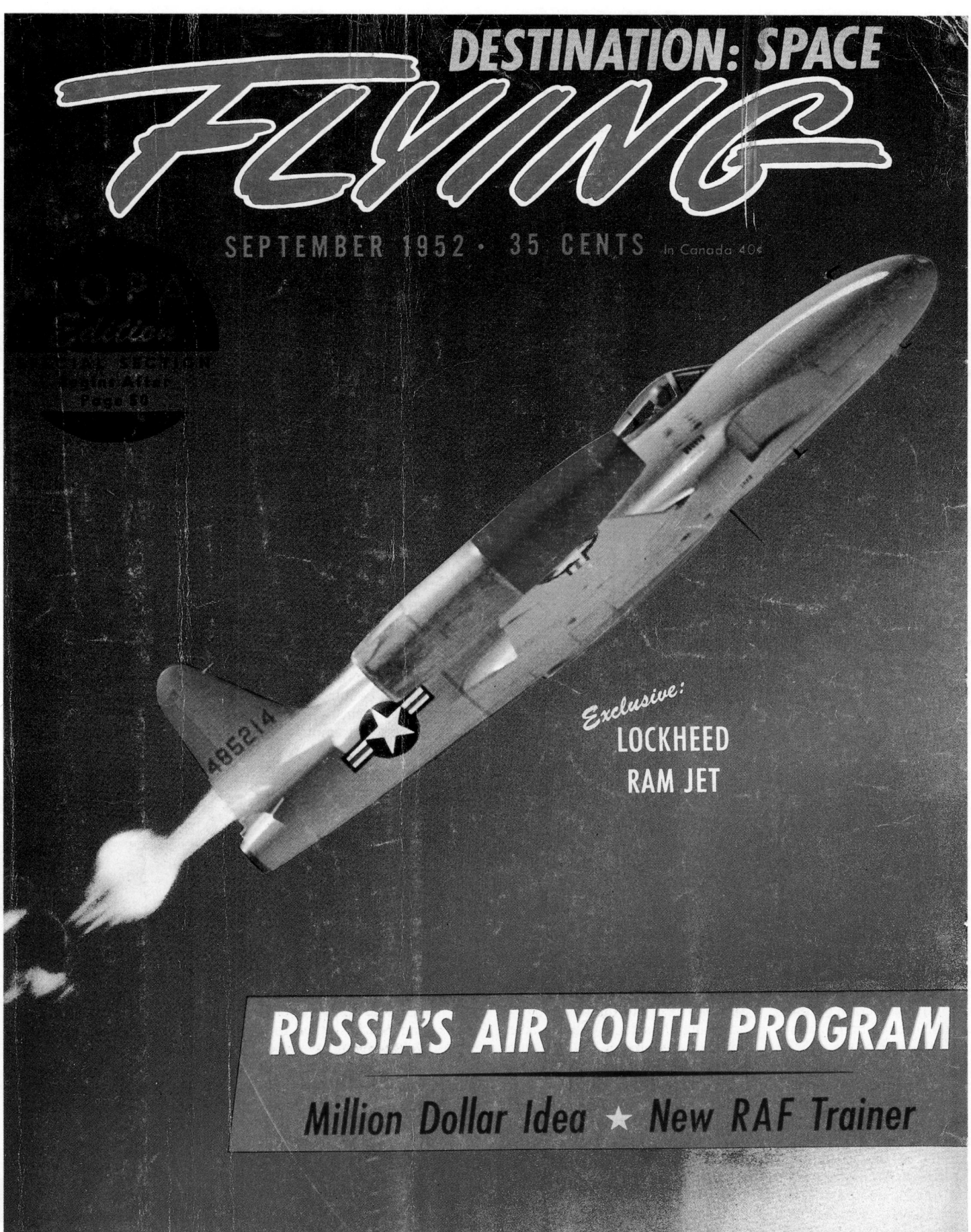

DESTINATION: SPACE

# FLYING

SEPTEMBER 1952 · 35 CENTS In Canada 40¢

*Exclusive:*
LOCKHEED
RAM JET

## RUSSIA'S AIR YOUTH PROGRAM

*Million Dollar Idea* ★ *New RAF Trainer*

# Bristol unveils its twin-rotor helicopter

*Bristol, England, January 3*
"Sox" Hosegood, principal helicopter test pilot of the Bristol Aeroplane Company, today completed the first air tests of the new Type 173. His comment: "I found it difficult to move in any direction except backwards!"

The 173 is Britain's first twin-engined helicopter. It uses two complete sets of 545-hp Alvis Leonides engines and rotors from the Syca-more, linked by a shaft with a freewheel clutch so that in the event of one engine failing, the other could drive both rotors. It has a tubular, stressed-skin fuselage, which in its production versions could seat 13 passengers.

The design team under Raoul Hafner expect to fit the 173 with wings to increase its cruising speed. It is hoped that production versions will interest BEA.

*The Bristol 173 helicopter is fitted with two 545-hp Alvis Leonides engines.*

# Newark airport is closed after crash

*Newark, New Jersey, February 11*
A National Airlines DC-6 with 62 people aboard crashed into a 50-family apartment block in heavily-populated Elizabeth, New Jersey, shortly after midnight last night. It is the third recent tragedy at Newark airport, and the Port of New York Authority has shut the airport pending an investigation.

Twenty-two died in the crash and four more people were reported to have died in hospitals which have about 40 other crash victims, many in critical condition. Twenty people from the rear of the aircraft are reported to have survived. The first crash in Elizabeth, on December 16, claimed 56 lives when a Miami Airlines Curtiss C-46 hit the Elizabeth river shortly after take-off. In the second, on January 22, an American Airlines Convair attempting to land in fog crashed into houses, killing seven residents and 23 on the plane (→ Nov 20).

# Boeing risks future on prototype model

*Seattle, Washington, April 22*
Today, just two weeks after the first de Havilland Comet jetliner was delivered to Britain's BOAC, Boeing announced that it is to invest $16 million of its own money in a jet transport. The airplane, the Model 367-80, is a speculative project which will be much bigger than the Comet. It will be a completely new design, but it will draw heavily on the company's experience in developing the B-47 Stratojet and B-52 Stratofortress jet bombers.

Boeing President William Allen initiated the project in 1950 after visiting Farnborough Air Show where he saw Britain's Comet jet airliner make its public debut. He saw an opportunity to put Boeing, which is known for its bombers but not competitive in the civil market, in contention with Lockheed and Douglas for the potentially huge market for America's first jet airliner (→ Jul 15, 1954).

# New queen flies in to a regal welcome

*Queen Elizabeth II emerges at Heathrow airport after the long flight home.*

*London, February 7*
Barely one week ago Princess Elizabeth waved goodbye to her father King George VI at London's Heathrow airport before leaving for a tour of Britain's East African colonies. Today, as Queen Elizabeth II, she arrived back at Heathrow aboard the BOAC Argonaut *Atalanta* to a country in mourning. The young queen, dressed entirely in black, was met among others by chairman of BOAC Sir Miles Thomas. The suddenness of her father's death meant that there was no time to arrange the normal procedure of an RAF VIP flight. In any case, BOAC had put the *Atalanta* at her disposal for the now abandoned tour with her husband Philip, Duke of Edinburgh.

Based on the Douglas DC-4, but built by Canadair in Montreal, the British airline's Argonauts are pressurized and powered by four Rolls-Royce Merlin engines.

# Pan Am tourist class packs in passengers

*New York, May 2*
Pan Am has opened its new transatlantic Rainbow service between New York and London. This takes advantage of the new tourist-class fares which has been established by the International Air Transport Association (IATA).

To maintain a high revenue on the new service despite offering low fares, Pan Am has opted to use its new 82-seat Douglas DC-6B, as this gives a particularly good cost per passenger mile. Pan Am's first-class transatlantic services will continue with the Boeing Stratocruiser and the Lockheed Constellation. Unlike other DC-6Bs which have so far been delivered, Pan Am's have been specially modified to have a 107,000-lb take-off weight and extra fuel capacity (→ May 3).

*Another attempt to win passengers.*

# Convair and Boeing vie for USAF's bomber role

*Boeing's YB-52, competing to be the USAF's first strategic jet bomber.*

*The Convair YB-60 is slower than the rival YB-52 but considerably cheaper.*

**Fort Worth, Texas, April 18**
The biggest jet airplane ever built, the Convair YB-60, today made a successful first flight at Carswell Air Force Base here. Alongside, in Convair's vast plant, there is a second YB-60 nearing completion.

Convair hopes to win a potentially enormous USAF contract for the first strategic jet bomber by basing the YB-60 on its existing B-36. Large parts of the fuselage, landing gear and other items are almost identical, although the new YB-60 has huge wings swept back at 35 degrees and a new swept tail. Housed in four twin pods under the wing are eight of Pratt & Whitney's new J57 turbojets. The same type of engine powers the YB-60's rival, the Boeing YB-52, which first flew three days ago.

The Boeing is totally new. Although the YB-60 is larger, Convair expects to sell it for less than the YB-52 and is trying to convince the USAF of the economies resulting from its similarity to the B-36. However, the USAF sees the global nuclear deterrent role of Strategic Air Command as so crucial that nothing but the best will do. Many consider that the YB-52 must be better than any derivative design; for example, it is likely to be almost 100mph faster than the Convair.

## Flying boat boosts US Navy hunt for subs

*The P5M Marlin flying boat can carry and launch both mines and torpedoes.*

**Norfolk, Virginia, April 23**
Building on its experience of anti-submarine warfare during the Second World War, the US Navy has invested in a new flying boat with a range of 2,000 miles. The boat, the Martin P5M-1 Marlin, was delivered today to its first operational unit, Patrol Squadron VP-44.

The Marlin uses the latest acoustic technology, including Jezebel, a passive sonar buoy dropped into the sea from a tube in the fuselage, to hunt its prey. The buoy automatically hoists an aerial and releases a sensor on an underwater cable to listen for noise coming from a submarine. Military scientists dream of an electronic data bank in which the aircraft carries a pre-recorded sonic identity of submarines for immediate comparison.

## Clouds save French DC-4 from Soviets

**Berlin, April 29**
Everything was peaceful at 6,500 feet as the Air France DC-4 – registration mark F-BELI – continued to descend. It was flying along the air corridor over East Germany, approaching Berlin's Tempelhof airport at the end of a scheduled flight from Frankfurt.

The tranquility was shattered by the sudden appearance of two Russian MiG-15 fighters. Passengers who had been fastening their seatbelts and extinguishing their cigarettes watched, stunned, as the stubby interceptors came very close alongside, then pulled away. Seconds later the MiGs fired two bursts of gunfire into the DC-4, injuring three people on board.

Captain Schvallinger dived into the clouds to avoid his attackers and made a safe landing with the DC-4. After the wounded were taken away, the aircraft was examined and found to be badly damaged. Enraged by the incident, France has protested to the Soviet Union (→ Jun 16).

## Air hostesses swap transatlantic roles

**Paris, May 3**
Air France's first tourist-class service from New York to Paris arrived today at Orly airport after a successful flight. On board were two women who are taking part in an unusual experiment.

American air hostess Jane Crocco, who works for Capital Airlines, was arriving in France to study the working practises of the stewardesses employed by Air France. She was accompanied on the flight to Paris by a hostess for Air France, Mademoiselle Rivet, who has been stationed in New Orleans over the past few weeks in order to gain some experience of the life of a stewardess working for Capital.

The exchange is part of a joint scheme arranged by Air France and Capital to discover ways of improving the service offered by their hostesses to the flying public. Both women will eventually file reports to their respective bosses on what they have seen and heard during the exchange (→ Apr 2, 1953).

# 'Yoke Peter' launches age of the passenger jet

*In December 1953 the world will celebrate the fiftieth anniversary of the Wright Brothers' first, tentative, powered flights at Kitty Hawk. Today the aviation industry celebrates the first passengers to fly seven miles above the Earth, in a luxurious, pressurized jet airliner, from one end of the world to the other in a few hours. Many people alive today, some of them on this flight, were born into a world in which even the idea of manned flight was an impossible lunatic dream. But the years between these two events have seen aviation progress at such a pace that such dreams are now a commonplace.*

*A great day for de Havilland and British aviation: the Comet G-ALYP "Yoke Peter" is about to fly to Johannesburg. It has already flown for over 500 hours.*

**London, May 3**
A new era in commercial air travel began yesterday when a BOAC de Havilland Comet 1, G-ALYP *Yoke Peter*, took off from London for South Africa on the world's first scheduled passenger flight by a jet airliner. During the flight, which inaugurates a regular jet service to Johannesburg, the Comet cruised at about 490mph to complete the staged journey of 6,724 miles today, after 23 hours 34 minutes. It is a great day for the de Havilland company and for all those in Britain who have shown faith in jet technology. Critics have been muted and many airlines are now beating a path to de Havilland's door.

So successful has been the development of the Comet that less than three years have passed since the prototype first took to the air. The second prototype was loaned to BOAC's Comet Unit at Hurn near Bournemouth, Hampshire, in April last year to begin a crew-training and route-development program.

Comet-proving flights were made to Beirut, New Delhi, Jakarta, Johannesburg and Singapore. The flights to South Africa, from January this year, carrying freight only, established future passenger schedules. The Comet's official Certificate of Airworthiness, the first for a commercial jet, was awarded on January 22. Initial production at Hatfield, Hertfordshire, has covered ten Comet 1s, all for BOAC. Deliveries to the airline started on April 8 this year; *Yoke Peter* was the first of these.

The flight has stolen much of the thunder from Pan Am's cheap transatlantic tourist-class Rainbow service, which began two days ago [see page 508]. Yet Pan Am's ability to carry 82 passengers from New York to London may not be lost on those debating the small (36-seat) capacity of the Comet 1 (→ Aug 11).

*Albert Henshaw, the first person to book for the flight, checks in at London.*

*Pressmen immortalize the moment as passengers board the historic flight.*

# US pilots give F-86 the edge over MiG-15

*Washington, DC, June 5*
A report presented to defense chiefs here today makes encouraging reading for students of the the air war in Korea. It is a detailed analysis of aerial combat between the two sides' best single-seat jet fighters: the USAF's F-86 Sabre and the Soviet equivalent, the lighter and better-armed MiG-15. The report shows that the "kill" ratio between the two is between 7:1 and 8:1 in favor of the Sabre. The results are not solely due to the aircraft; they owe an enormous amount to the quality and aggression of the US pilots, many of them veterans of the Second World War. These results are also despite being outnumbered in the air, being outgunned and having the handicap of fighting at the extreme range of the Sabre while the MiGs have a safe refuge in Chinese Manchuria.

The Chinese air force has 1,000 jet fighters, but as their losses rise in combat so, at last, the balance is tipping the UN's way. It cannot

*An F-86 test firing five-inch rockets.*

happen too soon for hard-pressed UN troops on the ground as well as pilots. Bombing has so far failed to cut Communist supply lines, and, with some exceptions, tactical air support has missed its targets.

# Flight of Princess nearly ends in tragedy

*The huge Princess skims over the water prior to take-off on another flight.*

*Hampshire, England, September 2*
Thousands cheered the huge, 105-seat Saunders-Roe SR.45 Princess as it flew low over the Farnborough Air Show today – unaware that the captain had been fighting furiously to avoid disaster.

Test pilot Geoffrey Tyson had put the 150-ton, ten-engined flying boat into a fast sustained bank at the climax of its display. Suddenly, as the huge machine swerved towards the crowd, its highly advanced electrical control systems

failed to respond properly. Tyson fought desperately with the controls until, with only seconds to spare, he wrenched the wings level and the Princess boomed over the unwitting crowd.

The SR.45, which first flew on August 21, is the largest all-metal airplane in the world. As flying boats fall out of favor, it faces an uncertain future, especially as the cost of each aircraft has soared from the £2.8 million estimated in 1946 to over £10.8 million.

# Two S-55 helicopters fly across Atlantic

*Prestwick, Scotland, July 31*
Two Sikorsky H-19s, designated S-55 by their American manufacturer, landed here today after setting a new world distance record for helicopters.

The first two machines to make a transatlantic helicopter flight left Westover, Massachusetts, on July 13 and flew via Maine, Labrador, Greenland and Iceland, in a total flying time of 42 hours 25 minutes. They covered the 920 miles of ocean between Keflavik, Iceland, and Prestwick in 11 hours.

The Sikorsky S-55 has become a familiar sight in both Europe and the USA. It figures prominently in

newsreel reports of rescue operations at sea and in mountain regions. Over the past three years, the Sikorsky S-55 has gained an excellent reputation among pilots. Structural modifications appear to have solved initial problems encountered with its stability in flight. Its Pratt & Whitney R1340 Wasp engine has been moved forward slightly, while the fuel tanks have been placed directly under the cabin floor. The S-55 is not a particularly light helicopter, weighing in at 7,975 lb. Its cockpit has been placed above the cabin, which has a large sliding door providing easy access and cargo loading.

*The blunt-nosed Sikorsky S-55 provides excellent visibility for the pilot.*

# France unveils first military jet trainer

*France, July 23*
The team behind the superb Fouga Cyclope jet-powered glider is again triumphant after today's first flight of its twin-engined Magister, the world's first jet-trainer aircraft. The two-seat Magister, developed by Robert Castello and Joseph Szydlowski, is fitted with two Turbomeca Marboré II engines each delivering 880 lb of thrust. The light, powerful airplane promises speeds as high as 400mph, combined with a range of some 600 miles. The first venture by Castello and Szydlowski into jet-powered flight, the Sylphe, first flew on July 14, 1949.

# Britannia aims to rule the airways

*Bristol, England, August 16*
The turboprop Britannia airliner destined for BOAC's long-haul routes, the Bristol Type 175, made a successful debut here today. The prototype is fitted with four Bristol Proteus 625 turboprops, but it began as a piston-engined design seating from 32 to 36 passengers. This was in response to BOAC's specification in 1947 for a medium-range transport. During development, the plans were revised and the prototypes are both fitted with Proteus turboprop engines. The resulting configuration will carry up to 90 passengers and have considerable range (→ Feb 4, 1954).

# Air show horror kills 28

*Part of the disintegrated D.H.110 hits the ground in an explosion of debris.*

*Hampshire, England, September 6*
Disaster hit the annual Farnborough Air Show today when the first prototype de Havilland D.H.110 disintegrated in flight above the main runway. More than 100,000 watched in horror as wreckage plowed into the crowd, killing 28 and injuring 60 others, many seriously. D.H.110 test pilot Squadron Leader John Derry, who four years ago became the first Briton to fly faster than the speed of sound, perished in the tragedy, together with observer Tony Richards.

All week Derry and Richards had been putting on a brilliant show in the twin-tailed, twin-engined D.H.110 second prototype. Their routine would begin with a dive from 40,000 feet, accelerating to beyond Mach 1 to cause a sonic boom. Then they would pull away at low level in a left-hand turn.

Today the second prototype was undergoing maintenance, and so the first prototype they collected from the de Havilland works at Hatfield, Hertfordshire, instead. The display began as usual, with the aircraft causing a sonic bang and then pulling round to begin the low-level routine. But then tragedy struck: the D.H.110 was heading for the densest part of the crowd when the leading edges of the outer wings began to buckle. In a split second the wings ripped from the fuselage, and then the tail and engines broke away and a cloud of lethal debris hurtled toward the spectators. Nearly all the casualties were caused by one engine.

An analysis of the disaster, which must surely put the D.H.110's future in doubt, will be helped by the fact that it was captured on film by amateur cameramen.

# Orders pour in for new Viscount airliner

*London, November*
In a move which may prove significant for the future of the Vickers Viscount turboprop airliner, Trans-Canada Air Lines has ordered 15 Type 724s, specially adapted for cold-weather operations. Canada has similar operating regulations to the US, and its acceptance of the Viscount could be a step toward the aircraft breaking into the difficult US market. The first airline to order the Viscount was Britain's BEA. Then, in November 1951, Air France became the first foreign airline to place an order, acquiring 12 Type 708s. Ireland's Aer Lingus ordered four Type 707s in the same month and Trans-Australia Airlines ordered six Type 720s in June this year. All these types can seat 47 to 53 passengers (→ Jan 3, 1953).

*A Vickers Viscount 701 in the livery of its first buyer, BEA.*

# US pilot breaks sound barrier in France

*Brétigny, France, November 12*
Piqued to learn that the first man to create a sonic "boom" in France was an American, French pilot Roger Carpentier today repeated the exploit at the controls of of a Dassault Mystère II. The flight was made near this airfield south of Paris. On October 28 US pilot Marion Davis, also flying a Mystère II jet, became the first to break the sound barrier in France. Davis's aircraft was about to go into service with the French air force and was therefore already armed with four 20mm cannon. He took off from the Melun-Villaroche air base, also south of the French capital, along with two fellow US pilots flying escort in their Sabres.

# SAS airliner is first to fly over North Pole

*Copenhagen, November 20*
After five years of intensive route proving, a scheduled passenger service over the Arctic between Europe and California is finally set to become a reality.

Today a DC-6B being delivered to Scandinavian Airlines System (SAS) landed here to complete the first ever flight over the polar regions by an airliner. The DC-6B took exactly 23 hours 38 minutes to fly the 5,852 miles from Los Angeles in a total journey time of just over 28 hours. It refueled twice, at Edmonton, Alberta, and at the new USAF base at Thule, Greenland. SAS has now formally asked US aviation authorities for permission to operate a regular service between Copenhagen and Los Angeles flying over northern Greenland and Canada.

Because of the route's proximity to the magnetic North Pole, compass navigation is impossible and Bendix Aviation is testing a gyroscope system. Ground-based radio beacons have also been set up along the polar route (→ Nov 16, 1954).

*Dassault's Mystère II, the first French-built jet to break the sound barrier.*

## 'The Sound Barrier' is top film of year

*Tragedy in "The Sound Barrier".*

*Britain, December 31*

The melodramatic efforts of a British aircraft manufacturer and his test pilot to break *The Sound Barrier* packed British fans into the cinemas this year. The film, released in the US as *Breaking the Sound Barrier*, stars top British actor Ralph Richardson as the manufacturer who is determined to prove that the barrier can be broken, and Nigel Patrick as his pilot. Directed by David Lean, it includes stunning air sequences.

## Heat no barrier for titanium Stiletto

*California, October 20*

Douglas test pilot Bill Bridgeman took off from Edwards Air Force Base today on the first flight of an unusual dart-like airplane. The Douglas X-3, aptly called the Stiletto, is 67 feet long, and it has a tiny 22-foot wing-span.

Powered by two Westinghouse J34 turbojets, the X-3 has been designed to exceed Mach 2. Its airframe is made mainly of titanium to withstand the heat caused by friction at such speeds. But the J34 engines may not be powerful enough to propel the X-3 even to Mach 1 and may be replaced by more powerful J46 engines. Alternatively, the X-3 may be fitted with rockets (two Bell X-1 engines) and dropped from a YB-60. Flight tests have already been delayed for over a year by cooling problems, tank leaks and structural modifications.

# Britain invests in V-bomber future

## Victor joins Valiant and Vulcan in fleet

*Wiltshire, England, December 24*

The third of Britain's V-bomber prototypes, the Handley Page Victor, took to the air today at Boscombe Down. It joins the Vickers Valiant, which flew on May 18 last year, and the Avro Vulcan, which made its maiden flight on August 30 this year. The trio will give RAF Bomber Command, which is equipped mainly with Lincolns, an all-jet backbone to carry Britain's nuclear deterrent. All three have a crew of five – two pilots, two navigator/bomb aimers and a radio communications and electronic countermeasures officer, all housed in a pressurized compartment.

The Victor and Vulcan are based on RAF specification B.35/46 for a four-jet bomber which can carry heavy loads, including nuclear weapons, over long distances at high subsonic speeds, in the stratosphere around 50,000 feet. The Valiant has four Rolls-Royce Avon RA.3 engines each giving 6,500 lb of thrust. Production aircraft will have Avons with 10,500 lb of thrust.

The Vulcan is a massive delta-wing. Research into the wing shape has been in hand since 1949 using the Avro Type 707 research airplanes, which confirmed that the delta shape offers good high- and low-speed flying characteristics, while providing a low wing-loading at high altitude and plenty of room for fuel tanks and the Avon engines, which are the same as the Valiant's.

Handley Page also tested its Victor wing shape on a small research airplane, resulting in a swept-wing which has less sweepback toward the tips. The pressurized crew compartment was originally intended to be jettisonable since ejecting at over 500mph at 50,000 feet is likely to be fatal. But as the problems proved too great, they will have ejection seats. The Victor can carry up to 35,000 lb of conventional bombs, and the bomb bay has to be big enough to carry a nuclear weapon which could be up to 6 feet in diameter and 30 feet in length. The engines are AS Sapphires.

*The delta wing marks out the Avro 698 Vulcan from its fellow V-bombers.*

*The Vickers Valiant has the most traditional appearance of the new trio.*

*The distinctive high tailplane characterizes the Handley Page Victor bomber.*

Hunting's P.66 Pembroke transport was developed from the civil Prince.

Italy's Nardi F.N.333 amphibian: powered by a 145-hp Continental.

The two-seat SIPA 300 Minijet flew only 347 days after design started.

The production Lockheed R7V-2 Super Constellations flew in 1952.

Douglas's X-3 lacked thrust, and failed to reach its design speed.

The Douglas XA3D-1 Skywarrior was a carrier-borne naval bomber.

Four Bristol Proteus turboprops powered the 90-seat Bristol 175 Britannia 100 long-range airliner when it entered service with BOAC in February 1957.

Convair's YB-60 was basically a B-36 with swept wings and jet engines.

The Saab A32 Lansen was a two-seat all-weather ground-attack aircraft.

Grumman's S-2 Tracker was designed as a carrier-borne ASW aircraft.

Tupolev's Tu-88 prototype became the Tu-16 ("Badger" to Nato) in service. Versatile and reliable, it was used in many roles and served for many years.

Piasecki's H-21 Workhorse picked up the nickname "Flying Banana".

The Mil Mi-4 (known as "Hound" to Nato), the first successful Soviet helicopter. Built in large numbers, it served in both civil and military duties.

Piper's PA-23 Apache 235 proved to be an enormously popular light twin.

Britain's Royal Navy bought 10 Sikorsky S-55 Whirlwind HAR.21s.

The 14-passenger CASA C 202 Halcon had two ENMA Beta engines.

The Cessna XL-19B Bird Dog: powered by a Boeing XT50 turboprop.

The Lockheed P2V-5 Neptune was a dedicated long-range maritime patrol and ASW aircraft which replaced aircraft like the Consolidated Privateer.

The US Navy's North American AJ-2P Savage reconnaissance aircraft.

Atar's 101C-powered Sud-Ouest SO 4050 Vautour prototype flew as a two-seat fighter; it was also planned as a single-seat attack and two-seat bomber.

The Max Holste M.H.1521 Broussard was developed for utility duties.

The giant Hughes XH-17 cargo helicopter remained only experimental.

Avro's prototype delta-winged 698 Vulcan, the second RAF V-bomber, entered service in February 1957; the last was delivered in January 1965.

The Cantinieau MC.101 was an experimental two-seat light helicopter.

The twin-engined Bristol 173 was developed into the RAF's Belvedere.

Macchi's MB.323 two-seat basic trainer, to replace NA's T-6 Texan.

The prototype eight-jet Boeing XB-52 Stratofortress seen here flew after the first production YB-52. The tandem crew cockpit was changed to side-by-side.

Handley Page's Marathon T.11: 28 were RAF navigation trainers.

Caproni's prototype Trento F.5 basic jet-trainer had wing-root intakes.

Saunders-Roe built three giant ten-engined SR.45 Princess flying boats.

The Fouga Cyclope, aerodynamic forerunner of the Magister trainer.

The Dassault M.D.453 Mystère de Nuit: a two-seat all-weather fighter.

The Boulton Paul P.120 was a single-seat delta-winged research aircraft.

The USAF paid for 225 Dassault M.D.452 Mystère IVAs under the Offshore Procurement Program. They had Hispano-Suiza Verdon jet engines.

# 1953

1,650mph
USA
Charles Yeager
Bell X-1A
Dec 12, 1953

23,093 miles
USA
James Gallagher
Boeing B-50A
Mar 2, 1949

83,253ft
USA
Marion Carl
Douglas D-558-2
Aug 21, 1953

420,000lb
USA
Boeing
B-52A Stratofortress

19,181lb thrust
USSR
Mikulin
AM-3D

**USA, January 1**
All-American Aviation changes its name to Allegheny Airlines.

**Oxfordshire, England, January 2**
The first of an order of about 430 US Sabre fighters, the RAF's first supersonic jet, arrives at RAF Abingdon.

**London, January 3**
British European Airways receives its first Vickers V.701 Viscount turboprop airliner (→ Apr 18).

**Cologne, Germany, January 6**
On the anniversary of its creation in 1926 as Deutsche Luft Hansa, the airline Lufthansa, which ceased to exist at the end of the Second World War, is provisionally revived as Luftag – Aktiengesellschaft für Luftverkehrsbedarf [Air Travel Services Limited] (→ Dec 20).

**Wichita, Kansas, January 15**
Mooney Aircraft moves its manufacturing plant from here to Kerrville, Texas (→ Sep 3).

**Sembawang, Singapore, February 1**
The RAF commissions its first helicopter squadron, 194 (Casualty Evacuation) Squadron.

**France, March 2**
The Sud-Ouest Aviation SO 9000 Trident jet and rocket-powered fighter makes its first flight, using just its two wing-tip-mounted Turbomeca jets; it also has a rocket engine in the fuselage.

**Germany, March 10**
A USAF F-84G Thunderjet is shot down near the Czech frontier by two Czech MiG-15s; the pilot ejects and lands safely in Czechoslovakia.

**Germany, March 12**
An RAF Avro Lincoln is shot down by MiG fighters while flying just inside (the British version) or outside (the Soviet version) the air corridor linking the cities of Hamburg and Berlin; six of the seven crew perish.

**The Hague, March 27**
The royal Netherlands air force is established as an independent service by royal decree.

**London and Paris, April 1**
BEA and Air France introduce tourist-class fares on their European routes.

**London, April 3**
BOAC inaugurates a weekly service to Tokyo with Comet 1s; the journey takes 33 hours 15 minutes (→ May 2).

**Atlanta, Georgia, May 1**
Delta Air Lines absorbs Chicago and Southern Air Lines, acquiring routes linking Chicago and New Orleans as well as international routes to the Caribbean.

**Canada, May 15**
Central British Columbia Airways is renamed Pacific Western Airlines after acquiring several smaller operators.

**Santa Monica, Calif, May 18**
The piston-engined Douglas DC-7 makes its first flight (→ Nov 29).

**London, May 21**
Dan-Air Services, a subsidiary of London shipping brokers Davies and Newman, is established as a charter airline operator.

**Yorkshire, England, June 14**
The Blackburn Beverley, the first British military aircraft built especially to carry heavy loads for airdrops, flies for the first time, at Brough; it is powered by Bristol Centaurus 173 engines.

**Japan, June 18**
In the first air tragedy to claim over a hundred lives, a USAF C-124 Globemaster II crashes on take-off from Tachikawa air base near Tokyo; all 129 military personnel aboard perish.

**Bonn, July 1**
The Western Allies hand over control of civil air traffic in West Germany to the Federal Republic.

**New York, July 8**
New York Airways, America's first scheduled passenger helicopter carrier, begins service between Idlewild, LaGuardia and Newark.

**Washington, DC, July 29**
Two days after the Korean War armistice, the USAF announces that it shot down 839 MiG-15s and probably destroyed 154 more in the 37-month conflict; UN air forces lost 110 aircraft in air combat, 677 to ground fire and 213 to "other causes".

**New Delhi, August 1**
Eight private carriers are nationalized as Indian Airlines Corporation.

**Australia, August 14**
The sound barrier is broken over Australia for the first time by Flight Lieutenant Bentleigh, RAAF, in the first Australian-built Sabre fighter at Avalon, Victoria.

**Paris, August 26**
Air France inaugurates its first regular Comet service, from Paris to Beirut via Rome (→ Aug 27).

**Hertfordshire, England, August 27**
The first production de Havilland Comet 2 makes its first flight at Hatfield (→ Jan 10, 1954).

**Brussels, September 1**
Sabena begins the world's first scheduled international passenger helicopter service, linking Brussels, Antwerp and Liège, Belgium, Maastricht and Rotterdam, The Netherlands, and Lille, France.

**Washington, DC, September 1**
The USAF carries out the first in-flight refueling of one jet by another; a Boeing KB-47B Stratojet, a tanker derived from the B-47 bomber, refuels a B-47.

**Kerrville, Texas, September 3**
Mooney Aircraft's M-20 model, a four-seater plane with a 150-hp Lycoming engine, makes its first flight. The "backwards" tail makes it easy to spot (→ Oct 15, 1960).

**Seoul, September 21**
A North Korean pilot lands his MiG-15 near the South Korean capital, earning a $100,000 reward offered by UN commander General Mark Clark.

**Sydney, October 1**
Following the withdrawal of British government backing, British Commonwealth Pacific Airlines is dissolved; Qantas will take over its transpacific route, allowing it to operate to North America for the first time (→ Apr 3, 1954).

**New Zealand, October 10**
The Christchurch Centenary air race from London to Christchurch is won by Squadron Leader R L E Burton and Flight Lieutenant D H Gannon in an RAF Canberra PR.7; they cover the 11,792 miles in 23 hours 50 minutes 42 seconds.

**New York, October 20**
A TWA Lockheed Super Constellation carrying 56 passengers completes America's first scheduled, non-stop transcontinental flight, flying from Los Angeles in 8 hours 17 minutes; westbound flights will still stop at Chicago.

**California, October 24**
Convair's YF-102A Delta Dagger fighter/interceptor prototype makes its first flight.

**New York, November 29**
American Airlines introduces the Douglas DC-7 on its scheduled New York/California Mercury service (→ Apr 4, 1954).

**Montreal, December 29**
The International Civil Aviation Organization says that 1953 is the first year in which the world's airlines (excluding the USSR and China) carried more than 50 million passengers (52,400,000).

*Gloster Meteor T.7s of the RAF Central Flying School's first jet aerobatic team, the "Meteorites", based in Gloucestershire, England.* ▶

# The Cessna 310 is a very fast light twin

*The Cessna 310 is almost twice as fast as a Cessna 120.*

**Wichita, Kansas, January 3**
Cessna's latest aircraft prototype took to the air for the first time today. The Model 310 is a lightweight, twin-engined airplane which seats a total of six. It is a typical example of the smaller aircraft which are favored by corporations and, given its impressive performance figures, it looks sure to put the Cessna company in a strong position in this lucrative market.

Powered by a pair of 230-hp Continental engines, the 310 is de-signed to reach a maximum speed of 238mph at sea level and 223mph while cruising at 7,500 feet. Its range is reckoned to be 1,740 miles. A pair of large wing-tip fuel tanks not only allow an extended range, but also serve to channel airflow over the outer wing, enhancing lift.

Initial tests have shown the airplane to be remarkably quiet in performance, which would be a key selling point. However, the 310 does not have a pressurized cabin. (→ May 9, 1961)

# Eastern's last DC-3 bows out of service

*One of Eastern's "Great Silver Fleet": the DC-3 has finally been retired.*

**Miami, January 31**
Eastern Air Lines has bid farewell to the last of its Douglas DC-3s, which made its final scheduled flight today. For so many years the stalwart of major airlines flying trunk routes, since the arrival of four-engined airliners, DC-3s have been moved to secondary local ser-vices. These routes are despised by some operators, who fly them principally to meet the requirements of their federal certifications. Others, such as Eastern, believe they generate passengers for their major routes. Eastern has bought Martin 4-0-4s as modern twin-engined replacements for its ageing DC-3s.

# American angled-deck carrier starts tests

**USA, January 12**
The US Navy today began operational flight tests of the world's first aircraft carrier with an angled flight deck, the USS *Antietam*. The Navy says that the angled deck, invented by Captain D R F Campbell of Britain's Royal Navy, revolutionizes carrier operations by allowing simultaneous take-off and landing.

Instead of landing along the line of the ship from stern to bow, aircraft land following a diagonal path from the rear starboard to the front port side. The pilot no longer faces rows of parked aircraft which could be hit if the aircraft's tail hook misses the arresting cables. The uncluttered deck allows the pilot a chance to take off again for another landing attempt if a miss occurs.

At the same time as the angled deck is used for landings, aircraft can be launched by catapult from the bow. Obscured vision, caused by ship's smoke trailing behind the ship along the line of approach, is eliminated (→ Dec 11, 1954).

*A Grumman Panther lands on the angled-deck carrier USS "Antietam".*

# Gander booms as a northern stopover

**Gander, Newfoundland, February**
As the nearest North American landfall from Europe, Newfoundland has been the start or finish of many historic Atlantic flights. With the growth in transatlantic passenger services, the little town of Gander, with 11,000 inhabitants, has become the main stopover point between Europe and the US.

Gander has a fairly temperate maritime climate and, despite winter snow, does not suffer extreme cold. Airline personnel based here include mechanics, flight operations officers and airline representatives, who handle aircraft making the two-hour refueling stop. If an airliner has serious problems, passengers transfer to another service and the troubled airplane flies to New York for repair.

# Cyprus flight marks turboprop's arrival

**Nicosia, April 18**
A Vickers-Armstrongs V.701 Viscount of British European Airways (BEA), the *Sir Ernest Shackleton*, arrived here this evening from London to launch the world's first sustained scheduled air service using turboprop aircraft.

Flying from Heathrow airport via Rome and Athens, the Viscount opens a new era of quiet, smooth, high-speed air travel. Powered by four 1,400-hp Rolls-Royce Dart engines, the 47 to 53-seat V.701 is proving especially popular because of its large elliptical passenger windows. As further V.701s are delivered, BEA will introduce them on all its domestic and European trunk routes. The Viscount is proving to be a hit with passengers, aircrews and engineers alike (→ Jun 3, 1954).

# Air reconnaissance helps rescue efforts as great floods hit England and Holland

*North Sea, February 5*
The value of helicopters in a disaster is being proved hourly in eastern England and the Netherlands, devastated over the last two days by hurricane-force winds and severe flooding. Over 1,000 people have died in the Netherlands, where dykes have burst, and at least 280 Britons have perished in low-lying areas. In the county of Norfolk, 12 US airmen were among 60 who drowned when giant waves swept over sea walls.

Working from dawn to dusk in terrible conditions, helicopters of the Royal Navy's 705 Squadron have winched more than 600 people to safety in the Netherlands and dropped vital drugs and two-way radios to doctors in isolated communities. Along a swollen Thames estuary east of London, helicopters have saved hundreds of people found clinging to rooftops.

All available fixed-wing aircraft are employed in the operation, with RAF Valetta transports delivering immersion suits to rescuers. Six Avro Ansons from the 2nd Allied Tactical Air Force in Germany are also involved in dropping supplies.

*Crews examine photographs of the flood damage taken by RAF Mosquitoes.*

# New President 'Ike' likes Constellation

*Washington, DC, January 22*
America's President has a new airplane, a USAF Lockheed C-121, the military version of the Constellation airliner. It replaces Truman's Douglas DC-6, the *Independence*, and is the third presidential aircraft. The first was Roosevelt's DC-4, the *Sacred Cow*.

President Dwight D "Ike" Eisenhower will call his plane *Columbine II*, after the Constellation he used as commander of Allied forces in Europe. The name and a blue columbine, official flower of Mamie Eisenhower's home state of Colorado, will be on the nose. As President-elect Eisenhower flew in the aircraft to Korea in November last year to fulfil his election promise to seek a speedy end to the war.

The airplane was delivered to the USAF in January 1949 and will be modernized for the President. A 20-foot area will become a suite with two couches which convert into beds. There will be special chairs for Ike and Mamie.

# Mystery Comet tragedy leaves 43 dead

*The fire-scarred wreck of the tail of the BOAC Comet after the crash in India.*

*Calcutta, India, May 2*
It is exactly a year since the Comet airliner entered commercial service, but the anniversary has given little cause for celebration. All 43 passengers and crew on board a BOAC Comet 1 were killed today when it crashed 25 miles west of Calcutta.

The cause has not yet been established, but a 14-year-old villager said he saw a red flash and what looked like a wingless airplane low over the trees. There were explosions and the airliner plummeted into a dried-up stream. A full investigation is already under way.

This is the third accident to strike the airliner. Doubts about the Comet's safety were first raised on October 26 last year, when a BOAC Comet 1 was wrecked during take-off at Rome. On March 3 this year, a Canadian Pacific Airlines Comet 1A crashed at Karachi during its delivery flight to Sydney to begin a transpacific service to Vancouver. Its place and that of its sister Comet were taken by DC-6Bs. Both accidents were found to have been caused by pilots lifting the nose too high on during take-off, preventing flying speed from being reached. Drooped leading edges, which increase lift at low speeds, have been adopted to prevent the problem recurring (→ Aug 26).

# Memoirs come out

*New York, June 1*
The secrets of three of America's greatest air pioneers are out. Two aviation volumes have hit the bookshops in time for the holiday rush: *The Papers of Orville and Wilbur Wright* and *The Spirit of St Louis*, Charles Lindbergh's story of his solo conquest of the Atlantic. Lindbergh's book is already a bestseller. The Wrights' story, appearing in the 50th anniversary year of their historic flight, is really a window on the brothers' early development work. It is a scientific and solid book, while *The Spirit of St Louis* is a dramatic and vivid account of pioneer distance flying in the 1920s, where even the slightest error could mean death.

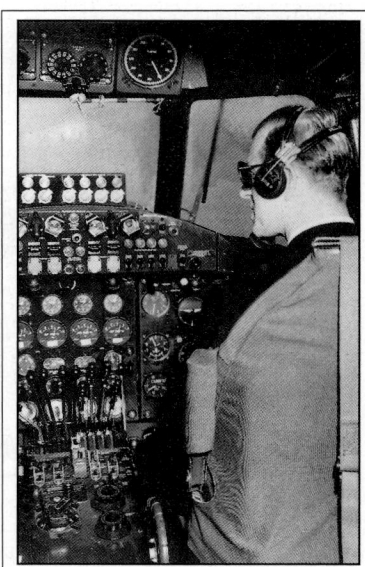

**The Duke of Edinburgh takes the controls of a Vickers Viscount.**

# New fighter hits Mach 1

*The YF-100 Super Sabre, which exceeded Mach 1 on its initial flight.*

*California, May 25*
George Welch, engineering test pilot for North American Aviation, was jubilant today after the YF-100 Super Sabre flew for the first time. Welch had bet Lieutenant-Colonel Pete Everest, chief of flight testing at Edwards Air Force Base, that he would break the sound barrier on the first flight. Everest, who accompanied the YF-100 in an F-86D, heard over the radio from Welch: "You owe me two beers."

Its ability to reach supersonic speed in level flight, rather than while diving, marks out the new fighter from all its predecessors. It is only five and a half years since Mach 1 was first exceeded by an air-launched research airplane. It has been done now by a fighter which is designed to go into regular squadron service. Originally North American hoped to base the Super Sabre on the existing F-86 Sabre. For a time it was called the Sabre 45 because the wing had to be swept more sharply, at 45 instead of 35 degrees. In the event, the F-100 is a totally new design, even bigger, heavier and more powerful than the F-86. A key to its design is its Pratt & Whitney J57 engine, rated at 10,000 lb thrust or 15,000 lb with afterburner. This is fed by a nose-inlet of a distinctive shape which, unlike that of a subsonic aircraft, is sharp-edged. The wing has no flaps; instead, there are full-span slats along the leading edge. The new fighter is armed with four of the new 20mm M-39 revolver cannon. The F-100 could prove to be very useful in Korea.

**A Republic F-84 Thunderjet is launched from a mobile platform in a test carried out at Edwards Air Force Base, California. The initial impetus is provided by the huge rocket attached beneath the fuselage of the fighter.**

## Jackie perfumed her Sabre's cockpit

*California, May 18*
Veteran pilot Jacqueline Cochran carefully perfumed the cockpit of a Canadian-built F-86E Sabre jet here today before flying off to join a supersonic "club" dominated until now by men. Cochran, who is now retired from full-time flying and is a successful executive in the cosmetics industry, has spent several weeks with "Chuck" Yeager – the first man to break the sound barrier – training at Edwards Air Force Base. The perfume, said Miss Cochran, was to disguise the smell

*Cochran descends from her Sabre.*

of kerosene in the cockpit, although some observers saw it as a useful piece of product publicity.

Her insurance was expensive – it cost her $10,000 for every flying hour – but she succeeded in flying at 652.5mph, establishing a new record for women. But sadly for the record-breaker and wartime organizer of women ferry-pilots for the USAAF, the record will not be recognized. Among her achievements, Miss Cochran undertook high-altitude aeromedical research in the 1930s. She flew in the Bendix trophy air race in 1935, winning it in 1938 in a Seversky SEV-S2; she nearly won it again in 1946 in a modified Mustang.

## Sikorsky tries out new 'jet helicopter'

*Bridgeport, Connecticut, July 24*
Sikorsky has become the latest company to experiment with gas turbines in helicopters. In December, 1951, Kaman was the first, by flying a US Navy K-225 fitted with a 175-hp Boeing 502-2 turboshaft option. Now Sikorsky has chosen a French powerplant, the 400-hp Turbomeca Artouste II turboshaft, for the experimental S-52-5, designated YH-18B by the military. The Artouste replaces the original 245-hp Lycoming piston engine, but it has been derated to 320hp because of airframe limitations.

The S-52-5 is a modification of one of four S-52/YH-18 four-seat helicopters which were evaluated by the US Army. The engine is bolted to the transmission gearbox on top of the fuselage. From the S-52-5, Sikorsky is now developing what it hopes will eventually be a production model, the S-59. In this, the engine, transmission and rotor-head will be packaged as a single unit for quick removal.

## Delta Sea Dart is hydroski first

*San Diego, California, April 9*
A new type of aircraft roared off the water here today and climbed into the sky. Convair test pilot E D "Sam" Shannon was at the controls for the first flight of the Convair XF2Y-1. Named the Sea Dart, it is the world's first "hydroski" fighter, the first potentially supersonic waterbased airplane, and the first jet of the new delta-winged species to fly from water.

The XF2Y-1 is expected to be the first of a whole new breed of US Navy airplanes. Built for the Navy Bureau of Aeronautics, the fighter is powered by two Westinghouse J34 turbojets, fed from inlets above the needle-nosed fuselage. At rest the XF2Y-1 floats low in the water, its wings level with the surface. On take-off, the hydroskis lift it clear until only the tails of the skis are in touch with the waves, and after take-off they are retracted like normal landing gear. Convair has tried out over 100 arrangements of single and double skis (→Aug 3, 1954).

# Records tumble as speed kings battle

## Sidewinder missile homes in on heat

## Duke of speed wins honors for Britain

*Littlehampton, England, Sept 7*
Hawker chief test pilot Squadron Leader Neville Duke has snatched the official world air speed record with a timed run of 727.48mph in the new Hunter fighter. Duke's record is still 33mph short of the sound barrier at sea level but beats by 12mph the time set on July 16 by USAF Lieutenant-Colonel W F Barnes in an F-86D Sabre.

The Hunter was ordered in 1948 to replace the RAF's Meteor and as the P.1067 first flew two years ago. The Hunter and the Supermarine Swift are planned as the RAF's first swept-wing supersonic fighters, and they should enter service

*Holiday-makers watch Duke fly by.*

some time next year. The first production model flew in May, but the British government has delayed acceptance for military service until an airbrake is fitted.

The Hunter is supersonic only in a shallow dive, though later models with more powerful engines will be able to fly supersonically in level flight. Hawker is impressed with the handling of the machine, even though early test results reveal some flaws which will need to be ironed out. These include, notably, its tendency to "pitch up" in some maneuvers, without warning, at high subsonic speeds.

## Crossfield is first pilot to exceed Mach 2

*Crossfield: flew to Mach 2.01.*

*California, November 20*
Civilian test pilot A Scott Crossfield today flew from Edwards Air Force Base here to over twice the speed of sound – Mach 2.01, or 1,291mph – at an altitude of 62,000 feet. Crossfield's Douglas D-558-2 Skyrocket was released in the thin upper atmosphere by a B-29. Crossfield called for a long burst of rocket power in level flight to reach his phenomenal speed. On

*Everest: set record in F-100.*

August 21 the same aircraft was flown by US Marine Lieutenant-Colonel Marion E Carl to a world record altitude of 83,825 feet, after being released at 37,000 feet. A new speed record for more orthodox runway-takeoff aircraft was set on October 29 by the F-100 Super Sabre, the first American supersonic fighter. At Salton Sea, California, it hit 754.99mph piloted by Lieutenant-Colonel Frank Everest.

## Yeager has bumpy ride to 1,650mph

*Edwards AFB, Calif, December 12*
USAF Major Charles E. "Chuck" Yeager has broken another remarkable barrier during an eventful flight in which he came close to being killed. Back in 1947 he became the first person to break the sound barrier and live – despite the handicap of broken ribs. Today he took a rodeo ride in a Bell X-1A as it tumbled end-over-end at 70,000 feet, reaching Mach 2.44 (1,650mph).

The trouble started when he tried to correct unwanted rolls. In the "wisp of atmosphere" at this altitude, his wings had almost no pressure to work on (Yeager later said it was "like driving on slick ice"). He was hurled at the control column and his helmet jammed onto it. He managed to put the aircraft into a normal spin, from which he recovered at 25,000 feet, half-conscious after his battering and exposure to exceptional G-forces. At 5,000 feet he lined up his approach to base (→ Aug 12, 1954).

## Proving flight for Japan's reborn line

*Tokyo, November 23*
A route-proving flight by Japan Air Lines (JAL) today has given notice of the company's intention to start scheduled intercontinental passenger services between Tokyo and San Francisco early next year. Facing no competition from other Far East airlines on the transpacific route, JAL is expected to clean up in an expanding market.

Two long-range Douglas DC-6A freighters were acquired from US operators, and these are assigned for modification to DC-6B passenger standard. Already looking ahead to future trends, JAL has ordered two Comet 2 jetliners from de Havilland in Britain. Japan Air Lines was founded last month out of the former Japanese Air Lines, created on August 1, 1951. The new carrier is 50 per cent owned by the Japanese government. Up to now, JAL operations have been domestic, using mainly airplanes and crews leased from Northwest Airlines of the US (→ Feb 2, 1954).

*China Lake, USA, September 11*
Early fighters were fitted with machine guns; then came cannon, firing explosive shells. Today the latest means of arming fighters was tested – a missile which homes on the engine heat of its prey. In today's test a US Navy pilot destroyed a pilotless Grumman Hellcat. The air-to-air killer is called the Sidewinder, after the deadly desert snake which detects the body heat of its quarry.

The missile is being developed by the US Navy on a shoestring budget, but the USAF is also interested. It is 9 feet long, has only 24 moving parts and is reliable for up to 2 miles, hitting its target at Mach 2.5. An infra-red heat-seeking unit is carried inside a spherical glass nose. One problem is how to prevent the guidance system from reacting to heat sources other than the target, such as protective flares or even the Sun. A theoretical solution might be to equip Sidewinder with a radar-homing system.

## Revived Lufthansa set to fly again

*Cologne, W Germany, December 20*
The three Western Allied occupying powers have agreed to allow "frozen" German airline Lufthansa to fly in competition with other world carriers. Reformed with the interim title of Luftag on January 6, the airline will be a West German airline only. It ordered four Super Constellations and has begun recruiting aircrew.

Today the airline demonstrated its determination to produce the "best pilots in the world" when it opened an intensive course for flying personnel at the university of Cologne. Students – many of them wartime Luftwaffe pilots – will work with machines that recreate the conditions and challenges expected in flight. The aim of the course is to develop the kind of reflexes essential in today's crowded skies. Practical and theoretical work will be carried out under the exacting eyes of instructors using electronic equipment devised in West Germany.

The 95-seat Douglas DC-7 used Wright Turbo-Compound engines; 120 were built to compete with the Super Constellation on US domestic trunk routes.

Cessna built over 6,200 examples of the Model 310 five-seat light twin.

Cessna sold more than 6,000 Model 180 Skywagon six-seater.

Custer made amazing claims for its CC-5 Channel Wing.

The Piaggio P.149 four-seat tourer was used as a military basic trainer.

The Sud-Ouest SO.1221 Djinn two-seat helicopter with a tip-drive rotor.

The Boeing RB-47E Stratojet multi-sensor reconnaissance aircraft.

The Beech Super 18 was an updated version of the pre-war feeder-liner.

The de Havilland Comet 2's fuselage was 3ft longer than the Mk 1's; it could carry 44 passengers 2,400 miles. Engines were four 7,000lb Avon turbojets.

Sikorsky S-56 prototype (US Army's H-37 Mojave/Marines' XHR2S).

Doman's LZ-5 had a hingeless main rotor; it was tested by the US Army.

The handsome Riley Twin-Navion.

The F-102 Delta Dagger, Convair's first "Century Series" fighter, was designed to fly all-weather supersonic interceptions using missiles rather than guns.

The US's Helio H-391 Courier.

The stub-winged SO. 1310 Farfadet.

Grumman's XF10F-1 Jaguar jet fighter researched variable sweep.

Sud-Ouest's aptly-named SO. 9000 Trident research aircraft was powered by wing-tip turbojets plus an SEPR liquid rocket-motor in the rear fuselage.

Lockheed's T-33 was developed into the T2V-1 SeaStar for the US Navy.

Italy's Sagittario experimental light jet aircraft was built by Ambrosini.

North American's first production F-86H Sabre with a GE J73 engine.

Armstrong Whitworth built the RAF 100 Meteor NF.14 night fighters.

*The Swiss air force used the two-seat Pilatus P 3 as a basic trainer.*

*Only a single Derwent-powered Avro 707C two-seat delta was built.*

*The Thrust Measuring Rig, or "Flying Bedstead", powered by Rolls-Royce Nenes, marked the beginning of British vertical take-off and landing research.*

*Canadair built 1,815 F-86 Sabres under license from North American, including the Sabre 5 and 6 with the more powerful Canadian Orenda engine.*

*Commonwealth Aircraft's CA-27 Avon-Sabre fighter for the RAAF.*

*The Bristol 170 Superfreighter 32 ferried cars across the Channel.*

*The USAF's twin-engined Piasecki YH-16 Transporter giant helicopter.*

*The Short SB.4 Sherpa research jet had elevon controls at its wing-tips.*

*Boulton Paul's P.111A delta-wing research aircraft featured airbrakes.*

*In the US Martin license-built English Electric's Canberras as B-57As.*

*Sud-Est's SE 5000 Baroudeur light jet fighter had no true landing gear.*

*Morane-Saulnier's MS.755 Fleuret was a two-seat armed jet trainer.*

*The first Blackburn-built Beverley transport, with Centaurus engines.*

*The turboprop Short SB.6 Seamew designed for anti-submarine work.*

*Ilyushin's Il-14 airliner ("Crate" to Nato), an improved Il-12: early versions only took 18 passengers. East Germany and Czechoslovakia also built some.*

*The Hispano HA-100 two-seat armed trainer had a 750-hp Beta engine.*

*The unusual Palas-powered Ikarus Type 452 twin-jet research aircraft.*

*North American's YF-100 Super Sabre was the first of the USAF "Century series" of supersonic fighters; it exceeded the speed of sound on its first flight.*

*Convair's XF2Y-1 Sea Dart twin-jet delta-winged fighter had hydroskis.*

*The pusher-engined Potez 75 was an early counter-insurgency aircraft.*

# 1954

1,650mph
USA
Charles Yeager
Bell X-1A
Dec 12, 1953

23,093 miles
USA
James Gallagher
Boeing B-50A
Mar 2, 1949

90,440ft
USA
Arthur Murray
Bell X-1A
Aug 26, 1954

420,000lb
USA
Boeing
B-52A Stratofortress

20,945lb thrust
USSR
Mikulin
AM-3M

**Italy, January 10**
After a study of the victims of the Comet crash near Elba, a medical examiner notes: "They showed no look of terror. Death must have come without warning."→

**Melun-Villaroche, France, Jan 22**
The Payen PA-49 delta-winged jet airplane makes its first flight; it is the smallest airplane of its type with a wing-span of just under 17 feet.

**Tokyo, February 2**
Japan Air Lines inaugurates its first international service: a twice-weekly route to San Francisco.

**South-west England, February 4**
The second prototype of the Bristol Britannia is lost when pilot A J Pegg is forced by a severe engine fire to land on the muddy bed of the river Severn; the aircraft is wrecked by the rescue cables. →

**San Diego, Calif, February 25**
The US Navy's Convair R3Y-1 Tradewind long-range patroller makes its maiden flight; it is the navy's only turboprop-powered flying boat (→ Apr 30).

**London, March 17**
BOAC announces an order for 19 new de Havilland Comet 4s, capable of taking full payloads on the transatlantic route (→ Apr 12).

**London, March 23**
BOAC's fleet of Comet 1 airliners resumes scheduled operations after an enquiry uncovers no evident design fault (→ Mar 31).

**Malaya, April 1**
One of the last Spitfires still serving in a front-line RAF unit makes the type's last operational flight, a photo reconnaissance mission.

**Colorado, April 1**
The US Air Force Academy is created; temporarily located at Lowry Air Force Base, it will teach officer cadets a curriculum of 2,178 hours in airmanship, 1,629 hours in sciences and 1,548 in humanities.

**Sydney, April 3**
Qantas introduces tourist-class-services on its Kangaroo route from Sydney to London.

**London, April 12**
In the wake of the crash of a BOAC D.H. Comet 1 which broke up and fell into sea south of Naples on April 8 – the second Comet crash in three months – the airliner's Certificate of Airworthiness is withdrawn.→

**Dallas, Texas, April 30**
The aircraft company Convair (Consolidated-Vultee Aircraft Corporation) is taken over by General Dynamics.

**USA, May 1**
Pan Am launches a new ticket which can be bought on credit: a down payment of 10 per cent of the cost is followed by 20 monthly payments.

**California, June 1**
A Grumman S2F-1 Tracker is launched from the USS *Hancock* in the first operational trial of the C-11 steam catapult; the *Hancock* is the first carrier with a steam catapult capable of launching high-performance jets.

**California, June 22**
The Douglas XA4D-1 Skyhawk prototype, intended for carrier service with the US Navy, makes its maiden flight.

**Valenciennes, France, June 27**
French pilot André Tesson is killed just after he has broken the sound barrier in his Mystère II at an air show: as he describes his reactions by radio over the loudspeakers, the spectators are horrified to hear him cry: "I have lost control of the airplane." He is unable to escape because his ejection seat jams.

**Tokyo, July 1**
The Japanese National Defense Force is formed, comprising air, sea and land units; this follows an agreement with the US covering the creation of Japanese defense forces.

**London, July 18**
BOAC, whose fleet has been depleted by the grounding of the Comet, begins service with the first of a number of Handley Page Hermes aircraft which it has recommissioned (→ Oct 19).

**South China Sea, July 26**
Two carrier-based US Navy Skyraiders down two Chinese MiG-15s off Hainan island; the US aircraft were searching for survivors of a Cathay Pacific DC-4, shot down by Chinese fighters three days ago with the loss of nine lives (→ Sep 28).

**San Diego, USA, August 3**
The Convair YF2Y-1 prototype breaks the sound barrier in a dive, becoming the first water-based airplane in the world to exceed the speed of sound.

**Hampshire, England, August 3**
The Rolls-Royce thrust-measuring rig (TMR), developed to test the capacity of the jet engine for powering vertical take-off and landing flights, makes its first free flight; the strangely-shaped vehicle is dubbed the "Flying Bedstead" by the British press.→

**USA, August 24**
The pilots of American Airlines return to work after a 25-day strike which has cost the company $19,000,000; they have failed to win a deal limiting flying time to eight hours a day.

**California, August 26**
After a launch by a Boeing B-29 motherplane, Major Arthur Murray flies the Bell X-1A to an altitude of 90,440 feet: a record for a piloted airplane.

**Colorado, September 1**
The USAF Air Defense Command is established, with HQ at Colorado Springs.

**Dublin, September 5**
A Lockheed Constellation of Dutch airline KLM crashes into the river Shannon, killing 28.

**Peking, September 28**
State radio announces that the People's Republic of China tested its first home-built aircraft on July 26; this marks the emergence of an indigenous Chinese aircraft industry.

**Wiltshire, England, October 6**
Peter Twiss makes the first flight of the experimental Fairey Delta 2, developed to investigate flight control at transonic and supersonic speeds.

**USA, October 17**
The Sikorsky XH-39 helicopter, piloted by US Army Warrant Officer Billy Wester, climbs to an altitude of 24,500 feet – a world record for rotary-winged aircraft.

**London, October 31**
British European Airways retires the Vickers Viking from scheduled service.

**Okinawa, Japan, November 1**
The USAF retires its last Boeing B-29 Superfortress bomber, based at Kadena, from front-line service; the type has now been supplanted by the B-47.

**Moffett Field, Calif, November 2**
Convair's XFY-1 vertical take-off and landing aircraft makes its first transition from vertical to horizontal flight and back again.

**USA, November 21**
Aviation pioneer Clyde Cessna, who in 1916 founded the Cessna Aircraft Compagny based in Wichita, Kansas, dies at the age of 74.

**Virginia, December 11**
The world's first carrier originally built with an angled flight deck, USS *Forrestal*, is launched at Newport News.

---

*The Grumman F-11, developed from the YF9F-9 Tiger prototype single-seat fighter, made its first flight on July 30, 1954.* ▶

# Comet in second tragedy

*Elba, Italy, January 10*
Death came in a clear blue sky today for the 35 passengers of the BOAC Comet I *Yoke Peter* when it apparently burst into flames at 30,000 feet and crashed into the Tyrrhenian Sea off Elba. The tragedy was witnessed by fishermen who described a "flaming, falling mass". The Comet had left Rome's Ciampino Airport at 9.31am on a scheduled flight to London.

After take-off, regular reports to Ciampino indicated that things were progressing normally. Just before 10am the captain called another BOAC aircraft, an Argonaut. His message began: "*How Jig* [the Argonaut's call sign], did you get my ..." and broke off. Even before accident investigators arrived here tonight BOAC ordered all Comets abroad to return to London empty. Experts are already speculating that the *Yoke Peter*, which was the first BOAC Comet in scheduled service, suffered a catastrophic loss of pressurization. Others who have flown in Comets over the same area are talking of a "cobblestone" sensation at high speed. Other theories are abundant. Previous Comet crashes – two have been lost in overshoot accidents and two while climbing to cruise altitudes – have been put down to "acceptable" hazards. Otherwise the jet has performed well (→ Mar 23).

# 'Yoke Peter' exhumed from watery grave

*Part of the Comet's mangled fuselage is hoisted up off the sea-bed near Elba.*

*Tyrrhenian Sea, March 31*
Today, after over two months of searching the sea bottom for fragments of the crashed BOAC Comet *Yoke Peter*, Britain's Royal Navy brought to the surface most of the forward section of the fuselage, the flight engineer's body still strapped into his seat. To recover the pieces from as much as 500 feet down, the navy used underwater television cameras and sonar to detect them; then divers guided giant grappling hooks to bring them to the surface.

The cause of the crash is still a mystery, though experts have recommended 50 modifications which they believe will prevent mid-air explosions. These are mainly concerned with preventing fire, which is thought to have been a factor in the disaster. The modified Comets started flying again this month, with full loads, their passengers apparently confident that there was no danger.

Meanwhile, at the Royal Aircraft Establishment at Farnborough, the remains of the *Yoke Peter* are being minutely examined by a team of experts for any clue as to what else could have gone wrong (→ Apr 12).

# Lockheed unveils its Mach-2 Starfighter

*The XF-104 has been dubbed "the missile with a man in it" by the US press.*

*Burbank, California, January 7*
The Lockheed XF-104 Starfighter, the USAF's dart-like, high-performance interceptor, made its first flight at the Air Force plant here today. The Starfighter, which was flown by Lockheed test pilot Tony LeVier, has air intakes on the side of a 55-foot fuselage and razor-edged wings which span just 22 feet. The wings are so sharp that protective covers are used when the XF-104 is on the ground. The maximum take-off weight is 20,000 lb, almost a third lighter than the F-100 Super Sabres it may replace. Yet it will reach Mach 2, twice the speed of the F-100, and operate above 50,000 feet.

It has a Buick-built J65, a version of the Armstrong Siddeley Sapphire engine, giving 11,500 lb thrust with afterburner. But production F-104s will have the General Electric J79, giving 15,000 lb thrust with afterburner.

# Japanese sign deal to build US warplanes

*The Lockheed F-94C Starfire, which is to be built under license in Japan.*

*Japan, March 1*
The Japanese aviation industry is facing a brighter future today. The recent lifting of the ban on the construction of military airplanes – imposed by the Allies at the end of the Second World War – has resulted in a firm contract between Lockheed and the Kawasaki Aircraft Company. Under the terms of the deal, which was signed today, the Japanese are to build two of the US company's jet aircraft under license, the F-94C Starfire and the T-33A jet trainer. Neither model represents the very latest state of the art; indeed, the Starfire is only an interim type, whose production was halted in February. But the Japanese are pleased to be able to familiarize themselves with the jet technology (→ Jul 1).

# DC-7 sets transcontinental speed record

*Los Angeles, April 4*
After only six months in service the latest Douglas airliner, the DC-7, demonstrated today that non-stop, coast-to-coast travel by American Airlines could become as routine as the legendary Greyhound bus. Eight hours 45 minutes is the target time for the journey from New York to Los Angeles, but today the DC-7 did it in 5 hours 51 minutes at an average speed of 420mph.

The DC-7 is basically a stretch and heavier DC-6B. It does however, have a totally new feature: 3,250-hp Wright R-3350 Turbo-Compound engines, a key factor in enhanced range and speed.

*The Douglas DC-7 has made a very impressive start in airline service.*

# Comet is grounded after mystery crash

*London, April 12*
Prime Minister Winston Churchill ordered all Comets grounded today following a third crash, off the island of Stromboli in the Mediterranean, on April 8. The Comet of South African Airways was on a flight to Cairo when it disappeared from radar after it left Rome; 14 passengers and the seven crew died.

For the British aviation industry, which had leapt far ahead of its competitors with this sleek aircraft, the loss of the Comet is a bitter blow. Orders had come from Air France, Air India, Canadian Pacific, Japan Air Lines, Pan Am, the Royal Canadian Air Force, South African Airways and Union Aéromaritime de Transport (→ Jul 18).

# US hydrogen bomb is exploded in Pacific

*Bikini Atoll, Pacific, March 1*
The frightening power of the first atomic bomb is a mere trigger for the latest nuclear weapon tested today. This fuzes hydrogen atoms under such explosive pressure that the blast is multiplied a hundredfold. Since the first atom-bomb test at Bikini 16 months ago, both superpowers have learned how to build the "thermonuclear" or "megaton" bomb. The British are working on one also. What was unclear was whether the device could be delivered by air. Today's bomb was

detonated on a pylon, but scientists describe it as "droppable" and say it could be refined for release from a B-52 bomber or as the warhead of a ballistic missile.

The new weapon could have the explosive power of two million tons of TNT (two megatons), or a hundred times the destructive potential of the atomic bomb which destroyed Hiroshima. As the Soviets race to perfect their own H-bomb, it is clear that the world is entering a dangerous era of staggering destructive power.

# Indo-China air drop fails

*A group of Helldiver bombers used in the attempt to save Dien Bien Phu.*

*Indo-China, May 7*
After an epic attempt to sustain a beleaguered army of nearly 11,000 in the jungle from the air, 190 miles from friendly territory, a humiliated French garrison at Dien Bien Phu has surrendered to the Communist Viet-minh insurgents.

Airmen had predicted that the army's effort to hold a fixed position with air power was doomed. The Communists defied attempts to cut their supply lines from the air and smuggled anti-aircraft guns

through dense jungle. There were not enough aircraft to fly the long distances from bases around Hanoi. In the later stages, air-to-ground support was impossible with opposing armies nose-to-nose.

Some of the air drops at Dien Bien Phu were made by US pilots of CIA-owned airline Civil Air Transport in USAF C-119s with French markings. One was shot down yesterday, and its pilots – James B McGovern, Jr, and Wallace A Buford – were killed.

**England, February 4: The second prototype of the Bristol Britannia was lost after being put down skilfully on the bank of the river Severn.**

# Sparkling debut for Boeing's 'Dash 80' airliner

*The "Dash 80" flies with Boeing chief test pilot A.M."Tex" Johnston.*

*Renton, Washington, July 15*
Movie director Cecil B De Mille could not have staged it better – dark skies, tension-building delay, then the parting of the clouds bathing the airfield in sunlight. So it was today as Boeing's $16 million prototype civil jet transport, the Model 367-80, the "Dash 80", flew for the first time. Originally scheduled to take off at 7am, Boeing chief test pilot "Tex" Johnston finally started up at 2pm. The four 9,500-lb thrust Pratt & Whitney JT3 turbojets lifted the "Dash 80" off the runway in 2,100 feet for a trouble-free 90-minute maiden flight.

"She wanted to climb like a rocket," said Johnston on touchdown. The name "Dash 80" refers only to the prototype; internally, the project is known as the 707 – the Seattle company's 707th Model. Boeing has a lot riding on the 707; so far it has borne the full cost of development – an investment that represents much of the company's net wealth. If it fails to win orders from the airlines, or from the USAF as an in-flight tanker, then Boeing could face bankruptcy – and so far there are no orders.

But Boeing is poised to forge ahead just as its nearest rival falters. "Tex" Johnston is embarking on his rigorous flight test program as the world's first jet airliner, Britain's Comet, remains grounded while investigations continue into three fatal crashes.

## USAF in largest-scale exercises since 1945

*Fort Bragg, NC, April 26*
The air was filled with 8,650 paratroopers today as the airborne phase of the week-long USAF Exercise Tac-Air 54-7 and US Army Exercise Flash Burn continued. These maneuvers, the biggest since the Second World War, involve 60,000 army and 30,000 air force personnel and 500 aircraft.

Today's jump, by the 82nd Airborne Division, was made from 180 Fairchild C-119 Flying Boxcars of the 18th Air Force, which made several flights to the drop zone over a ten-hour period. The exercise involves some of the latest equipment in both services. These include the Army's Honest John rockets, Corporal guided missiles, the 280mm atomic cannon and the USAF's North American F-86F Sabre and Republic F-84F Thunderjet tactical fighters, as well as C-119s, Douglas C-124 Globemasters and other support aircraft. The exercise will also simulate chemical, biological and atomic attacks.

## 'Flying Bedstead' flies on turbojet thrust

*Hucknall, England, August 9*
The strangest flying machine ever built began trials today near Nottingham, filling the sky with a thunderous noise. The Rolls-Royce thrust-measuring rig (TMR), known as the "Flying Bedstead", hovered precariously on the thrust of its engines. It is a research tool in the quest to find a way to build aircraft to take off and land vertically. The TMR is little more than two 5,000-lb thrust Nene engines mounted, with fuel tanks, controls and a pilot's seat, on a frame of steel tubes. Its jet pipes are turned 90 degrees downward to meet at the center, one pipe being divided into two smaller nozzles. Test pilot R T Shepherd flew the TMR today. An RAF test pilot will fly it soon.

*The unusual "Flying Bedstead".*

## Vickers Viscounts break into US market

*Viscount airliners being prepared for American buyer Capital Airlines.*

*Surrey, England, June 3*
Capital Airlines of the US today announced a firm order for three Viscount turboprop airliners, with options on a further 37. If the options are taken up, it will be the largest order for the airliner so far and a big boost for the Weybridge-based Vickers-Armstrongs.

The Viscount's selection by Capital has been greeted with great enthusiasm by Vickers. It is the first British aircraft to break into the US commercial market since US-built Airco D.H.4s were used as mailplanes in the 1920s. The Viscount will be operated on the airline's domestic routes, and Capital is satisfied that it will perform as well in the USA as it has for British European Airways (BEA). It will start service on Capital's Washington, DC/Chicago route next year.

The three Viscount Type 744s, modified from Type 701s which have been made available from production originally destined for BEA, seat 40. They are powered by turboprops – 1,400-hp Rolls-Royce Dart Mk 506s. However, airplanes now on option will, if they are required, be delivered or later fitted with more powerful 1,600-hp Dart 510 engines.

# 'The right stuff': pilots of the supersonic age

## Test crews bravely face the unknown

*Wiltshire, England, August 12*

English Electric chief test pilot Roland "Bee" Beamont dove the P.1 prototype fighter toward the test airfield at Boscombe Down today, making a deafening sonic bang. The unusual airplane, its engines superimposed one above the other, is another step toward a British double-sonic fighter for RAF Fighter Command.

In developed countries, the test pilots like Beamont are at the cutting edge of the quest to develop the next generation of jet fighters, even while the previous one is only just coming into service. Test flying has always been a dangerous and demanding job. This is especially so at the top level of research flying, where it takes the most of what laymen call "the right stuff", that rare combination of flying skill, technical understanding and sheer courage, to push back the frontiers of knowledge in speed, altitude and acceleration. Already at Boscombe is the Fairey Delta 2, which, although smaller than the P.1, is expected to be flown by test pilot Peter Twiss at well over 1,100mph. In France, Roland Glavany is getting ready to fly the Dassault Mirage fighter, while in Sweden Bengt Olow is looking forward to testing another fighter, the dart-shaped Saab 35 Draken [Dragon].

But it is in the US that the most stunning range of new jet airplanes is appearing, and where test pilots are not short of exciting work. In November last year A Scott Crossfield flew the Douglas Skyrocket faster than anyone had gone before, reaching Mach 2.05 at 62,000 feet. Then, the following month, Major Charles "Chuck" Yeager, first man to fly faster than sound, beat Crossfield's speed in the X-1A with Mach 2.44, or 1,650mph.

Bell has now produced two examples of an even faster airplane, the X-2. With a rocket engine of unprecedented power and thin swept-wings, it is designed to hit Mach 3. Colonel Frank Everest and Captain Mel Apt have been earmarked to fly it (→Oct 6).

*Six of America's top test pilots line up at Edwards Air Force Base, California, before some of the airplanes in which they made their names: (l to r) "Chuck" Yeager, the first man to fly faster than the speed of sound, in 1947; H G Russell, F J Ascani, J S Holtoner and Jack Ridley, who flew the B-29 which launched Yeager when he broke the barrier, and Arthur Murray.*

*Test pilot Glen Edwards (center left, in 1945), who was killed in the 1947 crash of a Northrop YB-49 and after whom Edwards Air Force Base is named.*

*Pilots Lithgow (l) and Colquhoun.*

*"Bee" Beamont, who flies the P.1.*

*Peter Twiss: pilots the Delta 2.*

# New machines lift off

*Moffett Field, California, August 1*
The quest for vertical take-off and landing (VTOL) aircraft is producing the weirdest flying machines seen for many years. The British "Flying Bedstead" [*see page 528*] is hardly a flying machine at all. Today an equally odd-looking machine, the Convair XFY-1 Pogo, hovered thunderously near the airship hangar here, supported by huge contra-rotating propellers.

The XFY-1 is intended to lead to a Navy fighter which, up-ended on the deck of a destroyer or even a fleet oiler, can take off vertically and then make the transition to horizontal flight; then, having made the transition back to vertical flight, it should be able to descend gently back onto the ship's deck. In other words, it could operate on ships other than aircraft carriers with their steel-deck runways and steam catapults.

Lockheed is experimenting with a similar design, the XFV-1. The key to both airplanes is the power of modern turboprops. The prototypes are fitted with a 5,850-hp Allison T40, and the definitive model is expected to have a 7,500-hp T54. Getting airborne and flying forward is the relatively easy part – the difficulty is landing the craft. The pilot has to look back over his shoulder with the airplane lagging in its response to the throttle. Convair had elected to begin in the hov-

*Convair's XFY-1 climbs straight up.*

ering, propeller-supported mode. Early tests were made inside the hangar on a test rig which allowed it to rise just a few inches; then today test pilot James "Skeets" Coleman made the first real flight up to 40 feet.

In contrast, Lockheed chose to start the XFV-1 in the horizontal mode, fitting temporary landing gear for fast taxi tests along the runway at Edwards Air Force Base. Test pilot Herman "Fish" Salmon says that the XFV-1 could reach 580mph. But the problem with these "tail sitters" is giving the pilot control over the rate of descent during landing (→ Nov 2).

*The Lockheed XFV-1, ready for vertical take-off from its mobile platform.*

## The LORAN system guides navigators

*Montreal, October 29*
The US's long-range navigation system (LORAN) has won the approbation of the world's airlines as the principal radio navigation system for use across the Atlantic. LORAN was first tested on US fishing boats in 1942, and a top-secret version of the system was used during the D-Day landings in 1944. LORAN operates on a radio electronic system based on the measure of the time differences between radio impulses transmitted by four transmitters. It gives a "fix" to an accuracy of less than 20 square yards. Today's decision is a blow to Britain's even more accurate Decca Navigator system.

## Colonel flies to a record by mistake

*Fairford, England, November 19*
Colonel David Burchinal of the USAF 43rd Bomb Wing based at Sidi Slimane, Morocco, and the crew of his B-47 Stratojet inadvertently found their way into the record books today.

They left their base on November 17 on a routine flight to Britain, but when they arrived over Gloucestershire bad weather prevented a landing, so back they went to Morocco. But the weather there had closed in, too, so they decided to stay aloft until the weather cleared, making nine in-flight refuelings, before landing after 47 hours 35 minutes in the air – a new endurance record for a jet airplane.

# Propeller-driven trainer becomes a jet

*The P.84 Jet Provost trainer: pilot and pupil sit forward of the wings.*

*Bedfordshire, England, June 26*
Today's first flight, at Luton, of the Hunting Percival P.84 Jet Provost opens a new chapter in pilot training. It is the first time an established piston-engined trainer has been converted into a jet.

The Jet Provost is not the first piston-engined aircraft to be converted into a jet, however. That credit belongs to the Swedes, who turned their J 21A fighter into the J 21R. Neither is the Jet Provost the first jet trainer, for the French Fouga CM.170 Magister has been in production since 1952. What is unusual about the P.84 is the extent of the conversion, which has effectively created a completely different aircraft. The side-by-side seats for instructor and pupil are now positioned ahead of the wing. Tricycle landing gear is fitted, and the turbojet engine, an Armstrong Siddeley Viper, is now at the back, fed via inlets on each side of the fuselage above the wing root.

The first prototype's ungainly landing gear will be shortened in production. It has neither a pressurized cockpit nor ejection seats, but it appears to be an interim development which will keep down technical problems and cost.

# YC-130 transport is an impressive vehicle

*The huge Hercules transport has a cruising speed of more than 350mph.*

**Burbank, California, August 23**
Lockheed's big YC-130 Hercules turboprop-driven tactical transport flew for the first time here today. The four-engined and high-winged cargo-carrier will replace the venerable C-47s and newer C-119s as the USAF's main paratroop and combat assault transport aircraft. The USAF asked for an aircraft which could carry 90 paratroopers over 2,000 miles, operate from rough runways and slow to 144mph for paradrops or even less for assault landings.

The Hercules has a 41-foot cargo area with rear-loading ramp which allows vehicles to drive into the airplane; heavy cargo can be slid down the ramp – on the ground or in flight. The YC-130 has four 3,250-hp Allison T56-A-1 turboprops and three-blade propellers and cruises at over 350mph.

# Streamlined YF-102A meets less resistance

**California, December 21**
The prototype of the YF-102A, the first US all-weather supersonic interceptor, exceeded Mach 1 for the first time today near Edwards Air Force Base. Convair redesigned the aircraft with a lengthened "Coke-bottle" fuselage [*see page 502*], correcting problems noted when it flew as the YF-102 earlier this year. The operational F-102 will employ an electronic fire-control system to search out enemy bombers at long range and select a course to attack them with missiles or rockets. When the target is in range and a proper firing attitude set up, the system fires automatically.

*The YF-102A prototype before being redesigned with a "Coke-bottle" waist.*

# Court of inquiry into Comet crashes points to metal fatigue

**Hampshire, England, October 19**
The court of inquiry into the Comet crashes ended today. Its findings have not been published yet, but it seems likely to name the cause of the disasters as metal fatigue due to repeated pressurization. The court met after the most remarkable and comprehensive investigation ever into an air accident. Members of the Royal Aircraft Establishment at Farnborough reassembled three-quarters of the wreckage of the BOAC Comet *Yoke Peter*, which crashed off Elba on January 10.

A complete Comet fuselage was then subjected to constant water-tank testing, which applied the kind of forces it would face during ascent to and descent from 40,000 feet. The inquiry is expected to find that no one was to blame. It is only through the Farnborough tests and the court of inquiry that the problem of metal fatigue in aircraft flying at great speeds at high altitude has been discovered.

# SAS flies over polar region to California

**Los Angeles, November 16**
A Scandinavian Airlines System (SAS) Douglas DC-6B landed here from Copenhagen today to complete the first scheduled passenger flight over the Arctic. The route cuts the journey time from Europe to California to 20 hours, one-third less than it takes other airlines, which follow a transatlantic route with a stopover at New York.

The historic flight, which set off from Denmark yesterday, included stopovers at Sondre Stromfjord, Greenland, and Winnipeg, Manitoba. SAS, which is the flag-carrier of Denmark, Norway and Sweden, received official approval to begin this service last month. The go-ahead followed a great deal of advance planning and route proving [*see page 512*].

The DC-6B offers sufficient range and carrying capacity, but problems of navigation near the magnetic pole have had to be overcome. Surprisingly, weather conditions over the Arctic were not a special difficulty.

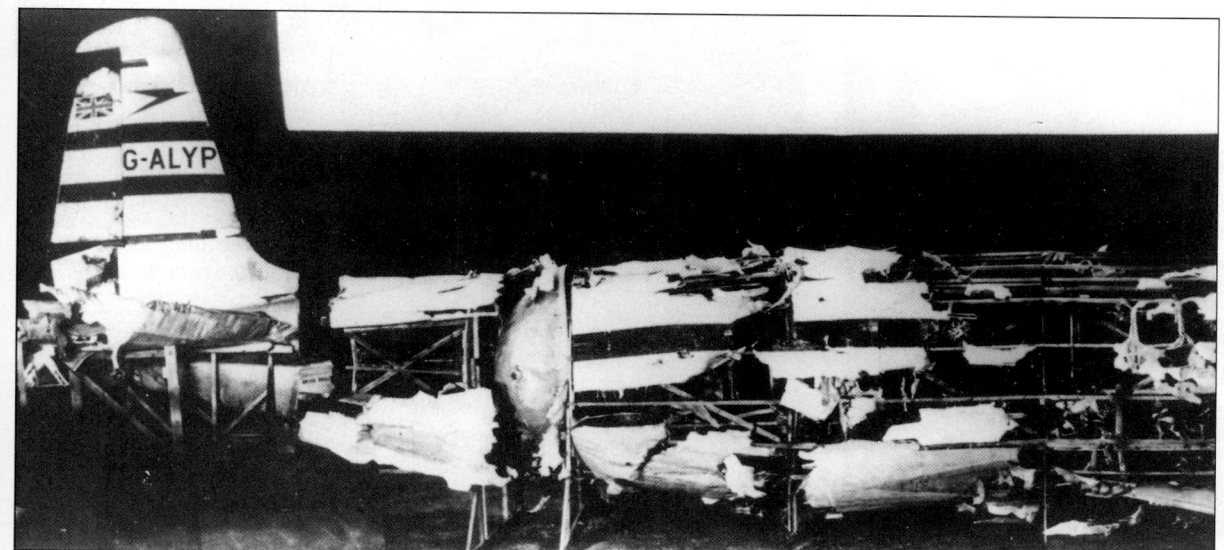

*The wreckage of the BOAC Comet "Yoke Peter" was pieced together to investigate the cause of the disaster.*

The Brochet 120 light tourer was one of eight 1954 Maurice Brochet types.

Sikorsky's S-58, here on pontoons, progenitor of a successful family.

The Morane-Saulnier MS.760 Paris, jet trainer and four-seater.

The Convair Tradewind, last and arguably the best USN flying boat.

The Nord 3201 trainer, with its distinctive trailing-link undercarriage.

Convair's C-131 Samaritan served long and hard with the USAF.

Boeing's Model 367-80 served as the prototype for the highly successful KC-135 and 707 airliner families and was repeatedly modified for research tasks.

The Fairey Jet Gyrodyne helicopter had a main rotor driven by tip-jets.

The Payen PA.49 was a dedicated delta-wing jet research aircraft.

Redesigned, the AOP.9 was the last Auster before Beagle took over.

The French SIPA 300 light jet was built as a tandem primary trainer.

The SFECMAS (later Nord) 1402 was designed for delta research.

The prototype Lockheed YC-130 Hercules, first of more than 2,000 to roll off the production line for a variety of roles, but chiefly as transports.

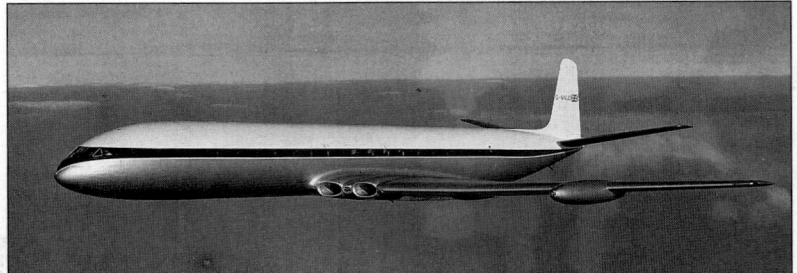

The prototype de Havilland Comet 3 during its maiden flight. The Comet 3 had none of the structural faults which plagued the original Comet I.

McDonnell's F-101A Voodoo: designed as a long range escort fighter, but versatile enough to be re-equipped for reconnaissance and interception.

The Grumman F11F Tiger exceeded Mach 1 without using an afterburner.

The S.E.5000 Baroudeur took off on a trolley and landed on three skids.

The prone-pilot Meteor, for research into high "G" force toleration.

The English Electric Canberra B(I).8, a dedicated night intruder.

The Supermarine 525 paved the way for the Scimitar naval strike fighter.

The Jet Provost T.Mk 1 was the RAF's first basic jet trainer.

The North American FJ-3 Fury, US Navy equivalent of the Sabre.

Douglas's B-66 Destroyer bomber and reconnaissance aircraft.

The English Electric P.1A led directly to the Lightning, although the two had hardly any parts in common. The two turbojet engines were superimposed.

The Soviet MiG-19 proved an effective interceptor and ground attack fighter. This MiG-19PMU is armed with four K-5M air-to-air missiles.

Short's S.B.5 research aircraft, with variable-position wing and tailplane.

The Fairey Delta 2 beat the World speed record by an amazing 310mph.

The prototype Douglas A4D-1 Skyhawk light carrier-based attack aircraft, designed by Ed Heinemann as a small ship-borne nuclear strike aircraft.

The first prototype of the Lockheed XF-104 Starfighter, with the original intake shape and short fuselage. The engine was a Wright J65 Sapphire.

The AS Viper-powered Folland Midge preceded the Gnat fighter.

The Cessna Model 318 (XT-37) a basic pilot trainer for the USAF.

# 1955

1,650mph
USA
Charles Yeager
Bell X-1A
Dec 12, 1953

23,093 miles
USA
James Gallagher
Boeing B-50A
Mar 2, 1949

90,440ft
USA
Arthur Murray
Bell X-1A
Aug 26, 1954

420,000lb
USA
Boeing
B-52A Stratofortress

22,047lb thrust
USSR
Lyulka
AL-7F TRD-31

**Pakistan, January 10**
Pakistan International Airlines is established, following nationalization air-transport.

**Warwickshire, England, January**
Britain's first V-bomber squadron, N° 138, equipped with Valiant B.1s, is formed at RAF Gaydon.

**London, February 11**
The findings of the inquiry into last year's Comet disasters state that both crashes were caused by structural failure owing to metal fatigue in the fuselage.

**Pacific Ocean, February 26**
Test pilot George Smith becomes the first man to survive an ejection made at supersonic speed when he abandons his North American F-100 Super Sabre at Mach 1.05.

**London, March 21**
BOAC announces an order for 19 de Havilland Comet 4 jet-airliners (→ Apr 27, 1958).

**Paris, April 1**
The ratification of the Treaty of Paris lifts the post-war ban on the construction of powered airplanes and the establishment of defensive air forces in Germany (→ Apr 15).

**Montreal, Canada, April 4**
Trans-Canada Air Lines introduces the Vickers Viscount on its route to New York, three days after it first used the airliner on the less important route to Winnipeg; this is the first British-designed aircraft in service with North American carriers since US-built DH-4s were used by the US Mail Service in the 1920s (→ Apr 17).

**London, April 17**
A BEA Viscount bound for Amsterdam makes the first operational departure from the new London Airport Central at Heathrow (→ Jun 16).

**Australia, May 3**
Qantas puts Lockheed Super Constellations into service on its route to Tokyo (→ Mar 2, 1956).

**Ottawa, May 5**
The US and Canada sign an agreement to begin constructing Distant Early Warning (DEW) radar stations across North America (→ Jul 31, 1957).

**New York, May 5**
Pan Am and TWA announce that their "fly now, pay later" schemes have proved a great success.

**California, May 10**
Douglas delivers the last of 448 C-124 Globemaster II transports, affectionately known as "Old Shaky", to the USAF.

**Iwakuni, Japan, June 1**
The US Navy's first Electronic Countermeasures Squadron, VQ-1, is commissioned; it is equipped with Martin P4M-1Q Mercators using combined piston and jet propulsion (→ Jan 17, 1956).

**Canada, June 4**
A Canadian Pacific Airlines DC-6B returns to Vancouver from Amsterdam via Greenland, launching the second scheduled passenger service between Europe and North America over the north polar region (after SAS's) (→ Feb 24, 1957).

**France, June 6**
French pilot Jean Moine lands a Bell 47G-2 helicopter on the summit of Mont Blanc at an altitude of 15,772 feet.

**Santa Monica, Calif, June 7**
Douglas says it is to build a jet-airliner, the DC-8, powered by four Pratt & Whitney JT3 engines.→

**Germany, June 8**
Re-established German airline Lufthansa opens its first transatlantic service, to New York (→ Jun 8, 1956).

**Chicago, June 9**
American Airlines orders 35 of the new Lockheed L-188 Electra four-engined turboprop transports, the US competitor to Britain's Vickers Viscount (→ Jan 12, 1959).

**Moscow, June 15**
The prototype of the Tupolev Tu-104 jet airliner makes its maiden flight (→ Mar 22, 1956).

**California, June 29**
The Boeing B-52 Stratofortress bomber enters USAF service with the 93rd Bomb Wing at Castle Air Force Base (→ Jan 18, 1957).

**Moscow, July 10**
The Tupolev Tu-95 bomber, powered by four turboprop engines each driving two contra-rotating propellers, makes a demonstration flight before invited foreign observers.

**Colorado, July 11**
The US Air Force Academy is dedicated at its temporary location at Lowry Air Force Base.

**Washington, DC, July 26**
Capital Airlines puts the British Vickers Viscount into service on its route to Chicago (→ Feb 14, 1958).

**Bulgaria, July 27**
An El Al Lockheed Constellation en route from Vienna to Tel Aviv is shot down by Bulgarian MiG-15 fighters near the Greek border; all 58 on board are killed.

**New York, August 3**
A Pan American Grace Airways' DC-7B lands after flying from Buenos Aires in 20 hours 2 minutes, a record time for an airliner on this route.

**Groom Dry Lake, Nev, August 4**
Tony LeVier pilots the Lockheed U-2 reconnaissance airplane on a 36-minute test flight; the U-2 first left the ground during a high-speed run on August 1 (→ Apr 1, 1956).

**England, August 29**
W F Gibb flies an Olympus-engined Canberra B.2 to a world record altitude of 65,889 feet.

**Melun-Villaroche, France, Sep 20**
André Turcat pilots the Nord 1500 Griffon I delta-winged airplane on its first flight (→ Feb 25, 1959).

**Australia, October 3**
Australian National Airlines and Trans-Australia Airlines introduce tourist-class services.

**Tampico, Mexico, October 10**
Helicopters from the carrier USS *Saipan* rescue 5,439 people stranded on the roofs of their homes in an area devastated by tropical rains.

**Seattle, October 13**
Pan Am announces an order worth $269 million for 25 Douglas DC-8s and 20 Boeing 707s (→ Jun 1, 1956).

**USA, October 16**
The Boeing 367-80 (707) flies from Seattle to Washington, DC, in 3 hours 58 minutes at an average of 592mph; it returns the same day in 4 hours and 8 minutes, an average of 567mph (→ Mar 11, 1957).

**California, October 22**
The prototype Republic YF-105A Thunderchief fighter-bomber exceeds Mach 1 during the course of its first flight (→ Mar 22, 1957).

**Washington, DC, November 1**
The USS *Boston*, armed with the Convair Terrier surface-to-air rocket, is commissioned by the US Navy; it is the world's first guided-missile cruiser.

**The Netherlands, November 24**
The prototype Fokker F.27 Friendship medium-range twin-turboprop transport flies for the first time (→ Sep 28, 1958).

**Baltimore, Md, December 4**
US aviation pioneer Glenn L Martin dies at the age of 69; in 1918 he developed the first major US bomber, the MB-1.

**Santa Monica, Calif, Dec 20**
Douglas's long-haul DC-7C makes its first flight (→ Jun 1, 1956).

*World in your hand: Spain's Iberia is trying to develop its international network; most of its post-war trade has been on domestic routes.* ▶

## Pan American carries out trials of weather radar

*USA, February 23*
Airline passengers and crew are likely to benefit from a new radar system tested today by Pan American aboard one of its DC-6B aircraft. The onboard radar system, built by Bendix Aviation, will give the pilot a clear picture of features on the ground, including mountain ranges and large stretches of water.

The benefit to passengers will come from the radar's capacity to detect storms ahead on the flight path, particularly at night when thunderclouds are often impossible to see. This ability will enable the captain to change course well in advance to avoid the storm, ensuring a smooth flight. The unit is housed in the aircraft's nose.

The tests follow the success of a similar radar manufactured by RCA, which is now being installed in United Air Lines' fleet.

## Idlewild airport is ready for a facelift

*New York, February 20*
The Port of New York Authority plans a multi-million-dollar project over five years to turn New York's Idlewild international airport into what it calls the "most beautiful, efficient, and functional" airport in the world. The first step will be a $60 million development of the passenger terminals. These will include a three-storey international arrivals building, flanked by two-storey buildings for foreign airlines, which will be finished in early 1957. There will also be seven terminals costing about $5 million each, on 11 or 22-acre sites, for US carriers, which will be completed by 1960. The terminals will front a 160-acre plaza with an artificial lagoon.

The extent of the planned improvements to Idlewild is evident from the new terminals' predicted capacity to handle some 140 airplanes a day. The authorities expect Idlewild to handle around 7 million passengers per year in 1960, and 8.5 million a year by 1965 (→ Aug 3).

# USAF deploys air-launched fighters

*Parasite: a Republic GRF-84 Thunderflash hooked beneath a GRB-36 ...*

*... and after release. The GRB-36 extends the GRF-84's range by 4,000 miles.*

*Great Falls, Montana, March 8*
America's strategic intelligence gathering capability was enhanced significantly today with the activation of the 91st Strategic Reconnaissance Squadron at Malmstrom Air Force Base. The squadron is equipped with modified Republic RF-84 Thunderflash fighters, which are carried aloft by modified Convair B-36 bombers, the GRB-36J.

The unit's 25 RF-84s have been given the designation GRF-84K after having a retractable hook fitted in the nose. This engages in a trapeze fitted in the bomb bay of the bomber. In flight, the cockpit, most of the rudder and the upper portion of the fuselage of the fighter are tucked inside the "mother" airplane. The mother then carries the fighter 4,000 miles to a release point within 1,000 miles of the area to be surveyed. The GRF-84 then uses its speed and maneuverability to penetrate the target area, make its observations or take photographs, then return to the GRB-36J and hook up in the bomb bay for the flight back to base. Details of the new unit's missions are shrouded in secrecy, but they could be used for missions over the Soviet Union.

Germany, Britain and the US experimented with this "parasite" concept using airships as aircraft-carriers before the war. Trials with larger airplanes carrying smaller ones aloft were also made in the USSR, Germany and Britain. In 1949 the USAF tested the McDonnell XF-85 Goblin parasite fighter intended to defend the bombers.

## Two-thirds of the US defense budget is allocated to air power

*Seattle, March 10*
The announcement today by Boeing president William Allen that last year was the first in which his company made sales worth $1 billion comes as no surprise to observers of the US aircraft industry. Business is booming for suppliers of military and commercial aircraft so that Boeing, with its bombers, tankers and missiles for the USAF, and its new 707 airliner, stands to do well in the future. Boeing can thank President Ei-

senhower for a large portion of the new orders: he gave the impetus to continued spending on military aircraft in his January State of the Union address. He said that the US military budget would place particular emphasis on the air power of the USAF, US Navy and Marines.

The Cold War is good for the aircraft business. Almost two-thirds of $34 billion proposed for the defense budget is allocated to air power, with half the budget assigned to the USAF alone.

"Ike" stressed in his address that the US would depend on its nuclear retaliatory power as "the principal deterrent to military aggression".

A good part of the USAF's budget will therefore go toward Boeing's strategic B-52 bomber and KC-135 tanker. It will also have to fund the Century Series of fighters from North American, McDonnell, Convair, Lockheed and Republic as part of what is aiming to be a 137-wing force.

# Lufthansa hopes for a post-war recovery

*The first photo-call for the cabin staff of West Germany's reborn airline.*

*A Lufthansa stewardess in training.*

**Bonn, April 15**
Airliners bearing the Lufthansa name are once again flying on European routes. On April 1, Lufthansa, now revived as the West German flag-carrier, began domestic services between Hamburg and Munich, taking in Frankfurt, Cologne and Düsseldorf. Its first international services, to London and Madrid, were launched today. As the Paris treaty restoring West German air sovereignty will not come into force until May 5, the Western Allies have granted Lufthansa special permission to begin flights. The airline has 44-seat Convair 340s, with British pilots. Their German co-pilots are eagerly learning the latest technical advances (→ Jun 8).

# Alouette II helicopter makes record start

**Buc, France, June 6**
Driven by a powerful gas turbine engine, a French Alouette II piloted by Jean Boulet set a helicopter altitude record of 26,934 feet today. The Alouette II, which made its first flight on March 12, differs considerably from piston-engined helicopters. It is smoother in flight, and the engine, small enough to be mounted on top of the aircraft, offers far more cabin space as well as being powered by inexpensive kerosene. Turbine helicopters are also being developed in the US.

Charles Marchetti, in charge of the production team, had the existing Alouette I redesigned around the more powerful Turbomeca Artouste II powerplant. The value of gas-turbine power was demonstrated today (→ Jun 13, 1958).

*Boulet with the Alouette's altimeter.*

# French Caravelle jet speeds to success

*Toulouse, France, May 27*
France's first jet airliner, the first prototype Sud-Est SE 210 Caravelle, flew for the first time today. The highly successful flight marks the full post-war rehabilitation of the French aircraft industry.

The Caravelle is the first short-haul jet airliner. It is also the first aircraft to have its engines mounted at the rear, on either side of the fuselage. It was originally planned to have three Atar engines, but the availability of the more powerful and fully-developed British Rolls-Royce Avon engine resulted in a redesign. The pressurized fuselage, which seats 80, is the same diameter as that of the Comet, and so the British jet's nose and cockpit design were also adopted. The Caravelle is intended to operate from today's airports and to cruise at 460mph for stage lengths up to about 1,200 miles. It is expected to have wide appeal (→ May 2, 1957).

*The engine control console is centrally located, between pilot and copilot.*

# Douglas announces its first civilian jet

*Santa Monica, Calif, June 7*
The Douglas Aircraft Company, renowned for its DC-3, DC-4, DC-6 and DC-7 airliners, has so far lagged behind its rival Boeing in going jet-powered. But it clearly picked up the challenge today with the announcement of a multi-million-dollar commitment to build its first civil jet – the DC-8.

It is widely believed in the industry that the move was prompted by a visit from Pan American executives who are anxious to see a competitor to Boeing, with its 707, so that the Seattle firm cannot call all the shots. Boeing is certain to produce the first American jet airliner, but Douglas is promising the airlines what it hopes will be a superior product. By giving the wing less sweepback Douglas hope the DC-8 will be easier to fly.

In planning the design, the team at Douglas took full account of the impact of the introduction of tourist-class fares on the North Atlantic routes in 1952. The DC-8 is just wide enough to seat six abreast, although the Boeing 707 can do the same. This should make operations considerably more profitable, provided that the airlines can fill the seats (→ Oct 13).

# British Viscount wins American orders

*Washington, DC, June 16*
The first of 60 Vickers Viscount 745 turboprop airliners was delivered here today to Capital Airlines. The occasion was remarkable on two counts: first, because no US airline has ever before had an airplane with gas-turbine engines (either turboprops or jets); second, because no US airline has ever used an airplane built outside the US.

The Viscount has won this big order – and dozens of others throughout the world – strictly on its merits. Its four 1,600-hp Rolls-Royce Dart engines give the airliner unprecedented speed, altitude and smoothness, and its appeal to passengers is further enhanced by its large elliptical windows.

Each Viscount in the new Capital fleet has a luxurious 40-seat interior, but the airliner can be adapted to take up to 59 passengers, and the future "stretched" Series 800 will seat as many as 80. Already the acclaimed British turboprop has been bought by over 20 airlines in 15 countries; its popularity shows no sign of abating (→ Jul 26).

*The Viscount, here in Aer Lingus colors, is winning orders around the world.*

# Mooney has built more than 340 Mites

*Kerrville, Texas, September*
First product of the new Mooney Aircraft company – set up by Al and Art Mooney in 1946 – the M-18 Mite is still selling well. More than 340 M-18s, an attractive single-seat light monoplane, have been built so far. The Mite is characterized by modern cantilever construction, an enclosed cockpit and a swept-forward vertical tail which seems likely to be a Mooney trademark. The first M-18 completed certification with a 25-hp Crosley engine. Mooney plans to market the M-18LA with a Lycoming engine and the M-18C with a Continental, both of 65-hp.

*The Mooney Mite M-18 serial number 336 was licensed on September 9.*

# French unveil a Mirage

*The Mirage: Dassault has concentrated on the aircraft's power:weight ratio.*

*Melun-Villaroche, France, June 25*
French aircraft designer Marcel Dassault pondered for some time before naming the slender, delta-winged MD.550 jet fighter which flew here for the first time today. He finally chose to name it the Mirage, because, as he said, "the enemy will see it, but he will not hear it or believe it".

The specification called for an interceptor which could fly at Mach 2 and climb to 57,600 feet in four minutes. Dassault appears to have achieved both with this small but powerful fighter powered by two 2,160-lb thrust Armstrong Siddeley Viper jets built in France under license. The Mirage is too small for military use in its present format, and Dassault is already working on a Mirage II development which he plans to power with two Turbomeca Gabizo jets fitted with reheat.

The French company is confident that the Mirage will attract foreign orders like its predecessor, the Mystère. One great strength of Dassault aircraft is their designers' concentration on achieving a good power to weight ratio, unlike many US aircraft which are often burdened by multiple systems redundancy and heavyweight equipment (→ Nov 17, 1956).

# Supersonic fighter snatches speed record

*California, August 20*
The USAF's latest jet fighter, the North American F-100 Super Sabre, took another record today at Edwards Air Force Base. Flown just feet the desert floor by Colonel H A Haines, an F-100C reached just over 822mph, which, when ratified by the International Aeronautical Federation (FAI), will be the first world speed record set by a production plane at over Mach 1.

The Super Sabre is the USA's first fighter capable of sustained supersonic speed in level flight. The YF-100A prototype set the previous world speed record in 1953. The Super Sabre is the first of the new Century series of fighters being built for the USAF. Others include the McDonnell F-101 Voodoo, the Convair F-102 Delta Dagger, the Lockheed F-104 Starfighter (intended to reach Mach 2) and the Re-

*English Electric's P.1A prototype.*

public F-105 Thunderchief. Supersonic jets look set to steal the limelight in the coming years.

In Britain, English Electric is aiming to produce a Mach 2 fighter from the prototype P.1 for the RAF; a prototype will be on display at the annual Farnborough Air Show next month. France is developing its Dassault Mirage, which flew for the first time in June [*see story above*].

## Women's record is to last for posterity

*France, May 31*
Airwoman Jacqueline Auriol succeeded in getting her name inscribed in the record books for ever today. The French pilot flew the Dassault Mystère IVN jet fighter to a speed of 715.2mph to wrest the women's world speed record back from veteran American flyer Jacqueline Cochran, who had set the previous record of 652.5mph in a Sabre [*see page 520*].

Cochran's record had been set to stand in the record books for all time after her own announcement – in her capacity as vice-president of the International Aeronautical Federation – that female flying records were to be abolished from tomorrow. Auriol's record beat the deadline by a matter of hours.

## US airports to get big federal cash aid

*Washington, DC, August 3*
US commercial aviation and communities which want a better airline service received a big boost today when President Eisenhower signed the Civilian Airport Modernization Bill into law. The legislation, which was originally opposed by the US Department of Commerce, breaks new ground in airport funding. For the first time it establishes a long-term program of federal government aid toward the construction of airports in the US. The new law initiates a program of airport construction and modernization over the next four years. It will involve the allocation of $252 million of federal money (→ Apr 3, 1957).

# Bomb kills 44 in mid-air explosion

*United Airlines' logo is still visible on the twisted wreckage of the DC-6B.*

*Denver, Colorado, November 14*
The FBI (Federal Bureau of Investigation) said today that a time bomb caused the mid-air explosion and crash on November 1 which killed all 44 aboard a United Air Lines DC-6B after it took off from Denver's Stapleton airport. The bomb had been placed in his mother's luggage by 23-year-old John Gilbert Graham. He had bought six 25-cent vending-machine insurance polices worth $37,500 on his mother's life minutes before the airplane took off, and admitted planting the device. Ironically, he could not have collected on the policies as his mother had not signed them (→ May 15, 1956).

## Financial restraints result in death of British jet transport

*Surrey, England, November 11*
Thousands of workers at Vickers in Weybridge were today stunned to learn of the cancellation of the V1000, Britain's 100-seater passenger jet with transatlantic potential.

Six V1000s were being built for the RAF, but the real significance of the cancellation is that it also ends the development of its commercial airliner derivative, the VC-7. Vickers managing director George Edwards commented: "We have handed to the Americans, without a struggle, the entire world market for big jet airliners."

The V1000 began life when air force chiefs realized the advantages in the combination of speed, range and short-field performace of the Vickers Valiant jet bomber. It seemed logical to produce a transport derivative which would have a bigger, all-pressurized fuselage and

*Another proposed 4-Conway transport, the HP.115, remains a brochure.*

engines with greater thrust and fuel economy. Rolls-Royce came up with the Conway bypass jet, the first turbofan.

The V1000 was killed by government pressure on the RAF to save money. The decision to scrap it was taken because it was one major project which could be dropped without causing the RAF great long-term damage. Nobody thought of the world jet market.

**A scene from British movie "The Dambusters", which opened May 16.**

# 'Coach-class' plan gets official go-ahead

*Washington, DC, September 9*
The US Civil Aeronautics Board (CAB) has given the thumbs-up to a request from the big three domestic airlines to offer a single "coach-class" fare of just $160 for round-trip coast-to-coast flights. American Airlines, TWA and United Air Lines will take advantage of the fare to expand coach-class services. A boom in coast-to-coast flying is also expected, with other airlines

likely to seek routes. Coach-class tariffs are not new on the transcontinental routes, however. American and TWA offered a $110 one-way fare at the end of 1949, on their stopping DC-4 services. TWA's slightly shorter New York/Los Angeles service was similarly priced in 1951. Fares were lowered further in 1952 at the behest of CAB, as airlines vied for shares of the transcontinental market.

*The Sud-Est SE.210 Caravelle was the first airliner with tail-mounted jet engines, reducing cabin noise levels and leaving the wing uncluttered.*

*The Scottish Aviation Twin Pioneer, a sixteen-place STOL transport.*

*The slender-winged Hurel-Dubois HD.32 was a moderate success.*

*Cessna's 172: for 20 years almost the standard four-seater for the whole non-communist world.*

*The Convair CV-440 was developed as a quieter, faster development of the previous CV-340.*

*The Handley Page HPR.3 Herald originally had four Leonides Major piston engines, before being given two turboprops in its production form.*

*The Westland Widgeon was basically an S-51 Dragonfly with five seats.*

*The bomber-derived Tupolev Tu-104 was the USSR's first jetliner.*

*The five-seat Sud-Est SE.313 Alouette II turbine-powered helicopter proved to be an enormous success for its makers. Just over 1,300 were built.*

*More than 600 Fokker F.27 Friendships were sold; the current Fokker 50 is a refined modern equivalent.*

*The Sapphire-engined Flug und Fahrzeugwerke FFA P-16 jet fighter jet fighter prototype, from Switzerland, never reached production status.*

*The experimental Nord 1500 Griffon I served as the prototype for an experimental light interceptor project intended to have a turbo-ramjet.*

The Yakovlev Yak-24 powered by two 1,700-shp ASh-82V piston engines, was an outstanding transport helicopter. Six military and civil versions were built.

The prototype Republic YF-105 Thunderchief strike fighter lacked the engine inlets and area-ruled fuselage of F-105Bs like the aircraft shown here.

The Gnat light fighter was exported to India, Finland and Yugoslavia.

Hispano's HA-200 Saeta jet trainer also had ground attack capability.

The Avon-engined Ryan X-13 Vertijet was an early experimental VTOL.

The Beech Model 73 Jet Mentor was an unsuccessful basic jet trainer.

Still in service today, the Saab J35 Draken has a distinctive double-delta wing and was Sweden's first supersonic fighter. Saab delivered 606.

The Martin XP6M SeaMaster jet-powered flying boat; 11 of these very fast T-tailed aircraft were built for mine-laying duties with the US Navy.

The Myasishchev M-4 "Bison" was destined to serve for 37 years.

The Mach-3 Bell X-2 made its first powered flight during 1955.

The Chance Vought XF8U Crusader fighter featured a variable-incidence wing to allow a lower nose attitude on approach; 1,281 were delivered.

The existence of the Lockheed U-2 spyplane was not acknowledged until 1960. It was used by the USAF and CIA for secret reconnaissance overflights.

# 1956

2,094mph
USA
Milburn Apt
Bell X-2
Sep 27, 1956

23,093 miles
USA
James Gallagher
Boeing B-50A
Mar 2, 1949

125,907ft
USA
Iven Kincheloe
Bell X-2
Sep 7, 1956

450,000lb
USA
Boeing
B-52C Stratofortress

22,047lb thrust
USSR
Lyul'ka
AL-7F TRD-31

**Washington, DC, January 17**
The US Department of Defense reveals the existence of the Semi-Automatic Ground Environment (SAGE) electronic system; it is a means of locating enemy airplanes and calculating the flight paths of interceptors.

**Sweden, January 26**
SAAB's prototype interceptor, the Draken J-35, breaks the sound barrier in a non-afterburner climb.

**Paris, February 6**
William Judd lands his Cessna 180 after a solo flight of 25 hours 15 minutes across the North Atlantic from the US.

**London, February 10**
Marshal of the RAF Viscount Trenchard, who spearheaded the creation of the service in 1918, dies at the age of 83.

**Hampshire, England, February 24**
The first Gloster Javelin delta-wing interceptor fighters enter RAF service, with 46 Squadron.

**Sydney, March 2**
Qantas introduces a route change on its Super Constellation service to London which cuts the flight time by more than 20 hours, to 54 hours 30 minutes westbound and 52 hours eastbound; the new service flies via Bangkok and Jakarta and eliminates the overnight stop in Singapore (→ Jan 14, 1958).

**Suffolk, England, April 1**
The first top-secret Lockheed U-2 spyplanes arrive at the USAF's Lakenheath base (→ Jul 4).

**Florida, April 2**
The USAF launches a Snark guided missile; its experimental flight covers over 1,500 miles.

**Bahamas, April 5**
An old B-25 bomber, converted for civilian use as a cargo airplane, disappears without trace in the area known as the "Bermuda Triangle" (→ Nov 9).

**Istres, France, April 17**
Michel Chalard pilots the SFECMAS Gerfaut II experimental delta-winged interceptor on its first flight.

**Santa Monica, Calif, April 20**
Link Aviation Company is commissioned by Douglas to build a "total test-flight simulator" for the DC-8, so that pilots can be trained to fly the new jet without leaving the ground (→ Jul 19, 1957).

**Melun-Villaroche, France, May 15**
The Dassault Super Mystère B.2 jet-fighter makes its first flight, piloted by Gérard Muselli.

**Australia, May 16**
Trans-Australia Airlines opens a weekly direct night service between Sydney and Darwin (→ Jan 3, 1958).

**New York, June 1**
Eastern Air Lines finally succeeds in its bid to take over US carrier National Airlines, thus ending a five-year-long leagal battle. National Airlines operated ailiners for a total of 25 years without a single accident.

**New York, June 1**
Pan Am introduces the long-range DC-7C on its transatlantic routes.

**Frankfurt, June 8**
Lufthansa introduces the Super Constellation on its transatlantic service to New York.

**USA, June 20**
The USS *Thetis Bay*, the US Navy's first helicopter assault carrier, is commissioned.

**Arizona, June 30**
A TWA Super Constellation collides with a United Air Lines DC-7 over the Grand Canyon, killing 128 (→ Jul).

**Lincolnshire, England, July 11**
The first Avro Vulcan delta-winged bombers to be operational with the RAF are delivered to 83 Squadron at Waddington.

**Yucca Flat, Nev, July 19**
A Northrop F-89J Scorpion fighter fires a Douglas MB-1 Genie, the first nuclear-armed air-to-air missile to be launched (→ Oct 10).

**Milan, Italy, August 9**
The Fiat G.91, produced for Nato as a light strike-fighter, makes its first flight.

**Washington, DC, August 24**
A US Army Piasecki H-21 helicopter lands here to become the first rotary-winged aircraft to fly non-stop across the US; it left San Diego, California, yesterday, and covered the 2,610 miles in 31 hours 40 minutes, with six air refuelings.

**USA, September 7**
USAF test pilot Iven Kincheloe is hailed by the US press as "the first of the spacemen" after he makes the first human flight over 100,000 feet, taking the Bell X-2 rocket airplane to a world record altitude of 125,907 feet (→ Sep 27).

**Moscow, September 15**
Aeroflot puts the Tupolev Tu-104 turbojet airliner into service for the first time, on its route to Irkutsk.

**Bonn, September 24**
The Luftwaffe is officially re-established as West Germany's air force; it is under the command of General Josef Kammhuber, responsible for the air defense of the Third Reich from summer 1940 until fall 1943 (→ Oct 31, 1958).

**Washington, DC, October 1**
NACA awards its Distinguished Service Medal to Richard T Whitcomb, inventor of the "area rule" concept, which provides for a "Coke-bottle" shaped fuselage to reduce high-speed drag.

**South Australia, October 11**
An RAF Vickers Valiant jet-bomber of 49 Squadron under the command of Squadron Leader E J G Flavell drops Britain's first atomic bomb, over Maralinga (→ May 15, 1957).

**Cornwall, England, October 15**
The RAF retires its last wartime Avro Lancaster bomber still in service from the School of Maritime Reconnaissance at St Mawgan.

**Wichita, Kan, October 24**
Boeing delivers the last of 1,373 production versions of the B-47 bomber; in all, 2,032 B-47s have been handed over to the USAF, the other 659 being built by Douglas and Lockheed.

**Antarctica, October 31**
The US Navy R4D-5 Skytrain *Que Sera Sera*, commanded by Rear-Admiral George Dufek, becomes the first airplane to make a landing at the South Pole.

**Egypt, November 5**
British and French paratroops make a successful airborne attack on Port Said during hostilities precipitated by Egypt's refusal to withdraw from the Suez Canal.

**Fort Worth, Tex, November 11**
The prototype Convair XB-58 Hustler supersonic bomber makes a 40-minute first flight.→

**London, November**
The Supersonic Transport Aircraft Committee is established to study the possibilty of building a supersonic airliner. It is made up of representatives of Britain's aircraft and engine manufacturers and the national airlines, as well as government officials and staff from the Royal Aircraft Establishment at Farnborough.→

**Washington, DC, December 1**
The US Army announces that the Fourth Field Artillery, a combat unit equipped with mules, based at Fort Carson, Colorado, is to be retired and replaced with helicopters.

*Marcel Dassault's Mirage III fighter benefited from the SNECMA Atar turbojet, developed by Hermann Oestrich and his team.* ▶

## Last DC-3 in service sold by subsidiary of Belgian airline

*Brussels, January 7*
Today Sobelair, the charter subsidiary of the Belgian national airline Sabena, sold its airliner OO-SBA, which is believed to be the last aircraft actually built as a Douglas DC-3 to be still flying.

Of course, this still leaves some 2,600 of the DC-3's C-47, C-53 and R4D versions in military service around the world, plus another 2,200 which were converted into civil transports. Thanks to the extremely strong wing-spars, which have a life well in excess of 40,000 hours' flying time, many of these aircraft could go on flying passengers for another 20 or more years, easily outlasting their supposed successors (→ Jan 3, 1958).

## Advanced seaplane developed for navy

*Baltimore, Md, March 8*
Modifications to the second of the US Navy's advanced jet seaplanes, the Martin XP6M-1 SeaMaster, are being made to correct flight control problems which caused the crash of the first prototype last December. The four-engined, swept-wing aircraft, which has a maximum speed of over 600mph, is the most advanced seaplane in the world.

The primary roles of the SeaMaster are expected to be minelaying and reconnaissance. It is equipped with a watertight rotary door in the hull on which mines, bombs, or a camera pod can be fitted. Additional funding of $120 million is expected for the XP6M-1.

**Advertising global connections.**

# Fairey jet smashes past 1,000mph

*Fairey's Delta 2 has added 310mph to the world speed record at a single blow.*

*Sussex, England, March 10*
Britain's experimental Fairey Delta 2 today became the first airplane ever to set an official record faster than 1,000mph. Piloted by Peter Twiss, it made the necessary two runs over a measured 9.7-mile course, within 30 minutes of each other, off the Sussex coast between Ford and Chichester. Twiss flew at an altitude of 38,000 feet, and the flight took a mere 23 minutes. It seems that the new world air speed record, awaiting ratification from the International Aeronautical Federation (FAI), will be recorded as 1,131.76mph, compared with the record of 822mph which was set last year by a USAF F-100C [*see story on page 538*]. Each run ended at well over Mach 2 (1,320mph), so with more fuel the FD.2 could go 200mph faster.

The Fairey Delta 2, built to investigate flight and control at transonic and supersonic speeds, has delta wings and a Rolls-Royce Avon engine.

*Record-breaking pilot Peter Twiss.*

## Tupolev Tu-104, Soviet jet transport, makes its debut in the West

*Pressmen at London airport get as close as they can to the Tupolev Tu-104.*

*London, March 22*
When the Tu-104 jet airliner flashed overhead through a gap in the clouds today, its shape was somehow familiar to those who had been waiting eagerly at London's Heathrow Airport for a glimpse of the first Soviet jet airliner making its first flight to the West. Aircraft buffs on the ground were in no doubt. They shouted: "It's a Badger!". This is the Nato designation for one of the most widely deployed of the Soviet Union's bombers.

After the airliner had landed, experts crowded round for a closer look. Serialed L-5400, it was, they were told, the Tu-104 prototype. It was bringing the head of the KGB to discuss security for the forthcoming visit to Britain of Soviet leaders, who will travel in three Tu-104s.

The Tu-104 does indeed appear to be a straightforward conversion of the Tu-16 "Badger", with the same RD-3M engines but a much bigger fully-pressurized fuselage seating 50 passengers. A 70-seat or even 100-seat version is planned.

While the Tu-104 is an economical way of turning a bomber into a jetliner, the result is very far from being high technology in Western terms, and would seem to have little chance of selling outside the Soviet bloc. Some features even date back to the Soviet-pirated Boeing B-29, although on the other hand the aircraft's external finish appears good.

Clearly the Tu-16, and the even larger Tu-95 "Bear" turboprop bomber, already in Soviet air force service in substantial numbers, can be regarded as wholly practical aircraft (→ Sep 15, 1956).

# Inflatable rubber airplane takes to air

*Bedfordshire, England, March 7*
Dan Perkins, engineer at Britain's Royal Aircraft Establishment, made his first flight today in an inflatable airplane. Weighing a mere 167 pounds, the rubberized-fabric craft was brought to the airfield at Cardington deflated and wrapped around its 4-foot propeller and wheel struts in a bundle 14 inches in diameter. It took 25 minutes to inflate it, using a large domestic vacuum cleaner. Then, with Perkins strapped into the inflatable cabin, the aircraft, which has a 6-hp engine and a delta wing of 160 square feet mounted on a tricycle frame, rose effortlessly into the air and made a smooth touchdown.

A similar airplane, made of rubber-coated nylon, developed by the Goodyear Aircraft Corporation in the US, flew for the first time on February 26.

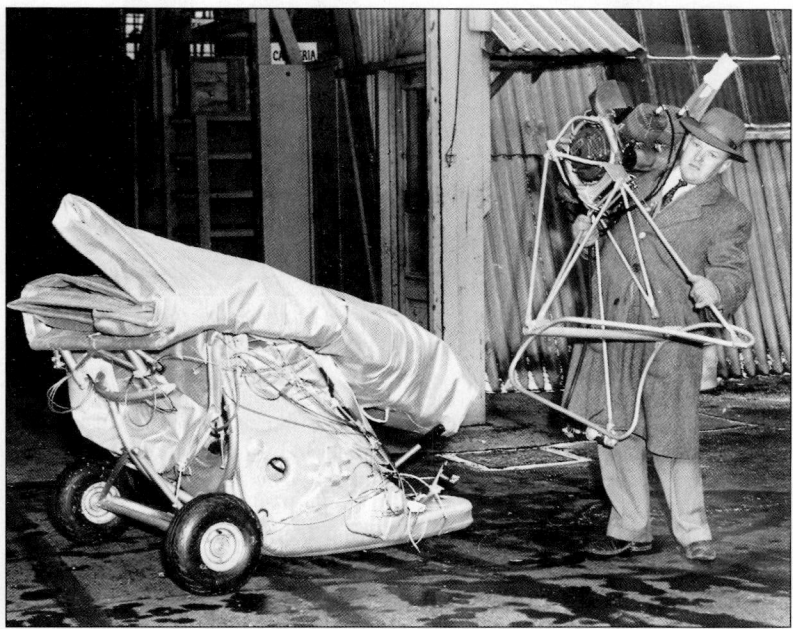

*An inflatable airplane produced by the Goodyear Corporation in the US.*

# US drops hydrogen bomb in Pacific trial

*Bikini Atoll, Pacific, May 21*
The nuclear edge enjoyed by the USSR for the past six months ended today when a USAF B-52B Stratofortress bomber piloted by Major David Critchlow dropped a hydrogen bomb more than twice as destructive as the one dropped by the Soviets in November.

While the Soviets succeeded in being the first to drop an H-bomb from an aircraft, their 1.6-megaton device was only half as powerful as today's air-dropped H-bomb, a 3.75 megaton device which was released from the Stratofortress at more than 40,000 feet above Bikini Atoll. US radio, television and newspaper reporters and civil defense officials aboard the USS *Mount McKinley* observed the explosion, about 4,000 feet over the atoll, at 5.50am.

*Major Critchlow in the B-52B.*

# Lockheed F-104 jet breaks new barrier

*California, April 27*
The aircraft which the US press dubbed the "missile with the man in it" has reached its highest speed to date. So called because of its slender, pointed fuselage, stubby wings and speed, the Lockheed YF-104A Starfighter reached Mach 2 in level flight today. Unlike the XF-104 prototype, which reached Mach 1.79 last year with a Wright J65 turbojet with afterburner, the YF-104A has a General Electric J79, offering 45 per cent more power also with afterburner. It has just been decided that when the Starfighter goes into service with the USAF, it will carry the Sidewinder air-to-air missile (→ May 16, 1958).

*An F-104 over Palmdale, Calif.*

# Boeing plans new medium-range jet

*Seattle, May 17*
To meet the demands for speed and comfort from travellers who fly from airports not big enough to handle its 707, Boeing is planning to develop a smaller jet transport designed to serve such terminals. The airliner may have three engines and seat about 70.

The plan is considered a risky venture by experts, who see it as a late response to the Douglas DC-9. This is at an advanced stage of development and has been ordered by several airlines for short-haul routes (→ May 7, 1957).

# Figures reveal big growth in airline passenger traffic

*Busy scene at London Heathrow.*

*New York, February 7*
Business is booming for the airlines, and it is set to grow ever faster as the jet-airliner comes into its own. Figures released here today show that at the end of 1955 world passenger traffic was growing at around 15 per cent a year, or doubling every five years. The total number of revenue passenger miles flown last year was 40 billion, and the world's scheduled airlines carried some 69 million passengers.

Around half the total is on US domestic routes. The most popular international route is the North Atlantic, where the most important factor in producing growth has been the price of tickets. People want to fly, and there has been constant pressure on the airlines to reduce fares. The year of biggest growth followed the introduction of tourist-class fares in 1952.

Looking to the future, the airlines are clearly planning for even greater growth. They are ordering new, bigger, faster jets from Boeing and Douglas in batches of ten and 20, and, if present trends continue, in another five years traffic will more than double. Sometime in the next two years the number of people traveling by air is likely to exceed those traveling by sea; then it will be possible to say that air travel has truly come of age (→ Sep 16, 1957).

# Piper Comanche makes its first flight

*Lock Haven, Penn, May 24*
Having broken with its high-wing tradition by creating the PA-23 Apache, the Piper Aircraft Corporation today unveiled a second low-wing light airplane, the PA-24 Comanche, which made its first flight today.

Indeed, the new four-seater Comanche might almost be mistaken for a wartime fighter because it is an all-metal, beautifully stream-lined aircraft with retractable tricycle landing gear and an almost fighter-like cockpit canopy. The prototype is powered by a 180-hp Lycoming engine, but future models could have various engines of up to 400-hp, giving the Comanche something akin to the performance of a wartime fighter too. Preparations for production are under way, and the first deliveries to customers are scheduled for next year.

*A new member of the Piper family, the streamlined Comanche tourer.*

# Secret US spyplane makes Soviet flight

*Wiesbaden, Germany, July 4*
The Lockheed U-2, a secret reconnaissance aircraft developed for the US Central Intelligence Agency, took off from here today on a mission to the USSR. The spyplane later returned with photographs of Soviet industrial facilities and military installations.

The single-engined aircraft, which carried only its pilot and camera equipment, has a 79-foot wingspan and looks ungainly, but is really of highly advanced design and construction. The U-2 can fly above 70,000 feet, well out of reach of any Soviet aircraft or ground-to-air missile, and has a range of over 3,000 miles. Today it flew over Czechoslovakia, Moscow and Leningrad before following the Baltic coast back to West Germany.

The U-2 undermines the Soviet refusal to allow aerial inspections in the interests of arms control and peace. The spyplane can also serve to trace nuclear "dust" at high altitudes (→ Feb 1, 1957).

# Arizona crash gives rise to huge claims

*Chicago, July*
Insurance claims for the worst commercial aviation accident in history, the collision on June 30 over the Grand Canyon between a United Air Lines DC-7 and a TWA Constellation, will top $5.5 million. There was $1.5 million coverage on the Constellation, about $2 million on the DC-7 and an estimated $2 million in travel life insurance for the 128 passengers who lost their lives in the tragedy.

With the US Civil Aeronautics Board due to start hearings into the cause of the accident due on August 1, finger pointing is rife. The Aircraft Owners and Pilots Association charges in an editorial for its magazine that both airliners, which were using visual flight rules (VFR), chose not to use the air traffic control system. Meanwhile, members of the US Airline Pilots Association say that the air traffic control system, which had its funding slashed by Congress in 1953 and 1954, is out of date.

# Thunderbirds step up to Super Sabres

*Four top US Air Force pilots put the supersonic Super Sabre through its paces.*

*New Hampshire, June 30*
With afterburners roaring, the USAF's aerial display squadron, the Thunderbirds, went through its paces today before 150,000 people at the dedication of Portsmouth Air Force Base. It was its first display in supersonic North American F-100 Super Sabres.

The switch from the Republic F-84F Thunderstreak to the F-100 allows the pilots, who are among the "best sticks" in the service, to show off the capabilities of one of the USAF's most modern combat aircraft. The Super Sabre makes the Thunderbirds the only supersonic flying team in the world. It is the third type flown by the squadron since it was formed in 1953, when it flew F-84Gs at Luke Air Force Base, Arizona (→ May 21, 1957).

**One of the USAF's latest meteorological balloons is inflated here with hydrogen through a 90-foot sleeve as technicians prepare it for launch. Scientists increasingly use data gathered by balloons on flights throughout the northern hemisphere for research into weather patterns.**

# Tragedy spells end of X-2 project

## American Airlines plans new training for stewardesses

*Fort Worth, Tex, July 25*
American Airlines announced today that it is to build a training facility for its stewardesses near Dallas-Fort Worth International Airport at a cost of $1 million.

The increasing use of large jet airplanes is placing new demands and responsibilities on airlines which operate them. The growing numbers of passengers per airplane complicates in-flight services and demands that they be provided with the utmost efficiency. American, in common with other US companies, sees itself as providing for a potentially enormous mass market and is thus seeking to ensure that it is in the strongest position to attract more customers and tend to their in-flight needs.

*The sleek, stainless-steel Bell X-2 was designed to fly faster than 2,000mph.*

### Research accident kills USAF test pilot

*California, September 27*
USAF Captain Milburn "Mel" Apt flew faster than any other pilot today, on the 13th flight of the X-2 rocket plane, and then died almost instantly. After release from the EB-50D "motherplane" he reached 72,000 feet, then nosed the X-2 over and accelerated to Mach 3.2 (2,094mph) before the motor cut out. He started a turn toward the Edwards Air Force Base, but he was going too fast and the X-2 careered out of control. He released the escape capsule at about 40,000 feet but was knocked unconscious by the shock of the capsule's parachute and, unable to bail out of the capsule, died when it hit the desert.

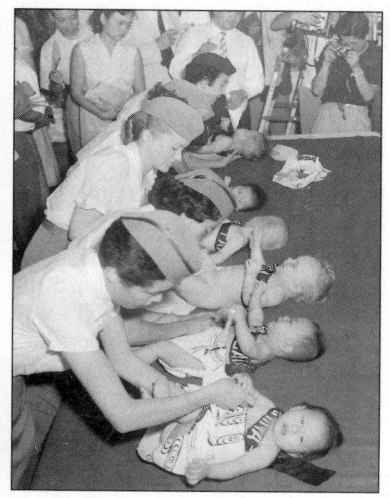

*An original contest for stewardesses.*

## Record-breaking research airplane shelved in wake of disaster

*California, September 27*
The death today of Captain Apt has almost certainly brought the X-2 program to a halt. It has also cast a shadow over the achievements of the X series of research aircraft. But in its aim of exploring the problems of flight around Mach 3.0, the project has been a success.

The X-2 was designed with a metal alloy fuselage and stainless steel wings swept back at 40 degrees. A jettisonable nose-capsule was devised to enable the pilot to escape from an emergency at high speed and high altitude. Ironically it was this feature which led to Apt's death today.

Gliding flights of the X-2 started in June 1952, with Bell test pilot Jean Ziegler at the controls. Captain Frank Everest of the USAF took over in October that year and flew the aircraft to supersonic speed last April. A month later it was former Korean jet ace Captain Iven Kincheloe's first turn to fly the X-2. He reached an unofficial record altitude of 125,907 feet on September 7, fully 35,000 feet higher than anybody had ever flown before, earning himself the title of "the world's first spaceman" from the press. In the thin air at that height he lost a great deal of the effectiveness of the X-2's controls, and on the downward dive he reached Mach 2.6 before regaining full use of them.

## New Boeing tanker

*Seattle, August 31*
USAF Strategic Air Command's potential need to keep its jet bombers airborne round the clock means that in-flight refueling has become an essential requirement. Boeing appears to have met the need with the first flight today of its KC-135A Stratotanker version of the 707. With tanks in its lower fuselage and wings holding 31,200 US gallons, refueling is carried out by a flying boom system. The KC-135A can also serve as a flying command post (→ Aug 22, 1957).

## US Navy's Vought Crusader fighter zips to new speed record

*The F8U-1 Crusader is due to undergo US Navy proving trials later this year.*

*Ridgecrest, Calif, August 21*
A Vought F8U-1 Crusader of the US Navy, piloted by Commander Robert W "Duke" Winslow, today established a world speed record for non-experimental aircraft. It hurtled across the Mojave Desert at China Lake Naval Ordnance Test Station at 1,015.428mph.

The record was set in an aircraft which was equipped with four 20mm cannon and weight equivalent to ammunition. The previous fighter record was held by a USAF F-100 Super Sabre. Following operational trials later this year, the Crusader is expected to begin full carrier service next March.

# Missiles launch new era of aerial combat

*Sparrow I missiles cluster beneath a US Navy F7U-3M Cutlass fighter.*

**Waltham, Mass, October 10**
Today's award to Raytheon of a $60 million US Navy contract for Sparrow III air-to-air missiles may finally spell the end of the days of guns-blazing, whirling, twisting aerial dogfight. Instead, aircraft will do battle by using highly accurate missiles launched at their foes from many miles away.

The Sparrow III admirably fulfills the US Navy's and USAF's need for a medium-range air-to-air missile. The 12-foot long, 8-inch diameter, 400-lb missile, which can be launched at a target more than 20 miles away, uses a radar homing guidance system to deliver its 60-lb warhead at speeds around Mach 4. It is a substantial improvement over the US Navy's Sperry Sparrow I, now with fleet air

units, which has a range of only five miles and, like the British Fairey Fireflash air-to-air missile, is equipped with a radar beam-riding guidance system.

The addition of the Sparrow III expands an already impressive US inventory of air-to-air guided missiles which have entered service since 1953. Among them are the USAF's Hughes GAR-1D, which is radar-guided, the GAR-2A, which uses infra-red homing and has a range of 5 miles, and the Philco GAR-8 Sidewinder, a heat-seeking missile with a 10-mile range used by both the USAF and the US Navy. This inventory will become much more formidable next year when the Douglas MB-1 Genie, with an atomic warhead, becomes operational.

**Who came down from Heaven: a helicopter delivers a gift to the pope.**

# BOAC takes the plunge and orders 707s

*London, October 24*
Another blow to the morale of British aircraft manufacturers was dealt today when the government gave BOAC the green light to buy Boeing 707 jet-airliners. Moreover, the order was for 15 707s rather than the expected six.

Observers cannot help noticing the irony that, despite British manufacturers' efforts with the Comet and the Britannia, the national airline continues to buy American. The withdrawal of the trouble-hit Comet 1, the delay in producing the transatlantic Comet 4 and the late

delivery of the Britannia have resulted in the stop-gap purchase of ten piston-engined Douglas DC-7Cs which are bound to have very short lives with the airline.

Britain's aircraft industry will feel this setback keenly. In November 1955 BOAC insisted that "our existing Comet and Britannia purchases will see us through to the 1960s". This policy contributed to the cancellation of the Vickers VC-7, yet now BOAC says that the 707s are needed "because no new British aircraft can be made available in time" (→ May 7, 1957).

*One of BOAC's Douglas DC-7Cs, part of a stop-gap order by the airline.*

# Israeli paras drop close to Suez Canal

*Sinai Peninsula, October 30*
Britain and France have threatened to mount an assault on key positions along the Suez Canal if fighting in the air and on the ground between Egypt and Israel in the Sinai continues and if the opposing forces do not stay at least 10 miles away from the canal. Reports suggest that Israel will accept the warning but Egypt will not.

Warplanes of both sides have been in action since early morning. The Israeli air force has flown hundreds of missions, most effectively against Egyptian ground forces moving toward Israeli paratroops and other units occupying the Mitla Pass.

In contrast, having opened air attacks at 7.30am with two MiG-15 jets, soon followed by four Vampire fighter-bombers and two more MiGs, Egypt has only flown some 50 armed sorties. This afternoon, six Israeli Dassault Mystère IVAs and six Egyptian MiG-15s fought over Kabrit. Lieutenant Tsuk's Mystère claimed a MiG but was itself damaged (→ Nov 5).

# Supersonic airliner planned by Britain

*Hampshire, England, November 1*
A first step toward creating a British supersonic transport (SST) was taken today when the Supersonic Transport Aircraft Committee (STAC) was set up at Farnborough to study its feasibility.

The STAC comprises nine representatives from British aircraft constructors and four from aero-engine companies, with scientists and engineers from the staff at the Royal Aircraft Establishment (RAE). The national airlines and the government will also be represented on the committee, which will be chaired by RAE director Morien B Morgan.

No decision has yet been taken to build an SST, and several factors make the STAC's deliberations of doubtful value, notably the long time (perhaps 15 years) which is likely to elapse between the committee's conclusions and an SST's entry into service. In this time there could be big developments in, for example, aerodynamic knowledge, new materials and fuel prices (→ Mar 1959).

# Brilliant Mirage appears over France

*The Mirage III, an improved version of the MD.550 which first flew last year.*

*Melun-Villaroche, France, Nov 17*
A stunning new French single-seat fighter made its first flight here today. The Mirage III has been designed to be the next-generation high-altitude interceptor and tactical support fighter for the French air force. It is said to be capable of operating from short and unprepared airfields and is expected to demonstrate a blistering Mach 2 performance. Unlike Marcel Dassault's previous jet fighters – the Ouragan and a succession of types called Mystère – the Mirage has delta wings and no horizontal tail surfaces. Power is provided by a SNECMA Atar 101G turbojet, offering 9,900-lb thrust with afterburner on. The airplane's light weight makes high performance possible on relatively low power.

The Mirage III is a development of the original prototype MD.550 Mirage delta-winged fighter, which first flew on June 25 last year. This aircraft was fitted with two British-designed Viper engines built under license, each offering only 2,160 pounds of thrust, but despite its high performance it was too small for military development. The next version, the Mirage II, remained a paper project only.

# Jet plane takes off vertically for first time

*The Vertijet maneuvers into position to "park" by hooking onto the tower.*

*California, November 28*
The USAF's Ryan X-13 Vertijet today made its first transition from vertical to horizontal flight. The X-13 is the first pure jet vertical take-off and landing (VTOL) aircraft with this capability. The US Navy's turboprop Convair XFY-1 Pogo had previously demonstrated the feasibility of the VTOL concept, but its design was impractical and it was canceled last year. The delta-winged X-13, which first took off, conventionally, on December 10 last year, will use a special trailer, raised vertically for launch and landing. The 24-foot-long aircraft has a 21-foot wingspan and a Rolls-Royce Avon engine. For stability while hovering it has a swiveling engine tailpipe and wing-tip nozzles (→Apr 2, 1957).

# Altitude record set in manned balloon

*Kennedy, Nebraska, November 6*
The US Navy's Project "Stratolab" today proved to be at the same time a success and a failure. A world record for manned balloon flight was set when Lieutenant-Commander Morton Lewis and Malcolm Ross ascended to 76,000 feet, but the men were unable to carry out the high-altitude experiments which were the principal purpose of the flight because a faulty valve forced an early descent. The two were encapsulated in a pressurized gondola which was suspended beneath the polythene balloon for the 175-mile flight.

The flight occurred 21 years to the month after the previous manned balloon altitude record of 72,395 feet was set by another US Navy balloon, the *Explorer II*. Both flights had two-man crews and originated from Rapid City, South Dakota. However, unlike pre-war balloon flights, today's was not merely to collect scientific data on the stratosphere's environment. The men themselves formed part of the experiment, each observing the other and sending information back to the ground about physical and mental capacities and limitations at stratospheric altitudes on the very fringes of space.

# Delta Dart promises to be on target as interceptor fighter

*California, December 26*
Convair test pilot Dick Johnson made the first flight of the F-106A Delta Dart today at Edwards Air Force Base. Originally designated F-102B, the F-106 has been derived from the F-102A Delta Dagger interceptor currently in production at Convair's plant at San Diego.

The fuselage has been completely redesigned and the J57 engine has been replaced by Pratt & Whitney's new J75, rated at 24,500 lb thrust with afterburner. The Delta Dart's maximum speed has been doubled to more than Mach 2.

# Another mystery in 'Bermuda Triangle'

*Sargasso Sea, November 9*
Another event has occurred to be added to the already lengthy list of inexplicable disappearances in what is called the "Bermuda Triangle". Today a US Navy Martin Marlin P5M and all six crew members have vanished without trace. The aircraft is regarded as among the best modern flying boats, and its loss is particularly ironic as it was engaged in an attempt to find and recover the aircraft which have gone missing since the "Triangle" disappearances began in 1947.

# Convair hustles in supersonic bomber

*Fort Worth, Tex, November 11*
The Convair XB-58 Hustler, the first supersonic bomber, made a successful first flight from Carswell Air Force Base today, adjacent to the giant factory where it was built. Inside the plant Convair is working on a second XB-58 and 11 YB-58As.

The bombers are capable of reaching Mach 2. Features include a tailless delta wing using a metal honeycomb sandwich structure, four GE J79 turbojets, a crew of three seated in tandem and a gigantic pod, which can be jettisoned carrying either conventional or atomic bombs and much of the fuel.

Ultimate version of the most attractive of all airliners was the extra long range version of the Lockheed Constellation, dubbed the L-1649A Starliner.

Cessna's 620 was a one off, six/ten seater executive transport prototype.

The Omega BS-12 was available in passenger (four) or cargo versions.

The Piper PA-24 Comanche was a four-seat 180hp touring aircraft.

Marcel Jurca designed the MJ.2 Tempête single-seat sporting aircraft.

The prototype Pasotti Sparviero was fitted with a Hirth air-cooled engine.

The SSSR L-5611 was the prototype Tu-114, the biggest and most powerful propeller-driven airliner in history, derived from the Tu-95 strategic bomber.

The Sud-Est SE.212 Durandal was an experimental delta interceptor.

Australia's Kingsford Smith PL-7 single-seat agricultural sesquiplane.

The Temco model 51 was known to the US Navy as the TT-1 Pinto.

The Mikoyan Ye-5 led to the world-famous MiG-21 fighter.

Precursor of what must be the best known of all helicopters, the "Huey", was the Bell XH-40 Iroquois with its distinctive lines and rotor layout.

Developed in accordance with NATO specifications, the Fiat G91 light strike aircraft was later developed into reconnaissance and training versions.

The Vertol H-21: also developed as the Model 44 commercial helicopter.

One Nord Noratlas was converted to N.2500 standard for test reasons.

The Douglas C-133A was more capable than the C-124 Globemaster.

The popular Beech 95 Travel Air was known, at first, as the Badger.

American helicopter manufacturers Kaman built the HH-43B Husky.

Intended initially as a supersonic interceptor, the Dassault Mirage III was developed as a fighter-bomber and also for reconnaissance and training.

Imposing in size, awesome in ability, the Convair B-58 was intended solely as a weapon for Strategic Air Command and fulfilled its task with distinction.

In many respects the pinnacle of the "Century series" aircraft: the Convair F-106 Delta Dart, a long-range interceptor that served for over three decades.

North American's FJ-4B Fury flew with a low-altitude bombing system.

The Hughes Model 269 was intended for both civil and military use.

The North American YF-107 was originally designated as the F-100B.

An aircraft of impressive performance, the Supermarine Scimitar was the first nuclear-capable strike fighter to serve aboard the Royal Navy's carriers.

The Nord Gerfaut II was fitted with an afterburning Atar 101G engine.

Based on the type 960 Vultur, the Breguet 1050 Alizé was a three-seat anti-submarine hunter-killer aircraft, powered by a Dart Mk 21 turboprop.

Carrying the Boeing company model number of 717, the KC-135 Stratotanker enabled Stategic Air Command bombers to refuel at jet height and speed.

# 1957

2,094mph
USA
Milburn Apt
Bell X-2
Sep 27, 1956

24,325 miles
USA
Archie Old Jr
Boeing B-52B
Jan 18, 1957

125,907ft
USA
Iven Kincheloe
Bell X-2
Sep 7, 1956

450,000lb
USA
Boeing
B-52C Stratofortress

27,008lb thrust
USSR
Lyulka
AL-21F

**Connecticut, January 30**
Sikorsky's HSS-1 S-58 piston-engined helicopter, developed for anti-submarine operations, makes its first flight.

**London, February 1**
The Bristol Britannia enters service on BOAC's route to Johannesburg; it is the world's first long-haul airliner (→ Dec 19).

**Washington, DC, February 5**
The US Civil Aeronautics Board directs that all testing of civil or military aircraft must be carried out over open water or sparsely-populated land.

**Copenhagen, February 24**
Scandinavian Airline Services (SAS) opens the first regular scheduled service from Europe to the Far East over the North Pole, with departures from Copenhagen and Tokyo; the DC-7C aircraft will circle the pole en route (→ Sep 11).

**USSR, March 7**
The Antonov An-10 Ukraina, powered by four Kuznetsov NK-4 turboprops, makes its first flight. It can carry 84 passengers and has a playroom for children.

**Baltimore, Maryland, March 11**
The prototype Boeing 707 jet lands after a press demonstration flight from Seattle during which it covered 2,350 miles in a record time of 3 hours 48 minutes (→ May 7).

**Boston, Mass, March 12**
Pioneer polar explorer Admiral Richard Byrd dies of heart failure at the age of 68.

**Manchester, England, March 14**
BEA's Vickers Viscount airliner *Discovery* crashes into houses near Ringway airport; all 15 passengers and five crew on the aircraft and two occupants of the houses are killed. An eye-witness reports having seen the airliner's starboard flap attachments buckle (→ Apr).

**Los Angeles, March 21**
A US Navy A3D-1 Skywarrior nuclear bomber lands after a record 9 hour 31 minute 35 second round trip to New York.

**Wiltshire, England, April 2**
The Short SC.1 jet-lift vertical take-off and landing (VTOL) aircraft flies for the first time, piloted by Tom Brooke-Smith at Boscombe Down (→ Apr 6, 1960).

**Washington, DC, April 3**
The US government approves a federal aid program which provides more than $52 million for airport building and improvement projects in 46 states.

**England, April**
BEA resumes services with Vickers Viscounts after the airliners were grounded on March 17 in the wake of the crash of *Discovery* in Manchester on March 14; investigators found that vital bolts had been incorrectly assembled, resulting in detachment of flap brackets (→ Jan 25, 1958).

**New York, May 2**
Air France's first Caravelle jet airliner lands at Idlewild airport from Miami on a tour of the US and Canada (→ Jul 27, 1959).

**Seattle, May 7**
Boeing president William Allen announces that the company has received 151 orders for its 707 airliner (→ Dec 21).

**Pacific Ocean, May 15**
A Vickers Valiant jet bomber, piloted by Wing Commander K G Hubbard, drops Britain's first ever hydrogen bomb in a test near Christmas Island (→ Oct 9).

**Manchester, England, May 29**
The first woman to win RAF wings, Jean Lennox Bird, dies when her Miles Aerovan crashes; she had accumulated over 3,100 hours' flying time in more than 90 types of aircraft.

**St Paul, Minn, June 2**
USAF Captain Joseph Kittinger ascends to an altitude of 96,000 feet in the balloon *Man High 1*; he stays at a height of more than 92,000 feet for 6 hours 34 minutes, and at 96,000 feet for 2 hours (→ Aug 20).

**Florida, June 6**
Two US Navy Skywarriors land on the carrier USS *Saratoga* just 4 hours and 1 minute after launch from the carrier USS *Bon Homme Richard* off California; this is the first transcontinental carrier-to-carrier flight.

**USSR, July 4**
The Ilyushin Il-18 medium-range turboprop transport makes its maiden flight, piloted by Vladimir Kokkinaki (→ Apr 20, 1959).

**Atlantic Ocean, July 5**
The captains of BOAC and Pan Am flights between Britain and the US exchange greetings when they pass each other in mid-flight; this gesture is to mark the 20th anniversary of the first passenger services flown across the North Atlantic (→ May 30, 1958).

**Washington, DC, July 13**
President Eisenhower becomes the first US president to fly in a helicopter when he is flown from the White House to an unnamed military post in a USAF Bell UH-13J.

**Athens, July 19**
New Greek airline Olympic Airways is reported to have ordered two Douglas DC-8 jet airliners for delivery in 1960.

**Washington, DC, July 31**
Official reports reveal that the US-Canadian Distant Early Warning (DEW) radar system is fully operational (→ Feb 1, 1959).

**Quebec, August 11**
In Canada's worst air crash, a Maritime Central Airways DC-4 crashes near Issoudon; all 79 people on board the airliner are killed.

**Gulf of Mexico, August 12**
A US Navy Douglas F3D jet makes the first "hands off" landing on an aircraft carrier, landing on the USS *Antietam* by means of the world's first automatic carrier landing system, built by Bell Aircraft.

**Bedfordshire, England, August 28**
An English Electric Canberra, in operation as a test-bed for the Napier Double Scorpion rocket engine, sets a new world altitude record of 70,310 feet during a flight from Luton.

**New York, September 4**
An Aeroflot Tupolev 104 carrying Soviet UN delegates is rerouted to a USAF base because it is too noisy for New York's airports.

**London, September 11**
Pan Am opens a London/San Francisco transarctic service, with Douglas DC-7s via Frobisher Bay and Baffin Island (→ Oct 2).

**London, October 2**
An L-1649 completes the first flight of TWA's Los Angeles/London service on the polar route, setting a new record for the longest non-stop flight by a scheduled airliner with its journey time of 23 hours 19 minutes (→ Oct 20, 1960).

**USSR, October 30**
A Mil Mi-6 helicopter, fitted with a five-blade 115-foot rotor and 5,500-hp Soloviev D-25V engines, makes its first flight.

**Italy, December 10**
Guido de Carestiato pilots the prototype Macchi MB.326 two-seat jet trainer on its maiden flight.

**California, December 12**
USAF Major Adrian Drew flies a McDonnell F-101A Voodoo fighter to an official world speed record of 1,207.6mph.

*Guarding the free world: the jet-fighter pictured in this advertisement defending air force supersonic "booms" is the Convair F-102A.* ▶

# Freedom Has a New Sound!

ALL OVER AMERICA these days the blast of supersonic flight is shattering the old familiar sounds of city and countryside.

At U.S. Air Force bases strategically located near key cities our Airmen maintain their *round the clock* vigil, ready to take off on a moment's notice in jet aircraft like Convair's F-102A all-weather interceptor. Every flight has only one purpose—your personal protection!

The next time jets thunder overhead, remember that the pilots who fly them are not willful disturbers of your peace; they are patriotic young Americans affirming *your New Sound of Freedom!*

PUBLISHED FOR BETTER UNDERSTANDING OF THE MISSION OF THE U.S.A.F. AIR DEFENSE COMMAND

## CONVAIR

A DIVISION OF GENERAL DYNAMICS CORPORATION

# B-52s fly non-stop around the world

*The round-the-world flight has proved an important point: the long-range B-52 can reach any target, however distant.*

## Brooklyn Dodgers baseball stars buy themselves a plane

*New York, January 8*
"Da Bums" are going to fly. The Brooklyn Dodgers today became the first US major league baseball team to have its own airplane when team president Walter O'Malley bought a twin-engined Convair 440. The Dodgers and their minor league farm teams will fly to games on the 44-seat airliner when the Dodgers' schedule makes train or bus travel difficult or impossible.

O'Malley experimented with a DC-3 in the past and found it too small to move a 25-player team, its coaches and equipment. He selected the Convair with the aid of Eastern Air Lines president Captain Eddie Rickenbacker, who was present when O'Malley announced the purchase. Eastern will service and maintain the plane for the Dodgers. The airplane is equipped as a standard airliner with reclining seats, but it also has tables for the players' favorite way (apart from baseball) of passing the time – poker.

*California, January 18*
Three USAF Strategic Air Command Boeing B-52B Stratofortress bombers landed at March Air Force Base today after flying non-stop around the world. The three eight-engined giants had been airborne for 45 hours 20 minutes, covering a distance of 24,325 miles at an average speed of 534mph. The USAF can now claim with justice that no target in the world is beyond the range of its bombers. Commanding the round-the-world flight, the first by jet airplanes, was Major General Archie J Olds, Jr.

The B-52Bs were from the 93rd Bomb Wing, which in November last year saw eight of its airplanes make a 17,000-mile flight round North America and over the North Pole in preparation for the circum-navigation attempt.

The B-52Bs set off from Castle Air Force Base on January 16. Because of the Stratofortress's range, the aircraft needed to be refueled in flight only three times, from Boeing KC-97 tankers. One tail gunner went round the world backwards.

## US Army trials for new Cessna helicopter

*Cessna's fast, lightweight Skyhook boasts an operational range of 310 miles.*

*USA, January*
Cessna, one of the world leaders in the field of light aircraft manufacture, has continued its recent flirtation with the helicopter industry in delivering the CH-1 Skyhook to the US Army for evaluation.

With a cabin layout remarkably similar to that of fixed-wing Cessna aircraft, the all-metal Skyhook (designated the YH-41 Seneca by the military) is a four-seater, light observation helicopter with two-bladed main and tail rotors. The power is provided by a 260-hp, six-cylinder Continental engine.

The CH-1 was made possible by Cessna's purchase of the Seibel company, owned by Charles Seibel, in 1952. The helicopter has a maximum operating range of 310 miles and climbs at 1,030 feet per minute to its hover ceiling of 9,600 feet while carrying a pilot, co-pilot as well as two fully-equipped infantrymen.

## Secret spy plane is for 'weather research'

*Washington, DC, February 1*
The US National Advisory Committee for Aeronautics (NACA) today revealed the existence of the U-2 spyplane when it released the first photographs of the aircraft. Officially the U-2 is on loan to NACA from the USAF, with civilian status and civilian NACA pilots.

The "U" designation stands for "Utility" and the U-2 is billed as a "general-purpose" aircraft. In particular, it is claimed that the U-2 is for meteorological research at very high altitudes. The airplane is certainly designed to fly at unprecedented heights, because it combines a large jet engine with light structure and wings like a glider. The U-2's real role – as a military spy plane – naturally remains top secret [see page 546].

*A later version of the Lockheed U-2: its true military role is top secret.*

# Bell rings in the era of the hovering jet

*Two Britsh Viper turbojet engines are fitted beneath the nose of the X-14.*

*Niagara Falls, NY, February 17*
Bell Aircraft test pilot David Howe today made the first hovering tests with the X-14 at the company's main plant here. The X-14 is the first jet-powered vertical take-off and landing (VTOL) airplane capable of taking off from a level position, with pivoted engine nozzles. The two Armstrong Siddeley Viper turbojets, each of 1,560 lb thrust, are mounted horizontally side by side under the nose.

The nozzles are thus near the X-14's center of gravity, and their thrust can be directed by diverters operated by the pilot to give lift for vertical take-off and hovering or thrust for forward flight. Special compressed-air nozzles for hovering control are fitted at the wingtips and tail (→ May 14).

## Eastern plans new electronic ticketing

*New York, March 3*
A quicker and more reliable reservation system for Eastern Air Lines passengers is on the way, thanks to a new Univac data-processing machine. The device will be the heart of a new $5 million electronic reservation center on the sixth floor of a building now being built in midtown Manhattan.

The center, scheduled to open in October, will occupy more than an acre of floor space, two-thirds of which will be filled with electronic equipment. Eastern's Thomas F Armstrong explained that it is being built because the airline's traffic is beyond the capacity of its current reservation system. The Univac will handle up to 60,000 reservations a day and keep track of one million seats on Eastern flights between New York and 120 cities, from Canada to Puerto Rico. The data-processor will initially be linked up to 135 booking agents in the New York area (→ Mar 6, 1958).

## New defense policy will slim down RAF

*London, April 4*
The British government's white paper [policy statement] on defense, published today, seems to spell the end of both the RAF and Britain's aircraft industry in their present forms. The paper, drawn up by minister of defence Duncan Sandys, describes a link between British economic strength and military spending, which absorbs 10 per cent of gross national product.

Future defense policy will be based on the concept of nuclear deterrence but with the stress on defensive ballistic missiles. The white paper calls for a smaller fighter force which "will progressively be equipped with air-to-air guided missiles". Most alarmingly for aircraft makers and the RAF, which believes that only piloted airplanes offer the flexibility to deal with all possible threats, the paper adds: "Fighter aircraft will in due course be replaced by a ground-to-air guided missile system" (→ Sep 16).

# Wraps come off Thunderchief warplane

*Farmingdale, NY, March 22*
The appearance of a new warplane, the Republic F-105 Thunderchief, was today disclosed by the USAF when it released the first photographs of the aircraft. Although it looks like a fighter and has an "F" designation, the powerful new aircraft is in reality an attack-bomber with an internal bomb bay.

The YF-105A prototype flew at Edwards Air Force Base, California, on October 22, 1955, exceeding Mach 1 on its first flight. Since then it has been considerably modified. The Pratt & Whitney J57 engine has been replaced by the larger J75, which gives 26,500 lb of thrust with afterburner, fed by unique "dog-tooth" inlets in the wing-roots (→ May 27, 1958).

*Low-temperature tests on the F-105.*

# Passenger is sucked out of plane window

*Istanbul, April 21*
An Air France Super Constellation flying from Tehran to Paris made an emergency landing here today after losing an American passenger in mid-air. The accident happened when the unfortunate passenger's window suddenly blew out as the airliner was flying at an altitude of 18,700 feet over the border between Turkey and Iraq. This caused the cabin to depressurize so quickly that the victim was literally torn from his seat and neither the crew nor other passengers could do anything to help.

# A Caravelle tours North American cities

*Orly, France, June 25*
A Sud-Aviation Caravelle with an Air France crew landed here today after a successful 68-day promotional tour of major South and North American cities.

The specially-refurbished aircraft began its 74,600-mile trip in Brazil, which it reached after brief stops in Dakar and Natal. It then flew to Uruguay, Argentina and Venezuela, each time carrying official guests and South American businessmen. Initial reaction to the twin-engined airliner has been very favorable. The Caravelle then made a 16-city tour of the US and Canada, where aviation experts were impressed by its stability and silent running. Sud-Aviation president Georges Hereil now hopes the tour will lead to firm orders.

*The Caravelle's cabin was equipped with gilt-trimmed seats and deep carpet.*

# Risner flies 'Lindy' route in seven hours

*M Renvoisé, the man who first greeted Lindbergh in 1927, welcomes Risner.*

*Paris, May 21*
On the 30th anniversary of the solo transatlantic flight by Charles Lindbergh from New York in a tiny single-engined monoplane, another young man has retraced the route of that historic crossing.

He too flew alone in a single-engined monoplane, but there the similarities end. For USAF Major Robinson Risner there was no question of a battle with fatigue or loneliness for 33 and a half hours, no problems of carburetor icing, and no groping through fog.

In his North American F-100 Super Sabre, Major Risner flew above the weather, had instruments and radio to guide him and, with the aid of aerial tanker planes to provide the fuel for his jet engine, took only 6 hours 40 minutes.

# France shows off vertical take-off jet

*The pilot sits in the nose of the craft.*

*Melun-Villaroche, France, May 14*
The chief French airplane-engine producer SNECMA today began free (untethered) flight trials with its Atar Volant C-400 P-2 vertical take-off and landing (VTOL) test rig. It comprises little more than an up-ended Atar turbojet with a fuel tank and an ejector seat on top with landing gear at the bottom. Test pilot was Auguste Morel.

SNECMA hopes to lead the rush to build VTOL airplanes which could operate from small ships or from ground hideouts where they would be much less vulnerable than when parked on airfields. The Atar Volant is providing vital experience in the control of jet engines in hovering flight, especially when near the ground.

Tethered testing of the original Atar Volant began on September 22 last year, when the device was remotely controlled. Today's "flight" was the first by the piloted C-400 P-2 version. Ultimately it is the company's intention to develop a VTOL fighter version of the Atar Volant, which will be called the Coléoptère (→ Jul 25, 1959).

# TWA Starliners offer last word in luxury

*New York, July 1*
The fierce battle between airlines to woo passengers on the lucrative North Atlantic route took another turn today, with TWA inaugurating its Jetstream service between New York and Paris. Competing with Pan Am's DC-7C Seven Seas service, which began last year, TWA now offers the luxury of Lockheed L-1649A Starliners, which can fly non-stop from the West Coast to most European capital cities. Starliners will also enter service with Air France next month.

The Starliner is the latest development of the Constellation series and still uses piston engines. The major difference to the airframe lies in the wings, which are of greater span and reduced thickness, and house some 50 per cent more fuel.

*Air France is getting its own Starliners to compete with US airlines.*

# Glenn makes three-hour crossing of US

*New York, July 16*
Major John H Glenn of the US Marines today set a new record for a coast-to-coast flight across the US when he landed at Floyd Bennett Field in a Vought F8U-1P Crusader. The flight from Los Angeles, the first supersonic west/east crossing of the country, took 3 hours 23 minutes 50 seconds – an average speed of 723.17mph for the 2,460-mile transcontinental dash. He slowed down for three in-flight refuelings of his photographic-reconnaissance version of the Navy's hottest fighter.

The US Navy is buying over 500 Crusaders for itself and the Marines; a difference between the F8U-1P and the F8U-1 fighter version is that the latter has four 20mm cannon (→ Aug 20, 1958).

*John Glenn at the controls of his Crusader during the record-breaking flight.*

# Cessna has a new plant to build its T-37s

*Cessna's two-seater trainer is easy to fly and has a top speed of 391mph.*

**Wichita, Kansas, September**
Like most demanding clients the Pentagon likes to receive the aircraft it has ordered on time. That is why Cessna has had to build a new plant here to cope with the USAF's growing demand for T-37 twin-jet trainers.

For the manufacturer the breakthrough came in December 1953 when the USAF chose Cessna's Model 318, powered by two Continental jet engines each with a thrust of 880 lb, over its competitors. In October of the following year a prototype of the Model 318, already designated XT-37 by the USAF, made its maiden flight. However, it soon became apparent that the small plane was difficult to pull out of a spin. Cessna corrected the problem by lengthening the fuselage and redesigning the vertical stabilizer.

Then, in September 1955, the USAF dropped the letter 'X' (for experimental) and designated the two-seater trainer T-37. The Pentagon ordered a first batch of the Cessna airplanes. This convinced the manfacturer of the need for a new plant to build T-37s.

# Airlines not keen on turboprop 'Connie'

*Air France finally decided to purchase piston-engined Lockheed Starliners.*

**Burbank, Calif, August**
Lockheed designers and engineers have been looking for a way of updating the Constellation. Two years ago they came up with the Model L-1249, a heavily modified Super Constellation powered by four turboprops instead of piston engines.

Also known as the *Elation,* this prototype, which has been undergoing tests with the US Navy under the designation R7V-2, was initially equipped with four Allison 501 D-13 turbines and later with Pratt & Whitney T34P-6s. Both of these powerplants however proved to be extremely thirsty engines and added fuel tanks had to be fitted. In January, an *Elation* flew across the USA in 4 hours 41 minutes. The USAF has also been testing the turboprop-powered Constellation, while Lockheed has so far been unable to convince airlines to purchase the civilian version of the aircraft, designated Model L-1249B. Carriers such as Air France, which has opted for the piston-engined Starliner, are hedging their bets, knowing that jet-engined airliners are just over the horizon.

# First US executive jet makes initial flight

**Burbank, Calif, September 4**
Just 241 days after the start of work on the project, Lockheed's CL-329, to be called the JetStar, made its first flight here today. It is the first executive jet built in the US.

The JetStar is designed to meet the USAF's desire for a utility transport experimental aircraft (UCX) to replace a motley collection of ex-wartime, piston-engined types. But the USAF is short of funds, and so Lockheed is looking mainly at the civilian business market. The prototype JetStar has two Bristol Orpheus turbojets, but these may be replaced by GE or Pratt & Whitney engines.

*The Lockheed JetStar is aimed at both the business jet market and the USAF.*

**A French Sud-Aviation Alouette II helicopter flies over Manhattan during a promotional tour of the United States.**

# USAF takes on massive new transport

*The Cargomaster: a new US workhorse to transport supplies or troops.*

*USA, August 22*
The USAF today took delivery of a cargo airplane which can carry twice the payload of its predecessor, the Douglas C-124 Globemaster. The new Douglas C-133 Cargomaster reflects the military's need for an aircraft with increased capacity and endurance. It made its first flight on April 23 last year.

The transport is powered by four Pratt & Whitney T34-P-7WA engines. Although it is not much big-

ger overall than the C-124, the Cargomaster can take twice as heavy a cargo, to a loaded weight of 275,000 tons. It can carry, for example, intercontinental ballistic missiles.

The main freight hold is 90 feet long and features two loading doors. Almost all types of military vehicle can drive up the ramp and between the main doors, which are situated at the rear. The aircraft can be adapted to transport more than 200 troops (→ Apr 8, 1958).

# British Army takes control of own flying

*London, September 1*
Earlier this year Minister of Defence Duncan Sandys told the British Army to take charge of its own light aircraft for reconnaissance, direction of artillery fire and general army liaison work. The result is the Army Air Corps (AAC), which came into existence today.

The AAC brings together and rationalizes two types of army

light-aircraft unit which until now have come under the control of the RAF. In the first of these, Air Observation Post (Air OP) squadrons, the pilots were officers in the Royal Artillery. Air Op units were supplemented by Light Liaison Flights, a group which was formed after gliders ceased to have an operational role, in order to train the best glider pilots to fly light aircraft.

*A British Army Auster AOP.9 taking off at the Farnborough show.*

# Hybrid airliner-helicopter flies at last

*Berkshire, England, November 6*
The dream of an airliner capable of vertical take-off and landing (VTOL) may be closer to reality after today's maiden flight of the Fairey Rotodyne at White Waltham. It combines the lift of a helicopter and the forward thrust of conventional engines. BEA sought such an aircraft and accepted Fairey's specification for a medium-haul "flying bus" capable of flying economical payloads between city centers.

Fairey's hybrid, which carries a crew of two and eight passengers,

is powered by two Napier Eland 2,800-hp turboprops. These also deliver compressed air to wing-tip jets on the 90-foot-diameter rotor blades, to assist take-off and landing. In flight, two high-mounted wings with a span of 46 feet 6 inches share the lift with the rotors. The Rotodyne's tail is mounted high on the fuselage with twin fins and rudders. The key feature is that behind each engine is an auxiliary compressor. When this is clutched-in it supplies air to the rotor. In cruising flight all power goes to the propeller (→ Jan 5, 1959).

*The Rotodyne takes off from a London heliport and heads over the Thames.*

# Airlines report big rise in passengers

*Washington, DC, September 16*
The number of people flying today has grown by a factor of 36 compared to two decades years ago. This worldwide surge in air travel is particularly evident in the United States. US domestic airlines are likely to carry a record 45 million or more passengers this year, more than all the world's other airlines combined, an IATA report says today.

Yet airline executives are not entirely happy. Despite the increase, airline profits are shrinking to a return below 2 per cent on gross revenues. This bodes ill for the future, especially next year when the transition to costlier jet aircraft is expected to intensify at an estimated cost to the carriers of $2.5 billion. Help in paying the bills is being sought in the form of fare raises of as much as 15 per cent (→ Dec 31, 1958).

# Spitfires end their operational service

*Kent, England, July 11*
Though the final operational mission by a Spitfire – a photo-reconnaissance by a PR.XIX version in Malaya – took place in 1954, various Spitfires continued to fly on RAF charge until today. Some have been used for high-altitude "met" (meteorological observation), while others have just been handy transports, for example for station and group commanders. Now all are struck off charge, the last three having today landed at Biggin Hill to join a ceremonial unit.

The celebrated Spitfire's passing ends a chapter of aviation and RAF history. An astonishing 20,351 examples of Britain's most famous wartime fighter were built after the airplane made its first flight at Southampton in March 1936. Nearly 20 years of continuous operational service followed.

# Boeing 707 heralds new travel era

*Seattle, December 21*
Boeing's 707-120, the first production example of the Model 707, made its first flight here today. The first commercial jet airliner to be built in the USA, it represents both the greatest financial risk ever taken by an aircraft manufacturer and also the biggest single success. It was in May 1952 that Boeing decided to risk over $16 million on building a prototype jet-transport, the Model 367-80 or "Dash 80". This first flew on July 15, 1954, and was instrumental in winning massive orders from the USAF for its derivative, the KC-135 Stratotanker. In 1955 the USAF sanctioned sales of a commercial version, the 707, with a larger fuselage and many other changes. The first sale, in October 1955, was to Pan Am, which next October introduces 707s on North Atlantic services (→ Sep 18, 1955).

*The Boeing 707's fuselage is wider and longer than that of the "Dash 80", and it is has more powerful engines.*

## Auto engine powers new Tipsy Nipper

*Charleroi, Belgium, December 3*
Powered by a modified Volkswagen car engine, the remarkable Tipsy Nipper took to the air here today amid high hopes from its makers that they have created a European "people's airplane". The minuscule Nipper, descended from the prewar Tipsy B Junior Trainer, is designed to be sold in cheap kit form, and flying clubs from as far apart as Austria, Belgium, Denmark, West Germany and South Africa are already showing interest.

The Nipper is the brainchild of the remarkable Ernest Tips; as general manager of Charleroi-based firm Avions Fairey, he oversaw the evacuation of staff and equipment to Britain in 1940, returning to Belgium to revive the factory in 1946. Société Anonyme Avions Fairey [Fairey Airplanes Ltd], an offshoot of Britain's Fairey Aviation, was formed to manufacture the British-designed Firefly fighter.

The little Nipper follows the company's early Tipsy B, the Avions Fairey Junior and the Tipsy Belfair

*The Nipper: a "people's airplane"?*

variant, built earlier in this decade. The Nipper is notable for its shoulder-height wings, tricycle undercarriage and basic controls. Due to go into full production at the end of next year, the makers describe it as "semi-aerobatic" – hence the interest from aero clubs in Europe and elsewhere.

## A flight simulator to train pilots

*Orly, France, June*
In the darkened cockpit of an Air France Super Constellation 1049G the flight crew is hunched over dozens of instruments and controls. Suddenly the silence is broken by an ear-splitting siren and the engineer shouts *"Fire in number two engine"*. The pilot quickly cuts fuel to the engine, initiates the fire extinguisher and begins to retrim the plane. Then a voice from the rear of the cockpit says calmly *"Very well gentlemen, let's try that again"*. The crew are being taught how to cope with every conceivable in-flight emergency, from a fire on the flight deck to a bird strike or catastrophic engine failure on take-off, while still firmly on the ground.

Increasingly realistic flight simulators are being used by a growing number of major airlines as a means of ensuring a high level of aircrew proficiency. Although very expensive, simulators are far more forgiving than real aircraft.

## Turboprop airliner flies the Atlantic

*Bristol Britannias under assembly.*

*New York, December 19*
BOAC today began its first regular service from London to New York using the Bristol Britannia turboprop airliner. It is the first time that passengers have flown the Atlantic in a gas-turbine powered aircraft.

Although the Britannia is a fine airplane, offering economical long-haul flights at over 400mph for up to 124 passengers, the British turboprop has faced several development problems which have delayed its appearance on air routes. As a result, many potential customers have instead bought the faster Boeing 707 or DC-8 jet airliners.

**Miss America 1957 leaves Paris by TWA after a short vacation.**

The production Boeing 707 civilian airliner made its first flight in 1957. The original 707-120 was smaller and less powerful than the later versions.

Powered by four 3,750-shp Allison 501D turboprops, Lockheed's Electra was plagued by structural problems. Lockheed were rescued by the P-3 Orion.

The Cessna 150 was the first of the world's best-selling lightplane family.

Tupolev's Tu-114 was a turboprop-powered airliner based on the Tu-20.

The Hurel-Dubois HD.34 was designed as a photo survey platform.

Lockheed's JetStar prototypes were powered by two Bristol Orpheus turbojets. The production version illustrated had four Pratt & Whitney JT12s.

The four-turboprop Ilyushin II-18 airliner proved a huge success; 565 were built, including 121 exported to 16 countries. This one is Polish.

Argentina's DINFIA IA 45 was a pusher-powered executive twin.

The Miles Student was designed as a minimum-cost jet basic trainer.

The Hollandair H.A. 001 was a piston-engined agricultural aircraft.

The Tipsy Nipper went on to become a very popular homebuilt aircraft.

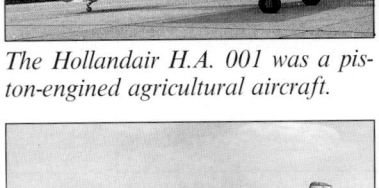

The German-built Blume Bl 500: a four-seat light cabin monoplane.

The Aviation Traders Accountant transport had twin Dart turboprops.

The 806-810 Series Vickers Viscount development aircraft had the Dart Mk 525 engines of the 810. Both families could cruise at up to 365mph.

The Fairey (later Westland) Rotodyne was a potentially outstanding twin-turboprop VTOL airliner, which suffered the fate of being cancelled in 1960.

The Sud Gouverneur, the single civil executive prototype of the Alouette.

The Mil-6 was for many years the largest helicopter in the world.

The Dassault Etendard IV was built to a French air force requirement, but ended up being ordered as a carrier-based fighter for the Aéronavale.

The Saunders-Roe SR.53 was a mixed powerplant interceptor, with a de Havilland Spectre rocket motor augmenting an Armstrong Siddeley Viper.

The English Electric P.1B was effectively the prototype for the Lightning interceptor, although RAF service entry remained over three years away.

The McDonnell XHJD-1 was an experimental twin-rotor helicopter.

The Thruxton Jackaroo was a four-seat conversion of the Tiger Moth.

The Bell X-14: an experimental VTOL with twin-jet deflection.

Breguet's Taon: designed to meet the same requirement as the G91.

The prototype of the best-selling MB.326 made its first flight in 1957.

Short's SC.1 featured four lift jets and one engine for forward flight.

The Vertol 76 was a turbine-powered tilt-wing twin-prop VTOL testbed.

The Westland Wessex was a British turbine-engined license-built S-58.

The Saab J32B Lansen of 1957 was an all-weather fighter variant of an established Swedish type. The prototype illustrated, however, flew in 1952.

Canadair's Argus was a long-range ocean patrol aircraft, derived from the Bristol Britannia but unpressurized and with Wright Turbo-Compound engines.

# 1958

2,094mph
USA
Milburn Apt
Bell X-2
Sep 27, 1956

24,325 miles
USA
Archie Old Jr
Boeing B-52
Jan 18, 1957

125,907ft
USA
Iven Kincheloe
Bell X-2
Sep 7, 1956

488,000lb
USA
Boeing
B-52G Stratofortress

27,008lb thrust
USSR
Lyulka
AL-21F

**Queensland, Australia, January 3**
Trans-Australia Airways begins to drop mail from DC-3s where airfields cannot be used because of flooding (→ Oct 31, 1960).

**Australia, January 14**
Two Qantas Super Constellations open the first regular round-the-world service: the *Southern Zephyr* leaves Sydney to fly westbound around the world and back to Australia via India, the Middle East and London, while the *Southern Aurora* leaves Melbourne to fly the other way via the Pacific (→ Jul 29, 1959).

**Chicago, February 14**
Continental Airlines becomes the second US airline to use the Vickers Viscount when it introduces the British turboprop airliner on its Chicago/Kansas City/Los Angeles route (→ Mar 31).

**USSR, February 26**
An agreement is signed by Britain and the Soviet Union, providing for a direct air link between them to be operated jointly by BEA and Aeroflot (→ Jun 2).

**Vienna, March 31**
Austrian Airlines resumes scheduled services for the first time in 20 years with a flight to London; equipped with a fleet of four Vickers Viscounts, it is the first all-jet airline in the world (→ Aug 11).

**California, April 18**
US Navy Lieutenant-Commander George Watkins flies from Edwards Air Force Base to a world record absolute altitude within the atmosphere of 76,932 feet in a Grumman F11F-1 Tiger (→ May 2).

**Hertfordshire, England, April 27**
The first de Havilland Comet 4 jet-airliner, the production version of the single Comet 3, makes its first flight, at Hatfield (→ Sep 14).

**Bedfordshire, England, April 30**
The prototype Blackburn B.103 low-level strike aircraft makes its first flight, at RAF Bedford.

**London, May 1**
BEA introduces services mixing first-class and tourist-class passengers.

**Istres, France, May 2**
Roger Carpentier beats Watkins' two-week-old world altitude record when he flies to 79,452 feet in a Sud-Ouest SO 9050 (→ May 16).

**California, May 6**
Flying the first service by a British airline to the US Pacific coast, a BOAC Bristol Britannia extends the airline's London/New York service to San Francisco.

**Colorado Springs, Colo, May 12**
The North American Air Defense Command (NORAD), which was activated informally on August 1 last year, is formally established at its headquarters here.

**Brunswick, Maryland, May 20**
A T-33 jet-trainer of the Air National Guard collides with a Capital Airlines Vickers Viscount airliner; all the crew and passengers on board the airliner are killed, but the military pilot survives the crash.

**Melun-Villaroche, France, May 21**
Jean-Marie Saget pilots the prototype Dassault Etendard IV-M fighter/bomber on its first flight.

**Eglin AFB, Florida, May 27**
The first Republic F-105B Thunderchief fighter/bomber enters USAF service with 335th Fighter Squadron; 64 feet long, the aircraft is the largest yet built for Tactical Air Command.

**Brussels, June 2**
Sabena inaugurates the first direct flights between a western European capital (excluding Scandinavia) and Moscow; the service is operated with DC-7Cs (→ Aug 3).

**Somerset, England, June 20**
The prototype Westland Wessex helicopter makes its first flight, at Yeovil.

**London, July 30**
British European Airways (BEA) retires its Airspeed AS.57 Ambassadors from scheduled service; the type, of which just 20 were built (for BEA's Elizabethan class), has flown more than 31 million miles since entering service in March 1952.

**Paris, August 3**
After a Franco-Soviet agreement, Air France and Aeroflot inaugurate regular passenger services between Paris and Moscow.

**Boston, Mass, August 11**
Northeast Airlines marks its 25th anniversary by flying its new Vickers Viscount along the airline's very first route, from Boston to destinations in Maine; the pilots on that first service, Milton Anderson and Hazen Bean, are aboard the commemorative flight.

**New York, August 14**
The Grumman G-159 Gulfstream executive airplane, powered by Rolls-Royce Dart turboprops, makes its first flight.

**Washington, DC, August 15**
Congress approves a bill creating a Federal Aviation Agency (FAA) to regulate all US commercial and military aviation (→ Oct 31).

**Dallas, Tex, August 20**
The first production Vought F8U-2 Crusader makes its first flight.

**Georgia, September 2**
A USAF RC-130A II on a spying mission along the Turkish-Soviet border is shot down by five Soviet MiGs; six of the 17 crew die, and the fate of the other 11 is unknown.

**USA, September 9**
The Lockheed X-7 pilotless test vehicle reaches a speed of Mach 4 after launch from a Boeing B-50.

**Hertfordshire, England, Sept 14**
A Comet 4 lands at Hatfield after a non-stop flight of 16 hours 16 minutes from Hong Kong.

**China, September 24**
The Beijing Nº 1 transport – the first airplane to be designed and built entirely in China – makes its maiden flight (→ Dec 16, 1959).

**Hampshire, England, Sept 30**
Aquila Airways, Britain's last commercial operator of flying boats, ends its service from Southampton to Madeira.

**Bonn, October 31**
The reborn Luftwaffe, the West German air force, buys 300 Lockheed F-104 Starfighters to serve as its primary fighter/interceptor (→ Feb 6, 1959).

**California, November 17**
Douglas delivers to Yugoslavia's state airline Jugoslovenski Aerotransport (JAT) the 704th and last DC-6 built.

**Ireland, November 29**
Irish flag-carrier airline Aer Lingus takes delivery of the first production Fokker F.27 Friendship twin turboprop airliner.

**New York, December 3**
An aircraft exchange, which will function like the stock markets and commodity exchanges, opens.

**New York, December 10**
National Airlines opens America's first domestic passenger jet service, using Boeing 707 airliners leased from Pan Am on its New York/Miami route (→ Jan 25, 1959).

**London, December 20**
BOAC inaugurates a passenger service to Montreal with the de Havilland Comet 4 (→ Jun 1, 1959).

**North Atlantic, December 31**
This year, for the first time, more passengers (1.2 million) have crossed the North Atlantic by air than by sea (→ Jun 15, 1959).

*Below the Pan Am Captain's wings is the 707 which has changed the face of air travel for all time. Already the big jets are in transatlantic service.* ▶

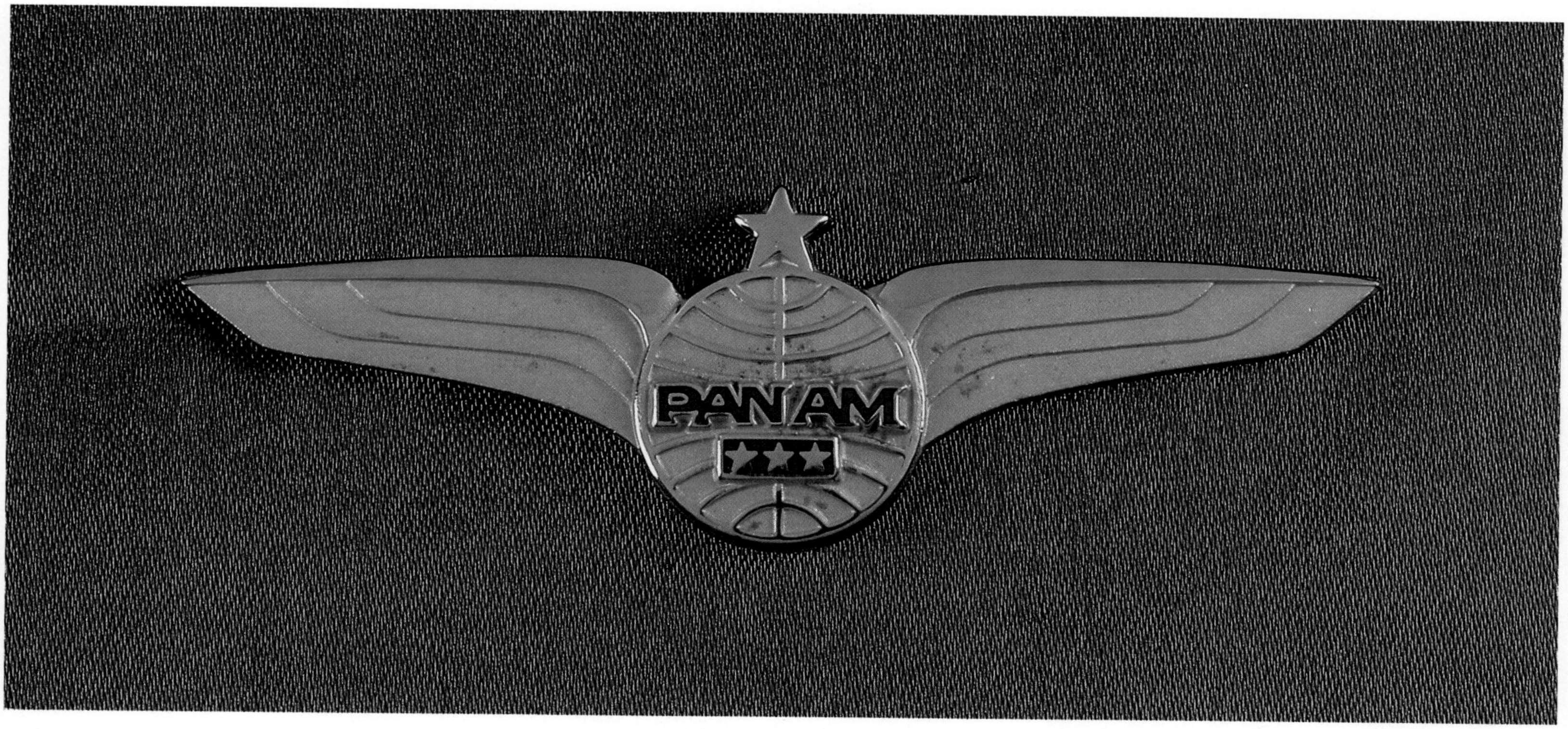
PAN AM

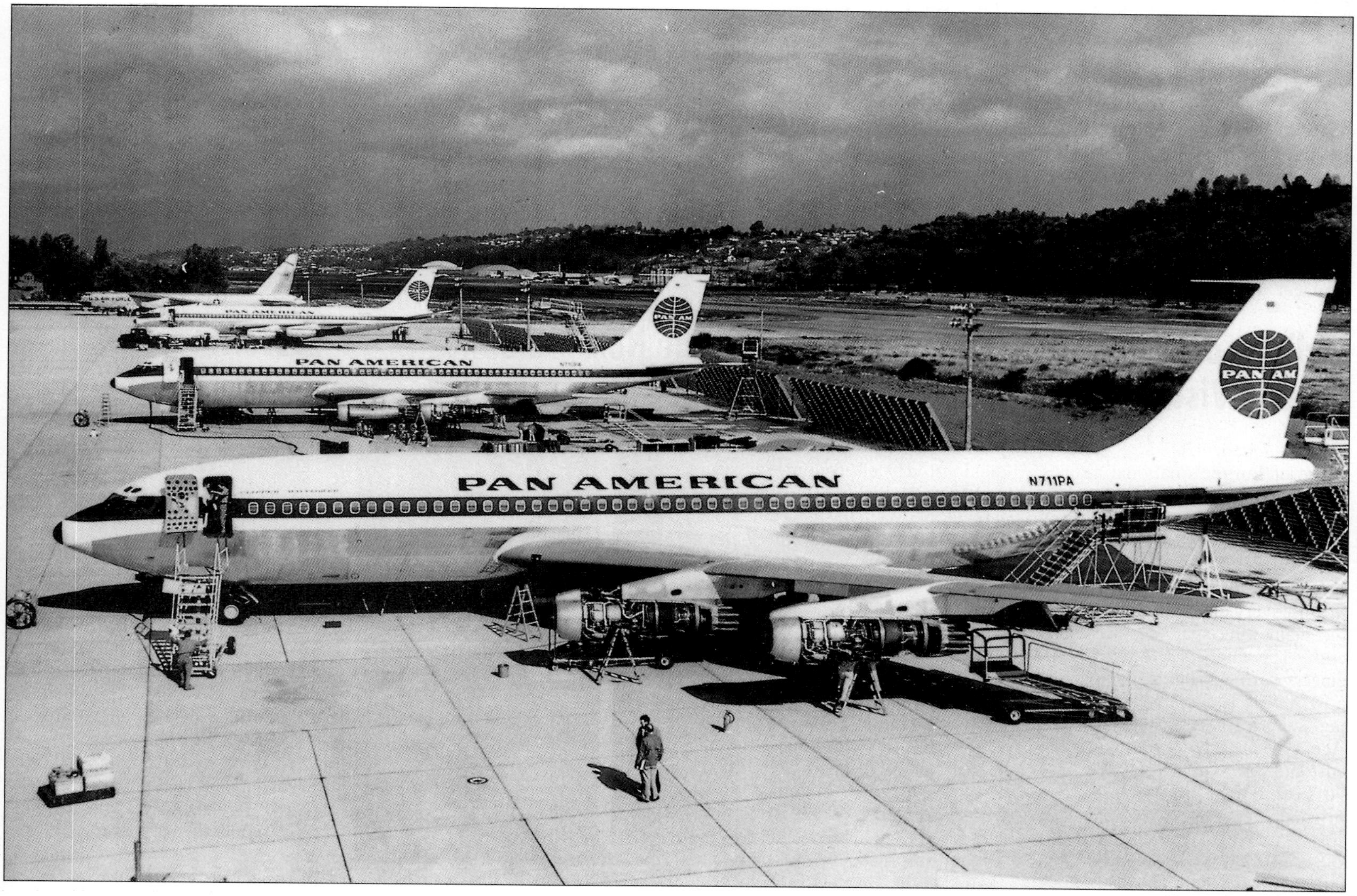
PAN AMERICAN
N711PA
PAN AM
PAN AMERICAN

# British soccer stars killed in air tragedy

*Snow falls to cover the wreckage of the BEA Ambassador airliner at Munich.*

*Munich, Germany, February 7*
Millions of British soccer fans are grief-stricken today by the news that one of their best teams has been virtually wiped out in an air crash. Manchester United was returning yesterday evening from victory against a Yugoslav team in Belgrade when their British European Airways (BEA) Airspeed AS.57 Ambassador, one of only 20 in BEA service, failed to leave the runway at Munich and crashed into a house. Twenty-three of the passengers were killed, including seven young soccer players – four of them international stars – and seven sports writers. The team manager Matt Busby is among the

21 survivors, most of whom are seriously injured.

It was snowing when Captain John Thain landed at Munich, but because the aircraft was in transit no attempt was made to de-ice the wings. When the Ambassador taxied for take-off once more the snow was described as "not the freezing sort". From his hospital bed, Captain Thain has told accident investigators that the runway was carpeted with slush, which hindered the aircraft's acceleration; when he could see that he was running out of runway and applied the brakes, it became like a ski-slope. Slush drag is now likely to be a major certification factor.

# Airlines ordered to ground Viscounts

*London, January 25*
Three of Europe's national airlines received a nasty shock today when they were ordered to ground their fleets of Vickers Viscount 701 turbo-prop airliners. The move, which severely disrupted services, follows the discovery of abnormal fatigue in the main wing spar of a BEA aircraft. The fault was found by engineers during a routine overhaul of a BEA 701. The temporary grounding affects BEA, Air France and Aer Lingus, three of the original customers for the Viscount, whose 701s were built in 1952. Vickers originally envisaged replacing the spars after 10,000 flights, a figure subsequently revised down to 6,000 and then down to 4,000.

# Jets usher in changes at world's airports

*New York, October*
With the launch this month of the first transatlantic passenger jet services the jet-airliner can finally be said to have come of age. But while jet flight is an attractive proposition for passengers, it is less so to the world's major airports, which as yet are completely unready to cope with the new era.

The most obvious challenge facing airports is to lengthen runways where necessary to allow heavy jets – loaded with record numbers of passengers and the fuel needed to cross oceans – to take off. At a cost of nearly $90 an inch, lengthening a runway by up to 2,000 feet is

no easy financial burden to absorb. The width of taxiways also has to be increased in many cases, to prevent low-slung engines in pods, a feature of the Boeing 707 and the DC-8, from sustaining damage. The airports are also faced with the need to provide hugely increased fuel storage capacity to feed the hungry jets, and many other essential maintenance facilities.

On the positive side, jets cannot be introduced any faster than they are built, so airports will probably have time for planned change. Manufacturers may also have to play their part by designing jets which can use short runways.

# Mayday ... Mayday

*Abilene, Texas, April 28*
USAF Major James Obenauf, aged only 23, landed his Strategic Air Command Boeing TB-47B Stratojet here tonight after risking his life to save his flying instructor.

The mid-air drama began when an engine caught fire. Fearing an explosion, Obenauf was about to eject with the navigator when he noticed the instructor had been knocked unconscious. He took the controls, radioed *"Stratojet 2278, Mayday, Mayday, Mayday"*, and managed to bring the crippled aircraft in safely.

# A record jump ...

*Rio de Janeiro, May 23*
Frenchwoman Colette Duval today set a new world record by parachuting into the Atlantic near here without oxygen from an altitude of 40,700 feet.

The jump nearly cost her her life as she came close to losing consciousness due to the lack of oxygen while still in free-fall. She clearly remembers screaming from the pain of a ruptured eardrum while passing through 20,000 feet. She did not pull on the ripcord until she was level with Sugar Loaf Mountain, about 1,000 feet from sea level.

# A cheaper way to fly the North Atlantic

*New York, April 1*
The cost of long-haul flights is tumbling once again with the introduction today of economy class on transatlantic flights. The main difference between the new fare and tourist class, introduced in 1949, is leg room. IATA has laid down that the seat pitch (the distance from the front edge of one seat to the next when both are in the upright position) for economy class can be 20 per cent less than tourist class, 34 inches compared with 42 inches in first class. Despite the discomfort, revenues have soared since the introduction of cheaper fares. Leading the change is Air France on its service to New York. It is the fifth largest transatlantic operator overall and third ranking European operator after BOAC and KLM.

*The airlines are in stiff competition.*

# Eastern comes top of US airline league

*Washington, DC, March 6*
Last year set new records for commercial aviation in the US with airlines carrying 49,339,000 passengers. Eastern Air Lines topped the domestic carriers with more than 8,145,000 passengers.

The airlines' passenger, mail and freight business generated a record $2 billion in earnings, but after the deduction of operating costs net profits stood at about $42 million, the lowest since 1950. The airlines are seeking fare increases of from 12 to 17 per cent from the US Civil Aeronautics Board to improve their profits. Earlier this year the carriers were granted an emergency increase in fares of 4 per cent plus a $1 per ticket service charge.

# USAF Stratotanker spans half the world

*Lajes Field, Azores, April 8*
A Boeing KC-135 Stratotanker of Strategic Air Command (SAC) arrived here today from Tokyo to establish a world straight-line, non-stop, unrefueled distance record for jet aircraft of 10,229.3 miles. The journey took 18 hours 48 minutes.

Brigadier-General William E Eubank, Jr, commander of SAC's 93rd Bomb Wing at Castle Air Force Base, California, piloted the Stratotanker. During the course of the flight, he set a speed record between Tokyo and Washington, DC, of 13 hours 45 minutes and 46.5 seconds.

Since entering service in 1956 the four-engined Boeing, derived from the same "Dash 80" prototype as the civil 707, has been replacing the USAF's piston-engined tankers. The KC-135 at last provides an aerial refueling platform to match the speeds and altitudes of the USAF's latest jet-warplanes.

*The KC-135 (left) extends Strategic Air Command's operational range.*

# Alouette II reaches record new heights

*Buc, France, June 13*
The growing success of the gas-turbine-engined Alouette II, designed by Charles Marchetti, has placed France's Sud-Aviation at the forefront of European helicopter development. Pilot Jean Boulet put the icing on Marchetti's cake today when he flew an Alouette II to a new world altitude record for helicopters, reaching 35,150 feet. The French army has already ordered this general-purpose helicopter, originally developed for agricultural use; other countries are also showing serious interest. The versatility of the Alouette II is shown in its many roles, ranging from casualty evacuation aircraft to flying crane. A new seven-seater, the Alouette III, is likely to be airborne shortly (→ Feb 28, 1959).

*France's pride: the Alouette II helicopter meets the Caravelle jet at Orly.*

# Starfighter shoots to two new records

*California, May 16*
The USAF's newest and fastest interceptor, the Lockheed F-104A Starfighter, has set another absolute world record in under a fortnight. Hot on the heels of Major Howard C Johnson's magnificent world altitude record of 91,243 feet, set on May 7, Captain Walter W Irwin today flew the aircraft nicknamed the "manned missile" to an average speed of 1,403.19mph over Edwards Air Force Base during two level dashes, flying the prescribed 15-25km course [c.10-16 miles].

This beats the previous record, set by a Voodoo last year, by nearly 200mph. For both records the Starfighter was a YF-104A, a service evaluation version.

*Johnson grins after his record flight.*

# NASA, aviation and space body, set up

*Washington, DC, July 29*
A new federal agency, the National Aeronautics and Space Administration (NASA), was created today as President Eisenhower signed the National Aeronautics and Space Act. NASA's stated goal is to enable the US to lead the exploration of space for peaceful purposes to benefit humanity. NASA will replace and absorb the National Advisory Committee for Aeronautics (NACA). The president said: "the combination of space exploration responsibilities with NACA's traditional aeronautical research functions is a natural evolution."

# US concern as China beefs up air force

*Washington, DC, June*
US defense chiefs are worried that a recent strengthening of Communist Chinese air power means that an invasion of the Nationalist-held isle of Taiwan is imminent. The communist air force now has 2,000 airplanes, half of them jets, and has built or modernized five air bases across from Taiwan, from which it is operating Soviet-made MiG-17 jet-fighters.

Until now, with only about 300 jet aircraft, the Nationalists have held their own. Their well-trained pilots in US-built F-86 Sabre jets have kept up that aircraft's superiority over the MiG-15, established by US pilots in Korea. The MiG-15 is the best aircraft the Nationalists have had to face, but the MiG-17 is faster than the Nationalists' F-86s and totally outclasses their F-84 Thunderjet fighter/bombers.

Two courses are being considered to stop Communist China using the MiG-17 to gain the air superiority needed for an invasion. The Nationalist government of Chiang Kai-shek could be given more advanced aircraft, such as the F-100 Super Sabre. Or, more probably, an advanced air-to-air missile now in production, which can be mounted on either the F-86 or F-84 with little or no modification, will be provided to counter the MiG-17. A likely candidate is the easy-to-use and effective Sidewinder (→ Sep 24).

**A chef and a stewardess add the finishing touches to a meal in the galley of a Tupolev Tu-114.**

# Douglas DC-8, a rival to the 707, makes its debut

*Douglas's first venture into the jet-airliner market: the prototype DC-8, powered by four Pratt & Whitney JT3C-6 turbojets each giving 13,500 lb thrust.*

*Long Beach, California, May 30*
The prototype DC-8 today made its maiden flight. It took off from the Douglas Aircraft airfield here, which is also Long Beach airport, black smoke pouring from its four Pratt & Whitney JT3C-6 turbojets, at full thrust with water injection. After the planned program of tests the landed at Edwards Air Force Base 2 hours and 7 minutes later.

The prototype is known simply as the Douglas DC-8. It is crucial because, compared with rival Boeing, Douglas has a bigger financial risk and no chance of massive sales to the US Air Force. Both Donald Douglas and his son Donald, Jr, were on board today. Much will depend on how the new airplane performs. In most respects it is similar to its Boeing rival, the 707. The wing is different, with less sweepback, more conventional flight controls and an unusual "upside-down" profile at the root. The fuselage is shallower, though cabin width is the same, and passengers have fewer, but larger, windows. Unlike the 707, all flight controls are fully powered. Like Boeing, Douglas plans longer-ranged versions powered by the JT4A (or RR Conway) engine. Unlike Boeing, these advanced DC-8s will be the same size as today's, with a length of 150 ft 6 in and seat up to 176 passengers six-abreast. These new DC-8s should enter flight test next year (→Sep 18, 1959).

## Phantom fighter unveiled by McDonnell

*Planned as an attacker, the F4H-1 has emerged as an all-weather interceptor.*

*St Louis, Missouri, May 27*
McDonnell test pilot Robert Little flew the YF4H-1 Phantom II, probably one of the most powerful and versatile fighters yet built, on its first flight today. It began life in 1953 as the F3H-H, a private venture for McDonnell to supply the US Navy with a Mach 1.5 single-seater, powered by two Wright J65 engines and armed with 20mm cannon and 11 external pylons for other weapons. Then in 1955 the Navy asked for it to be revised from an attack aircraft into a radar-equipped, all-weather, two-seater interceptor armed solely with air-to-air missiles. The result was the Phantom II, now powered by two 15,000-lb thrust General Electric J79 jets with afterburner, giving it a top speed exceeding Mach 2 and overall performance making it a world-beater (→Dec 15, 1959).

## American puts its faith in the Convair 600

*Chicago, July 30*
American Airlines, in one of the biggest commercial jet orders so far, is to buy 25 Convair 600 Golden Arrow airliners from the drawing board with options on 25 more of the four-engined planes. American's airplane has been designated the 990. It will use General Electric's new turbofan version of its CJ-805 turbojet engines to reach a top cruising speed of around Mach 0.9. TWA is sponsoring an earlier version of the 600, the 880.

**A USAF Douglas C-124 Globemaster transport takes on board a Thor medium-range ballistic missile to transport it to an RAF base in England.**

# World of European aviation mourns the passing of five of its greatest pioneers

*Henry Farman joking with friends.*

*British pioneer Alliott Verdon-Roe.*

*Ernst Heinkel at a British air show.*

*Paris, July 17*

With the death here today at 84 of Henry, or Henri, Farman, European aviation has lost one of its great pioneers. Farman, born in Paris of English parents, flew Europe's first circuit in 1908, in a Voisin biplane. His own biplane won countless prizes in those pre-war days, and Farman aircraft played major roles as bombers, reconnaissance aircraft and trainers in the First World War. Farman became a French citizen, and when his factory was nationalized in 1937 (it became SNCAC, closed down in 1949), he returned to his first passion, painting.

Last year French aviation lost Robert Esnault-Pelterie, 76, who died in Nice. Among his innovations were ailerons and the single "joystick" control lever. He became a leading figure in space research, but a 1912 paper foreseeing space flight met with skepticism. His 1927 paper on the use of rockets for space exploration is a classic. With the launch of Sputnik 1 last year he had the satisfaction of seeing his predictions begin to come true.

A great British pioneer died aged 80 on January 1 at Cowes in England. Sir Alliott Verdon Roe's outstanding career began when he won a £75 prize for his model of a biplane and put the money towards a full-sized aircraft, which he "hopped" on June 8, 1908. Verdon Roe, founder of Avro, had an innovative approach to construction which led to the Avro 504, thousands of which were built during the First World War. He later diversified into motor cars, but without success, and in the late 1920s he lost control of Avro but with S E Saunders formed the Saunders-Roe, or Saro, company to manufacture marine aircraft.

Italy and Germany have also lost pioneers. Count Gianni Caproni, designer of a wide range of aircraft including bombers and giant flying boats, died in Rome on October 27 last year at 71. Ernst Heinkel, builder of the world's first jet aircraft, the He 178, died in January at Stuttgart, aged 70. He made his first airplane in 1911 and went on to design a remarkable dynasty of seaplanes, fighters and bombers.

# Friendship binds Fokker and Fairchild

*USA, September 28*

The Fairchild FH-227 Friendship turboprop airliner entered service with West Coast Airlines today. Fairchild, which is licensed to build and market the Dutch-designed aircraft in the USA, has orders for 75. So far 62 have gone to 16 airlines, including Bonanza, Pacific, Piedmont and West Coast. The remaining orders are from private corporations. Fairchild is also offering a military version.

Fokker began work on the 40-seat F.27 in 1950 as a mid-range transport to replace the DC-3. The pressurized aircraft has two Rolls-Royce Dart engines.

*One of the Fairchild F-27s, which are proving popular with US airlines.*

# Boeing's 707 engines undergo noise tests

*Seattle, September 18*

Boeing was today notified by the US Federal Aviation Agency that its 707-120 jet airliner has been certificated for service. Pan Am will begin transatlantic flights with the aircraft next month. One of the last tests was the measurement of noise at Le Bourget airport, Paris. The Pratt & Whitney JT3 engines have multi-pipe nozzles to make the aircraft quieter, but a problem remains. The bigger 707-320 will be even louder (→Oct 26).

*Multi-tube noise reducing nozzles on a Pratt & Whitney JT3C turbojet.*

# London gets a new airport at Gatwick

*The Queen just before the ceremony.*

*Sussex, England, June 9*
Queen Elizabeth II today cut a tape to open the new £7.8 million Gatwick Airport near Crawley, about 35 miles south of London. Heathrow was becoming seriously overcrowded. At Gatwick, the existing pre-war terminal building has been redesigned to allow aircraft to park a few yards from customs facilities. The new terminal has a 900-foot pier and includes a train station offering express trains to central London. A second stage will allow for the airport's expansion to twice its size, with two more piers. The 7,000-foot runway will be extended to 8,100 feet.

*The main pier and terminal at Gatwick shortly before the airport's opening.*

# A Cessna stays in the air for 1,558 hours

*Las Vegas, Nevada, December 4*
Two Americans landed here today after setting an unusual endurance record: flying a small Cessna 172 for 64 days 22 hours 19 minutes and 5 seconds without once touching down. The fliers, Robert Timm and John Cook, broke a record set last September by two other Americans, Jim Heth and Bill Burhart, who stayed in the air over Dallas, Texas, for a total of 50 days. For over two months, Timm and Cook flew over the airport here. Twice a day, they would fly low and slow over the runway. Then, using a rope and grapnel, they would pick up jerrycans of fuel as well as fresh supplies of food and water from a speeding, open-topped car.

*The four-seater Cessna 172 has a cruising range of approximately 600 miles.*

# Nationwide agency for aviation formed

*Washington, DC, October 31*
Tough new rules for flyers, both professional and private, are now being imposed by the newly formed Federal Aviation Agency (FAA), which aims to regulate all commercial and military aviation in the United States.

No longer will both pilots be able to leave the controls to chat to passengers while the automatic pilot flies the aircraft. This rule follows several near-accidents in areas of clear-air turbulence, with one airliner dropping more than 10,000 feet while the crew fought their way back to the flight deck. One pilot must now remain at the controls at all times. Aircraft manufacturers and airlines are also required to answer to the FAA.

# Royal Navy fighter

*Lossiemouth, Scotland, June*
Royal Navy fighter-pilots of 803 Squadron have started operational training on the RN's first swept-wing fighter, the Supermarine Scimitar. Originally designed as a single-seater fighter, it has been redesigned as a low-level strike aircraft, capable of carrying a nuclear bomb. It is supersonic in a shallow dive, useful when trying to clear the target area after an atomic strike. It can also carry auxiliary fuel tanks which other aircraft can use for in-flight refueling. The squadron is expected to embark on HMS *Victorious* next September.

# Missing airplane is found in Australia

*Remains of the "Southern Cloud".*

*Australia, October 27*
The 27-year-old mystery of the *Southern Cloud*, the aircraft which disappeared on a routine flight from Sydney to Melbourne in March 1931, was finally solved today when highway engineers came across its wreckage in Tooma Gorge, high in the Snowy Mountains. More than 20 aircraft and thousands of police took part in a massive search for the aircraft when it failed to arrive.

Experts who studied today's find are convinced that the aircraft was thrown off course in bad weather and was banking to avoid a mountain when it plowed into the gorge, killing the two pilots and six passengers instantly.

**Britain's first supersonic, all-weather fighter is christened the English Electric Lightning at the Royal Aircraft Establishment, Farnborough.**

# 'Clipper' 707 launches Pan Am Atlantic jet service

*Before the 707's first Atlantic crossing, the 45 Pan Am air hostesses who have been trained on the type line up before one of the airline's 707s.*

*Paris, Le Bourget, October 27*
With high-pitched whine, heralding the jet age, a Pan Am Boeing 707 (N711PA) landed here this morning. Dignitaries, led by the Mayor of Paris, were on hand to greet 111 passengers and 11 crew.

In New York, after a "Bon-voyage" party hosted by Juan Trippe, Capt. Sam Miller (Chief Pilot) announced, "Clipper *America* is now prepared to inaugurate the jet age for the United States." Flight 114 departed Idlewild at 7:20 pm and flew 2 hrs and 42 min before landing at Gander, Newfoundland, for

provisioning and fuel. The second leg was 5 hrs and 23 min duration at 31,000 ft. The 707-121 is not quite capable of NY-Paris non-stop with a full load. Capt. Miller and acting first officer, Capt. Waldo Lynch, under intense scrutiny from the US Civil Aeronautics Adminis-

tration, have been involved in proving flights since September. The sleek new jet was delivered to Pan Am on October 16 and christened "Clipper *America*" by Mamie Einsenhower. Introduction of daily jet service will shrink our world by 40 per cent (→ Oct 10, 1959).

## Britain's Comet 4 is the first jet to fly the transatlantic route

*London, October 4*
Britain's national overseas airline BOAC has become the first carrier to fly the Atlantic route by jet-airliner. It has beaten Pan Am with its Boeing 707, which is still making proving flights. Today two de Havilland Comet 4s made simultaneous departures – one from London's Heathrow airport (commanded by Captain R E Millichap) and one from Idlewild, New York (commanded by Captain T B Stoney). Both Comets carried a full complement of fare-paying passengers.

The race to be first has made no impact on the true progress of commercial aviation. Although much longer, heavier, more powerful and more capable than the ill-fated Comet 1, the Comet 4 was never designed for the North Atlantic, and the westbound flight today had to refuel at Gander, Newfoundland. BOAC will replace the Comet on the route once its own Boeing 707s are delivered.

First flown on April 27 this year, the Comet 4 is powered by four Rolls-Royce Avon turbojets, each

*Passengers boarding the first transatlantic Comet service at London airport.*

of 10,500-lb thrust. It can carry 60 to 76 passengers, depending on the seating arrangement, at 500mph for a little under 3,000 miles. In contrast, the 707-320 can carry 100 more passengers a greater distance and 100mph faster. At

least passengers can be assured that the British jet is structurally sound. The Comet metal-fatigue problem has been overcome by design changes; the Comet 4 has round windows, and it should have a long life on shorter routes (→ Dec 20).

## US jet airliners set to dominate sales

*New York, December 31*
Although Britain can be pleased that the de Havilland Comet 4 made the first direct commercial crossing of the Atlantic by jet, its airliner faces formidable competition. Pan Am may have been three weeks later with its first Boeing 707 flight from New York to Paris, but as the year ends it is the 707, not the Comet, which points the way.

In the end it is aircraft sales round the world which are going to matter. Here Boeing already has a substantial advantage, with orders from Air France, Braniff, Continental, Pan Am, Qantas, Sabena and TWA – even one from Britain's BOAC, which is the main customer for the Comet. It will be extremely difficult for the Comet to catch up in the sales war. Britain's only serious competitor, namely the Vickers 1000, was foolishly cancelled in 1955. The recent arrival of the Douglas DC-8 means that US airliners are set to corner the market.

*The Gulfstream I RR Dart-powered pressurized executive transport.*

*A four-seat development of earlier variants was the French Jodel D.140.*

*The prototype Douglas DC-8 was completed to the initial Series 10 standards, but was updated to Series 50. Here it makes its first flight at Long Beach.*

*The de Havilland Comet 4C was the major production version of the Comet 4, a lengthened version for oceanic work. 29 were built, almost all for export.*

*Breguet's Br.765 Sahara was a military version of the famous Br.763 "Deux Ponts". The type could air-drop up to 150 paratroops or carry a light tank.*

*Later versions of the Jodel D.140 featured a more conventional tail.*

*Antonov's An-14, a light feeder liner code-named "Clod" by NATO.*

*The Hindustan HUL-26 Pushpak, powered by a 90-hp Continental.*

*The Saunders-Roe P.531 acted as prototype for the Wasp and Scout.*

*The de Havilland Canada DHC-4 Caribou 32-seat STOL transport.*

*The Sikorsky S-62 was a single-engined helicopter with boat hull.*

*The PZL M-2 light trainer/tourer was designed by Warsaw students.*

*North American's Sabreliner was completed to the USAF's UTX specification, but found more fame as a civilian executive jet than as a T-39.*

*The Doak model 16 had tilting ducted propellers for VTOL research.*

*The Andersson BA-7 was the forerunner of the Malmö MFI-9.*

*Handley Page's Herald was re-engined with only a pair of Dart turboprops instead of its original four piston engines to become the HPR.7 Dart Herald.*

*First flying this year, the Antonov An-12BP was to become the "Soviet Hercules", used in huge numbers and many variants around the world.*

*The Gannet AEW.3: airborne early warning for Royal Navy carriers.*

*One of the Morane-Saulnier MS. 1500 Epervier prototypes.*

*North American's T2J design is better known as the T-2 Buckeye.*

*A major Boeing B-52 variant was the B-52G, introducing the short fin.*

*The Douglas A3D-2P Skywarrior was later redesignated the RA-3B.*

*The Ryan VZ-3RY was a V/STOL research aircraft with blown flaps.*

*Another STOL research vehicle, the Dornier Do 29 had tilting propellers.*

*Two Piasecki VZ-8s were delivered to the US Army for VTOL research.*

*Named Vigilante, the North American A3J was initially used as a nuclear bomber, with a single weapon housed in a tunnel between the engines.*

*McDonnell's classic XF4H-1 became the F-4 Phantom II, one of the world's greatest fighters. They set new standards of flight and radar performance.*

*Dassault's private-venture Etendard evolved through several prototypes. The IVM was the full naval version, entering service in January 1962.*

*Avro Canada's mighty CF-105 Arrow Mach 2.5 interceptor was cancelled with six aircraft completed, despite the enormous potential the design showed.*

*With the company designation B.103, the Blackburn Buccaneer was to become a highly successful carrier- and land-based low level strike platform.*

# 1959

2,094mph
USA
Milburn Apt
Bell X-2
Sep 27, 1956

24,325 miles
USA
Archie Old Jr
Boeing B-52B
Jan 18, 1957

125,907ft
USA
Iven Kincheloe
Bell X-2
Sep 7, 1956

488,000lb
USA
Boeing
B-52G Stratofortress

27,008lb thrust
USSR
Lyulka
AL-21F

**USA, January 1**
The 702nd Strategic Missile Wing is activated and assigned to the Eighth Air Force; this is the first time missile and bomber forces have been integrated in this way.

**Berkshire, England, January 5**
The Fairey Rotodyne, piloted by W P Gellatly and J G P Morton, sets a world speed record for convertiplanes of 190.9mph over a 62-mile circuit (→ Feb 26, 1962).

**Leicestershire, England, January 8**
The Armstrong Whitworth Argosy turboprop transport makes its first flight, piloted by Eric Franklin, at Bitteswell aerodrome.

**North America, February 1**
The RCAF takes over operational control of the North American Distant Early Warning (DEW) air-defense scheme from the USAF (→ Sep 10, 1960).

**[West] Germany, February 6**
The Luftwaffe orders 66 Lockheed F-104G Starfighters, the aircraft which will form the basis of its fighter force (→ Dec 6, 1966).

**Fort Worth, Tex, February 12**
The last Convair B-36 bomber in operational USAF service is retired to Amon Carter Field, where it is put on display; Strategic Air Command is now equipped with an all-jet bomber force.

**Ottawa, February 20**
Prime minister John Diefenbaker announces the cancellation of the Avro CF-105 Arrow; unveiled on October 4, 1957, the high-performance, supersonic, delta-winged interceptor, of which six were built, was the most ambitious aircraft produced by the Canadian industry, to which its cancellation comes as a bitter blow.

**Istres, France, February 25**
André Turcat sets a speed record of 1,018mph over a 100-kilometre [62.14-mile] closed circuit in the Nord 1500 Griffon, powered by a combined turbojet/ramjet unit.

**France, February 28**
Jean Boulet pilots the prototype of the Alouette III helicopter on its first flight, at Marseille-Marignane (→ Nov 5, 1960).

**Beijing, China, February**
China signs an agreement with the USSR providing for Soviet aid in the development of the aircraft industry in its provinces (→ Dec 16).

**England, March**
The Supersonic Transport Aircraft Committee proposes three designs for a supersonic transport: one with wings forward-swept then swept back to the tips, capable of Mach 1.2 and a 1,500-nautical mile range; one with a slender delta wing, able to reach Mach 1.8 with a 3,500-nautical-mile range; and a huge steel and titanium aircraft capable of Mach 3 and a range also of 3,500 nautical miles.

**Czechoslovakia, April 5**
The prototype of the Aero L-29 Delfin two-seat jet trainer, the first jet aircraft to be designed and built in Czechoslovakia, makes its maiden flight.

**USSR, April 20**
Aeroflot puts the 84 to 110-seater Ilyushin Il-18, its first turboprop, into service from Moscow to Alma Ata, Kazakhstan, and Adler, now Sochi on the Black Sea.

**Seletar, Singapore, May 15**
The RAF's two remaining flying boats, both Short Sunderlands, make their final operational flight.

**London, June 1**
BOAC puts the de Havilland Comet 4 jet airliner into service on its route to Singapore (→ Nov 1).

**France, June 4**
French aero-engine makers SNECMA and American United Aircraft Corporation (UAC) of the USA announce an agreement under which SNECMA will be licensed to build and market all engines by Pratt & Whitney, the US manufacturer controlled by UAC.

**California, June 8**
Scott Crossfield pilots the North American X-15 research airplane on its first free (gliding) flight, at Edwards Air Force Base (→ Sep 17).

**Somerset, England, July 2**
The Royal Navy's first operational unit equipped with de Havilland Sea Vixen swept-wing fighters, 892 Squadron, Fleet Air Arm, is commissioned at Yeovilton Royal Naval Air Station.

**USSR, July 14**
Major V Ilyushin takes the world absolute altitude record when he pilots the Sukhoi T-431 to an altitude of 94,659 feet.

**France, July 27**
Air France puts the new Caravelle jet airliner into service on its route to London.

**Pacific Ocean, July 29**
Qantas flies its first scheduled jet service across the Pacific when it puts the Boeing 707 into service on the route between Sydney and San Francisco (→ May 27, 1960).

**California, July 30**
The Northrop N-156F (F-5) prototype supersonic fighter exceeds Mach 1 on its first flight, from Edwards Air Force Base.→

**Alaska, August 7**
Two USAF F-100F fighters land at Eielson Air Force Base to complete Operation Julius Caesar, the first flight by jet-fighter aircraft over the North Pole; they had left Wethersfield, Essex, England, 9 hours 37 minutes earlier.

**France, August 26**
French flyer Jacqueline Auriol, piloting a Mirage III, becomes the first woman to attain the speed of Mach 2 (→ Jun 22, 1962).

**Sydney, September 5**
Qantas Boeing 707-138 *City of Melbourne* takes off to fly the airline's first jet service to London, via Fiji, Honolulu, San Francisco and New York.→

**USA, September 18**
The Douglas DC-8 enters service with Delta Air Lines and United Air Lines.

**Croydon, England, September 30**
Croydon airport, London's main terminal between the wars, is closed; the final service is a flight to Rotterdam by a de Havilland Heron of Morton Air Services, piloted by the aptly-named Captain Geoffrey Last.

**USSR, October 31**
Colonel Georgi Mossolov sets a world speed record in the Mikoyan Ye-66 tailless delta, reaching 1,483.8mph at Sidorovo Tyumenskaya (→ Apr 28, 1961).

**London, November 1**
BOAC introduces the de Havilland Comet 4 jetliner on its service to Sydney (→ Apr 1, 1960).

**Olathe, Kansas, December 15**
Ed King, dissatisfied with the products offered to private pilots, formed the King Radio Corporation to engineer and manufacture light aircraft avionics. He designed and made the first low-cost, 90-channel, crystal-controlled VHF transceiver for light aircraft, the KY 90, selling for $895. As business is booming, he now sets up for mass production in an old dairy farmhouse on the outskirts of Kansas City (→ Feb 5, 1961).

**Taiwan, December 16**
China Airlines is set up by the Nationalist government to operate domestic services (→ Aug 10, 1964).

**Hertfordshire, England, Dec 17**
The famous de Havilland Aircraft Company is forced to merge with Hawker Siddeley.

*The X-15 research airplane clings beneath the wing of the B-52 bomber which will carry it to an altitude of 35,000 feet for launching.* ▶

# Convair test-flies medium-range jetliner

*The elegant Convair 880: intended as a competitor to the 707 and the DC-8.*

**San Diego, Calif, January 27**
As they watched the prototype Convair 880 airliner take to the skies for the first time today, experts were already questioning the commercial future of this long and elegant jet. No one questioned the beauty of the aircraft; the problem is that Boeing can sell the 720 considerably cheaper.

With its successful 240/340/440 series behind it, Convair is firmly in the aviation market place and sees the 880 as a competitor to the

Boeing 707 and the Douglas DC-8. Despite its similarity to the 707, the 880's design – five-abreast seating, rather than six in the 707 – means that its passenger capacity is limited to 88 to 110, compared with the 707's 150 to 200. Convair hopes that speed – the 880 cruises at 615mph – will be the selling factor, together with its range of 2,880 miles. Four General Electric CJ-805-3 turbojets power this elegant newcomer to the US's aviation scene (→ Feb 12, 1960).

# Cessna's best-ever best-seller

*Wichita, Kansas, January*
Whatever else they have manufactured over the years, the main products of the Cessna Aircraft Company have been high-wing cabin monoplanes. Of these, more than 90 per cent have been either two-seaters or four-seaters. And today's two-seater, the Model 150, is selling like the proverbial hot-cakes both in the USA and overseas.

Immediately after World War II Cessna produced the de luxe 140 for touring and the austere 120 model for training, both with two seats placed side by side. Surprisingly, no two-seater was produced from 1950 until 1959. Then the Model 150 hit the market, basically a modernized

120/140 with tricycle landing gear and a 100-hp Continental engine. It has appeared in three versions, all with flaps, a square vertical tail and the option of wheel or float gear, radio and various other extras. The Trainer has the Standard version's equipment plus dual controls and additional instruments and fittings, while the Inter-City Commuter is further upgraded for cross-country flying "in weather".

Demand from flying clubs and private owners everywhere is unprecedented. The Cessna Aircraft Company now has ideas for upgrading the 150's appearance, and perhaps producing an aerobatic version (→ Feb 15, 1960).

*The Cessna Model 150 boasts a cruising speed of 112mph at 7,000ft.*

# Lockheed Electra is new buy for Eastern

**New York, January 12**
Britain's Vickers Viscount, for long the only turboprop airliner flying in the US, now faces competition. Today Eastern Air Lines introduced the new Lockheed 44 to 88-seat Electra on its route between here and Miami and will begin flying it to Puerto Rico on February 22. The day after that, American Airlines is scheduled to introduce Electras on its New York/Chicago route.

Braniff, National, Northwest and Western Air Lines will start using the Electra later in the year. The plane, which cruises at 405mph, can be operated profitably on routes where pure jets would be uneconomical. It poses a major challenge to Capital and other airlines still flying the older British airliner (→ May 17, 1960).

# Igor Sikorsky's 'Hiss-Two' opens up a new era for helicopters

*A US Navy Sikorsky HSS-2 winching a Ryan Firebee drone from the sea.*

**Stratford, Connecticut, March 11**
Already known as *Hiss-Two*, from its US Navy designation HSS-2, the S-61 began its flight test program today at the Sikorsky Aircraft

plant. It is the first helicopter to combine all available new technology. Like the small S-62 flown last year the *Hiss-Two* has the General Electric T58 turboshaft engine of

1,250-hp, whose compactness and very light weight make it possible to put the power plant above the cabin, next to the rotor gearbox. Unlike the S-62 the S-61 has two engines, and can fly on one. It also has an amphibious hull, with stabilizing floats into which the twin-wheel main landing gears retract. The 62-ft main rotor has five blades, and together with the complete tail section can be folded for deployment aboard ships. The HSS-2 is an anti-submarine hunter-killer, packed with avionics, but other versions will be used for transport, rescue and civil airline operations. There are bound to be many versions of this machine, licenses for which are likely to be obtained by Westland (UK), Agusta (Italy) and Mitsubishi (Japan). Production machines for the Navy may be named Sea King (→ Feb 5, 1962).

# Air crash in Iowa kills Buddy Holly

*Death-trap: the wreck of the Bonanza after it crashed in an Iowa snowstorm.*

*Singer Buddy Holly, a tragic loss.*

*Mason City, February 3*
Buddy Holly, the Big Bopper and Ritchie Valens, three of rock-and-roll music's biggest stars, died early today when a single-engined Beechcraft Bonanza crashed on a farm 5 miles from Mason City airport. Its pilot, Roger Peterson, was a fourth victim of the crash. News of the tragedy has stunned millions of fans this morning. Holly, 22, with the group The Crickets, had numerous hits, notably "That'll Be the Day", "Oh Boy!" and "Peggy Sue". The big hit for 24-year-old Big Bopper (real name J P Richardson) was "Chantilly Lace", while Valens, just 17, will be most remembered for "Donna". The three performers appeared before more than 1,000 teenagers at Clear Lake last night and had chartered the airplane to fly them to Fargo, North Dakota, for an engagement tonight. Their backing musicians traveled by bus. The authorities are blaming the crash on weather conditions. The aircraft took off at about 1am in sub-zero conditions, when heavy snow was falling.

## Manchester United crash: ice blamed

*Munich, Germany, March 9*
A report on the air crash in February last year which killed many of the Manchester United soccer team [*see page 564*] has concluded that ice on the wings was the principal cause. British European Airways (BEA), the airline involved, has hit back with a vigorous rebuttal, citing thick slush on the runway. The aircraft's captain, James Thain, who has been grounded since last August, as well as several eye-witnesses, maintain that ice formed on the wings between the time of the crash and the arrival of the airport officials.

Whatever the case, it seems unlikely that ice on the wings alone could have stopped the Airspeed Ambassador taking off. Slush on the runway seems to be the more probable cause of the disaster. It slowed the airplane at a critical point in its take-off run. There are as yet no regulations making it compulsory for airports to clear snow from their runways.

## 707 plummets over Atlantic Ocean

*Gander, Newfoundland, Feb 4*
Captain Waldo Lynch sits quietly sipping coffee after a terrifying fall over the Atlantic. Coffee may be what caused him to be in the "bathroom" of Clipper 115 when the autopilot tripped off. The Paris-New York 707 was being flown by the copilot. He was flying too fast and entered a high-speed stall, throwing Lynch and others to the floor. Lynch was able to crawl forward and get back to his seat. "I saw pieces flying off the plane; we were almost on our back," he said. They had been flying at over 30,000 ft, and Lynch was able to right the ship at only 4,000 ft. "The airspeed indicator was pegged, she shook and bucked like a wild bronc."

Post-flight inspection shows missing fairings, wrinkled skin and the horizontal stabilizer bent unbelievably. Mechanics report bolts that attach the engine to the wings are bent at crazy angles, indicating a "G" force near seven. Passengers cheered Lynch on landing.

# Seven top Service pilots are selected to be first US Astronauts

*The first of America's Astronauts, with an F-106 used for training.*

*Washington, DC, April 6*
Seven of the US's best pilots, chosen to be the first Americans in space, were today introduced to the press and public. The men, one of whom will ride the Mercury spacecraft being built for the National Aeronautics and Space Administration (NASA) by McDonnell Aircraft, are: USAF Captains Virgil I Grissom, Leroy Gordon Cooper, Jr, and Donald K Slayton; Navy Lieutenant-Commanders Alan B Shepard, Jr, and Walter M Schirra, Jr, and Lieutenant Malcolm Scott Carpenter; and from the US Marines, Lieutenant-Colonel John H Glenn, Jr.

The criteria for selection as an astronaut, to orbit the Earth and investigate human reactions and abilities in space, were stringent. Candidates had to be or have been military test pilots, trained in observing scientific and technical phenomena and able to react calmly to high-stress situations never before experienced. They had to be physically fit, between 25 and 40 years old and, because of the spacecraft's small size, no more than 5 feet 11 inches tall. The seven, chosen from over 450 possible candidates, will begin training at NASA's Langley Research Center in Hampton, Virginia.

Military rockets will power the Mercury capsule. NASA plans to begin the manned space flights with sub-orbital launches using the US Army's Redstone rocket. Orbital flights, using the USAF's more powerful Convair Atlas intercontinental ballistic missile, will follow.

# Istanbul flight marks Caravelle's debut

*Istanbul, May 6*
The Sud-Aviation Caravelle jet airliner, France's remarkable contender in the short-haul market, landed here from Paris today at the end of its first scheduled flight.

The debut of the Caravelle follows intensive competition by designers of six companies for a French government award. Sud-Aviation came up with an unconventional scheme in which the two engines were placed at the rear of the airplane, giving passengers mush a quieter ride.

The Caravelle has excellent maneuverability, as was shown during a demonstration flight for aviation writers on April 15, when Captain Marcel Guibbert took off entirely on one engine.

He then climbed up from Orly airport until he reached an altitude of almost 40,000 feet, shut down both of the 10,500-lb thrust Rolls-Royce Avon engines and brought the gently gliding aircraft down to land at Dijon, southeast of Paris, just 46 minutes and 200 miles later (→ Jul 27).

*Air France's first regular Caravelle service to Istanbul is planned for May 6.*

# British flag-carrier's first 707 is flying

*BOAC's first 707 lands at Boeing Field, Seattle, after its 71-minute test flight.*

*Seattle, May 19*
The first Boeing 707-436 Intercontinental destined for BOAC made its maiden flight today, landing at Boeing Field, Seattle, after 1 hour 11 minutes in the air. BOAC ordered 15 Intercontinentals in 1956.

This airplane is the 35th 707 to be built at Boeing's Renton plant. As part of the deal, BOAC's 707s will be powered by Rolls-Royce Conway engines, spending some of the purchase price in Britain.

Another major development in British commercial aviation took place five days ago when BEA began the first London/Moscow service using Viscounts, and today the first jet service between South America and Britain was inaugurated by Aerolineas Argentinas using Comet 4s (→ Apr 29, 1960).

# Grandfather sets a lightplane record

*Los Angeles, June 4*
A 56-year-old grandfather and father of 10 Max Conrad set a light-aircraft flight-distance record of 7,668 miles when today he landed here 58 hours 38 minutes after taking off from Casablanca, Morocco. He had covered the distance alone, non-stop, in a single-engined airplane; a perfectly standard Piper Comanche with added tankage. He had originally intended to land at El Paso, Texas, but, after a low pass for the welcoming committee, he carried on to California.

*Conrad on arrival in Los Angeles.*

# Supersonic Freedom Fighter soars aloft

*California, July 30*
Northrop test pilot Lew Nelson today flew the diminutive N-156F Freedom Fighter on its first flight, at Edwards Air Force Base. The N-156F is a single-seat version of the USAF's T-38 Talon supersonic trainer, also under development and powered by two afterburning General Electric J85 engines. It has two cannon and two missiles.

From the start, in 1956, of the Fang fighter project, chief engineer Welko Gasich planned both trainer and fighter versions. The N-156F has not been ordered by the USAF, but will go to friendly nations as the F-5A and the two-seater F-5B.

*The neat lines of the N-156F (F-5).*

# US firms fly record number of air miles

*Washington, DC, June 15*
The first four months of 1959 saw substantial growth in business for most airlines in the US. Figures released today by the International Air Transportation Association of America (IATA) show airlines reporting 8.5 billion revenue passenger miles, an 8.9 per cent increase over the same period last year, despite a wave of strikes which hit the industry early this year.

The public's eager acceptance of the new jet-airliners is cited as one of the reasons for the increase in traffic and advance reservations which have led the ATA to predict that 1959 will be a "banner year" in travel. TWA lends credence to that optimism. Since the first jet went into service in March, its fleet has been averaging 96 per cent of passenger capacity. TWA flew 374,000 passenger miles in May, 13 per cent above the April total and 213 per cent greater than in May 1958.

Cargo services are doing well, too. Airlines which carry cargo showed a 19.3 per cent increase to 12 million-ton miles compared with the first quarter of 1958.

# Man flies English Channel – upside down

*Lympne, Kent, England, June 27*
It can be a topsy-turvy world for an aerobatic pilot. But flying the English Channel upside-down in a slow biplane is quite another matter, and no easy feat.

For Britain's Elwyn McAully, who today piloted the inverted de Havilland Tiger Moth *Archbishop* from Lympne, Kent, to Le Touquet, France, the feat marked a double anniversary. It was 50 years, bar a few weeks, since Louis Blériot became the first person to fly the Channel and 25 years since a Tiger Moth first flew over upside-down.

The flight had demonstrated just what the aircraft can do. The *Archbishop* is one of four Tiger Moths modified to see off overseas competition for the Lockheed International Aerobatic Trophy (→ Jul 25).

# Flight of bizarre Coléoptère is flop

*Melun-Villaroche, France, July 25*
Entomologists know all about "coleopterous" insects – beetles whose wings are sheathed beneath hardened wing-covers to protect them when not in use. SNECMA in France took a leaf out of their book when it named its C.450-01 circular-winged, vertical take-off and landing research aircraft, which made its test flight today, the Coléoptère: its wings form a "shield" around the fuselage.

Test pilot Auguste Morel knew that he would need all his experience to fly the strange machine. The pilot's position is very unusual, standing upright on take-off, then lying prone once the transition has

*The craft is positioned for take-off.*

been made to horizontal flight. From the moment of take-off he found that the Coléoptère behaved very differently from the way that the makers had anticipated. Morel wrestled valiantly to control the unruly machine but, once fuel began to run low, he decided to land. He managed to hold the Coléoptère in stable horizontal flight, but in doing so lost a lot of height. When he was just 45 feet off the ground, he decided to eject. It was probably a prudent decision, considering the behaviour of the airplane. He was fortunate to survive, suffering severe internal injuries from the ejection which have probably ended his career as a test pilot.

# Qantas opens jet route Sydney to London

*Flying westbound to London, Qantas can take advantage of favorable winds.*

*London, September 5*
The last word in fashionable holidays will soon be to set off for a restful trip to Australia. Australian overseas airline Qantas this morning landed its Boeing 707 on British soil, thus inaugurating the first jet service between Sydney and London. The route offers some tantalizing stopovers: Fiji, Honolulu, San Francisco and New York.

Qantas is using a model 707-138 Boeing equipped with Rolls-Royce turbofans for this long flight. The 707-138 is a special version of the 707-120B series. Instead of the standard fuselage length of 144 feet 6 inches, the 707-138 has a fuselage that has been shortened 10 feet aft

of the wing. The plane can carry 181 passengers, but at present it is being operated in a way that puts comfort before everything else – and at first-class standards. Qantas is using it on its regular service from Sydney to San Francisco. This route, which was opened on July 29, was the first transpacific connection to be made by an airplane of this category. It also had the distinction of being Qantas's first regular jet service. Today's flight is the culmination of almost exactly three years' planning. It was on September 6, 1956, that Qantas ordered a total of seven Boeing 707-138s, at a cost of £A1.8 million each (→ Nov 26, 1964).

# Supersonic bomber makes first outing

*Melun-Villaroche, France, June 17*
Test pilot Roland Glavany, who has been specially seconded to Dassault from the French air force for the purpose, made the first flight of the prototype Dassault Mirage IVA today. The new supersonic bomber has been designed specifically to carry an atomic bomb, and it will go into production as the backbone of France's nuclear deterrent, the air force's Force de Frappe [Strike Force], equivalent to Britain's V-bomber force or the USAF's Strategic Air Command.

The new delta-winged Mirage is powered by two SNECMA Atar 09 turbojets with afterburners. It looks like a big fighter, with two seats one behind the other. The original plan was for a bigger aircraft with Pratt & Whitney J75 engines, but this was rejected on grounds of cost. The prototype which flew today was a scaled-up version of Dassault's superb Mirage III fighter. Production models will be rather larger, and with in-flight refueling will be able to reach most targets in the USSR. Some Mirage IVAs will be equipped to carry extra fuel so that they can operate in pairs, one carrying a 60-kiloton atomic bomb under the fuselage, the other the extra fuel. France is also buying a fleet of Boeing KC-135 tankers. Production Mirage IVAs will also be able to carry 16 conventional 1,000-pound bombs.

# Easy to fly, but lacking power, the Rallye makes its maiden flight

*Villacoublay, France, June 10*
Anyone, say Joseph Rostaing and his team of designers, should be able to fly the MS-880 Rallye, a three-seater tourer fitted with a 90-hp Continental motor which today made its first flight. This all-metal, low-winged aircraft, which the makers plan to produce in large numbers, is not designed for speed.

Today's test pilot, Jean Cliquet, was not satisfied with the power available, however, and experts are dubious about Rostaing's claim that the Rallye will carry three people. A larger power plant will have to be installed if the Rallye is to stand a chance in the competitive private aircraft market.

*The makers of the all-metal Rallye plan to mass-produce it like an automobile.*

# Eisenhower follows Soviets and gets a jet

*Eisenhower stands before his new jet as he receives an RAF salute in London.*

**Washington, DC, August 26**
The leader of the US will no longer look second best to the premier of the USSR when his airplane arrives in a foreign capital. President Eisenhower, currently on his way to meet with West German chancellor Konrad Adenauer, is flying on board his new USAF VC-137A, a specially adapted version of the Boeing 707 jet-airliner.

By replacing the old presidential Lockheed Super Constellation *Columbine III* with a jet, "Ike" will be able to cut his travel time in half while enjoying greater comfort. The switch to a 707 is also a propaganda coup against the Soviets, who have been trying – unsuccessfully – to market their Tu-104, a jet-transport version of the Tu-16 bomber, which has been flying Soviet premier Krushchev since 1956. It was the arrival of Soviet ministers in Washington aboard a Tu-104 which prompted Eisenhower's determination to go one better and get a 707. Following the stop in Germany, the president's

*At work on the Soviet Tu-104.*

new airplane will take him to London and Paris before he goes to Scotland for some golf and relaxation prior to his return. During the whole trip he will cover almost 9,000 miles in less than 20 hours flying time.

**The Fairey Rotodyne is in the course of a series of demonstration flights around Britain, but is unfortunately failing to drum up many orders.**

# Rocket-plane is tested

**California, September 17**
The second of three examples of the North American X-15, designed to fly to previously unexplored speeds and altitudes, made the type's first powered flight today, from Edwards Air Force Base, in the hands of company test pilot Scott Crossfield. The flight went well, Crossfield modestly saying: "This is Harrison Storm's day" – a reference to the leader of the design team.

Douglas and the US Navy had earlier planned the D-558-III, to fly even faster and higher than the X-15, but no money was made available. Instead the X-15 was launched, mainly by NACA (now NASA, the National Aeronautics and Space Administration) and the USAF.

The X-15 is a black aircraft with tiny, straight wings. Two RMI four-barrel rocket engines are fitted as an interim measure until the same company's very powerful LR99 is

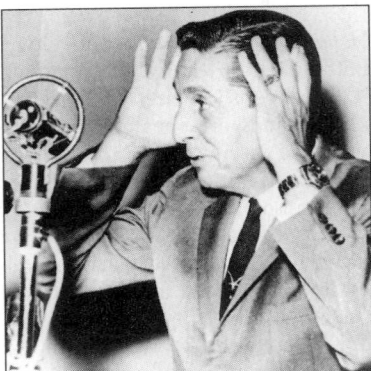

*A lively Crossfield describes the test.*

ready. It is designed to reach Mach 7, about 4,600mph, and fly higher than 200,000 feet (38 miles). On each flight it will be carried up to about 35,000 feet by an NB-52 parent aircraft, slung under the right wing. The rocket engine is ignited as the X-15 drops from the NB-52 (→ Aug 12, 1960).

*Like a black bullet: the X-15 is designed to reach speeds as high as Mach 7.*

# First come, first served on regional airline

**Philadelphia, October 4**
If you are willing to take a chance, from today Allegheny Airlines will fly you from here to Pittsburgh or vice versa for much less than other passengers on the same airplane. Its new non-reserved fare on its Penn Commuter route offers a 36 per cent discount over normal fares.

Thrifty travelers simply go to Allegheny's counter at the airport and buy a time-stamped ticket. When the flight is called, passengers with advance reservations who have paid the full fare are boarded first. Any

remaining seats are filled by non-reserved ticket holders standing by – first come, first seated.

This move by Allegheny, a small, regional airline, is a direct challenge to giant TWA, which operates the same route. Allegheny expects to cut reservation operation costs and fill more seats with the unique non-reservation system. It estimates that only about 5 per cent of passengers who buy the heavily discounted tickets at the airport will not get seats on the flights they particularly want.

# Pan Am begins round-the-world flights

*New York, October 10*

Pan Am's newly-acquired Boeing 707-321, *Clipper Windward*, inaugurated the company's first all-jet, round-the-world service today. It is scheduled to encircle the globe in slightly more than two days. The service, routed via San Francisco, Honolulu, Manila, Karachi and Rome, has put Pan Am very much at the forefront of the world's airlines. The 707 is clearly a winner. Only BOAC's Comet 4s offer real competition on the lucrative transatlantic route, overtaking TWA, whose piston-engined L-1649As are no match for the jets. While the British and US giants battle it out over the Atlantic, the race is on among other airlines to buy the 707 and the DC-8. If deliveries are kept up, at least 11 airlines will be using jets between Europe and North America next year, something BOAC said would not happen (→ Aug 20, 1960).

Pan Am's fleet of sleek 707 jets has helped the airline edge ahead of its rivals.

# French jet pilots to wear masks in flight

*Paris, November 27*

Prompted by the serious consequences of sudden cabin decompression at high altitudes, France's transport ministry has today issued a decree that whenever any French aircraft flies higher than an altitude of 9,000 metres [29,500 feet], the flight crew must all have serviceable oxygen masks immediately available, with the pilot currently in control of the aircraft actually wearing his. It has been shown that at over 30,000 feet sudden decompression renders the average pilot unconscious in about half a minute.

**September 30: a D.H.114 Heron flies the last service from Croydon.**

# Records just keep tumbling as US pilots fly higher and faster than ever before

*Rogers flew a Convair F-106 interceptor to set today's world speed record.*

*California, December 15*

A ten-day assault on speed and altitude records by USAF and US Navy pilots ended today at Edwards Air Force Base with Major Joseph W Rogers setting a world speed record at 1,525.9mph. Five of the six records were set here.

Commander Lawrence E Flint began the record-busting binge on December 6, when he pushed the second prototype of the US Navy's new McDonnell F-4H Phantom II fighter to 98,556 feet. The second record, also for altitude, was made at Bloomfield, Connecticut, by USAF Major William J Davis and Captain Walter J Hodgson. They piloted a turbine-powered Kaman H-43B Huskie rescue helicopter to 29,846 feet to break the heavy-lift helicopter record of 21,982 feet held by a Soviet Mi-1. On December 11 Brigadier-General Joseph H Moore, the commander of USAF Fourth Tactical Fighter Wing, set the speed record for 100 kilometers [62.14-miles] closed-circuit at 1,216.48mph in a Republic F-105B Thunderchief.

Three days later, Captain Joe B Jordan eclipsed Flint's altitude record when he climbed to 103,395.9 feet in a Lockheed F-104C Starfighter, climbing from take-off to 98,424 feet in an unprecedented 15 minutes 4.92 seconds.

These flights prove the advances in technology and performance achieved by the USAF's impressive "Century Series" of fighters (so called from their type numbers in the low 100s) and the US Navy's second generation of Phantoms, which strengthen the defensive capabilities of the US military.

*Joe B Jordan aboard the F-104 Starfighter he took to a world altitude record.*

The prototype Boeing 707-320 Intercontinental long-range four-jet airliner, which provided new, shorter trip times for long-range passengers.

The prototype Convair 880 airliner, first of an unprofitable family.

The Sikorsky S-61N helicopter was a stretched civil HSS-2 Sea King.

Sud-Aviation's SE. 3160 Alouette III enjoyed a long and successful production run, and huge numbers of this versatile helicopter remain in use.

The Beech 33 Debonair was virtually a conventional-tail Bonanza.

The French SIPA S.261 Anjou remained as a single prototype.

Dassault's M.D.415 Spirale twin turboprop remained a prototype.

Italy's Procaer F15 Picchio, an aerobatic four-seat light monoplane.

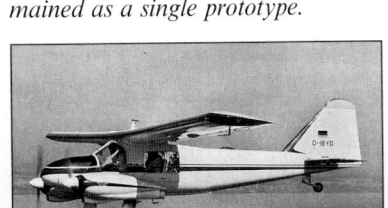

Dornier's Do 28 STOL utility aircraft enjoyed considerable success.

Max Holste's 250 Super Broussard was made for civil and military use.

Morane-Saulnier's MS.880 Rallye Club, first in the Rallye series.

Yugoslavia's UTVA-56 was a four-seater utility airplane.

Argentina's Aero Boero 95: a lightweight three-seat touring aircraft.

The Australian Victa Airtourer 100, later transferred to New Zealand.

The Lake LA-4 Buccaneer, intended to be an affordable amphibian.

The Westland Westminster, a flying crane based on Sikorsky technology.

The prototype Vickers Vanguard: the Vanguard was powered by four Rolls-Royce Tynes and featured a 139-seat double-bubble pressurized fuselage.

The Handley Page Victor B.2, the very last of Britain's V-bombers.

Wassmer's WA-40 Super IV four-seater was sold in three versions.

The prototype Boeing 720, a much lightened intermediate-range 707.

India's prototype HAL Krishak, a two/three-seat multi-role aircraft.

*Dassault scaled up its delta-wing layout for the Mirage IVA prototype.*

*The Canadair CL-44, a long-range four-turboprop transport.*

*English Electric designed the side-by-side Lightning T.4 as a conversion trainer for its jet fighter (rear). Previous pilots trained on Hawker Hunters.*

*The civil variant of the twin-boomed, Dart-engined Armstrong Whitworth A.W.650 Argosy freighter/transport had a full-width door at each end.*

*The Northrop N-156F (later designated the F-5A) Freedom Fighter.*

*The Folland Gnat T.1 replaced the RAF's DH Vampire T.11.*

*Devised from the civil Electra, Lockheed's P-3A Orion maritime patrol and anti-submarine-warfare aircraft proved a worthy successor to the Neptune.*

*The twin-turboprop Hiller X-18 was designed for V/STOL research.*

*The trainer predecessor of the Northrop N-156 was the T-38A Talon.*

*Dassault's Mirage IIIB: two-seat trainer version of the IIIC fighter.*

*Czechoslovakia's Aero L-29 Delfin, the Warsaw Pact's jet-trainer.*

*The Grumman OV-1 Mohawk, a STOL tactical observation aircraft.*

*The remarkable North American X-15, designed for Mach 6 research.*

*The first Sikorsky HSS-2 Sea King anti-submarine-warfare helicopter, founder of an important dynasty, all of whose members have twin GE T58 engines.*

*The prototype Kaman YHU2K-1 (later SH-2) Seasprite helicopter.*

*The turbine-engined (licensed T58) Westland Whirlwind Series 3.*

# 1960

 2,196mph
USA
Joseph Walker
North American X-15
Aug 4, 1960

 24,325 miles
USA
Archie Old Jr
Boeing B-52B
Jan 18, 1957

 136,500ft
USA
Robert White
North American X-15
Aug 12, 1960

 488,000lb
USA
Boeing
B-52G Stratofortress

 27,008lb thrust
USSR
Lyulka
AL-21F

**Ankara, January 19**
An SAS Caravelle airliner crashes into a hill as it begins its landing approach, killing 42.

**Dallas, Texas, February 1**
Universal commences operations as the Universal Weather Service.

**New York, February 10**
Douglas and Sud-Aviation sign an agreement under which Douglas will represent the French company in large areas of the world and has an option to build the Caravelle jet airliner under license.

**Miami, Fla, February 12**
A Delta Air Lines Convair 880 lands from San Diego to set a new transcontinental speed record over the route of 3 hours 31 minutes.

**Reims, France, February 15**
Cessna acquires a 49 per cent shareholding in Max Holste's aircraft company; Holste gains the right to build the majority of Cessna models under license.

**Dallas, Tex, February 16**
The Vought F8U-2N Crusader interceptor makes its maiden flight.

**Hamburg, [W] Germany, March 2**
Lufthansa takes delivery of its first Boeing 707.

**Amsterdam, March 16**
KLM opens its first inter-continental jet service, by Douglas DC-8 to New York.

**Tell City, Indiana, March 17**
A Northwest Airlines Lockheed Electra crashes, killing 63; as with the crash on September 29 last year of a Braniff Electra at Buffalo, Texas, structural failure is suspected (→ Mar 20).

**Washington, DC, March 20**
The US Federal Aviation Agency orders Lockheed Electras to fly no faster than 275 knots (315mph) up to 15,000 feet and at slower speeds above that, while the causes of the two recent disasters are investigated (→ Dec 31).

**Montreal, Canada, April 1**
Trans-Canada Air Lines flies its first Douglas DC-8 service, to Vancouver (→ Mar 1, 1963).

**USA, April 19**
The Grumman A-6A Intruder all-weather attack aircraft makes its first flight, in the hands of Robert Smythe.

**England, May 2**
Westland Aircraft takes over the aviation interests of the Fairey company; it took over the helicopter division of Bristol Aircraft on March 23.

**Florida, May 21**
The USAF retires its last B-25 Mitchell bomber, converted for use as a staff transport, from active service, at Eglin Air Force Base.

**London, May 27**
BOAC opens its first service with the Boeing 707, between London and New York.

**Washington, DC, May 31**
At the capital's overcrowded National Airport, Butler Aviation is now handling 120 business aircraft movements a day.

**Australia, June 10**
The Trans-Australia Airlines' Fokker Friendship *Tasman* crashes into the sea with four crew and 25 passengers aboard; it is the airline's first accident in which passengers have died in almost 14 years of operation.

**England, July 1**
New independent carrier British United Airlines begins operations.

**Chicago, July 5**
United Airlines puts the first Boeing 720 medium-range jet-airliner into service, on its route to Los Angeles via Denver (→ Jul 28).

**USA, July 6**
Sikorsky's S-62 amphibious helicopter wins federal approval for operation as a commercial passenger aircraft.

**Washington, DC, July 28**
United Airlines and Capital Airlines announce that they are seeking federal permission for a merger (→ Jun 1, 1961).

**Tokyo, August 12**
Japan Air Lines (JAL) opens its first jet service, by Douglas DC-8 to San Francisco (→ Oct 4, 1962).

**USSR, August 17**
Gary Powers, pilot of the American U-2 reconnaissance airplane shot down on May 1, is sentenced to ten years in a labor camp for espionage (→ Feb 10, 1962).

**USA, August 20**
Pan Am sells its last 14 Boeing Stratocruisers to a scrap-metal merchant for the modest sum of $105,000; most of Pan Am's Stratocruiser fleet became Boeing property in 1958-9 when they were traded in for 707s (→ Apr 25, 1962).

**Kerrville, Texas, October 15**
Mooney Aircraft introduces the first all-metal Mooney, M-20B.

**London, October 16**
A BOAC Comet 4 lands from New York at the end of the type's last scheduled transatlantic service for the airline.

**London, October 20**
BOAC flies its first service to Los Angeles by the polar route.

**Surrey, England, October 21**
Hawker Siddeley's P.1127 experimental vertical/short take-off and landing (V/STOL) aircraft makes its first tethered flight at Dunsfold, piloted by Hawker test pilot Bill Bedford (→ Sep 12, 1961).

**Birmingham, England, October 31**
A Douglas DC-3 flies in from London on the type's last scheduled flight for BEA (→ May 11, 1962).

**Canada, November 16**
The prototype Canadair CL-44D-4 freighter, the first cargo airplane designed with a hinged tail-section to facilitate rear loading, makes its first flight.

**USA, December 5**
Boeing announces that orders for its Boeing Model 727 short-to-medium-range airliner, which is under development, stand at 40 for Eastern Airlines with 20 firm orders plus 20 options for United Airlines.

**Connecticut, December 6**
The Sikorsky S-61L transport helicopter makes its maiden flight, at Stratford.

**Melbourne, December 20**
The first commercial heliport in Australia is opened, on the river Yarra.

**Middle River, Md, December 20**
Martin hands over its last airplane, a P5M-2 Marlin flying boat, to the US Navy; Martin is ending aircraft production – after 51 years and 12,400 airplanes – to concentrate on missiles, electronics and space research.

**Washington, DC, December 31**
The Federal Aviation Agency lifts speed restrictions which it had imposed on the Lockheed Electra, following modifications to the airliner to prevent the structural failure behind both recent tragedies.

**USA, December 31**
This year American Airlines has stolen a march on its competitors by introducing its Semi-Automated Business Research Environment (SABRE) system, which cuts the average time taken to make a reservation from 45 minutes to three seconds.

*A French mountain rescue Alouette III helicopter equipped with a powered winch, homing radio and both skis and wheels.* ▶

# Cherokee signals a success for Piper

*Vero Beach, Florida, January 14*
The first flight of the prototype PA-28 Cherokee today heralds the arrival of another mass-production light airplane from Piper Aircraft. The Cherokee is designed to be the successor to the Tri-Pacer as the company's standard four-seater light airplane. It differs in being of all-metal construction and having a low-mounted wing and a more streamlined appearance.

The engines offered will all be Lycomings, of 150, 160 or 180hp, and everything is being done at the Vero Beach development office to cut costs. For example, the Cherokee has only 1,200 parts, compared with over 1,600 for the Tri-Pacer.

The Cherokee signals the end of the Cub family, whose ancestry goes back to 1931. If it proves as popular, the new low-wing machine can expect a long production run and a profusion of different versions. At the moment customers already have a choice of a wide range of configurations. Cherokees will be available with wheels or floats, or with agricultural spraying equipment (→ Jan 24, 1963).

# Hercules on skis are Antarctic lifeline

*The landing skis of the C-130 are covered in the non-stick material Teflon.*

*Antarctica, January 23*
Life at Byrd Station changed today when the first of seven USAF Lockheed C-130D Hercules transports equipped with ski undercarriages landed with several tons of supplies which would previously have been dropped by parachute.

The C-130Ds can land almost anywhere on the ice, and their huge capacity means drops need be made only every seven months, rather than every two. Research bases will no longer be isolated over the winter, making it easier to entice top scientists who do not want to leave jobs for lengthy periods to work here. Substantial savings on the cost of delivering supplies – $1 million per year on parachutes alone – are expected from ending the old-style air drops, in which instruments and supplies were sometimes damaged or lost.

# BEA starts new jet services with Comet

*London, April 1*
British European Airways (BEA) is making an all-out effort to hold on to its reputation as the preferred airline operating in Europe. BEA's success, built around the turboprop Vickers Viscount, had come under threat from the French Caravelle, forcing the British airline to look for a rival short-haul jet. The answer was the de Havilland Comet 4B. The first Comet was delivered to BEA last November, and today the type entered service. One is flying to Nice, France, two are operating between London and Tel Aviv, and a fourth replaces the Viscount on the Moscow service (→ Oct 16).

# American pilots are told to retire at 60

*Washington, DC, April 22*
The US Court of Appeals today upheld the Federal Aviation Agency's decision to bar pilots over the age of 60 from flying commercial airliners. The US Air Line Pilots Association has expressed its disappointment at the ruling, which stems from medical advice that with advanced age comes physical and psychological deterioration, which could put the flying public at risk. About 40 pilots over 60 now fly for the airlines, and there would have been about 250 in eight years' time.

# First 707s arrive to boost BOAC's fleet

*London, April 29*
A new era in the operation of Britain's national intercontinental airline, BOAC, opened today with the arrival at Heathrow Airport of the first of a fleet of 15 Boeing 707-436 long-haul jets. They were ordered in 1956 soon after the airline had rejected Britain's very similar VC7 design (which was subsequently canceled), stating that it would not need any long-range jets for many years. All 15 707-436s are either finished or nearing completion at Boeing's factory in Seattle. Crew training has been taking place at Tucson, Arizona (→ May 27).

# Swedish plane flies to twice sonic speed

*Linköping, Sweden, January 14*
Sweden's powerful Saab J 35D Draken [Dragon] proved its worth today by reaching twice the speed of sound. Deliveries of the aircraft, with its unique stepped ("double-delta") wing configuration, began late last year, with the first customer for the impressive fighter – it is designed to counter bombers at transonic speeds – being the Swedish air force.

The wing is configured in two parts. The front section is broad and thick, allowing for air intakes, undercarriage, fuel and armaments. The rear part is slender and has an 80-degree sweep. The configuration allows for both very high and very low speeds because the inner wing is offering low drag and enhancing low speed flight. The first prototype Draken flew in October 1955, and achieved Mach 1 in a climb without afterburner.

# Chicago is busiest US airport, says agency

*Snow-clearing equipment keeps flights running at the world's busiest airport.*

*Chicago, March 14*
Within a year of completion of a major expansion program, Chicago's O'Hare International airport has become the busiest terminal in the US, handling 10.2 million passengers in 1959, the Federal Aviation Agency reported today. In the same year it handled 431,600 take-offs and landings.

The Windy City has had an airport ever since 1927, when it was simply known as Chicago airport. It was named Midway in 1942 in recognition of the famous Battle of Midway.

However, this is far too small today and the airport cannot be enlarged as it is surrounded by buildings. Therefore, the giant new airport, named for wartime US ace "Butch" O'Hare, was built far out to the north-west of downtown Chicago.

# Cold War crisis after Soviets down US spyplane

## U-2 is hit by guided missile over Siberia

*Moscow, May 5*

Superpower relations have plummeted to a new low following the downing of a US spyplane over the USSR on May 1. Soviet premier Nikita Khrushchev announced today that a ground-launched guided missile hit a US airplane which was on a mission of "aggressive provocation" over the USSR, and that pilot Francis Gary Powers is being held in custody. The intercepted aircraft was a Lockheed U-2 high-altitude reconnaissance plane – a plane hitherto thought to be invulnerable to anti-aircraft missiles.

The U-2 left Peshawar in northern Pakistan on a route to Bodo, Norway, which would allow it to photograph key strategic airfields and industrial areas in the USSR, including a missile test center. The missile hit the U-2 at 65,000 feet near Sverdlovsk [Yekaterinburg]. Cameras and film have been recovered from the wreckage (→ Aug 17).

*The true purpose of the U-2 – reconnaissance – was a closely-guarded secret.*

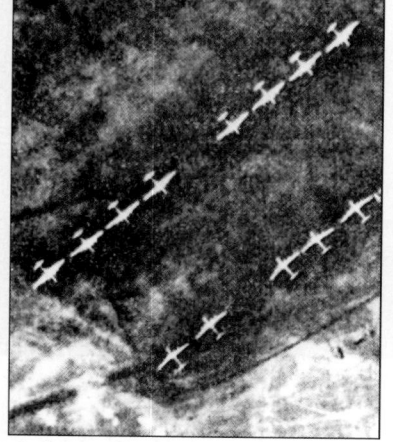

*A photo taken from a U-2 spyplane.*

*Khrushchev is shown the mangled wreckage of the downed U-2.*

## Incident is blow to US airborne espionage

*Washington, DC, May 5*

The U-2 shot down over Sverdlovsk is the most visible example of the multi-million-dollar high-technology espionage war that the US is waging against the USSR. The US has gotten around the difficulty of intelligence-gathering by humans by turning to electronic and photographic surveillance from ships and airplanes, including the U-2.

Conventional aircraft have long plied their trade along the Soviet borders at highly vulnerable low altitudes in order to gather military intelligence. Several of them have disappeared over the Baltic, the Bering Sea and north of Japan. But the U-2, designed to cruise at 70,000 feet, out of reach of intercepting aircraft and known anti-aircraft weaponry, laid bare the USSR to US intelligence for four years with impunity. The real job of the U-2, described to the public as a general-purpose "utility" aircraft, was a closely guarded secret. Now that secret is out, the Americans must find another way to keep an eye on the Soviets.

## Vertol becomes part of Boeing's empire

*Philadelphia, June 13*

The Vertol International Corporation has become part of the Boeing empire and already the main Delaware County plant here is being extended. The new Boeing Center will cover more than two million square feet devoted to the manufacture of helicopters.

The main factory area covers 1.25 million square feet. The plant will include a whirling tower for testing rotor blades and also Boeing Vertol's wind tunnel, one of the biggest in the world. The company's flight test center, 25 miles away at Wilmington Delaware Airport, houses computers and automatic data acquisition equipment to monitor helicopter capacity. The center will also be able to test four helicopters simultaneously.

# British VTOL research aircraft is first to show get up and go

*The five turbojets are opened up.*

*Four engines provide vertical lift ...*

*... the fifth powers forward flight.*

*Bedfordshire, England, April 6*

After almost two years of flight testing in both the vertical take-off and landing (VTOL) mode and the forward flight mode, the Short SC.1 today combined both modes in a full transition. It took off as a conventional airplane down the runway at Bedford, was brought to a halt and hovered in the sky down to a height of 20 feet, before it climbed away and accelerated back into wingborne flight.

The SC.1 is the first aircraft with separate lift and propulsion engines ever to accomplish this transition. Its five engines, four for lift and one for propulsion, are all basically of the same Rolls-Royce RB.108 turbojet type. Each has a thrust of 2,130 pounds and the two pairs of lift jets can swivel fore and aft through 35 degrees to assist braking or acceleration. For control in hovering flight the pilot can control high-pressure air jets at the wing tips and at the nose and tail. To assist the pilot, the SC.1s – two have been built – have automatic control systems (→ May 27, 1961).

# Soviet airliner sets propeller speed record

*The Tu-114 Rossiya, which is soon expected to enter service with Aeroflot.*

*USSR, April 9*
The Soviets are celebrating today after setting a new world speed record for propeller-driven airplanes of 545.07mph. The giant Tupolev Tu-114 Rossiya [Russia] was carrying a 55,116-pound payload at the time and flew around an official 3,107-mile closed circuit.

At the controls was test pilot Ivan M Sukhomlin, who had previously smashed six speed records (with and without payload) in the Tu-114 on March 24, adding another speed record, over a 1,242-mile circuit, at the start of this month. The airliner – which can be viewed as a direct development of the Tu-95 bomber – was designed for long-range domestic flights, but is also clearly suited to non-stop intercontinental services, when its maximum capacity of 220 passengers would be cut to about 120. It should enter Aeroflot service shortly (→ Apr 24, 1961).

# RAF receives its first supersonic fighter

*Norfolk, England, June 29*
RAF Fighter Command, until now equipped entirely with Hawker Hunters and Gloster Javelins, has begun to move into the supersonic era. Today 74 "Tiger" squadron, based at Coltishall, a key station in Britain's air defenses, received the first of a consignment of 12 supersonic English Electric Lightning F.1 all-weather interceptors.

The Lightning is a totally redesigned development of the P.1, which first flew on August 4, 1954. Powered by two Rolls-Royce Avon afterburning turbojets, it is armed with two Firestreak missiles and two 30mm cannon and is capable of exceeding Mach 2, although for the moment it is restricted to Mach 1.9. Only 20 Mk. 1 Lightnings have been built. The next single-seater version is the 1A, with an in-flight refueling probe and other changes. Other types, such as the T.4 two-seater trainer, are in production.

The high-speed interceptor was christened "Lightning" at Farnborough on October 23, 1958, when after a special ceremony test pilot "Bee" Beamont carried out a superb demonstration flight.

*Tests on the Lightning's turbojets; the incandescent jets are supersonic.*

# Pilot lands jetliner after roof is ripped off in a mid-air collision

*With just one engine functioning and several electrical circuits destroyed, the Air Algérie pilot managed to land safely.*

*Paris, May 19*
A tragedy was narrowly avoided today at Orly airport. As the Air Algérie Caravelle F-BONI was on final approach of the airports's west runway, the airliner's captain was ordered to divert to another runway to allow the aircraft taking Soviet leader Nikita Khrushchev back to Moscow to take off. As the Air Algérie airplane was veering right to line up with the south-west runway, it suddenly found itself in the path of the Stampe F-BDEV. The light plane was flying at an altitude of 1,000 feet from Chelles, east of Paris, to Toussus-le-Noble, west of the capital. The two aircraft collided in mid-air, killing the pilot of the Stampe. A gaping hole was torn out of the top of the Caravelle's fuselage and it lost one engine. Despite this, the Air Algérie pilot landed safely, although one passenger was killed. An investigation is under way to determine how the light plane happened to overfly Orly.

# Altitude record for US rocket airplane

*California, August 12*
Dropped from the wing of its B-52 "motherplane", North American's X-15A rocket airplane today climbed from Edwards Air Force Base to an astonishing 136,500 feet and set a new world altitude record. Piloted by Major Robert White, the black aircraft broke the record of 126,200 feet set four years ago by Captain Iven Kincheloe's Bell X-2.

The $150 million X-15 program is a joint NASA, US Navy and USAF effort to study the flight conditions humans are likely to meet beyond the Earth's atmosphere. The project's first powered flight was on on September 17 last year. At altitudes where the air is so thin that aircraft control surfaces are ineffective, the X-15 is controlled by small jets on its nose and tail. To conserve the X-15's fuel, a B-52 bomber is used to carry it up to 40,000 feet (→ Apr 21, 1961).

# Boeing 707s take out 300 at a time in big Congo airlift

*Congo [Zaïre], July 28*
Following the independence of the Belgian Congo on June 30, French and Belgian airlines have been co-operating in evacuating Europeans from this troubled land. The airlift operation began on July 9 and ended today with over 15,000 people having being brought out safely.

Helping Belgian airline Sabena have been French carriers Air France and UAT. Local airlines first took evacuees to Dakar, Fort-Lamy, Abidjan, Douala, Pointe-Noire and Niamey. Five Sabena Boeing 707s then ferried them to Europe. As many as 300 people left on each 707.

Evacuation has not come a moment too soon for Europeans caught up in the bloody birthpangs of the former Belgian colony. Fundamental to the success of the evacuation plan has been a remarkable regional air network, established by Sabena for over 40 years.

# TWA slips from the control of Hughes

*Wilmington, Del, December 30*
A new future for TWA, which has been hit by severe financial troubles, beckoned tonight as all the stock of owner Howard Hughes was transferred to a voting trust dominated by creditors. Ernest R Breech, the retired executive who effectively rebuilt Ford, has been appointed to help reshape the bankrupt airline's top management.

Hughes actually lost control of TWA on December 15, when his stock was confiscated. Breech must now undo the damage Hughes has done. This includes speeding up the re-equipping of TWA with the Convair 880 jets that were impounded from the production line during Hughes' financial maneuvering, and improving its management and operations so capital can be raised at favorable rates. TWA, which under Hughes became derisively referred to as an "unscheduled airline", saw its domestic passenger market share slip to 20 per cent in 1960, a loss of 3 per cent.

# Parachutist jumps from 20 miles up

*Tularosa, N Mex, August 16*
Captain Joe Kittinger took a really big step today – a 102,800-foot one, to be precise. The USAF officer set two records when he stepped out of an open gondola suspended from a balloon: the greatest altitude from which a parachute descent had been made, and the longest delayed parachute jump.

After leaving the gondola, Kittinger, wearing a pressure suit, fell for 4 minutes 38 seconds at a top speed of 614mph, with only an experimental stabilization chute to prevent him from going into a fatal spin. His main parachute opened at 17,500 feet and he then took another 9 minutes 7 seconds to reach the ground.

*Safe on the ground after the jump.*

# Tragedy over New York

*The shattered fuselage of United's DC-8 where it came down in Brooklyn.*

*New York, December 16*
A United Air Lines Douglas DC-8 jet airliner, waiting to land at New York International Airport, and a TWA Lockheed Super Constellation, waiting to land at LaGuardia, collided over the harbor today, killing 127 passengers and crew. The wreckage was scattered over Staten Island and Brooklyn, killing at least five people on the ground.

Only one person on the two airplanes, an 11-year-old boy who was hurled from the tail section of the United jet into a snowbank in Brooklyn, survived. Ten apartment buildings, shops, a funeral home, and an empty church in Brooklyn were destroyed by a fire started by the UAL airplane's wreckage. On Staten Island, 11 miles away, people and buildings were spared as pieces of the TWA Lockheed fell on open areas of Miller Army Air Field or into the water around the island. At the time of the tragedy the two airplanes should have been several miles apart and at different altitudes, but the TWA Super Constellation seems to have wandered off course. The death toll of 132 so far makes this the US's worst commercial air disaster since the Arizona crash of June 30, 1956, when 128 lives were lost in a mid-air collision over Grand Canyon.

# Alouette helicopter sets altitude landing record in the Himalayas

*Boulet, with mechanic Robert Malus, who accompanied him on the flight.*

*India, November 5*
Jean Boulet, who set the record for high-altitude landing in an Alouette III helicopter in June this year when he landed on the top of Mont Blanc, broke that record today when he brought the same aircraft down on the 19,690-foot peak of Deo Tibaa in the Himalayas.

The seven-seater Alouette III, which also carried engineer Robert Malus and some 550 lb of cargo, is generally agreed to be a great improvement on the Alouette II. It is also safer in operation, not least because its pilots can rely on the powerful 870-hp Turbomeca Artouste III turbine. The Alouette III first flew in February last year.

*The Cessna Model 185 Skywagon was a structurally strengthened 180.*

*AESL of New Zealand improved the Airtourer.*

*The Enstrom Model F-28 three-seat light piston-engined helicopter.*

*Dassault's M.D.410 Spirale multi-role turboprop military aircraft.*

*Hawker Siddeley launched the 748 inherited from Avro without orders, but Skyways soon ordered three for the Lympne-Beauvais shuttle.*

*Partenavia's P.59 Jolly two-seater was built only in prototype form.*

*The single-seat Bowers Fly Baby 1-A, designed for amateurs to make.*

*The DINFIA IA 45B Querandi Lycoming-engined light transport.*

*The Fauvel AV.45 single-seat tailless motor glider, with 40-hp engine.*

*Originally with conventional side-loading doors, the D4 version of the Canadair CL-44 introduced a hinged tail to facilitate straight-in loading.*

*Sud-Aviation built Yves Gardan's GY 80 Horizon metal four-seater.*

*A Turbomeca Marboré II powered the Procaer Cobra 400 two-seater.*

*Los Angeles Airways, the first customer for Sikorsky's enlarged (up to 28 passengers) S-61L non-amphibious development of the S-61A, ordered four.*

*The prototype Tupolev Tu-124 was configured for 44 passengers, but production aircraft seated up to 56. It replaced Ilyushin Il-14s with Aeroflot.*

*Australia's 250-hp agricultural airplane, Yeoman's YA-1 Cropmaster.*

*The Canadair CL-66/540 featured Napier Eland turboprops.*

A 24-ft-diameter radome is a feature of the Grumman E-2 Hawkeye carrier-based early-warning airplane, originally flown with the designation W2F-1.

Side-by-side seating was provided in the Grumman A-6 Intruder for optimum use of the Digital Integrated Attack Navigation Equipment (DIANE).

Canadair CL-41 Tutors flew with the Canadian Armed Forces Snowbirds aerobatic team - the CAF designation was CT-114. Engine was a GE J85.

Flight Refuelling developed the Meteor V.16 pilotless target drone.

Beriev's Be-12 amphibian, with nose radome and MAD stinger, was designed to replace the earlier Be-6 patrol flying boat. Engines are 4,190-ehp AI-20s.

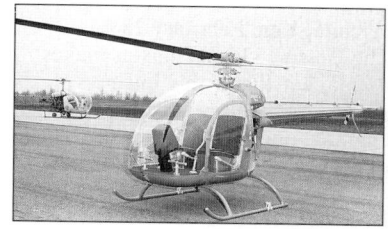

A single prototype of the Italian Agusta A 104 Helicar was built.

The first post-war jet aircraft of entirely Japanese design was the Fuji T1F1, and 20 of this tandem two-seat basic trainer were built for the JASDF.

The MiG Ye-152A experimental jet-fighter was larger than the MiG-21.

Hawker's P.1127 prototypes pioneered the vectored thrust concept.

The OKL TS-11 Iskra [Spark] two-seat tandem jet trainer was produced for the Polish air force as a replacement for the piston-engined TS-8 Bies.

Boeing Vertol's Model 107 became the US Army's/Marines' H-46.

Fiat evolved the G.91T two-seat trainer development of the G.91R.

# 1961

 4,093mph
USA
Robert White
North American X-15
Nov 9, 1961

 24,325 miles
USA
Archie Old Jr
Boeing B-52B
Jan 18, 1957

 217,000ft
USA
Robert White
North American X-15
Oct 11, 1961

 488,000lb
USA
Boeing
B-52G Stratofortress

 27,008lb thrust
USSR
Lyulka
AL-21F

**Toulouse, France, January 23**
The double-deck Breguet Universel [Universal], equipped to carry vehicles, freight or passengers, begins flight tests.

**Olathe, Kansas, February 5**
King Radio's NAV/COMM radios are installed in almost every type of US-built light aircraft.

**Brussels, February 15**
Members of a US skating team are among 73 killed when a Sabena Boeing 707 crashes during its landing approach.→

**Wichita, Kan, February 28**
The Cessna 336 Skymaster makes its maiden flight; this business airplane is equipped with two engines, one in the nose, the other behind the cabin.

**Bedfordshire, England, March 13**
The Hawker Siddeley P.1127 experimental vertical/short take-off and landing fighter makes its first conventional flight. The government allows the project to go ahead on the understanding that it will not be a combat aircraft.

**Texas, March 17**
The first Northrop T-38 Talon jet trainer to enter service with USAF Air Training Command is delivered to Randolph Air Force Base.

**Cartierville, Canada, March 18**
The first production Lockheed CF-104 Starfighter, built under license by Canadair, is rolled out.

**Laos, March 23**
A USAF EC-47 is shot down over the Plain of Jars in northern Laos; it was checking radio frequencies used by Soviet aircraft delivering arms to Communist rebels.

**Caracas, April 1**
Venezuela's new national airline, Viasa, starts scheduled services with the flight of a Douglas DC-8, leased from Dutch airline KLM.

**New Mexico, April 7**
A B-52 bomber is downed by a Sidewinder missile fired automatically from an F-100 Super Sabre when the fighter's security system short-circuits; three of the B-52's crew die (→ Jan 11, 1962).

**California, April 21**
USAF Major Robert White pilots the X-15A research airplane from Edwards Air Force Base on its first flight at full throttle, reaching a speed of 3,074mph at an altitude of 79,000 feet, before climbing to 105,100 feet (→ Jun 27, 1962).

**USSR, April 24**
The Tupolev Tu-114 turboprop airliner enters Aeroflot service between Moscow and Khabarovsk.

**New Zealand, April 27**
Australia's 50 per cent holding in Tasman Empire Airways is purchased by the New Zealand government.

**USA, May 10**
A Convair B-58A cruises at a speed of 1,302mph [2,095kph] and wins the Blériot trophy, created 30 years ago for the first airplane to maintain a speed of more than 2,000kph for more than 30 minutes in a closed circuit (→ May 26).

**Algeria, May 10**
An Air France Lockheed L-1649 crashes in the Sahara desert; all 79 people on board are killed.

**Paris, May 26**
A Convair B-58A Hustler delta-winged supersonic bomber lands at Le Bourget for the 24th air show after flying from New York in 3 hours 19 minutes 41 seconds at an average speed of 1,103mph (→ Jun 3).

**Paris, May 27**
The Short SC.1 experimental vertical take-off and landing (VTOL) aircraft, piloted by Alex Roberts, arrives at Le Bourget airport after the first flight across the English Channel by a VTOL airplane.

**Paris, June 3**
The Convair B-58A bomber which flew here last week crashes after taking off from Le Bourget during the air show; its three crew members are killed.

**Paris, June 15**
An Air France air hostess who was sacked because she married loses a court appeal against her dismissal; the judge rules that a hostess who weds has broken her contract of with the airline (→ Jul 5, 1963).

**India, June 17**
The HF-24 Marut supersonic fighter makes its maiden flight; it was designed by German engineer Kurt Tank, the creator of the Second World War Focke-Wulf Fw 190, who has been hired by Hindustan Aircraft.

**London, June 21**
The Air Transport Licensing Board withdraws BOAC's monopoly on its North Atlantic route, granting British independent airline Cunard Eagle the right to operate a scheduled daily service to New York (→ Nov 29).

**Washington, DC, June 28**
The Secretary of the Navy gives the go-ahead to plans to end the service's lighter-than-air operations, which began in 1915 (→ Dec 31, 1962).

**Kuwait, July 1**
The RAF deploys Hawker Hunters as part of a British defense force in the newly independent emirate, which has been threatened by neighboring Iraq.

**Cornwall, England, July 4**
The first Westland Wessex anti-submarine helicopters enter RAF service with 815 Squadron at Culdrose.

**USA, July 10**
In a test of radar and instruments, a Tactical Air Command pilot flies a Republic F-105D Thunderchief for more than 1,500 miles with no external vision.

**Fort Bragg, NC, August 8**
Some 7,500 paratroopers are dropped nearby during joint USAF and US Army exercise Operation Swift Strike (→ Jan 22, 1962).

**USA, August 16**
The Bell Model 205 UH-1D troop transport helicopter, built for the US Army, makes its first flight.

**Dallas, Texas, August 16**
Ling-Temco Electronics merges with the Chance Vought Corporation to form the Ling-Temco-Vought Corporation.

**Chamonix, France, August 30**
A Mirage III jet slices through the supporting wire of a cable car carrying tourists 12,600 feet above Blanche valley; six die.

**N Rhodesia [Zambia], Sept 18**
UN Secretary-General Dag Hammarskjöld dies when his Douglas DC-6B crashes near Ndola; there is only one survivor among the 14 passengers.

**USA, October 14**
All commercial flights are grounded for 12 hours as thousands of USAF aircraft take part in the air defense exercise Operation Sky Shield II.

**Wichita, Kansas, October 23**
The Beech Model 23 Musketeer low-cost light airplane makes its maiden flight.

**California, November 22**
Lieutenant-Colonel R B Robinson flies a McDonnell F4H-1F Phantom II to a new world speed record of 1,605.51mph at Edwards Air Force Base.

**Washington, DC, December 4**
The National Air and Space Museum receives the Douglas C-54 transport *Sacred Cow* used by Presidents Roosevelt and Truman.

*An advertisement issued in 1961 to commemorate 50 years of US Navy aviation since the first Navy pilots were trained by G Curtiss in 1911.* ▶

### Electronics for the Fleet's Fastest

Collins has served Naval Aviation for more than twenty years. Typical of this service are the Collins communication-navigation-identification (CNI) systems aboard all the Fleet's newest jet aircraft, including these illustrated.

*From left: Grumman A2F, North American A3J, McDonnell F4H.*

# COLLINS RADIO COMPANY

# Wraps are taken off new airborne missile

*Wichita, Kan, January 5*
Boeing today showed how the GAM-87A Skybolt air-launched, intermediate-range ballistic missile will be carried by a B-52. It rolled out a Stratofortress which had four mock-ups of the missile suspended from wing pylons between the fuselage and the inboard engines.

The two-stage, solid-propellant-powered Skybolt is being developed by Douglas. The British government has also decided to use it, so Douglas, in addition to working closely with Boeing to ensure B-52 compatibility, is collaborating with Avro, which manufactures Vulcan bombers for RAF Bomber Command, to make the 38-foot-long, 11,000-pound missile equally compatible for operational use with British aircraft (→Oct 28, 1962).

*Night display: a B-52 bomber, now designated to carry the Skybolt missile.*

# Sabena Boeing 707 crashes near Brussels

*Berg, Belgium, February 15*
A Boeing 707 of Belgian airline Sabena crashed just before landing today at Brussel's Zaventem airport on its return from New York. In all 73 people died, including 11 crew members and a farmer working in his field. The OO-SJB had made several circuits above the airport's runway beacon: poor visibility required all incoming aircraft to wait.

At exactly 10.05am the pilot began his approach and, at about 350 feet, opened the throttle and raised the undercarriage. It was then that the plane pulled up too sharply and went into a stall that ended in disaster. All Sabena's Boeing 707s have been accident-free since coming into service with the company in January 1960. Today's accident is being put down to pilot error.

*Sabena's 707 fleet had given a year's accident-free service before this crash.*

# Eastern launches no-frills shuttle flights

*Eastern has chosen the 95-seater "Super Connie" for its trial shuttle service.*

*New York, April 30*
Eastern Air Lines today launched a new venture into cheap mass air travel with its no-frills, first-come-first-served shuttle services between New York and Boston and New York and Washington, DC. The two services will initially run for a six-month trial period.

Eastern plans to operate eight flights daily (fewer at weekends) out of New York's LaGuardia airport to both cities, using densely packed 95-seat Super Constellations. Flights should last an hour to an hour and a half. Rather than handing over baggage at a ticket counter in the terminal, passengers must carry it to the boarding gate, where boarding passes will be issued 45 minutes before the aircraft leaves. The passes, which are also seat reservations, can be bought by latecomers from stewardesses on the airplane. There will be no food or drink served on the flights.

The shuttle fares ($12 one-way to Boston, $14 one-way to Washington) are between $1 and $5 lower than current air fares. They are only a little more expensive than the cheapest rail fares ($11.58 to Boston, $10.65 to Washington), which the airline hopes will prove attractive to those who normally travel overland. Whether expenses-paid business travelers will prefer less comfort in a crammed, slow airliner to a first-class seat in a jet remains to be seen (→Apr 1, 1963).

**A Viking airliner perched atop a home in Gloucester, England, after a forced landing. Both the pilot and co-pilot were killed.**

# Gagarin first in space

*Baikonur, Kazakhstan, April 12*
At 9.07am today, Moscow time, the Soviet rocket Vostok 1 took off from Tyuratam in central Asia, launching Flight-Major Yuri Alexeyevich Gagarin into space and the history books. After a single orbit, the first human in space landed safely back at the space center here in eastern Kazakhstan to a hero's welcome. NASA chief James Webb called the 108-minute flight "a fantastic achievement". Gagarin, a 27-year-old military reserve pilot, had orbited at over 17,000-mph, 174 miles up. He observed the Earth through the four-and-a-half-ton spacecraft's portholes, transmitting the first words from space by radio.

Among his comments later was: "Visibility is good, one can see everything. Some areas are covered with patches of cloud." Vostok 1 was guided by automatic ground control, with emergency manual control if needed. A parachute on the re-entry vehicle was used to bring Gagarin safely back.

*Soviet air force pilot Yuri Gagarin, the first person in space, is acclaimed.*

## Second man in space is US Navy pilot

*Cape Canaveral, Fla, May 5*
Commander Alan B Shepard, Jr, US Navy, 37, today became the second man to explore space when he rode his Mercury Freedom 7 capsule, blasted aloft by a Redstone missile, to 115 miles above the Earth. It is three weeks since Yuri Gagarin's historic first manned space flight [*see story above*].

Commander Shepard's flight did not circle the Earth as Gagarin's did, but it did show that the US can also put a man into space. Unlike Gagarin, Shepard, a trained test pilot, was able to maneuver his spacecraft. After the capsule parachuted to the ocean's surface 302 miles from here, it and Shepard were picked up and flown by helicopter to the aircraft carrier USS *Lake Champlain*. Aboard the carrier, Shepard was toasted with champagne, but had to forego the bubbly himself because doctors did not want it to upset the results of

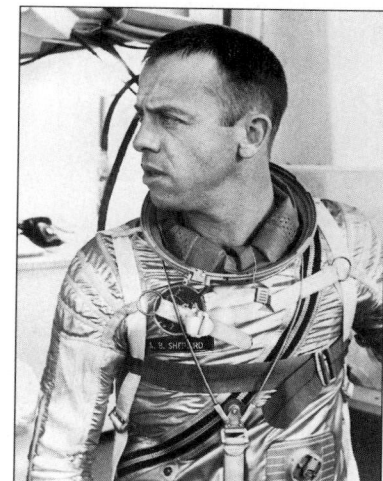

*Shepard: also a trained test pilot.*

his extensive post-flight medical tests. President Kennedy called the carrier to congratulate the "astronaut", who had trained for two years for today's flight of 15 minutes 22 seconds.

## New flight rules set to increase safety

*Paris, April 1*
The International Air Transport Association (IATA) has made new rules for air traffic over Europe and the Mediterranean. All planes of member airlines will have to fly under Instrument Flight Rules (IFR), whatever the weather conditions, under constant supervision by air-traffic control.

Their altitude, or flight level, is fixed according to their heading. On a north/south heading they will fly at odd-numbered flight levels – for example, 19,000 feet will be flight level 190. On a south/north heading they will fly on even flight levels, thus ensuring at least 1,000 feet of separation. IATA is also requesting business and military airplanes to follow these rules in all air space under air-traffic supervision. Visual Flight Rules (VFR) will apply to light aircraft.

## General LeMay to head US Air Force

*Washington, DC, May 22*
Gruff, no-nonsense General Curtis E LeMay, who made the Strategic Air Command (SAC) into the deterrent nuclear shield of the USA and its allies, has been nominated by President Kennedy to succeed General Thomas D White as the USAF's next chief of staff.

General LeMay has been deputy chief of staff since 1957. His service dates back to the prewar US Army Air Corps, and he was a pioneer of strategic bombing. During the Second World War he was most noted for organizing low-level B-29 incendiary raids on Japanese cities. After the war he built up the SAC with propeller-driven B-29s, B-50s and B-36s and then with the current jet KC-135s, B-47s, B-52s and B-58s. He encouraged the development of intercontinental ballistic missiles.

## Antiquated looks no bar to Swiss success

*Despite old-fashioned looks, Pilatus airplanes are attracting wide interest.*

*Stans, Switzerland, May 2*
The small factory of Pilatus Flugzeugwerke, nestling here in the Swiss Alps, is likely to have plenty of work in the foreseeable future. This is because of the success of the PC-6/A Turbo-Porter, which flew for the first time today.

When the original PC-6 Porter prototype flew just two years ago many observers thought it looked like something from the 1920s. The squared-off wings and tail, clumsy fixed landing gear and strange, rounded cabin windows contrasted with most of today's airplanes. But there is no doubt that the Swiss firm has come up with a smash hit.

Even the piston-engined version has sold quite well, but the transformation brought about in the Turbo-Porter is generating interest with military and civilian customers all over the world. Many versions are available. Most can carry ten passengers and pilot, or a 1.5 tons of cargo. Other options include versions of the PC-6/A equipped for agricultural spraying or for water-bombing forest fires. The standard engine is likely to be the Pratt & Whitney Canada PT6A.

## Skyknight offers comfort to executives

*Wichita, Kansas, May 9*
The Cessna Company has had to modify its manufacturing installations. On one hand, its Military Aircraft Division has received fewer orders ever since the Pentagon decided to spend more on missiles than on airplanes. Also, the Light Aircraft Division is running out of space. Therefore, the production facilities for the Model 310 twin were transferred last year to the Military Aircraft Division. That is where the Model 310F Skyknight executive airplane is being built. Like the Cessna's 172, 175 and 182 models, the Skyknight has a new vertical stabilizer. The USAF has ordered 35 Skyknights for delivery this year. The Skyknight is a Model 310 powered by turbosupercharged engines, and with a higher and longer cabin. It can fly at 27,200 feet and cruise at up to 245mph and has a well-appointed interior for between four and six people.

*The Cessna Skyknight business twin offers a top cruising speed of 245mph.*

# United is biggest airline

*United is introducing 20 Caravelle VIR short-haul jets from July 14.*

*USA, June 1*
In the largest merger of air operators in aviation history, United Air Lines today formally took over Capital Airlines. The deal has been on the cards since July last year, when United publicly expressed interest in such a merger.

Capital had been suffering severe financial problems for some time, culminating in a bid by major shareholders to sack the board of directors in May last year, following a first-quarter loss of $5 million. The merger has made United the biggest airline outside the Communist bloc, exceeded in size only by Soviet giant Aeroflot. It serves 116 cities, including 17 of the 20 most important in the US. Its huge fleet of 267 airplanes cover 18,000 miles of routes, and it now carries the largest number of passengers of any western airline.

## Ex-RAF mechanic Laker unveils Carvair, for passengers and cars

*Essex, England, June 21*
Air entrepreneur Freddie Laker today unveiled his latest venture, the Aviation Traders ATL.98 Carvair, which made its first flight at Southend. Designed to a 1959 specification from another Laker company, Channel Air Bridge, it has been developed to replace the Bristol Freighter on mainly cross-Channel flights.

The development of the Carvair has been assisted by technical help from Douglas Aircraft in the USA. To reduce the cost of development and production, the Carvair is based on surplus Douglas DC-4s. The main design change is the entirely new bulbous forward fuselage, incorporating an elevated flight deck and a nose-loading door. Except for the vertical tail, the rest of the DC-4 airframe is unchanged. The aircraft can carry up to 5 vehicles, plus 22 passengers in the rear cabin, or 19,335 pounds of freight and 65 to 85 passengers. The first Carvairs will join British United Air Ferries early next year. Freddie Laker's company Aviation Traders was formed in 1949 as an airplane overhaul and maintenance center, particularly important to associated airplane operator Air Charter. This was also founded by Laker, a one-time RAF mechanic who saw the opportunities offered in buying surplus transport airplanes after the war. The Berlin Airlift in 1949 was a chance to maximize their use. In 1949 Airwork acquired Air Charter (later Channel Air Bridge), and Laker became a director. Last year Airwork and Hunting-Clan united to form British United Airways (→ Feb 8, 1966).

*Carvair: vehicles or freight are loaded at the front through the hinged nose.*

## US airliner hijacked on flight to Dallas

*Miami, Fla, July 24*
An unidentified man armed with a pistol today hijacked an Eastern Air Lines flight which left here at 10.05am bound for Dallas. He forced the pilot to fly to Cuba, and the turboprop Lockheed Electra, with 33 passengers and five crew, landed in Havana at 12.25pm.

Air-traffic controlers knew something was up when radar showed the airplane flying off course, toward Cuba. North American Air Defense Command in Colorado Springs sent an F-102 fighter from Tampa to investigate. The F-102 pilot intercepted the Electra but his signals to turn back were ignored. Its only transmission was one radio message saying "proceeding to Havana at pistol point".

This is the second US airliner hijacked to Cuba since the failed Bay of Pigs invasion in April. The first, a National Airlines Convair, was seized on May 1.

# New Boeing transport is version of tanker

*Seattle, June 9*

The USA's Military Air Transport Service (MATS) entered the jet age today when it took delivery of the first of 30 Boeing C-135A Stratolifter transports. MATS will use the new aircraft for cargo and troop transport missions.

Although based on the design of the proven KC-135 tanker, the C-135A is a very different aircraft. The absence, beneath the tail, of the in-flight refueling boom and the housing for the boom's operator is immediately noticed. Inside the C-135A, there is more sound-proofing than in the tankers, better lighting and two air conditioning units to make it more comfortable for the upward of 126 troops or, on medical evacuation flights, the 44 stretcher and 54 sitting patients it can carry. For cargo handling the C-135A has a metal floor, with a special transfer plate to allow maneuvering of pallets.

Boeing C-135A Stratolifter: the USA's first jet-powered military transport.

# British plane unveiled to test delta wing for supersonic airliner

*Bedfordshire, England, August 17*

Handley Page test pilot Jack Henderson landed at Bedford today full of enthusiasm after taking the H.P.115 aloft on its 31-minute first flight. The flight's success suggests that Britain is along the right lines in advocating a slender delta-wing configuration for the proposed supersonic transport (SST).

A delta wing has an extremely low aspect ratio, being very long from front to rear in relation to its short wingspan. A crucial feature of such a wing is that it generates a strong vortex along the leading edge. This rolls back across the upper surfaces at high angles of attack, greatly increasing lift. No such wing has ever been flown before, and the H.P.115 has been especially built by Handley Page to test the concept. It has a wing with the amazing leading-edge sweep angle of 74.7 degrees. The wing is 40 feet long at its root but only 20 feet wide, and its aspect ratio is 1.0. A special feature is that the leading

The HP.115 flies side by side with a Gloster Gladiator fighter of the 1930s.

edges are made of plywood so that they can quickly be changed on the ground for components of different shape. The H.P.115 is not intended for high speeds, although it does have a turbojet, a Bristol Siddeley Viper of 1,900 pounds thrust. Bristol Aircraft is rebuilding the Fairey F.D.2 record-breaker to test the delta wing at high speeds. When finished the former F.D.2 will be called the BAC.221. Together with the H.P.115 it should make the proposed SST wing a known quantity.

# Belgians aid birth of Congolese airline

*Congo [Zaïre], June 28*

Today, Africa's newest airline was born in this former Belgian colony. The Belgian airline Sabena holds 30 per cent of the new carrier, Air Congo, with the new republic holding 65 per cent. Sabena will also help Air Congo set up its routes and operations.

Just under a year ago Belgians working and living in the former Belgian Congo were fleeing for their lives from a bloody revolution. The tens of thousands who escaped were assisted by a domestic airline network in the former African colony which had been painstakingly established over four decades and proved vital to the success of their rapid evacuation.

Sabena's network of routes created in the Congo in the 1920s has left a sound legacy for Air Congo, including airdromes and other facilities. Major routes include the one which links Boma with Leopoldville, the Congolese capital, and Elisabethville, some 1,420 miles long and bringing together the nation's biggest cities (→Oct 16).

(→Oct 16)

# Passengers reach for the sky as the airline fares fall

*International, June*

As civil air transport enters its fifth decade two clear trends are emerging: a steady reduction in the price of airline tickets, and a steady increase in the number of people buying them. The total number of individual air journeys exceeded 100 million for the first time last year.

Before the war, only the very rich or those traveling at company or government expense could afford to travel by air. Then in 1948 came the first coach-class fares, followed in 1952 by tourist-class and in 1958 by economy. Each time the fares went down the number of people flying went up, and today only about a third of passengers fly first class.

Yet more innovative schemes to attract passengers are being introduced. On November 1 this year BEA will put on a night service between London and Glasgow using 130-seater Vanguards. The price will be £3 3/-, or 2.2d [1p] per mile, the cheapest rate anywhere in the world. As the major airlines buy the new big jets, so a great many propeller-driven airplanes are available for shorter routes. Rather than being scrapped, they have been used to provide new, cheap services such as Eastern's "Shuttle" which began on April 30. Passengers who want to travel between New York, Washington DC, Newark and Boston turn up at the airport without reservations and buy tickets on the spot. If the aircraft is full another follows. Allegheny Airlines pioneered the no-booking system in 1960 with offers of a 36 per cent discount.

Looking ahead, a new area of growth may be the "package holiday", where people buy a ticket and hotel well in advance, which means the operator is certain of a full load and can offer low fares. If this catches on, air travel will truly have become a mass, rather than an exclusive, means of travel (→May 5, 1962).

(→May 5, 1962)

# Cochran, at 55, is still a record-breaker

*Age is not slowing Jackie Cochran.*

*California, August 24*
Veteran US aviator Jacqueline Cochran, now 55, today shattered the women's speed record for a 15-km [9-mile] straight course by 127.3mph. She flew a Northrop T-38 Talon jet trainer at an average speed of 842.6mph (Mach 1.3) from Edwards Air Force Base.

Cochran, one of the US's most famous flyers, holds more speed records than any other pilot in the world. In addition to today's record, she holds the propeller-driven aircraft speed record over 15km for both men and women, the women's jet aircraft speed records over 100km and 500km, and the women's propeller-driven aircraft speed records over 3km, 100km, 500km and 1,000km (→ Jun 22, 1962).

# Traffic helicopter makes wrongful arrest

*Washington, DC, October 20*
Today a single incident simultaneously revealed the possibilities and the limitations of helicopter surveillance. For a month Washington police have been using a local radio station's helicopter to gain an overview of traffic conditions to broadcast to drivers. This morning an armed man held up an Arlington bank and made off in a car with $12,730. A car fitting the given description was seen from the helicopter, and the driver was promptly arrested. Unfortunately, it became clear that although it might have looked like the right car, it was certainly not the right man.

*Keeping watch, the traffic surveillance Bell 47J used by Washington police.*

# African states create international airline

*Paris, October 16*
Independent Africa took a bold new step into the international airline business today with the first scheduled service, between Paris and Douala, of a new airline, Air Afrique. The weekly service, with Lockheed Super Constellations, is also the first regular air connection between the two cities. Air Afrique, based at Abidjan, Ivory Coast, was founded on March 28 at Yaoundé, Cameroon, by 12 francophone states independent since last year: Cameroon, Central African Republic, Chad, Congo-Brazzaville [Congo], Dahomey [Benin], Gabon, Ivory Coast, Mauritania, Niger, Senegal, Togo and Upper Volta [Burkina Faso].

# 'Jump-jet' is a reality

*The P.1127 makes a vertical take-off before moving into forward flight.*

*Surrey, England, September 12*
At Dunsfold today test pilots Bill Bedford and Hugh Merewether made the first complete transition from vertical to horizontal flight in the British experimental Hawker Siddeley P.1127. It is the only vertical take-off and landing (VTOL) airplane so far to achieve both high-speed flight and the ability to hover, all with a single engine.

The originator of the idea was retired French aircraft designer Michel Wibault. In 1956 he suggested building for NATO a small tactical attack fighter powered by a 7,000-hp Bristol Orion turboshaft engine geared to four centrifugal compressors. These compressors would have outlets which could rotate so as to blow the jets of air from the compressors either downwards, to generate lift, or to the rear, to generate thrust. The four scrolls would have to rotate in unison.

Bristol Aero-Engines saw that it would be much simpler to use one large fan, and examined the possibility of an Orion driving two stages from an Olympus low-pressure compressor. This study, the BE.48, was followed by a neater engine with Olympus LP and Orpheus HP (high-pressure) compressors. This, the BE.53, gave way to the Pegasus, with four nozzles (two cold, from the fan, and two hot, from the jet).

It is the Pegasus which powers the P.1127. The engine's thrust is just enough, at 11,000 pounds, for the lightweight P.1127. The Pegasus will need to be upgraded to about double its current thrust for any future VTOL combat airplane, which could carry a wide range of weapons (→ Feb 11, 1963).

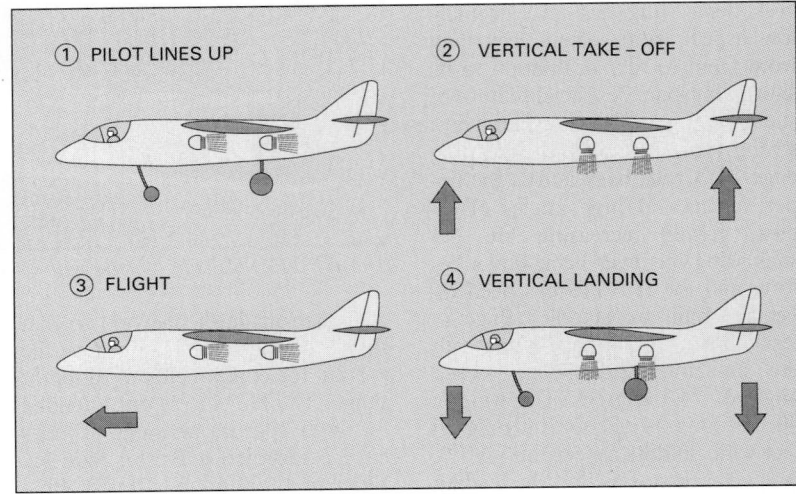

① PILOT LINES UP
② VERTICAL TAKE-OFF
③ FLIGHT
④ VERTICAL LANDING

# JFK's 707 can't land at most US airports

*Washington, DC, September 1*
From this month President John F Kennedy will use a seven-year-old military version of the Douglas DC-6 airliner, the C-118, as the official presidential aircraft for short flights within the US. The piston-engined, propeller-driven airplane was chosen from those already in the USAF's Special Air Missions unit, because the larger, jet-powered Boeing VC-137s, the military version of the Boeing 707

airliner, cannot yet operate from most of the country's airports.

The C-118 has been modified with communications equipment to allow it to operate as a "flying White House" and its interior has been refurbished to accommodate the president and his staff. Kennedy, however, prefers the Boeing VC-137s and is expected to use them for overseas trips and for flights within the US to airfields which can handle them.

*President Kennedy's VC-137s are too big for most airports in the country.*

# US airliner crashes in Ireland – 86 killed

*Shannon, Ireland, September 10*
A DC-6 operated by US carrier President Airlines plunged into the Shannon estuary moments after take-off here last night. The six crew and all of the 77 passengers were killed. The airliner, which had stopped to refuel en route from Germany to the US, took off from Shannon airport at 3.53am. The

roar as it climbed from the runway was followed by an awful silence when its engines cut, and then a thud as it smashed into the water. Rescue workers hurrying to the scene found that only the plane's tail was visible, sticking out of the estuary. One dazed woman survivor was picked up, but she died later in hospital.

# US deploys first helicopters in Vietnam

*Saigon, December 11*
American involvement in a southeast Asian guerilla war deepened today when 32 Piasecki H-21 helicopters and 400 men of the US Army's 57th and Eighth Transportation Companies arrived here by ship. They will provide airlift capability for South Vietnamese troops battling Communist Vietcong insur-

gents. President Kennedy decided to send them after US Army General Maxwell Taylor reported that poor roads and an inability to move forces rapidly were hindering efforts to stop the rebels. The president approved sending the helicopters, as well as military advisors and support from the US Army, US Navy and USAF (→ Feb 4, 1962).

# Breguet Atlantic sea patrol aircraft flies

*Toulouse, France, October 21*
With its lengthy coastline and commitment to European defense, it was inevitable that France should develop its own long-range maritime reconnaissance aircraft. It flew for the first time today, in the form of the Breguet 1150 Atlantic, a twin-engined maritime patrol aircraft, with a range of 5,590 miles and facilities for both a crew of 12 and a relief crew. Although a more sophisticated version is planned, 40 Atlantics have been ordered by the French navy, with further orders coming from the navies of West Germany, the Netherlands and Italy (→ Dec 10, 1965).

# Smaller British airlines get bite of cherry

*London, November 29*
This has been a momentous day for the small British airlines trying to expand their very limited share of scheduled services. Britain's Air Transport Licensing Board, which first met in June, has awarded British United Airways (BUA) and Cunard Eagle Airways the opportunity to fly scheduled services in Europe over some routes monopolized up until now by British European Airways (BEA).

In submitting their cases, BUA and Cunard were careful not to overlap each other's interests. Fol-

lowing the June meeting, the board had awarded Cunard the chance to compete with BOAC to launch scheduled Atlantic flights – but on a one service a day basis. Despite the breaking of BOAC's and BEA's complete stranglehold, both BUA and Cunard view the awards as not being nearly sufficient.

The move flies in the face of opposition from the two big national carriers. In one counter-measure, on November 1 BEA began new 63-shilling [£3.15] night flights from London to Edinburgh, Glasgow and Belfast.

# Air travel increase grows more slowly

*Chicago, December 29*
Worldwide commercial air traffic has reached a new peak this year despite a slackening in the rate of growth, the International Civil Aviation Organization revealed today. International and domestic scheduled airlines carried 112 million passengers and flew 72 billion passenger miles, the UN agency reported. The figures suggested a 6 per cent growth over 1960 figures, the smallest increase in 15 years.

Meanwhile the International Air Transport Association reported that growth was picking up on the American internal network and the North Atlantic routes.

*Three BEA Vanguards at Heathrow – now the airline is losing its monopoly.*

The Beagle A.109 Airedale continued the long-running Auster series.

Morane-Saulnier's MS.885 Super Rallye had a 145-hp Continental.

The first prototype of the Potez 840 feeder-liner was powered by four 530-shp Turbomeca Astazou turboprops: only six series aircraft were built.

Sud-Aviation's Caravelle VIR was similar to the VIN but featured a modified windscreen and more powerful 12,600-lb st Rolls-Royce Avon 532R turbojets.

The Fiat 7002 featured a low-noise cold-jet blade-tip propulsion system.

Contra-rotating rotors were fitted to the Gyrodyne Model 2 helicopter.

Cessna's 337 "push-pull" twin: no asymmetric power problems.

Aermacchi built the Lockheed AL.60 under license at Varese.

A 562-hp Turbomeca Astazou drove the Pilatus PC-6/A Turbo-Porter.

The Beech 23 Musketeer, designed as a low-cost four-seat light aircraft.

The Kamov Ka-22 Vintokryl was a large compound helicopter.

Mil's Mi-8 prototype combined the rotors and transmission of the Mi-4 with a new fuselage. Powered by a single engine, it later had two Isotov turboshafts.

The Ryan Flex-Wing tested the Rogallo sail-like flexible delta wing.

The original customer for the Vanguard, BEA, changed the livery.

Aviation Traders took a standard Douglas DC-4 airframe and added a new cockpit section with a nose-loading door to produce the Carvair vehicle ferry.

Bell used a longer fuselage, increased rotor diameter and fuel capacity and an uprated Lycoming T53-L-11 engine in the Model 205 UH-1D Iroquois.

Breguet developed the 1150 Atlantic to meet a Nato requirement for a long-range maritime patrol aircraft to replace the Lockheed Neptune.

The Breguet 941 STOL transport featured trailing-edge slotted flaps.

The Lockheed C-130E was an extended-range version of the C-130B.

The Gyrodyne DSN-3 (QH-50C) pilotless anti-submarine drone.

Yakovlev's Yak-28 was a supersonic replacement for the Ilyushin Il-28.

Neiva built 80 U-42 Regente utility aircraft for the Brazilian air force.

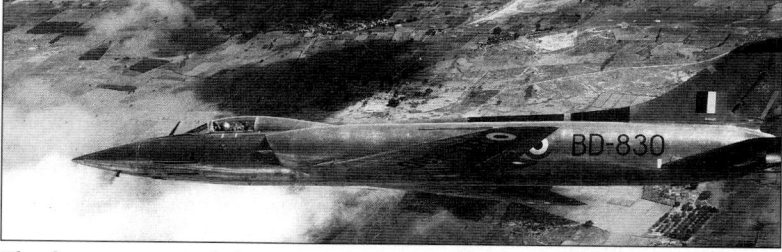

The first supersonic fighter aircraft designed by an Asian manufacturer, the HAL HF-24 Marut was used by the Indian Air Force for ground attack.

The Avro VZ-9V Avrocar VTOL research aircraft: a "flying saucer".

Mitsubishi was prime contractor for the license-built Lockheed F-104J.

Dassault's Mirage IIIE long-range fighter/bomber (a Cyrano II radar).

Yugoslav Soko's G2-A Galeb [Seagull]: armed two-seat jet-trainer.

The Bell HUL-1M was powered by an Allison T-63 turboshaft engine.

Armstrong Whitworth designed the A.W.660 Argosy tactical transport for the RAF, which – by ordering 56 – rescued a flagging civil program.

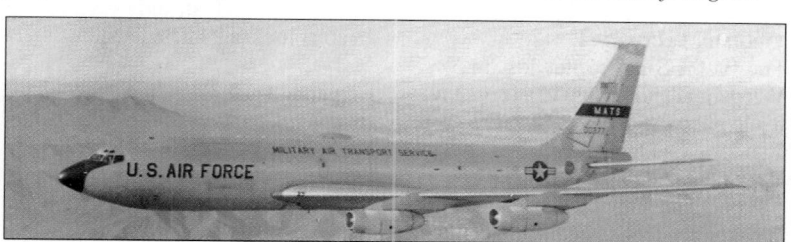

The USAF Military Air Transport Service received 18 Boeing C-135 jet transport versions of the KC-135A tankers minus the refueling equipment.

Handley Page built the H.P.115 as a research aircraft to investigate low-speed characteristics of the slender delta wing proposed for the Concord(e).

Convair received a launch order from American Airlines for 20 of its Model 990 medium-range airliner with General Electric CJ805-23B turbofan engines.

The Mil Mi-10 crane used closed-circuit TV to assist its load handling.

Canadair built Lockheed's F-104G under license as the CF-104.

# 1962

4,104mph
USA
Joseph Walker
North American X-15
Jun 27, 1962

24,325 miles
USA
Archie Old Jr
Boeing B52-B
Jan 18, 1957

314,750ft
USA
Robert White
North American X-15
Jul 17, 1962

488,000lb
USA
Boeing
B-52G Stratofortress

27,008lb thrust
USSR
Lyulka
AL-21F

**Armenia, January 7**
A Sabena Caravelle on a scheduled service from Tehran to Brussels departs from its flight path and is forced down by Soviet MiG fighters at Erevan.

**South-east Asia, January 12**
The USAF begins Operation Ranch Hand, using Fairchild C-123 Providers to spray defoliating herbicides on vegetation and expose roads and trails used by the Vietcong; the most common of the defoliants used is known from its metal-containers as Agent Orange (→ Feb 2).

**[West] Germany, January 22**
The USAF completes Operation Long Thrust II, a seven-day exercise in which 5,273 troops have been airlifted from the US.

**Vietnam, February 2**
A C-123 taking part in Operation Ranch Hand crashes for reasons which are unclear; three of the crew die – the first USAF fatalities in Vietnam.

**Vietnam, February 4**
The first US helicopter lost in Vietnam is shot down at Hong My while carrying troops against the Vietcong (→ Dec).

**Connecticut, February 5**
A Sikorsky HSS-2 Sea King of the US Navy sets a world helicopter speed record of 210.6mph, in the course of a flight between Milford and New Haven.

**Berlin, February 10**
American U-2 pilot Gary Powers, shot down and arrested in the USSR in May 1960, is released in exchange for Soviet spy Colonel Rudolf Abel.

**London, February 26**
Britain's Conservative government cancels backing for the Westland (formerly Fairey) Rotodyne vertical take-off and landing airliner, despite its many good performances in trials, because of the costs involved.

**Gloucestershire, England, Feb**
The first Hawker Siddeley Gnat jet trainers enter RAF service with the Central Flying School, Little Rissington; they replace the Vampire T.11 as the standard advanced trainer (→ May 14, 1965).

**California, March 1**
Los Angeles Airways becomes the first airline to put the Sikorsky S-61L helicopter into commercial service.

**Cameroon, March 4**
A Douglas DC-7C of British airline Caledonian Airways crashes near Douala, killing all 111 on board; this is the worst accident to date involving a single airliner.

**Switzerland, March 9**
The Convair CV-990, a larger and faster version of the 880 airliner, makes its commercial debut when Swissair introduces it on its route to Tokyo.

**Bristol, England, April 14**
The Bristol 188 stainless-steel, supersonic, high-altitude research aircraft makes its first flight.

**England, April 21**
British air pioneer and businessman Sir Frederick Handley Page, 77, dies.

**Seattle, April 25**
Pan Am orders 15 Boeing 707-321Cs, a cargo or passenger airplane which can be converted from one use to the other in a few hours (→ Jun 4, 1963).

**Florida, April 27**
USAF Tactical Air Command establishes the Special Air Warfare Center at Eglin Air Force Base.

**Okinawa, Japan, May 11**
Eddie Webber, 18-year-old mechanic refused entry to the USAF as a pilot, steals a DC-3 from the USAF base here and takes off in it, although he has never flown; he is frightened to land, and only succeeds in setting the airplane down at his fifth attempt.

**Paris, June 3**
An Air France Boeing 707 crashes on take-off at Orly airport, killing 130 (→ Jun 21).

**North Carolina, June 7**
A Boeing B-52H bomber commanded by Captain William Stevenson lands at Seymour Johnson Air Force Base to complete a 11,337-mile round-flight to Anchorage, Alaska, during which it has set a world closed-circuit distance record (→ Oct 26).

**Guadeloupe, June 21**
An Air France Boeing 707 en route from Paris to Santiago crashes into a hill near Pointe-à-Pitre; all 113 passengers and crew aboard are killed.

**Istres, France, June 22**
French flyer Jacqueline Auriol, piloting a Mirage IIIC, sets a new unofficial women's speed record of 1,149.7mph (→ Jun 14, 1963).

**Hanover, [W] Germany, June 22**
US aviator Jacqueline Cochran lands from New Orleans in her Lockheed JetStar *Scarlett O'Hara* after the first Atlantic jet crossing by a woman (→ May 1, 1963).

**California, June 27**
Joe Walker takes the X-15A rocket research aircraft from Edwards Air Force Base to a speed of 4,159mph, more than six times the speed of sound (→ Jul 19, 1963).

**Melbourne, June 30**
On the last day that the Avro Anson is certificated for service, a local company stages a fly-by of three of the machines.

**Sidorovo, USSR, July 7**
Colonel Georgi Mossolov sets a new world absolute speed record for airplanes, flying the Mikoyan Ye-166 at 1665.89mph.

**Marietta, Georgia, July 7**
The Lockheed VZ-10 two-seat vertical take-off and landing research vehicle makes its first conventional flight.

**Japan, August 30**
The Nihon Airplane Manufacturing Company's twin-turboprop, medium-range YS-11, Japan's first post-war commercial airplane, makes its first flight.

**USSR, October 2**
The Tupolev Tu-124 airliner enters service with Aeroflot on its route from Moscow to Tallinn, Estonia; it is powered by two D-20P turbofans.

**Japan, October 4**
Japan Air Lines inaugurates its "Silk Road" service to Europe via south-east Asia and the Middle East; flown with Convair 880 airplanes, it takes in Hong Kong, Bangkok, Calcutta, Karachi, Kuwait, Cairo, Rome, Frankfurt and London.

**Wichita, Kansas, October 26**
The last of 744 Boeing B-52 Stratofortress bombers is delivered to the USAF.

**Marietta, Georgia, November 2**
The Lockheed Model 186 research helicopter, which features a rigid main rotor, makes its maiden flight.

**Seattle, November 27**
The first B-727, a three-engined short-to medium-range jet airliner with all engines mounted at the rear, is rolled out (→ Feb 2, 1963).

**USA, December 8**
The Bell Model 206, developed to a US Army specification for a light observation helicopter, makes its first flight.

**Melun-Villaroche, France, Dec 24**
The Nord 262 Frégate, a twin-engined light transport which is a pressurized and more powerful version of the Nord 260 Super Broussard, flies for the first time.

*Boeing 707 long-range jet airliners load and unload at the new TWA terminal at New York's ever-busier Idlewild airport.* ▶

## Piper, a pioneer of private flying, is 80

*Miami, January 8*

William Piper, one of the greatest names in aviation, sat on a Miami beach today to watch an impromptu fly-past by owners of the much-loved aircraft which bears his name – the Piper Cub. Floridian Cub-owners were paying tribute to him on his 80th birthday.

After some years in oil exploration, Piper entered the aircraft industry with an investment of $400 in the 1932 Taylorcraft E-2 Cub, which is still in production at the Piper plant. The Cub's ancestry goes back to the two-seater Chummy made by Taylor Brothers, one of whom, C Gilbert Taylor, became Piper's first partner in 1929. They built the E-2 Cub, which with its 20-hp Brownback Kitten engine was underpowered. By 1939 more powerful engines were being used, and the Cub had surpassed its rivals in sales. During the war the Cub was turned out in thousands to meet the demand for front-line observation aircraft.

# British Trident hailed on first flight

*BEA is hoping for a great future with the new Trident, but there are some fears that the airliner may prove too small.*

*Hertfordshire, England, January 9*

The first of 24 Hawker Siddeley Trident three-engined jet transports built for British European Airways (BEA) made its first flight at Hatfield today. The test crew of five, headed by John Cunningham, were delighted at the way it behaved.

The Trident began life as the de Havilland D.H.121 and was exactly tailored to BEA's requirements. The original D.H.121 was to have been capable of carrying 111 passengers on stages of up to 2,070 miles, powered by three Rolls-Royce Medway engines.

But in 1959 BEA said that the D.H.121 should be less ambitious, carrying 88 passengers up to 930 miles. Rolls-Royce had to scrap the 14,000-lb thrust Medway and produce the 9,850-lb thrust Spey for the Trident.

The Trident promises well. But by following BEA's cautious line the de Havilland team – now part of Hawker Siddeley – may have risked handing the world market to the Trident's forthcoming rival, the Boeing 727 (→ Mar 11, 1964).

## Stratofortress stretches distance record

*The record-breaking Stratofortress crew after landing at Torrejon, Spain.*

*Madrid, January 11*

The USAF has wrested the world record for a non-refueled, non-stop flight from the US Navy by taking a Boeing B-52H Stratofortress from Okinawa in the Ryukyu Islands to Madrid. The distance covered was 12,532 miles.

In command of the strategic bomber, which took off yesterday, was Major Clyde P Evely. The B-52H, which first flew in March last year, is the latest variant of the highly successful B-52 Stratofortress bomber. It differs from its predecessors in being the first version to use turbofan engines, and its armament is also new. It was originally intended to carry the Skybolt air-launched nuclear missile [*see page 592*], but this was canceled, and its main offensive armament became the Hound Dog supersonic, strategic stand-off missile (→ Jun 7).

## Lear opens for business at Wichita base

*Wichita, Kan, January 31*

William P Lear has set up a drawing office here and aims to build his own jet airplanes. He has sold his electronics business for $100 million and has invested $11 million of the proceeds in developing a twin-engined jet for use by business executives. The wing design of the Lear Jet is based on that for a prototype strike fighter which Lear worked on at the Swiss-based Swiss American Aviation Corporation. Bill Lear, an electronics genius, designed the world's first successful jet autopilot (→ Oct 7, 1963).

**New York, February 20: commuters at Grand Central Station watch the launch of US Marine Lt-Col John H Glenn, first American in orbit.**

# Man powers airplane for half-mile flight

*Hertfordshire, England, May 2*
Pedal-powered aviation may sound ridiculous, but Britain is leading the field in developing human-powered airplanes which are capable of sustained flight.

Today, to the jubilation of the Hatfield Man-Powered Aircraft Club (HMPAC), its Puffin monoplane has managed a straight flight of 2,988 feet, the first time an airplane of this type has ever exceeded a distance of half a mile. The pilot today was the HMPAC chairman and professional aerodynamicist John Wimpenny. The Puffin has been built to mount a challenge for the £50,000 Kremer prize to be awarded to the first human-powered airplane to fly a figure-of-eight round two pylons placed exactly half a mile apart. The HMPAC team consists of approximately 40 members, including engineers from de Havilland Aircraft (now Hawker Siddeley). The balsa-wood airplane weighs just 265 pounds at take-off.

*Pedal-pilot John Wimpenny in the saddle of the remarkable Puffin airplane.*

# Giant transport Sikorsky Skycrane flies

*The powerful Sikorsky Skycrane is capable of lifting loads weighing 10 tons.*

*Stratford, Connecticut, May 9*
The S-64A Skycrane, possibly the most powerful helicopter outside the USSR, today began its flight-test program at the plant of the Sikorsky Aircraft division of United Aircraft Corporation. It is the only crane-type helicopter in the Western world.

Crane helicopters are designed to pick up and position heavy loads, but not necessarily to transport them over long distances. Typical tasks can include putting air-conditioners on the roofs of skyscrapers or positioning freight containers. Sikorsky developed today's machine in stages. The S-56, with two 1,900-hp piston engines, flew in 1953. The same five-blade main rotor, tail rotor and engines were then used in the first Sikorsky crane helicopter, the S-60, of 1959. Many similar parts are used in the S-64A, but this has a six-blade main rotor and two 4,050-hp Pratt & Whitney T74 turbine engines.

Production S-64As will be supplied to the US Army as the CH-54A Tarhe. They can carry loads weighing 10 tons, including a pod with 68 troop seats.

# New US spyplane, A-12, takes to sky

*Groom Dry Lake, Nevada, April 26*
Today, in utmost secrecy at this remote airfield, the first Lockheed A-12 made its first flight. It marks another extraordinary development program by the Lockheed Advanced Development Projects secure plant at Burbank, California – the so-called "Skunk Works" – headed by C L "Kelly" Johnson.

The A-12 is the first of a family of top-secret spyplanes. Somewhat sinister in appearance, it is coated overall with a matt black finish which dissipates heat and helps make the aircraft invisible to radar. They are designed to fly at unprecedented speeds and altitudes in spying missions over hostile territory, carrying giant cameras and other special sensors (→ Aug 7, 1963).

# Euravia offers first inclusive tour holiday

*Bedfordshire, England, May 5*
At 9.20am a former El Al Lockheed Constellation, now in the livery of Euravia, sped down the runway at Luton on a short flight to Manchester's Ringway airport. Shortly after 11.00am it was airborne once more, destined for Palma, Majorca, via Perpignan, France.

On board were passengers about to participate in a new experience, an inclusive tour holiday organized by an operator with its own airline. Euravia is the brainchild of Ted Langton, whose Universal Sky Tours package holiday company has previously relied on chartered airliners. The company, which has a fleet of three Constellations in 82-seat configuration, was registered on December 1 last year, with John Ernest Derek ("Jed") Williams as the managing director.

Williams was instrumental in Euravia's conception. Independently, he too had evolved the idea of an integrated tour-airline operator and had been approached by an airplane dealer to help find a buyer for three Constellations. He then sought Langton and everything fell into place. With a reliable airline at its calling, Universal Sky Tours may hold the key to the future of cheap holiday packages.

If others follow suit, it may force scheduled airlines to revise their flight charges. They may even establish their own dedicated charter branches.

# Air and sea giants linked by a merger

*London, June 6*
The world of air transport was astonished today when British minister of aviation Peter Thorneycroft announced the formation of a new company, BOAC-Cunard Ltd. Seventy per cent of the capital is to be held by BOAC, Britain's national long-haul carrier, the remainder by the Cunard Steamship Company.

Cunard already has an air transport subsidiary, Cunard-Eagle, a rival of the national airline, although this is not affected by the new joint venture which links BOAC with its parent. BOAC-Cunard intends to use its parents' resources in marketing throughout eastern North America, Central America and the Caribbean and northern Latin America.

# Vickers VC10 is a short-field 707

*Surrey, England, June 29*
The prototype Vickers VC10 long-range jet-airliner made its first flight today at Weybridge. Manned by a test crew led by G R "Jock" Bryce and his co-pilot Brian Trubshaw, the powerful jet easily took off from the tiny runway in the center of the old Brooklands racetrack and landed a short distance away at Wisley, the test airfield of Vickers-Armstrongs (Aircraft), now part of British Aircraft Corporation.

The flight was watched by new minister of aviation Julian Amery as well as company managing director Sir George Edwards and customer managing director Sir Basil Smallpeice. The VC10 is impressive technically, with an uncluttered high-lift wing and four very powerful Rolls-Royce Conway turbofans mounted on the rear fuselage, but politically it is in trouble. Because of supposed overcapacity BOAC, the VC10's customer, has cut its order from 15 to 12 and is set to cut its order for the heavier, longer-range Super VC10 from 30 to only 17, with a possibility of ordering a few more after 1967. Much of this retrenchment is due to BOAC's "buy US" faction, say cynics. In 1955 BOAC rejected the VC7 in favor of the Boeing 707, and it is now claiming that the 707 must be better than the VC10, which can use short runways (→ Apr 29, 1964).

*The VC10's super-powerful Conway turbofans make a huge roar on take-off.*

*For these ground tests, special silencers were connected to the four engines.*

## De Havilland unveils D.H.125 executive jet as successor to Dove

*The D.H. Jet Dragon, with Viper turbojets, has replaced the outmoded Dove.*

*Hertfordshire, England, August 13*
What will almost certainly be the last aircraft to bear the famous de Havilland name made its first flight today at Hatfield, headquarters of the British company absorbed by the Hawker Siddeley group in 1960. Test pilot Chris Capper said he was very pleased with the aircraft, which lifted off from a runway just 2,000 feet long. The D.H.125 Jet Dragon is an executive jet. Initially, the company was not eager to risk a large amount of its own money on what was a quite new type of airplane. It was prompted to do so by two facts: first, that the piston-engined D.H.104 Dove executive aircraft was obsolescent, and, second, that the cancellation last year of Britain's Blue Streak long-range missile had left a large number of technical staff unemployed. The company's final spur to proceeding with the D.H.125 project was the reassurance by Britain's RAF that it would buy a batch of D.H.125s for use as navigation trainers.

The D.H.125 is a neat, low-wing aircraft with two Viper turbojets of 3,000-lb thrust each mounted at the rear. Up to eight passengers can be carried.

# Radar development leaps to new levels

*Baltimore, Maryland, September 5*
The development of radar is reaching new heights of sophistication. The Westinghouse Electric Corporation, for example, is now producing the most advanced fire-control radar in the world, the AWG-10, for the F-4B and other versions of the Phantom II. And well advanced in testing is the next generation, the AWG-9, for the F-111B fighter of the US Navy; this can track 24 aerial targets at once and guide missiles to any six, while also scanning the airspace out to 120 miles looking for fresh targets.

Another completely new capability is automatic terrain-following radar (TFR). Now nearing its first flight, the USAF's F-111A will have a TFR made by Texas Instruments enabling it to attack at treetop height, even in dense fog or at night, in mountainous country. For ultra-long-range, high-power vision, no airborne radar can equal the giant installations now on Super Constellations and the new E-2 Hawkeye; the latter has a streamlined rotating dish for an antenna. Many groups in the US, western Europe and the USSR are working on high-power airborne early-warning (AEW) radars.

Westinghouse, Hughes and Northrop are leaders in high-definition mapping radars using such new technologies as side-looking airborne radar (SLAR), synthetic apertures and doppler-beam sharpening. Impetus for such radars has come from space reconnaissance.

*GE makes the E-2 Hawkeye radar.*

# Pilot rockets into space

*The X-15 drops free an instant after release from its B-52 "motherplane".*

**Nevada, July 17**

The USAF got its fifth astronaut aloft today in an airplane rather than a rocket. Major Robert M White flew the North American X-15 rocket-airplane to a height of almost 59 miles after taking from Edwards Air Force Base.

Major White's flight set a world altitude record of 314,750 feet for winged aircraft and qualified him to wear USAF astronaut wings, which are awarded to those who fly to at least 50 miles above the Earth. The other four pilots authorized to wear the wings are Mercury astronauts Alan B Shepard, John H Glenn, Vir-

gil I Grissom and Malcolm Scott Carpenter. The flight began when the X-15 was dropped from a B-52, 45,000 feet over the Nevada desert. The 57,000-pound thrust engine was ignited and burned for 81 seconds. The top speed reached in the ascent was 3,784mph, below the X-15's record of 4,159mph. White saw strange, flaky, gray objects, one as large as his hand, floating near the X-15 as he began re-entry. Tomorrow he will join fellow X-15 pilots Joe Walker, Scott Crossfield and Forrest Peterson in Washington, DC, to be honored at the Collier trophy presentation.

**Space-age design: the new TWA flight center at Idlewild, New York.**

# Bizarre-looking 'Pregnant Guppy' flies

**Van Nuys, Calif, September 19**

On getting out of the aircraft John Conroy was asked by a reporter how the "Pregnant Guppy" had performed during its first flight. "Well," he replied, "we knew it would fly. It is really the next one – which will be much longer – that is worrying us." So what will the authorities at Van Nuys do for the next flight, when this one has already caused deep anxiety? After Conroy announced that he was go-

ing ahead with a test flight, all the town's firemen and police officers were put on red alert. Already famous for the many modifications he has made to the DC-3, Conroy has rebuilt a Boeing 377 Stratocruiser and carried out tests on it. With partner Lee Mansdorf he founded a private company, called Aero Spacelines Inc, aiming to carry rocket parts for NASA. Conroy uses old Stratocruisers from the 1950s, which he modifies.

*An extraordinary shape in the sky: the "Pregnant Guppy" cargo-airliner.*

# De Gaulle urges Anglo-French air alliance

**Paris, October 26**

Last month French President Charles de Gaulle made a impassioned plea for Britain and France to cooperate in building civil aircraft, using the joint resources of their two aircraft industries to counter what he calls "American colonization of the skies".

It is not difficult to see why, in the light of statistics released today, the fourth anniversary of the first revenue-earning flight by the Boeing 707. Since October 26, 1958, the 707 has become known as "the master of the skies", penetrating the international market for civil airliners in a spectacular way. At 11pm today there were 167 707s airborne, carrying a total of 10,210 passengers. The record of the last four years is even more impressive: a total of 26 airlines have bought 300 707s, using them to carry 30 million passengers over 750,000 miles. The routes on which they now operate include 175 towns in 83 countries. On the back of this success, Boeing is planning a whole

family of airliners, ranging from short-haul versions, such as the 720 and 727, to much larger jets.

That is not the policy favored in Europe. The French leader wants Britain and France to concentrate on speed rather than increased size, and he wants to build a supersonic transport. Such a project would be too expensive for either the French or British alone, and so cooperation is essential. The question is whether the idea of greater speed is right. US companies have also studied the possibility of building a supersonic transport (SST), but some in the industry see speed as the wrong way to go. They argue that the growth in passenger traffic has been built largely on the introduction of lower fares, bringing air travel within the pockets of more and more people, and they do not see a market for a supersonic airliner, with much higher operating costs, as the way ahead. The European proposal, if it goes ahead, will need heavy government subsidy to make it financially viable (→ Nov 29).

# Air reconnaissance spots Cuba missiles

*A spyplane's shot of MiG-21 fighters with air-to-air missiles in Cuba.*

*Washington, DC, October 28*

The threat of nuclear war receded today with Soviet premier Khrushchev's promise to order the dismantling of the USSR's SS-4 missiles in Cuba and to ship them back home. President Kennedy, who has taken a strong stance throughout a dangerous fortnight, has greeted the decision as "statesmanlike" and he will now order the US naval blockade of Cuba to be lifted.

Speculation that Soviet nuclear ballistic missiles and Ilyushin Il-28 bombers had been shipped to Cuba, as a forward base very near the US mainland, had been circulating in Washington, DC, since September. Lockheed U-2 spyplanes flown by the CIA had detected what looked like missile sites being prepared.

Two flights in October brought back evidence of more advanced construction of sites.

Such was the alarm that USAF crews helped the CIA to gather more evidence, which came on October 14 when a U-2E of 4028th Strategic Reconnaissance Squadron photographed SS-4s near San Cristobal. Within a few days nine sites had been found. Low-level reconnaissance flights by USAF RF-101 Voodoos and naval RF-8A Crusaders confirmed missile sites plus about 40 bombers at Holguin and San Julian. On October 22 Kennedy broke the news publicly. The world waited as the two superpowers looked on the brink of conflict; only yesterday a U-2 was shot down over Cuba by a Soviet missile.

# New US military aircraft designations

*Washington D.C., June 30*

US military aircraft now have common designations. These are generally based on those of the US Air Force. Aircraft of the Navy and Marine Corps have totally new designations.

The former Navy practice of including a letter for the manufacturer is scrapped. And most of the categories have had the existing number sequence terminated, and a new sequence has been started at 1. Thus, the F-111 remains the F-111, but the F-110 becomes the USAF's F-4C. The FJ-4B Fury becomes the AF-1E (AF, attack fighter).

The AD Skyraider series become A-1 versions, the A3D Skywarriors are now A-3s, the A4D Skyhawks are A-4s, the A3J Vigilantes are A-5s and the A2F Intruders are A-6s. There are F-2 Banshees (ex-F2H), F-3 Skyknights (F3D), F-4 Phantom IIs (F4H), F-5 Freedom Fighters (no prior US code), F-6 Skyrays (F4D), F-8 Crusaders (F8U) and F-9 Cougars (F9F). It is pure chance that most retain the same number. In other categories the changes are complete. The W2F Hawkeye is now the E-2, and WV-2 Constellations are various sub-types of EC-121.

# First flights leave stylish Dulles airport

*Architect Eero Saarinen thought the futuristic Dulles airport his best work.*

*Herndon, Va, November 17*

Before 60,000 people, President Kennedy today dedicated Dulles International Airport, the first US airport designed from the outset to handle jet aircraft. Dulles, twice the size of New York International Airport, is on 10,000 acres among farms in the Virginia countryside, 27 miles from Washington, DC.

For the ceremony, the president was joined by former President Eisenhower and the widow of John Foster Dulles, the US Secretary of State for whom the airport is named. They and other dignitaries stood before the soaring white terminal which, with the control tower and service buildings, was designed by the late Eero Saarinen.

At most airports passengers walk long distances to airliners parked at extensions of the terminal. At Dulles, aircraft are parked away from the terminal, reducing noise and fumes. Mobile lounges, which can be raised and lowered, move passengers from 12 boarding points right to the airplane door. There are two 11,500-foot runways and one 10,000-foot runway, which will enable Dulles to handle all jets with ease.

# 'Huey' helicopter wins spurs in Vietnam

*The Bell UH-1 "Huey" is changing the face of helicopter warfare in Vietnam.*

*Saigon, December*

US Army crews using armed Bell UH-l Iroquois to support South Vietnamese troops have written a new chapter in the history of helicopters at war. The Utility Tactical Transport Helicopter Company, based at Tan Son Nhut airport, received 15 UH-1As in September and equipped them with two .30-in machine guns and 16 2.75-in rockets each. These "gunships" have proved a lethal escort for helicopters carrying troops into action. In November, 11 more powerful and heavier-armed UH-1Bs arrived. Each had four M-60 machine guns and the 2.75-in rockets in clusters of eight.

Since both models of the armed UH-1, known to its crews as a "Huey", have been in use, losses of troop-carrying helicopters to ground fire have decreased and the scope of operations has expanded because of the "Huey's" firepower.

# Anglo-French deal agreed for supersonic airliner

*London, November 29*

A supersonic airliner will soon be a reality. After long negotiations the British and French governments have at last decided to embark on one of the greatest adventures in the history of aviation. Representatives from the two countries, British minister of aviation Julian Amery and French ambassador Jouffroy de Courcel, have today signed an historic draft treaty for collaboration in the building of a supersonic transport aircraft.

Never before have two countries committed themselves to such close cooperation. The treaty stipulates that France and Great Britain "must in all aspects of the project make an equal contribution regarding both the costs to be taken on and the work to be carried out, and to share equally proceeds from sales". Four companies have been entrusted with bringing the project to fruition. The British Aircraft Corporation and France's Sud-Aviation are to build the airframe, while the four Olympus 593 jet engines for the plane will be manufactured by both Bristol Siddeley and SNECMA (→ Jan 13, 1963).

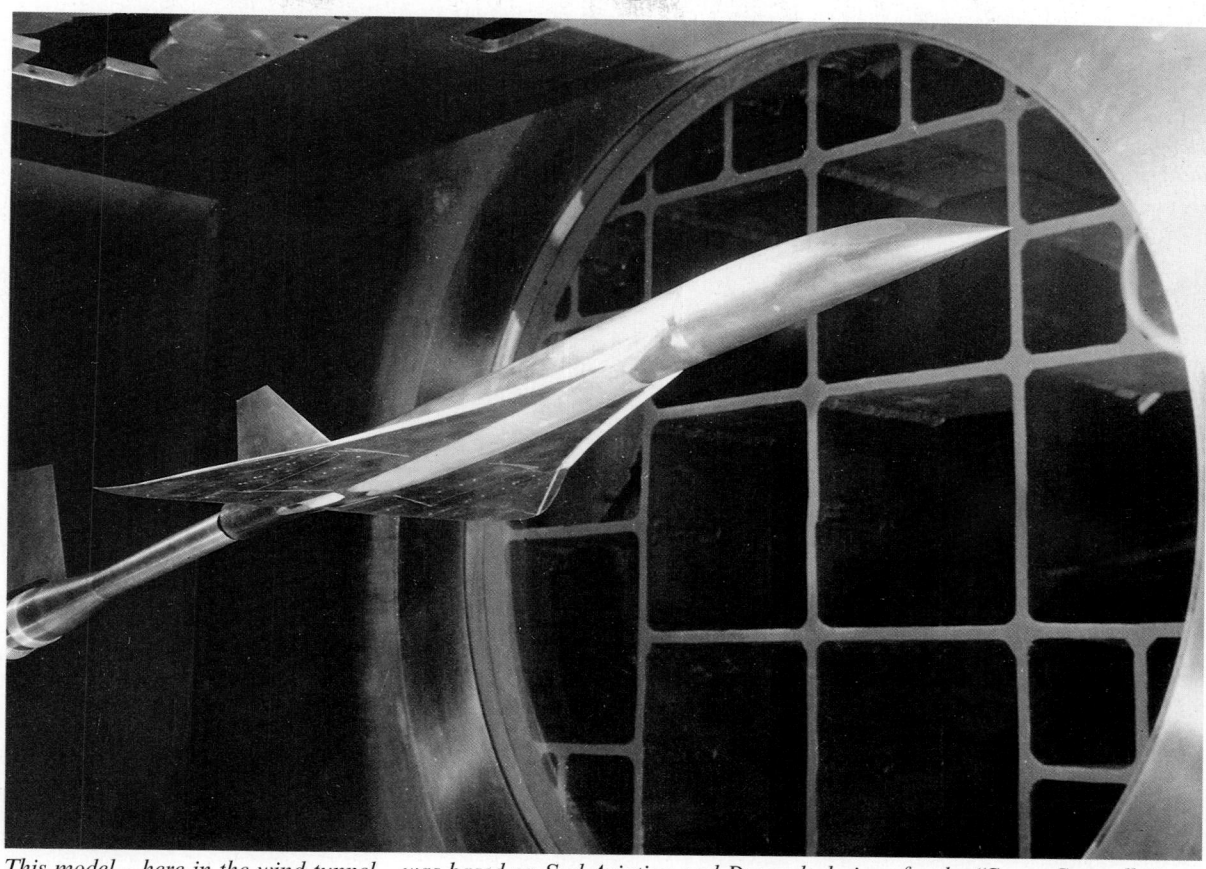

*This model – here in the wind tunnel – was based on Sud-Aviation and Dassault designs for the "Super Caravelle".*

## Vulcans equipped with Blue Steel bombs

*Lincolnshire, England, December*

The famous 617 "Dambuster" Squadron of Britain's RAF, based at Scampton and renowned for its wartime "Bouncing Bomb", is to get a new weapon: Blue Steel. This is the name given to the stand-off missile for 617's Avro Vulcan B.2 bombers. Blue Steel is also made by Avro, now part of Hawker Siddeley. It resembles a miniature tail-first airplane, 34 feet long and weighing 15,000 lb; it carries fuel for the rocket engine, a complex guidance system and a nuclear warhead. Blue Steel Mk I can fly up to 200 miles at supersonic speed, and so the carrier aircraft need not approach heavily defended targets, hence the term "stand-off".

The Vulcan B.2 is powered by 20,000-lb thrust Olympus engines, giving it the higher load-carrying capacity needed for the Blue Steel missiles, and the combination of the two is intended to extend the deterrent role of the RAF's V-bomber until 1969/70 (→ Sep 9, 1966).

*The Blue Steel missile is carried beneath the Vulcan bomber's main fuselage.*

## French VTOL fighter begins flight trials

*Melun-Villaroche, France, Oct 18*

Six days after making its first tentative, tethered, vertical take-off, the Dassault Balzac V 001 today began its free-flight trials program at Melun-Villaroche test airfield.

The Balzac, developed in collaboration with Sud-Aviation, is basically a Mirage III prototype fitted with four pairs of Rolls-Royce RB.108 lift jets, each of 2,200lb thrust. They draw in air through louvered doors in the top of the fuselage and can be directed forward or backward from the vertical to assist in braking and forward acceleration. The engine for forward flight is a 4,850-lb thrust Bristol Siddeley Orpheus. Using separate propulsion systems for lifting and forward flight, rather than using the same engine, as in Britain's Hawker Siddeley P.1127, is favored by Rolls-Royce which is working with Dassault (→ Mar 18, 1963).

## US Navy winds up airship operations

*Lakehurst, NJ, December 31*

A chapter in US naval aviation history which began in June 1915 ended today with the announcement that all lighter-than-air operations have finished. The last airship flew on August 31.

In 47 years the navy's airships achieved moments of glory and tragedy. The rigid models of the 1920s and 1930s were a source of pride for their crews, but their vulnerability to violent weather took its toll in a series of crashes. The brightest period for the navy's "blimps" was the Second World War. The 134 K-class airships proved ideal for both anti-submarine patrols and convoy escort and were credited with shepherding 89,000 surface ships safely across the oceans. But now the advent of very effective patrol-bombers such as the P-2 Neptune and new P-3 Orion have made the huge airships redundant.

Douglas's DC-8 Series 54 was also designated the DC-8F Jet Trader.

NAMC's YS-11 52/60-passenger twin-RR-Dart transport sold well.

Merville's D.63 tricycle-landing-gear-version of the Druine D.62.

On-Mark Engineering converted a standard Boeing 377 Stratocruiser into the Model 377-PG "Pregnant Guppy" outsize freighter for Aero Spacelines.

Piaggio's P.166: bigger landplane version of the pusher-engined P.136.

The Nord 262: a pressurized development of the 250 Super Broussard.

The Fuji KM-2, a two/four-seat Japanese version of the Beech Mentor.

BAC built standard VC10s for British Overseas Airways Corporation, Ghana Airways and British United Airways as well as 14 for the Royal Air Force.

Hawker Siddeley's D.H.121 Trident 1 was designed to meet a British European Airways requirement for a 103-seat short/medium-range tri-jet airliner.

Totally redesigned: PZL's 104 Wilga 35 utility aircraft and glider tug.

Cessna's Model 411 six/eight-seat private-owner and business aircraft.

The Piper PA-30 Twin Comanche, a twin-engined version of the PA-24.

The Scintex CP.1310-C3 Super Emeraude with a revised canopy.

The Jurca M.J.5 Sirocco two-seat development of the M.J.2 Tempête.

Aero Commander's 680FL five/seven-passenger transport.

Hawker Siddeley's HS.125 jet business aircraft was designed for a variety of other roles, including military communications and pilot/navigator training.

The Dinfia IA.50 (FA.1) Guarani 10/15-passenger light transport.

The Beagle 206Y with 310-hp RR Continental GIO-470-A engines.

Plastics were used in non-stressed areas of the Beagle M.218 airframe.

The SIPA S.251 Antilope used a Turbomeca-Astazou II turboprop.

Dassault converted the prototype Mirage III into the Balzac development aircraft used to develop the control system for the Mirage III-V VTOL fighter.

The Wing Derringer: planned as a twin-engined high-speed two-seater.

The Sikorsky Skycrane carried large underslung or podded loads.

Lockheed's VZ-10 Hummingbird direct (ejector) lift research aircraft.

The LTV TF-8A two-seat trainer, a conversion of the F-8E prototype.

The prototype Sud-Aviation SA 321 Super Frelon troop carrier was powered by three Turbomeca Turmo III C2 turboshafts. A naval version followed.

Three of the 18 Lockheed A-12 research aircraft ordered by the USAF were completed as YF-12A interceptors although no production was intended.

Sud-Aviation converted a standard license-built H-34 to the H-34 Bi-Bastan with two Turbomeca Bastan IV turboshaft engines in a coupled installation.

Lockheed's XH-51A compound helicopter with auxiliary J60 turbojet.

The Heinkel CM.191, a four-seat development of the Fouga Magister.

The Bell Model 206 OH-4A later became the Kiowa or JetRanger.

The Westland Wasp anti-submarine helicopter for Royal Navy frigates.

Bristol built the Type 188 high-speed research aircraft from stainless steel to explore effects of prolonged kinetic heating (which it could not achieve).

# 1963

 4,104mph
USA
Joseph Walker
North American X-15
Jun 27, 1962

 24,325 miles
USA
Archie Old Jr
Boeing B-52B
Jan 18, 1957

 354,200ft
USA
Joseph Walker
North American X-15
Aug 22, 1963

 488,000lb
USA
Boeing
B-52G Stratofortress

 27,008lb thrust
USSR
Lyulka
AL-21F

**Ap Bac, Vietnam, January 2**
In the first major battle involving US forces, US helicopters carry 2,500 South Vietnamese troops in an assault on a 300-strong enemy force at Ap Bac; the assault fails, raising questions about the fighting ability of Saigon's army.

**Reykjavik, January 10**
The Icelandic airline Loftleidir offers fares lower than those fixed by the International Air Transport Association (IATA) on its North Atlantic services; companies which are members of IATA decide to lower their fares as a result.

**Paris, January 13**
In a speech, French President de Gaulle makes use of the word *"concorde"* with reference to the Anglo-French supersonic transport project (→ Jun 4).

**Belfast, Ulster, January 17**
The prototype Short Skyvan transport makes its first flight, in the hands of Denis Tayler at Sydenham; it is powered by two 390-hp Continental GTSIO-520 piston engines but may later have turboprops.

**Paris, January 23**
French engineer-designer Michel Wibault, first Frenchman to develop the all-metal airplane, dies at the age of 65.

**Canada, March 1**
Trans-Canada Air Lines opens a freight-only service to Europe with Douglas DC-8F Jet Traders.

**Melun-Villaroche, France, Mar 18**
The Dassault Balzac V 001 vertical take-off and landing airplane makes its first successful transition from vertical to horizontal flight.

**London, April 1**
British European Airways introduces the first "stand-by" fares, under which passengers arriving at the airport on the chance of an available seat are given one-third off the full price.

**California, April 8**
Douglas Aircraft, having decided not to proceed with its option to make the French Caravelle under license, announces that it is to develop its own short-range jet, the DC-9 (→ Feb 25, 1965).

**California, May 1**
Jacqueline Cochran takes off from Edwards Air Force Base to set a 100-km [62-mile] closed-circuit world speed record for women of 1,203.7mph in a Lockheed Starfighter (→ May 11, 1964).

**USA, May 7**
Death of Prof. Theodor von Karman, celebrated Hungarian aerodynamicist who for the past 20 years has been the closest air advisor to US presidents.

**England, May 8**
The last six D.H. Mosquitoes in RAF service are retired.

**Brisbane, Australia, May 12**
American flyer Betty Miller lands to complete the first transpacific flight by a woman; she left Oakland, California, on April 30.

**New York, June 4**
Pan Am announces that it has taken out options to buy six Anglo-French Concordes (→ Oct 24).

**Paris, June 6**
Air France opens a non-stop Paris/Los Angeles service with Boeing 707s; it is the longest route without stops in the world – 5,660 miles in 12 hours.

**Istres, France, June 14**
Jacqueline Auriol wins the 100-km closed-circuit women's speed record from Jacqueline Cochran, flying the Dassault Mirage IIIR, to a speed of 1,261.4mph.

**New York, June 24**
A peaceful demonstration takes place at Idlewild airport to mark the first year of a flight engineers' strike against Eastern Air Lines over who should occupy the third cockpit seat in jet airliners.

**Sweden, June 29**
The prototype Saab 105 twin-jet attack-trainer makes its first flight, piloted by Karl-Erik Fernberg.

**North Pole, July 4**
Bob Fisher and Cliff Aldefer make the first landing by a single-engined airplane at the pole; they flew their Cessna 180, fitted with extra fuel tanks and skis, from Point Barrow, Alaska.

**Paris, July 5**
Air France introduces new rules under which air hostesses are permitted to marry, but must be willing to be sent away from home for two weeks at a time.

**USA, July 19**
Joe Walker pilots the North American X-15A research aircraft to an unoffical altitude record of 347,800 feet (→ Aug 22).

**Canada, July 20**
A total eclipse of the Sun is filmed from a specially equipped Douglas DC-8-53 piloted at an altitude of 42,000 feet by astronaut Malcolm Scott Carpenter.

**Israel, August 20**
Two Israeli Mirage jets shoot down two of a group of eight Syrian MiG-17 fighters over Lake Tiberias, forcing the other six to flee.

**Berlin, September 1**
The East German national airline, hitherto known by the pre-war name of Deutsche Lufthansa, renames itself Interflug to avoid confusion with West German airline Lufthansa.

**Zurich, September 2**
A Swissair Caravelle jet flying to Rome crashes near here shortly after take-off; all 74 passengers and six crew on board the airliner are killed.

**Nagoya, Japan, September 14**
The prototype Mitsubishi MU-2 light utility transport makes its maiden flight (→ Jul 1, 1966).

**[West] Germany, September 20**
The Entwicklungsring Süd GmbH vertical take-off and landing supersonic jet VJ 101C makes its first transition from vertical to horizontal flight.

**Hampshire, England, October 22**
The British Aircraft Corporation One-Eleven prototype crashes during a test flight, killing a very experienced seven-man crew; the aircraft suffered a "deep stall", thought to have been caused by its T-tail configuration (→ Apr 9, 1966).

**Bristol, England, October 24**
An experimental model of the Anglo-French Concorde supersonic transport is shown to British and French journalists (→ Mar 1, 1964).

**Atlantic Ocean, October 30**
A US Marine Corps KC-130 Hercules tanker transport achieves a remarkable feat when it lands on the carrier USS *Forrestal* without the help of a restraining hook.

**England, November 11**
Britain's Fleet Air Arm establishes a Small Ship Flight of Westland Wasp helicopters, capable of operating from platforms on frigates and small naval vessels.

**Florida, November 20**
The USAF's first two McDonnell F-4C Phantom II fighters are formally accepted into service, at MacDill Air Force Base.

**England, December 21**
The prototype Hawker Siddeley HS.748MF military transport, called the Andover by the RAF, makes its maiden flight.

**New York, December 24**
New York International Airport is rededicated as John F Kennedy Airport in honor of the murdered president.

*The marketing study carried out by Boeing before building the 727-100 showed that the company should be able to sell 300 of the trijets.* ▶

# Il-62, Soviet VC10 lookalike, flies

*The Aeroflot Ilyushin Il-62 jet airliner is a big hit with spectators when it is displayed at the Paris air show.*

*Moscow, January*
Under the inevitable shroud of Soviet secrecy, aviation engineers have spent more than three years developing a long-range turbojet airliner. The prototype Ilyushin Il-62 made its maiden flight this month, although the West is unlikely to see the Soviet giant for some time. Nato has already given the designation "Classic" to this latest addition to the Soviet fleet.

The Il-62 has incorporated several features familiar in the West, the most arresting being the siting of the four 19,180-pound Mikulin AM-3M turbojets; these have been mounted in pairs on either side of the fuselage, as in the British Vickers VC10, to which the Il-62 bears a striking superficial resemblance. Kuznetsov is now developing more powerful engines for use in later versions of the aircraft.

The wings are swept back at 35 degrees, like the Boeing 707's. The airliner has a projected cruising speed of 559mph and a range of 4,971 miles. It is planned to carry 195 passengers.

## English magazine's statistics show that jet airliners are safe

*London, January 10*
A report published today by British journal *The Aeroplane* suggests that, in the age of the jetliner, air travel is getting safer. The survey reveals that the number of crashes involving jets rose in 1962. But it also shows that the total number of jet crashes since the new airliners were first introduced represents just one in every 160,000 passenger hours in commercial service. Of the 18 jet-airliners which have been lost since the jet was introduced, eight were lost in crashes in 1962. Of the total of 18, 11 were Boeings – four of which were lost on training flights and did not involve passengers – and seven were DC-8s.

Over the service history of these airliners, the death rate for each 100 million passenger miles flown proves to be just 0.88 for the Boeing and 0.78 for the DC-8. Last year the world's commercial jet fleet flew 4,240,000 hours, including freight flights.

# 1,000th Cherokee light airplane rolls out

*The Piper Cherokee, a single-engined four-seater, is good value for money.*

*Vero Beach, Florida, January 24*
The Piper Aircraft Corporation reached a milestone today by delivering the 1,000th Cherokee off the production line. The Cherokee was designed and developed at the company's new facility at Vero Beach, and is the only airplane in production here. Other Piper airplanes are produced at the manufacturer's original plant at Lock Haven, Pennsylvania. The Cherokee was always expected to do well as the standard low-price four-seater lightplane to replace the TriPacer.

An all-metal, low-wing airplane, the Cherokee is available in several versions, the latest of which is the PA-28-235 with a 235-hp engine. Others are planned (→ Dec 6).

# P.1127 is first VTOL to fly from carrier

*Dorset, England, February 11*
The first prototype Hawker P.1127 "jump jet" today made the first test flights by a vertical take-off and landing (VTOL) jet airplane from a ship at sea, aboard the carrier HMS *Ark Royal*. It was piloted by Bill Bedford, manufacturer's chief test pilot. Over the next five days he and colleague Hugh Merewether are to tackle taking-off, hovering, landing and general deck operations to see if any problems arise. These will be done off Portland, with the ship both under way and at anchor. Unlike normal airplanes, the P.1127 needs no wind over the deck to take off (→ Mar 7, 1964).

*The P.1127 makes the first vertical landing by any jet on a carrier.*

# Boeing sets sights on mid-range market with 727

*Seattle, February 2*
The first flight of the new Boeing 727 here today makes it clear that the company plans to dominate both short-range and medium-range jet-transport markets. In the 727, Boeing has taken the comfort and speed of its successful four-engined 707s and 720s and put them into a quieter, three-engined plane which can fly from shorter runways and has the economy to generate profits on short flights.

The Boeing 727 can operate from the 5,000-foot landing strips used by piston-engined Constellations, DC-6s, DC-7s and turboprop Electras. It will bring jet services to older airports in densely populated areas which have short runways and noise restrictions, such as New York's LaGuardia airport. Its impressive ability to take off and land in a short distance results from new triple-slotted, trailing-edge flaps, retractable leading-edge slats outboard and Krueger flaps inboard.

*The 727 on its maiden flight over Seattle: already it promises to transform jet travel by opening up the smaller airports.*

Up to 129 passengers can be carried by the 727. It has a self-contained stairway which lowers below the T-tail, another plus for small airport operations. Unlike the bigger Boeing jets and the Douglas DC-8 – which have four engines slung from wing pylons – the 727 has two engines in pods on the aft fuselage and a third in its tail. This reduces take-off noise for passengers, except those in the very rear of the cabin, and reduces trim problems if an engine has to be shut down in flight (→ Feb 11, 1964).

## First Blackburn Buccaneers embark in HMS 'Ark Royal'

*English Channel, February 20*
The first operational Blackburn Buccaneer S.Mk.1s embarked on board HMS *Ark Royal* today in the English Channel. Squadron 801 was commissioned at Lossiemouth, Scotland, on July 17 last year. Forty S.Mk.1s were ordered in October 1959, and production will continue throughout this year.

The Buccaneer is a weapons system which is unique, perhaps years ahead of competition. It was designed to make high-subsonic and low-level penetration attacks with nuclear or conventional weapons, making use of the vulnerable airspace beneath an enemy's radar defenses. It has a tactical radius of action of over 500 miles, allowing the aircraft carrier to remain in relative safety.

The heart of the airplane lies in its integrated navigation and control system, bringing together the functions of the navigation and attack avionics, autopilot, radar and instruments.

# France, West Germany cooperate to produce military airlifter

*On this test flight one of the two 6,100-hp Rolls-Royce Tyne turboprops was stopped and the propeller feathered.*

*Melun-Villaroche, France, Feb 25*
Despite thick snow on the ground, dignitaries from France and West Germany watched today as Jean Lanvario took the first prototype Transall C-160 skyward from Melun-Villaroche for a 55-minute first flight. Everything went well, although Lanvario reported some difficulty with the flaps.

Transall is a good demonstration of the new era of cooperation between these former antagonists.

The Arbeitsgemeinschaft Transall organization was founded in 1959, just three years after the West German government took the first practical steps towards the creation of its post-war air force.

Transall has the backing of two German companies and one French one, of which Vereinigte Flugtechnische Werke is overall manager of the program. The French Nord-Aviation company, responsible for wings and engine assemblies, con-structed the first prototype. The C-160 is a medium twin-turboprop transport designed to the requirements of the German Luftwaffe and French air force. A commercial version will be available. Maximum payload is 35,270 lb, which can consist of, for example, cargo, missiles, tanks, armored or other vehicles, 81 troopers or paratroopers and 62 stretchers with four accompanying doctors. Loading is done via a ramp under the tail.

# Kennedy backs the SST

*Kennedy: the US needs the SST.*

*Colorado Springs, Colorado, June 5*
With the US already about two years behind the Anglo-French Concorde effort, President Kennedy today backed the development of a US supersonic transport (SST) which would be even better. In an address to 30,000 people attending graduation exercises for the Air Force Academy, the US president said: "It is my judgement that this government should immediately commence a new program, in partnership with private industry, to develop at the earliest practical date the prototype of a commercially successful supersonic transport superior to that being built in any other country of the world."

He pledged his administration to make every "reasonable effort" to maintain the US's world leadership in long-range commercial aircraft. Referring indirectly to the Concorde, he admitted that he had been "spurred by competition from across the Atlantic".

The president expects the US aircraft industry to design "an aircraft capable of transporting people and goods, safely, swiftly, and at prices the traveler can afford and the airlines find profitable". He said the government would "rely heavily on the flexibility and ingenuity of private enterprise", but added that the SST would be pushed forward only if the initial design and development work showed it would be commercially feasible. He is expected to ask Congress for an extra $100 million in this year's budget to spur the SST program forward (→ Oct 14).

# Phantom F-4C, new tactical fighter, flies

*The F-4C Phantom II is fitted to fill a variety of roles in USAF service.*

*St Louis, Missouri, May 27*
The first USAF version of the US Navy's F-4 Phantom II fighter took to the air today. The air force model – originally to be the F-110 but now designated F-4C – retains the folding wing and arresting gear found on the Navy F-4Bs, and externally the two airplanes look alike. The USAF will fly the Phantom with two pilots instead of a pilot-radar operator combination, and so the rear cockpit is fitted with flight controls. The USAF version has a receptacle for in-flight refueling by boom instead of a retractable probe. Because the USAF will use the Phantom as an air-superiority fighter, a fighter/bomber and as a nuclear strike aircraft, it will have a different avionics array, and many minor changes (→ Nov 20).

# Atlantic hero Lindbergh impressed by Mystère 20 executive jet

*The Mystère 20 has a bright future if, as Charles Lindbergh urges, Pan Am buys it for its business fleet.*

*Bordeaux, France, May 4*
The Dassault Mystère 20 executive jet prototype made its first flight today at the Merignac airfield near here. It is the first such aircraft to be built in France, although Dassault planned a business jet named the Mediterranée ten years ago.

The prototype has two 3,300-pound thrust Pratt & Whitney JT12A turbojets, but production Mystère 20s will have the quieter, more fuel-efficient General Electric CF700. The aircraft seats eight passengers, or 12 without tables.

A short time before the Mystère 20s flew today, the aircraft was examined by a delegation from Pan Am led by none other than veteran flyer Charles Lindbergh. Pan Am is setting up a Business Jets division and has sent Lindbergh to examine European types. Although he was unable to see the aircraft fly, he was impressed enough to telegraph Pan Am: "Have found your bird!"

The French airplane is dearer than its main European rival, Britain's D.H.125, partly because it is slightly larger and has powered flight controls. But these features should help the Mystère 20 penetrate the US market (→ Jul 10, 1964).

# Tereshkova is first woman cosmonaut

*Kazakhstan, June 16*
The USSR pulled off another space coup today by putting the first woman into space. Twenty-six-year-old pilot Lieutenant Valentina Vladimirovna Tereshkova was launched at 12.30am (Moscow time) in Vostok 6 from the Baikonur space center in eastern Kazakhstan.

In orbit she joined Lieutenant Valery Bykovsky, blasted into space two days ago on Vostok 5. They are in radio communication, with call signs "Seagull" (Vostok 6) and "Hawk", and have sent joint messages to Soviet premier Khrushchev. He replied: "Now you see what women are capable of."

Tereshkova is orbiting every 88 minutes at about 18,000mph, at altitudes of between 112 and 143 miles above the Earth. This is the second two-craft mission, following Vostoks 3 and 4 last year. They came within miles of each other, a rehearsal for link-ups in the future.

# Airlines impressed with BAC One-Eleven

*Hampshire, England, August 20*
The British Aircraft Corporation's BAC One-Eleven made a successful first flight at Hurn airfield near Bournemouth today. It is the first really modern, short-haul jet.

The One-Eleven began life as the Hunting H.107. When Hunting was taken over by BAC it was enlarged, the number of seats rising from 32 to 59 and finally to 89. Instead of BS.75 turbofans, the engines are Rolls-Royce Speys, each of 10,400-lb thrust. These have the advantage of having been tried and tested for the three-engined Trident. Already the One-Eleven has attracted favorable comment from airlines around the world. BAC sees it as "the jet successor to the Viscount", and like its turbo-prop predecessor it will be developed in different versions; so far BAC has announced the Series 200, the more powerful and longer-ranged Series 300, and the Series 400 tailored to the US market, with lift-dumpers and drop-down passenger oxygen masks.

With France's Caravelle jet obsolescent, and no US competitor in sight, the jet's future looks rosy. Sales forecasts point to the Viscount's figure of 445 (→Oct 22).

*The promising BAC One-Eleven comes in to land after its maiden flight.*

# X-15 pushes altitude record higher still

*New heights: Walker and the X-15.*

*California, Aug 22*
NASA test pilot Joe Walker today took the North American X-15 rocket airplane from Edwards Air Force Base to 354,200 feet – just over 67 miles. It is a new record for flight in a winged aircraft.

Despite the record, eclipsing the one of 348,700 feet he set on July 19, Walker was not satisfied. His goal was 360,000 feet, and he feels he missed it because of the inaccuracy of a new instrument, an altitude predictor, used for the first time today. It is designed to tell the pilot when to shut the X-15's engine or lower the angle of climb to avoid overshooting the test objective. Walker said: "Near the top of the climb I had an altitude prediction of 362,000 feet, so I nosed her over a little. It looks like the predictor was off" (→Nov 18, 1966).

# Short Skyvan transport proves its worth

*Belfast, N Ireland, October 31*
Since exchanging its former piston engines for two 520-hp Turbomeca Astazou turboprops and flying in this form on October 2, the prototype Short Skyvan has aroused huge interest the world over. A major sales tour begins next year.

In order to develop a light and rugged transport, Short Brothers established a Light Aircraft Division in Belfast in 1959. The SC.7 Skyvan, featuring a perfectly square section box fuselage and rear loading-ramp, was developed with company funds and first flew on January 17. To ensure rigidity, most of the fuselage has a double skin, the outer flat or single-curved, bonded to an inner corrugated skin.

*Short's box-like Skyvan transport, which is winning orders all over the world.*

# Six die in a helicopter crash at Idlewild

*New York, October 15*
Three passengers and three crew died today when a New York Airways (NYA) Boeing Vertol 107 helicopter crashed and burst into flames shortly after take-off from Idlewild airport. Five men were injured trying to save the victims, who are the first fatalities for the airline. NYA has grounded the three remaining helicopters in its fleet, all twin-rotor 107s, pending an inquiry into the disaster.

An initial federal investigation indicates that a 4-foot section of a rotor blade broke off in flight. The noise this would make would be loud enough to account for the reports of some eye-witnesses who said they heard an explosion.

**The flight director clears a Tu-114 for take off at Moscow Vnukovo.**

# Interceptor version of spyplane tested

*USA, August 7*
In 1960 a design competition was held for a strategic reconnaissance airplane which could fly faster than Mach 3 at over 80,000 feet. The idea was a spyplane which could fly fast and high enough to be impervious to anti-aircraft missiles, thus escaping the fate of Gary Powers's U-2 [*see page 585*]. Boeing, North American and General Dynamics each submitted designs, but it was the genius of Clarence "Kelly" Johnson and his team at Lockheed's "Skunk Works" which won the contract for the project.

The A-12 flew for the first time on April 26, 1962. It was so successful that a prototype interceptor version, the YF-12A, was ordered, and it was this which flew for the first time today (→ Feb 29, 1964).

*Parts of the YF-12A's skin heat up to 1,060ºF (570ºC) at speeds of Mach 3.*

# Pan Am and TWA put weight behind the SST

*Washington, DC, October 14*
Many US airlines have said that they want to buy the supersonic transport, (SST), which is being developed as a rival to the Anglo-French Concorde in a joint government-industry program. So today two huge carriers, Pan Am and TWA, put $2.1 million on the table to back their words. Pan Am has put down $1.5 million with the Federal Aviation Agency on 15 SSTs and TWA $600,000 on six. This will be used to defray the estimated $1 billion SST development costs, which are being shared by the aircraft industry, airlines and the federal government (→ Jan 28, 1964).

# Transport takes off

*Marietta, Georgia, December 17*
After a remarkably fast design and development timetable, the first C-141A StarLifter built by Lockheed-Georgia made a successful first flight here today. It is seen as the first of 284 for the USAF's Military Air Transport Service (MATS). The C-141 is urgently needed to modernize the MATS fleet – virtually all piston-engined aircraft. The military's specification called for a 60,000-pound payload and a range of over 3,500 nautical miles. The C-141 Starlifter is powered by four Pratt & Whitney TF33 turbofans (→ Nov 14, 1966).

**The new way to go water-skiing.**

# Business rivalry hots up

*The pacy Learjet 23 began life as a design for a fierce-looking warplane.*

*The Mitsubishi MU-2, a seven-seater turboprop, can reach speeds of 350mph.*

*The Jet Commander eight-seater business jet first flew on January 27.*

*Wichita, Kansas, October 7*
While the giants of the aviation world are fighting for supremacy in the stratosphere, an equally fierce battle is under way among smaller companies in the lucrative executive aircraft market. William Lear's $11 million investment in his rakishly lined Learjet 23, N 801L, which first flew today, is clearly about to pay off, with orders on the company's books for more than 14 aircraft at a cost of $600,000 apiece.

Businessmen do not seem to mind the cramped interior of this ten-seater, the wing of which started life as a design for a fighter/bomber. Lear makes no excuses for it; he tells potential buyers: "You can't stand up in a Jaguar, either." Slower but more spacious than the Lear Jet is the twin-jet Aero Commander, which first took to the skies in January. It can seat eight comfortably.

It was almost inevitable that the renascent Japanese aircraft industry should become involved in the business airplane market, and Mitsubishi has produced the impressive MU-2, a high-winged aircraft with pressurized fuselage and two wing-mounted turboprop engines. It made its first flight on September 23. Not least, the big, rear-engined Jet Commander is now flying (→ Jul 31, 1964).

# Long-haul airline formed by merger

*France, October 1*
French overseas airlines UAT and TAI merged today to form a new long-haul carrier: UTA, l'Union des transports aeriens. The new company will employ 4,900 people, including 630 aircrew, operating a fleet of 29 aircraft comprising two de Havilland Herons, six DC-8s, two DC-7Cs, 13 DC-6As and Bs and six DC-4s. It inherits a route network of some 118,000 miles covering most of the countries of Africa as well as the Middle East, the Far East, Indonesia, New Caledonia, New Zealand, Fiji, French Polynesia, Australia, Hawaii and the west coast of the US.

*France's unified long-haul airline.*

# 'Big Lift' trial tests US army's mobility

*[West] Germany, October 25*
Despite its commitment to Nato, the US has never before demonstrated its capacity for rapid reinforcement of its army in Europe. Now in Operation Big Lift, which ended today, a fleet of Lockheed C-130 Hercules transporters with fighter escorts has done so, moving the entire US Second Armored Division from Fort Hood, Texas, to West Germany. In-flight refueling was provided by Strategic Air Command KC-135 Stratotankers.

# British airlines face probe of finances

*London, November 22*
Sir Giles Guthrie has replaced Sir Matthew Slattery as BOAC chairman. Minister of aviation Julian Amery suggested in a BBC interview that there had been "very serious weaknesses of management". There has been a probe into BOAC's deficit of £12.9m for 1962-63. This compares favorably with £14.4m for 1961-62, but the accumulated deficit is now £77m. A worldwide slump in ticket sales, and the British government's insistence that BOAC buy British aircraft when it would rather buy American, are cited as reasons. Sir Matthew said last year, over using BOAC as an instrument of national policy: "To expect a company to do something which is not commercial and then, when it has lost money doing it, to expect it to pay interest on the money, is crazy."

# Britain's secret TSR.2 is shown to press

*First glimpse of the TSR.2 bomber.*

*Surrey, England, October 28*
Selected pressmen were today allowed in to see the prototype TSR.2 supersonic bomber at the Weybridge works of Vickers-Armstrongs, now part of British Aircraft Corporation. Photographs of the plane were released a week ago. Powered by two Bristol Siddeley Olympus turbojets, each rated at 30,610-lb thrust with afterburner, TSR.2 is designed to take off from short unpaved strips. It will, the makers hope, penetrate enemy airspace at about Mach 2.5 and, to escape detection by radar, fly closer to the ground than any other aircraft. It carries a crew of two.

The TSR.2 will carry nuclear or conventional weapons and special reconnaissance sensors, such as side-looking radar. Even without spare fuel tanks it will have a very long range of operation. Because of its speed, it will not need defensive armament (→ Sep 27, 1964).

# For business or pleasure, business is booming for light airplanes

*Vero Beach, Fla, December 6*
Yet again the Piper Cherokee, based here at the Piper research and development center, is in the news. Today saw the first flight of the enlarged and more powerful Cherokee Six, which instead of seating four adults can carry seven.

The Cherokee Six is only one of more than 20 new light-aircraft models, or new versions of older models, to have flown for the first time this year. The number of customers for light airplanes in the US and Canada has soared more than anywhere else, but almost every country is experiencing brisk sales; this is also the case in Britain, which has very little in the way of a light-airplane industry of its own. Apart from the US, the big producers are found in France, Italy, Brazil and Czechoslovakia, with Poland, Romania and Japan growing rapidly. Piper, Cessna, Beech and Mooney, in the US, and Reims, Socata and Robin, in France, have been particularly hard-pressed to meet the demand. For example, last year Cessna delivered 3,124 aircraft, and total deliveries for this year will exceed 3,200.

For the increasing numbers who can afford them, light aircraft are becoming accepted as almost essential for business, pleasure and tourism. As demand grows yearly, so too does the quality of the aircraft. Today very few are sold without at least communications radio, and a high proportion have navigational aids for flying in all weathers.

*Home take-off: houses at Fresno, California, have one area to leave your airplane and another for your car.*

With a total of 1,832 produced, Boeing's Model 727 short/medium-haul airliner became the best-selling commercial transport aircraft in the world.

SOCATA's MS.881 Rallye-Club was a popular trainer and tourer.

Piper's PA-32 Cherokee Six was a PA-28 with a 30-in fuselage stretch.

The DINFIA IA.50 Guarani II was a 10/15-seat turboprop transport.

The Riley Dove Executive 400, a re-engined conversion of the D.H.104.

France's entry in the growing business-jet market was the Dassault Falcon 20, first flown under the name of Mystère XX. It was selected by Pan Am.

Another Argentinian DINFIA light-plane design was the IA.51.

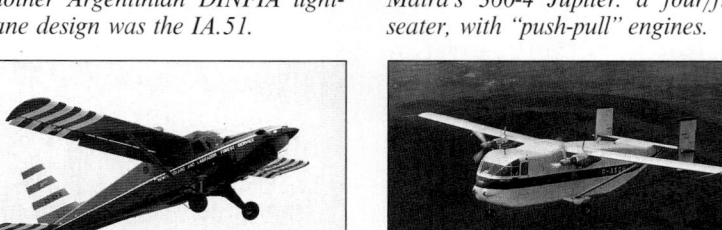

Matra's 360-4 Jupiter: a four/five-seater, with "push-pull" engines.

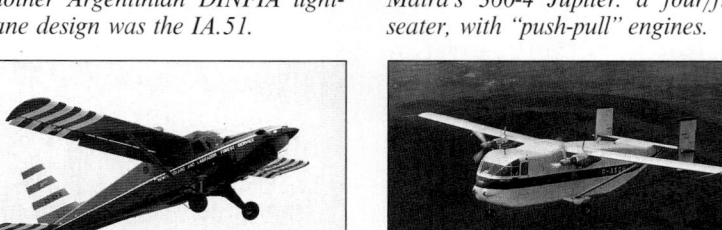

The DHC-2 Mk.III Turbo-Beaver was powered by a PT6A turboprop.

Shorts' SC.7 Skyvan was intended as a "go anywhere" cargo aircraft.

Mainstay of the Soviet long-haul fleet was the four-jet Ilyushin Il-62.

India's first indigenous jet trainer was the HAL Kiran II (Viper II).

The BAC One-Eleven Series 200 was one of several early designs aimed at producing a short-range jet-airliner, and it sold well around the world.

Fast, stylish and much in demand, the Learjet 23, using the wing of the Swiss FFA P.16A fighter, paved the way for a large family of Learjet designs.

The long-lived Jet Commander ultimately spawned the IAI Westwind.

The Tupolev Tu-134 is roughly equivalent to the BAC 1-11 or DC-9.

The five-seat Navion Rangemaster sold in small numbers in 1961-63.

Many Cessna Model 206 Super Sky-wagons can still be found in service.

Sweden's Saab 105 military jet-trainer has a tactical attack role.

Powered by Astazou engines, Mitsubishi's MU-2A had up to nine seats.

The initial Phantom II model for the USAF was the McDonnell Douglas F-4C, which brought with it a revolution in jet-combat thinking.

The all-round performance and range of the Blackburn Buccaneer were considerably improved in the Rolls-Royce-Spey-engined S.2 version.

The RF-4C Phantom supplied tactical reconnaissance for the USAF.

Hawker Siddeley's Andover military transport was fitted with a ramp.

The Franco-German-designed Transall C-160 was originally developed as a military transport, but some did find their way into commercial service.

First of the USAF's jet-powered strategic transports was the Lockheed C-141A StarLifter, which serves with Military Airlift Command; 285 were built.

Sikorsky's S-61R was known as the CH-3C in USAF transport service.

Germany's EWR-Süd VJ 101C X-1 tilt-wing VTOL research aircraft.

Northrop's F-5A Freedom Fighter, intended as a simple combat aircraft.

The Hughes OH-6A Cayuse, winner of a giant US Army competition.

The Hunting H.126 blown-flap research aircraft used an Orpheus jet.

The privately-funded Curtiss-Wright X-19A, a high-speed VTOL.

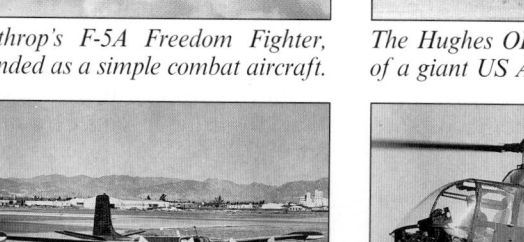

On Mark B-26K Counter Invader: a rebuilt Second World War design.

The US Army's Hiller OH-5A was developed into the civilian FH-1100.

# 1964

 4,104mph
USA
Joseph Walker
North American X-15
Jun 27, 1962

 24,325 miles
USA
Archie Old Jr
Boeing B-52B
Jan 18, 1957

 354,200ft
USA
Joseph Walker
North American X-15
Aug 22, 1963

 550,000lb
USA
North American
XB-70A Valkyrie

 32,500lb thrust
USA
Pratt & Whitney
JT1 1D-20B

**Amman, January 4**
Pope Paul VI lands in Jordan in a special Alitalia DC-8; it is the first time that a pope has used an airplane for an official visit.

**Wichita, Kansas, January 20**
The Beech King Air 90 makes its first flight; it is powered by two PT6A engines built by Pratt & Whitney Canada.

**Victoria, Australia, Jan 29**
The Royal Australian Air Force at Avalon receives its first two Mirage IIIO jet fighters; they are part of a batch built under license.

**Oklahoma City, February 3**
The Federal Aviation Agency launches Operation Bongo Mark 2 to investigate the effects of supersonic flight; over the coming months, a Convair B-58 will fly through the sound barrier at low altitude over the city (→ Jul 10).

**Paris, February 25**
French aviation pioneer and aircraft manufacturer Maurice Farman, 87, dies.

**USA, February 29**
President Johnson reveals the A-12 (he calls it the A-11) high-altitude reconnaissance plane, which first flew in 1962; it is capable of 2,000mph and will be operated by the CIA (→ Dec 22).

**London, March 11**
BEA puts the Trident airliner into scheduled passenger service for the first time on its route to Copenhagen (→ Nov 2).

**London, April 29**
BOAC introduces the VC10 jet airliner into regular passenger service, on its route to Lagos, Nigeria.→

**Cornwall, England, May 2**
BEA Helicopters Ltd opens the first helicopter passenger service in Europe with multi-engined machines, from Land's End to the Scilly Isles, using Sikorsky S-61Ns (→ Oct 6).

**California, May 7**
A Pacific Airlines Fairchild F-27 crashes near San Ramon, killing all 44 passengers and crew on board, after the pilot is shot by an intruder in the cockpit.

**England, May 7**
The British Aircraft Corporation Super VC10 makes its first flight; it is a version of the VC10 which has a longer fuselage, more powerful engines and greater fuel capacity (→ Apr 1, 1965).

**USA, May 11**
Jacqueline Cochran sets a new women's speed record, flying a Lockheed F-104G Starfighter at 1,429.2mph over a course of 15-25km [9-15 miles].

**USA, May 12**
American flyer Joan Merriam Smith lands her Piper Apache to complete the second round-the-world flight by a woman; she took 56 days.

**Washington, DC, May 21**
Boeing and Lockheed are asked by the government to prepare design-concept documents for the airframe of the US supersonic transport (SST); General Electric and Pratt & Whitney will do the same for the engine (→ Dec 31, 1966).

**Paris, May 21**
British actor Roger Moore, star of James Bond films, *The Saint* and *Ivanhoe*, is Air France's eight-millionth Caravelle passenger when he flies from London to Nice.

**English Channel, June 6**
Silver City Airways, which established the first British cross-Channel car ferry service by air in June 1948, carries its one millionth passenger on this route.

**Antarctica, June 26**
An LC-130 aircraft of US Navy Air Development Squadron 6 lands at McMurdo Sound to complete the first flight to Antarctica in the winter season.

**California, July 16**
Ryan's Model 43 (XV-5A) experimental VTOL airplane makes its first vertical take-off and landing, at Edwards Air Force Base.

**Wichita, Kansas, July 31**
The Learjet, the world's first aircraft developed specifically for the business market, receives full federal certification in record time, just nine months after its maiden flight (→ Jun 21, 1965).

**Vietnam, August 5**
The first naval air strike on North Vietnam is carried out from the carriers USS *Constellation* and USS *Ticonderoga*; one pilot is killed and one captured, the US Navy's first combat losses in Vietnam.→

**Cyprus, August 9**
The United Nations intervenes to end Turkish air attacks, which have taken place over the past two days on Greek-Cypriot positions.

**Washington, DC, August 10**
US officials report that China has delivered MiG-15 and MiG-17 fighters to Hanoi, together with pilots to train North Vietnamese airmen how to fly them.

**Stratford, Conn, October 14**
The prototype Sikorsky CH-53A Sea Stallion heavy assault helicopter makes its first flight.

**England, November 2**
The Hawker Siddeley Trident 1E, a "stretched" version of the Trident airliner capable of carrying 115 passengers, makes its first flight.

**London, November 19**
Britain's new Labour government announces its withdrawal from the Anglo-French Concorde supersonic transport project (→ Jan 20, 1965).

**[West] Germany, November 20**
Two large aircraft manufacturers, Heinkel and VFW, agree to merge; Heinkel will become a subsidiary of VFW but will keep its corporate identity.

**Sydney, November 26**
Qantas inaugurates its "Fiesta" service from Australia to London, by way of Fiji, Tahiti, Acapulco, Mexico City, the Bahamas and Bermuda (→ Mar 7, 1965).

**Congo [Zaïre], November 26**
Belgian paratroops are dropped from US airplanes at Kamina to launch a land attack on the capital, Stanleyville, where Westerners are being held hostage by anti-government troops; the operation is largely successful, although 30 hostages and seven paratroopers are killed in the operation.

**Washington, DC, December 8**
A United Air Lines Caravelle makes the first landing in the USA completely controlled by computer (automatic touchdown).

**Laos, December 14**
USAF tactical fighters launch Operation Barrel Roll, an attack on the vital Communist supply route in northern Laos known as "the Ho Chi Minh Trail".

**Washington, DC, December 22**
President Johnson approves the development of the Lockheed CX-HLS heavy logistic transport for the USAF.

**USA, December 22**
The SR-71A long-range reconnaissance airplane flies for the first time; developed from the A-12, it is capable of flying at 3.2 times the speed of sound and as high as 100,000 feet.→

**St Petersburg, Fla, December 26**
Max Conrad lands his Piper Twin Comanche light airplane here after a non-stop flight of 7,878.26 miles from Cape Town, setting a new world non-stop-flight distance record for an aircraft in this category.

*A Boeing KC-135F of the French Armée de l'Air refueling Dassault Mirage IVA bombers. It can deliver six tons of gas in six minutes. ▶*

## Pilots are specially trained to help the Vietnamese to fly

*Vietnam, February*
Most USAF pilots fly modern aircraft such as the F-105 Thunderchief attack bomber, the Mach 2 B-58 Hustler bomber or a modern transport or aerial tanker. But there are also USAF pilots who fly propeller-driven airplanes of Second World War vintage. They are the advisors to the South Vietnamese air force (VNAF).

In one form or another they have been here since November 1960, helping the VNAF by showing them how to fly observation, strike, close-air-support and supply missions – in short, how to run an air force. The training takes place under the codename Farm Gate.

The advisors are from the USAF's Special Air Warfare Center, run by Tactical Air Command at Eglin Air Force Base (biggest in the USAF), Florida. They have been trained to live and work in primitive environments and to use aircraft not requiring the support equipment and facilities of modern combat airplanes – planes such as the Douglas B-26 Invader and A-1 Skyraider, the North American T-28 Trojan and Cessna O-1 Bird Dog. Their contribution to the war, as pilots, maintenance men and communications officers at the same time, is significant.

**Minister of aviation Julian Amery, Britain's representative in talks with France over the Concorde supersonic transport.**

# American firms compete for the SST

*SST designs: (top) from Lockheed and (below) from North American.*

*An artist's conception of Boeing's SST design, Model 733, coming in to land. Its variable-sweep wing is forward, allowing operation from a shorter runway.*

*Washington, DC, January 28*
Several of the biggest firms in the US aerospace industry are rushing to take the lead in a gigantic contest to build the supersonic transport (SST) launched by the late President Kennedy last year. The administration has set up a special SST Program Office of the Federal Aviation Agency (FAA) to evaluate bids. Back in 1959 Convair was in the lead in this field, basing its proposals on the existing B-58 bomber. This was knocked out by the consensus that, unlike the Anglo-French Concorde, the US's SST should be a steel airplane capable of cruising at Mach 3. This stipulation gradually eliminated most contenders, while NASA carried out exhaustive tests to determine the best configuration.

Today the front-runners are: Boeing's SCAT-16 variable-sweep (swing-wing) Model 733; Lockheed's CL-823; and North American's NAC-60 (→ May 21).

## Boeing's 727 makes a smooth debut for Eastern and United

*Boston, February 11*
Boeing's 727 has had a smooth and untroubled debut in airline service. Both Eastern, which introduced the airliner on February 1, and United Airlines, which introduced it on February 6, report minimal teething problems and excellent economics. United says that it is delighted with the performance of the 727. At this stage, however, the 727 is tailored to the needs of these two airlines, and Boeing will need to attract a wider range of operators if it is to reach the 300 hoped-for sales. So far there are 127 on the order book.

The 727 closely resembles the 707, the main difference being the rear-engined layout with two engines in pods on either side of the fuselage and a third mounted in the fuselage, a configuration similar to its British equivalent, the Hawker Siddeley Trident, which will receive its certificate of airworthiness this month and will enter passenger service with British European Airways (BEA) in April.

*The Trident may pay a high price for being made smaller and short-ranged.*

*The 727 carries all three JT8D engines on or inside the rear fuselage.*

# All hands to pump for Concorde project

*Toulouse, France, March 1*
No special company has been formed to build the Anglo-French Concorde SST. Instead, a rather loose management structure has been created of officials from the two governments, from BAC and Aérospatiale for the airframe, and for Rolls-Royce and SNECMA for the Olympus 593 engine. In turn, these companies are already signing contracts with hundreds of British, French and US suppliers.

Following discussions with possible airline customers, the design has been enlarged, matching the growth in thrust of the engine. Concorde will have a bigger wing and longer body, seating 118 (→ May 1).

*Lifting a spin model Concorde.*

# Crack strike force is formed in France

*Taverny, France, January 14*
A new strategic air force (Force Aérienne Stratégique, or FAS) has been created within the structure of the French air force. The FAS is under orders to maintain itself at the highest state of readiness and be capable of striking immediately on the direct command of President Charles de Gaulle.

Its headquarters will be in a secret location in a forest in the Val d'Oise, and its force of Mirage IV jets will be situated at nine French air bases – four aircraft at each. The aircraft will be maintained at a central depot in Bordeaux.

# Kestrel jump jet, built for Nato, lifts off

*The V/STOL Kestrel can take off at night without any ground lights.*

*Surrey, England, March 7*
The Kestrel vertical/short take-off and landing (V/STOL) airplane, developed from the Hawker Siddeley P.1127, made its first flight today at Kingston. But with the RAF still pressing for a supersonic V/STOL and the British government looking for military economies, its future rests on the opinion of the Nato Tripartite Evaluation (TES) Squadron – with pilots from Britain, the US and West Germany – which will begin tests this year. The P.1127 was the outstanding design tendered for the Nato competition for a V/STOL tactical support aircraft. Yet it might have been dropped but for American Larry Levy, who persuaded Nato to conduct an evaluation. The Kestrel has a more powerful Pegasus 5 engine than the P.1127, and a swept wing (→ Oct 15).

# Belfast firm unveils bulky cargo airplane

*Short brothers: the enormous Belfast beside the compact, box-like Skyvan.*

*Belfast, Northern Ireland, Jan 5*
With flying boats now consigned to the aviation history books, Short Brothers have turned their skills in large aircraft manufacture to producing a long-range, heavy-lift cargo aircraft.

The result is the Short Belfast, which flew from the company's Northern Ireland works for the first time today. It is a hybrid, owing much of its design and many of its parts to other aircraft. In collaboration with the Bristol Aeroplane Company and Canadair, Short examined several projects before the Belfast – based largely on the Britannia, with parts from the Canadair CL-28 and Vickers Vanguard – reached the drawing board. Early versions will go to the RAF and they will initially ferry Blue Streak missiles to Woomera, Australia, for testing (→ Jan 20, 1966).

# Jerrie Mock is first woman to fly solo around the world

*Columbus, Ohio, April 17*
A speck appeared in the sky. As it grew larger, the high-pitched drone of the Cessna 180's Continental piston engine became audible to the thousands of well-wishers at Port Columbus. They waited and watched, murmuring at every twitch of the wings. Tiny against the vastness of the runway, the monoplane touched down at 9.36pm and the crowd roared its approval. A message from the control tower went to the pilot: "Jerrie, we've got a cold one on the rocks waiting for you."

Housewife Geraldine "Jerrie" Mock, 37, had made history. Since

*Jerrie Mock during a stop in Cairo.*

March 19, she had flown 23,103 miles in just under 29 and a half days with 21 stops, making her the first woman ever to complete a solo flight around the world. As she stepped from her red and white airplane, named *Spirit of Columbus* in recognition of that earlier heroic airplane *Spirit of St Louis*, her husband, Russell, and their three children rushed up to hug and kiss her. Meanwhile, American airwoman Joan Merriam Smith, 27, is in Australia on her own solo global flight. She set off two days before Mock from Oakland and will next fly to Papua (→ May 12).

# DHC-5 Buffalo follows DHC-4 Caribou

*The DHC-5 Buffalo, essentially an uprated version of the company's Caribou.*

**Canada, April 9**
It was inevitable that the enterprising de Havilland Canada company should seek to repeat the outstanding success of the versatile Caribou, which has been sold to armies and police forces in 14 countries as well as to several airlines.

A longer and uprated version of the Caribou, the DHC-5 Buffalo, which flew for the first time today, has similar capabilities, except that it will carry more troops (41 troopers, or 35 paratroopers), or civil passengers and freight. Its predecessor carried a 8,740-pound payload.

With its General Electric T64 turboprop engines offering 3,133hp, the Buffalo can lift 18,000 pounds over 691 miles. With this vast country's numerous remote outposts, many with rudimentary landing strips, there has always been a need for an aircraft with a short take-off and landing capacity. So de Havilland Canada's new Buffalo should find a home market.

On the other hand it is unlikely to repeat the success of its predecessors, the Beaver, Otter and Caribou, all of which were bought in large numbers by US services.

# Hansa jet features forward-swept wings

**Hamburg, [W] Germany, April 21**
Distinguished by its striking forward-swept wings, the prototype HFB 320 Hansa executive jet made its first flight today at Hamburg's Finkenwerder airfield. Construction of the prototype began two years ago. The forward-swept configuration was pioneered in Germany during the war and enables the strong spars to pass behind the cabin. Thus, the cabin is not cut into above or below and provides accommodation for four to 12 passengers. Two GE CJ610-1 turbojets of 2,850-lb thrust are fitted.

*The Luftwaffe has ordered a version of the HFB 320 Hansa as a jet trainer.*

# Research plane tests wings for Concorde

*The BAC 221 is to test the ogival "Gothic delta" wing to high angle of attack.*

**Bristol, England, May 1**
The British Aircraft Corporation's experimental "mini-Concorde", the BAC 221, flew here for the first time today. It will do its testing in the Bordeaux region in the south of France where the weather is better and the sparsely-populated country is more suited to frequent sonic booms. In France, it is possible for supersonic flights to be conducted at levels down to 3,500 feet. Since 1957, the British government has only allowed supersonic flights at altitudes below 30,000 feet over a limited route in East Anglia between Bedford and the Wash. After years of research, British engineers are happy that the projected delta-wing configuration and the "droop nose" are suitable for the Anglo-French airliner.

The BAC 221 is by no means a new airplane. It is, in fact, one of the most famous aircraft in the world. It was built in 1953 as the first Fairey FD.2, WG774, which on March 10, 1956, set a new world speed record of 1,132mph. The rebuilt aircraft will be slower because the engine inlets are less direct (they start under the wing roots and curve inwards and upwards), the fuselage is longer and the wing area appreciably greater. Only the afterburning Rolls-Royce Avon engine has remained substantially unaltered (→ Nov 19).

*The 221's landing gear is far higher than before, for added clearance.*

# Supersonic boom is cause for complaint

**Oklahoma City, July 10**
A six-month test of the effects of sonic booms has ended with mixed reactions from the 800,000 inhabitants of this area. Supersonic USAF aircraft have created a total of 1,253 booms to simulate the effect of supersonic airliners regularly crossing the US. The Federal Aviation Authority recieved 8,335 telephone complaints and the USAF 5,036 claims for damages, but many people were late for work today; they had come to rely on the first boom of the day, promptly at 7am, to wake them up.

# The BAC VC10 goes into airline service

*London, England, April 29*
BOAC added a new British airliner to its fleet today: the BAC VC10. The inaugural service was from London to Lagos, Nigeria. The VC10 has been tailored to the airline's long-distance routes, especially to Africa, Australia and the Far East, where conditions are hardest: temperatures can be very high, and runways short and at high altitude, where a great deal of power is needed to get airborne. Typical are the airports of Johannesburg, Nairobi and Singapore. Nevertheless, a 35,000-lb payload was required and a still-air range of 4,000 miles. It was, therefore, essential that the airplane was de-signed to be at the very forefront of modern civil aviation technology.

The resulting airliner is in fact suitable for all BOAC's long-haul routes, including over the Atlantic. An unusual feature of the VC10 is the four Rolls-Royce 22,500-lb thrust Conway Mk 540 turbofan engines, mounted in pairs at the rear of the fuselage, which make it very quiet in the 135-seat cabin. BOAC has ordered 12 of the standard version and 30 of the Super which has a fuselage 13 ft longer to accomo-date 163 passengers. The first Super should fly next month. It will have a cruising speed of 580mph and a range of 4,450 miles even when fly-ing from short runways.

*The well-laid-out flight deck of BOAC's new VC10 long-haul airliner.*

**The twin-turboprop King Air 90 business airplane is rolling off the production lines at Beechcraft's Wichita factory. The compact transport can carry two crew and six passengers at a speed of over 250mph.**

# Pan Am modifies its fleet of Mystère 20s

*The Mystère 20 as modified for Pan Am, with new General Electric turbofans.*

*Melun-Villaroche, France, July 10*
Pan Am observers were today re-ported to be well satisfied by the first flight of a Dassault Mystère 20 prototype, which has been specially modified at their request.

It is a year since the US airline signed a contract to buy a number of these twin-engined executive jets (capable of seating up to 14) for its Business Jets division. Having ta-ken the airplane on a number of test flights, the airline concluded that better efficiency and reduced noise would be achieved by replacing the two Pratt & Whitney JT12A-8 turbojets with General Electric CF 700 aft-fan turbofans. The air-craft's internal circuitry has also been substantially modified.

# Tilt-wing vertical take-off transport flies

*The remarkable XC-142A tilts its wing to fly foward after a vertical take-off.*

*Dallas, Texas, September 29*
The first – conventional – take-off of the XC-142A vertical take-off and landing (VTOL) transport took place today at the former US Navy plant of LTV Corporation (formerly Chance Vought). The aircraft has been produced in partnership with two other firms, Hiller and Ryan. The companies won a design com-petition in September 1961 for a VTOL transport which could be used by the US armed forces. All three services are interested in the XC-142A, which bears the word "Tri-Service" on its tail.

The aircraft is unique in that its four 2,850-hp General Electric T64 turboprops are mounted on a wing which can pivot upward through 90 degrees to permit vertical take-off and landing (→ Jan 11, 1965).

# Valkyrie rides in the skies at Mach 3

*North American warrior: the huge, ultra-modern Valkyrie bomber can cruise for hours at 2,000mph or Mach 3.*

*Palmdale, California, September 21*
The first prototype of the North American XB-70A Valkyrie took off today from the airfield here, where it was built, and flew to the test airfield of its prospective customer at Edwards Air Force Base. A few mishaps occurred: one of the six 30,000-lb thrust GE J93-3 engines oversped and had to be shut down, and on landing the brake computers malfunctioned and locked the two left main landing-gear tires, which exploded. But these are

trivialities compared with the fact that the program to put a gigantic Mach 3 (2,000mph) bomber into the sky has succeeded.

The colossal airplane is made almost entirely of stainless steel. The huge (6,300-square-foot) wing is very thin, with a sharp leading edge, and has an enormous outer section which can be turned down in cruising flight to box in the airflow past the 110-foot-long engine housing. At the front is the four-man cockpit, with short foreplanes

sprouting on each side. Behind the cockpit and giant electronics bays are huge ammonia and water tanks into which the Freon refrigeration system carries excess heat. Between the engine ducts is the bay for the Valkyrie's future weapons.

Whether the USAF will ever deploy the Valkyrie is another matter, however. Controversy surrounds the 265-tonner; its cost will be phenomenal, and missiles of various kinds may render it both vulnerable and unnecessary (→ May 19, 1966).

## Britain's state-of-the-art TSR.2 bomber faces uncertain future

*Wiltshire, England, September 27*
After agonizing delays, the British Aircraft Corporation's new supersonic tactical strike and reconnaissance (TSR) bomber finally made its first flight today, at Boscombe Down. Called the TSR.2, it flew in the hands of test pilot Roland "Bee" Beamont and test observer Don Bowen. "I thoroughly enjoyed this flight," Beamont said.

Problems remain, however, the most immediate being the two 33,000-lb thrust Bristol Siddeley Olympus Mk 320R engines, which suffer from a "bell-mode" vibration. This is a resonance in the main shaft which at a certain rate of revolutions per minute can cause the whole engine to disintegrate.

Far more serious for the airplane is that Britain's Labour Party says it will cancel the entire program if it wins next month's general election. Its reason is basically one of

*The TSR.2 supersonic bomber is one of the most advanced aircraft ever built.*

cost, despite the fact that the TSR.2 has been given all the money it needs to make up for eight years of an official government policy of seeing the future in terms of missiles rather than manned military air-

craft. The TSR.2 is one of the most advanced and complicated aircraft ever built. Novel features include terrain-following and side-looking radar, and rough-terrain landing gear (→ Apr 6, 1965).

## US Navy warplanes carry out big raid on North Vietnam

*Vietnam, August 5*
Warplanes from the carriers USS *Ticonderoga* and USS *Constellation* in the Gulf of Tonkin today attacked torpedo-boat bases and oil-storage facilities in a five-hour raid along a 100-mile stretch of the North Vietnamese coast. The raid was in response to recent torpedo-boat attacks on two US destroyers.

The US Navy said F-4 Phantoms, F-8 Crusaders, A-4 Skyhawks and A-1 Skyraiders flew 64 sorties. About 25 patrol boats were destroyed or damaged at Queng Khe, Hongay, Loc Chau and Phuc Loi. In addition, 90 per cent of a fuel-storage facility at Vinh is now destroyed, and seven anti-aircraft

*US Navy air power close to Vietnam.*

installations in the area have been destroyed or severely damaged. Smoke belching from the blazing tanks rose to 14,000 feet.

An A-4 from the *Constellation* was shot down by anti-aircraft fire during the attack on Hongay, and pilot Lieutenant Everett Alvarez, Jr, was captured by the North Vietnamese. An A-1 from the *Constellation* was also shot down, and two other aircraft returned to their carriers with damage.

During the earlier North Vietnamese attacks on US destroyers, F-8s from the *Ticonderoga* helped drive off the attackers.

# USAF's controversial F-111 makes debut

*Fort Worth, Texas, December 21*
Ten days ahead of schedule the first of 18 prototypes of the General Dynamics F-111A tactical strike aircraft made its first flight near here today at Carswell Air Force Base.

Carswell adjoins the huge plant of General Dynamics, which won the F-111 program in November 1962, despite the preference of customers for a rival Boeing design. US defense secretary Robert McNamara insisted that General Dynamics, aided by Grumman, pro-duce F-111As for the USAF and F-111Bs for the US Navy. This flew in the face of service experts, who say the aircraft is too heavy (21 tons empty) and will be too costly.

The airplane does have original points. It has swing-wings (with the F-111B having a greater wingspan), which pivot from 16 to 72.5 degrees. On today's flight they were locked at 26 degrees. It also has Pratt & Whitney TF30 afterburning turbofan engines, giving 18,500 lb thrust each (→ Aug 23, 1965).

*The F-111 is unveiled before a large crowd at General Dynamics, Fort Worth.*

# Three air forces in tests of 'jump jet'

*Surrey, England, October 15*
Pilots, engineers and scientists of three nations – Britain, the US and West Germany – are cooperating here on the development of the Hawker Siddeley Kestrel. The aircraft, which first flew in March [*see page 623*], is set to become the world's first operational vertical take-off and landing jet warplane.

The Tripartite Evaluation Squadron (TES), formed today at Dunsfold under the command of Wing Commander D M Scrimgeour, includes air-force pilots of all three nations. It was first mooted two years ago when official interest in the project, then designated P.1127, had appeared to be running out of steam. The TES, which is jointly funded by the member countries, will begin evaluation of the Kestrel next year at RAF West Raynham.

# New helicopter can fly in all weathers

*USA, October 6*
The new Sikorsky S-61R (CH-3C to the USAF) today received the first all-weather airworthiness certificate awarded by the Federal Aviation Agency to a helicopter.

In its CH-3C military version, the aircraft, which is based on the highly successful SH-3A, meets many of the USAF's requirements for a helicopter which can remain self-supporting in a battle zone. New features of the CH-3C include the provision of a hydraulically operated rear ramp for straight-in vehicle loading, and a powerful cargo winch. An auxiliary gas-turbine power supply for engine starting and systems checking during maintenance makes the new helicopter independent of ground power supplies. The CH-3C first flew on June 17 last year.

# SR-71A will be top-secret eye in the sky

*The SR-71A, believed to be capable of reaching a speed of over Mach 3.*

*Burbank, California, December 22*
One of the most sophisticated and unusual-looking aircraft ever built made its maiden flight today. Designed and built here at Lockheed's secret plant (the so-called "Skunk Works"), the SR-71A strategic reconnaissance aircraft is intended to supersede the U-2 spyplane.

Developed from the A-12 over the past two years, it can survey more than 100,000 square miles of territory in an hour, using cameras and other sensors. Five different sensor payloads will be available.

The internal structure, airframe and skin-coating all inhibit detection by radar. Details are shrouded in secrecy, but the SR-71A is believed to be capable of Mach 3.3 and altitudes of up to 120,000 feet, making interception virtually impossible. Power comes from two massive afterburning Pratt & Whitney JT11D-20B jet engines, each of 32,500-lb thrust. To extend operational range it can be refueled in flight by the KC-135Q Stratotanker, which carries the SR-71A's special JP-7 fuel (→ Jan 7, 1966).

**Yul Brynner tends to one of the pilots on the "Flight From Ashiya".**

In the US, Beech developed a turboprop successor to the successful Queen Air business aircraft in the form of the seven/ten-seat Model 90 King Air.

Piper's roomy and comfortable PA-31 Navajo six-seat business aircraft.

Agusta's A 105, powered by a Turbo-meca-Agusta TAA 230 turboshaft.

SIAI-Marchetti's S.205: designed for engines in the 180/300-hp range.

The Aérospatiale Super Caravelle, powered by P & W JT8D turbofans.

The Hamburger Flugzeugbau HFB 320 Hansa executive transport – also offered as a 12-seat feeder-liner – featured an unusual swept-forward wing.

Piper's PA-32-260 Cherokee Six: a private single-engined six-seater.

Vying for a US Army tactical transport aircraft contract, De Havilland Canada made the DHC-5 Buffalo, a stretched, turboprop-powered Caribou.

The clipped-wing Champion Model 7ECA Citabria for aerobatic use.

SOCATA's MS.892 Rallye-Commodore was a full four-seater.

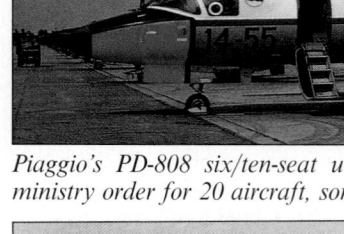

Piaggio's PD-808 six/ten-seat utility jet transport won an Italian defense ministry order for 20 aircraft, some to be used for navigation aid checking.

Vickers' stretched-fuselage Super VC10 could seat 174 passengers.

Agusta's A 101G powered by three Bristol Siddeley Gnome turboshafts.

Miles's M.100 Student Mk 2: re-vamped jet-trainer/liaison aircraft.

The Aviamilano F.260 was produced by SIAI-Marchetti as the SF.260.

Hawker Siddeley's HS.121 Trident 1E had more powerful Spey engines.

LTV/Hiller-Ryan's XC-142A tilt-wing experimental VTOL aircraft.

Erco's between-wars Ercoupe led to the Alon Model A-2 Aircoupe.

The Beagle B.242: developed from the B.218 four-seater light aircraft.

The STOL turboprop Helio Stallion Model H-550: a utility aircraft.

Convair's 48 Charger, designed to perform counter-insurgency work.

*The Vought F-8E (FN) Crusader, with blown flaps and other high-lift devices to enhance its performance at low speeds, was built for the French Navy.*

*Northrop's F-5B trainer version of the successful F-5 Freedom Fighter.*

*Bölkow's Bo 46 was fitted with Derschmidt's high-speed rotor system.*

*The Potez CM.173 served as the development aircraft for the Potez 94.*

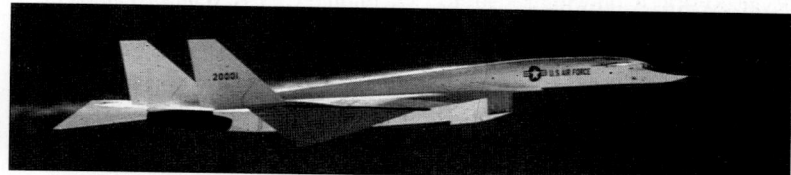

*North American was awarded a contract to develop a Mach 3 strategic bomber which appeared as the XB-70A Valkyrie, a replacement for the Boeing B-52.*

*The prototype Helwan HA-300 supersonic fighter, built near Cairo.*

*Two Ryan XV-5A VTOL lift-fan research aircraft were built.*

*The US Marine Corps used the Sikorsky CH-53A Sea Stallion.*

*The Short SC.5 Belfast heavy military transport; ten were constructed.*

*Lockheed developed the amazing SR-71 high-altitude strategic reconnaissance aircraft to replace the U-2 in service with Strategic Air Command units.*

*Hawker Siddeley's VTOL Kestrel, for US/UK/German evaluation.*

*The HAL HJT-16 Mk II Kiran trainer for the Indian Air Force.*

*BAC 221: modified Fairey Delta 2 with Concorde ogival wing planform.*

*General Dynamics gave the F-111 variable wing sweep-back to provide good take-off and landing performance and high-speed dash combat capability.*

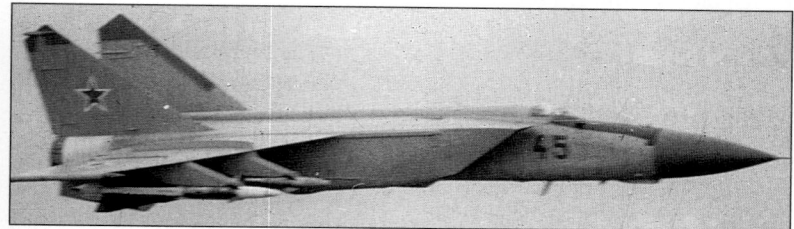

*Originally developed to counter the threat of the USAF B-70 Valkyrie, the MiG-25 became a widely-used Soviet fighter and reconnaissance aircraft.*

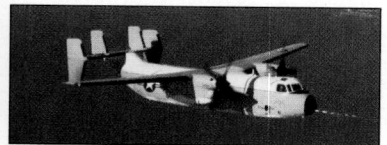

*Grumman's C-2A Greyhound was a transport version of the E-2A.*

*Hughes' XV-9A was a hot-cycle propulsion system research helicopter.*

*A supersonic replacement for the English Electric Canberra bomber, the BAC TSR.2 (Tactical Strike and Reconnaissance) was cancelled in April 1965.*

# 1965

4,104mph
USA
Joseph Walker
North American X-15
Jun 27, 1962

24,325 miles
USA
Archie Old Jr
Boeing B-52B
Jan 18, 1957

354,200ft
USA
Joseph Walker
North American X-15
Aug 22, 1963

551,147lb
USSR
Antonov
An-22 Anteus

32,500lb thrust
USA
Pratt & Whitney
JT1 1D-20B

**Fort Worth, Texas, January 11**
The Ling-Temco-Vought/Hiller/ Ryan XC-142A tilt-wing research vertical take-off and landing transport makes its first full transition from vertical to horizontal flight and back.

**London, January 20**
Britain will not, after all, withdraw from the Concorde supersonic transport project; the intention to pull out was announced by the incoming Labour government on November 19 last year (→ Sep 11).

**USA, January 20**
The Boeing Airplane Company is reorganized into the Commercial Airplane Company at Seattle and the Military Airplane Company at Wichita, Kansas.

**London, February 2**
Prime Minister Harold Wilson announces that the Hawker Siddeley P.1154 vertical/short take-off and landing strike aircraft and the HS.681 tactical transport are to be canceled; in place of the P.1154, the RAF will be equipped with a mix of Harrier and Phantom jets (→ Apr 6).

**Vietnam, February 11**
For the first time, USAF and USN aircraft have escorted VNAF A-1 Skyraiders. They were making attacks on barracks at Chanh Hoa and Vit Thulu. The A-1s, from the 514th (formely the 1st) Fighter Squadron, flew their first mission against Vin Linh three days ago (→ Feb 18).

**Medford, NJ, February 15**
Mrs Guy Maher arrives from Culver City, California, in a Hughes 300 to complete the USA's first transcontinental helicopter flight by a woman.

**Vietnam, February 18**
In the first air strike in the Vietnam conflict in which no South Vietnamese pilots take part, USAF jets attack Communist guerillas in Bin Dinh Province in support of South Vietnamese troops.

**Mayport, Florida, March 6**
A Sikorsky SH-3A Sea King piloted by J R Williford lands on the USS *Franklin D Roosevelt* after a 2,116-mile flight from the carrier USS *Hornet* at San Francisco of 15 hours 52 minutes; it is the first non-stop helicopter flight across the US.

**Los Angeles, March 25**
Pioneer Zeppelin engineer Dr Wolfgang Klemperer, 76, who became a designer for Douglas Aircraft, dies.

**Australia, March 29**
Qantas puts the Boeing 707-338C airliner into service on its route to London (→ Apr 27, 1967).

**London, April 1**
BOAC introduces the BAC (Vickers) Super VC10 on its Monarch service to New York.

**Chicago, April 6**
United Air Lines places the world's largest airliner order to date, signing contracts worth $750 million to buy, lease or have options on 144 DC-8s, 727s and 737s.

**Marignane, France, April 15**
The prototype Sud-Aviation SA 330 Puma, a medium-size transport helicopter for the army, makes its debut (→ Jun 12, 1972).

**California, May 1**
Colonel Robert L Stephens sets a world speed record of 2,062mph flying a Lockheed YF-12A.→

**England, May 14**
Hawker Siddeley delivers the 105th and last Gnat trainer of an order for the RAF; it has proved an excellent teaching airplane.

**Canada, May 20**
The de Havilland Canada DHC-6 Twin Otter STOL twin turboprop makes its maiden flight.

**England, May 26**
Pioneer British aviator and aircraft designer and manufacturer Sir Geoffrey de Havilland, 82, dies.

**Isle of Wight, England, June 13**
The prototype Britten-Norman BN-2 Islander lightweight ten-seat multirole transport makes its first flight (→ Dec 20, 1969).

**Vietnam, July 10**
USAF pilots score their first air-to-air victories of the war: Captains Thomas S Roberts and Ronald C Anderson in one F-4 and Captains Kenneth E Holcombe and Arthur C Clarke in another down two MiG-17s.

**Utica, NY, July 15**
Mohawk Airlines, which covers much of the north-eastern USA, introduces seven BAC One-Eleven airliners on its route to Newark, New Jersey; this is the first pure jet service by a US regional carrier and cuts the current flight time from 64 minutes to 36 (→ Jun 20, 1968).

**Hampshire, England, August 1**
Britain's Army Air Corps, established on September 1, 1957, is renamed Army Aviation.

**Fort Worth, Texas, August 23**
General Dynamics' F-111 fighter/ bomber makes its first flight at Mach 2, while at an altitude of 40,000 feet (→ Dec 31, 1967).

**England, August 26**
BEA signs a contract worth £30 million for 15 Hawker Siddeley Trident 2E airliners, with options on ten more (→ Jun 3, 1966).

**USA, September 27**
The first of seven Ling-Temco-Vought A-7A Corsair II attack aircraft built for evaluation by the US Navy makes its first flight.

**USA, September 30**
Fairchild-Hiller completes its acquisition of Republic Aviation for $17.6 million in cash and $1.5 in shares, as well as assuming $12.2 million of Republic's liabilities.

**Vietnam, October 23**
The Northrop F-5A Freedom Fighter arrives in Vietnam with the 4,503rd Tactical Fighter Squadron.

**Vienna, October 28**
Representatives of the International Air Transport Association (IATA) authorize the showing of in-flight movies aboard airliners.

**Dallas, Texas, November 1**
Braniff Airways unveils two brightly-colored new members of its airliner fleet: a BAC One-Eleven painted orange and a Boeing 720-027 painted lavender.

**Salt Lake City, Utah, November 12**
A United Air Lines Boeing 727 smashes into the runway here after making its descent too quickly, killing 41 out of 85 passengers and crew on board; this is the second crash involving a 727 in three days and the third in less than three months.

**USA, November 30**
The first Convair 600, a turboprop version of the piston-engined Convair 240, equipped with Rolls-Royce Dart engines, enters commercial service, with Central Airlines.

**Vietnam, December 2**
The aircraft carrier USS *Enterprise* launches air sorties against Viet Cong guerilla positions near Bien Hoa in South Vietnam, thereby becoming the first nuclear-powered carrier to take part in a hostile engagement.

**Atlanta, Georgia, December 8**
Delta Air Lines puts the Douglas DC-9 into service, just nine months after the airliner made its first flight (→ Jun 17, 1968).

**Wichita, Kansas, December 14**
A Learjet 23 executive transport shows off its impressive capabilities by climbing to 40,000 feet in 7 minutes 21 seconds with seven people aboard (→ May 23, 1966).

*Douglas Aircraft is experiencing severe cash-flow problems, largely because of the success of the new DC-9 airliner!* ▶

# Douglas launches its short-haul DC-9

## Boeing gets in first with news of 737

*The DC-3 (l) and the DC-9 (r) outside the Douglas plant at Long Beach.*

*The DC-9 resembles the Caravelle.*

**Seattle, February 19**
With the first flight of the Douglas DC-9 airliner imminent, Boeing today stole some of its rival's thunder by announcing its intention to enter the short-haul jet-airliner field with a new model, the 737. Boeing is already serving long and medium-range needs with its 707 and 727, and the short-haul 737 completes its family of airliners.

Boeing hopes that the delay in fielding a short-haul jetliner will not lose it customers. Unusually for the American company, the launch customer is not US, but foreign: Lufthansa placed the first order, for 21. The initial version, the 737-100, was intended to have 60 to 85 seats, but Lufthansa prefered seating for 100, which led to it being configured for 103 to 115 passengers. The 737 has much in common with the 727; the fuselage section is virtually identical, and about 60 per cent of components and assemblies are the same (→ Apr 9, 1967).

**California, February 25**
Donald Douglas, Jr, who has followed his father at Douglas Aircraft, has set himself a difficult goal: to find a successor to a legendary airplane. Almost 30 years after the maiden flight of the Douglas DC-3, the California manufacturer - now moving from Santa Monica to Long Beach - has launched the DC-9. This short/medium-haul jet is original. Although Douglas at first thought of a smaller version of the DC-8, it gave up that project in view of the success of Aérospatiale's Caravelle. Instead it has opted for a machine with a capacity of 90 passengers, fitted with two Pratt & Whitney JT8D-5 turbofans mounted on the rear fuselage, each with a thrust of 12,000 lb. Having already received 58 orders, Donald Douglas, Jr, is optimistic. The first airline to show interest was Delta, in April 1963. TWA followed in 1964, and Eastern has also just signed up (→ Dec 8).

# Air Canada wins the vote in name wrangle

*All the company's ground vehicles are decorated with the Air Canada logo.*

**Canada, January 1**
What's in a name ? A great deal it seems, if you are Canadian and love your national airline. After over a decade of argument, the controversy over the name of Canada's largest airline finally ended today.

Since 1952 Trans-Canada Air Lines has been able to use the name Air Canada, and that is how it has been known in Europe. Those in favor of the name pointed out that it was bilingual, short, easy to remember and followed an established formula for national airline names (Air France, Air India and so on). But it was still thought too French by the Canadian English-language press, and the prolonged row blocked its usage at home.

Now, after a long and stormy debate in the Canadian parliament, the airline will be known by the same name at home and abroad.

# French vertical fighter makes first flight

*On the fuselage the air inlets are open on the eight jet engines providing lift.*

**Melun-Villaroche, France, Feb 12**
It was bitterly cold and snow lay everywhere when Henri Deplante reported today for trials of the vertical take-off and landing (VTOL) Mirage III-V-01, the operational prototype of the Balzac. At the controls was René Bigand, since his colleague Jean-Marie Saget had broken his leg out walking. Bigand achieved a highly satisfactory hovering flight. The 12-ton aircraft he flew is powered by a SNECMA TF-104 jet engine, derived from a Pratt & Whitney JTF10, and eight Rolls-Royce RB.162/1s, which provide lift. Within the context of the Cold War it has become important for an air force to deploy machines that can take off from airfields that are easy to conceal and hence as small as possible. Conventional 6,500-foot runways will be prime targets for enemy attack.

# Giant Soviet transport astounds Paris

*Le Bourget, Paris, June 16*
Like so many Soviet aircraft, little was known in the West about the Antonov An-22 other than its Nato codename (Cock) and the fact that it was supposed to be big. But just how big became clear today, when the An-22 appeared at the Paris Air Show today.

With a wingspan of over 211 feet and an almost 190-foot-long fuselage, the An-22 is truly massive, without doubt the largest transport aircraft in the world. The aircraft's capacity is equally astonishing.

With its 176,350-lb maximum payload, the Antonov leviathan is already in use – five months after the first flight of the prototype – ferrying complete mobile power stations to Siberia. It is the only Soviet transport capable of lifting the 64-ton T-62 tank. Soviet technicians who flew with the aircraft are talking of a stretched version that will carry 724 passengers on two decks. The An-22 Antei is powered by four 15,000-hp Kuznetsov NK-12MA turboprops, and its range is 6,800 miles.

*The An-22 would be capable of carrying 724 if it were fitted for passengers.*

# Britain abandons TSR.2 bomber program

*People at Warton around the plane.*

*London, April 6*
After years of threats, Britain's Labour Party has finally killed the TSR.2. Its cancelation was announced today in the first Budget speech of Harold Wilson's Government.

TSR.2 was started in 1959 and was the only military aircraft permitted at that missile-minded period. It was used to force English Electric and Vickers-Armstrongs to link into British Aircraft Corporation, and this supersonic attack aircraft was by far BAC's biggest project. The first prototype flew on September 27 last year, and has proved brilliantly successful. On February 22 test pilot "Bee" Beamont and observer Don Bowen flew supersonically to the plant at Warton, where half of it had been built. The Government intends to replace TRS.2 by an outright purchase of 50 F-111Ks.

# Qantas is first non-stop across Pacific

*The 707 powered by JT3D turbofans has transformed Qantas's operations.*

*San Francisco, March 7*
A Boeing 707-338B of Australian airline Qantas landed here today at the end of the first non-stop commercial flight across the Pacific. The four-turbofan airliner took just 14 hours 33 minutes to fly the 7,424 miles from Sydney.

A little under six years ago, when Qantas took delivery of its first Boeing 707-138A at the end of July 1959, it was the first non-American airline in the world to operate the type. At that time it was preparing itself for a ruthless battle with its international competitors – with the prize for the winner nothing less than control of the principal air routes in the Pacific region. The Boeing 707s then in service on the route took more than 16 hours for the journey from Sydney to the Californian coast.

Then the airline hoped to steal a march on its rivals by putting the 707-138A into service. The performance of the new -338B, which made today's flight and which is a good deal quicker and more economical on fuel than the -138A, is giving Qantas new cause for confidence (→ Mar 29).

**A montage photograph showing how the changing angle of the engines on the tilt-wing of the LTV/Hiller/Ryan XC-142A aircraft allows a vertical take-off followed by a transition to horizontal flight.**

# Laker's BUA introduces BAC One-Eleven

*BUA managing director Freddie Laker before the inaugural flight to Genoa.*

*London, April 9*
British United Airways (BUA) today inaugurated commercial services with the BAC One-Eleven airliner, flying a service from Gatwick to Genoa, Italy. BUA's order for ten was originally announced simultaneously with the news of the start of One-Eleven development.

All BUA's airplanes are to be of the Series 200 type, designed for operators flying on both short- and medium-range routes. The Series 200 can seat up to 89 passengers in single-class layout, or 65 in a mixed first and tourist-class arrangement. Two 10,330-lb thrust Rolls-Royce Spey 25 Mk 506 turbofan engines provide a cruising speed of 541mph at 21,000 feet. Interest in the airliner from US operators began with an order for six from Braniff, which will start using the airplane this month (→ Jul 15).

**British air pioneer Sir Geoffrey de Havilland, who died on May 26. He built his first biplane in 1908 with the help of a £500 loan from his grandfather, and went on to found an aircraft company which became very successful. He was knighted in 1944.**

## Cool-headed pilot is hailed as a hero

*Travis AFB, California, June 28*
Pan Am Flight 843 from San Francisco to Hawaii was at 700 feet and climbing today when the outer starboard engine exploded. Horrified passengers watched as flames began to spread along the wing. A child's voice was heard to say: "Mommy, the fire is coming toward me."

The fire was not visible on the flight deck, where Captain Charles Kimes felt the 707 shudder and begin to yaw to the right. Using the rudder and left aileron trim tab, Kimes managed to steady the bucking plane and make a wide turn back toward the mainland.

Kimes considered ditching but chose to land at the air base here. With the wing still burning, he told passengers: "Folks, we have a little problem." Through his sheer skill, Flight 843 landed safely.

# Learjet sets three records in one trip

*Los Angeles, June 21*
No less than three world records for business jet airplanes were established when a twin-engined Learjet Model 23 today streaked from here to New York – and back.

The total time of 10 hours 22 minutes for the 5,005-mile flight, an average of 485.45mph, set a record for the round trip.

In addition the eight-seater airplane, piloted by John M Conroy, set both a Los Angeles/New York record, and a New York/Los Angeles one. Demand for the jet is high. Deliveries of the aircraft began in October last year, and the company is producing 23 aircraft per month (→ Dec 14).

# Pilots in airborne telephone link-up

*Atlantic Ocean, June 9*
As millions of airline passengers will no doubt testify, one of the pleasures of flying is freedom from the telephone – whether it be the office or a nagging partner at the other end. The end to this freedom is in sight from today, when the crew of a Pan Am 707 were able to chat to their head office in New York's 44th Street on a link via the newly launched orbiting Early Bird satellite.

Despite technical problems, the system will almost certainly supplant the use of existing high- and low-frequency radio systems; but the cost to customers may turn out to be excessive when it becomes a passenger facility.

# Warplane sets two speed records in a day

*California, May 1*
New world speed records were set at Edwards Air Force Base today by a Lockheed YF-12A interceptor of the USAF. Commander of the 4786th Test Squadron Colonel Robert L "Fox" Stephens and Lieutenant-Colonel Daniel Andre set a new record of 2,070.102mph over a straight course at a record height of 80,258 feet. Meanwhile, Major Walter F Daniel and Captain James P Cooney set a record of 1,688.891-mph over a 1,000-km [621.4-mile] circuit. To assist optical tracking, the black YF-12 was painted with a white cross from wing-tip to wing-tip and from nose to tail.

*Andre (l), Stephens and the YF-12A.*

# 707 takes in both poles on world flight

*Los Angeles, Calif, November 15*
Resplendent in its red and blue livery, a 707-320C of the Flying Tiger line landed here today after an historic flight which took it over the North and South Poles. The airline is celebrating a crucial decision by the US Civil Aeronautics Board which cuts the amount of charter cargo which may be carried by scheduled airlines, giving cargo airlines a huge increase in business.

The scheduled airlines' appeals were dismissed by the US Supreme Court, which was good news for Flying Tigers. The company, which is now 21 years old, has just moved from its headquarters at Burbank to a fine new building at Los Angeles International Airport. Its directors, all of them war veterans, have every cause to be happy: their operating profit last year clocked in at more than $20 million.

This is not bad for an airline which once worried when it spent $90,000 on buying two Conestoga freighters, not knowing quite how it was going to fill them. The company has just leased two 707-349C jets and added two more CL-44Ds to its fleet (→ Jun 5, 1967).

# Only the sound could betray the autoland

*Hands-off approach: the pilot and co-pilot for the historic automatic landing.*

*London, June 10*
The world's first automatic landing by an airplane in normal commercial service took place today at Heathrow airport, to the astonishment and acclaim of those on board. It was made by Hawker Siddeley Trident 1C G-ARPG of British European Airways (BEA) on Flight BE 393 from Paris.

Captain E L R Poole sat at the controls but did not touch them.

Britain has led the world in developing advanced autopilots and flight-control systems which can be linked to an airport's instrument landing system so that a landing can be made blind, such as in thick fog. The Trident is equipped with Smith's Autoland; the VC10 has Elliott-Automation/Bendix equipment. Such a system must have a reliability rate of one failure in ten million landings (→ Aug 26).

# Top stunt pilot dies in movie set tragedy

*Yuma, Ariz, July 8*
Veteran stunt pilot Paul Mantz died this morning when the airplane which he was flying as double for actor James Stewart crashed and disintegrated.

The cobbled-together airplane, designed by Mantz and Otto Timm for the movie *Flight of the Phoenix*, hit a sand dune during filming of a scene from the film. Stuntman Buddy Rose was thrown clear and is now in hospital. Mantz, 61, flunked his US Army Air Corps pilot training in 1926 but learned to fly anyway. His first movie was *Airmail* (1930) when he flew an airplane in one end of a small hangar and out of the other. Mantz, who won the Bendix transcontinental race three times, was to have been Amelia Earhart's co-pilot on her last flight but could not go because of a movie commitment.

*Stunt pilot Mantz was flying as movie "double" for Jimmy Stewart (centre).*

# Britain and France to share construction of supersonic airliner

*Bristol, England, September 11*
Work is now going ahead at the Filton division of the British Aircraft Corporation (BAC) on Britain's 40 per cent share of the airframe for the Anglo-French Concorde supersonic transport (SST). The other 60 per cent is the responsibility of France's Sud-Aviation.

Britain's share is mainly the forward fuselage and tail, the French handling the wings, controls and the rear cabin section.

Overall the program is meant to be shared 50/50, but Britain has the biggest share of the engines, which are an existing type.

Much of the fuselage may be made at BAC's Weybridge factory. Most of the airframe will use a British aluminium alloy RR58, which is called AU2GN in France. If Concorde was designed to fly faster it would have to be of steel or titanium, making it more costly and taking longer to build (→ Sep 9, 1966).

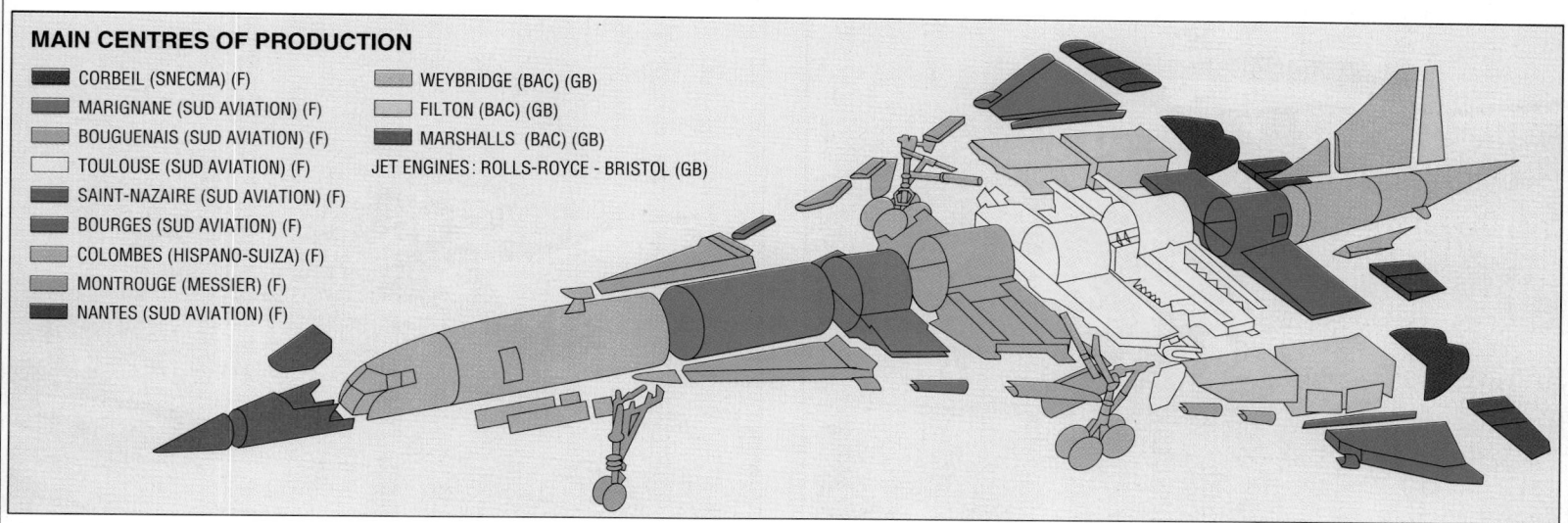

**MAIN CENTRES OF PRODUCTION**

- CORBEIL (SNECMA) (F)
- MARIGNANE (SUD AVIATION) (F)
- BOUGUENAIS (SUD AVIATION) (F)
- TOULOUSE (SUD AVIATION) (F)
- SAINT-NAZAIRE (SUD AVIATION) (F)
- BOURGES (SUD AVIATION) (F)
- COLOMBES (HISPANO-SUIZA) (F)
- MONTROUGE (MESSIER) (F)
- NANTES (SUD AVIATION) (F)
- WEYBRIDGE (BAC) (GB)
- FILTON (BAC) (GB)
- MARSHALLS (BAC) (GB)
- JET ENGINES: ROLLS-ROYCE - BRISTOL (GB)

# American flyers learn new tricks in Vietnam War

*USAF RF-101C Voodoos are taking perfect photos of combat damage.*

*Four UC-123 "Ranch Hands" hit the jungle with defoliating chemicals.*

## Bridge bombed on key supply route

*Korat Air Base, Thailand, April 4*
For the second day running US Air Force F-105 Thunderchief fighter/bombers based here have attacked the Thanh Hoa bridge 76 miles south of Hanoi, on a key supply route from north to south.

Yesterday's attack with Bullpup air-to-ground missiles was unsuccessful. Today 750-lb bombs were used, and photographs show about 300 bomb-hits either on or near the bridge, which has railroad tracks running down its center. It was not destroyed, but sufficient damage was done to close it for a month or more.

## 'Ranch Hands' seek to strip vegetation

*Saigon, April*
No parachutes for the aircrews: when you attack by flying in formation, straight and level 100 feet above the ground at about 150mph, they are useless. But extra flak vests are carried to sit on for protection from small arms fire.

Such is life for the "Ranch Hands", the USAF Special Operations aerial spray unit which uses herbicides to prevent the Viet Cong from growing food or using the jungle for cover. It flies twin-engined UC-123 transports fitted with large tanks with spray nozzles on the wings to disperse the defoliants.

## Huge B-52s pound Communist forces

*Guam, June 17*
The USAF's biggest bomber was used in war for the first time today. Twenty-seven Boeing B-52 Stratofortresses, flying with the mission code name "Arc Light" from Andersen Air Force Base here, rained both 750-lb and 1,000-lb bombs on enemy forces in a heavily forested area of just one by two miles, 30 miles north of Saigon. The exact amount of bombs used was not disclosed, but it is estimated that as many as 500 tons were dropped. Thirty B-52s left on the raid; two collided and were lost, and a third was unable to drop its load.

## New Cobra will add venom to US attack

*Fort Worth, Texas, September 7*
The new Bell helicopter Model 209 HueyCobra, designed to meet the need identified in Vietnam by the US Army for a specialized attack helicopter, flew for the first time today. Unlike the army's Huey (officially the UH-1 Iroquois), which can carry eight infantrymen, a pilot, co-pilot and two gunners, the new HueyCobra only carries a crew of two: a pilot and a gunner.

While the Army is anxious to get its hands on the new helicopter as quickly as possible, it will be about two years before production models are ready for delivery (→ Mar 1967).

*"Flying horsemen" of the US First Cavalry drop in to spearhead an assault.*

*A Skyhawk jet in action on board the nuclear-powered carrier "Enterprise".*

# 'Magnificent Men' recalls the early days

*England, June*
It was a challenge no aircraft manufacturer could resist. The call went out from the movie company not merely for reproductions of five early aircraft but for ones which would actually fly.

The movie *Those Magnificent Men in their Flying Machines*, starring Benny Hill, Red Skelton, Sam Wanamaker and many others, required some robust airplanes. Bits had to fall off, one had to be shot

down by a blunderbuss, another had to land on a train – all in the course of a hilarious race from London to Paris.

The models selected for the movie were a 1908 Antoinette, a 1909 Roe Triplane, a 1911 Eardley Billing Biplane, a 1909 Blériot monoplane and a 1910 Bristol Boxkite. For the record, the pilots – most of them trained on modern jets – agreed that the Boxkite, built by Miles Engineering, flew the best.

*British director Ken Annakin had 25 antique airplanes rebuilt for the film.*

# Atlantic deal unites France and Germany

*Static experiments in the hangar test the strength of the Atlantic's fuselage.*

*France, December 10*
In a ceremony at Nîmes-Garons today the French navy took delivery of its first operational Breguet 1150 Atlantic maritime patrol aircraft. The navy's air arm (Aéronavale) is to get 40 Atlantics to equip three squadrons. West Germany is taking 20.

The Atlantic was one of 25 contending design studies submitted to the Nato Armaments Committee by manufacturers from many different countries. Each company hoped to be chosen to develop the succes-

sor to the widely-used Lockheed P-2 Neptune. In the event, the Breguet was selected and two prototypes were ordered six years ago. The first flew on October 21, 1961.

The Atlantic program is supervized and financed by the governments of Belgium, France, West Germany, the Netherlands and the USA. A consortium to construct the airplanes includes companies from all these nations except the USA, which supplies the avionics. The Rolls-Royce Tyne turboprops are built in France and W Germany.

# Sun sets on Japan Air Lines' old image

*Tokyo, October 1*
From today the emblem of the Rising Sun is to be replaced on Japan Air Lines aircraft by the *tsuru*, the crane, which to the Japanese is a symbol of long life, courage and good luck. To add a unique feature to its service, JAL has also decided that its stewardesses will wear traditional kimonos (→ Mar 6, 1967).

# Utility Islander dispenses with cabin aisle

*The Britten-Norman Islander, designed for low-cost, short-haul operations.*

*Isle of Wight, England, June 13*
A small utility transport airplane with great potential made its first flight at Bembridge today. It is the Islander, produced by the small firm of Britten-Norman Ltd. Company chiefs John Britten and Desmond Norman were on board for the flight, along with flight observer A J Coombe.

The Islander has a high wing, fixed tricycle undercarriage and two

210-hp piston engines. Previous aircraft in this class have needed a central aisle so that passengers could reach their seats, but by providing doors by each seat row the Islander dispenses with an aisle, and the fuselage can be narrower for the same width of seat. A tough, rough-field airplane, the Islander can carry ten people or 2,300 lb cargo. It should prove ideal for short-haul work in difficult terrain.

# Pan Am and Boeing agree on a 'Jumbo'

*Seattle, December*
After much talking to establish the right product, Boeing and Pan Am have agreed to back the building of a jumbo-sized airliner – the Model 747. It will dwarf every airliner currently operating. Known as a wide-body because it will have an internal cabin width of about 20 feet, almost twice that of the 707, it may provide 490 seats.

But why build such a giant? Over the past decade passenger traffic has been rising at some 15 per cent a year. To keep pace airlines have coped by streamlining operations, buying more and larger airplanes and flying faster jetliners which allow increased use. However, airports are becoming congested, and the future, so Boeing and Pan Am believe, lies in carrying more people per flight. This should achieve lower operating costs (→ Apr 13, 1966).

*Japan's Fuji FA-200 Aero Subaru four-seat light touring aircraft.*

*Champion's Model 7GCAA Citabria, powered by a 150-hp Lycoming.*

*Cessna's first foray into the agricultural aviation field: the AGwagon.*

*Aero Spacelines' B-377SG Super Guppy: a Boeing C-97 conversion.*

*Canadair stretched the swing-tail CL-44D cargo transport by inserting new sections fore and aft of the wing, providing room for 189-214 passengers.*

*Transavia's PL-12 Airtruk utility/ agricultural aircraft from Australia.*

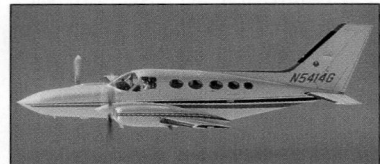

*Cessna's 421 Golden Eagle pressurized six-passenger business aircraft.*

*General Dynamics' RR-Dart-engined Convair 600, a conversion of the piston-engined Convairliners.*

*Swearingen changed engines to turboprops to produce the Merlin II.*

*The prototype Douglas DC-9 was the first of 976 aircraft which were delivered to the world's airlines and military customers between 1965 and 1982.*

*The Britten-Norman Islander ten-seat utility aircraft: prototype.*

*Kamov originally developed the Ka-26 for agricultural use, but it was also put to work on geophysical survey, ambulance and passenger operations.*

*Mitsubishi's MU-2B was powered by two Garrett TPE331 turboprops.*

*Lockheed's experimental Model 286 with rigid rotor and retracting skids.*

*The Distributor Wing DW-1 was designed as an agricultural aircraft.*

*The de Havilland Canada DHC-6 Twin Otter STOL transport.*

*Fairchild built the Swiss Pilatus Porter as the AU-23A Peacemaker.*

RAF Transport Command ordered 14 Vickers VC10 C.1 transports.

North American's OV-10A Bronco was a counter-insurgency airplane.

Canadair developed the CL-84 Dynavert tilt-wing aircraft to evaluate the V/STOL concept for use in a variety of military and civilian support roles.

McDonnell's RF-4B reconnaissance Phantom for the US Marine Corps.

The McDonnell F-4D Phantom II: in total, 825 were built.

Antonov's An-22 Antaeus long-range heavy transport aircraft, powered by four Kuznetsov NK-12MA turboprop engines, dwarfed others in its class.

Aérospatiale originally developed the SA 330 Puma to meet a French army all-weather transport helicopter requirement, but it also serves worldwide.

General Dynamics' F-111B, made for US Navy fleet defense duties.

The Agusta A.106 anti-submarine helicopter built for the Italian navy.

The Sikorsky S-61F high-speed experimental helicopter with jet thrust.

Bell's Model 209 AH-1 HueyCobra gunship: the dynamic train of the UH-1C Iroquois plus a streamlined fuselage and tandem seating for two crew. The Emerson Electric turret housed a multi-barrel GAU-2B/A 7.62mm Minigun.

McDonnell Douglas's TA-4E two-seat trainer, for the US Navy.

Ling-Temco-Vought's A-7A Corsair II won the US Navy competition for a carrier-based light-attack aircraft to replace the Douglas A-4E Skyhawk.

Dassault's Mirage III-V single-seat V/STOL fighter, fitted with a SNECMA TF-104 propulsion engine and eight Rolls-Royce RB.162 lift engines.

# 1966

4,250mph
USA
Pete Knight
North American X-15
Nov 18, 1966

24,325 miles
USA
Archie Old Jr
Boeing B-52B
Jan 18, 1957

354,200ft
USA
Joseph Walker
North American X-15
Aug 22, 1963

551,147lb
USSR
Antonov
An-22 Anteus

32,500lb thrust
USA
Pratt & Whitney
JT1 1D-20B

**Washington, DC, January 1**
The USAF directs the Military Air Transport Service (MATS) to change its name to Military Airlift Command (MAC).

**California, January 7**
USAF Strategic Air Command receives its first Lockheed SR-71 supersonic reconnaissance airplanes, at Beale Air Force Base.

**Spain, January 17**
A USAF B-52 bomber collides with a KC-135 tanker while refueling over the Mediterranean coast, killing seven; four hydrogen bombs fall from the B-52, all of which are recovered intact after a land-and-sea search.

**Oxfordshire, England, January 20**
RAF Transport Command takes delivery of its first operational Short Belfast transport, at Brize Norton.

**Japan, February 26**
The Nihon University NM-63 Linnet man-powered airplane makes its first flight.

**France, March 7**
President Charles de Gaulle announces that France is to leave Nato; the US demands the return of aircraft it has supplied to the French.

**Vietnam, March 10**
Major Bernard F Fisher of 1st Air Commando Squadron lands an A-1E Skyraider on the A Shua airstrip after it has been overrun by North Vietnamese troops; he rescues Major Dafford Myers (→ Jan 19, 1967).

**Kingston, England, March 12**
Sir Sydney Camm, 72, aircraft designer responsible for the Hawker fighters, dies.

**Long Beach, Calif, March 14**
The Douglas DC-8 Super 61, a "stretched" DC-8 capable of seating 251 passengers, makes its first flight.

**USA, March 17**
The Bell X-22A vertical/short take-off and landing tilting-duct research aircraft flies for the first time.

**Issoire, France, March 22**
The world's first glass-fiber production airplane, the Wassmer WA.50, is piloted by Gérard Tahon on its first flight.

**London, April 1**
The British Airports Authority is established.

**London, April 4**
BOAC opens its first scheduled service to Mexico, flying to Mexico City via Bermuda and Kingston (Jamaica).

**USA, April 11**
A new policy is introduced under which USAF pilots and crews will be limited to a Vietnam tour of duty lasting 12 months or 100 combat missions; the limits do not apply to US Navy and US Marine Corps flyers.

**Vietnam, April 12**
USAF Strategic Air Command Boeing B-52 Stratofortress bombers hit targets in North Vietnam for the first time when they attack the Mu Gia pass.

**Seattle, April 13**
Boeing announces an order worth $525 million from Pan Am for 25 Model 747 jumbo jets (→ Sep 1).

**Cheyenne Mountain, Colo, Apr 20**
The combat operations center of the North American Air Defense Command (NORAD) moves into its new heavily protected underground complex; the nerve center for US-Canadian defense, it can identify and track aircraft or missile threats to the entire North American continent.

**Britain, May 2**
BEA opens the first jet service between London Heathrow and Glasgow, using de Havilland Comet 4Bs.

**Rogers Dry Lake, Calif, May 3**
A Lockheed HC-130H equipped with a Fulton recovery system is tested here and "rescues" Captain Gerald T Lyvere.

**USA, May 19**
North American's XB-70 Valkyrie maintains a speed of Mach 3 over a period of 32 minutes (→ Jun 6).

**Wichita, Kansas, May 23**
A Learjet with four on board returns after circling the world in 50 hours 20 minutes' flying time (a total elapsed time of 65 hours 40 minutes) (→ Apr 10, 1967).

**California, June 6**
A wide-ranging investigation of jet noise and sonic booms is launched at Edwards Air Force Base using XB-70, B-58, F-194 and KC-135 aircraft; the results will be applied to the development of supersonic transports (→ Jun 8).

**Hertfordshire, England, July 1**
A Mitsubishi MU-2B executive transport is demonstrated to the press; it is the first Japanese-built aircraft to visit England since 1936.

**London, August 2**
British minister of aviation Fred Mulley quashes an attempt by BEA to acquire US airliners, ruling that the airline should buy British One-Eleven aircraft.

**Moscou, August 11**
An Aeroflot Tupolev Tu-114 takes off on a proving flight to Tokyo, preparatory to the joint operation of this route by the Soviet airline and Japan Air Lines.

**Sion, Switzerland, August 26**
Mountain-rescue pilot Hermann Geiger, who saved hundreds of lives by making daring landings high in the Alps, dies in a collision between his airplane and a glider.

**Surrey, England, August 31**
The first of six Hawker Siddeley Harrier jump jet development aircraft makes an initial hovering flight at Dunsfold (→ Mar 19, 1969).

**London, September 1**
BOAC places an order for six Boeing 747s (→ Sep 30, 1968).

**Germany, September 15**
Reinhold Platz, 80, designer of a number of excellent German aircraft (especially Fokker) of the First World War, dies.

**Paris, September 19**
Air France opens a direct service to Shanghai; it is the only Western company to fly services to the People's Republic of China.

**USSR, October 21**
A three-jet mid-range transport, the Yakovlev Yak-40, makes its first flight; it is intended to replace the Lisunov Li-2, the Soviet version of the DC-3.

**Paris, November 4**
An Air France Boeing 707, equipped with stalls and a special ventilation system, carries 31 racehorses to London.

**Antarctica, November 14**
A USAF Military Airlift Command Lockheed C-141 StarLifter commanded by Captain Howard Geddes puts down at McMurdo Sound to become the first jet aircraft to land in the Antarctic.

**USA, November 18**
Major Pete Knight pilots the North American X-15 to 4,250mph (Mach 6.33) (→ Oct 3, 1967).

**Germany, December 6**
The Luftwaffe grounds the 770-strong fleet of Lockheed F-104G Starfighters; 65 of them have been lost in accidents (→ Jan 4, 1967).

**Melun-Villaroche, France, Dec 23**
The Dassault Mirage F1 single-seat supersonic fighter prototype makes its maiden flight.

---

*To reduce passenger boredom on long-haul flights, the major airlines introduced in-flight movies in 1966. The show begins after the meal.* ▶

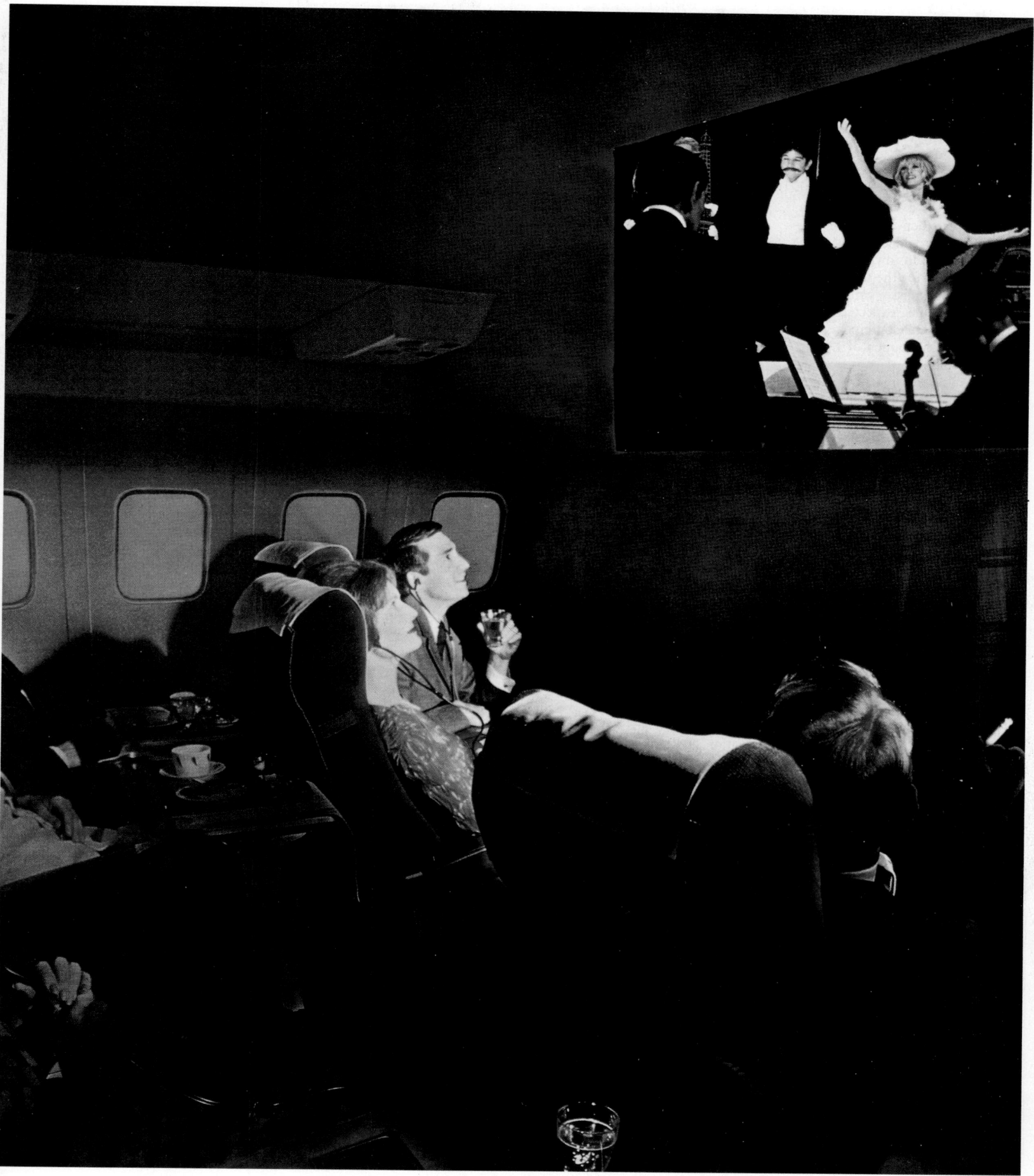

# Laker sets up cheap charter airline

## US ends massive airlift to Vietnam

*Sussex, England, February 8*
When Freddie Laker does something, he does in it style. A year ago, when British United Airways (BUA) took delivery of the BAC One-Eleven, 50 representatives of the travel media gathered at Gatwick airport for a flight to Genoa, where Laker, then BUA's managing director, provided refreshment at the best hotel in town.

Today, ready for the usual Laker surprises, journalists gathered at Gatwick for the expected good lunch and a press conference. The occasion was the launch of Laker's own airline, Laker Airways. Based in the tax haven of Jersey, Laker Airways has been formed as the vehicle to express Laker's ideas of cheap and easy air travel. It is a contract-hire and ad hoc airline, operating two Bristol Britannias from Gatwick to deal mainly with inclusive tour holidays. Setting his sights on greater things, Laker,

*Laker Airways' initial fleet consists of two Britannias bought from BOAC.*

after his experience with BUA, has no doubt that he needs to acquire three of the new BAC One-Eleven Series 300 airliners as the nucleus of a modern fleet of state-of-the-art, short-haul jet-transports.

Although departed from BUA, Laker remains a man bursting with drive, always ready to take a cal-

culated gamble. Sometimes, as with the 1948 purchase by his Aviation Traders of the ex-BOAC Handley Page Haltons just as the Berlin Airlift got under way, all goes well. On other occasions, as with Percival Prentice conversions or development of the ATL.90 Accountant, things do not (→ Jun 25, 1971).

*Pleiku, Vietnam, January 23*
Operation Blue Light, the longest combat airlift in history, ended today as the final elements of the 3rd Brigade of the US Army's 25th Infantry Division arrived here in the central highlands from their home at Schofield Barracks, Hawaii. USAF Lockheed C-141 StarLifter transports, covering the 7,000 miles between here and Hawaii in 14 hours, were the principal aircraft used to move the troops.

The airlift of the brigade, reinforced with artillery and engineer battalions and a cavalry squadron, began when its advance element arrived on December 28. With the later reinforcing units the airlift of the brigade moved 3,000 troops and 4,700 tons of equipment in some 231 sorties. The remainder of the 25th Infantry Division, which carries the name "Tropic Lightning", will follow later (→ Feb 22, 1967).

# Soviets show off gigantic Mil helicopter

## French use fighter as Concorde simulator

*Marseilles, France, April 1*
The world's largest helicopter, the Mil Mi-6, landed at Marignane airport here today. The Soviet giant is known to the Western military by its Nato codename "Hook".

As well as providing a great tool for the Soviet armed forces, the helicopter's tremendous ability to lift a 19,840-lb slung load enables it to support oil and other industries in eastern Europe. In 1963 it was used to carry heavy oil-rig components for assembly at Zhyrnovsk in the

transVolga steppes, and it has been used to fight forest fires. In 1961 it became the first helicopter to exceed 300kph [186.4mph].

The Mi-6 appeared today as part of a demonstration tour of Western Europe. Its pilots Kolochenko and Garnaeyev, had arrived with Sud-Aviation's Roland Coffignot on board, the French pilot helping to navigate while learning about the machine. Soon it is off to the south of France for fire-fighting demonstrations (→ Feb 12, 1969).

*Paris, June 25*
In contrast to Britain, which has built three special research aircraft for aerodynamic tests in support of the Anglo-French Concorde program, France has adapted military aircraft. The latest French development is the adaptation of a Mirage IIIB fighter to be used as a flying Concorde simulator to give pilots the feel of the controls of the supersonic airliner. It was used for the first time today. It is essential that pilots know how the airliner will

behave before it flies, because one of the conditions of its certification is that it can be handled in a fashion identical to that used for existing subsonic transports.

A computer aboard the Mirage IIIB modifies the commands transmitted to the control surfaces in such a way that the pilot has the impression of flying a much heavier supersonic aircraft. Meanwhile, the research center at Toulouse is also conducting flight-control tests with a ground simulator (→ Sep 9).

*The Mi-10 is a special 'crane' version of the huge Mi-6; here it lifts a bus.*

*Using a French fighter, pilots are learning how to fly a supersonic airliner.*

# Close encounters over Vietnam for USAF

*Crusaders and Skyhawks are readied for action on board the "Ticonderoga".*

*Vietnam, March 4*
North Vietnamese MiG-17 fighters challenged US warplanes today for the first time in more than a month. Neither side suffered any damage or losses in two separate incidents.

The first incident occurred 80 miles north of Hanoi when USAF F-4 Phantoms, flying cover for aircraft attacking rail and highway bridges, were attacked by three North Vietnamese MiGs. These MiGs, firing their cannon, made a single diving pass on the Phantoms and fled toward Hanoi. The US warplanes pursued their attackers but

the MiGs disappeared into the clouds before the Phantom crews could manage to get any kind of missile lock.

In the second incident, F-105 Thunderchief pilots returning from a strike on a railroad bridge 120 miles north-west of Hanoi spotted two North Vietnamese MiGs above and behind them. The F-105s turned to meet the MiGs, which then fled toward Hanoi. The F-105 pilots broke off the chase because they were running low on fuel and returned safely to their base across the border in Thailand (→ Apr 26).

# Trident test flight ends in tragic crash

*Hatfield, England, June 3*
Hawker Siddeley Trident 1C G-ARPY, 23rd of 24 being built for British European Airways (BEA) crashed today during its routine production test flight. All on board were killed, including George Errington, who had been a test pilot for 40 years.

Thanks to his calm radio transmissions the cause is not in doubt. At one point in the flight it is normal to check the stall-warning system. This is naturally done at high altitude. As angle of attack approaches the stall, the warning system first sounds an aural alarm and then triggers a stick-shaker which slams the pilot's yoke to and fro. On this occasion the aircraft entered a "deep stall" regime in which it was falling through the sky in a level attitude but with near-zero forward speed.

There was nothing the pilot could do to recover. Selecting flaps or maximum asymmetric thrust had no effect. There was no useful slipstream past any of the control surfaces. This crash calls into question the basic design of rear-engined jets with T-type tails. A similar deep-stall recently destroyed a BAC One-Eleven (→ Mar 1, 1971).

# British airwoman in record world flight

*Sheila Scott, a triumphant return.*

*London, June 20*
Record-breaking airwoman Sheila Scott touched down at Heathrow airport today after completing the first-ever solo flight around the world by a British pilot. Flying alone in her Piper Comanche 260, she chose to complete the 29,055-mile flight the hard way, by following the equator, the longest route to take and the most difficult. Scott's Comanche *Myth Too* was a standard production model, modified only by the addition of two 65-US-gallon fuel tanks in the cabin (→ Aug 4, 1971).

# Fighter collides with bomber in tragic end to publicity flight

*California, June 8*
One of the US Air Force's two North American XB-70 Valkyrie supersonic advanced jet bombers today crashed in flames after a mid-air collision with a Lockheed F-104 Starfighter. The disaster occurred during a five-plane formation flight from Edwards Air Force Base to provide publicity photos for General Electric, manufacturer of the aircraft's engines.

Two people died in the accident: NASA X-15 test pilot Joe Walker, who held world speed and altitude records of 4,104mph and 354,200 feet respectively, who was flying the F-104, and Major Carl Cross, co-pilot of the XB-70. The XB-70's pilot, North American's Al White, survived the collision, ejecting in a seat capsule.

The USAF said that the F-104 appeared to hit the two vertical sta-

*The Valkyrie XB-70 jet-bomber: millions of dollars were lost in today's crash.*

bilizers of the 500,000-lb bomber while they were flying together at 25,000 feet. The other planes in the tight formation were a McDonnell F-4 Phantom fighter, a Northrop F-5 Freedom Fighter and a T-38

Talon trainer. The two XB-70s cost $1.2 billion, but US defense secretary Robert McNamara rejected putting it into production. It is the first aircraft of its size to reach 2,000mph and 70,000 feet.

# In-flight films are set to start rolling

*USA, May*
International airlines are introducing yet another attraction, in-flight movies, to take the boredom out of long-distance flying. Cabins are being equipped with 16mm projectors fitted in the ceilings and films will be shown on retractable screens. The movies are contained in cassettes which can be changed by cabin staff with little trouble. Passengers who do not wish to see a movie will not be disturbed – the soundtrack is only heard through headphones plugged into their armrests.

The US Bureau of Aviation has approved an IATA recommendation for a $2.50 charge for the headphones. The leading airlines are competing hard for first-run Hollywood movies, which are proving to be an excellent sales gimmick.

# Vietnam war intensifies

## US pilots score first victory over MiG-21

*Saigon, April 26*
The first North Vietnamese MiG-21 to be shot down fell today to a Sidewinder heat-seeking missile fired by a USAF F-4 Phantom. Major Paul J Gilmore and First Lieutenant William T Smith, who were escorting F-105 Thunderchiefs near Hanoi, were credited with the kill after they were attacked by two MiG-21s. The second aircraft fled.

Yesterday two Phantoms engaged a pair of the Soviet-designed aircraft 85 miles north-west of Hanoi. About a dozen Sidewinders and radar-guided Sparrows were

*Gilmore (r) and Smith demonstrate just how they downed the MiG-21.*

fired off, but none hit. With a top speed in the 1,500-mph range, the MiG-21 is a much more formidable adversary than the slower MiG-17. In most engagements so far it has appeared capable of outmaneuvering the Phantom.

## Helicopters play leading role in combat

*New face of air war: "Slicks" land troops to overpower front-line resistance.*

*Vietnam, November*
"Slicks", "Hogs" and "Dust-Offs" have changed the face of ground warfare for US forces here. Today every major unit has its own helicopter companies, and the foot soldier is more likely to fly into battle than walk. Helicopters play a vital part in all major operations.

Troops usually ride into an LZ (landing zone) on a Bell UH-1 Huey "Slick", which is unarmed except for two door-mounted machine guns. It carries eight infantry,

while the larger Boeing CH-47 Chinook can carry up to 40. They are protected by UH-1 "Hog" gunships with their forward-firing guns and/or cannon, grenade launchers and rockets as well as the door guns found on the "Slicks".

With the troops in place, the "Hogs" provide support fire and the "Slicks" and CH-47s become supply ships bringing in ammunition, food and artillery. Wounded are evacuated by the UH-1 "Dust-Off" unarmed medical helicopters.

# Sturdy Twin Otter leaves Canadian stable

*The Twin Otter's cabin is typically furnished with 19 passenger seats.*

*Toronto, August 1*
Some pilots find it a rather ugly machine with its fixed landing gear and strut-braced wing. On the other hand, they agree that the de Havilland Canada DHC-6 Twin Otter, which enters service this month with the Ontario Department of Lakes and Forests, is one of the most sturdy, pleasant to fly and versatile aircraft around.

Like its predecessors from the de Havilland Canada menagerie – the DHC-2 Beaver, DHC-3 Otter, DHC-4 Caribou and DHC-5 Buffalo – the Twin Otter has remarkable short take-off and landing (STOL) capabilities suited to Can-

ada's terrain. The airplane is powered by two Pratt & Whitney Canada PT6A-20 turboprops, each of about 578hp. It has a maximum speed of 210mph; the range depends on the aircraft's payload. The Twin Otter may be fitted with either skis or floats, enabling it to operate just about anywhere. It is, of course, unpressurized.

Orders for the Twin Otter are now pouring in, from both civilian and military customers. This spacious and powerful short-range Canadian airplane is set to make an impact in particular on small companies as one of the best light transports of its class.

**A Lockheed HC-130H hauls in two airmen it has rescued from the sea using the Fulton system, shown folded back, on the aircraft's nose.**

# Boeing wins supersonic airliner contract

*Lockheed's delta-winged L-2000.*

*A scale model of the Boeing SST.*

*Seattle, December 31*
Boeing's swing-wing design and General Electric's engine have beaten Lockheed's delta wing and Pratt & Whitney's engine as the US's late entry in the supersonic transport (SST) race. The prototype of the Anglo-French Concorde is now 90 per cent complete, with flight testing scheduled for early 1968 and passenger service planned for 1971.

The selection of the Boeing-General Electric combination for the design and development of the American SST does not guarantee it will ever be produced. The decision to proceed with production will be made by the President and subject to funding by Congress.

Assuming a decision to build a test plane is made soon, and production is given the go-ahead at the right time, the US prototype SST will not fly until 1970, and production aircraft will not begin to reach the airlines until mid-1974. Recognizing the competitive disadvantage they will face if they wait for the Boeing-GE SST, US airlines have begun expressing an interest in buying the European rival.

Boeing's SST, which is expected to carry a price tag of $35 million per aircraft, will be a 306-foot-long, 338-ton airliner capable of 1,800mph. Its swing-wing is at right angles to the fuselage at take-off to provide best lift and good low-speed handling. As the SST climbs, the wings are swept back, and as its speed increases, they continue to move back until they meet the horizontal tail surfaces to produce a delta wing. (→ Feb 22, 1968).

# Wingless aircraft glides safely home

*California, July 12*
Wingless and unpowered, the Northrop/NASA M2-F2 looked like nothing on Earth as it dropped through the sky today during its first test glide. Released from under the wing of a Boeing B-52 "motherplane" at 45,000 feet, the pilot successfully practised a "flare-out" at about 25,000 feet, a maneuver he would need to land safely.

The maneuver completed, the aircraft increased speed to 350mph, needed to allow it to "flare out" again at lower altitude, to decrease the rate of descent at touchdown from 250 feet per minute to under 5 feet per minute. Just four minutes from release, the M2-F2 had dropped 45,000 feet to land on the bed of Rogers Dry Lake near Edwards Air Force Base. Built as a lifting-body, re-entry research vehicle, the M2-F2 will help in spacecraft development.

*The wingless M2-F2 (l.) during tests.*

# Three leading air pioneers bow out

*USA, December 31*
After eight years and one of the longest lawsuits in US history, one of the great names in aviation, Howard Hughes, has sold out his TWA shares this year for $566 million. Hughes will be remembered as a record-breaking pilot, a significant aircraft builder in the Second World War, the constructor of the hugh "Spruce Goose" flying boat and a great movie maker.

One by one the giants are leaving the aviation scene. Bill Patterson, once a cabin boy, recently retired as head of United Air Lines, which he ran from 1933. Eastern has lost Eddie Rickenbacker, former racing driver and First World War air ace, who made the airline number four in the world (→ May 7, 1968).

# State takes over

*London, November 21*
Britain's Labour government today proposed the nationalization of the British Aircraft Corporation and Hawker Siddeley Aviation, which would almost monopolize the British aerospace business. It would leave only Beagle, Britten-Norman, Handley Page, Westland, Short Brothers, and a handful of other smaller companies as independent aircraft producers.

**Marina Solovyeva, from the USSR, who set a women's closed-circuit world speed record of 1,281mph on September 16.**

# Supersonic engine for Concorde is flight tested on a Vulcan

*For the tests, the Olympus 593 was fixed beneath the fuselage of the Vulcan.*

*Bristol, England, September 9*
Attached to the underside of a converted RAF Vulcan bomber, the engine which one day will power Concorde began flight tests today. It is the Rolls-Royce (formerly Bristol Siddeley) Olympus 593, the most powerful version of the Olympus range. The flight tests, are limited by the Vulcan to a speed of Mach 0.98, while the airliner is designed to cruise at Mach 2. Launched in 1953, the Olympus 101 gave around five tons of thrust. The version for Concorde will furnish over 15 tons. The airborne tests will be compared with ground bench tests (→ Dec 11, 1967).

The Gates Learjet Model 25 Transporter was some four feet longer than the earlier Model 24, and accommodated eight passengers instead of six.

The BAC One-Eleven Series 300.

The Argentinian DINFIA IA 53 piston-engined agricultural airplane.

Hants & Sussex Aviation re-engined a Chipmunk with a Rover turboprop.

Wassmer's WA-50: a one-off four-seater of all-plastic construction.

Beech's Duke Model 60: a fast pressurized executive transport aircraft.

The IMCO CallAir B1 was an improved version of the earlier A-9.

The Andreasson BA-4B prototype was built by MFI apprentices.

The Dornier Skyservant inherited the basic configuration of the Do 28.

The prototype Neiva IPD-6201 Universal trainer, constructed in Brazil.

The 19-seat Beech C.99 was designed for the scheduled air-taxi market.

The Douglas DC-8 Super 61 had an extended fuselage with accommodation for 251 passengers but retained the wing of the standard Series 50 DC-8s.

The American Alon A-4: an unsuccessful attempt to improve the A-2.

The McDonnell Douglas DC-9-30, first of the family to be stretched.

The Russian Yakovlev Yak-40 - "Codling" to Nato - is a three-engined 31-passenger jet transport used widely by civilian and military operators.

The Cessna Model 177 Cardinal was originally designated 172J.

The Fiat G91Y was a twin-engined version of the original G91 fighter.

The Bell 206A JetRanger was to become the world's best known small helicopter, spawning numerous sub-variants through the following decades.

The Grumman Gulfstream II was the first jet-engined Gulfstream executive airplane and was powered by a pair of Rolls-Royce Spey turbofans.

Fairchild Hiller's FH-227 was a license-built and slightly lengthened version of the successful Fokker F.27 Friendship turboprop commercial transport.

Carstedt's Jetliner was based on the airframe of the de Havilland Heron.

The Pilatus PC-7 Turbo-Trainer: basically a turbine-powered P-3.

The KA-6D tanker version of the Grumman A-6 Intruder made its maiden flight during 1966. The aircraft is equipped with a centerline refueling pod.

The first Hawker Siddeley Harrier was originally the P.1127 (RAF).

The Soko P-2 Kraguj was a piston-engined light-attack/COIN aircraft.

The Japanese-built version of the Lockheed P-2 Neptune maritime patrol aircraft was initially known as the Kawasaki P2V Kai, then later as the P-2J.

Northrop-NASA's M2-F2, a wing-less "lifting body" research aircraft.

The Bell X-22A featured tilting ducted fans on wings and foreplanes.

The prototype Mirage F1 fighter first flew six months after the larger two-seat Mirage F2, from which the variable-geometry Mirage G was derived.

# 1967

 4,534mph
USA
Pete Knight
North American X-15
Oct 3, 1967

 24,325 miles
USA
Archie Old Jr
Boeing B-52B
Jan 18, 1957

 354,200ft
USA
Joseph Walker
North American X-15
Aug 22, 1963

 551,147lb
USSR
Antonov
An-22 Anteus

 32,500lb thrust
USA
Pratt & Whitney
JT1 1D-20B

**[West] Germany, January 4**
The Luftwaffe lifts the operational ban on its Lockheed F-104G Starfighters, which was imposed last year in the wake of a series of crashes (→ Jun 24, 1971).

**USA, January 19**
Major Bernard Fisher becomes the first USAF pilot to win the Medal of Honor, the US's highest valor award, in the Vietnam War; on March 10 last year he rescued a colleague from A Shua airfield, which has been captured by enemy forces, under heavy fire (→ Dec 15).

**USA, February 3**
USAF Strategic Air Command (SAC) airborne command posts, whose crew would direct SAC bombers if the command's regular facilities were put out of action, complete six years of round-the-clock operations.

**Sweden, February 8**
Saab chief test pilot Erik Dahlstrom takes the prototype of the Saab AJ37 Viggen combat aircraft on its first flight.

**Vietnam, February 22**
Paratroops of the US 173rd Airborne Brigade are airlifted by 23 C-130s from Bien Hoa to take part in Operation Junction City, a concentrated offensive against Viet Cong bases near the Cambodian border (→ Nov 17).

**Vietnam, February 26**
Commander A H Barrie leads seven US Navy A-6 Intruder aircraft from the aircraft carrier USS *Enterprise* on a mission to plant mines at the mouths of the Song Ca and Son Giang rivers in an effort to prevent enemy barges from moving supplies; this is the first airborne minelaying mission of the Vietnam war.

**USSR, March 3**
The Beriev Be-30, a short take-off and landing turboprop intended to replace the Antonov An-2 in service with state airline Aeroflot, makes its first flight.

**Japan, March 6**
JAL opens a round-the-world service from Tokyo to London via Honolulu, San Francisco and New York, returning along the airline's Silk Route via the Middle East and south-east Asia (→ Apr 18).

**Vietnam, March 10**
USAF Captain Max Brestel, flying an F-105 Thunderchief, shoots down two MiG-17 fighters in a single mission. The F-105 is really an attack bomber.

**Britain, March 18**
RAF and Royal Navy aircraft bomb the tanker *Torrey Canyon*, which has foundered off Land's End; the purpose is to burn off oil before it reaches the coast.

**Bangalore, India, March 29**
The first Indian-designed fighter, the Hindustan Aeronautics HF-24 Marut, makes its initial flight.

**USA, April 6**
TWA becomes the first US airline to have an all-jet fleet.→

**Marseilles, France, April 7**
French airplane manufacturer Sud-Aviation launches an all-new helicopter, the SA 340 Gazelle.

**Wichita, Kansas, April 10**
William Lear's Learjet Corporation is sold to the Gates Rubber Company (→ Feb 20, 1968).

**Moscow, April 18**
JAL and Aeroflot open a jointly-operated service between Moscow and Tokyo (→ Jun 16, 1968).

**Vietnam, April 20**
Haiphong suffers its first bombing raid of the war as it is hit by 86 US airplanes from the carriers USS *Kitty Hawk* and USS *Ticonderoga*.

**Sydney, April 27**
Qantas introduces Lockheed Electras on its service to Johannesburg, slicing almost six hours off the time taken by the Super Constellation (→ Aug 1).

**England, May 23**
The prototype Hawker Siddeley Nimrod maritime reconnaissance aircraft – a development of the D.H. Comet 4 – begins flight trials (→ Oct 2, 1969).

**Manchester, June 4**
In the second disaster involving British holidaymakers in two days, a British Midland Airways Argonaut bringing tourists home from the island of Majorca in the Mediterranean crashes near the airport, killing 72; yesterday, 88 died when a chartered DC-4 bound for Spain's Costa Brava crashed in the Pyrenees.

**Middle East, June 5**
The Israeli air force launches pre-emptive strikes against Egypt, Syria and Jordan.→

**Seattle, June 6**
Boeing delivers its 1,000th jet airliner, a 707-323 for American Airlines (→).

**France, June 28**
One of France's oldest airplane manufacturers, Breguet, is taken over by Dassault.

**Wiltshire, England, July**
The first Lockheed C-130K Hercules to enter service with the RAF are delivered to N° 36 Squadron at Lyneham.

**Sydney, August 1**
Qantas, which has been formally called Qantas Empire Airways since 1934, adopts the title Qantas Airways Ltd (→ Sep 17, 1971).

**Spain, August 7**
Iberia and Aerolineas Argentinas jointly launch the world's longest non-stop air route, between Madrid and Buenos Aires, a total of 6,462 miles.

**Seattle, August 8**
Boeing's 737-200, 6 feet longer than its 737-100 predecessor and capable of carrying up to 130 tourist-class passengers, makes its maiden flight (→ Feb 4, 1968).

**Moscow, September 15**
Aeroflot introduces the Ilyushin Il-62 jet airliner into international service on its route to Montreal (→ Aug 14, 1972).

**Kobe, Japan, October 5**
The prototype Shin Meiwa SS-2 flying boat begins flight tests.

**Moscow, October 5**
M Komarov sets a world closed-circuit speed record of 1,852mph, in a Mikoyan Ye-266 (MiG-25).

**Lagos, Nigeria, October 7**
Four (allegedly drunk) white mercenary airmen, hired by Biafran separatists, decide on the spur of the moment to bomb the Nigerian high command, but their airplane explodes in mid-air when it is hit by anti-aircraft fire.

**New Zealand, November 5**
Air New Zealand reopens weekly services to Tahiti, which ended following the termination of air rights in February 1964; the route is envisaged as the first leg of a new service to Los Angeles.

**Middle East, November 8**
British troops are withdrawn from Aden by 50 transport aircraft flying the RAF's biggest airlift operation since the Berlin Airlift.

**Istres, France, November 18**
The Dassault Mirage G becomes the first European-designed swing-wing jet aircraft to fly.

**West Germany, December 16**
The Dornier Do 31E vertical/short take-off and landing aircraft makes its first transition from vertical to horizontal flight.

**Nebraska, December 29**
US Strategic Air Command retires its last Boeing B-47 Stratojet from service, at Offutt Air Force Base.

---

*The Bell UH-1 is the most widely-used helicopter in Vietnam. Its official US Army name is Iroquois, but it is known as the "Huey".* ▶

# Dornier launches a ten-engined vertical take-off and landing transport airplane

*The Do 31E is being test-flown from Dornier's airfield at Oberpfaffenhofen.*

**Bavaria, West Germany, Feb 10**
The largest vertical/short take-off and landing (V/STOL) aircraft currently under development, West Germany's Dornier Do 31E, made its first flight today. Two prototypes were ordered by the West German defense ministry and built with the assistance of VFW and Hamburger Flugzeugbau.

The Do 31E is an experimental transport, hence its large size, with accommodation for 36 troops, 24 litters, vehicles or cargo. The characteristic which distinguishes it most from conventional transports is its small, upright lift-jets housed in removable wing-tip pods. Each pod accomodates four 4,400-lb thrust Rolls-Royce RB.162-4D turbojets in a row, each of them fitted with deflector nozzles to allow thrust to be directed.

The main horizontal thrust is provided by two Pegasus turbofans of Harrier jump-jet type, which can also be vectored to provide lift. Should one fail in the vertical-lift phase, the wing-tip lift-jets help check roll movement (→ Dec 16).

**Sikorsky's S-64 Skycrane heavy-lift helicopter performs one of its many functions, rebuilding a bridge in South Vietnam. The S-64, called the CH-54A Tarhe by the US Army, is equipped with interchangeable pods and can be used as a troop transport, a field hospital or a minelayer.**

# HueyCobra ordered for action in Vietnam

*Fort Worth, Texas March*
The US Army has ordered 529 new helicopters of a type yet to see active service, and the first ones are due to begin operations in Vietnam by September. The type is Bell's new AH-1G HueyCobra: a helicopter designed solely as a gunship which is fast, maneuverable and packs a lot of firepower to protect assault troops.

The AH-1G can reach close to 200mph. The tandem seating for a pilot and co-pilot/gunner in a fighter-like cockpit gives an all-round field of view. This enhanced visibility affords the gunner maximum effectiveness from the six-barrel, 4,000-rounds a minute 7.62mm Minigun mounted in a turret below the aircraft's nose. As the gunner tracks the target with his sight, the gun swivels through a 230-degree field of fire which can be raised 25 degrees or lowered 50 degrees. This enables the AH-1G to avoid hovering while allowing a gunner to keep firing on a target.

The HueyCobra carries additional weapons on its stubby wings, including 78 2.75-inch rockets in four 19-tube rocket pods, which can be fired in pairs from opposite wing-stations. The number of pairs of rockets to be fired can be preselected from one to 19 by the gunner. The rockets can be replaced by other pods containing 7.62mm Miniguns or 20mm cannon and their ammunition.

*From the top: UH-1D troop transport; UH-IB gunship; AH-IG HueyCobra.*

# Ailing Douglas agrees McDonnell merger

*St Louis, January 13*
The fourth largest company in the US aerospace industry was created today when the financially ailing Douglas Aircraft Company agreed to merge with the McDonnell Company to form the McDonnell Douglas Corporation.

Based on 1965 data, the new company will rank behind Boeing, North American and Lockheed with sales of $1.7 billion and assets of approximately $951 million.

Douglas was forced to seek a merger when delays in the delivery of jet engines for its highly successful DC-8 and DC-9 airliners, allied to a shortage of skilled workers and its volume of business, outstripped its capacity to deliver. This forced operating costs up, and despite $3 billion in orders Douglas is expected to lose $40 million this fiscal year. McDonnell, whose main business is military aircraft and space vehicles, was one of five suitors.

# Jet transport moves into a new era

## TWA has first all-jet fleet of airliners

*St Louis, Missouri, April 6*
An era closed today when the last of what was once the industry's largest fleet of Lockheed Constellations completed a farewell flight for TWA from New York's John F Kennedy International Airport to St Louis. Because of TWA owner Howard Hughes's links with Lockheed, the Constellation and TWA almost became synonymous from the close of the war until the development of jets. TWA is the first US airline to have a fleet entirely of jets, made by Douglas (now McDonnell Douglas), Boeing and Convair.

*Boeing's 737 is winning orders with its promise of cheap short-haul operations.*

## USAF helicopters fly the Atlantic

*Le Bourget, Paris, June 1*
Spectacular proof that helicopters are not merely short-range aircraft came today when two Sikorskys HH-3Es landed at the Paris airshow here after flying non-stop from New York. Refueled nine times in flight, the HH-3Es had succeeded in flying 4,271 miles in 30 hours 46 minutes – three hours less than it took Charles Lindbergh when he flew the same route 40 years ago.

These turbine-powered helicopters, based on the CH-3E, are made for rescue work and used by the Aerospace Rescue and Recovery Service. Their top speed is 162mph and operating ceiling 11,000 feet.

## Carriers cast their vote for new Boeing 737

*Seattle, April 9*
The first "baby Boeing", the Model 737, started its flight-test program this morning. It plugs a gap in the company's product range for a short-haul airliner, and production deliveries are scheduled to begin later this year, after certification.

With an initial order from Lufthansa, the 737 has the distinction of being the first US airliner launched by a foreign airline. Total sales to date stand at well over 100 and are growing rapidly, mainly on the backs of United Air Lines and Western Air Lines, which together ordered 60 initially. The United

order is for the 737-200. This is similar to the 737-100 but lengthened by 6 feet to carry 115-130 passengers. It is fitted with more powerful Pratt & Whitney JT8D-9 turbofan engines. United is currently discussing a deal to buy around 60 more airliners from Boeing, of which nearly half will be 737s.

The success of the 737 and Douglas DC-9 has been a not unexpected blow to Britain's BAC One-Eleven short-haul jet, which was hoping to break into the US market in a big way. However, it has useful orders from American Airlines, Braniff and Mohawk (→Aug 8).

*TWA is leading the way with its ultra-modern, all-jet fleet.*

*Igor Sikorsky (l) and the two pilots who made the transatlantic flight.*

## Boeing delivers its 1,000th jet airliner

*Seattle, June 6*
American Airlines took delivery of a new Boeing 707-323 today – the 1,000th jet airliner to leave the factories of the great Seattle manufacturer. While Boeing and American Airlines were celebrating today, champagne was not being drunk at United Air Lines, which had lost the "war for the 1,000th Boeing". Minutes after American got its 707, United took delivery of a Boeing 727. This machine, which left the Renton factory in Seattle on April 20, was supposed to be the 1,000th Boeing to be delivered. United was pipped at the post.

# Dassault unveils the first of 50 Mirage V fighters for Israel

*The Mirage V's fuel capacity allows a 35 per cent greater range over the IIIE.*

*Melun-Villaroche, France, May 19*
For some time the Israeli air force has worked closely with French manufacturer Dassault to develop a simpler, cheaper version of the Mirage IIIE fighter, designated the Mirage V. An order for 50 such aircraft was placed last year.

The Mirage V flew for the first time today. It is a single-seat ground-attack aircraft, capable of speeds in excess of Mach 2, and has the ability to operate on rough airfield surfaces. The maintenance of the Mirage V will be easier than that of the IIIE, as it has fewer electronics. This fact and its longer fuselage give a much increased storage and fuel capacity (→Jun 5).

# Israeli air power is decisive in Six-Day War

## Pre-emptive strike destroys Egyptian aircraft on the ground

*Middle East, June 5*

Israel and its Arab neighbours are at war. At 8.45am, after days of rising tension, the Israeli air force delivered a bold pre-emptive strike against the Egyptian air force. Nine Egyptian airfields came under simultaneous attack from Israeli fighter/bombers including Mirage III CJs and Mystère IVAs carrying anti-runway "dibber" bombs, Vautours with 1,000-pounders and Super Mystères loaded with 500-pounders. They cratered the runways and hit parked aircraft before making repeated strafing runs, hitting aircraft and ground installations with cannon fire.

A few Egyptian fighters got airborne, but ten were shot down in aerial combat and more were lost landing on the damaged runways or crashed after running out of fuel with nowhere to land. At 9.30am, the Israelis were back, having returned to base where in ten minutes they were refueled and rearmed, and some had battle damage repaired. By 1.00pm they had destroyed half Egypt's aircraft including most

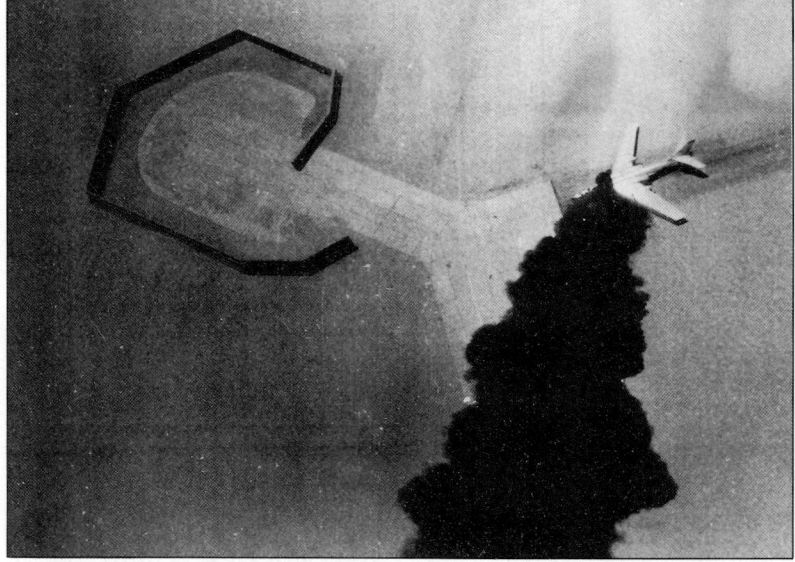

*A Tupolev Tu-16 heavy bomber, destroyed on an Egyptian airfield.*

of the Tu-16 and Il-28 bombers, which could have been used to strike back at Israel, and most of the MiG-21 and MiG-19 fighters.

Attacks were also made against the Syrian and Jordanian air forces, and by this evening 25 Arab air-

fields were out of action and 350 aircraft had been destroyed, all but around 24 on the ground. Israel lost 19 aircraft, with eight aircrew killed and 11 missing, but its pilots have won air superiority and can turn their attention elsewhere (→ Jun 10).

## Mirage wins battle honors in the air

*Israel, June 10*

Destroying Arab air power on the ground was the key to Israel's air superiority, but Israeli fighter pilots outperformed their Arab counterparts in the air too. The most advanced Israeli fighter, the Dassault Mirage IIICJ, though marginally less maneuverable than the best Arab fighter, the MiG-21F, carried the major honors. Israeli Mirage pilots accounted for 48 Arab fighters in aerial combat, losing eight Mirages to ground fire and one in the air, caught alone by eight MiGs.

The Mirage comes out of the war with a much enhanced reputation, meaning increased foreign sales for Dassault, which is ironic, since it was at least in part the embargo on further sales of Mirages to Israel by French President de Gaulle, when he backed the Arabs, which precipitated the war by cutting of the flow of spare parts for them. It is also ironic, since most of the credit for the Mirages' performance is down to the Israeli pilots who flew them.

# Israel's 'air umbrella' gave key to victory for its land forces

*Air superiority: an Israeli Mirage in the empty skies over Amman, Jordan.*

*Sinai Desert, June 10*

At 6.30pm, after six days of intensive fighting, Israel agreed to a cease-fire, having taken the Sinai Desert from Egypt, the West Bank from Jordan and the Golan Heights from Syria. Without the Israeli air

force it could not have been done. Having achieved air superiority on day one, Israel quickly established an air umbrella over its own ground forces, enabling transport and liaison aircraft, helicopters and reconnaissance aircraft to fly unmolested

by Arab fighters. Then the air force provided "flying artillery" for the Israeli army, flying hundreds of sorties every day to ground units.

The Egyptian army started retreating across Sinai toward the Suez canal on the second day of fighting, but without air cover the convoys were sitting ducks for the Israeli air force. Restricting them to three roads, two of them through the Giddi and Mitla passes, the Israelis turned the desert into a graveyard of burnt-out vehicles.

On the fourth day the air force turned its attention to supporting the Israeli force which had the task of taking the strategically important Golan Heights to the north. More ground attack sorties were flown on this front than on any other, hitting the defenders and cutting off Syrian reinforcements as the armored brigades inched their way up the steep slopes and, after a fierce battle, took the summit.

**Israeli air force commander-in-chief Brig-Gen Mordecai Hod oversaw a brilliant display of air strategy during the Six-Day War. Israel destroyed 452 Arab aircraft (all but 79 were hit on the ground) in the conflict for the loss of just 46 Israeli aircraft.**

# Joanne Fletcher is Eastern's first black stewardess

*Miami, Florida, July 1*
It has taken Joanne Fletcher eight long months to get a job as an airline stewardess. Few applicants were better qualified than Joanne, a fully trained nurse and linguist. The only thing against her was the color of her skin, which US airlines reckoned was just too dark at a time when the nation is recovering from major urban race riots.

In the end it was Eastern Air Lines which gave her a job, but only after three interviews with its personnel department. Most airlines deny vehemently that they operate any kind of color bar, but very few US airlines have hired a black stewardess since Mohawk Airlines became the first to do so in 1957.

It is hoped that more black women may follow "Joni" Fletcher's example. She is a battler and refuses to take "no" for an answer. This paid off today, as it also did when she became the first black woman to work for the Agricultural Credit Union in Washington.

# USAF steps up attacks on Vietnam

*Haiphong after a bruising B-52 raid.*

*A C-141 StarLifter takes off from the US Air Force base at Tan Son Nhut.*

*Takhli, Thailand, August 11*
Following US President Lyndon B Johnson's approval of a new group of targets in North Vietnam, US Air Force fighter/bombers based here and elsewhere in Thailand today attacked the Paul Doumer bridge, Hanoi, for the first time. The go-ahead from the President was a response to congressional criticism of target restrictions, particularly from Senate Preparedness Subcommittee chairman John Stennis and other committee members.

The President's action marks the first intensification of the air war since the spring, when targets in Hanoi and Haiphong were first struck. The new target list includes transportation centers and industrial installations in both Hanoi and Haiphong and along the railroad between Hanoi and China. The Doumer bridge crosses the Red river from the north-east edge of Hanoi. Its targeting is significant because four of the five major rail lines in the country meet there and it carries about 26 trains each day.

Closing it should severely disrupt rail and road traffic carrying supplies to the south. Despite heavy flak, today's raid – by F-105 Thunderchiefs using 3,000-lb bombs – succeeded in closing the bridge by destroying two sections.

# Soviets put new fighters through paces before Western visitors

*Visitors were most impressed by the first MiG swing-wing prototype, the 23-11/1, with its K-23 missiles.*

*Moscow, July 9*
Several previously unknown Soviet fighters and research aircraft were publicly displayed at the Aviation Day Air Show at Moscow's Domodedovo airport today. It was the first such display in six years. Western observers were impressed by the thunderous flyby of four MiG fighters, faster than any previously known. They were MiG-25s, called "Foxbats" by Nato; as the Ye-266 one of these has gained many world records. Both the MiG and Sukhoi teams showed modifications of existing fighters, some with lift-jets in the fuselage and others with pivoted swing wings. These aircraft are designed to carry heavier loads from shorter airstrips. Even more of a surprise was the Yakovlev Yak-36. Two of these vertical take-off and landing jet airplanes were on view, one of them in flight.

The Yak-36s are not fighters but research aircraft from which a production combat airplane will probably be developed. In contrast, the other airplanes appear to be almost ready for service (→ Oct 5).

# Sonic boom 'causes death of workers'

*Mauran, France, August 1*
Three Breton farmworkers died today when the barn in which they were working collapsed. The cause was alleged to have been a boom from a supersonic aircraft, although no such aircraft were over Brittany at the time.

Since SSTs (supersonic transports) began to be developed, the subject of the sonic boom has generated intense media interest, most particularly in English-speaking countries. There have been countless articles, interviews and tests designed to highlight the dangers of aircraft sonic booms to people and property, even though the loudest and most widespread of all booms is natural thunder.

A series of tests flown by Lightning fighters over England failed to cause expected damage to buildings, but prolonged tests in 1964 over Oklahoma City in the US aroused much public hostility.

# Europeans sign accord for new Airbus

*Paris, September 26*
Today the governments of France, West Germany and Britain signed a memorandum of understanding (MoU) for development of the Airbus A300 wide-bodied jet airliner. The designation reflects the proposed capacity of 300 seats.

The MoU runs until July 31 next year, providing the authority for design studies and project definition to be continued. Sud-Aviation of France, Deutsche Airbus of West Germany and Hawker Siddeley of Britain will be partners in the development and production of the airframe, with Sud-Aviation as project leader. Rolls-Royce (Britain), SNECMA (France) and MAN-Turbo (West Germany) will look after the engines. Airframe costs will be shared as follows: 37.5 per cent France, 37.5 per cent Britain and 25 per cent West Germany. Britain will meet 75 per cent of the engine costs, with France and West

Germany paying 12.5 per cent each, reflecting Rolls-Royce's leadership in development of the expected RB.207 advanced turbofan. Discussions on the development of a short-to medium-range wide-bodied European airliner date from 1965, when British and French representatives first met. With West German interest high, no time was lost in including that country, too, in the discussions, leading to the first official tripartite agreements last year (→ Mar 1, 1969).

*Tunnel tests on a model Airbus.*

# F-111 prepares to enter combat service

*Nellis AFB, Nevada, December 31*
The 474th Tactical Fighter Wing of the USAF is gradually beginning to build up its strength in readiness for the deployment of some of its new F-111A airplanes to Thailand next year. The first of the large swing-wing bombers was received last July, and fully operational aircraft have been arriving since October.

The F-111A is the controversial twin-jet made at Fort Worth, Texas, by General Dynamics. The

F-111B Navy version is currently experiencing such trouble that it is likely to be canceled. The USAF models are also troubled but are considered so important that they are likely to go ahead. In the pipeline are the F-111C for Australia, the FB-111A for USAF Strategic Air Command and the improved F-111D, E and F for Tactical Air Command. No other airplane can fly blind missions against point targets (→ Mar 17, 1968).

*Breaking new ground: the General Dynamics F-111A fighter/bomber.*

# Rocket plane soars to record 4,534 mph

*California, October 3*
Piloted from Edwards Air Force Base by USAF test pilot Major William J "Pete" Knight, the North American rocket-powered research airplane X-15A-2 flew today at 4,534mph, or Mach 6.72. This is the highest speed reached in the X-15 program and the fastest any airplane has ever flown.

The original X-15 did not carry sufficient propellant for its powerful rocket engine to reach the maximum speed of which it was capable. The A-2 version carries giant under-wing tanks, one holding liquid oxygen and the other ammonia. These extend the time the rocket burns, although the extra weight prevents it from reaching an even higher speed (→ Jan 29, 1968).

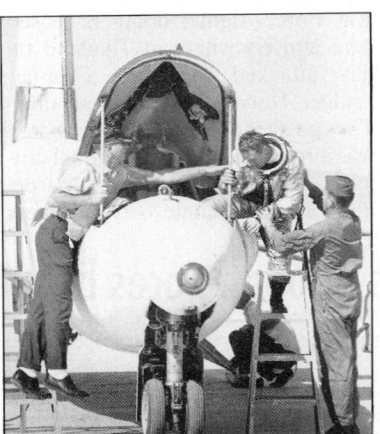
*Major Knight after the record flight.*

# Water-bomber set to take on forest fires

*Montreal, Canada, 23 October*
The Canadair CL-215 fire-fighting amphibian took to the air today for the first time. At a symposium on forest-fire control in Ottawa in December 1963 it was recognized that a new aircraft was needed to take the "water-bomber" role until then filled by the Catalina. The CL-215, which was committed to production early last year, meets the needs identified at that time. It can lift 1,462 US gallons of water in two fuselage tanks which are filled, through retractable inlets under the hull, as the aircraft taxis across the surface of a convenient stretch of water. A load can be dropped every ten minutes (→ Aug 31, 1974).

# Hero wins prize for services to aviation

*Robin Olds, Vietnam air strategist.*

*Washington, DC, December 15*
The man who led the USAF's most effective anti-MiG unit in Vietnam, Colonel Robin Olds, has won this year's Kitty Hawk memorial award for achievement in military aviation. Colonel Olds commanded the 8th Tactical Fighter Wing "Wolf Pack" at Ubon Royal Thai Air Force Base. The wing's F-4 Phantom aircrews shot down 25 MiGs in the course of the year.

Colonel Olds designed missions to lure the MiGs into the air so that the threat to bomb-laden USAF aircraft attacking heavily defended targets in North Vietnam could be reduced. It proved a highly effective tactic, which saw its greatest success on January 2, when seven MiG-21s fell to the "Wolf Pack".

*The CL-215 drops its unusual load.*

# France takes wraps off the first Concorde airliner

*The 001 prototype is rolled out at Toulouse. It has not yet been fitted with engines; a thorough schedule of ground tests is planned before the first flight.*

*Toulouse, France, December 11*
In the presence of over 1,100 guests from almost every group associated with the aircraft, the first prototype Concorde was ceremonially rolled out here today. It marks what everyone at Sud-Aviation and the British Aircraft Corporation hopes will be the dawn of the age of the supersonic transport (SST), when long-haul flight times will be cut by more than half.

The aircraft unveiled today is called Concorde 001. Almost completed at BAC's factory north of

Bristol is 002. British technology minister Anthony Wedgwood Benn resolved a minor controversy today when he announced at Toulouse that from now on the British aircraft would be called Concorde, like the French one, and not Concord. The extra "e", he said, stood for "excellence, England, Europe and *entente*".

In overall shape, aerodynamics, flight controls, environmental system, propulsion and auxiliary systems Concorde is a generation ahead of all other civil transports.

One obvious new feature is the "droop-snoot" nose, with a sliding vizor, which enables the pilots to have a good view ahead on take-off and landing, yet adjust the nose to a perfect streamlined form suitable for Mach 2. The planned cruising speed of Mach 2.2, or 1,450mph, is the practical limit for an aluminum aircraft. In service, airlines may choose the slightly slower speed of Mach 2 to avoid any thermal fatigue problems. Inevitably Concorde has to be extremely long and slender, and the

cross-section of the 128-seat passenger cabin is similar to that of a DC-3. Opponents of the SST have compared the somewhat cramped interior unfavorably with the forthcoming 747. But the designers will make it as comfortable as possible, and, in any case, passengers will be on board for only half the current journey time for long-haul flights.

Yet to be resolved are the overall economics of SST transportation, and, especially, the vexed question of noise, both from sonic booms and at take-off (→ Sep 19, 1968).

# Cathay Pacific halts Saigon flights as US steps up war airlift

*Hong Kong, November 17*
Cathay Pacific has halted all flights from Hong Kong's Kai Tak airport to Saigon while the USAF borrows it for Operation Eagle Thrust, a massive airlift of men and material to Vietnam.

Set up with a few DC-3s after the Second World War by Roy Farrell and Sydney de Kantzow, Cathay Pacific has grown from the maverick cargo carrier nicknamed "Syd's Pirates" of the late 1940s (motto: fly anything, anywhere) into one of the best organized airlines of the Far East. Based in this British colony, it has built up an impressive Asian network (→ Mar 1, 1968).

*Part of the runway at Hong Kong airport is on land overhanging the sea.*

# US plans a reusable plane to orbit Earth

*Washington, DC, December 31*
Officials of the US National Aeronautics and Space Administration (NASA) have been involved in talks with the federal government and US industry aimed at laying down the guidelines for a future space transportation system which is reusable by being capable of landing intact on its return to Earth.

The main problem with today's rockets is that they are lost on every launch. A "space shuttle", by being used many times like an airplane, should slash the costs of the US space program (→ Jan 5, 1972).

*The Pilatus P-8 Twin Porter, a twin-engined development of the Porter.*

*Canada's Found Centennial 100, designed as a six-seat utility aircraft.*

*Fokker's F.28 Fellowship was a twin-jet successor to the Friendship. It made its maiden flight on May 9, 1967, and went into service two years later.*

*Advance orders ensured that the twin-jet Boeing 737 short-range transport was a success before it flew; it became the all-time best-seller.*

*The Beriev Be-30 light turboprop transport did not enter production.*

*The Ted Smith Aerostar six-seater was manufactured in three variants.*

*SIAT 223 Flamingo production was taken over by MBB and then CASA.*

*SOCATA's ST 10 Diplomate was originally known as the Provence.*

*Volpar's Turboliner development: new life for Beech's Model 18.*

*The One-Eleven 500: a stretched version of BAC's successful short/medium-range airliner, with extended wing-tips and seating for 119 passengers.*

*Dornier Do 31E: four Rolls-Royce lift engines in each wing-tip pod.*

*The agile Rollason Beta single-seat aircraft for competition aerobatics.*

*Jetstream production was taken over by Scottish Aviation and then British Aerospace following the demise of the originating company, Handley Page.*

*The Zlin 42 was a two-seat trainer and tourer from Czechoslovakia.*

*From Italy: SIAI-Marchetti's S.208 all-metal five-seater.*

*The Taylor J.T.1 was popular with the builders of homemade aircraft.*

*When the Beagle Pup was taken over by Scottish Aviation, the new manufacturer developed it as the Bulldog trainer, which entered RAF service [p.679].*

The first prototype of the Dassault Mirage G two-seat variable-geometry fighter was lost in an accident on January 13, 1971. Two more were built.

Jim Bede's unconventional BD-2 pusher was destined for obscurity.

The McDonnell Douglas DC-9-40 was specially designed for SAS use.

The smart Robin DR.253 was superseded by the DR.400/180 Régent.

The McDonnell Douglas DC-8-60 series made ideal freight transports.

The Hughes' 500 series has found many civil and military applications.

The USSR's widely used MiG-23 variable-geometry fighter.

Powered by a J75, and with a saiplane-like wing of over 103ft span, the U-2R weighs more than twice as much as the first Lockheed U-2 of 1955.

The RAF's McDonnell Douglas F-4M has Rolls-Royce Spey engines.

Canadair's CL.215 amphibian water-bomber wars on forest fires.

Westland's Sea King used the Sikor-sky SH-3D's airframe and rotor.

The Sikorsky HH-53B Super Jolly rescued combat aircrew in Vietnam.

The Aérospatiale SA 341 Gazelle helicopter first flew on April 7, 1967.

The BAC Jet Provost T.5 continued the line of Percival military trainers.

Boeing Vertol's CH-47C had more power and fuel than earlier variants.

The MBB Bo 105, a successful twin turbine helicopter.

The Grumman TC-4C was used to train A-6A Intruder navigators.

Argentina's FMA IA.58 Pucará was designed for counter-insurgency.

The multi-mission Saab 37 Viggen, with its canard foreplane, has been adapted to serve in attack, interception, reconnaissance and training roles.

Aeritalia's AM.3C, for army co-operation over the battlefield.

Only ten Lockheed YAH-56 fire-support helicopters were built.

# 1968

4,534mph
USA
Pete Knight
North American X-15
Oct 3, 1967

24,325 miles
USA
Archie Old Jr
Boeing B-52B
Jan 18, 1957

354,200ft
USA
Joseph Walker
North American X-15
Aug 22, 1963

769,000lb
USA
Lockheed
C-5A Galaxy

44,095lb thrust
USSR
Kouznetsov
NK-144

**England, January 5**
The RAF's № 24 Squadron makes a ceremonial formation flight from Colerne to Aldershot and back to mark the retirement of the Handley Page Hastings transport after 20 years in service.

**London, January 15**
The British government announces the cancellation of its order for 50 General Dynamics F-111Ks, which were to have replaced the canceled TSR.2 (→ Mar 17).

**Washington, DC, January 15**
Air Defense Command is redesignated Aerospace Defense Command (ADC).

**Greenland, January 21**
A Strategic Air Command B-52 carrying four nuclear bombs crashes on approach to Thule Air Force Base; the bombs are all destroyed in the ensuing fire.

**USA, January 29**
Officials announce that the successful North American X-15 program will be terminated at the end of the year.

**Wichita, Kansas, February 20**
A standard Learjet 25 sets a new "time-to-climb" record by climbing to 40,000 feet in 6 minutes 29 seconds (→ Aug 30, 1970).

**Marietta, Georgia, March 2**
President Johnson attends the roll-out of the USAF's Lockheed C-5A Galaxy transport, the world's largest aircraft (→ Jun 30).

**Vietnam, March 3**
A patrol of USAF AC-47 aircraft, codenamed "Spooky", repels a Viet Cong night attack; since the Tet Offensive, launched on January 31, these airplanes, armed with three SU-11A Miniguns, have been keeping a constant watch over US bases in Vietnam.

**Istres, France, March 9**
René Leduc, 70, renowned for his development of ramjet-powered aircraft, dies.

**Vietnam, March 17**
The General Dynamics F-111A makes its first operational flight of the war (→ Mar 31).

**Moscow, March 27**
Yuri Gagarin, in April 1961 first man in space, is killed in the crash of a MiG-15UTI trainer near the Soviet capital.

**London, April 26**
The *Daily Mail* newspaper announces that it will sponsor an Atlantic air race in 1969 to mark the 50th anniversary of the first transatlantic flight; prize money will total £45,000 (→ May 11, 1969).

**Somerset, England, April 29**
The Fleet Air Arm takes delivery of its first McDonnell Douglas F-4K Phantom II carrier-based fighter-interceptors at Yeovilton air station (→ Jan 14, 1969).

**USA, April 29**
United Air Lines becomes the first carrier to put the Boeing 737-200, a larger-capacity version of the standard 737, into service.

**London, May 16**
A BOAC Super VC10 on a routine service from Chicago and Montreal makes the airline's first fully automatic approach and landing.

**Norwegian Sea, May 25**
A Soviet Tu-16 "Badger-F" reconnaissance airplane crashes into the water 8 miles from the carrier USS *Essex* after making low passes over the ship.

**London, June 8**
Barnes Wallis, developer of the R.100 airship, the bouncing bombs used in the Second World War raid on the Ruhr dams, and also of the geodetic airframe of the Wellington bomber, receives a knighthood for services to aviation.

**Berkshire, England, June 14**
To mark the 50th anniversary of the creation of the RAF, Queen Elizabeth II reviews the service at Abingdon.

**Tokyo, June 16**
Japan Air Lines opens a non-stop service to San Francisco using the longest-range version of the DC-8, the DC-8-62 (→ Mar 30, 1969).

**Long Beach, California, June 17**
The first C-9A Nightingale, a version of the McDonnell Douglas DC-9 adapted for use by Military Airlift Command as an aeromedical transport, is rolled out.

**Vietnam, June 18**
USAF B-52 bombers complete three years of war operations; they have flown more than 25,000 sorties, dropping over 630,000 tons of conventional bombs.

**Bucharest, June 20**
Romanian airline Tarom, which has bought six British BAC One-Eleven short-haul jet airliners, puts the type into service between here and Frankfurt.

**Hertfordshire, England, June 28**
A formation fly-past by six Avro Ansons at RAF Bovingdon marks the type's withdrawal from service after a record 32-year career.

**Aldergrove, N Ireland, July 20**
The RAF's first McDonnell Douglas Phantom FGR.2 ground-attack and tactical-reconnaissance aircraft is delivered (→ May 7, 1969).

**Costa Rica, August 1**
Two USAF helicopters assist in efforts to evacuate people threatened by the eruption of the Arenal volcano.

**Nigeria, August 13**
Swedish pilot Count Carl Gustav von Rosen braves Nigerian air defenses to fly in supplies to Biafran separatist rebels whom the Nigerian government is attempting to starve into submission.

**New York, August 14**
TWA convenes a meeting of air-transport companies in the area to discuss problems of congestion at airports, especially JFK.

**Paris, August 28**
French pioneer aircraft manufacturer Robert Morane, 82, dies.

**Derbyshire, England, August 31**
Rolls-Royce carries out the first successful bench test of its RB.211 turbofan engine (→ Aug 29, 1969).

**Istres, France, September 8**
The Anglo-French Jaguar E.01 warplane prototype flies for the first time.→

**Auckland, September 11**
To mark the 40th anniversary of Charles Kingsford Smith's epic flight across the Tasman Sea, an Air New Zealand DC-8 flies to Sydney carrying T H Williams, the navigator who flew with "Smithy" on his record-breaking trip.

**Mediterranean Sea, September 11**
An Air France Caravelle jet carrying 95 passengers from Ajaccio, Corsica, to Nice, France, catches fire and crashes off Antibes.

**Seattle, December 19**
The Boeing Company receives its first order, from Israeli airline El Al, for a long-range version of the 747 Jumbo Jet, production of which was announced just under a month ago (→ Feb 9, 1969).

**Beirut, December 28**
In reprisal for an attack against an El Al airliner at Athens two days ago by two Palestinians, an Israeli commando destroys eight airplanes of Middle East Airlines, three of Lebanese International Airlines and two of Trans Mediterranean Airlines (→ Oct 31, 1969).

**Seattle, December 31**
This year Boeing has delivered a record 378 airliners: 111 707s, 160 727s and 107 737s.

---

*The Soviet Union's Tu-144 makes its first flight on the last day of 1968. It is slightly bigger than the Anglo-French Concorde.* ▶

# Air power enters crucial phase in Vietnam War

## Air drops send aid to Marines in siege

*Khe Sanh, Vietnam, March 1*
Air power is the only thing keeping almost 7,000 isolated US Marines and South Vietnamese army troops here from being annihilated by an estimated force of 40,000 North Vietnamese and Viet Cong surrounding this plateau.

Every day since the siege began, on January 21, USAF transports and US Army and US Marine helicopters have come with supplies for the main garrison and its outposts. At first the C-130 Hercules would land on the short strip here, but this became too dangerous as rockets and artillery fire showered the field when they were present. So the landing of supplies and troop replacements, together with the evacuation of wounded, was left to the C-123 Providers and the helicopters, which do not need as much ground time. The C-130s, which initially dropped their loads by parachute, now use low-altitude parachute extraction system (LAPES) techniques to get the supplies in. Fighter/bombers, fixed-wing and helicopter gunships, and even B-52s with 54,000-pound bomb-loads, add their firepower to that of ground artillery at Khe Sanh, providing cover for resupply missions and also suppressing the enemy's artillery.

Some predicted that Khe Sanh would be the US's Dien Bien Phu; others put their faith in airpower and said it would not happen. They appear to be right: a massive air strike today drove the Viet Cong back into the hills.

*A US Navy F-8 Crusader launches rockets at besiegers around Khe Sanh.*

*Sky fire: an artist's view of a US AC-47 gunship blasting ground targets.*

## Comeback for C-47 as lethal gunship

*Vietnam, March*
The tracer fire between the Viet Cong and the outpost which they were attacking was clearly visible from the air at night. When the outpost asked for illumination, a parachute flare was dropped. Viet Cong tracer fire then rose like small phosphorescent globes toward the aircraft. The pilot put the airplane into a turn, flipped three switches, positioned his sight and pressed the trigger. Three six-barreled 7.62mm Miniguns, capable of firing up to 6,000 rounds per minute, hummed for about three seconds, and what looked like a red neon line stretched from the airplane to the ground. The Viet Cong tracer stopped. The 25-year-old military version of the DC-3 airliner, the C-47, rejuvenated as an AC-47 night-attack gunship, had done its job.

## Bad start for F-111

*Takhli Air Base, Thailand, Mar 31*
Spirits are low here today as Detachment 1 of the 428th Tactical Fighter Squadron, 474th Tactical Fighter Wing, gets down to planning its next mission over North Vietnam. Of the detachment's six aircraft, two have vanished in the first five days of deployment, without being fired on by the enemy. Everyone here wants the aircraft concerned, the new General Dynamics F-111A, to give the lie to its detractors, but nobody knows what downed the aircraft.

## First 'baby Boeings' arrive at Lufthansa

*Hamburg, [West] Germany, Feb 4*
Lufthansa maintained its loyalty to Boeing today when the West German flag-carrier took delivery of 21 of Boeing's new "baby" jet-airliner, the 737. This was the first 737 to be ordered and delivered, making Lufthansa the first foreign airline to launch a US airliner.

This new short-haul transport has 100 seats and is powered by two 14,500-lb thrust Pratt & Whitney JT8D-9A turbofans. Clearly a member of the Boeing family, the fuselage owes much to the 727, and the tail unit is derived from the larger 707. Nonetheless, this is a very different aircraft from its fellows. Boeing has accepted the twin-jet layout for the first time in this generation of its aircraft, and the interior design gives a surprisingly spacious feel to the short passenger cabin (→ Apr 29).

## Hostesses get new uniforms – of paper

*USA, January 1*
The public relations men have never doubted the value of a pretty face in selling an airline. What the traveling public does not know, however, is that the attractive hostess who serves them cocktails and plastic food trays is usually a highly trained professional, who speaks at least one foreign language and is able to cope with in-flight medical problems or even a full mid-air emergency. The PR people, however, are more concerned with appearance. TWA has just launched an idea in which its stewardesses change from formal uniform into costumes appropriate to the route – togas for Rome, chic cocktail dresses for Paris and somewhat sober gear for London. Unfortunately, the clothes are made of paper, a potential fire hazard. The idea may not last (→ Jan 31, 1970).

# Gargantuan Lockheed Galaxy, the world's biggest airplane, impresses on first flight

*Lockheed's C-5A Galaxy is capable of airlifting 750 infantry in a single load.*

**Marietta, Georgia, June 30**
The US's ability to move military forces rapidly anywhere in the world received a big boost today when the world's largest aircraft, the USAF's Lockheed C-5A Galaxy transport, completed a successful 94-minute first flight here.

The Galaxy looks like the highly successful Lockheed C-141A Star-Lifter, the long-haul workhorse of the USAF. But if the two aircraft were to be parked side by side the C-141A would be dwarfed by the C-5A, which has a wingspan more than 60 feet greater (222 feet) and is almost 100 feet longer (247 feet). The Galaxy is designed to carry

oversized, heavy cargo such as 50-ton tanks and 74-ton mobile bridge-launchers for the US Army. Its cargo compartment is 121 feet long with a minimum height of 9 feet 6 inches and a maximum height of 13 feet 6 inches. It has a usable volume of 34,796 cubic feet. A cargo ramp lowers to the ground at the aircraft rear; its nose can be opened to produce a ramp for straight-through loading of vehicles.

The Galaxy can fly 2,875 miles with a 265,000-lb load, or 6,325 miles with a 100,000-lb one, while cruising at over 500mph. If the whole aircraft is used, it can airlift up to 750 troops (→ Nov 15, 1969).

**Women's Royal Air Force officer Vivienne Whyer, in a Lightning, becomes the 1,000th member of the "Ten-Ton Club", for pilots who have flown at 1,000mph, during a flight with Grp Capt Mike Hobson.**

# Passengers escape Heathrow 707 blaze

**London, April 8**
In an amazing escape from a raging inferno, 110 passengers were evacuated from a blazing BOAC Boeing 707 jet airliner at Heathrow today. Tributes have been made to the skill and bravery of the crew.

All seemed normal as the airliner prepared for take-off, the 126 passengers settling down for a flight expecting it to be just another of thousands taking place safely the world over. It was not to be.

Just seconds after lift-off the number two engine failed catastrophically. Some of its compressor blades severed fuel pipes. The crew reacted immediately, but in their efforts to keep the airplane in the air the fuel pump was left on and the engine burst into flames. This is the second time a 707 engine has broken up.

With all the skill needed to captain a large jet, the pilot assessed the situation and told the control tower at Heathrow he needed to land immediately on the nearest runway. Every second counted. The airport's emergency services were alerted as the 707 prepared to touch down, while on board the passengers were readied for an emergency landing. Strong crosswinds hit the flaming airplane as it came in to land, and on the runway a wing burned through, spewing fire around the fuselage, through which the crew helped 110 of the passengers to escape.

*The crew's quick reactions saved 110 passengers from the blazing BOAC 707.*

# Hijacker forces pilot to fly him to Cuba

**Havana, February 21**
Apart from his white cowboy hat, there was nothing unusual about the customer in row 14 on Delta Air Lines' Flight 843 from Chicago to Miami – until he drew a gun on the stewardess and ordered her to take him to the flight deck. There, holding the pistol to the woman's head, he ordered the captain to divert to Havana. Captain J D Gainey had no choice but to obey. Over the cabin intercom, he told passengers calmly: "Folks, there's been a kind of change in our plans" and explained the situation.

On arrival in Cuba the hijacker disappeared into the airport building. The American passengers are being well looked after by the Cuban authorities (→ Jul 23).

# US scales down air attacks on Vietnam

**Washington, DC, March 31**
President Lyndon B Johnson told a nationwide television audience tonight that he would not seek re-election this year, and announced that air and naval attacks on most of North Vietnam would be halted immediately. The President said: "Tonight, in the hope that this action will lead to early talks, I am taking the first step to de-escalate the conflict. We are reducing – substantially reducing – the present level of hostilities. And we are doing so unilaterally and at once."

He said attacks would continue only in the demilitarized zone between North and South Vietnam, where a continuing build-up plus re-supply activities clearly threatened allied forces (→ Oct 31).

# Rolls-Royce gains big US engine order

*Derby, England, March 29*
Lockheed and Rolls-Royce jointly announced today that development of the L-1011 TriStar wide-bodied airliner is to go ahead. Lockheed already has orders for 144 aircraft, for which Rolls-Royce will provide engines. The Rolls-Royce RB.211 advanced three-shaft turbofan engine is essential to the airplane, offering a potential 25 per cent reduction in fuel consumption, lower weight, reduced noise on approach through lower fan speed while maintaining constant thrust by increasing the rpm of the compressor, easier maintenance and lower operating costs than its competitors. It is also less expensive, owing to a transatlantic price war to gain the order and the weakness of the pound (→ Aug 31).

# Last naval fighters

*Yeovilton, Somerset, April 29*
Three McDonnell Douglas F-4K Phantom interceptors arrived here today, destined for 892 Squadron, Fleet Air Arm, which has designated them FG.1. They will serve on Britain's last big carrier, HMS *Ark Royal*. As the last naval air superiority fighters, each of these aircraft will carry an Omega symbol on the tail, signifying the last of the line (→ Jan 14, 1969).

**Four twin-boom Sea Vixens lead a Buccaneer into a turn. They took part in this year's Farnborough, England, air show.**

# First executive jet flies Atlantic non-stop

*The Gulfstream II: from New Jersey to Gatwick in just 6 hours 55 minutes.*

*London, May 5*
A Grumman Gulfstream II today became the first executive jet to fly over the Atlantic non-stop. Taking off from Teterboro, NJ, it flew the 3,500 miles to London's Gatwick airport in six hours 55 minutes.

With no separate prototype built, the Gulfstream II made its first flight on October 2, 1966. Certification was granted on October 19 last year and the first airplane, the one which made today's historic flight, became the property of National Distillers & Chemical Corporation on December 6.

The Gulfstream II, which uses two Rolls-Royce Spey turbofan engines, is an entirely different airplane from the earlier turboprop-powered Gulfstream I. Nineteen passengers can be carried at speeds of up to 585mph. The aircraft's normal maximum range is 3,460 miles.

# Washington delays supersonic program

*Washington, DC, February 22*
Discussions between Federal Aviation Agency officials and the Boeing Company culminated today in the decision to delay the schedule for building the US's supersonic transport (SST) by one year. This is almost entirely because of unprecedented technical problems with the structurally overweight swing-wing Model 2707-200.

Boeing is expected to abandon the swing-wing formula entirely, even though it was this configuration which resulted in Boeing being chosen to build the SST over its rival Lockheed. Ironically, Boeing may now switch to a design resembling the Lockheed concept, but with a horizontal tail.

Congress will not now vote the earmarked $225 million for the project for US fiscal year 1969. This leaves Boeing's suppliers unable to continue work unless funds are quickly made available. Many of them, like Boeing itself, will incur extra costs in redesigning their systems and equipment (→ Dec 31).

# Juan Trippe retires after 41 years at the helm of Pan American

*New York, May 7*
Juan T Trippe, last of the pioneers who built the US's major airlines, announced his retirement today at the annual meeting of Pan American World Airways, the airline which he founded 41 years ago. Trippe, 68, follows Captain Eddie Rickenbacker, who retired from Eastern Air Lines at 73 in 1963, William A Patterson, who relinquished the helm of United Air Lines at 67 in 1966, Howard Hughes, who sold his last shares in TWA in the same year [*see page 645*], and C R Smith, 68, who left American Airlines in January.

Acting upon Trippe's recommendation, the Pan Am board of directors elected Harold E Gray, 62, to move up from president to replace Trippe as the airline's chairman and chief executive officer. Gray joined Pan Am in 1929 as the company's tenth pilot and made the first scheduled transatlantic flight in 1938. The senior vice-president Najeeb E Halaby, 53, former Administrator of the Federal Aviation

*Juan Trippe (c) hands over control of Pan Am to Gray (l) and Halaby (r).*

Agency – called the Federal Aviation Administration since last year – will take over the presidency. Trippe, who started Pan Am in 1927 with funds from friends Cornelius Vanderbilt Whitney and John T Hambleton and a contract from the US Post Office to fly mail from

Florida to Havana, has seen the airline grow into a carrier serving a total of 83 countries on six continents today. In his 41 years running Pan Am, Trippe opened up Latin America for other airlines as well as his own and provided the first reliable transoceanic routes.

# Britain rolls out the second Concorde

*Bristol, England, September 19*

The first Concorde supersonic airliner to be assembled in Britain was rolled out today from the so-called Brabazon hangar at the British Aircraft Corporation (BAC) plant at Filton, Bristol.

Registered G-BSST, Concorde 002 is fully painted and could fly in a few weeks, but it has already been decided that the French prototype will fly first. On its first flight 002 will take off from Filton, captained by company test pilot Brian Trubshaw, and land at Fairford RAF base in Gloucestershire, which has been equipped as the main Concorde flight-test center.

Although 002 was assembled at Filton, about half of it was made in France. In the same way, half of Concorde 001, the French prototype, was made in Britain. Currently nearing completion in the Brabazon hangar can be seen the first production aircraft, Concorde 01. Registered G-AXDN, the 01 incorporates numerous modifications, including a fuselage lengthened from an original 184 feet to 193 feet (but the final production aircraft will be 204 feet), a new "droop-snoot" nose with a fully transparent vizor, and increased weight and engine thrust. Other enhancements are planned for subsequent aircraft.

Technically, the future looks clear. But nobody can predict just how many Concordes will be sold, or how they will perform once they are in service (→ Dec 31).

*The Concorde prototype 002 at Filton, Bristol, before engine-running tests.*

*Putting it all together: at work on the forward fuselage of the 002 prototype.*

## Anglo-French co-operation bears fruit in versatile Jaguar fighter

*The Anglo-French Jaguar, designed to be used as both a trainer and a fighter.*

*Istres, France, September 8*

First Concorde and now Jaguar: a sure indication that cooperation between Britain and France is beginning to pay dividends. It was in 1965 that Breguet and British Aircraft Corporation design teams set out to meet a joint requirement from the RAF and the French air force and navy for a lightweight dual-role trainer and operational fighter. The first to be built was the French version, which flew for the first time today. It will be followed by operational-trainer versions, including the British Jaguar S and an export variant (→ Oct 12, 1969).

## Arabs hijack 707 of 'most secure airline in the world', El Al

*Algiers, July 23*

Dinner had just been served on the El Al flight from Rome to Tel Aviv when a shot was heard from the 707's flight deck, and the captain emerged with blood streaming from a headwound. Three Palestinian terrorists had accomplished what many thought impossible; they had hijacked an aircraft belonging to the Israeli airline, thought to be the most secure in the world.

The crew of ten and 12 Israeli nationals are being held as hostages in Algiers tonight; 20 other passengers have been flown to France. In Beirut, terrorist leader George Habash claimed that El Al was an auxiliary of the Israeli air force and had been used to ferry mercenaries to the Arab-Israeli Six-Day War last year.

One passenger said that the captain had bled onto a dinner plate. One of the hijackers dipped his thumb in the blood and said: "Not bad for an Israeli" (→ Dec 28).

## US and USSR begin new direct flights

*Moscow, July 15*

The first direct airline service between the Soviet Union and the US was inaugurated today, ten years after negotiations started. An Aeroflot Il-62, flown by Captain Boris Yegerov, landed at JFK after a 13 hour 17 minute flight with a stopover at Montreal. Pan Am used two 707s for its simultaneous service to Moscow's Sheremetyevo airport, one to carry VIPs, the other for fare-paying passengers. Among the VIP guests was Pan Am ex-president Juan Trippe, for whom the flight was the culmination of plans laid 35 years ago.

Deputy minister for Aeroflot Major-General Boris Bugayev welcomed the American party, thanking officials of both airlines for their "persistent endeavours" in negotiating the agreement and hoping that the service would "contribute to mutual understanding and co-operation between the Soviet Union and the United States".

▷

# Boeing rolls out its first 747 and opens a new era

*The assembly line for 747 "Jumbo Jets" at Boeing's new plant at Everett.*

*The 747 was decorated with the insignia of the airlines which had ordered it.*

*Everett, Washington, September 30*
To great acclaim Boeing today rolled out the first Model 747 "jumbo jet" from its specially built plant here, 35 miles north of Seattle at Paine Field. That the Boeing company had been developing a giant wide-bodied transport was well known, as was the fact that Pan Am had placed a $525 million order for 25 plus spares as far back as April 13, 1966. The surprise today was the sheer bulk of the new airliner.

Weighing 710,000 lb laden, with an overall length of 231 feet and height of over 63 feet, the 747 looks too big to fly. Boeing has built it with bulk cargo in mind as well as the hundreds of passengers who will sit in the wide twin-aisled cabin. The flight deck is perched high above the 8-foot-4-inch-high front cabin, permitting a freighter version to have a through-loading opening nose. To the rear of the flight deck, and accessible from the cabins via a spiral staircase, is an upper-deck lounge.

Most of the 747 jet's technology breaks no new ground in the sciences of aerodynamics or airframe structure. To lift the huge weight, Pratt & Whitney has provided just the usual four podded engines, but each JT9D turbofan is capable of 43,500 lb or more of thrust.

Knowing how a huge wingspan would create difficulties at some airports and when using hangars, Boeing has kept the 747's span to under 200 feet by adopting special Boeing wing airfoil sections and an angle of sweep of just over 37 degrees. Each of the wings has triple-slotted trailing-edge flaps, ten variable-camber leading-edge flaps and also three-section Krueger leading-edge flaps to provide high lift.

A unique feature of the 747 is the undercarriage. The designers had to distribute the weight in such a way that it did not impose any greater loads on existing runways and taxiways. The 18 wheels are only slightly bigger than those on the 707. They are on four widely-spaced bogies whose tracks do not overlap with each other, giving the aircraft the widest track of any commercial airliner (→ Feb 9, 1969).

## USAF makes record airlift from Europe

*Washington, DC, October 1*
The four-month airlift from West Germany of two brigades of the US 24th Infantry Division, the 3rd Armored Cavalry Regiment and some USAF units – a record 33,000 military personnel, 3,700 tons of cargo, and 15,000 dependants in one operation – is over.

Following a 1967 plan, under which US-based forces committed to Nato go to Europe periodically for training, early next year approximately 12,000 troops will go back to West Germany for Exercise Reforger I (Redeployment of Forces from Germany). This will be a simultaneous airlift and fighter-deployment exercise.

## Knight receives trophy for record flight

*Washington, DC, October 19*
USAF test pilot Major William J "Pete" Knight has won this year's Harmon international aviators' trophy. Major Knight was singled out as "the world's outstanding pilot for exceptional individual piloting performance". On October 3 last year he flew the North American X-15A-2 rocket airplane at 4,534mph, a record for fixed-wing aircraft [*see page 654*]. He earned his astronaut's wings on another flight when the aircraft reached an altitude of 280,000 feet.

The X-15 program is gathering data on flying conditions at the fringe of the Earth's atmosphere. The knowledge gained may be used to build aircraft that will fly at more than five times the speed of sound.

*The President congratulates Knight, outstanding pilot of the year.*

## LBJ ends bombing of North Vietnam

*Washington, DC, October 31*
In a television broadcast tonight, President Johnson announced that he is halting all US bombing of North Vietnam from tomorrow at 8am, Eastern Standard Time. The President said he had taken the decision "on the basis of developments in the Paris talks" and "in the belief that this action can lead to progress toward a peaceful settlement of the Vietnamese war ... in an atmosphere conducive to peace".

US air power has reduced the North Vietnamese capacity to conduct the war, despite restrictions on what targets US pilots could attack. US losses to date are 915 fixed-wing aircraft (→ Jun 5, 1969).

# Soviet 'Concordski' is first supersonic airliner aloft

*The Soviets' supersonic Tupolev Tu-144, which beat Concorde into the skies.*

*Edward Elyan, one of the two test pilots for today's 38-minute maiden flight.*

*Moscow, December 31*

The first supersonic transport (SST) to fly, the Tupolev Tu-144, took off for the first time today from the long runway beside the Zhukovski factory where it was built. The USSR has fulfilled – just – its promise that the Soviet SST would fly in 1968. Like Concorde, which it resembles sufficient-ly for the West to have nicknamed it "Concordski", the Tu-144 has four large afterburning turbojets under a slender delta wing, a "droop-snoot" nose and a single fin, but no tailplane.

In detail, however, there is little similarity between the two SSTs. The Tu-144 is slightly larger and more powerful than Concorde, with 44,090-lb thrust NK-144 engines and a take-off weight of 150 tons. It can carry 121 passengers (fewer than Concorde) for 4,040 miles at a cruising speed of Mach 2.35. The most obvious difference between the two aircraft is that the Tu-144 has all four engines close together underneath the aircraft. To some degree this is dictated by the length of the NK-144 engine, including the variable inlet and duct and variable nozzle. The engines could not be positioned further out under the wing without projecting in front of the leading edge. In any case, designer Andrei Tupolev claims that the Tu-144's engine arrangement causes the least drag (→ Mar 2, 1969).

## New NASA 'lifting body' aircraft flies

*California, November 13*

The HL-10 research aircraft made its first powered flight today. It was dropped from an NB-52 "mother" airplane near to Edwards Air Force Base. The HL-10 is one of a series of bizarre, wingless "lifting bodies" – airplanes designed by NASA and built by Northrop to investigate the possibility of building a reuseable space vehicle which could be put into orbit by a rocket, then re-enter the Earth's atmosphere and land like an airplane.

The previous craft, the M2-F2 [*see page 645*], was designed at NASA's Ames Research Center; the HL-10 was designed by NASA Langley, on the East Coast. The M2-F2 has a flat top, bulging underside and projecting cockpit; the HL-10 is more streamlined with a cambered bottom, round top, three fins instead of two, and a flush cockpit in the nose.

# Overheated fuselage poses problem for aircraft flying at Mach 3

*The SR-71's specially-developed JP-7 fuel helps to cool the aircraft in flight.*

*Seattle, December 31*

Engineers at Boeing are not only bothered by the continuing structural problems of the US supersonic transport (SST); they are also worried that at the planned cruising speed of Mach 3 (2,000mph), kinetic heating caused by air friction will heat up the entire aircraft. In particular, this means that colossal air-conditioning capacity must be installed to keep the cabin cool.

Similar problems have been encountered by the Soviets with the MiG-25, Lockheed with the A-12 Blackbird and successor SR-71, and, most severely, North American with the XB-70 Valkyrie. This is the only aircraft so far built which can maintain Mach 3 for long enough to "soak" at high temperatures. It is impossible to insulate the SST passenger cabin thermally; a great deal of heat will also be generated by engines and avionics. Disposing of all this heat is a problem (→ Sep 23, 1969).

Tupolev's Tu-144 was the first supersonic airliner to enter service, but the aircraft experienced only a short and intermittent working life with Aeroflot.

The Nord 500 ducted propeller research aircraft was a single-seat design fitted with an ejector seat for the pilot and two 317-shp Allison turboshaft engines.

Intended to be marketed as a civil commuter aircraft and military crew-trainer, Dassault's M.D.320 Hirondelle never got beyond the prototype stage.

Built as a replacement for the L-29 aircraft, Aero's L-39 Albatros was the standard Warsaw Pact trainer, also available in an armed version.

American Aviation's AA-1 Yankee, a simple, rugged and functional training aircraft, formed the basis for the later and very successful AA-5 family.

Developed as a Brazilian government project, the EMBRAER EMB-110 Bandeirante has sold worldwide in numerous civil and militiary variants.

The Filper Beta 400 was an unusual looking four-seat private owner's helicopter with tandem three-blade rotors, based on the earlier two-seat Filper 200.

Despite being inadequate by comparison with contemporary Western aircraft, the Tupolev Tu-154 served widely with the airlines of Soviet client states.

The final model of the Lockheed F-104 Starfighter was the F-104S, 245 of which were built by Aeritalia with improved avionics and weapons systems.

Already in service with the USAF as the A-7A, the A-7D Corsair from Vought was fitted with much expanded electronics and an Allison TF41 (Spey) engine.

Grumman EA-6B Prowlers are used exclusively on electronic warfare and signals intelligence missions with a pilot and three electronics officers.

The Lockheed P-3C Orion offered a significant improvement in ability over previous models; many earlier survivors have been upgraded to this standard.

The SEPECAT Jaguar evolved from the Breguet 121, to meet a joint French and British requirement for a multi-role attack and reconnaissance aircraft.

The McDonnell Douglas DC-9-10 was adopted for service as an aeromedical evacuation aircraft by the USAF under the designation C-9A Nightingale.

Beating Boeing for the order, Lockheed was chosen by the USAF as prime contractor for a new strategic airlifter which became the C-5A Galaxy.

Though based on the Comet airliner, the Hawker Siddeley Nimrod anti-submarine aircraft has Spey engines and is very capable in its new role.

# 1969

4,534mph
USA
Pete Knight
North American X-15
Oct 3, 1967

24,325 miles
USA
Archie Old Jr
Boeing B-52B
Jan 18, 1957

354,200ft
USA
Joseph Walker
North American X-15
Aug 22, 1963

769,000lb
USA
Lockheed
C-5A Galaxy

46,950lb thrust
USA
Pratt & Whitney
JT9D-7AW

**Somerset, England, January 14**
The Royal Navy's first McDonnell Douglas F-4K Phantom II training unit, 767 Squadron, is established at Yeovilton Royal Naval Air Station (→ Feb 24, 1970).

**Stockholm, January 24**
Scandinavian airline SAS puts the Douglas DC-9-20 into service; this version of the DC-9 – with a short fuselage and wider wingspan – is designed for short runways.

**Britain, February 26**
The death is announced of George Carter, who designed the Allies' first jet aircraft, the Gloster E.28/39, which first flew on May 15, 1941, and the Meteor fighter.

**Toulouse, March 2**
The French-built Concorde prototype, 001, makes its first flight (→ Apr 9).

**Washington, DC, March 19**
The US secretary of defense announces an initial order for 12 Hawker Siddeley Harriers for the US Marine Corps (→ Dec 15, 1970).

**Japan, March 30**
Japan Air Lines retires its last DC-6Bs and becomes an all-jet airline (→ May 28, 1970).

**London, March 31**
All BOAC flights are grounded as pilots strike over pay and productivity.

**Norway, April 10**
The Royal Norwegian Air Force is the first European air service to take delivery of the Lockheed P-3B Orion (→ Jan 22, 1971).

**California, April 17**
Major Jerauld Gentry pilots the X-24 lifting-body research airplane on its first free flight, at Edwards Air Force Base (→ Mar 19, 1970).

**Surrey, England, April 24**
The Hawker Siddeley Harrier T.2 prototype, a two-seat trainer version of the jump jet, makes its first flight (→ May 11).

**London, April 30**
RAF Bomber Command and Fighter Command are united to form RAF Strike Command.

**London, May 5**
BOAC opens a service to Tokyo via Anchorage, Alaska, following the polar route; previously it had flown via India.

**Vietnam, May 18**
A tragic crash occurs over Phu Bai when a KC-130 Hercules, refueling two US Marine F-4B Phantom fighters, collides head-on with a third Phantom.

**Paris, May 29**
Before going on display at Le Bourget air show, the French Concorde prototype makes a low-level flight over the city (→ Oct 1).

**USSR, June 5**
The Tupolev Tu-144 Soviet supersonic transport exceeds the speed of sound for the first time.

**Vietnam, June 5**
US bombers make their first attacks on bases here since the cease-fire ordered by President Johnson on October 31, 1968.

**Germany, June 19**
The death is announced of Siegfried Günter, who designed most of the famous Heinkel aircraft produced in 1930-45.

**London, June 25**
Westward Airways inaugurates a shuttle air service linking London's international airports, Gatwick and Heathrow, using a Britten-Norman Islander.

**London, July 21**
Officials announce that although the British government is to play no part in the development of the European Airbus airliner, British company Hawker Siddeley will act as consultant on the Franco-German project and build the wings for the airliner under contract, entirely at the company's own risk.

**Sweden, July 22**
The Saab-90 Scandia is withdrawn from airline service; conceived as a replacement for the DC-3, it never sold internationally.

**Turin, Italy, July 22**
Fiat and Rolls-Royce sign an agreement to cooperate on the development of a new series of Viper turbojet engines.

**USSR, August 6**
The giant Mil V-12 helicopter lifts a record payload of 88,636 lb to an altitude of 7,398 feet.

**Radlett, England, August 8**
One of Britain's oldest aircraft manufacturers, Handley Page Ltd, announces that it is to go into voluntary liquidation.

**London, August 29**
The British government decides to supply "launching aid" for the RB.211 engine: in a decision having effect retrospectively from January 1, 1967, it agrees to cover up to 70 per cent of certain costs, to a maximum of £47,130,000.→

**Manchester, England, October 2**
The RAF takes delivery of its first Hawker Siddeley Nimrod MR.1 maritime reconnaissance airplane, originally based on the de Havilland Comet 4.→

**Warton, England, October 12**
The first Anglo-French SEPECAT Jaguar to be completed in Britain makes its first flight, on which it exceeds Mach 1 (→ Nov 14).

**Washington, DC, October 29**
USAF Strategic Air Command announces that the B-58 Hustler strategic bomber is to be phased out of service as an economy measure.

**Seattle, October 31**
To celebrate his 20th birthday, Italian-born US Marine Raphael Minichiello hijacks a TWA Boeing 707 en route from Los Angeles to New York and forces it to fly to Rome – diverting it 6,900 miles out of its way (→ Sep 12, 1970).

**New Mexico, November 6**
A 34-million-cubic-feet balloon – twice as tall as the Washington Monument and the largest balloon ever launched – lifts a payload of 13,800 lb over Holloman Air Force Base.

**USA, November 10**
James Bede completes an unrefueled world-record closed-circuit class distance of 8,973.4 miles in his BD-2 *Love One*.→

**Toulouse, France, November 12**
Concorde makes its first night landings; Air France, BOAC, Pan Am and TWA pilots take turns at the controls (→ Sep 13, 1970).

**Melun-Villaroche, France, Nov 14**
The naval version of the SEPECAT Jaguar makes its first flight, piloted by Jacques Jesberger; it differs from the land-based model in having an arrester hook, among other features.

**Washington, DC, November 15**
The US Department of Defense reduces its order for C-5A Galaxy transports from 115 to 81; the reduction is caused by rising costs.

**Nigeria, November 20**
A Nigeria Airways VC10 crashes in the jungle: 87 die.

**USA, December 1**
The first legislation to limit aircraft noise at airports, Federal Air Regulation Part 36, comes into force.

**Wichita, Kansas, December 2**
Following a takeover, Lear Jet becomes Gates Learjet Corp.

**USA, December 17**
The USAF closes Project Blue Book, its 22-year investigation into sightings of unidentified flying objects, or UFOs.

*The French-assembled Concorde 001, F-WTSS, seen here on an early test flight. It is almost identical to "British" 002.* ▶

# Boeing 747 launches age of mass jet transport

*The first Boeing 747, giant of the skies, during its maiden flight; the 315-ton "Jumbo" was filled with measuring equipment to assess its initial performance.*

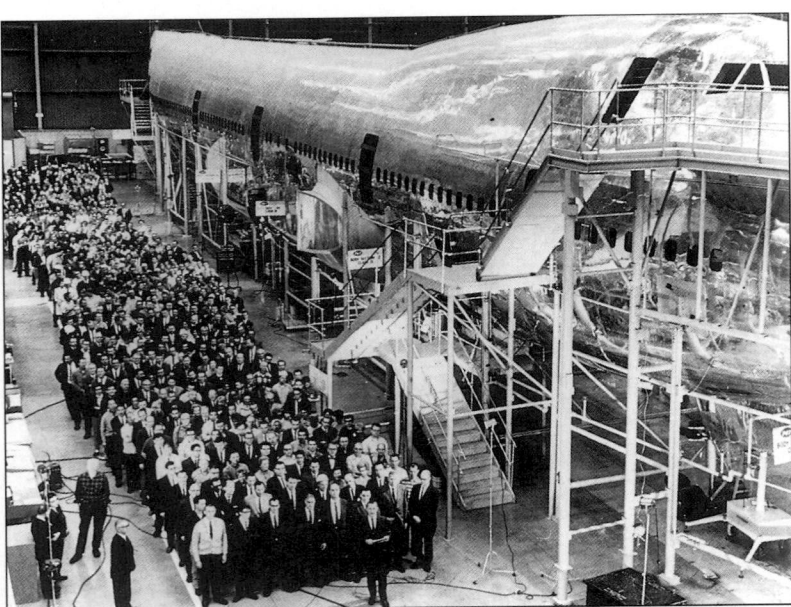

*The company president addresses his staff alongside the second 747 prototype.*

| | | | |
|---|---|---|---|
| | Douglas DC-3 | 1936* | 28 passengers |
| | Douglas DC-4E | 1939 | 52 " " |
| | Lockheed Constellation Model 049 | 1945 | 51 " " |
| | De Havilland D.H.106 Comet | 1952 | 36 " " |
| | Boeing 707-100 | 1958 | 179 " " |

*Dates = receipt of ATC

*Seattle, February 9*

From Everett, 20 miles to the north of Boeing's original Seattle plants, a miracle of modern technology took to the air today on its first flight. Weighing well over twice as much as the largest Boeing 707, the huge aircraft lifted easily, even gracefully, off the runway after a run of perhaps as little as 4,500 feet.

It was the first Boeing 747, emblazoned with the emblems of the many airlines already committed to buying the "Jumbo Jet". At the controls was 747 project pilot Jack Waddell, while in the cabins many tons of measuring and recording instruments were busily working to assess the flight.

If ever there was an airplane finally to dispel the belief that flying is only for the rich, this is it. Just to fill its cavernous cabins it needs to appeal to the traveling masses. The airlines must be equally convinced that this third-generation jetliner, the world's first "wide-bodied" passenger jet, will make money. A growing demand for seats had left little option but to produce something either faster or bigger.

Yet filling seats is not all that the 747 is about. It is a long-haul airliner with a very long range, perhaps 5,700 miles with 374 passengers on board. That opens up new parts of the world to the holiday-maker on a limited budget. In producing an airplane with seating for well over 400, Boeing has been careful not to make it so large that it will pose a storage or maintenance problem. But airport services may prove a different matter. Can they cope if one 747 arrives after another, each filled with hundreds of impatient passengers wanting to pass quickly through customs and gather their baggage? Airport terminals could be forced to adapt to the demands of the new aircraft.

The 747 has not been created overnight, and the initial 747-100 will not be the only version of the airliner. It took Boeing five years to research the market for its "Jumbo Jet", and as usual the decision to launch into full development depended on an early commitment to buy the aircraft from a major airline. Even having won an order for 25 from Pan Am in 1966, the manufacturer's agreement to supply was conditional on other airlines ordering to make production practical.

However, the company was certain enough of its position to begin work on a new plant here at Everett, beside Paine Field, to build 747s. It is, in fact, the world's largest building. This enabled Boeing to divide its Commercial Airplane Division into four separate branches in July 1966, with Everett assigned to work on the 747. The prototype took 30 months to build from the cutting of the very first metal part (→ Jun 1969).

# French and British Concorde prototypes airborne

*Brian Trubshaw, chief 002 pilot.*

*Trubshaw "greases" the Concorde onto the runway despite the fact that the two radar altimeters were not working.*

*Toulouse-Blagnac, March 2*
Today aviation entered a new era, with the start of flight testing of Concorde prototype 001. As part of a 50/50 project with Britain, aircraft 001 has been assembled here at the Aérospatiale plant from components made in both countries. It bears appropriate resgistration F-WTSS. Today's flight-test crew comprised: André Turcat, chief test pilot; Jacques Guignard, copilot; Michel Rétif and Henri Perrier, engineer observers. Packed with ten tons of instrumentation, 001 had waited through several days of foul weather, until at last,

Turcat was able to start the first takeoff run at exactly 11 seconds past 3.40 pm. With afterburners lit on the 4 Rolls-Royce/SNECMA Olympus 593 turbojets acceleration was brisk, and Turcat, flying manually throughout, rotated after a run of 4,700 feet at 205 knots, climbing steeply away but leaving gear down and the "droop snoot" nose lowered. There followed the planned test points, accompanied by two chase aircrafts, one taking film and video and the other serving to calibrate the Concorde's airspeed-indication systems. At 4.08 pm 001 made a perfect landing.

*Fairford, England, April 9*
Five weeks after the start of the Concorde flight-test program with 001, the British-assembled prototype 002 has now completed a successful first flight. It has also been produced from parts made in both countries; there is duplication of assembly lines, but not of manufacture. Again, 002 has an appropriate registration: G-BSST. It is almost identical to 001, though the on-board test intrumentation is different. It was assembled at the Filton (Bristol) plant of British Aircraft Corporation (BAC). Today's flight crew comprised: Brian Trubshaw, chief test pilot for

commercial aircraft of BAC; John Cochrane, copilot; and Brian Watts, engineer observer. As at Toulouse on March 2 a crowd had gathered at Filton to see 002 smoothly leave the huge runway less than half-way along, as its rotation reached an angle of attack of 6°. After covering the specified test items G-BSST made its approach to RAF Fairford, its future flight-test base some 50 miles from Filton. Both radar altimeters failed, which could have made the landing difficult in view of the 35-ft height of the pilots as the main gears touch the runway. "Trubby" made an impeccable landing (→ May 29)

*André Turcat (r) with Michel Rétif.*

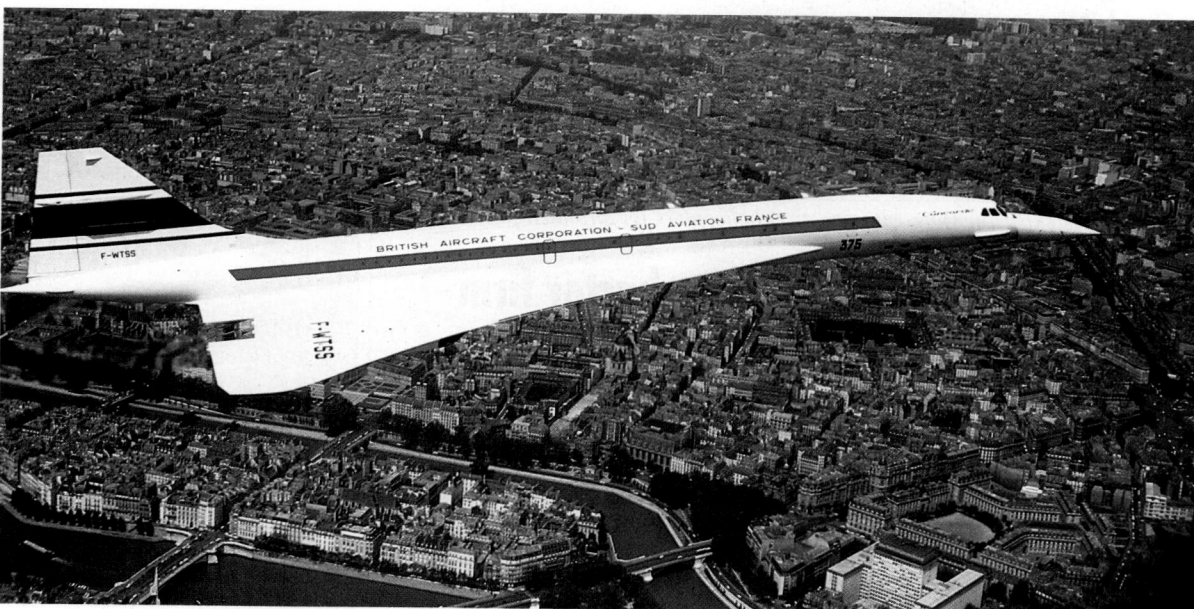

*A few days after the maiden flight, the French prototype flies low over Paris as it makes its way to Le Bourget.*

# Silent flyer aids US mobility in Vietnam

*Tests are under way with the QT-2PC, a glider fitted with a near-silent engine.*

*Saigon, May 25*
It flies by night, quietly surveying the countryside for enemy movement. It is said that it can pass right over you and you will not hear it. Nobody will tell you who it belongs to. It is, in fact, another product of the people who made the U-2 spyplane: the Lockheed QT-2PC.

It has been operating in Vietnam since December 1967. During the Tet Offensive the two QT-2PCs in Vietnam were used in the Mekong delta for night surveillance. These stealthy aircraft began life as the Schweizer SGS 2-32 sailplane. A need arose in Vietnam for a superquiet night surveillance aircraft; the Defense Advanced Research Projects Agency gave Lockheed the task of making it.

Lockheed put a muffled engine driving a very efficient, low-speed propeller onto the low-noise Schweizer, added a sensor package and a few other features and produced the Quiet Thruster single seater, or QT-1. After initial testing the two QT-1s became QT-2PCs with an observer's seat.

*The USAF is experimenting with one-man helicopters for stranded pilots.*

# BEA sets up its own holiday charter firm

*England, April 24*
BEA Airtours has been established as a division of British European Airways to meet the airline-charter requirements of its holiday-tour business. BEA's current profitability, compared with a loss of about £1.75 million in the fiscal year from April 1967, makes the expansion a sound proposition. BEA has for some time been in business outside normal airline operations. It formed Airport Catering Services with hoteliers Forte; together they then founded the subsidiary BEA Forte's Hotels.

The company was a logical extension to their business, and now has hotels in Britain, Malta, France, Cyprus and the Netherlands. It is also part of the European Hotel Corporation (→ Mar 6, 1970).

# Soviet Union unveils giant helicopter

*Moscow, February 12*
In 1957 the Mil design bureau unveiled the Mi-6, a helicopter which dwarfed all others. Today the Soviet Union designers showed off another giant, in effect twice as big as the Mi-6 since the new helicopter has two complete Mi-6 engine-rotor groups, measuring over 219 feet across. It is the world's largest helicopter. First flown on July 10, 1968, the Mil V-12, or Mi-12, has lifted a load of 68,410 lb (over 31 tons) to 9,678 feet. With two pairs of Soloviev D-25VF 6,500-hp turboshaft engines, the Mi-12 helicopter weighs 231,480 lb when laden and has a hold 92 feet long.

*The record-breaking Mi-12 has a hold 92 feet long and over 14 feet wide.*

# British drop out of European Airbus scheme

*London, March 1*
In what many experts believe may be a mistake by the present government, Britain has pulled out of the European Airbus wide-bodied airliner program. British technology minister Anthony Wedgwood Benn has been advised that the Airbus will not sell. Following a series of at times acrimonious meetings between representatives of Britain, France and West Germany, the remaining two partners in the project will now proceed alone. However, the Airbus could still end up being partly British: Hawker Siddeley is considering financing a private share in the project (→ May 28).

**The Queen, with Sir Peter Masefield, opens Heathrow's Terminal 1.**

# Jump jet gives air force new options

## RAF puts the first Harriers into service

*Northamptonshire, England, April 9*
The Hawker Siddeley Harrier GR.1 jump jet, the world's only combat-ready vertical/short take-off and landing (V/STOL) aircraft, became operational with the RAF at Wittering today. It joined 1 Squadron, Britain's oldest airplane unit, currently celebrating the 57th anniversary of its formation.

Two aircraft will shortly be detached from the unit to take part in a transatlantic air race. The remainder will continue with intensive training, exploring the ways in which an aircraft which needs no airfield can be used in simulated front-line conditions.

The Harrier is used primarily as a close-support ground-attack airplane, carrying bombs and rockets and with two hard-hitting 30mm cannon. In addition there are indications that, by using the vectoring (swiveling) capability of the four nozzles of its 21,500-lb thrust Rolls-Royce Pegasus turbofan engine, the Harrier could prove a very effective fighter (→ Apr 24).

*Sqn Ldr Lecky-Thomson taking off near the Post Office Tower, London.*

## Harrier steals limelight from a Phantom

*New York, May 11*
The *Daily Mail* transatlantic air race to mark the 50th anniversary of the first direct flight across the Atlantic by Alcock and Brown in 1919 was won by Lt-Commander Brian Davis, RN. He traveled from the top of the Empire State Building, Manhattan, to the top of the Post Office Tower, highest building in London, in 5 hours 11 minutes 22 seconds, crossing the Atlantic in an air-refueled F-4K Phantom.

But the most spectacular take-off was from the heart of London by a Harrier jump jet of 1 Squadron, RAF, flown by CO Squadron Leader Tom Lecky-Thomson. His flight, in the opposite direction, took 6 hours 11 minutes.

## Airports prove too small for Boeing's 'Jumbo Jets'

*New York, June*
When the first Boeing 747 "Jumbo Jets" crowd into airports next year it could be like three 50-passenger buses arriving simultaneously at a ten-seat coffee shop. Airport designers are looking at how to deal with the up to 500 passengers, plus their luggage, who will pour from each 747 that lands. The 747 is 79 feet longer, has a wingspan 53 feet wider and a tail 20 feet higher than the widely used 707. It can also carry 300 more passengers.

Four 747 jumbos arriving in a 15-minute period, combined with people waiting to greet passengers, could easily jam a terminal with 3,000 or more people. Luggage-handling facilities, already a sore point with many travelers, could be totally overwhelmed. Ground safety is another concern. Airport managers around the US and overseas are looking at taxiways, parking ramps and hangars to determine how to maneuver and service the 747s. TWA's solution is to build an extension to its terminal at New York's John F Kennedy Airport just to handle 747s (→ Jan 12, 1970).

## US Navy opens 'top gun' pilot course

*San Diego, March 1*
Unhappy with its aircrews' performance in combat over North Vietnam, the US Navy today opened a postgraduate course in fighter weapons, tactics and doctrine at Miramar Naval Air Station here. The new course will teach the aircrews of Navy F-4 Phantoms how to use their aircraft to maximum advantage in both air-to-ground and air-to-air combat, with the emphasis on the latter.

The course lasts for four weeks. One week is used for the tactics and delivery of weapons on ground-targets, and three weeks are devoted to air-to-air tactics and weapons employment. Both portions of the course involve classroom instruction and flying training missions in order to practice the theories and tactics being taught.

# North Korean fighter shoots down US Navy Super Constellation

*Since jet aircraft became standard, Super Constellations have flown missions where speed is of less importance.*

*Sea of Japan, April 14*
Thirty-one crew were aboard a US Navy EC-121 reconnaissance aircraft shot down today by a North Korean MiG while on a routine patrol. Search and rescue operations for the missing plane and its crew are now under way in the Sea of Japan. The airplane, one of a fleet of highly modified versions of the Lockheed Super Constellation now flown by both the USAF and the US Navy for intelligence-gathering purposes, was said to have been on a frequently used course 60 miles off the Korean coast when it was attacked by two MiGs. A North Korean broadcast claimed the aircraft, which was based in Japan, had intruded into its airspace and was dispatched with one shot.

# Anglicized Phantom fighters join the RAF

*A Phantom pilot looks on as colleagues create a "Diamond 9" formation.*

**Lincolnshire, England, May 7**
Pilots of 6 Squadron, RAF, based at Coningsby became the envy of other RAF pilots today when they took delivery of the first McDonnell Douglas Phantom IIs, the US-built fighters capable of over Mach 2. Like the Royal Navy Phantoms, they are powered by two Rolls-Royce Spey turbofans, rated at 20,515 lb of thrust with afterburner in operation.

The first RAF Phantoms are FGR.2s – the "fighter, ground-attack and reconnaissance" version of the versatile American fighter, which can be armed with 11 1,000-pound bombs, 128 SNEB 68mm armour-piercing rockets in six pods and one 20mm Vulcan gun in a pod. The first interceptor versions of the Phantom for the RAF, designated F.G.1, will go to 43 Squadron in September, replacing its Hawker Hunters. They will be armed with four Sky Flash or Sparrow air-to-air, radar-guided missiles or four infra-red air-to-air missiles. The total order for Phantoms is now standing at 170.

**Pan Am is planning to introduce a new form of in-flight entertainment – television. Screens on this trial flight were placed on the baggage racks.**

# Britain is out, but A300 show goes on

**Paris, May 28**
Despite Britain's decision to pull out of the Airbus program [*see page 672*], it is full steam ahead for the remaining partners. Today, France and West Germany signed a new agreement which covers continued work on the airliner and establishes a company to manage the program, Airbus Industrie.

The first Airbus A300 design was reworked during the final months of last year into the A300B, essentially because of doubts as to when the very powerful new Rolls-Royce engines might be ready. The new A300B is shorter and narrower than the original concept. But it is still wide-bodied, while being much lighter, and can use existing US engines if needed (→ Feb 1970).

# Man flies Atlantic in landing-gear bay

**Madrid, June 4**
Ground crew watched with amazement here today as a young man fell from a main-gear compartment of one of Iberia's DC-8s as it came to a standstill after a transatlantic flight. The man was unconscious and frostbitten, and it was not until he came to that his story emerged.

Armando Socarras told doctors that he and another man had been determined to leave Cuba and had concealed themselves in the landing-gear well shortly before take-off from Havana. After 15 minutes in the air he lost consciousness and knew nothing more until now. Doctors who examined Socarras believe he literally hibernated, at a temperature of around -35ºC. His friend must have fallen to his death.

# Air support saves US lives in Vietnam War

*Air ambulance: a casualty is rescued from a tiny clearing in the A Shua valley.*

**Vietnam, May**
For the ground soldier wounded in Vietnam, survival and the road to recovery usually begin with the arrival of a UH-1 Huey "Dust-Off" air-ambulance helicopter. Its crew, ignoring enemy fire, lands or sometimes hovers at the rice paddy or patch of jungle where the soldier is to take him to a field hospital.

If his wounds are bad enough to require extensive medical care at a hospital outside Vietnam, a C-141 StarLifter with complete medical team will carry him on the next leg of his journey. The rule of thumb is that if he is to be in hospital for less than 60 days he goes to the Philippines, Okinawa, mainland Japan or Hawaii; if over 60 days, he returns to the US, to a military hospital. This leg of his trip is likely to be the slowest, as piston-engined C-118s or C-131s are used within the US.

Speedy treatment of wounded soldiers, particularly the aid provided by the "Dust-Offs", coupled with more advanced medical techniques, has significantly reduced the number of deaths caused by wounds compared with previous conflicts (→ Jun 2, 1972).

# First US troops fly home from Vietnam

*The first troops leave the C-141 StarLifter which returned them to the US.*

## Vietnam, July 8

As part of the overall plan of "Vietnamization" – handing over to the South Vietnamese – coupled with the phased withdrawal of US forces from Vietnam, the first combat unit to return to the US departed today. Troops boarded Lockheed C-141A StarLifter transports of USAF Military Airlift Command (MAC) at Tan Son Nhut airbase and are to land at McChord Air Force Base, Washington.

Throughout the war in Southeast Asia the C-141 has been the workhorse on the long hauls across the Pacific. Carrying troops and equipment on the westward flights and casualties on the return, the big jet-airlifters have operated around the clock. Lockheed-Georgia delivered 284 production aircraft, powered by Pratt & Whitney TF33 turbofans of 21,000-pound thrust.

They entered MAC service on April 23, 1965. One of their advanced features is an all-weather landing system (AWLS), enabling almost blind landings to be made.

Under President Nixon's proposed plan, 25,000 US troops will be sent home by the end of this month. And more will follow if the South Vietnamese appear capable of holding their own. It is hoped that all US forces will be withdrawn by 1972. Progressively this will involve Lockheed-Georgia's current production USAF transport, the enormous C-5A Galaxy, which first flew on June 30 last year. The C-5A has the reputation of being the world's largest airplane, with a wingspan of nearly 223 feet and length of nearly 248 feet. The huge aircraft will carry just about all the cargo and equipment used by the US military, from troops to tanks.

# White House backs SST

## Washington, DC, September 23

After many months of hesitation, President Nixon today reaffirmed government backing for the US's supersonic transport (SST). He still has to get the vote for funds through both houses of Congress, but he and other supporters of the project appear quietly confident of success. At a news briefing this morning, the president said: "The SST is going to be built." The US aircraft will be the world's third SST, after the Soviet Tu-144 and Anglo-French Concorde.

The chosen design is Boeing's 2707-300, a simplified fixed-wing version of the original swing-wing 2707-200 concept, which proved impractical. It will carry up to 234 passengers on long-haul flights at Mach 2.7, or 1,785mph. Its engines will be four General Electric GE4 turbojets of 67,000-lb thrust. The administrations of Presidents Kennedy and Johnson poured over $500 million into the design and planning of the SST, and well over $1.2 billion of federal funds will be needed to get the first one flying in 1972. No administration has previously voted such lavish federal support of an industrial product. The SST has enemies, however, some of whom disagree with federal funding. Others, such as Senator William Proxmire, say the fate of the SST "should be decided in the market-place, not in the councils of government". Another reason for opposition is the sonic boom. US transportation secretary John A Volpe said today the SST would not fly over the US (→ May 20, 1970).

# Government funds Rolls-Royce's engine

*Tested August 31, 1968: RB.211.*

## Derby, England, August 29

Rolls-Royce's new RB.211 turbofan engine, which is to power Lockheed's L-1011 airliner, is proving a costly venture for the company and the British government. Launch costs are put at £65.5m, and today the government agreed to pay 70 per cent of certain costs backdated to January 1, 1967, up to a maximum of £47.13m. The government will receive repayments from levies on engine sales. The funding is intended to keep Rolls-Royce in the forefront of jet-engine technology, the only serious competitor to US giants Pratt & Whitney and General Electric (→ Nov 11, 1970).

# US pilots make giant leap onto Moon

*Crossing the final frontier ...*

## The Moon, July 20

The world watched and held its breath today as, with consummate skill, former fighter-pilot Neil Armstrong landed the lunar module *Eagle* on the surface of the Moon. At 10.56pm Eastern Daylight Time (3.56am British Summer Time) Armstrong stepped off the ladder of the module and told the world the memorable words: "That's one small step for a man, one giant leap for mankind." Armstrong reported that the Moon's surface was fine powder. He was joined by fellow astronaut Colonel Edwin "Buzz" Aldrin, USAF, and together the two men demonstrated the problems of moving about in the Moon's low gravity. A third astronaut, USAF Lieutenant-Colonel Michael Collins, remains in the circling Command Module. A million people watched from the neighbourhood of Cape Kennedy as the Apollo 11's Saturn V rocket blasted off from the Florida Space Center on July 17.

*... Aldrin discovers a new world.*

# Concorde smashes the sound barrier

*Toulouse, France, October 1*
Today, on its 45th test flight, the French-assembled Concorde prototype 001 exceeded Mach 1 for the first time. It held about Mach 1.05 for 9 minutes from 11.29am some 75 miles from Toulouse at an altitude of 36,000 feet. When it enters airline service, Concorde will go twice as fast at over 60,000 feet, but the test program must proceed meticulously, stage by stage.

On landing, Sud-Aviation test director and chief pilot André Turcat said the aircraft was magnificent, and no future problems were expected. Although a small degree of reheat is used on the Rolls-Royce/SNECMA Olympus 593 engines, to accelerate to supersonic speed, the reheat fuel is shut off in cruising flight. It is believed that the rival Soviet Tu-144 has to keep reheat fuel burning throughout each supersonic flight, drastically reducing its range. From now on the test flying of both Concorde prototypes will proceed up the Mach scale, eventually reaching beyond the maximum cruising speed of Mach 2.2. Later tests will measure long-range payloads (→ Nov 12).

# Racehorse gives new name to Cessna jet

*The Cessna Citation can reach 41,000 feet and fly at speeds of over 400mph.*

*Wichita, Kansas, September 15*
Just after the first flight today of the Cessna Fanjet 500, Cessna sales director Jim Taylor, judging that the name Fanjet would not mean much to passengers, suggested that the name be changed to the more euphonious Citation, after a champion racehorse which has been winning a lot of races. The idea was not new: when he was director of Pan Am's Business Jets division, Taylor proposed the name for the Dassault Mystère 20, which was bought for Pan Am's executive fleet.

The Citation's circuits and hydraulics are quite simple, but its maneuverability is astonishing, although it is slower than the Learjet with only a slightly greater range. The twin Pratt & Whitney Canada JT15A turbofans each produce 2,500 lb of thrust. The Citation seats eight, including the crew.

# Finnair navigators acquire new skills

*Helsinki, October 20*
Navigators of Finnish national airline Finnair are claiming to be the first in the world to use an inertial navigation system (INS) in scheduled passenger service. The INS, which will be used on Finnair's regular services from today, is the first navigational aid able to read out the precise position of an object in three dimensions with no external aid.

The first airplane designed to be equipped with an INS as standard equipment is the Boeing 747, the first wide-bodied airliner. This is normally equipped with the Carousel IV INS, triplicated for safety in view of a mean time between failures (MTBF) of only about 1,250 hours. The supplier is AC Spark Plug, now Delco. In due course Finnair is certain to buy wide-body airplanes. These will thus have triple INS installed from the start.

In the meantime, Finnair has bought the Sperry SGN-10. Sperry, which began INS work with nuclear submarines, was a natural choice for Finnair. It also produces the SP-30 autopilot for the airline's DC-8-62CFs, which fly long-haul polar routes to the US.

# Air crash downs invicible boxer Marciano

*Marciano at the height of his career.*

*Des Moines, Iowa, August 31*
Former undefeated world heavyweight boxing champion Rocky Marciano died tonight when a light airplane carrying him and two companions crashed in wooded country 2 miles south of Newton airport.

Details of the crash are sketchy, but it seems that the pilot called up Newton's control tower to say he was going to land, after which nothing was heard.

Marciano, who would have been 46 tomorrow, was planning to visit friends here in Des Moines. His companions were insurance executive Frank Farrell, 28, and building contractor Glenn Bells who was piloting the aircraft.

The champion, born Rocco Marchegiano in Brockton, Massachusetts, began his boxing career in the Army and went on to beat such previously invincible fighters as Joe Louis and Jersey Joe Walcott. The death of one of the great US sporting heroes highlights growing fears surrounding private flying in the US. Commercial airliner pilots are becoming increasingly concerned at the number of near misses involving small airplanes, particularly close to major airports.

**The McDonnell 188, which is making demonstration flights with American Airlines, is the Breguet 941. McDonnell may make it under license.**

# Engineer Bede sets world distance record

*Bede's BD-2 "Love One" features a three-blade pusher propeller at its tail.*

**Kansas City, November 10**
The world distance record for a non-stop, unrefueled flight in a piston-engined airplane in a closed circuit was broken today by Jim Bede. He landed here after having covered 8,973 miles from Columbus, Ohio, in three days in his BD-2 *Love One*. Bede Aircraft specializes in the manufacture of highly original sports airplanes, and the 30-hp *Love One* is clearly in that category.

Based on the front section of a Schweizer glider, the BD-2 weighs very little. It has a 30-hp engine which drives a high-performance, three-blade pusher propeller at the rear of the aircraft (→ Sep 13, 1971).

# Bearcat speeds to record for piston aircraft

**California, August 16**
The 30-year-old world speed record for a piston-engined aircraft flying in a straight line was finally broken today. The new mark of 482.462mph was set today at Edwards Air Force Base, the giant test center in the desert, by Darryl F Greenamyer, flying a much modified Grumman F8F-2 Bearcat fighter of 1944 vintage, powered by a Pratt & Whitney R-2800 radial engine. The old record of 469.2mph was set by Fritz Wendel, in the Messerschmitt Me 209 V1, at Augsburg, Germany, on April 26, 1939.

# Comet is reincarnated as the Nimrod, the RAF's new maritime reconnaissance jet

**Cornwall, England, October 2**
RAF Coastal Command is on the way out. From late next month it is to be combined into Strike Command, itself formed from the old Bomber Command and Fighter Command in April. With it is going the RAF's last armed piston-engined warplane, the Shackleton, which will be replaced by the Hawker Siddeley Nimrod MR.1 jet, deliveries of which began today.

The Nimrod, Britain's newest anti-submarine and maritime patrol airplane, is being operated initially by Nº 236 Operational Conversion Unit based at St Mawgan, Cornwall. After crew training, the first operational Nimrod unit will be 201 Squadron, Strike Command, at Kinloss, Scotland, which will be re-equipping next year.

The Nimrod is derived from the Comet 4C airliner, with airframe changes including an unpressurized lower fuselage for weapons, other mission equipment and radome. Equipment includes sonar, ship detection equipment and a magnetic anomaly detector in the protruding tail as well as electronic countermeasures. Spey turbofans replace the Comet's Avon turbojets. As a fast jet with 12-hour endurance, the Nimrod can respond quickly to threats, flying low to search and patrol for over 8 hours, to a radius of 1,150 miles.

*The first Hawker Siddeley Nimrod is christened before entering RAF service.*

# Speedy Islander wins commemorative England/Australia race

**Sydney, Australia, December 20**
A Britten-Norman BN-2A Islander, piloted by Captains W J Bright and F L Buxton, won the England-to-Australia commemorative air race today. It landed in Sydney 76 hours and 41 minutes after leaving London's Gatwick airport.

The race, marking the 50th anniversary of the first flight between the two countries, gave the BN-2A the chance to show its mettle. Aerodynamically more advanced and better equipped, it superseded the BN-2 only a few months ago and is set to become a model of low-cost reliability (→ Sep 11, 1970).

*Race-winners Bill Bright and Frank Buxton just before taking off for Sydney.*

# New US rules will control noise of jets

**Washington, DC, December 1**
Regulations setting out acceptable levels of aircraft noise around airports were published today by the Federal Aviation Agency (FAA). The regulations, FAR 36, apply only to subsonic aircraft and favor large jets. Noise levels, expressed in terms of decibels (dB) of Equivalent Perceived Noise (EPN), are calculated as a function of aircraft weight. Thus, according to the formula used, a VC10 weighing 147.6 tons produces 106dB although the measurable level is 114dB.

Boeing's 747 "Jumbo Jet", the first, biggest and best-selling of the wide-bodies, was launched with an order for 25 from Pan American World Airways.

Japan's Mitsubishi MU-2J turbo-prop-powered utility transport.

Cessna's Model 207 Skywagon: a stretched, seven-seat Model 206.

Wassmer's WA-51 Pacific had an unconventional all-plastic airframe.

The Bölkow BO 209 Monsun, developed from the Mylius MHK-101.

An appropriately registered Cessna Citation Model 500 eight-seat executive twin-jet, originally launched as the Fanjet 500, displays its elegant lines.

The Britten-Norman BN-3 Nymph four-seat light aircraft: prototype.

Saab's Safari two-seat trainer prototype had a generously large canopy.

The aerobatic Mudry CAP 20, a single-seat version of the CAP 10.

Antonov's An-28, an enlarged turbo-prop-powered version of the An-14.

The prospects for the supersonic Aérospatiale/BAC Concorde, of which only 16 production examples were built, were ruined by the 1974 oil crisis.

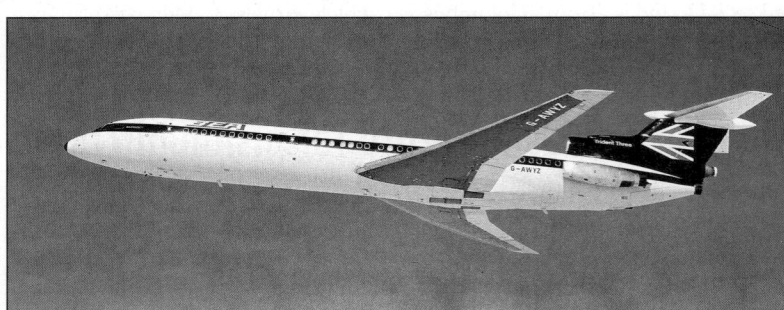

A Trident 3B in the markings of BEA. Hawker Siddeley built 26 for the airline as well as two Super 3Bs for CAAC (Civil Aviation Administration of China).

The Aviation Traders/Vickers Vanguard Merchantman freighter.

The prototype Let L-410 Turbolet, powered by PT6A-27 turboprops.

The Fairchild (later Fairchild-Swearingen) Metro turboprop transport was a 20-passenger commuter development of the Merlin executive aircraft.

*The prototype Gazuit Valladeau GV-103L private two/three-seater.*

*Conroy's CL-44-O conversion of Canadair's long-range freighter.*

*The Anglo-French Sud Aviation (now Aérospatiale)/Westland Puma; the SA 330B version was built for service with France's l'Armée de l'Air.*

*The Reims-Cessna FA150 Aerobat, an aerobatic derivative of the 150 built under license in France and powered by a 100-hp Continental engine.*

*SEPECAT's single-seat Jaguar M prototype eventually lost out to the Super Etendard for the French navy shipboard fighter/attack aircraft contract.*

*Hawker Siddeley's Harrier T.2 operational two-seat trainer.*

*Argentina's FMA IA.58 Pucará entered service carrying external stores.*

*SIAI-Marchetti's SM.1019 powered by Allison 250-B15G turboprop.*

*The improved CH-54B version of Sikorsky's odd Skycrane helicopter.*

*Beagle's Bulldog side-by-side two-seat piston-engined trainer, production of which was undertaken by Scottish Aviation at Prestwick airport, Scotland.*

*The E-2B version of Grumman's Hawkeye carrier-borne AEW and control aircraft, fitted with an improved Litton Industries general-purpose computer.*

# 1970

4,534mph
USA
Pete Knight
North American X-15
Oct 3, 1967

24,325 miles
USA
Archie Old Jr
Boeing B-52B
Jan 18, 1957

354,200ft
USA
Joseph Walker
North American X-15
Aug 22, 1963

775,000lb
USA
Boeing
B-747 200B

46,950lb thrust
USA
Pratt & Whitney
JT9D-7AW

**London, January 12**
A Pan Am Boeing 747, on a proving flight from New York, is the first wide-bodied airliner to make a landing at Heathrow Airport (→ Jan 21).

**USSR, January 31**
Helicopter designer Mikhail Mil, 61, dies.

**England, February 15**
Air Chief Marshal Lord (Hugh) Dowding, 87, commander-in-chief of RAF Fighter Command during the Battle of Britain, dies.

**Akrotiri, Cyprus, February 16**
Harrier jump jets of 1 Squadron, RAF, arrive after the type's first overseas proving flight, from Wittering, England.

**Laos, February 17**
USAF B-52s begin the first bombing raids against North Vietnamese and Pathet Lao troops threatening the Plaine des Jarres in the north of the country.

**Amsterdam, February 18**
KLM, Swissair, SAS and UTA form KSSU to place a bulk order for the new Douglas DC-10 plus parts; the group will also cooperate over the maintenance of the airplanes (→ Aug 29).

**Britain, February 24**
The aircraft carrier HMS *Ark Royal* is recommissioned after a £30 million refit to equip it as a base for F-4 Phantom IIs and Hawker Siddeley Buccaneers.

**Palma, March 6**
The first service of BEA Airtours Ltd, the airline's charter-tour arm, arrives from London Gatwick.

**Boston, March 17**
An Eastern Air Lines DC-9 from Newark lands safely after an attempted hijacking in which the co-pilot was shot and fatally wounded and the captain was shot in both arms; the hijacker was also shot during a struggle in which he was overpowered.

**Tokyo, March 28**
Japan Air Lines opens a service to Paris via Moscow, becoming the first international airline to fly the trans-Siberian route which was recently approved by the Soviet authorities.

**Hamburg, [W] Germany, Mar 30**
Lufthansa receives the first Boeing 747 to be handed over to a European airline (→ Nov 30, 1971).

**England, April 4**
The RAF retires its last Douglas DC-3 Dakota cargo airplane.

**Washington, DC, May 18**
National Airlines, the sixth largest US carrier, agrees a deal to end a 108-day strike under which 3,600 ground staff will get a 33 per cent raise, backdated to May 1 last year.

**Washington, DC, May 20**
A 12-man committee reporting to President Nixon recommends the cancellation of the US supersonic transport project (→ May 18, 1971).

**USSR, May 26**
The prototype Tupolev Tu-144 supersonic airliner reaches a speed of 1,335mph, becoming the first commercial transport in the world to exceed Mach 2.

**Melbourne, July 1**
A new international airport opens at Tullamarine, close to the city.

**New Orleans, July 17**
New Orleans airport introduces the first airport-wide screening system designed to prevent hijackings; suspicious-looking passengers are asked to pass through one of 13 metal-detecting magnetometers.

**Vietnam, August 22**
Two USAF Sikorsky HH-53s land at Da Nang from the US after the first non-stop air-refueled helicopter Pacific crossing.

**Los Angeles, August 30**
A Learjet 25C flies to New York and back in 11 hours 23 minutes, setting a new round-trip speed record for all classes of commercial aircraft.

**France, September 3**
Air France announces an order for six Airbus A300s (→ Dec 18).

**London, September 13**
The British Concorde prototype lands at Heathrow for the first time; local residents complain about the noise (→ Nov 12).

**Hurlbert Field, Fla, October 2**
The first Bell UH-1N helicopter to enter USAF service is delivered to the Special Operations Force.

**India, October 19**
The first MiG-21 built under license by Hindustan Aeronautics is delivered to the Indian Air Force.

**California, October 21**
The X-24A lifting-body research airplane, which first flew on March 19, makes its first supersonic flight, at Edwards Air Force Base.

**London, November 11**
The British government agrees to provide troubled Rolls-Royce with further funds to develop the RB.211; it will provide 70 per cent of the increased costs to a maximum £42 million (→ Nov 16).

**Fairford, England, November 12**
The British Concorde prototype 002 flies at Mach 2 for the first time; the French prototype did so eight days ago (→ Apr 22, 1971).

**Britain, November 30**
British United Airways and Caledonian Airways merge to form British Caledonian Airways.

**USSR, December 15**
Artem Mikoyan, founder of the dynasty of MiG fighters, dies.

**Washington, DC, December 15**
Congress decides against funding licensed production of the Hawker Siddeley Harrier by McDonnell Douglas (→ Jan 26, 1971).

**France, December 18**
Airbus Industrie is formally established to develop the Airbus A300: it comprises Aérospatiale, Deutsche Airbus, Fokker and Hawker Siddeley (→ Nov 9, 1971).

**USA, December 20**
Reports indicate that with zero growth the US's 21 scheduled airlines could show a collective pre-tax loss of over $130 million this year, with only Continental, Delta and Northwest of the 11 trunk carriers making a profit; the recession is blamed for the worst year in American commercial aviation history.

## Factfile

World revenue passenger miles: 285,844 million
Passengers through Chicago O'Hare: 13.6 million
Passengers through New York (JFK/Newark/LaGuardia) 14.2 million:
Passengers through London (Heathrow/Gatwick): 19.2 million
Price of a single ticket coach-class New York/Los Angeles (Apr): $142
Price of a ticket London/New York: $316
World air freight (ton miles): 40,344.4 million
Average salary of long-haul pilot and co-pilot (US): $33,199
Average salary of cabin crew (US): $8,674
Price of a Boeing 747: $20 million
Price of a Concorde: $31.2 million
Price of a Falcon 20: $1.9 million
Price of 1,000 US gallons of Jet A1 fuel (average for July): $96.27
Average exchange rate: £1 = $2.396.

*Up front: the nose of Boeing's huge 747 "Jumbo Jet", which made a successful debut in airline service with Pan Am on January 21.* ▶

# Spacious 'Jumbos' launch new era in air transport

*The Pan Am crew for the first scheduled 747 flight, from New York to London. Take-off was held up by engine trouble.*

*First "Jumbo" arrives in London.*

## Pan Am launches 747 on Atlantic route

*New York, January 21*
At 1.52am today a Pan Am Boeing 747 called *Clipper Young America* thundered down the runway at New York's John F Kennedy Airport and lifted into the sky. It was bound for London on the historic first scheduled service by a wide-bodied jet airliner.

Pan Am originally planned to launch its 747 transatlantic services at the end of last year, but engine problems forced a postponement. All was prepared for the rescheduled start date of January 21 when fate struck again. The instrument panel in the cockpit of the jumbo indicated that one of the JT9D turbofan engines was overheating, and once more the flight had to be delayed. This time the trouble took just a few hours to put right. Almost as much interest has greeted the return London/New York flight this evening, with crowds gathering to watch the giant airliner land. TWA is to introduce the 747 on its transcontinental route between New York and Los Angeles next month (→ Jan 23).

## 'Jumbo' to enjoy two years with no rivals

*USA, January 23*
The Boeing 747, which began passenger service two days ago, will be the only US wide-bodied jet around for some time. The US's two other big airliner makers, McDonnell Douglas and Lockheed, will unveil their own jumbos later this year, but it will probably take two years for them to reach certification. The McDonnell Douglas DC-10's first flight is planned for August and that of the Lockheed L-1011 Tri-Star for November. Both have three engines and are about four-fifths the size of the 747 (→ Feb 25).

## TWA flies first 747 in US domestic service

*New York, February 25*
TWA became the first airline to fly "Jumbo Jets" within the US today when it inaugurated a Boeing 747 service between Los Angeles and New York with an almost perfect flight. This occasion makes TWA the second airline to put the world's largest jet-airliner into scheduled service, following Pan Am last month [*see story left*].

Passengers heaped praise on the giant 747 as they came into the terminal, where a champagne party for the 311 passengers who would board the airliner for the return flight to Los Angeles was in progress. Today's inaugural flight was the first to use TWA's new $20 million building at John F Kennedy airport, which the airline says is the only terminal in the country fully able to handle the Boeing 747s.

There was only one hitch on the flight to New York: the failure of one of the in-flight movie projectors. Passengers changed seats (only 258 of 342 seats on the plane were filled) to see the film from one of the other projectors (→ Mar 30).

## Europeans wait for wide-bodied Airbus

*Europe, February*
Work on Europe's A300 Airbus is well behind the three American wide-bodied airliners. Construction of the first airplane started in September last year, and it is not expected to fly until 1972. Unlike the US aircraft, it is intended for short/medium-range rather than long-haul routes. Backed by the French and German governments, and by Britain's Hawker Siddeley, the idea of a multinational European airliner has not captured the imagination of either the public or the airlines like Concorde (→ Sep 3).

*Inside the 747: a mock-up of the cabin made when the jet was being developed.*

# Aircraft-cum-space vehicle starts tests

*California, March 19*

USAF Major Jerauld R Gentry today completed the first successful powered flight of the X-24 lifting body at Edwards Air Force Base. Seven days ago Major Gentry was presented with the Harmon aviation trophy for his work on the X-24 program.

The X-24 is a joint USAF and NASA research program to test the flight characteristics of a vehicle which is designed to fly as both a spacecraft and a wingless airplane. Data from flights of the bulb-shaped vehicle will be used in the design of future spacecraft. The Apollo spacecraft, like its Gemini and Mercury predecessors, cannot be controlled by the astronauts as they re-enter the Earth's atmosphere. The X-24 is exploring handling characteristics for extended near-Earth flight and conventional runway landing (→ Oct 14).

# Huge Guppy transport passes flight test

*Aero Spacelines 101, the smallest member of its family of giant Guppies.*

*California, March 13*

Onlookers watched amazed today as the hefty bulk of the Guppy-101 lifted into the sky, powered by four Allison 501-D22C turboprop engines. It is the latest airplane in the outsized Aero Spacelines Guppy series to fly and, at 180,000 lb, the heaviest. Despite its weight, it is the smallest of the series. "Smallest" applies to an airplane with a cargo cabin 15 feet 6 inches high and 18 feet 4 inches wide, with a swing-nose entrance. Somewhere lost in the Guppy's airframe is the original Boeing Stratocruiser C-97 body on which its "bubble" fuselage is based (→ Nov 23, 1971).

# Boeing wins AWACS airplane contract

*Kent, Washington, July 23*

Boeing has been awarded an initial contract today to develop an airborne warning and control system (AWACS) aircraft for the USAF. The project is expected to cost several billion dollars over the next decade.

The AWACS will be based on the airframe of the Boeing 707 jet-airliner, but will carry a unique radar system with a giant rotating antenna dish high above the fuselage. Westinghouse beat Hughes for the contract to develop the radar, while Boeing beat McDonnell Douglas to develop the aircraft.

The test aircraft will be modified 707s designated EC-137D, but the production AWACS will be called the E-3A. The USAF expects to buy 34, to keep watch on vast tracts of airspace. Most will be operated by the 552nd AWAC Wing at Tinker Air Force Base, Oklahoma.

# Skirts for hostesses get shorter in Jumbos

*Paris, January 31*

It is only the very beginning of the 70s, but already there is such a mood of change in the air that one small revolution can mask another. First came the arrival of the Boeing 747 "Jumbo" amid great publicity. It is a machine with many fine qualities: it is beautiful to look at; it is powerful; it is comfortable, and it has a certain charm. In short, those who work on board it should have nothing to complain about. Most of the great airlines – Pan Am, Air France, British Airways and Sabena – have accordingly wanted to change the appearance of their hostesses. The length of skirts and dresses is to be shortened to reveal more leg than before – especially on the other side of the Atlantic. Pan Am, for instance, prefers its hostesses to wear mini-skirts, while Belgian Sabena favors more modest hemlines that come to just above the knee.

*An Air France hostess in a B-747.*

*Modern look: Pan Am's mini-skirt.*

# Close call for top British aerobatic pilot

*The Zlin is a specially designed aerobatic airplane built in Czechoslovakia.*

*Wiltshire, England, June 3*

Veteran British aerobatic pilot Neil Williams landed his Zlin 526 at Hullavington today - in spite of having an entire wing about to part company with the aircraft. Williams, who had no parachute, had completed his fifth maneuver in a practise flight before a competition when he noticed that the left wing was beginnng to fold upwards. Showing great presence of mind, he turned the aircraft over and approached the ground inverted. In a feat of prodigious skill, he rolled the aircraft the right way up at the last moment and touched down safely (→ Dec 19, 1971).

# Four airliners blown up by hijackers

*Jordan, September 12*

The vulnerability of airliners to hijack was graphically illustrated this week when Palestinian terrorists blew up a TWA 707, a Swissair DC-8 and a BOAC VC10 after seizing them six days ago and ordering them to fly to "Liberation Airport" – an old RAF airstrip called Dawson's Field.

Many of the 255 passengers were Americans en route to New York from Europe. Most were released before the explosions after days of sweltering confinement, but 56 are still being held at a secret location. A fourth aircraft, a Pan Am 747, was ordered to fly to Cairo where it was blown up after all on board had been freed.

The attempted hijack of an El Al 707 as it left Amsterdam for New York failed when two hijackers were overwhelmed by crew, who killed one and captured Palestinian Leila Khaled. She is being held in London where the 707 landed. Israel wants her extradition, but the British government faces a demand for her release in exchange for the 56 passengers still held (→ Sep 30).

*A bomb blasts the BOAC VC10 – empty of people – at Dawson's Field.*

## Leila Khaled swapped for hostages

*London, September 30*

An RAF Comet left Britain today bound for Beirut; on board is Palestinian terrorist Leila Khaled. It will call at Munich and Zurich to pick up three other terrorists held by the German and Swiss governments as part of a swap deal arranged with the Popular Front for the Liberation of Palestine. All the hostages taken in the mass hijack [*see story left*] have been released. There is great relief in many quarters that the incident has ended without great loss of life, but many in the airline industry are dismayed at the capitulation of Western governments to the demands of hijackers.

*Hertfordshire, England, November*

From the small town of Letchworth, north of London, Richard Wiggs runs the Anti-Concorde Project (ACP), which has grown from nothing to a major worldwide organization. In the USA his opposite number is William A Shurcliff, who is the director of the Citizens' League Against the Sonic Boom (CLASB).

These organizations have proved to be rallying points for hundreds of thousands of protesters who, for a variety of reasons, are determined to kill off the supersonic transports (SSTs). Some hate them on the supposed ground that they will benefit only a few rich passengers (as did the first cars), while others are afraid that SSTs will damage the environment, although there is as yet little firm evidence of this.

In addition to popular concern over the idea of SSTs, there are also financial worries. The cost of building Concorde has risen steadily, and some economists are now fearing that operating costs will be prohibitively high.

# McDonnell Douglas decide on three jet engines for the DC-10

*Long Beach, August 29*

The first flight of the DC-10 has just taken place, but it has failed to cheer up the financiers of McDonnell Douglas. The new aircraft's profitability is far from assured, thanks to its competitor Lockheed. Since the beginning of the project in March 1966, Douglas has opted for a machine whose basic structure allows it to be adapted to several versions. The DC-10-10 has been designed to carry 255 to 270 passengers on inland routes over a distance of 620 miles. The long-haul version, meanwhile, could take up to 380 passengers. This plane, along with the Lockheed L-1011 TriStar, is the main competitor of the Boeing 747. The machine has three General Electric CF6-6 turbofans, each with a thrust of 41,664 lb. The DC-10 poses a problem of choice to those airlines flying the TriStar. United Air Lines, its technical management not in agreement with the general management, has ordered 60 DC-10s, half on option. American Airlines is taking 50, 25 of them on option (→ Aug 5, 1971).

*Isle of Wight, England, Sep 11*

Britten-Norman's latest airplane, the Trislander, pulled off a double display today. It made its maiden flight, and it put in an appearance at the Farnborough air show.

The Trislander, as its name implies, is a three-engined derivative of the successful Islander transport. The fuselage has been stretched by seven feet six inches, reinforcing the rear and altering the tail unit to carry the third 260-hp Lycoming O-540 engine and a high tailplane. The Trislander also has raked wingtips as standard, whereas on the Islander they are an optional extra, which increases the wingspan by 4 feet. The result is a 17-seater capable of 180mph and a still-air range of 1,000 miles. The similarity between the Islander and Trislander is essential to Britten-Norman's integrated production line. Either type can be built from the same basic airframe (→ Oct 22, 1971).

*McDonnell Douglas's DC-10-10 is the first of the new breed of wide-bodied "Jumbo Jets" to have three engines.*

# Tomcat, replacing US Navy's F-111B, flies

*Calverton, NY, December 21*
What better Christmas present for the US Navy than its first sight of a Grumman F-14A Tomcat prototype fighter in flight, more than a month ahead of the scheduled date? All agree that the aircraft made an awesome sight as it thundered away from Calverton in the hands of test crew Bob Smyth and Bill Miller.

The speed with which Grumman has produced the prototype, built to a contract awarded in February last year – after winning the Navy's VFX carrier-based fighter design competition the month before – is indicative of its earlier preparations. The Tomcat's design has followed a series of logical steps. By the time Congress brought development of the naval F-111B version of the USAF's General Dynamics F-111 to a halt in 1968, Grumman had already seen the writing on the wall and begun its own design for a replacement.

Recognizing as assets the F-111B's swing-wings, Pratt & Whitney TF30 engines, long-range Phoenix missiles and AN/AWG-9 weapons-control system, Grumman put these ideas into a new Mach 2-plus two-seater. It suits naval carrier operations better, having a 20mm cannon and short- and medium-range missiles. The degree of wing sweep is automatically selected to optimize performance.

*Awesome sight: Grumman's variable-wing F-14A Tomcat prototype in flight.*

# Lockheed TriStar makes flawless debut

*Palmdale, Calif, November 16*
Lockheed's entry in the wide-bodied airliner stakes, the L-1011 TriStar, made a flawless first flight here today. The three-engined airliner, which superficially resembles the DC-10, flew with a test crew comprising pilot H B "Hank" Dees, co-pilot R C Cokeley, engineer G E Fisher and research and development engineer R C Bray. A key feature of the aircraft is its Rolls-Royce RB.211 engines. Derated on this occasion to only 36,500-lb thrust, they appeared reliable and quiet, but the British company is committed to deliver engines of 42,000 lb for the initial L-1011-1. Future heavier models will need even higher power (→ Apr 26, 1972).

*The L-1011 TriStar during its first flight over California's Mojave Desert.*

# Air-and-space test vehicle tops Mach 1

*The X-24A's high-altitude launch.*

*California, October 14*
Today, on one of the routine flights in the USAF/NASA lifting-body program, the X-24A flew to a speed of Mach 1.19 at 68,000 feet from Edwards Air Force Base. Later the bulbous craft is expected to fly both faster and higher.

Whereas previous lifting bodies have been designed (at least as far as external shape is concerned) by NASA and built by Northrop, the X-24A has been produced by Martin Marietta; it was previously known as the SV-5P. Pilots currently assigned to it are Jerauld Gentry and John Manke of NASA and Major Cecil Powell, USAF. The X-24A has proved tricky to fly, although it can make precision landings on Runway 18 of the Edwards test center. On the same power as the Bell X-1 (an RMI rocket engine with four 1,500-lb thrust chambers) the X-24A is 200mph faster, even though it looks unstreamlined (→ Oct 21).

# Holm is first female general in the USAF

*Washington, DC, December 31*
Colonel Jeanne M Holm, a professional silversmith before she chose a military career, will be the USAF's first woman general. She was among 73 air force officers nominated for promotion to brigadier-general by President Nixon and confirmed by the US Senate.

This is not the first time that the 49-year-old director of Women in the Air Force (WAF) has set such a precedent. On February 28, 1968, she and Colonel Helen O'Day became the first women to be promoted to the rank of colonel, under a law which removed restrictions on the promotion of women to the higher ranks of the military.

Colonel Holm, who enlisted in the Women's Army Auxiliary Corps in 1942 and since October 1965 has been director of the WAF, has sought to expand women's roles and career opportunities in the USAF (→ Mar 2, 1971).

*Jeanne Holm: historic appointment.*

# Daring Vietnam PoW rescue raid misfires

*Washington, DC, November 23*
US secretary of defense Melvin R Laird said today that an attempt on November 20 to rescue US prisoners of war from the Son Tay prison camp, 28 miles northwest of Hanoi, had failed. The US Army and USAF rescue force landed in the camp by helicopter but found that the prisoners had been moved.

President Nixon, who had received reports that the American PoWs were dying, approved the raid, which involved all three services. The key to allowing the HH-3 and HH-53 helicopters to reach Son Tay lay in neutralizing enemy radar and air defenses. F-105 Wild Weasel radar-suppression fighter/bombers were used against surface-to-air missile sites in the Son Tay area, while EC-121 Big Eyes in Laos kept watch on enemy airfields. Meanwhile, US Navy aircraft moved through the Hanoi/Haiphong area to divert radar.

Designed to the same requirements that gave birth to the TriStar, the McDonnell Douglas DC-10 widebody airliner was first powered by CF6 engines.

Only 40 of the Sud-Aviation SN.601 Corvette bizjets were constructed.

Brazil's EMBRAER named its EMB-200 crop sprayer "Ipanema".

When fitted with PT6 turboshafts, the Sikorsky S-58 became the S-58T.

The Lockheed TriStar, with room for up to 400 passengers, was one of the first airliners introduced to meet the growing demand for capacity in the 1970s.

The BAe 125-600 series was noticeably longer than previous models.

MBB's Bo 105 twin-turbine helicopter sold all over the world.

Rockwell's 112 and later 114 Commanders proved to be very popular.

The Martin X-24B was used for lifting-body research by NASA.

Following the brisk sales of its Falcon 20 executive jet, Dassault decided to produce a smaller version with 7/9 seats, and so the Falcon 10 was born.

Adding a third engine to the BN-2 resulted in the BN-2A-III Trislander.

The IAI 1123 Westwind: an improved version of the Commodore.

Italy's Aeritalia (now Alenia) built the G.222 tactical military transport.

Longest-lived of all the Guppy conversions, the Aerospacelines Guppy 201 now flies for Airbus Industrie, delivering components to the Toulouse factory.

A Robin DR.300/140 Petite Prince fitted with a sliding cockpit canopy.

The Dassault Milan operational prototype displays its small foreplanes.

Grumman developed the YF-14A Tomcat for the US Navy to fulfil the need for a carrier-borne fighter/interceptor able to defend the fleet at great range.

Training for Sweden's Saab Viggen is provided by the two-seat SK-37.

Produced by SOKO in Yugoslavia, the Galeb 3 is a basic jet trainer.

The Mil Mi-24 "Hind" combined awesome firepower, including underwing rocket pods, with the ability to carry a sizeable number of troops into combat.

Sikorsky's first Black Hawk, the S-69 high-speed combat helicopter.

A single T55 turboshaft engine provided the power for the Bell 214.

The Saab 35XD was the export version of the Draken fighter-bomber.

Austria's Air Force received a special model of the Saab 105, the 105ö.

Boeing-Vertol's Model 347 research helicopter was a modified CH-47A.

The Israeli Aircraft Industry's Arava twin-engined, twin-boom transport.

Belgium's Air Force operates the Mirage VBA ground-attack aircraft.

The Aermacchi MB.326K is a jet trainer which has attack capability.

The McDonnell Douglas A-4M was fitted with a J52 engine and a braking parachute, a larger cockpit canopy and increased ammunition provision.

The Kawasaki C-1 medium transport was developed to fulfil the Japanese Air Self Defense Force's CX requirement, for a Curtiss C-46 replacement.

# 1971

4,534mph
USA
Pete Knight
North American X-15
Oct 3, 1967

24,325 miles
USA
Archie Old Jr
Boeing B-52B
Jan 18, 1957

354,200ft
USA
Joseph Walker
North American X-15
Aug 22, 1963

833,000lb
USA
Boeing
B-747 200F

50,400lb thrust
USA
General Electric
CF6-50C

**Washington, DC, January 2**
Official figures reveal that in 1970 US scheduled airlines had their lowest number of fatalities since federal accident records began in 1938, with no deaths on scheduled domestic flights and only two on scheduled international flights; the 117 fatalities on non-scheduled flights (in just two accidents) represents the lowest annual figure since 1957.

**France, January 13**
The Dassault Mirage G fighter prototype – the first European swing-wing aircraft to fly, on November 18, 1967 – is destroyed in a crash.

**Gloucestershire, England, Jan 20**
Four members of the top RAF aerobatic display team, the Red Arrows, are killed at Kemble when the two Folland Gnats collide while practicing a maneuver.

**Patuxent River, Md, January 22**
A US Navy P-3C Orion lands after a flight of 15 hours 21 minutes from Atsugi, Japan, setting a non-stop distance record for a turboprop-powered aircraft of 7,010 miles.

**Derby, England, February 4**
Rolls-Royce, close to financial ruin owing to difficulties with the development of the RB.211 engine, publicly requests the appointment of a receiver; this is despite the fact that bench tests as recently as last night show that the engine is now performing well (→ May 22).

**London, March 1**
BEA introduces the Hawker Siddeley Trident 3B airliner on its route between here and Orly airport, Paris (→ Jun 18, 1972).

**Washington, DC, March 2**
A new policy is made public under which women in the USAF who become pregnant are allowed to request a waiver to remain on active duty, or alternatively may ask to be discharged and then return to duty within 12 months.

**Somerset, England, March 21**
The Westland WG.13 Lynx helicopter prototype makes its first flight at Yeovil (→ Jun 29, 1973).

**Beaufort, SC, April 15**
The US Marine Corps's first squadron equipped with Hawker Siddeley AV-8A Harriers, VMA-513, becomes operational.

**London and Paris, April 22**
Britain and France give the go-ahead for four more Concordes, bringing the total to ten (→ May 13).

**Bordeaux, France, May 8**
Jean-Marie Saget pilots the Dassault Mirage G8 swing-wing fighter prototype on its first flight.

**Dallas, Texas, June 18**
A new US carrier, Southwest Airlines, based at Love Field, begins operations with three B-737s (→ Feb 7, 1973).

**Bonn, June 24**
The West German government announces an order for 175 F-4E Phantoms to replace Fiat G.91s and Lockheed F-104s.

**Nagoya, Japan, July 20**
The first supersonic aircraft to be designed and built in Japan, the Mitsubishi XT-2 jet trainer, makes its first flight; the two Rolls-Royce Turbomeca Adour engines are its only non-Japanese features.

**Benghazi, Libya, July 26**
A BOAC VC10 flying from London to Sudan is forced to land here by two Libyan government agents.

**Japan, July 30**
An All Nippon Airways Boeing 707 collides with a fighter; 162 die.

**London, August 5**
The British Civil Aviation Authority (CAA) is officially established (→ Apr 1, 1972).

**Los Angeles, August 5**
The McDonnell Douglas DC-10 enters airline service, on American Airlines' route between here and Chicago (→ Jun 18, 1972).

**Montreal, August 12**
An Advanced Purchase Excursion fare (APEX), available for a trip lasting between 22 and 45 days and paid for three months in advance, is established (→ Sep 28, 1972).

**Brazil, September 3**
The first Brazilian-built jet aircraft EMBRAER's EMB-326GB Xavante trainer (a licensed Aermacchi 326), makes its first flight (→ Apr 16, 1973).

**USA, September 13**
James Bede pilots his Bede BD-5 Micro on its first flight; it is a single-seater light airplane designed to be built by amateurs from a kit.

**Nicaragua, September 16**
Three USAF aircraft complete a relief mission flying food, medical supplies and fuel to victims of Hurricane Edith.

**USA, September 28**
Concorde test pilots André Turcat and Brian Trubshaw are awarded the Iven C Kincheloe trophy by the US Association of Test Pilots.

**Manchester, England, Sep 30**
The Hawker Siddeley Shackleton AEW.Mk. 2 airborne early warning aircraft makes its first flight, at Woodford.

**Belgium, October 2**
A BEA Vanguard flying from London to Salzburg, Austria, partially breaks up, crashing near Aarsele; all 55 on board die.

**Paris, November 9**
Air France orders six Airbus A300Bs, with options on a further ten (→ Feb 3, 1972).

**Isle of Wight, England, Nov 23**
Britten-Norman (Bembridge) Ltd is formed to carry on the activities of the financially beleaguered Britten-Norman company which requested the appointment of a receiver on Oct 22 (→ Jan 24, 1979).

**Seattle, November 30**
The Boeing 747-200F cargo version of the 747 airliner, ordered by Lufthansa, makes its maiden flight (→ Mar 9, 1972).

**Pakistan and India, December 12**
In the last two days, during fighting between India and Pakistan, RAF C-130 Hercules have evacuated 909 British and other nationals from Karachi to Masirah, off the Arabian peninsula; in the same period, 474 people have been flown from Dacca, East Pakistan [Bangladesh], to Calcutta, India.

---

## Factfile

World revenue passenger miles: 307,058.596 million
Number of passengers through Chicago O'Hare: 13.2 million
Number of passengers through New York airports: 16.0 million
Number of passengers through London: 20.8 million
Price of a single coach ticket New York/Los Angeles (April): $154
Price of the cheapest return ticket London/New York: $361
World air freight (ton miles): 43,689.6 million
Average salary of a long-haul pilot (US): $32,603
Average salary of cabin crew (US): $8,835
Price of a Beech 100: $695,000
Price of a Cessna 414: $197,430
Price of a Gulfstream II: $3.95 million
Price of 1,000 (US) gallons of Jet A1 fuel (average for July): $97.02
Average exchange rate: £1 = $2.4417

*Miniskirts and cowboy boots do nothing to harm the attractions of Southwest's first stewardesses, seen at their June 18 inaugural.* ▶

# Hawkeye's vision and hearing improved

*The Grumman Hawkeye is capable of flying for six hours without refueling.*

*Bethpage, NY, January 20*
The first of two prototypes of the Grumman E-2C Hawkeye made its first flight today at the company's main production plant here on Long Island. Although it is externally almost indistinguishable from the original Hawkeye, which first flew on October 21, 1960, the E-2C boasts a totally different array of avionics packages which merely happen to fit the same airframe.

All the E-2 family have been designed as the most effective possible airborne early warning (AEW) airplanes which can operate from an aircraft carrier. This means not only that the aircraft have folding wings, but also that they have a retractable main antenna as well as the ability to make catapult take-offs and arrested landings.

By far the most important technological improvement in the C model is the General Electric APS-120 main radar, the units of which occupy the entire mid-fuselage. The radar antenna, located inside the revolving Randtron rotodome, is the new APA-171, with identification friend or foe (IFF) antennas on the opposite side. Grumman confidently expects the E-2C to stay in production for many years as the standard AEW aircraft of the US Navy.

**January 29: the first SA 330 Puma built by Britain's Westland under an Anglo-French agreement enters service with RAF Air Support Command.**

# USAF 'haylift' helps snowbound farmers

*Great Bend, Kansas, February 24*
Cattle marooned in deep snow in this area were bombed today – with bales of hay dropped from USAF C-130 Hercules transports. The airlift of fodder follows a blizzard two days ago which dumped up to 30 inches of snow across a wide belt from Oklahoma to Iowa.

The snowstorm came on the heels of weekend floods which have cut off towns and stranded an estimated 70,000 head of cattle. Army National Guard troops are using trucks and "snowmobiles" to carry food to people in isolated communities, where 10-foot drifts surround some of the farmhouses.

The American Humane Society has purchased the 35,000 bales of hay which it is estimated will be needed to keep the cattle alive until the snow melts and they can resume foraging. The first load of 250 bales was dropped to the cattle today. Five of the C-130s are expected to be in the air tomorrow when the operation gets into full swing.

*Friendly bomber: a C-130 Hercules drops bales of hay to snowbound cattle.*

# Harrier jump-jet is ready for Marines

*South Carolina, January 26*
The first vertical/short take-off and landing warplanes to enter US service, the Marine Corps Hawker Siddeley AV-8A Harrier jump jets, arrived in the US today, following a formal handover in Britain on November 20 last year. The Marines will soon have the backing of the new close-support jet during beach-landing amphibious operations. The Harrier needs no hard runway or large navy carrier. The first squadron will be VMA-513, which will shortly become operational at Beaufort, South Carolina.

The 21,500-lb thrust Rolls-Royce Pegasus 11 vectoring turbofans are specified as standard. However, the first ten Harriers are being delivered with 20,000-lb thrust Pegasus 10s. Twelve AV-8As were funded in fiscal year 1970 by canceling 17 F-4J Phantoms; 18 more have been ordered (→ Apr 15).

# London gets a new air traffic center

*Middlesex, England, January 31*
The new London Air Traffic Control Centre (LATCC) at West Drayton, not far from Heathrow airport, became operational today. It represents a milestone in the drive to improve air safety, and its controllers face an awesome task.

LATCC takes control of all air movements over land and sea in a vast area south of an imaginary line drawn between the southern tip of Ireland and a point in the North Sea not far from the Dutch coast, and running through Aberystwyth, Wales, and Norwich, Norfolk.

Details of any aircraft approaching this southern sector, one of the busiest in the world, are received by LATCC from the last take-off point. Aircraft are contacted by LATCC, which advises the route they must follow at what speed and altitude, and whether stacking is necessary.

# Spain launches sturdy Aviocar transport

*The Aviocar is powered by two 750-hp Garrett TPE331 turboprops.*

**Spain, March 26**

There are no frills on the CASA 212 Aviocar, the first turboprop aircraft from Construcciones Aeronauticas, which made its first flight near Madrid today.

Functional rather than elegant, it had to conform to the demands of the general staff of the Spanish air force, the Ejercito del Aire: they

wanted a 2-ton "truck" which was able to operate in the rugged Spanish hinterland. It needed to be able to take off from rough surfaces and runways no longer than 1,641 feet. The prototype can take off within 1,215 feet and land within 800 feet. A civilian version, with 2 tons of rear-loaded freight, can carry 21 passengers.

# US supersonic airliner project is ditched

**Washington, DC, May 18**

Hopes of reviving the US supersonic transport (SST) program, fading since the Senate axed funding for it on March 24, finally died tonight when the senators reaffirmed their earlier decision in two votes.

Tonight's first vote killed a House of Representatives appropriation of $85 million for further SST development by 58 to 37, a wider margin than in March. Senators sealed the fate of the SST by voting to make

termination payments of $155 million to the airlines and manufacturers who have participated in the program. The politicians who have backed the SST have now given up hope of raising funds.

President Nixon's press secretary Ron Ziegler blamed the failed revival effort on the SST prime contractor Boeing, which would not budge from its call for $500 million to $1 billion in government funds to restart the program (→ May 1973).

*Millions were poured into the SST project, but the dream has come to nothing.*

# BOAC steps up 747 services to New York

**London, May**

BOAC has increased the frequency of its Boeing 747 services between London and New York to daily flights this month. Until now the airline has only flown a twice weekly service with the 747 since putting the jumbo into service on April 14.

Since Pan Am became the first airline to inaugurate Boeing 747 services on January 22 last year on the route, the aircraft has carried over

ten million passengers with all its operators. Flying hours for the entire fleet now exceed 250,000 and more than 115 million miles have been accumulated.

BOAC has ordered 12 747-36s, deliveries of which are continuing. The airline and the British Air Line Pilots' Association are to assess two-man operation of the 747, following the negotiation of a new pay structure (→ Sep 17).

*One of BOAC's present fleet of six Boeing 747 jets at the moment of take-off.*

# Fare farce exposed by 'Left Hand Club'

**Atlantic, May 1**

The great Atlantic Affinity Charter fiasco is in full swing with airlines offering ridiculously low fares to "clubs" being formed all over the UK and USA. The only requirement for a cheap London/New York/London trip is that club members share a common interest.

With full flights guaranteed, the airlines are delighted. It could be a flight filled with "bird fanciers" – many of whom would not know an eagle from a Times Square pigeon – which lands at Heathrow today; or a planeload of American football "supporters" for whom a gridiron is something to press their pants. This is coming to an end, with IATA carrying out spot checks this month on a so-called Left Hand Club (who held martinis in their right hands). In addition, Britain's Freddie Laker plans a "Skytrain" with fares to match any "club" flight (→ Jun 25).

# 'Sierra' flights test Concorde prototype

**France, May 13**

Opponents of Concorde claim that the sonic booms it generates will cause unacceptable damage. Four years ago, tests using supersonic fighters over London brought 4,000 protests, even though a 73-year-old Londoner who had been deaf since 1954 had his hearing restored by the boom.

In France today, Concorde completed a series of flights, dubbed Sierra, to measure the effects of supersonic flights over populated areas. The aircraft crossed France from Brittany to Provence at Mach 2 and 52,500 feet. Recording machines were placed at various points along the flight path and observers noted people's reactions. Tests performed at Istres showed that, flying at 49,000 feet, Concorde created a pressure of 1.02 millibars at ground level, whereas laboratory tests showed that it took 8 millibars of pressure to shatter glass (→ Sep 18).

# Rolls-Royce reborn after troubled time

*Derby, England, May 22*
Today is the first full day of a new company, Rolls-Royce (1971) Ltd, securing the jobs of some 63,000 people. The intention to transfer the aero-engine, marine gas turbine and industrial divisions from the receiver and manager of the old company was announced by the British government on May 10, following the registration of the new state-owned company on February 23. The transfer, which does not affect the famous luxury car business, has now taken effect.

The government has formed the new company to take over those parts of Rolls-Royce considered essential to Britain's defense, to save collaborative programs underway

*The RB.211 engine caused the crisis.*

with foreign partners and to support the many commercial and military aircraft manufacturers and operators which rely on products made by Rolls-Royce. Twelve days ago Rolls-Royce (1971) signed a new contract with its customers. Turnover in the first year is anticipated to be about £250 million.

Rolls-Royce got into financial difficulties over the development of the RB.211 engine chosen by Lockheed for its TriStar. An aid package was put together by the government and banks, but the threat of penalties, which Lockheed and airlines were entitled to invoke in the case of delays, required still more cash. It was too much, and on February 4 this year Rolls-Royce called in the receiver.

# Laker unveils new, low Atlantic fares

*England, June 30*
Those who want cheap travel across the Atlantic have found a champion in the form of a Briton with a London accent and a flair for publicity. Freddie Laker said today that his company, Laker Airways, has applied to the British Air Transport Licensing Board (ATLB) to launch a low-cost scheduled service between London and New York with a lowest single fare of £32.50. The cheapest seat on any other airline is currently £94.20.

Laker said that the low prices would be made possible "by cutting out the traditional costly frills of international air travel". There would be no reservation system and meals during the flight would be extra. The £32.50 fare would apply in the winter and rise to £37.50 in the summer months.

The application will be heard before the ATLB with BOAC and Caledonian/BUA expected to raise strenuous objections to the new service (→Aug 12).

# Adaptability is key to new Ilyushin 76

*Le Bourget, Paris, June 6*
Short or makeshift runways will not present any obstacle to the Ilyushin Il-76, which is designed to operate from every sort of airfield. At present on view at the Paris Air Show as a civil airplane, it answers to the need for wide-bodied aircraft that can be used in Siberia. Equipped with high-lift devices, thrust reversers on each of the four very powerful (26,455-lb) D-30 turbofans and brakes that are reliable and powerful, the plane's tricycle undercarriage has an unusual feature.

The pilot can modify, in flight, the pressure on the 20 tyres in order to suit both the surface of the ground where he will land and the load he is carrying. Military versions have a tail turret. With a payload of 88,200 lb, the Ilyushin has a range of 3,000 miles and an average speed of 500mph at an altitude of 29,500 feet. In trials it has been demonstrated that a runway of less than 3,300 feet is sufficient for the Ilyushin.

# Federal Express founded for fast delivery

*Fred Smith: promising fast delivery.*

*Memphis, Tennessee, April 17*
Federal Express, a new air freight service which guarantees overnight delivery anywhere in the USA, began operating tonight – in a less than ostentatious manner. Its fleet of Dassault Falcon 20s carried only 18 packages.

The company is the brainchild of Yale-educated former US Marine pilot Fred Smith. He has staked his $4 million inheritance, plus $72 million of investors' money, in a company which aims to meet business demand for overnight delivery. His airplanes, modified for cargo, fly packages here each night where they are sorted for delivery to the airport nearest their destination before dawn. Trucks then take the packages from the airport to customers.

# USAF pilots launch attack on fatal virus

*Texas, July 22*
For two weeks, six USAF Fairchild UC-123K spray planes have been battling a new and unusual foe: a virus called Venezuelan equine encephalomyelitis which has killed more than 100 Texans since it was first detected in Brownsville early this month. The disease is spread among horses, and from horses to humans, by mosquitoes.

With outbreaks reported in Oklahoma, Louisiana and Arkansas, the spraying program is now to be boosted by the addition of eight C-47s and another UC-123K. The airplanes are being used to spray the insecticide malathion along the Rio Grande river to kill the culex and salt water mosquitoes which carry the disease; it is hoped that this, together with the inoculation of horses, will contain the epidemic.

The UC-123Ks use the same spraying techniques which they employed in the Vietnam defoliation campaign. The aircraft now being added to the spray effort have to be modified to dispense the correct mixture of malathion to water. Only three ounces of the insecticide are needed to cover one acre.

**Hi-tech design: the long-haul departure terminal at London Heathrow.**

# Scott flies 34,000 miles via North Pole

*Shiela Scott: set several records.*

**London, August 4**
British aviatrix Sheila Scott landed her twin-engined Piper Aztec D at Heathrow today at the end of an epic 34,000-mile journey. Leaving on June 11, she made the first light airplane circumnavigation from the Equator, over the North Pole, then back across the Equator, finally returning home via the southern hemisphere.

Scott is the first woman to fly over the pole and the first person to fly over it solo. Among the records she set during her journey is a new time from Darwin, Australia, to London of three and a half days, knocking fully a day and a half off the previous record. This was her 100th flying record and the seventh of this particular trip. It was not her first epic flight, though: in 1966 she was the first British pilot to fly solo around the world.

During the journey, Scott conducted research on behalf of British and US organizations, including NASA. "It was a great flight and I was glad to help scientific research as well," she said on her arrival. Her airplane, the Aztec, is one of the most popular models from the Piper stable and is currently being produced at the rate of one machine a day.

# Italy's Hirundo helicopter graces the skies

*Agusta's sleek A-109C Hirundo helicopter has retractable landing gear.*

**Italy, August 4**
What is perhaps the world's most beautiful helicopter, the A-109A Hirundo (Swallow) made its first flight today.

The 109A is distinguished by its streamlined fuselage and its fully retractable tricycle landing gear. Originally planned with a single Turbomeca Astazou engine, it is now powered by two Allison 250-C20B engines of 400 hp each. The Hirundo provides comfortable accomodation for a pilot and seven passengers, although orders are being taken for medevac, search/rescue and various other special versions.

Agusta are also hoping to market highly specialized and armed 109 versions for army and navy use. With a sustained speed of 165mph, this helicopter has few equals on the international market.

# Singapore is first stop for Qantas 747s

*Qantas is one of many airlines redrawing its plans to accommodate the 747.*

**Australia, September 17**
Qantas today inaugurated its first Boeing 747 service with a flight from Australia to Singapore. The 747 will be the flagship of the airline's modernization over the coming years, which includes holding options to buy four Anglo-French Concorde supersonic airliners.

Alongside the first of its new 747s, the company has a fleet of Boeing 707-338Cs, which entered service in 1967. The development of the 747 gave rise to a radical review of future plans by the airline in the mid-1960s. Projections in 1966 envisaged a fleet of 33 Boeing 707s up to 1972, comprising both new and existing models. But a shortage of crews saw daily utilization fall, with consequently lower income and worsening costs.

With the new 707s delivered, the old 707-138Bs were sold. In May 1966, Qantas turned down Boeing's offer to provide three of the high-capacity 747s for 1970 delivery. But with more and more airlines showing an interest in the new wide-bodied airliners Qantas decided that, as Australia's national airline, it did not want to be left behind. Operating costs would also be lower than for the new 707s. So, on June 18, 1967, after a loss-making year, Qantas decided to buy four 747s, subject to government approval. In that year, too, "Empire" was dropped from its name, making it just Qantas Airways.

**The BD-5 Micro low-wing monoplane was conceived by designer James Bede to be put together by amateur constructors using home-assembly kits. A jet-powered model, the BD-5J, is under development, although even the piston-engined version is capable of speeds as high as 220mph.**

# NASA tries 60-year-old French invention

*Here the flaps – beneath the rolling cylinders – have been fully extended.*

**Mountain View, California, Nov 6**
Flight trials have just started of a special high-lift flap system at the NASA Ames Research Center. The system has been installed aboard a North American Rockwell OV-10A Bronco light attack airplane, redesignated the YOV-10A.

Originally proposed by French officer Colonel Lafay in 1910, and first applied to an airplane by engineering scientist Professor Favre at Marseilles in 1938, the system involves fitting a rapidly rotating cylinder in front of each flap. This helps the airflow to remain "attached" to the flap, increasing lift when the flaps are fully down. The aircraft can thus fly slower without stalling, but at very low speeds some augmentation to the flight controls may be needed. There is no plan to put the system into immediate production, but NASA's research might be useful for future aircraft development.

# Ungainly Super Guppy flies Airbus parts

*Toulouse, France, November 23*
This great swollen giant of a transport looks like a tropical fish, although with its center of gravity so far forward on landing, some pilots say it flies like a submarine. It is the Super Guppy, two of which are playing a crucial role in the construction of the European Airbus which is being assembled here by Airbus Industrie. Their role is to fly components in from all parts of Europe, including complete wings from Hawker Siddeley Aviation in Britain.

Guppies were created in the US by Aero Spacelines, which was set up by ex-USAF bomber and transport pilot John M "Jack" Conroy. They were first built to fly space boosters between NASA contractors and the launch pads. The Super Guppy Model 201, designed to carry complete DC-10 fuselage sections and TriStar wings, is ideal for this European operation.

*The huge Super Guppy 201's hold has a usable volume of 38,850 cubic feet.*

# Concorde carries out South American tour

*During the tour, Concorde flew at low-altitude over the bay at Rio de Janeiro.*

**Toulouse, France, September 18**
Concorde 001 arrived back here today after a triumphant tour of South America. It left Europe two weeks ago on its first transatlantic voyage, with André Turcat and Jean Pinet at the controls. The airliner flew for a total of 29 hours 52 minutes, of which 13 hours 30 minutes were at supersonic speed; the latter included 9 hours 21 minutes at Mach 2.

Concorde had arrived in Rio de Janeiro via the Cape Verde islands, Cayenne and Sao Paolo, where it was highlight of the France '71 exhibition, and made several demonstration flights (→ May 25, 1972).

# Japanese get hitched in a German Jumbo

*Pacific, November 5*
Twenty Japanese couples made their marriage vows 36,000 feet up in the sky today aboard a Lufthansa Boeing 747. The ceremony, which was carried out in strict conformity with Shinto custom, took place in front of family and friends as well as the captain of the 747 and a number of Japanese stewardesses who were on board especially for the occasion, wearing traditional kimonos.

The cabin had to be extensively rearranged for the ceremony. Several rows of seats were taken out to enable the Shinto priest, in full traditional robes, to officiate in front of a tiny altar.

*Apart from the unusual setting, the ceremony was traditional in every way.*

# Hijacker escapes plane by parachute

*A composite picture of an Air Canada DC-8-40; Cini, who tried a hijack similar to today's, was too slow to jump.*

*Mexico City, November 24*
All was going smoothly on Northwest Airlines' flight from Portland, Oregon, to Seattle today when passenger D B Cooper in the rear section rang for the stewardess. He casually showed her two red cylinders wired together and told her it was a bomb. The stewardess took it calmly and went forward to tell the captain. None of the other passengers had any inkling of what was

happening. The 727 landed normally at Seattle and the passengers filed off. Only the hijacker and the crew remained aboard and waited until $200,000 was loaded on board.

The refueled aircraft took off again and set course for Mexico. When it landed here there was no sign of either Cooper or the ransom money. He had locked the crew on the flight deck and parachuted from the rear door. The FBI

has begun a nationwide hunt for the hijacker, who was probably inspired by Paul Cini, who hijacked an Air Canada DC-8 two weeks ago. Declaring himself an IRA member, Cini demanded a $1.5 million ransom. After the passengers had been let off at Great Falls the DC-8 took off again. Cini had planned to jump from a rear door, but was overwhelmed by cabin staff and crew as he tried to strap on his parachute.

## Egyptian MiGs cock a snook at Israelis in flight over Sinai

*Tel Aviv, November 6*
Two Soviet-built Egyptian air force MiG-25s flew with impunity over the Israeli-held Sinai peninsula today. Reconnaissance versions of the most advanced Soviet fighter, they flew above 70,000 feet at a maximum speed of Mach 2.3, well beyond the capabilities of Israel's F-4 Phantoms.

The Egyptian spyplanes flew from near Sabkhet el Bardawil on the Mediterranean coast south to Ras Sudar on the Gulf of Suez, in order to observe fortifications which Israel has built near the Suez Canal. This is Egypt's second use of MiG-25s to observe Israeli defenses; on October 10 they flew along the southern coast of Sinai.

Tension between the countries has heightened since September 11, when Israel downed an Egyptian Su-7 fighter-bomber. An Israeli Stratocruiser transport fell to an Egyptian missile a week later. Israel has made a formal complaint about today's flight to United Nations truce supervisors in Jerusalem.

## France likely to pay back Israeli money

*Israel, November 20*
Since 1967, the matter of 50 Mirage Vs, ordered and paid for by Israel, but not delivered by France because of an embargo imposed by President de Gaulle, has cast a heavy shadow over relations between the two countries. But the latest news is that Tel Aviv might accept reimbursement for the machines.

Israel doubtless believes that the Mirage Vs will never be delivered, and wishes to acquire instead more modern American equipment that corresponds better to its present needs. Quite apart from the sales loss, things look bad for the French, who do not know what to do with the machines, stockpiled at the Chateaudun base. Built specially for the needs of the Israeli military, they could only be used by the French after modifications that would be too costly. Negotiations are set to continue (→ Apr 14, 1975).

## Czech pilot flies to West with family

*[West] Germany, December 19*
In 1968 Czechoslovak Airlines pilot Ladislaw Bezak decided to defect to the West. That was when Soviet tanks invaded his country. This morning, he arrived at the airport of Kladno, near Prague, and said he would be taking a little Zlin aircraft on a short trip.

As soon as he had taken off, he headed towards a clearing where his wife Marie and four children were waiting. But when he had crammed the family in beside him, Bezak found he could not take off from the rough ground. He flew back to the airport. His family made their way to the airport and eventually were able to climb aboard the Zlin. When the Bezaks at last took off for West Germany, a Czech MiG-17 fighter spotted them and opened fire, but the Zlin climbed into the clouds, to land in Bavaria and freedom.

**A few staff of Beirut-based Middle East Airlines (MEA). In 1971 MEA, serving 36 cities on three continents, carried more than 200,000 passengers. Its fleet consists of Boeing 707s for long-haul flights, supplemented by Boeing 720s (a 707 derivative) for the shorter-range routes.**

VFW-Fokker's VFW 614 had overwing pod-mounted Rolls-Royce/SNECMA
M45 Mk 501 turbofans. It was used by Touraine Air Transport/Air Alsace.

Dassault's Mercure 124/150-seat short-haul transport was optimised for
ranges of between 100 – 1,000nm; Air Inter, the only operator, bought ten.

The Stelio Frati-designed Italair
F.20 Pegaso five/six-seat light twin.

An upward-opening nose loading door was a feature of the Boeing 747-200F
freighter, the first production example of which was delivered to Lufthansa.

Robin's second production all-metal
airplane – the two-seat HR.200.

Agusta's A.109 Hirundo, powered by two Allison 250-C20 turboshaft engines,
has been widely used as an executive transport and for various military roles.

The prototype Bede BD-5 Micro single-seat sport aircraft, powered by a 40hp
three-cylinder Kiekhaefer Aeromarine engine. A 70hp version was available.

Ilyushin's Il-76 heavy transport, powered by four Soloviev D-30KP turbofan
engines, was designed to operate from short unprepared strips, as in Siberia.

The Maule M-5 Lunar Rocket development of the M-4 Strata Rocket featured
increased flap and tail surface areas for improved field/climb performance.

CASA's C.212 Aviocar, powered by two Garrett TPE331 turboprop engines,
replaced the Spanish Air Force Junkers Ju 52/3ms and CASA.207 Azors.

A lengthened and strengthened fuselage was a feature of the Bell 309 King Cobra, and changes to the nose to accept a stabilized multi-sensor gunsight.

A counter-insurgency aircraft based on the North American P-51 Mustang, the Piper Enforcer was powered by a Lycoming T55 turboprop engine.

Two Allison 250-B17 turboprops powered the Government Aircraft Factory's Nomad utility transport, operators of which included the Australian Army.

VFW-Fokker's H3 Sprinter had tip-driven rotors and a butterfly tail.

Cerva's CE.43 Guepard was an all-metal version of Wassmer's WA 421.

The Mitsubishi XT-2, designed as a supersonic jet trainer and light-attack aircraft for the JASDF, was powered by two Rolls-Royce Turbomeca Adours.

The prototype variable-geometry Mirage G.8, powered by two SNECMA Atar 9K-50 engines, attained Mach 2.03 only four days after its maiden flight.

The Japanese Defense Agency chose McDonnell Douglas's F-4EJ to be the main JASDF air defense fighter, license-built by Mitsubishi Heavy Industries.

Westland's W.G.13 prototype, powered by Rolls-Royce BS.360 engines, was flown with the skid landing gear chosen for the British Army Lynx AH.1.

Twelve Avro Shackleton MR Mk2 airframes were converted by Hawker Siddeley for airborne early warning duties and renamed Shackleton AEW.Mk2.

Chin-mounted search radar was a feature of the US Kaman SH-2D produced under the LAMPS (Light Airborne Multi-Purpose System) program.

# 1972

4,534mph
USA
Pete Knight
North American X-15
Oct 3, 1967

24,325 miles
USA
Archie Old Jr
Boeing B-52B
Jan 18, 1957

354,200ft
USA
Joseph Walker
North American X-15
Aug 22, 1963

833,000lb
USA
Boeing
B-747 200F

50,400lb thrust
USA
General Electric
CF6-50C

**Washington, DC, January 5**
President Nixon announces that $5.5 billion will be spent to develop a 'Shuttle' capable of flying both in space and in the Earth's atmosphere (→ Dec 2, 1976).

**Marietta, Georgia, January 21**
The prototype Lockheed S-3A Viking carrier-based, anti-submarine airplane makes it first flight.

**Ottawa, January 27**
The Canadian government and leaders of the country's 1,600 air traffic controllers agree to go to arbitration, ending a strike which since January 12 has paralyzed 116 airports and all but emergency and humanitarian services; the controllers, who earn an average $9,135 a year, want a pay rise and shorter hours because of the increased stresses of controlling modern airport traffic.

**France, January 30**
French domestic airline Air Inter orders ten Dassault-Breguet Mercure short-range jet airliners; it is the first firm order for the aircraft (→ Dec 19, 1975).

**Spain, February 3**
Iberia orders three Airbus A300Bs with options on six more (→ Oct 28).

**London, April 1**
The British Airways Board, established under last year's Civil Aviation Act, takes over BEA, BOAC and their subsidiaries; the airlines still trade under their existing names (→ Apr 1, 1974).

**Philippines, April 2**
Members of the USAF's 31st Aerospace Rescue Squadron pick up Charles Lindbergh and a scientific team from the jungle on Mindanao island after their helicopter crashed while on an anthropological survey.

**[West] Germany, April 25**
Hans-Werner Grosse sets a world sailplane distance record of 907.7 miles flying a Schleicher ASW 12.

**Miami, April 26**
The first Lockheed L-1011 TriStar enters scheduled service, with Eastern Air Lines, on its route to New York.

**Vietnam, April 27**
Four USAF aircraft destroy the Thanh Hoa bridge with Paveway laser-guided "smart" bombs; 871 earlier missions against the bridge using conventional bombs have all failed (→ Dec 26).

**St Louis, Missouri, April 29**
An experimentally-equipped McDonnell Douglas YRF-4C Phantom II becomes the first aircraft in the US to fly with a "fly-by-wire" control system, in which the aircraft's ailerons, tailplanes and rudder are controlled electronically, rather than mechanically by cables.

**London, May 25**
BOAC places an order for five Concordes (→ Oct 26).

**Istres, France, June 21**
Jean Boulet pilots an Aérospatiale SA 315 Lama to a helicopter world altitude record of 40,820 feet.

**California, June 21**
The McDonnell Douglas DC-10-30, a version of the DC-10 with a greater fuel capacity developed for intercontinental operations, makes its maiden flight.

**USA, August 1**
Delta Air Lines absorbs Northeast Airlines; the merged company will operate as Delta Air Lines.

**Texas, August 10**
Entrepreneur Frank Lorenzo takes control of Texas International Airlines.

**California, August 11**
The Northrop F-5E Tiger II single-seat tactical fighter makes its maiden flight, at Edwards Air Force Base (→ Apr 6, 1973).

**Berlin, August 14**
An Ilyushin Il-62 airliner crashes with the loss of 156 lives.

**Vietnam, August 28**
Captain Richard S Ritchie downs his fifth MiG-21 and becomes the first USAF ace of the war while flying a protection mission with co-pilot Captain Charles 'Chuck' DeBellevue for aircraft bombing North Vietnam.

**Wolverhampton, England, Aug 28**
First cousin of Queen Elizabeth II Prince William of Gloucester is killed with his co-pilot when their Piper Cherokee Arrow 200 crashes during the Goodwood Trophy race.

**Seattle, September 22**
Delta Air Lines orders 14 Boeing 727s, bringing total sales of the airliner to a record 1,000.

**Washington, DC, September 28**
The US Civil Aeronautics Board announces that rules covering charter flights are to be liberalized on a trial basis: after December 31, it will no longer be necessary to be a member of a club to benefit from reduced fares; it will be enough to pay a non-returnable fee 90 days in advance of the flight.

**Chicago, October 26**
United Air Lines decides not to take up options on six Concordes which were due to expire in February 1973 (→ Feb 28, 1973).

**Turkey, October 29**
A Lufthansa Boeing 727 flying from Beirut to Ankara is hijacked by a terrorist, who demands the return of three Palestinians held for murdering Israeli athletes at the Munich Olympic Games in the summer.

**Vietnam, December 18**
Sergeant Samuel Turner becomes the first B-52 gunner to shoot down an enemy aircraft when he hits a MiG-21 near Hanoi.

**Hertfordshire, England, Dec 23**
The Hertfordshire Pedal Aeronauts (HPA) Toucan two-man-powered aircraft makes a first flight of just over 2,000 feet (→ Aug 23, 1977).

**Vietnam, December 26**
A force of 117 USAF B-52 bombers hit Hanoi in the largest raid of the war to date, part of Operation Linebacker II, a concentrated offensive ordered by President Nixon on December 18.

**Uruguay, December 29**
It is revealed at a press conference in Montevideo that the survivors of a Uruguayan airliner crash in the Andes on October 13 were forced to eat those who were killed in order to stay alive.

---

## Factfile

World revenue passenger miles: 348,033.712 million
Passengers through Chicago O'Hare: 14.7 million
Passengers through New York (JFK/Newark/LaGuardia): 17.8 million
Passengers through London (Heathrow/Gatwick): 23.6 million
Price of a coach class ticket New York/Los Angeles (April): $163
Price of the cheapest return ticket London/New York: $219
World air freight (ton miles): 49,120.2 million
Average salary of long-haul pilot (US): $35,612
Average salary of cabin crew (US): $9,939
Price of a Falcon 20: $1.9 million
Price of an HS.125: $1.25 million
Price of a Learjet 25 B: $957,000
Price of 1,000 (US) gallons of A1 fuel (average for July): $116.73
Average exchange rate: £1 = $2.5038

*Several of Europe's aircraft manufacturers are pinning high hopes on the Airbus A300B, the world's first twin-engined, wide-body transport.* ▶

698

# European tour shows off Cessna Citation

*The Cessna Citation: offering high altitude performance at a low price.*

*France, February 29*
As part of a sales tour around Europe, the Cessna C-500 Citation was in France today for a lightning visit. Already sales in Europe are expected to live up to the manufacturer's forecasts, and delivery of Citations are supposed to begin in April. Cessna is touring round all its agents to introduce them to the C-500, which ought to prove attractive to a large number of twin-jet owners. And users of the Cessna 310, 421, 401 and 414 are unlikely to remain blind to the advantages of the C-500. Even if some of these propeller-driven aircraft are, like the C-500, pressurized, the differences remain great. The flight level, which is over 33,000 feet, changes the whole ball game – and that is without taking into account the speed, which can increase from 220 to 400mph. The price is also attractive, since it less than that of other executive jets. All that remains is for pilots to gain a new qualification in order to fly this new jet.

# Helicopters go to the rescue in Vietnam

*Saigon, June 2*
At noon today, 23 days of evading North Vietnamese forces ended for Captain Roger C Locher when a USAF Sikorsky HH-53 helicopter flew deep into North Vietnam on a daring daylight rescue mission. "I was never so happy in my life when I hooked myself to the rescue cable and they hoisted me up to that Jolly Green Giant chopper," Captain Locher said. About 100 US aircraft from bases in Thailand – fighter-bombers, command and control and jamming aircraft, as well as the helicopter – were used in the rescue. They flew through heavy fire to the vicinity of Yen Bai, northwest of Hanoi and within 60 miles of the Chinese border, to reach the stranded airman.

Locher lost 15 lb during his ordeal, which began on May 10 when his F-4 Phantom was shot down during a mission against the rail link between China and Hanoi. The other member of the F-4's crew is still missing.

*Sikorsky's "Jolly Green Giant" rescue helicopter can carry up to 38 people.*

# Lufthansa buys first 747 built for cargo

*The hinged nose on Boeing's 747-200F allows for easy front-loading of cargo.*

*Seattle, March 9*
The first Boeing 747-200F (the F stands for freight) was delivered today to Lufthansa.

The cargo giant weighs a massive 410 tons. It can carry a cargo of 100 tons, and 118 tons of fuel. This capacity, superior to that of the 747-100, is made possible by using JT9D or CF6 engines of 51,000-lb thrust. The West German airline expects to haul a 100-ton load between Frankfurt and New York every day of the year with this one aircraft. In 1966, Boeing put the 747 cockpit on top so that cargo could be loaded through the aircraft's nose.

# Allegheny is sixth in the US after merger

*Washington, DC, April 12*
The merger of Allegheny and Mohawk Airlines, which was agreed in December last year, was completed today after approval by President Nixon and the US Civil Aeronautics Board. The absorption of Mohawk makes Allegheny the sixth largest passenger airline in the US.

Allegheny was founded in 1937 as All-American Airways and within a year began an airmail service to 58 small communities in Delaware, Maryland, Ohio, Pennsylvania and West Virginia. That service ended in June 1949, three months after the airline was certificated to take passengers. The name was changed to Allegheny Airlines in 1951. The merger with Mohawk, which has served upstate New York and New England for 26 years, will give Allegheny routes to 20 States and Canada, as well as a fleet of 62 jet and 40 turboprop airliners.

# Soviets fly spying mission from Cuba

*USA, February 13*
The Soviet Union has started to use Cuba as a base from which to spy on the US. The first mission was flown today by two Soviet Tu-95 turboprop reconnaissance aircraft (called Bear by Nato) which surveyed part of the east coast.

The Tu-95s took off from Havana and headed for Florida, flying at between 50 and 100 miles off the coast. South-east of the Norfolk, Virginia, naval base, home of the Atlantic fleet, an F-4B Phantom and an A-7 Corsair II from the aircraft carrier USS *Forrestal* intercepted the Bears and escorted them from the area.

Long-range Soviet aircraft have been operating along the US east coast since 1968, gathering information on US air defenses and space activities, but they have previously only stopped over in Cuba before returning to the USSR.

# Fairchild puts faith in anti-tank A-10

*Farmingdale, NY, May 10*
The first of two YA-10 prototypes made its first flight here at the plant of Fairchild Republic Company this morning. Located in central Long Island, New York, this factory has produced fighters for the air force for nearly 40 years. Everything now depends on the A-10.

The A-10 is the first aircraft designed from the outset to give close air support on the battlefield, especially against enemy armor. It carries a General Electric GAU-8A, seven-barrel, 30mm cannon – the most powerful gun ever fitted to an airplane, which fires armor-piercing shells of depleted uranium.

It also has ten pylons for missiles, bombs or electronic-warfare pods. Unusual features of the new attack plane include twin General Electric TF34 turbofans mounted on the rear fuselage, and a cockpit housed inside a "bath" of thick titanium armor. The A-10 is designed to survive hostile fire, even up to 37mm caliber.

# Pilots strike to publicize hijack problem

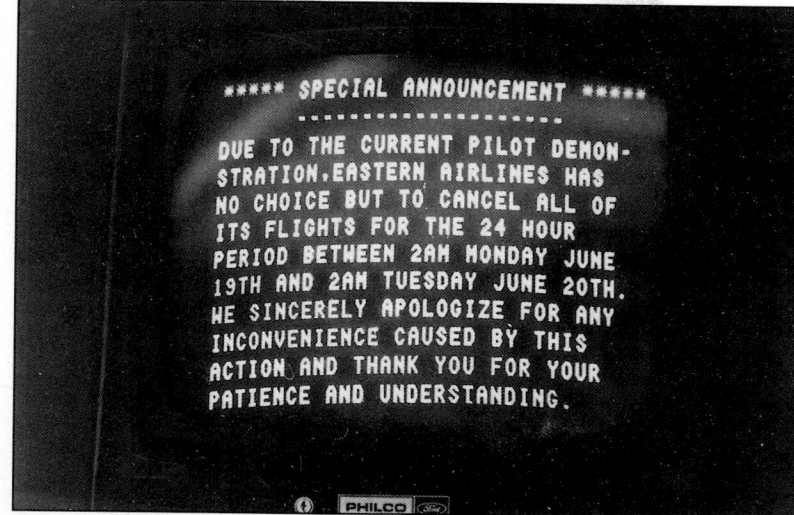
*The message displayed by Eastern Air Lines at New York JFK on June 19.*

*International, June 20*
Airliners in locations as far apart as Canada, India and New Zealand stood idle today as pilots around the globe went on strike to call for tougher anti-hijack measures.

In the US, some flights operated normally, but many were canceled. The Eastern Air Lines Washington/- New York/Boston shuttle did not fly, leaving 5,000 daily passengers to find space on other airlines or take the train. At New York's JFK airport, a pilot dressed as a pirate carried a sign with the words: "The Next One Killed by an Air Pirate May Be You." He said that he was afraid every time he took off.

# Navy fliers become the first US aces of the Vietnam war

*Saigon, May 10*
Lieutenant Randy Cunningham and Lieutenant Junior Grade William Driscoll of the US Navy shot down North Vietnam's top ace and two other MiG-17s today to become the first US aces of the Vietnam war. Shortly afterward, their F-4J Phantom was hit by a surface-to-air missile, but they nursed the crippled airplane as far as the Gulf of Tonkin before ejecting and being picked up by US Marine helicopters. Tonight they are back aboard the carrier USS *Constellation*.

Overall, ten MiG-21s and MiG-17s fell to USAF and US Navy pilots today, while three US aircraft were lost. Cunningham and Driscoll began the day with two "kills" to their credit: a MiG-21 on Jan-

*Cunningham: three hits in one day.*

# Terrorists slaughter 25 fellow passengers at Tel Aviv airport

*Tel Aviv, May 30*
Three Japanese men walked off an Air France airliner at Tel Aviv's Lod airport today, pulled automatic rifles and grenades from their luggage and began a brutal massacre in which 25 died and 72 were injured, many seriously. The three men, who had boarded the Paris/Tel Aviv flight at Rome, retrieved their luggage from customs before heading for the main terminal hall.

The Israelis believe that the murderers were Arab terrorists. One assassin is said to have killed himself with a grenade and another was captured; troops are hunting the third. The atrocity is sure to mean tighter airline security worldwide. Earlier this month a Sabena jet was hijacked by Black September terrorists; 92 passengers were freed after the plane was stormed by Israeli troops (→Oct 29).

uary 19 and a MiG-17 on May 8. As in the past, they used Sidewinder missiles for their victories today. Cunningham said later he might have achieved three more if the Phantom had also had a gun.

Their last encounter of the day was with North Vietnamese ace Colonel Toon, who had downed 13 US aircraft. In several minutes of tight maneuvering, the MiG-17 and the F-4 each sought a chance to fire. Finally, as both aircraft were climbing, Cunningham throttled back and braked hard; Colonel Toon overshot him, then pitched earthward. Cunningham followed, and fired his missile (→Aug 28).

*On May 8, a Boeing 707 operated by Belgian airline Sabena was hijacked by terrorists just after it landed at Vienna.*

# US Phantom aircrew shoot down MiG-21

*Shortly after the kill, the two aircrew pose on the canopy rail of their F-4.*

**Pacific, August 10**

Lt-Cdr R E "Gene" Tucker and radar intercept officer Lieutenant Junior Grade Bruce Eden have just returned to "Trap" aboard the USS Saratoga after an aerial contest between their F-4J Phantom II and a MiG-21 of the North Vietnamese air force. The unlucky MiG pilot will not be returning to his base, however.

Lt-Cdr Tucker had been doing routine paperwork while serving on catapult "alert status". The silence was shattered by the "launch the alert aircraft" command given over the carrier's flight deck public address system. The carrier's combat information center had detected a "bogey" (enemy threat) and it was Tucker's mission to intercept the intruder. The F-4J was launched into the gathering darkness and its flight crew was disappointed to learn that radar contact had been lost. However, after a tricky night refueling by a KA-6D tanker, the Phantom was again vectored toward a re-acquired target.

Eden was able to find the "bogey" on his own intercept radar and the afterburners were lit to close the 12-mile distance between them. At a speed of 650 knots, at 8,000 feet the target was lost again. Descending to 3,500 feet, the MiG emerged once more in the vicinity of Vinh, near the Kart mountains.

With only 2 miles between the two jets, Tucker quickly fired two Sparrow missiles. Blinded by rocket motor exhaust Tucker's eyesight recovered just in time to see the MiG-21 explode.

# Worries about air-travel safety increase

**London, June 18**

A fatal crash in Britain and a near thing in the US have focused attention on the safety of air travel again. On June 12, just after take-off from Detroit, as the cabin was being pressurized, the cargo door of an American Airlines DC-10 blew off, damaging its hydraulic control lines, though luckily leaving the pilot with just enough control to land. An investigation into the cargo doors is under way.

Just after take-off from Heathrow today, all 118 passengers and crew aboard a BEA Trident died in Britain's worst air disaster. The cause has yet to be confirmed, but it appears there is a human factor. Captain Stanley Key was in command with two junior second officers. He was known to be hostile to strike action planned by flight crews for tomorrow, which had led to graffiti being scrawled in the Trident's cockpit. This could have made him angry and, unknown to BEA, he also had a heart condition. It seems that he had a heart attack shortly after take-off which led to confusion on the flight deck, which in turn led to the crash (→ Mar 3, 1974).

# Laker takes delivery of his first DC-10

**London, November 12**

Freddie Laker, aviation entrepreneur and thorn in the side of the big established airlines, took delivery of his first DC-10 today. It will go into service on the "sunshine" routes flying holidaymakers to the Mediterranean area.

The aircraft is the first of two McDonnell Douglas DC-10-10s, which rival any airplane of the big carriers. A second DC-10 is due for delivery in two days' time. Meanwhile, Laker is still battling to get his no frills, no advanced booking transatlantic "Skytrain" service off the ground.

The DC-10s would be ideal to replace the 707s first listed when his Skytrain application was submitted to the British Air Transport Licensing Board last year. With the 707s Laker could offer tickets at roughly a quarter of the existing economy fare. DC-10s could bring prices down even further.

*Laker discusses the company's first DC-10 with chief pilot Alan Hellery.*

# Eagle points way to future fighter forces

**California, July 27**

Test pilot Irving Burrows smiled as he brought the McDonnell Douglas F-15A Eagle to a halt on the apron at Edwards Air Force Base today. After a 50-minute flight at the controls of the air superiority fighter, he knew that he had been handling a thoroughbred of the skies. The Eagle, which is designed to replace the F-4 Phantom as the workhorse fighter of the USAF, is equipped with two Pratt & Whitney F100 afterburning turbofans.

At over 18 tons it is a heavy aircraft, but it is also the first fighter to achieve a thrust greater than its weight, enabling it to accelerate faster than any other fighter. Its top speed is Mach 2.5 (→ Feb 1, 1975).

*Thoroughbred of the skies: the McDonnell Douglas F-15 can reach Mach 2.5.*

# Multinational Airbus challenges monopoly of USA

*Toulouse, France, October 28*
The first real challenge to the US domination of the subsonic airliner market in many years took to the air here today, and even the most staid of British, Dutch, French, German and Spanish technicians felt this should be the beginning of a new era. It is three years since construction work began on the Airbus Industrie A300B1 here and in four other factories in Europe. The first multinational European airliner exists at last, and now the burning question is: will the Airbus prove a commercial success?

The Airbus story goes back to the mid-1960s when French and West German manufacturers met at the Paris Air Show and set up a working party to examine the feasibility of building a 200-seater short-to-medium-range airliner as a joint venture.

At the same time, Britain's BEA was looking for a successor to its Vanguard fleet, and over the next few months a number of proposals were considered. Finally, an agreement was reached that a consortium

*The A300B: Europe's first multinational airliner and the first in the world to challenge the near-monopoly of the US.*

should be formed to build a 200-300 seater based on the HBN100, designed jointly by Hawker Siddeley, Breguet and Nord Aviation. Much of the fuselage was to be built in West Germany by the newly created company Deutsche Airbus; the wings would be made in England by Hawker Siddeley and the moving wing parts by Fokker in Holland, while the horizontal tail surfaces would come from Construcciones Aeronauticas (CASA) in Spain. The aircraft would be assembled by Sud Aviation in Toulouse under the generic name of Airbus Industrie. The Airbus is powered by two General Electric CF6 turbofans each giving 52,500 pounds thrust which are built under licence by SNECMA in France, giving a maximum cruising speed of 566mph at 25,000 feet. Passenger accomodation will be for up to 296 people (→ Jan 18, 1973).

## Two great Russian designers are dead

*Universally acknowledged "father of the helicopter" Igor Sikorsky.*

*Moscow, December 23*
The great Soviet aircraft designer Andrei Nikolayevich Tupolev died today at the age of 86. Born on November 11, 1888, Tupolev was a major force in the Central Aero-Hydrodynamics Institute in Moscow from its inception in 1920. He will be remembered for his incredible variety of aircraft, exceeding the output of any any other designer in history. He was also a deputy to the Supreme Soviet and was awarded Stalin prizes in 1943 and 1948 and the Order of Lenin.

Tupolev's death comes just two months after that of Russian-born pioneer Igor Sikorsky, who died on October 26, aged 83. When his early helicopter designs failed he turned to airplanes, building the first four-engined airplane in 1913. After the 1917 revolution he fled to the USA, where in 1923 he established Sikorsky Aero Engineering to build flying boats. But from the late 1930s his main concern was the helicopter, his greatest achievement.

## Helicopters find new role in the North Sea

*Aberdeen, Scotland, November 15*
A new passenger terminal which opened here today includes a hangar for four Sikorsky S-61N helicopters. Normally equipped for 26 passengers, the S-61N is one of the workhorses used in support of the oil and gas drilling rigs and the production platforms in the North Sea. This traffic has grown in five years to 40,000 passengers this year and is forecast to reach 250,000 by 1981 with over 80 helicopters then in use.

Unlike those serving other offshore oil installations, helicopters here frequently to fly in appalling weather. So precision navigational aids and X-band radar are essential, as is emergency flotation gear and all-weather de-icing systems.

*One of BEA's S-61Ns operating from an oil rig in the North Sea, off Scotland.*

The Sabreliner 75A was powered by a pair of CF700 turbofan engines.

Sikorsky's XH-59A was an Advancing Blade Concept coaxial helicopter.

The Beech 100 King Air was a development of the popular Model 90.

The Fokker F.28 Fellowship developed in several new versions.

With seating for up to 300 passengers, the Airbus Industrie A300B1, built by France, Britain, Germany, Holland and Spain, was powered by two GE CF6s.

Built in Argentina, the Aero Boero AG.260 was an agricultural aircraft.

The Saab Supporter is the military version of the civil two-seat Safari.

The Ted Smith Super Star 700 had a longer fuselage than its forebears.

Closely resembling the Piper PA.36, is India's Hindustan HA.31 Basant.

The final model of Boeing's immensely successful 727 was the advanced Series 200, which featured uprated JT8D engines, more fuel and greater range.

The DC-10-20 was the first to be optimized for long-range operations.

Australia's AESL Airtrainer was a two-seat aerobatic military trainer.

Best-selling version of the McDonnell Douglas DC-10 was the Series 30, with its CF6-50A engines, which was also available in a pure freighter version.

The first of Aérospatiale's Dauphin twin-engined helicopters, the ten-seat SA.360 was aimed at customers requiring a blend of speed and comfort.

The Beech 200 Super King Air pressurized turboprop-powered twin.

MiG-27 ground-attack aircraft equipped Soviet Frontal Aviation.

Although expensive, the McDonnell Douglas YF-15A Eagle offered unprecedented increase in air combat ability over aircraft such as the Phantom.

Almost the complete antithesis of aircraft such as the Eagle, Northrop's F-5E Tiger II (and the two-seat F-5F) was a cheap but effective multi-role fighter.

Lockheed's S-3A Viking was designed to incorporate all the equipment needed to locate and destroy enemy submarines in a single carrier-borne aircraft.

Vought's YA-7H Corsair II tandem-seat naval trainer, later the YA-7E.

Northrop's YA-9A ground-attack aircraft did not go into production.

Fairchild's A-10A anti-armor and ground-attack aircraft serves with the USAF, its primary armament being the GAU-8/A 30mm cannon in the nose.

The Sukhoi T-4, or T-100, experimental bomber was a supersonic research airplane made of titanium, which incorporated early fly-by-wire controls.

# 1973

4,534mph
USA
Pete Knight
North American X-15
Oct 3, 1967

24,325 miles
USA
Archie Old Jr
Boeing B-52B
Jan 18, 1957

354,200ft
USA
Joseph Walker
North American X-15
Aug 22, 1963

833,000lb
USA
Boeing
B-747 200F

51,800lb thrust
USA
General Electric
CF6-50E

**Paris, January 18**
Max Fischl lands the Airbus A300B at Orly airport after a flight doubling as a delivery and a demonstration that the airliner is capable of operating at low noise levels which are less disturbing to local residents (→ May 8).

**USA, February 7**
A "$13 war" begins between Braniff and Southwest Airlines; Braniff offers a $13 Dallas to Houston ticket and Southwest responds by offering a bottle of whiskey (→ Jun 18, 1974).

**Tanzania, February 18**
Daniel Bauchart and Didier Potelle land 19,568 feet up on the summit of Mount Kilimanjaro in an SA 319 B Alouette II helicopter.

**USA, March 29**
Continental Airlines decides against taking up its options to buy three Concordes.

**Nepal, March**
Britain's RAF launches Operation Khana Cascade, its biggest airlift operation since Berlin in 1948-9, to drop nearly 2,000 tons of grain, maize and rice to Himalayan villagers.

**Arizona, April 6**
The first Northrop F-5E Tiger II is delivered to the USAF, at Williams Air Force Base.

**Seattle, Washington, April 10**
The T-43A navigation trainer, developed for the USAF from the Boeing 737-200, makes its first flight.

**Tallahassee, Florida, April 16**
The state senate votes unanimously to restore the name Cape Canaveral to the NASA establishment which was renamed Cape Kennedy shortly after the President's assassination.

**Toulouse, France, May 8**
The Airbus A300B prototype makes the type's first fully-automatic landing (→ Oct 18).

**Sweden, May 21**
The all-weather armed overland photographic reconnaissance version of the Saab Viggen, the SF 37, makes its first flight.

**Scotland, May 30**
The first production SEPECAT Jaguar GR.1 single-seat tactical support aircraft for RAF service is delivered to the Jaguar Operational Conversion Unit at Lossiemouth (→ Mar 29, 1974).

**Britain, June 29**
The Westland Lynx twin-turbine helicopter makes its first deck landing at sea, on board the Royal Fleet Auxiliary *Engadine*.

**Paris, July 11**
A Boeing 707 of Brazilian airline Varig flying from Rio de Janeiro to Orly airport, is forced to make an emergency landing when a fire breaks out on board; 123 die from asphyxiation by the fumes.

**USSR, July 25**
Alexander Fedotov flies a Mikoyan Ye-266 to a world record altitude of 118,898 feet (→ Aug 31, 1977).

**California, August 1**
The Martin Marietta X-24B lifting-body research airplane makes its first unpowered flight, gliding to Edwards Air Force Base after launch at 40,000 feet from an NB-52 motherplane (→ Nov 15).

**Cambodia, August 15**
US bombing attacks cease; a peace treaty ending the war in Vietnam was signed in Paris in January, but USAF B-52's have remained in action because of cease-fire violations (→ Apr 30, 1975).

**Wichita, Kansas, August 22**
The prototype Learjet Model 35 eight-seat business jet makes its first flight (→ Apr 5, 1975).

**England, August 29**
Hawker Siddeley announces that it has received a grant from the British government of £46 million to support the development of the company's HS.146 turbofan-powered airliner (→ Oct 18, 1974).

**Somerset, England, September 12**
The Westland Commando military helicopter, a development for Egypt of the Sea King, makes its first flight, at Yeovil.

**Washington, DC, September 20**
President Nixon presents the annual Harmon trophy for a substantial contribution to aeronautics to Concorde chief test pilots Brian Trubshaw and André Turcat (→ Mar 31, 1976).

**Paris, September 26**
The second production Concorde lands after a flight from Washington, DC, taking just 3 hours 33 minutes (→ Jun 17, 1974).

**Tokyo, October 7**
Japan Air Lines puts the Boeing 747SR, a short-range, large-capacity version of the Jumbo Jet capable of carrying 498 passengers, into service on its domestic route between here and Okinawa.

**Israel, October 14**
Seven USAF C-5A Galaxy transports arrive from the US with supplies to help the Israeli war effort against Egypt (→ Oct 24).

**Toulouse, France, October 18**
The Airbus A300B returns from a promotional tour of the Americas; it has covered almost 25,000 miles in 53 hours 35 minutes flying time, with 23 stops (→ May 23, 1974).

**Linz, Austria, October 21**
The Militky MB-E1 becomes the first electrically-driven piloted airplane to fly; it is powered by an electric motor driven by rechargeable batteries.

**Istres, France, October 26**
The Dassault-Breguet Dornier Alpha Jet trainer prototype makes its maiden flight (→ Oct 28, 1975).

**London, October 31**
BEA Airtours flies its last scheduled service with a D.H. Comet 4B (→ Feb 12, 1974).

**USSR, November 24**
The death of pioneer helicopter designer Nikolai N Kamov is announced.

**Renton, Washington, Nov 29**
The 1,000th Boeing 727 rolls off the production line.→

**London, December 1**
British inclusive tour operators impose a surcharge on fares to cover increases in fuel prices which have occurred in the wake of the Arab-Israeli war.→

---

*Side-mounted jets boost forward speed on the Sikorsky S-69 two-seat research helicopter; it features two contra-rotating, coaxial rotors.* ▶

## Factfile

World revenue passenger miles: 384,137.052 million
Passengers through Chicago O'Hare: 15.5 million
Passengers through New York (JFK/Newark/LaGuardia): 17.9 million
Passengers through London (Heathrow/Gatwick): 26.1 million
Price of a single Coach ticket New York/Los Angeles (April): $176
Price of the cheapest return ticket London/New York: $233
World air freight (ton miles): 54,263.4 million
Average salary of a long-haul pilot (US): $36,146
Average salary of cabin crew (US): $9,769
Price of a Beech 100: $744,500
Price of a Falcon 10: $1.48 million
Price of a Gulfstream II: $4.1 million
Average exchange rate: £1 = $2.4479
Price of 1,000 (US) gallons of Jet A1 (average for July): $150.08

# JAL flies luxurious 747 over North Pole

*Paris, January 24*
The Japan Air Lines Boeing 747 *Celestial Garden* is a true ambassador of the air. It landed at Orly airport today at 3pm, after carrying out a special kind of reconnaissance flight on the polar route from Tokyo to Paris.

Although JAL has been flying this route for ten years, it has never flown it with a 747 before. Today's flight was also the first made by JAL on the route without a navigator. This left just two pilots and a flight engineer. The service enabled JAL to evaluate the problems posed by operating the Boeing Jumbo on this route, and showed that gains of up to 45 minutes could be made over schedules operated at present by DC-8s.

But speed is not the only advantage of the *Celestial Garden*. The luxurious interior has been thought out with great care: there is a bar decorated with rising Sun motifs, while first class contains the Pine, Wisteria, Maple and Wild Orange Tree gardens, each in approporiate colors (→ Sep 29, 1974).

*The flight from Paris to Anchorage is ten hours; it is another seven to Tokyo.*

# Balloon firm launches first hot-air airship

*Bristol, England, January 4*
An unusual aircraft, the D96, the world's first hot-air airship, made its first flight here today at the works of its makers, Cameron Balloons. The light tubular-metal gondola was made by a group headed by Dr E T Hall at Oxford.

The fabric envelope is 100 feet long and has a volume of 96,000 cubic feet, hence the designation D96. The gondola carries the pilot, a passenger, propane burner and gas bottles, and the 45-hp Volkswagen engine, which drives a shrouded pusher propeller.

It is expected that the D96 could have various uses, although its normal cruising speed of only 11.5mph will preclude its operation in anything more than a gentle breeze. It has not been decided whether the airship will go into production or remain unique.

# US airlines give thumbs down to Concorde

*Toulouse, France, February 28*
While the Concorde prototypes, pre-production and production aircraft continue to perform faultlessly, the decision of two of the main potential customers not to take up their options is likely to mean that no more will be sold beyond the 16 production aircraft ordered for BOAC and Air France. This will make the overall programme financially unprofitable.

The airlines backing out are Pan Am, TWA and other operators, such as Qantas and JAL, are likely to follow their lead. The loss of Pan Am as a customer was the biggest blow; it had always been seen as the most important US customer. Pan Am's options ran out at the end of last month, and despite strenuous efforts by the BAC sales team to convince Pan Am's executives, in the end the economics just did not add up. A Concorde was going to cost the airline $65m (compared with $21m for a 747) and though it could carry passengers much faster, its operating costs are much higher; Pan Am was unconvinced that there would be sufficient demand (→ Mar 29).

# Israelis down Libyan airliner: 104 dead

*The wreckage of the airliner is searched for the bodies of missing passengers.*

*Egypt, February 21*
A Libyan Airlines Boeing 727 carrying 104 passengers was shot down today by Israeli fighters. At least 74 people died when the aircraft was hit and forced to crash-land in a portion of the Sinai desert controlled by Israel.

An Israeli statement claimed that the airplane, en route to Cairo from Benghazi, Libya, had flown 50 miles into an occupied area of the Sinai, passing over its forces along the Suez Canal and a military airfield. It said that when attempts to contact the intruder by radio failed, fighters intercepted the airliner and instructed it to land using international signals which were ignored, as were several subsequent warning shots. Israeli Prime Minister Golda Meir expressed Israel's "deep sorrow at the loss of life". Cairo radio denounced the tragedy as "an act of mass murder violating all international laws" (→ Oct 6).

# NASA tries out a new 'supercritical' wing

*The "supercritical" wing is flatter on top and more curved on the underside.*

*California, March 31*
Flight testing began at Dryden Flight Research Center today of the "supercritical" wing fitted to a Ling Temco Vought F-8A Crusader supersonic fighter. A wing of this type was first tested on a Rockwell T-2 Buckeye jet trainer in November 1970. It has a flatter upper surface than other wings, but a lighter structure, thicker leading edge, bulging underside and down-curved trailing edge. It offers more volume for fuel and less drag at speeds of around Mach 0.8 to 0.9.

The "supercritical" wing was invented by Richard Whitcomb of NASA and the entire test program is NASA-managed. The next stage is to refit a swing-wing F-111.

# Bandeirante proves a commercial success

*Brazil, April 16*
The EMBRAER Bandeirante entered service today on the airline Transbrasil's internal routes. The state has ordered 80 models of this versatile light transport airplane, which is the first of a large Brazilian aircraft-building program. The government set up EMBRAER in 1969. Based at São José dos Campos, the

company is Brazil's leading aircraft builder, with the state retaining 51 per cent ownership.

The success of the Bandeirante depends largely on the patronage of all state enterprises. But foreigners have lent a hand. It was designed by Frenchman Max Holste and its engines are Pratt & Whitney Canada turboprops (→ Oct 10, 1976).

*Brazilian export: Bandeirante in service in the USA with Allegheny Airlines.*

# Supersonic Soviet airliner crashes: 14 die

*Paris, June 3*
The northern Paris suburb of Goussainville is in a state of shock tonight following the crash there this afternoon of a Soviet Tu-144 supersonic transport during the Paris Air Show. All six aboard the aircraft, including a French cameraman, died, as did eight on the ground.

Aircraft 77102, the second in the initial production batch, had been almost completely redesigned com-

pared with the prototype seen at the last Paris Air Show two years ago. Most notable were the new retractable canards or foreplanes at the front of the aircraft, which were to aid control at low speeds. In its last moments pilot M V Kuzlov had appeared to pull up to avoid a Mirage fighter, dive and pull up again. On the last maneuver the aircraft lost a wing and broke apart, plummeting to earth (→ Dec 26, 1975).

*The doomed Tu-144 wrecked this part of the Paris suburbs when it came down.*

# Anglo-French Jaguar stars at Paris show

*The Jaguar shows off its wide range of weaponry at this year's Paris Air Show.*

*Paris, May*
The Anglo-French Jaguar tactical fighter-bomber, which will go into service with the RAF soon, has been one of the stars of the Paris Air Show. It was originally designed by Breguet in France as the Br.121 trainer, with limited attack capability, but following an agreement between Britain and France, it was redesigned, mainly by the British Aircraft Corporation (BAC), to be a far more potent

ground-attack aircraft, with a speed of Mach 1.6 and the ability to carry 10,000 lb of bombs. Production is being handled by the international company formed by BAC and Breguet, SEPECAT.

RAF pilots will start training on them in September and the first squadron to get them will be Nº 54 which should be operational next year. The RAF and the French air force have ordered 402, including dual-control trainers (→ May 30).

# US supersonic fails to reach starting gate

*Washington, DC, May*
When a French Concorde supersonic transport (SST) arrives for the dedication of Dallas-Fort Worth airport this fall, many Americans will ask: "Where is our SST?" The answer is: "Nowhere." And it isn't likely to be for a long time.

When the Anglo-French Concorde was announced, the US launched a joint industry-government program to build its own SST. Boeing and General Electric were chosen to build the airframe, and engine costs rose just as sharply as they did with Concorde. The only difference was that, despite the backing of the President and strong lobbying by some of its members, Con-

gress killed off the program because it did not want to become a perpetual subsidizer of the US SST, not just during construction, but also throughout its time with the airlines.

When Pan Am and TWA canceled their options on the Anglo-French Concorde in February this year [*see opposite*], the Congress action was vindicated. Airlines are hard-nosed businesses and neither Pan Am nor TWA believed that they could make money with the Concorde. Why fly an immensely expensive airplane just because it is faster if it can carry only 128 passengers at a time, when you can make more money with a Boeing 747 with 400 seats?

# French produce world's smallest twin

*Colomban's Cri-Cri: the prototype was powered by two chain-saw engines.*

*Versailles, France, July 19*

The French have a predilection for tiny aircraft – especially the sort which can be built and flown by amateurs. The Flying Flea was a forerunner of an entire line of aircraft ranging in size from the very small to the positively minuscule. Now, looking for sales in the build-it-yourself market, comes hopeful inventor Michel Colomban with his Cri-Cri, which he claims to be the smallest twin-engined aircraft ever built.

Certainly, it seems unlikely that any other aircraft is powered by two Stihl-Rowenta 9-hp chain saw engines, pull-started like a lawn-mower and reliant on two-stroke

fuel to keep the airplane in the air. Cri-Cri flew for the first time today with 68-year-old test pilot Robert Buisson, who has more than 12,000 flying hours in his log-book, taking a run of a little over 200 feet to get into the air.

Before he applies for certification, however, Colomban will instal two 15-hp engines, which will give the Cri-Cri a fuel consumption of approximately 4 (US) gallons per 60 hour. He is aiming at a cruising speed of 124mph with a maximum weight of 374 lb. The cost of construction was an astonishingly low 5,000 francs (£500). Colomban has sold 42 sets of plans to US enthusiasts (→ Jan 25, 1975).

# Sikorksy's latest flies without tail-rotor

*Connecticut, July 26*

The two-seat S-69 research helicopter made its first flight today. Sikorsky hopes to sell it to the US Army, which has given it the designation XH-59A.

The pilot tested the Advancing Blade Concept (ABC), in which two three-blade rigid rotors contra-rotate on the same axis. This new breed of rotor offers better maneuverability and higher speeds and dispenses with the need for the torque-canceling tail rotor. Power comes from a 1,825-shp Pratt & Whitney Canada Turbo-TwinPac and two 3,000-lb Pratt & Whitney Canada turbojets on the sides of the fuselage. The S-69 can reach a speed of over 280mph.

*Sikorsky's S-69 – with no tail rotor – has a sleek, streamlined appearance.*

# Drama at Heathrow

*London, June 26*

The cool nerves of a Pan Am flight crew on a routine service from the US to Britain today saved 220 lives and averted a dramatic tragedy. Over the Atlantic, one of the airline's 747s was hit by a violent thunderstorm which damaged the flight deck windshield and cut off forward vision. But by using the aircraft's automatic approach systems, the pilots landed safely.

# Concorde becomes flying observatory

*View of the eclipse from Concorde.*

*Fort-Lamy, Chad, June 30*

Concorde has found a new use: as a flying observatory. Today's solar eclipse – which astronomers had predicted would be the longest for 1,000 years – was watched by seven scientists on board a specially-modified Concorde flying at 55,000 feet. The scientists, from the USA, Britain and France, viewed the eclipse for 74 minutes during a flight from Las Palmas, Canaries, to Ndjamena (Chad) (→ Sep 26, 1973).

**Progress in flying machines: France's pedal-powered Aviette races past Concorde 001 at Le Bourget, Paris.**

# Concorde makes first entry to US airport

*Concorde parks alongside a 747 during Dallas-Fort Worth's dedication.*

*Dallas, September 20*
The Anglo-French Concorde was under the spotlight today at the dedication of Dallas-Fort Worth International Airport. Concorde was here to gain the trust of US officials and the public. It was the first visit of a supersonic airliner to the US.

The French Concorde 02 flew here today from Caracas, on a flight which served as a demonstration of the difference between ordinary jet airliners and this one. Some 32 officials and newsmen had been flown to Venezuela on a Braniff International 707. That flight took more than four and a half hours; today they flew back on the same route on Concorde in about two and a half hours. The airplane limited itself to flying supersonic only over water, because, according to Aérospatiale chairman Henri Ziegler: "We don't want to disturb the authorities of New York now."

Thousands of sightseers turned out in Dallas to get a glimpse of the Concorde, and local dignitaries were taken for supersonic rides over the Gulf of Mexico. BOAC and Air France hope to begin Concorde services to the USA in late 1975.

# Conference unable to combat hijacking

*Rome, September 21*
Delegates to the International Civil Aviation Organization are breaking up today after three weeks of discussions, no nearer to finding any solutions on a world-wide scale to the problems of air terrorism and hijacking.

Among the dangers associated with aviation, that of coming into contact with a terrorist is the most recent and the least easily controlled legally. On their own, measures such as screening hand luggage with X-ray equipment or confiscating certain prohibited objects – whether a pair of scissors or a hair-spray canister – can do little good.

Of course, every country wants to retain sovereign control of its skies. But in the face of a mushrooming problem, what is increasingly necessary is an international agreement on the measures to be taken against the hijackers.

# Pioneer pathfinder Alan Cobham dies

*England, October 21*
One of the great old men of British aviation, Sir Alan Cobham, died today at the age of 79. Born on May 6, 1894, Cobham was a grammar school boy of unremarkable origins. Working first as a farm-hand and then in a warehouse, he enlisted in the British Army in 1914.

Persistent attempts to join the forerunner of the RAF, the Royal Flying Corps, led to his transfer in 1917 and the start of a long relationship with the air. After the war he started a joy-riding business and got involved in air photography.

He often chose de Havillands for his famous route-proving flights of the 1920s and 1930s, which laid the basis for many of BOAC's long-haul routes. His National Aviation Day barnstorming circuses followed, as did his work to extend the range of airplanes in flight through his firm, Flight Refuelling, now an international giant.

# Arabs shock the Israelis

*Tel Aviv, October 6*
Israeli air force commanders are urgently studying the first day's air fighting in a war launched today by the Arab nations to coincide with the Jewish festival of Yom Kippur – the day of atonement. They attacked on two fronts: over the Suez Canal and in the Golan Heights. In previous wars, Israel's air force has had command of the air, but now it is hard pressed.

The Egptian air force hit Israeli air bases in the Sinai as its armies crossed the canal. As the Egyptians advanced, they took effective mobile air defenses with them, foremost amongst them the Soviet SAM-6 system. The missiles are mounted on a tank chassis with a separate radar and fire control vehicle. The SAM-6 is fast, with a range of 17 miles, and the Israelis have no effective electronic countermeasures against it. Another deadly AA weapon is the radar-guided ZSU-23-4 mobile four-barrel gun, which can track fast, low-level aircraft at a range of 2 miles. On day one of this war, Egyptian ground defenses have the upper hand (→ Oct 20).

*In the front line: crack Egyptian MiG-21s take off to hit Israeli bases.*

# Israeli air force overcomes early losses

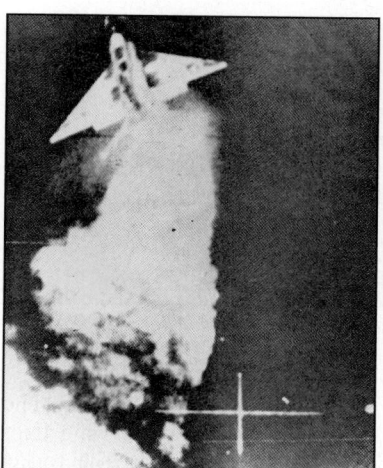

*Kill: an Arab MiG-21 is shot down.*

*Tel Aviv, October 20*
After two weeks of fighting, the Israeli air force has now gained the upper hand in the air after losing around 80 aircraft in the first week of the war and 38 in the second, all but a few to ground-based, anti-aircraft systems. In addition to the SAM-6 and ZSU-23-4 guns, it also had to face the larger SAM-2 and SAM-3s and the shoulder-launched SAM-7s, but gradually it found out how to avoid them and now, with its customary superiority in aerial combat, has begun to inflict heavy losses on the Arab air forces. They also managed to shoot down a Tu-16 bomber which was attempting to launch a stand-off cruise missile against Israel.

Since the Six-Day War in 1967, the Israeli air force has been largely re-equipped with US aircraft and missiles, including the F-4 Phantom and A-4 Skyhawk, the Hawk ground-to-air missile and the Sidewinder air-to-air missile. US and Soviet analysts will be eager to see how their systens have performed in this war and what the long-term implications of the effectiveness of anti-aircraft systems are, particularly at low level (→ Oct 24).

# Air power turns Yom Kippur war

## Boeing celebrates enduring success of the 727 airliner

*Syrian Su-7Bs over the war zone.*

*Three Israeli Dassault Mystères make a daring low-level raid with napalm.*

*Tel Aviv, October 24*
Air power has once again been decisive in the Middle East. Israel is dominant today as its airforce continued to attack Egyptian forces right up to the cease-fire.

Aircraft from both superpowers have also played an important role by flying in war materiel for their client states. Tel Aviv's Lod international airport was one of several used during the past 15 days to handle the US airlift of weapons, spare parts and munitions. Israel requested help on October 7, once it was clear that the Soviets were giving massive assistance to the Arabs. Washington went into high gear: the first supplies were flown in El Al aircraft, but soon large numbers of C-141A and giant C-5A jets of Military Airlift Command were flying in everything including battle tanks. A-4 Skyhawks and F-4 Phantom fighters were flown direct. Further assistance was provided by reconnaissance flights over the war zone by USAF SR-71s which provided Israel with valuable intelligence. These were paralleled by Soviet MiG-25Rs, which are now based in Egypt. Such assistance helped the combatants, but it also gave the superpowers leverage with their clients when it came to brokering the cease-fire.

*Seattle, November 29*
The 1,000th Boeing 727 airliner rolled out of the Renton factory today and into the pages of aviation history. It is the first commercial airliner to be produced in such a large quantity. The 727 made its first flight more than ten years ago on February 9, 1963, and there are plenty more 727 orders to be filled after today's airplane is delivered to its customer, Delta Air Lines.

The 727 has stayed in production so long because Boeing did not let the model stagnate: it has been continually modernized and updated to meet the needs of both airlines and airports. The first 727s were delivered to United Air Lines. They were 133 feet two inches long, with a wingspan of 108 feet, 14,000-lb-thrust JT8D engines and capacity for 131 passengers. The Advanced 727 rolled out today has the same wingspan as the first models, but is powered by 16,000-lb-thrust engines and, 20 feet longer, can take 189 passengers.

# Martin's hypersonic X-24B makes debut

# Papua New Guinea's Air Niugini takes off

*The X-24B lifting-body aircraft: a radical redesign of the earlier "A" model.*

*California, November 15*
The successful flight research program of the Martin Marietta X-24 lifting-body aircraft, took a major step forward at Edwards Air Force Base today with the first flight under rocket power of the X-24B.

The B model is a major redesign of the original X-24A, which made its first free flight on April 17, 1969, and first went supersonic on October 14, 1970 [*see page 685*]. The X-24A was egg-shaped, whereas the X-24B has a long, pointed nose with a flat underside. The rear end has been modified with wing flaps and inset vertical fins. The rocket powerplant remains an XLR11.

The pilot on today's flight was NASA's John Manke, who made 12 flights with the X-24A. The X-24B is expected to approach Mach 2 and to achieve a better ratio of lift to drag at hypersonic speeds. Such speeds cannot be reached by the X-24A.

*Port Moresby, November 1*
The latest Third World country to found its own national airline is Papua New Guinea. Air Niugini is mainly government-owned, with a limited number of shares in private hands. Still a dependency of Australia, Papua New Guinea will use its airline to help in the development of backward regions as well as the promotion of tourism.

Air transportation is bringing benefits to those living at subsistence level in remote inland areas, allowing the delivery of goods in a matter of minutes to places which were once accessible only by trekking along jungle paths.

*Speeding development and helping tourism, Papua New Guinea's Air Niugini.*

# Sabena adopts high-fashion profile

## Oil price increases shock the airlines

*Sabena, on its 50th birthday, has introduced the stylish new logo seen here on the vertical stabilizer of its first DC-10.*

*Zaventem, Belgium, September 12*
Belgian flag carrier Sabena, which is still celebrating the 50th anniversary of its creation in May 1923, has chosen to mark the occasion by updating its company image and adopting a new livery for its fleet of aircraft. A new logo will now adorn the tail of all Sabena's airliners: a white circle containing a stylized "S". At the same time, the airline's female staff are to get new uniforms which have been designed by French couturier Louis Féraud and made by fashion company Butch.

Stewardesses will continue to wear red and navy blue uniforms, while women ground staff will wear costumes in maroon trimmed with orange or green. In adopting the new color scheme, staff will be able to choose between a number of designs, ranging from the traditional skirt with tailored blazer to flared trousers accompanied by a white blouse with a collar which can be knotted like a tie.

*International, December 1*
Without fuel, airplanes cannot fly. The decision by the Arab oil-producing countries to increase the price of oil by 70 per cent and reduce production by 5 per cent per month in the aftermath of the Yom Kippur war, sent shivers through most boardrooms in the Western world. But one of the most immediate effects will be on the world's airlines, who are today grappling with the prospect of reducing services, grounding aircraft, slashing payrolls and surcharging passengers.

Scheduled airlines want to keep their business customers happy, and so the first to suffer will be package holiday-makers where the margins are already small. From midnight tonight, British Midland is cutting services by 10 per cent to save 120,000 gallons per month. Its holiday customers will be surcharged £3.75 a head on flights to Spain.

# Pan Am opens a huge new terminal at JFK

*Pan Am has enlarged its terminal at JFK to cope with Boeing 747 operations.*

*New York, September 30*
The Boeing 747 is dramatically changing airline operations, and no airline is more aware of this than Pan Am, which has 33 Jumbo Jets in service – more than any other carrier in the world. It has now expanded its facilities at John F Kennedy International Airport to meet the requirements of big jets.

Pan Am, which saw a 59 per cent increase in New York-London passengers when it put the 747s into operation last year, has spent $50 million on its terminal here. The expanded terminal, five times the size of the original, began operation this summer. It has six positions for 747s and six for the older 707s, an integral road system and greatly improved amenities for travelers. Earlier this year Pan Am opened a $73 million maintenance complex which can accomodate four 747s.

**Five of France's supersonic planes, from bottom: the Mirage G8 swing-wing aircraft; the Mirage F1 interceptor; the Jaguar dual-role tactical support/trainer; the Mirage IIIB trainer; and the Mirage IVA bomber.**

Produced by the Franco-German Transporter Allianz consortium, the C-160 Transall military transport is also used by Air France (Postale de Nuit).

Radically modified Boeing 747-200Bs were delivered to the USAF as E-4A command posts, their tasks being to direct a nuclear war from the air.

Although the Model 26 was very popular, the Gates Learjet 26 with TFE-731 engines never entered production and appeared only as a prototype.

After the success of the earlier Mentor series the Beech YT-34 Turbo Mentor saw the fitting of a Pratt & Whitney Canada PT6A to the tested airframe.

Powered by a Wankel rotary piston engine, RFB/Grumman American Fanliner was a radical attempt at producing a lightweight touring or training aircraft.

Providing a unique ability to control and command the battlefield, the Boeing E-3A Sentry features a Westinghouse radar mounted above a 707 airframe.

The SZD.45A Ogar, which means "Seagull", is a Polish-built two-seat, side by side pusher trainer which first entered service with the state aeroclubs.

The Saab SH.37 Viggen, recognizable by its radarless, chisel-edged nose, is the version of the Viggen family optimized for overland reconnaissance.

*Serving with the USAF as a "fly-ing classroom": the Boeing T-43A.*

*Powered by a pair of Turbomeca Astazou turboprops, the Scottish Aviation Jetstream T.1, developed from the original Handley Page design, fulfils the multi-engined pilot and navigator training role in the Royal Air Force.*

*To provide secondary training capability for the Taiwanese Air Force, the indigenous AIDC XT-CH-1A, resembling North American's T-28, was chosen.*

*Despite its small size the carrier-borne McDonnell Douglas A-4S Skyhawk can carry a war load, in addition to its pair of cannon, of nearly 8,200lb.*

*Providing advanced training for F.15 Eagle pilots, the dual-control McDonnell Douglas TF-15A (later designated F-15B) retains combat capability.*

*The Westland Commando was a fixed-gear version of the successful Sea King transport helicopter which dispensed with the latter's amphibious capability.*

*English Electric Canberras modified by the addition of the Blue Parrot radar to train Buccaneer strike aircraft crews became known as Canberra T.22s.*

*Dassult Breguet of France and Dornier of Germany teamed up to produce the Alpha Jet, trainer and light strike aircraft, which gained sizeable sales.*

*The Grumman YF-14B Tomcat was the first of several attempts at improving the basic F-14, on this occasion by the addition of F401 turbofans.*

*Developed especially for the Soviet Navy from the Mi-8, the Mil Mi-14 "Haze" is a shore-based anti-submarine helicopter with an amphibious hull.*

# 1974

4,534mph
USA
Pete Knight
North American X-15
Oct 3, 1967

24,325 miles
USA
Archie Old Jr
Boeing B-52B
Jan 18, 1957

354,200
USA
Joseph Walker
North American X-15
Aug 22, 1963

833,000lb
USA
Boeing
B-747 200F

51,800lb thrust
USA
General Electric
CF6-50E

**South Pacific, January 30**
Queen Elizabeth II opens the new international airport on the island of Rarotonga.

**Hertfordshire, England, Feb 12**
The last de Havilland Comet 4 in service with a major operator (Dan-Air) makes a farewell flyby at Hatfield airfield, where it first flew 15 years ago, on its way to RAF Duxford for preservation.

**Atlantic Ocean, February 21**
US Army reservist, Colonel Thomas Gatch, disappears during an attempted balloon crossing of the North Atlantic; he left Pennsylvania three days ago.

**Corpus Christi, Texas, Feb 22**
Lieutenant Junior Grade Barbara Ann Allen receives her Gold Wings at the naval air station here to become the US Navy's first woman pilot; she will fly transports because women are barred from piloting combat aircraft (→ Jun 4).

**Stratford, Connecticut, March 1**
The prototype Sikorsky YCH-53E multi-purpose helicopter, a development of the S-65A powered by three up-rated turboshaft engines, makes its first flight.

**Nitray, France, March 12**
Bernard Chauvreau pilots the Fournier RF-6B aerobatic mono-plane on its first flight.

**Morayshire, Scotland, March 29**
The first RAF squadron equipped with Jaguars, Nº 54, is formed at Lossiemouth (→ May 19, 1976).

**London, March**
Trade and industry secretary in Britain's new Labour government, Peter Shore, announces a halt to plans for a third London airport at Foulness, Essex.

**Leicestershire, England, May 22**
RAF Cottesmore hosts a celebration to mark the 25th anniversary of the first flight of the Canberra; 33 Canberras of 19 versions are present.

**Fort Rucker, Alabama, June 4**
Second Lieutenant Sally D Woolfolk becomes the US Army's first woman pilot when she graduates from the US Army Aviation Center.

**California, June 9**
The Northrop YF-17 fighter prototype makes its first flight.

**Love Field, Texas, June 18**
Southwest, which flew its 1,000,000th passenger on January 23, becomes the "Love" airline, serving "love potions" instead of drinks and "love bites" instead of peanuts (→ Jun, 1976).

**Marseilles, France, June 24**
The Aérospatiale AS 350 Ecureuil [Squirrel] helicopter prototype makes its first flight, at Marignane; it is to be marketed in North America with an Avco Lycoming LTS 101-600A2 turboshaft engine as the AS 350C Astar.

**Sussex, England, July 13**
Britain's first national hang-gliding championships is held at Steyning Hill.

**Europe, July 19**
President Valéry Giscard d'Estaing of France and Prime Minister Harold Wilson of Britain agree to continue the Concorde programme, but to limit production of the airliner to 16 (→ Sep 14).

**Cyprus, July 26**
Since the Turkish invasion of Cyprus six days ago, Britain's RAF has airlifted 13,430 civilians off the island, using Hercules, VC10, Britannia, Belfast and Comet transports; also, on July 22, helicopters from the USS *Inchon* evacuated 466 people in a five-hour operation.

**London, August 17**
British Airways, Dan-Air, Laker Airways and British Caledonian Airways join forces to fly home 49,000 tourists stranded overseas by the collapse of the charter operator Court Line.

**Surrey, England, August 21**
Hawker Siddeley's Hawk jet trainer makes its first flight, at Dunsfold.→

**Belfast, Northern Ireland, Aug 22**
The prototype Short SD3-30 twin-turboprop commuter transport makes its maiden flight, in the hands of the company's chief test pilot Don Wright (→ Aug 24, 1976).

**Hampshire, England, Sep 1**
The Sikorsky S-67 Black Hawk helicopter crashes during the Farnborough air show.

**Phan Rang, Vietnam, Sep 15**
An Air Vietnam Boeing 727 crashes after being diverted here by a hijacker; all 76 on board are killed.

**Tokyo and Peking, September 29**
Japan Air Lines (JAL) and the Civil Aviation Administration of China (CAAC) open services between the two capitals with a JAL DC-8 and a CAAC 707. The services are part of a deal which also allows CAAC to fly from Tokyo to Canada and the US – the People's Republic's first air links with the West; in return JAL has the (less lucrative) right to fly from Peking to Karachi and the Middle East (→ Aug 9, 1975).

**Stratford, Connecticut, Oct 17**
The prototype Sikorsky UH-60A transport helicopter, which has been developed for the US Army, makes its first flight.

**Hatfield, England, October 18**
Hawker Siddeley announces that it is to halt development of the HS.146 short-range transport because the economic recession has severely damaged its sales prospects (→ Jul 29, 1976).

**Istres, France, October 28**
The Dassault Super Etendard 01 carrier-based attack prototype makes its first flight, piloted by Jacques Jesberger; it is a development of the Etendard IVM powered by an Atar 8K50 turbojet.

**Belize, November 28**
Belize Airways is formed as the national airline of this British territory in Central America.

**Istres, France, December 22**
The Dassault Breguet Mirage F1-E makes its first flight, in the hands of Guy Mitaux-Maurourard.

**Toulouse, France, December 26**
The Airbus A300B4, a development of the European wide-body airliner with increased range, makes its maiden flight (→ Jun 1, 1975).

---

## Factfile

World revenue passenger miles: 407,911.816 million
Passengers through Chicago O'Hare: 16.4 million
Passengers through New York (JFK/Newark/LaGuardia): 17.0 million
Passengers through London: 25.2 million
Price of a single coach-class ticket New York/Los Angeles (April): $176
Price of the cheapest return ticket London/New York: $303
World air freight (ton miles): 55,670.0 million
Average salary of a long-haul pilot (US): $39,437
Average salary of cabin crew (US): $10,991
Price of a Learjet 25 B: $1,071 million
Price of an HS.125: $1.68 million
Price of a Falcon 20: $2.55 million
Price of 1,000 (US) gallons of Jet A1 fuel: $335.79
Average exchange rate: £1 =$2.3401

*A Lockheed TriStar wide-body airliner during tests over the Mojave desert, California. On top of the fuselage is an engine inlet duct.* ▶

## Helicopters save oil crew in sea drama

*North Sea, January 1*
Braving storm-force winds, helicopters succeeded in rescuing the 50-man crew of a North Sea oil-rig tonight minutes before the rig overturned and sank. The rig *Transocean III* was under tow to Norway when the first Mayday calls were received in Scotland.

Tonight's dramatic rescue was yet another demonstration of the value of helicopters in oil-rig emergencies in the treacherous North Sea. Unlike the generally good weather of the Gulf of Mexico, conditions between the Shetland Islands and Norway call for large and powerful machines, such as the Aérospatiale AS.332 Super Puma and the Sikorsky S-76. The real workhorse in these waters, however, is still the Sikorsky S-61N, which acts as a crew ferry, equipment carrier and ambulance. It is often expected to fly as far as 250 miles from bases at Aberdeen, Scotland, and in the Shetlands to the oilfields.

# World's worst air disaster kills 346

*Hellish scene: the mangled remains of Flight 981 of THY Turkish Airlines.*

*Ermenonville, France, March 3*
A DC-10 dived into the forest of Ermenonville, north of Paris, today, killing all 346 people on board, in the world's worst air disaster. The aircraft, a McDonnell Douglas DC-10-10 which had only just been delivered to THY Turkish Airlines, had taken off about 10 minutes earlier from Paris Orly en route for London. The captain, Nejat Berkoz, did not transmit any message indicating an abnormality. Thus, the cause was one of extreme suddenness. All three CF6 engines were operating normally and almost the whole aircraft was intact until impact.

Among the jet's passengers were about 200 English rugby supporters, flying home from yesterday's France-England match in Paris. A strike at Heathrow had prevented them leaving on an earlier flight. At 11.40am, the DC-10 was 11,480 feet above the village of Saint-Pathus, when it suffered a catastrophic failure. Eye-witnesses say it went straight down in flames. Part of it cut a swathe a mile long through thick forest, but part of the fueslage and seven bodies were found some 7 miles away, a sure sign that it suffered a structural failure in the air. Captain Berkoz was clearly powerless to prevent the aircraft's death dive.

The cause is unknown, but the damaged "black box" flight recorder has been recovered (→ Mar 17).

## Lightweight YF-16 makes its debut flight

*The lightweight YF-16 is designed to sustain a crushing 9G in maneuvres.*

*California, February 2*
General Dynamics' YF-16 made its official first flight today at Edwards Air Force Base, two weeks after test pilot Phil Oestricher lifted it briefly into the air during a taxi test. The YF-16 is the first of the two entrants in the USAF's lightweight fighter (LWF) competition. Its rival, the Northrop YF-17, is expected to fly in June.

The USAF is developing the LWF as a possible complement to its force of McDonnell Douglas F-15 Eagles. The LWF, at around 20,000 lb loaded weight (about 20,000 lb lighter than the F-15), will not have all the capabilities of the Eagle in terms of avionics and overall performance. But its smaller and less complicated design has the advantage of making it a cheaper airplane.

The General Dynamics YF-16 has one P&W F100 engine, the same as fitted to the twin-engined F-15. Northrop's YF-17 follows the F-15 and F-14 Tomcat in having two engines and twin stabilizers (→ Jan 13, 1975).

## FAA demands changes to Douglas DC-10

*Washington, DC, March 17*
It has now been established that the Turkish DC-10 tragedy was caused by a cargo door bursting open. This created a decompression stress which buckled the cabin floor, making it cut into control cables.

The tragedy would not have happened if the US Federal Aviation Authority (FAA) had taken tougher action after a similar DC-10 incident nine months ago, when the pilot landed safely. The US National Transportation Safety Board had requested a directive demanding corrective action by makers and users. The FAA put out a directive to makers only; McDonnell Douglas had not modified the Turkish airplane before delivering it.

## Charles de Gaulle airport opens for Paris

*Paris, March 13*
Apart from the fact that it is an ultra-modern international airport, created for passenger convenience as well as efficiency, the notable thing about Paris's new Charles de Gaulle airport, which opened today, is that only one house had to be demolished to enable its construction to proceed.

Work began on the 7,670-acre site on a plateau between the rivers Seine and Marne at Roissy-en-France in 1966. It was named after the late French President and war leader in October last year. Charles de Gaulle is designed to relieve the passenger and cargo burden on Le Bourget and Orly airports in Paris.

In addition to the existing new runway, another is planned so that the airport can cope with as many as 150 movements an hour by 1990. The airport differs from others in its provision of underground walkways for passengers from a central terminal, which includes departure, arrival and transfer lounges and four levels of car parking. The airport is on the Paris/Lille/Brussels motorway. Charles de Gaulle and Orly are the first airports in the world to be equipped with the Turboclair fog dispersal system.

# Air France puts Airbus into service

*Europe's great hope: the A300B2 coming in to land at London Heathrow after the type's first service flight, from Paris.*

**Paris, May 23**
At precisely 11.22am the Airbus A300B2, gleaming in the livery of Air France, took off from Roissy-Charles de Gaulle airport. It landed at Heathrow 41 minutes later. Exactly 53 years ago to the day Joseph Portal flew this same route, Paris/London, in his Breguet XIV – in 3 hours 50 minutes. This veteran pilot was among the 250 specially invited passengers on board for today's flight. With this first commercial flight the Airbus, which is also the first twin-jet, wide-bodied aircraft, has made an auspicious beginning. Captain Jean Massoti, who is head of the center for medium-haul flights and of the Airbus division, has stated that the jet gives the pilot no problems. He has also pointed out that it has features that should prove attractive to customers: low noise levels, comfortable seating, spacious accomodation for overhead hand luggage and main cargo and baggage in standard 747-type containers. The A300 has not so far won many orders, but its European manufacturers are convinced that it will eventually do well, even in the US market (→ Dec 26).

# Super-quick Concorde 'laps' a 747 on Atlantic service to Boston

*A British Airways Concorde touches down at Boston on a promotional tour.*

**Boston, Massachusetts, June 17**
Air France, eager not only to promote its own use of Concorde, but also to support the makers of the Anglo-French supersonic airliner, today put on the most dramatic demonstration yet of the airliner's superior speed.

At 8.22am Eastern Standard Time an Air France Concorde took off from Boston's Logan airport and set course for Paris. The take-off was timed to coincide with the departure from Paris's Orly airport of an Air France 747 bound for Boston. When the two flights passed (the Concorde flying at twice the 747's altitude) the Jumbo had covered 620 miles and the SST 2,400. The Concorde landed at Paris, spent one hour 8 minutes on the ground, then headed back to Boston. It arrived 11 minutes before the 747. Such an impressive feat goes down well with the media and public. But it may cut little ice with airlines, who put economic considerations first (→ Jul 19).

# British Airways will fly flag for Britain

**London, April 1**
The two biggest British airlines, BOAC and BEA, were replaced today by a single national carrier. It adopts the name of one of the two companies from which BOAC was originally created in 1939: British Airways (BA). The two old airlines were formally dissolved yesterday under the government Air Corporations (Dissolution) Order 1973.

BA combines the long-haul operations of BOAC with the European network of BEA, as recommended by the British Airways Board in 1972. The board, formed under the 1971 Civil Aviation Act, assumed ownership and control of the airlines on April 1, 1972. In its subsequent reports, it recommended their dissolution and the adoption of a single name for the unified carrier. BA now has the world's most comprehensive route network of half a million miles with as many as 200 destinations in 84 countries.

But the immediate problem facing the airline is its fuel costs, which have risen from £70m to £110m since last year (→ Feb 2, 1975).

# Lindbergh, hero of Atlantic flight, dies

*American hero: "Lucky Lindy".*

**Maui, Hawaii, August 26**
The Lone Eagle finally came to rest today. Charles Lindbergh, one of the greatest names in all aviation, died here today of lymphatic cancer at the age of 72. "Lucky Lindy", who hated publicity, achieved international fame when he made the first non-stop solo Atlantic crossing from New York to Paris in May 1927, in a single-engined Ryan NYP monoplane, the *Spirit of St Louis*. He continued working in aviation for the rest of his life.

# Tornado strike aircraft storms aloft

## Hawker Siddeley's Hawk leaves perch

*Manching, [West] Germany, Aug 14*
Its two Turbo-Union RB.199 turbofans in full afterburner, the first swing-wing Panavia Tornado tactical strike aircraft took to the air today. At the controls of the German-assembled, two-seat prototype was British Aircraft Corporation (BAC) chief military test pilot Paul Millett. The Tornado, formerly known as the Multi-Role Combat Aircraft (MRCA), is the latest product of European collaboration and advanced technology.

The three-nation development team comprises MBB of West Germany, BAC and Aeritalia of Italy, whose national air forces, as well as the German navy, plan to deploy the type in the early 1980s.

Development has so far cost the sponsor nations about £345 million, with £166 million as Britain's share. Current thinking is that each

*The Panavia Tornado is fitted with the very latest terrain-following radar.*

Tornado will cost under £5 million. The aircraft is expected to deliver its warload with pinpoint accuracy in all weather conditions and around the clock, using terrain-following radar to fly at treetop height. With Britain's RAF it will take over the tactical penetration role still exercised by the last of the force's ageing V-bombers, the Vulcan, which is ill-suited to low-level operations (→ Jul 29, 1976).

*Surrey, England, August 21*
Chief test pilot of Hawker Siddeley Aviation at Dunsfold Duncan Simpson piloted the new Hawk on its first flight here today. Originally called the HS.1182, the aircraft is designed to replace the same company's Gnat and Hunter as the standard advanced jet trainer for Britain's RAF.

Powered by a single non-afterburning Rolls-Royce Turbomeca Adour turbofan of 5,340 lb thrust, the Hawk seats pupil and instructor in tandem ejection seats, and can exceed 600mph. A particular feature of its design is its ability to carry 5,000 lb of bombs or other weapons, as well as a 30mm cannon. Hawker Siddeley is optimistic that the new aircraft will prove appealing to many customers worldwide, apart from the RAF.

## SR-71 sets stunning Atlantic speed record

## All places great and small are linked by the flourishing US commuter airlines

*The sleek SR-71 touches down at Farnborough at the end of its record flight.*

*Hampshire, England, September 1*
Of all the records set by the Lockheed SR-71A Blackbird, none has better illustrated its amazing ability to devour distance than today's flight by aircraft 64-17972 on its way to the international Air Show at Farnborough. It landed after crossing the North Atlantic in less than two hours. After they arrived the crew were called to the telephone – to be congratulated by President Gerald Ford. Crewed by pilot Major James V Sullivan and systems officer Major Noel F Widdifield, the

menacing black airplane took off from its home base, Beale Air Force Base, California, refueled in flight from a KC-135Q near the US east coast and set course for England. The result was a recorded distance of 3,490 miles across the Atlantic to Hampshire in 1 hour 55 minutes 42 seconds. The actual distance covered was appreciably more, because of the need to pass accurately through radar "gates" a known distance apart. On its return trip, the SR-71A is expected to set a record between London and Los Angeles.

*USA, October*
How do you get from a big place, say New York or Los Angeles, to a small one, say Lebanon, New Hampshire, or Mojave, California? The answer is simple: by commuter airline.

Commuter airlines now run more than 1,000 airplanes, serving 725 airports throughout the US. Almost two-thirds of those airports serve cities with populations of under 50,000 people; one-fifth of them are based in towns with fewer than 10,000 people. Frequently, they are affiliated to a major airline, such as Delta or Braniff, serving communities where major carriers cannot make a profit.

The US's 222 commuter airlines represent the third tier of air travel, behind the big national trunk airlines such as United or American, and the regional carriers such as Allegheny and Piedmont, which cover a number of States.

As with the major airlines, the commuters are certificated by the US Civil Aeronautics Board as carriers which fly a regular

schedule. The Federal Aviation Administration (FAA) tests and certificates the planes and licenses their pilots, who are required to meet FAA physical standards and undergo retraining and a flying proficiency test every six months.

While a commuter flight will not be on a big airliner (federal regulations prevent these airlines from carrying more than 30 passengers at a time), travellers do not have to worry about climbing up on to the wing to get into an open cockpit biplane. Except for some old and reliable Douglas DC-3s, they will be boarding a modern, small transport which has been specifically designed for passenger or executive travel; airplanes like the Fokker F.27, Convair 240, Short SD3-30, Nord 262, Cessna 402 or the Learjet.

The commuter business is still growing. For 1974 the number of flights is up by 15.9 per cent on last year and passengers up by 14.3 per cent to 6.3 million. Cargo trade has gone up by 30 per cent.

# Canadair water-bomber proves its worth

*The CL-215 water-bomber in action.*

*Marignane, France, August 31*
A carelessly dropped match or cigarette can start a series of fires in the tinder-dry forests along the French Riviera, causing millions of dollars' worth of damage and wreaking havoc in the tourist industry. Firemen in the region have a specialized tool at their disposal – the Canadair CL-215, a purpose-built amphibian designed as a firefighter, capable of "bombing" fires with water.

There has been a water-bomber base here at Marignane since 1963, initially equipped with Convair Canso and Catalina aircraft. The CL-215, first flown on October 23, 1967, has since replaced the Canso and proved itself one of the best airplanes of its type.

The CL-215 is usually land-based, but in action it will land on sea or lake, scooping up over 5 tons or water which can be dropped in less than a second, an operation which can usually be repeated every ten minutes. The tanks can also be refilled on land with water "spiked" with fire-retardant fluid.

The province of Quebec, where forest fires are prevalent, ordered 20 CL-215s, and a further ten went to the French *Protection Civile*. Although firefighting is the principal role of the CL-215, the aircraft is also used as an observation platform and for air-sea rescue.

# Kenya air crash is first for a Boeing 747

*Nairobi, November 20*
Fifty-five passengers and four crew died today when a Lufthansa Boeing 747-130, en route from Frankfurt to Johannesburg, crashed on take-off here. It was the first-ever crash of the Boeing Jumbo Jet. During take-off the crew felt vibration and buffeting, and the co-pilot, who was controlling the aircraft, noticed a total lack of acceleration. The aircraft hit the ground 1,225 yards beyond the end of the runway, skidding a further 372 yards and then catching fire. There were 97 survivors (→ Mar 29, 1977).

*The charred remains of the 747 after the crash; remarkably, 97 survived.*

# Concorde flies east for tropical trials

*Singapore, September 14*
Having successfully completed cold climate tests at -40°C at Fairbanks, Alaska, last February, Concorde has now come through tropical trials with flying colors. The second production aircraft, 202, with a crew headed by Brian Trubshaw, departed London Heathrow on August 7 for a fast run to Tehran.

Having offloaded passengers, aircraft 202 then went to Bahrain for prolonged hot-weather trials, under the most severe conditions. These were followed, from August 27, by demonstration flights at Abu Dhabi, Qatar, Kuwait, Dubai and Muscat.

On September 3, Concorde 202 left Bahrain for further runway trials here at Singapore's Paya Lebar airport. These again proved satisfactory. And on September 12, news came that Concorde flight testing had passed the 3,000-hour mark. Having been proved at temperatures over 47°C, 202 will now return to England (→ Sep 1, 1975).

# Rockwell's sleek and powerful B-1 bomber makes its entrance

*The B-1's four jet engines give it a thrust of over 50 tons; empty, it weighs just over 85 tons. Its top speed is Mach 1.25.*

*California, December 23*
The prototype of the USAF's new intercontinental B-1 bomber landed at Edwards Air Force Base today after a successful first flight of 1 hour 16 minutes. The aircraft had taken off from the Palmdale base of its manufacturer, Rockwell International, and flew at subsonic speed over the Mojave Desert, reaching a maximum altitude of 10,000 feet.

The swing-wing B-1 will be capable of supersonic flight and is due to replace the ageing Boeing B-52 as the USAF's strategic bomber. While it is about two-thirds the size of the B-52, the B-1 will be able to carry four times its bomb load. Critics say that, given the development of intercontinental ballistic missiles, the purchase of 244 B-1s at $76 million per plane, already $14.5 million over budget, is unnecessary (→ Jun 30, 1977).

The A300B2 wide-body airliner was Airbus Industrie's first project and gradually became a successful challenger to the dominance by the United States.

The Fournier RF.6B lightplane is powered by 100hp O-200A engine.

The Helicopter Technik Sky-trac 3 was designed and built in Germany.

Shorts' SD3-30, later the Shorts 330, powered by two 1,156shp PT6A-45B turboprops, can carry 30 passengers or up to 7,500lb in the all-cargo mode.

Bell's 206L LongRanger, a seven-seat development of the JetRanger, can be fitted with skis, floats or skids as shown. The engine is a 500hp Allison C25B.

The Piper PA-32R-300 Cherokee Lance lightplane combines the fuselage of the earlier Cherokee Six with the retractable gear of the Piper Seneca.

Since its introduction as a successor to the Alouette family more than 1,400 Aérospatiale AS.350 Ecureuils (French for squirrels) have been delivered.

The Saunders company was formed in Canada in 1968 to produce the ST-27 twin-PT6 turbine conversion of the four-Gipsy-engined DH.114 Heron.

In the US Army's UTTAS competition to find a replacement for the ubiquitous Bell UH-1 "Huey", victory went to the Sikorsky YUH-60A Black Hawk.

In competition with the YF-17, the prototype General Dynamics YF-16 Light Weight Fighter was later developed into the Fighting Falcon family.

The Rockwell B-1A supersonic bomber, intended as a B-52 replacement, first canceled and then resurrected, was later redesigned as the B-1B Lancer.

Failing to beat the Sikorsky Black Hawk, the rival UTTAS design for the US Army was the Boeing YUH-61A helicopter. Three prototypes were constructed.

Northrop's F-5E and two-seat F-5F Tiger II gained many export orders.

FFV's AS.202/18A Bravo trainer is a successful 2/3-seat Swiss design.

The three-engined Sikorsky CH-53E Super Stallion provides heavy-lift capability for the US Navy and Marine Corps. It has a seven-blade main rotor.

The Northrop YF-17 Light Weight Fighter contender, which led to the F/A-18 Hornet, an aircraft which recently saw its 1,000th production example.

Produced by Germany, Italy and Britain, the Panavia MRCA (Multi-role Combat Aircraft) became the Tornado, and saw much service in the Gulf War.

Dassault's Super Etendard, developed from the Etendard IV-M, is a subsonic attack aircraft designed to operate from the carriers "Foch" and "Clemenceau".

The Hawker Siddeley (now BAe) P.1182 Hawk jet trainer is powered by a non-afterburning Rolls-Royce Turbomeca Adour turbofan of 5,200lb thrust.

# 1975

4,534mph
USA
Pete Knight
North American X-15
Oct 3, 1967

24,325 miles
USA
Archie Old Jr
Boeing B-52B
Jan 18, 1957

354,200ft
USA
Joseph Walker
North American X-15
Aug 22, 1963

833,000lb
USA
Boeing
B-747 200F

51,800lb thrust
USA
General Electric
CF6-50E

**Cleburne, Texas, January 7**
The Mohawk 298 – a development of the Nord 262 light transport with Pratt & Whitney Canada turboprops – makes its first flight, in the hands of Fred Frakes.

**Baghdad, January 20**
A Boeing 707 commandeered by three terrorists and flown by a crew of Air France volunteers lands here; the terrorists forced the French airline to fly them out of Paris by taking ten travelers hostage yesterday, at Orly airport.

**London, January 21**
The RAF announces that its search-and-rescue (SAR) helicopters flew 1,018 missions during the course of 1974 and rescued 319 people.

**New Zealand, February 6**
Air Chief Marshal Sir Keith Park dies; under Lord Dowding he was responsible for the air defense of London and neighboring counties in the Battle of Britain, and later in the war he was in command of the air defense of Malta.

**USA, March 2**
A route exchange agreement is implemented by TWA and Pan Am; under its terms, TWA is to suspend services on certain Pacific routes.

**Japan, March 5**
The first Shin Meiwa SS-2A air-sea-rescue amphibian is delivered to the Japanese Maritime Self-Defense Force, under the designation US-1; it is a development of the PS-1 maritime surveillance and anti-submarine flying boat.

**USSR, March 7**
The Yaklovlev Yak-42 short-range transport makes its first flight; it is fitted with three Lotarev D-36 turbofans.

**France, March 18**
The noted aviatrix Adrienne Bolland, the first pilot to fly over the Andes in 1921, dies at the age of 90.

**Wichita, Kansas, April 5**
A standard Learjet 36 lands after a non-stop 3,833-mile flight from Hawaii (→ May 19, 1976).

**London, April 6**
Some 105 South Vietnamese orphans arrive after an airlift organized by charity (→ Apr 30).

**Lyons, France, April 12**
French President Valéry Giscard d'Estaing opens the new airport of Lyons-Satolas.

**Dallas, Texas, May 6**
Jim Read begins tests of the first of 60 Vought Corsair A-7H all-weather attack aircraft ordered by the Greek air force.

**London and Auckland, May 7**
British Airways and Air New Zealand open a joint service between the two cities via Los Angeles, using McDonnell Douglas DC-10s (→ Aug 6, 1976).

**[West] Germany, June 1**
The first Airbus A300C4 long-range cargo version of the European airliner enters service, with Germanair (→ Apr 1, 1976).

**Japan, June 3**
The Mitsubishi FST-2kai single-seat twin-turbofan supersonic fighter prototype makes its first flight; the aircraft is a development of the T-2 jet trainer.

**Brussels, June 7**
The Belgian government chooses the US F-16 fighter over the French Mirage F1-E when it places an order for 102 fighters.

**London, June 26**
British Airways signs a contract for four Boeing 747-236 airliners powered by Rolls-Royce RB.211-524 engines.

**Paris, July 16**
The last Lockheed Constellation in airline service goes into retirement at Le Bourget.

**Israel, July 21**
Israel Aircraft Industries begins flight tests of its IAI 1124 Westwind II, a turbofan version of the 1123 Westwind transport.

**Oshkosh, Wisconsin, August 4**
The 23rd meet of the US amateur airplane builders' Experimental Aircraft Association ends; 1,200 machines and 6,800 visitors were present (→ Sep 29, 1980).

**Tokyo, August 9**
Japan Air Lines establishes a wholly owned subsidiary, Japan Asia Airways, to operate a service between Japan and Taiwan.

**Long Beach, California, August 26**
The prototype McDonnell Douglas YC-15 short take-off and landing transport makes its first flight.→

**London, September 1**
The fourth production Concorde makes two return flights to Gander, Newfoundland, becoming the first aircraft to make four Atlantic crossings in a single day (→ Dec 5).

**USA, October 1**
The Bell Model 409, produced to compete for the US Army's armed attack helicopter program, makes its first flight; its rival, the Hughes Model 77, first flew yesterday.

**Washington, DC, October 8**
President Gerald Ford announces plans to cut government economic controls over US domestic airlines; the administration believes federal regulation forces US air travelers to pay too much (→ Feb 23, 1977).

**Chartres, France, October 28**
In a demonstration of the maneuverability of the French Alpha Jet, Jean-Marie Saget lands on and takes off from a stretch of the *autoroute* [freeway] linking Paris and Le Mans (→ Nov 4, 1977).

**Hertfordshire, England, Nov 29**
British former world champion racing driver Graham Hill and five passengers are killed when his twin-engined plane crashes in fog near Elstree airport; he was 46.

**London, December 5**
Concorde is awarded its British certificate of airworthiness; the French certificate was awarded on October 9 (→ Dec 18).

**Istres, France, December 19**
The last Dassault-Breguet Mercure airliner – one of just ten built – is delivered to the French internal airline Air Inter; the company's disappointment at the failure of the Mercure was tempered yesterday by the decision of the French defense ministry to back the Mirage 2000 fighter program.

---

## Factfile

World revenue passenger miles: 433,339.504 million
Passengers through Chicago O'Hare: 15.9 million
Passengers through New York (JFK/Newark/LaGuardia): 16.4 million
Passengers through London (Heathrow/Gatwick): 26.6 million
Price of a single coach class ticket New York/Los Angeles: $194
Price of the cheapest return ticket London/New York: $350
World air freight (ton miles): 59,302.6 million
Average salary of long-haul pilot (US): $44,202
Average salary of cabin crew (US): $11,303
Price of a Beech 100: $845,000
Price of a Falcon 10: $1,850 million
Price of a Gulfstream II: $4.8 million
Price of 1,000 (US) gallons of Jet A1 fuel: $429.41
Average exchange rate: £1 = $2.2222

*A Concorde cockpit; the four engine controls are located between pilot and copilot, with engine indicators just forward of them.* ▶

## Strike curtails BA's no-booking shuttle

*London, February 2*

Cheap British Airways (BA) shuttle flights are in jeopardy today – at the very moment of the service's success. Since introducing Europe's first shuttle service on January 12, on its London/Glasgow route, BA has been overwhelmed by the response. But having taken the idea to its logical next stage – the selling of tickets on board the airplanes themselves – 450 BA workers have walked out on strike in protest at the extra administrative work. Today the airline's European division has virtually ground to a halt and many would-be passengers are angry and disappointed.

The shuttle service is a no-booking operation, but still guarantees accommodation for every passenger. With departures each hour, if an airplane is fully loaded, the airline merely provides another, even if it is for a single passenger. In the first week of shuttle flights, 11,716 passengers took advantage of the 150 allotted flights, forcing BA to provide no fewer than 45 additional airliners to meet demand.

Competing airlines are less happy with the service, suggesting that BA is using its financial muscle to fly unprofitably and thereby offer unfair competition (→ May 7).

## YF-16 wins USAF light fighter competition

*John McLucas presents a model of the YF-16 at a Pentagon news conference.*

*Washington, DC, January 13*

US Secretary of the Air Force John L McLucas, announced today that General Dynamics' YF-16 has won the multi-billion dollar lightweight fighter competition over the rival Northrop YF-17. The USAF will buy 650 YF-16s at $6.7 million per aircraft.

Among the many factors which has influenced the selection of the single-engined YF-16 was General Dynamics' use of the same powerplant as that of the F-15 Eagle. The USAF hopes to control the engine's price, which has risen over the past two years from $800,000 to $1.5 million, by using it in the YF-16. Northrop's YF-17 had two smaller engines.

Secretary McLucas said that, compared with the YF-17, the YF-16 has better visibility, superior maneuverability and acceleration at transonic and supersonic speeds, and better deceleration. He also said that it would be 8 per cent cheaper to produce and would not cost as much to develop because of the use of the F-15 engine (→ Jun 7).

## Birdman is lightest airplane in the sky

*Daytona Beach, Fla, January 25*

The world's lightest powered airplane, the 100-lb Birdman TL-1, took to the air today for the first time. The TL-1, which has been in development for almost six years, is intended as a strong, lightweight, inexpensive aircraft that can be easily assembled from a kit.

The ultra-lightweight TL-1 has a single-spar wing with wooden ribs and foam leading edge covered with Monocote film. It is powered by a 15-hp Tally Aircraft air-cooled engine. Two alloy tanks hold 4 gallons of fuel which give the TL-1 a range of 200 miles. The aircraft's most economical cruising speed is 35mph, but it can cruise at a maximum of 54mph. Its maximum level speed is 60mph.

## Mid-air emergency as 140 become ill

*Copenhagen, February 10*

A fleet of ambulances lined up at Kastrup airport here two days ago to meet a Japan Air Lines flight from Tokyo via Anchorage, Alaska. A mid-air emergency had been declared as the 747 flew over the North Pole with passengers in agony, clutching their stomachs.

By the time it was cleared for landing more than 140 passengers were clearly suffering from food poisoning. With limited medical supplies available, cabin staff were finding it hard to cope. Cold meat served at dinner is believed to be the cause. All the passengers soon recovered and were able to continue their journey to Paris.

Inquiries in Tokyo revealed that one of the catering workers had a cut on his hand which had turned septic. What no one expected was the reaction of one of the directors of the restaurant service that produced the meal. He went home tonight and committed *hara kiri*.

## First woman pilot of Airbus takes off

*Danièle Décuré and Pierre Balmain.*

*Villegénis, France, April 7*

Air France's Danièle Décuré became the first woman Airbus pilot today when she took off from here. She joined Air France in 1973 when the airline held a competitive entry examination open to women. She was one of seven winners.

**Bombers come here when they die: a huge "graveyard" at Walnut Ridge, Arkansas, containing Boeing B-17 Flying Fortresses and Consolidated B-24A Liberators. Their career with the US air forces ended long ago.**

# De Havilland Dash 7 leaps into action

*The quiet, maneuverable Dash 7 is designed to fly from city center airports.*

*Downsview, Ontario, March 27*
The de Havilland Canada DHC-7 (Dash 7) flew for the first time today, landing at an angle of 7.5 degrees, three times the normal angle of approach. The turboprop aircraft is equipped with Fowler flaps, which increase the wing area and the camber to create higher lift; it can take off and land in less than 2,000 feet and comes to a halt in spectacular fashion, by reversing its propellers. This enables it to operate from airports in town centers. Today, the Dash 7 reached 126mph at 1,057 feet, but it is expected to reach a crusing speed of 260mph at 8,750 feet. It will carry 50 passengers, or the equivalent in freight, or a mixture of the two. Less polluting than a car, it makes much less noise than most transport aircraft, qualities which might enable it to fly at night over built-up areas.

# Israel reveals Mirage-derived warplane

*Tel Aviv, April 14*
The existence of an Israeli supersonic fighter was disclosed today when the first production example was publicly displayed at Tel Aviv's Ben-Gurion International airport.

The new fighter, made by Israel Aircraft Industries (IAI) and called the Kfir [Lion Cub], is obviously derived from the French Dassault Mirage III. A major difference is that the engine is a US-supplied General Electric J79, giving greater power and better fuel economy than the French Atar engine of the Mirage. The Kfir can also carry a heavier load of weaponry.

In the future, IAI expects to produce improved versions. For example, a fixed canard (foreplane) will be added in a version to be designated Kfir C2. IAI also plans to upgrade the avionics, for better weapons delivery (→ Jul 20, 1976).

*The Kfir is well equipped to take on the latest Soviet-supplied Arab fighters.*

# Sea Harrier points way to the future for British naval aviation

*London, June 15*
The Royal Navy today came a step closer today to becoming the first naval force in the world to fly vertical/short take-off and landing (V/STOL) warplanes. The British government announced last month that it had approved the development of a maritime version of the Hawker Siddeley Harrier; now an order has been placed for three development airplanes and 21 full production Sea Harrier FRS.1s, the designation meaning fighter, reconnaissance strike.

Few will doubt the wisdom of the move, because of the proven versatility of the Harrier family. It is also not a moment too soon, as the whole future of large aircraft carriers within the Royal Navy is looking rather bleak. Only V/STOLs operating from much smaller carrier-cruiser vessels can guarantee that the Fleet Air Arm will have fixed-wing combat jets at sea in the

*HMS "Ark Royal" carries Phantom, Buccaneer and Gannet aircraft.*

1980s. Already laid down at the Vickers shipyard in Barrow-on-Furness is the first "through deck" carrier-cruiser, HMS *Invincible*. The small fleet carrier HMS *Hermes* was withdrawn from active service in June 1970 and placed in reserve. HMS *Eagle* has also since been withdrawn, leaving only HMS *Ark Royal*, which was recommissioned on February 24 1970, after a £30 million refit to allow Phantom and Buccaneer operations in what is expected to be its final service.

# Streak Eagle soars to series of records

*Grand Forks, N Dakota, February 1*
Operation Streak Eagle, a 16-day assault on time-to-altitude records, has resulted in eight world bests falling to a USAF F-15 Eagle.

Today it reached 30,000 meters [98,000 feet] in just three minutes 27.8 seconds. The Mach 2.5 McDonnell Douglas F-15 is the Air Force's latest fighter and the most advanced aircraft of its type in the world. The one used today was specially prepared for the flights. The new records are:
Jan 16 3,000m 27.57 sec
Jan 16 6,000m 39.33 sec
Jan 16 9,000m 48.86 sec
Jan 16 12,000m 59.38 sec
Jan 16 15,000m 1 min 17.02 sec
Jan 29 20,000m 2 min 02.94 sec
Jan 26 25,000m 2 min 41.02 sec
Feb 1 30,000m 3 min 27.80 sec
Conversion note: 1 meter = 3.281 feet (→ Apr 27, 1977).

▷

# Helicopters fly last US missions of Vietnam war

*Flight to safety: evacuees scramble to board an Air America helicopter preparing to take off from a Saigon rooftop.*

## Over 100 orphans die in Saigon crash

**Saigon, April 4**
The first flight in a USAF airlift of 2,000 Vietnamese children to the US ended tragically today when a giant C-5 Galaxy transport with 243 orphans aboard crashed and burst into flames shortly after taking off from Saigon's Tan Son Nhut airport. As rescue work continues, more than 100 of the children and 25 of their adult escorts are reported to have been killed.

The C-5 carried 305 people when it left here; a crew of 16, 2 flight nurses, 44 escorts, and the children. About 100 orphans and 20 others survived the crash, which strewed aircraft wreckage, baby bottles, bedding and bodies over rice paddies 5 miles north-east of the airport. The escorts were secretaries from the US embassy and wives of staff members.

Galaxy pilot Captain Dennis Traynor was one of the survivors. The aircraft was over the South China sea, about 40 miles from Saigon, when the trouble started. Traynor said a loss of pressurization blew out the rear door, which he believes struck the tail. With the elevator stuck, only partial control of the aircraft was possible, he said. He tried to return to the airport but was descending too rapidly to reach the runway (→ Apr 30).

*Desperate means to clear the doorway of an overcrowded refugee airplane.*

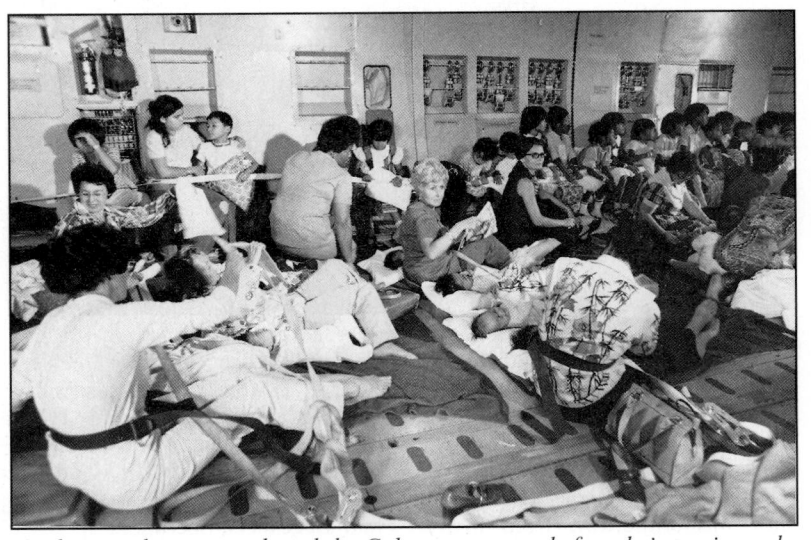

*Orphans and escorts on board the Galaxy, moments before their tragic crash.*

## Helicopter airlift of 7,000 personnel as Saigon is captured

**Saigon, April 30**
The US closed the book on the Vietnam war today when the last 11 US Marines scrambled from the roof of the US Embassy here into an HH-53 helicopter to end an amazing feat of aerial evacuation. In all, 7,014 US and South Vietnamese military, diplomatic and government officials were taken out in the final days before the North Vietnamese captured the city.

Helicopters of the USAF, US Marines and the CIA-run airline Air America moved evacuees from the American Defense Attaché Office, formerly MACV Headquarters, and the US Embassy to the US and allied task force gathered off the Vietnamese coast. President Gerald Ford ordered them into action after Saigon's Tan Son Nhut airport was forced to close by rocket and artillery fire.

The armada of about 80 USAF HH-53s and US Marine CH-46s, CH-53s and Cobra gunship escorts flew more than 660 sorties. Meanwhile, USAF and US Navy fighter-bombers, attack aircraft, KC135s and its command-and-control airplanes from bases in Thailand and the carriers USS *Kitty Hawk* and *Enterprise* provided cover for the evacuation. Despite the intense air traffic and enemy fire, only three aircraft and two crewmen were lost.

On the whole, however, the US did not use airpower wisely or effectively – except for helicopters and close air support – during its 12 years of heavy involvement in Vietnam. Too much politics entered into the selection of weapons and targets for US raids in North Vietnam. There were too many sanctuaries and rules of engagement, which cost aircrews their lives, and too many pauses in the bombing, which allowed the Communists to recover and convince themselves that the US commitment was not real. Surgical strikes in a high-threat air defense environment without "smart" weapons proved mostly ineffective and costly.

## UTA establishes a 747 freight shuttle

*Lyon, France, May 18*
French airline UTA has launched an ambitious new cargo shuttle operation, mainly using 747s. The service will link the brand new Lyon-Satolas airport with Kano in northern Nigeria. It will supply the big assembly plant recently set up by French car manufacturer Peugeot at Kaduna, at the junction of the railroads to Lagos and Port Harcourt. On each trip the 747s will carry the parts for no fewer than 120 cars.

Freight, an important but often unsung aspect of air transportation, has long played a significant part in the activities of UTA, which serves Africa, the Middle and Far East, Australasia and North America. Since the Paris-based company was created in 1963, its cargo business has developed steadily and has enabled UTA to weather troubled times, especially periods of steep fuel price rises and stagnation in passenger traffic.

# Long-haul Boeing 747SP is unveiled

*Long-distance performer: the Special Performance 747 is not only shorter but also has a taller vertical tail.*

*Seattle, July 4*
The Boeing 747 Jumbo Jet appears to have shrunk. The latest model to come from the Everett plant, near Seattle, is a Boeing 747 with a fuselage shortened by 48 feet 4 inches and the tailplane span increased by nearly 10 feet. This means a significant reduction in the aircraft's weight. Other modifications from which the 747SP ("Special Performance") benefits include the adoption of single-slotted flaps and lighter landing gear.

The 747SP is designed to operate from short runways at high altitudes and in hot climates. It will also travel very long distances – the changes will enable the new airplane to transport between 288 and 331 passengers over a distance of 6,740 miles. Orders for the 747SP have already been received by several of the big US airlines, among which Pan Am envisages putting it into service on the non-stop New York/Tokyo route (→ Mar 24, 1976).

## Mystery New York disaster kills 109

*New York, June 24*
Some 109 people are feared dead after this afternoon's crash of an Eastern Air Lines Boeing 727. Flight 66, on a flight from New Orleans, struck Rockaway Boulevard, near John F Kennedy International Airport, and burst into flames. The 727 was trying to land in a thunderstorm.

Rescuers doused the flames within minutes. Doctors and priests moved among the bodies, looking for survivors and giving last rites. Two children were among the 16 who were thrown out alive on to the boulevard. Two survivors have since died.

An eyewitness reported that the 727 was flying too low and struck several of the 35-ft-high lighting towers marking the runway approach. There is speculation that the airliner may have been struck by lightning. But experts point to the aircraft's ability to cope with lightning strikes, and a more likely explanation is windshear – sudden reduction in wind caused by local variations in air pressure.

## Sales of Corvette get off to a slow start

*France, September 9*
Aérospatiale came late to the executive jet market, launching the SN 600 Corvette seven years after the appearance of the Dassault Falcon 20. The 19 Corvettes which have so far left the factory have now clocked up 10,000 hours in the air in under a year of operation, which represents 40,000 passengers carried. However, despite a promising early career, it may not share the commercial success of its rivals. Designed for the US market as a general-purpose aircraft, the Corvette first flew in July 1970, the prototype powered by two Pratt & Whitney Canada JT15D-4 turbofans rated at 2,200 lb thrust each. The engines were upgraded to give 2,300 lb of thrust on the Corvette 601, which followed in 1972. The 601 has a longer fuselage than the prototype and carries up to 14 passengers and two crew. An 18-seater version is on the drawing board and a three-engined version, the Corvette 300, is also planned.

*Five years after its first flight, the Corvette is not yet a commercial success.*

## New aerobatic Zlin combats g-forces

*Czechoslovakia, July 18*
Drawing on the knowledge gained in 40 years of building competitive aerobatic airplanes, the Zlin company today began flight testing the new Z 50L. The testing is based at the small airport of Otrokovice, adjacent to the factory.

The Z 50L is an all-metal, low-wing single-seater, with fixed tailwheel landing gear. Unlike previous Zlin aerobatic aircraft, it has a US-built engine, a 260-hp Avco Lycoming. The pilot is seated leaning well back, the better to resist g-forces, and wearing a back-type parachute. The cockpit is enclosed by a bubble canopy, which can be jettisoned in an emergency.

The Z 50L is designed to be a superior performer to the latest aerobatic aircraft to be developed in the USSR, the Su-26 and Yak-55. To enhance the accuracy with which it can be flown, the Z 50L has two-section ailerons, which extend along most of the trailing edge of the wings; the inboard section has an automatic trim tab.

# YC-15, possible heir to the Hercules, flies

*McDonnell Douglas YC-15: aiming to replace the C-130 Hercules transport.*

**California, August 26**
Today saw the first flight of McDonnell Douglas's YC-15, its entry in the USAF's advanced medium short take-off and landing transport (AMST) competition to replace the 20-year old turboprop Lockheed C-130 Hercules. Boeing's YC-14, which will be completed next year, is the other competitor. Both of the new airplanes are powered by jets.

The four-engined McDonnell Douglas AMST, which flew from Long Beach to Edwards Air Force Base, is the first large transport to use the NASA-developed "supercritical" wing, which significantly reduces fuel consumption. The YC-15 also has an efficient high-lift system in which the four Pratt & Whitney JT8D engines blow through heat-resistant titanium triple-slotted flaps to improve the aircraft's short take-off performance. The Boeing YC-14 design is different. Its engines will blow over the top of the wings.

From their experiences in Vietnam, where getting large loads of troops and cargo into and out of short, rough airfields was critical, the USAF and US Army concluded that they needed even better performance than that offered by the excellent C-130. AMST requirements are for an aircraft which can operate from a 2,000-foot runway compared to the 3,500-foot strip needed by the C-130. It will be able to carry two and a half times the load of the Hercules, and its greater length (26 feet in the case of the YC-15) and wider fuselage mean it can carry more oversize equipment.

**Waging war against terrorists: X-ray systems to detect metal objects in passengers' baggage are now in use in airports across the world.**

# Hughes launches Apache attack helicopter

**Los Angeles, September 30**
Hughes Helicopters today staged the first flight of its contender in the US Army's Advanced Attack Helicopter (AAH) competition. Its YAH-64 Apache lines up against Bell's YAH-63 to succeed the Bell AH-1 Cobra as the Army's attack helicopter.

Today's flight of the Hughes AAH was by one of two prototypes which will be turned over to the Army for a competitive trial with the Bell AAH next May. Between now and then, the two YAH-64s will undergo 850 hours of flight and ground trials, which will examine such areas as rotor flutter and vibration. There will also be firing tests of the aircraft's turret-mounted XM-230 30-mm Chain gun, rockets, and TOW missiles.

Hughes is teamed with Teledyne Ryan Aeronautical, the manufac-

*Apache: four weapon mountings.*

turer of the prototypes' fuselage, and 12 other major subcontractors. The 49-foot-long YAH-64 is powered by two General Electric 1,536-hp turboshaft engines (→ Oct 1).

# Airplane found in desert after 42 years

*The wreckage of "Southern Cross Minor" after 42 years in the Sahara.*

**Algeria, November 17**
Forty-two years after crashing in the Sahara desert, the wreckage of Avro Avian 5 *Southern Cross Minor* has been rediscovered by members of the Wylton Dickson expedition. Only the fuselage structure, a wing bare of covering fabric, engine and fuel tanks are whole among the debris, its broken tail pointing skyward some feet above the ground.

The Avro Avian was being piloted by Englishman Captain William N Lancaster at the time of the crash on April 12, 1933. He had left Lympne, England, the previous day in an attempt to set a new London/Cape Town record. He was last seen alive at In Salah on the Trans-Saharan track.

Lancaster's long-time friend and fellow pilot Mrs K Miller had been expected to mount her own search, but abandoned plans. The French colonial authorities failed to find Lancaster or the smashed airplane, their efforts being hampered by sandstorms lasting days.

Nearly 30 years later, in March 1962, a French desert patrol came across the airplane and Lancaster's mummified body about 170 miles south of Reggane. The Avian was left in the desert.

# Braniff flies the flag for US bicentennial

*Washington, DC, December*
To celebrate the USA's 200th birthday next year, Braniff, the "Flying Colors" airline, will add a red, white, and blue airplane to its already distinctive and kaleidoscopic fleet. Painted by the noted modern artist Alexander Calder, the Boeing 727 will have an abstract design inspired by the Stars and Stripes in motion which is called "The Flying Colors of the United States". As in 1973, when Calder did the "Flying Colors of South America" for a Braniff DC-8, there will be no airline logos on the bicentennial 727, only Calder's signature, because it is a work of art.

In its effort to differentiate itself from other airlines, Braniff will also offer "Good Taste of America with Flying Colors" menus in 1976. They will feature items from the period around 1776.

*Calder's brightly colored airliner pays homage to the American flag.*

# USAF tests its new long-range bomber

*Edwards AFB, September 19*
Major George W Larson today became the first pilot from the USAF's Strategic Air Command to fly the USA's latest, deep penetration bomber, the variable geometry Rockwell B-1. Alongside Rockwell pilots Charles Bock and Richard Abrams, he was at the controls for about two hours out of the six and a half hour flight.

The B-1 is the US response to the Soviet Union's similar, large, variable-geometry aircraft, the Tupolev Tu-26, known in the West as the "Backfire". The Soviets are very cagey about the Tu-26. They insist on calling it the Tu-22M, implying that it is merely an update of a 1950s aircraft. But US intelligence sources, who have photographed the "Backfire" from espionage satellites, insist that it is a new bomber capable of hitting the USA – justifying the B-1.

# Congress backs ban on Concorde flights

*Washington, DC, December 18*
In what some view as tweaking the nose of the British and French aviation industry, the US House of Representatives voted by 199 to 198 tonight to put a six-month ban on landings by the Concorde supersonic airliner in the USA. British Airways and Air France want to fly Concorde six times a day to both New York's John F Kennedy airport and Washington's Dulles.

Opponents of the ban warned that it invited retaliation from Concorde's builders and would hurt the US's own aviation industry. Ohio representative Wayne Hays scoffed at fears that the Concorde flights would lead to increases in skin cancer or produce damaging noise. Senator Clarence J Brown, also of Ohio, said: "I see no reason to oppose the SST just because we were stupid enough to get out of the SST business ourselves" (→ Mar 11, 1976).

# Soviet supersonic airliner goes to work

*Soviet Tu-144 supersonic transport and officials at Moscow Sheremetyevo.*

*Moscow, December 26*
After its horrific crash at the Paris Air Show in 1973 [*see page 709*], many doubted that the Soviet supersonic Tu-144 – unfairly nicknamed "Concordski" in the West – would ever be any more than a symbol of Iron Curtain technology. But Aeroflot proved the doubters wrong today when one of the sleek airliners left Moscow's Domodedovo airport for Alma Ata, 1,864 miles away in Kazakhstan.

The flight time between the two airports is under two hours, although passengers wanting to fly the route have to take conventional aircraft – the Tu-144 carries only mail and freight. However, it is reported that the occasional VIP will fly in a luxury suite built forward in the cabin.

Plans are in hand for an improved version of the Mach 2 airliner, including new Kolesov turbojet engines and accommodation for more than 200 passengers. Like much aviation news from the USSR today, the details are inevitably sketchy. Nothing much has been seen of the aircraft outside the USSR since the Paris tragedy (→ Nov 1, 1977).

**Future surveillance: the E-3A Sentry airborne warning and control system (AWACS) aircraft is under development at Boeing for the USAF. The disc above the rear fuselage is a 30-foot rotating pulse-doppler radar antenna capable of tracking aircraft at a radius of more than 200 miles. The airframe is a derivative of military versions of the Boeing 707.**

Seen on its rollout from Boeing's Everett factory, the 747SP (Special Performance) offered airlines extremely long range without excessive capacity.

Intended as a Tu-134 replacement for Aeroflot, the Yakovlev Yak-42 can carry up to 120 passengers over a distance of up to 2,000km (1,242 miles).

The Beech Model 58TC Baron twin was unpressurized but turbocharged.

Fuji's Commander 700 6/8-seater was a joint venture with Rockwell.

Despite owing its ancestry to the Jet Commander, the Israel Aircraft Industry's IAI-1124 Westwind executive jet is a considerably updated design.

The Robinson R-22 is a light and affordable two-seat helicopter.

Intended as an executive transport the Cessna 441 could carry up to ten.

Beechcraft's entry in the light trainer market was the Model 77 Skipper.

Factory-built Pitts Specials came from the premises of Aerotek in Wyoming run by Pitts aerobatics since 1977. Single- and two-seat models are built.

The last two BAe Tridents to be constructed were Super 3Bs for China.

With its ability to carry freight or up to 50 passengers into the smallest of airfields, the DHC Dash 7 offers true STOL performance at airline standard.

While basically a stretched Model 402, the Continental GTSIO-520-powered Cessna 404 Titan has become a popular commuter and freight aircraft.

*By rebuilding F-111As, Grumman produced the EF-111 Raven, an electronic warfare aircraft able to identify and jam all hostile tactical surface radars.*

*Designed for the battlefields of Northern Europe, the Hughes YAH-64 Apache brought a formidable anti-tank capability by virtue of its 16 Hellfire missiles.*

*The Atlas C.4M Kudu is a sturdy six- to eight- seat transport.*

*The DHC-5 Buffalo's T-tail and high wing made it the ideal aircraft for the NASA Augmentor-wing jet STOL research aircraft program which involved the fitting of two Rolls-Royce Spey turbofans ducted to blow through the flaps.*

*The two to four seat Valmet L-70 Vinka/Miltrainer was produced to meet a basic requirement of the Finnish Airforce to replace its Saab Safirs.*

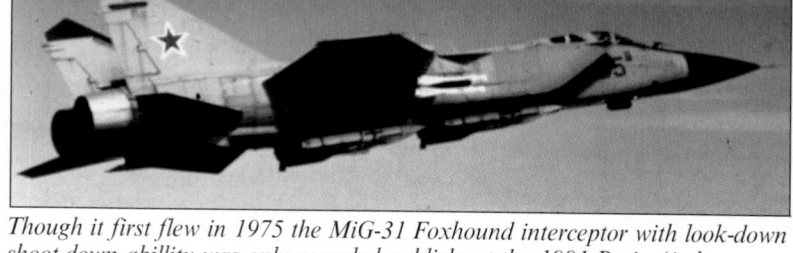

*Though it first flew in 1975 the MiG-31 Foxhound interceptor with look-down shoot-down abillity was only revealed publicly at the 1991 Paris Airshow.*

*The McDonnell Douglas DC-10-40 was originally designated the -20, and was built for Northwest Orient Airlines with Pratt & Whitney JT9D engines.*

*Displaying an obvious ancestry with the Yak-18, the Yak-52 has a semi-retractable main landing gear. It equipped the former Soviet DOSAAF.*

*A contender for the USAF Advanced Medium STOL Transport fly-off was the JT8D-powered McDonnell Douglas YC-15 with externally blown flaps.*

*Boeing's YC-14 was the other AMST competitor in the search for a C-130 Hercules replacement, but neither it nor the YC-15 ever entered production.*

# 1976

4,534mph
USA
Pete Knight
North American X-15
Oct 3, 1967

24,325 miles
USA
Archie Old Jr
Boeing B-52B
Jan 18, 1957

354,200ft
USA
Joseph Walker
North American X-15
Aug 22, 1963

833,000lb
USA
Boeing
B-747 200F

53,230lb thrust
USA
Pratt & Whitney
JT9D-59B

**New York City, March 17**
A Japan Air Lines Boeing 747 lands after the first non-stop flight from Tokyo to New York; it covered the 6.300 miles in 11 hours 30 minutes.

**Bordeaux, France, March 18**
Bernard Monnier and Olivier Dassault land after a 33-day, 55,240-mile demonstration tour of the Far East and Australia with the Falcon 10 bizjet.

**South Africa, March 24**
A Boeing 747SP, developed for long-haul flights, lands at Cape Town after setting a world non-stop distance record for a civil aircraft of 10,290 miles on its delivery flight from Paine Field, Washington (→ May 3).

**Frankfurt, April 1**
Lufthansa's first two Airbus A300Bs enter service (→ Dec 22).

**Pennsylvania, April 1**
The 100,000th Piper airplane, a turboprop PA-31T Cheyenne II, is rolled out of the company's Lock Haven plant (→ Aug 13, 1980).

**Paris, April 9**
Air France opens its second supersonic service, to Caracas, Venezuela; Concorde takes six hours, including a stop at the Azores (→ May 24).

**New York, May 3**
Pan Am's 747SP *Clipper Liberty Bell* returns after a world record for a round-the-world flight of 1 day 22 hours 26 minutes: it took off on May 1 and refueled in Delhi and Tokyo.→

**Toulouse, France, May 19**
The French Armée de l'Air takes delivery of its 100th SEPECAT Jaguar.

**Los Angeles, May 19**
Champion golfer and businessman Arnold Palmer lands his Learjet 36 to set a round-the-world record for a business jet of 57 hours 26 minutes flying time.→

**Zamboanga, Philippines, May 24**
Filipino troops attack a Philippines Airlines DC-9 which was seized with its passengers yesterday by six terrorists; three of the hijackers are among ten people killed in the ensuing battle, which ends when the three remaining terrorists are captured.

**Le Mans, France, June 12**
An SA.360 Dauphin helicopter is used to shoot aerial views of the Le Mans 24-hour car rally.

**Britain, July 1**
Clive Canning lands his Thorp T-18 Tiger to complete the first flight from Australia in a home-built aircraft.

**Italy, July 3**
Italian manufacturer Piaggio's P.166-DL3 twin-engine transport makes its maiden flight.

**Hatzerim, Israel, July 20**
The Israeli air force unveils its IAI Kfir-C2 fighter; it is a modified version of the Kfir (which first flew last year) with fixed foreplanes to improve maneuverability.

**Washington, DC, July 22**
The US State Department licenses Pratt & Whitney to develop the JT10D turbofan engine in collaboration with Fiat, MTU and Rolls-Royce.

**Wiltshire, England, July 22**
The Royal Navy retires its last piston-engined helicopter, a Whirlwind HAS.7, from service at its Old Sarum base.

**London, July 29**
The British government announces that production of the BAC One Eleven and the Hawker Siddeley 146 airliners will be supported by a loan (→ Jul 11, 1978).

**Europe, July 29**
The governments of Britain, Italy and West Germany sign a memorandum for the production of 809 Panavia Tornados for their air forces (→ Oct 27, 1979).

**Seattle, August 9**
The Boeing YC-14 prototype, which has been designed for testing as part of the USAF's advanced medium/short take-off and landing (AMST) transport development program, makes its initial flight.

**Fort Worth, Texas, August 13**
The Bell 222 prototype, the first light twin-turbine commercial helicopter to be built in the US, flies for the first time (→ Jan 18, 1981).

**Alberta, Canada, August 24**
The Short SD3-30 commuter transport begins its first commercial service, with the airline Time Air.

**Warsaw, August 27**
The 1,000-hp PZL-Mielec M-18 Dromader, equipped for crop spraying and other agricultural duties, completes flight tests.

**Oxfordshire, England, Sep 14**
The RAF's Short Belfast heavy transport unit, 53 Squadron based at Brize Norton, is disbanded as part of government defense cuts.

**Auckland, September 29**
Air New Zealand introduces a new uniform for its female cabin staff, created by top fashion designer Nina Ricci.

**São José, Brazil, October 10**
EMBRAER's EMB-121 Xingu transport prototype makes its first flight (→ Mar 16, 1982).

**Connecticut, USA, October 12**
The first Sikorsky Model 72 rotor systems research aircraft (RSRA) helicopter prototype begins flight tests; the experimental aircraft can be fitted with wings and turbofan engines and is capable of flying as a conventional airplane.

**USA, December 2**
The Boeing 747 SCA, an ex-American Airlines airliner which has been adapted to carry the US reusable space shuttle, makes its first flight (→ Feb 18, 1977).

**Cadiz, Spain, December 9**
Spain's first jump jet unit, 008 Squadron of the Arma Aerea de la Armada Española, becomes operational; it is equipped with AV-8A/TAV-8A Matadors.

**Lyons, France, December 22**
An Airbus A300B of the French internal airline Air Inter lands in Category IIIA weather conditions to complete the first fully automatic landing of the type in commercial service (→ Nov 18, 1977).

---

## Factfile

World revenue passenger miles: 474,556,966 million
Passengers through Chicago O'Hare: 18.1 million
Passengers through New York (JFK/Newark/LaGuardia): 17.6 million
Passengers through London (Heathrow/Gatwick): 29.0 million
Price of a single coach ticket New York/Los Angeles (April): $194
Price of the cheapest return ticket London/New York: $295
World air freight (ton miles): 65,149.1 million
Average salary of a long-haul pilot (US): $47,147
Average salary of cabin crew (US): $12,671
Price of a Learjet 25 B: $1.3 million
Price of an HS 125: $2 million
Price of a Falcon 20: $2.99 million
Price of 1,000 (US) gallons of Jet A1 fuel (average July): $447.98
Average exchange rate: 9c 1 = $1.8061

*The three-engined Falcon 50 marks a firm move by Dassault-Breguet in the direction of long-range trans-oceanic business jets.* ▶

# Concorde opens era of supersonic passenger flight

*Air France has trained seven crews to fly passenger services on Concorde.*

*Concorde carries 97 tons of fuel, stored both in the wings and the fuselage.*

*Rio de Janeiro, January 21*
"Passengers for Air France flight 085 are requested to proceed to the departure gate." For 100 travelers this midday announcement at satellite 5 of Paris's Charles de Gaulle airport heralded the start of one of the most exciting events in aviation history. Flight 085, which left Paris for Rio via Dakar at 12.40pm, was no ordinary flight: it was the first commercial flight of Concorde and the world's first scheduled flight for fare-paying passengers operated by a supersonic airliner. To symbolize 13 years of Anglo-French collaboration on the project, a British Airways Concorde took off at the same time from London Heathrow for Bahrain. Around 60 of the French Con-

corde's first paying passengers were French, and there were eight Americans, six Germans, four Italians, two Spaniards, two Scandinavians and one Swiss. The oldest passenger was an 82-year-old woman from Toulouse.

Pierre Chanoine, the captain of the French Concorde, landed his aircraft at Dakar at 3.27pm. The airliner was greeted by Senegal's President Leopold Sedar Senghor before taking off at 4.45pm for the last leg of its flight. It arrived at Rio's Galeao airport at 8.06pm Paris time. The Air France Concorde had traveled the 6,000 miles between Paris and Rio in just 7 hours 26 minutes. The era of supersonic flight has arrived (→ Mar 11).

## US Concorde ban sparks a legal row

*New York, March 11*
The Port Authority of New York and New Jersey today banned the Anglo-French Concorde supersonic airliner from using its airports. The move is a tough blow for British Airways and Air France, since the aircraft was designed largely with the North Atlantic route in mind.

A long legal battle is now set to begin. The question is whether the Port Authority's ban will prevail over the decision of the federal authorities in Washington, DC. On February 4 Transportation Secretary William Coleman gave the go-ahead for Concorde to fly to New York and Washington for a trial period of 12 months, each airline being allowed three flights per day. The government envisaged two of these daily flights landing at New York's John F Kennedy airport. Judge Milton Pollack will decide the case (→ Apr 9).

## Two Concordes land together at Dulles

*Washington, DC, May 24*
Two Concorde supersonic airliners – one in British Airways colors, the other in those of Air France – landed at Washington's Dulles International Airport today. They are the first Concordes to visit the USA.

After taking off at the same time from London and Paris respectively, the two aircraft co-ordinated their flights so that they both appeared simultaneously in the skies over the US capital. They made parallel approaches just a few hundred yards apart and touched down together on the runway. The British Concorde landed on runway 01 left and the French aircraft on 01 right.

Dulles airport is the property of the Federal Aviation Administration, which is run by the US Department of Transportation. Transportation Secretary William Coleman gave special permission for today's flights (→ May 21, 1977).

*Three Concordes have been delivered to Air France; two to British Airways.*

## Test pilot Turcat to hang up his spurs

*Toulouse, France, March 31*
Andre Turcat, the Marseille-born pilot whose name is inextricably linked with Concorde, has left the cockpit of "his" supersonic airliner for the last time. Turcat, 55, director of flight testing at Aérospatiale, is facing his retirement with good humor: his engineer friends have made him a member of the "King's Own Grease Monkeys"!

Since receiving his pilot's license in 1947, Turcat has clocked up some 6,500 hours in the air in 110 types of aircraft and flown 4,000 hours of test flights, including 720 at the controls of Concorde. In 1954, André Turcat became the first French pilot to break the sound barrier in level flight, and he developed the first all-weather automatic landing system to be installed aboard a commercial airplane. He will be succeeded by test flight engineer Henri Perrier.

# Lufthansa begins services with the Airbus

# Pan Am Jumbo sets world-circling record

*The economics of the Airbus must make it attractive to the world's airlines.*

*The Boeing 747SP can fly 15 hrs at a height of 45,000 feet (13,750 meters).*

*Frankfurt, April 1*

The latest additions to the Lufthansa fleet, two Airbus A300B2 airliners, entered service today. They will fly on the West German flag-carrier's routes between here and Düsseldorf, Hamburg, Stuttgart and London.

Lufthansa chose the European airliner because, in the airline's view, it is the most economical jet airliner in scheduled service over any distance, in terms of cost per passenger per mile. The twin-engined, medium-range Airbus has a fuel consumption 35 to 40 per cent lower than that of other wide-body airliners. This is a crucial factor for airlines facing financial difficulties, which could not afford an airplane that lost them money.

Another point in the Airbus's favor is its ability to carry 30 tons of freight in standard containers such as those with which cargo transports are equipped (→ Dec 22).

*New York, May 3*

A new round-the-world record for commercial transports was set today when a Pan Am Boeing 747SP (Special Performance) returned to New York's John F Kennedy International Airport, 46 hours 26 minutes after it had departed.

The trip would have been even quicker but for a two-and-a-half hour delay owing to a labor dispute in Tokyo. En route the Pan Am Clipper, with 100 passengers aboard, made the longest non-stop commercial aircraft fight, covering 8,088 miles from the US to New Delhi in 13 hours 31 minutes. The 747SP's range, up to 3,000 miles greater than that of other 747s, comes from the weight saved in a fuselage nearly 50 feet shorter than a standard 747's. Pan Am 747SPs began regular non-stop service between New York and Tokyo on April 25. Japanese airlines, without the 747SP, must refuel at Anchorage.

# Howard Hughes dies from a stroke

*Houston, Texas, April 5*

On board a chartered Learjet, reclusive billionaire Howard Hughes died at 1.27pm today. He suffered a stroke en route from Acapulco, Mexico, to the Methodist Hospital here, his home town, for emergency treatment. He was 70.

The colorful Hughes made most of his billions in oil. He produced movies and was also a daredevil pilot, breaking several records – and bones – for his pains. For many years boss of TWA, he was an air pioneer, although his huge "Spruce Goose" flying boat was a flop. If he spent much of his early career surrounded by movie stars and admiring fans, for the last 30 years of his life Hughes lived as a recluse, allegedly never cutting his hair or nails and obsessive about hygiene. Armed guards escorted him on his rare ventures into the world outside his palatial estate.

# British Airways turns its back on Europe

*London, August 6*

British Airways (BA) is experiencing vast growth in its holiday business within Europe, and revenues on its routes to Australia and the Far East now far exceed those on routes to the US. It must therefore be asked: why has BA turned its back on Europe's airliner industry in favor of even more US types?

Already committed to making the Boeing 747 its standard long-haul airliner, BA has again snubbed Europe today with its decision to favor the Lockheed TriStar over the Airbus A300 to replace its ageing Tridents and One-Elevens. Critics point to Air France's support for the Airbus and to McDonnell Douglas's offer of a deal on its DC-10 which would have been worth around £300 million to the British economy. BA's decision is a blow to Hawker Siddeley, which plays a key part in manufacturing the A300Bs (→ Apr 1, 1977).

*The choice of the TriStar over the Airbus has provoked bitter controversy.*

# Golfing star Palmer sets a flying record

*Denver, Colorado, May 19*

Arnold Palmer is never happier than when he takes up a challenge. Champion golfer and successful businessman, he also became a record-breaking pilot today.

Palmer set a record for flying round the world in a business jet when he and three companions touched down here in his personal Learjet after covering 23,000 miles in 57 hours 25 minutes 42 seconds. This was nearly 29 hours better than the previous record.

Powered by two Garrett TFE731 turbofans, Palmer's Model 36 is a 35 with two seats removed to allow more fuel. Flying at a maximum altitude of 45,000 feet, the 36 will normally seat four passengers and two crew. Its range of over 3,100 miles makes it capable of crossing the Atlantic – a good sales point. On this trip the aircraft flew at around 405mph.

# C-130 raid frees Entebbe hostages

*The Israeli commandos receive a hero's welcome on their return to Tel Aviv.*

*Captain of the A300B Michel Bacos.*

*Entebbe, Uganda, July 4*
Israeli commandos pulled off an astonishing rescue last night when they stormed the airport here and freed over 100 hostages, passengers from a hijacked Air France Airbus.

The Ugandan government, which had allowed the hijackers to land eight days ago, was taken by surprise when three C-130E Hercules transport planes flew in at dead of night. In a sharp 35-minute battle, 20 Ugandan soldiers and all seven hijackers were killed. Three hostages and one commando – the raid commander – also died. The hijack began on June 27 at Athens when 258 passengers were about to disembark from the A300B2 Airbus. The aircraft was boarded by five Palestinian terrorists and two German members of the Red Army Faction, who forced the pilot to head for Entebbe and demanded the release of 53 Palestinian terrorists held in Israel. Ugandan dictator Idi Amin promptly began negotiating with the hijackers and backed their demands.

Meanwhile, the Israelis, while appearing willing to negotiate, were planning their daring expedition. There were only hours to go until the deadline for the execution of the hostages, most of whom were Jews or Israeli citizens, when the three transport airplanes arrived at Entebbe. A black Mercedes emerged from the first airplane and Ugandan guards took it for their president. But within moments the Israeli commandos had neutralized the control tower, destroyed 13 Soviet-made MiG fighters on the ground – a quarter of the Ugandan Air Force – and were storming the terminal to release the hostages. Loading them on to the C-130 Hercules, the Israeli force returned home via Kenya, where the wounded were taken to a waiting hospital airplane. A few hours later hostages and rescuers were welcomed by a jubilant crowd at Tel Aviv.

## Top-secret Tomcat is lost from carrier

*Scotland, September 14*
A Soviet cruiser is circling an area north-west of Scotland where a US Navy F-14A Tomcat with super-secret advanced weapons and electronic gear rolled off the deck of the carrier USS *John F Kennedy* and into 1,890 feet of water today. The F-14 had the Phoenix missile system, AWG-9 radar and some other equipment not included on models sold to other countries.

The US Navy considers the presence of the Soviet warship not unusual, because it was following the carrier during Nato exercises. It said that raising the aircraft would be a difficult task for anyone.

*F-14: a top-secret weapons system.*

# Soviet military pilot defects to the West with MiG-25 fighter

*Hakodate, Japan, September 6*
Officials at the airport here on the northern island of Hokkaido got a surprise at 1.57pm today. Without any advance notice, a MiG-25 jet fighter landed, almost overshooting the end of the runway, and shut down its two huge jet engines. Out of it stepped Soviet Lieutenant Viktor Belenko.

He asked airport workers to cover his airplane with tarpaulin, because it contained secret equipment. Then he said he was seeking asylum in the USA. The MiG-25 is the fastest fighter in service in the world. Little is known of it except its outward appearance. It is certain to be carefully studied by Western experts before being returned to the Soviet Union.

*Japanese police examine the Soviet MiG-25 fighter in which Belenko defected.*

## Mid-air crash over Zagreb kills 176

*Croatia, Yugoslavia, September 10*
A British Airways Trident jet and a Yugoslav DC-9 of Inex Adria collided in clear skies at 33,000 feet today, killing 176 people in the worst-ever mid-air disaster. The British jet was carrying 54 passengers and nine crew on a scheduled flight from London to Istanbul. The DC-9 was heading north from the Yugoslav resort of Split to Cologne, with 108 German holiday-makers and a crew of five. Errors made by air traffic controllers in Zagreb seem the likeliest cause of the crash.

# Falcon 50 jet has intercontinental range

*The Falcon 50: its three turbofans give it an impressive range of 3,400 miles.*

*Mérignac, France, November 7*
The Dassault-Breguet Mystère 50, which flew for the first time today here at Mérignac, is an executive jet which embodies some of the experience of the Mystère 20 while retaining the wing design of the Mystère 10, updated with every technological innovation.

The Mystère 50 is intended to satisfy the demands of the business market in the US, where it will be known as the Falcon 50 and distributed by the Falcon Jet Corporation. In the de luxe version for eight passengers, the cabin comprises a bar, a cloakroom and a lavatory in which you can stand up. Its three Garrett TFE731 turbofans plus a large fuel capacity, give the airplane a range of just over 3,400 miles at 500mph. Its maximum take-off weight is more than 37,500 lb. The Falcon 50 is just as comfortable as the Falcon 20, but its range enables it to travel coast to coast, a vital qualification for the US market. Some modifications are expected after a few problems on the first flight (→Apr 1, 1978).

**An Airbus carries out water aquaplaning tests on a flooded runway. Researchers film the patterns of spray thrown into the aircraft's engines.**

# Aeroflot takes on Il-86, Soviet jumbo jet

*The Ilyushin Il-86's passengers carry their own luggage on and off.*

*Moscow, December 22*
The USSR's own jumbo jet flew for the first time today. The wide-body Ilyushin Il-86 passenger aircraft has a fuselage nearly 19 feet in diameter and is powered by four Kuznetsov turbofans, each of 28,650 lb thrust, two on each wing. It is designed to fly at 594mph, at an altitude of 33,000 feet, and its navigation equipment is highly sophisticated.

The cockpit of the Il-86 will hold three or four crew, while the cabin takes up to 350 and is divided into three sections.

One of the great novelties of this aircraft is the way passengers get on and off. Instead of waiting for gangways to be brought up to the doors, the Il-86 has three built-in staircases which unfold at the touch of a button. Passengers climb to the lower deck, leave luggage and coats and then climb further staircases to reach the main deck, where the seats are. They will also carry off their luggage upon arrival.

Aeroflot hopes to use the Il-86 to carry passengers to the Moscow Olympics in 1980 (→Oct 2, 1978).

**"Southwest Flyers Have More Fun". During the summer, Southwest personnel will dress in shorts, colorful T-shirts and tennis shoes.**

*Dassault's first attempt at a long-range executive jet was the Falcon 50 tri-jet, powered by Garrett TFE731 engines and with capacity for up to ten passengers.*

*In an attempt to improve the Bulldog trainer, Scottish Aviation flew a single example of the retractable-gear Bullfinch, but it failed to gain any orders.*

*Two further overwing exits and a lengthened fuselage indicate the high density seating -4000 version of the Fokker F.28 Friendship aft-engined airliner.*

*Until the Model 800, the best-seller of the BAe 125 bizjet family was the Series 700, which used the Garrett TFE731 turbofan instead of R-R Viper turbojets.*

*The first commercial twin-engined light helicopter to be built in the USA, the Bell 222 featured a fully retractable undercarriage and night/IFR capability.*

*Intended as a simple passenger/cargo aircraft, the Ahrens 404, built in Puerto Rico, ultimately failed to enter production. The engines were four Allisons.*

*Operated by a crew of 13, the Lockheed L-1011-200 TriStar offered greater range over earlier models, courtesy of its up-rated Rolls-Royce RB211 engines.*

*Despite offering sparkling performance and load factors of +12g to -9g the Flight Invert/Cranfield A.1 aerobatic and training aircraft was not a success.*

*A pressurized 5/6-seat business transport, the Brazilian Embraer EMB-121 Xingu has been bought by both commercial and military operators.*

*Built originally to a USAF specification, and the original "biz-jet", the Lockheed 1329 Jetstar II's JT12 engines were replaced by TFE 731 turbofans.*

*Although outwardly an ex-American Airlines Boeing 747-123, the NASA 747 Shuttle Carrier was extensively modified, upgraded and re-engined.*

*The popular family of Robin lightplanes gained a new member with the one off Robin HR.100/180, powered by a 180hp Lycoming O-360 piston engine.*

*Equipped with the rotors of an S-61 and a pair of General Electric turbofans, the Sikorsky S-72 was known as the Rotor Systems Research Aircraft.*

*Based on its predecessor, the MB.326, the Aermacchi MB.339A basic/advanced trainer has a redesigned forward fuselage and the ability to carry 4,000lb of weapons.*

*The HAL Kiran II (R-R Viper) is a weapons trainer/COIN aircraft.*

*Developed from license-produced versions of the Folland Gnat, the Hindustan Aeronautics Ajeet Trainer serves only with the Indian Air Force.*

*The size of the Lockheed S-3A Viking made it an eminently suitable aircraft for the carrier on-board delivery role, in which the US-3A now serves.*

# 1977

4,534mph
USA
Pete Knight
North American X-15
Oct 3, 1967

24,325 miles
USA
Archie Old Jr
Boeing B-52B
Jan 18, 1957

354,200ft
USA
Joseph Walker
North American X-15
Aug 22, 1963

833,000lb
USA
Boeing
B-747 200F

53,230lb thrust
USA
Pratt & Whitney
JT9D-59B

**Washington, DC, January 5**
The US Coast Guard is authorized to order 41 Dassault Falcon 20G twin-jets for surveillance use. (→ Apr 1, 1978).

**Washington, DC, January 10**
Alfred Kahn is head of the Civil Aeronautics Board (→ Mar 15).

**USSR, February 7**
The aircraft designer Sergei V Ilyushin dies at the age of 83.

**Woodford, Britain, February 18**
Hawker Siddeley's Coastguarder maritime reconnaissance aircraft, a development of the HS.748, makes its first flight.

**California, February 18**
The converted Boeing 747 space shuttle carrier makes its first flight with the shuttle *Enterprise* on its back, at NASA's Dryden Flight Research Center (→ Aug 13).

**Washington, DC, March 15**
The US Civil Aeronautics Board approves American Airlines plan to offer "super-saver" fares between New York and the West Coast from 35 to 45 per cent lower than standard, effective April 24; United Air Lines and TWA say they will match the discounts, which mean a return fare between New York and Los Angeles/San Francisco from $227 to $268.

**Georgia, March 24**
The Lockheed YC-141B StarLifter, a "stretched" conversion of the C-141A with an air-refueling socket, flies for the first time.

**Wichita, Kansas, March 31**
The 10,000th Beechcraft Bonanza is rolled out of the company's plant, more than 31 years after the prototype's first flight in December 1945.

**London, March 31**
The British government gives the go-ahead for the full development of an airborne early-warning version of the Hawker Siddeley Nimrod (→ Aug 23, 1979).

**London, April 1**
British Airways opens its Shuttle service to Belfast (→ Aug 10, 1978).

**USA, April 14**
US defensive radar chiefs are embarrassed by a Soviet Tupolev Tu-95 Bear which appears south of Charleston, South Carolina, then dives beneath the radar and only turns up again 60 miles from Jacksonville, Florida (→ Oct 10).

**[West] Germany, April 27**
The first USAF squadron of McDonnell Douglas F-15 Eagle fighters to be stationed in Europe arrives at Bitburg.

**Paris, May 21**
Concorde makes a special trip from New York to Paris to mark the 50th anniversary of Charles Lindbergh's historic flight on the same route in the *Spirit of St Louis*; the airliner takes just 3 hours 44 minutes, compared with Lindbergh's time of 33 hours 29 minutes (→ Nov 22).

**Britain, May 26**
The Norman NDN-1 Firecracker two-seat sporting and training aircraft makes its first flight; it is the product of a new company set up by Desmond Norman, one of the two co-founders of the Britten-Norman company of the Isle of Wight, which went bankrupt in 1971 (→ Jan 24, 1979).

**USA, June 13**
President Jimmy Carter gives British airline entrepreneur Freddie Laker the go-ahead for a one-year trial of his proposed low-cost Skytrain service across the North Atlantic (→ Sep 26).

**Alexandria, Virginia, June 16**
German rocket pioneer Wernher von Braun dies.

**Bermuda, June 22**
A few minutes before the expiry of the existing Anglo-US agreement covering air rights between the two countries, the two governments come to a new agreement, known as Bermuda 2.

**Washington, DC, June 30**
President Carter cancels development of the Rockwell B-1 bomber in favor of a cruise missile program.

**Tampa, Florida, July 4**
Patricia Undall and Nan Gaylord arrive from Palm Springs, California, in their Cessna 177 to win the 30th and last annual women's transcontinental air race, which is nicknamed the Powder Puff Derby.

**[West] Germany, July 14**
Lufthansa places the largest order in its history, for five long-distance Boeing 747s and six medium-range "stretched" 727s.

**USSR, August 31**
Alexander Fedotov climbs to 123,524 feet in his Mikoyan Ye-266M, a world record altitude for air-breathing, rather than rocket-powered, aircraft.

**Komaki, Japan, September 16**
The first Mitsubishi F-1 single-seat fighter is handed over to the Japan air self-defense force.

**Atlantic Ocean, October 10**
Two Soviet Tupolev Tu-95 Bears drop metal foil over the destroyer USS *Spruance* in an attempt to confuse US radar.

**London, October 23**
British Caledonian Airways opens daily flights to Houston, Texas.

**San Francisco, October 31**
A Pan Am Boeing 747SP lands after a round-the-world flight over both poles to celebrate the airline's 50th anniversary.

**Kazakhstan, November 1**
A Tupolev Tu-144 supersonic airliner arrives at Alma Ata from Moscow at the end of its first Aeroflot passenger service.

**Istres, France, November 4**
First production Dassault-Breguet-Dornier Alpha Jet twin trainer makes its first flight.

**Memphis, Tennessee, November 9**
Deregulation allows Federal Express to begin use of larger aircraft for their package/cargo.

**London, December 13**
A Concorde service between London and Singapore, jointly operated by British Airways and Singapore Airlines and inaugurated just six days ago, is suspended because the Malaysian government bans the supersonic airliner from its airspace (→ Jan 24, 1979).

## Factfile

World revenue passenger miles: 505,390.834 million
Passengers through Chicago O'Hare: 19.2 million
Passengers through New York (JFK/Newark/LaGuardia): 18.9 million
Passengers through London (Heathrow/Gatwick): 30.0 million
Price of a single coach ticket New York/Los Angeles (April): $206
Price of the cheapest return ticket London/New York: $290
World air freight (ton miles): 70,396.3 million
Average salary of long-haul pilot (US): $52,353
Average salary of cabin crew (US): $14,275
Price of a Boeing 747-100: $42 million
Price of an A300 B4: $24 million
Price of a Boeing 727: $11 million
Price of 1,000 (US) gallons of Jet A1 fuel (average July): $504.45
Average exchange rate: £1= $1.7454

*The Boeing 747 space shuttle carrier lifts off from Edwards Air Force Base to launch the Space Shuttle "Enterprise" on flight tests.* ▶

# President endorses airline deregulation

*Washington, DC, February 23*
Airline deregulation was backed today by President Jimmy Carter and the General Accounting Office (GAO). The President said he would be sending a message to Congress in support of a less tightly regulated airline industry.

Deregulation would substantially change a system under which the federal government has had the responsibilty of assigning routes to airlines and approving ticket prices since 1938. The system has put carriers in the position of competing on routes flown by several airlines, using increased services, amenities, or gimmicks to attract customers.

The White House position follows proposed legislation introduced on February 10 by Senators Edward M Kennedy of Massachusetts and Howard W Cannon of Nevada. Their bill would give carriers the right to start or stop services on routes and would seek to create a competitive fare environment. It would also provide for anti-trust safeguards.

The GAO, which is Congress's investigative agency, proposed that Congress and the Civil Aeronautics Board permit price competition and make it easier for new airlines to get started. The report said that between 1969 and 1974, without government control of fares, domestic airlines could have cut operating costs and saved passengers nearly $2 billion a year. It pointed out that without regulation, first-class and coach-class tickets would probably have been 22 to 52 per cent cheaper.

The GAO said its study did not have answers to all the consequences of deregulation and that transition periods would be needed to avoid "undue disruption of the air transportation system" as the rules were changed (→ Oct 27).

*Airlines face an uncertain future as they come to terms with deregulation.*

# Four aircraft firms form British Aerospace

*Surrey, England, April 29*
From today Britain boasts the largest aerospace company in Europe, employing about 67,000 people and with an expected annual turnover of £800 million. This has come about through the merger of the British Aircraft Corporation, Hawker Siddeley Aviation, Hawker Siddeley Dynamics and Scottish Aviation into a new, nationalized corporation, to be known as British Aerospace (BAe), with headquarters at Weybridge, Surrey.

British Aerospace has been set up under the Labour government's Aircraft and Shipbuilding Act 1977. For the rest of this year, the four component parts will continue to function and trade under their existing names, although owned by BAe. From January 1 next year a new company organization will be implemented, with activities divided between the Aircraft Group and the Dynamics Group. The latter group will be concerned mainly with missiles, including the Sea Skua and Sky Flash.

The chairman of the new corporation's board is Lord Beswick, while F W Page and G R Jefferson are expected to take up appointments as chairman and chief executive of the Aircraft and Dynamics groups respectively. The merged company has wide-ranging activities outside Britain, with subsidiaries in Australia, the Middle East, Scandinavia and the USA. It also has key stakes in European collaboration, such as the SEPECAT Jaguar and Panavia Tornado warplanes, Concorde and the Airbus (→ Jan 1, 1978).

# AWACS is latest military eye in the sky

*With in-flight refueling, AWACS can keep a permanent watch in the sky.*

*Oklahoma City, Okla, March 23*
The first production Boeing E-3A Sentry, the USAF's airborne warning and control system (AWACS) arrived today at Tinker Air Force Base. It is the first of 24 surveillance and aerial battle management aircraft which will fly all over the world in the hands of Tactical Air Command's 552nd Airborne Warning and Control Wing.

The aircraft is based on a modified Boeing 707 with new TF33 turbofan engines. It is easily recognized by its 30-foot diameter rotating radar which looks like a giant frisbee mounted above the rear fuselage. The E-3A is equipped with Westinghouse AN/APY-1 pulse-doppler look-down radar, with high and low-level search capability over land or water. This will

*Nothing in the sky can elude them.*

prevent hostile aircraft avoiding detection by the tactic of hugging the surface of the Earth, in the blind spot of ground-based or ship-borne radar (→ Mar 10, 1979).

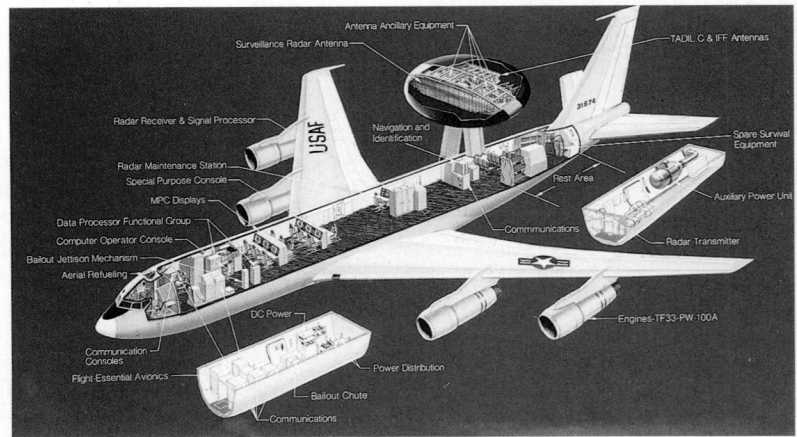

*A rest area fitted with bunkbeds is provided at the rear of the E-3A's cabin.*

# Two 747 Jumbo Jets collide at Tenerife: 575 dead

*The horrific scene after the world fell apart for those aboard the two 747s.*

*Both jets were destroyed by impact, and most victims died in the fire.*

*Tenerife, Canary Islands, March 27*
"There it is ... look at the sonofabitch, the goddam sonofabitch, it's there! Get the hell outta here!" These were the last words today from the cockpit of a Pan Am 747, four seconds before it was struck by the full force of a KLM 747 speeding at 160mph down the runway of Los Rodeos airport. Of the 637 aboard both aircraft 575 were killed, including everyone on the KLM Jumbo. It is the worst accident in aviation history.

The irony is that neither aircraft was supposed to be at this small airport at all. Both had been diverted after a terrorist bomb had gone off at Las Palmas on the neighboring island of Gran Canaria, and were preparing to make the short hop to their original destination when tragedy struck. Los Rodeos was in a state of some chaos at the time owing to thick fog and the unusual amount of traffic. At around 5.40pm the control tower – where only one controller spoke English – requested Pan Am Flight 1736 and KLM Flight 4805 to proceed to the main runway.

Halfway down the runway, the Pan Am aircraft was supposed to take slip runway C3 in order to clear the main runway. For reasons as yet unclear, the 747 taxied toward the more distant slip runway C4. Meanwhile, despite much radio interference, the KLM pilot believed he had been cleared for take-off. He applied full thrust and the 350-ton airliner hurtled down the runway, straight at the Pan Am Jumbo taxiing across its path.

## Thunderbolt II carries death into the skies

*Myrtle Beach, SC, May 1*
Named the Thunderbolt II in honor of its famed predecessor, the P-47 Thunderbolt made by Republic Aviation, the Fairchild Republic A-10A entered service with the USAF's 354th Tactical Fighter Wing here today. A formal ceremony marking the event will be held at this South Carolina airbase on June 10. Noted for its devastating firepower, which comprises the hardest-hitting aircraft gun in history and up to ten anti-armor missiles, the A-10A is designed to destroy enemy tanks and other hard-skinned battlefield targets. It is also designed to withstand hostile gunfire.

## XV-15 flight rewards 25 years hard work

*Fort Worth, Texas, May 3*
Bell Helicopters' XV-15 tilt-rotor aircraft, which has been under development since 1951 for NASA and the US Army, made its first hovering flight today at the company's Arlington Flight Research Center here. The XV-15 looks like a conventional two-seater, high-winged airplane, except for the swivelling 1,550-hp Lycoming LTC1K-4K turboshaft engines mounted at the wingtips. These drive 25-foot propeller/rotors, which can swivel from the horizontal position to give the speed of an airplane, to the upright, which gives the vertical lift and maneuverability of a helicopter.

*The Thunderbolt II is not a fast airplane, but it packs a devastating punch.*

*The wings of the XV-15 span 35 feet, and have propeller/rotors at the tip.*

# Pedaling pilot takes off

*Cyclist-pilot Bryan Allen at the Condor's controls on an earlier trial flight.*

*Shafter, California, August 23*
The £50,000 Kremer prize for man-powered flight has been won at last. British industrialist Henry Kremer originally offered £5,000 over 15 years ago, for a flight by a human-powered airplane on a figure-of-eight course around two points at least half a mile apart.

Today's flight, at Shafter airport, was by cyclist Bryan Allen, pedaling the Gossamer Condor designed by Dr Paul B MacCready. The flimsy airplane has a wingspan of 97 feet, but it is ultra-lightweight. In flight, the pedals turn a large pusher propeller, while a stabilizer is carried on a long boom in front.

Dr MacCready, a well-known sailplane designer, is now working on his next man-powered airplane (MPA). It will be even lighter than the Gossamer Condor through the use of carbon fiber material. Today Gossamer Condor was in the sky for about six minutes, but MacCready is certain an MPA could stay up longer. For example, he believes one could be pedaled across the English Channel (→ Jun 5, 1979).

# Space shuttle glides home for first time

*California, August 13*
The prototype US space shuttle *Enterprise* glided to Earth today after separating from a specially modified Boeing 747 "motherplane" and landed smoothly on a dry lake bed in the Mojave Desert. Today's flight, from Edwards Air Force Base, was a major accomplishment in NASA's $6.9 billion shuttle development project. It showed that the unpowered shuttle can be brought to Earth safely after it leaves orbit because of the glide and braking characteristics of its 75-foot span wing and flat-bottomed fuselage.

Explosive charges at three connection points separated the shuttle from the 747 at 24,100 feet and the descent, by pilots Fred W Haise, Jr, and USAF Lieutenant-Colonel C Gordon Fullerton, lasted five and a half minutes. This was the sixth time that the 747, with the carrying gear on its upper fuselage and two additional small vertical stabilizers on the horizontal stabilizer, had taken to the air with the 75-ton, 122-foot-long *Enterprise*. On the first five flights the stability and handling of the two vehicles combined was established and procedures for separation checked.

NASA is planning a fleet of five shuttles – excluding *Enterprise* – which in the 1980s could be making weekly trips to position and service satellites, as well as moving people and supplies to orbiting space laboratories (→ Apr 14, 1981).

*According to plan, "Enterprise" is freed from its "motherplane" at 24,100 feet.*

# Three-way military operation takes hijackers by surprise in Africa

*Mogadishu, Somalia, October 17*
Eighty-six hostages aboard a hijacked Lufthansa Boeing 737 were freed today when the aircraft was stormed by West German commandos. With the aid of stun grenades supplied by Britain's élite SAS, troops of the GSG-9, a recently formed anti-terrorism unit, rushed the 737 and killed four German terrorists, two men and two women of the Red Army Faction.

Apart from one injured soldier, the only casualty in the hijacking and rescue was pilot Captain Jürgen Schumann. The hijackers seized the airplane on a flight from Majorca to Frankfurt last week. Before arriving in Somalia the crew had been forced to fly to Rome, Cyprus, Bahrain, Dubai, and then South Yemen. They shot Captain Schumann in Aden.

*Captain Jürgen Schumann is threatened with a gun; he was later murdered.*

# Committee says yes to deregulation bill

*Washington, DC, October 27*
President Jimmy Carter has hailed today's decision by the Senate Commerce Committee to give the green light to an airline deregulation bill. The president sees this as a big breakthrough in his administration's efforts to bring regulations more into line with the needs of the American traveling public.

The law would allow routes to change and fares to be altered without approval from the Civil Aeronautics Board, and give incentives for airlines to maintain services to small communities. Airlines with well-established routes could protect them from competition for a limited period. Carriers would have to give two months' notice before ending a service (→ Oct 24, 1978).

# Freddie Laker toasts launch of low-cost Skytrain

*Sussex, England, September 26*

At 5pm today, dead on time, the Laker Airways DC-10 *Eastern Belle* left London's Gatwick Airport for New York. It marked the successful conclusion of a six-year battle by owner Freddie Laker to offer cheap fares on long-distance routes, in the face of opposition from his giant rivals.

Known as Skytrain, the no-frills Laker service costs passengers only £59 ($102) for a one-way ticket, or about $236 for a round-trip, compared with $626 for a normal economy ticket offered by Laker's rivals – prior to today. Now, having lost the fight to stop Laker despite years of court action, the major, scheduled airlines, are suddenly offering

*Hero of the skies: Laker is making air travel affordable for young people.*

their own cut-price fares, which are just a few dollars higher than Laker's. Laker's tickets are sold on a first-come, first-served basis on the day of departure only. On this first service, hundreds of passengers queued for up to 48 hours to buy one of the 345 seats available. The return flight from New York tomorrow is believed to be fully booked. It remains to be seen if Laker can fill his aircraft for each flight.

Freddie Laker has always been the champion of the less affluent traveler, who would probably not be able to fly at all except for lower fares. He may be hated by the big airlines, but he is loved by his passengers, who see him as champion of the underdog (→ Jun 3, 1978).

## Europe's Airbus finds foothold in the US

*New York, November 18*

Eastern Air Lines today began operating the first of four leased European Airbus A300B2 airliners. Today's flight from Newark, New Jersey, to Miami marks the first serious flirtation by a major US carrier – Eastern is the second largest airline in the world, by passenger volume – with a foreign manufacturer of transports. If the planned six-month trial period and evaluation is a success, Eastern says it

may buy 19 aircraft from the makers Airbus Industrie. Privately, sources at Eastern say that as many as 50 A300Bs could be purchased over the next five years. Eastern is interested in the A300B because of its low fuel consumption, its size (200-250 passenger seats) and quiet engines. The latter may be especially important given the advent of new, stringent regulations introduced by the Federal Aviation Administration (→ Apr 6, 1978).

## Two Concordes arrive at last in New York

*New York, November 22*

Two Concorde supersonic airliners arrived at John F Kennedy International Airport today to start what is officially a 16-month test of their suitability to operate here.

The two airplanes, one each from British Airways and Air France, arrived following a 19-month delay caused by protesters who invoked local anti-noise ordinances. A New York court ruled against the objectors last month after sensitive noise-measuring instruments showed that a Boeing 707 was a bit louder than Concorde and a Boeing 727 was a

bit quieter. Small groups of pickets at the entrances to JFK were the only evidence of the previously vociferous anti-Concorde campaign.

Air France plans one flight a day from Paris while British Airways will operate from Heathrow twice a week, building to daily flights by January next year. This is the route for which Concorde was built: high-density traffic with business travelers who will pay a premium for speed, completely the opposite trend to Skytrain, where price is of the essence. It remains to be seen which flourishes (→ Aug 10, 1978).

*A European triumph: the Airbus flying in the colors of Eastern Air Lines.*

*Air France (l) and British Airways Concordes finally reached JFK airport!*

The Space Shuttle Orbiter made its first flight on a converted Boeing 747 from the NASA Dryden Research Facility at Edwards AFB, California.

Quickie Enterprises Q-2 is a popular homebuilt of canard (tail first) layout.

A SOCATA Rallye 235A Agricole, with spraybar and chemical hopper.

Only a single example was built of a Britten-Norman BN.2 Islander fitted with Dowty Rotol ducted propellers (driven by the original piston engines).

Rockwell's Sabre 65 incorporated a supercritical wing, Garrett TFE731 fan engines and increased tailplane area. It offered transcontinental range.

Hundreds of Brazil's Embraer EMB-110 Bandeirante twin-turboprop commuter aircraft are in service around the world, each seating up to 21 people.

First of a family of SOCATA lightplanes was the TB 10 Tobago 4/5-seater which, along with the TB 9 Tampico, has become a popular club aircraft.

With space for a further three passengers, the Cessna 550 Citation II offers a longer cabin (20ft 11in) than the Model 500 Citation I (17ft 6in).

This clipped-wing version of the Pitts Special was intended to have a higher rate of roll than the original (and very popular) S-2 model.

Italy's Procaer F.15F lightplane with one-piece moulded canopy.

The Ball-Bartoe Jet Wing single-seat blown-wing research aircraft.

*After several years of redesign Sukhoi's T-10 prototypes emerged as the Su-27, probably the best all-round fighter. Engines remained twin D-30F6 turbofans.*

*Modified Dassault Falcon 20s serve with the United States Coast Guard as the HU-25A Guardian surveillance aircraft. Engines are Garrett ATF3-6s.*

*Companion to the General Dynamics F-16A Fighting Falcon is the combat capable two-seat F-16B trainer. The added rear seat reduces internal fuel.*

*The Antonov An-72 STOL multi-role twin-turbofan transport.*

*The German RFB AWI-2 Fantrainer was intended for military use.*

*The Bell 301 was an attack helicopter that failed to enter production, having lost out to the rival Hughes (later McDonnell Douglas) YAH-64A Apache.*

*The TFE731-powered CASA-101 Aviojet is the Spanish Air Force's primary jet trainer but it can also fulfil a close support, reconnaissance or ECM role.*

*The Hindustan Aeronautics HPT-32 trainer serves only the Indian AF.*

*The NDN.1 Firecracker trainer was an unsuccessful RAF candidate.*

*One of the new breed of Soviet combat aircraft, the MiG-29 fighter proved to have a generally trouble-free development and entered service in 1983.*

*The Bell XV-15 combined the wing of an aeroplane with tilting proprotors, and was flown jointly and very successfully by Bell, NASA and the US Army.*

*Sperry converted retired F-102 interceptors to PGM-102 target drones, and they were the first such USAF conversion to have no provision for a pilot.*

# 1978

4,534mph
USA
Pete Knight
North American X-15
Oct 3, 1967

24,325 miles
USA
Archie Old Jr
Boeing B-52B
Jan 18, 1957

354,200ft
USA
Joseph Walker
North American X-15
Aug 22, 1963

833,000lb
USA
Boeing
B-747 200F

53,330lb thrust
USA
Pratt & Whitney
JT9D-7Q1

**Bombay, India, January 1**
An Air India Boeing 747 explodes in mid-air, killing 213.

**Britain, January 1**
British Aerospace takes control of the assets and business of British Aircraft Corporation, Hawker Siddeley Aviation, Hawker Siddeley Dynamics and Scottish Aviation; the new corporation was established on April 29 last year, but the four constituent companies have continued to trade under their original names (→ Jul 23, 1979).

**USA, January 11**
The American Jet Industries' Hustler executive transport makes its first flight.

**Somerset, England, January 26**
The first Royal Navy unit equipped with the Westland Lynx helicopter, the n° 702 Naval Air Squadron, is commissioned at the Yeovilton Royal Naval Air Station (→ Sep 28).

**London, January 31**
Britain signs a contract with Boeing Vertol for 30 CH-47 Chinook helicopters for the RAF.

**USA, April 4**
Pan Am orders $500 million worth of Lockheed L-1011-500 TriStars (→ May 7, 1979).

**Miami, Florida, April 6**
Eastern Air Lines orders 25 Airbus A300B4 airliners (→ Jul 7).

**Reno, Nevada, May 14**
William "Bill" Powell Lear, founder of the Learjet Corporation, dies of leukemia (→ Jan 1, 1981).

**USSR, June 1**
The Tupolev Tu-144 supersonic airliner is withdrawn from service with Aeroflot in the wake of a fatal crash involving a Tu-144 which was not in airline service.

**London, June 3**
Freddie Laker is knighted for services to aviation in the Queen's Birthday Honours (→ Oct 29).

**London, June 9**
British Caledonian and British Airways Helicopters open a helicopter service linking Heathrow and Gatwick airports.

**Britain and Romania, June 15**
British Aerospace (BAe) comes to an agreement with Grupul Aeronautic Bucuresti for the construction of 80 BAe (formerly BAC) One-Eleven airliners under license in Romania.

**France, June 28**
The French navy receives the first of an order for 71 Dassault-Breguet Super Etendard carrier-based strike aircraft.

**Munich, July 7**
The development of the Airbus A310 is launched; the improved aerodynamics of the wing and the use of composite materials are designed to produce a more economical airliner (→ Aug 31).

**London, July 11**
The British government approves full development of the HS.146 airliner, which was unveiled five years ago; it is now known as the BAe 146 (→ Sep 3, 1981).

**Europe, July**
Britain, France, Italy and West Germany agree to develop a new range of helicopters for anti-tank, transport and reconnaissance roles.

**London, August 10**
British Airways carries the 100,000th passenger to fly on Concorde (→ Sep 20).

**USA and Italy, August 14**
Aeritalia signs a contract to become a partner with Boeing in the development of the Model 767 wide-bodied jet (→ Dec 10, 1979).

**Georgia, USA, September 1**
American Jet Industries acquires the Grumman American Corp and changes its name to the Gulfstream American Corporation.

**Zimbabwe [Rhodesia], Sep 3**
An Air Rhodesia Viscount carrying 56 passengers is shot down by a Soviet-made SAM-7 missile launched by members of Joshua Nkomo's Patriotic Front, near Lake Kariba; ten of the 18 survivors are shot dead by the guerrillas, who claim that the airplane was carrying armed government troops.

**France, September 13**
The Aérospatiale AS 332 Super Puma helicopter makes its first flight; based on the Puma, it is fitted with twin Turbomeca Makila 1A turbines.

**Paris, September 20**
Air France extends its Concorde route to Washington, DC, as far as Mexico City (→ Jan 13, 1979).

**USSR, October 2**
Aeroflot begins route-proving trials with the Ilyushin Il-86 on its route between Moscow and Mineralnye Vody (→ Dec 26, 1980).

**USA, October 17**
TWA announces an order worth $300 million for 10 Boeing 727-200s and 3 long-range 747SPs, for delivery in 1980.

**New York, October 29**
A Mooney 201 sets a new non-stop record as the first single engined plane to fly from North America to Denmark direct. The 2,762 miles took 13 hrs and 13 min.

**Paris, November 1**
Air France opens a business-class service on its to New York.

**St Louis, Mo, November 9**
The McDonnell Douglas YAV-8B Harrier II prototype, an improved version of the British Aerospace Harrier jump jet, makes its first flight (→ Jun 25, 1981).

**Sri Lanka, November 16**
An Icelandic Airways DC-8 crashes, killing 202.

**Birmingham, England, Nov 26**
Tour operator Horizon Travel establishes its own airline, Orion Airways, to fly inclusive-tour holiday-makers out of East Midlands airport (→ May 5, 1979).

**London, November 27**
In the wake of the success of his Skytrain service to New York, Sir Freddie Laker opens a new low-cost service to Los Angeles, using DC-10s (→ Apr 10, 1979).

**Dallas, Texas, December 11**
Deregulation allows expansion for Southwest Airlines. New Orleans is first city outside of Texas to be served (→ Dec 3, 1980).

---

*McDonnell Douglas's F-15 Eagle was designed as an air superiority fighter, but can be developed to fly ground attack missions.* ▶

## Factfile

World revenue passenger miles: 581,854.104 million
Passengers through Chicago O'Hare: 21.5 million
Passengers through New York (JFK/Newark/LaGuardia): 21.2 million
Passengers through London (Heathrow/Gatwick): 34.3 million
Price of a single coach ticket New York/Los Angeles (April): $213
Price of the cheapest return ticket London/New York: $256
World air freight (ton miles): 78,603.4 million
Average salary of long-haul pilot (US): $56,810
Average salary of cabin crew (US): $16,300
Price of a Boeing 747-100: $46 million
Price of an A300 B4: $27 million
Price of a Boeing 727: $12 million
Price of 1,000 (US) gallons of Jet A1 fuel (average July): $483.60
Average exchange rate: £1 = $1.9197

# Sandra Scott is first woman in SAC crew

*California, March 23*

The US Air Force had a notable "first" today when Sandra M Scott became the first woman pilot to fly on alert duty in Strategic Air Command. Captain Scott is temporarily assigned to the 904th Air Refueling Squadron, which flies KC-135 tankers from Mather Air Force Base. The USAF has recently launched a test program to select six enlisted women as KC-135 refueling operators and ten others as C-141 flight engineers. Also this month another 40 USAF woman officers and enlisted women began training as members of crews operating Titan II intercontinental ballistic missiles.

*Captain Scott (l) and First Lt Mary Livingston inspect a T-38 jet trainer.*

# Soviet pilot forces down wayward 707

*USSR, April 20*

A Korean Air Lines 707 has crash-landed on a frozen lake in a snow-covered forest region of the USSR after being strafed by a Soviet MiG fighter. It is known that a Japanese and a South Korean were killed by the fighter and 13 others wounded.

Flying from Paris, the 707 had strayed way off course, ending up near the highly secret Soviet Kola Peninsula military area. After the attack, the airplane dropped from 30,000 feet to 6,000 feet. The pilots regained control and flew it on for 90 minutes. Once down, helicopters arrived to lift the wounded to hospital, while the others have been taken by road to Kem.

# US Coast Guard plumps for the Falcon 20

*The US Coast Guard has placed an order for 41 French Falcon 20G jets.*

*USA, April 1*

The US Coast Guard's (USCG) HU-25 Guardian prototype was delivered to the service today. The Guardian, which made its first flight on November 28 last year, is a version of the Dassault-Breguet Mystère 20 business jet, sold in the US as the Falcon 20 by the Falcon Jet Corporation. The USCG model is designated Falcon G.

The USCG has been looking for a number of years for an aircraft to replace its Grumman HU-16 Albatross amphibians. It evaluated the Grumman Gulfstream I, IAI Westwind 1123, Cessna Citation I, and looked at the Rockwell Sabre 75A before opting for the HU-25.

The Guardian will have provisions for carrying four stretchers, a drop hatch in the fuselage and four points to carry supply or rescue packs. It will also have four points on the wings for sensors or other loads (→ Apr 15, 1981).

# Microlight crosses the English Channel

*Calais, France, May 5*

Captain Matthew Webb started the fashion back in 1875 when he swam it. Blériot hit the headlines when he flew it in 1909; since then, hundreds have crossed the narrow seas between England and France in every conceivable form of transport.

The growing popularity of hang-gliding made it inevitable that sooner or later someone would seek to fly from England to France. Today it was Englishman Dave Cook who landed here – appropriately, on Blériot Beach – after a flight lasting just over an hour. Cook had waited several days for the right wind to take his microlight, a powered VJ-23 hang-glider, from the beach at Walmer Castle, Kent.

With a rescue boat below threatening to break up as it raced to keep up with him, Cook maintained a steady altitude of 300 feet for most of the journey. The biggest hazard he faced – apart from the possibility of running out of fuel – was losing contact with support boat *African Queen* in the choppy seas.

Approaching France, Cook, now seriously worried about his fuel, banked quickly to starboard and made a long descent to the coast from three and a half miles out. Despite running low, the 9-hp engine consumed less than a quarter of the fuel used by Blériot.

# Cessna family grows with the launch of the uprated Citation jet

*Cessna's twin-jet Citation II has a greater range than its predecessor.*

*Wichita, Kansas, March 31*

The new Cessna Citation II was awarded its certificate of airworthiness today, 14 months after it first flew. Compared with the Citation I, the II has undergone several modifications. The fuselage has been stretched to accommodate another two passengers. Its wingspan has also been extended by four and a half feet, which increases its range and fuel-carrying capacity. Maximum take-off weight is 5.7 tons.

The Model 550 has a cruising speed of 420mph and can fly at an altitude of 41,000 feet. As with the Model 500, Cessna also provides a version for a single pilot. Costing under $1 million, the twin-jet Citation II is an affordable business jet, plain but comfortable.

# US balloon is the first to cross Atlantic

*Evreux, France, August 17*
The first Atlantic crossing by balloon ended in triumph for three US crewmen today, 5 days 17 hours 6 minutes after they lifted off from Presque Isle, Maine. The balloonists had hoped to touch down, like Charles Lindbergh in 1927, at Paris's Le Bourget airport, and had jettisoned much of their equipment over the French countryside.

Hundreds had followed their balloon *Double Eagle II* since it crossed the French coast, and the roads here were jammed for a good half hour before the crew finally hung the Stars and Stripes and the French tricolor from the gondola and came in to land gently in a field. Captain Ben Abruzzo, 48, said that they were beginning to run short of food.

*Descending at the end of the flight.*

# Three's company, French crews insist

*Paris, May 2*
The pilots and technical staff of Air France are refusing to accept a cockpit crew of two for the Boeing 737. Even small jets have traditionally carried three crew, including a flight engineer. The size of crews is certain to be an issue when Air France decides whether to buy 13 Boeing 737s. For the unions, it is not just a matter of jobs, but also of safety. The management, on the other hand, insist that as other airlines have reduced the crew to two pilots, Air France cannot afford to be the exception. US carriers have the advantage of having already resolved a similar dispute. Henceforth three in the cockpit will seem uneconomical.

# Boeing's answer to Airbus gets a boost

*Seattle, July 14*
An order from United Air Lines for 30 Boeing 767 wide-body, twin-engined transports has launched the new jet, of which Boeing will now start full-scale development and production.

The 767 closely resembles the successful European Airbus A310, but with a bigger wing and narrower cabin. Now that it has a firm future there is little doubt it will be bought by British Airways (BA), which favors US airplanes. BA has sought permission to buy two other Boeings, the 737 (instead of the British 1-11) and the projected 757. It has shown no interest in the British Aerospace 146, which was launched three days ago (→Aug 14).

# Violence flares at new Tokyo airport

*Tokyo, May 22*
A huge pall of black smoke greeted the first passenger flight to land at Tokyo's Narita airport today when thousands of environmental demonstrators burned motor tires in protest at the building of the airport. A huge balloon was flown at the end of the runway in an attempt to prevent landings. Security is awesome: the first passengers to pass through the immigration hall were greeted by thousands of riot police in black protective clothing, armed with batons and shields. Visitors are barred; so are friends and relatives. Airport staff, aircrews and passengers are searched twice.

*A protestor at Narita is engulfed in a blaze caused by his own firebomb.*

# France's up-to-the-minute Mirage 2000 has an electronic brain

*The Mirage 2000's fly-by-wire flight controls make it highly agile. It can climb to 50,000 feet in just 4 minutes.*

*Istres, France, March 10*
The Mirage 2000, the latest high-tech fighter from Dassault, made its first flight today in the hands of test pilot Jean Coureau. The delta-winged, single-engined jet, which is already being rated by many experts as the best combat aircraft of its generation, is the first French aircraft to be equipped with electronic "fly-by-wire" controls.

The pilot is no longer mechanically connected to the elevons and rudder. Although these surfaces are still activated by hydraulic power units, the nerves which prompt them are electric signals triggered by the stick and rudder pedals.

Electronic control allows a faster response to uncommanded divergences from an aircraft's flight path as, for example, in the case of flying in turbulence. There is another advantage: the removal of mechanical controls reduces the weight of the aircraft. The 2000 is powered by a SNECMA M53 bypass turbojet.

# Collision over San Diego: 144 die

*San Diego, September 25*
Bodies and flaming debris rained on to houses three miles from San Diego's Lindbergh Airport today following the mid-air collision of a Pacific Southwest Boeing 727 and a two-seat Cessna light aircraft.

The death toll of 144 makes this the worst accident in US aviation history. All of the 136 passengers and crew in the airliner, which was coming in to land, and the instructor pilot and student in the Cessna, perished. The other deaths were on the ground, caused by falling wreckage and fires started when the 727 tore through part of a residential neighborhood near the airport.

Both pilots had acknowledged a warning from air traffic controllers that they were on a collision course; but the Cessna took no action to avoid the 727, while the airliner's pilots were looking at another airplane. The Cessna hit the starboard

*The stricken 727's last moments, snapped by an amateur photographer.*

wing of the 727, which burst into flames. A witness said that the pilots apparently tried to pull the 727 up, but the wing began to break up and the airliner plummeted to the ground. One body crashed through the windshield of a car carrying a mother and daughter, who were treated for minor injuries and shock. Police have arrested 22 people at the crash site for looting and interfering with rescue efforts.

## US airlines set for era of deregulation

## US airlines set for era of deregulation

*Washington, DC, October 24*
United, Eastern, and American headed the 20 airlines represented at the Civil Aeronautics Board (CAB) today. They were applying to CAB chairman Alfred E Kahn and colleagues for routes which are now up for grabs following President Carter's signature of the bill deregulating the US airline industry. Extensive hearings prior to airline certification are no longer required; airlines can be formed by showing they are "fit, willing, and able". Until 1983, airlines will be able to cut fares by up to 50 per cent without federal approval (→ Jan 7, 1980).

## Aviation designer Messerschmitt dies

*Munich, September 15*
Dr Willy Messerschmitt died in hospital here today after an operation; he was 80. Messerschmitt began gliding (the only flying then permitted in Germany) in 1922. He went on to head several companies, culminating in the Bayerische Flugzeugwerke (BFW), at Augsburg, where the prototype of his Bf 109 fighter, one of the best aircraft of the Second World War, flew for the first time in 1935.

## Price war on Atlantic routes hits Sabena

*Brussels, June 30*
Belgian airline Sabena has been experiencing serious financial difficulties, partly due to cut-throat competition on Europe/New York routes. For years it has been attempting to gain other US destinations without success. The latest round of discussions paid off today when it began a service to Atlanta, Georgia. The new route will be flown by its Boeing 707-320Cs, as the airline's two 747s are fully occupied on its routes to New York and Zaïre. With the director general and president both about to retire, new managers are being appointed and extra capital raised.

*CAB chairman Alfred E Kahn.*

## Sea Harrier, navy version of British jump jet, makes first flight

*Surrey, England, August 20*
Today the first of 34 Sea Harrier FRS.1 jump jet multirole fighters for the Royal Navy made its first flight at the former Hawker Siddeley (now British Aerospace) airfield at Dunsfold. It should have flown in July last year, but has been delayed by industrial unrest and other non-technical factors.

Ordered in 1975, the Sea Harrier will equip squadrons embarked in "through-deck cruisers" – small 15,000-ton carriers. Two of these are being built and a third is expected to be ordered. The FRS.1 has radar and will carry Sidewinder air-to-air missiles as well as a range of other ordnance. The manufacturers hope the aircraft will find export customers (→ Jun 18, 1979).

*Prof Dr Willy Messerschmitt (l).*

*The radar-equipped Sea Harrier jump jet ordered by Britain's Royal Navy.*

# BA 'Club Class' hits back against Laker

*London, October 29*

British Airways (BA) has struck a blow against any airline likely to reduce its revenues by offering very cheap, no-frills fares, with Laker's Skytrain service in particular in its gunsights. From today, BA passengers paying the full economy class fare on transatlantic flights can fly in a new "Club Class".

This provides for a three-class system similar to that in the US. First class remains as before, but to a new "Discount" economy class is added "Club". At the airport of departure Club passengers will enjoy their own check-ins. They have wider seat-spacing, and receive free drinks, a choice from a special menu, and entertainment. They can also take advantage of exchange services and stopovers. In another move to protect its market share, BA has reached agreement with IATA to slash prices on the airline's 18 European services from next month (→ Nov 27).

*Canadair is proposing a launch price of $4 million for the twin-jet Challenger.*

# Canadair pins its hopes on the Challenger

*Montreal, November 8*

The Canadair Challenger executive jet completed its first flight today, landing at Cartierville airport, near here, after 50 minutes in the air. The prototype was structurally complete in the spring, and should have been in the air by the summer, but ground testing delayed its maiden flight until now.

Ironically, this aircraft which will compete with US business jets should have been a Learjet. The Challenger was designed by "Bill" Lear who sold exclusive production rights to Canadair in 1976. Two 7,500 lb Textron Lycoming ALF-502 turbofans on the rear fuselage give a range of 3,170 miles and a speed of Mach 0.8.

It is a relatively wide-bodied aircraft in which people can stand up and walk about. The cabin space allows all sorts of internal arrangements including luxurious seating for 11 passengers.

# Britain returns to the Airbus program

*London, August 31*

Tonight the British government has announced that it has rejoined the Airbus consortium, with a 20 per cent share and a voting seat on the board. British Aerospace (BAe) will build the wings for the new A310 and will be able to participate in future Airbus programs.

Britain was a full member of Airbus at its inception in 1967, but for some reason thought the original product, the A300B, would not sell, and pulled out. Showing great commercial courage, Hawker Siddeley (now part of BAe) joined the project and put its own money into building the wings for the A300B.

The British industry has had to overcome an almost universal reluctance among politicians to get involved – they still regard the Airbus venture as doubtful. BAe has also had to convince its Airbus partners of Britain's good faith, despite British Airways's preference for US aircraft (→ Mar 14, 1979).

# Navy's new Hornet fighter packs a sting

*The Hornet is to replace the F-4 Phantom and A-7 Corsair in US Navy.*

*St Louis, Missouri, November 18*

Jack Krings, chief engineering test pilot of McDonnell Aircraft, today made a successful 50-minute flight in the YF-18. Named Hornet, the white-painted prototype even has symbolic hornets painted on it. The US Navy launched the VFAX program in 1974 to find a low-cost aircraft to replace the F-4 fighter and A-7 Corsair attack aircraft aboard its carriers. Congress directed it to choose one of the USAF light fighters as a basis, and it picked the McDonnell Douglas sub-mission of a development of the Northrop YF-17. The YF-18 has a wider fuselage to accomodate a bigger radar, greater fuel capacity, a larger wing, carrier equipment and 16,000-lb General Electric F404 turbofans instead of YJ101 turbojets.

Northrop becomes an associate contractor, responsible for the rear fuselage and tail. Eleven development aircraft, one of which will be a two-seater, are being built. McDonnell Douglas is hoping for good export sales (→ Oct 20, 1981).

# First solar-powered airplane rises in sky

*Hampshire, England, December 19*

Piloted by David Williams, *Solar One* has just made a brief hop at Lasham gliding airfield. Designed in London by Freddie To, *Solar One* is similar to a glider, with a wingspan of 68 feet, but above the nose is a strut carrying a propeller. This is driven by a 1-hp electric motor, which is powered by solar cells fitted above the wing.

Today's flight is believed to be the first by any solar-powered airplane. Another, the Solar Riser biplane, has been built in California by Larry Mauro, but it is not yet ready. Another is being built by Dr Paul B MacCready (→ Aug 7, 1980).

**A Canadian tourist, into his third day of queueing for a cheap flight home from London aboard Freddie Laker's Skytrain, takes a well-earned nap.**

*Powered by a trio of Rolls-Royce RB.211 turbofans, the tell-tale feature of the extended-range Lockheed L-1011-500 TriStar is its shortened fuselage.*

*NASA's Quiet Short-Haul Research Aircraft was a DHC C-8A Buffalo, rebuilt by Boeing with upper-surface blowing from four YF102 turbofans.*

*Rockwell's Sabreliner 80A, based on the earlier Model 75, had a Raisbeck supercritical wing and other changes, known as the Mark Five system.*

*The Zlin 142 two-seat trainer and touring aircraft from Czechoslovakia is a higher powered version of the Zlin 42M, fully stressed for all aerobatics.*

*Cessna's 303 Crusader, at first only a four-seater, was introduced as a fast and comfortable successor to the popular Cessna 310 with up to six seats.*

*A commercial development of the ill-starred Peregrine military jet trainer, the American Jet Industries Model 400 Hustler too, failed to find customers.*

*Designed by William P Lear of Learjet fame, the Canadair CL-600 Challenger was the base model of the company's successful line of executive jets.*

*Powered by two 310hp Lycoming TIO-540 piston engines and with a fixed tricycle landing gear, the General Avia F.600 Canguro had room for ten.*

*Mitsubishi's MU-300 Diamond I executive jet, initially powered by two JT15D-4s, gave a poor performance and received several changes of engine.*

The McDonnell Douglas F/A-18 Hornet was developed from the Northrop YF-17, and can perform both air combat and attack missions with ease.

The Fouga 90A was intended as a successor to the CM.170 Magister with a raised rear (instructor) cockpit, but it failed to gain any production orders.

Switzerland's PT6 powered, fully aerobatic, Pilatus PC-7 Turbo Trainer is fitted with six underwing hardpoints and can carry over 2,000lb of stores.

The Royal Navy's latest strike fighter is BAe's Sea Harrier FRS.1, designed to serve aboard the "Invincible" class carriers, requiring vertical landings.

The Mirage 2000 air superiority fighter is the latest in a long line of classic delta-winged designs from Dassault, a great improvement on the Mirage III.

Yugoslavia's SOKO G-4 Super Galeb, which means "seagull", is an armed trainer powered by a single Rolls-Royce Viper turbojet uprated to 4,000lb.

The McDonnell Douglas YAV-8B Harrier II prototype is a second-generation V/STOL attack aircraft used by the US Marines in a close air support role.

There is room for 19 passengers inside Aérospatiale's AS.332 Super Puma, a stretched version of the AS.330 equipped with higher-powered engines.

# 1979

**France, January 1**
The French government takes a 21 per cent interest in Dassault-Breguet.

**London, January 24**
British Airways and Singapore Airlines' London/Singapore Concorde service, suspended because of political difficulties, reopens (→ Nov 1, 1980).

**Isle of Wight, England, Jan 24**
Switzerland's Pilatus Aircraft takes over British-based Britten-Norman (Bembridge) Ltd; the new subsidiary company is called Pilatus Britten-Norman Ltd.

**Belgium, January 26**
The first European-built General Dynamics F-16 Fighting Falcons go into service, with the Belgian air force (→ Jul 21, 1980).

**London, February 12**
Queen Elizabeth II and Prince Philip, the Duke of Edinburgh, fly by Concorde to Kuwait at the start of a three-week royal tour of the Middle East (→ Sep 21).

**Kitty Hawk, NC, February 21**
Former astronaut Neil Armstrong climbs to 50,000 feet in just over 12 minutes in a Gates Learjet Longhorn 28, breaking five world records for business jets (→ Apr 19).

**London, March 2**
British Airways places an order for 19 Boeing 757 narrow-body airliners (→ Mar 23).

**France, March 9**
Dassault-Breguet's Mirage 4000 delta-wing multi-role combat aircraft makes its first flight; a bigger twin-engined development of the Mirage 2000, it is equipped with canard foreplanes and, like its predecessor, has "fly-by-wire" control.

**Riyadh, March 10**
Two USAF E-3A Sentry AWACS aircraft arrive to monitor current fighting between North and South Yemen (→ Dec 12, 1980).

**Switzerland, March 14**
Swissair orders ten Airbus A310s with options on ten more (→ Apr 2).

**Seattle, March 23**
Boeing orders its Model 757 into production (→ Nov 12, 1980).

**Sydney, March 25**
Qantas flies its last Boeing 707 service and becomes the world's only airline with a fleet entirely made up of 747s.

**[West] Germany, April 2**
Lufthansa orders 25 Airbus A310s with options on 25 more (→ Apr 10).

**Britain, April 10**
Sir Freddie Laker signs an order for ten Airbus A300Bs (→ Jan 6, 1981).

**Sussex, England, May 5**
Inclusive tour operator Air Europe flies its first service, from Gatwick Airport to Las Palmas, Canary Islands, with a Boeing 737-200.

**Kerrville, Texas, May 7**
Mooney Aircraft rolls off its 1,500th aircraft. It is the Model 231 (→ Oct 22).

**London, May 7**
British Airways is the first airline to operate the Lockheed L-1011-500, a long-range version of the TriStar with shorter fuselage, more powerful engines and improved aerodynamics (→ Aug 19, 1980).

**USA, June 5**
The Massachusetts Institute of Technology Chrysalis man-powered biplane makes its first flight (→ Jun 13).

**Los Angeles, June 13**
Air New Zealand charters a Pan Am Boeing 747 to operate six extra round-trips between Los Angeles and Auckland over the next fortnight, to cope with congestion caused by a backlog of 1,000 passengers resulting from the grounding of the McDonnell Douglas DC-10 (→ Jul 13).

**Somerset, England, June 18**
The Royal Navy's first BAe Sea Harrier is delivered to the Fleet Air Arm at Yeovilton.

**Toulouse, France, July 5**
French aviation pioneer and aircraft manufacturer Emile Dewoitine dies at the age of 87.

**Fort Worth, Texas, July 24**
The Bell XV-15 tilt-rotor research aircraft's first transition from hovering to forward flight is made by the second of the two XV-15s which have been built.

**Scotland, Aug 23**
The RAF's first rebuilt British Aerospace Nimrod MR reconnaissance aircraft is delivered to 201 Squadron of RAF Strike Command at Kinloss (→ Jul 17, 1980).

**USA, September 28**
The North American Rockwell RA-5C Vigilante is withdrawn from US Navy service when Squadron RVAH-7 is disbanded.

**California, October 18**
The McDonnell Douglas DC-9 Series 80, a "stretched" version of the DC-9 with a greater wingspan, increased fuel capacity and refanned JT8D engines, makes its first flight (→ Dec 17, 1980).

**Kerrville, Texas, October 22**
Mooney introduces its 231 model, able to cruise at 220 mph at 24,000 feet. Seating four people in its narrow cockpit, it is the fastest single-engine production airplane in the world (→ Jan 7, 1980).

**Britain, October 30**
Sir Barnes Wallis, the engineer behind the R.100 airship, Wellington bomber, dambuster and Earthquake bombs dies at the age of 92.

**London, November**
The British government announces that the Vulcan bomber will be phased out of RAF service from 1981.

**Marietta, Georgia, December 4**
The USAF takes delivery of its first C-141B StarLifter transport, a stretched version of the C-141A with in-flight refueling capability.

**USA, December 10**
TWA announces an order for ten Boeing 767 airliners with options on a further ten, and also two Lockheed L-1011s (→ Sep 26, 1981).

**London, December 16**
A British Airways Concorde lands after flying from New York in less than three hours (2 hours 58 minutes) at an average speed of 1,172mph (→ May 31, 1980).

## Factfile

World revenue passenger miles: 652,625.350 million
Passengers through Chicago O'Hare: 21.1 million
Passengers through New York (JFK/Newark/LaGuardia): 21.8 million
Passengers through London (Heathrow/Gatwick): 36.6 million
Price of a single coach ticket New York/Los Angeles (April): $170-227
Price of a ticket London/New York: $495
World air freight (ton miles): 86,309 million
Average salary of a long-haul pilot (US): $61,162
Average salary of cabin crew (US): $17,445
Price of a Boeing 747-100: $47.4 million
Price of an A300 B4: $27.5 million
Price of a Boeing 727: $12.5 million
Price of 1,000 (US) gallons of Jet A1 fuel (average July): $713.28
Average exchange rate: 9c 1 = 2.1222

*An air traffic controller in the tower at Orly airport, Paris, communicates with one of the many aircraft he is responsible for.* ▶

## Braniff launches its Concorde services

# DC-10s grounded after Chicago crash

*Dallas, Texas, January 13*
Braniff International Airways today inaugurated Concorde services between here and London/Paris via Washington, DC. The flight between Dallas and Washington will be at subsonic speed (Mach 0.92), because of restrictions on supersonic flight over the US.

The aircraft are really chameleons. They in fact belong to British Airways and Air France and only become Braniff's for the section between Washington and Dallas, as US law forbids US airlines from using planes owned by foreign airlines. To get around this, when they land at Washington the Concordes are transferred to the ownership of the Delaware Corporation, a US-registered company owned by the British and French airlines which leases the airplanes to Braniff. Braniff crews then fly the Concordes between here and Washington, DC, with special adhesive US titles on the airplanes (→ May 31, 1980).

*The Chicago crash: the American Airlines DC-10 rolls after losing an engine.*

*The DC-10's engine lies where it fell.*

*Washington, DC, June 6*
All of the 138 McDonnell Douglas DC-10 wide-body jets flown by US airlines were grounded indefinitely today by the Federal Aviation Administration (FAA). Checks carried out in the aftermath of the May 25 American Airlines crash at Chicago's O'Hare airport, which killed 279, have revealed flaws in more of the aircraft. This is the third grounding of DC-10 aircraft. FAA chief

Langhorne Bond said that the DC-10s would be grounded until tests either identified basic design flaws or proved the DC-10 to be basically sound. Bond said he will also prohibit flights into the US by DC-10s of foreign airlines.

Most foreign carriers have already complied with the domestic grounding order. McDonnell Douglas, however, objected strongly to the FAA's action against its $35

million airplane, calling it "extreme and unwarranted". The FAA acted when more cracks, which could not be blamed on bad maintenance, were found in the engine pylons of two DC-10s. In the Chicago crash, the world's worst involving a single aircraft, faulty maintenance may be the reason why an engine pylon tore loose and damaged the hydraulics, causing the slats on one wing to retract (→ Jun 13).

## First F-16A fighters enter USAF service

*Utah, January 6*
After first scorning it as an inferior aircraft, the USAF today welcomed the first of what will certainly be more than 1,000 General Dynamics F-16 Fighting Falcons. The first recipient is the 388th Tactical Fighter Wing, based at Hill Air Force Base near Ogden, Utah.

With the two-seat F-16B, the new fighter represents a new peak in terms of cost effectiveness, being lighter than the F-4 as well as cheaper and a better air-combat fighter – reputedly the most agile warplane in the world. It has a long range and can carry a heavy load of air-to-ground ordnance (→ Jan 26).

**May 7: Mooney Aircraft rolls off its 1,500th aircraft at the Kerrville plant. It is a four-seater Mooney 231. (→ Oct 22).**

## Powerful Longhorn hits business market

*The "winglets" at the Longhorn 50's wing-tips are designed to reduce drag.*

*Tuscon, Arizona, April 19*
The Gates Learjet executive aircraft company announced its latest project at the Paris Air Show nearly two years ago. Today that project came to fruition when the Longhorn 50, the prototype of the latest 50 series of the Learjet, made its first flight.

The aircraft was built in the firm's Wichita workshops. Compared with previous models, the

Longhorn 50 is bigger and more powerful. It has "winglets" on each wing-tip, which were perfected by NASA to reduce drag and improve performance. Powered by two Garrett TFE731 turbofans, the Longhorn 50, which will be sold in three versions (the 54, 55 and 56), can fly at 534mph, and carry 11 passengers for more than 2,500 miles. It will be manufactured at the company's new Tucson plant (→ Aug 11, 1980).

# Pedal power matches Blériot's feat

*Throughout the flight, the Gossamer Albatross was shadowed by a lifeboat.*

*Bryan Allen: a 20th-century Icarus.*

**Cap Gris-Nez, France, June 13**
Bryan Allen has crossed the English Channel – on a flying bicycle. The *Gossamer Albatross* left the shores of Kent, England, at 7am and arrived here three hours later.

Sixty years ago, Blériot took 37 minutes to cover the same stretch in the opposite direction. But his aircraft had a motor, whereas Allen, a 26-year-old Californian, had to pedal all the way across, to turn the propeller and keep his machine about 16 feet above the sea. Allen's reward for this extraordinary feat is £100,000, offered by British industrialist Henry Kremer, who is fascinated by the idea of human-powered flight. The *Gossamer Albatross* was conceived by the famed American glider pilot and designer Dr Paul B MacCready, 53. Its success depends on its weight of less than 71 lb and a wingspan of more than 95 feet. The main structure of tubes and cables is covered by Mylar, a material of phenomenal strength-to-weight ratio.

In August 1977, MacCready's *Gossamer Condor* won another Kremer prize by performing a figure of eight around two pylons half a mile apart [*see page 746.*]

# Britain to privatize aviation companies

**London, July 23**
Hot on the heels of the announcement two days ago by British trade and industry secretary John Nott of plans to privatize British Airways, comes news today that Margaret Thatcher's new Conservative government plans to give private investors a chance to buy into the state-owned aerospace conglomerate, British Aerospace (BAe), which was nationalized by the previous Labour government.

These moves are in line with the government's election pledges to "sell back to private ownership the recently nationalized aerospace and shipbuilding concerns". Planned legislation will make British Aerospace a limited liability company, and a minority of shares is expected to be offered for sale when market conditions are appropriate, which is viewed as still being a long way off. Wrangling continues over the compensation that should go to former shareholders in the companies from which BAe was formed. Elsewhere, it is thought that the new government will continue to fund military programs, but that finance for civil projects will have to be raised on the open market (→ Feb 13, 1981).

# F-15 Eagle makes a first combat killing

**Tel Aviv, Israel, June 27**
Widely regarded as the best fighter in the world, the McDonnell Douglas F-15 Eagle had never shot down another aircraft in anger until today. Now its combat efficiency is proven; in the space of a few moments F-15As of the Israeli air force has shot down four MiGs.

Israeli US-built F-15s and home-built Kfirs were escorting Phantom attack aircraft over Sidon in the Lebanon when they encountered six Syrian MiG-21PFMAs flying at 15,000 feet. Using Shafrir missiles the US-built Eagles destroyed four of the Syrian aircraft within seconds. The fifth was shot down by a Kfir and the sixth fled into cloud.

The Israeli air force has received 25 F-15s, which were all delivered in 1976-7. This is the first time they have seen combat (→ Jun 4, 1980).

# Dornier's TNT tests a new design of wing

*Dornier's Dieter Thomas was impressed with the TNT's reduced-drag wing.*

**[West] Germany, June 14**
The Dornier Tragflügel Neuer Technologie [New Technology Wing] (TNT) wing-demonstrator aircraft flew for the first time today at Oberpfaffenhofen. The tips of the "supercritical" 56-foot span wing are designed to minimize drag. It has been installed on a modified Skyservant with a stretched fuselage, powered by two Garrett TPE331-5 turboprops. On the strength of today's 50-minute flight, Dornier chief test pilot Dieter Thomas confirmed that the wing does indeed provide very low drag rates. He added that the aircraft had displayed outstanding handling characteristics.

# DC-10s can return to airline service

**Washington, DC, July 13**
The Federal Aviation Administration (FAA) today lifted the 37-day grounding of the 138 McDonnell Douglas DC-10s in service with US airlines. The grounding followed the American Airlines crash at Chicago on May 25 which killed 279.

FAA boss Langhorne Bond said that safety questions arising from the crash had been answered and that steps were being taken to ensure that such an accident would never recur. These include adherence to maintenance procedures by the airlines, inspection by field inspectors and modification of the engine pylon assembly – on which the crash was blamed – by the makers. Frequent checks of the pylons are required until redesigned units, eliminating the possibility of damage during maintenance, are fitted (→ Nov 29).

# Tornado detects enemy 115 miles away

*The first production Tornado was a dual-control trainer, flown on July 10.*

*Lancashire, England, October 27*
The first air-defence fighter variant (ADV) of the Tornado made its first flight today at Warton. Aircraft A.01 is intended only for exploring the basic aerodynamics (and for testing the Frazer-Nash missile ejector-release units). It has no radar.

About 80 per cent of the ADV is the same as the Interdiction Strike (IDS) version. The main differences are a longer fuselage to allow four Sky Flash missiles to be carried (this automatically provides space for another 200 gallons of fuel), as well as a forward extension of the fixed wing-root gloves. The airplane's weapon system is based on Foxhunter track-while-scan pulse-doppler interception radar, capable of detecting enemy aircraft over 115 miles away and of tracking several at once. The nose radome is more pointed than in previous Tornados.

Today's ADV prototype is one of three ordered under the first production contract for 40 Tornados, mainly IDSs. Since the first Tornado flew in 1974, the program has moved ahead well. All six pre-production IDSs have flown, and on July 10 the first production Tornado flew. This was an RAF Tornado GR.1 trainer, which was followed 17 days later by a West German machine (→Jul 1, 1980).

*The first ADV, unveiled at British Aerospace's Warton plant earlier this year.*

# Supersonic production lines will be short

*Paris, September 21*
At a meeting here today of the British and French transport ministers, it was agreed that no more Concordes would be built after number 216, the 16th production aircraft. This means there will be 20 Concordes in all, counting two prototypes (001 and 002) and two pre-production aircraft (01 and 02). A total of 88 Rolls-Royce Olympus 593 engines have been produced.

On February 22 the British government agreed to write off the cost to British Airways of their first five aircraft, and a similar arrangement has been worked out in France. At today's meeting it was agreed that a notional charge of one franc each would be the price to Air France of its final three aircraft (203, 213 and 215) and to British Airways of its last two (214 and 216).

It is unlikely that, given present traffic forecasts and availability of routes, that either airline will actually operate all their Concordes. The last three aircraft assigned today to Air France were laid down to meet preliminary purchase agreements by Iran and China. These are now understood to have been canceled and there seems virtually no chance of other sales.

There are many reasons why Concorde has not sold widely, but foremost among them has been the rising cost of oil (→Dec 16).

*The keys to one of the French Concordes are handed over by André Turcat (l).*

# Mustang bolts to a new speed record

*Nevada, August 14*
When Darryl Greenamyer set a new speed record for piston-engined airplanes of 477.98mph in 1969 – breaking a mark which had stood for 30 years – many said that was the limit for piston engines.

They were wrong: today a new record has been set, just a whisker short of 500mph. Steve Hinton hit 499.047mph in his North American P-51D Mustang *Red Baron*. Almost every part of the Mustang, which has a 3,800-hp Rolls-Royce Griffon engine, has been specially rebuilt for high speed.

# Canada gets early taste of Beaujolais

*Montreal, November 15*
For the first time, thanks to Air Canada and the time difference between Canada and France, this year's new Beaujolais arrived on both sides of the Atlantic on the same day. Some 70,000 bottles of this fruitiest of young wines, which does not have a reputation for traveling well, were aboard of an Air Canada Boeing 747F cargo jet.

The consignment is a new venture in Air Canada's freight operation which, after doubling in size over the last decade, is now having a vintage year.

# New DC-10 crash raises fresh doubts

*Antarctica, November 29*
Following a 17-hour search by two ski-equipped US Navy Lockheed KC-130 Hercules and two US Navy helicopters, plus a USAF Lockheed C-141A StarLifter transport, the mangled wreckage of an Air New Zealand Douglas DC-10 which crashed yesterday has been found. All 237 passengers and 20 crew are dead.

The DC-10 left Auckland at 8.21am yesterday for a routine eight-hour sightseeing flight over the Antarctic costing $359. The aircraft was about 38 miles north of McMurdo US scientific station when the pilot radioed that he was descending from 10,000 feet to 2,000 feet. This would have given the passengers an excellent view of Mount Erebus, an active volcano.

It is not yet known whether the crash was caused by the weather or mechanical failure on the DC-10. There is speculation that the airplane was well off course and flew into a mountain in "white out"

*Wreckage of the ill-starred DC-10 litters the side of an Antarctic mountain.*

weather conditions, when the snow makes ground and sky indistinguishable. The DC-10 hit the lower slopes at about 1,500 feet. Rescue operations began three and a half hours later, hampered by the difficult terrain and low cloud. Three

climbers were flown in from New Zealand but saw no sign of life. Apart from engendering new fears about the safety of the DC-10, the tragedy raises the question of facilities in Antarctica to deal with major disasters (→Apr 27, 1981).

## NASA's AD-1 tests new slewed wing

*California, December 21*
Today, NASA's AD-1 experimental oblique-wing aircraft flew for the first time at Dryden Flight Center. The twin-jet research airplane is designed to determine whether a pivoting wing can achieve the benefits of drag reduction and high speed given by more conventional symmetrical swept-back wings, without suffering from the deficiencies of such designs at low speed. The research team contends that the AD-1 will be capable of pivoting its wing in flight to a maximum angle of 60 degrees from the conventional position. For today's maiden flight, however, the wing was configured normally.

Tests to pivot the AD-1's wing in flight are due to begin early next year, after several further conventional flights. The researchers are planning to carry out the pivot-wing tests at altitudes of between 7,000 and 13,000 feet and at speeds of between 120mph and 175mph.

# Optica observation plane offers clear view

*Humbug: the super-quiet Optica features an insect-eye observation cockpit.*

*Bedfordshire, England, Dec 14*
The first flight of the new Edgley Optica at Cranfield today brought the term "humbug" to mind, but not in the derogatory sense – quite the opposite. "Hum", because of the low noise of the 160-hp piston engine driving a five-blade fan in the ducted propulsor unit, and "bug" because the three-person cockpit looks

like an insect's head. Optica was conceived by John Edgley as a small, slow, observation airplane with short take-off and landing (STOL) capability, with the all-round vision of a helicopter but none of the high costs. It is suitable for pipeline and powerline inspection, forestry patrol and aerial photography, among other uses.

**December 25/26: five Soviet military regiments are airlifted to Afghanistan and the Soviet/Afghan border region in over a hundred flights by Antonov An-22 and An-12 transport aircraft. The Soviet government's move is thought to be in response to a perceived threat from Muslim insurgents in these areas. The number of Soviet combat troops in Afghanistan is now estimated to be between 4,000 and 5,000.**

Instead of the odd Polish M-15 jet biplane the USSR simply produced a turboprop conversion of the An-2, designated the An-3. It may be Polish-made.

First of the Citation business jets to offer true intercontinental range, the Cessna 650 Citation III can cross the Atlantic with ten passengers.

Undisputed king, in its day, of executive transports, the Gulfstream III combined speed with extended range. Performance was enhanced by winglets.

Although bearing a resemblance to the Lynx, the Westland WG.30 transport helicopter offers much greater cubic capacity to civil and military operators.

Pooling their helicopter experience, Kawasaki and MBB jointly designed and built the BK 117 twin-engined helicopter aimed chiefly at the civil market.

The American-built Gossamer Albatross, powered and piloted by Bryan Allen, completed the first crossing of the English Channel by a man-powered aircraft.

The Aérospatiale AS.355F Twin Squirrel, powered by a pair of Allison 250 turboshaft engines, was a new addition to the AS.350 Squirrel/Astar family.

Although outwardly similar to the SA.365C, Aérospatiale's SA.365N featured extensive use of composites in its construction and retained little commonality.

The Dornier TNT research aircraft for evaluating new wing technology.

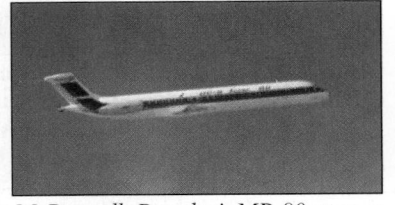

McDonnell Douglas' MD-80 was a stretched and re-engined DC-9.

Plagued by management problems throughout its life, the unusual Edgley Optica offered an airborne observational capability that was unparalleled.

*Standard primary trainer for the French Air Force is the Aérospatiale TB.30 Epsilon, an armed version of which is also available for combat duties.*

*Winner of the US Navy's Light Airborne Multi-purpose System (LAMPS) competition was the Sikorsky SH-60B Seahawk anti-submarine helicopter.*

*Developed in conjunction with Allison of Indianapolis, the PZL-Swidnik Kania, or Kitty Hawk, was a turbine conversion of the Russian Mil Mi-2.*

*The Bell 412 is intrinsically a Bell 212 fitted with a four-bladed rotor.*

*Dassault's Mirage 50 has a higher powered engine than the Mirage III.*

*Produced independently of the Tornado program by BAe, the Tornado ADV (Air Defence Variant) was intended as a Lightning and F-4 replacement.*

*The Dassault-Breguet Mirage 4000 was a privately funded, scaled-up development of the Mirage 2000 with twin M53 engines and fly-by-wire controls.*

*Delivered solely to the Canadian Armed Forces, the Lockheed CP-140 Aurora is basically a P-3 Orion with a large quantity of Canadian equipment.*

*The Boeing-Vertol YCH-47D Chinook offers more than twice the useful load capability of the earlier CH-47A and 100 per cent increase in performance.*

# 1980

4,534mph
USA
Pete Knight
North American X-15
Oct 3, 1967

24,325 miles
USA
Archie Old Jr
Boeing B-52B
Jan 18, 1957

354,200ft
USA
Joseph Walker
North American X-15
Aug 22, 1963

833,000lb
USA
Boeing
B-747 200F

54,840lb thrust
USA
Pratt & Whitney
JT9D-7Q2

**San Francisco, January 7**
A single-engined Mooney 231 sets a non-stop coast-to-coast record in 8 hours 4 minutes using only 105 gallons of fuel.

**Britain, January 16**
British Island Airways and Air Anglia merge to form Air UK; the new airline is the country's largest scheduled operator after British Airways and British Caledonian.

**Zimbabwe, April 18**
Air Zimbabwe is created; it was founded as Air Rhodesia in September 1967, and took the name Air Zimbabwe-Rhodesia during the country's independence negotiations.

**St Louis, Missouri, June 4**
The first of 92 McDonnell Douglas F-15J Eagles for the Japan Air Self-Defense Force makes its first flight; with the exception of eight machines, the order is to be filled by Japanese manufacturers working under license.

**Britain, June 13**
The 16th production Concorde is delivered to British Airways.

**Connecticut, June 19**
Sikorsky Aircraft delivers its 136th and last S-61 commercial helicopter; in 19 years of production, more than 1,100 have been produced in all variants.

**Delhi, June 23**
The eldest son of Prime Minister Indira Gandhi and her likely successor, Sanjay, dies when his Pitts aerobatic biplane crashes.

**Britain and Italy, June**
Westland and Agusta form European Helicopter Industries to design and produce the EH 101.

**Leicester, England, July 6**
The Popular Flying Association annual international rally ends; some 750 airplanes have attended over two days, making it the world's largest light airplane meet outside the USA (→ Sep 9).

**Long Beach, California, July 12**
The McDonnell Douglas KC-10A Extender transport/tanker makes its first flight (→ Mar 17, 1981).

**Devon, England, July 17**
Captain Geoffrey Whittaker of British charter airline Alidair makes a successful emergency landing in a field when all four engines on his Viscount airliner fail because of fuel starvation; the 58 passengers and four crew escape with a few minor injuries.

**Utah, July 21**
The USAF's new fighter, the General Dynamics F-16, is officially named the Fighting Falcon in a ceremony at Hill Air Force Base (→ Jul 3, 1982).

**France, July 23**
The Aérospatiale AS.366G Dauphin II helicopter makes its first flight; it is to enter service with the US Coast Guard as the HH-65A Dolphin.

**Tucson, Arizona, August 11**
The first production Gates Learjet Longhorn 50 makes its first flight. The 1,000th Learjet was delivered to Eaton Corporation on March 28.

**Riyadh, August 19**
A Lockheed TriStar of the Saudi national airline Saudia bursts into flames as it lands. Passengers had a fire in the cabin! (→ Dec 7, 1981).

**Australia, August 27**
Hawker de Havilland Pty will build Airbus wing components.

**Mediterranean Sea, September 16**
A USAF RC-135 electronic surveillance airplane from Hellenikon airbase near Athens is forced to take evasive action to avoid an attack by Libyan MiG-23 fighters during an electronic intelligence (Elint) flight along the Libyan coast.

**Middle East, September 22**
Iraq launches an attack on Iran; there are air raids on military bases, the oil wells at Abadan and Tehran.

**North Sea, October 2**
A Westland Sea King helicopter rescues 22 passengers and crew from the blazing wreck of the Swedish freighter *Finneagle* and flies them to Kirkwall in the Orkney Islands.

**Sussex, England, November 9**
A Dan-Air de Havilland Comet 4 makes the type's last commercial flight, a round-trip for enthusiasts from London's Gatwick airport; it is 31 years since the Comet made its maiden flight.

**Tarbes, France, November 14**
The Socata TB.20 Trinidad touring airplane flies for the first time.

**Shafter, Calif, November 20**
Dr Paul B MacCready's *Solar Challenger* makes a first solar-powered flight; it made its first flight, on battery power, on November 6 (→ Dec 6).

**Hampshire, England, December 2**
The RAF's first Boeing Vertol Chinook helicopter is delivered to its first operational squadron at Odiham (→ Jul 1, 1981).

**Dallas, Texas, December 3**
Southwest Airlines adds 22 Boeing 737 aircraft to its fleet. One is christened in honor of Rolling King, co-founder of the airline. Herbert Kelleher is president since February 23, 1978 (→ May 23, 1988).

**Arizona, December 6**
The MacCready *Solar Challenger* covers 18 miles on solar power between Tucson and Phoenix, before a heavy rainstorm brings the flight to an end (→ Jul 7, 1981).

**Peking, December 7**
Pan Am's Boeing 747 *China Clipper* arrives from New York via Tokyo to complete the first official flight between China and the USA since shortly before the 1949 Communist takeover.

**Middle East, December 16**
Saudi Arabian Airlines announces an order for 11 Airbus Industrie A300-600s, the first order for this increased-capacity variant of the Airbus (→ Jan 6, 1981).

**San Francisco, December 17**
The McDonnell Douglas DC-9 Series 80 enters service, on Pacific Southwest Airlines' route to Los Angeles (→ Sep 3, 1981).

**USSR, December 26**
Aeroflot puts the Ilyushin Il-86 into service on its Moscow-Tashkent route (→ Jul 3, 1981).

---

*The RAF's crack aerobatic display team, the Red Arrows, has swapped its Folland Gnats for British Aerospace Hawk trainers.* ▶

## Factfile

World revenue passenger miles: 676,785.382 million
Passengers through Chicago O'Hare: 19.2 million
Passengers through New York (JFK/Newark/LaGuardia): 21.7 million
Passengers through London (Heathrow/Gatwick): 37.2 million
Price of a single coach ticket New York/Los Angeles (Apr): $154-317
Price of a ticket London/New York: $595
World air freight (ton miles): 88,266 million
Average salary of long-haul pilot (US): $71,311
Average salary of cabin crew (US): $18,879
Price of a Boeing 747-200: $57.8 million
Price of a DC-10-30: $46.1 million
Price of a Lockheed L-1011: $43 million
Price of 1,000 (US) gallons of Jet A1 fuel (average July): $1,122.59
Average exchange rate: 9c 1 = $2.3269

# Merger gives Pan Am internal US routes

*The winners in the battle of the airlines are those which can fill their planes.*

**New York, January 7**
Pan Am acquired Miami-based National Airlines today and got what it has long wanted – routes within the USA. The merger with National gives Pan Am 8,500 more employees, a fleet of Boeing 727s and McDonnell Douglas DC-10s, and a route system which covers most of the eastern and southern USA. Pan Am has long contended that it needed domestic routes to feed passengers into and from its international flights from the major east coast cities. Pan Am had to bat-tle two competing airlines, Eastern and Texas International, for control of National. The financial side of the deal was completed on December 21 last year, when Texas International sold its last 1.31 million shares of National to Pan Am for $65.5 million.

Immediately after the deal was clinched, Pan Am announced its intention to challenge Eastern in the New York/Washington air shuttle market with routes between Newark International and Washington National airports (→ Jun 6).

# French Dauphin speeds to world records

**Issy-les-Moulineaux, February 8**
An Aérospatiale Dauphin II helicopter has beaten the record Paris/London/Paris time achieved by a Sikorsky S-76 on January 8. Bernard Pasquet and Max Jot flew the SA 365N between Issy-les-Moulineaux, Paris and Battersea, London, on February 6 and again today.

The first return flight took ten passengers and did not touch down at Battersea. The outbound journey was made at an average speed of 186.3mph and took 1 hour 7 minutes, while the return trip was flown at an average of 177.5mph and lasted 1 hour 11 minutes. The S-76 had taken 1 hour 11 minutes and 1 hour 15 minutes respectively. Today's flight included touchdown at Battersea heliport. The average outbound speed was 200mph and the return run, with a headwind, was at 174.6mph (→ Jul 23).

*The Dauphin's performances are arousing interest in the United States.*

# RAF shows interest in Jetstream transport

*BAe's Jetstream 31 is a development of Handley Page's H.P. 137 Jetstream.*

**Prestwick, Scotland, March 28**
Test pilots Len Houston and Angus McVitie made a 1 hour 22 minute handling flight in the British Aerospace (BAe) Jetstream 31 here today. A representative of Garrett, the maker of the Jetstream's turboprops, and a BAe engineer were also on board. The aircraft's two Garrett TPE331 engines, rated at 900hp, drive Dowty Rotol four-blade propellers. Garrett describes this combination as the quietest they have known.

Britain's RAF has expressed interest in the Jetstream 31. It will meet the service's requirements for a replacement for Devon and Pembroke liaison aircraft and, unlike the Beech Super King Air 200, which the RAF regards as a possible alternative, will satisfy the government's current "Buy British" policy.

# Beechcraft C99 makes its flawless debut

**Wichita, Kansas, June 20**
With the C99, the prototype of which flew for the first time today, airplane manufacturers Beech are re-entering the regional traffic arena from which they bowed out in 1975. The original Beech Model 99 Airliner, the largest of the company's range of twin-engined aircraft, flew for the first time in July 1966 and was certificated on May 2 1968. It carried up to 15 passengers and was intended primarily for commuter airline use. The later 17-seat B99 was also unpressurized, and was designed for the scheduled airline and air-taxi market. The C99 is a 19-seat improvement of previous models, with two 750hp PT6 turboprops and a cruising speed of 286mph at 8,000 feet.

Demand for this type of aircraft is likely to be high, not least because with the final withdrawal from service of ageing DC-3s, many provincial towns in the USA have lost their connection into the main air traffic network. The first deliveries of the C99 are expected to be made in the course of next year.

*Beechcraft is confident of orders for the C99 in the US short-haul market.*

# Helicopters fail in Iran rescue fiasco

*Washington, DC, April 25*

A complex and risky attempted rescue of the 53 Americans currently held hostage in Tehran has ended in fiasco. A rescue force of 208 personnel was to fly in six C-130 Hercules from Egypt to a remote spot codenamed Desert One in the desert 200 miles south-east of Tehran.

There, they would rendezvous with eight RH-53D Sea Stallion helicopters flown in 600 miles from the carrier USS *Nimitz* in the Gulf of Oman. At Desert One they were to refuel and then take the assault force 135 miles to a mountain hideaway 65 miles south-east of the capital. The force would rest until nightfall, when it would travel in trucks to Tehran, storm the US embassy and the foreign ministry, free the hostages and take them to a spot where the helicopters would fly in and pick them up.

The plan ended in disaster. One helicopter had to turn back and another to land short of the rendezvous. Of the remaining six RH-53s, the minimum needed for the rescue, one had developed a leak in its flight controls and could not be repaired. Washington was notified and President Carter ordered the force back to its bases. But as they prepared to take off, an RH-53 collided with a C-130, killing eight men and badly burning three more. The other helicopters were abandoned and the rescue team left on the five remaining C-130s.

*Two of the RH-53 helicopters had to drop out because of mechanical problems.*

*Charred wreckage of one of the US helicopters at an Iranian desert oasis.*

## Braniff to abandon Concorde services

*Dallas, Texas, May 31*

Braniff International Airlines' brief love affair with Concorde is over. The airline announced that today's flight will be the last because of a lack of passengers and an increase in fuel costs.

Despite the fanfares and optimism which accompanied the start of Braniff services from Dallas to London and Paris, via Washington, DC, on January 12, 1979, the Concorde never caught on here. An average of only one-third of its seats were filled. At Mach 2 its engines gulp four times the fuel of a Boeing 747 on a transatlantic flight. With US regulations restricting the Concorde to less efficient subsonic speeds between Dallas and Washington, operating costs for Braniff soared (→ Nov 1).

## Tornado roars in

*Leicestershire, England, July 1*

A thunderous roar heralded a new shape in the sky over Cottesmore RAF base today, as the first Tornado flew in. Another followed. The two aircraft, BT 002 and BS 002, are the initial equipment of the three-nation Trinational Tornado Training Establishment (TTTE). Eventually the TTTE will have 50 of these warplanes. Weapons training will take place at RAF Honington (→ Jan 6, 1982).

## Japan's new Jumbo will fly 550 at once

*Tokyo, February 14*

Japan Air Lines (JAL) today flew its first service with the first of an eventual fleet of seven Boeing 747SR Jumbo Jets. The 747SR can seat 550 passengers, more than any other airplane in history.

SR stands for Short Range. This means more take-offs and landings than on long-haul services, and the SR has an airframe specially modified to avoid the fatigue caused by frequently applied loads. Today's flight took off from Haneda airport for Okinawa. The return flight tomorrow is fully booked, with 550 passengers (→ Oct 5, 1982).

## Eastern set to face shuttle competition

*New York, June 6*

Texas International Airlines (TIA) president and chief executive Frank Lorenzo is said to have his eye on the New York/Washington air shuttle market which Eastern Air Lines has had to itself. That view is strengthened by Lorenzo's creation today of Texas Air Corporation, which only has TIA now but is expected to spawn another airline soon. The new airline, New York Air, will compete on the shuttle routes which deregulation has opened to other carriers. Lorenzo turned round the sickly TIA from a $70 million loss in 1970 to a $46 million profit last year.

## Record-breaker Cochran hits end of road

*Indio, California, August 9*

Jacqueline Cochran, the first woman to fly faster than the speed of sound and breaker of over 200 flying records, died today aged 74 of a heart attack in her desert home.

Jackie Cochran broke the sound barrier in 1953 in an F-86 Sabre, and in 1964 set a women's world speed record of 1,429mph in an F-104G Starfighter. She began flying at the age of 22 and in 1935 was the first woman to enter the Bendix Trophy race. Early in the Second World War she served with Britain's Air Transport Auxiliary before being appointed as the head of the US Women's Air Force Service Pilots (WASPs).

*Cochran: set more than 200 records.* ▷

# Piper hails delivery of its 500th Cheyenne

*USA, August 13*

Today's delivery of the 500th Cheyenne is testimony to the success of its manufacturer, Piper. For the past three years Piper has continued to improve the range of its models, for comfort as much as safety.

Since 1978, the family of twin-engined Cheyennes has comprised three models. The Cheyenne I takes seven passengers and has long been recognized as one of the most economical twin-turboprop aircraft in the world in the business traveler market. The cabin has seats facing each other, with work tables in between. Just over 4 feet wide, and fractionally higher, it is paneled with cherry wood, and there is a bar at the rear. Each seat has its own lighting, ventilation and armrest. The latest model, the Cheyenne III, can take ten people. It is faster and, above all, quieter.

*Like many small business aircraft, the Cheyenne III has PT6A turboprops.*

# Flyers hit Oshkosh in record numbers

*Oshkosh, Wisconsin, September 9*

An estimated 7,000 pilots flew in with their aircraft to Wittam field here today to join over 200,000 spectators on the ground for the second day of the Experimental Aircraft Association's 28th annual convention, the biggest aviation gathering anywhere in the world.

The annual "fly-in" has also become America's greatest aviation showcase, with over 270 commercial exhibitors from the world of avionics and aviation accessory manufacturers represented. More than 150 aviation seminars are also planned. More than 1,200 entries have been made in the homebuilt, warbird, antique and classic classes, and each evening spectators can watch competitors from around the world practising for the 10th World Aerobatic Championships, which will be held at the end of the convention in two weeks' time. Three people have died in two separate crashes involving visiting light aircraft.

# 'Ark Royal' leaves on its last voyage

*Devon, England, September 22*

Tugs today began to tow HMS *Ark Royal* out of its home port of Plymouth for the beginning of its final journey. Its destination and last landfall will be a breaker's yard at Cairnryan, near Stranraer on the south-west coast of Scotland. Many small craft, crowded with spectators, escorted the vessel into Plymouth Sound.

The decommissioning of *Ark Royal* in 1979 signaled the fact that the maintenance of a credible Carrier Air Group at sea, resting as this does upon the operation of the fleet carrier, is more costly than most politicians are willing to countenance. It remains to be seen whether the refusal to pay for this asset represents a wise decision. Royal Navy carriers in recent years have increasingly been seen as costing a great deal but delivering no essential benefits. They have had no real strategic role, since even the largest could not sustain a long-range nuclear bombing capability.

# An 'ugly sister' gives RAF early warning

*Woodford, Britain, July 17*

Britain took a major step towards a new airborne early warning (AEW) aircraft today with the first flight of the latest BAe Nimrod. It is based on the Comet 4C airliner, but the bulbous new lines hide a complex new radar system made by Marconi Avionics, which should be able to see anything that moves below it or in front of it for 200 miles over the horizon. The RAF has ordered 11 AEW Nimrods, the first entering service in 1982. No costs have been released, but each aircraft is expected to cost around £20 million.

*Nimrod's bulbous nose has earned it the nickname of the RAF's "ugly sister".*

# Microjet light trainer wins flying colors

*The tiny, twin-engined Microjet is capable of speeds as high as 288mph.*

*Toulouse, France, June 24*

The prototype Microjet has just completed its first test flight in the hands of Jacques Grangette, who designed it. Jean-Gabriel Bayard, the president of Microturbo, which specializes in making very small turbojets, invited Grangette to design a small trainer aircraft for the French army. The whole project was financed privately. The tiny aircraft's take-off weight is 2,205lb and it is powered by two jets, each giving 243 lb thrust. The Microjet can reach a cruising speed of 288mph and can fly as high as 30,000 feet. Its construction enables it to perform aerobatics.

Microturbo, which has no aircraft building workshops of its own, will entrust any ensuing production of the Microjet to Marmande-Aéronautique. The potential market could be large.

# 'Penguin' flies on power of Sun's rays

*Flying into history: the world's first flight entirely powered by the Sun's rays.*

**California, August 7**
The Sun was the downfall of the earliest aviation casualty, Icarus the son of Daedalus, according to ancient Greek mythology. That same Sun brought triumph today for Janice Brown, who succeeded in flying *Gossamer Penguin*, a solar-powered monoplane for two miles at Edwards Air Force Base, the first sustained flight using solar power.

After some weeks of intense dieting, Janice got her already diminutive frame down to 99 lb before taking off on a windless day when the Sun was at its most powerful. *Gossamer Penguin*, a scaled down model of the *Gossamer Albatross* – winner of the Kremer prize for the first man-powered crossing of the English Channel last year – is fueled by no fewer than 16,128 solar cells in the extra-light wing fabric. These provide enough solar energy to drive the 3hp engine which turns a 7-foot propeller.

*Gossamer Penguin* flew earlier under solar power, in May this year, and this time had a tow-assis-

ted take-off before it achieved a short climb along the runway. The next stage in designer Dr Paul B MacCready's solar program will be another attempt on the English Channel. Other attempts at "pure" solar flight have been made by British engineers [see page 755].

*The pilot's weight had to be kept low.*

# Delta places largest ever order for airliners

**Atlanta, Georgia, November 12**
Delta Air Lines has ordered 60 Boeing 757s, the largest order in airline history for a single type of aircraft. The purchase, including the aircraft, spare parts, simulators, and ground equipment, is expected to cost Delta about $3 billion by the time it is completed in 1990. The

largest previous deal was United Air Lines' purchase of 30 Boeing 767 wide-bodies in July 1978 for $1.2 billion. Delta's 60 757s alone will cost $1.5 billion. Delta will replace its fleet of 727s and DC-9s with new-generation, fuel-efficient, quiet, twin-engined Boeing 757s, which seat 180 passengers.

# Concorde pulls in horns

**Singapore, November 1**
British Airways (BA) flight crews, mainly captains, are sadly packing their bags here to return to Britain. Today the airline ended its scheduled Concorde services to Singapore from London via Bahrain, mainly because of falling traffic and changed financial arrangements between BA and Singapore Airlines.

The Concorde service was run jointly by the two airlines. Cabin staff were drawn from both, and Concorde G-BOAD, which operated this route, is painted with BA livery on one side and Singapore

Airlines livery on the other. Back in June, another joint Concorde operation was wound up. Braniff had flown BA Concordes (subsonically) between Washington, DC, and Dallas. The US airline had hoped eventually to operate at Mach 2 to South America, but again falling traffic stretched Braniff's resources.

At great financial risk a Concorde stewardess recently chartered her airplane to sell short flights to friends. This is fast becoming big business and many organizations are now chartering Concordes, for fun or for profit.

# Australian woman sets world flight record

*Chisholm: flew the world in 15 days.*

**London, December 3**
Judith Chisholm claimed the world record today as the fastest woman to fly solo round the world. She has spent 15 days 22 minutes 30 seconds since leaving here on 21 November and arriving back, flying via Port Hedland in Australia.

Chisholm's feat eclipses a record held for 44 years by Jean Batten [see page 340]. Judith Chisholm had certain advantages: sophisticated systems for navigation and storm detection. In her single-piston-engined turbo Centurion from Cessna, the young Australian had already broken the record for her flight from England to Australia. Having got her record, Judith Chisholm now has one overwhelming desire – to sleep.

# Boeing prepares its AWACS for service

**Seattle, December 12**
The first of 18 E-3A Sentry airborne warning and control system (AWACS) aircraft being built by Boeing for Nato flew here today from the Renton plant to be fitted with its rotating rotodome and other equipment. Following completion of testing in March it will go to Oberpfaffenhofen in West Germany where, in accordance with the contract for the E-3As, the German firm of Dornier will instal the advanced avionics equipment. AWACS will monitor the activities of Warsaw Pact forces.

# Art Mooney leaves firm to brother Al

**Marble Falls, Texas, December 29**
Art Mooney, co-founder of Mooney Aircraft, died here today at the age of 76. His younger brother, Al, 74, is now in charge of the firm they set up in July 1946. The Mooney manufacturing plant, which moved from Wichita, Kansas, to Kerrville, Texas, in 1953, will continue to produce successful light aircraft such as the Mooney 201, named Airplane of the Year in 1977, and the 231, which earlier this year set a new, single-engined, nonstop coast to coast record of 8 hours 4 minutes (→Aug 1, 1984).

*The Nash Petrel is a British designed and built two-seat light aircraft based on the Procter Kittiwake, and was originally intended for glider towing.*

*The original Scottish Aviation Jetstream was handicapped by its Astazou engines. The Jetstream 31 used Garrett engines and was much more successful.*

*The Dassault Falcon 200 was originally known as the Falcon 20H and featured new wingroot fairings, Garrett turbofans and other improvements.*

*The production standard MD-81 first flew in 1980. It was delivered to Swissair. The MD-80 series are all stretched and modernised DC-9 variants.*

*The McDonnell Douglas DC-10 Series 15, for "hot and high" airfields, had uprated engines. It was ordered by Mexicana and Aeromexico.*

*Dornier loosely based their commuter and utility twin, the Do 228, on the piston-engined Skyservant, but with an entirely new, advanced design wing.*

*The Gulfstream II-B conversion combined the wing of the Gulfstream III with the fuselage of the Gulfstream II to produce a new variant of the type.*

*Similar in appearance to the Boeing 707, the Shanghai Y-10 was China's first indigenous jet airliner, but the design was an anachronism in 1950s style.*

*The dimunitive Microjet 200 was designed as an ultra-economical military pilot trainer, but the concept turned out to be too much of a compromise.*

*The Mudry CAP.21 was designed as a single-seat competition aerobatic aircraft, and has enjoyed some success both nationally and internationally.*

The trainer version of Dassault's Mirage "Deux Mille", the Mirage 2000B, which had two seats in tandem, retained virtually full operational capability.

The HH-65A (SA.366) Dolphin is a version of the Aérospatiale SA.365 Dauphin designed for the US Coast Guard for patrol and air sea rescue.

The Fournier RF6B, which first flew in 1980, was later license-built in Britain as the T-67 and T-67M Firefly by Slingsby, the famous glider manufacturer.

The SOCATA MS.892, from France: a light piston-engined tourer displaying the distinctive lines of the popular and widely-used Rallye series.

The Grob 109, the most successful Grob light aircraft design to date.

Boeing Vertol's Model 234 was a commercial version of the Chinook.

The McDonnell Douglas KC-10A Extender is a military freighter and inflight refueling tanker derivative of the company's DC-10 wide-bodied airliner.

Britain attempted unsuccessfully to produce an indigenous Airborne Early Warning aircraft using the Nimrod's airframe for the Nimrod AEW.Mk 3.

The AIDC AT-3 was developed as an indigenous military jet trainer for the Taiwanese Air Force. The Northrop Corporation assisted in the design.

Brazil produced one of the most successful military training aircraft of the decade in the shape of the turboprop-powered Embraer EMB-312 Tucano.

The Aermacchi MB.339K Veltro 2 is a single-seat light-attack and advanced trainer derivative of the basic MB.339 jet trainer, with built-in cannon.

# 1981

4,534mph
USA
Pete Knight
North American X-15
Oct 3, 1967

24,325 miles
USA
Archie Old Jr
Boeing B-52B
Jan 18, 1957

354,200ft
USA
Joseph Walker
North American X-15
Aug 22, 1963

833,000lb
USA
Boeing
B-747 200F

54,840lb thrust
USA
Pratt & Whitney
JT9D-7Q2

**USA, January 3**
Pan Am retires the Boeing 707 from its fleet (→ May 24, 1982).

**Toulouse, France, January 6**
Laker Airways receives the first of an order for ten Airbus A300 airliners (→ Apr 1).

**New York City, January 7**
A Boeing 747 of the Civil Aviation Administration of China (CAAC), China's state airline, arrives at John F Kennedy Airport from Beijing via Shanghai and San Francisco, piloted by Captain Xu Bai Ling; this is the first scheduled flight between China and the US since 1949 and inaugurates a weekly CAAC service.

**USA, January 18**
Bell delivers its 25,000th production helicopter, a Model 222.

**Stratford, Conn, February 6**
The Sikorsky YEH-60B army reconnaissance helicopter, a development of the UH-60A Black Hawk, makes its maiden flight.

**London, February 13**
Britain's Conservative government puts 50 per cent of the shares in British Aerospace up for sale; there are three and a half times more applications than shares available.

**Japan, March 2**
Japan Air Lines puts its newly-delivered Redifon Boeing 747 flight simulator, the first in the world to make use of computer-generated images, into use for crew-training (→ Apr 10).

**Paris, France, March 28**
Captain Michel Breton flies Air France's last service with the Caravelle jet, a return flight from Paris's Charles de Gaulle airport to Amsterdam; the aircraft, F-BHRY *Touraine*, has clocked up 43,855 hours' flying time.

**[West] Germany, March 28**
The Dornier 228 commuter transport makes its first flight.

**New York City, April 1**
Pan Am resumes its service to Paris after a break of six years.

**Mérignac, France, April 15**
The first of five Dassault-Breguet Gardian maritime patrol aircraft for the French navy makes its first flight.

**New Zealand, April 27**
The report of a royal commission on the crash of an Air New Zealand DC-10 in Antarctica on November 29, 1979 [*see page 763*], exonerates the crew from blame, laying responsibility for the tragedy on the company itself (→ Dec 16, 1984).

**France, June 6**
Air France announces an order for 25 Airbus A320s with options on a further 25 (→ Oct 6).

**Iraq, June 7**
Eight Israeli General Dynamics F-16s bomb the Iraqi nuclear reactor at Osirak, near Baghdad, hitting the target with 15 of the 16 bombs dropped; an accompanying force of six McDonnell Douglas F-15s provides cover.

**London, June 25**
The British government announces that the McDonnell Douglas AV-8B Harrier II, an improved development of the British Harrier, is to be ordered for the RAF as the Harrier GR Mk 5 (→ Nov 5).

**USA, June 26**
To ease financial difficulties caused by the current economic recession, Pan Am sells eight of its fleet of Boeing 747 Jumbo Jets to a credit corporation (→ Feb 25, 1982).

**Moscow, July 3**
Aeroflot opens its first international service with the Ilyushin Il-86, on its route to East Berlin.

**Beirut, Lebanon, July 17**
Israeli jets attack the city center in reprisal for Palestinian terrorist acts.

**Mediterranean Sea, August 19**
Two US Navy Grumman F-14A Tomcats from the aircraft carrier USS *Nimitz* shoot down two Soviet-built Su-22 fighter/bombers of the Libyan air force with Sidewinder missiles over the Gulf of Sidra after the Su-22s opened fire on them.

**England, September 3**
The prototype of the British Aerospace 146 four-turbofan transport makes its first flight, at Hatfield, Hertfordshire.→

**USA, September 3**
McDonnell Douglas delivers its 1,000th DC-9; it is a Super 80 model, later to be redesignated MD-80 ordered by Switzerland's Swissair.

**Britain, September 10**
British Airways (BA) chief executive Roy Watts tells staff that BA, in the worst crisis in its history, is losing £200 a minute.

**Washington, DC, October 2**
President Ronald Reagan announces an order for 100 Rockwell B-1B strategic bombers for the USAF (→ Sep 4, 1984).

**Canberra, October 20**
The Australian government says the McDonnell Douglas F-18 Hornet has been selected for the RAAF as a tactical fighter.

**USA, November 1**
Pan Am introduces new fares on the North Atlantic which undercut all competitors (→ May 27, 1983).

**St Louis, Mo, November 5**
The McDonnell Douglas AV-8B Harrier II jump jet makes its first flight (→ Jan 30, 1985).

**Washington, DC, November 21**
The government bans Aeroflot flights to and from the USA after a routine Moscow/Washington return service on November 8 strayed from its usual flight path and overflew military installations.

**USA, December 7**
Lockheed says it is to phase out production of the L-1011 TriStar.

**USA, December 17**
The Hughes experimental NOTAR (no tail rotor) helicopter, in which the anti-torque tail rotor is replaced by a jet of pressurized air released through an adjustable slit, flies for the first time.

**North Atlantic, December 25**
USAF Lieutenant Thomas Tiller is picked up by a rescue boat a week after ejecting from his McDonnell F-4E Phantom II on December 18.

---

# Factfile

World revenue passenger miles: 695,346.6 million
Passengers through Chicago O'Hare: 16.3 million
Passengers through New York (JFK/Newark/LaGuardia): 21.1 million
Passengers through London (Heathrow/Gatwick): 37.1 million
Price of a single coach ticket New York/Los Angeles (Apr): $147/438
Price of the cheapest return ticket London/New York: $620
World air freight (ton miles): 90,791.7 million
Average salary of long-haul pilot and co-pilot (US): $76,873
Average salary of cabin crew (US): $22,912
Price of Boeing 747 Combi: $71 million
Price of an Airbus A300B4: $44.3 million
Price of a Boeing 737: $14.2 million
Price of 1,000 US gallons Jet A1 fuel (July): $1,253.73
Average exchange rate: £1 = $2.0283

*It looks real, but these Alitalia pilots are on the ground; they are being trained on a Rediffusion McDonnell Douglas DC-9 Super 80 simulator.* ▶

# Lear Fan is designer's elegant bequest

*His and Hers: "BL" stands for Bill Lear and "ML" for Maya Lear.*

**Reno, Nevada, January 1**
Maya Lear fought back the tears this morning as she watched the new aircraft from the Lear Avia factory take off for the first time. She was carrying out the last wishes of her husband Bill, who conceived the project in 1976, when he was 73, and died of leukemia three years ago. Maya used her $100 million inheritance to finance the Lear Fan 2100. It is a revolutionary business airplane, made almost entirely from composite materials, notably fibers reinforced with Kevlar. Powered by twin turboprops driving a rear propeller, it weighs only 4,000 lb. It can carry six passengers and uses 209 gallons of fuel to fly to the limit of its 1,988-mile range.

# Tanker based on DC-10 joins USAF fleet

**Louisiana, March 17**
The McDonnell Douglas KC-10A Extender joined the USAF at Barksdale Air Force Base this morning. It is one of the largest and most powerful airplanes to see service with the military.

The KC-10A's primary role is that of in-flight refueling tanker, to extend the range of fighters and attack aircraft. Derived from the commercial DC-10, it can fly 2,200 miles, transfer 200,000 lb of fuel and then return to its base. It transfers fuel via a single high-speed operator-controlled boom. The eventual total order by the USAF could run to as many as 60.

The KC-10, which can itself be refueled in flight, is alternatively capable of carrying a wide range of cargoes; for example, with a 100,000-lb load it can fly almost 7,000 miles non-stop. The maximum cargo load is 169,000 lb. When carrying this load the range is about 4,370 miles. The maximum range is 11,500 miles.

*Hi-tech tanker: the KC-10A Extender has a range of nearly 7,000 miles.*

# Laker takes on the authorities as he launches services to Europe

**Manchester, England, April 1**
Sir Freddie Laker, chairman of Laker Airways, is now taking on Europe in his bid to deregulate air tariffs. As a first move, he has inaugurated a Skytrain-type cheap no-frills scheduled service between Manchester and Zürich, Switzerland. Called the Metro service, it is Laker Airways' first foothold in Europe. The Airbus A300B4-200 used on Metro is one of ten ordered for delivery by 1984.

Sir Freddie Laker is sure he will eventually create a big European scheduled and charter network, but his ideas still encounter official opposition. For two years he has campaigned for licenses to operate up to 630 routes at cheap rates. Last year his applications were turned down by the commercial aviation authorities, and an appeal to Britain's Department of Trade and Industry (DTI) fared no better.

Now Sir Freddie is to take the British Civil Aviation Authority (CAA) and the DTI to court, hoping to establish that their opposi-

*Flying the flag: Freddie Laker sets his sights on European destinations.*

tion breaches Article 85 of the Treaty of Rome – the founding document of the European Community (EC) – which he claims forbids anti-competitive agreements. It seems likely that Britain's High Court will refer the action to the European Court, in which case it is likely to have far-reaching implications for the flag-carriers of all EC nations. Hearings could start in the fall, with judgement later this year. Laker thinks the action will clear up misunderstandings in European law. The DTI will defend its earlier decision (→ Feb 6, 1982).

# Three great names in US aviation die

**New York City, April 3**
Juan Trippe, founder of Pan American World Airways, died today. He is the third giant figure of aviation to die recently, after Jack Northrop, on February 18, and Donald Douglas, on February 1.

Trippe founded Pan Am in 1927 with a contract to deliver mail to Havana, Cuba, from Key West, Florida. Pan Am's flying boats pioneered Latin American, Pacific and transatlantic services.

Northrop designed the fuel tanks for the Douglas World Cruisers, played a key role in the Lockheed Vega transport and helped Douglas design the DC-1, DC-2 and DC-3 airliners. His own Northrop Aircraft built the P-61 Black Widow night fighter during the Second World War, and the XB-35 and YB-49 "flying wings".

Douglas, whose career began with Glenn Martin, brought safe, reliable air travel to the USA and much of the world with the DC-3.

## 'Best airline' JAL flies 100 millionth internal customer

*Japan, April 10*

Japan Air Lines (JAL), recently voted airline of the year, carried its 100 millionth domestic passenger today on board flight JL903 from Tokyo to Okinawa. The passenger was Tokyo housewife Mrs Fumiko Hayashi.

Partly owned by the Japanese government, JAL has become a runaway success both domestically and internationally. It has a domestic scheduled route network covering about 6,365 miles and an international scheduled network totalling 148,320 miles.

Its greatest business remains domestic; 8,818,611 passengers were carried within Japan, according to the latest figures. This compares with the 3,483,971 passengers who were flown internationally by the airline over the same period.

With a modern fleet of US-built jet airliners and almost 21,000 employees, JAL flies to Australia, Brazil, Britain, Canada, Denmark, France, Greece, Italy, Mexico, the Netherlands, Switzerland, the US, the USSR and West Germany. The most numerous airplane type is the Douglas DC-8, of which JAL has 37. More importantly, it operates 33 wide-bodied Boeing 747s, including seven 747SRs for high-capacity short-range flights, and ten wide-bodied Douglas DC-10-40s, plus two short-range Boeing 737-100s.

JAL came into being in October 1953 as a reorganization of the former Japanese Air Lines, which itself had existed as a private company only since 1951. Its predecessor in turn was the Greater Japanese Airways Company, founded in 1938 by the merger of two other carriers. The operations of Greater Japanese were suspended at the end of the Second World War.

Only days ago the law governing JAL's operations was revised to give it greater commercial freedom. It simultaneously appointed its first six female chief pursers (→ Jun 1, 1983).

# Shuttle craft 'Columbia' soars aloft

*Take-off: the Space Shuttle is blasted into space by rocket boosters.*

*Landing: "Columbia" returns to earth like an airplane, on to a runway.*

*California, April 14*

The first operational flight of the USA's Space Shuttle ended with a perfect landing at Edwards Air Force Base this morning. The orbiter, OV-102 *Columbia*, was crewed by only two men, NASA astronaut John W Young (commander) and US Navy Captain Robert L Crippen (pilot). The mission went exactly according to plan, the Shuttle lifting off from Cape Canaveral on April 12 and then orbiting the Earth 36 times in 54 hours and 22 minutes.

The Space Shuttle system is designed to effect a dramatic reduction in the cost of putting payloads such as satellites into space, by using launch vehicles that are largely reusable. Previous launch vehicles have been destroyed on their one-way missions. Many arrangements for a reusable vehicle were studied. The system finally chosen has an orbiter about as big as a DC-9 but with a curiously blunt shape. The bluff body has a pressurized forward section with three decks, the top level being the two-man cockpit, with mission specialists behind. The latter can leave via air locks to enter the large payload bay amidships. The bay is 60 feet long and can carry any satellite or other space payload at present contemplated. The roof of the bay opens like giant bomb doors to enable payloads to be taken out or picked up from space, using a powerful but delicate manipulator arm.

At lift-off the orbiter points vertically towards the sky, fastened to a tank holding liquid oxygen and liquid hydrogen for the three main engines, each with a maximum vacuum rating of 512,300 lb. Attached to each side of the tank is a giant solid boost motor with a sea-level thrust of 3,300,000 lb.

The combined thrust of nearly eight million pounds lifts the assembly off vertically. About two minutes into the flight, at an altitude of 27 miles, the boosters burn out, separate and parachute into the sea to be reused. In orbit the Shuttle can maneuver like a space vehicle. On return to the atmosphere it changes back to an airplane, complete with aerodynamic controls for an unpowered but otherwise normal runway landing (→ Jan 28, 1986). ▷

# Boeing introduces 767 to challenge Airbus A300 and A310

*United Airlines ordered 30 Boeing 767s while the airliner was still under development in September 1978.*

**Seattle, September 26**
Fuel saver: this is the image Boeing wants associated with its latest airliner, the 210-seat medium-range 767, which made its first flight today. The fuel economy of the twin-engined jet could prove a decisive sales factor for airlines, for which aviation fuel accounts for some 50 per cent of direct operating costs.

Boeing says the 767 should consume from two to eight per cent less fuel than the rival European Airbus A310, partly because of having a narrower fuselage.

On the 767 the classic dials of the cockpit instrument panel have given way to six computer screens showing the key flight parameters (speed, altitude and so on). The 767's state-of-the-art flight deck has about 90 per cent in common with that of the Boeing 757, a short-range airliner developed in parallel with the 767 and unveiled today. Computer-assisted design, another original feature, has been used for 35 to 40 per cent of the new airliner, compared with the 20 per cent originally envisaged (→ Feb 19, 1982).

# BAe 146 proves itself a quiet operator

**Hertfordshire, England, Sep 3**
Instead of the usual racket created by aircraft engines, a low murmur was heard overhead at the Hatfield factory of British Aerospace (BAe) today. It came from the BAe 146, – the end result of a project dating back to 1973, when it was planned as the Hawker Siddeley 146 – which was making its first flight and proving that it could overfly urban areas near airports without causing excessive noise.

The 146's quiet operation is a trump card for the 80 to 100-seat short-range transport, which is specially designed to operate from runways which are short or difficult to get to. The manufacturer, which stresses the low cost of the 146's operation, has its sights on the US regional market (→ Nov 16, 1983).

*The BAe 146: fruit of the HS 146 project which began on August 23, 1973.*

# Defiant air-traffic controllers strike

*Washington, DC, August 3*
Despite warnings from President Ronald Reagan that they were breaking the law and would lose their jobs, more than 13,000 of the US's 17,000 air-traffic controllers struck today. The action caused the cancellation of almost half the airlines' 14,200 daily flights, leaving stranded passengers to clamber onto trains and buses instead.

Union chief Robert E Poll warned that government plans to use 2,500 supervisors and military air-traffic controllers during the strike would be dangerous because many of them were unqualified. A federal judge has found the union in contempt for ignoring his back-to-work order. The judge orderd it to comply by tomorrow or face a fine of up to $1 million per day.

The traffic controllers believe the stress of the job entitles them to higher wages, a working week shortened from 40 to 32 hours and retirement after 20 years in the job on 75 per cent of highest gross pay.

# Sun-powered plane flies across Channel

*Kent, England, July 7*
An all-American team has waited four weeks for cloud over northern Europe to clear before their solar-powered aircraft, the *Solar Challenger*, could be wheeled out on the airfield at Cormeilles-en-Vexin, near Paris, to attempt to fly the English Channel.

Flown by 28-year-old Stephen Ptacek, the *Solar Challenger* took five hours and 25 minutes to reach RAF Manston in Kent. It was an almost faultless flight, marred only by turbulence from an escorting helicopter. The monoplane, 30 feet in length with a wingspan of 47 feet, was powered by 16,000 solar cells. It reached an altitude of 12,000 feet over France and cruised at 37mph. The *Solar Challenger* was the latest design by Dr Paul MacCready.

*A concave wing was found to be the best design to catch the rays of the Sun.*

# Sophisticated Airbus has crew of only two

*After the trial flight, Garuda placed a firm order for the two-crew Airbus.*

*The two-person cockpit of the Airbus: computers have replaced the engineer.*

**Toulouse, France, October 6**
Is there a pilot in the plane? Yes, but for how much longer will there be a flight engineer on board? That is the question being faced by the world of commercial aviation. The debate continues to set at odds with each other manufacturers, operators and various aircrew unions. One airline company, Garuda, has already come to a decision. Two pilots of the Indonesian national airline have just carried out the first two-man flight in a wide-bodied aircraft. Setting off from Toulouse, they flew without an engineer on a certification flight, lasting nearly 4 hours, for an Airbus A300. Garuda is opting for a two-man crew for the nine A300s it has ordered which will be delivered from next January. Garuda's president considers the aircraft's systems are such that the workload does not warrant the presence of the engineer. In order to make it possible to fly the A300 with just two men, Airbus has all the controls the engineer formerly used placed in the front. In the side space that used to be reserved for him, there remain only the systems necessary for ground maintenance. Airlines that want to, however, will be easily able to go back to the old arrangement. The concept of the forward-facing crew cockpit (FFCC) has been made possible by technological progress in computer science being applied to airplanes (→ Jan 8, 1982).

## Lockheed launches latest US spy plane

**Palmdale, California, August 1**
More than a decade after it went out of production, a new version of the Lockheed U-2 high-altitude reconnaissance aircraft made its first flight today. The reincarnated spyplane is known as the TR-1.

It is specifically intended for use in tactical reconnaissance in Europe in support of ground and air forces of the US and its Allies. The TR-1 has both electronic sensors for day or night all-weather observation. While retaining the basic design of its predecessor, the U-2R, the TR-1 has an advanced side-looking airborne radar (SLAR) and an electronic countermeasures suite. With its high-altitude and extended loiter capability, the TR-1 can "see" as far as 300 miles across the Iron Curtain (→ Feb 12, 1983).

## British Airways takes on Boeing Chinook

**Aberdeen, Scotland, July 1**
A Boeing Vertol Model 234 helicopter has opened an air link to the Brent oilfield in the North Sea. British Airways Helicopters has chosen the Model 234 (a commercial version of the military Chinook) for its range. It can fly the 373 miles to Brent and then return within five hours. The old journey – by plane to Shetland, then helicopter – is six hours longer.

Shell, which is exploiting the Brent field, has concluded a £70 million seven-year agreement with British Airways (→ May 20, 1982.)

*High-altitude reconnaissance: the TR-1, seen here on an early flight.*

*A Chinook helicopter lands on an oil rig in an unusually calm North Sea.*

Shown here wearing the company livery is the prototype Boeing 767 airliner, a wide-body, 230-passenger, twin-engined medium- to long-range airliner.

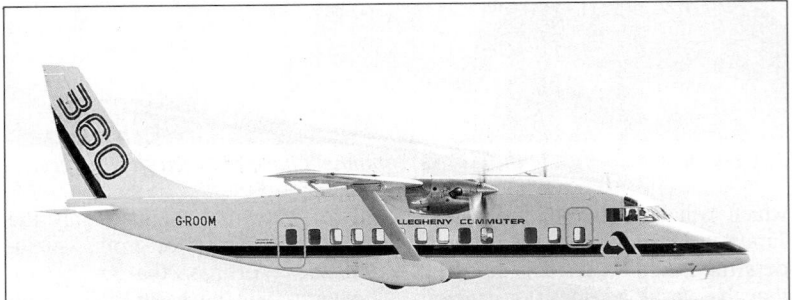

Developed from the earlier SD-330, the stretched and more powerful short-haul Shorts 360 is a 36-seat, twin-turboprop airliner, built in Belfast.

The NDN.6 Fieldmaster, a large agricultural aircraft powered by a Pratt & Whitney Canada PT6A turboprop, which can be used for firefighting.

The OMAC-1, built by the "Old Man's Airplane Company", is an unconventional canard configuration business aircraft produced in the USA.

The Fairchild Metro 111A from the USA is a pressurized high-speed commuter airliner and business aircraft based on the original Swearingen design.

The McDonnell Douglas DC-8 Super 71 prototype fitted with CFM56s.

The LET Turbo Cmelak prototype: a Czech agricultural aircraft.

The PZL-106 Kruk (Raven), a crop sprayer originating from Poland.

China's Harbin Y-12 Turbo-Panda general-purpose STOL transport, a truly indigenous Chinese airplane designed to operate from local airstrips.

The prototype British Aerospace 146 series 100 airliner. This remarkable airliner is nicknamed the "Whisper Jet" because its four turbofans are so quiet.

The unsuccessful Lear Fan Model 2100, a composite business aircraft of unusual configuration, powered by a rear-mounted pusher twin-turboprop.

Originally designed by Grumman, the Peregrine military jet trainer, based on the 1978 Hustler 500, was developed and built by American Jet Industries.

The Chilean Enaer T-35 Pilan two-seat piston engined trainer was based on the Piper Cherokee. It was powered by a 300hp Avco Lycoming AEIO-540.

Hughes' (McDonnell Douglas') revolutionary NOTAR helicopter uses a jet of air through its tailboom slot in place of a conventional anti-torque tail rotor.

Sperry converted many North American Super Sabres to serve as QF-100 unmanned target drones to assist US military pilots with weapons training.

Dassault's Atlantique 2 is an updated version of the original Atlantic long-range maritime patrol aircraft, with a fatigue life in excess of 20 years.

The multi-faceted Lockheed F-117 stealth fighter remained top secret and was unseen in public (but increasingly talked about) during the 1980s.

The Lockheed TR-1A is a long-range, ultra-high-altitude reconnaissance aircraft based on the U-2R, but fitted with advanced radar.

A production McDonnell Douglas AV-8B Harrier II. This aircraft featured a new forward fuselage with a raised canopy, and extensive lift devices.

# 1982

4,534mph
USA
Pete Knight
North American X-15
Oct 3, 1967

24,325 miles
USA
Archie Old Jr
Boeing B-52B
Jan 18, 1957

354,200ft
USA
Joseph Walker
North American X-15
Aug 22, 1963

833,000lb
USA
Boeing
B-747 200F

56,000lb thrust
USA
Pratt & Whitney
JT9D-7H1

**Suffolk, England, Jan 6**
The first Panavia Tornado GR.1 strike aircraft to enter RAF combat service is delivered to 9 Squadron at Honington (→ Jul 2).

**Europe, January 8**
The Airbus A300 becomes the world's first wide-bodied airliner to be certificated for operation by a flight crew of two (→ Apr 3).

**Teterboro, NJ, January 10**
The Gulfstream III *Spirit of America* sets a round-the-world record for an executive jet of 43 hours, 39 minutes and 6 seconds.

**Tokyo, January 11**
Engineer Jiro Horikoshi, 78, chief designer of the Mitsubishi A6M Zero fighter in 1939, dies.

**[West] Germany, January 22**
Nato's first Boeing E-3A Sentry AWACS aircraft is handed over at Oberpfaffenhofen.

**Wichita, Kansas, January 27**
Cessna delivers its 1,000th business jet; it has built 349 Citations, 293 Citation Is and 358 Citation IIs.

**USSR, February 3**
A Mil Mi-26 helicopter sets a world record, lifting 125,153.8 lb to a height of 6,562 feet.

**Europe and USA, February 5**
Fokker and McDonnell Douglas announce that because of the recession they have decided to end development of the joint-project MDF-100 airliner they launched last year.

**Tokyo, February 13**
Investigators into the crash of a Japan Air Lines DC-8 on February 9 say there was a cockpit struggle before the airliner hit the sea 900 ft short of Tokyo's Haneda airport, killing 24 of the 174 on board. It seems Captain Seiji Katagiri, who has had mental problems, may have had a breakdown and put an engine into reverse; the co-pilot and engineer battled to restrain him.

**Renton, Washington, February 19**
The Boeing 757 airliner, a twin-jet designed as a replacement for the 727, featuring a new-technology wing and accommodation for 186 to 228 passengers, makes a successful first flight.→

**USA, February 25**
Feeling the bite of the recession in airline traffic, American Airlines cancels an order for 15 Boeing 757s and options on 15 more (→ May 13).

**France, March 16**
Brazilian manufacturer EMBRAER delivers the first EMB-121 Xingu general purpose transport/trainer for the French navy and air force (→ Jun 27, 1983).

**Devon, England, March 29**
Brymon Airways inaugurates a passenger service from Plymouth to London Heathrow using de Havilland Canada DHC-7 Dash-7s.

**Paris, April 1**
Air France closes its Concorde services to Rio de Janeiro and Caracas (→ Oct 29).

**Hampshire, England, April 5**
The carriers HMS *Hermes* and HMS *Invincible* set sail for the South Atlantic with the British task force, following the invasion of the Falkland Islands by Argentinian forces three days ago (→ Apr 12).

**South Atlantic, May 9**
The crew of the Argentine vessel *Narwhal*, which is shadowing the British South Atlantic task force, surrenders after the ship comes under attack by two Sea Harriers of the Royal Navy (→ Jun 3).

**USA, May 18**
American Airlines carries its 500 millionth passenger (→ May 19).

**USA, May 20**
The US Army receives its first production Boeing Vertol CH-47D Chinook helicopter (→ Jun 1, 1990).

**London, May 24**
British Airways retires the Boeing 707; its last scheduled flight is from Cairo to Heathrow (→ Oct 28).

**Falkland Islands, June 14**
The Argentine forces surrender; 109 of their airplanes have been shot down or captured, while the British have lost just ten.

**Wichita, Kansas, June 14**
Beechcraft's Model 38P Lightning four/six-seater transport makes its first flight; the fuselage and wings are those of the Model 58P Baron, but the 38P is fitted with a single turboprop engine.

**[West] Germany, July 2**
The federal German navy takes delivery of the first of 112 Panavia Tornados (→ Nov 5, 1984).

**New Orleans, July 9**
A Pan Am Boeing 727 carrying 137 passengers, the majority of whom are gamblers leaving for a weekend in Las Vegas, crashes in the city suburbs; a freak thunderstorm is blamed for the accident (→ Jun 30, 1984).

**Dallas, Texas, September 30**
H Ross Perot Jr and J W Coburn land their Bell 206L LongRanger II, *The Spirit of Texas*, to complete the first round-the-world helicopter flight; their voyage lasted 29 days, 3 hours and 8 minutes.

**Seattle, October 5**
Boeing begins flight-tests of its Boeing 747-300, a variant of the 747 with provision for 69 extra passengers seated on the upper deck (→ Mar 28, 1983).

**London, October 25**
British Midland Airways opens a service to Glasgow in direct competition with British Airways.

**Paris, October 28**
Air France withdraws the Boeing 707 from passenger service; the last scheduled flight is from Tunis to Paris.

**Paris, October 29**
Air France ends its Concorde service to Washington; it now flies the airliner to just one destination, New York (→ Mar 27, 1984).

**Los Angeles, November 4**
Pan Am opens the longest non-stop commercial service in the world, 7,487 miles between here and Sydney, with long-range Boeing 747SPs (→ Jan 30, 1988).

**England, December 21**
The last V-bomber squadron of Britain's RAF, 44, is disbanded at Waddington, Lincolnshire.

## Factfile

World revenue passenger miles: 709,377.8 million
Passengers through Chicago O'Hare: 16.0 million
Passengers through New York (JFK/Newark/LaGuardia): 23.0 million
Passengers through London (Heathrow/Gatwick): 37.6 million
Price of a single coach ticket New York/Los Angeles (Apr): $148/488
Price of the cheapest return ticket London/New York: $579
World air freight (ton miles): 92,895.4 million
Average salary of long-haul pilot and co-pilot (US): $83,185
Average salary of cabin crew (US): $25,155
Price of a Boeing 747 Combi: $81 million
Price of an Airbus A300B4: $47.1 million
Price of a Boeing 737: $15.5 million
Price of 1,000 US gallons of Jet A1 fuel (average July): $1,206.36
Average exchange rate: £1 =$1.7506

*Airbus Industrie's A310 is a little shorter than its predecessor, the A300, and has a newly-designed wing providing high efficiency.* ▶

# Nearly 80 perish as 737 hits the Potomac

*Several of the victims survived the crash only to perish in the icy river.*

*Washington, DC, January 13*
"It stalled. I said to my friend next to me "We're going in"," recalled private pilot Joseph Stiley, one of the survivors of an Air Florida Boeing 737 which, as it was taking off from Washington National Airport in a snowstorm, hit one of the bridges that connects Washington and Virginia before plunging into the icy Potomac river.

Stiley was lucky; despite two broken legs he survived the crash, which killed 78 passengers and

people in vehicles on the bridge. An eye-witness said the airliner had its wheels down and the pilot seemed to be trying to pull up the nose when it struck vehicles on the bridge. The airplane had been de-iced with glycol anti-freeze solution, but the formulation had been mixed for minus 2°C, when the actual temperature was minus 4°C. Moreover, the Boeing 737 had been standing at National for 30 minutes, gathering ice that made flight impossible.

# Laker's dream collapses

*Laker Airways' staff stage a final protest to try to keep the airline alive.*

*London, February 6*
Sir Freddie Laker's dream of cheap air travel has come to an untimely end. Receivers have been called in to wind up Laker Airways. At just after 10am yesterday all operations by the rebel airline were suspended. The airline's planes were grounded immediately.

One flight on its way to Tenerife with 300 passengers on board was recalled as it passed over the Bay of Biscay. About 6,000 holidaymakers have been stranded abroad by the

collapse, and other airlines are organizing rescue schemes. A fighting fund has been set up by the public to try to save Sir Freddie's ailing company. Offers already amount to about £1 million; they include £1,000 left at Laker's offices by a 76-year-old woman.

Healthy profits had been anticipated for the coming year, and loan repayments had been deferred. Exchange rates between the earned pound and dollar debt exacerbated the financial crisis (→ May 27, 1983).

# Three phases of the 30-year 'Jet Age'

*International, May 2*
The Jet Age is 30 years old today. What defines that age is the way the jet engine has increased the productivity, or "utilization", of airliners. This has come about in three distinct phases, the first one based on speed. After the false start of Britain's Comet in the 1950s, the US's Boeing and Douglas halved journey times in the 1960s with the 707, 727, 737, DC-8 and DC-9.

The second phase was based on size. The US led the way again, by doubling passenger loads in the 1970s with the Boeing 747, Lockheed 1011 and Douglas DC-10. Now a third phase is based on efficiency, more economical engines and better aerodynamics. It was pioneered in Europe with the Airbus A300, and now the A310, competitors for Boeing's 757 and 767.

# Europeans counter the Boeing challenge with new Airbus A310

*Toulouse, France, April 3*
The Airbus A310 left the ground for the first time at 8.30am today, at the beginning of what will be an extensive test program. The airspace within the triangle of Toulouse, Bayonne and Quimper was closed to all traffic, while radar stations at each point of the triangle watched very closely.

Airbus Industrie (AI) believes that, with the medium/long-range A310, it has created a viable competitor to the Boeing 767, representing the company's intention to break into the long-haul market. Its hopes are built on an already full order book; 44 airlines have made 88 orders and placed options on a further 90 aircraft.

Today's performance has served to confirm AI's view that the A310 is a winner. It is shorter than its predecessor, the A300, and has a new wing which it is hoped, with its

*An Airbus A310 in the livery of one of its many customers, Swissair.*

3-D curvatures and completely clean external profile, will provide fuel economy and thus permit a highly competitive payload and range. Boeing, the giant rival, has

poured criticism on the A310 and is predicting that it will have poor performance. Time and the rigors of the marketplace will show which view is right.

# Britain learns lessons of air war in the Falklands

## Harriers hit Stanley in first British raid

*Port Stanley, Falkland Is, May 1*
At 8.10am today, four and a half hours after the airfield here was hit by an RAF Vulcan bomber, a force of Royal Navy Sea Harriers followed up the attack. Four aircraft flew in very low from the north-east and released 12 1,000-lb bombs, which exploded over Argentinian anti-aircraft positions nearby.

Five more Sea Harriers meanwhile went for the airfield. They came in from the north, carrying cluster weapons and parachute-retarded 1,000-lb bombs; they dropped these on airport buildings and parked aircraft. One Harrier was damaged by anti-aircraft fire, but it made off south-eastward at wavetop height.

Small Argentinian formations have been aloft several times today, but there was no aerial combat until late this afternoon, when there was a dogfight between two Harriers and two Argentinian Mirages. One Mirage was shot down; the pilot baled out and landed in the sea off West Falkland (→ May 4).

## New Nimrod type is up in three weeks

*Ascension Island, April 12*
Since April 5, Nimrod MR.1s of 42 Squadron of Britain's RAF have been operating from here on patrol around the British task force to the Falklands as well as around Ascension itself. Their task is to counter any possible threat from Argentinian submarines which could attack British ships or land commandos to blow up vital installations here.

But today even more effective Nimrod MR.2s arrived to take over the work. To give them some self-protection they are now carrying two Sidewinder missiles under each wing. Normally these aircraft have a range of 5,800 miles, but they have been hastily fitted with air-to-air refueling probes to stay in the air almost indefinitely. They have a vital role in protecting British forces (→ May 1).

*A Sea Harrier prepares for action on one of the Task Force's two carriers.*

*Brazilian aircraft fly low over the RAF's Vulcan bomber at Rio de Janeiro.*

*Marines wait to be picked up by Sea King HC.4 helicopters of the Royal Navy.*

## Destroyer wrecked by air/sea Exocet

*Falkland Islands, May 4*
In a surprise air attack this morning the Royal Navy destroyer HMS *Sheffield* was hit by an Exocet anti-ship missile and has since sunk. The *Sheffield* was on radar picket duty to the west of the British flagship, HMS *Hermes*, when two Super Etendards of the Argentinian navy came in at low level.

It has been known from the start of the Falklands operation that the most deadly threat to British ships is this French-built combination of Super Etendards and Exocets. Argentina is believed to have only five aircraft of this type, but their top speed at sea level of over 650mph gives very little time for reaction. The Exocets which they carry can be launched more than 20 miles from their targets to skim the waves at over 700mph, guided by radar. There are two answers to an Exocet attack: shoot the missile down, or fire off a cloud of "chaff" which the missile mistakes for a ship. In the case of HMS *Sheffield*, neither was adopted (→ May 9).

## Vulcan ends up in Brazil after mishap

*Rio de Janeiro, Brazil, June 3*
A Vulcan bomber of Britain's RAF made an emergency landing here today. Operating from Ascension Island, these aircraft have made several attacks on the Falkland Islands, refueling in the air no less than six times during the 7,860-mile round trip. They are by far the longest bombing raids in history.

Although more than 25 years old and soon to be scrapped by the Royal Air Force, Vulcan bombers are the only land-based ones that can reach the islands. Today's northbound aircraft was trying to refuel off the coast of Brazil when the probe broke off. The only hope for the aircraft, by now very short of fuel, was to head for the nearest airfield, some 400 miles away at Rio. The crew only just made it (→ Jun 14).

# Braniff falls prey to deregulation

*Braniff's fleet is parked folornly at Dallas-Fort Worth airport.*

*Braniff chief Howard D Putnam.*

*Dallas, Texas, May 13*
Braniff International Airlines to-day became the first major airline in the US to fall victim to airline deregulation when it filed for protection under bankruptcy laws. A sombre Howard D Putnam, Braniff chairman, gave the news on TV. Passengers with reservations have been told to find space on other carriers

as Braniff's 71 aircraft have been ordered back to Dallas. The airline's 9,500 staff are now jobless.

The airline has not shown a profit since 1978, the year deregulation came in. It made $45.2 million that year but since then has lost nearly $400 million, including almost $41.5 million just this year. It owes over $733 million to 38 banks and

insurance companies. It could not reduce operating costs fast enough to remain competitive. Braniff said that today's action was triggered by declining passenger numbers, a problem in meeting the next payroll of about $12.5 million and concern that, without the filing, creditors might seize its airliners and force it into liquidation (→ May 19).

## American Airlines sees bright future

*Dallas, Texas, May 19*
With rival Braniff no longer operating and offering cheap discount fares and ticket giveaways on routes which the two carriers shared, American Airlines' boss Robert L Crandall was optimistic when he addressed stockholders today.

His optimism is based on a number of factors. First, American flew its 500 millionth passenger yesterday. Second, he is hopeful that fares will rise from the non-profit levels they were at when Braniff was pressed for cash. Third, American, by taking over Braniff's non-stop Dallas/London route, finally has a link between its base here and Europe. Starting today it is offering five Boeing 747 flights per week, to become daily from June 1.

Even with Braniff out of the Dallas-Fort Worth market, American still faces stiff competition that has become even stronger since the Federal Aviation Administration's recent award of six terminal slots to the nation's largest internal carrier, United Air Lines (→ Jul 3, 1984).

# Boeing 757 aims to repeat success of 727

*British Airways and Eastern Air Lines are the first customers for the 757.*

*Seattle, February 19*
The market for short-range airliners designed to carry around 180 passengers on flights lasting less than two hours is one of the biggest and thus, for manufacturers, one of the most potentially lucrative. Boeing carved out the lion's share of this market for itself with the triple-engined 727 and now hopes to repeat its success with the new twin-engined 757.

The 757 flew for the first time today, five months after being un-

veiled at the Boeing factory here. Developed in tandem with the 767 [*see page 778*], the 757 is abstemious in its thirst for fuel. Boeing has calculated that the airliner's modern turbofans allow a 20 per cent reduction in the consumption of fuel, at the same time as providing much more power.

For the 757 to be profitable the manufacturer has to sell 300 within five years. Eastern Air Lines and British Airways are first in line for the new jet (→ Feb 9, 1983).

# Composite-wing F-16XL put through paces

*Fort Worth, Texas, July 3*
General Dynamics, in its bid for the contract for an advanced air-to-air and air-to-ground fighter, is modifying two USAF F-16s. One is a single-seater with a Pratt & Whitney F100-PW-102 engine, made its first flight today. The other is a

two-seater with a General Electric F110 engine. The main difference from the basic F-16 is the wing, of cranked-arrow shape and made mainly of graphite/epoxy composite. With a longer fuselage the XL has much greater range with twice the weapon load.

*The F-16XL's wings reduce runway distances and increase agility.*

# Soviet strike-power is boosted by Flanker

*USSR, August 22*
The Soviets have developed a new fighter which has startled Western experts. The Sukhoi Su-27 (Nato codename: "Flanker") may be the best fighter in the world. Implications for Nato's attack tactics are far-reaching.

The Su-27, which first flew in production form on April 20 last year and is now entering service, is different from the T-10 prototypes which have flown from 1977. Deve-

lopment was protracted, and the airframe was redesigned. The result is significantly larger and more powerful than the USAF's similar F-15. The large track-while-scan pulse Doppler radar has a range of 150 miles. The pilot's helmet carries what is called a slaved target designator, so that when he turns his head towards the target, the radar, infra-red search/ track and laser rangefinder follow. Up to 10 missiles can be carried, of four types.

*The Su-27 is replacing the MiG-21 at the Soviet Kola peninsula base.*

# United starts services with the first 767s

*The 767 on a proving flight: roomy for passengers, miserly with fuel.*

*Denver, Colorado, September 8*
Everybody was smiling here today when United Air Lines' new Boeing 767 wide-bodied, twin-jet airliner completed its first passenger flight. The 767 offers more passenger room, double-width doors and a quiet ride. But what passengers do not see is what really makes airlines

happy. Fuel consumption is one-third better than current airplanes'. "It's so fuel efficient that the sooner they are in the fleet, the sooner we'll save money," said United chairman Richard Ferris, who has ordered 39 767s. A computerized cockpit and a two-person crew also help to cut costs (→ Mar 16, 1983).

# Weather radars become more capable

*Here the radar display is superimposed on the pilot's HSI.*

*France, December 31*
As recently as 1960 weather radar was a bulky, heavy and expensive installation suitable only for large transports. Today far more versatile radars are compact, light and cheap enough for business aircraft and up-market private machines.

Today's radars do not need a separate display. Information can be presented on the HSI (horizontal situation display), the primary navigation display of all except the very simplest private aircraft. The

received echoes from atmospheric precipitation, ice crystals and electrostatic charges is digitized and converted into colors denoting, for example, the likely severity of turbulence. Thomson-CSF in Paris is competing with six main suppliers in the USA and one in Britain. All have agreed on red for severe storm centers, some radars having a purple or white option for exceptional severity. A few can be switched to display vertical "slices", sections through storm clouds ahead.

# Rolls-Royce furious at P&W engine deal

*USA, October 1*
Sparks are flying across the water as the British firm Rolls-Royce and the US's Pratt & Whitney fight for the right to supply engines for Boeing 757s for American Airlines. The 535C engine from Rolls-Royce is closely similar to its rival's PW-2037.

But rather than admit defeat, Pratt & Whitney has offered to compensate American Airlines to the tune of $40 million if the PW-2037 does not prove to burn seven per cent less fuel than the competition. If confirmed, this would be an unprecedented deal.

**Clint Eastwood stars in the movie "Firefox" as an undercover US pilot out to thwart the Soviets.**

The Hughes (later McDonnell Douglas) 500E featured a lengthened nose, giving more leg room, as well as improved soundproofing and fuel capacity.

The Cessna 208 retains the traditional high-winged layout of smaller single-engined Cessnas, combining this with an underfuselage baggage/freight hold.

Originally known as the A300B10, the A310 is a shortened derivative of the A300B with a new advanced-technology wing designed by British Aerospace.

The German glider manufacturers Grob Werke GmbH designed the Grob 110 as a two-seat sporting aircraft using all-composite construction.

Boeing's 757 combined advanced aerodynamics and engines with a fuselage of conventionally "thin" cross-section to keep drag down to a minimum.

The Canadair CL-601 Challenger introduced winglets to the design series, and was powered by General Electric instead of Textron Lycoming engines.

Valmet's neat PIK-23 Towmaster was originally known as the Suhinu, and was designed as a two-seat sporting, training and glider-towing aircraft.

The Beech 1900 is a twin-turboprop, 19-seat commuter airliner which is in some respects a scaled-up derivative of the successful King Air series.

The first homebuilt Sequoia Falco F.8L (based on the Italian Falco F.8 of 1955) first flew on June 14, 1982. The plans were marketed by a US company.

Based on the airframe of the pressurized model 58P Baron, the Beech 38P Lightning was fitted initially with a PT6A turboprop, first flying on June 14.

General Dynamics' F-16 Advanced Fighter Technology Integration program used a modified Fighting Falcon airframe to test fly-by-wire maneuvering.

Northrop's privately funded F-20 was a development of the earlier F-5 series, but with greatly improved avionics, weapons capability and powerplant.

Deployment of RAF aircraft to the South Atlantic for the Falklands conflict meant the hasty conversion of a handful of Vulcan K Mk1 tanker aircraft.

Developed from the successful Piel Emeraude lightplane family, the Mudry CAP side-by-side two-seat trainer is piston-engined and fully aerobatic.

Shorts was selected by the USAF, in a hard-fought competition, to supply an inter-theater transport version of the SD-330 airliner, the C-23A Sherpa.

Known to Nato under its codename "Condor", and to its builders as the Ruslan, the Antonov An-124 was, for a while, the largest aircraft in the world.

Another F-16-based project into advanced flight regimes was the "cranked-arrow" winged F-16XL, which also had a conspicuously stretched fuselage.

The Romanian-built ICA IAR-825TP Triumf tandem-seat military trainer shares its ancestry with the IAR-823, but was redesigned for its new role.

Re-engining the USAF's fleet of KC-135 tankers with CFM56 turbofans saw them redesignated as KC-135Rs, and with great performance improvements.

# 1983

4,534mph
USA
Pete Knight
North American X-15
Oct 3, 1967

24,325 miles
USA
Archie Old Jr
Boeing B-52B
Jan 18, 1957

354,200ft
USA
Joseph Walker
North American X-15
Aug 22, 1963

833,000lb
USA
Boeing
B-747 200F

56,000lb thrust
USA
Pratt & Whitney
JT9D-7H1

**USA, January 25**
The Swedish-US Saab-Fairchild 340 transport, the first aircraft built by this collaboration, makes its first flight (→ Jun 15, 1984).

**Seattle, February 3**
Boeing announces that it is winding up production of its 727 airliner; 1,832 of the type have been built (→ Aug 14, 1984).

**France, February 3**
The Dassault Mirage 2000N, an all-weather nuclear-attack version of the Mirage 2000, makes its first flight (→ Jul 2, 1984).

**Marietta, Georgia, Feb 9**
A version of the USAF's Lockheed C-5A Galaxy transport fitted with newly-designed wings in order to overcome fatigue problems which have been encountered with the existing model makes its maiden flight (→ Dec 17, 1984).

**London, February 9**
British Airways introduces the Boeing 757 short/medium-range airliner, on its shuttle service from Heathrow to Belfast (→ Aug 30).

**Cambridgeshire, England, Feb 12**
The first operational squadron of USAF TR-1 spyplanes to be based in Europe arrives at Alconbury.

**Seattle, March 16**
A Boeing 767 lands after a non-stop flight of 5,499 miles from Lisbon to set a distance record for a twin-jet airliner in commercial service (→ Apr 1, 1986).

**Washington, DC, March 25**
The government bans flights in US airspace by Cuban airline Cubana de Aviacion for 14 days after two Cubana Il-62M airliners departed from their pre-arranged course on March 4 and 5.

**USA, April 9**
Piper's PA-48 Enforcer fighter prototype makes its first flight; it is a turboprop-powered development of the Second World War P-51 Mustang.→

**Britain, April 26**
Henry Kremer offers a prize of £20,000 to be awarded for the first human-powered flight of less than three minutes around a 1-mile circuit (→ Apr 23, 1988).

**Miami, Florida, May 5**
An Eastern Air Lines Lockheed L-1011 en route to the Bahamas is forced to return to the airport here when one of its engines fails 37 minutes out. As it makes its way back both the other engines fail in turn, so that at one point the airliner is completely unpowered; it lands on one of the engines which pilot Richard Boddy manages to coax back to life (→ Jul 23, 1984).

**Los Angeles, May 10**
Airspur Helicopters introduces the Westland 30 helicopter into scheduled airline service.

**Paris, May 26**
A Learjet 55LR business jet lands at Le Bourget airport from Los Angeles, setting a world speed record of 12 hours, 37 minutes and 40 seconds for an aircraft in its class; its average speed over the 5,655-mile flight was 448.5mph.

**London, May 27**
US airline People Express launches a new low price of £99 for a return ticket to New York; this is £76 cheaper than a standby ticket from British Airways.→

**Sao Paulo, June 27**
EMBRAER's EMB-120 Brasilia prototype regional airline flies for the first time (→ May 15, 1984).

**Tarbes, France, June 29**
The first production Aérospatiale Epsilon trainer for the French air force flies for the first time.

**Toulouse, France, July 8**
The Airbus A300-600, an increased capacity freight/passenger version of the A300, makes its first flight (→ Oct 11).

**USA, July 11**
By special arrangement with the CBS TV network, American Airlines introduces a special 30-minute in-flight news program.

**Phoenix, Arizona, August 1**
America West Airlines begins service, serving Colorado Springs, Kansas City, Los Angeles, Phoenix and Wichita (→ ).

**London, August 24**
A Canadair Challenger 601 arrives here from Calgary, Alberta, to set a world distance record for business jets of 4,364.2 miles.

**Moscow, September 6**
Soviet officials admit that military chiefs ordered the attack on a Korean Air Lines 747 which penetrated deeply into Soviet airspace on September 1.

**Japan, September 29**
Japan Air Lines places an order worth £560 million for nine Boeing 767-300 290-seater airliners, with options on a further six (→ Aug 13, 1985).

**Paris, October 7**
To celebrate its 50th anniversary, Air France announces that for one day films, music and all drinks including champagne will be provided free to economy-class passengers on long-haul flights.

**Britain, October 11**
British Caledonian places an order for seven Airbus Industrie A320 airliners (→ Mar 2, 1984).

**USA, October 18**
Pan Am agrees to swap 15 DC-10s for eight Boeing 747s owned by American Airlines; it is the first fleet-swapping deal of its kind in the history of aviation.

**New York, October 26**
Pan Am celebrates the 25th anniversary of its first Boeing 707 flight from New York to Paris – the first American commercial jet service – by flying a one-of-a-kind service with the 707 along the same route.

**USA, November 16**
Pacific Southwest Airlines places an order for 20 British Aerospace 146-200 airliners, with options on 25 more (→ Nov 11, 1986).

**Libya, December 4**
A group of 28 US Navy Grumman A-6E Intruders carries out a raid against terrorist bases in reprisal for an attack against a US military base in Beirut.

**Renton, Washington, December 9**
Boeing rolls out its 1,000th Model 737 jet-airliner; it is for Delta Air Lines (→ Feb 24, 1984).

---

*This rocket-assisted launch of a Martin-Baker ejection seat tests the seat's ability to blast through the fighter's Perspex cockpit canopy.* ▶

## Factfile

World revenue passenger miles: 737,359.454 million
Passengers through Chicago O'Hare: 18.1 million
Passengers through New York (JFK/Newark/LaGuardia): 24.8 million
Passengers through London (Heathrow/Gatwick): 39.2 million
Price of single coach ticket New York/Los Angeles (Apr): $189/502
Price of the cheapest return ticket London/New York: $395
World air freight (ton miles): 97,427.1 million
Average salary of long-haul pilot and co-pilot (US): $90,933
Average salary of cabin crew (US): $27,782
Price of a Boeing 747 Combi: $85.2 million
Price of an Airbus A310 300: $48.3 million
Price of a Boeing 737: $16.9 million
Price of 1,000 US gallons of Jet A1 fuel (average July): $1,060.44
Average exchange rate: £1 = $1.5166

# Crop-duster joins the drive against drugs

*Belize, January 31*
The Ayres Turbo-Thrush NEDS is a very special crop-dusting airplane. NEDS stands for "Narcotics Eradication Delivery System". With NEDS aircraft, crop dusting, once intended to eliminate harmful insects or apply chemicals beneficial to plant survival and growth, is now a weapon in the war on drugs.

Ayres bought the Turbo-Thrush from Rockwell International in 1977. The NEDS aircraft, based upon its crop-duster design, was built to meet a US State Department requirement for an anti-drug herbicide spray plane. Because in the drug war it is subjected to ground fire, its two-seat cockpit and 20-gallon self-sealing auxiliary fuel tank are armored. To handle the increased weight of the armor, its 1,376-hp Pratt & Whitney Canada PT6A-65R turboprop engine is one-third more powerful than the standard model (→ May 21, 1989).

*A deadly spray for deadly drugs: the Ayres Turbo-Thrush goes into action.*

# Swissair is first customer for bigger 747

*The Jumbo gets bigger: the clue is in the extra length of the upper deck.*

*Geneva, March 28*
Swissair has taken delivery of a Jumbo Jet with a difference. This 570th Boeing 747 also happens to be the first of a new model – the 747-300. The airliner is also known as the 747-SUD, the initials standing for Stretched Upper Deck.

In this new version, the upper cabin level has been "stretched" by 23 feet, allowing Boeing to use the space for either 26 additional first-class seats or a further 85 economy seats. To the untutored eye, the only differences between this model and the standard Boeing 747 are the 21 upper portholes and the extra door. The aircraft's overall capacity has been increased by ten per cent, although this is at the cost of five per cent less leg room.

Several other 747-300s are to be delivered to Swissair. Meanwhile, Belgium's Sabena is planning to take one on trial, and other airlines seem bound to take an interest.

# Agency combats bird threat to airplanes

*One bird-deterrent: a falcon.*

*Paris, April 1*
A 4.5 lb gull carries a punch of 2.5 tons when it hits an aircraft travelling at 150mph. At 300mph the impact is equal to 9 tons. The body of a bird, small and light though it may be, can still make a hole in a metal fuselage, damage an engine or smash a windscreen. The risk cannot be ignored, and it is significant that of 10,000 incidences of bird damage reported each year, 8,000 occur around airports.

There are several reasons why birds congregate around airports: these great expanses of flat ground have no human habitation; there is a good chance of food discarded by air travelers; and the concrete runways provide warmth in winter. The European Bird Strike Committee, founded in 1966, is looking at various ways of getting rid of them. This is not an easy task: both ornithologists and naturalists never cease to wonder at the ability of birds to adapt, for example to scarecrows or to new methods of cultivation.

In the USA, experts are trying to undermine their habitats and deprive them of sources of food. One project aims to remove worms from the earth around airports.

# Dornier amphibian revives seaplane era

*The amphibious Do 24TT has three Pratt & Whitney turboprop engines.*

*[West] Germany, April 25*
The Do 24TT made a successful first flight today from the Dornier flight-test center at Oberpfaffenhofen, near Munich. It is a much-modified version of a Second World War Dornier Do 24, bought in 1980 from Spain. Whereas the Do 24 was a flying boat with three piston engines, the 24TT is an amphibian (able to operate from land or water) with three Pratt & Whitney Canada PT6A-45 turboprops. In addition, the 24TT has a completely new wing, of a patented Dornier high-lift type.

Many other parts are also new: they include an elevated cockpit, new sponsons and the landing gear. The 24TT will be used for research.

# The Mustang is reborn

*Pennsylvania, April 9*
Piper Aircraft's "tank killer" today started its flight trials. Christened "Enforcer", it is derived from the P-51 Mustang fighter of the Second World War, whose Rolls-Royce piston engines have been replaced with a modern turboprop. The Enforcer carries on its wings two 30mm Gepod anti-tank cannons. The Gepod fires the same ammunition as the GAU-8A of the Thunderbolt A-10, whose devastating effect the US Air Force has been able to test on Soviet armor. According to the Piper company, the Enforcer is an economical complement to the ultra-powerful A-10.

*The Enforcer has been fitted with additional gas tanks on the wing-tips.*

# Pierre Robin's two-seater offers the last word in light airplanes

*The heat of an iron shrinks the fabric.*

*Dijon, France, June 17*
Aircraft builder Pierre Robin is determined to set new standards of economy. His ATL (Avion Très Leger – Very Light Airplane) prototype, which made its first flight today, does just that. This tiny two-seater, with fixed undercarriage, slender rear fuselage and butterfly tail, weighs just 700 lb empty.

Robin was inspired by techniques used in modern gliders to develop the necessary lightness and aerodynamic qualities of the ATL. He then added the 65-hp JPX engine, a simple yet modern air-cooled flat-four with direct drive. It is both remarkably cheap to buy and uses very little fuel. The Robin factory in central France uses traditional methods and materials in its airplanes, with wood for the main structure. The fabric covering is sewn by hand.

*The lightweight ATL takes off at 65mph and will cruise at 95mph.*

# New executive jet is launched by BAe

*Chester, England, May 26*
The British Aerospace 125, one of the world's most successful mid-sized business jets, began a new chapter in its history today with the first flight of the Series 800. Still unpainted, it took off after a short run, climbed to 43,000 feet and stayed aloft for three hours. The chief new feature, apart from all-round improved appearance, is a new wing of greater span, reduced drag, higher efficiency and an increased fuel capacity.

The US-built Garrett TFE731 turbofans are more powerful, and other changes include low-drag cockpit windshields, sophisticated electronics and a redesigned cabin giving greater comfort. Nearly 600 have been sold of the earlier versions, which began as the de Havilland Jet Dragon and was then the Hawker Siddeley 125.

The Series 800 is much the best, and several have been ordered; the largest market is certain to be the US, where the coast-to-coast range of the new jet will be a great advantage (→ Jun 16, 1990).

# Singapore orders signal the rise of Far East carriers

*Seattle, June 1*
A $1 billion package purchase of Boeing aircraft by Singapore Airlines (SIA) is indicative of the continued growth of air travel around the Pacific rim. SIA has ordered four 757s and six 747-300s, the extended upper deck version of the Jumbo.

The deal is very significant for Boeing. It is the first penetration by the 757 of the Asian market, which until now has favored the European Airbus A300. To clinch the deal, Boeing had to agree to take back ten of the airline's older wide-bodied aircraft – two 747-200s, three McDonnell Douglas DC-10-30s and five Airbus A300s. With the sale to Singapore, Boeing now

*The Airbus: in eastern favor.*

has nine customers for the 757, who have ordered 127 aircraft.

The air travel explosion across the Pacific rim is phenomenal. Carriers such as Japan Airlines and Korean Air Lines are facing a heavy demand for internal flights and services to other nations in the region. While these airlines continue to order the ocean-spanning Boeing 747 and McDonnell Douglas DC-10, they are wanting to modernize and expand their shorter-haul fleets. For example, Japan Airlines is reportedly looking to buy either Boeing 767s or Airbus A310s (→ Sep 29).

# Soviets down strayed Korean airliner: 269 perish

*Moscow, September 2*

A Korean Air Lines Boeing 747 carrying 269 passengers and crew was shot down yesterday by a Soviet fighter. The airliner was hit with an air-to-air missile at 35,000 feet. The crippled airliner dropped to 19,000 feet in just four minutes, and it was another eight terrifying minutes before it smashed into the sea. There were no survivors.

The 747 had apparently strayed into Soviet airspace on a flight from New York to Seoul, flying near the highly sensitive Sakhalin Island military installation to the north of Japan. US secretary of state George Shultz said intelligence sources believe the strayed airliner was tracked by Soviet defenses for two and a half hours.

At 6.12pm GMT yesterday one of several missile-carrying fighters dispatched, a Sukhoi Su-15, reported it had made visual contact with the 747. Fourteen minutes later the pilot radioed that the target had been destroyed and he confirmed seeing fuel on the sea. According to Moscow, which claims it

*Nikolai Ogarkov, Soviet chief of air staff, gives Moscow's explanation of how the Korean 747 was shot down.*

was on a spying mission, the 747 first flew over the Kamchatka peninsula and then Sakhalin, with no navigation lights showing, while an electronic-reconnaissance EC-135 flew nearby. Soviet forces say the airliner ignored warnings. Whether or not the 747 ignored attempts to contact it, a row is inevitable over whether there can ever be any justification for shooting down what was clearly a commercial airplane. The navigational "error" is unbelievable, just as it was with a Korean 707 in April 1978 (→6).

## Scenic Airlines gives tourists grandstand view of Grand Canyon

*Las Vegas, Nevada, July 20*

On leaving the Scenic Airlines airplane, the tourist receives a certificate. It serves as a reminder that he or she now belongs to the select few who have had the good fortune to see one of the world's most stunning natural phenomena, Arizona's Grand Canyon, from the air.

Based at Las Vegas's McCarran airport, Scenic Airlines is one of the best known operators of this type of excursion flight. The most frequently flown route takes tourists to Grand Canyon airport after a 90-minute flight over the gorges of the Colorado plateau. The passengers are taken by bus for lunch before returning to the aircraft for the flight back.

Always on the lookout for ways to improve its service, the airline has just introduced a modified de Havilland Canada DHC-6 Twin Otter. This 19-seater is fitted with much bigger windows reaching to the floor of the cabin. Tourists can now take pictures of the Grand Canyon to their hearts' content.

*Capt Chemel, an editor of this book, flew this "Tin Goose" for Scenic.*

## Atlantic fares are cut to below £100

*New York, May 27*

The price war over the Atlantic continues to work in favor of the passenger. Today, a £99 one-way transatlantic fare was offered by American airline People Express. A license from the UK Department of Trade was gained just 12 hours before the jet left New York.

Speculation grows that permission was linked to delicate negotiations between the British and US governments over the collapse of Laker Airways, a pioneer of cheap air travel. British Airways and British Caledonian are reportedly facing questions over their part in an alleged fare-cutting conspiracy to force Laker out of business, against US anti-trust laws. A host of US and European airlines and builders are facing separate civil actions. The first People Express flight landed at Gatwick early this morning, with the first return flight some hours later. Five return flights are permitted weekly (→Jun 22, 1984).

# Sleek StarShip is latest Beech enterprise

*The distinctive StarShip boldly goes into new worlds of design.*

**Wichita, Kansas, August 29**
A dramatic new shape appeared in the sky over Wichita today. It was the eight to 11-seat Beech StarShip, making its first flight.

One of the many unusual things about this new twin-turboprop is that today's flight was made by a prototype slightly smaller than the production StarShip. It is an air-plane 85 per cent of full size, design-ed and built by Burt Rutan's firm Scaled Composites Inc. The en-gines, however, are fully rated Pratt & Whitney Canada PT6A-27s of 1,000hp each. They are positioned right at the rear of the aircraft, mounted above the aft-positioned swept-wing and driving four-blade pusher propellers (→ Feb 15, 1986).

# Italian army orders new attack helicopter

**Cascina Costa, Italy, September 15**
The first prototype Agusta A.129 Mangusta [Mongoose] helicopter made its official first flight today. This follows two unofficial flights four days ago.

Powered by two Rolls-Royce Gem turboshaft engines, each in the 1,000-hp class, the A.129 is an anti-tank gunship capable of firing up to eight TOW or HOT guided missiles, as well as batteries of rockets or pod-mounted guns. As in similar American helicopters pilot and gunner sit in armored cockpits, with the pilot being be-hind and higher than the gunner. It has all-weather avionics.

*Agusta's Mangusta helicopter adds a powerful punch to Italy's air power.*

# Piper Malibu outperforms Cessna rival

*The Piper Malibu poses a potent challenge in the light-aircraft market.*

**USA, November 1**
The Piper Aircraft Corporation has unveiled its latest creation, the single-engined PA-46-310 P Mal-ibu. Equipped with a 300-hp Con-tinental turbosupercharged engine, it has room for six passengers in its pressurized cabin. The Malibu is a direct challenge to the Cessna Cen-turion, currently the only pressur-ized single-engined light aircraft on the market.

The Malibu is a better performer in all the key areas. It can carry a load of 1,600 lb (60 lb more than the Cessna), has a cruising speed of 240mph (20mph faster) and can climb at a rate of 200 feet per min-ute more. Its range is twice that of its rival (→ Feb 21, 1984).

# Alitalia looks to future with the MD-82

**Italy, December 9**
After 20 years of service, Alitalia's McDonnell Douglas DC-9s are fi-nally being retired, to be replaced in the Italian flag-carrier's fleet by the McDonnell Douglas MD-82 (pre-viously called DC-9 Super 82). The airline ordered 30 MD-82s on Nov-ember 3 last year, and the first two arrived today. The purchase of this 150-seat short-haul airliner is one manifestation of Alitalia's desire to expand. Although a relative new-comer among European airlines (it was created in 1946), Alitalia has grown to become one of the biggest, carrying 13 million passengers an-nually (→ Feb 29, 1984).

*The Douglas MD-82, with a fuselage some 103 feet long, in Alitalia colors.*

The Airbus A300-600 became the major production version of the first-generation Airbus from early 1984. Various improvements increased capacity.

Following the successful Bandeirante, Embraer produced the slightly larger 30-seat EMB-120 Brasilia twin-turboprop passenger and cargo transport.

An ex-Spanish Dornier Do 24T, retired from SAR duties in 1971, was converted to serve as the ATT (Amphibian Technology Testbed) with new wing/engines.

The revolutionary looking Beech Starship was designed by Burt Rutan, and an 85 per cent size proof-of-concept prototype first flew in 1983.

Two CASA/Nurtanio CN-235 prototypes were simultaneously rolled out in Spain and Indonesia: delays in Indonesia prevented synchronous first flights.

The Reims/Cessna 406-5 Caravan II was jointly developed, but marketed and manufactured solely by the French company, using Cessna-built wings.

The Saab-Fairchild SF-340 is a true joint venture, with Fairchild building the wings, tail and nacelles for final assembly with Saab parts in Sweden.

Powered by a single turbosupercharged Teledyne Continental piston engine of 310 hp, the Piper PA-46-310P Malibu seats six in pressurized comfort.

Capable of 400 mph, the Piper Cheyenne IV was basically similar to the Cheyenne III, but was fitted with a new powerplant and various refinements.

*Minesweeping is the primary role of the triple-engined Sikorsky MH-53E Sea Dragon. Enlarged sponsons house extra fuel, and systems are improved.*

*In 1983 British Aerospace flew the first BAe 125-800, which, compared with the preceding Dash-700, has a new wing and greater fuel capacity.*

*The NDN-1T Turbo Firecracker was developed from the piston-engined Firecracker: an unsuccessful contender for the RAF's trainer requirement.*

*Robin's ATL (Avion Très Léger) was designed as a very lightweight, economical two-seat private and club trainer, in the tradition of the Jodel D.112.*

*Funded by a Cornish businessman, the Trago Mills SAH.1 is a twin-seat aerobatic trainer with superb handling qualities and a spacious cockpit.*

*The two-seat training version of the Mirage 2000, the 2000B, made its maiden flight in 1983. The basic two-seat airframe formed the basis of the later 2000N.*

*The Skyfox was a radical upgrade of the Lockheed T-33 with podded twin turbofan engines but retaining 70 per cent of the T-33's basic structure.*

*This Mitsubishi T-2 was converted as a control configured vehicle testbed, with triplex digital fly-by-wire controls and large canard foreplanes.*

*The Agusta A.129 Mangusta is a tandem-seat attack helicopter influenced by the larger AH-64 Apache. The prototype first flew on September 15.*

# 1984

**Dallas, Texas, January 2**
UVair, a division of Universal, issues ID cards to clients allowing them to purchase aviation fuel at a discount at over 260 domestic and international airports.

**USA, February 4**
The prototype of the Sikorsky HH-60D Night Hawk all-weather combat/rescue helicopter for the USAF makes its first flight.

**Paris, February 21**
Racing driver Henri Pescarolo and Air France pilot Patrick Fourticq land their Piper Malibu after a flight from New York, setting a speed record of 14 hours 2 minutes for a single-engined light aircraft across the North Atlantic.

**USA, March 2**
The USAF announces it has selected the Short 330-200 Sherpa to fulfill its requirement for a European Distribution Systems Aircraft. Designation: C-23A.

**London, March 27**
British Airways opens a Concorde service to Miami (→ Jan 21, 1986).

**Canada, April 9**
Air Canada offers old-age pensioners a 65 per cent reduction on all its domestic routes.

**New York, April 29**
TWA opens services from JFK International Airport to Atlanta, Memphis, Raleigh-Durham, Norfolk, Milwaukee, Jacksonville, Amsterdam, Brussels, Munich, Zürich and Kuwait in the largest single route expansion in the company's history (→ Sep 26, 1985).

**USA, June 9**
Northwest Orient opens a direct passenger service to Dublin; it is the only US airline to serve the Irish capital.

**Somerset, England, June 14**
The Westland Lynx 3 prototype combat helicopter makes its first flight, at Yeovil (→ Aug 11, 1986).

**Basel, Switzerland, June 15**
Swiss airline Crossair is the first to put the Saab Fairchild SF340 into service, on its routes to Frankfurt and Paris.

**California, June 22**
The Rutan *Voyager* light airplane, designed for a projected unrefueled round-the-world flight, makes its first flight (→ Dec 23, 1986).

**New Orleans, June 30**
A court orders Pan Am to pay $11 million damages to a couple whose baby girl was killed in the New Orleans crash of July 9, 1982 [*see page 782*]; it is the largest award of damages ever made against an airline.

**Dijon, France, July 2**
The first Dassault-Breguet Mirage 2000s are welcomed into the French air force in a special ceremony (→ Feb 19, 1987).

**Fort Worth, Texas, July 4**
The Bell Model 400 TwinRanger helicopter makes its maiden flight.

**Gimli, Ontario, July 23**
An Air Canada Boeing 767 flying from Montreal to Edmonton runs out of fuel because of a mistake in calculation by members of the ground crew; pilot Robert Pearson is an amateur glider pilot, and brings the 767 down, though the nose gear collapses.→

**Paris, France, August 1**
A group led by Alexandre Couvelaire of Euralair, SA, and Michel Seydoux, known as Groupe MSC, purchase the stock of Mooney Aircraft Corporation.

**Toulouse, France, August 16**
The Avions de Transport Régional (ATR) 42 twin-turboprop airliner, a joint development by France's Aérospatiale and Italy's Aeritalia, makes its first flight (→ Dec 2, 1985).

**Hampshire, England, September 4**
A de Havilland Canada DHC-5 Buffalo performing at the Farnborough Air Show in the hands of Bill Loverseed crashes while landing; the pilot and crew escape unhurt.

**Mérignac, France, September 21**
The Dassault-Breguet Mystère-Falcon 900 three-turbofan executive jet makes its first flight; it can accommodate 19 passengers.

**Florida, October 4**
Elaine Yadwin, 61, never having piloted an airplane before, takes the controls of her husband's Piper Cherokee Warrior II when he dies of a heart attack in mid-air; she lands the machine safely at Dade-Collier airfield after being talked down by an instructor on the ground.

**Palmdale, California, October 18**
Rockwell's first production B-1B variable-geometry bomber flies for the first time (→ Jul 4, 1987).

**London, October 25**
The British government orders airlines to halt the sale of low-cost transatlantic tickets, declaring void 130,000 which have been issued.

**England, November 5**
The RAF's first Panavia Tornado F.2 all-weather interceptors are delivered to Nº 229 Operational Conversion Unit at Coningsby, Lincolnshire (→ Sep 26, 1985).

**Cornwall, England, November 9**
The first helicopter airborne early-warning unit in the world, 849 Squadron, Fleet Air Arm, is established at Culdrose.

**Dallas, Texas, December 7**
The Boeing 737-300, a stretched development of the 737, enters airline service with Southwest Airlines.

**New Zealand, December 16**
Air New Zealand winds up its DC-8 freighter service to the US because of new American noise regulations (→ Oct 3, 1988).

**USA, December 17**
A USAF Lockheed C-5 Galaxy sets a national record for the greatest take-off weight, becoming airborne with a total weight of 920,836 lb (→ Sep 10, 1985).

**Long Beach, Calif, December 17**
The McDonnell Douglas MD-83 airliner, one of the MD-80 series which has been developed from the DC-9, takes to the air for the first time (→ Nov 4, 1985).

**USA, December 18**
Pan Am takes delivery of its first Airbus A300 (→ Mar 15, 1985).

---

*The Falcon 900 is at the peak of Dassault's range of business airplanes. Its wings were designed by computer in three dimensions.* ▶

## Factfile

World revenue passenger miles: 789,563.268 million
Passengers through Chicago O'Hare: 19.0 million
Passengers through New York (JFK/Newark/LaGuardia): 31.7 million
Passengers through London (Heathrow/Gatwick): 43.1 million
Price of a single coach ticket New York/Los Angeles (Apr): $199/433
Price of the cheapest return ticket London/New York: $579
World air freight (ton miles): 105,621.9 million
Average salary of long-haul pilot and co-pilot (US): $95,789
Average salary of cabin crew (US): $27,865
Price of a Boeing 747 Combi: $89.5 million
Price of an Airbus A310-300: $51.5 million
Price of a Boeing 737: 18.3 million
Price of 1,000 US gallons Jet A1 fuel (average July): $972.51
Average exchange rate: £1 = $1.3365

# Apache is latest US warrior whirlybird

*The Apache is seen by the US Army as the best attack helicopter yet built.*

*Mesa, Arizona, September 30*
The first of what are expected to be about 1,000 battlefield helicopters, each costing $13.2 million, rolled out of the McDonnell Douglas plant here today. It is the first production AH-64A Apache for the US Army.

The McDonnell Douglas (formerly Hughes) product was chosen over a rival from Bell after a fly-off competition back in 1975/76. Then followed seven years of modifications. The result is judged the most formidable attack helicopter ever built. Powered by two 1,696-hp General Electric T700 engines, the Apache can reach 184mph even though it weighs up to 17,343 lb. Its weapons include a powerful 30mm gun with 625 rounds, up to 16 Hellfire laser-guided missiles, and batteries of rockets. The pilot and gunner have all-weather avionics and weapon-aiming systems. The whole helicopter is designed to withstand heavy-caliber enemy gunfire (→ Oct 1, 1986).

# Record commercial order by American

*Dallas, Texas, February 29*
American Airlines today ordered 67 McDonnell Douglas MD-80 airliners at a cost of more than $1.3 billion and took options on an additional 100 aircraft. If the options are exercised, the total value of the deal would exceed $3 billion. American will receive 25 of the fuel-efficient MD-80s in 1985, 25 in 1986, and the final 17 in 1987.

The order will give McDonnell Douglas's commercial aircraft business a much-needed new lease of life. The airliner division has been losing money for almost 15 years, and there had been speculation that the firm, with only 80 MD-80s on its order books before today, would abandon the airliner business entirely to concentrate on military and space enterprises (→ Dec 17).

# New Airbus project gets the green light

*Toulouse, France, March 2*
At an estimated cost of $US1.7 billions, Airbus Industrie (AI) has been given the go-ahead to produce the Airbus A320 – proving without a doubt that Europe's aircraft industry has not merely arrived but has become a serious challenger to American aviation might.

The finance ministers of Britain, France, West Germany and Spain will underwrite the venture, accepting that AI will need to sell 600 in order to break even. What makes this single-aisle 150-seater a particularly attractive proposition is passenger appeal. With its internal cabin width of just over 12 feet it offers significantly more seat room than any comparable Boeing. Its capacity for a quick turnaround will equally appeal to airlines.

# First flight for Boeing's 'stretched' 737

*Seattle, February 24*
The latest Boeing 737 took to the air this morning. The 737-300 is aimed at the new market for short-range airliners with around 150 seats and is expected to be faster and cheaper than the rival products of its Airbus and McDonnell Douglas competitors. Based on the 737-200, it has cost far less to develop than a new model. The plane has two CFM56 engines, built by General Electric and SNECMA, providing 20 per cent better fuel efficiency than the P&W engines in the 737-200. Carbon fiber has been used for the rudder, flaps and engine nacelles, which are closer to the wing. Boeing hopes to begin deliveries by the end of the year (→ Dec 7).

*The new (and longer) Boeing 737-300 can carry up to 150 passengers.*

# Italy, Brazil collaborate on new warplane

*Rio de Janeiro, Brazil, May 15*
A remarkable transatlantic collaboration between Italian and Brazilian aircraft makers has succeeded in producing an all-weather fly-by-wire AMX attack aircraft.

Aeritalia and Aermacchi SpA in Italy joined up with EMBRAER in Brazil to create the single-seat AMX, which flew for the first time today, and further prototypes will fly in Brazil next year. The AMX has powered controls (with manual reversion). The engine is an RR Spey 807 turbofan of 11,200 lb thrust.

*Computerized flight controls help improve the performance of the AMX.*

# Airbus A310 makes debut for Air France

*Paris, May 12*
Air France's first Airbus A310 has taken off for Milan. The aircraft, which has been on a tour of France, is powered by two GE CF6-80 engines of 50,500 lb thrust. Thanks to their efficiency, and that of the British-designed wing, the 310 burns 31 to 34 per cent less fuel per passenger-seat than the Boeing 727s previously used by Air France. The 310 has the advanced two-seat cockpit, all information being presented to the two pilots. In the 210 to 250-seat class, the 310 is becoming a long-range airplane, with future potential to operate sectors up to 5,000 miles. Airbus Industrie is marketing the A310-200 and ultra-long-haul 310-300s (→Sep 13).

*The A310 could soon be a familiar sight on the runways of Europe.*

## More women take the helm in the air

*Denver, Colorado, June 17*
Women are making their presence felt in the cockpit. Last month Captain Lynn Rippelmeyer became the first woman to fly a Boeing 747 on a transatlantic passenger run. Rippelmeyer, 33, commanded a People Express flight from Newark, NJ, to London's Gatwick airport. Now Frontier Airlines has claimed the first all-woman commercial airliner cockpit crew. Frontier said it was just normal scheduling when Captain Emily Warner and First Officer Barbara Cook took the controls for the flight from Denver to Lexington, Kentucky. The occasion was a personal landmark for Warner, who originally wanted to be a stewardess (→Oct 31, 1987).

*Captain Rippelmeyer at the helm.*

# Maiden flight for Virgin

*Champagne launch: Richard Branson celebrates the first Virgin flight.*

*London, June 22*
Amid great hype, Virgin Atlantic today joined the cut-price airlines competing over the Atlantic. Its one-way fare from London Gatwick to Newark, NJ, on its single 747 jet leased from Boeing, is £99 [about $132].

Richard Branson, 33, owner of the highly successful Virgin Group, said he aimed to make flying "a memorable, enjoyable experience". American lawyer Randolph Fields, chairman of Virgin Atlantic, added: "Airlines have got awfully boring. With us, flying will be a fun experience." The first passenger list reads like a page from *Who's Who*. For entertainment Branson engaged a pop group, a magician, and illusionist Uri Geller.

From September 16 the standard fare will be £110 [about $147] one-way. Apart from "quiet zones" away from the "good films and music", Virgin offers family areas and, for £1,013 [about $1,353] return, a seat in the eight-place first-class sleeping lounge, with a personal steward, helicopter and limousine connections, plus food by Maxim's of Paris.

## SimuFlite Training center soothes nerves

*Dallas, Texas, March 19*
Featuring a beautiful atrium and an indoor waterfall that efficiently masks the noises asociated with powerful hydraulic simulators, SimuFlite Training International today opened a 164,000 sq ft facility here.

This state-of-the-art facility includes the first non-airline phase II simulator to be licensed by the US Federal Aviation Administration (FAA). The popular Learjet 35/36 simulator will be kept busy, since the full rating certification can now be granted in the simulator with no requirement to fly the actual aircraft. In order to cope with expected demand SimuFlite Training International has decided to bring a new simulator on-line every two months for the next two years.

The company was funded with $135 million of asset-based financing, making it the largest start-up venture in aviation history.

▷

# Twin-engined jets get Atlantic go-ahead

*El Al plans to fly its Boeing 767 between Tel Aviv and Montreal.*

*USA, July 1*
The Atlantic, hitherto off-limits to twin-engined commercial jets, is now open to the Airbus A310-300 and the Boeing 757 and 767. Until 1970, piston engines and the first jets lacked the power and reliability to permit transatlantic flights by twin-engined aircraft. But today's engines are in a different cate-gory. For many years airlines flying the A300B and A310 had asked the US Federal Aviation Administration (FAA) to change its rules, but the FAA insisted twin-engined aircraft stay within one hour of an air-field. With US-built big twins the limit is now extended to two hours, allowing direct transatlantic flights (→ Feb 1, 1985).

# The last Boeing 727 rolls out of factory

*Renton, Washington, August 14*
In a ceremony marking the end of a 22-year production cycle, Boeing today rolled out its 1,832nd and fi-nal Model 727 airliner. This is a 727-252F freighter for Federal Ex-press, the express postal deliveries firm. Federal Express has added 15 of these new freighters to its fleet since last year, having already op-erated 53 second-hand 727s.

The enormously successful 727 is the only commercial jet transport to have exceeded 1,500 sales.

**General Dynamics' F-16 has proved itself in many roles with the USAF.**

# Air Florida is victim of stiff competition

*New York, July 3*
The third major US airline bank-ruptcy since 1978 came today when Air Florida filed for protection. It follows Braniff, which filed in May 1982 [*see page 786*], and Continen-tal, which filed last September.

Air Florida grew after deregula-tion from a regional carrier to one having routes to Costa Rica, El Salvador, Guatemala and Hondur-as as well as London. Its $5.1 mil-lion profit in 1981, as other carriers were losing $500 million, made it the darling of investors. Braniff and Continental could fly again, but, with $134.8 million losses in the past three years, it is doubtful Air Florida will (→ Nov 23, 1987).

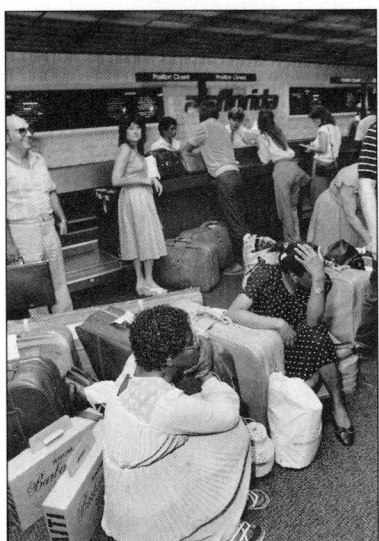

*Stranded passengers in Miami.*

# Airships fly in the skies over London

*Nostalgic: airships over London.*

*London, July 17*
Not since the First World War have two or more airships been seen together over London. Today two modern craft built by Airship Indus-tries flew gracefully over the city, hovering above Tower Bridge be-fore making their return journey to Cardington, Bedfordshire.

The smaller craft was the Sky-ship 500-02, the company's first production airship, which first flew in 1981. The other was the world's largest airship, the Skyship 600, which made its maiden flight last March. The 13-passenger Skyship 600 has a top speed of 64mph. The envelope is made of polyester, coated with titanium dioxide-loaded polyurethane and with an inner polyvinylidene chloride film.

# Air Canada airliner glides home safely

*Gimli, Manitoba, July 23*
Robert Pearson is an accomplished glider pilot, and glider pilots love the hushed serenity that accompan-ies the muted rush of air flowing past the cockpit of a sailplane. However, there is nothing serene about it when the sailplane is a 150-ton Boeing 767 airliner. Air Canada Captain Pearson discover-ed this today when he used all his skills as a commercial airliner and glider pilot to bring his powerless 767 and its 61 passengers down to a safe landing on the 7,200-ft run-way here. The airplane was power-less because the twin-jet wide-bodied airliner had run out of fuel 1,000 miles short of its destination. The ground crew had miscalculated the weight of the jet fuel when they converted the volume to pounds.

The emergency had occurred as Captain Robert Pearson, piloting the 767 from Montreal to Edmon-ton, reached Red Lake, Ontario, before crossing into Manitoba. He picked his landing site for the 767 – now the world's largest glider – and lined up with the runway at Gimli as his co-pilot lowered the landing gear manually. The 767 landed safely, but the nose gear collapsed.

# New strategic bomber is rolled out

*Palmdale, California, September 4*
The USAF's first production B-1 bomber, reborn under President Ronald Reagan's build-up of the US military, made its debut today at a Rockwell International plant.

Although it looks like the B-1As built before President Carter canceled their production in 1977, this is a different aircraft, designated the B-1B. Some refinement of external features and the use of radar-absorption materials have reduced the B-1B's radar cross-section to one per cent of that of a B-52. While the variable-sweep wing of the B-1A has been retained, the top speed requirement has been reduced from Mach 2 to Mach 1.25, which allows a higher gross weight and eliminates the need for variable engine inlets.

The B-1B will replace the B-52 in the US's nuclear strategic triad of intercontinental ballistic missiles, ballistic missile submarines, and bombers. For strategic missions it

*The B-1B bomber: rescued by Reagan, it offers a more flexible attack force.*

can carry various combinations of nuclear air-to-ground missiles and free-fall bombs and auxiliary fuel. Provisions are being made to incorporate a rotary launcher for the air-launched cruise missile (ALCM).

The B-1B will be able to carry 84 500-lb bombs and will perform anti-submarine patrol, long-range maritime surveillance and mine-laying duties now undertaken by the B-52 (→Oct 18).

## Nations airlift aid to starving Ethiopia

*Ethiopia, November 1*
With the full extent of the current famine in Ethiopia brought to the West's attention last month, a rush of international relief got under way yesterday. But diplomats still warn of the possibility of 900,000 deaths by Christmas.

So far, over 30 foreign heavy-lift airplanes have been pledged to carry in food and help distribution – mostly from the West, but Eastern Bloc offers now include vital helicopters and 300 trucks. Britain has been fast to react. The government has chartered two Boeing 707s to carry in supplies today, while a British Airways TriStar will fly in ten tons of high-protein biscuits tomorrow. RAF Hercules transports left Lyneham last night for Addis Ababa as part of Operation Bushel, initially airlifting staff, field kitchens, supplies and vehicles to set up operations. Distribution sorties to Assab will start shortly.

# Pan Am places big order for the Airbus

*Bernard Lathière of Airbus Industrie with a model in Pan Am's livery.*

*Miami, Florida, September 13*
Pan Am has agreed to buy a fleet of Airbus airliners in a deal worth about $780 million. The deal represents a significant breakthrough by the European consortium into the American market, which has been dominated by Boeing, McDonnell Douglas and Lockheed. Pan Am has agreed in principle to lease 12

ready-built A300-B4s and four A310-200s until 12 new A310-300s and 16 A320s can be delivered. The most significant part of the order is the choice of the new 150-seat A320, which was launched earlier this year. The Pan Am deal, forged against bitter competition from Boeing, takes firm orders for the A320 to 71 (→Dec 18).

# Futuristic Grumman is a computer triumph

*California, December 14*
The first of two Grumman X-29A research airplanes made its maiden flight at Edwards Air Force Base today. The pilot, Charles "Chuck" Sewell, had no trouble on the 66-minute flight and landed without a single snag to report.

Some had predicted that this pioneer forward-swept wing (FSW) aircraft would be impossible to handle. Not only does the wing try to tear itself off, but the X-29A is totally unstable in design. As a result the pilot has to fly it via three computers which correct the flight path 40 times per second. On the other hand, FSW airplanes are in several ways more efficient than those with backswept wings. The X-29A will be carefully reviewed to see whether future fighters should be FSW airplanes. If so, Grumman might be well placed to build them.

*Test pilot Charles "Chuck" Sewell after the X-29A's inaugural flight.*

The Boeing 737-300 first flew on February 24. It features a stretched fuselage and CFM56 turbofan engines for greater economy and enhanced performance.

The Franco-Italian ATR program was launched in 1981, yielding a first flight on August 16, 1984. The ATR 42 is a twin-turboprop regional transport.

The Airbus A300-600C was a convertible passenger/freight aircraft with a strengthened cabin floor and a large freight door for a 46-ton load.

Schweizer's Model 300C (ex-Hughes) first flew in 1984.

The NAC-1 Freelance was based on the airframe of the BN-3 Nymph.

Dornier's Seastar used the same basic configuration as pre-war Dornier flying boats but with new technology in many areas and modern turboprop engines.

The Dassault-Breguet Mystère-Falcon 900 is similar in overall configuration to the Falcon 50, with a larger fuselage and more powerful engines.

The Rutan Voyager: designed for a non-stop round-the-world flight.

The lone Fournier RF.10 prototype featured a carbon-fibre main spar.

The Pratt & Whitney Canada JT15D-5 engined Mitsubishi Diamond II had improved performance, payload and range. It was made in the USA.

The RAF's VC10 K. Mk 3 is an inflight-refueling tanker conversion of the Super VC10 airliners originally delivered to East African Airlines.

This white-painted B-1A was flying intensively in 1984 in support of the B-1B Lancer, a completely upgraded aircraft for different (low-level) missions.

*Argentina's indigenous FMA IA.63 Pampa jet trainer bears a striking resemblance to the Dassault-Dornier Alpha Jet (Dornier assisted throughout).*

*Grumman built two X-29A research aircraft for NASA to study the handling of a totally unstable Forward Swept Wing aircraft with fighter-like qualities.*

*Westland's Lynx 3 has greater firepower and more advanced avionics than the standard model. It was c.27 per cent heavier but used the same dynamics.*

*The Pilatus PC-9 is an up-engined and much improved derivative of the PC-7 with stepped cockpits, light Mk11 ejection seats and a ventral airbrake.*

*The Fuji KM-2B was fitted with a turboprop to become the KM-2D.*

*The prototype RF-18 "Recce Hornet" had a deepened camera nose.*

*Lockheed's HTTB: a modified C-130H used for high-lift research.*

*Cessna's T-47A: a Naval Flight Officer training model of the Citation.*

*The Lockheed S-3B Viking incorporated many improvements over the S-3A, most notably provision for new avionics and the Harpoon cruise missile.*

*The SIAI Marchetti S.211 is a lightweight low-cost jet trainer designed for basic and advanced jet training and light attack missions (JT15D turbofan).*

*Lockheed put a Hawkeye's AN/APS-138 radar atop an ex-RAAF P-3B to produce the prototype P-3(AEW&C) for airborne early warning and control.*

# 1985

4,534mph
USA
Pete Knight
North American X-15
Oct 3, 1967

24,325 miles
USA
Archie Old Jr
Boeing B-52B
Jan 18, 1957

354,200ft
USA
Joseph Walker
North American X-15
Aug 22, 1963

892,859lb
USSR
Antonov
An-124 Condor

59,000lb thrust
USA
General Electric
CF6-80C2A1

**Geneva, January 3**
IATA announces that lost baggage costs its member companies $180 million each year in direct costs alone.

**USA, January 14**
Twelve airlines being sued by Laker Airways for having conspired against the British independent airline and brought it to bankruptcy offer $50 million to end the action (→ Aug 21).

**Boston, February 1**
TWA becomes the first US airline to fly a twin-engined jet across the Atlantic on a scheduled passenger service when it introduces the Boeing 767 on its route to Paris and Zürich (→ Feb 1, 1990).

**Bilbao, Spain, February 19**
An Iberia Boeing 727 collides with a television mast and crashes, killing 148.

**Pacific Ocean, February 20**
All four engines of a China Airlines Boeing 747 fail when it encounters clouds of volcanic ash, and it plunges 30,000 feet before the pilot is able to restart them; there are a number of injuries among the passengers, but no deaths.

**USA/Britain, March 4**
A General Dynamics F-16 carries out the first flight trials of the British Aerospace terrain profile matching (TERPROM) navigation system.

**Isle of Wight, England, March 11**
ARV Aviation's ARV Super 2 light airplane makes its first flight, at Sandown; it is initially to be sold in kit form for assembly at home.

**Miami, March 15**
Pan Am puts the Airbus A300B airliner into service, on its route to Mexico City (→ Apr 22).

**Dallas, Texas, March 15**
New US commuter airline American Eagle begins operations; its first service is by Jetstream 31 to Wichita Falls, Kansas.

**London, March 21**
The British government announces that the Brazilian-developed EMBRAER Tucano has been chosen as the new RAF trainer; it will be built under license by Shorts at Belfast (→ Feb 14, 1986).

**Paris, April 22**
Air France places an order for 25 Airbus A320s with an option on a further 25 (→ May 24).

**USA, April 22**
Pan Am sells its Pacific division to United Air Lines for $750 million; the deal includes all Pan Am's Pacific routes as well as its complete fleet of long-range 747SPs, half its TriStars and one DC-10 (→ May 24).

**Warsaw, April 24**
Polish airline LOT opens a service to New York using the Ilyushin Il-62M (→ May 9, 1987).

**Austria, May 21**
The Austrian government orders 24 Saab J35 supersonic fighters from Sweden.

**Istres, France, May 21**
The Falcon V 10F business jet, jointly developed by Dassault-Breguet and Aérospatiale, makes its first flight; it is the first civil aircraft to be made of composite materials, carbon fiber and epoxy resin.

**Dallas, Texas, August 2**
A Delta Air Lines TriStar explodes on impact with the ground after a microburst (violent downdraft) knocks it out of the sky as it is coming in to land at Fort Worth airport; 133 perish.

**Europe, August 2**
West Germany's Messerschmitt-Bölkow-Blohm, Italy's Aeritalia and British Aerospace agree on the joint development of the European Fighter Aircraft (EFA), intended to enter service in the mid-1990s (→ Apr 25, 1988).

**Britain, August 21**
On the day of a deadline set by British Airways, Sir Freddie Laker makes a private settlement worth £8 million to end his court case against the British airline; Laker employees say they will fight on alone (→ Nov 1).

**Fort Worth, Texas, August 30**
The Bell D-292 composite airframe helicopter takes to the air for the first time.

**USA, September 26**
TWA signs a merger agreement with US businessman Carl C Icahn and his associates; Icahn's group initially acquired 23 per cent of the airline's common stock in May this year, and today's agreement provides for it to acquire the remainder.

**Riyadh, September 26**
Saudi Arabia finalizes a major defense order for European aircraft: 24 Panavia Tornado ADVs, 48 Tornado IDSs, 30 BAe Hawks, 30 Pilatus PC-9s and two BAe Jetstream 31s (→ May 3, 1990).

**Washington, DC, October 18**
An official of the US National Transportation Safety Board says evidence from fragments of the Air India 747 which crashed off Ireland on June 23 point to a bomb as the cause of the tragedy.

**USA, November 4**
TWA orders ten McDonnell Douglas MD-80s (→ May 1, 1987).

**USA, November 18**
Cessna, the USA's last independent general aviation company, becomes a subsidiary of General Dynamics Corporation.

**Malta, November 24**
An Egyptair airliner, hijacked yesterday shortly after take-off from Athens, is stormed by a group of Egyptian commandos; 60 people are killed in the ensuing gun battle.

**France, November 26**
Air Inter orders ten Airbus A320s with ten options (→ Feb 22, 1987).

**France, December 2**
The first production ATR 42 airliner is delivered, to France's Air Littoral (→ Oct 27, 1988).

**Newfoundland, December 12**
A chartered DC-8 carrying men of the US 101st Airborne Division returning for Christmas leave crashes after take-off from Gander, killing 250.

**Saint-Cloud, France, December 14**
Dassault-Breguet unveils the new Rafale experimental combat airplane (→ Jul 4, 1986).

*McDonnell Douglas's AV-8B Advanced Harrier, a version of the British combat jet developed for the US Navy and US Marine Corps.* ▶

## Factfile

World revenue passenger miles: 849,671.290 million
Passengers through Chicago O'Hare: 48.4 million
Passengers through New York (JFK/Newark/LaGuardia): 78.0 million
Passengers through London (Heathrow/Gatwick): 46.2 million
Price of single coach ticket New York/Los Angeles (Oct): $240/490
Price of the cheapest return ticket London/New York: $579
World air freight (ton miles): 112,468.1 million
Average salary of long-haul pilot and co-pilot (US): $98,822
Average salary of cabin crew (US): $28,303
Price of a Boeing 747 Combi: $93.3 million
Price of an Airbus A310-300: $54.7 million
Price of an Airbus A320: $30.1 million
Price of 1,000 (US) gallons of Jet A1 fuel (average July): $867.53
Average exchange rate: £1 = $1.2961

# US Marines take on updated VTOL Harrier

*Yuma, Arizona, January 30*
The first operational squadron to deploy the new AV-8B Harrier II light attack aircraft, VMA-513, was commissioned at Yuma Marine Corps Air Station today. Three squadrons flying older AV-8As and AV-8Cs and four Douglas A-4M Skyhawk units will be converted to the upgraded Harriers in the next four years. The US Marines are the only users of the vertical take-off and landing (VTOL) Harriers in the US armed forces.

The AV-8B incorporates a Mc-Donnell Douglas supercritical wing made of graphite composites, large flaps and improved engine inlets and nozzles to increase lift. The aircraft also has 50 per cent more fuel capacity and greatly improved avionics and weapons capability.

*The Harrier II will transform the combat capabilities of the Marine Corps.*

# Tests open for improved version of Galaxy

*Marietta, Georgia, September 10*
Despite its failure to produce a commercial version of the Galaxy – which, it said, could carry 87 Volkswagens from Frankfurt to New York in one hop – Lockheed is going ahead with an even better version of the world's biggest aircraft. The first of them, a C-5B, flew for the first time today. After previous problems with the Galaxy's wings, Lockheed is taking no chances this time. The 222-foot wings of the C-5B have been put through a cyclic test of 105,000 hours, including simulated battle damage, representing three and a half "lifetimes" of the aircraft, which is able to lift an amazing 922,000 lb (→Jan 8, 1986).

*A Lockheed worker in Georgia is dwarfed by the Galaxy's rear fuselage.*

# Air India crash kills 329

*Part of the Air India 747 seen floating in the sea after its mysterious crash.*

*London, June 23*
Air India staff waited in vain at Heathrow airport today for the arrival of a flight from Montreal. It has now become clear that the Boeing 747 vanished from radar screens about 120 miles west of Ireland. All 329 on board are feared dead.

Something happened to the Air India 747 so suddenly that the crew could send no radio message, and it is widely feared that the flight was the victim of a terrorist bomb. Investigators see a possible link between the loss of the Air India 747 and an explosion just 55 minutes earlier which killed two baggage handlers unloading a Canadian Pacific 747 from Vancouver at Tokyo's Narita airport. The Canadian airplane had arrived early, while the Air India Jumbo was running late (→Jul 11).

# India spurns British aid on 'black boxes'

*Hampshire, England, July 11*
Experts at the Royal Aircraft Establishment (RAE) at Farnborough are amazed today at India's rejection of the RAE's offer to analyse the tapes from the two "black boxes" carried by the Air India 747 which crashed into the Atlantic last month. The vital boxes were at last recovered today after an intensive search of the ocean, which at that point is 6,700 feet deep.

The boxes are in fact seldom black, but usually bright orange. They are more properly called FDRs (flight data recorders). Their task is to record continuously all the parameters which might assist an accident investigation. These include flight altitude, airspeed and heading, engine power settings, control-surface positions, slat/flap position, rates of rotation about the three axes, fuel flow and cabin pressure. Investigators would also look

*Do the "black boxes" hold the key?*

for the CVR (cockpit voice recorder) which records what the flight crew say to each other.

The RAE is shocked at India's attitude because the special equipment at Farnborough could extract much more information from the FDR tapes than could any normal playback equipment, such as that available in India (→Oct 18).

# Tragedy claims 520 aboard JAL Boeing 747

*Rescue was difficult in mountains.*

*Japan, August 13*
It was only this morning, some 12 hours after the worst catastrophe involving a single airplane, that rescuers reached survivors of the horrific crash 70 miles north-west of Tokyo. There were only four, out of 524 aboard Japan Air Lines Flight 123, which left Tokyo's Haneda airport yesterday under the command of Captain Takahama.

There was a happy atmosphere among the 509 passengers on board the Boeing 747SR when it took off at 6.12pm. They were leaving the hot, humid capital to celebrate the great Japanese festival of Bon with their families in Osaka. But 12 minutes after take-off, as it was approaching its cruising altitude, the Jumbo was shaken by an explosion. Panic spread among the helpless holiday-makers as the cabin depressurized rapidly. At the same time the captain radioed he was getting no response from his controls as a result of a total loss of hydraulic pressure. A flight engineer reported the rear hold had blown and door number five was open.

After several minutes the captain somehow managed to bring the aircraft under some sort of control by juggling with the four throttle levers. Some of the passengers, sensing the closeness of death, scribbled harrowing farewell notes to their families which were later found scattered about the crash site. With extraordinary coolness the pilot avoided first one mountain, then a second. But the airliner was losing too much height, and at 6.53pm, when it was below 11,000 feet, Mount Otsuka loomed unavoidably ahead. The impact scattered wreckage over a wide area. That anyone survived at all is a miracle (→ 22).

*Only four people survived the crash.*

## Sixteen days of hell end for US hostages

*Beirut, July 1*
Sixteen days of hell came to an end for the 39 passengers and crew of a TWA Boeing 727 today when gunmen of the Iranian-backed Amal guerilla movement summoned the world's press to Beirut airport before disappearing into the suburbs.

During the hijack, one man, a US sailor, was shot in front of fellow passengers and his body thrown onto the runway. Angry President Ronald Reagan had already ordered an aircraft carrier to the area, and retaliation seemed certain until Israel announced it was meeting the terrorists' demand for the release of many of 700 Shi'ite prisoners. For much of the hijack, which began in Rome and continued via Algiers, Beirut, Algiers again and finally Beirut, world attention was focussed through TV cameras on Captain John Trestrake – talking from the flight deck of the 727 with a pistol held to his head.

*Captain John Trestrake stayed in the cockpit with a gun at his head.*

## Third major crash in a month – 54 killed

*Firemen tackle the smoking wreck of the 737 after it exploded in flames.*

*Manchester, England, August 22*
A British Airtours Boeing 737 was about to become airborne here today when its port Pratt & Whitney JT8D engine exploded, causing the aircraft to veer off the runway and burst into flames.

In the ensuing fire, 54 vacationing passengers were killed by dense smoke or flames, while a further 80 escaped via the escape chutes. Already there are calls for the provision of smokehoods as a compulsory safety measure.

This has been the world's worst-ever month for aviation disasters. In Japan, a 747 packed with 524 passengers and crew crashed into a wooded mountainside near Tokyo; only four survived [*see above*]. And in the US, 133 died when a Delta Air Lines Lockheed TriStar crashed when landing at Dallas-Fort Worth airport was knocked out of the sky by a violent downdraft. There were 41 survivors.

The shorter-fuselaged, reduced-capacity Airbus A310, with a smaller high-efficiency wing, has now been developed into the long-ranged A310-300.

The Fokker 50 was an advanced derivative of the original Friendship with Pratt & Whitney Canada PW120 engines and a variety of other improvements.

The Tay-engined Gulfstream IV long-range bizjet also featured an advanced "glass cockpit", a structurally redesigned wing and an extended fuselage.

The Sikorsky Helicopter Advanced Demonstrator of Operator Workload (SHADOW): an S-76 with a single-pilot advanced cockpit grafted in front.

The NAL Asuka was a STOL testbed based on the Kawasaki C-1 with a new wing and upper surface blowing from four FJR710 turbofan engines.

Avions Mudry failed to dent Soviet leadership in the field of advanced aerobatic aircraft even with their excellent CAP 230, derivative of CAP 21.

The ARV Super 2 featured a revolutionary two-stroke engine, with three liquid-cooled cylinders. Sadly, this machine has been hit by repeated bankruptcy.

Like the C-18A transport, the Boeing EC-18B ARIA (Advanced Range Instrumentation Aircraft) was based on the airframe of the Boeing 707-320C.

Lockheed's C-5B Galaxy was almost identical to the earlier variant externally, but it incorporated all the improvements and changes added to the C-5A.

*The Italo-Brazilian Aeritalia/Embraer AMX: a lightweight strike fighter made jointly for both countries' air forces. The engine is a RR Spey turbofan.*

*Upgraded avionics, larger tip tanks and compatibility with new weapons make the Aermacchi MB.339C a more capable aircraft than its predecessors.*

*The Changhe Z-8 is basically a Chinese-built version of the Aérospatiale Super Frelon. The initial batch comprised ten aircraft for naval missions.*

*The RAF's Lockheed TriStar K.Mk1 has two hose drum units on the center-line and two underwing. An inflight refueling probe was also fitted.*

*Bell's D292 was built under the US Army's Advanced Composite Airframe Program (ACAP) as part of an effort to reduce helicopters' weight and cost.*

*The ill-fated Fairchild T-46A Next Generation Trainer was defeated by financial pressures, although it was in itself an excellent little aircraft.*

*This General Dynamics F-111 received a Mission Adaptive Wing, whose camber could be varied in flight, as part of the USAF's AFTI programme.*

*To replace the Fuji T-1 in JASDF service, Kawasaki developed the XT-4 advanced jet trainer. Engines are twin Ishikawajima-Harima F3 turbofans.*

# 1986

4,534mph
USA
Pete Knight
North American X-15
Oct 3, 1967

24,987 miles
USA
Jeager and Rutan
*Voyager*
Dec 23, 1986

354,200ft
USA
Joseph Walker
North American X-15
Aug 22, 1963

892,859lb
USSR
Antonov
An-124 Condor

59,000lb thrust
USA
General Electric
CF6-80C2A1

**London, January 8**
Armed police begin patroling Heathrow airport.

**Oklahoma, January 8**
The first production Lockheed C-5B Galaxy transport is delivered to the USAF at Altus Air Force Base (→ Apr 17, 1989).

**London, January 9**
British defense secretary Michael Heseltine resigns after a row over the future of Westland Helicopters: he is in favor of the company becoming part of a European consortium, while trade and industry secretary Leon Brittan wants greater US participation (→ 24).

**India, January 11**
The first MiG-27M fighter built under license by Hindustan Aeronautics Ltd is delivered to the Indian Air Force.

**Britain and France, January 21**
British Airways and Air France complete a decade of Concorde operations, in which their fleet has flown 71,000 hours at supersonic speeds (→ Dec 2).

**London, January 24**
British trade and industry secretary Leon Brittan resigns as the Westland row continues.

**Canada, January 31**
Boeing buys nationally owned de Havilland Aircraft of Canada.

**London, February 6**
The Heathrow/Gatwick helicopter link is terminated.

**Mediterranean Sea, February 12**
US Sixth Fleet carriers embark 240 F-14 Tomcat and F/A-18 Hornets and set sail for exercises in the Gulf of Sidra, off Libya.

**USA, February 15**
The Beech Model 2000 StarShip 1 eight to 11-seater business airplane, which features wing-tip stabilizers and variable-geometry foreplanes, makes its first flight.

**Iran, February 20**
An Iraqi fighter downs an Iranian Fokker 28 civil aircraft flying from Tehran to Ahwaz; there are no survivors among the passengers, who included members of the Iranian parliament and Ayatollah Khomeini's personal representative.

**Wichita, Kansas, March 3**
A stretched variant of the Cessna Model 208 Caravan I, developed for courier company Federal Express, makes its first flight.→

**Frankfurt, March 6**
Japan Air Lines embarks the world's heaviest man, an 880-lb Austrian, as a passenger; 16 seats are removed from the cabin to make room for him.

**Kuwait, April 1**
An extended-range model Boeing 767-200 lands from Seattle, to set a new distance record of 7,892 miles for a twin-engined airliner.

**Japan and Australia, April 2**
Japan Air Lines and Qantas inaugurate a joint passenger service between Tokyo and Brisbane, via Cairns (→ Mar 23, 1987).

**[West] Germany, April 6**
A pre-war Junkers Ju 52/3m transport takes to the air once more after two years' careful restoration by Lufthansa.

**Neuilly, France, April 18**
Marcel Bloch, 94, dies. Under his professional name of Marcel Dassault he was the most famous of France's airplane designers.

**New York, April 28**
Pan Am resumes its service to the USSR, with a Boeing 747-200 taking off from JFK Airport bound for Leningrad by way of Frankfurt and Moscow.

**Colombo, May 3**
A bomb planted by Tamil separatists kills 20 people on board an Air Lanka TriStar which is about to take off for Madras, India.

**Dallas, Texas, May 7**
Al Mooney, co-founder of Mooney Aircraft, dies at the age of 80.

**Surrey, England, May 19**
The British Aerospace Hawk 200 combat aircraft, a private venture by the company, makes its first flight, at Dunsfold (→ Jul 2).

**Paris, May 25**
Nadin Vaujour, flying an Alouette II helicopter, helps her husband to escape from the city's Santé jail.

**Kent, England, August 30**
Lydd airfield, the nearest in Britain to France, is threatened with closure. Home of England's oldest flying club, the Cinque Ports, it became a major airport in 1948.

**Genoa, Italy, September 23**
The Piaggio P.180 Avanti executive jet flies for the first time; its radical design features two wing-mounted turboprop engines, each driving a pusher propeller.

**Calverton, NY, September 29**
The Grumman F-14A Plus Super Tomcat prototype, powered by General Electric F110-GE-400 turbofans and advanced avionics, begins flight tests.

**London, October 21**
The British government launches the sale of British Airways to the public (→ Jun 27, 1987).

**Shetland Isles, November 6**
A Boeing 234 Chinook helicopter ferrying oil-rig workers crashes; just two of the 47 on board survive, making it the world's worst civilian helicopter crash.

**Britain, November 22**
BAe's Experimental Aircraft Programme (EAP) technology demonstrator is mothballed because of a lack of funds to continue tests.

**St Louis, Missouri, December 2**
Lockheed delivers its 1,800th C-130 Hercules; over 32 years, the sturdy transport has been exported to 56 countries.

**Paris, December 2**
A Concorde airliner carrying 94 passengers returns to Charles de Gaulle airport after an 18-day round-the-world journey; total flying time amounted to 31 hours 51 minutes (→ Apr 12, 1989).

**USA, December 31**
The current crisis in the country's civil aviation industry has led to a dramatic reduction in average crew salaries this year *(see Factfile)*.

---

*Boeing's E-3A Airborne Warning and Control System (AWACS) is easily distinguishable by its 30-foot-diameter rotating radar dome.* ▶

## Factfile

World revenue passenger miles: 902,310.084 million
Passengers through Chicago O'Hare: 53.3 million
Passengers through New York (JFK/Newark/LaGuardia): 78.8 million
Passengers through London (Heathrow/Gatwick): 47.6 million
Price of a single coach ticket New York/Los Angeles (Apr): $240/490
Price of the cheapest return ticket London/New York: $468
World air freight (ton miles): 120,320.7 million
Average salary of long-haul pilot and co-pilot (US): $81,913
Average salary of cabin crew (US): $25,953
Price of a Boeing 747 Combi: $97 million
Price of an Airbus A310-300: $58 million
Price of a Boeing 757: $50 million
Price of 1,000 (US) gallons of Jet A1 fuel: $564.71
Average exchange rate: £1 = $1.4671

# People Express follows expansion road

*Newark, NJ, January 31*
People Express today bought the nation's oldest commuter airline, Provincetown Boston Airlines. The upstart low-fare airline, which began with services to three cities in May 1981, now flies to more than 50 US cities, as well as to London, and is flying more than 1.1 million passengers per month. The recent growth by People came through challenging Eastern Air Lines' dominance in Florida with $79 fares to Miami and Orlando. The acquisition of Denver-based Frontier Airlines last November provided a second main operating base at Stapleton airport for People's fleet of 50 Boeing 727-200s, 22 737s and six 747s (→ Feb 2, 1987).

*Low fares have enabled People Express to serve over 50 US cities.*

# Americans stunned by Challenger tragedy

*Cape Canaveral, Fla, January 28*
TV viewers round the world today watched, horrified, as the space shuttle *Challenger* exploded shortly after blast-off – the first fatal in-flight accident in NASA's manned space program. It was the 25th shuttle mission, and the tenth by *Challenger*. The mission was not especially demanding, and the crew of seven included several experienced astronauts and schoolteacher Christa McAuliffe.

The vehicle exploded just 72 seconds into the flight. Two seconds later the Mission Control commentator announced: "Velocity 2,900 feet per second, altitude 9 nautical miles, downrange distance 7 nautical miles." The pilot had just throttled up the three space shuttle main engines (SSMEs) from 65 per cent to 104 per cent, but these seem to have played no part in the disaster. There is no doubt that the fireball was made by the explosion of the huge fuel tank, loaded with a high proportion of its original load of 795 tons of liquid oxygen and liquid

*"Challenger's" moment of tragedy.*

hydrogen. But the tank could not have been ruptured except by externally inflicted damage. Increasing suspicion is falling upon the solid rocket boosters. One may have exploded.

# Shorts to build Brazilian trainer for RAF

*Brazil, February 14*
The first flight of an EMBRAER Tucano with a 1,100-hp Garrett TPE331 turboprop engine, as specified by Britain's RAF for its forthcoming T.Mk 1s, took place today.

In control of the Brazilian-designed prototype was test pilot Alan Deacon of British manufacturer Shorts. The Garrett replaces the 750-hp Pratt & Whitney Canada PT6A of standard Tucanos, allowing a higher speed, particularly at low altitude, and better rate of climb. RAF Tucanos, to be built under license by Shorts, will also have redesigned cockpits and structural strengthening. The prototype will be airfreighted to Britain after initial trials (→ Jan 20, 1987).

*The EMB-312 Tucano trainer is to be built under license by Shorts in Belfast.*

# FedEx is set to fly the mail by Caravan

*Wichita, Kansas, March 3*
Cessna's Model 208 Caravan I was designed to supersede the Beaver and Otter as a rough-terrain airplane. Because it is above all an economical aircraft, international courier Federal Express (FedEx) decided to acquire the Caravan I in large numbers. Powered by a 590-hp Pratt & Whitney Canada turbo-prop, it can also carry a ton of cargo and requires only light maintenance. A modified version for FedEx flew for the first time today; the fuselage has been "stretched" by 4 feet, and the cabin windows have been taken out. The Model 208 comes in various versions, for both civil and military use, with either wheel, ski or float undercarriage.

*The Caravan, modified for Federal Express, can carry a ton of freight.*

# Reagan unleashes his bombers to 'punish' Libya

*Tripoli, April 15*
US Air Force and Navy aircraft made surprise pre-dawn attacks on military installations in Libya today, "executing a series of carefully planned air strikes against terrorist targets", according to presidential spokesman Larry Speakes. These targets were part of the terrorist infrastructure, he claimed, including training facilities.

The attacks, which began at 1am GMT, are said to be in retaliation for alleged Libyan-backed terrorist activities against the West, including the bombing of a German discotheque ten days ago in which two died and 230 others were injured. Early reports suggest perhaps 15 Libyans have been killed and 60 to 100 injured. The dead are believed to include Colonel Gadaffi's adopted daughter, Hana, who suffered a brain hemorrhage. Eighteen USAF F-111s – chosen for

their bombing accuracy – and 15 US Navy A-6 Intruders and A-7E Corsair IIs took part in the attacks, supported by 30 in-flight refueling tankers and three EF-111A Raven electronic warfare airplanes. The only US loss was one General Dynamics F-111 bomber and its crew. The mission began in Britain at Mildenhall air base, Suffolk, from which tanker airplanes took off to position themselves to refuel the F-111s which were later to leave Upper Heyford, Oxfordshire, and Lakenheath, Suffolk. The French government's refusal to allow the F-111s to overfly France forced a 2,400-mile detour and two in-flight refuelings.

Next, the US Navy's Sixth Fleet went into action, sending light bombers to attack Libyan radar. The first US strikes were against the airport, Sidi Bilal naval harbor and Tripoli's Al Azziziyah bar-

*US Defense Department photos show Soviet planes under attack at Tripoli.*

racks. Stray bombs are said to have damaged five foreign embassy buildings. Meanwhile, Navy airplanes hit Benghazi, bombing the Benina airfield and airplanes and Jumahi-

riya barracks. Yesterday a Libyan vessel fired two missiles against a US radar site on the Italian island of Lampedusa, but failed to find their target (→ Jan 5, 1989).

## Terrorist bomb blasts TWA 727 in mid-air

*The Boeing 727 bears the scars of the bomb after it landed at Athens.*

*Athens, Greece, April 2*
A TWA Boeing 727 en route from Rome to Athens landed safely here today despite a mid-flight explosion which had ripped a 9-foot-by-3-foot hole in its fuselage. Four passengers were sucked through the hole and nine were injured when a bomb blasted the aircraft as it began its let-down.

The bodies of three of the dead, including a child, were found on a mountainside near the town of Argos; the fourth body was found in the sea. Security experts are certain

that the bomb was placed by terrorists in the pay of Libyan leader Colonel Gadaffi seeking revenge for the US Navy's action in the Gulf of Sirte last week in which Libyan fighters were shot down. Most of the 114 passengers had transferred from a flight from New York, only ten joining in Rome.

Experts agree the aircraft was saved by its low altitude. Had it been a few thousand feet higher, rapid depressurization would almost certainly have caused it to disintegrate.

## New terminal opened at Heathrow Airport

*London, April 12*
Champagne was flowing in jet-fuel measures at Heathrow today when, with American-style razzmatazz, the British Airports Authority opened a much-needed fourth terminal at the world's busiest international airport. The stylish building, to be used mainly by British Airways (BA) long-haul flights, should increase Heathrow's capacity by about eight million to 38 million passengers a year.

The first of these, who arrived on a BA flight from Tokyo at 5.45am, were greeted by bagpipes, free Concorde tickets and teddy bears – with the added bonus of unhindered passage through Customs, which were enjoying a typically British strike to mark the occasion.

*Terminal Four before opening.*

## Only BAe Hawk 200 is destroyed in crash

*Surrey, England, July 2*
An impressive demonstration of the private-venture Hawk 200 by the deputy chief test pilot at British Aerospace's Dunsfold airfield ended abruptly in tragedy today.

The apparently problem-free aircraft looped at low altitude and then dived into the ground. Pilot

Jim Hawkins, 47, died instantly. The Mk 200 is a new version of the proven Hawk trainer, hundreds of which are flying. The new airplane is a single seater, with comprehensive avionics equipment and weapons for a wide range of roles; these include battlefield interdiction and close air support (→ Jan 14, 1987). ▷

# 'Unducted fan' engine is tested on 727

*The "unducted fan" is seen here mounted on the right of the fuselage.*

*California, August 20*
General Electric started flight-tests of its GE36 "propfan" engine, better known as the UDF ("unducted fan"), at Edwards Air Force Base today. A single GE36 engine has been mounted on the right pylon on the rear fuselage of a Boeing 727 airliner. The 727's other two engines, P&W JT8D turbofans, remain.

The supposed advantage of a propfan is that, by driving extremely thin scimitar-like blades, it can achieve jet speed with the fuel consumption of a turboprop. General

Electric has made a bigger effort, and spent more money, on this new class of engine than anyone else.

In the GE36 the complications and potential problems of a reduction gearbox are solved by not having one; the contra-rotating sets of blades are instead mounted directly on extra turbine stages at the back of the engine. It is too early to assess gains in fuel economy, but today's flight has answered one worrying question. The radically new engine proved no noisier than modern turbofans and turboprops.

# Dassault unveils hi-tech Rafale A fighter

*Istres, France, July 4*
The 92nd prototype to be produced by Avions Marcel Dassault made its first flight here today, at the French national flight test center. It is perhaps the most important of the 92, for the new Rafale [Hurricane] is slated to replace virtually all the fighters in both the French air force and navy.

Production versions of the new aircraft, which will be different for each service, will be powered by new French engines, a pair of SNECMA M88s. The prototype now flying has US-supplied General Electric F404 afterburning turbofans, similar to those of the F/A-18 Hornet, each giving 16,000 lb of thrust.

Like all new fighters, the Rafale is a basically unstable design, flown only with the aid of computers. Features include a large aft-mounted delta wing, forward controlable canard foreplanes, a single fin and twin engine-air inlets on the flanks of the forward fuselage.

Chief test pilot Guy Mitaux-Maurouard expressed full satisfaction with the aircraft, which France is boldly developing alone. In contrast, its rival, the European Fighter Aircraft, is being produced by four nations (→ Jan 26, 1988).

*The Rafale: an important future?*

# Futuristic British EAP tests the very latest combat technology

*England, August 8*
The Experimental Aircraft Programme (EAP) airplane built by British Aerospace (BAe), which has made its first flight today at Warton, is potentially the most important new airplane in Europe. Although the EAP is a unique example made to demonstrate new technology, its performance could lead to a huge program to build 1,000 new fighters.

The new fighter is simply known as the EFA (European Fighter Aircraft) and is a joint project by BAe, MBB of West Germany, Aeritalia of Italy and CASA of Spain. All four national air forces urgently need a modern combat fighter.

The EFA will be packed with new technology and powered by new engines, but the EAP is powered by the same pair of Turbo-Union RB.199 engines as the Tornado. Its large, single vertical tail is

*The experimental EAP could lead to a potential 1,000-plane order.*

also modified from that of a Tornado, but in other respects the EAP is totally new. Features include a huge delta wing mounted at the rear, a pair of downsloping fore-

planes and a large rectangular air inlet underneath. Even on this first flight the speed of sound was exceeded. The flight itself lasted 1 hour 7 minutes.

# United's hub makes more connections

*Washington, DC, May 1*
United Air Lines opened its new $15 million passenger hub at Dulles International Airport today. It could spell trouble for smaller carriers such as Dulles-based Presidential Airlines, which do not have as extensive a route network.

Hubs are designed to keep passengers from changing airlines to reach a destination, and to get maximum use from aircraft at maximum capacity. They cut down on long, nonstop flights with empty seats. Instead, someone going, for example, from New York to Jacksonville, Florida, would fly to Washington, DC, on a full airplane with people going to New Orleans, Houston, and other destinations. In Washington, they would board other planes from the same airline to reach their final destinations (→ Dec 10, 1987).

# Voyager lightplane flies the world

## US Army takes on Apache helicopter

*Killeen, Texas, October 1*
The 3rd Squadron of the 6th Cavalry Brigade, based here at Fort Hood, is the first unit in the US Army to have been fully trained, equipped and fielded with the Mc-Donnell Douglas AH-64 Apache advanced attack helicopter. Developed by Hughes Helicopter before the company was acquired by Mc-Donnell Douglas, the Apache will be the Army's primary attack helicopter. With its 30mm Chain Gun and rockets it is designed to provide 24-hour fire support to units in the field. Eventually it will be equipped with 16 laser-guided Hellfire anti-tank missiles.

## Tourists saved from a towering inferno

*Puerto Rico, December 31*
At least 80 people died when a horrifying fire swept through the 21-storey Dupont Plaza hotel at San Juan today, but the death toll would have been much higher had it not been for the efforts of the US Coast Guard HH-65A Dolphins and Sikorsky H-3 Sea Kings of the US Navy, which made repeated flights through the smoke to rescue people who had managed to find their way to the roof. They were even able to rescue some people from rooms in which they had become trapped. One crew alone succeeded in rescuing 13 people.

*Rescue under way at the hotel.*

*The record-breaking "Voyager": conquering aviation's last frontiers.*

**2 - OIL PUMP.** An adapted version of the tiny pump used in open-heart surgery supplies oil to the engines.

Warm air directed towards the cabin

Radiator

Oil pump

Air sucked in from outside

Canopy

Parachutes

**1- HOT MEALS.** Precooker in sealed packages and reheated on the radiator of the rear engine. A small immersion heater is used to heat liquids.

Radio and intercom

Food store

Forward fuel tank

**5 - TOILETS.** Feces are put into bags and stored away in one of the wings. The pilots' urine is evacuated via a funnel connected to a tube which goes across the fuselage.

**3 - WATER.** 10.5 US gallons in individual plastic sachets, each of which contains one glass.

**4 - OXYGEN.** A supply for flying above 16,500 ft.

*California, December 23*
In what Dick Rutan called the "last major event in atmospheric flight", a trimaran-configured Magnamite graphite and Hexcel paper honeycomb Voyager light airplane today became the first aircraft to fly non-stop and unrefueled around the world. A crowd estimated at 50,000 gathered at the giant Edwards Air Force Base in the Californian desert to see the historic airplane land on a runway which is normally reserved for the NASA space shuttle.

Voyager was designed by Dick's brother, Burt Rutan, and cost about $2 million of sponsored and donated money. Fuel was always going to be the greatest problem. It took off with 1,208.9 (US) gallons on board, and after 24,986 miles it landed with just 37 gallons remaining.

The weather had demanded so many route detours over Africa that on occasions Rutan believed he might run out of fuel early. In a tiny, unpressurized fuselage pod just 2 feet wide, Dick Rutan and co-pilot Jeana Yeager lived for 9 days 3 minutes 44 seconds, snatching sleep in the bunk area.

The epic voyage began at 7.59am local time on December 14, the 110-foot wingspan *Voyager* taking 14,200 feet of runway to lift off. A westbound course was chosen. The aircraft and its crew completed their remarkable circumnavigation today at 8.05am.

## Composite blades help Lynx helicopter to set world speed record

*England, August 11*
The Westland Lynx demonstrator set a world speed record for helicopters today. Its average speed over a 15/25-km [9.3/15.5-mile] course was 249.09mph, making it the first helicopter to exceed 400 kilometers per hour [248.95mph]. Piloting was Trevor Egginton. Subject to FAI ratification, the Lynx has beaten the old record, held by the A-10 special version of the Soviet Mil Mi-24 gunship, by over 20mph.

For the record flight the Lynx was fitted with advanced British Experimental Rotor Programme (BERP) III main rotor blades; the airframe was cleaned up to aid streamlining; a water-methanol in-

*The Westland Lynx helicopter seen here before its record flight today.*

jection system and tuned jetpipes were added to the normal Gem 60 turboshaft engines; the gearbox was uprated, and new tail surfaces were installed. The BERP blades are said to improve rotor efficiency by up to 40 per cent. They are built of composite materials, with paddle-like tips. Airfoil section and planform vary along their length.

*The Fokker 100 is a substantially upgraded and improved stretched-fuselage derivative of the F.28 Fellowship. Engines are two Rolls-Royce Tay turbofans.*

*The Boeing 767-300 is slightly stretched, to accommodate 269 passengers, and has a strengthened airframe. The fuselage is narrower than an A300.*

*Production examples are manufactured by Beech, but the Model 2000 Starship I's prototype (see 1983) was built by Burt Rutan's Scaled Composites.*

*The Piaggio Avanti is powered by a pair of pusher turboprops. A six-to-ten seat executive aircraft, the Avanti was developed in conjunction with Gates.*

*Canadair's Challenger CL601-3A had a "glass" cockpit and upgraded GE CF34-3A engines for improved hot day and high-altitude airfield performance.*

*The MD-87 is a short-fuselage member of the MD-80 family, with accommodation for up to 130 passengers. It has various low drag modifications.*

*The Mil Mi-34 will be a lightweight two/four seater with a piston engine.*

*Italy's Partenavia P.86 Mosquito was transferred to the firm of Aviolight.*

*BAe's ATP is an advanced technology regional turboprop loosely based on the proven airframe of the BAe 748, but with a 16 foot fuselage stretch.*

*The Polish PZL-130 Orlik (Spotted Eagle): intended for target towing, reconnaissance and even ground attack, as well as tandem pilot training.*

*The dedicated ground attack Eagle, the McDonnell Douglas F-15E, was originally known as the Strike Eagle, although this name was later dropped.*

*Dassault's next-generation fighter aircraft is the Rafale (meaning Hurricane). The original Rafale A was larger than the intended production version.*

*Britain's EAP (two RB.199 engines) was built as a technology demonstrator for the similarly configured Anglo-German-Italian-Spanish Eurofighter.*

*The little-known Kamov "Hokum" first flew on July 27, 1982.*

*The high-tech IAI Lavi was canceled due to financial problems, but was intended as an indigenous F-16 replacement, with the accent on ground attack.*

*The single-seat BAe Hawk 200 was derived from the Hawk trainer.*

*The PZL I-22 Iryd is a tandem-seat advanced trainer, reconnaissance aircraft and ground-attack fighter, built as a twin-jet successor to the TS-11 Iskra.*

*Finland's Valmet Redigo: a 500-hp Allison-engined turboprop trainer.*

*The Cessna Caravan, a versatile and tough 14-seat utility transport.*

*Cranfield Institute of Technology converted the ASTRA (Advanced System Training Aircraft) Hawk as a variable-stability platform for the ETPS.*

# 1987

4,534mph
USA
Pete Knight
North American X-15
Oct 3, 1967

24,987 miles
USA
Jeager and Rutan
*Voyager*
Dec 23, 1986

354,200ft
USA
Joseph Walker
North American X-15
Aug 22, 1963

892,859lb
USSR
Antonov
An-124 Condor

61,500lb thrust
USA
General Electric
CF6-80C2A5

**Chad, January 7**
French Jaguar fighters hit radar installations at the Libyan base at Ouadi Doum in reprisal for a Libyan raid on January 4 against French positions at Arada.

**Beirut, January 8**
The airport is closed after a bomb planted on a Middle East Airlines Boeing 707 explodes during ground maintenance.

**Switzerland, January 14**
Switzerland chooses the British Aerospace Hawk to replace its Vampire trainers.

**Belfast, January 20**
The first production Short Tucano T.1 turboprop trainer, designed in Brazil by EMBRAER and produced under license, rolls out.

**New York, February 2**
People Express flies its last service, from Newark; it has been taken over by Continental Airlines (→ Nov 23).

**Mont-de-Marsan, France, Feb 19**
The first Dassault-Breguet Mirage 2000N is delivered to the French air force, to replace the Mirage IIIE and the Jaguar (→ Mar 30, 1988).

**Paris, February 26**
France orders three Boeing AWACS E-3A Sentry reconnaissance airplanes.

**Washington, DC, March 9**
The airline USAir announces that it is taking over Piedmont Airlines for $1.59 billion (→ Aug 8, 1989).

**Japan, March 23**
Japan Air Lines announces that it is to fit its airliners with a new off-course alert system to warn crew-members when they stray from the correct flightpath.

**France, March 31**
Flight tests begin of a version of the Mirage III fitted with a voice decoder, by means of which the pilot can give spoken instructions to the computer which is controlling the airplane.

**Sweden, April 26**
The first full-scale prototype of Saab's hi-tech JAS 39 Gripen fighter is unveiled.

**Bristol, England, May 1**
Paramount Airways begins operations, with a fleet of two McDonnell Douglas MD-83s.

**Warsaw, May 9**
One hundred and eighty-three die when an Ilyushin Il-62M of Polish airline LOT, bound for New York, crashes when two of its engines catch fire shortly after take-off.

**Paris, June 21**
Air France pilot Patrick Fourticq and racing driver Henri Pescarolo land their Lockheed 18 *Spirit of J & B*, sponsored by whisky manufacturers J & B, at Le Bourget to complete a round-the-world flight in 88 hours 19 minutes, beating by just under 3 hours the record of 91 hours 8 minutes set by Howard Hughes in 1938 with almost the same type.

**Buckinghamshire, England, Jun 21**
The last airworthy Bristol Blenheim bomber – a Mark IV rebuilt by the British Aerial Museum – is damaged beyond repair while attempting a touch-and-go landing during an air show at Denham; the shaken crew-members escape with only minor injuries.

**Palmdale, California, July 4**
A Rockwell B-1B bomber sets four unofficial world records for speed, distance and payload; taking off with a 66,140-lb payload, it flies two legs, the first of 620 miles at an average speed of 678.48mph, and the second of 1,240 miles at 669.52mph average (→ Sep 28).

**Zürich, July 10**
Swissair, British Airways, KLM and United Air Lines launch the Galileo ticket reservation system (→ May 15, 1989).

**Britain, July 16**
British Airways announces it is buying Britain's second largest airline, British Caledonian, for £237 million (→ Aug 6).

**Britain, July 16**
The British Airports Authority (BAA) is privatized.

**London, August 6**
The British government says it will refer British Airways' takeover of British Caledonian to the body which regulates Britain's anti-trust laws, the Monopolies and Mergers Commission (→ Apr 14, 1988).

**Detroit, August 16**
A Northwest Airlines McDonnell Douglas MD-80 crashes onto a freeway when one of its engines catches fire shortly after take-off from Detroit; 154 die.

## Factfile

World revenue passenger miles: 987,149.826 million
Passengers through Chicago O'Hare: 26.1 million
Passengers through New York (JFK/Newark/LaGuardia): 32.6 million
Passengers through London (Heathrow/Gatwick): 54.1 million
Price of a single coach ticket New York/Los Angeles (May): $270/530
Price of the cheapest return ticket London/New York: $398
World air freight (ton miles): 130,074.6 million
Average salary of long-haul pilot and co-pilot (US): $87,420
Average salary of cabin crew (US): $30,027
Price of a Boeing 747 Combi: $100.7 million
Price of an Airbus A340: $85.5 million
Price of an Airbus A320: $31.2 million
Price of 1,000 (US) gallons of Jet A1 fuel: $635.20
Average exchange rate: £1 = $1.6392

**La Junta, Colorado, September 28**
A USAF B-1B bomber on a high-speed, low-altitude training flight crashes after it collides with a 15/20-lb bird, probably a large pelican; three of six servicemen on board are killed (→ Nov 18, 1988).

**Japan, October 21**
Japan Air Lines is to use General Electric engines in its Boeing 747-400 airliners (→ Nov 18).

**Britain, October 31**
British Airways takes on its first women pilots.

**Japan, November 18**
Japan Air Lines changes status, becoming an entirely privately-owned company (→ Dec 14, 1988).

**Washington, DC, November 19**
A US Department of Defense contract worth $2 billion is awarded to Northrop for production of the forthcoming B-2 bomber (→ Jul 17, 1989).

**New York, November 23**
Figures published today reveal that of 128 new, mainly low-cost airlines certified after US deregulation (from 1978 through July this year), only 37 are still operating; large, established carriers control 90 per cent of US commercial traffic.

**Denver, Colorado, November 25**
A Continental Airlines DC-9, caught in a snowstorm, turns over while attempting to take off, killing 26 and injuring 56; some survivors are trapped in the wreckage for six hours before being rescued.

**USA and Britain, December 10**
United Air Lines and British Airways launch a worldwide marketing partnership; they will share facilities and coordinate schedules (→ Jul 18, 1989).

*Thousands of amateur flyers flock each summer to the Experimental Aircraft Association's annual meet at Oshkosh, Wisconsin.* ▶

# Enter the A320: the airliner flown by computer

*Toulouse, France, February 22*
The latest of Airbus Industrie's progeny, the Airbus A320, took to the air today. More than any previous airliner, the short/medium-range A320 owes both its existence and its performance to the latest information technology.

It is the first airliner to make extensive use in its development of not only computer-assisted design (CAD) but also computer-assisted manufacture (CAM). CAD is responsible for no less than 100 per cent of the design, and CAM for 80 per cent of the realization, of the A320. When it enters service next year it will be the first commercial aircraft to make full use of the all-electronic "fly-by-wire" concept. Even before the A320 leaves the factory its performance is pre-programed. It "knows" not to fly too fast or too slowly, a fact which should, for instance, rule out the possibility of an A320 stalling.

The A320's cockpit is designed for a flight crew of only two. The

*The A320 has a small sidestick.*

*Jean Pierson gives Princess Diana the bottle of champagne.*

pilots have "sidesticks" instead of the time-honored "joystick" control columns; the A320 dispenses with the cables of previous airliners, since most of the control surfaces are operated by electronic signals from the sidesticks. The only cable, to the rudder, has a trim function. Electronic controls give none of the customary feedback sense of air acting on aerodynamic surfaces. There are seven on-board computers handling all flight control functions such as pitch, roll/attitude and changes of flight level, and also thrust-control functions.

Even the throttles are based on computer logic and do not move in the traditional manner. Six interactive color monitor screens (two in front of each pilot and two centrally) provide primary flight and navigational data and total-systems information (→ Apr 29, 1988).

## Privatization nears for British Airways

*London, January 27*
British Airways chairman Lord King has welcomed another move today toward privatization of the airline. The British government has announced a share price of £1.25. With 720 million shares available, this puts the value of the airline at £900 million. One in five shares will be offered abroad (→ Jul 16).

*Glad to go private: Lord King (r).*

## German pilot lands Cessna in Red Square

*Mathias Rust's Cessna 172 on his audacious flight to the Soviet capital.*

*Moscow, May 29*
Shoppers, tourists and guardsmen watched amazed today as a Cessna 172 buzzed the Kremlin, made a tight turn around the multi-colored domes of St Basil's Cathedral and then made a perfect landing on the hallowed flagstones of Red Square. They were even more bemused when the pilot climbed out and began signing autographs.

To the huge embarrassment of Soviet military authorities, West German pilot Mathias Rust, 19, had outwitted one of the most sophisticated defense systems in the world. Taking off from Helsinki, the tiny Cessna had ducked under Soviet radar and flown, often at rooftop height, to the USSR's capital, which is ringed with anti-aircraft missiles.

Rust, who gained his pilot's license only a year ago, had originally taken off from Hamburg and flown via various North Sea islands to Finland. Helsinki air-traffic control had watched him flying toward Moscow but failed to contact him. As he sits in a Moscow jail tonight, charged with violating Soviet airspace, Rust can be sure that he will have ample time in which to contemplate his historic flight.

## Hijacker captured by own hostages

*Geneva, July 24*
Members of the crew of an Air Afrique DC-10 turned the tables on one hijacker today when they overpowered a Lebanese terrorist after he had killed a French passenger. An airline steward was critically wounded in the struggle, and 30 other people were hurt.

The flight began at Brazzaville and then stopped in Rome before taking off for Geneva. Hussein Ali Mohamed Hariri bided his time, taking control only on the last leg of the journey. He announced that he had a score to settle with France and he demanded the release of Lebanese Shi'ite brothers Mohamed and Abbas Hamadei, currently jailed for terrorism in West Germany. Once the DC-10 landed at Geneva, he isolated the 64 French passengers from the other 99 in preparation for negotiations with the French and German authorities, but when a passenger opened the back door of the aircraft chaos ensued, in the midst of which the hijacker was seized.

# Entrepreneur Branson turns balloonist

*The largest-ever hot-air balloon.*

*Limavady, Northern Ireland, July 3*
Richard Branson, owner of the Virgin group, and balloon manufacturer Per Lindstrand have been rescued after a dramatic end to the first-ever transatlantic flight by hot-air balloon. During their 31-hour 41-minute trip, a distance record of 3,075 miles and a speed record of 153mph were set by entering a jetstream at 27,000 feet.

The *Virgin Atlantic Flyer* is the largest hot-air balloon ever built. As it set off from Sugar Loaf Mountain, Maine, at 8.10am GMT yesterday, a snagging ballast line ripped off two fuel tanks, but they were not needed. The balloon hit ground at Limavady, lifting again to come down in the Irish Sea.

# United opens huge terminal at Chicago

*Chicago, August 4*
United Air Lines has opened the world's largest single-airline terminal at its main hub at Chicago's O'Hare International Airport. The $500 million structure will handle airplanes and people quickly and efficiently to help relieve congestion at an airport designed for 20 million passengers a year, but which last year served 55 million.

The hub has 48 gates and can handle up to 18 wide-bodied airliners at a time. Inside there are 46 ticket counters. Laser-read baggage tags are used, and automatic sorters process 480 pieces of baggage a minute. Two soaring glass concourses are connected by an avant-garde underground passage.

# Soviet fighter hits a Nato patrol aircraft

*Andoya, Norway, September 13*
The Lockheed P-3 Orion maritime-patrol aircraft based here with Squadron 333 of the Royal Norwegian air force encounter Soviet airplanes on most missions. They often come close enough to wave to one another, but today a Sukhoi Su-27 (Nato codename: "Flanker") got a little too intimate.

The port vertical tail of the giant fighter collided with the propeller of the P-3's starboard outer turbo-prop engine. Severe damage was caused to both, although the P-3 returned here and made a normal landing, and there is no reason to doubt that the fighter also got home safely. Such a near-tragedy is most unlikely to happen again.

# Ten-year-old boy pilots Piper across US

*Christopher: all his own work.*

*Florida, July 23*
At an age when most other children are playing with model aircraft, little Christopher Marshall has crossed the US at the controls of a single-engined Piper Warrior. The ten-year-old took off from Oceanside, California, the town of his birth, and landed, without the help of the instructor who was accompanying him, at Fort Lauderdale. Including stops, the young pilot has been flying his aircraft continuously for five days (→Jul 13, 1988).

# New city-center airport opens in London

*A BAe 146 approaches London's new airport in the old docklands area.*

*London, November 5*
London City Airport, in the heart of the city's old docklands, was opened today by Queen Elizabeth II. How well this bold concept works will be watched closely by other British and European cities, which will assess the environmental impact and economic benefits of flying short/medium-range airliners into the heart of a conurbation. The airport was seen as crucial to the docklands' regeneration. But the environmental battle was won only by the quietness and short take-off and landing capability of the four-turboprop 50-seat de Havilland Canada DHC-7 (Dash 7).

The Dash 7 takes off steeply and very quietly. Louder turboprops are permitted only at the expense of several Dash 7 movements. The battle to allow the quiet BAe 146 jet to fly in looms large.

**New color-coding helps air-traffic controlers distinguish flightpaths.**

Airbus Industrie's short-medium range, single-aisle Airbus A320 introduced digital FBW controls, sidestick controllers, and extensive use of composites.

The A300-600R is an extended-range version of the Airbus A300-600 with a tailplane trim tank, increased maximum weights and other detail changes.

The MD-88 has EFIS cockpit displays, a flight management system, onboard windshear detection and a host of other improvements. It can seat 142.

MacAvia's firefighting conversion of the BAe 748 releases a load of retardant. This conversion has not sold, despite having an outstanding performance.

The Dash Eight was the last DHC design, Boeing then taking over the company. The DHC-8-300, pictured, is a stretched version.

The BAe 146-300 has a stretched fuselage, allowing 100 passengers to be carried (five abreast), or up to 128 in various six-abreast configurations.

This McDonnell Douglas MD-80 served as a demonstrator for an Ultra High Bypass (UHB) or propfan engine developed by GE Aircraft Engines.

The Boeing Model 360 is a private-venture research vehicle and demonstrator for a new, high-technology utility helicopter able to cruise at 230mph.

The original Egrett proof of concept high-altitude surveillance aircraft, which has been followed by more highly developed pre-production versions.

With the Grumman F-14A (Plus) (now the F-14B) the Tomcat at last got a reliable engine, removing the US Navy's frontline fighter's main handicap.

Promavia's Jet Squalus (one F109 turbofan) was designed as an "all-through" jet trainer, and was marketed as a possible alternative to the T-46.

The Night Attack version of the AV-8B Harrier II has a FLIR (forward-looking infra-red) above the nose, and a night vision compatible cockpit.

A military version of the Beechcraft Model 400 was developed to meet the USAF's TTBTS (Tanker Transport Bomber Training System) requirement.

The IAI Phantom 2000 (Kurnas) upgrade involved structural strengthening, re-wiring, improved aerodynamics and redesign of the hydraulic system.

The Grumman A-6F Intruder II: an upgrade for the A-6E, with new avionics in a redesigned cockpit and new non-afterburning GE F404 engines.

Boeing's E-6A: developed to replace the EC-130Q in the TACAMO role, to communicate between SSBNs and the shore-based command structure.

The Sikorsky SH-60F was designed as a CV Inner Zone ASW helicopter to replace the SH-3H Sea King. LAMPS (p.697) installations were removed.

The Anglo-Italian EH-101 was originally designed as the Westland WG34 three-engined ASW helicopter for the RN and Italian Navy.

4,534mph
USA
Pete Knight
North American X-15
Oct 3, 1967

24,987 miles
USA
Jeager and Rutan
Voyager
Dec 23, 1986

354,200ft
USA
Joseph Walker
North American X-15
Aug 22, 1963

892,859lb
USSR
Antonov
An-124 Condor

61,500lb thrust
USA
General Electric
CF6-80C2A5

**Canada, January 1**
The Canadian airline industry is deregulated (→ Oct 9, 1990).

**Paris, January 26**
The Dassault-Breguet Rafale is chosen to equip the Armée de l'Air and Aéronavale.

**Seattle, January 30**
Boeing's long-range 747SP *Friendship One* returns to set a round-the-world record of 36 hours 54 minutes 15 seconds.

**Washington, DC, February 8**
The FAA retires an aircraft registration number for the first time – that of Amelia Earhart's airplane, which disappeared over the Pacific in July 1937.

**West Sussex, England, March 18**
The new North Terminal of London's Gatwick Airport is opened by Queen Elizabeth II.

**Paris, March 28**
Celebrating its delivery to Air France, the first Airbus A320 to reach a customer flies at 1,500 feet down the Champs-Elysées in the heart of the city with Prime Minister Jacques Chirac on board.

**Luxeuil, France, March 30**
The first Mirage 2000N is delivered to the French air force.

**London, April 1**
Caledonian Airways is established as a wholly owned subsidiary of British Airways; it will operate charter flights for British Airtours and British Caledonian (→ Apr 14).

**London, April 14**
Following approval of the takeover by Britain's Monopolies and Mergers Commission, all of British Caledonian's business is transferred to British Airways (→ Jan 15, 1990).

**Long Beach, California, April 16**
The McDonnell Douglas T-45 Goshawk naval trainer, developed from the British Aerospace Hawk, makes its first flight.

**Algiers, April 20**
The last hostages are freed from a Kuwaiti Boeing 747 which was hijacked over on April 5.

**London, April 25**
The British government announces funds of £6 billion for the RAF's Eurofighter program (→ Nov 1).

**Hawaii, April 30**
The FAA bars older Boeing 737s from flying above 23,000 feet after an Aloha Airlines 737's fuselage ripped open here two days ago.

**Arkansas, May 26**
Blytheville Air Force Base is renamed in honor of General Ira C Eaker, the first commander of the US Army Eighth Air Force in the Second World War.

**Elmira, NY, June 14**
Robert Golden takes the Schweizer 330 helicopter on its first flight.

**Paris, July 13**
American Chris Marshall, 11, lands here in a Mooney airplane after a flight from San Diego, which he left on July 8.

**France, September 14**
Michel Asselline, pilot of the Airbus A320 which crashed on June 26, is sacked after an inquiry reveals it was flying too low; the crew were flying manually, and were inattentive (→ ).

**New Zealand, October 3**
Air New Zealand imposes a ban on smoking on board all its domestic flights (→ Dec 20).

**USA, October 4**
Scandinavian airline SAS acquires 10 per cent of the capital of Texas Air Corporation, parent of Continental Airlines and Eastern Air Lines (→ Oct 12).

**Seattle, October 9**
Boeing Advanced Systems begins tests of the Condor, a large twin-engined robotic airplane capable of flying entire missions according to information pre-programed into on-board computers.

**Pennsylvania, October 12**
A Bar Harbor Airlines ATR 42 is involved in a "close call" with the official presidential Boeing when it approached to within 1,000 feet of *Air Force One*.

**New York, October 12**
Real estate developer Donald J Trump agrees to buy the Eastern Air Lines shuttle service, including 17 ageing Boeing 727s, from the Texas Air Corporation for $365 million; the deal bars Trump from selling the shuttle to another airline for ten years.

**Britain, October 20**
Record-breaking British airwoman Sheila Scott, 61, dies.

**China, October 21**
Grumman signs a contract with China to develop the Super 7 fighter, an advanced version of the F-7; it is the first true joint project between China and the West.

**London, October 26**
A British Airways Boeing 747 arrives from Tokyo with one passenger, a Japanese woman; when a technical hitch delayed take-off, all the other passengers made new arrangements, giving the woman the choice of 353 seats.

**Toulouse, France, October 27**
The ATR 72 64/74-seat airliner makes its first flight; it is the first airliner to have major parts of its wings made out of carbon fiber.

**Britain, October 27**
Air UK becomes the first non-US carrier to fly the Boeing 737-400 airliner (→ Dec 14).

**South Dakota, November 18**
A B-1B of 28th Bomb Wing, USAF, crashes near Ellsworth Air Force Base; ten days ago a B-1B of 96th Bomb Wing crashed at Dyess Air Force Base, Texas; no one was injured in either accident.

**Japan, December 14**
Japan Air Lines says its future Boeing 747-400s will be fitted with personal video screens in first and business class (→ May 17, 1989).

**New Zealand, December 20**
The New Zealand government announces the sale of Air New Zealand to a consortium headed by Brierley Investments Ltd.

**Scotland, December 28**
An analysis of the wreckage of the Pan Am Boeing 747 which crashed at Lockerbie a week ago reveals that a bomb had been planted in the jet's luggage hold (→ Jan 5, 1989).

---

*The US's "invisible" airplane: the F-117A stealth attacker's radar-evading shape was so secret that for years photographs were banned.* ▶

## Factfile

World revenue passenger miles: 1,059,872.268 million
Passengers through Chicago O'Hare: 26.5 million
Passengers through New York (JFK/Newark/LaGuardia): 32.7 million
Passengers through London (Heathrow/Gatwick): 58.3 million
Price of a single coach ticket New York/Los Angeles (Apr): $239/560
Price of the cheapest return ticket London/New York: $508
World air freight (ton miles): 143,838.1 million
Average salary of long-haul pilot and co-pilot (US): $93,193
Average salary of cabin crew (US): $26,930
Price of a Boeing 747 Combi: $103.6 million
Price of an Airbus A340: $94.3 million
Price of an ATR-42: $14.5 million
Price of 1,000 (US) gallons of Jet A1 fuel (average July): $614.37
Average exchange rate: £1 = $1.7812

# Federal Express delivers to the world

*A DC-10 of Federal Express: part of a fleet larger than most airlines, yet one without passengers.*

**Memphis, Tennessee, April 1**
Just 15 years after its creation, the name of Federal Express (FedEx) is so well known that Americans have turned it into a verb: to FedEx. On its first day the Memphis-based company had transported a mere 18 packages. Nowadays it delivers more than a million a day in 100 countries, thanks to its fleet of over 380 aircraft, led by 20 Boeing 747s, 124 Boeing 727s and 26 McDonnell Douglas DC-10s.

This fleet, larger than those of most airline companies, flies only at night to avoid cluttering up already congested airports. At the height of its success, Federal Express prom-ised its customers any package weighing up to 73 lb would be delivered anywhere in the country before midday the following day. Chief pilot and operations director Jerry Wolfe was one of the first to back Fred Smith's idea for a competitor to the US postal services. Smith's gamble has paid off.

# Boeing launches 747-400 'super Jumbo', world's heaviest airliner

*The 747-400 stretches a fully loaded Jumbo's range to over 7,520 miles with reserves of fuel to spare.*

**Everett, Washington, April 29**
The world's heaviest commercial airliner, the Boeing 747-400, took off from Paine Field here today. Capable of weighing in for take-off at 870,000 lb, the new "super Jumbo" development of the 747 can carry an extra 3,300 (US) gallons of fuel in the tail.

The fuel capacity, when married to the improved fuel consumption of its advanced turbofan engines, structural weight reductions and extended wing-tips, permits an incredible range. Loaded with 412 passengers and flying at optimum cruising speed, the 747-400 can cover over 7,520 miles non-stop with reserve fuel remaining, which must be just about the ultimate range required of a commercial jet-airliner. Winglets on the wings alone mean about a 3 per cent range increase. Other characteristics include a two-crew digital avionics flight cabin, as developed by Boeing for its 757 and 767. This allows 60 per cent fewer gauges and instruments on the flight deck.

Advanced aluminum alloys are used in the 747-400's construction, and it incorporates a 747-300-type extended upper deck (→ Oct 27).

## Smoking is banned on short US flights

**USA, April 23**
Today is the day "No Smoking" signs will remain lit on 80 per cent of domestic airline flights in the US as the government's ban on smoking on flights of two hours or less goes into effect. Flight attendants are to be armed with gum and candy for those in anguish.

Passengers on the around 13,600 flights affected by the ban who refuse to comply face stiff sanctions. Violations carry fines of up to $1,000, and those who believe they can sneak a puff in the bathroom had better think twice. Smoke detectors have been installed, and tampering with them to satisfy the craving for a drag carries a penalty of up to $2,000. Those who ignore the ban and refuse to put out their cigarettes are likely to be greeted by police when the airplane lands.

The ban also applies on flights longer than two hours total if they are made in shorter segments – a flight is defined as a segment between two stops. Even if weather or air-traffic delays keep a flight in the air beyond its scheduled two hours the ban remains in effect (→ Jun 10).

## British Airways to swallow rival BCal

**London, May 24**
British Airways, the national flag-carrier and already bigger than all its British rivals combined, has today taken over the largest of those rivals, British Caledonian. BA has reputedly paid £246 million (about $450 million) for the Gatwick-based airline.

One interesting facet of the deal is that British Caledonian was the original launch customer for the Airbus A320, the first single-aisle product from the European consortium and the most advanced aircraft in its class. BCal bought a fleet of ten, the first of which has been painted at Toulouse in BA livery and is about to be delivered (story opposite). With BA's notorious preference for American equipment this relatively small fleet looks vulnerable to being replaced by more primitive but less costly 737s. In any case the merger gives BA a major base at Gatwick.

# Greek flyer recreates mythical exploits

*Pedal power and high-tech materials provide success for this "Daedulus".*

**Crete, April 23**
A modern-age Daedalus has today recreated Greek mythology by flying by human muscle power from Crete to the island of Santorini. The pilot, 31-year-old Greek cycling champion Kanellos Kanellopoulos, did not flap wings of feathers and wax but used pedal power to propel his hi-tech airplane *Daedalus*, designed at the Massachusetts Institute of Technology. The *Daedalus* has a 112-foot wingspan and is made of advanced and exceedingly light materials. It flew the 74 miles in 3 hours 54 minutes, helped by tail winds.

However, when Kanellopoulos attempted to turn for the landing, the tail boom and then the wings collapsed, leaving him to swim the final few feet to shore.

# Airbus demo ends in tragedy at Habsheim

*Aftermath of a low-level demonstration flight which went tragically wrong.*

**Habsheim, France, June 26**
Charred debris is all that remains today of the *City of Amsterdam*, a brand new Airbus A320. Rescuers retrieved four bodies and 30 injured people from the wreckage. The Air Charter International A320 took off from Paris to fly over Mont Blanc, then changed course for an air show at Mulhouse-Habsheim to perform two low-level passes. Approaching Habsheim, 100 feet from the ground with flaps and wheels down, it hit trees at the end of the runway and plunged into the wood, catching fire in seconds. Pilot Michel Asseltine and co-pilot Pierre Mazières, flying manually, managed to defeat all the A320's ultra-safe systems.

These systems are more comprehensive than those in any other airplane in the world. They naturally include a GPWS (ground-proximity warning system) plus extras which guarantee that the aircraft will neither stall nor hit the ground even in the most extreme atmospheric conditions of windshear (headwind quickly becoming tailwind) or microburst (violent downdraft). On this occasion the pilots switched off the GPWS for a steep letdown and flypast at a very low level, and then simply failed to look ahead (→ Sep 14).

# Airbus A320 joins British Airways fleet

**West Sussex, England, April 29**
Today Captain John Duncan flew the first British Airways (BA) service to be operated by the Airbus A320 when he took off from London's Gatwick airport for Geneva.

BA did not buy its fleet of A320s. It inherited them from British Caledonian, which the bigger airline has lately swallowed up. In fact, BA never acquired any of the Airbus range, preferring older-technology US-built aircraft such as the 737. But the unique qualities of the European airplane have already endeared it to BA flight crews, cabin staff and maintenance engineers, who would certainly fight any attempt to replace it by US airliners.

In almost every respect the A320 is a generation ahead of any rival. The whole airplane is packed with avionics, and careful design and development have made these systems highly reliable. Powered by two

*British Airways' first Airbus A320.*

CFM56 or V.2500 engines in the 25,000-lb thrust class, the A320 seats from 150 to 179 passengers in a cabin wider than those of its competitors (→ Jan 15, 1990).

# Southwest Airlines is flying killer whales

**Houston, Texas, May 23**
Shamu One, a Southwest Airlines B-737-300 painted to look like a 110-foot killer whale, landed here this morning.

It has been dubbed "Shamu" in honor of the star of Sea World in San Antonio. This is the first jet aircraft to be painted in the likeness of an animal. Houston's Mayor, Kathy Whitmire, was on hand to greet Shamu One, as were special guests Herb Kelleher, chairman of Southwest, and George Becker, chairman of Sea World of Texas. The men were dressed in tuxedos to match the black and white livery of the airliner. Once again, it seems that Southwest has lived up to its reputation of being a "fun" airline.

*Three Southwest Boeing 737s display their new killer-whale livery.*

# US cruiser downs Iranian Airbus; 290 die

*Washington, DC, July 3*
The tense cat-and-mouse game in the Persian Gulf and the Strait of Hormuz between the US and its allies – who are protecting oil tankers in the area – and Iran claimed the lives of 290 Iranian civilians today. The tragedy occurred when the guided missile cruiser USS *Vincennes* shot down an Iran Air Airbus A300 which it mistook for a hostile F-14 fighter. President Ronald Reagan said the US regretted the loss of life. Iran denounced the action and vowed to "avenge the blood of our martyrs".

The downing occurred while the warship was being engaged by Iranian gunboats. Admiral William Crowe, chairman of the US Joint Chiefs of Staff, said that radar had tracked the Airbus, which was not following normal civil air corridors from Iran. No signal was received from the transmitter it should have carried to identify it on radar screens as a civilian aircraft, and

three warnings on civilian and four on military radio frequencies were ignored. The airliner was hit because the captain of the *Vincennes* believed it was a combat aircraft which was endangering his ship.

USS *Vincennes* and her sisters are equipped with the Aegis electronic system which is the most advanced in the world for the detection, identification and "prioritization" of aerial targets. It seems incredible that this astronomically expensive system proved unable to distinguish between a fighter and a 300-seat wide-body transport. In a hastily arranged press conference in Washington, Admiral William Crowe, chairman of the US Joint Chiefs of Staff, explained that "one of the most difficult problems is from a radar blip, particularly from a head-on target, to identify the type of aircraft". President Reagan, who backs the admiral in insisting that *Vincennes* is not to blame, has ordered a full inquiry.

# USAF tests more maneuverable F-15 Eagle

*The F-15 Eagle: designed for shorter take-offs and more maneuverability.*

*St Louis, Missouri, September 7*
An indication that the USAF is not completely unaware of the need to move away from vulnerable airfields is shown by the start today of some 150 hours of flight testing by the F-15 S/MTD. The letters stand for STOL (short take-off and landing) maneuvering technology demonstrator. The objective is to develop an F-15 which can safely operate from a 1,500-foot runway at night or in bad weather.

Among the many changes made to this McDonnell Douglas fighter are: controllable two-dimensional nozzles on the two F100 engines,

not only for shorter landings but also for enhanced flight maneuverability; two large controllable canard surfaces (modified F-18 tailplanes), and a digital "fly-by-wire" flight-control system. One extra on this particular airplane is that the wing skin is made of a new aluminum-lithium alloy, both stronger and lighter than those on other F-15s. The new skins were made in Britain by Alcan.

But despite the test program, there is as yet no suggestion that the S/MTD modifications will see service with the USAF, or be used in some totally new US fighter.

# Nato Air Show horror kills 33, injures 60

*The moment of impact when the doomed airplanes became deadly fireballs.*

*[West] Germany, August 28*
One of the most horrific accidents ever to occur at an air show took place at 3.35pm today. The scene was Ramstein, one of the biggest Nato airbases, which was hosting an Air Show attracting over 100,000 spectators.

Italian national aerobatic team Frecce Tricolori was performing in its MB.339 jets. Suddenly a crossing maneuver went wrong, and solo lead pilot Lieutenant-Colonel Ivo

Nutarelli collided with the main formation. The result was a huge fireball and a lethal shrapnel bombardment from disintegrating aircraft. Three pilots died, and 30 spectators; another 60 spectators are critical.

The crossing maneuver was not only highly dangerous in itself but also violated a basic airshow rule in that the solo airplane flew towards the crowd. The routine was an accident waiting to happen.

# A secret cigarette costs man $3,000

*Washington, DC, June 10*
Derryl Seigel's sudden craving for a cigarette while on a 90-minute flight from Seattle to Reno has cost him dear. A Washington State tribunal fined him $1,000 today for the first offense of smoking and a further $2,000 for putting the smoke alarm out of action so that he could enjoy his clandestine cigarette to the full in the bathroom.

Two months ago Northwest Airlines became the first airline to forbid smoking on US internal flights lasting less than two hours – a move now reinforced by a government ban [*see page 828*]. The airline then enforced the same rule on flights to Mexico, Canada, Jamaica and the Cayman Islands. Northwest Airlines says the ban was the clear wish of 89 per cent of its passengers, who said they were upset by the smell of tobacco smoke.

# European fighter to use Eurojet engines

*Munich, November 1*
Eurojet Turbo GmbH, whose head office here is next to that of Turbo-Union, is today celebrating the signing of the main production contract for the EJ200 engine. This engine was specially designed to power the forthcoming twin-engined European Fighter Aircraft (EFA).

Eurojet was formed in August 1986 by Rolls-Royce of Britain, Fiat of Italy, MTU of West Germany and Sener of Spain. Their shareholdings reflect the percentages of costs agreed on the EFA, which in turn reflect likely purchases by the four national air forces. More than 2,000 engines are expected to be ordered.

The EJ200 is a remarkably light (2,000-lb) and compact afterburning turbofan in the 20,000-lb thrust class, with a small number of parts compared with other engines.

# USAF unveils secret Nighthawk stealth aircraft

*Las Vegas, Nevada, November 10*
The shadowy form appearing in photographs taken from the perimeter of nearby Nellis Air Force Base and published in aviation magazines was finally identified by the USAF today as its F-117A Nighthawk "stealth" aircraft. It is a product of Lockheed's top-secret so-called "Skunk Works", the source of the U-2 and SR-71 spyplanes.

The USAF has worked very hard to keep the F-117 hidden from view by flying it only at night from a remote part of Nellis. The Pentagon said that the airplane, which is powered by two General Electric engines and constructed of special radar-absorbing material, flew for the first time in 1981 and became operational in 1983.

Sources familiar with the program say it has been operated outside the US and has occasionally flown to Britain for training exer-

*First sight of an airplane designed not to be seen: the F-117 stealth attacker intended to be invisible to enemy radar.*

cises. The aircraft is not designed to engage other airplanes. Its primary job is to avoid detection by radar and penetrate enemy defenses to destroy high-value targets such as command posts. The somewhat less than revealing photograph which was distributed today shows a boxy, angular vehicle which is a distinct departure from the USAF's sleek F-15 Eagles and F-16 Fighting Falcons. The USAF has accepted 52 of the F-117s, and seven more are scheduled to be delivered by 1990.

## Aerial traffic jams plague Europeans

*Europe, December*
The way things are going, the skies above Europe will soon become as congested as those of the USA. According to the European Airlines Association, tourists flying over the bank-holiday weekends in May this year suffered delays of at least six hours – when their flights were not canceled altogether. Several paying passengers were obliged to spend the night huddled in airport waiting rooms.

In Britain, where air traffic is densest, jets have more than once passed within 30 feet of each other, and the authorities have lost count of the number of near collisions. In France the annual number of flight movements has almost doubled in ten years and has just passed the 1.6 million mark. For the whole of Europe, air traffic increased by 13 per cent this year. The sky, already marked with the trails of Jumbo Jets and other large carriers, is increasingly criss-crossed with the plumes left by business aircraft, which fly round the clock, and military airplanes which, in the view of several firms, are colonizing ever more airspace (→ Jul 16, 1989).

## Pan Am Jumbo Jet crashes on small Scottish town, killing 270

*Investigators examine the cockpit section of Flight 103 in a Scottish field.*

*Shattered houses at Lockerbie.*

*Lockerbie, Scotland, December 21*
In the worst air disaster in British history, a Pan Am Boeing 747 fell from the sky this evening onto Lockerbie, a small town in southwest Scotland with a population of just 3,000. Flames hundreds of feet high lit the sky, an eye-witness said. All on board the 747 perished.

More than 40 homes were destroyed by the falling wreckage of the airliner, adding a number of residents to the list of dead. Several on the ground were also badly injured. Two rows of houses were flat-tened by the airplane's engines. Experts have not ruled out structural failure, but all the indications point to a mid-air bomb blast. It is known that US and Japanese diplomats were on board, along with US servicemen flying home for Christmas. Pan Am Flight 103, with 258 passengers and crew, left London's Heathrow airport at 6.25pm today, on a routine seven-hour flight to New York's John F Kennedy airport. Flying the usual northerly route at 31,000 feet and 550mph on Blue Three airway for the Atlantic, the pilot made radio contact with the air-traffic control center at Prestwick airport at 7.15pm. Four minutes later the airplane suddenly disappeared from radar screens.

The 747 had disintegrated in mid-air, scattering pieces of shattered airplane over 10 miles. The blazing main section struck a hill to the east of Lockerbie, hurling tons of metal over a nearby trunk road and spraying fuel over a wide area. Investigators have arrived to recover the "black box" and cockpit voice recorders (→ 28).

The ATR 72 is a stretched derivative of the original ATR 42, accommodating between 66 and 74 passengers. Engines are PW124s or 127s of up to 2,880ehp.

Russia's Airbus is the Ilyushin Il-96-300, derived from the earlier Il-86, and identifiable from the Il-86 by its short body and long-span wing with winglets.

The Boeing 737-400 incorporates two fuselage plugs and accommodates up to 170 passengers. Further new technology is included in the design.

The LET 610 was designed for short-haul operations on stages of between 650 and 1,000 miles. It was built to Soviet airworthiness standards.

The Soviet Union's Buran Shuttle orbiter made its first flight unmanned, under control from the ground. It is transported on the Antonov An-225.

The Boeing 757-200M retains all passenger windows and doors, but has an upward opening cargo door to allow Combi passenger/cargo operation.

The Extra 300 is a two-seat version of the original Extra 230 unlimited aerobatic monoplane. The Textron Lycoming piston engine is rated at 300hp.

The TBM 700 was jointly developed by Socata of France and Mooney of the USA as a pressurized single-engined six/eight-seat business aircraft.

The MBB Bo 108 features a bearingless main rotor, a new tail rotor, and more powerful Allison, Turbomeca or Pratt & Whitney Canada engines.

*Latest version of the Jumbo Jet is the Boeing 747-400, which has a two-crew cockpit and extended wings which are tipped by drag-reducing winglets.*

*The Chichester Miles Leopard is an interesting cheap and small bizjet.*

*The FFV Aerotech BA-14 Starling is a two-seat multi-purpose lightplane.*

*The LoPresti Piper Swift Fire is a turbine version of the Globe Swift.*

*The Teledyne Ryan Model 410: developed for long-endurance missions.*

*The Antonov An-225 Mriya (Dream) was derived from the original An-124 Ruslan, with a stretched fuselage, two extra engines and end-plate tailfins.*

*BAe's 146 STA (Small Tactical Airlifter) prototype: a military side-loading freighter evolved from the Quiet Trader. Inflight refueling probe optional.*

*The Royal Navy's Sea Harrier FRS.Mk1s are being upgraded to FRS.Mk2 standard with a new radar, longer fuselage and AMRAAM capability.*

*Britain's Hawk trainer was completely redesigned for US Navy service as the T-45 Goshawk with McDonnell Douglas, St Louis as the prime contractor.*

*Saab's Gripen is intended to augment and eventually replace the multi-role Viggen. Development was delayed by an accident to the first prototype.*

*Sikorsky's HH-60H and HH-60J Jayhawk are versions of a dedicated combat rescue and special-forces support helicopter developed from the Seahawk.*

*The Tornado ECR is a dedicated reconnaissance and defense suppression aircraft. Guns are removed, but the aircraft can carry HARM missiles.*

4,534mph
USA
Pete Knight
North American X-15
Oct 3, 1967

24,987 miles
USA
Jeager and Rutan
*Voyager*
Dec 23, 1986

354,200ft
USA
Joseph Walker
North American X-15
Aug 22, 1963

1,120,370lb
USSR
Antonov
An-225 Mriya

61,500lb thrust
USA
General Electric
CF6-80C2A5

**USSR, January 2**
Tupolev's Tu-204, the Soviet Union's first airliner fitted with a fly-by-wire control system, makes its maiden flight.

**Libya, January 4**
Two US Navy F-14 Tomcats shoot down two Libyan MiG-23 fighters about 70 miles off the Libyan coast; US officials say the Tomcats fired in self-defense, but Libyan President Gadaffi denounces the act as one of "premeditated aggression".

**Kegworth, England, January 8**
A British Midland Boeing 737-400 crashes onto the M1 motorway near here while attempting an emergency landing after reporting an engine fire; 32 people are killed (→ Feb 1).

**Washington, DC, January 24**
The Pentagon lifts a ban on the use of pin-ups to decorate the fuselage of USAF aircraft; feminist groups protest against the decision.

**USA, February 1**
The Federal Aviation Administration orders Boeing to carry out checks on the plumbing and wiring aboard all 1,755 jets delivered by the company since December 31, 1980; this results from widespread concern in Europe following suggestions that the crash of a Boeing 737-400 near Leicester, England, on January 8 was caused by faulty wiring (→ Oct 18, 1990).

**Azores, February 8**
A chartered Boeing 707 crashes into the Pico Alto mountain after a misunderstanding in radio communications between the crew and the ground; the airplane was 21 years old and had been restored seven times.

**Hawaii, February 24**
A United Air Lines Boeing 747 loses part of its fuselage while flying over the island; 11 business-class passengers are sucked out of the depressurized cabin.

**Athens, February 28**
The Greek carrier Olympic Airways is forced to ask 12 overweight passengers to get off one of its airliners which proves to be too heavily loaded.

**Wichita, Kansas, March 1**
Brian E Barents is elected president of Learjet Corporation.

**USA, April 13**
The first flight-tests of the Pratt & Whitney/Allison propfan engine are carried out.

**Marietta, Georgia, April 17**
The last C-5 Galaxy transport produced by Lockheed is delivered to the USAF.

**Paris, April 24**
French carrier Heli Union puts a Sikorsky S-76A helicopter, F-GIFT, into service to ferry businessmen around.

**Dallas, Texas, May 15**
American Airlines is connected to the computerized reservation system Amadeus, which now services 19 of the world's airlines.

**Japan, May 17**
Japan Air Lines adopts a new spelling – Japan Airlines – and a new logo based on the letters JAL.

**Paris, May 22**
Air France orders 12 Boeing 737-500 airliners, to be delivered from 1991.

**Belgium, July 4**
A pilotless Soviet MiG-23 jet crashes near Courtrai killing an 18-year-old man; after its pilot had ejected over Poland because of technical problems, the airplane continued over Germany and was then picked up and escorted by two USAF F-15s, which were ordered not to attack the MiG unless it was about to crash on a town.

**Europe, July 16**
Strikes by French air-traffic controllers over the weekend July 15-16 cause delays for thousands of tourists throughout Europe.

**USA, July 18**
United Air Lines announces plans to open passenger services to Europe in 1990 (→ May 15, 1990).

**Sioux City, Iowa, July 19**
A United Air Lines DC-10 flying from Denver to Chicago crashes while attempting an emergency landing; 107 die. Explosion of the center engine left the crew with no control of any of the the tail surfaces, and to reach an airport was a miracle.

**Moscow, August 22**
Soviet airplane designer Alexander Yakovlev, 84, dies.

**Brazil, September 3**
A Varig Boeing 737 flying from Sao Paulo to Belem crash-lands in the jungle when it runs out of fuel, killing 12 of the 53 passengers; the crew had set the flight on automatic pilot because they were engrossed in radio coverage of a soccer match, but the pilot deviated by 180 degrees from the planned track.

**New York, September 20**
A USAir Boeing 737 skids into the East River after the pilot tries to "accelerate stop" out of a failed take-off from LaGuardia; two die and 45 are injured.

**Ténéré Desert, Niger, Sept 20**
A DC-10 of French carrier UTA is destroyed in mid-air by a terrorist bomb; all 117 people on board die.

**California, November 12**
The world's first human-powered helicopter, made of balsa wood, plastic and carbon materials, flies for the first time – for just 2 seconds – at California Polytechnic State university, in the hands of pedal-pilot Greg McNeil.

**Phoenix, Arizona, November 16**
America West Airlines initiates flights to Honolulu, Hawaii; the airline's fleet includes DHC-8s and Boeing 737s, 757s and 747s.

**London, November 21**
A British Airways Boeing 747 piloted by Captain William Stewart narrowly misses the Penta hotel near Heathrow in very poor visibility (→ May 12, 1991).

**Lyon, France, Nov 23**
An Airbus A310-300 opens Air France's new direct Lyon/New York service (→ Jan 15, 1990).

---

## Factfile

World revenue passenger miles: 1,107,583.360 million
Passengers through Chicago O'Hare: 59.1 million
Passengers through New York (JFK/Newark/LaGuardia): 74.4 million
Passengers through London (Heathrow/Gatwick): 60.7 million
Price of a single coach ticket New York/Los Angeles (April): $588
Price of the cheapest return ticket London/New York: $528
World air freight (ton miles): 151,176.8 million
Average salary of long-haul pilot and co-pilot (US): $95,558
Average salary of cabin crew (US): $26,685
Price of Boeing 747-400: $118.4 million
Price of an Airbus A-310: $65.2 million
Price of an Airbus A-320: $38.9 million
Price of 1,000 (US) gallons of Jet A1 fuel (average for July): $640.1
Average exchange rate: £1 = $1.6397

---

*The Northrop B-2 stealth bomber, a "flying wing" designed to evade radar detection with long-range nuclear capability, makes its debut.* ▶

# 'Sydney Tower, please say again...'

*Despite a badly damaged rudder section, the Concorde landed safely.*

**Sydney, Australia, April 12**
"Speedbird Concorde Alpha Fox, you have lost half of your tail." An incredulous Captain David Leney immediately radioed back: "Say again Sydney Tower". The control tower's message was not a joke, the British Airways Concorde that landed here today from Christchurch, New Zealand, was indeed missing half of its top rudder section. A piece of rudder skin had become detached from the honeycomb section to which it was glued and had peeled back. That explained the small 'thud' and vibration felt by crew and passengers after take-off, as Concorde was climbing through 43,000 feet and accelerating to Mach 2 (→ Mar 21, 1992).

# Northwest introduces the Jumbo 747-400

*The 747-400's 6 ft high winglets improve fuel and aerodynamic efficiency.*

**Minneapolis, Minnesota, Jan 31**
Less than a year after the Boeing 747-400 made its first flight, Northwest Airlines today began its first Dash-400 on the short route between its HQ here and Phoenix, Arizona. For such routes Northwest would usually use smaller aircraft, such as the A320 of which 100 are being delivered. Northwest is buying an initial fleet of 16 of the monster 747-400s, to back up earlier 747s and DC-10-40s on transoceanic routes. All these long-haulers have Pratt & Whitney engines, but for the future the airline is talking to Boeing, Airbus Industrie and McDonnell Douglas in order pick the best of the next generation (→ Oct 12).

# Paris is stunned by Soviet 'Cobra' stunt

*The flying prowess of the Sukhoi Su-27 impressed visitors to Le Bourget.*

**Paris, July 1**
Soviet airplanes have hogged the limelight at this year's Paris air show, and none more so than the Sukhoi Su-27 ("Flanker" as codenamed by Nato) fighter.

Among its novel features is a maneuver dubbed "Cobra". Slowing to 270mph in level flight, the pilot switches off the electronics, heaves back the control column and the aircraft abruptly rears up; the full expanse of its underside is applied to bring it almost to a halt before, just as abruptly, the pilot lurches the fighter into forward flight again.

The twin-jet's innovations also include a target-finding system integrated into the pilot's helmet; a movement of the head points the aircraft in the right direction. Unusually for a warplane, a soft female voice warns of any malfunctions.

# Antonov carries 250 tons on its back

**Paris, June 7**
With the 250-ton Buran [Snowstorm] Soviet space shuttle on its back, the Antonov An-225 Mriya [Dream] is one of the Soviet sensations of this year's Paris air show. The six-engined An-225 is the biggest airplane in the world, and it made its debut in the USSR last year in front of thousands of spectators. Its first flight took place at Kiev, Ukraine, on December 21, and the West learnt of the existence of the gigantic six-engined jet-transport shortly after.

Derived from the An-124 Ruslan, with a "stretched" fuselage and two extra engines, the An-225 is remarkable for its enormous twin-rudder tail, which allows it to carry very heavy loads on its back, attached to large securing clamps. The aircraft can cruise at 530mph over a range of 2,800 miles.

*The world's biggest plane, the An-225, has the Buran space shuttle on its back.*

# Soviet pilot ejects from just 400 feet

*Paris, June 8*

Only the cool head of pilot Anatoli Kvochur prevented the first full day of the Paris air show from being marred by tragedy. All began well for Kvochur and his MiG-29 (Nato codename: "Fulcrum-A"). Its low-level maneuvers had delighted the crowd. But then, when he applied full thrust after a steeply-angled pass, his starboard engine suddenly cut out, and the aircraft hurtled to earth. Kvochur, anxious to prevent the crippled MiG from hitting the crowd, only ejected – horizontally – 400 feet from the ground, 2.1 seconds before impact (→ Jul 1).

# New stealth bomber is 'flying wing'

*The airplane designed to be unseen by enemy radar: the stealth bomber reveals its distinctive shape on its first flight.*

*At a height of 400 feet the pilot of the MiG-29 ejects - horizontally.*

*The moment of impact, as the pilotless Soviet plane hits the ground.*

*The MiG-29 explodes in a ball of flame, away from any spectators.*

*Palmdale, California, July 17*

The tailless Northrop B-2 stealth bomber, which took off from here on its two-hour first flight at 6.37am, is only fractionally longer than that of an F-15 Eagle fighter, but the aircraft has all the capability of a B-52 and then some. Like the Lockheed F-117A stealth bomber, the B-2 has a striking profile, although more rounded than its starkly angular fellow. The new aircraft represents a return to the concept of the "flying wing", with no separate fuselage or tail.

The USAF has ordered a fleet of 132 B-2s at $500 million each, or more than ten times the cost of an F-15. The aircraft, which can carry 23 tons of nuclear and conventional armaments and has a greater range than the B-52, is designed for low- and high-altitude (around 50,000 feet) strategic operation. Powered by four General Electric F118-100 engines, it is the most complex aircraft ever built.

# Alaska Airlines, the 'fog busters'

*Seattle, Washington, October 9*

Utilizing the HGS-1000 head-up guidance system, Alaska Airlines Captain Paul Zaborowski today became the first airline pilot manually to land a commercial Boeing 727 aircraft in less than 800 feet of forward runway visibility. Alaska Airline's $12 million investment in this innovative and efficient "anti-fog" system is already paying dividends.

Although some military pilots have enjoyed the benefits of this advanced technology for years, Alaska Airlines has become the first commercial carrier to install such a system fleet-wide. All its B-727s are scheduled to be equipped with the HGS-1000 by the time the heavy winter fogs arrive.

Paradoxically, while the trend over the last few years has been away from "hands-on" flying, this system is certified by the Federal Aviation Administration (FAA) to be flown manually down to 700 feet visibility.

# Qantas flies London to Sydney non-stop

*Sydney, August 18*

At 4.23am today (Universal time) Qantas Boeing 747-400 *Spirit of Australia* touched down here a little over 11,100 miles and 20 hours after leaving London Heathrow. It was the longest non-stop flight by a four-engined jet airliner. The Jumbo left at 9.13am yesterday with just 23 on board for the first direct flight between Europe and Australia. Flights now take over 24 hours, but Qantas has shown – even allowing for favorable winds on this proving flight – that the time can be cut considerably.

*The four captains of Qantas prepare to leave Heathrow in their 747-400.*

# The V-22 Osprey goes to horizontal flight

*The tilt-rotor V-22 Osprey is translating from vertical to horizontal flight.*

*Arlington, Texas, September 14*
After successfully completing its vertical-flight tests, the V-22 Osprey, developed jointly by Bell and Boeing Vertol, today began a series of tests of its horizontal flying capabilities. A cross between an airplane and a helicopter, the Osprey is a tilt-rotor aircraft powered by an Allison T406 turboprop engine – developed from those of the Lockheed C-130 – mounted at the tip of each wing.

The two engines, which tilt from vertical to horizontal and back, drive huge 'proprotors', each 38 feet in diameter. This allows the Osprey to take off vertically and then, once the engines have tilted forward, to fly like a normal airplane to a maximum speed of 300-mph. Another feature of this amazing aircraft is that it can fold to fit easily on to ships.

The Pentagon is planning to purchase more than 1,200 Ospreys: 552 for the Marines, 350 for the Navy, 251 for the Army and 80 for the USAF. Each aircraft costs $16 million (→ Jan 11, 1990).

# Satellite gives warning of storms ahead

*Miami, Florida, September 20*
The island of Guadeloupe may now be in the eye of a cyclone, but the cyclone itself is in the eye of a satellite. Thanks to its super-radar,

*A satellite picture of the cyclone.*

the Miami meteorological center has been closely monitoring the course of Hurricane Hugo - at the very low pressure of 923 millibars the most violent storm recorded since 1928 - since it struck the French territory on September 15.

All Hugo's movements and its changes of shape or direction are followed minute by minute, and the information is passed on, especially to pilots in the area, who then know whether to alter course or which airport has been hit.

But if the hurricane which culminates at over 37,000 feet has now come under the watchful eye of the satellite, the methods of studying it at close quarters are fairly simple: taking off from, for example, Paramaribo, Surinam, airplanes penetrate into the depression and then make their reports.

# USAir, Piedmont Airlines in big merger

*Washington, DC, August 5*
Potentially one of the USA's largest carriers was born today as USAir merged with Piedmont Airlines. Both share a heritage of small community service. In 1953, when USAir's name changed from All American Aviation to Allegheny Airlines, its fleet was composed of 13 DC-3s. In 1966, the first pure jet DC-9 was introduced, and in July 1968 it merged with Lake Central Airlines. It became the USA's 6th largest passenger carrier in 1972 after integration of Mohawk Airlines and was the first local service carrier to be removed from government subsidy in 1974. In October 1979, Allegheny changed its name to USAir.

Following today's deal, USAir operates a fleet of more than 400 modern jets and boards 60 million passengers a year.

*USAir was on July 24 the US launch customer for the Fokker 100.*

# Beechcraft introduces the King Air 350

*Atlanta, Georgia, October 2*
The National Business Aircraft Association today played host for the introduction of the new Super King Air 350 business turboprop, powered by two Pratt & Whitney Canada PT6A-60A engines.

Charles Dieker, Beech executive vice president of marketing, reports that the aircraft, at 34 inches longer and with the new wider 57 foot 11 inch wing span, is "the most comfortable and capable Super King Air ever built". This model has 7 polarized windows compared to 5 on other King Airs, and most distinctive are the two-foot high winglets for drag reduction. The seating capacity is an impressive 11 passengers and a crew of two.

*The twin-engined Super King Air 350 flies at a maximum speed of 360mph.*

# Speedbird Concorde 001 ready to start, gate V14

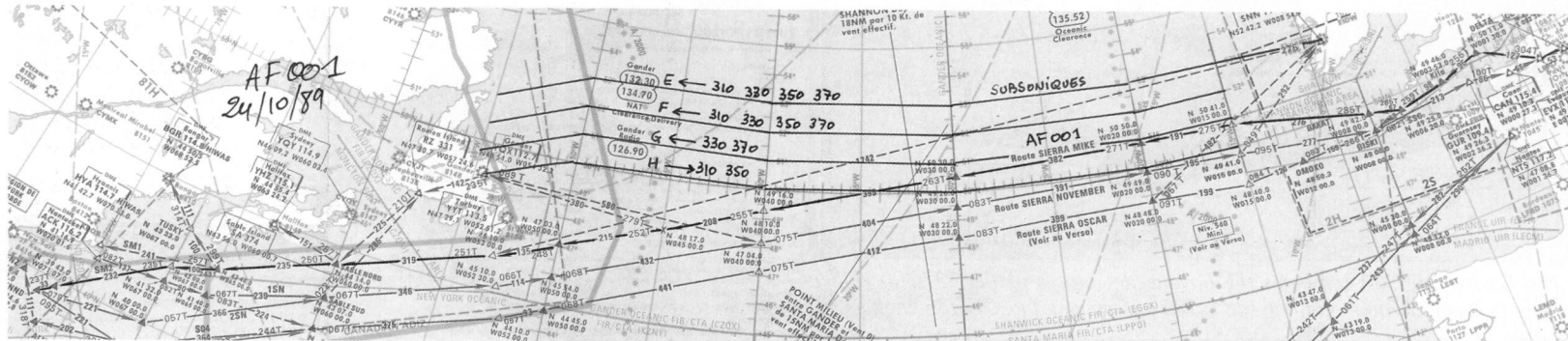

*This Air France map shows Concorde routes over the Atlantic. On the way to New York the route is known as Sierre Mike. The return route is called Sierra Oscar. Winds determine the route for subsonic airliners. Concorde, flying at 60,000 ft, is not troubled by winds.*

## Power checked

**Heathrow, September 25**
"Speedbird Concorde 001 is cleared to line up and take off runway 27 right." Captain Dave Leney rapidly opens the throttles and the four Olympus engines accelerate to full power, causing Concorde to leap forward. Copilot Tony Yule calls "100 knots" and Flight Engineer Dave Macdonald confirms "power checked". At 195 knots Concorde rotates towards the sky.

## Passing Mach 1.00

**Over the Bristol Channel**
"Speedbird Concorde 001 cleared to flight level 600 to JFK." Level at 28,000 feet, Dave Leney tells the passengers that they are about to start the acceleration and climb to Mach 2 and 60,000 feet. The Engineer switches on the reheats and carefully monitors all the engine parameters. In a few moments Concorde is passing the magic figure of Mach 1, the speed of sound.

## Temperature 130° C

**20° West, 60 minutes into the flight**
"Good morning Shanwick this is Speedbird Concorde 001 passing Sierra Mike two zero West." Tony tells Shannon the aircraft's position crossing the meridian 20° West on the track SM. Concorde is passing 52,000 feet in a slow climb and the speed is Mach 2, or 1,350 mph. Due to friction of the air on the skin of the plane, the temperature on the nose reaches 130° Celsius.

---

### BEFORE TAKE-OFF CHECK-LIST

| | | |
|---|---|---|
| Briefing Take-off Data | *Updated* | C |
| Transponder | *Set* | P |
| Master Warning | *Recall/inhibit* | P |
| Take-off Monitor | *Armed* | P |
| Reheat | *ON* | E |

### TRANSONIC CHECK-LIST

| | | |
|---|---|---|
| **M = 0.95** | | |
| Reheat | *ON* | E |
| Fuel transfer | *Transfer aft* | E |
| **M = 1.1** | | |
| Secondary nozzles | *0-5 deg* | E |
| **M = 1.7** | | |
| Reheat | *OFF* | E |
| **50,000 feet** | | |
| Engine Flight Rating | *Cruise* | E |

### LANDING CHECK-LIST

| | | |
|---|---|---|
| Landing gear | *4 greens* | ALL |
| Nose | *Down, green* | PE |
| Brakes | *Checked/Normal* | P |

*(A part of the sixteen pages of Concorde check-lists.)*

---

## Subsonic again

**Nantucket, 2h50 after take-off**
"Concorde 001 cleared to descend to 12,000 feet, altimeter 1014." The Captain asks for the Deceleration and Descent Check-List, and Dave Macdonald begins to pump fuel forward to bring the center of gravity forward to prepare for subsonic flight. In the cabin, Tom Hunt and Sue Groves complete the meal service and give the passengers their Concorde gifts.

## It's a visual

**Long Island, 3h05 after take-off**
"This drawn-out approach could lose us 5 minutes." Dave Leney is always keen to get there on schedule. Tony lowers the nose and visor at 270 knots. Concorde now weighs 110 tons and Dave Macdonald begins the approach checks. The drizzle does not help. The three men look out for the flashing lights which denote the final turn onto the runway.

## Over the runway

**JF Kennedy, 3h20 after take off**
"Speedbird Concorde 001 cleared to land runway 13 left." The final right turn is complete and the runway lies ahead, the speed is approaching 160 knots. All is set for landing and Dave Leney adjusts for the crosswind. Dave Macdonald calls 40 feet, auto throttles out, and at 15 feet the throttles are closed and, nose high in the air, Concorde touches down smoothly.

The Boeing 737-500 combines the advanced features of the 737-400 with a short fuselage accommodating 108 – 132 passengers and CFM56 engines.

The CL-215T is little more than a turboprop version of the tried and trusted Canadair CL-215, although other minor improvements are incorporated.

The Tupolev Tu-204 is similar in size, performance, and, most notably, in appearance to the Boeing 757. It will fly with Russian, US and UK engines.

The Beechjet 400A has improved avionics, soundproofing and cabin volume, and enjoys a higher certificated ceiling and increased payload over the 400.

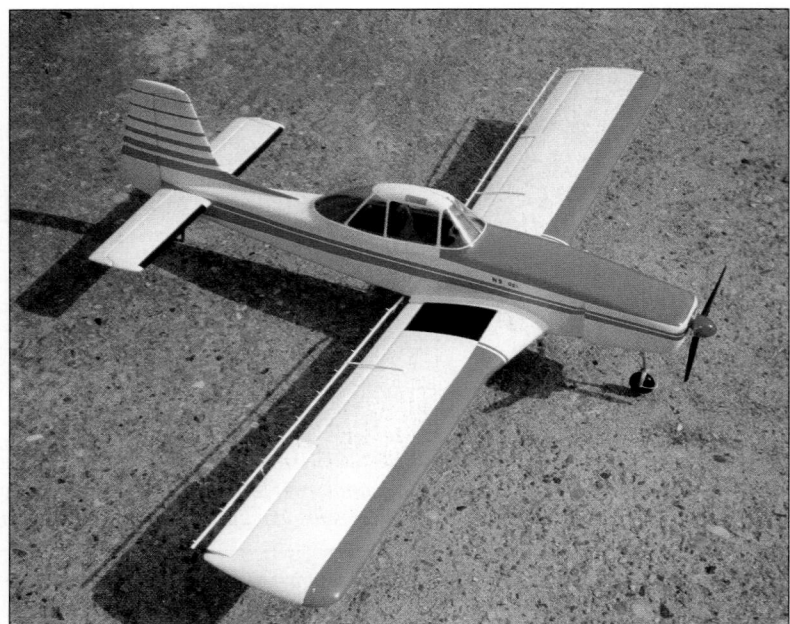

The NAMC N-5A is a specialised agricultural aircraft designed and built in China, which has a domestic market for roughly 300 such aircraft.

The Australian MAC Mamba has hardpoints to suit it for military roles. The production aircraft will have a 160hp engine, adequate for many roles.

The Bell/Boeing V-22 was designed to meet US Joint Services Advanced Vertical Lift Aircraft requirements; funding for production was later withdrawn.

Socata's Omega is essentially a turboprop-powered version of the earlier Epsilon, with better fatigue tolerance and a wider operating envelope.

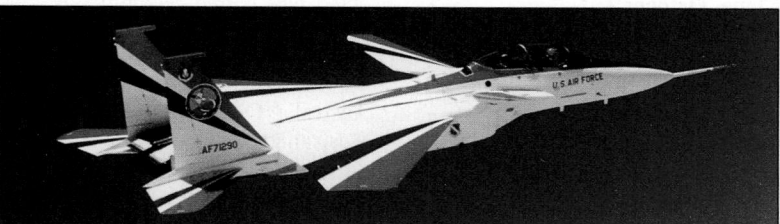

The McDonnell Douglas F-15 S/MTD is basically an F-15B with integrated controls for its canard foreplanes and limited-vectoring engine nozzles.

The Westland Lynx AH.Mk 9 (also known as the Battlefield Lynx) features a wheeled landing gear and prominent exhaust infra-red suppressors.

The Jaffe/Swearingen SA-32T Turbo Trainer, derived from Swearingen's SX300 light aircraft as a military trainer and FAC-reconnaissance platform.

The flying-wing configuration returned in 1989 in the shape of Northrop's awesome B-2 "Stealth Bomber" or ATB (Advanced Technology Bomber).

Taiwan's indigenous AIDC Ching Kuo fighter, designed with US help.

Designed to replace the Yak-38 "Forger", the Yak-141 "Freestyle".

Two LTV YA-7Fs were produced to serve as prototypes for a major upgrade for the Corsair to enable it to fulfil the USAF's close air support requirement.

Aero's L-59 was first known as the L-39MS, and is an up-engined version of the Czech L-39 Albatros, the Warsaw Pact's standard advanced jet trainer.

A single AH-1W undertook extensive trials with a four-blade main rotor as the AH-1 4BW. This may be procured as an upgrade for USMC AH-1Ws.

# 1990

 4,534mph
USA
Pete Knight
North American X-15
Oct 3, 1967

 24,987 miles
USA
Jeager and Rutan
*Voyager*
Dec 23, 1986

 354,200ft
USA
Joseph Walker
North American X-15
Aug 22, 1963

 1,322,754lb
USSR
Antonov
An-225 Mriya

 61,570lb thrust
USA
Pratt & Whitney
4060A

**Washington, DC, January 11**
The US Defense Department awards a contract worth $123.1 million to Boeing Vertol and Bell Helicopter Textron for the development of the V-22 tilt-rotor (→ Dec 12).

**Kerrville, Texas, January 12**
Mooney Aircraft introduces its latest model, the TLS; it has a 270-hp Lycoming engine, replacing the current Continental engine.

**New York, January 25**
An Avianca Boeing 707 from Medellin, Colombia, crashes while attempting to land at John F Kennedy airport; 72 of the 161 persons on board are killed; initial reports indicate the aircraft may have run out of fuel.

**Minneapolis, Minnesota, Jan 30**
Connie Walker, aged 70, the oldest flight attendant ever to work for Northwest Airlines, ends 42 years of airline service.

**Bangalore, India, February 14**
An Indian Airlines Airbus A320 on a routine flight from Bombay crashes while attempting to land here; 89 people, including both pilots, are killed.

**Washington, DC, February 25**
Smoke-free flights become mandatory throughout North America for all US airlines.

**Wichita, Kansas, March 6**
Beech Aircraft delivers its first Super King Air 350 to the Tecumseh Products Company.

**Italy, April 21**
Aeritalia becomes a partner in the Airbus programme when it signs an agreement to build fuselage sections for the A321 (→ Oct 1).

**[West] Germany, May 3**
The Luftwaffe takes delivery of the first of an order of 35 Panavia Tornado ECRs, a version equipped for electronic combat and reconnaissance.

**USA, May 10**
Pan Am pays out £10 million in compensation to families living in the town of Lockerbie, Scotland, where a Pan Am 747 crashed on December 21, 1988, after a terrorist bomb exploded in mid-flight.

**USA, May 15**
United Air Lines opens services to Frankfurt, [West] Germany, from Chicago's O'Hare airport and Dulles International Airport, Washington, DC.

**[West] Germany, May 22**
The Luftwaffe flies the Lockheed F-104 Starfighter for the last time before it is withdrawn from service; the airplane was nicknamed "the widow-maker" because of its terrible safety record - in its first five years of service, 110 Starfighter pilots were killed.

**USA, June 1**
The Boeing Chinook MH-47E helicopter, a version developed for special operations with the US Army, makes its maiden flight.

**Nagasaki, September 1**
The first landing of a chartered Concorde supersonic airliner in Japan is watched at the offshore airport of Omura by more than 15,000 people.

**Hong Kong, September 27**
United Airlines Flight 805 arrives here from San Francisco; it is the first commercial carrier to use satellite data communications in flight, allowing quick and uninterrupted communications between cockpit and ground. Soon all long-haul flights will use Satcoms.

**China, October 2**
A Boeing 737 which had been hijacked on an internal Chinese flight collides at White Cloud Airport, Canton, with two airliners on the ground, one empty and one containing 150 passengers which was waiting to take off for Shanghai; 127 persons are killed.

**Europe, October 3**
Swissair orders 19 Airbus A321s and seven A320s with 26 options on the same types (→ Oct 10).

**London, October 4**
A First World War pilot's log-book which could fuel the controversy over who downed German ace Baron von Richthofen fetches £3,080 at a public auction at Christie's here; the log-book, belonging to Lieutenant Lionel Lomas, RFC, says Canadian pilot Captain Roy Brown of 209 Squadron, RFC, was responsible for ending the German's superb career.

**Canada, October 9**
Air Canada makes 2,900 employees redundant and closes three international routes.

**London, October 18**
The official report into the Kegworth disaster – in which a British Midland 737 crashed near East Midlands airport on January 8, 1989, killing 47 – says the pilots acted hastily and recommends improvements to onboard instruments and pilot training.

**Australia, October 31**
Australian airlines are deregulated; subject to safety regulations set by Australia's Civil Aviation Authority, carriers are now free to choose their routes and set their own fares (→ Dec 1).

**Dallas, Texas, November 7**
Lone Star One, a new flagship in Southwest Airlines' fleet of Boeing 737s, enters service. Painted to resemble a Texas flag, the 737-300 joins a fleet of three such specially-painted aircraft.

**Brisbane, December 1**
Taking advantage of the new deregulated regime, Compass Airlines opens services to Sydney, Melbourne and Perth.

**Seattle, Washington, December 7**
An Alaska Airlines Boeing 727-200 piloted by Captain Duane Tibbles takes off from Seattle/Tacoma International Airport in fog that grounded other aircraft; with a visibility of just 500 feet, it is the lowest-visibility take-off for a scheduled commercial jetliner in US aviation history.

**USA, December 19**
Northwest Airlines buys a 25 per cent stake in Hawaiian Airlines for $20 million, thus gaining its first services to Australia.

## Factfile

World revenue passenger miles: 1,176,310.2 million
Passengers through Chicago O'Hare: 59.9 million
Passengers through New York (JFK/Newark/LaGuardia): 74.8 million
Passengers through London (Heathrow/Gatwick): 63.7 million
Price of a single coach ticket New York/Los Angeles (April): $623-646
Price of the cheapest return ticket London/New York: $462
World air freight (ton miles): 143,825.9 million
Average salary of long-haul pilot and co-pilot (US): $102,726
Average salary of cabin crew (US): $26,852
Price of a Boeing 747-400: $123 million
Price of an Airbus A340: $104.5 million
Price of an ATR 42: $16.2 million
Price of 1,000 (US) gallons of Jet A1 fuel (average for July): $638.2
Average exchange rate: £1 = $1.7850

*A Spitfire from the Second World War joins Concorde over the cliffs of Dover to mark the 50th anniversary of the Battle of Britain.* ▶

# McDonnell Douglas updates the DC-10

*The first Douglas MD-11 nears completion at the Long Beach factory.*

*Long Beach, California, January 11*
With its own DC-10 and the Lockheed TriStar both 20 years old, McDonnell Douglas felt it was high time to launch a new three-engined jet-airliner. The fruit of the company's labors, shown off today for the first time, is the MD-11.

The MD-11 is less a brand-new concept than an improved and technologically updated development of the DC-10, with its capacity slightly increased. As such it is intended as a competitor to the long-range European Airbus A330 and A340 which, being completely new designs, burn less fuel per passenger-mile and have several other advantages such as longer range.

So far McDonnell Douglas has received a total of 118 firm orders for the 350-passenger version of the MD-11 and options on a further 194. Each airliner costs a cool $90 million.

# Airbus flies in BA colors for the first time

*London, January 15*
Having become the unwilling owner of a fleet of Airbus A320s through its takeover of British Caledonian (BCal), British Airways (BA) is now singing the airliner's praises – well, to the skies.

BA – which for so long shunned the Airbus in favor of its transatlantic competitors – has now taken delivery of six of BCal's order for ten A320s. It has put the new airliner into service to 66 destinations. The A320's advanced technology and big capacity are key points appreciated by pilots, engineers and passengers. Trials have been conducted to study how the airliner's complex systems would be affected by lightning and electromagnetic interference. The verdict: not at all. Its blind landing systems enable it to land with only 250 yards visibility (the distance covered by the Airbus in one second at its speed of approach).

*An Airbus bought by British Caledonian, now flying for British Airways.*

# Twin engines spell long-haul success

*International, February*
In the space of around five years long-haul transoceanic and trans-desert flights by twin-engined airliners have become established as a technically safe and economically efficient means of travel.

Originally only manufacturers Boeing and Airbus Industrie were in favor of extended-range twin-engine operations (ETOPS), seeing them as a way to boost sales of their 757/767 and A310 respectively. On 125,000 ETOPS flights recorded since 1985, there have been only five instances of an engine failing in flight. With safety fears silenced, national authorities will surely follow the International Civil Aviation Organization (ICAO), which has progressively extended from one to three hours the maximum time it would take a twin-jet airliner to reach the nearest airport if one engine failed.

# Universal Weather is now 30 years old

*Weather forecasting at any time.*

*Houston, Texas, February 1*
From a humble beginning in 1959 Universal has grown to a globe-spanning expert on aviation and marine weather forcasting. Founded by the late Tom Evans, the company began by serving 35 flight crews and last year found weather and flight planning solutions for over 7,000 clients. In the 1960's Universal began a metamorphosis which found it transitioning from a basic supplier of weather-related services to offering computerized flight planning for its customers as well. Not only does Universal keep a staff of meteorologists, but also provides support services as over-flight permits, customs assistance, catering, hotel reservations, fueling, ground transport and helping determine the complex "gratuities" that must be paid at many foreign destinations. This would make many corporate pilots turn in their wings and go fishing, but thanks to Universal, it's just not a problem.

Flight crews located anywhere can contact Universal via HF (High Frequency) "patch" services provided through Aeronautical Radio, of Annapolis, Maryland.

# America West gains Major Carrier rank

*Phoenix, Arizona, January 1*
America West announced today that it has just gained the coveted "Major Carrier" status as a result of last year's revenues. America West began service on August 1, 1983 serving Colorado Springs, Kansas City, Los Angeles, Wichita and Las Vegas.

Its founder, Edward Beauvais, belives in "customer service". His employees are cross-trained in the jobs of their fellow workers, and they are given every opportunity to implement their own ideas. Most innovative are the company's displayed concerns and provisions for the child care of its workforce. This year America West earned the Labor/Management Relations Award from *Air Transport World* Magazine, and *Traveler* Magazine recognized the airline as one of only three US carriers among the world's top 20 rated carriers.

# Learjet has joined the Bombardier family

*Maya Lear with Brian Barents (Learjet), left, and L Beaudoin (Bombardier).*

*Wichita, Kansas, June 29*
Learjet today became the newest member of the Bombardier family, in a $75-million purchase by the Montreal-based business from the bankrupt Integrated Resources of New York.

The courts approved the deal on April 26, and negotiations were finalized on June 22. Laurent Beaudoin, president of Bombardier, said that Learjet will continue to function under its name as an autonomous entity within the Bombardier group. Learjet should be able to hold its own under the Bombardier umbrella as 1989 sales totalled $264 million and there continues to be a substantial backlog of orders. Bombardier, the world's leader in snowmobiles, also controls companies involved in railroad/monorail systems.

Bombardier acquired Canadair, Canada's leading integrated aircraft manufacturer in 1986. Its products center around the Challenger wide-bodied business aircraft and the CL-125 amphibian intended to fight forest fires. The Canadair RJ is a newly-launched project aimed at the 50-passenger regional air-carrier market. In 1989, Bombardier acquired Short Brothers of Belfast, maker of a wide range of airplanes and parts.

**Greg Morse, president of Morse Aviation & Racing, shown here in the cockpit of "Bad Juju", the T-6 (Harvard) racer in which he competed in the 1990 National Championships Air Races at Reno, Nevada.**

# US-German X-31 explores low speeds

*Palmdale, California, October 11*
The dogfights of the year 2000 will not necessarily be won by the fastest warplanes but by the most maneuverable ones, xhich can turn in the smallest space with the most power at their disposal.

A fighter with the capacity to slow from 500 to 100 knots in a few seconds will be leader of the supersonic pack, and could well be assisted by the X-31A, developed jointly by Rockwell of the US and MBB of Germany. The X-31A began its flight-tests at very low speeds and steep angles of attack here today. These tests will probe the limits to which a warplane will go when pulled up in flight, below its lift threshold.

The X-31's vectored-thrust engine plays a crucial role in controlling the aircraft's pitch and sharp turns. An integral digital system allows the pilot to alter the direction of the engine's thrust.

*The X-31A, designed for maneuverability of speed and angle of attack.*

# BAe launches long-range business jet

*Chester, England, June 16*
The first prototype of a new twin-engined executive jet, the British Aerospace BAe 125-1000, made its maiden flight here today. BAe has concentrated on developing the range of the new jet, which is designed to fly for nearly 4,200 miles at Mach 0.77 with six passengers.

This represents a 21 per cent increase in range over the BAe 125-800. Powered by two Pratt & Whitney Canada PW305 engines, the new aircraft also has a greater capacity than the 125-800 owing to a fuselage "stretched" by nearly 3 feet. Another bonus is the price: $12 million, 20 per cent cheaper than one of its likely future rivals, the French-built Falcon 2000. British Aerospace's Chester plant, most of which is in Wales rather than England, also makes Airbus wings.

*The BAe 125-1000 will be in service before France's rival Falcon 2000.*

▷

# Pilot sucked from cockpit escapes death

*An artist's impression of Captain Lancaster being held by his colleagues.*

*Southampton, England, June 10*
A BAC One-Eleven of British Airways carrying tourists to Malaga, Spain, touched down perfectly today at Southampton after a dramatic flight from East Midlands airport. Not long into the flight, 23,000 feet over Oxfordshire, there was a sudden loud bang as the left front windscreen, replaced only yesterday, blew out, causing a violent rush of air from the cockpit which sucked out every loose object – including Captain Tim Lancaster.

In the nick of time a steward and the co-pilot grabbed his legs, and he was held tight for 18 minutes, half out of the aircraft, while the co-pilot brought the airliner down at Southampton. There had been little alarm among the 81 passengers. Amazingly, Lancaster escaped with only frostbite, bruises and a broken elbow, wrist and thumb.

# New Air Force One is based on a Jumbo

*Andrews AFB, Maryland, August 23*
The first of two VC-25 transports for use by President George Bush was delivered today. Based on the Boeing 747-200, they will replace the two Boeing VC-137s that have been Air Force One since the 1960s.

Airline 747s can carry more than 400 passengers, but the VC-25s, with living and sleeping quarters for the President, and staff offices, will handle 70 passengers and a crew of 23. Communications gear, a baggage-loading system, stairs and auxiliary power units make them virtually self-sufficient. The VC-25s can cruise at 560mph with a range of 7,200 nautical miles and are equipped for in-flight refueling. The total cost for the two aircraft, parts, ground equipment and their hangar is $410 million.

*One of the two new airplanes specially adapted for the US President.*

# Royal opening for new airport computer

*London, June 18*
A £22 million IBM computer is the centrepiece of a modernization drive under way at the London Air Traffic Control Centre. The center's upgraded computer facilities, which were formally opened today at RAF West Drayton, near Heathrow airport, by the Princess Royal, enable 650 controlers to monitor all airline operations from the coast of France to the Scottish borders and from the North Sea to Northern Ireland.

*The princess inspects the center.*

# A Concorde facelift is a 40,000-hour job

*The fuselage of Concorde F-BVFA has been entirely stripped and checked.*

*Paris, August 1*
The old man had aged well, but it was time for a new lease of life. The fifth production Concorde, registration F-BVFA, emerged from a hangar the size of a cathedral at Roissy-Charles de Gaulle airport here today. For the past year staff at this huge maintenance hangar have subjected the 14-year-old supersonic airliner to a massive inspection and overhaul.

F-BVFA, which entered service on January 21, 1976, and has flown for 11,650 hours, covering 12 million miles, is the first of the six French Concordes to undergo this treatment. The gargantuan task required 40,000 of work and began at Orly, where the aircraft was thoroughly stripped down to the bare metal. It was then repainted khaki at Roissy to prevent corrosion before being mounted on jacks and dismantled down to its basic skeleton. Everything was then X-rayed down to the last square inch, from the 94 portholes to the 200 inspection covers and 13 fuel tanks, to discover any cracks. Even the tiniest crack could be a fatal structural weakness (→ Sep 1).

# CBA-123 set to be South American success

*Sao José dos Campos, Brazil, Jul 18*
Brazil faces an almost constant battle against economic setbacks and hyper-inflation, but this has not stopped state-owned aircraft manufacturer EMBRAER producing a healthy balance sheet. The latest fruit of the company's dynamism is the CBA-123, which made its first flight here today. CBA stands for Cooperacion Brasil-Argentina.

Developed jointly with Argentinian company FAMA, the new aircraft has two rear-mounted 1,250-hp Garrett TPF-351 turboprop engines. It has a cruising speed of 400mph and a ceiling of 30,000 feet and is of largely metal construction, although it also employs composite materials.

The choice of a 19-seat cabin means the CBA-123 is well placed to compete in the regional airliner market as well as in that for business airplanes. At a single stroke Embraer has produced what could prove a successor to both its Bandeirante and its Xingu.

*Employees of Embraer surround the CBA-123 after its maiden flight.*

# Battle is on for fighter of the 21st century

*The Northrop YF-23.*

*Lockheed's challenger: YF-22.*

*California, August 27*
The competition to find the US Air Force's fighter of the future is well under way. The victorious Advanced Tactical Fighter (ATF) might go into service in 1998. Congress would like the Navy to adopt a shipboard version.

The first of the two competitors, the YF-23 – developed jointly by Northrop assisted by McDonnell Douglas – successfully made an hour-long first flight today from Edwards Air Force Base, several weeks ahead of the launch of its rival, the YF-22, developed by Boeing, General Dynamics and Lockheed. The YF-23, of similar dimensions to the F-15 Eagle, has been conceived with stealth operation in mind: rounded forms, integrated engine nacelles, recessed air intakes and angled tail-fins. Like the YF-22, the new YF-23 is a twin-engined single-seater weighing in at about 22 tons and designed to have a maximum speed of around Mach 2.5.

The stakes are extremely high in the ATF battle, since the total cost of the program could be somewhere in the region of $140 billion, with each aircraft expected to cost $100 million.

# Future looks bright for Europe's Airbus

*Toulouse, France, October 1*
Last year was a good one for Airbus Industrie, and the prospects for 1990 are excellent. In 1989 Airbus sold 421 airliners for a total of $28.2 billion. As of June 8 the European consortium had sold 1,442 aircraft to 91 customers and delivered 602, including 500 A300s and 310s. Airbus airliners notched up seven million hours of commercial flights.

The A300s now have the lion's share (56 per cent) of the world market for 210/250-seat airliners, ahead of Boeing's 767-200 and 300. This dominance is greater in the Middle East (80 per cent), Africa (71 per cent), Europe (66 per cent) and the Far East and Australasia (63 per cent). Boeing leads in North America (60 per cent) and South America (53 per cent) (→ Oct 3).

# The dual-use V-22 Osprey tilt-rotor aboard the USS Wasp

*A spectacular view of the V-22 Osprey coming in to land on the USS Wasp.*

*USS Wasp, December 12*
Two remarkable V-22 Osprey tilt-rotor technology aircraft (numbers 3 and 4) have completed sea trials with the US Navy aboard the USS Wasp (LDH-1). The V-22s participated in shipboard compatability tests including landings, take-offs, tie-downs, emergency procedures and wing/blade folding evaluations. Prior to the tests the aircraft had been flown to Patuxent River Naval Air Station for airspeed calibration flights and electomagnetic vulnerability testing, a prerequisite for shipboard operations.

The Osprey is being developed as a dual-use aircraft with a wide range of civilian tasks. City-center to city-center commuter operations, disaster relief, medical fast-response, evacuation, rescue, drug interdiction, border patrol and express package delivery are a few.

# Airbus gets new factory to boost output

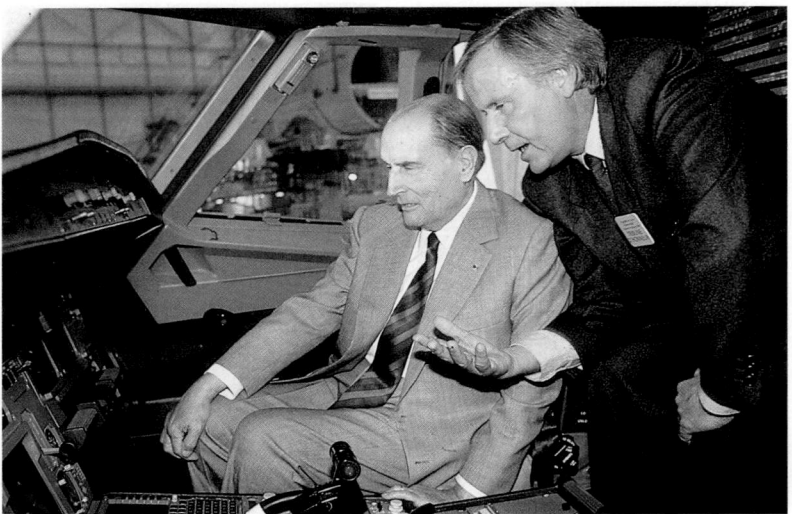

*The controls of an Airbus A320 are explained to President Mitterrand.*

**Toulouse, France, October 10**
A massive metal structure, called "Clément Ader" in honor of the early French air pioneer, was opened here today by French President François Mitterrand. The building, which covers nearly 130 acres, is the new factory for the European Airbus consortium and has been constructed by France's Aérospatiale over three years at a cost of around a billion francs.

Some 550 yards long by 330 wide and 50 high, the assembly hall is subdivided into an area for unloading aircraft sections, two paint shops, a technical center, a huge restaurant and various service buildings. Close to 650 workers will work here on the assembly of the long-range Airbus A330 and 340 airliners. They face the task of setting up the production line and then rapidly increasing output. By 1995 seven A330/A340s should be leaving the factory every month. In 1975 Airbus output stood at just one aircraft a month.

**An Apache helicopter, the first of 18 arriving in Israel, stands on its tail.**

# United grabs Pan Am's London routes

*New York, October 23*
United Air Lines, taking advantage of Pan American World Airways' need for cash, today completed a $400 million deal that will give it Pan Am's valuable routes to London's Heathrow Airport. The deal also calls for schedules to be co-ordinated so that United's domestic flights will feed passengers into Pan Am's routes from Los Angeles and Miami to Latin America.

Customers will participate in the "frequent-flyer" programs of both airlines. Selling the profitable New York, Washington, San Francisco, Los Angeles and Seattle routes to London, as well as its Dallas/Paris route and Dallas facilities, continues the downward spiral for Pan Am. It is now only a carrier in the Latin American and East Coast shuttle markets – and it is trying to unload the latter. Its cherished Pacific routes were sold to United in 1985, and its Inter-German Service is being transferred to Lufthansa for $150 million. Pan Am posted a $239 million loss for the first half of this year alone.

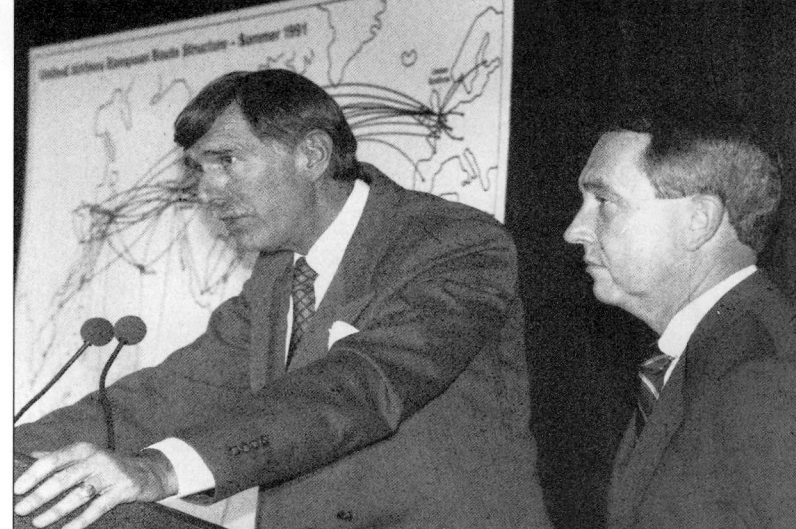

*United's Stephen Wolf (l) and Pan Am's Thomas Plaskett reveal the deal.*

# Osaka airport opens on artificial island

*Osaka, Japan, November 9*
Japan's first 24-hour airport is being constructed in Osaka Bay. Built on a 1,260-acre artificial island two and a half miles offshore, Kansai airport is far enough from urban centers to permit acceptable noise levels all day long. It has a 2.2-mile runway as well as three passenger and two cargo terminals. A 2.3-mile road and rail bridge links the new airport to the mainland.

*Surrounded by sea, Kansai airport has no neighbors to be upset by noise.*

# Simulators reach new heights of realism

*A 747 simulator, reproducing the sound, images and sensations of flight.*

# Allies prepare for war

*A Lockheed Galaxy transport disgorging troops after the flight to the Gulf.*

*Vilgénis, France, November 1*
The aircraft is descending toward New York's JFK airport, and the Atlantic swell is now visible. Under an early morning sky the pilot, on his final approach, sees the sky-scrapers in the distance and the lights of the cars on the freeways. The noise of the jet engines responding to the pilot's commands and the movement of the cabin complete the impression of being at the controls of an Air France Boeing 747-400 coming in to land.

However, Air France will not take delivery of its first 747-400 until February. The pilot is in fact at the controls of one of the new flight simulators at the Vilgénis instruction center, surrounded by images produced by the SP-X 500 Wide, made by the British company Rediffusion.

Stored in the memory of this huge computer are over 30 remarkably realistic airport scenarios. The principal technical innovation is in the image creation. The picture is

*San Francisco 28R, by simulator.*

projected by three generators on top of the simulator onto a 180-degree concave mirror in front of the "cockpit". With such convincing practise, pilots should be better prepared for the real thing when the time comes.

*Saudi Arabia. December 31*
As 1990 draws to a close, the prospects for peace in the Gulf diminish. The Allies, led by the USA, are preparing for war, and in the initial stages great use is likely to be made of their vastly superior air power. Overall Allied commander General Norman Schwarzkopf has formidable air assets: 1,350 US combat aircraft ranging from the latest F-117 stealth fighters, F-14 Navy Tomcats, USAF F-15 air-superiority fighters, A-10 Thunderbolt II anti-tank aircraft to ageing B-52 strategic bombers, AWACS airborne radar and control aircraft and around 1,500 helicopters.

Schwarzkopf also has six US Navy aircraft carriers in the Gulf and Red Sea. Other major air forces come from Saudi Arabia with 140 combat aircraft, including F-15s and Tornados, Britain with 75 Tornados (of both IDS and ADV types) and Jaguars, and 70 helicopters, Italy with Tornados of the IDS type, and France with 50 combat aircraft and 120 helicopters.

Any correlation of air forces must give the Allies the upper hand, not only in numbers but also in the effectiveness of their weapons systems; most were designed for combat against a much more technically advanced enemy than Iraq. Air superiority should be gained quite quickly, then sustained by attacks on Iraqi airfields. This would be followed by a long period in which air forces would "prepare the battlefield" by bombing Iraqi forces and cutting their lines of communication prior to any ground assault.

# Johnson, king of the Skunk Works, dies

*Burbank, California, December 21*
"Be quick, be quiet, be on time." This was the motto of great US aircraft designer Clarence L "Kelly" Johnson, 80, who died today. Head of the Lockheed Advanced Development Company for thirty years, Johnson played an essential role in the creation of over 40 aircraft, including the piston and turboprop Electras, the Constel-

lation, and the first US jet-fighter, the XP-80 Shooting Star prototype, completed in just 143 days. Johnson was also the originator of the noted U-2 spyplane and TR-1, the amazing YF-12/SR-71 Blackbird, which exceeded 2,000mph high in the stratospere at 85,000 feet, and the F-104 Starfighter, the first production aircraft to reach Mach 2.

*Lethal weapons: Sikorsky Black Hawk helicopters on exercise in the desert.*

The first prototype McDonnell Douglas MD-11 trijet widebody airliner. The MD-11 is essentially a re-winged, up-engined, new-technology DC-10.

The BAe 1000, an uprated version of the best-selling 1960s vintage BAe (originally de Havilland, and then Hawker Siddeley) 125 business jet.

Embraer's revolutionary looking CBA-123 Vector commuterliner features rear-mounted, rear-facing propfan powerplants.

The prototype Beech 1900D was based on the 1982 Model 1900, but is liberally covered with an amazing number of aerodynamic improvements.

The Taylorcraft Model F-22A Classic is a two/three-seat sporting aircraft which harks back to the immortal 1930s Taylorcraft (E-2 Cub) designs.

The first Boeing E-3D Sentry early warning aircraft for the RAF features CFM56 fan engines, wingtip ESM pods and an inflight-refueling probe.

The Boeing Sikorsky Fantail Demonstrator, a modified Sikorsky H-76 used in support of the LHX Comanche program, with a Fenestron tail rotor.

Rockwell/MBB's X-31A EFM is designed to investigate enhanced fighter maneuvrability, breaking what has been called the "Alpha Barrier".

*The prototype Boeing MH-47E, a dedicated special-operations variant of the Chinook with more power, night capability and an inflight-refueling probe.*

*Rutan's Model 151 ARES, a low-cost single-seat close-support aircraft which features an unprecedented asymmetric arrangement of gun and engine.*

*One of two Boeing VC-25As, selected to serve as US Presidential transports to replace the "Air Force One" VC-137s. The basis, of course, is a B-747.*

*The Atlas Rooivalk, an indigenous South African armed attack helicopter which followed on from the Alpha and Beta technology demonstrators.*

*Lockheed's YF-22 Advanced Tactical Fighter, successful contender for the USAF's requirement for an F-15 replacement able to serve beyond 2020.*

*The Northrop YF-23, unsuccessful rival to the YF-22 in the USAF's ATF competition, despite being faster and (some say) having other advantages.*

*An early example of the Italian/Brazilian AMX close-support aircraft, a highly capable light strike fighter sometimes dubbed the "Pocket Tornado".*

# 1991

4,534mph
USA
Pete Knight
North American X-15
Oct 3, 1967

24,987 miles
USA
Jeager and Rutan
*Voyager*
Dec 23, 1986

354,200ft
USA
Joseph Walker
North American X-15
Aug 22, 1963

1,120,370lb
USSR
Antonov
An-225 Mriya

61,570lb thrust
USA
Pratt & Whitney
4060A

**China, January 25**
A Chinese Tupolev Tu-154 airliner on a flight from Shanghai is grounded during a stopover at Taiyun after eight white mice are found roaming about the aircraft; local aviation authorities fear the rodents may have damaged wiring aboard the aircraft.

**San Antonio, Texas, February 13**
Probably the world's smallest bizjet, the Swearingen SJ-30, makes its first flight. Configured for two in the cockpit and (typically) four in the cabin, it is powered by two Williams-Rolls FJ44 engines.

**Edwards AFB, February 14**
Flight testing of the MBB/Rockwell X-31A, possibly the world's most maneuverable airplane, has now progressed to vectoring the jet from the engine, using three surrounding paddles. The Nos 1 airplane is being used, though No 2 has been flying since January 19.

**USSR, March 15**
Flight testing begins of the Yak-42ELL, a Yak-42 civil jetliner with the Nos 1 and 3 engines replaced by D-236 tractor contra-rotating propfans. Soviet opinion holds that the West is shortsighted to put propfans on the back-burner.

**Mojave, California, March 22**
Powered by two Electro-Motive V-6 turbocharged and intercooled engines, the Pond Racer makes its first flight. Created by Burt Rutan's Scaled Composites company, it is designed to break the world piston-engined speed record, at over 530 mph.

**Bogota, April 10**
The Aviones de Colombia AC-05 Pijao ag-plane makes its first flight.

**Cartierville, Canada, May 10**
The first of hundreds of RJs (Regional Jets) makes its maiden flight. Derived by stretching the Challenger bizjet, the RJ is in the 50/56-seat class.

**Stans, Switzerland, May 31**
Designed to replace King Air type airplanes, with one engine instead of two, the PC-12 pressurized 8/10-seater began its flight-test program today. Price could be only $1,630,000.

**New York, June 1**
A passenger on Delta flight DL236 from Orlando, Florida, discovers a python in one of the overhead baggage lockers.

**Paris, July 17**
Nearly $1 million in cash carried by a scheduled Air France flight from Bastia, Corsica, is found to be missing when the aircraft lands here; the thief hid inside a trunk in the aircraft's hold before breaking into two sealed Brink's sacks and escaping shortly after arrival.

**London, July 26**
British Airways and Aeroflot jointly announce the formation of a new airline, Air Russia; initially to be equipped with Boeing 767s, it will open up air routes between Russia and the West; headquarters will be in Moscow.

**Seattle, September 1**
Boeing announces final termination of production of the B-707, continuously manufactured for 37 years.

**Warsaw, Poland, September 18**
To the 27 types of turboprop trainer already flying can be added the South African Atlas TP, first flown on April 29; the Brazilian Tucano H stretched (September 9); and the PZL Turbo-Orlik 130-TB, flown today.

**Prestwick, Scotland, September 25**
Already ordered to a total of close to 100 aircraft, the British Aerospace Jetstream 41 makes its first flight; it carries about 29 passengers, ten more than its parent Jetstream 31.

**Long Beach, California, Nov 7**
McDonnell Douglas decides to split its Douglas Aircraft Company into separate commercial and military segments.

**USSR, November 8**
An Aeroflot Yak-40 crashes near Makhachkala, in the Caucasus mountains, killing all 34 people on board.

**Xian, China, November 23**
First flight of the Xian 200B turboprop transport, with greater power provided by PT6A engines, follows the successful flight yesterday of the Korean Air Lines Chang Gong 91 utility transport. Few details have yet been released of China's latest fighter, the Chengdu J-9, first flown on September 5.

**Oberpfaffenhofen, Germany, Dec 6**
Having sold more than 200 20-seat Do 228s, Dornier has today begun flight-testing the pressurized 30/33-seat Do 328.

**Istres, France, December 12**
Today saw the start of flight testing of the Rafale M. This is the carrier-equipped version of the latest Dassault fighter, for the French Aéronavale (navy air force). This follows the first flight last May 19 of the Rafale C, first with the definitive M88-2 engines.

**St Louis, Missouri, December 19**
McDonnell Douglas Corporation announces that the Swiss government has formally submitted a $2.6 billion acquisition bill to the parliament to buy 34 F/A-18 Hornet fighters.

**Moscow, December 19**
Aeroflot reports that about 40 per cent of its total fleet of aircraft are currently grounded by fuel shortages due to the nation's economic crisis.

**Heidelberg, Germany, Dec 22**
A chartered DC-3 on a "nostalgia" flight from Frankfurt organized by Classic Wings crashes into a hillside near here, killing 26 people.

**Bloomfield, Connecticut, Dec 23**
Kaman has returned to the "eggbeater" formula with two intermeshing rotors with the K-Max high-lift crane/transport first flown today.

**Ontario, Canada, December 26**
Northwest Airlines signs a $190 million deal to buy 20 Dash 8 Series 100 commuter aircraft from Boeing's de Havilland division for use by its Northwest Airlink affiliated carriers.

---

*End of an era: Captain Mark Pyle brings "Clipper Goodwill" into Miami to end 64 years of Pan Am operations.* ▶

## Factfile

World revenue passenger miles: 1,125,000 million
Passengers through Chicago O'Hare: 58.4 million
Passengers through New York (JFK/Newark/LaGuardia): 68.3 million
World air freight (ton miles): 139,908.4 million
Passengers through London (Heathrow/Gatwick): 60.8 million
Price of a single coach ticket London/New York: $499
Price of a Boeing 747-400: $126 million
Price of an Airbus A340: $108.2 million
Price of a Boeing 737-500: $30 million
Price of an ATR 42: $18.1 million
Average salary of long-haul pilot: $107,044
Average salary of cabin crew (US): $27,979
Price of 1,000 (US) gallons Jet A1 fuel (July average): $712.15
Average exchange rate £1 = $1.6890

# First 727 is retired after 64,492 hours

*N7001U was the first of 1,832 Boeing 727s, all built at Renton.*

**Seattle, Washington, January 13**
Following an extraordinary career spanning a quarter of a century, the first Boeing 727-100 ever built was retired here today. N7001U (Spirit of Seattle) flew more than 64,492 hours and completed 48,057 cycles (one take-off and landing constitutes a cycle), carried more than 3,000,000 passengers and generated over $300 million in revenue during its operation by United Air Lines. Not a bad investment for an aircraft originally costing $4.4 million.

The old workhorse will now become part of the Museum of Flight, fulfilling a promise made by United president Stephen M Wolf on January 23, 1988. It is not without some pride that United traces its history as an airline to Boeing and the Seattle-Tacoma area. The delivery ceremony is likely to evoke feelings of nostalgia, as the Spirit of Seattle has been repainted in its original 1964 livery.

# Cessna's Citation VII has extended range

**Wichita, Kansas, February 2**
The protoype Cessna Citation VII, a more powerful version of the Citation III, today made a successful first flight of 1 hour 10 minutes, climbing to an altitude of 41,000 feet. The prototype constists of a Citation III to which two Garrett TFE731-4 engines have been fitted. Each powerplant develops a thrust of 4,000 lb. The new Cessna aircraft is to be priced at $8.6 million and is designed for improved performance. Its avionics and other equipment is more sophisticated than the Citation III.

Both aircraft seat eight, but the VII has a slightly shorter range than the III. (2,250 nautical miles compared to 2,345 nmi).

*Citation VII matches the new wing of the III with upgraded engines.*

# American celebrates 1 billionth passenger

*Raleigh, North Carolina, March 27*
When he boarded American Flight 1637 to Dallas here today, Howard A Laffler, of Raleigh, became the carrier's billionth passenger. Laffler, chairman and chief executive of RCA Business Telephone Systems, received a free vacation for two in London and other gifts. He has been a member of American's A-Advantage frequent-flyer program since 1981. American touts the program as the industry's first, and on May 1 they will celebrate its 10th anniversary. During the anniversary celebrations, American plans to give away over $2 million in awards and prizes, including 10 years of free air travel and Fly AAway vacations.

*American is proud of its service.*

# The changing of the guard at Heathrow

*United's distinctive livery is now familiar at London's Heathrow.*

*London Heathrow, April 4*
Today Buckingham Palace will not be the only place in London where the old guard will be replaced by the new. Venerable Pan American, after serving London for 45 years, is being replaced by another airline with a historic past.

United Air Lines Flight 918, a Boeing 747 aircraft from Dulles International Airport, Washington, DC, is scheduled to land at 7.40am today, closely followed by a 747 from New York's JFK airport. Later flights will arrive from San Francisco, California, and Miami, Florida.

United completed a $715 million deal for Pan Am's Pacific routes in February 1986 and appears to be, to all intents and purposes, heir to Pan Am's pioneering past. These recent setbacks are fueling speculation about Pan Am's ability to survive.

# The EH101 helicopter enters production

*Cascina, Italy, January 16*
Today the Italian Agusta company made the first flight of the PP.9, the ninth and last prototype of the most powerful helicopter ever built in Western Europe. The EH 101 is a 50/50 project with Westland of the UK. All versions are powered by three engines, either the 1,714-hp GE T700 or the 2,312-hp Rolls-Royce Turbomeca RTM322. The Royal Navy expects to operate 50 (named Merlin), the Italian Navy 42 and the Canadian Navy up to 35. The RAF requires 25 of a utility transport version. With full engine-out performance, all-weather avionics and a 184mph cruising speed, the EH 101 could be in a class of its own, apart from the USSR's Mi-38 which is unlikely to begin flight testing until 1993, whereas the first EH 101 flew in October 1987.

# 'Desert Storm', the highest-technology war

## AWACS plays crucial role over the Gulf

*The E-3A Sentry proved its worth in managing the Middle East airspace.*

**Saudi Arabia, January 18**
Radar officers from USAF E-3 Sentry Airborne Warning and Control System (AWACS) aircraft this morning confirmed their complex role in last night's "Desert Storm" operation. The most intricate of air assaults began under the cover of darkness when waves of allied aircraft took off from air bases and carriers heading for Iraq.

Never have so many different aircraft with such diverse capabilities, from so many nations, fallen under the command of one leader. In large measure it was the coordination of the AWACS that made such a mission possible. Captains Patterson and Chewning of the 552nd Air Control Wing of Tinker AFB, Oklahoma, reported the need for AWACS personnel to know capabilities of every allied aircraft and the weapons systems it carries. AWACS radar was responsible for the coordination of each ingress and egress of every allied aircraft during the long night.

All allied pilots received initial strike coordination from USAF AWACS aircraft as well as continuing "threat awareness" information. Chewning, who assisted in two MiG kills, stressed the importance of the AWACS role in command and control.

## RAF Tornados take out Iraq's airfields

*Tornado attack aircraft of the RAF peel off over their Saudi base.*

**Saudi Arabia, February**
Probably the world's best low-level all-weather attack aircraft, with a clean sea-level speed of 800 knots (902mph), the Panavia Tornado has done brilliantly in its first test in actual warfare.

Though the European airplane has flown only a small fraction of the overall allied missions, its contribution to the night-time low-level sortie rate was almost 50 per cent. It repeatedly demonstrated its ability to place ordinary "iron bombs" exactly on target even in the face of the heaviest Iraqi defenses. Tornado is the biggest-ever international aircraft program. Well over 900 have been delivered, flying more than a million hours. Both the IDS (interdiction strike), and ADV (air-defence variant) have been used since hostilities broke out in the Gulf last month. They were flown by the air forces of Britain, Italy and Saudi Arabia. The two-seat, swing-wing (variable sweep), twin-engined airplane has two cannon, a flight-refueling probe, and very comprehensive radar and defensive avionics. Other defensive equipment includes the Alarm anti-radar missile, seen as a gray tube under the nearer aircraft in the photograph. Under the nose can be seen the laser ranger and marked-target seeker.

## Air Force pilot Jon Kelk downs MiG-29

*Jon Kelk was credited with first kill.*

**Saudi Arabia, January 17**
Flying an F-15C, USAF Captain Jon Kelk, 31, and three other aircraft left here tonight to cover the withdrawal of F-117 stealth bombers and F-15E attack aircraft which had launched earlier to try to catch Iraqi defenders by surprise. Shortly after 3am, Kelk spotted an "unknown" on his APG-63 air-to-air radar. The enemy aircraft was climbing from 6,000 to 18,000 feet and the F-15's systems told Kelk he was being hunted. From a distance of 20 miles, he fired an AIM-7 Sparrow missile and scored a hit. Later, AWACS aircraft confirmed Kelk had been credited with the first kill of "Desert Storm", an Iraqi MiG-29 Fulcrum fighter.

**The Lockheed F-117A and the McDonnell Douglas KC-10 Extender proved a winning combination. This photograph emphasises the sheer size of the tanker which carries over a hundred tons of fuel.**

# McDonnell Douglas tries harder on MD-11

*AA is one of the most important customers for the big MD-11.*

Long Beach, California, Nov 29
A razzmatazz ceremony to celebrate delivery of the first McDonnell Douglas MD-11 to Finnair did not disguise the desperate struggle the manufacturer is having to speed up production whilst at the same time achieving the promised range with full payload.

No customer is more important than American Airlines, with 15 firm orders and 35 options, yet AA President Robert L Crandall said he was "very, very unhappy" with the first to be delivered, last February 1, and threatened to refuse to take delivery of the second of the MD-11s on order. He later said AA would claim $7.3 million in damages per year per aircraft, be-

cause of the airplane's inability to fly some long-distance routes with a full payload.

Powered by Pratt & Whitney, General Electric or Rolls-Royce engines in the 55,000-65,000-lb class, the MD-11 is an upgraded and improved DC-10, typically seating 323 passengers. McDonnell Douglas has a total of approximately 175 firm orders, but the manufacturer is suffering severe competition from the basically newer Airbus A330/340, and even from the larger Boeing 747-400. The main board of McDonnell Douglas may before long take the giant decision to go ahead with a completely new MD-11 successor (→ Apr 30, 1992).

# Alaska opens first service to Soviet Union

Anchorage, Alaska, June 17
Alaska Airlines today became the first US passenger carrier to offer regularly scheduled flights to the Soviet Union from the West Coast, as Flight 29 left with 144 passengers and crew. The Boeing 727 with the striking Eskimo livery departed at 6.30pm enroute to Magadan and Khabarovsk. This first flight included 60 people on a trade mission sponsored by the Alaska State Chamber of Commerce and the US-USSR Trade and Economics Council. Magadan is a city of 150,000 on the Sea of Okhotsk. A closed city for decades, it is now an administrative center and major port. Khabarovsk, near China, is a large river port of 700,000.

*Alaska Airlines flies 32 MD-80s.*

# Boeing admits B-767 reverser problems

*On May 26, a Lauda Air B-767 crashed in Thailand after a reverser operated inadvertently in flight.*

Washington, DC, August 16
The Federal Aviation Administration today ordered all operators of Boeing 767s to disconnect the thrust reversers on the aircraft. Recent tests carried out by the Seattle-based manufacturer have shown that reversers could deploy in flight, causing a catastrophic loss of control.

A thrust reverser problem is one of the possible causes of the May 26 crash in Thailand of a Lauda Air 767, in which the 223 people on board were killed. Boeing is now likely to have to modify the reverser systems on its 767 fleet.

**The sleek, smooth and fast Learjet 60, which made its first flight on June 13, is the first Lear to be powered by Pratt & Whitney engines. Priced at $7.9 million, it is scheduled for certification in late 1992.**

**Butler Aviation provides service to Airforce 1 Boeing VC-25B as President Bush visits Palm Beach to meet his ailing mother in February. Starting in 1948, Butler today is the biggest US fixed-based operator.**

# Cessna's CitationJet, a predictable winner

*The prototype and a pre-production CitationJet will fly over 1,000hr this year.*

*Wichita, Kansas, April 29*
Today's maiden flight of the latest member of the large Cessna family was nearly spoilt by freak storms and tornados.

The CitationJet had been due to take off at precisely 9am, but the 400 guests waited patiently for the conditions to improve. Cessna test pilots Bob Leonard and Bob Carnahan were finally able to take off at 5.38pm, climbing quickly to 10,000 feet for the start of a 45-minute flight. The CitationJet, with a cruising speed of 380 knots and a maximum range of 1,730 miles, is powered by two Williams-Rolls FJ44 jet engines each of 900 lb thrust. Priced at $2.85 million, the CitationJet is designed to carry four passengers and one pilot. FAA certification of the aircraft is expected in November 1992. Even though the new jet's career has hardly begun, its manufacturer has already received 100 orders.

# Most pilots could not fly without the FBOs

*Denver, Colorado, June 25*
For the past 15 consecutive years the AMR Combs fixed-base operation (FBO) here has been awarded the number one rating by *Professional Pilot Magazine*. The annual award is the result of a survey poll taken of more than 30,000 professional pilots. FBOs are rated in specific categories and overall.

Known to professional and private pilots as FBOs, fixed-base operators provide "soup to nuts" services for every aspect of corporate and general aviation. To the corporate pro, his choice of FBO can mean the difference between a successful or a failed flight.

FBOs handle vital details such as lounges for passengers, inflight meals, rental cars and executive conference rooms. They provide flight planning and weather services as well as aircraft fueling and maintenance when the inevitable mechanical or avionics problems occur. There are over 5,000 FBOs in the USA alone.

*AMR Combs FBO of Denver is again awarded the Nº 1 by Professional Pilot.*

# TWA sells Heathrow rights to American

*Dallas, Texas, May 2*
American Airlines announced today that all the remaining obstacles to the TWA purchase had finally been overcome.

The American carrier said it would buy three of TWA's routes to London at the same price it originally agreed to pay TWA for six. American has agreed to pay $445 million for the routes to Heathrow Airport that originate in New York, Los Angeles and Boston. Route authority from these three cities to the coveted destination of London Heathrow will begin on July 1.

American Airlines Chairman Robert L Crandall said that "it is extremely important to AA to operate those three key routes, plus Chicago-Heathrow and Miami-Heathrow during the peak summer 1991 season." TWA's Heathrow employees will be offered jobs.

# West discovers East at Paris Le Bourget

*Paris, June 13*
More than ever before, the Soviet Union's aviation industry is lifting the veil of secrecy, openly displaying its wares and answering questions. For example, the previously almost unknown MIG-31 (until now written MiG) was not merely displayed but shown with the radome off to reveal the advanced Zaslon phased-array radar, which General Constructor Rostislav Belyakov described in detail. Next year Tupolev's Tu-204 and Ilyushin's Il-96 jetliners will fly with British and US engines.

*For several months MIG has been written thus, so the above is a MIG-31.*

# British law court convicts BA captain

*London, May 12*
In an unprecedented civil trial a British Airways captain has been found guilty of "negligently endangering his aircraft and the 273 people aboard". He was cleared of the charge of "negligently causing his aircraft to endanger people and property on the ground". On November 21, 1989, Captain Glen Stewart was flying a 747-100 making an approach in very poor visibility to London Heathrow. The autopilot failed to lock on the ILS, and a manual go-around was initiated at 75 feet, missing the Heathrow Penta hotel by about 12 ft. Flight data records showed that at 200 ft localizer deviation must have shown full deflection, with deviation warning lights indicating. The British Air Line Pilots' Association says that "the criminal prosecution of a pilot in these circumstances is wholly inappropriate".

# American operates Fokker 100 Luxury Jet

*American's F 100s perpetuate the tradition of polished aluminum all over.*

*Chicago, Illinois, August 1*
Fokker's Chairman, Erik Jan Nederkoorn, today delivered the first of 75 Fokker 100 luxury jets to American Airlines President Robert Crandall. Eleven are scheduled for delivery this year, and 24 more in 1992. American has options on 75 additional F 100s, representing the largest single industrial order ever placed with the Dutch manufacturer.

This first aircraft begins service on August 15, on the Chicago-Milwaukee and Chicago-Cincinnati routes. These aircraft "will be the quietest jets we operate", said Crandall. The Fokker F 100 is designed for the medium to small market and has a full-payload range of 1,100 miles in an eight first-class and 89 coach seat configuration. Although design and assembly are done in Holland, it is very much an international jet as the engines are built by Rolls-Royce (Tay 650 turbofans), the fuselage sections by MBB of Germany, the wings by Short Brothers of Belfast, and avionics and systems by US manufacturers such as Honeywell, Sperry, Grumman, Bendix, PPG Industries, Garrett, Goodyear and Loral. The cockpit is state-of-the-art with fully integrated digital flight systems.

Fokker has been a strong player on the US market since the 1920s, when it helped pioneer early American aviation.

# C-17 USAF airlifter begins flight testing

*Edwards AFB, California, Sept 15*
The McDonnell Douglas C-17 first prototype made its first flight here today.

Powered by four PW F117 turbofans, the T-tailed giant can carry a load of nearly 90 tons, and can use rough strips. It is expected to fly at speeds from 95 to 590mph. The USAF hopes to buy 120, with the first squadron operational by the end of 1994, but at $294 million each the prospects for completing the whole program look uncertain. Already the overall program has been cut from its original level of 210 aircraft, and the Air Force is fighting hard to keep it at 120.

*The C-17 is built at Long Beach.*

# Harrier family grows for many customers

*Dunsfold, England, December 31*
While workers are finishing the design of the Harrier II Plus, the British Aerospace plant here is assembling the first Sea Harrier FRS.2 aircraft. The Mk 2 version of the Royal Navy's Harrier will be the first aircraft to be armed with the AMRAAM missile, for BVR (beyond visual range) "look up and look down" interceptions. It can carry an 8,000-lb weapon load, including Sea Eagle anti-ship missiles. The land-based Harrier II family has been joined by the McDonnell Douglas Night Attack version for the US Marine Corps, and the Harrier GR.7 for the RAF. Both have a pimple above the nose for housing an FLIR (forward-looking infra-red). With night-vision goggles, a digital map and various other updates it enables high-speed low-level attacks to be made against point targets at night with great precision. Perhaps the most important is the II Plus, developed by BAe and McDonnell Aircraft. This mates the redesigned Harrier II airframe with a host of updates, including the Hughes APG-65 radar. The II Plus has been sold to the US Marines and the Spanish and Italian navies.

# Europe's Tiger joins rivals to the Apache

*The AH-1W is a twin-turbine helo.*

*Marignane, France, April 27*
Today, 28 years after the Franco-German helicopter program started, the Eurocopter Tiger has flown. The MBB/Aérospatiale battlefield helicopter, powered by two 1,285-hp RR-MTU-Turbomeca MTR 390 engines, is envisaged in different anti-tank, scout and escort versions. Service entry is due in 1997-98. It emerges into a crowded market. IBM, GEC Avionics and Honeywell are working with Bell on upgrades of the AH-1W SuperCobra. McDonnell Douglas has the Longbow Apache, Britain the T800 Lynx, Italy the A129 Mangusta, the USSR the Mi-28, South Africa the Rooivalk, and for the year 2000 is the Boeing/Sikorsky RAH-66 Comanche. They cannot all sustain viable programs.

*British Aerospace is now delivering the night/all-weather Harrier GR.7.*

# Delta swallows almost all of Pan Am's operations

*Delta's 757s will now operate throughout the previous Pan Am system.*

*Pan Am's famous global emblem will now be seen only in Central America.*

**New York, August 12**
Pan Am, which has been operating under court protection from its creditors since January, has paid a heavy price for years of strategic and tactical errors. Today at 12.04am Pan Am's creditors agreed to a Delta Air Lines offer of about $1.4 billion that will leave the carrier in business, primarily flying routes between the USA and Latin America. Delta outbid three rival suitors, American Airlines, TWA and United. Lawyers for Pan Am said the agreement will enable the airline to meet its administrative and priority claims, and preserve about 13,500 jobs out of a current payroll of 17,000. Atlanta-based Delta agreed to pay $416 million for Pan Am's routes between the USA and Europe, its Northeast shuttle, planes and equipment. Delta is also to make a $305 million investment in a reorganized Pan Am which would move its headquarters from New York to Miami and be owned 45 per cent by Delta and 55 per cent by Pan Am's creditors. Delta is also to assume about $669 million in Pan Am's liabilities. The deal will make Delta one of the biggest international airlines. Delta currently serves about 148 US cities and has 26 overseas destinations. Its overseas routes include Mexico, the Bahamas and Canada. The Pan Am purchase will give it a much larger overseas presence, especially in Europe (→ Dec 4).

## Airlines to offer satellite phone services

**International, August 1**
A growing number of leading airlines are gearing up to launch satellite phones for passengers on their long-haul flights. Plans to offer passenger phones are well advanced with at least three carriers, British Airways, Northwest Airlines and United Airlines. The satellite phone system calls for about six bulkhead-mounted handsets in the cabin so that travelers do not have to wait too long to place a call. The equipment will be programmed to seek the cheaper terrestrial system first. When this is out of range, the passenger will hear a recorded message telling him that the call can be completed via satellite and informing him of the higher rates.

## Piper applies for Chapter 11 protection

**Vero Beach, Florida, July 1**
Faced with a $28 million debt, Piper Aircraft, once one of the leading builders of light planes, today filed for Chapter 11 protection. The manufacturer hopes that this move will reassure potential investors so that it can continue operations. Piper had survived a string of setbacks, but the final blow came last March when one of its top sellers, the piston-engined Malibu business aircraft, was banned from flying in bad weather following a series of crashes. However, Piper Aircraft's management has not abandoned hopes of saving the ailing company, as its order books currently show potential sales of nearly $200 million (→Apr 1, 1992).

On October 31, after 30 years of service, United Airlines retires the last of its once-huge fleet of DC-8s. The last service is flown by Capt. Dennis Darida, First Officer Dale Richter and Flight Engineer John Eddins.

American Airlines has spent $38 million on TRAAM at Dallas/Fort Worth, Texas, the world's biggest airport. It saves passengers having to carry baggage tens of miles when checking-in or changing planes.

# Airbus A340 opens new era for European aircraft manufacturing

# Rolls and Pratt still locked in combat

*After exploring initial handling, the test crew retracted the gear and tested Mach numbers up to 0.85 over the Atlantic.*

*Toulouse, France, October 25*
With the completion of a perfect 4 hour 47 minute first flight here today, flight testing of the first Airbus A340 is moving into high gear.

With its partner, the A330, the new airplane adds significantly to the product range of the European partnership. After years of planning, in 1984-88, it was found possible to make the twin-engined A330 virtually identical to the four-engined A340, because the bending loads on the slender high-efficiency wings are almost the same. This is despite the fact that the A340 carries more fuel, making it almost 50 tons heavier and needing an extra main landing gear on the centerline. Both aircraft grew in weight and power during development, so that while the A340 has four CFM56-5 engines of 31,200 lb thrust, the 330 has two engines (GE, PW or RR) in the 66,000 to 80,000 lb class. Already, 29 airlines have signed for 258 of the new Airbus family, almost guaranteeing that by the year 2000 the total will be well beyond 600. This is the first time that airlines have had the option of a high-capacity twin and an ultra-long-range four-engined airplane which in almost all other respects are the same aircraft.

*Greenwich, Connecticut, Dec 18*
In one of the biggest about-faces in aviation history, the package-delivery giant United Parcel Service (UPS) has selected the Rolls-Royce 535E4 engine to power 20 757PF cargo aircraft ordered from Boeing. The new fleet will be delivered in 1994-97.

The remarkable feature of the deal is that UPS already operates 20 757PFs, all powered by the rival Pratt & Whitney PW2040 engine. For a major operator to change from one engine to another is unprecedented. The costs are huge. Pratt & Whitney were eager to be launch supplier of engines on the 757. They lost out to Rolls-Royce on the launch customers, Eastern and British Airways, but won massive orders with Delta and United. Their engine has the edge in fuel economy (though not by the 7 per cent they promised), but the Rolls engine has set such an impressive record of low-cost reliability that for many years it has been the preferred choice. The PW2037 and PW2040 claims "half the total of 757s", but Rolls claims "80 per cent of the customers".

# United invites you to 'Connoisseur class'

# Jet Aviation moves to West Palm Beach

*Chicago, November 1*
United Air Lines today inaugurated a new class for the international business traveller, the "Connoisseur Class".

This luxury service applies to its long-distance routes world-wide. It offers gourmet food, vintage wines, piped compact-disk, rather than audio-cassette, music, as well as a non-smoking section. Seating in "Connoisseur Class" aircraft will be roomier and more comfortable (seven seats per row in Boeing 747s and six in DC-10s and B-767s), and all seats will have foot-rests. The new class is available on 586 United flights every week.

*West Palm Beach, Florida, Oct 1*
Thomas M Hirschmann, Chairman and CEO of Jet Aviation, today announced the completion of the transfer here of the organization's headquarters from Zurich, Switzerland.

Hirschmann sees the company's move to the USA as a step towards globalization. "I believe that the US market presently offers the greatest opportunity for further expansion and growth," he said. The group's Zurich-based FBO was recently honored with Europe's number 2 ranking, making good on their motto, "special people serving special people".

*The 'Connoisseur class' is offered on 586 of UAL's flights each week.*

*Jet Aviation's corporate headquarters were based in Zurich, Switzerland.*

# 'Clipper Goodwill' is the last of Pan Am's Clippers

*Miami, Florida, December 4*
Today marks a sad end to a proud American saga. The dream of Juan Trippe, Pan American World Airways, now belongs to the history it helped to make. At 5.23pm today the final Pan American flight, Clipper 436 from Bridgetown, Barbados, landed at Miami International Airport (ironically developed by Pan Am).

Under the command of Captain Mark S Pyle, of Liberty, Missouri, this flight of passage departed New York's JFK International Airport at 7.30am, and the crew was not advised of the demise until after arrival at the gate in Barbados.

First Officer Robert Knox, of Greensboro, North Carolina, had remarked at the start of the trip: "What a beautiful day to go flying." Who would have thought that such a sunswept day would hold such dark events for pioneering Pan

```
QX 170408 12041429 0055
QX QWAAWPA QWBAWPA QWCAWPA CDGEJPA LGWEJPA MIAEDPA MIASRPA
MIAEHPA MIAVSPA MIAMWPA MIANVPA NYCEQPA NYCFOPA NYCIOPA
MIAPBPA NYCLWPA CPYXXXX MIAEKPA
.MIAEKPA 041415 DEC91

SUSPENSION OF SERVICES - STATUS NBR 1

SUBJECT/ ANNOUNCEMENT

PAN AM PRESIDENT AND CEO REGRETS TO ANNOUNCE THAT PAN AM
CORP HAS WITHDRAWN IT/S MOTION FOR CONFIRMATION OF THE
CHAPTER 11 PLAN OF REORGANIZATION FWR PAN AM AND IT/S
AFFILIATED COMPANIES CMA AND THAT CMA AS A RESULT IT IS
CEASING FLIGHT OPERATIONS EFFECTIVE IMMEDIATELY.

FURTHER INFORMATION REGARDING THE SPECIFICS RELATED TO THIS
WITHDRAWAL WILL BE PROVIDED THROUGH A COMPANY PRESS RELEASE.

PAN AM MANAGEMENT HAS BEEN DIRECTED TO IMPLEMENT A SHUTDOWN
PLAN GUIDED BY THE FOLLOWING PRINCIPLES CLN

 . IMPLEMENT SUSPENSION OF SERVICES IN A SAFE AND
   PRGFESSIONAL MANNER.

 . ENSURE CUSTOMER-DRIVEN ACTIONS THAT MINIMIZE INCONVENIENCE
   TO THE TRAVELING PUBLIC CMA SHIPPERS AND OTHER CUSTOMERS.

 . PRESERVE AND PROTECT THE ASSETS OF THE COMPANY.

SPECIFIC SUSPENSION OF SERVICE STATUS BULLETINS WILL BE
ISSUED BY THE CENTRAL COMMAND POST.

WANGERIEN
```

American. Upon arrival in Miami, Pan Am made a request that Pyle make a low pass over the field in a final gesture of goodbye. The taxiways were lined with police, fire and ground equipment as well as men and women in military formation. As the B-727 roared over historic Dinner Key, more than a few tears were shed by those on the ground. The cockpit decorum was maintained until the fire equipment's water cannon paid final tribute to the once great airline by showering *Clipper Goodwill* (N368PA) with impressive sprays of water. It was then that the finality of the moment "slammed my senses", said Pyle, adding, "this last salute by men and machine was to all the Pan American history this ship represents." There were no dry eyes among the crew and very few among the passengers of the "Last Clipper".

## Cessna delivers 500th Caravan to FedEx

*Wichita, Kansas, December 17*
Ted Wise, Federal Express vice-president for air operations, today took delivery of the 500th Cessna Caravan I. During a ceremony held here, Cessna vice-president for marketing Roy Norris, handed over the aircraft, a model 208B Super Cargomaster, to FedEx. A total of 250 Caravan Is had been ordered by FedEx, and the last of these is due to be delivered by the manufacturer by the end of the year. Over the past six years, Cessna has ben producing an average of 70 Caravan Is per year. These aircraft have accumulated a total of one million hours' flying time, half of which has been for FedEx, which reports a reliability rate of 99.8 per cent. Thanks to FedEx, the Caravan I has been authorized to ferry cargo in IFR conditions to Canada and several European countries.

## Ice made both engines stop after take-off

*Stockholm, December 27*
In what Swedish Prime Minister Carl Bildt called a "Christmas miracle", all 129 passengers and crew of an SAS MD-80 today survived when the aircraft crashed into a field near here. The pilot, Danish Air Force veteran Stefan Rasmussen, reported he had lost power in both engines shortly after take-off from Arlanda International Airport at 8.45am. Flying at an altitude of only 2,000 feet, he glided the aircraft past a village, cutting through the tops of a forest of tall trees at 155mph to slow the plane down. The MD-80 hit an icy meadow, broke into three pieces and slid about 100 yards before coming to rest. About 40 people were injured, seven of them seriously. But most of the 122 passengers and seven crew walked away from the wreckage unaided.

*In the Super Cargomaster version, the Cessna Caravan can carry 4,285 lb.*

*Despite several injuries, all aboard the SAS MD-80 survived the crash.*

With the A340, Airbus have finally flown an airliner that can compete with the Boeing 747 on the world's long-distance routes. Engines are CFM56-5s.

The twin-turboprop Dornier 328 is a high-tech pressurized commuter airliner designed to carry up to 33 passengers into the smallest of airports.

The Regional Jet or "RJ", ensures that Bombardier's Canadair leads the way in opening up a whole new market for the short-range jet for commuter airlines.

Based on the ATL airframe but with room for four passengers, the Robin X4 is a new touring design powered by a Textron Lycoming O-235 engine.

The Swearingen SJ30 six-seat business jet was the first of an emerging class of small jet aimed at replacing executive turboprop aircraft.

A brand-new design from the Swiss firm of Pilatus, the PC-12 is aimed at those seeking a fast, large-capacity utility transport.

Cessna's radical Model 525 Citationjet offers jet style and performance to customers who would otherwise have bought propeller-driven aircraft.

Capable of limited aerobatics, the FFT Eurotrainer is being built in Germany and can seat up to four as a light multirole touring or training aircraft.

With the distinctive Learjet characteristics of a T-tail and sharply pointed nose, the Learjet 60 is a medium-range business jet, newest of the family.

Building on the successful Jetstream family, British Aerospace's new Jetstream 41 is a bigger and more advanced commuter aircraft seating 29/30 passengers.

*Bell Helicopter's Model 230 is a re-engined and significantly improved version of the company's earlier Model 222 six-seat twin-turbine helicopter.*

*Budding aerobatic pilots can now train in a high-performance aircraft in safety, now that Sukhoi have developed the two-seat version of the Su-29.*

*A millimetric-band radar on top of the rotor mast gives the McDonnell Douglas AH-64 "Longbow" Apache a vastly improved all-weather attack capability.*

*Embraer's EMB-312 Tucano H is a stretched and far more powerful version of the Brazilian company's strongly selling military turboprop trainer.*

*The new Rafale C development aircraft will be used by Dassault to assist in integrating the new fighter's complex weapons systems and avionics.*

*Intended as the new attack helicopter for both the French and German armed forces, the Tiger is a product of the joint Eurocopter consortium.*

*McDonnell Douglas' C-17 high-technology transport will be the new-generation tactical airlifter for the US Air Force. Engines are PW 2000-series.*

*Mirage 2000D is an all-weather, two-seat, deep-strike version of the Mirage 2000 fighter. The 2000D is now entering service with the Armée de l'Air.*

# 1992

4,534mph
USA
Pete Knight
North American X-15
Oct 3, 1967

24,987 miles
USA
Jeager and Rutan
Voyager
Dec 23, 1986

354,200ft
USA
Joseph Walker
North American X-15
Aug 22, 1963

1,120,370lb
USSR
Antonov
An-225 Mriya

61,570lb thrust
USA
Pratt & Whitney
4060A

**Gosselies, Belgium, January 13**
SABCA, the primary Belgium aircraft producer, delivers the first of 48 locally assembled Agusta A-109HO helicopters under a contract valued at US $216 million. Destined to replace the Belgian Army's fleet of ageing Sud Alouette IIs, 28 of the new machines will be the A-109HA version, equipped for anti-tank duties and carrying the Hughes TOW-2A anti-armor missile system, while the remaining 20 A-109HOs are equipped for day or night reconnaissance.

**Strasbourg, France, January 20**
87 of 96 people aboard Air Inter Flight IT5148 are killed when their Airbus A320 crashes into Mount Saint Odile en route from Lyon to Strasbourg.

**Burbank, California, February 21**
Lockheed announce that they are to modify a fourth ex-US Navy P-3B Orion into an Airborne Early Warning (AEW) configured aircraft for use by the US Customs Service. Due for delivery in mid-1993, this machine will join its brethren in the task of tracking illicit – mainly drug-carrying – flights which are attempting illegally to sneak across the borders of the southern states of the USA.

**Dunsfold, England, February 29**
British Aerospace's latest Hawk demonstrator, Hawk Mk 102D, ZJ100, takes to the skies for the first time. The Hawk 100 is an enhanced two-seater ground-attack version with a modified wing and incorporates many improvements to its onboard sensors and weapons system.

**Wichita, Kansas, March 23**
Founded on April 1, 1932 and now a subsidiary of Raytheon, Beechcraft celebrates the delivery of its 50,000th aircraft, a King Air 90B. Current Beechcraft types in production range from the seemingly evergreen single-engined Bonanza of late 1940s origins to the twinpusher-engined, canard-configured Starship.

**Long Beach, California, May 18**
Maiden flight of first production McDonnell Douglas C-17A Globemaster III.

**Minneapolis St Paul, May 20**
Today SAAB deliver their 300th SAAB 340. In this instance, a 340B goes to Express Airlines 1, a code-sharing associate of Northwest Airlines' Airlink regional services.

**Paris, May 27**
The French Air Force receives the first of six Socata TBM 700 six/seven seat, pressurized multi-role aircraft. Powered by a 1,580-shp turboprop – which is manufactured by the firm Pratt & Whitney as the Canada PT6A-64 – the TBM 700 will be used by the French military in the liaison and high-priority dispatch role. Capable of a maximum speed of 300 knots at an altitude of 26,000 feet, this militarized business aircraft has a range, with reserves, of 1,242 miles when cruising at 234 knots.

**Long Beach, California, June 11**
McDonnell Douglas delivers their 2,000th twinjet, an MD-83 for American Airlines, 27 years after the first flight of the prototype Douglas DC-9-10 in 1965. Since then, the company has delivered 976 DC-9s, prior to switching to the MD-80 series, originally known as the DC-9-55 or DC-9 Super 80.

**Bangalore, India, June 29**
Hindustan Aeronautics Ltd, the Indian State-owned aircraft manufacturer, rolls out the first prototype of its Advanced Light Helicopter. It is the fruit of a joint development contract drawn up with the Indian Government and the German company of Messerschmitt Bolkow-Blohm back in July 1984. Five prototypes of this new twin turboshaft-powered military, multi-role machine will be built.

**Norfolk, Virginia, July 4**
The sixth 'Nimitz'-class nuclear-powered super carrier, USS *George Washington* comes into service today. With its standard carrier air wing of approximately 90 aircraft, this one ship alone carries far more air power than most of the world's air forces.

**Potomac River, Virginia, July 20**
The fourth prototype of the tilt-wing Bell Boeing V-22 Osprey prototype assault transports for the US Marine Corps crashes into the Potomac River about half a mile short of the runway at Quantico, Virginia. The large convertiplane is reported to have been transitioning from cruise to hovering flight. All seven aboard, comprising four Boeing crew members and three Marines, are killed. This is the second V-22 to be lost; previously, the fifth prototype was lost during its first flight on June 11, 1991 (→ June 17, 1993).

**Seattle, August 6**
Boeing announces that the order-book for their 737 twinjet has surpassed the 3,000 mark with an order for 34 737-300s from the Texas-based Southwest Airlines. The 737 is the first commercial jetliner in history to have reached this figure.

**Arabian Gulf Region, August 27**
Acting to implement United Nations Resolution 688, around 300 (mainly American) aircraft have returned to the area to mount 'Operation Southern Watch' which takes effect from today. 'Operation Southern Watch' establishes a 'No-Fly' zone for Iraqi military aircraft south of the 32nd Parallel. Besides the US Air Force, US Naval and US Army aircraft that have been flown in, the British and French air forces are also providing small contingents of combat and support aircraft. The operation has been mounted in an endeavour to protect the Shi'ite Muslims of Southern Iraq from continuing attacks by Iraqi forces, both on the ground and from the air.

**Rome, October 31**
The Italian Government has contracted to buy 13 McDonnell Douglas/BAe AV-8B Harrier II Plus jumpjets for use aboard the Italian Navy's helicopter carrier *Garibaldi*. Although the option to purchase these machines has been held for some time, the only Harrier II currently operated by the Italians are two TAV-8B two-seaters, predominantly used for pilot type-conversion training.

**Czech Republic, December 18**
Maiden flight of the Let L-610G twin-turboprop regional airliner. The L-610G variant is powered by two 1,750shp General Electric CT7-9D turboprop engines and incorporates largely American avionics.

---

## Factfile

World revenue passenger miles: 1,000,000 million
World revenue passengers: 1,130 million
World air freight (ton miles): 42,000 million
Passengers through London (Heathrow/Gatwick): 60 million
Total airline employees: 1,861,460
Total jetliners employed: 10,447
Total turbo-prop liners employed: 3,836
Total piston engined liners employed: 878
Total scheduled service helicopters employed: 89
Average salary of long-haul pilot: $111,500
Average salary of cabin crew (US): $29,000
Price of 1,000 (US) gallons Jet A1 fuel: $600
Average exchange rate: £1=$1.82

*Work is underway on the joint NASA/ESA Cassini/Huygens space probe destined to survey Saturn and her satellites.* ▶

# Short Sherpas for the US Army

*One of the 16 Short C-23Bs operated by the US Army.*

*Belfast, N. Ireland, February 13*
Short Brothers, the Queen's Island-based aircraft manufacturer have just delivered the first of a previously unannounced order from the US Army for six more C-23B Sherpas. There are now 52 of these Short 330 in its militarized version operating with the US military, of which 30 C-23As are in place with the US Air Force, and 16 C-23Bs are in place with the US Army, which also operates six ex-civilian C-23Bs.

The Sherpa is the latest success in a story that began back in April 1901, when the brothers Oswald and Eustace Short first set up in business at Hove in Sussex, England as manufacturers of aerial balloons. In 1908, they were joined by their brother Horace, and at a new base at Shellbeach on the Isle of Sheppey near London began building, under licence, six of Wilbur and Orville Wright's biplanes. The main production facilities were moved to Belfast in Northern Ireland in the late 1930s. Production began with a contract to build 50 Bristol Bombay bomber/transports for the RAF; then came production runs that included over 1,200 four-engined Stirling bombers and 130 Sunderland flying boats. With the factory located in Belfast, Short has been a major employer in Ulster for many years. The Sherpa is used for light transport duties, and also as a CASEVAL aircraft.

## Trans World Airlines find themselves in trouble

*One of the McDonnell Douglas MD-80s that form the backbone of TWA's fleet.*

*New York, January 31*
Trans World Airlines, or TWA, one of the most famous pioneering US airlines, has filed today for protection from its creditors under Chapter 11 provision of the US Bankruptcy Court. For many years under the sole control of eccentric tycoon Howard Hughes, Trans World Airlines has sunk from a leading position to its current seventh-place ranking among American carriers. Last year, TWA's major stockholder, Carl Icahn, announced plans to file for the airline to go into pre-planned bankruptcy early this year. However, in the light of today's development, it now looks as if Icahn's talks with the major creditors have allieviated the financial pressure – for the time being.

## US Air disaster at LaGuardia

*New York, March 22*
A Fokker F28 Fellowship 4000 of US Air crashed today, killing 27 of the 47 passengers and four crew aboard after stalling back onto the runway after take-off during a snowstorm. Such was the violence of the crash that the aircraft's nose section, left wing and one of its two engines separated from the burning fuselage, which continued upside-down into Flushing Bay. Ice build-up in the 30 minutes between de-icing and take-off is blamed.

## American breakthrough for Tampico

*Daytona Beach, Florida, March 15*
The first of 14 Socata TB9 Tampico Club 4-seat touring and training machines is today formally handed-over to Embry-Riddle Aeronautical University. Embry-Riddle, who train over 6,000 student pilots each year, placed the order for these 160hp Textron Lycoming O-320 D2A-powered aircraft on February 13, following months of evaluations of the range of American and other training aircraft available. Embry-Riddle expect to place follow-on orders for the TB9 to replace out-of-production Cessna and Piper singles.

*The first of 14 Socata Tampico trainers at its March 15 hand-over.*

# 'Wild Weasel' Phantom II not finished yet

*F-4G 'Wild Weasel' Phantom II in operation during Operation Desert Storm.*

**Washington, DC, May 9**
In an about-face from the US Department of Defense's 1990 decision to retire the McDonnell F-4G 'Wild Weasel' Phantom II, it has been decided that the type will now be kept in service, probably until around the turn of the century. The reversal stems in part from the F-4G's success in last year's Operation Desert Storm and the abandonment of plans to modify General Dynamics F-16s with the emitter location system pod needed to fly 'Wild Weasel' ground defense suppression missions. In the longer term, the F-4G's replacement is likely to be a 'Wild Weasel' version of the McDonnell-Douglas F-15E Eagle.

The 'Wild Weasel' concept originated in the Vietnam War, when US strike aircraft began to suffer unacceptable losses from radar-directed AAA and SAMs. In 1965, a number of two-seat F100F Super Sabres were fitted with a compact radar frequency receiver/direction finder and given the task of locating and destroying North Vietnamese SA-2 sites. The F-100s were soon replaced by F-105s armed with Shrike anti-radar missiles, and the role was named 'Wild Weasel'. For much of the Vietnam War, 'Wild Weasel' activity was constrained by rules of engagement that restricted attacks to SAM sites presenting a direct threat to American strike formations, but the concept was firmly rooted and the task was inherited by the F-4G in 1978. Royal Air Force tornados also operate in the 'Wild Weasel' role, using the ALARM anti-radiation missile. This loiters under a parachute after launch, and selects a target automatically.

# Quiet Engines for the Boeing 727

**San Antonio, Texas, April 18**
Dee Howard, the San Antonio, Texas-based aircraft maintenance and modification specialists, send their re-engined Boeing 727-100 aloft on its maiden flight today. Expected to receive its supplemental certification in November 1992, covering the retro-fitting with 15,100lb s.t. Rolls-Royce Tay 650s, these re-engined trijets meet the more demanding Stage 3 noise requirements. Dee Howard are to fit the Tay to all 40 of the UPS-operated 727 parcel carriers, as well as undertaking a flight deck refit with modern avionics.

# French lightplanes take increasing market share

**Tarbes, France, January 31**
Socata, the Aerospatiale light aircraft subsidiary previously known as Morane-Saulnier, today delivered a total of 203 of its Caribbean range of touring/training aircraft, which include the TB9 Tampico and the TB10 Tobago, along with the TB20 and TB21 Trinidad. Just how much Socata are currently benefiting from the virtual cessation of lightplane production within the US can be gathered from the fact that deliveries have more than doubled since 86 aircraft were delivered five years ago. In 1986 punitive Californian product liability laws caused the big US manufacturers Beech, Cessna and Piper to cease production of single-engined lightplanes. Socata have now taken complete control of the TBM700, jointly developed with Mooney in the US. To date, 28 of these large single-turboprop aircraft have been produced in a new facility at Tarbes.

# Textron buys Cessna Aircraft

**Wichita, Kansas, January 24**
Textron Inc, the giant automotive and aerospace comglomerate, has bought Cessna Aircraft from General Dynamics for US $600 million. Recent problems have meant that Cessna, along with other US manufacturers, have been forced to stop building their light single-engine aircraft lines. Despite this, Textron envisage that Cessna will still produce both a range of business jets and utility turboprops, as complimenting its Bell Helicopter and Lycoming Engines activities.

# Prototype fighter wrecked in crash

*An in-flight view of the ill-fated second prototype YF-22 fighter.*

**Edwards AFB, USA, April 25**
The second of the two Lockheed/Boeing/General Dynamics YF-22 prototype stealth fighters was partially destroyed by fire here today after it had encountered 'porpoising' – severe pitching – problems as it attempted to touch down. Happily, the pilot, Tom Morgenfeld, only suffered minor injuries and managed to jump clear of the aircraft as it careened to a stop before the fire took hold. Competent eyewitnesses note that both the fighter's tailerons and engine thrust-vectoring nozzles were moving up and down in quick succession as the machine was settling to land. While confirmation will clearly have to await the board of inquiry's findings, all the indications point to a flight-control computer command-law software problem as being the culprit.

▷

## South Africa's new attack chopper

*South Africa's Rooivalk makes much use of existing French technology.*

*Gauteng, South Africa, June 30*
Reliable sources here indicate that an improved model of the two-seat Denel AH-2 Rooivalk attack and ground support helicopter has been flown. This second example of the Rooivalk is believed to be the weapons development machine, but little more reliable information is available. The Rooivalk uses the 'dynamic raft' (rotors and trans- mission) of the Aerospatiale AS 330 Puma and proves the old helicopter designer's maxim that you can do anything you like with what hangs beneath the rotors, so long as they themselves are left alone. Bell demonstrated this long ago, when they took the dynamic raft of their tubby UH-1 and hung the totally new, slender, two-man AH-1 Cobra gunship beneath it.

## New British lightplane takes wing

*Gamston, England, September 12*
Something of a rarity in itself these days, a smart new British two-seat cabin lightplane has taken to the sky on its maiden flight. Designed by pilot Ivan Shaw, who was at the controls today, the Europa employs modern day glass-fiber reinforced plastic as its basic constructional material. Powered by a fuel-thrifty 80-hp Rotax 912, Europa is aimed squarely at the homebuilder market and as such has wing-folding and is sized to fit into most home garages. Assembly or dissasembly time for the Europa is put at four to five minutes. An unusual feature is a single semi-retractable main wheel.

*A British newcomer to the lightplane scene is the two-seat Europa.*

# German EFA doubts

*Bonn, Germany, June 30*
In a not totally unexpected development, Germany's Defense Minister, Volker Ruhe, announced today that Germany is to withdraw from the multi-national European Fighter Aircraft, or EFA, program at the end of the current develop- ment phase. In a virtually instant response, British Prime Minister, John Major, said that Britain would hold urgent talks with Italy and Spain, the remaining partner nations in the EFA project. Ruhe, a long time opponent to Germany's participation in the EFA program on the grounds of its cost, has for some time now been alluding to a possible alternative to EFA in the shape of a joint Franco-German light fighter. Where this would leave the French with their Das- sault Rafale leads seasoned indus- try observers to dismiss this proposal as little more than a pipedream. Certainly, the rising cost of the EFA program has been the focus of much German public attention of late, including sugges- tions that the number of EFAs required by the Luftwaffe be reduced from the original 250 planned to around 138 machines. The first prototype EFA, a German- built example, is essentially com- plete. It had its interim twin R.B.199 turbofan engines run up for the first time earlier this month.

# Cassini to make maiden Titan voyage

*Huygens, depicted after separation from Cassini, seen descending by parachute.*

*Paris, September 17*
Aerospatiale, prime contractors for the European Space Agency's Huygens interplanetary probe, have today released basic data on the craft. Built as part of the joint NASA/ESA Cassini/Huygens program, Huygens will be 'piggy- backed' on Cassini for its nearly seven-year journey from Earth to Saturn and its largest moon, Titan. The task Huygens will face is to descend through Titan's extremely hostile atmosphere using a system of parachutes acting as aerody- namic brakes to slow descent speed. Opened at an altitude of 112 miles above Titan's surface, the parachute is designed to cope with re-entry speeds of 4.35 miles per second at an altitude of 62 miles. The overall time of the descent is estimated as being two and a half hours. Other Huygens features include an overall diameter of 9.8ft, along with a mass of 518lb. Huy- gens is not expected to survive for longer than a few minutes after its arrival on Titan's surface, thanks to the extreme corrosiveness of the local environment. The interplane- tary probe is named after the Dutch astronomer who discovered Titan in March 1655 (→ October 15, 1997).

# Europe or bust: balloons race across the Atlantic

*Europe, September 22*
Taking a decade to plan and organize, the Chrysler Trans-Atlantic Challenge balloon race set off from Bangor, Maine, in the early hours of September 16. The five two-man teams competing are using identical Roziere 77 type hot air balloons produced by the Bristol, England-based Cameron Balloons Ltd. The Belgian crew in balloon No.1 are Wim Verstaeten and Bertrand Piccard, the Germans in No. 2 are Eric Krafft and Jocken Maas, the British (No. 3), are Rob Bayly and pilot/designer/builder Don Cameron. The Dutch team, in balloon No. 4, consists of Evert Louwman and Gerhard Hoogeslag, while Richard Abruzzo and Troy Bradley form the US team in No. 5. Delayed for a month awaiting the right weather conditions, the balloons made their night-time departure eastwards at five-minute intervals. Sadly, the German team – whose balloon picked up much rainwater en route for Corpus X Christi, Texas – were compelled to

*The five Cameron-built balloons at their Bangor, Maine, starting point.*

make a night 'ditching' in mid-Atlantic and high seas close to the tanker, MV *Granite*, who took them aboard. Two others to get their feet wet were Louwman and Hoogeslag in balloon No. 4, who ditched close to Lands End, England and were rescued by the Falmouth Lifeboat crew. The first to make landfall were the Belgium team – made up of Wim Verstaeten and Bertrand Piccard – who landed near Peque in Spain. Next to come ashore were Cameron and Bayly, who put down on the beach near Monte Real in Portugal. Finally came the US team of Abruzzo and Bradley, who touched down in Morocco. Although they were the last to land, the Americans at least stole some of the glory of the event by establishing a new world duration record for balloons of 144 hours and 16 minutes. This time significantly beat the previous record of 137 hours five minutes and 50 seconds which was set by the first-ever transatlantic balloon flight made by *Double Eagle II* on August 17, 1978.

## Eastwood's piloting proficiency

*Paris, September 2*
The star of numerous Westerns and the *Dirty Harry* films, Clint Eastwood today departed the Paris heliport for the Deauville American Film Festival piloting a Eurocopter Ecureuil, loaned to him by the company. As a 450-hour helicopter pilot, with experience of flying 10 helicopter types, Eastwood is already familiar with the Ecureuil as he flies his own Astar – the American name

for the Ecureuil – around the US and Canada from his Carmel, California, home. The film star had a bad introduction to flying in the 1950s when the US Navy Douglas Skyraider – in which he was hitching a lift – ditched off the California coast. Luckily for him, the young Eastwood was at the time serving as an Army swimming instructor and was able to make it ashore, albeit with some difficulty.

## British Airways buys Dan Air for £1

*London, November 8*
An agreement was reached today whereby British Airways will acquire the financially failing mixed scheduled and charter airline Dan Air for just £1. British Airways, however, will meet all of Dan Air's outstanding debts, estimated at around £58 million. Since both the British Monopolies and Mergers Commission and the European Community appear

not to have any strong objections to the take-over, it is very likely to go through. This is despite an outcry from a number of other British airlines, who are currently claiming that it will give British Airways a stranglehold on services in and out of both Heathrow and Gatwick. At the moment Dan Air employ a workforce numbering around 2,000 and operate a fleet made up of 38 aircraft.

## European 'Jumbos' prepare to enter service

*Blagnac, France, December 22*
The Airbus A340-200, along with the stretched -300 version, received their Type Certification from the 18 nation-strong European Joint Airworthiness Authority (JAA)

today. The first examples of both the A340-200 (typically 253 passengers) and 295-passsenger A340-300 are each set to enter service with launch airline customer Lufthansa in January 1993.

*The Airbus A340 is one of only two large four-engined airliners in production.* ▷

Known as the Harrier II Plus, the first radar-equipped AV-8B Harrier II V/STOL strike aircraft is pictured during its flight trials.

The SAAB 2000 50-seat high-speed regional airliner embodies advanced 21st-century technology in its design.

Seen at the hover over desert terrain, the first prototype McDonnell Douglas AH-64D Longbow Apache advanced attack helicopter.

The development program of the McDonnell Douglas C-17 was beset by continual delays, and flight testing did not get under way until 1992.

The attack version of the BAe Hawk, the Hawk 200 – seen here in company with a Hawk 100 in the foreground – was equipped with radar in 1992.

The first production Learjet 60 seen over the Kansas landscape on its first flight from Wichita Mid-Continent Airport, June 15.

An uprated version of the SIAI-Marchetti S.211 turbofan-powered light attack aircraft, the S.211A (seen here at Le Bourget, Paris).

*The A340-200A is a longer-range version of the Airbus A340-300, but with the same powerplant and a shorter fuselage.*

*The McDonnell Douglas Explorer was the first new twin-turbine helicopter to enter production in nearly a decade.*

*Powered by two General Electric CF6-80E-1 turbofans, the first Airbus A330 is pictured on roll-out. The aircraft's maiden flight was on November 2.*

*Developed as an off-the-shelf replacement for helicopters like the UH-1H, the Eurocopter 800 Panther began its test flight program in June.*

*The McDonnell Douglas/Beech T-1A Jayhawk, is a military version of the Beechjet 400T, flew for the first time this year.*

*The 40-passenger LET L610G is among the latest of an ever growing number of regional turboprops on offer.*

*The turbo-fan powered Tupolev Tu-204 was designed as a replacement for the aging Tu-154.*

*Climbing out on its maiden flight on March 23, the first development British Aerospace 146 RJ85 seats 85-112 passengers and has uprated LF507 turbofans.*

*Seen here in its typical operational environment, the Fokker F.50 Maritime Enforcer first flew on December 10.*

# 1993

4,534mph
USA
Pete Knight
North American X-15
Oct 3, 1967

24,987 miles
USA
Jeager and Rutan
Voyager
Dec 23, 1986

354,200ft
USA
Joseph Walker
North American X-15
Aug 22, 1963

1,120,370lb
USSR
Antonov
An-225 Mriya

61,570lb thrust
USA
Pratt & Whitney
4060A

**Manching, Germany, January 15**
Today, a new German-US jet takes to the skies. The first of two Rockwell/DASA Ranger 2000 two-seat jet trainers makes its maiden flight. The Ranger 2000 is one of the competitors for the potentially lucrative US Air Force/US Navy JPATS, or Joint Primary Air Training System.

**Linkoping, Sweden, March 4**
SAAB company test pilot Lars Radestrom takes the first production JAS 39 Gripen aloft on its 32-minute maiden flight. SAAB are developing a two-seat operational trainer version of the supersonic multi-role Gripen, the JAS 39B, set to make its first flight in 1996, with service deliveries following in 1998.

**London, March 25**
The first woman Concorde pilot makes her first flight as First Officer of the daily supersonic London–New York route. British, born Barbara Harmer is one of only 17 co-pilots in the British Airways Concorde fleet.

**Canberra, Australia, March 31**
The two government-controlled airlines, Qantas and Australian Airlines (previously TAA) were merged today, with Qantas as the surviving identity.

**Schiphol, Netherlands, April 2**
Fokker have provided proof that even jetliners can be 'recycled' as their prototype Fokker 100 re-emerges in somewhat abbreviated form to make its first flight as the Fokker 70. Converted by the removal of two fuselage sections fore and aft of the wing, the now 79-seat twin turbofan is expected to be granted its Type Certification in October 1994, following an extensive 480-hour certification program.

**Seattle, Washington, May 7**
Today saw the first flight of Boeing's 747-400F freighter version. Unlike other 747-400s, this new model has no winglets.

**Sao Jose dos Campos, Brazil, May 15**
An improved version of EMBRAER's successful Tucano two-seat military turboprop basic trainer, the EMBRAER EMB-312H Super Tucano, makes its first flight today.

**Farnborough, England, June 1**
In pursuit of its declared policy of concentrating on its core businesses, British Aerospace (BAe) announce the sale of its Corporate Jets Division to Raytheon in the US for £250 million. For this, Raytheon – who already own Beech Aircraft – get the BAe 125 range of business jets, of which over 800 have been delivered. Included is Arkansas Aerospace Inc of Little Rock, Arkansas, a fully owned BAe subsidiary, which specializes in installing customized interiors to business jets.

**Arlington, Virginia, June 17**
Bell Boeing resume flight testing of their V-22 Osprey convertiplane, modified after last year's fatal crash of the fourth development aircraft.

**Paris, June 18**
An Airbus A340-211 sets a new Great Circle Distance Without Landing record of 11,814.9 miles, when it flies from Paris to Auckland, New Zealand. After refuelling, the jetliner returned non-stop to Paris, setting a new around the world, eastbound record speed of 490.8mph.

**Huntington Beach, June 26**
The US Air Force successfully launches the last of the NAVSTAR satellites to provide the complete three-dimensional global coverage required for the Global Positioning System's initial operating capability. A McDonnell Douglas Delta II rocket was used to boost the satellite into orbit, which also carried a second, tethered Plastic Motor Generator experimental satellite.

**Wichita, Kansas, July 26**
All three test crew members on the first prototype Canadair RJ feederjet were killed when this regional jetliner development of the CL-601 Challenger bizjet crashed.

**Seattle, Washington, September 10**
Boeing roll-out their 1,000th 747 just a month under 26 years after the program launch.

**Wichita, Kansas,, September 15**
Cessna roll-out their new Citation X business jet, set for mid-1995 initial deliveries. The first customer is believed to be retired golfer Arnold Palmer.

**Paris, October 8**
The Turkish Government place a contract for 20 Eurocopter AS 532UL Cougars.

**Blagnac, France, October 21**
The Airbus A330 receives both US and European Type Certification.

**Paris, October 22**
The Dutch Government orders 17 Eurocopter AS532 U2 Cougars, taking the total orderbook for the Super Puma/Cougar family to 442 helicopters.

**Las Cruces, USA, October 25**
McDonnell Douglas halts flight testing of the DC-X experimental reusable launch vehicle after being notified that the sponsoring Ballistic Missile Defense Organization cannot provide further funds.

**London, November 16**
Italy's Defence Minister, Fabio Fabbri, while visiting London, announces that Italy will lease 24 surplus Panavia Tornado F3s from the RAF for a 10 year period, pending delivery of Eurofighter, in a deal worth up to £110 million to Britain.

**Blagnac, France, December 2**
First flight of Airbus A300-600F, the specialized freighter version of the A300-600 jetliner. FedEx have ordered 25, and hold a further 50 options.

**Central America, December 6**
Central American Airlines (CAA) is the umbrella identity adopted by five of the region's main airlines: Aviateca of Guatemala, COPA of Panama, LACSA of Costa Rica, NICA of Nicaragua and TACA of El Savador. CAA is to pool shareholdings, sales, administration, engineering and insurance.

**Novosibirsk, Russia, December 12**
Today saw the first flight of the first production Sukhoi Su-34,which is a side-by-side, two-seat supersonic all-weather bomber aircraft, derived from the Su-27IB. This extremely long-ranged aircraft is designed to replace the Su-24 'Fencer'.

---

## Factfile

World revenue passenger miles: 1,240,000 million
World revenue passengers: 1,170 million
World air freight (ton miles): 44,000 million
Passengers through London (Heathrow/Gatwick): 67.7 million
Total airline employees: 1,480,360
Total jetliners employed: 9,420
Total turbo-prop liners employed: 3,293
Total piston engined liners employed: 567
Total scheduled service helicopters employed: 27
Average salary of long-haul pilot: $117,000
Average salary of cabin crew (US): $30,000
Price of 1,000 (US) gallons Jet A1 fuel: $550
Average exchange rate: £1=$1.57

*An Avions Transport Regional ATR 72 is shown here climbing out against the stunning backdrop of the Pyrenees.* ▶

# 'Super Jumbo' joint project starts to take shape

*Seattle, Washington, January 27*
The entire history of the Boeing Company (previously the Boeing Airplane Company) has been a succession of bold decisions. Decisions to go ahead and build a new transport or bomber far more advanced than any in existence, in advance of definite orders and risking far more than the net worth of the company. Perhaps the biggest gamble of all came in 1966 when the company went ahead with the Boeing 747. Admittedly, that time it did have an order, from Pan American; but the risk on that occasion was probably the greatest any industrial company has ever accepted. In the event, the colossal gamble came off, and Boeing changed the face of air transport for ever.

Now, another giant leap forward into the unknown is on the horizon, as Boeing and the four national shareholder companies that form Airbus Industrie sign a Memorandum of Understanding launching a joint 12- month study into a next generation jetliner with

*An artist's impression of the proposed Very Large Commercial Transport under joint study.*

a staggering capacity of between 550 and 800 passengers; to include shopping and exercise facilities. The Very Large Commercial Transport study will look at market prospects, technical, environmental, regulatory and financing aspects of a 'Super Jumbo' to enter service early in the 21st century. One noticable corporate absentee from the study group is McDonnell Douglas, whose own MD-12 project already encroaches into this seating capacity region (→ January 26, 1996).

## A Dassault Rafale built for two

*Dassault test pilot, Jean Fremond.*

*Istres, France, April 30*
Dassault company test pilot, Jean Fremond, makes the maiden flight of prototype two-seat Dassault Rafale B. A potential rival to the Eurofighter, this French-developed supersonic combat aircraft continues to outstrip its multi-national competitor in terms of development progress. This is in spite of all the doubters who, for years, have been constantly insisting that no one nation would be able to afford the cost of developing such a front-line combat type.

## Buying a fighter-building business

*Los Angeles, California, March 12*
In a demonstration of the old addage that 'there's more than one way to skin a cat', Lockheed Corporation get to 'bolt on' a complete and instant in-house fighter design, development and production capability, thanks to today's take-over of the

former General Dynamics' Military Aircraft Division. Having paid US $1.525 billion in December 1992 for this Fort Worth-based operation, Lockheed are now back in the fighter business as the new proud owners of the extremely successful and highly exportable General Dynamics F-16 fighter.

## Taiwan unveils its Indigenous Defense Fighter

*Taiwan, February 10*
Taiwan goes in for high-tech flag waving when its Republic of China Air Force (RoCAF) publicly unveils the AIDC Ching Kuo IDF, its first indigenously designed and developed fighter today. The type was developed with the help of General Dynamics, producers of

the similar looking F-16. The IDF differs in its use of twin International Turbine TFE-1042-70 reheated turbofans, fed from underwing intakes, rather than the F-16's ventral scoop. First flown in prototype form on May 28, 1989, the IDF is now in full-scale production for the RoCAF.

*Lockheed acquire the fighter business, as well as the F-16 Fighting Falcon.*

# First Gripen handed to Swedish Air Force

*Satenas, Sweden, June 8*
The first of SAAB's JAS 39A Gripen supersonic, multi-role combat aircraft was ceremonially handed over to the Royal Swedish Air Force today in the presence of Lars-Erik Englund, its Commander-in-Chief. The Gripen (Griffon) lightweight fighter concept was conceived during the late 1970s as a replacement for the AJ, SH, SF and JA versions of the Saab 37 Viggen. Its configuarion follows Saab's tried and tested format, featuring an aft-mounted delta wing and swept canard foreplanes. The flying surfaces are controlled by a fly-by-wire system. Advanced avionics, including pulse-Doppler search and acquisition radar, pod-mounted FLIR, headup and head-down displays (replacing normal flight instruments), plus excellent ECM and navigation systems, give the aircraft a multi-role, all-weather capability. Like its predecessors, the Viggen and Draken, the Gripen was designed to meet a threat from the former Soviet Union, whose air bases were only a few minutes' flying time away, so short take-off and rapid climb were particular requirements. The aircraft can also operate from certain stretches of motorway. The Gripen is set to become operational in 1996 and will ultimately replace the SAAB Viggen as Sweden's front-line combat aircraft.

*Lars-Erik Englund, Commander-in-Chief from the Royal Swedish Air Force.*

## New workhorse joins the ranks

*The bulky C-17A needs agility in order to be effective in its assault role.*

*Charleston AFB, USA, June 14*
The US Air Force takes delivery of its first McDonnell Douglas C-17A Globemaster III when the sixth production aircraft, 89-1192, is handed over to the 17th Airlift Squadron of the 437th Airlift Wing today. The C-17A is powered by four 40,440-lb s.t. Pratt & Whitney F117-PW-100 turbofans, enabling it to haul 85 tons of cargo over intercontinental distances and land on a fairly austere 3,000-feet airstrip. Of these workhorses, 120 are set to be delivered to the US Air Force by June 2001 as replacements for the Lockheed C-141 StarLifter.

## Experience saves the day after inflight break-up

*Kings Lynn, England, June 7*
The quick-witted skill of Captain Ed Wyre, a former RAF Tornado pilot, saved the day today when the Piper Navaho he was flying started to break up in mid-air. Flying Prospair's scheduled evening Birmingham to Norwich service, 5,000ft above King's Lynn he heard a bang. The control column was suddenly snatched from his hand. Taking instant stock of the situation, Captain Wyre saw that his righthand engine had parted company with the rest of the aircraft, damaging the nose and left-hand engine as it departed. The eight-seater Navaho entered a vicious righthand spiral, heading for the ground. Ed Wyre finally regained control at a height of around 1,750ft, managing to avoid overhead power lines as he glided the aircraft down to a skidding halt in a barley field. Only one passenger was slightly injured.

## Latest from Long Beach

*Long Beach, February 22*
The most recent son of the Douglas DC-9 family, the McDonnell Douglas MD-90, climbed away on its maiden flight today. Powered by twin IAE V2525-D5 turbofans – weighing in at 25,000lb s.t. – this latest short/medium-haul jet-liner has a typical two-class capacity for 153 passengers, which it can carry over distances of up to 2,600 miles.

*The MD-90 shows its ancestry; descended from the Douglas DC-9 and MD-80.* ▷

# RAF say goodbye to the 'Banana Bomber'

*Lossiemouth, Scotland, September 30*
At RAF Lossiemouth, the last of the RAF's Blackburn Buccaneers retires today. It will be replaced by Panavia Tornado GR1Bs. The RAF initially rejected the Buccaneer in the 1950s but went on to take over the former Royal Navy Buccaneer S.2s after the decommissioning of the last of the Navy's aging conventional aircraft-carriers. As history shows, the RAF's Buccaneer proved to be not just a superb naval strike aircraft but, during the air strikes of the Gulf War last year, the machine found itself serving both as a very effective strike aircraft and laser target seeker/marker for accompanying bombers. Much underestimated by other than specialist maritime strike crews, the Buccaneer had only one real contemporary, the US Navy's much bigger and less agile Grumman A-6 Intruder. Perhaps one of the finest tributes the 'Bucc' could be paid came from a US Navy Rear Admiral long involved in A-6 development who, having flown both types, praised the British machine as having superior high subsonic ride quality and handling 'down on the deck' – the natural domain for both aircraft.

*The last of the RAF's – sometimes underestimated – Buccaneer S2s bows out for the last time today.*

# V-bomber era ends

*RAF Marham, England, October 15*
The RAF today retires the last of its Handley Page Victors, ending the 36-year operational career of this, the last remaining member of the service's trio of 'V' bombers. Long since relegated from its original role as a stand-off nuclear weapon carrier, the Victor soldiered on as a airborne fuel tanker, a role in which it served during both the 1982 Falklands War and the 1991 Gulf War. The last unit to operate the Victor was No. 55 Squadron which, from now on, will be disbanding. The Victor was the last of the RAF's trio of V-bombers (the other two being the Valiant and Vulcan) to become operational, the first squadron – No. 10 – forming at Gaydon in Warwickshire in April 1958. Two Victor squadrons, Nos 100 and 139, later switched from the free-fall bombing role and were armed with the Avro Blue Steel stand-off bomb, which had a range of about 100 nautical miles. The RAF's V-Force maintained Britain's nuclear deterrent posture for some 12 years, each V-bomber station holding three or four bombers at permanent readiness on Operational Readiness Platforms set at an angle to the main runway, enabling the aircraft to become airborne from a standing start in about two and a half minutes. The British nuclear deterrent role was assumed by the Royal Navy's Polaris submarines in 1968–69. In its heyday, the Victor also performed a vital strategic reconnaissance role, operating from RAF Wyton with No. 543 squadron.

# Son of 'Tweety Bird' flies

*Wichita, Kansas, December 20*
Today, Cessna fly the first prototype of their two-seat CitationJet. The only US Joint Primary Aircraft Training System (JPATS) trainer submission to have been specifically developed against the JPATS need instead of using an adaptation of an existing aircraft, to have twin engines and also to be produced by a single manufacturer rather than a team. Power for the CitationJet is provided by twin William International F129 turbofans. Unlike many other JPATS contenders, Cessna have a wealth of experience with this type of trainer, having produced the T-37 'Tweety Bird', the standard US Air Force's basic jet trainer from the 1960s onward. The T-37 was also used in the light strike role as the A-37.

**July 6. Olive Beech, who died today, co-founded the Beech Aircraft Company in 1932 along with her husband.**

December 17. Stealth salutes the Wright Brothers. The first of 20 Northrop B-2 Spirit operational stealth bombers is delivered to the Whiteman Air Force Base to coincide with the 90th anniversary of the Wright Brothers' first powered flight.

# 'Jimmy' Doolittle dies, aged 96

'Jimmy' Doolittle and the Gee Bee Sportster Model R.

# 'Space junk' poses real threat

*Jerusalem, Israel, October 29*
A conference of international space scientists were today warned of the threat from potentially lethal space debris. Since the launch of the first Sputnik in 1957, more than 11,000 satellites have been sent into space. The leading debris contributor is Russia, with 1,274 pieces from former satellites, to which must be added 2,359 pieces of Russian rocket cases. This compares with the American contribution of 617 satellite bits, plus 2,676 rocket case fragments. To emphasize the danger, it was noted that a 1.2-in object travelling at 5 miles per second would have the same impact as a bowling ball moving at a speed of 62mph. The problem appeared so severe that in the 1980s several schemes were proposed to build robot junk collectors that would use lasers to carve up the larger pieces of debris. But far fewer satellites have been launched into space since the end of the cold war, so that existing junk is not being replaced by new debris as it falls out of orbit. Some of the latest satellites, however, are nuclear-powered, and this poses its own set of problems. Russia's Radar Ocean Reconnaissance satellites – ROR-SATS – carry nearly a ton and a half of nuclear fuel between them.

As a safety measure, the Russians fire their RORSATS into a higher orbit when their mission is completed. The fuel core is then ejected from the satellite's nuclear reactor and 'stored' in space at a safe distance from the Earth's upper atmosphere. However, some nuclear debris has plunged to Earth as a result of launch failures. The most famous was the RORSAT that failed to go into orbit and broke up over Canada in 1978. The Canadians spent a lot of time and money looking for radioactive debris, which was eventually found. They received $2.6 million in compensation from the Soviet Union.

How long a piece of debris remains in space before being pulled into the Earth's atmosphere by gravity depends on how high its orbit is. Some fragments will remain in orbit for millions of years. But the record for the shortest time in space for any piece of debris must surely be held by US astronaut Ken Mattingly's wedding ring. When he left Apollo 16 for a spacewalk in 1972, the ring, which he had lost inside the spacecraft earlier, drifted out of the hatch after him. It bounced off his helmet and was deftly fielded by his colleague, Charlie Duke, who handed it back to him.

*Pebble Beach, USA, September 27*
James 'Jimmy' Doolittle died today, aged 96. By the time the planner and lead pilot played his part in the daring April 1942 carrier raid on Tokyo, 'Jimmy' Doolittle had already contributed massively to the advancement of aviation. He went on to head the US Army's mighty 8th Air Force. As a young US Army officer, Doolittle became the first man to fly across the United States in less than a day on September 4, 1922. In October 1925 he was to win the Schneider Trophy and, in September 1929, he demonstrated the value of instrument flying, when he 'soloed' a Consolidated trainer from beneath a blind flying hood. In 1932, he set a new world landplane speed record of over 294mph in the lethal Gee Bee R Sportster. In the postwar era, Doolittle sat for a number of years in the position of Chairman of the USAF's Scientific Advisory Committee.

# Celebrating the '125'

*Brasilia, Brazil, November 25*
Brazil's Forca Aerea Brasileira (FAB) today marked 25 years of Hawker Siddeley (now BAe) 125 operations. The FAB took its first delivery of these airplanes on October 15, 1968. With a total of 12 of these twin jets currently in service, the FAB now has the largest single fleet of 125s outside Britain. BAe 125s are now in service with some 40 countries worldwide.

*One of Brazil's Forca Aerea Brasileira 12 H.S. 125s.*

The British-built Slingsby Firefly basic trainer has been the subject of a large USAF order. The first USAF aircraft is seen flying in trials.

The Block 50/52 is the latest version of the Lockheed F-16 Fighting Falcon. The first aircraft, serial 91-0360, was delivered to the USAF in May.

Seen against an Alpine background, the prototype Grob G-520T (D-FDST) high-performance powered glider makes its first flight.

The Aero L-139, the latest Czech light jet trainer and strike aircraft.

The Boeing 747-400F is a freight-carrying version of the 747 series.

Derived from the Fokker 100, the Fokker 70 is a new-generation fanjet with a standard capacity of 79 passengers.

The Dassault Falcon 2000 is powered by two General Electric/Garrett Engines CFE 738 turbofans – silent and cost-effective.

The SAAB JAS 39A Gripen lightweight all-weather fighter, pictured on the occasion of its handover to the Royal Swedish Air Force.

The Pilatus PC-9 Mk II advanced training system is being produced under licence by Beech Aircraft. The first US-built machine flew in December.

*The Sukhoi Su-34 two-seat strike aircraft will replace the Su-24 'Fencer'.*

*The Canadair CL-415 fire fighter can hold 1350 gallons of water.*

*The Airbus A321 can carry 185 passengers in a lengthened fuselage.*

*The McDonnell Douglas MD-90, seen here on its first flight, shares many common components with its predecessor, the MD-80.*

*The Socata TBM 700 became the first single-engined aircraft to fly around the world in under 80 hours, covering 22,860 miles.*

*The Cessna Model 750 Citation X is designed to cruise at Mach 0.88.*

*The Embraer 313H Super Tucano, a turboprop-powered trainer.*

*Built of all-composite materials, the South African Denel/Atlas trainer was granted its civil registration this September.*

*The Dassault Rafale B 01, development aircraft for the two-seat Rafale B multi-role combat aircraft is launched this year.*

*The first Service delivery of the US Air Force's latest stealth technology acquisition, the sinisterly sculptured Northrop B-2 'Stealth' bomber was made to the 509th BW at Whiteman Air Force Base, Missouri, on December 17.*

# 1994

**Linkoping, Sweden, January 26**
A Swedish Air Force order for five SAAB 340AEWs takes the order-book for all versions of this twin turboprop 37-passenger feederliner past the 400 mark to 403.

**Yeovil, England, January 29**
Nine new Westland Super Lynx naval helicopters are ordered by Brazil, while five of Brazil's original nine Lynx will be upgraded to Super Lynx standard.

**Paris, January 29**
Eurocopter announced that it has increased its market share to 54 per cent of the 260 civil helicopters sold globally.

**Cape Canaveral, February 3**
The Space Shuttle *Discovery* blasted off today carrying the commercially developed SPACE-HAB research laboratory module. The pressurized module fixed within *Discovery*'s cargo bay carries 14 experiments aimed at the development of space-based manufacturing processes and products.

**Ottobrun, Germany, February 15**
First flight of the Eurocopter EC 135 twin-engined, five-to-seven seat civil helicopter.

**Cape Canaveral, March 9**
A McDonnell Douglas Delta II launches the 24th and last Block II NAVSTAR global positioning system (GPS) satellite, completing the GPS constellation to bring the system to full operational capability.

**Los Angeles, California March 29**
Northrop Corporation beats Lockheed Martin's US $1.93 billion bid for the acquisition of the 64-year-old Grumman Corporation, with a bid of US $2.17 billion. Following US Government approval, the new entity will be known as the Northrop Grumman Corporation (→ May 18).

**Warton, England, April 6**
First flight of second Eurofighter 2000 prototype and first to come off the British assembly line.

**Warton, England, April 7**
Maiden flight of the first of 13 BAe/McDonnell Douglas Harrier T 10 night-attack trainers for the RAF.

**Yeovil, England, April 10**
Westland Helicopters have been acquired by GKN, becoming GKN Westland Helicopters.

**Zhukovsky, Russia, May 17**
Powered by a 210hp Teledyne Continental IO-360-ES2B, the prototype Ilyushin Il-103 low-wing, fixed-landing gear trainer and two-to-five seat tourer makes its maiden flight from the flight test center.

**Los Angeles, California, May 18**
Northrop Grumman Corporation comes into existence.

**Ottowa, Canada, May 23**
Today, Air Canada selects the Airbus A319 as its replacement, on a one-to-one basis, for its 35 Douglas DC-9-30s.

**Paris, June 21**
The French Air Force is, in future, to accept women as fighter pilots. The service has had women pilots flying non-combat aircraft since 1983.

**Novosibirsk, Ukraine, June 23**
First flight of Antonov An-38. The 26-passenger high wing, twin-finned transport is powered by two 1,500-shp Honeywell TPE-14GR-801E turboprops.

**Wichita, Kansas, June 25**
Cessna's Citation Ultra, a seven/eight seat improvement of the Citation V bizjet, gains Federal Aviation Administration Type Certification. Powered by two 3,045-lb s.t. Pratt & Whitney Canada JT15D-5D turbofans, the Citation Ultra has a range of up to 1,960 nautical miles with five passengers.

**London, June 29**
The British Parliamentary Public Accounts Committee is told that the joint Eurofighter 2000 program has slipped by a further four months, giving a supposed initial service delivery date of December 2000.

**Singapore, July 9**
Today, Singapore's Defense Minister announces the purchase of 18 Lockheed Martin F-16C/D Fighting Falcons.

**St Louis, Missouri, July 17**
McDonnell Douglas deliver the last of 209 F-15E Eagles to the US Air Force.

**Wichita, Kansas, August 17**
Roll-out of 350th Beech 1900 twin turboprop feederliner, introduced in 1983.

**Osaka, Japan, August 29**
Japan opens its new international airport at Kansai, the culmination of eight years' work and an investment of around $15 billion.

**Bethesda, Maryland, August 30**
Lockheed Corporation and Martin Marietta Corporation will merge to become Lockheed Martin Corporation. The $10 billion deal is said to favor Lockheed, whose Chairman and Chief Executive Officer, Daniel Tellep, will head the new organization.

**Blagnac, France, September 13**
First flight of Airbus A300-600ST Super Transporter. Four of these 'pregnant guppy' jets are being built to fly outsize components to and from Airbus's various multi-national sites. After this four hour plus baptism to flight, Gilbert Defer, Aerospatiale's Flight Test Director and Chief Test Pilot, who flew this extremely bulbous aircraft, summed up by noting that "This balloon is fully steerable!".

**Toulouse, France, September 16**
First flight of the ATR42-500 twin turboprop regional airliner. Expected to enter service in June 1995, Avions Transport Regional currently hold 10 firm orders, plus 10 options for the type.

**Florida, November 1**
Today, the NASA-developed WIND spacecraft was launched by McDonnell Douglas Delta II.

**Washington DC, November 4**
US Secretary for Commerce, Ron Brown announces a US $1.6 billion contract for McDonnell Douglas to supply 40 MD-80s and MD-90s to China. Half of these aircraft will be assembled in the industrial region of Shanghai.

**London, November 21**
Rolls-Royce have bought the US Allison Engine Company for the total sum of US $525 million. The vendor was Clayton, Dubilier and Rice, well-known as a US investment group.

---

*A serenely evocative portrait of an Airbus A340, seemingly suspended above the clouds, between the earth and the sky.* ▶

## Factfile

World revenue passenger miles: 1,260,000 million
World revenue passengers: 1,190 million
World air freight (ton miles): 53,000 million
Passengers through London (Heathrow/Gatwick): 72.4 million
Total airline employees: 1,770,388
Total jetliners employed: 10,843
Total turbo-prop liners employed: 3,936
Total piston engined liners employed: 521
Total scheduled service helicopters employed: 59
Average salary of long-haul pilot: $123,000
Average salary of cabin crew (US): $31,000
Price of 1,000 (US) gallons Jet A1 fuel: $460
Average exchange rate: £1=$1.49

# Air battle over the Balkans 'No-Fly' zone

*United States Air Force General Dynamics F-16s leave their Italian base to provide high-level fighter cover.*

*Bugojno, Bosnia, February 28*
Four out of six Soko G-4 Super Galeb light strike aircraft were today downed by missiles fired by a flight of US Air Force General Dynamics F-16s. The Super Galebs – which were bombing townships in this United Nations designated 'No-Fly' zone – were detected initially by a German-based Boeing E-3 operating over Hungary. Three of these Serbian jets were shot down by Captain Bob 'Wilbur'

Wright of the 555th Fighter Squadron; the two surviving aircraft escaped to land at Banja Luka. Patrols by NATO fighters have reduced Yugoslav air activity to a minimum; even so, small subsonic aircraft and helicopters are still able to make 'hit-and-run' raids under cover of terrain and bad weather. The bulk of the former Yugoslav Air Force has remained under Federal Government (Serbian) control throughout the civil war. Now

known as the Federal Air Force, it is divided into three corps, one for air defence, a second for all other flying and a third for logistics and maintenance. It was the Federal Air Force's increasing involvement in operations against the independent states, in particular striking at Croatian towns, positions and supply routes, that prompted the United Nations to set up a no-fly zone, which is currently patrolled by combat aircraft from

the United States, United Kingdom, France and Italy. An unknown number of Federal aircraft and helicopters have been lost to opposition ground forces. The Bosnian Serb Air Arm, Croatian Air Force and Slovenian Air Arm all operate small numbers of aircraft or helicopters, which were either captured or defected from the former Yugoslav Air Force. Much of this equipment is believed to suffer from low serviceability.

## German-assembled Eurofighter aloft at last

*Manching, Germany, March 27*
The maiden flight of the first Eurofighter EF2000, a German-assembled machine, took place today. The British-assembled second prototype is expected to fly shortly. Both of these two prototype Eurofighters are powered by a pair of RB199 engines, as employed in the Panavia Tornado, but this is an interim solution pending the availability of the definitive 20,000-lb s.t. Class Eurojet EJ200 turbofans. The Eurofighter programme has already slipped very badly, due in the main to German prevarication over funding, and the type is not likely to be in service until 2001.

*The German-built first prototype Eurofighter EF 2000 prior to its first flight.*

## Deadly mistake

*Northern Iraq No-Fly Zone, April 14*
In a catastrophic 'friendly fire' incident, two US Air Force F-15 Eagles shoot down two US Army UH-60 Blackhawk helicopters today, mistaking them for Russian-built 'Hinds'. All 26 aboard the two helicopters were killed, including some US and British Army personnel and several Kurdish officials. An investigation is under way to establish the cause of the tragedy, in particular to determine whether there was a malfunction in the helicopters' IFF (identification friend/foe) systems, or whether the aircraft systems may have been subjected to Iraqi jamming.

# Freighting with Federal Express

*The Airbus A300-600F – scheduled to enter service with Federal Express.*

*Blagnac, France, April 23*
Airbus have delivered the first of 25 Airbus A300-600F dedicated freighters to the specialized package carrier, FedEx. Powered by two 58,000-lb s.t General Electric CF6-80C2A5 turbofans, this all-cargo version can carry up to a maximum payload of 120,855lb over a range of 1,900 nautical miles.

# Pre-teen pilot's 3,000 mile oceanic leap

*Vicki van Meter, with her Cessna 210.*

*Glasgow, Scotland, June 7*
The sight of Vicki van Meter, a bubbly 12-year-old American schoolgirl and her adult flying instructor, Curt Arnspiger, climbing out of a single-engined Cessna 210 is not likely to attract much attention at an airport used to light aircraft comings and goings. However, this is an arrival with a difference, completing, as it does, an epic three-stage, 3,000 mile flight during which Vicki was at the controls the whole of the way. Setting off on Sunday from Augusta, Maine, Vicki and Curt – aboard for both safety and legal reasons – made their first stop at Goose Bay, Newfoundland. From here they routed Narsarsuaq, Greenland to Reykjavik, Iceland and Glasgow. Ironically, while the flight makes Vicki the youngest girl pilot to fly the Atlantic, her age and lack of a licence debars her from gaining any form of official acknowledgment of her feat.

# DC-X reusable launch vehicle enters new test program

*Las Cruces, USA, June 20*
Following the May 3 receipt of a $3.5 million contract from the Ballistic Missile Defense Organization to resurrect their DC-X reusable launch vehicle, McDonnell Douglas flew the first of between three and five more test flights today. The latest flight of the 42-ft craft saw the DC-X reach 2,600ft and cover 1,050ft across the ground. The 136-second long flight surpassed the three made last year.

**March 30. The Pilatus PC-12 single-turboprop business aircraft gains its Swiss Type Certificate. The orderbook for this pressurized nine-seater stands at 21 firm, plus 23 options.**

# New giant Boeing twinjet takes to the skies

*Seattle, USA, June 12*
The first Boeing 777 long range, widebodied twin turbofan jetliner makes its maiden flight here today. Many see it as the successor to the four-engined 747, thanks to the general adoption of Extended-range, Twin-engined OPerationS (ETOPS) flying rules. Current orders for the 777 stand at 147 from 16 airlines plus 108 options. The world's largest twin-engined jetliner to date, the 777 is scheduled to receive Type Certification by May 1995, a process speeded by the involvement of five aircraft within this intensive flight test program. Following Type Certification, the first 777s will go to launch customer United Airlines. Powered by two 75,000-lb s.t. class turbofans from models being offered by General Electric, Pratt & Whitney and Rolls-Royce, the 777 has accommodation for up to 400 passengers in a three-class cabin layout and has a full-payload range in excess of 3,500 nautical miles.

*Ushering in an era of trans-continental, wide-bodied twins is the Boeing 777.*

# Rise of the Remotely Piloted Vehicles

*San Diego, USA, July 3*
The General Atomics Predator made its maiden flight today. An unmanned, piston-engined machine, the Predator is designed to carry an electro-optical and synthetic aperature radar sensor package aloft to provide long duration, medium altitude tactical reconnaissance. A range of satellite and radio data links provide a two-way flow of vehicular guidance commands and real-time target intelligence to and from the ground station. This is the first of 10 to be manufactured under a US Department of Defense Advanced Concept Technology Demonstration contract. It is likely that, before too many years have passed, Remotely Piloted Vehicles (RPVs) will be at the forefront of the air combat arena. There is already a vast library of experience behind the development of such vehicles, which were first used to test

*The functionally contoured, unmanned General Atomics Aeronautical Division Predator.*

weapon systems and to train gunners. Their next application was as reconnaissance systems; Teledyne Ryan Firebee RPVs, launched by C-130 Hercules aircraft, were used in the Vietnam War to overfly heavily-defended targets in the north.

Drones are being developed to destroy tanks and radar stations, and there is no technological reason why they should not ultimately perform all the tasks currently in the domain of manned combat aircraft. Because they carry no pilot, RPVs can be made very small and can be subjected to accelerations and forces that would be unacceptable to a human being.

## Col. Hubert 'Hub' Zemke dies, aged 80

*Colonel Hubert 'Hub' Zemke.*

*Oroville, USA, August 30*
'Hub' Zemke died today aged 80. He was the battling commander of the US Army Air Force's UK-based 56th and 479th Fighter Groups of the 8th Air Force, stationed in England between 1943 and late 1944. Zemke preferred the North American P-51D to the Republic P-47D, but the decision was made that the 56th should remain with the P-47. Although Zemke did get to fly the P-51D on taking command of the 479th Group, his loyalty for his original 56th Group later led him to argue that this unit could have been the top scoring European-based US fighter group had they not stayed with the P-47. Shot down, towards the close of 1944, Zemke ended his war in a German prisoner of war camp. Zemke remained with the post-war US Air Force until his retirement in 1967.

## Double-decker Airbus unveiled

*Blagnac, France, June 22*
Airbus Industries today revealed their A3XX range of next-generation, double-decker outsize jetliners. The baseline A3XX-100 carries between 530 and 570 people, while the A3XX-200's capacity is for 630 to 670 seats, with as many as 965 passengers being carried in a single class layout. The seating capacity figures quoted for the A3XX are some 30–40 per cent greater than today's largest airliner, the Boeing 747-400. The A3XX's shape is abbreviated, if not downright squat, in order to meet the requirements of the taxiway and gate of the average international airport.

*Double-decker buses give scale in this artist's impression of the Airbus A3XX.*

## Bidding for the next-generation fighter

*St Louis, USA, November 1*
McDonnell Douglas announced today that they will lead an industrial team, partnered by Northrop Grumman and British Aerospace, to compete for the upcoming Joint Advanced Strike Technology program. Both companies had previously been working together under a $27.7 million contract covering Phase II of the Advanced Short Take-Off and Vertical Landing (ASTOVL) study, which has now been merged into JAST under US Congressional direction. It is thought that the designation X-32 or X-35 has been allocated to the ASTOVL aircraft.

# Allies mount air strikes to little avail

*Croatia, November 18-December 5*
Following the bombing of Bosnian forces by Serbian Air Force light strike aircraft, NATO air forces mounted a protracted aerial onslaught against Serbian airfields. On November 21, NATO mounted its initial air strike. Taking part in this raid were 39 aircraft from five Italian bases, all to make or support a single strike against the Ubdina airbase. Matters took a further ugly turn on November 23, when two Royal Navy BAe Sea Harrier FRS 1s were targeted by Serbian SAM-2 missiles that, happily for the jump jet pilots, both missed their targets. The NATO response was to dispatch 20 aircraft to attack the offending SAM site on the morning of November 24. Again, the results were disappointing, as post-strike aerial reconnaissance showed that while the ground radars had been hit successfully,

*F-16 fighters depart Aviano in Italy on an air strike against Serbian forces.*

the SAMs were still operational. By the start of December it was clear that these NATO air strikes were failing to halt the Serb campaign. The protracted search for a diplomatic solution began, with the United Nations somewhat belatedly requesting a scaling-down of NATO's air strikes. After a

brief cooling-down period, lasting a day or two, NATO rebuffed the UN by re-imposing their own overflights a part of Operation 'Deny Flight'. A high-level NATO investigation is under way to determine why so many of the precision-guided bombs appear to have malfunctioned.

## British Hercules deal threatens FLA

*London, England, December 16*
The Ministry of Defence today announced its intention to purchase 25 Lockheed Martin C-130Js as an immediate solution to its pressing Hercules Replacement Program, while following up with an order for 40 to 50 Future Large Aircraft (FLA) early in the next century. The FLA is a proposed European medium-lift military transport, capable of carrying cargoes that are beyond the capacity of the C-130. The FLA, whose chief protagonists are the French, is to be a C-130 replacement and, as such, the British decision brings the FLA program launch no nearer. However, the UK armed forces have an urgent requirement for a Hercules replacement to support the new Airmobile Brigade.

# Co-axial Kaman ready for service

*One of four K-Max 'flying cranes' used in certification flying.*

*Bloomfield, USA, August 30*
Kaman's novel K-Max single-seat, co-axial rotored, utility helicopter, first flown at the end of 1991, received its Federal Aeronautics Administration (FAA) Type Certificate. Designed specifically for external load-hauling, the K-Max is aimed at the construction industry, power line work, log-hauling

and fire-fighting, and can carry a maximum underslung load of 6,000lb. Power for the K-Max is provided by a single Textron Lycoming T53-17A-1, de-rated to 1,500shp. The final 50-hour phase of certification flying was completed within just 19 days, with only one unscheduled maintenance stoppage – to change a light bulb.

# Rinaldo Piaggio is staying afloat Italian-style

*Genoa, Italy, November 21*
An Italian Court, using the so-called Prodi Law, has put the Rinaldo Piaggio company under bankruptcy protection. Under this law, Piaggio's $200 million debt will be frozen for up to two years, while the firm will

qualify for state aid as a strategic, high-technology national asset with a sizable workforce. Piaggio's problems revolve around the P.180 Avanti, a futuristically styled canard pusher business aircraft that has elicited little market interest.

# Brazil's EMBRAER privatized

*Brazil, December 7*
The Brazilian Government today sold a controlling 55.4 per cent of EMBRAER, the country's leading aircraft builder, into the private sector. The sale, valued at $182 million, saw Brazilians take two

thirds, while foreign investors gained a third of the released stock. Foremost among the Brazilian shareholders are Companhia Bozano, Simonsen, along with the country's largest pension fund, Previ e Sistel.

# Ukrainian heavyweight turbo-prop unleashed

*Kiev, Ukraine, December 16*
Today Antonov's latest An-70 four-turbo-pop heavy widebody cargo transport made its maiden flight. As with many things in the former USSR, the An-70 program has

suffered its share of delays due to a considerable lack of finances. Despite this, Antonov are confident that their latest massive offering will be adopted as the successor to their smaller, earlier An-12 'Coke'.

*Antonov's An-70 prototype climbs out on its maiden flight.*

First deliveries of the 185-seat A321, the stretched version of the Airbus A320, were made to Lufthansa, Alitalia and Air Inter at the beginning of 1994.

The military variant of the third prototype of the Hindustan ALH helicopter for the Indian Army and Air Force. .

The Jetstream 61 (formerly the Advanced Turboprop Airliner) seats 70 people and is powered by PW127D engines.

Airbus's A300-600ST. Four of these transports will be used to carry bulky airframe parts between Airbus's widely separated supplier facilities.

Maiden flight of the first of 13 BAe/McDonnell Douglas Harrier T.10, a night-attack trainer for the RAF.

Delivieries of the CH-146 Griffon began to the Canadian Armed forces.

The Bell 407 concept demonstrator first flew on April 21.

The Cirrus Design ST-50, a pressurized single, pusher-arranged turboprop engined, five-seater.

*Poland's Iryda M-93V combat trainer, powered by twin Rolls-Royce Viper engines, made its first flight from the PZL-Mielec flight test centre.*

*In January the Westland Mk 8 Super Lynx became the subject of overseas orders, nine aircraft being acquired by Brazil.*

*Neatly filling the gap between the Boeing 747 and 767 airliners, the twin-turbofan Boeing 777 takes off on its inaugural flight.*

*The Ilyushin Il-103 is powered by a Teledyne Continental engine.*

*The Eurocopter EC five-seven seat helicopter.*

*Developed to meet Sweden's air defense needs at a modest price, is this airborne early warning and control version of the SAAB 340 airliner.*

*The Eurocopter EC 135 light twin helicopter can carry seven passengers. It is seen here indulging in an 'aerial ballet'.*

4,534mph
USA
Pete Knight
North American X-15
Oct 3, 1967

24,987 miles
USA
Jeager and Rutan
Voyager
Dec 23, 1986

354,200ft
USA
Joseph Walker
North American X-15
Aug 22, 1963

1,120,370lb
USSR
Antonov
An-225 Mriya

71,100lb thrust
UK
Rolls Royce
Trent 772

**Mindelheim, Germany, March 31**
First flight of the one-off Grob G-820 Strato 2C high-altitude environmental research aircraft. The aircraft's cabin has accommodation for two crew and two scientists, with power being supplied by two 400-hp liquid-cooled Teledyne Continental TSIOL-550 Voyager engines (→August 4).

**Prague, Czech Republic, April 11**
The Czech Government give the go-ahead for the development and production of 72 Aero L-159 light strike/trainers for the Czech Republic Air Force.

**Mitchelville, Florida, April 11**
T. Keith Glennan dies. Glennan was the first head of NASA following its formation in 1958.

**Moscow, Russia, April 26**
A Mikoyan MiG-29 sets new a FAI Class C-1h world altitude record of 90,092ft.

**Warsaw, Poland, April 26**
Today saw the first flight of the Yalo GM-01 Gniady single radial-engined glider tug.

**Elmira, New York, May 31**
First flight of the Schweizer RU-38A Twin Condor long-range surveillance aircraft.

**Mull of Kintyre, Scotland, June 2**
All 29 aboard an RAF Boeing Vertol Chinook survive when the helicopter flies into rising ground. The 26 passengers include senior Northern Ireland-based officials going to a security conference.

**London, June 2**
British Aerospace sign an agreement with SAAB to globally market their SAAB JAS 39 Gripen.

**Seattle, Washington, June 20**
First flight of the Boeing 767-300F freighter version.

**Seattle, Washington, June 26**
Boeing announce the launch of the stretched Boeing 777-300 twin-engined widebody airliner.

**Gioia del Colle, Italy, July 5**
The first of 24 Panavia Tornado F 3s, to be leased from the RAF, is handed over to the Italian Air Force's 12th Fighter Squadron today. These two-seater Tornado F 3s replace aging Fiat-built single seat Lockheed F-104S Starfighters.

**Edwards AFB, California, July 10**
Hover testing of an 86 per cent-scale model of Lockheed Martin's Joint Advanced Strike Technology design has started at NASA Ames where such matters as jet thrust and ground pressures can be assessed. Vertical-to-horizontal flight transition testing in the large, low-speed wind tunnel will follow in September.

**Paris, July 25**
Jean Macaigne dies, aged 90. One of France's foremost early airline pioneers, he joined Aéropostal in 1927. Here he was responsible for setting up Aéropostal's flights between Europe and Brazil during the 1928 to 1932 period.

**Edwards AFB, California, July 26**
Personnel from the US Air Force's 9th Reconnaissance Wing begin a month-long work-up on the first two of the three refurbished Lockheed SR-71s that have been brought back into service. These aircraft are scheduled to restart their careers as operational craft on September 1.

**Mindelheim, Germany, August 4**
The G-820 Grob Strato 2C high-altitude environmental research aircraft sets a new FAI world altitude record for manned, piston-engined aircraft, at a height of 60,867 feet.

**Irkutsk, Siberia, August 15**
The first flight of the Beriev Be-32K twin turboprop feederliner takes place.

**Toronto, Canada, 15 August**
Clennell Haggerston 'Punch' Dickens, one of Canadian aviation's earliest 'bush pilots' died today.

**New York, August 16**
An Aerospatiale-BAC Concorde, chartered from Air France, returns to JFK International Airport, just 31 hours 27 minutes after setting off from there, to set a new around-the world speed record. Traveling eastwards, the Concorde staged through Toulouse, Dubai, Bangkok, Guam, Honolulu and Acapulco.

**Hamburg, Germany, August 25**
First flight of the 150-passenger Airbus A319 jetliner, orders for which stand at 81.

**St Louis, USA, September 12**
McDonnell Douglas hand-over the first of 72 F-15Ss to the Royal Saudi Arabian Air Force. Delivery will be made at a rate of one a month and will keep the Eagle production line open for several years.

**Cherry Point, USA, September 21**
After months of 'work up' training on their new McDonnell Douglas/BAe TAV-8B and AV-8B Plus Harriers, the first Italian Navy fixed-wing air group in 66 years departs for Italy. They are being transported to Italy aboard the *Guiseppe Garabaldi,* an aircraft carrier.

**London, October 3**
Boeing representatives at the public inquiry on expansion of London Heathrow airport confirm that Boeing is studying a further stretch of their basic 747, the -600X, with up to 550 passengers, or over 700 in a single class layout.

**Nagoya, Japan, October 7**
The latest Japanese fighter takes to the skies on its maiden flight. This is the prototype Mitsubishi FS-X single seat multi-role fighter aircraft, which is an altogether larger development of the General Dynamics F-16 Fighting Falcon.

**Wichita, Kansas, October 7**
On the 32nd anniversary of the maiden flight of the prototype Learjet 23, Learjet's 45 business jet makes its maiden flight, lasting 2 hours 2 minutes.

**Glasgow, Scotland, October 16**
Launch of the Royal Navy's newest helicopter carrier, HMS *Ocean.*

**Seattle, Washington, November 14**
Boeing announce a massive $12.7 billion order for 77 Boeing 777-200Bs from Singapore Airlines, and options a further 43.

**Savannah, November 28**
First flight of Gulfstream Aerospace Gulfstream V. With a fully equipped price tag of around $32 million, the current orderbook is for these luxury long range business jets stands at 60.

## Factfile

World revenue passenger miles: 1,400,000 million
World revenue passengers: 1,300 million
World air freight (ton miles): 60,000 million
Passengers through London (Heathrow/Gatwick): 76.5 million
Total airline employees: 1,838,331
Total jetliners employed: 11,469
Total turbo-prop liners employed: 4,235
Total piston engined liners employed: 638
Total scheduled service helicopters employed: 79
Average salary of long-haul pilot: $128,000
Average salary of cabin crew (US): $32,000
Price of 1,000 (US) gallons Jet A1 fuel: $500
Average exchange rate: £1=$1.56

*The US Air Force's Lockheed U-2R continues to play an active part in flying reconnaissance missions for their current Balkans operations.* ▶

# The first 500 and going strong

*The Chicago-based United Air Lines receive their 22nd Airbus A320 making the 500th in total.*

*Blagnac, France, January 25*
After successes with its large A300 and A310 airliners, Airbus hoped that the smaller A320 would equal the sales of these reliable carriers, it has become easily the most advanced airliner currently in service, with sales racing ahead. The extremely successful A320, launched in March 1985, had attracted 439 commitments from 16 customers before it first flew in February 1987. The A320 has followed the design example of modern jet fighters such as the F-16 in dispensing with a conventional control column; a sidestick relays pilot input commands to the fly-by-wire system. The cockpit is state of the art, featuring multi-display screens and few dials. A central fault-finding system displays impending faults to the crew.

## Lightplane with its own parachute

*Duluth, Minnesota, March 31*
Today saw the first flight of the Cirrus SR-20 lightplane. Powered by a 200-hp air-cooled Teledyne Continental IO-360-ES, this four-seater cruises along at 160 knots and has a maximum range of 800 nautical miles, despite having a fixed, tricyle landing gear. Making extensive use of composite materials in its sleekly contoured construction, the SR-20 has one quite unique advantage over any of its competitors. In flight, when all else fails, either the pilot or the front seat passenger can save the day by simply deploying an integral onboard parachute that permits the machine to descend gently to earth.

**Xichang Space Centre, China, January 26. A Long March 2E booster with its Hughes-built Apstar 2 communications satellite explodes and is destroyed 45 seconds into its ascent.**

## Cessna 182 selling singles again

*The prototype new-build Cessna 182 takes to the air again.*

*Wichita, Kansas, April 19*
Today, was the first flight of the first Cessna 182 to be produced since the draconian California Product Liability Law brought about the virtual total cessation of single-engined lightplane manufacturing in the US for the last decade. The recent neutralization of the catastrophic impact of the Liability Law is largely attributed to the efforts of President Clinton.

## High Hopes for Japanese Space Shuttle

*Tokyo, Japan, February 20*
Japan's National Space Development Agency (NASDA) today announced that its budget for 1995-1996 has been increased to $2.3 billion. One central thrust of spending is aimed at developing a small unmanned 8.8-ton space shuttle craft called Hope, which stands for H-II Orbiting PlanE and alludes to the H-II orbital rocket atop which it is mounted.

# Luftwaffe back over the battlefield

*Berlin, Germany, June 30*
The German Government today agreed to deploy German troops and aircraft in support of United Nations forces in Bosnia, this commitment ending a long-standing parliamentary and public debate. It will lead to German forces entering a combat zone for the first time since the end of World War II, some 50 years ago. The air element sees the deployment of six Luftwaffe Panavia Tornado ECRs for ground defense suppression – followed by a further eight Luftwaffe Tornado IDSs for strike missions – before the end of July 1995. Initially these machines will be based at Piacenza in the north of Italy. The German Navy will also participate, supplying two Atlantic maritime patrol aircraft. Fourteen Atlantics have been modernized by Dornier with new search radars, navigation systems and electronic surveillance measures for the maritime patrol role. Five more are used for

*For the first time in 50 years, the German Air Force is set to go in harm's way.*

electronic intelligence missions. Some 12 home-based C.160 Transalls will be involved in carrying reinforcements to the Croatian city of Split, where Germany will set up a field hospital manned by between 400 and 600 personnel. The Franco-German-developed Transall can carry 35,270lb of

cargo over 1,150 miles. The Transalls are being progressively refurbished to allow thm to remain in service until 2010. The Luftwaffe's transport force has also been strengthened by the acquisition of Russian transport aircraft operated by the former East German Air Force.

## Human shields halt air NATO strikes

*Near Pale, Bosnia, May 25-26*
A second NATO air strike against Bosnian Serb forces was called off today after Bosnian Serbs take more than 90 United Nations troops and observers hostage, using some as human shields to protect fuel dump supplies. The US Navy has rushed a carrier group and Marines to the Adriatic. Incidentally, the air strikes of yesterday and this morning are the first to be carried out since late November 1994.

## Prop beats the jets

*Washington DC, June 22*
Today the US Department of Defense selected as winner of the JPATS joint service trainer 'fly-off' competition the Beech/British Aerospace team, with a version of the Pilatus PC-9 turboprop. The aircraft will be known as the Beech T-6 Texan II.

# Designer Ben Rich dies, aged 69

*Ben Rich, seen here with his brainchild, Lockheed's stealthy F-117A.*

*Los Angeles, California, January 5*
Ben Rich, designer of the F-117 died today aged 69. Rich succeeded Clarence 'Kelly' Johnson as head of Lockheed's 'Skunk Works' from 1975 until his retirement in 1991. During this time Rich led development of the F-117 stealth aircraft. Previously, as Johnson's deputy at the top-secret 'Skunk Works', Rich had worked closely with his team leader in the develop-

ment of the SR-71 Blackbird, a program that called upon all of his earlier aero-thermodynamics training. The kind of man-manager that got results by encouraging his team – rather than harassing them – Rich modestly attributed much of his team's success in the field of stealth technology to a 1975 Russian scientific paper, openly published in the West after the Soviet military had dismissed its potential.

# Westland to build new US helicopter

*The formidable McDonnell Douglas AH-64D Longbow Apache.*

*London, England, July 13*
Today the British Government formally announced its selection of the McDonnell Douglas AH-64D Longbow Apache as the Army Air Corps' new attack helicopter.

Valued at £2.5 billion, the deal involves the purchase of 67 Longbow Apaches, assembled under licence by Westland, from parts supplied by McDonnell Douglas Helicopters.

# Britten is Britain's top aerobatic pilot

Britten holding the 1995 British Aerobatics Championship Trophy.

*Sywell, England, September 9*
Diana Britten's central dedication to competition aerobatics paid off today when she was announced overall British aerobatic champion and, incidentally, the first female holder of the title. This success however, was not won lightly, representing the culmination of competition flying that started in 1981, the year after Diana gained her Private Pilot's Licence. From 1982-85, Diana campaigned the aerobatics circuits of England, France and Holland flying a Cap 10b, which from 1983 was her own G-BKUC. Her skill received full recognition in 1985, when she switched to flying the single seat CAP-21, G-BLZZ, gaining a place in the British Aerobatics Team for the following year and becoming the first British female team member since 1970. Between 1987 and 1991 Diana competed in both hemispheres, often as the sole representative British pilot and mainly in her own Extra 230, G-DIAN. During 1991, Diana upgraded to an Extra 260, G-EXTR, the machine she was to compete in during the 1992 World Aerobatics Championship.

## Fiat's 'Gina' retires

The Fiat G-91T, has now been retired.

*Foggia, Italy, September 30*
The Italian Air Force finally retired the last of its Fiat G-91 strike fighters today. Initially placed in operations during 1964. and replaced by the Aermacchi-Embraer AMX, the last of the breed to fly – a G-91T two seater – carries a suprisingly gaudy paint scheme commemorating, among other things, the 289,000 flying hours the Fiats had managed to accumulate in Italian service. The Fiat G-91 resulted from a NATO requirement for a lightweight strike fighter.

## US-Russian Heavenly accord

*Cape Canaveral, USA, June 27–July 7*
The era of the US–Soviet space race saw some wonderous events, but few as remarkable as those that have occurred with Earth-orbit within the past few days. Commanded by Robert 'Hoot' Gibson, the Space Shuttle *Atlantis* lifted off from Cape Canaveral on June 27 to rendezvous with the Russian *Mir* space station. *Atlantis* docked with *Mir* on June 29 for five days to form a giant 231-ton orbiting linked spacecraft. Part of *Atlantis'* mission involved ferrying up two Russian cosmonauts to relieve two previously orbiting Russians. Also retrieved was US astronaut, Dr Norman Thagard, who had flown a 115-day mission aboard *Mir*, exceeding by a fair margin the previous longest US space mission duration of 84 days, set by the four-man Skylab crew in 1974. Dr Thagard's major problem while aboard *Mir* stemmed from a feeling of acute cultural isolation. As he put it 'You are the one American on a Russian craft and no one else really speaks English.' Sometimes, Thagard went days without talking in English or hearing news. Further missions to *Mir* are planned, involving US and other foreign crew members.

## Reflections of a former warrior

*Tokyo, Japan, August 18*
Saburo Sakai, a leading Japanese World War II fighter ace with 64 victories and 2,000 hours of combat flying, is unstinting in his criticism of the Japanese establishment's conduct during the war and the 10 years leading up to it. Sakai points to folly of launching a war against a foe with a far greater economy and of the stupidity of the *Kamikaze* tactic.

## EMBRAER'S Brazilian beauty

The attractively proportioned EMB-145 is the latest offering from EMBRAER.

*Sao Jose dos Campos, Brazil, August 11*
EMBRAER's 50-passenger EMB-145 twin jet feederliner makes its maiden flight today. The aircraft has survived initial design vacillations, cut-backs and competition, all against a background of major corporate uncertainty. Currently, EMBRAER has firm orders for 18 EMB-145s, plus 127 letters of intent. Type certification is planned for the third quarter of 1996. Total development cost of the program so far is put at $180 million. Between another $140 million and $200 million is also required. The EMB-145 carries a price tag of $14.5 million for the basic airframe and engines; this is without the furnishings and engine thrust reversers that EMBRAER are offering as an option.

# Eastern jets get Western upgrades

*Manching, Germany, October 16*
As the efforts of the 'Bottom-Liners' bite deep into both defense and airline procurement budgets everywhere, manufacturers are paying more and more attention to maximizing cash returns from maintenance and product support. Today, for example saw the arrival, for refurbishment, of the first of the 24 Mikoyan MiG-29s of the German Air Force's 73rd Fighter Squadron (JG 73) at the Daimler-Benz Aerospace (DASA) maintenance facility. The work is to be carried out by MAPS, a joint ownership operation in which DASA has a 50 per cent interest, while three Russian companies – ANKP-MiG, MAPO and Rosvooruzhenie – have the rest. MAPS is aggressively promoting its maintenance/product support capability to MiG-29 users worldwide, as well as offering its unique blend of East-West 'know-how' in modernization upgrades.

*One of the German Air Force's Mikoyan MiG-29s undergoes maintenance.*

## UPS pass the parcel with new Boeing freighers

*Seattle, Washington, October 12*
United Parcel Service (UPS), one of the leading new-breed express delivery operators, today took delivery of the first of the 30 Boeing 767-300 Freighter's ordered by the carrier, who also hold a further 30 options. Powered by two 57,900-lb s.t. General Electric CF6-80C2s, this particular workhorse can haul an impressive 60-ton payload over a distance of 3,000 nautical miles.

Boeing announced the go-ahead for the basic 767-300 in February 1983, the aircraft retaining the basic structure of the series 200 but with a lengthened fuselage. By placing a 10 feet 1in plug forward of the wing, and an 11 feet plug aft, Boeing achieved a far more capacious aircraft with little change to the systems and construction. Necessary modifications included a strengthened landing gear.

## Two new Russian trainers at Paris Air Show

*Le Bourget, France, June 12*
Today both contenders for the Russian Air Force's next generation jet trainer requirement came to the Paris Air Show inside Antonov transports, fresh from their factory roll-outs and as yet unflown. Mikoyan's MiG-AT was officially unveiled a couple of weeks ago, on May 18, while Yakovlev's Yak-130 is even more recent, having rolled-out on May 29. Both designs incorporate Western equipment and are being offered for export with European partners, Dassault for the MiG and Aermacchi for the Yak.

## Extended-range Airbus twin

*Blagnac, France, November 24*
At a glittering ceremony Airbus Industrie announce the launch of the Airbus A330-200 extended range variant today. Shorter by 14 feet 4.75in than the standard A330-300, the A330-200 seats 253 passengers, compared to the A330-300's 295 pasengers in conventional three-class cabin layouts. By trading passengers for extra fuel, the A330-200's range with 253 passengers is 6,400 nautical miles, which is a significant improvement upon the A330-300's 4,800 nautical miles full load capability.

## 'Super Bug' promises more sting

*St Louis, Missouri, November 29*
The first flight of the bigger, better McDonnell Douglas F/A-18E Super Hornet took place today. Physically larger and heavier than its predecessor, the Super Hornet has two 22,000-lb s.t. General Electric F414-GE-400 engines, providing nearly 40 per cent more power than that of the standard Hornet. More fuel and superior avionics will improve its strike range and capability, while the Super Hornet's flight control system will benefit from McDonnell Douglas's extensive development of their more battle damage-tolerant systems.

## Set the controls for the heart of the sun

*Cape Canaveral, December 2*
A NASA Atlas IIAS launcher successfully thrust the 1.6-ton European Space Agency SOHO space probe out of the Earth's atmosphere today. The name stands for SOlar and Heliospheric Observatory, whose job it will be to study the sun in unprecedented detail. To carry out its task, SOHO is equipped with instruments with which to survey the Sun's hidden interior and its solar atmosphere, as well as radiated solar winds. SOHO will take up an orbit at a point around 932,055 miles from Earth, where Earth and Sun gravities cancel each other out.

*The first prototype of the McDonnell Douglas F/A-18E Super Hornet.*

The Fokker 60 Utility, seen here during its first flight, can be quickly converted to different transport configurations.

Based on the F-16 Fighting Falcon, the first prototype of the Mitsubishi XF-2A, also called the FS-X, made its maiden flight.

The three-engined Dassault Falcon EX is the latest executive jet aimed at both civil and military markets.

The Grob Strato 2C high altitude surveillance aircraft is claimed to be the largest composite type in the world.

Converted from the second Pilatus PC-12, the PC-12 EC Eagle was developed for electronic countermeasures work.

The attractive Cirrus SR-20 can, if necessary, be brought gently, and safely, to earth by emergency parachute.

The Beech JPATS advanced training aircraft, the US version of the Pilatus PC-9 Mk II, making a very steep climb-out.

Boeing employees gather at Everett, Washington, to watch the roll-out of the first Boeing 767-300F Freighter.

*Developed in Indonesia and powered by two Allison AE2100 turboprops, the IPTN N-250 regional airliner first flew on August 10.*

*After the success of the Citation X, Cessna went on to develop yet another executive variant, the luxuriously appointed Citation Bravo.*

*The Tu-334 was designed as the successor to the Tupolev Tu-134.*

*The Ilyushin Il-76MF has excellent shortfield performance.*

*The Eurocopter EC120 Colibri has been developed in co-operation with companies in China and Singapore.*

*Seen here in Japanese Air Self-Defence Force markings after handover in March, these B.Ae 125-800 series aircraft are marketed as the Hawker 800.*

*The NH Industries NH90 transport helicopter, seen here on a test flight over the French countryside.*

*The first Airbus A319, assembled in Hamburg, seen taking off on its first flight on August 25. The A319 can carry up to 124 passengers.*

*The Augusta A119 Koala is the fastest wide-body single turbine helicopter, and has an exceptionally roomy cabin.*

# 1996

4,534mph
USA
Pete Knight
North American X-15
Oct 3, 1967

24,987 miles
USA
Jeager and Rutan
Voyager
Dec 23, 1986

354,200ft
USA
Joseph Walker
North American X-15
Aug 22, 1963

1,120,370lb
USSR
Antonov
An-225 Mriya

77,000lb thrust
UK
Rolls Royce
Trent 877

**Toulouse, France, January 1**
Aero International (Regional) or AI(R), which was registered on June 11, 1995, begins operations.

**In Earth Orbit, January 15**
NASA astronaut Leroy Chiao becomes the 100th person to take a space walk when he exits from the Space Shuttle *Endeavour*.

**Schiphol, Netherlands, January 22**
Fokker, the Dutch aircraft manufacturer, faces serious financial difficulties following the decision of its major shareholder, Daimler Benz Aerospace, to withdraw financial support.

**Dominican Republic, February 6**
All 189 aboard a Boeing 757 are killed when the jet stalls and crashes into sea. (The subsequent inquiry blames the pilot's lack of basic flying skills, including how to react to stick shaker.)

**Madrid, February 20**
The Spanish Army selects the AS 532UL Cougar as its new transport helicopter with plans to order 15.

**Bordeaux, France, February 26**
The first production Dassault Mirage 2000-5 for the French Air Force makes its maiden flight.

**Moscow, March 16**
The first flight of the Mikoyan MiG-AT takes place, lasting five minutes. At the controls of this twin jet trainer is Mikoyan test pilot, Roman Taskayev.

**Moscow, March 17**
The Tupolev Tu-144LL supersonic flying test bed is rolled out, preparatory to initiating a $15 million joint NASA/Tupolev flight test program this April.

**Gifu, Japan, March 22**
Mitsubishi deliver the prototype of their single seat XF-2A fighter (formerly known as FX-X) to the Japanese Air Self-Defense Force's Air Development and Test Wing today.

**Marietta, USA, April 5**
First flight of the Lockheed Martin C-130J Hercules. Computer problems are given as the reason for the three-month slippage in the aircraft entering flight testing.

**Moscow, April 25**
First flight of Yakovlev Yak-130 military two-seat jet trainer, with test pilot Aleksandr Sinitsyn at the controls.

**Wichita, Kansas, June 3**
Today, Cessna's fast Citation X (ten) business jet receives Federal Aviation Administration (FAA) Type Certification following a three aircraft, 3,000-hour test program. Capable of carrying up to 12 passengers, the luxurious Citation X can cruise at up to Mach 0.91 at 37,000 feet and range out to 3,430 nautical miles.

**Wichita, Kansas, June 24**
Raytheon delivers their 5,000th Beech King Air business turbo-prop, in this particular instance a top-of-the-range -300 model. Outstripping its nearest rival by more than two to one in terms of sales, the first Beech King Air took to the skies in 1964.

**Seattle, Washington, July 2**
Boeing and the General Electric Company announce the formation of Boeing Business Jets as a joint venture to build lavishly appointed Boeing 737-700s as the BBJ.

**Washington DC, July 3**
NASA announces that Lockheed Martin's Venture Star is the winner of the X-33 orbiter competition.

**Washington DC, July 10**
The US Air Force terminates its development of the Lockheed Martin F-22B two-seat operational trainer version of the F-22A fighter.

**Tokyo, Japan, July 29**
First flight of Mitsubishi MH2000 multi-role seven-to-12 seat civil helicopter. This machine is powered by two 800-shp MG5-100 turboshaft engines manufactured by Mitsubishi.

**Toulouse, France, August 3**
AI(R), the jointly owned European regional aircraft producer today announces that recent orders for 11 aircraft have taken the total ATR 42/-72 order book to the 500th aircraft mark. This event comes 11 years after the first ATR 42 entered service.

**Japan, August 6**
The first flight of the Kawasaki OH-X two-seat reconnaissance helicopter takes place today. Power for this tandem-seater is provided by two 884-shp Mitsubishi XTS1-10 turboshafts. The development of the OH-X for the Japanese Ground Self-Defense Force was initiated by Kawasaki four years ago in August 1992.

**Baltimore, Maryland, August 9**
Sir Frank Whittle dies aged 98. Whittle is considered by many to be the father of the jet engine.

**Orlando, Florida, August 26**
Roll-out of the first prototype of the Bombardier Global Express large business jet.

**Getafe, Spain, August 31**
Maiden flight of first two-seat Eurofighter 2000. Assembled in Spain, this is the sixth of seven development aircraft programs.

**Seattle, Washington, September 2**
Boeing launch their 757-300, with a fuselage stretched by 23ft 4in to seat 243 passengers in a two-class layout. This represents a 20 per cent increase in seating capacity over the standard 757-200.

**Washington DC, November 6**
US Air orders another 120 of the A319/A320/A321 family of twin engined, narrowbody jetliners and places intents to purchase an additional 120, as well as reserving options on a further 160.

**Australia, November 27**
Today, the Australian Government has selected the BAe Hawk 100 as its next Lead-In Fighter Trainer (LIFT). The Hawk's advanced cockpit instrumentation will simulate the Australian-operated F/A-18 Hornet.

**Cape Canaveral, December 4**
NASA's Mars Pathfinder space probe is today launched atop a McDonnell Douglas Delta II.

**China, December 26**
First flight of the Jingdezhen Z-11, China's first indigenously designed and manufactured helicopter, a six/seven-seat, general-purpose machine compatible for either civil or military use.

---

*With production now switched to Canada, Bell's Model 206 JetRanger still continues to sell – it first took to the skies in 1962.* ▶

## Factfile

World revenue passenger miles: 1,500,000 million
World revenue passengers: 1,380 million
World air freight (ton miles): 64,000 million
Passengers through London (Heathrow/Gatwick): 79.8 million
Total airline employees: 1,842,777
Total jetliners employed: 11,340
Total turbo-prop liners employed: 3,954
Total piston engined liners employed: 1,115
Total scheduled service helicopters employed: 372
Average salary of long-haul pilot: $134,000
Average salary of cabin crew (US): $34,500
Price of 1,000 (US) gallons Jet A1 fuel: $600
Average exchange rate: £1=$1.49

# Starship design plans published

*Derby, England, January 27*
Charles Osmond Frederick, a recent employee of British Rail in Derby, has startled the scientific world by publishing plans today, first proposed in 1972, for an inter-stellar space vehicle. Presently, traveling as fast as is physically possible, a starship would take about a decade to make a round trip to the nearest star. The plodding, chemical-fuel rockets in use today would take 50,000 years. But that has not stopped far-sighted inventors like Charles Frederick from coming up with designs that might just work. In the 1950s, American physicists Theodore Taylor and Freeman Dyson developed and patented Project Orion, a nuclear-powered spacecraft designed for interstellar travel. Taylor believed that nuclear fuel, which is a million times more powerful than chemical fuels, was the key to deep space flight. The idea was that Orion would be powered – in reality blasted forward – by a series of nuclear explosions, each with the strength of the bomb that destroyed Hiroshima. Every second, one nuclear charge would be ejected rearward from the spaceship and detonated. The shockwaves from the powerful atomic blasts would act on a large 'pusher plate' attached to the rear end of the ship by huge shock absorbers that would translate what would otherwise be a very jerky flight into a smooth ride.

With a supply of 300,000 bombs, Orion would accelerate to 3 per cent of the speed of light – in other words, 5,580 miles per second – and reach Alpha Centauri, the nearest star to our own Sun, in 130 years. In 1977 the British Inter-planetary Society entered the fray again and produced Project Daedalus, a two-stage, 54,000-ton craft propelled by high-energy electron beams that fuse pellets of heavy hydrogen and light helium. With a top speed of 24,000 miles per second – 13 per cent of the speed of light – the ship could reach Barnard's Star, just under six light years away, in 50 years. Barnard's star is seen as a solitary 'wanderer' in space.

# Famous Fokker firm finally fails

*Schiphol, Netherlands, March 16*
Fokker, the Dutch aircraft builder, is declared bankrupt by the District Court of Amsterdam, thus ending 77 years of aircraft manufacture since Anthony Fokker set up the present company in 1919. Parts of the Fokker organization involved in maintenance – such as Product Support and Aircraft Services – will continue to operate under the new identity of Fokker Aviation BV. Of the workforce of 5,664 prior to the collapse, around 2,500 are expected to continue working under the new regime.

**Berlin, Germany, February 9. General Adolf Galland dies, aged 83. After flying with the German Kondor Legion in the Spanish Civil War, Galland went on to become a top World War II Luftwaffe fighter ace with 104 'kills'.**

# Where's the tail

*St Louis, March 19*
McDonnell Douglas and NASA Ames today unveiled their X-36 tailless, unmanned, advanced research vehicle. Lacking either vertical or horizontal tail surfaces, the X-36 uses split ailerons and engine thrust vectoring to maintain flight control. Designed and built in just 28 months at the company's 'Phantom Works', the sole X-36 prototype, which is unmanned, cost $14 million and will shortly enter a six-month, 25-flight program at NASA's Dryden facility at Edwards AFB.

*The NASA/McDonnell Douglas X-36.*

# C-17A Globemaster IIIs for the USAF

*USAF are taking delivery of C-17As.*

*Washington DC, February 2*
The US Department of Defense awarded a single, mammoth $16.6 billion multi-year contract covering the manufacture of 80 more McDonnell Douglas C-17As to bring the fleet to its full strength of 120 aircraft. A versatile aircraft, the C-17A has had a protracted development history, with its flight test program a year behind schedule. The go-ahead for full-scale engineering development was given in December 1985.

# First 'Air Force One' retires to museum

*The long-serving Boeing VC-137 presidential transport.*

*Washington DC, June 29*
The Boeing VC-137 transport, used by US presidents since 1959 as 'Air Force One,' has touched down for the last time and is now in storage for the Smithsonian Institution's National Air and Space Museum at Dulles Airport, Washington. Three Boeing VC-137A aircraft, military versions of the Boeing 707-153, were originally ordered by the USAF as VIP transports, being refited with a 22-seat VIP interior and extremely comprehensive communications for use as airborne command posts; they were later fitted with turbofan engines and redesignated VC-137Bs. Later, a VC-137C (Boeing 707-320B) was added to the fleet and delivered to the Special Air Missions Squadron of the USAF Military Aircraft Command, but was later handed over to the 86th Military Airlift Wing. It was this aircraft that was mainly used to carry the President and other US government officials.

# CAA reveal potential peril over the Atlantic

*London, August 7*
In a report released today, the UK Civil Aviation Authority has admitted that two French airliners came within seconds of colliding over southeast London in May 1995. Only the alertness of an air traffic controller averted a disaster. Airliner safety over the Atlantic may be in jeopardy because some crews who stray badly off course try to cover up the fact, or simply fail to report it. The danger was highlighted in 1990, when two Boeing 747s carrying hundreds of people missed each other by about 200 yards off Iceland – because one of them was 60 miles off course and the crew had not told the oceanic air controllers. The 747s, one belonging to British Airways and the other to El Al, the Israeli Airline, were both en route to the United States. They had left

*The Civil Aviation Authority admits airline safety could be in jeopardy when planes stray off their original course.*

London Heathrow and were flying at about 500mph. The British Airways 747 was on its correct course and was flying at 33,000 feet off the coast of Iceland, 58 miles

from the capital, Reykjavik, when its crew saw the El Al airliner about to cross its path. The crew took sharp avoiding action, turning away and informing Icelandic Control

what they had seen. Later, it turned out that the Israeli aircraft was having trouble with its navigational equipment. The crew had not bothered to tell anyone.

## Asymmetry in the ascendence

*The Boomerang carries the stamp of a design created by Burt Rutan.*

*Mojave, USA, June 17*
Burt Rutan, creator of many unusual designs, has excelled himself with the Scaled Composites 202-11 Boomerang, which set off on its maiden flight today. The Boomerang is an 89 per cent-scale prototype for a twin piston-engined light transport, palpably designed to 'cock a snook' at its more conventional brethren. Scaled Composites is based at Mojave Airport close to

Edwards AFB and specializes in producing proof-of-concept designs for a diversity of customers, ranging from NASA to aspirant manufacturers. Among other early efforts, Scaled Composites produced the initial sub-scale demonstrators that led to Fairchild Republic's T-46A and Beech's Starship. The company's most famous product is the 1986 non-stop round-the-world *Voyager* aircraft.

## Record-setting Mir astronaut returns

*Kazakhstan, February 29*
European Space Agency (ESA) astronaut Thomas Reiter has returned aboard Soyuz TM-22 after spending a record-setting six months on the Russian space station *Mir*. Sharing the confines of *Mir* with Reiter were Russian cos-

monauts Yuri Gidzenko and Sergei Avdeev. Mission highlights include the first ESA astronaut to make a 'spacewalk', participating in the 'docking' with the Space Shuttle *Atlantis* and conducting several significant experiments onboard as part of the Euromir 95 program.

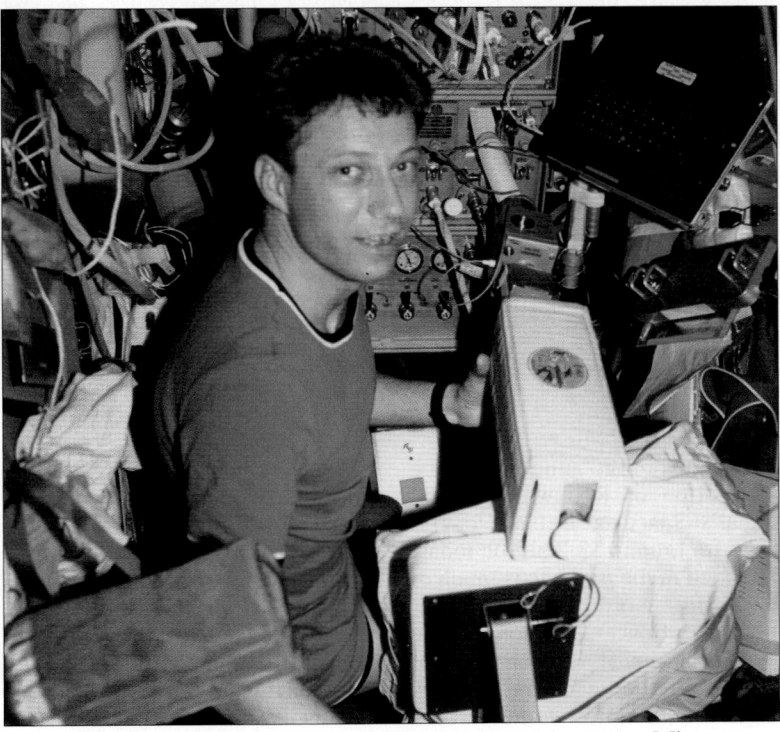

*Astronaut Thomas Reiter, seen aboard the Russian space station* Mir.

# Next century's Nimrod

*London, July 25*
Britain's Ministry of Defence elected today to modernize 21 BAe Nimrods, all well over 30 years old, up toNimrod 2000, or MR4 standard, rather than buy new equipment. The long-awaited announcement, made by Defence Secretary Michael Portillo, values the overall Replacement Maritime Patrol Aircraft (RMPA) at £1.8 billion. Of the aircraft themselves, the airframes are to be completely rebuilt by Flight Refuelling Aviation at Bournemouth Hurn, under sub-contract to British Aerospace.

As part of this work, the existing engines will be replaced by BMW Rolls-Royce BR710s, rated at 15,500lb s.t., providing the Nimrod MR4 with a 30 per cent increase in thrust, while burning around 25 per cent less fuel. At the project's heart is the installation of Racal's Searchwater 2000MR radar and new mission management suite. Each aircraft conversion will take 15 months, with no more than six being rebuilt at any one time. Service entry date for the first Nimrod MR4 is set for 2002, with all being delivered by 2005/2006.

*An impression of the modernized BAe Nimrod MR4, set to enter service in 2002.*

## Boeing AWACS for Japan

*Seattle, August 9*
The first of four Boeing 767 AWACS, Airborne Warning And Control System aircraft with the distinctive, saucer-like 30 feet rotating radome above the aft fuselage made its maiden flight today. The foursome are set for delivery to Japan's Air Self-Defense Force. Previously, all Boeing AWACS had used the four- engined 707 airframe as the basis.

*The first of four Boeing 767 AWACS for Japan's Air Self-Defense Force.*

## Boeing buys Rockwell

*Seattle, August 15*
Today, Boeing announced the acquisition of Rockwell International's Space & Defense operations for around $3.2 billion today. Included in the package is much of the former North American Aviation and Space Division assets, including the B-1B bomber and the Space Shuttle, along with the large rocket motor, strategic missile and global positioning satellite business. The acquisition is expected to push Boeing's space and defense annual turnover to around $9 billion, or roughly one-third of their total annual business. While the acquisition will significantly strengthen Boeing's defense-related business, it still leaves the Seattle-based jetliner manufacturer as third-placed US defense supplier behind Lockheed Martin and McDonnell Douglas.

## More Super Lynx for German Navy

*Yeovil, England, September 30*
GKN Westland Helicopters announced the sale of seven Westland Super Sea Lynx Mk 88As to the German Navy to augment their existing 17 Sea Lynx Mk 88s. The placement of this contract reflects the now significant slippage apparent in the earliest operational deployment date for the Franco-German NH90 helicopter. Production of these new Lynx will start in 1997, with the first delivery being made in 1999. Discussions are currently underway with the German Navy relating to the refurbishment of the existing 17 machines to Mk 88A standard. This sale takes the overall Lynx series orderbook to over 370.

## Plug pulled on persistent interplanetary probe

*Villafranca, Spain, September 30*
As a result of the withdrawal of NASA support funding, scientists of the ESA reluctantly shut down their International Ultraviolet Explorer (IUE) space probe after nearly two decades of contributing to the world's astronomic knowledge. Launched on January 26, 1978, and only intended to function for three years, the 1,540-lb IUE carried a 17.5-in (45cm) UV telescope that witnessed many things from black holes and supernova to the impact of comet fragments on Jupiter.

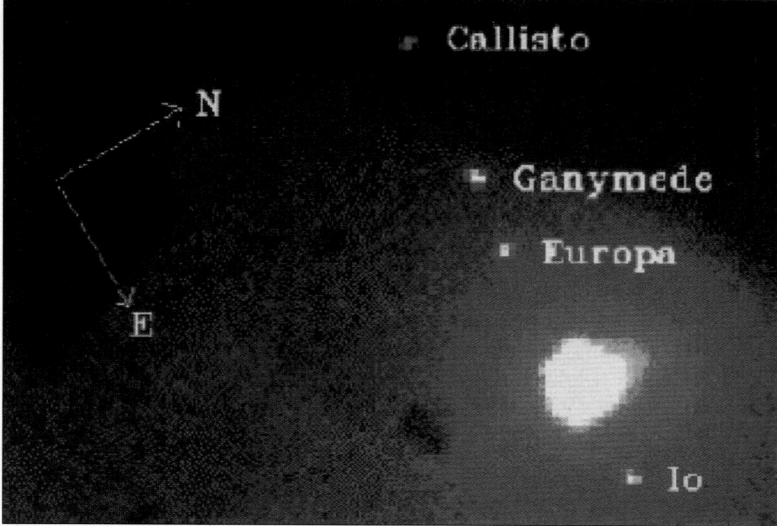

*Deep space imagery provided by the Ultraviolet Explorer.*

# Joint STARS arrives for European operations

*Specialist tactical analysts monitor target movements aboard JSTARS.*

*Rhein-Main , Germany, December 29*
Two highly-modified Boeing 707 radar platforms, 400 US Air Force personnel and some vehicles have arrived here and in the Balkans on detachment for a minimum of two to three months. Collectively known as the 4,500th Joint Stars Squadron (Provisional), the operation is spearheaded by two Northrop Grumman E-8 JSTARS, or Joint Surveillance and Target Attack System. Stuffed with very powerful and discriminating radars and other electro-optical sensors that feed their information to banks of equally impressive data processors, these E-8s and their crews are the airborne eyes, ears and brain of a system that gathers battlefield information and distributes it to the ground commanders virtually as it happens. To do this, the E-8s downlink their radar information to the dedicated JSTARS ground station vehicles, which provide the ground forces with an up-to-the-minute situation report of virtually anything that moves in the area under surveillance. Some idea of JSTARS capability can be gathered by the fact that an E-8 team can readily detect covert, slow vehicular movement from a height of 25,000 feet and distances in excess of 100 miles. Dispatched to aid NATO and allied troops in the former Yugoslavia, the E-8s operate their missions of up to 10 hours from southern Germany, passing their intelligence to ground station vehicles distributed around Bosnia and Croatia. The E-8 JSTARS was rushed into service during the 1991 Gulf War well before it had completed its assigned test program. However, its presence undoubtedly helped in the enormous task of directing the thousands of sorties flown every day and the massive movement of troops throughout the theater.

## Boeing buys out McDonnell Douglas

*Seattle and St Louis, December 15*
Philip Condit and Henry Stonecipher, the respective Chief Executive Officers of Boeing and McDonnell Douglas, today announced their agreement to merge the two corporations, with Boeing being the surviving entity. Thus, in one fell swoop, Boeing has now digested its only US jetliner manufacturing rival, while simultaneously acquiring a substantial fighter building and development capability centered around the F-15 Eagle and F/A-18 Hornet and Super Hornet programs. The estimated value of the deal is set at a staggering $13.3 billion and will bring about a combined payroll of around 200,000 employees, operating across 27 US states with estimated 1997 revenues in excess of $48 billion. Despite the extensive legal formalities that such a massive merger will involve, the actual integration of the two organizations could well occur as early as mid-1997.

## Mars Global Surveyor on its way

*Cape Canaveral, November 7*
NASA's Mars Global Surveyor spacecraft is boosted into space by a McDonnell Douglas Delta II. The Mars Global Surveyor is the first of two NASA space probes to be launched towards Mars in 1996, the other being the Mars Pathfinder. As its name implies, the Mars Global Surveyor will have the task of mapping the entire Martian surface. One of its primary missions is to establish whether water once flowed freely on the red planet, and whether there may stil be major deposits deep underground. The presence of water on Mars will give fresh impetus to plans, as yet tentative, to colonise the planet in the 21st century.

## Joint Strike Fighter contracts awarded

*Washington DC, November 16*
Today's Department of Defense announcement revealed that Boeing and Lockheed Martin have both won contracts worth $660 million to proceed into the Concept Demonstration Program (CDP) phase of the Joint Strike Fighter (JSF). McDonnell Douglas are dropped from the program. The JSF is aimed at providing an essentially common, affordable multi-service combat aircraft for the US Air Force, US Marines, US Navy and Royal Navy. The 51-month long CDP will see the two companies each build and flight test two aircraft, one with Conventional Take-Off and Landing (CTOL) characteristics for the USAF and USN, and the other with Short Take-Off and Vertical Landing (STOVL) performance to meet the USMC and RN requirements.

*Boeing's JSF STOVL proposal is proceeding to the demonstrator phase.*

The first of 34 Swiss-assembled F/A-18 Hornets, seen here against an Alpine background, successfully completed its first flight at Interlaken.

Computer problems having caused a three-month delay in the flight test schedule for the Lockheed Martin C-130J Hercules.

SAAB's first two-seat Gripen. The JAS 39A Gripen first became operational with the Royal Swedish Air Force in 1995.

With the delivery of the first A319 in April 1996, Swissair became the first airline to operate all three members of the single-aisle Airbus family.

The Kawasaki OH-X two-seat reconnaissance helicopter has formed part of the Japanese Ground Defence Force. Trials took place at Gifu, Japan.

The powerful Sukhoi Su-37, first flown on April 2, incorporates three-dimensional vectoring nozzles to provide extra air combat agility.

Grumman's Gulfstream V is the world's first ultra-long-range, large cabin business jet, with certification and deliveries expected in 1996.

*The Airbus A319 is powered by International Aero Engines V2524 turbofans. The A319 is the smallest aircraft in the Airbus family.*

*The Cessna 182S is the latest in the famous Cessna Skylane series of light two-seater touring aircraft.*

*The Bombardier Global Express completes a test flight of 2 hours 46 mins.*

*The Boeing Sikorsky KAH-64 Comanche attack helicopter.*

*Shown here in test phase with Mikoyan test pilot Roman Taskayev, the MiG-AT is designed to make its impact on the advanced jet trainer market.*

*On June 24, 1996 Raytheon delivered their 5,000th Beech King Air business turboprop, in this instance a model 300 for JeldWen of Oregon.*

*Seen here at Farnborough in September 1996, the Tupolev Tu-214 is the latest addition to Russia's domestic airliner fleet.*

*Yakovlev's Yak-130 military jet trainer seen here in trials with company test pilot Aleksandr Sinitsyn at the controls.*

*The first two-seat Eurofighter 2000 takes to the air for the first time. This is the first example to be assembled in Spain.*

4,534mph
USA
Pete Knight
North American X-15
Oct 3, 1967

24,987 miles
USA
Jeager and Rutan
Voyager
Dec 23, 1986

354,200ft
USA
Joseph Walker
North American X-15
Aug 22, 1963

1,120,370lb
USSR
Antonov
An-225 Mriya

84,000lb thrust
UK
Rolls Royce
Trent 884

**France and Seattle, January 8**
Figures published today show that during 1996 Airbus gained 326 firm orders, compared with an improved 559 firm orders for Boeing, the values of the two being put at $23.6 billion and $42.8 billion respectively. During the year, Airbus delivered 126 jetliners, while Boeing delivered 215.

**Detroit, Michigan, January 9**
All 29 aboard a Comair EMB-120 Brasilia are killed when it plunges from 4,000 feet.

**Bechar, Algeria, January 9**
Balloonist Per Lindstrand and Richard Branson, members of one of the teams attempting to circle the globe non-stop in hot air balloons, are forced to withdraw just over 20 hours into their flight as the *Virgin Global Challenger* develops a leak in its vital buoyancy-providing, hydrogen gas cell. The venture started at Marrakesh, Morocco (→ January 12).

**Marignane, France, January 11**
Eurocopter, the subsidiary of Aerospatiale and DASA, retains the crown of being the world's largest exporter of civil helicopters in 1996, with a total orderbook for the year – including military machines – of 228 helicopters. These comprise 29 Super Pumas/Cougars, 21 Dauphins/Panthers, 5 BK117s, 23 Bo105s, 18 EC135s, 23 AS355s and 109 AS350s.

**Sultanpur, India, January 20**
American millionaire Steve Fossett fails in his latest attempt to circumnavigate the Earth non-stop in his hot air balloon, *Solo Spirit*, but sets a new Absolute Distance record for balloons of 10,363 miles, having departed from St Louis, USA six days earlier, on January 14.

**Bangkok, Thailand, February 23**
Helicopters battle against strong winds to rescue 93 construction workers stranded on the roof of the blazing 36-storey President Towers in central Bangkok, which caught fire during building work.

**Darmstadt, Germany, March 17–19**
Today, the European Space Agency holds its second conference on the growing threat of space debris.

**Warton, England, April 4**
First flight of the first of 142 Panavia Tornado GR.4s, a major up-grade of the GR.1. At the controls were BAe Tornado Project Pilot, Graham Wardell, accompanied by Phil Compton acting as navigator (→ October 31).

**Marietta, Georgia, April 9**
Today saw the roll-out of the first of nine production Lockheed Martin/Boeing F-22A Raptor air dominance fighters. Two further airframes are to be built for static and fatigue testing.

**Savannah, Georgia, May 5**
Gulfstream Aerospace announce a United States Air Force contract, valued at $68.9 million, for two C-37As, a militarized version of the long-range Gulfstream V business jet. The C-37As will join the 89th Airlift Wing at Andrews Air Force Base, Maryland.

**Moscow, May 16**
Maiden flight of the Ilyushin Il-96T, the freighter version of the Il-96M passenger jetliner, which it precedes. Both the Il-96T and IL-96M are derivatives of the shorter fuselaged Il-96-300, but powered by four 37,000-lb s.t. Pratt & Whitney PW2337 turbofans.

**Bethesda, Maryland, May 8**
Lockheed Martin announce that Northrop Grumman, previously part of the losing McDonnell Douglas JSF submission, has now joined their JSF team.

**Edwards AFB, May 17**
First flight of the McDonnell Douglas X-36 tailless fighter technology demonstrator, power for which is provided by a 700lb s.t. Williams International F112 turbofan.

**Bunia, Zaire, June 6**
All 27 aboard die after a chartered Vickers Viscount crashes after pilot reports technical problems.

**Le Bourget, France, June 15**
Airbus use the 1997 Paris Air Show to announce the launch of their A319CJ, a corporate jet version of the basic A319 twin-engined jetliner. The A319CJ is being developed as a counter to Boeing's earlier BBJ.

**Australia, June 24**
The Australian Government place an order for 33 BAe Hawk 100s for use by the Royal Australian Air Force as lead-in fighter trainers for those student pilots destined to fly F/A-18 Hornets.

**Tokyo, June 26**
The Mitsubishi MH200 helicopter receives Japanese Type Certification, following an extnesive flight test program.

**Seattle, Washington, June 30**
Roll-out of the first Boeing 737-800. Capable of carrying up to 189 passengers, at 129.5ft this latest version is also the longest available to date. It also happens to be the 2,906th 737 to be built.

**Mars, July 4**
NASA's Mars Pathfinder, with its 22-lb rover buggy 'Sojourner', lands safely on the surface of Mars after its six-month journey from Earth.

**Seattle, Washington, July 31**
Boeing confirms delivery of all relevant merger documentation to the incorporating State of Maryland, and thus McDonnell Douglas ceases to be as of midnight.

**Miami Airport, August 7**
All four crew and four on the ground are killed when a Fine Air cargo DC-8 crashes just yards outside the airport.

**Moscow, September 25**
Today, saw the maiden flight of the Sukhoi S-37, the forward-swept winged, twin turbofan, supersonic fighter demonstrator.

**Moscow, October 30**
Sukhoi, who manufacture piston-engined single-seat aerobatic aircraft as well as supersonic combat jets, are now delivering their aerobatic Su-31M equipped with the new $35,000 SKS-94 lightweight ejection seat.

**Bonn, Germany, December 22**
The defense ministers of Germany, Italy, Spain and the United Kingdom have today sanctioned the go-ahead of production on the program for the Eurofighter 2000. The four participating nations have requirements for over 600 of the aircraft, and all seven development aircraft have now flown.

---

## Factfile

World revenue passenger miles: 1,555,000 million
World revenue passengers: 1,440 million
World air freight (ton miles): 63,000 million
Passengers through London (Heathrow/Gatwick): 84.6 million
Total airline employees: 2,101,033
Total jetliners employed: 11,722
Total turbo-prop liners employed: 4,034
Total piston engined liners employed: 926
Total scheduled service helicopters employed: 256
Average salary of long-haul pilot: $140,000
Average salary of cabin crew (US): $35,000
Price of 1,000 (US) gallons Jet A1 fuel: $760
Average exchange rate: £1=$1.66

*The first of the low-scale production Lockheed Martin/Boeing F-22A Raptor two-seat, air-dominance fighters.* ▶

# Fuel leak brings watery end to *Breitling Orbiter*

*Betrand Piccard and Vim Verstraeten shortly after take off, in the* Breitling Orbiter *hot air balloon used in the ill-fated round-the-world record attempt.*

*Off Montpellier, France, January 12*
Swiss psychiatrist and balloonist, Bertrand Piccard, and Vim Verstraeten, a Belgian balloonist, were compelled to ditch in the Mediterrean today while attempting to fly their *Breitling Orbiter* hot air balloon non-stop around the Earth. This happened only six hours into their flight. It appeared that the problem stemmed from a leak of kerosene, used to power the burners, that found its way into the pressurized gondola, leaving the pair sick and dazed. This incident comes just three days after balloonists Per Lindstrand and Richard Branson, another of the teams attempting to circle the globe in a hot-air balloon, were forced to withdraw from the contest after their *Virgin Global Challenger* developed a leak in its hydrogen gas cell, losing vital buoyancy (→ August 16, 1998).

## Bartered deal will help to build a Space Station

*Paris, March 7*
The European Space Agency (ESA) revealed today that some fairly sophisticated bartering took place two days ago concerning the International Space Station (ISS). In a heads of agreement between NASA and ESA, ESA will provide two essential additional ISS elements, known as Nodes 2 and 3, along with further high technology equipment in return for NASA launching ESA's Columbus Orbital Facility (COF) space laboratory, a part of the ISS, at no charge. The COF is due to be launched in late 2002.

## Cosmonaut nearly pulls the plug on Mir

*In Earth Orbit, July 17*
The three-man crew of the damaged Russian space station *Mir*, including Michael Foale, are plunged into a further crisis today with the unplugging of a wrong cable connection that sends the craft into a spin, while simultaneously further depleting energy vital to its life support systems

## When spacecraft collide

*NASA astronaut Dr Mike Foale.*

*In Earth Orbit, June 25*
*Mir*, Russia's space station launched in 1986, was today damaged in a collision with its Progress re-supply craft. British-born NASA astronaut Michael Foale and his two Russian colleagues, Valily Tsibliyev (*Mir*'s commander) and Alexander Lazutkin, are currently safe, but most of *Mir*'s systems are in shut-down mode. Dr Foale is not due to be relieved by another NASA astronaut until October when David Wolff is due to arrive. If the damage turns out to be worse than it now appears, a rescue mission may have to be launched sooner (→ July 17).

# Tilting into production

*Washington DC, April 28*
The US Department of Defense take delivery of the initial five production Bell Boeing V-22 Osprey tiltrotor convertiplanes for the US Marines. These machines are set to be followed by production of another five in 1998, seven in 1999 and eight in 2000, against a total US Marine requirement of 425 V-22s. The V-22 Osprey lies at the end of a long line of tiltrotor helicopters, more correctly called convertiplanes, whose development stretches back to the 1950s, and even beyond if some German wartime designs are to be taken into account. One promising design was the LTV XC-142A, a V/STOL tilt-wing military transport developed for use by all three US services by LTV, Hiller and Ryan. Five prototypes were built, the first flying on 29 September 1964. During the test program, the XC-142As carried out successful carrier trials, flew at speeds between 35 and 400mph and reached heights of up to 25,000 feet. Despite the aircraft's promise and versatility, it was expensive and the program was abandoned for economic reasons.

*Bell Boeing's V-22 Osprey tiltrotor convertiplane to be delivered to the marines.*

# Phones, fax and paging in space

*Vandenberg AFB, May 5*
The first five of an ultimate 66-satellite constellation of low Earth-orbit Iridium communication satellites were boosted into space aboard a McDonnell Douglas Delta II today. Planned for introduction into service in late 1998, the Iridium system should provide a space-based network that will permit voice, data, fax and paging to reach any part of the world.

# BAe to end Scottish aircraft production

*Farnborough, England, May 29*
In a further down-sizing of its loss-making civil aircraft activities, British Aerospace today announced that it will close down its Prestwick-based Jetstream Aircraft division at, or around, the end of this year. This step is likely to bring about the loss of 380 jobs out of the current 600 employed in Jetstream assembly. It was in 1993 that Jetstream 31 production ended, followed in 1995 by the closure of the Jetstream 61 (formerly ATP) line. This latest development brings aircraft production in Scotland to an end, although it is hoped that the 1,000 employed on aerostructure work at Prestwick will remain, while a further 150 to 200 people will be kept busy providing technical support for the existing Jetstream fleet.

## New British Airways designs annoy 'Iron Lady'

*A bold new image for BA.*

*London, June 10*
British Airways revealed a controversial £60 million corporate image revamp today that, among other things, involves the replacement of the existing stylized Union Jack flag on all BA's aircraft, except Concorde. In place of the national flag will appear a series of colorful ethnic art designs. At a preview of the new imagery, former Prime Minister Lady Thatcher made her feelings very clear by frowning and pointedly covering the fin of a nearby model Concorde with a tissue handkerchief.

## Around the world, Boeing 777-style

*Seattle, April 2*
A Boeing 777, powered by twin Rolls-Royce Trent 892 turbofans, returned here today to set a new Eastbound speed around the World record of 553mph. En route, the twinjet set a Great Circle distance without landing record of 12,455.34 miles when flying from Seattle to Kuala Lumpur, Malaysia.

## Airlifter resurrection

*Kiev, Ukraine, April 24*
The second Antonov An-70 four-prop-fan transport made its maiden flight today. The cash-strapped Russian Government agreed to fund support for the construction of a second example in the immediate wake of the first prototype's destruction following a mid-air collision on February 10, 1995. This support increases the likelihood that the An-70 will be selected as the Russian and Ukrainian replacement for the An-12, giving a home market potential of over 500 machines.

## Woman adds high-altitude hang gliding record to tally

*Wye Valley, England, September 10*
Judy Leden, Women's World Hang Gliding Champion, has added a seventh record to her tally by gaining a new altitude record of 16,800ft for two-place hang gliders. Hoisted aloft below a hot air balloon, Judy's companion on the flight was Lucy Armour, a registered blind person, who had only made one previous hang glider flight before today.

**Guam International Airport, Guam, August 6. Of the 254 aboard Korean Airlines' Boeing 747 flight KAL 801, 229 are killed when the airliner crashes into a hill on its approach to land.**

# Next-generation fighter comes closer

*Paul Metz boards the first F-22.*

*Marietta, USA, September 7*
A further milestone was reached today with the maiden flight of the first pre-production Lockheed Martin/Boeing F-22 Raptor. Accompanied by two F-16 'chase planes', the F-22 stayed aloft for just under an hour in the hands of F-22 Chief Test Pilot, Paul Metz. During the flight, Metz felt sufficently confident to fly close formation on one of the F-16s. Constructor's number 4001, this aircraft will continue its initial trials here at Dobbins AFB, prior to being transported to Edwards AFB for comprehensive performance testing in the spring of 1998, where it will be joined in mid-1998 by aircraft 4002. Service deliveries of the F-22 Raptor are set to begin in 2002. Powered by two 35,000-lb s.t. Pratt & Whitney F119-100 turbofans, which can vector their exhaust through a vertical range of plus-or-minus 20 degrees, this stealthy air dominance fighter – the successor to the McDonnell F-15 Eagle – can cruise at above Mach 1 and has already demonstrated its ability to achieve Mach 1.7 at 30,000 feet. As with all 'stealthy' aircraft, the F-22 necessarily carries both its defensive and offensive armament stowed internally to prevent tell-tale radar reflections. While the Raptor's primary hitting power comprises AMRAAM and Sidewinder air-to-air missiles, this single-seater is also equipped to carry a rapid-fire 20-mm Vulcan cannon.

**Denham, England, August 15** Jennifer Murray, a 56-year old grandmother, and her co-pilot, Quentin Smith land after completing a 97-day circumnavigation of the world in a four-seat Robinson R 44 helicopter. This is the first around the world piston-engined helicopter flight.

## International space station comes together

*Korolev, Russia, October 28*
The European Space Agency (ESA) today formally delivered the first flight computer hardware and software for the Russian Service Module of the International Space Station (ISS). This Data Management System performs the vital navigation and guidance function for the whole of the ISS, not only during its initial assembly phase, but also for the Russian module throughout its expected 10- to 15-year life. The ESA-supplied gear should be launched in a Russian Proton booster in December 1998.

## Long, longer, longest airliner yet from Boeing

*Seattle, September 8*
With an overall length of 242ft 4 in, the latest Boeing 777 version, the 777-300, is the longest jetliner yet and looks it, beating the 747-400 into second place by 10.5ft. This stretched twin jet can accommodate between 328 and 550 passengers, depending upon cabin layout. As of August 8, the company had announced orders for 323 Boeing 777s to 25 airlines, with deliveries of 85 already having been made to 13 carriers.

*Invited guests gather around the newly rolled-out Boeing 777-300.*

# NASA sends probe to explore Saturn

*An artists impression of the 5.5-ton Cassini-Huygens space probe.*

*Cape Canaveral, October 15*
Today, NASA launches a Titan IVB rocket carrying the Cassini-Huygens combination space probe, aimed at exploring the planet Saturn and its largest moon, Titan. For the 5.5-ton Cassini-Huygens probe, this is the start of a 932,055 million mile journey that will take seven years to complete. On arrival at Saturn, the ESA/Aerospatiale-built Huygens probe will part company from NASA's Cassini, to whose side it has previously clung, to plunge into the dense atmosphere of Titan. Having parted from its smaller relative, the Cassini spacecraft will then enter orbit around Saturn for the next four years, from where its sensors will study and relay data on the planet back to earth. If all goes well, the 772-lb parachute-braked Huygens will commence its descent through Titan's atmosphere in late November 2004, sampling and radioing data back during its retarded descent. It will hopefully survive for a few moments on the surface, long enough to provide information on Titan's surface make up.

# Latest from Sukhoi

*The Sukhoi S-37 Berkut (Golden Eagle) makes its appearance.*

**Moscow, September 25**
The first flight today of Sukhoi's forward-swept supersonic agile fighter demonstrator, the S-37, has brought Russian aircraft design to the cutting edge of technology. According to reports, design began in 1987. The S-37 originally had no tailplane, having shallow, broad, flat surfaces extending back from the wing trailing edge; these later developed into very narrow-span tailplanes. Russian sources have repeatedly denied that the S-37 is a fighter prototype, although a twin-engined version, thought to carry the designation S-237, is said to be under development. However, the Russian Air Force newspaper, *Red Star*, has stated that the project has zero priority for the Russian Air Force. Funds for the program, it appears, have been made available from foreign sales of the Su-27 Flanker air superiority fighter. First flight of the prototype was made from the Zhukovsky test establishment near Moscow. Major components of the aircraft, such as tailfins, canopy, windscreen and landing gear, appear to be common with those of the Su-27. The S-37, as yet, is not equipped with radar, weapons or mission systems, but there is provision for these to be fitted later.

# More Dassault Mirages in the desert

**Abu Dhabi, UAE, December 16**
The United Arab Emirates (UAE) awarded today Dassault Breguet a $2.9 billion contract to supply 30 Dassault Mirage 2000-9 fighters. To be delivered between 1998 and 2001, these machines, specifically tailored to UAE requirements, will replace the UAE Air Force's Dassault Mirage 5s. As part of the current deal, the UAE's existing fleet of 33 Mirage 2000-5s will be upgraded to the standard of the Mirage 2000-9.

*The UAE is the latest customer to buy Dassault Mirage 2000's.*

**Blagnac, France, November 3. US Airways places an order for 124 Airbus 320s and 319s, taking the manufacturer's order intake to 607 jetliners over the past 18 months. As well as the firm orders, the airline has already taken options on a further 276 A320-series delivery positions.**

# New Panavia Tornados for old

*The first of 142 refurbished RAF Tornado GR.4s is handed over to the RAF.*

**Warton, England, October 31**
The first of 142 RAF Panavia Tornados to be upgraded to GR.4 standard was today officially accepted from Mike Rouse, BAe's Managing Director, by Air Chief Marshal Sir Richard Johns, Chief of Air Staff of the Royal Air Force. At the heart of the GR.4 upgrade are a series of significant improvements to the aircraft's sensors, computers and weapons systems, including the addition of a Forward Looking Infra-Red (FLIR) system, better cockpit displays and the ability to carry a greater range of weapons. These will include the British Aerospace Sea Eagle for antishipping operations, a role assumed by the Tornado since the last Buccaneers were withdrawn from service in 1993, the Sidewinder AAM for self-defence. The mid-life update now under way, to be completed by the end of 2002, will also give the Tornado GR.4 the capability to carry advanced weapons such as the Brimstone anti-armor weapon and the Storm Shadow stand-off attack missile.

*The CASA C-295 prototype tactical transport, pictured on its maiden flight. The C-295 is the latest in a long line of CASA transports.*

*The MiG-29SMT is to form the basis for ongoing upgrades to meet the requirements of potential customers worldwide.*

*Latest offspring of the Artem I. Mil design bureau is the formidable Mi-28 attack helicopter, seen here on its first flight.*

*The US Navy's newest strike fighter, the McDonnell Douglas F/A18E/F Super Hornet, pictured on board the aircraft carrier USS John C. Stennis.*

*Seen here taking off on its first flight is the new-generation Boeing 737-700. The new 737s will fly higher, faster and farther than existing models.*

*Millionaire Steve Fossett begins his second try at a non-stop flight around the globe in his STL02 balloon Solo Spirit on January 13.*

*The Ilyushin Il-96T is the freighter version of the Il-96M passenger jetliner. Both are powered by Pratt & Whitney turbofans.*

*The first flight of a second prototype Antonov An-70. This aircraft has suffered considerable delays due to Russian lack of finances.*

*The AASI JetCruzer brings a new dimension to executive air travel.*

*The Aero L159 was developed under a Czech Air Force contract.*

*'Action Man' was one of the more bizarre and inventive hot air balloon designs produced by Cameron Balloons in 1997.*

*By mid-1997, Airbus Industrie was able to offer customers three different versions of its single-aisle Airbus family, the A319, A320 and A321.*

*The first Lockheed Martin F-22 Raptor, seen at its roll-out ceremony at Lockeed Martin Aeronautical Systems, Marietta, in April 1997.*

*The Grob G115TA advanced trainer has generated huge interest. It was first delivered to the United Arab Emirates AF early in 1997.*

*The latest Eurofighter prototype DA5, is equipped with the new EJ200 engines and ECR90 radar.*

*The Malaysian Airlines' Boeing 777-200 that set new World Distance and Speed records on the Seattle-Kuala Lumpur-Seattle route in June 1997.*

*The Hughes 500 helicopter of the type used by Good and Smith to circumnavigate the globe in a journey covering 19,800 miles.*

4,534mph
USA
Pete Knight
North American X-15
Oct 3, 1967

24,987 miles
USA
Jeager and Rutan
Voyager
Dec 23, 1986

354,200ft
USA
Joseph Walker
North American X-15
Aug 22, 1963

1,120,370lb
USSR
Antonov
An-225 Mriya

84,000lb thrust
UK
Rolls Royce
Trent 884

**Ottawa, Canada, January 5**
The Canadian Government orders 15 European Helicopter Industies EH 101 Cormorant helicopters for search and rescue (SAR) duties.

**Seattle, Washington, January 8**
Boeing bring the McDonnell Douglas MD-95 into their family of jetliners by renaming it the Boeing 717-200. The non-stop range of this 100-passenger twin is up to 2,230 miles and the first is set for delivery to AirTran Airlines (formerlyValuejet) in June 1999.

**Northern Australia, January 28**
A Bristow Helicopters' Eurocopter Super Puma, being operated in the area on behalf of BHP Petroleum, lifts a total of 43 people, comprising two crew and 41 women and children flood victims during one emergency rescue flight. The normal Super Puma complement is two crew, plus 18 passengers. Even with all these people aboard, the helicopter was still being flown within its maximum permissable payload limits.

**Stansted, England, January 30**
Launch of Go, British Airways' subsidiary low-fare airline. To be equipped with Boeing 737s, Go is expected to commence operations in the spring.

**Munich, Germany, January 30**
Today, the NATO Eurofighter and Tornado Management Agency, the industrial group, Eurofighter Jagdflugzeug GmbH, and Eurojet GmbH sign contracts covering the production and maintenance of 620 Eurofighter aircraft and 1,500 EJ 200 turbofan engines.

**Tarbes, France, March 3**
Today saw the first flight of the Socata/Renault TB 20 powered by new a Renault MR200 diesel engine.

**Seattle, Washington, March 11**
The first two of four Boeing E-767 airborne warning and control systems (AWACS) aircraft were officially handed over to the Japanese Air Self-Defense Force.

**Dayton, USA, March 13**
Hans von Ohain, an aircraft propulsion engineer and contemporary of Britain's Sir Frank Whittle, dies.

**The Hague, Netherlands, April 7**
The Dutch Government selects the McDonnell Douglas Helicopters AH-64D Longbow Apache as its new attack helicopter, of which 30 will be bought for operations with the Dutch Air Mobile Brigade.

**Seattle, Washington, May 21**
First Boeing 777-300 was delivered today. This aircraft is the first of six ordered by Cathay Pacific. To date, the total 777 orderbook stands at 392 aircraft.

**Sao Jose dos Campos, Brazil, July 4**
First flight of the EMBRAER ERJ-135 regional jet. The ERJ-135 is some 11.6 feet shorter than the earlier ERJ-145 from which it derives, giving it a cabin capacity of 37 seats.

**Coral Sea, Pacific Ocean, August 16**
After taking off from Mendoza, Argentina, on August 7, Steve Fossett lands his *Solo Spirit 3* hot air balloon on the wrong side of the Pacific in the Chesterfield Reef and is unable to gain the accolade of being the first balloonist to fly non-stop around the world. However, as is getting routine with his flights, he sets a new Absolute Distance record for balloons of 14,239 miles (→ March 21, 1999).

**Patuxent River, USA, August 20**
Navy Air Test Center trials with the Bell-Boeing V-22 Osprey set a new unofficial world record when the tilt-rotor convertiplane flies at 220 knots, carrying a large underslung load of 10,000lb.

**Blagnac, France, August 25**
British Airways places the biggest Airbus contract ever from a non-US airline with orders and options for 188 of the A320 family of single-aisle jetliners. To be delivered over the next seven years, 59 are firm orders, while the other 129 are optioned. All of the airliners are to be powered by the IAE V2500 turbofan engine.

**London, England, September 2**
The name Typhoon is to be given to Eurofighter aircraft sold into export markets from 2002.

**Irkutsk, Siberia, September 25**
First flight of the twin-turbofan Beriev Be-200 amphibious flying boat. It is designed for aerial fire-fighting, among other roles.

**Warton, England, September 28**
The last of 974 Panavia Tornados is delivered today. While this concludes the production of new aircraft, the Warton-based Tornado facility will be kept occupied until early 2003 at least carrying out major upgrading programs on both strike and fighter versions operated by the RAF.

**Gardermoen, Norway, October 7**
King Harald of Norway officially opens Oslo's new airport. The airport, with the capacity to handle up to 17 million passengers a year, has caused controversy thanks to its being sited almost 32 miles from Oslo, some 26 miles further away than the old airport.

**Hamburg, Germany, October 17**
The First Airbus A319 is delivered; it is also the initial A319 ordered by US Airways as part of the 276 Airbus aircraft contract placed by the airline. This is the biggest single order in civil aviation history.

**Seattle, Washington, October 29**
Boeing's BBJ business jet receives Type Certification jointly from the US FAA and European JAA. Boeing holds orders for 56 BBJs.

**Seattle, Washington, November 3**
Boeing and British Airways mark the delivery of the airline's 50th Boeing 747-400 with a further seven set for delivery by April 1999. To date, the company has delivered 448 Boeing 747-400s.

**St Louis, Missouri, November 9**
First flight of the first production Boeing F/A-18E Super Hornet. The single seat 'E' model is backed up by a two-seat operational trainer version, carrying the 'F' suffix.

**County Durham, England, Dec 18**
The pilot of an RAF BAe Harrier GR7 is killed after his aircraft hits overhead power lines.

**Yeovil, England, December 24**
First flight of a production European Helicopter Industries EH 101 Merlin HC 3 for the RAF.

**Huambo, Angola, December 26**
Fourteen United Nations personnel are feared killed when their Lockheed C-130 is shot down by rebels.

## Factfile

World revenue passenger miles: 1,655,000 million
World revenue passengers: 1,480 million
World air freight (ton miles): 70,000 million
Passengers through London (Heathrow/Gatwick): 89.3 million
Total airline employees: 1,620,968
Total jetliners employed: 12,055
Total turbo-prop liners employed: 4,098
Total piston engined liners employed: 880
Total scheduled service helicopters employed: 291
Average salary of long-haul pilot: $145,000
Average salary of cabin crew (US): $35,500
Price of 1,000 (US) gallons Jet A1 fuel: $336
Average exchange rate: £1=$1.69

*An image of Boeing's 'Next Generation 737' family with the 737-600 leading the formation, followed by the 737-700 and 737-800.* ▶

# France and Germany unleash Tiger

*Berlin, Germany, May 20*
French and German Defense Ministers, Jean-Yves Helmer and Gunnar Simon, today signed a Memorandum of Understanding giving the go-ahead for the Franco-German Tiger combat helicopter. Developed by Eurocopter, the initial production batches will comprise 80 each for the two countries with deliveries from 2001. The total program requirement is 215 Tigers for the French Army, while the German Army needs 212. The Tiger twin-engined anti-tank and ground support helicopter has been under development since 1985, when Eurocopter GmbH was formed by France and Germany for the purpose of developing a common combat helicopter. The program has been subjected to

*Eurocopter's Tiger gets the production go-ahead from the partner governments.*

considerable delay, mainly because of German funding constraints. Eurocopter was previously teamed with British Aerospace Defence Dynamics Division in a bid to provide 91 combat helicopters for the British Army at a cost of £25 billion, the UK Government considering full membership of the Tiger programme, but in July 1995 Tiger was rejected in favour of the AH-64A Apache.

## New German JETS

*Berlin, Germany, May 19*
Fairchild Dornier used the venue of this year's Schonefeld Air Show to launch a new family of 55- to 100-seat regional jets, their planned 528-JET and 928JET, based on their proposed 728JET low-wing, 70 to 75 passenger design. Using the generally accepted practice of either inserting or removing sections of an aircraft's circular cross-sectioned fuselage, Fairchild Dornier are offering an abbreviated 55 passenger 528JET for initial delivery in mid-2002 – along with a stretched 928JET, with a capacity for between 80 and 100 passengers, available from mid-2003. Knowing that the market is well-served by Canadair and EMBRAER, Fairchild Dornier are promoting their 'wide-body' cabin width of 11ft 2in as a prime feature.

# Giant Global Hawk takes to the skies

*The robot Ryan RQ-4A Global Hawk.*

*Edwards AFB, USA, February 28*
A wide-winged robot took to the skies today with the maiden flight of the first of two prototype Teledyne Ryan RQ-4A Global Hawk unmanned air vehicles (UAV). The Global Hawk is being developed to fulfil the same type of high altitude, long-range reconnaissance missions currently being flown by manned Lockheed U-2s. As a

vehicle, the RQ-4A is impressive enough, 2ft shorter than the AV-8B Plus Harrier II. Using a mix of composite-clad aluminum fuselage structure, married to all-composite materials for wings and tail surfaces and powered by a single Rolls-Royce Allison AE3007H turbofan, the Global Hawk's mission is to carry a 1,900-lb package of extremely effective sensors over a distance of 6,400 nautical miles. At mid-point, a 24-hour loiter at 65,000 feet is possible from where it can monitor an area of 40,000 square miles. For this, the RQ-4A has a take-off weight of 25,600lb, of which 14,500lb is fuel! Testing of this unmanned aircraft will be exhaustive, as the Global Hawk needs to show its ability to mix safely with both military and civil aircraft en route.

# Famed test pilot Tony LeVier dies, aged 84

*Top gun – Tony LeVier.*

*Los Angeles, California, February 8*
Anthony W. 'Tony' LeVier, former Lockheed, California Division test pilot died today. Tony LeVier had made his mark in US air racing circles during the late 1930s, prior to joining Lockheed in April 1941 as a ferry pilot. By 1942 he had moved into the company's Flight Test Department and stayed to retire as Director of Flying Operations in 1974. LeVier logged 20 prototype first flights, including those of the TF-80 (T-33) trainer, XF-94 Starfire, XF-104 Starfighter and U-2 spyplane. He survived eight crashes, along with a mid-air collision.

# From the voice of God into the hands of the law

*Salisbury, England, March 12*
John Holme, a computer software sales manager and lay evangelist preacher, was fined £1,050 plus £250 costs at Salisbury Magistrates Court this week for flying too close to a populated area and straying into the air space above an airfield. Holmes had embarked upon this, his first unsupervised flight of his foot-launched, motorized paravane on August 8, 1997, after only two training lessons. Hoping to emulate the 'voice of God', the confident salesman launched himself aloft, aiming to overfly a local council

estate, booming his message down through a megaphone he was carrying with him. Only once he was aloft did the inexperienced airman realize he had not quite grasped the basics of flying his paravane, and he spent a frightening initial 15 minutes flying between the houses, rather than over them. Perhaps, one of the most surprising facts to emerge from the proceedings was that, in Britain, it is perfectly legal to strap on one of these motorized, glorified parachutes and go flying, without any form of training or licence.

# Space station 'lifeboat' test launched

*Edwards AFB, USA, March 12*
The first of three NASA Johnson-devised, Scaled Composites-built X-38 Crew Return Vehicles (CRV) underwent its first free, unpowered flight, when dropped from beneath its Boeing NB-52 motherplane today. Although all went well initially, the test ended dramatically when the parafoil – which forms no

part of the definitive X-38, but is used to recover these first-phase, non-space going craft – was ripped away by greater than expected turbulence during opening. The second phase will involve building a space-going demonstrator to be 'piggy-backed' into orbit within the cargo hold of a Space Shuttle early in the next decade.

# RAF goes non-nuclear

*London, April 1*
To coincide with the 80th Anniversary of the Royal Air Force's foundation, it was confirmed today that the RAF's stockpile of several hundred WE.177 freefall tactical nuclear weapons, carried by the Panavia Tornado GR 1, are to be withdrawn from front-line service with immediate effect. This leaves the Royal Navy's submarine launched Trident missiles as Britain's sole nuclear deterrent.

The 950lb WE.177B freefall retarded bomb has been the RAF's standard tactical nuclear weapon since the 1970s, and was deployed with the Vulcan squadrons assigned to SACEUR after these assumed a tactical role. Before that, the RAF mostly used tactical nuclear weapons of American origin, the Mk 7 or Mk 43; the exception was the British-designed 'Red Beard', which armed the RAF's Canberra B(I)6 aircraft.

# Programed to self destruct

*Paris, May 18*
The European Space Agency revealed today that its Infra-red Space Observatory (ISO) switched itself off two days ago, as it had been instructed to do. ISO was also programed to alter its orbit in such a way as to ensure that it will burn up and self destruct on re-entering the atmosphere some 20 days from now. During its 10-month operating life ISO had made more than 26,000 observations, including analysing Comet Hale-Bopp's tail, and probing far into the depths of the universe to view the remnants of supernova and the dusty precursors of stars and planets.

# Russian airlines drastically reduced

*Moscow, January 16*
In a statement indicative of the poor state of the Russian economy, Ivan Valov, first deputy head of the Russian Aviation Service, announced plans to improve safety and service by cutting the number of Russian airlines from the current 315 to 53. Valov revealed that many of the so-called 'babyflots' that sprang up following the end of Aeroflot's monopoly in 1992 have been poorly operated and under-resourced financially. Valov stated that in 1997, while 36 new airlines had commenced operations, 65 existing airlines had become bankrupt.

**Munich, Germany, January 23. Eurofighter milestone. Eurofighter 2000 has passed its 500th flight test hour, with seven development aircraft now having amassed 570 flights. Other milestones achieved include reaching Mach 2.0, proving its air-to-air refueling capability, carriage of external fuel tanks and missile launching.**

# Texan II trainer takes off for testing

*Raytheon's first production T-6A Texan II gets airborne on its maiden flight.*

*Wichita, Kansas, July 15*
Still in its primer finish and wearing a US civil registration, the first production Raytheon T-6A Texan II made its first appearence over Kansas today, with a maiden flight that provided no surprises for experimental test pilot, Bob Newsom. Winner of the Joint Primary Aircraft Training System (JPATS) program, initial deliveries of the T-6A are set to be made to the US Air Force's Randolph AFB in April 1999, followed by the first for the US Navy in 2002. One reason why the aircraft currently wears civil markings is that, besides carrying out its normal military qualification testing, the machine is also being used to gain civil US Federal Aviation Administration (FAA) Type Certification which, in the future, will open the door for export sales.

# Prototype Proteus is built for special missions

*The curiously shaped Rutan-designed Scaled Composites 281 Proteus.*

*Mojave, USA, July 26*
A creation from the fertile mind of Burt Rutan, the Multi-role twin jet, twin-boomed fuselage Scaled Composites 281 Proteus made its maiden flight. Designed for high-altitude, long-duration flight today, the Proteus has accommodation for a pilot and relief pilot in its pressurized cabin, enabling it to conduct atmospheric research, reconnaissance/ surveillance, or act as a orbiting relay link for area, rather than continental-coverage mobile telephone systems. With two 2,293-lb s.t. Williams FJ44-2 turbofans as propulsion, the Proteus is capable of loitering for up to 14 hours at an altitude of around 61,000 feet over an area of some 1,000 nautical miles.

# Undaunted aerobatic champion

*Huddersfield, England, September 30*
Company director and pilot John Askew is in a wheelchair and will be for the rest of his life, the result of a horse-riding accident in 1994. Determined that his disability was a challenge, not a millstone, John went to work to prove the point. Already the holder of a Private Pilot's Licence, John first had to retake his licence in the light of his injury, then started looking around for something a little more adventurous than his old Beagle Pup. His eyes fell upon a Yakovlev Yak-52, a 360-hp fully aerobatic two-seater. The Yak was modified so that John could control the rudder by hand, rather than foot, and John set off to show the world just what they could do. Some measure of John's success can be seen in his treasure chest of trophies won this year.

*The wheelchair-bound John Askew and his Yakovlev Yak-52.*

Among these are the 'Shaggy Cow' Trophy, awarded to the Yak pilot with the highest total points scored during the season, and the Standard-level British National Aerobatic Championship Cup.

# Through the Boeing looking glass

*Nebraska, September 25*
The last five Boeing EC-135 Looking Glass strategic airborne command and control posts flown by the US Air Force were today officially retired after almost 40 years in service. Their mission is now being flown by US Navy Boeing E-6B Mercurys. Ironically, the service provider may have changed, but the EC-135 and the E-6B are variations on the basic Boeing 707 airframe.

# Boeing offers the ultimate, luxurious executive toy

*Seattle, Washington, September 4*
The BBJ, or Boeing Business Jet makes its first flight today. A luxuriously customized version of the Boeing 737-700, the BBJ cruises at up to Mach 0.82, or around 550mph over distances of up to more than 6,000 miles. If your pocket can take it, the price tag for a BBJ which has been styled to your liking is put at between $40 million and $45 million.

**Wichita, USA, August 19. Raytheon roll-out their first Premier I bizjet amid a carnival atmosphere. The six-passenger Premier I is the smallest of Raytheon's range of business jets.**

# International space station begins to take off

*Paris, France, November 24*
The European Space Agency (ESA) placed contracts today with Aerospatiale and Daimler Chrysler Aerospace (DASA) to develop and build eight to 12 Automated Transfer Vehicle (ATV) space transporters, designed to re-supply the International Space Station (ISS). As prime contractor, Aerospatiale will be responsible for design and development, while manufacture of the ATVs will take place at DASA's Bremen facility. The first of a planned 45 missions to assemble the ISS was succesfully executed four days ago with the launch of a Russian-built Proton launcher from Baikonur, Kazakhstan carrying 'Zarya', the Russian-supplied control module that forms the first element of the ISS.

# South Africa selects SAAB's Gripen

*South Africa, November 18*
The South African Air Force announced today that they will buy 28 SAAB JAS 39 Gripens – the first export order for the Swedish fighter – and 24 BAe Hawk trainers from British Aerospace. Delivery of the first fighters is set to occur in 2002. GKN Westland are to supply four Super Lynx 300 helicopters for the Navy. Delivery of the first fighters is set to begin in 2002, with both the Gripens and Hawks being supplied by BAe, who are acting on SAAB's behalf as prime contractor to the South African Government. As well as fighter aircraft and naval helicopters, this massive arms deal involves the supply of battle tanks and patrol craft.

*SAAB's JAS 39 Gripen.*

# Baby business jet for beginners

*Wichita, Kansas, December 22*
The prototype Raytheon Premier I twin-engined light business jet rolled out in August, made its maiden flight today, lasting 62 minutes. The Premier 1 is described as an 'entry-level' business jet, meaning that it is aimed directly at the corporate user who is stepping up from using a turboprop, or piston-engined aircraft into the jet category. Powered by two 2,300-lb s.t. Williams FJ44-2A turbofans, the Premier 1 can accommodate up to six passengers, in addition to its single- or two-pilot crew. Its range, with single pilot and four passengers, is cited as 1,500 nautical miles. To expedite certification flight testing, Raytheon will employ four fully production-representative aircraft. Currently, Raytheon hold orders for over 140 Premier Is.

# From Douglas DC-9 to Boeing 717

*Long Beach, California, September 2*
The first flight of Boeing's 717-200 short-haul jetliner today lasted four hours and seven minutes. At the controls were Captains Ralph Luczak and Tom Melody. Departing from Long Beach, California, the aircraft landed at Yuma, Arizona, where it will be joined by three more 717s to complete a nine-month flight test and Type Certification program. Deliveries of the 717 are set to begin in the third quarter of 1999 to launch customer AirTran, who hold orders for 50, with a further 50 options. The aircraft, with a cabin capacity for up to 106 passengers, had previously been known as the McDonnell Douglas MD 95, and is a development of the 1960s-vintage Douglas DC-9. It is powered by two 18,500-lb s.t. BMW Rolls-Royce BR715 turbofans.

*The first Boeing 717-200 climbs out from Long Beach on its maiden flight.*

**Vero Beach, August 21. First flight of Piper's seven-place Malibu Meridian. Powered by a 400-shp Pratt & Whitney PT6A-42A, it competes with the Pilatus PC-12 and Socata TBM 700.**

# Splashdown for European day tripper

*Kourou, French Guiana, October 21*
Today, Ariane 503, the third of Europe's massive launcher vehicles, behaved impeccably, launching the ARD capsule and Maqsat 3 mock-up satellite it was carrying into orbit. ARD stands for Atmospheric Re-entry Demonstrator, a prototype for a European re-entry vehicle. On release it also flew successfully, splashing down in the Pacific, between the Marquises Islands and Hawaii, 1 hour 43 minutes after the launch. ARD, similar in size and configuration to the earlier US-developed Gemini capsule, was retrieved by the French Navy vessels, *Revi* and *Pereal*.

# Lt-Col Robert 'Bob' Johnson dies

*Tulsa, Oklahoma, December 27*
Lt-Col Robert 'Bob' Johnson died today, aged 78. With 28 confirmed 'kills', Bob Johnson was joint top-scoring US fighter ace in the European theater of World War II, sharing honors with Lt-Col Francis Gabreski. Johnson was another one of the many US fighter aces who built their score flying with the Republic P-47D Thunderbolt-equipped 56th Fighter Group. He initiated his victory tally on June 13, 1943 and concluded it just a little under 11 months later, with two 'kills' on May 8, 1944. As a youth in his home town of Lawton, Oklahoma, Johnson worked in a cabinet-making shop for just four dollars a week, one-third of which went to pay for a 15-minute flying lesson every Sunday morning. Thirty-nine dollars and six and a half hours' flying time later he made his first solo flight, and he joined the US Army Air Corps in November 1941 as an aviation cadet. He was a natural pilot, but in other subjects he came close to failure, and at one point he was almost transferred to twin-engined aircraft to train as a bomber pilot. But he worked hard to remedy his deficiencies, and eventually applied successfully to train on single-engined fighters.

*'Bob' Johnson and his P-47,* Lucky.

*Sailors from the French Navy recover the ARD from the Pacific Ocean.*

# International space station plugged together

*Cape Canaveral, December 15*
Space Shuttle *Endeavour* today returned after carrying 'Unity', the first US supplied element of the International Space Station. 'Unity' and 'Zarya', the first Russian element, were mated on December 6. During the rendezvous, two astronauts made three space walks, totalling 21 hours 22 minutes over a five-day period, making 40 different electrical and data connections. ▷

*A neat formation of GKN Westland Merlin HC Mk 3 helicopters. The first RAF squadron to equip with this range is No 28.*

*Boeing brought the McDonnell Douglas MD-95 into their family of Jetliners by renaming the aicraft the Boeing 717-200.*

*The Europa homebuilt kit plane can be fitted with either standard wings or glider wings, the latter fitted with trailing edge airbrakes.*

*The first production Augusta Heliliner pictured here in the livery of the Tokyo Metropolitan Police who use this helicopter effectively.*

*Chief Test Pilot Paul Metz is the first to fly Raptor 4002, the second Lockheed Martin-Boeing F-22. He takes it for a spin over northern Georgia.*

*Twenty five of the formidable twin jet strike fighters Boeing (McDonnell) F-15I Eagles have been ordered by the Israel Air Force.*

*One of Boeing's 'Next Generation 737' jet airliners . All of this series use a new and larger wing, along with a more powerful -7 version of the CFM 56 engine.*

*The curiously designed Rutan Scaled Composites 281 Proteus is built for high-altitude, long-duration flight.*

*Over 500 of de Havilland Canada's sleek Dash-8 regional airliner had been sold by mid-1998.*

*First flown on January 28, the Fairchild Dornier 328JET is aimed at the lucrative short-range commuter-jet market.*

*The Boeing 757-300 lifts off for its maiden flight on August 2. By the end of June 1998 Boeing had received orders for 920 757s.*

*The new Sikorsky S-92 helicopter. The helicopter will assure rapid point-to-point air links.*

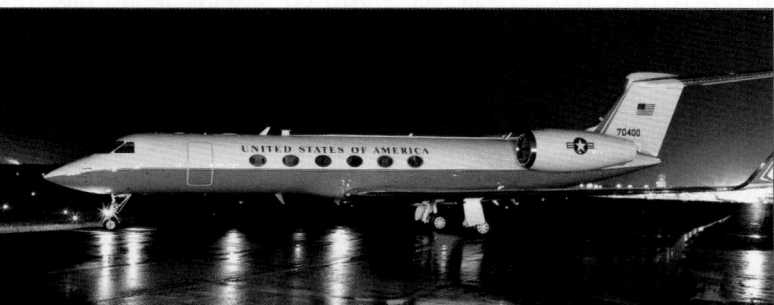

*Latest in the Gulfstream line, the Gulfstream V's military version, the C-37A, was delivered to the USAF in 1998. The aircraft has a variety of applications.*

*The Kamov Ka-60 multi-purpose helicopter can carry up to 16 infantry troops or six stretchers and three attendants.*

# 1999

4,534mph
USA
Pete Knight
North American X-15
Oct 3, 1967

24,987 miles
USA
Jeager and Rutan
Voyager
Dec 23, 1986

354,200ft
USA
Joseph Walker
North American X-15
Aug 22, 1963

1,120,370lb
USSR
Antonov
An-225 Mriya

84,000lb thrust
UK
Rolls Royce
Trent 884

**Cape Canaveral, January 3**
NASA's Mars Polar Lander (MPL) is launched aboard a Boeing Delta II booster. The MPL is scheduled to touch down in the Martian southern polar region in December.

**Cape Canaveral, January 21**
The first space launch of 1999 takes place using an Atlas II booster to launch the US Air Force DCCS III B8 satellite into orbit.

**Kourou, French Guinea, January 24**
Arianespace uses a Ariane 42L booster to place PanAmSat's large Galaxy XR communications satellite into geostationary Earth orbit.

**Avalon, Australia, February 16**
British Aerospace use the Australian Air Show as the platform to announce the conditional launch of their Avro RJX. This long-awaited BAe 146 derivative is to be powered by four 7,000-lb s.t. Allied Signal AS977-1A turbofans and will have the same range of cabin layouts as the Avro RJ family.

**Moscow, Russia, March 9**
First flight of Sukhoi Su-30MKK, Su-27 with thrust vectoring deleted (advanced strike variant for China).

**Edwards AFB, USA, March 29**
One of the two Ryan RQ-4A Global Hawk unmanned reconnaissance vehicles is destroyed in a crash at China Lake Naval Air Station. The more than $13 million unmanned air vehicle carries a suite of synthetic aperture radar, infrared and electro-optical sensors, the output from which is sent back to base via US military communications satellites.

**Meza, USA, March 30**
Today Boeing delivered the 1,000th AH-64 Apache combat helicopter. Apaches, in service with the US Army over the past 15 years, have played a prominent part in operations as far apart as Bosnia and Korea. It fell to the Apache to fire the first US shots in Operation Desert Storm, when it flew against Iraqi troops occupying Kuwait.

**Chicago O'Hare Airport, April 1**
Three hundred passengers aboard a Korean Air Boeing 747-400 escape death by a reported 25 feet when their pilot, with barely sufficent flying speed, hauls the huge jetliner aloft, banking to the right in an effort to avoid colliding with an Air China cargo Boeing 747F. The freighter had got into the airliner's path by taking the wrong taxiway.

**Long Beach, California, April 10**
First flight of first Boeing MD-10 freighter conversion, commencing a 10-month flight test program.

**Australia, April 14**
A taxing Boeing 737 was badly damaged by hailstones measuring up to more than 1.5in.

**Lanseria, South Africa, April 22**
All 66 aboard a Boeing 727 approaching to land at Johannesburg survived an encounter with a severe hailstorm, although on landing safely, the jetliner was declared a 'write-off'.

**Moscow, April 29**
First flight of Sukhoi Su-27KUB (Su-33B) tandem-seat carrier-going combat trainer.

**Northern Albania, May 5**
Today, the leading Boeing AH-64 Apache of a five-helicopter training flight suddenly rears up, rolls to the right and hits the ground, killing both crew members.

**Arlington, May 14**
The first production Bell Boeing MV-22B Osprey tilt-rotor completes its acceptance test flight today and is handed over to the US Marine Corps, who will ultimately have 360 Ospreys.

**Sao Jose dos Campos, Brazil, May 22**
Maiden flight of EMBRAER EMB-145SA, or Airborne Early Warning and Control (AEW & C) variant, five of which have been ordered for delivery to the Greek Air Force starting in June 2001.

**Hamburg, Germany, May 25**
First flight of Airbus A319-133X ACJ, or Airbus Corporate Jet, airliner-sized business jet.

**Ottobrun, Germany, May 31**
First flight of NH Industries NH-90 TTH, the tactical transport version of this multi-role helicopter.

**Little Rock, USA, June 1**
Eleven of 145 aboard an American Airlines' MD-80 die when the jetliner overruns the runway in a night landing, breaks up and burns. NTSB suspect fatigue, as the crew had been on duty for 13.5 hours.

**Lobutu, Zaire, August 17**
The crew of a De Havilland Canada Twin Otter are uninjured after the pilot misidentified the section of road he uses as a landing strip, shearing off the wings when he landed between embankments.

**Arizona, USA, September 29**
First flight of Groen Hawk 4 gyroplane after 13 years of development.

**Shanghai, China, October 4**
Maiden flight of first Chinese-built McDonnell Douglas MD-90-30 TrunkLiner.

**London, October 5**
The British Ministry of Defence merge all Army, Royal Navy and RAF attack and support helicopters under a new Joint Helicopter Command.

**Subic Bay, Philippines, October 17**
A FedEx MD-11 freighter overruns the runway, falling into the sea. The crew members are slightly injured but the tri-jet is demolished.

**Paris, October 18**
In the wake of the formation of the Franco-German EADS Company, its two partners, together with Britain's Marconi Electronics Systems, agree to form Astrium; who will become Europe's largest space company with a workforce of 8,000.

**Czech Republic, October 20**
First flight of Aero L-159A Advanced Light Combat Aircraft fitted with its new F124 turbofan.

**Berlin, October 20**
First flight of 'Joey', an eighth scale model of the CargoLifter CL-160 airship.

**Pristina, Kosovo, November 12**
All are killed, including US Assistant Secretary of Defense, when a UN-chartered ATR42 impacts a ridge.

**Stanstead, England, December 22**
All four aboard a Korean Air Boeing 747 freighter are killed in a crash soon after take-off as a result of EFIS, or Electronic Flight Instrument System-induced controlled flight into ground.

## Factfile

World revenue passenger miles: 1,725,000 million
World revenue passengers: 1,600 million
World air freight (ton miles): 74,000 million
Passengers through London (Heathrow/Gatwick): 92.4 million
Total airline employees: 1,863,431
Total jetliners employed: 13,102
Total turbo-prop liners employed: 3,937
Total piston engined liners employed: 935
Total scheduled service helicopters employed: 396
Average salary of long-haul pilot: $148,000
Average salary of cabin crew (US): $36,000
Price of 1,000 (US) gallons Jet A1 fuel: $336
Average exchange rate: £1=$1.48

*A dramatic underside image of a Panavia Tornado GR4A, carrying a mix of 'iron' bombs inboard and air-to-ground missiles outboard.* ▶

# Around the world in twenty days

*Mut, Egypt, March 21*
After nearly three weeks aloft, Swiss psychiatrist and balloonist, Bertrand Piccard, and Englishman Brian Jones, a balloon instructor and Project Manager of this event, bring their their Cameron-produced hot air balloon, *Breitling Orbiter 3* to earth in the Egyptian dessert, exhausted but happy in the knowledge that they have just become the first balloonists to successfully fly non-stop around the globe. This milestone flight sets three major new records, including the Absolute Distance record for any kind of aircraft at 25,360.6 miles, the Absolute Duration record for balloons of 19 days, 21 hours, 47 minutes and the Fastest (and First) balloon flight around the world at 15 days, 10 hours 24 minutes. The pair also established four other records pertaining to the type of balloon they were flying, a Roziere, including a new Altitude record of 38,506 feet. The balloonists had departed from Chateau d'Oex, Switzerland three weeks earlier, on March 1. During

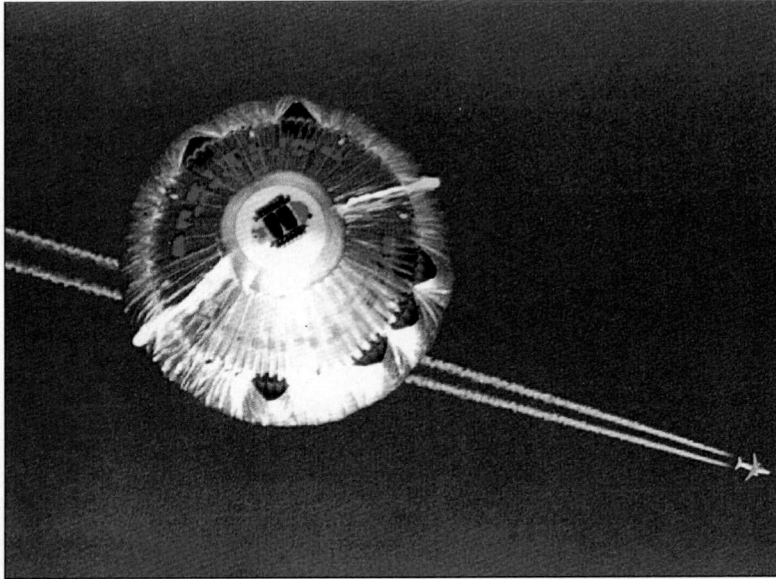

*The* Breitling Orbiter *takes off from the Alpine village of Chadeau-D'Oex.*

this flight, it was not possible for the official from the FAI's International Ballooning Commission to maintain visual contact; the balloon's track was monitored by Inmarsat-C satellite links. For Bre-

itling Watches, sponsors of the attempt, this unique achievement represents the successful climax to many years of effort and, on occassion, failure, as evidenced by the 'ditching' of *Breitling Orbitor 2.*

*Seattle, Washington, April 23 –24*
A Boeing Business Jet (BBJ) completed the longest ever Boeing 737 non-stop flight today, flying a 'round- Robin' of the USA in 13 hours 51 minutes 42 seconds, travelling 6,252.5 nautical miles for an average speed of 451 knots. Equipped with standard BBJ fuel tankage of 10,695 US gallons, the aircraft departed Martin State Airport, near Baltimore, heading northeast for Kennebunkport, Maine. Here it turned west towards Seattle, from whence it headed south for San Diego, then on to Miami and back to Baltimore. Overhead Baltimore, the BBJ went into a 'holding pattern' to use up fuel, prior to landing at Sussex County Airport, near Georgetown, Delaware. The two pilots making this trip were Boeing Business Jet's Chief Pilot, Michael Hewett, and former United Airlines Boeing 747 pilot, Clay Lacy. As a derivative of the Boeing 737-700, the BBJ has already notched up a total of 46 orders.

# MD-10 freighter rejuvenates DC-10

# 'Smart' bullets revealed by USAF

*A Boeing-modified McDonnell Douglas DC-10.*

*Long Beach, California, March 19*
Boeing today rolled-out the first of 79 MD-10 freighter conversions ordered by Fedex. MD-10 is the name given to the Boeing-modified McDonnell Douglas DC-10 that

incorporates the Boeing Advanced Common Flightdeck (ACF) 'glass' cockpit, identical to that fitted in the (Boeing) McDonnell Douglas MD-11, of which Fedex has 26, with more to be added (→ April 10).

*Washington DC, July 6*
USAF sources have revealed that scientists are developing smart bullets – Barrel Launched Adaptive Munitions (BLAMS) – that will follow the twists and turns of a target after they have left the barrel of a gun. Each bullet has a nose that can swivel, changing the angle it makes with the airflow. At supersonic speed, very small angles generate huge amounts of lift, so angling the nose towards the target causes the bullet to veer in that direction. The nose of the 'smart' bullet is connected to the body by a number of rods, or tendons, which change length when a voltage is applied to them. Increasing the length of a rod on one side of the bullet while shortening its opposite number changes the angle of the nose by up to 0.1° in any direction. Simple actuators of this kind are ideal for bullets because they can withstand the huge forces generated during firing, being able to survive accelerations of more than 17,000g. They are also able to expand and contract hundreds of times a second, an

important factor, because a spinning bullet travels at several times the speed of sound and any control mechanism must be able to act quickly to compensate. It has been demonstrated in wind tunnel tests that the actuators can produce good control of a round travelling at more than Mach 3.0. Much of the work on BLAMS has concentrated on large-calibre (20mm or 30mm) ammunition, the accuracy of which drops off with distance because of the effect of the wind on the round and the fact that it follows a parabolic trajectory. The only way a hit can be guaranteed is to use a multi-barrel gun with a high rate of fire. BLAMS, on the other hand, generate lift and so overcome the combined effects of wind and gravity, giving them at least twice the range of conventional rounds. To guide the smart bullets to their target, the latter would be 'painted' with a laser beam and the bullets equipped with a sensor, stressed to withstand the massive acceleration involved, that would home in on the objective, just like a smart bomb.

# Global Hawk gathers impetus

*Washington DC, July 7*
A third Ryan RQ-4A Global Hawk has been built to replace the vehicle lost in the March 29 crash. This machine is set to enter flight test later this month. Two further RQ-4As will hopefully join the program before the end of this year. Also revealed are plans to build up 40 or more Global Hawks as replacements for the manned Lockheed U-2 spyplane.

# Echoes of war in Iraq with air combat

*Southern Iraq, January 5*
The first air-to-air combat between US and Iraqi fighters in just over seven years took place in the southern Iraqi no-fly zone today. In two separate incidents, a pair of US Air Force Boeing F-15 Eagles launched one AIM-7 and three AIM-120 AMRAAM medium-range missiles at two Iraqi MiG-25 'Foxbats', while later in the day, two US Navy Grumman F-14 Tomcats fired two AIM-54 Phoenix long-range missiles at a pair of MiG-25s. However, all six of these missiles happened to miss their targets. The Iraqi Air Force has 10 MiG-25 Foxbats on its inventory. Other combat types still in service include 36 MiG-21PFMs, 60 MiG-23s, 60 Mirage F.1s and around 40 Chengdu F-7s. The latter started life as a Chinese copy of the MiG-21, but have since been developed significantly.

# The man who made Mustang great dies aged 90

*Taupo, New Zealand, May 30*
Today saw the passing of Ronald Harker (90), famed wartime Rolls-Royce test pilot. Harker was the man mainly responsible for turning one of America's good World War II fighters into their greatest. After testing a standard Allison-powered Mustang at the end of April 1942, he instantly grasped the benefits of fitting the fighter with a Rolls-Royce Merlin. With the sole exception of support from the influential Sir Wilfred Freeman at the Air Ministry, Harker found himself facing a mountain of home-based opposition. Despite this, his advocacy ultimately won the day and the superbly agile, long-ranged North American P-51D Mustang was born. Ronnie Harker joined Rolls-Royce as an apprentice in 1925, but the recession of 1930 left him without a job, so he spent his time in learning to fly. He was invited to return to the company when work began on the engines for the Schneider Trophy racing seaplanes, then being designed by Supermarine. Harker flew the Hawker biplanes, most of which were powered by Rolls-Royce Kestel engines, so his background of engineering and flying stood him in good stead when he was assigned to liaise with the RAF on high-performance engine development. His first project was the 'R'

*Ronnie Harker, dies aged 90.*

engine, which after much initial trouble took the Supermarine S.6 to a record speed of 407.5mph on 29 September 1931. Harker was soon approved by the Air Ministry to fly Service aircraft for test purposes, and was appointed as a test pilot with the handsome salary of £4.10s per week. His encounter with the Mustang came when he was sent to the Air Fighting and Development Unit at Duxford to evaluate Allied and enemy aircraft. Harker was commissioned in the Royal Auxiliary Air Force, with the rank of flight lieutenant.

**Dorval Airport, Canada, May 27. The first flight of Bombardier (Canadair) CRJ-700 turbojet feederliner.**

# The French merger trail

*Paris, June 11*
Aerospatiale Matra was formally created today. With a workforce of 52,000 and a market split 65 per cent civil and 35 per cent military, the new organization ranks second in Europe after British Aerospace, and fifth in the world after Boeing, Lockheed Martin, British Aerospace and Raytheon, for annual sales turnover. Control is 48 per cent by the French Government, 33 per cent by Matra former owners, Lagardere SCA, 17 per cent by investors and 2 per cent by the salaried staff.

# Sea Launch proves new system works

*Pacific Ocean, March 27*
Sea Launch – the joint US-/Russian-owned, California-based operation in which Boeing have a 40 per cent interest – today successfully launched its first demonstrator Zenit 3SL geostationary-capable booster supplied by Russian partners. This took place from aboard its Anglo-Norwegian 'Odyssey' launch ship and orbiter assembly and command ship 'Sea Launch Commander'. Boeing provide both overall mission management and the necessary payload fairings (→ October 9).

**Hamburg, Germany, April 15. Airbus deliver the 1,000th narrow-bodied A320 series jetliner, an Airbus A319, to Air France.**

# Fairchild Dornier 328JET into service

*Fairchild Dornier's 32-passenger 328JET receives certification today.*

*San Antonio, USA, August 9*
During the first half of last month, not only the European Joint Airworthiness Authorities (JAA) but also the US Fedreal Aviation Administration (FAA) were responsible for the awarding of Type Certifications to the company Fairchild Dornier. Today, Fairchild Dornier delivered its first two 328JETs to Skyways Airlines of Milwaukee, which is one of its launch customers. The current combined orders and options held by the Fairchild Dornier company – according to latest orderbook reports – number a total of 162 aircraft.

## Sad fate of golfer Payne Stewart

*South Dakota, October 26*
All five passengers aboard a Learjet 35, including star US golfer Payne Stewart, were killed today when the aircraft crashed having flown almost 1,440 miles from its point of departure in Orlando, Florida – seemingly on autopilot. US Air Force fighters, sent to check on the business jet, fail to make contact with its occupants, who are believed to have fallen unconscious after a total pressurization fail. This has been the cause of several accidents over the years.

## Franco-Russian helicopter collaboration

*Moscow, Russia, August 18*
Mil, Kazan Helicopters and Eurocopter today signed a joint contract to develop a 'proof-of-concept' demonstrator of the 15-ton, 30-passenger Mil-38 helicopter, powered by twin Pratt & Whitney Canada PWC127 turboshaft engines. Mil will take responsibility for general design and flight testing, while Kazan Helicopters will build the fuselage and rotor blades, and Eurocopter have charge of cockpit, avionics and equipment design, along with the layout of the different versions. First flight of the Mil-38 should take place during the first half of 2001.

## Cheaper spacecraft launches

*Huntsville. October 7*
NASA have revealed that it has completed an experimental 50-feet electrically powered, magnetic levitation track. This will enable the testing of the feasibility of accelerating a single-stage-to-orbit spacecraft to high speed prior to engine ignition, considerably reducing overall structure through fuel tankage shrinkage and hence vehicle cost.

## Super-stretched 767 takes to the air

*Boeing's 767-400ER has the capacity to carry 15 per cent more passengers.*

*Seattle, USA, October 9*
Depending on your viewpoint, the stretched Boeing 767-400ER – whose first flight lasted 5 hours 5 minutes today – can be seen to fill a gap in the market between Boeing's 767-300 and their 777-200. Alternatively, it can be seen as a market opponent to the Airbus A330-200. This latest offering from Boeing was launched in March 1997, with an order for 21 from Delta Air Lines. In terms of size, this version of the 767 is bigger than either the existing 767-200 or the 767-300, being 21ft longer and spanning 14ft more than the 767-300. A typical 304 passenger payload in a two-class layout can be carried over distances of up to around 6,500 miles. The orderbook for this particular variant currently stands at a total of 54 aircraft.

**Near Christmas Island, Pacific, October 9. Sea Launch successfully launches into orbit its second Zenit booster and the first to inject a commercial payload, the DIRECTV 1-R broadcast satellite.**

# RAF boosts its Jaguars, making the big cats better

*The Jaguar is to receive an extra 10 per cent thrust with the engine upgrade.*

*Warton, England, November 16*
The SEPECAT Jaguar pilot community – which currently has its base on RAF Coltishall – will soon get that extra little bit of reassurance. This is thanks to an engine upgrade program due to be carried out on the SEPECAT's Rolls-Royce/Turbomeca Adour. The work undertaken on this program will boost the engine's thrust by as much as 10 per cent, and such an increase in power will bring the SEPECAT Jaguar level with the standard of the Mk 106. As far as the airframe is concerned, British Aerospace (BAe), based at Warton, will be responsible for the development flying of the Adour Mk 106. During this development, British

Aerospace will be carrying out around 50 flights as specified in a contract that has a value of more than £100 million. Testing will be conducted with the first Warton-assembled production single seater, the S1. This machine recently made a comeback to the airfield after a break of nine years. The contract covers plans for the conversion of 122 existing Adours, as well as for carrying out the necessary modifications to 62 of the current Jaguars. Following the hours of development flying, BAe will then go on to sub-contract the modification work. This will be undertaken by the Defense Aviation Repair Agency, which is currently based at RAF St Athan.

## Boeing's JSF is under starter's orders

*Palmdale, December 14*
Boeing unveil their two Joint Strike Fighter demonstrators, the X-32A and X-32B. The three objectives that the X-32 demonstrators will be used to prove are: highlight commonality across the variants, including design/build processes; Boeing's direct-lift propulsion concept for Short Take-Off/Vertical Landing; and low-speed carrier approach flight handling qualities. Specifically, the X-32A will concentrate on Conventional Take-Off and Landing for the US Air Force, along with carrier approach han-

dling for the US Navy. The X-32B is to be used to explore the STOVL requirements for the US Marines, RAF and Royal Navy. The two X-32s are set to make their first flights in the spring and summer of 2000.

The Joint Strike Fighter program originated in the Common Affordable Lightweight Fighter projects of the early 1990s, which were investigated by the USAF and USN on the one hand and the Defense Advanced Research Project Agency on the other. The designation X-32 was applied to a planned CALF demonstrator.

## X-ray probe orbits

*French Guiana, December 10*
Today witnessed the launch of the third Ariane 5 rocket carrying the European Space Agency's impressive XMM space-probing X-ray telescope. The 32.8 feet tall-when-stowed satellite weighed 8,298lb at

its launch and was placed precisely into its highly elliptical orbit. Built for the ESA by DASA/Dornier Satelliten Systeme, the XMM has three telescopes, each consisting of 58 concentric tubular mirrors, and it has a design life of 10 years.

## Official surrender ends violent hijacking

*Afghanistan, December 24*
Five Islamic fundamentalists hijacked an Indian Airlines' Airbus A300 with 150 aboard en route from Katmandhu, Nepal to New Delhi, India today. After several stops for fuel and one killing – to demonstrate the hijackers'

resolve – the aircraft landed at Kandahar. Here all the highjackers, plus three fundamentalists who were previously imprisoned in India, were allowed to go free when the Indian Government was forced to partly capitulate to the hijackers' demands.

**Lynham, England, November 23. The RAF accepts the first of 25 Lockheed Martin C-130J Hercules it has on order.**

*The Islamic fundamentalists walk away from the Indian Airways Airbus A300.* ▷

*The ATR 42MP Surveyor is optimized for maritime missions, from patrol work to anti-pollution detection and control.*

*The EMBRAER ALX is a special-application version of the Super Tucano trainer/light attack of which 100 have been ordered by the Brazilian Air Force.*

*The Alenia C-27J Spartan tactical transport demonstrates its ability to operate from short, rough airstrips.*

*The Ilyushin Il-114-100 is the latest in a line of Ilyushin transports stretching back to the Il-12 of 1946.*

*The first of five EMBRAER EMB-145SA Airborne Early Warning and Control aircraft, ordered by the Greek government is seen here.*

*Production version of the Mitsubishi MH2000 seen here in Mitsubishi colors flying over Shinjuku, Tokyo.*

*Galaxy intercontinental business jet developed by Israel Aircraft Industries at their Tel Aviv facility.*

*The fourth prototype of the four-nation NH90 tactical transport helicopter is seen here in the markings of the German armed forces.*

*The Boeing Business Jet (BBJ), a derivative of the 737-700, made the longest non-stop flight of any 737 variant, completing 14 hours on April 23-24.*

*This Boeing 737-200 was adapated as an avionics flying laboratory to flight test the avionic systems for the forthcoming Joint Strike Fighter.*

*The second Boeing Sikorsky YRAH-66 Comanche began flight testing in May. One of the aircraft is 'clean' and one shows the undercarriage extended.*

*Making its appearance in 1999, the Airbus A319 Corporate Jet offers luxury travel and long range for business enterprises.*

*Production of the Tu-334 short-haul airliner was well under way in 1999, this being the responsibility of the MiG Corporation.*

*First production flight of the European Space Agency's Ariane 5 rocket on 10 December from Launch Zone No 3 at Kourou, French Guiana.*

4,534mph
USA
Pete Knight
North American X-15
Oct 3, 1967

24,987 miles
USA
Jeager and Rutan
Voyager
Dec 23, 1986

354,200ft
USA
Joseph Walker
North American X-15
Aug 22, 1963

1,120,370lb
USSR
Antonov
An-225 Mriya

95,000lb thrust
UK
Rolls Royce
Trent 895

**Warton, England, January 5**
Maiden flight of the first BAe Hawk Mk 127 Lead-In Fighter (LIF) trainer for the Royal Australian Air Force.

**France and Seattle, January 7**
Figures published today reveal that rivals Airbus Industries and Boeing delivered 294 and 620 jetliners respectively during 1999.However, in terms of total firm order intake, 1999 saw Airbus overtaking the US giant for the first time in its 30-year history, taking 476 against Boeing's 391,

**Seattle, Washington, January 27**
Boeing's 737, the world's most widely used twin jet, becomes the first jetliner in history to amass more than 100 million flying hours. Clearly, much water has passed under the bridge since the 737 was launched onto the market in 1965.

**Blagnac, France, March 21**
US Airways accepts the first of 10 Airbus A330-300s it has on order. The 335-passenger big twin with its two 67,500-lb s.t. General Electric CF6-80E1A4 turbofans is set to enter Trans-Atlantic service with the carrier in May of this year.

**Blagnac, France, April 3**
Today British Aerospace Systems' Regional Aircraft SA announced their launch order for the Avro RJX program, with a contract for two 82-seat Avro RJX-85s, placed by Druk Air of Bhutan in the Himalayas. These regional jets are scheduled to enter service in November 2001 and January 2002 and will replace the pair of BAe 146-100s currently operated by the carrier.

**Seattle, Washington, April 14**
The first of the Boeing C-40As, slated to replace the US Navy's fleet of C-9s made its maiden flight today, lasting 2 hours and 15 minutes. Like the C-9, which was a navalized Douglas DC-9, the C-40A is a navalized version of the 737-700C convertible passenger/cargo carrier.

**Rome, April 14**
Finnemeccanica, the Italian state-owned industry financial backers, who have a controlling interest in Agusta, Alenia and ATR, have signed a Memorandum of Understanding with EADS to form a joint company involved with both civil and military aeronautics.

**Toulouse, France, April 14**
Avions Transport Regional, or ATR, deliver their 600th ATR turboprop feederliner, an ATR72-500 for the Italian carrier, Air Dolomiti, the airline's 17th ATR.

**Marignane, France, April 19**
Eurocopter deliver their 100th EC 120B Colibri, with 170 ordered to the end of March 2000.

**Fort Worth, April 28**
Lockheed Martin deliver their 4,000th F-16 Fighting Falcon.

**Lyon-Satalos, France, June 29**
Lyon-Satalos International Airport becomes Lyon Saint-Exupery, marking the 100th anniversary of Antoine de Saint-Exupery, the famous French aviator's birth.

**Dorval, Canada, July 23**
Bombardier announce deliveries of 116 Challenger and Learjet business jets during the first half of 2000, ending June 30, compared with the delivery of 84 Bombardier business jets during the same period of 1999.

**Seattle, Washington, July 23**
The roll-out of first Boeing 737-900 is attended by thousands of people from Boeing and Alaska Airlines, the latter being the launch customer for this, the longest and largest version so far.

**Sao Jose dos Campos, Brazil, July 24**
EMBRAER announce that the orderbook for the ERJ-145 stands at 461 firm, plus 257 options, of which 224 have been delivered. Contracts for the shorter ERJ-135 are 164 firm, plus 157 options, of which 39 have been delivered.

**Kazakhstan, August 28**
Russia launches a military communications satellite, Cosmos 2,372, using a Proton booster.

**Japan, September 25**
Mitsubishi Heavy Industries handover the first production F-2A single-seat fighter to the Japanese Air Self-Defense Force. Of the 130 ordered, 45 have been purchased to date, as is usual under the incremental procurement system employed by the Japanese Government.

**Reynosa, Mexico, October 6**
An AeroMexico Douglas DC-9-31 overshoots the runway during heavy rainstorm. Despite severe damage to the jetliner, only three passengers are injured of the five crew and 83 passengers aboard. Tragically, however, the careening airliner kills five people on the ground.

**Czech Republic, October 24**
Let AS, the Czech aircraft manufacturer of light transport aircraft is declared bankrupt by the Regional Court today. The event was not totally unexpected as relations between Let and its American partner Ayres had been deteriorating for some time. Coupled with this a significant factor was that their 40-passenger Let L-610G had failed to sell in any numbers.

**Seattle, Washington, Nov 28**
After already committing to buy the Airbus A3XX, today Boeing announced that Australian carrier QANTAS has ordered six of their Longer-Range 747-400, formerly known as the 747-400X, for service entry with the airline in 2002. This appears to commit the American manufacturer to a head-on contest with Airbus for the next generation of Jumbos.

**Blagnac, France, December 19**
Airbus Industrie announce the launch of their A380, formally known as the A3XX. The program launch decision was taken after Virgin Atlantic's commitment to acquire six of these aircraft, for which Airbus hold 50 firm orders, plus 42 options. Estimated to cost around £8.5 billion to develop, Boeing and US officials, claim that the A380's EC funding is an unfair subsidy and breaks the terms of US-European trade pacts.

**Moscow, 29 December**
During 2000, Russian and Ukranian aircraft manufacturers delivered a mere four jetliners, comprising three Tupolev Tu-204s and one Antonov An-124. Yuri Koprev, head of the Russian Aviation and Space Agency is looking for industrial mergers as part solution to the commercially catastrophic outlook facing the Russian aircraft industry.

*XMM, the European Space Agency's deep-space probing x-ray telescope, was recently boosted on its way aboard Ariane 503.* ▶

## Factfile

World revenue passenger miles: 1,760,000 million
World revenue passengers: 1,580 million
World air freight (ton miles): 77,000 million
Passengers through London (Heathrow/Gatwick): 96.2 million
Total airline employees: 2,156,620
Total jetliners employed: 13,204
Total turbo-prop liners employed: 3,952
Total piston engined liners employed: 657
Total scheduled service helicopters employed: 44
Average salary of long-haul pilot: $150,000
Average salary of cabin crew (US): $36,500
Price of 1,000 (US) gallons Jet A1 fuel: $767
Average exchange rate: £1=$1.60

# Bombardier's regional Jets soar

*A 70-passenger Bombardier CRJ 700 in Delta Connection livery.*

**Dorval, Canada, March 29**
Bombardier today received a Delta Connections Inc. contract for 104 CRJ firm orders, plus a further 396 CRJ optional delivery positions. Value of this latest order for CRJs is in excess of $2.2 billion and represents the largest single regional aircraft contract placed to date. Delivery of these feederjets will commence in December 2000 and end in November 2004, with the optional deliveries extending into 2010. The firm CRJ order comprises 25 of the 70-seat CRJ700 and 79 CRJ100s and CRJ200s with a mix of 40, 44 and 50-seats. They will be operated by Atlantic Southeast Airlines (ASA) and Comair, wholly owned subsidiaries of Delta Air Lines. Including earlier orders, ASA and Comair have placed firm orders for 291 Bombardier CRJs, of which 132 have been delivered.

# Joint ventury improves Boeing 777

**Seattle, USA, February 29**
A further development in the Boeing versus Airbus saga emerged today with a joint Boeing and engine manufacturer General Electric communique launching two ultra-long-range versions of the 777, namely the 777-200X and stretched 777-300X. The aircraft are aimed at competing directly with the Airbus A340-500 and -600, and Boeing Chairman, Phil Condit, puts the cost of developing the two new 777 versions at $1 billion. Service entry date for the 777-200X is planned for September 2003, compared with the April 2001 first-flight date set for the A340-600. The A340-500 is scheduled for a maiden flight in December 2001. Both versions of the Boeing will be exclusively powered by GE90-115B turbofans, which are from General Electric.

**Fort Worth, USA, April 28. Lockheed Martin deliver the 4,000th F-16 Fighting Falcon, in this particular case a single seat F-16C, one of a batch produced for the Egyptian Air Force.**

# Boeing 747 still going strong

**Seattle, USA, January 21**
Boeing celebrate the 30th anniversary of the Boeing 747's introduction into commercial service with Pan American World Airways. Since then, 1,238 of these widebodies have been delivered, of which around 1,100 remain in service and of these, approximately 500 are of the latest 747-400 version.

# Gulfstream leads the world in high-end business jets

**Savannah, USA, April 25**
Gulfstream Aerospace today held symbolic simultaneous roll-out of the 400th plus Gulfstream G IV (the 400th G IV actually having been rolled out in February) and 100th Gulfstream G V business jets. Yet to be equipped with their 'customized' interiors, both aircraft will be delivered to their customers later this year. The Gulfstream G IV, first introduced in 1985 and capable of cruising at 45,000 feet, has accumulated a fleet milage in excess of 1.2 million flying hours. First flown in 1995, the Gulfstream G V cruises at an altitude of up to 51,000 feet. While operating at these heights, well clear of the commercial jet traffic below, both aircraft maintain their internal cabin pressure to the equivalent of flying at an altitude of 6,500 feet. To date, 79 Gulfstream Vs have now been delivered to customers.

# Airbus beat Boeing to the draw

*Airbus's mammoth double-decker A3XX 'Super Jumbo'.*

**Blagnac, France, June 23**
The on-again, off-again, long awaited emergence of the next-generation giant jetliner came considerably closer today, as Airbus Industrie partners approve 'Authorization to Offer', enabling the company's sales team to make firm commercial offers relating to the all-new 550-seat A3XX-100. Eight potential cutomers have already expressed interest in 52 of these super-jumbos. These customers are Air France (10), Emirates (7), ILFC (5), Singapore Airlines (10), Virgin Atlantic (5), plus one each for 15 undisclosed customers. Airbus Industrie Chief Executive Officer, Noel Forgeard is convinced the program's industrial launch will be approved late this year, or early in 2001. The current program milestones call for a first flight in 2004 and first deliveries in the last quarter of 2005. Of the aircraft, itself, the initial 100, powered by four turbofans of 70,000lb s.t., will carry its 555 three-class passenger compliment, plus 30 metric tonnes of cargo, over a range of 6,000 nautical miles. Boeing's current ploy is to emphasize the early availability of their 747X, while their problems appear to revolve around a lack of customer interest in a thirty-something year-old aircraft.

# Concorde crash disaster kills over 100

*The doomed Air France Concorde vainly attempts to reach safety at the nearby Le Bourget airport.*

*Gonesse, France, July 25*
An Air France Concorde today crashed 90 seconds after take-off, killing all 109 aboard, plus four on the ground. Air France promptly grounded its Concorde fleet. Trailing a plume of flame nearly as long as the aircraft itself, the doomed Concorde appears to have been making for the nearby Le Bourget airfield prior to crashing onto a hotel. Numerous observers have been astonished by the minimal size of the post-crash debris field that would seem to indicate that the airliner fell to earth almost vertically. Within hours of the disaster, the French Transport Minister stated that Air France would suspend all Concorde operations, pending the findings of an inquiry. While British Airways suspended Concorde services for the rest of the day, a spokesman said that they intended to continue running their Concorde services until further notice. Although too early to identify the cause of the crash, investigators are already concentrating on two main theories: either the aircraft suffered a sudden and catastrophic engine failure, leading to the rupture of fuel lines and a major fire outbreak, or the aircraft's main undercarriage struck an object on the runway, causing a tyre to shred and puncture a fuel tank.

# Russians boost US space effort

*Cape Canaveral, USA, May 24*
Today's successful launch of a Lockheed Martin Atlas III that was carrying a telecommunications satellite – the $150 million, 7,000-lb Eutelsat W4 – set a number of 'firsts' today. The most notable of these firsts was that this was the first US booster to employ a Russian-built rocket engine, namely the throttlable NPO Energomash RD-180, which is rated at a thrust of 860,000lb. It also happened to be the first launch of a Titan III. A third 'first' comes from the fact that the RD-180 is the first throttlable engine to be employed on a US expendable booster. In this instance, the booster had a launch weight of 243 tons. The RD-180 is proving to be a popular choice for future projects; it is also to be fitted in Lockheed Martin's Atlas V boosters, the first of which is set to be launched in early 2002. Inspite of funding problems, Russian boosters have proved to be extremely reliable.

# NH 90 production go-ahead given

*The European-collaborative NH 90 multi-role helicopter.*

*Paris, France, June 30*
Contracts for the NH Industries NH 90 multi-role helicopter were placed today, covering 116 for Italy, 80 for Germany, 27 for France and 20 for the Netherlands, the total value of which is cited as 6.6 billion Euros. This follows the signing of the Memorandum of Understanding by the governments of France, Germany, Italy and the Netherlands earlier this month, which effectively launched the NH 90 production program. The number of production NH 90s that the four governments plan for procurement is 595, with deliveries spread over the period 2003-2022.

# EMBRAER's latest RJ baby is born

*Brazil, June 27*
EMBRAER's ERJ-140 made its maiden flight today. Certification of this 44-seater is set for late in the first half of 2001. In fact, the prototype ERJ-140 was a conversion of one of the earlier ERJ-135 prototypes, using two fuselage plugs to stretch the aircraft's length by 6.96 feet. That the convertion was done with a total workforce of 93 and needed only around four months to complete was made possible by EMBRAER's initial decision to employ a circular sectioned, largely cylindrical fuselage that, in turn, allows the design team to insert fuselage sectional plugs of various lengths almost at will and with minimal impact in terms of production and assembly.

**Farnborough, England, July 25. British Aerospace Systems announce the delivery of the first of their Hawk Mk 115s for the North Atlantic Treaty Organization's Flying Training in Canada (NFTC) program, based in Moose Jaw, Saskatchewan.**

# First foray for baby Boeing X-32A JSF

*Palmdale, USA, September 18*
Today saw the first flight of the Boeing X-32A Joint Strike Fighter (JSF) demonstrator, with company Chief JSF Test Pilot, Fred Knox, at the controls for this transit to Edwards AFB, where the aircraft will be based for an initial 100-hour, five-month flight test program. The X-32A is designed to operate as a Conventional Take-Off and Landing (CTOL) for the US Air Force and to be used to check out US Navy carrier approach flight handling. This first machine will later be modified, gaining larger tail surfaces and flaperons. The second of the pair of Boeing JSF demonstrators, the X-32B, will undertake exploration of the aircraft's Short Take-Off and Vertical Landing (STOVL) handling to meet US Navy, US Marine and Royal Navy operational requirements. It is set to make its long-awaited maiden flight in the first quarter of 2001. The delay is technical, but also reflects Department of Defense policy vacillations.

*Boeing's X-32A Joint Strike Fighter demonstrator climbs away on its maiden flight with test pilot at the controls.*

## 20,000 hours for armchair pilots

*The USAF are making increasing use of unmanned RQ-1 Predators.*

*San Diego, USA, August 1*
Tactical reconnaissance was the very first mission of the military heavier-than-air flying machine. In the wake of the Gulf War, the US looked at the possibility of producing unmanned intelligence-gathers – one of the first of this new breed, General Atomics Aeronautical Systems RQ-1 Predator, passed the 20,000 flying hour mark today. Designed to give optimum endurance while flying at medium altitude, the Predator's power is provided by either a fuel thrifty 85-hp Rotax 912 or 105-hp Rotax 914 turbo-charged engine either of which gives a cruising speed of around 70 knots along with a typical 40-hour flight endurance. Predator weighs in at a meagre 2,300lb maximum take-off weight, of which 650lb is fuel and 450lb is the vital sensor/data link package. While it may have taken more than 30 years to achieve, it would appear that machines such as the RQ-1, with their ability to make major reductions in the time between gathering the information and its exploitation by the battlefield managers, are, at last, being taken seriously.

## Swedes show stealthy UAV SHARC

*Linkoping, Sweden, September 1*
SAAB today revealed that they have been developing a 26.2-ft wingspan stealthy unmanned air vehicle (UAV). This is in collaboration with the FFA and Ericsson as part of the National Aeronautics Research Program. Known as SHARC – or Swedish Highly Advanced Research Configuration – studies leading to this aircraft were initiated in April 1998.

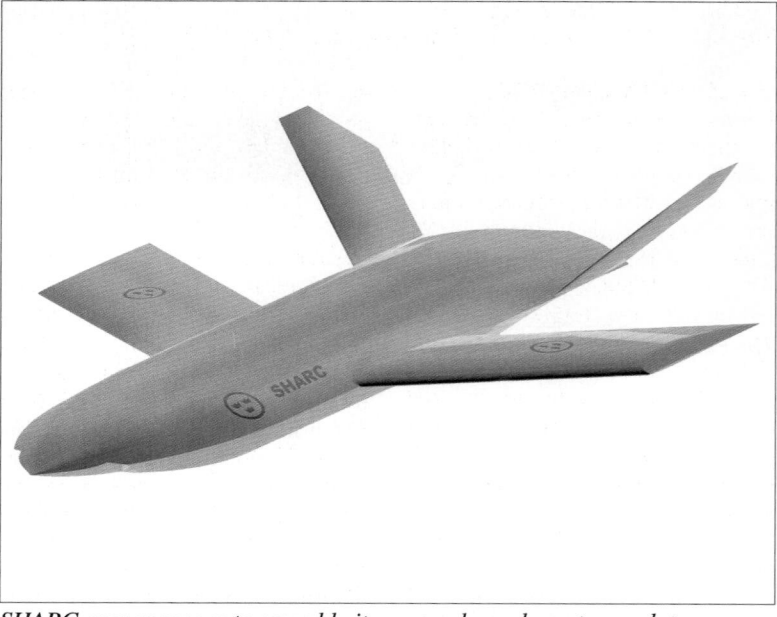

*SHARC even manages to resemble its namesake underwater predator.*

# Sea Launch are back in business

*Pacific Ocean, October 21*
Sea Launch, the internationally owned commercial space launch company who, like everyone else in the aircraft business, it seems, suffers the occassional setback, proved their corporate resilience today with the successful launch of the Thuraya-1 satellite. Made by the former Hughes, now Boeing Satellite Services, this 11,261-lb telecommunications spacecraft, claimed to be the heaviest commercial satellite yet built, is boosted into its geo-stationary orbit by its Zenit 3SL rocket. Costing $960 million and sched-

uled to commerce operating in the first quarter of next year, Thuraya-1 belongs to a United Arab Emirates company and will provide mobile telephone services across a wide swath of the eastern hemisphere, stretching from India to Eastern Europe. Besides producing Thuraya-1, Boeing Satellite Services (BSS) have assembled a second satellite as a ground spare as well as holding an option for the delivery of a third. Responsible for bringing the overall system fully into operation, BSS also furnishes the ground stations and mobile phones.

# Joining the Joint Strike Fighter joust

*The X-35A JSF demonstrator is taken aloft for its first flight.*

*Palmdale, USA, October 24*
Lockheed Martin's X-35A, the first of their two Joint Strike Fighter (JSF) demonstrators, made a maiden flight of 22 minutes today in the hands of the company's JSF Chief Test Pilot, Tom Morgenfeld. As with its rival, Boeing's X-32A, the primary purpose of this initial flight is to ferry the aircraft from Palmdale to nearby Edwards Air Force Base, where the testing and evaluation of the rival machines will be conducted. The X-35A never got to retract its landing gear as a result of a minor problem, which was believed to involve a landing gear door switch. This transit flight starts a month of flight testing in which the X-35A will

accumulate around 20 hours, prior to the machine being grounded towards the close of November 2000 for modification from its current conventional take-off and landing (CTOL) configuration into its short take-off and vertical landing (STOVL) form as the X-35B. Evaluation of the machine in its X-35B guise is set to start with ground testing over a grated pit, to check out engine performance, in January 2001. Meanwhile, Lockheed Martin's second JSF demonstrator, the X-35C – which features larger wings and which is aimed at meeting the requirements of the US Navy – is expected to make its first flight around the end of next month.

# The more, the merrier

*An impression of Raytheon's latest bizjet, the eight-passenger Hawker 450.*

*New Orleans, USA, October 9*
New Orleans and this year's National Business Aircraft Association Show are the venue for Raytheon Aircraft's Chairman and Chief Executive Officer, Hansel Tookes' announcement of the launch of a new, light mid-size business jet, the Hawker 450. Positioned in capacity terms between Raytheon's best-selling

Hawker 800XP and Raytheon's Beechjet 400A, this new 'bizjet', typically seating eight passengers, will have a 2,000 nautical mile range and carry a $7.8 million to $9 million price tag. Raytheon can now go to the one source, Honeywell Inc, for items as diverse as the Hawker 450's TFE731-40 turbofan engines and its Primus Epic avionics.

# Up, up and away

*London, England, October 24*
Today, Don Cameron, founder and Chairman of Cameron Balloons, received this year's Prince Philip Designers Prize. Presented to him at the Design Council by Prince Philip, the award recognizes his 35-year career, one in which, virtually single-handedly, Cameron managed to focus public awareness on the hot air balloon's design potential. Cameron's achievements include his designs of the first balloon to cross the Atlantic in 1986 and the Breitling Orbiter III that circumnav-

*Don Cameron and Prince Philip.*

igated the globe in 1999, and his pioneering design work of the mid-1970s into 'special shape' balloons.

# Russian averts spacecraft disaster

*In Near-Earth Orbit, November 18*
The first three-man crew of the International Space Station (ISS), comprising US Navy Capt. Bill Sheppard, Russian Air Force Lt. Col. Yuri Gidzenko and Sergei Krikalev today faced the real prospects of losing vital supplies ferried up to them by one of Russia's 7.5-ton Progress re-supply vehicles in an incident that could readily have ended in a collision between the two spacecraft. Having guided the Progress into close proximity with the ISS, the Rus-

sian-built automatic guidance system developed problems that required former fighter pilot Gidzenko to take over the 'docking' manually. To complicate his task, during this critical final phase he found himself staring directly into the sun's glare, while a vital sighting system misted up, which left him blinded, creating a second dangerous situation. Composed and with the help of his colleagues' advice, he backed the Progress out to a safe distance until the ISS passed into night-side orbit.

▷

*The first of six Boeing C-40A transports on order for the US Navy Reserve taking off on its maiden flight.*

*The A380 is a double-deck variant of the Airbus, launched on December 19. It is seen here in the livery of the Emirates airline.*

*A multi-use and special mission transport aircraft, the Ae270 Propjet from Ibis Aerospace.*

*Trials conducted on a Europa company demonstrator fitted with new 'speed kit' have recorded a 9-knot increase on the XS Monowheel.*

*The X-32A, concept demonstrator for the Boeing Joint Strike Fighter, takes off for its maiden flight from Palmdale, California, on September 18.*

*A Sea Lynx is seen here in the colours of the German Navy. The helicopter is optimised for the AS and ASW roles.*

*The comfortable, well-equipped interior of the new Gulfstream V ultra-long-range business jet.*

*The EC-135, the new twin-engined helicopter developed by Eurocopter, used by mountain rescue teams.*

*A Tupolev Tu-204-120 delivered to Air Cairo in 2000. The Tu-204 is appealing to customers because of its relatively low cost.*

*Latest version of the EMBRAER regional passenger jet family, the ERJ-140. This prototype was built by stretching an ERJ-135.*

*Lockheed Martin's X-35A is their submission for the potentially lucrative Joint Strike Fighter market, seen here at the start of a month's trial testing.*

*The first of 67 WAH-64 Apache helicopters, licence-built by GKN Westland, was handed over to the Army Air Corps in March 2000.*

*Undergoing trials in 2000, the MiG 1.42 MFF's design benefits from earlier experiences with the MiG-29 air superiority fighter.*

# General Index

# Picture Credits

## Cover

The position of the pictures is indicated by the following letters:
B: bottom, T: top, M: middle, L: left, R: right, X: middle left, Y: middle right, C: centre, FP: full page

When "RR" appears with a picture credit in the following pages,
It means "All rights reserved".

### Front cover
The All Transport Media Picture Library – TM, TR, CTX, CTY, Associated Press – BR, Aviation Images – CBR, Flight International – CBM, BX, Hulton Getty – TL, TY, CTL, CTR, CBL, Popperfoto – TX, BY, Topham Picturepoint – BL

### Back cover
The All Transport Media Picture Library – BL, Mary Evans Picture Library – TL, Popperfoto – CR

### Spine
Popperfoto

3 – DK Picture Library – M

5 – Corbis – M

6 – Hulton Getty – BM

7 – Hulton Getty – T

8 – Hulton Getty – TL, BR

9 – Hulton Getty – TL, Corbis – BR

10 – Hulton Getty – TL, Aviation Images – BM

11 – Aviation Images – TL, BR

12 – MR Chronicle Communications Ltd – ML Ann Ronan Picture Library – BY Royal Aeronautical Society

13 – TL Aspect Picture Library – MX, MR Mary Evans Picture Library – TR Syndication International

14 – TY Ancient Art and Architecture – MR Chronicle Communications Ltd – BM Royal Aeronautical Society

15 – TL Mary Evans Picture Library – TR Peter Newark's Pictures – BR Chronicle Communications Ltd

16 – TR Mary Evans Picture Library – BR Royal Aeronautical Society

17 – ML Popperfoto – TR, MX Aspect Picture Library

18 – TX, TY TRH Pictures – TR National Portrait Gallery, London – MM Mary Evans Picture Library – BR Topham Picture Library

19 – TX E T Archive – MR Mary Evans Picture Library – BM Peter Newark's Pictures

20 – All pictures from Peter Newark's Pictures

21 – ML Topham Picture Library – TR, MR Ann Ronan Picture Library – BR Mary Evans Picture Library

22 – TR RR/Coll. musée de l'Air et de l'Espace – MR E T Archive

23 – ML RR/Coll. musée de l'Air et de l'Espace – TR Royal Aeronautical Society – BL, BR E T Archive

24 – BM Private Collection

25 – FP Peter Newark's Pictures

26 – TL Mary Evans Picture Library – MY RR/Coll. Chemel – BX Royal Aeronautical Society – BL Hulton Deutsch

27 – TX Boireau – TR Photo X – BR RR/Coll. Chemel

28 – BM Kharbine Tapabor

29 – FP Kharbine Tapabor

30 – TM Library of Congress – MR RR/Coll. musée de l'Air et de l'Espace – BL RR/Coll. Larousse – BY Kharbine Tapabor

31 – TL Wright State University Archives – TR, MR RR/Coll. Chemel – BL Topham Picture Library

32 – BM RR/Coll. musée de l'Air et de l'Espace

33 – FP RR/Coll. Chemel

34 – TL, MR Topham Picture Library – MX Royal Aeronautical Society

35 – TM, ML Wright State University Archives – MR Royal Aeronautical Society

36 – BM RR/Coll. musÈe de líAir et de líEspace

37 – FP Royal Aeronautical Society

38 – TM Royal Aeronautical Society – ML TRH Pictures – BR RR/Coll. Chemel

39 – TM Wright State University Archives – BM Chronicle Communications Ltd

40 – BM Wright State University Archives

41 – FP Aspect Picture Library

42 – TR Hulton Deutsch – ML, BR RR/Coll. Chemel

43 – TM Chronicle Communications Ltd – MM Wright State University Archives – ML RR/Coll. Chemel – BR Royal Aeronautical Society

44 – BM RR/Coll. Chemel

45 – FP RR/Coll. Chemel

46 – TL Library of Congress – TR Coll. Joy – MR RR/Coll. Chemel – BL Robert Opie

47 – TM RR/Coll. musée de l'Air et de l'Espace – ML Royal Aeronautical Society – BR National Archives of Canada

49 – FP Kharbine Tapabor

50 – BX Royal Aeronautical Society – MR Popperfoto – TR RR/Coll. Chemel

51 – TL, BL RR/Coll. musée de líAir et de l'Espace – TR, BR RR/Coll. Chemel

53 – FP Royal Aeronautical Society

54 – TL Tallandier – MR Popperfoto – BL Royal Aeronautical Society

55 – TM RR/Coll. Chemel – MM Tallandier – MR Philip Jarrett

56 – TL Tallandier – BX Sygma/Illustration – MR Royal Aeronautical Society – BY, BR Robert Opie

57 – TR Tallandier – MR Tallandier, Smithsonian Inst

59 – FP Tallandier

60 – TM RR/Coll. musée de l'Air et de l'Espace – BR Topham Picture Library – ML Philip Jarrett

61 – TL, TR Library of Congress – BM National Archives of Canada

62 – TL Private Collection – MR Kharbine Tapabor

63 – TL, TR, BL RR/Coll. Chemel – MX Kharbine Tapabor – BR Sygma/Illustration

64 – TL Smithsonian Inst – MR Hulton Deutsch – BX TRH Pictures – BR Royal Aeronautical Society

65 – TL RAE, Farnborough – TM Hulton Deutsch – BL National Archives of Canada – MR Popperfoto

67 – FP Kharbine Tapabor

68 – TL, MR RR/Coll. Chemel – ML Coll. Jackson – BR Chronicle Communications Ltd

69 – TL Royal Aeronautical Society – TR, MR, BR Coll. Joy

70 – TR RR/Coll. Chemel – MR, TL, ML, BL Royal Aeronautical Society

71 – TR Chronicle Communications Ltd – TL RR/Coll. musée de l'Air et de l'Espace – BX Robert Opie – MR Tallandier

72 – TL Smithsonian Inst – BL RR/Coll. musée de l'Air et de l'Espace – BR Popperfoto

73 – TL Library of Congress – BL, BY Tallandier – BR Robert Opie

74 – TL TRH Pictures – TR Library of Congress – BL Aspect Picture Library – BX Royal Aeronautical Society – BR Peter Newark's Pictures

75 – ML Popperfoto – BR RR/Coll. musée de l'Air et de l'Espace

79 – FP Peter Newark's Pictures

80 – TX Library of Congress – TR, ML RR/Coll. Chemel – BR RR/Coll. musée de l'Air et de l'Espace

81 – MR Chronicle Communications Ltd – TR Kharbine Tapabor – MM Mansell Collection

82 – TM Topham Picture Library – BL Tallandier – MR Royal Aeronautical Society

83 – ML Topham Picture Library – TM, BX Royal Aeronautical Society – MR The Age, Melbourne

87 – FP Kharbine Tapabor

88 – TM Library of Congress – ML Sygma/Illustration

89 – TX, TY Royal Aeronautical Society – BL Library of Congress

90 – TM Coll. Meurisse – MM, BM Hulton Deutsch

91 – TL, ML, MR, BL Hulton Deutsch – TR Philip Jarrett – BR Popperfoto

92 – TX, ML Kharbine Tapabor – TR Robert Opie – MR RR/Coll. Chemel – BR Topham Picture Library

93 – TM Chronicle Communications Ltd – MM TRH Pictures – BR RR/Coll. musée de l'Air et de l'Espace

97 – FP Royal Aeronautical Society

98 – TY Kharbine Tapabor – MR NASM

99 – TM RR/Coll. Chemel – ML Royal Aeronautical Society – BR Boox Sale

100 – TM The Age, Melbourne – BL Mary Evans Picture Library – MY Chronicle Communications Ltd – BR Philip Jarrett

101 – TL SHAA – TR Hulton Deutsch – BM RR/Coll. Chemel – BR Robert Opie

105 – FP Bridgeman Art Library

106 – TM RR/Coll. Chemel – ML Library of Congress – MR Royal Aeronautical Society

107 – ML Bettmann Archive – TR Sygma/Illustration – BR Chronicle Communications Ltd

108 – TL RR/Coll. musée de l'Air et de l'Espace – MY Hulton Deutsch – TR Smithsonian Inst – BR Sygma/Illustration

109 – ML Novosti – BX Hulton Deutsch

113 – FP Bridgeman Art Library

114 – TL State Photographic Archive – MR, MM Hulton Deutsch

115 – TL Bain Collection – MM, MR Royal Aeronautical Society – BR Hulton Deutsch

116 – TL SHAA – TR Robert Hunt

117 – ML, TR Peter Newark's Pictures – MX Popperfoto – BR TRH Pictures

118 – TL, TR, BR SHAA – BL Chronicle Communications Ltd

119 – TX Hulton Deutsch – ML Popperfoto – MR Chronicle Communications Ltd

120 – TR Bridgeman Art Library – BR, MX Peter Newark's Pictures – BL Sygma/Illustration

121 – ML Royal Aeronautical Society – TR RR/Coll. musée de l'Air et de l'Espace – MR Kharbine Tapabor

125 – FP Peter Newark's Pictures

126 – TL Topham Picture Library – TR Sygma/Illustration – BL Popperfoto

127 – MK Kharbine Tapabor – TR TRH Pictures – BL Royal Aeronautical Society – BR SHAA

128 – TL SHAA – TR Royal Aeronautical Society – MY Kharbine Tapabor

129 – TR Hulton Deutsch – ML Peter Newark's Pictures – MR Chronicle Communications Ltd – BR Bettmann Archive

130 – TL Bettmann Archive – MR TRH Pictures – BR Hulton Deutsch

131 – TM SHAA – MM Royal Aeronautical Society – BR Hulton Deutsch

135 – FP Peter Newark's Pictures

136 – TR RR/Coll. Chemel – MM Tallandier

137 – TL, BL Popperfoto – MR RR/Coll. Chemel

138 – TM Imperial War Museum – MM Hulton Deutsch – BM Chronicle Communications Ltd

139 – TL Royal Aeronautical Society – TY Topham Picture Library – ML Bettmann Archive – BR RR/Coll. Chemel

140 – TL Imperial War Museum – MR National Archives of Canada

141 – TL Popperfoto – TR Peter Newark's Pictures – BR TRH Pictures

145 – FP Library of Congress

146 – TM Imperial War Museum – TR TRH Pictures – BL Hulton Deutsch – BR Bridgeman Art Library

147 – TM SHAA – MR RR/Coll. Larousse – MM Topham Picture Library

148 – TM Topham Picture Library – MM Chronicle Communications Ltd, Hulton Deutsch

149 – ML Library of Congress – TR Coll. Jackson – MR RR/Coll. musée de l'Air et de l'Espace

150 – TL Topham Picture Library – TR TRH Pictures – BL Sygma/Illustration

151 – TR Dornier – ML Bettmann Archive

155 – FP Peter Newark's Pictures

156 – TM Popperfoto – MM Peter Newark's Pictures – MR Hulton Deutsch

157 – TL Peter Newark's Pictures – MX Royal Aeronautical Society – TR Bettmann Archive, Tallandier

158 – TL DITE – MR Topham Picture Library – MM Royal Aeronautical Society

159 – TR Kharbine Tapabor – ML Royal Aeronautical Society – BR Topham Picture Library

160 – TM Bettmann Archive – ML RR/Coll. Larousse – BR Philip Jarrett

161 – ML Philip Jarrett – TR Chronicle Communications Ltd – BR Bettmann Archive

162 – TL Aspect Picture Library – TR Bettmann Archive – ML National Archives of Canada – MR, BX Imperial War Museum – BL Royal Aeronautical Society – BY Popperfoto – BR Hulton Deutsch

163 – MM Chronicle Communications Ltd

167 – FP Aspect Picture Library

168 – ML Ivan Rendall – TR Lufthansa – MR Sygma/Illustration

981

# Picture Credits

**169** – ML Royal Aeronautical Society – TX Private Collection – MY Topham Picture Library – BX Bettmann Archive – BR Sygma/Illustration
**170** – ML Bettmann Archive – BL Chronicle Communications Ltd – BR, TR Hulton Deutsch
**171** – ML RR/Coll. musée de l'Air et de l'Espace – TM, BM Royal Aeronautical Society – MR Topham Picture Library
**172** – TL Sygma/Illustration – MR Musee de la Poste – BX Topham Picture Library
**173** – TR Topham Picture Library – ML Chronicle Communications Ltd – MR Hulton Deutsch
**177** – FP Peter Newark's Pictures
**178** – TY, BM Sygma/Illustration – MR Topham Picture Library
**179** – TL Sabena – MR Sutton Library – ML Sygma/Illustration
**180** – TL McDonnell Douglas – BL Bridgeman Art Library – MR Air France
**181** – TL Hulton Deutsch – TM Topham Picture Library – MM RR/Coll. musée de l'Air et de l'Espace – BL Robert Opie
**185** – FP Peter Newark's Pictures
**186** – TL, MR, BR Kharbine Tapabor – ML Sutton Library
**187** – TL RR/Coll. Chemel – TR Smithsonian Inst – ML, MY TRH Pictures
**188** – ML, BL, BX RR/Coll. Chemel – TR Sygma/Illustration – MR Royal Aeronautical Society
**189** – TL, ML Philip Jarrett – TR Bettmann Archive – BR Chronicle Communications Ltd
**193** – FP Air France
**194** – TL Kharbine Tapabor – MR Popperfoto – ML Sygma/Illustration
**195** – TR Hulton Deutsch – BL, BR Sygma/Illustration
**196** – TR Bettmann Archive – ML National Library of Australia – MM Topham Picture Library
**197** – ML, BL, BR Hulton Deutsch – TM, TR Qantas – MR Chronicle Communications Ltd
**201** – FP Robert Opie
**202** – TM RR/Coll. musée de l'Air et de l'Espace – MM Chronicle Communications Ltd – ML Hulton Deutsch – MR Philip Jarrett
**203** – TR Kharbine Tapabor – MR Chronicle Communications Ltd – MM Harenberg
**204** – TM RR/Coll. musée de l'Air et de l'Espace – BR Hulton Deutsch – BL Sygma/Illustration
**205** – TL Chronicle Communications Ltd – BL RR/Coll. Larousse – MR Bettmann Archive, Hulton Deutsch
**206** – ML Royal Aeronautical Society – TR Sygma/Illustration – MR DITE
**207** – TL Sygma/Illustration – ML Harenberg
**211** – FP Peter Newark's Pictures
**212** – TL Chronicle Communications Ltd – TR Royal Aeronautical Society – MR Hulton Deutsch – MM National Archives of Canada
**213** – TL Sygma/Illustration – MY RR/Coll. musée de l'Air et de l'Espace – MR Boeing
**214** – TL Royal Aeronautical Society – TY Kharbine Tapabor – MM Chronicle Communications Ltd – BR Hulton Deutsch
**215** – TR Chronicle Communications Ltd – ML RR/Coll. musée de l'Air et de l'Espace – BM Topham Picture Library
**216** – TL Sygma/Illustration – MR, BL RR/Coll. musée de l'Air et de l'Espace – BR Chronicle Communications Ltd
**217** – TL Sygma/Illustration – ML Bettmann Archive – BR Royal Aeronautical Society
**221** – FP Royal Aeronautical Society
**222** – TL USAF – MR Sygma/Illustration – BL Bettmann Archive
**223** – ML Hulton Deutsch – TM RR/Coll. musée de l'Air et de l'Espace – TR Topham Picture Library – BM Kharbine Tapabor
**224** – TY Royal Aeronautical Society – MR Keystone, Paris – MM US Navy
**225** – TL Topham Picture Library – MR, BM Bettmann Archive
**229** – FP Topham Picture Library
**230** – TL Topham Picture Library – TR TRH Pictures – MM Chronicle Communications Ltd
**231** – TL, TR Sygma/Illustration – MY, BR Topham Picture Library – MR Library of Congress
**232** – TL McDonnell Douglas – MY RR/Coll. musée de l'Air et de l'Espace – BR Kansas State Historical Society – BL Topham Picture Library
**233** – ML Kharbine Tapabor – TR Chronicle Communications Ltd – MM Hulton Deutsch – BR NASM
**237** – FP Hulton Deutsch
**238** – TM RR/Coll. musée de l'Air et de l'Espace – MM Sygma/Illustration
**239** – TY Encyclopaedia of Posters – MR Bettmann Archive – BR Hulton Deutsch – BL Topham Picture Library
**240** – ML Pan Am – TR Coll. Nungessor – BR RR/Coll. musée de l'Air et de l'Espace
**241** – TR Popperfoto – ML, MR Peter Newark's Pictures
**242** – TL Keystone, Paris – TR Hulton Deutsch – BM Sygma/Illustration
**243** – ML, TR Sygma/Illustration – BL, MR Bettmann Archive
**244** – TL Royal Aeronautical Society – MR De Havilland – MY Hulton Deutsch
**245** – TM Sygma/Illustration – MR Robert Opie – BL National Archives of Canada
**246** – TL Kobal Collection – MR Air France – BL, BX Royal Aeronautical Society
**247** – TM, BL Chronicle Communications Ltd
**251** – FP Royal Aeronautical Society
**252** – ML State Library of New South Wales – TM The Age, Melbourne – BY Royal Aeronautical Society – BL Robert Opie
**253** – TR Keystone, Paris, Chronicle Communications Ltd – BR Hulton Deutsch – ML Qantas
**254** – BL Sygma/Illustration – TL, TR National Library of Australia
**255** – BM Pan Am – MM Sygma/Illustration – BL Sutton Library – BR Lufthansa
**256** – TL Courtesy of Boeing – MY Royal Aeronautical Society – MX Peter Newark's Pictures, Hulton Deutsch – BL Sygma/Illustration – BR Hulton Deutsch
**257** – ML Sygma/Illustration – TR Topham Picture Library – MR Chronicle Communications Ltd – BR Hulton Deutsch
**261** – FP Peter Newark's Pictures
**262** – TL Los Angeles Public Library – MR Royal Aeronautical Society – ML Sygma/Illustration
**263** – TM TWA – MM Chronicle Communications Ltd – ML Philip Jarrett
**264** – TL, MY Sygma/Illustration – BL, BX, BY Robert Opie
**265** – TL Royal Aeronautical Society – TR Robert Opie – MR Hulton Deutsch – BL RR/Coll. Chemel
**266** – TL Lufthansa – ML Peter Newark's Pictures – MR Sygma/Illustration – BM Sabena
**267** – TM, TR Hawaiian Airways – BL Chronicle Communications Ltd
**271** – FP Mary Evans Picture Library
**272** – TL, TR Sygma/Illustration – MM Hulton Deutsch
**273** – ML United Airlines – MR Topham Picture Library, Royal Aeronautical Society – BR Boeing
**274** – ML Northrop Corporation – TR Kobal Collection – BM Sygma/Illustration
**275** – TM Peter Newark's Pictures – BL, BR Royal Aeronautical Society
**276** – TR Chronicle Communications Ltd – MX Sygma/Illustration – BR Kharbine Tapabor – BL Robert Opie
**277** – TX Peter Newark's Pictures – TR, MR Hulton Deutsch – ML Sygma/Illustration
**278** – ML Pan Am – TR Royal Aeronautical Society – BY Chronicle Communications Ltd
**279** – ML Hulton Deutsch – BL, TR Sygma/Illustration – MR Popperfoto – BR CD Collection
**282** – FP Robert Opie
**284** – TL, TR Royal Aeronautical Society – BY Chronicle Communications Ltd
**285** – ML Popperfoto – MM TRH Pictures
**286** – TL Topham Picture Library – TR RR/Coll. Chemel – ML Hulton Deutsch – TL CD Collection – BL Chronicle Communications Ltd
**287** – All pictures from Sygma/Illustration
**288** – TM, MM Hulton Deutsch – BL Peter Newark's Pictures
**289** – TM Peter Newark's Pictures – MM Keystone, Paris
**293** – FP Kharbine Tapabor
**294** – TM Royal Aeronautical Society – BL Keystone, Paris
**295** – TL Keystone, Paris – MR J L Charmet – BR Sygma/Illustration
**296** – TL, TR Topham Picture Library – MM Keystone, Paris – BL Robert Opie
**297** – ML Chronicle Australasia – TM Topham Picture Library – BL Kharbine Tapabor – BR Hulton Deutsch
**298** – TL Topham Picture Library – TR, BM Sygma/Illustration
**299** – ML Sutton Library – TR Jacques Legrand s.a. – BR Hulton Deutsch
**303** – FP Mary Evans Picture Library
**304** – TL RR/Coll. musée de l'Air et de l'Espace – TR Popperfoto – MR Royal Aeronautical Society – BL Sygma/Illustration
**305** – ML Popperfoto – TR Topham Picture Library – BL Sygma/Illustration – BR Royal Aeronautical Society
**306** – TM American Airlines – MR, MM Sygma/Illustration
**307** – BX Topham Picture Library – MR Peter Newark's Pictures – BL Sygma/Illustration
**308** – TL, TR Tallandier – BL McDonnell Douglas – MR Sygma/Illustration
**309** – TM Sygma/Illustration – MM Hulton Deutsch
**313** – FP Peter Newark's Pictures
**314** – TL Sygma/Illustration – MR Michael Taylor
**315** – TL Private Collection – TR Topham Picture Library – BL Mary Evans Picture Library – BR Royal Aeronautical Society
**316** – MR Lockheed – BR Topham Picture Library – BL Sygma/Illustration
**317** – TL McDonnell Douglas – TR Topham Picture Library – BM Popperfoto
**318** – TL Keystone, Paris – TM, MY, BL Royal Aeronautical Society – BR Mary Evans Picture Library
**319** – ML Topham Picture Library – TR, MR Robert Opie – BL Sygma/Illustration
**323** – FP Royal Aeronautical Society
**324** – TR Mary Evans Picture Library – BR DeSelav-Tapabor – BL Bettmann Archive
**325** – TL American Aviation Historical Society – TR RR/Coll. musée de l'Air et de l'Espace – ML, MY Royal Aeronautical Society
**326** – TR, MR, BL Sygma/Illustration – TL Popperfoto
**327** – TR E T Archive – ML UTA
**328** – TM Topham Picture Library – MR Sygma/Illustration
**329** – TM Keystone, Paris – BL Pan American – BR RR/Coll. musée de l'Air et de l'Espace
**333** – FP Peter Newark's Pictures
**334** – MY Peter Newark's Pictures – ML Sygma/Illustration – BR Royal Aeronautical Society
**335** – TX Chronicle Communications Ltd – TR, ML Topham Picture Library – BR Royal Aeronautical Society
**336** – ML, BL Sygma/Illustration – TR Royal Aeronautical Society – MR Smithsonian Inst
**337** – BR RR/Coll. musée de l'Air et de l'Espace – ML Keystone, Paris – MY Topham Picture Library – MR Tallandier – BM Royal Aeronautical Society
**338** – MR Royal Aeronautical Society – TL Eastern Airlines – BL United Airlines
**339** – TL Sygma/Illustration – TR Royal Aeronautical Society – MR RR/Coll. musée de l'Air et de léEspace
**340** – MR Royal Aeronautical Society – TM Pan Am – MM Chronicle Communications Ltd – TR US Navy
**341** – TL, BL Keystone, Paris – MR Sygma/Illustration – BR RR/Coll. Chemel
**345** – FP Robert Opie
**346** – TL Topham Picture Library – MR Sygma/Illustration – BR Keystone, Paris
**347** – TL Zentral Bild, Berlin – TR Private Collection – BM Sygma/Illustration
**348** – TL Popperfoto – MR Lockheed, Royal Aeronautical Society – BL Topham Picture Library
**349** – TL Chronicle Communications Ltd – MY, ML Sygma/Illustration – MR Smithsonian Inst
**350** – TL Coll. Bauer – TR, BR, BL Sygma/Illustration
**351** – TR, BL Sygma/Illustration – BR Sutton Library
**355** – FP Peter Newark's Pictures
**356** – TL Sygma/Illustration – BL Popperfoto – MR Keystone, Paris
**357** – TL Royal Aeronautical Society – MR Lockheed – BL Library of Congress – BY Hulton Deutsch
**358** – TL E T Archive – MR Latécoère – BL Royal Aeronautical Society
**359** – TR McDonnell Douglas – ML E T Archive – BR Peter Newark's Pictures
**360** – ML Topham Picture Library – TR Michael Taylor – MR The Age, Melbourne
**361** – TR Lufthansa – BR Boeing – BL Mary Evans Picture Library
**365** – FP Topham Picture Library
**366** – TL Lockheed – BL SHAA – TR DITE – BR National Archives of Canada
**367** – ML Keystone, Paris – TR Coll. Lorant – BR National Library of Australia
**368** – TM Pan Am – MM, BM Keystone, Paris
**369** – ML Chronicle Communications Ltd – TR, BL Aerospace Publishing – BR Hulton Deutsch
**370** – TL Imperial War Museum – TR Royal Aeronautical Society – BR Coll. J. Boulet
**371** – TL Popperfoto – ML SHAA – TR Bettmann Archive – BR RR/Coll. musée de l'Air et de l'Espace
**372** – TL Topham Picture Library – MM Robert Hunt – BL Popperfoto – MR Hulton Deutsch
**373** – TL Topham Picture Library – MX Popperfoto – TR Peter Newark's Pictures – BR Kobal Collection
**377** – FP Tallandier
**378** – TL Peter Newark's Pictures – MR Popperfoto – BL Kharbine Tapabor
**379** – TL, TR SHAA – BR Aerospace Publishing – BL Sygma/Illustration
**380** – TL RR/Coll. Larousse – MR UCPA – BL RR/Coll. musée de l'Air et de l'Espace
**381** – TL SHAA – TR Keystone, Paris – BL Jacques Legrand s.a.
**382** – TL Topham Picture Library – MR Imperial War Museum – BR RR/Coll. musée de l'Air et de l'Espace – BL Robert Opie
**383** – TL Aerospace Publishing – MR, MM Topham Picture Library
**384** – TL Popperfoto – TR Imperial War Museum – BL Tallandier – MR Topham Picture Library
**385** – ML, BX, BR Topham Picture Library – TR Popperfoto
**386** – BL, MM Peter Newark's Pictures – TL Imperial War Museum – BR Coll. Lorant
**387** – TL Aspect Picture Library – MR Popperfoto – BR Jacques Legrand s.a.
**391** – FP Imperial War Museum
**392** – TL Naval and Military Club, London – TR Keystone, Paris – BL Coll. Lorant – MR Michael Taylor
**393** – TL, BR Aerospace Publishing – TR Peter Newark's Pictures – BL Newark
**394** – TL Hulton Deutsch – TR Imperial War Museum – MR Michael Taylor – BL Aspect Picture Library
**395** – TR Robert Hunt – ML Popperfoto – BR SHAA
**396** – BL RR/Coll. musée de l'Air et de l'Espace – TL Chronicle Communications Ltd – MR Topham Picture Library – BR Peter Newarkís Pictures
**397** – TL Aerospace Publishing – TR DITE
**401** – FP Imperial War Museum
**402** – TL, BR TRH Pictures – MR Topham Picture Library – TR Aerospace Publishing – MX Peter Newark's Pictures
**403** – TL USAF – MR TRH Pictures – BR Aerospace Publishing
**404** – MR TRH Pictures – TL, BR Peter Newark's Pictures – BL CD Collection
**405** – All pictures from Aerospace Publishing
**406** – TL, TR DITE – BL Imperial War Museum
**407** – TL SHAA – MX Imperial War Museum – MR Topham Picture Library – BR Aerospace Publishing
**408** – TM Keystone, Paris – ML Bundesarchiv, Deutschland – MM Camera Press
**409** – TL CD Collection – TY Topham Picture Library – BR Popperfoto
**413** – FP Kharbine Tapabor
**414** – ML Popperfoto – BL DITE – BR Aerospace Publishing – TR Chronicle Communications Ltd
**415** – ML Imperial War Museum – TX Topham Picture Library – MR Tallandier – TM USAF
**416** – TL DITE – TR Kharbine Tapabor – MY John Philipps
**417** – TM Peter Newark's Pictures – MM Chronicle Communications Ltd – BL Popperfoto – BR Robert Opie
**418** – TL Robert Hunt – TR Imperial War Museum – ML Peter Newark's Pictures – BR Aerospace Publishing

**419** – TM McDonnell Douglas – BL Keystone, Paris – BR Associated Press/Topham
**420** – BL Hulton Deutsch – TL USAF – TR Imperial War Museum – MY Popperfoto
**421** – ML, BR Aerospace Publishing – TR Imperial War Museum
**425** – FP Peter Newark's Pictures
**426** – TL, BL RR/Coll. musée de l'Air et de l'Espace – BR RR/Coll. Larousse – TR DITE
**427** – TL, ML Coll. Bauer – TR RR/Coll. Larousse – BR Jacques Legrand s.a.
**428** – TL RR/Coll. musée de l'Air et de l'Espace – TR RR/Coll. Larousse – BR McDonnell Douglas
**429** – TL, TR DITE – BR Aerospace Publishing – BL Michael Taylor
**430** – TL Aerospace Publishing – MR Michael Taylor – BR Peter Newark's Pictures
**431** – TL CD Collection – TM Royal Aeronautical Society – BM DITE
**432** – TL Aerospace Publishing – BR DITE – ML Aerospace Publishing
**433** – TL Aspect Picture Library – MR USAF – BL DITE
**437** – FP Peter Newark's Pictures
**438** – TL Boeing – MR RR/Coll. musée de l'Air et de l'Espace – ML, BL Keystone, Paris
**439** – TL Sabena – BR RR/Coll. musée de l'Air et de l'Espace – TR Kharbine Tapabor – BL Aerospace Publishing
**440** – TL Popperfoto – ML CD Collection
**441** – TM Topham Picture Library – MR Keystone, Paris – BR CD Collection
**442** – TL Imperial War Museum – TR Bettmann Archive – BL, BR Kobal Collection
**443** – TR, MR Topham Picture Library – ML TRH Pictures
**444** – MR Royal Aeronautical Society – BR McDonnell Douglas – BL DITE – TL Aerospace Publishing
**445** – TL, BR Keystone, Paris – MY Royal Aeronautical Society – BL Michael Taylor
**446** – All pictures from the Imperial War Museum
**447** – All pictures from the Imperial War Museum
**451** – FP Popperfoto
**452** – ML RR/Coll. musée de l'Air et de l'Espace – TR TRH Pictures – MR Michael Taylor – BL The Age, Melbourne
**453** – TM Lockheed – ML Keystone, Paris – BR Michael Taylor
**454** – TL Pan Am – MR Private Collection, Royal Aeronautical Society – ML Royal Aeronautical Society
**455** – ML Topham Picture Library – TM E T Archive – MR Roger Schall
**456** – TL Royal Aeronautical Society – MM TRH Pictures – BL USAF
**457** – TL Michael Taylor – MR British Aerospace – ML RR/Coll. musée de l'Air et de l'Espace
**458** – TL Lockheed – MR Lockheed, Kobal Collection – BL Peter Newark's Pictures
**459** – TL RR/Coll. musée de l'Air et de l'Espace – ML Chronicle Communications Ltd – TR Michael Taylor
**463** – FP Air France
**464** – TM, ML Sabena – MR Topham Picture Library
**465** – TL Michael Taylor – MR Private Collection
**466** – TL Topham Picture Library – MM, BR Royal Aeronautical Society
**467** – TL RR/Coll. musée de l'Air et de l'Espace – TR Topham Picture Library – MM Royal Aeronautical Society
**468** – TM TRH Pictures – TR Peter Newark's Pictures – BY Royal Aeronautical Society – BL Popperfoto
**469** – TL, ML RR/Coll. musée de l'Air et de l'Espace – BL Royal Aeronautical Society – MR Keystone, Paris
**473** – FP Bettmann Archive
**474** – TX Topham Picture Library – MR Philip Jarrett – BR RR/Coll. musée de l'Air et de l'Espace – BL Royal Aeronautical Society
**475** – TL, MR Royal Aeronautical Society – ML Topham Picture Library
**476** – TM, TR Topham Picture Library – BM Hulton Deutsch
**477** – TR TRH Pictures – BL Royal Aeronautical Society – BR Hulton Deutsch
**481** – FP Royal Aeronautical Society
**482** – TL Topham Picture Library – MR RR/Coll. musée de l'Air et de l'Espace – BR Topham Picture Library
**483** – TL, TR, BL Popperfoto – MR Hulton Deutsch – BR Topham Picture Library
**484** – MR Topham Picture Library – BR TRH Pictures – BL Peter Newark's Pictures
**485** – TL Peter Newark's Pictures – MR Popperfoto – BX Keystone, Paris
**489** – FP Lockheed
**490** – All pictures from Keystone, Paris
**491** – TM, MM Popperfoto – BL, BR Topham Picture Library
**492** – TL Hulton Deutsch – BX Popperfoto
**493** – TL DITE – ML Peter Newark's Pictures – BR Popperfoto
**497** – FP Royal Aeronautical Society
**498** – ML Popperfoto – TR RR/Coll. musée de l'Air et de l'Espace – BL SNCASO
**499** – ML, MR TRH Pictures – BL Topham Picture Library
**500** – TM Photo X – ML National Library of Australia – BR Popperfoto
**501** – TL Royal Aeronautical Society – TY Topham Picture Library – BM Hulton Deutsch
**502** – TL Hulton Deutsch – TR Keystone, Paris – MR Royal Aeronautical Society – BL Chronicle Communications Ltd
**503** – ML E T Archive – BR Keystone, Paris
**507** – FP Royal Aeronautical Society
**508** – ML RR/Coll. musée de l'Air et de l'Espace – TR Topham Picture Library – BY Royal Aeronautical Society
**509** – TL, TR RR/Coll. musée de l'Air et de l'Espace – ML Coll. Bauer
**510** – MM Hulton Deutsch – BL Popperfoto – BR Topham Picture Library
**511** – TX Topham Picture Library – TR, ML Popperfoto
**512** – TL Popperfoto – MR Royal Aeronautical Society – BR RR/Coll. Larousse
**513** – TL Hulton Deutsch – TR TRH Pictures – MR Hulton Deutsch – BR ECPA
**517** – FP Royal Aeronautical Society
**518** – TL RR/Coll. Chemel – MR Topham Picture Library – ML Royal Aeronautical Society
**519** – ML Popperfoto – TR, BR Topham Picture Library
**520** – TL TRH Pictures – MY, BL RR/Coll. musée de l'Air et de l'Espace
**521** – ML Popperfoto – TX, TY Topham Picture Library
**525** – FP TRH Pictures
**526** – TR Coll. Bauer – ML Popperfoto – MR Michael Taylor
**527** – ML Royal Aeronautical Society – TR Popperfoto – BR Topham Picture Library
**528** – TL Boeing – MR TRH Pictures – BX Royal Aeronautical Society
**529** – TM Bettmann Archive – TR, BM, BR Topham Picture Library – MR Popperfoto
**530** – TX, MR Royal Aeronautical Society – BL DITE
**531** – TL Topham Picture Library – MR Royal Aeronautical Society – BL Aerospace Publishing
**535** – FP Royal Aeronautical Society
**536** – All pictures from TRH Pictures
**537** – TL Lufthansa – ML Hulton Deutsch – MR RR/Coll. musée de l'Air et de l'Espace – BX Topham Picture Library
**538** – TR Keystone, Paris – ML RR/Coll. musée de l'Air et de l'Espace – MR Peter Newark's Pictures – BL Mooney
**539** – TM, BL Topham Picture Library – MR TRH Pictures
**543** – FP RR/Coll. Larousse
**544** – TM, TR TRH Pictures – MM Hulton Deutsch – BL Robert Opie
**545** – ML Popperfoto – MY, BX Topham Picture Library – TR Popperfoto
**546** – ML Piper – TR Royal Aeronautical Society – BR Bettmann Archive
**547** – ML Popperfoto – TM Topham Picture Library – BM Royal Aeronautical Society
**548** – TL Topham Picture Library – MR Royal Aeronautical Society – BL Popperfoto
**549** – TL Royal Aeronautical Society – ML TRH Pictures
**553** – FP Peter Newark's Pictures
**554** – ML, BR TRH Pictures – MR Royal Aeronautical Society
**555** – TL Hulton Deutsch – TR Topham Picture Library – BR Coll. Bauer
**556** – TL Keystone, Paris – MR, BL Popperfoto – BR Royal Aeronautical Society
**557** – TL Cessna – TR RR/Coll. Chemel – BL Lockheed – BR Keystone, Paris
**558** – TM, BL Michael Taylor – TR Fairey Aviation
**559** – TM Keystone, Paris – TR, MX Popperfoto – MX Royal Aeronautical Society
**560** – RR/Coll. musée de l'Air et de l'Espace
**563** – FP Robert Opie
**564** – TY Hulton Deutsch – TL Associated Press – BY Robert Opie
**565** – ML Boeing – MY Topham Picture Library – BL RR/Coll. musée de l'Air et de l'Espace – BR Popperfoto
**566** – TM Coll. Bauer – ML McDonnell Douglas – BR Keystone, Paris
**567** – TL ADP – ML Royal Aeronautical Society – BL Topham Picture Library – MR RR/Coll. musée de l'Air et de l'Espace – BR Keystone, Paris
**568** – TL, ML Topham Picture Library – TR Herald & Weekly Times, Melbourne – BL Cessna – BR Hulton Deutsch
**569** – TM RR/Coll. musée de l'Air et de l'Espace – MM Popperfoto
**573** – FP TRH Pictures
**574** – TL Coll. Bauer – MR, MM RR/Coll. musée de l'Air et de l'Espace
**575** – TL, TY, MM Topham Picture Library
**576** – ML Keystone, Paris – TR Boeing – BL Topham Picture Library – MY Royal Aeronautical Society
**577** – TM Qantas – ML, BR RR/Coll. musée de l'Air et de l'Espace
**578** – TL Hulton Deutsch – TX Popperfoto – TR Topham Picture Library – MR Michael Taylor – BL RR/Coll. musée de l'Air et de l'Espace
**579** – ML Agence France Presse – TR TRH Pictures – BR Topham Picture Library – BL Croydon Library
**583** – FP Robert Opie
**584** – TM Coll. Bauer – MM Bettmann Archive
**585** – TR Peter Newark's Pictures – ML Topham Picture Library – MX Jacques Legrand s.a., RR/Coll. Larousse – MY, MR RR/Coll. Larousse
**586** – TL BSI – MR Michael Taylor – ML Keystone, Paris
**587** – MX Topham Picture Library – TR Bettmann Archive – BM RR/Coll. musée de l'Air et de l'Espace
**591** – FP Peter Newark's Pictures
**592** – ML DITE – TR Michael Taylor – BL Sabena – BR Bettman Archive
**593** – ML Hulton Deutsch – MX Keystone, Paris – MR Pilatus
**594** – ML Coll. Bauer – TR Coll. Yannick Delamarre – MM Aerospace Publishing
**595** – ML Michael Taylor – MM Topham Picture Library
**596** – TL Bettmann Archive – TR Keystone, Paris – BR Chronicle Communications Ltd – ML WMAL
**597** – ML Bettmann Archive – BR Royal Aeronautical Society
**601** – FP TWA
**602** – TR Coll. Bauer – ML Topham Picture Library – BR Bettmann Archive
**603** – ML Popperfoto – TR Sikorsky
**604** – TM Hulton Deutsch – MM Popperfoto – BR Michael Taylor – ML Coll. Bauer
**605** – TL DITE – MR TRH Pictures – BL Popperfoto
**606** – TL, BL, TR Bettmann Archive – MR Coll. Bauer
**607** – TR Private Collection – BL Royal Aeronautical Society
**611** – FP Coll. Bauer
**612** – TL Photo X – ML Piper – BR Hulton Deutsch
**613** – TR Peter Newark's Pictures – MR RR/Coll. Larousse
**614** – TL Bettmann Archive – TR RR/Coll. Larousse – ML Dassault/Larousse
**615** – ML, BL Topham Picture Library – MR RR/Coll. musée de l'Air et de l'Espace – BR Popperfoto
**616** – ML TRH Pictures – TR Lear – MR Mitsubishi Aircraft, Coll. Bauer – BL Keystone, Paris
**617** – TY Topham Picture Library – TL UTA – BR Keystone, Paris
**621** – FP Coll. Bauer
**622** – TX, TR Topham Picture Library – MR Coll. Bauer – BR United Airlines – BL Popperfoto
**623** – ML Hulton Deutsch – TM RR/Coll. musée de l'Air et de l'Espace – MR Bettmann Archive – MM Coll. Bauer
**624** – TL, BM Coll. Bauer – TR, MR RR/Coll. musée de l'Air et de l'Espace
**625** – ML Peter Newark's Pictures – TR Dassault – MR Bettmann Archive – BL Coll. Bauer
**626** – MR Bettmann Archive – TL Peter Newark's Pictures – MM TRH Pictures
**627** – ML, TR Bettmann Archive – BR Kobal Collection
**631** – FP Bettmann Archive
**632** – TL, ML RR/Coll. musée de l'Air et de l'Espace – TY McDonnell Douglas – MR RR/Coll. Larousse
**633** – ML Novosti – TR Qantas – BL Keystone, Paris – BR DITE
**634** – TL Hulton Deutsch – MR Peter Newark's Pictures – BL Popperfoto
**635** – TL Hulton Deutsch – MR Kipa, Paris – BM Chronicle Communications Ltd
**636** – TL Hulton Deutsch – TR, BL, BR Bettmann Archive
**637** – ML Kobal Collection – TR Coll. Bauer – BL Chronicle Communications Ltd – MM Topham Picture Library
**641** – FP Air France
**642** – TM Aerospace Publishing – BL Keystone, Paris – BR RR/Coll. musée de l'Air et de l'Espace
**643** – TL Bettmann Archive – TR Topham Picture Library – MM RR/Coll. Larousse
**644** – MX, ML Bettmann Archive – TR Coll. Bauer – BR Peter Newark's Pictures
**645** – TL, BL Keystone, Paris – TX Coll. Bauer – MY TRH Pictures – BR Hulton Deutsch
**649** – FP Australian War Memorial, Canberra
**650** – TL Coll. Bauer – MR, BL Peter Newark's Pictures
**651** – TM TRH Pictures – ML Michael Taylor – MR Bettmann Archive – BM Coll. Bauer
**652** – MM, BR Topham Picture Library – ML Bettmann Archive
**653** – TX, TR Coll. Bauer – ML Air et Cosmos
**654** – MX RR/Coll. Larousse – MY, TR Bettmann Archive – BL, BR Peter Newark's Pictures
**655** – TM Peter Newark's Pictures – BM Cathay Pacific
**659** – FP Peter Newark's Pictures
**660** – TM Bettmann Archive – MM Peter Newark's Pictures
**661** – TL TRH Pictures – MR, BL Keystone, Paris
**662** – TM Peter Newark's Pictures – MR Bettmann Archive – BL Popperfoto
**663** – TM, MM Royal Aeronautical Society – BL Coll. Bauer
**664** – TL Coll. Bauer – TR Boeing – BX Bettmann Archive
**665** – TL Roger Demeulle – TR Topham Picture Library – BR Lockheed
**669** – FP RR/Coll. Chemel
**670** – TM TRH Pictures – ML Keystone, Paris – BL Chronicle Communications Ltd
**671** – BL Tallandier – BR Sud Aviation – TL Keystone, Paris – TR Hulton Deutsch
**672** – TL Lockheed – ML Keystone, Paris – MR RR/Coll. Larousse – BR Hulton Deutsch
**673** – TM Royal Aeronautical Society – MR Keystone, Paris
**674** – TL Hulton Deutsch – MR Bettmann Archive – BL Keystone, Paris
**675** – TL Bettmann Archive – MY Royal Aeronautical Society – BL TRH Pictures – BR Peter Newark's Pictures
**676** – TM, BR Coll. Bauer – ML Peter Newark's Pictures
**677** – TL RR/Coll. musée de l'Air et de l'Espace – MR Hulton Deutsch – BM Royal Aeronautical Society
**681** – FP Ernoult, France
**682** – TL Pan Am – TR Popperfoto – BM Hulton Deutsch
**683** – TM Michael Taylor – BL, BX Keystone, Paris – MR RR/Coll. musée de l'Air et de l'Espace
**684** – TM Popperfoto – BL Coll. Bauer
**685** – ML, TY TRH Pictures – MR, BL Bettmann Archive
**688** – FP Bettmann Archive
**690** – TL Coll. Bauer – MR Bettmann Archive – BL Hulton Deutsch
**691** – TL RR/Coll. musée de l'Air et de l'Espace – MR Hulton Deutsch – BL RR/Coll. Larousse
**692** – ML Coll. Bauer – TY Bettmann Archive – BR Hulton Deutsch
**693** – TL Keystone, Paris – TR Royal Aeronautical Society – ML Coll. Bauer – BR Roger Demeulle
**694** – TL Private Collection – MR Airbus Industrie – ML Keystone, Paris – BR Lufthansa
**695** – TL Air Canada – BR Keystone, Paris

# Picture Credits

699 – FP Coll. Bauer
700 – TL, MR Coll. Bauer – ML Boeing
701 – TM, MR Bettmann Archive – BM Jacques Legrand s.a.
702 – MR Hulton Deutsch – TL Tucker Group – BR Coll. Bauer
703 – TM Coll. Bauer – BR Royal Aeronautical Society – BL Simon Danger
707 – FP TRH Pictures
708 – ML Keystone, Paris – TR Popperfoto – MR TRH Pictures
709 – ML Coll. Bauer – TR Hulton Deutsch – BL Sipa Press, Paris
710 – TL Keystone, Paris – MR Aerospace Publishing, DITE – BL Topham Picture Library
711 – TL Bettmann Archive – MR Popperfoto – MY TRH Pictures
712 – TL Gamma, Paris – TM, ML Keystone, Paris – BR TRH Pictures
713 – TL Sabena – ML Pan Am – BR Keystone, Paris
717 – FP Topham Picture Library
718 – TM Sipa Press, Paris – ML Hulton Deutsch
719 – ML Keystone, Paris – BL, MR Bettmann Archive
720 – TM Topham Picture Library – ML Bettmann Archive
721 – TL Canadair – MR Hulton Deutsch, Coll. Bauer
725 – FP Hulton Deutsch
726 – TM Bettmann Archive – MR, BL Keystone, Paris
727 – TL TRH Pictures – MR Keystone, Paris – MM Topham Picture Library
728 – All pictures from Bettmann Archive
729 – TR Coll. Bauer – BM RR/Coll. musée de l'Air et de l'Espace
730 – TL TRH Pictures – TR McDonnell Douglas – MR Royal Aeronautical Society – BL Keystone, Paris
731 – ML, BR Bettmann Archive – TR Novosti
735 – FP TRH Pictures
736 – TL RR/Coll. musée de l'Air et de l'Espace – TR Hulton Deutsch – BM Air France
737 – TL Keystone, Paris – TR Pan Am – BM Lockheed
738 – TL Private Collection – TY Popperfoto – MR TRH Pictures – BM Bettmann Archive
739 – TL Dassault – TR Keystone, Paris – BL Airbus Industrie – BR Southwest Airlines
743 – FP Sipa Press, Paris
744 – ML RR/Coll. musée de l'Air et de l'Espace – TR, BR Coll. Bauer – MR Keystone, Paris
745 – TL Gamma, Paris – TR Sipa Press, Paris – BL Associated Press/Topham – BR DITE/NASA
746 – TL Bettmann Archive – MR Keystone, Paris – BM Topham Picture Library
747 – TM Popperfoto – BL, BR Ernoult, France
751 – FP TRH Pictures
752 – ML Bettmann Archive – TM Ernoult, France – BM Coll. Bauer
753 – TX Bettmann Archive – BL Topham Picture Library – MR AMD-BA/Aviaplanes
754 – TM Sipa Press, Paris – MR Bettmann Archive – BL Peter Newark's Pictures – BR Hulton Deutsch
755 – TM David Mondey – ML Coll. Bauer – BR Popperfoto
759 – FP RR/Coll. Larousse
760 – TM Sygma/Illustration – TR Bettmann Archive – MR Coll. Bauer – BL Mooney
761 – TL, TY DITE – MM Coll. Bauer
762 – TL Hulton Deutsch – BL TRH Pictures – MR RR/Coll. Chemel
763 – TM Popperfoto – ML Coll. Bauer – BR Novosti
767 – FP Ernoult, France
768 – TL Ernoult, France – MR Air et Cosmos – ML Aerospace Publishing – BR RR/Coll. musée de l'Air et de l'Espace
769 – TM TRH Pictures – MM, BR Bettmann Archive
770 – ML Piper – BL, MR Keystone, Paris
771 – TL Bettmann Archive – MX Keystone, Paris – MY Topham Picture Library
775 – FP Royal Aeronautical Society
776 – TL Lear – MR Ernoult, France – MM Popperfoto
777 – TM TRH Pictures – BM Peter Newark's Pictures
778 – TL, BL Coll. Bauer – BR Associated Press/Topham
779 – TR, TL Airbus Industrie – BL Lockheed – BR Boeing
783 – FP Airbus Industrie
784 – TL Pereira/Sipa Press – TR Popperfoto – MR Airbus Industrie
785 – TM, MM Topham Picture Library – BY Associated Press/Topham
786 – TL, TY Bettmann Archive – ML Coll. Bauer – BR Sipa Press, Paris
787 – ML Ernoult, France – TR Coll. Ferry – ML TRH Pictures – BR Peter Newark's Pictures
791 – FP Royal Aeronautical Society
792 – ML Cessna – TR Ernoult, France – ML Sipa Press, Paris – MR RR/Coll. musée de l'Air et de l'Espace
793 – ML Piper, Pierre-Yves Grasset – MM RR/Coll. musée de l'Air et de l'Espace – MR Royal Aeronautical Society
794 – TR Associated Press – BM RR/Coll. Chemel
795 – TL DITE – TR RR/Coll. musée de l'Air et de l'Espace – BL Ernoult, France – BR Alitalia
799 – FP Coll. Bauer
800 – TL TRH Pictures – MR Boeing – BR Coll. Bauer
801 – ML Air France – TR Popperfoto – BX Topham Picture Library
802 – TL El Al – MY Bettmann Archive – TR Hulton Deutsch – BL TRH Pictures
803 – TM Sipa Press, Paris – ML, BR Bettmann Archive
807 – FP Coll. Bauer
808 – ML McDonnell Douglas – TR Topham Picture Library – BL Bettmann Archive – MR Rex Features
809 – TL, TR Keystone, Paris – BL Agence France Presse, Paris – MR Topham Picture Library
813 – FP Royal Aeronautical Society
814 – ML, BR Ernoult, France – TR Associated Press/Topham – BL Embraer, France
815 – TR TRH Pictures – ML Sipa Press, Paris – MR Topham Picture Library
816 – TL, MM Coll. Bauer – TR TRH Pictures
817 – TM, MR Topham Picture Library – MM Jacques Legrand s.a. – BL Fernandez/Sipa Press
821 – FP Rex Features
822 – TX Ernoult, France – TR Meauxsoone/Sygma – MM Sipa Press, Paris – BL Topham Picture Library
823 – TL Associated Press/Topham – TR London City Airport – BL Sipa Press, Paris – BR Royal Aeronautical Society
827 – FP Aviation Picture Library
828 – TL Ernoult, France – ML Boeing
829 – TL Rex Features – TR Associated Press/Topham – MX Topham Picture Library – BR Southwest Airlines
830 – TR Associated Press/Topham – ML Coll. Bauer
831 – TR Lockheed – MM Associated Press/Topham – MR Press Association/Topham
835 – FP Coll. Bauer
836 – TL Capt Chris Norris – TR Northwest Airlines – ML Sipa Press, Paris – BR Ernoult, France
837 – ML, BL Sipa Press, Paris – TR Coll. Bauer – BR Press Association/Topham
838 – TL Coll. Bauer – MR USAir – MY Sipa Press, Paris
839 – All pictures from Chronicle Communications Ltd
843 – FP Press Association/Topham
844 – TL, MR Sipa Press, Paris – MX Universal
845 – TL AMR Combs – MR Coll. Bauer – ML Learjet – BR British Aerospace
846 – TL Sipa Press, Paris – TR Press Association/Topham – BL Associated Press/Topham – MR Ernoult, France
847 – ML Embraer, France – TY, TR Sipa Press, Paris – BM Mark Pyle
848 – TL Sipa Press, Paris – MR, BL Bettmann Archive – BR Kansai
849 – TL Lufthansa – MX McDonnell Douglas – TR Associated Press – BR TRH Pictures
854 – TL, MY United Airlines – BL Cessna – BR American Airlines/International Flagship Service
855 – TL, BR USAF – TR JM Guhl, Sipa Press – BL Jon Kelk
856 – TL American Airlines – TR Alaska Airlines – MY Ernoult, France – BL Learjet – BR Butler Aviation
857 – TL Citation – MR AMR Combs – BM Alain Ernoult/Ernoult Features
858 – TL American Airlines – TR Courtesy of McDonnell Douglas – BR British Aerospace – BL Courtesy of Bell
859 – TL, TR Ernoult, France – BL United Airlines – BR American Airlines
860 – TL Coll. Yannick Delamarre – BL, BR Courtesy of United
861 – TM Pan Am – BL Courtesy of Federal Express – BR SipaPress, Paris
865 – FP Lockheed Martin/Hugh W Cowin
866 – TR McDonnell Douglas/Hugh W Cowin – TL Short/Hugh W Cowin – BR Socata/Hugh W Cowin
867 – TL TRH Pictures – BR Hugh W Cowin
868 – TL TRH Pictures – Y ESA/Hugh W Cowin –BL Keith Wilson/Hugh W Cowin
869 – T Cameron Balloon Ltd/Hugh W Cowin – B Airbus/Hugh W Cowin
870 – TL TRH Pictures – TR British Aerospace/TRH Pictures – X SAAB/Hugh Cowin – MX Westland/TRH Pictures – Y Aerospace Publishing – BL McDonnell Douglas/TRH Pictures – BR Austin J Brown/APL
871 – TL Austin J Brown/APL – TR Raytheon/Hugh W Cowin – X McDonnell Douglas/TRH Pictures – Y Hugh W Cowin – MX Airbus/TRH Pictures – MY TRH Pictures – BY Austin J Brown/APL – BL LTV Aerospace Defence/TRH Pictures – BR N.V. Fokker/APL
873 – FP Aerospatiale/Hugh W Cowin
874 – T British Aerospace/Hugh W Cowin – L Dassault/Hugh W Cowin – B Lockheed Martin/Hugh W Cowin
875 – T SAAB/Hugh W Cowin – M, B McDonnell Douglas/Hugh W Cowin
876 – T TRH Pictures – B Beech/Hugh W Cowin
877 – TR TRH Pictures – TL Northrop/Hugh W Cowin – B Raytheon/Hugh W Cowin
878 – TL Slingsby/TRH Pictures – TR Lockheed/TRH Pictures – X Grob /TRH Pictures – MM TRH Pictures Y Boeing/Hugh W Cowin – MX Fokker/TRH Pictures – MY Dassault/Hugh W Cowin – BL SAAB/Hugh W Cowin –BR Raytheon/Hugh W Cowin
879 – TL Canadair/TRH Pictures – TM Austin J Brown/APL – TR McDonnell Douglas/TRH Pictures – MT Airbus/Hugh W Cowin – X Socata/Hugh W Cowin – M Cessna Aircraft Company/APL – Y Embraer/TRH Pictures – BL, BR TRH Pictures – B Northrop/Hugh W Cowin
881 – FP Airbus/Hugh W Cowin
882 – T TRH Pictures – B Daimler Chrysler Aerospace/Hugh W Cowin
883 – TL Airbus/Hugh W Cowin – TR TRH Pictures – BL PA Photos – BR Boeing/Hugh W Cowin
884 – T General Atomics/Hugh W Cowin – M USAF/Hugh W Cowin – B Airbus/Hugh W Cowin
885 – T POPPERFOTO – M Kaman/Hugh W Cowin – B Antonov/Hugh W Cowin
886 – TL, BX, M, Y TR TRH Pictures – X Hindustan Aeronautics Ltd/APL – BL Airbus/Hugh W Cowin – BR Cirrus Design/Hugh W Cowin
887 – TL Rolls Royce/TRH Pictures – TM Dave Willis/TRH Pictures – TR Bell/TRH Pictures – Y TRH Pictures – X Westland/Hugh W Cowin – BL Boeing/TRH Pictures – BR Eurocopter/TRH Pictures
889 – FP Lockheed Martin/Hugh W Cowin
890 – TL Airbus/Hugh W Cowin– – BL POPPERFOTO – R Cessna/Hugh W Cowin
891 – TM Daimler Chrysler Aerospace – Y Rolls Royce/Hugh W Cowin – X Lockheed Martin/Hugh W Cowin
892 – TL Diana Britten/Hugh W Cowin – TR Hugh W Cowin – MR Embraer/Hugh W Cowin
893 – T Daimler Chrysler Aerospace/Hugh W Cowin – B McDonnell Douglas/Hugh W Cowin
894 – TL N.V.Fokker /APL – TR Lockheed Martin/Hugh W Cowin – TX Dassault/Hugh W Cowin –TY Keith Wilson/Hugh W Cowin – BX TRH Pictures – BY Cirrus Design/Hugh W Cowin – BL Raytheon/TRH Pictures – BR Boeing/TRH Pictures
895 – TL Rolls Royce/TRH Pictures – TR, TY TRH Pictures – X Cessna/TRH Pictures – BX, M Dave Willis/TRH Pictures – BL Eurocopter/J. Deulin – BR Augusta/TRH Pictures – MY Airbus/Hugh W Cowin
897 – FP Hugh W Cowin
898 –T The Cowin Collection – TR Mc Donnell Douglas/TRH Pictures – MR TRH Pictures – BM Boeing/Hugh W Cowin
899 – TR Austin J Brown/APL – M Scaled Composites/Hugh W Cowin – BR ESA/Hugh W Cowin
900 – T BAe/Hugh W Cowin – M Boeing/Hugh W Cowin – B ESA/Hugh W Cowin
901 – TL Hugh W Cowin – BR Boeing/Hugh W Cowin
902 – TL Boeing/APL – TR Kawasaki/TRH Pictures – TX Lockheed Martin/TRH Pictures – Y, BR, BL TRH Pictures – BX SAAB/TRH Pictures
903 – TL, TY, BR, BL TRH Pictures – TR Raytheon/TRH Pictures – BY Aerospace Publishing – BX Bombardier/TRH Pictures – MM Boeing Sikorsky/TRH Pictures – TX Austin J Brown/APL
905 – FP Lockheed Martin/Hugh W Cowin
906 – T Boeing/Hugh W Cowin – B POPPERFOTO
907 – T E Partridge/TRH Pictures – M TRH Pictures – B POPPERFOTO
908 – TL Lockheed Martin/Hugh W Cowin – TR POPPERFOTO – Y ESA/Hugh W Cowin – B Boeing/Hugh W Cowin
909 – TL Dave Willis/TRH Pictures – TR Daimler Chrysler Aerospace/Hugh W Cowin – Y British Aerospace/Hugh W Cowin – B Dassault/Hugh W Cowin
910 – TL CASA/TRH Pictures – TR Robert Hewson/APL – TY Boeing/Hugh W Cowin – BY POP-PERFOTO – BR TRH Pictures – BL Hugh W Cowin – BX McDonnell Douglas/TRH Pictures – TX Austin J Brown/APL
911 – TL, MT TRH Pictures – TR Cameron Balloons Ltd/Hugh W Cowin – TY Lockheed Martin/TRH Pictures – BY Daimler Benz Aerospace/TRH Pictures – BR Hugh W Cowin – BL Boeing/TRH Pictures – BX Grob/TRH Pictures – TX British Aerospace/TRH Pictures
913 – FP Boeing/Hugh W Cowin
914 – T Eurocopter/Hugh W Cowin – X Northrop Grumman/Hugh W Cowin – M Lockheed Martin/Hugh W Cowin
915 – T Raytheon/Hugh W Cowin – Y Scaled Composites/Hugh W Cowin – BL Daimler Chrysler Aerospace/Hugh W Cowin
916 – John Askew/Hugh W Cowin – M SAAB/Hugh W Cowin – B Raytheon/Hugh W Cowin
917 – T Piper/TRH Pictures –X Boeing/Hugh W Cowin – BL USAF/Hugh W Cowin – BR ESA/Hugh W Cowin
918 – TR TRH Pictures – TL Lockheed Martin/TRH Pictures – Y, BR Boeing/TRH Pictures – BL Augusta/TRH Pictures – BX Keith Wilson/Hugh W Cowin –TX Boeing/Hugh W Cowin
919 – TL Austin J Brown/APL – TR Sikorsky/TRH Pictures – Y Gulfstream/TRH Pictures – BR Sergey Sergeyev/APL – BL Boeing/Hugh W Cowin – BX Fairchild Aerospace/Hugh W Cowin TX de Havilland/TRH Pictures
921 – FP Sgt Jack Pritchard RAFRR/Hugh W Cowin
922 – T POPPERFOTO –B Boeing/Hugh W Cowin
923 – T Bombardier/Hugh W Cowin – M Rolls Royce/Hugh W Cowin – B Daimler Chrysler Aerospace/Hugh W Cowin
924 – L Boeing/Hugh W Cowin – T Fairchild Aerospace/Hugh W Cowin –B Boeing/Hugh W Cowin
925 – T BAE Systems/Hugh W Cowin – BR POPPERFOTO – BL Lockheed Martin/Hugh W Cowin
926 – TL, Y TRH Pictures – TR, TX Embraer/Hugh W Cowin – BR Israel Aircraft Industries Ltd/APL – BL E Nevill/TRH Pictures – BX Lockheed Martin/TRH Pictures
927 – TL, TX, BX TRH Pictures – TR Boeing/Hugh W Cowin – Y Sikorsky/Hugh W Cowin – BR ESA/Hugh W Cowin – BL Robert Hewson/APL
929 – FP ESA D Ducros
930 – T Bombardier/Hugh W Cowin – Y Airbus/Hugh W Cowin – BR Lockheed Martin/Hugh W Cowin
931 – T.POPPERFOTO – X NHI/Hugh W Cowin – BR BAE Systems/Hugh W Cowin
932 – T Boeing/Hugh W Cowin – BR SAAB/Hugh W Cowin – X General Atomics/Hugh W Cowin
933 – T Raytheon/Hugh W Cowin – Y Design Council/Hugh W Cowin – X Lockheed Martin/Hugh W Cowin
934 – TL, Y Boeing/Hugh W Cowin – TR Keith Wilson/Hugh W Cowin – BR, BL, X TRH Pictures
935 – TL, TR, MR, BR TRH Pictures – BL Sergey Sergeyev/APL – BX Lockheed Martin/Hugh W Cowin – TX Austin J Brown/APL